SOMETHING ABOUT THE AUTHOR®

Something about
the Author *was named
an "**Outstanding
Reference Source**,"
the highest honor given
by the American
Library Association
Reference and Adult
Services Division.*

ISSN 0276-816X

something ABOUT THE AUThor®

**Facts and Pictures about Authors
and Illustrators of Books for Young People**

volume 181

THOMSON

GALE

Detroit • New York • San Francisco • New Haven, Conn. • Waterville, Maine • London

Something about the Author, Volume 181

Project Editor
Lisa Kumar

Editorial
Dana Ferguson, Amy Elisabeth Fuller, Michelle Kazensky, Kathy Meek, Jennifer Mossman, Joseph Palmisano, Mary Ruby, Robert James Russell, Amanda D. Sams, Marie Toft

Permissions
Scott Bragg, Kelly Quin, Tracie Richardson

Imaging and Multimedia
Leitha Etheridge-Sims, Lezlie Light

Composition and Electronic Capture
Tracey L. Matthews

Manufacturing
Drew Kalasky

Product Manager
Peg Knight

Contents

Authors in Forthcoming Volumes vii

Introduction ix

SATA Product Advisory Board xi

Illustrations Index 199

Author Index 229

A

Ada, Alma Flor 1938- 1

Akib, Jamel 13

Aveni, Anthony 1938- 14

Aveni, Anthony Francis
  See Aveni, Anthony 14

B

Banta, Susan 19

Bardoe, Cheryl 20

Bennett, Holly 1957- 20

Berglin, Ruth Marie 1970- 22

Bernard, Patricia 1942- 23

Bernard, Trisha
  See Bernard, Patricia 23

Blankenship, LeeAnn 1944- 25

Boyne, John 1971- 27

Brown, Charlotte Lewis 29

Bruchac, Margaret M.
  See Bruchac, Marge 30

Bruchac, Marge 30

C

Callan, Jim 1951- 33

Campoy, F. Isabel 1946- 33

Ceccoli, Nicoletta 38

Cole, Henry 1955- 40

Cooney, Doug 45

Cooper, Michael L. 1950- 46

D

Darrow, Sharon 50

Day, Larry 1956- 52

Denton, Kady MacDonald 1942- 53

Derby, Ken 1956- 57

Derby, Kenneth R.
  See Derby, Ken 57

Dunbar, Polly 1980- 59

Duval, Kathy 1946- 61

E

Erlbruch, Wolf 1948- 64

F

Fine, Howard 1961- 67

Fletcher, Susan 1951- 69

Fletcher, Susan Clemens
  See Fletcher, Susan 69

Fox, Helen 1962- 74

G

Goodman, Susan E. 1952- 76

Gray, Serena
  See Sheldon, Dyan 162

Guibert, Emmanuel 1964- 80

Gwaltney, Doris 1932- 82

H

Hammond, Andrew 1970- 84

Hasler, Eveline 1933- 85

Heinz, Brian J. 1946- 86

Heinz, Brian James
  See Heinz, Brian J. 86

Helgerson, Joseph 1950- 88

J

Janisch, Heinz 1960- 90

Jarvis, Robin 1963- 93

K

Klise, Kate 96

Krommes, Beth 1956- 99

L

LaReau, Jenna 103

LaReau, Kara 103

Larson, Kirby 1954- 105

Litty, Julie 1971- 108

Lobel, Gillian 109

López, Lorraine M. 1956- 110

M

MacRae, Tom 1980- 112

Matlin, Marlee 1965- 113

McCormick, Patricia 1956- 115

Miura, Taro 1968- 117

Montserrat, Pep 118

N

Nelson, Kadir 121

Nelson, S.D. 125

Nickle, John 127

P

Pitzer, Susanna 1958- 130

Q

Quintano, D.M.
    See Sheldon, Dyan 162

R

Redlich, Ben 1977- 131

Rosen, Michael 1946- 132

Rosen, Michael Wayne
    See Rosen, Michael 132

Roth, Susan L. 143

Rubel, Nicole 1953- 147

Ruby, Laura 153

S

Sapergia, Barbara 1943- 156

Schlesinger, Arthur M., Jr. 1917-2007
    Obituary Notice 157

Schlesinger, Arthur Meier, Jr.
    See Schlesinger, Arthur M., Jr. 157

Schneider, Howie 1930-2007 158

Schubert, Leda 1945- 160

Scot-Bernard, P.
    See Bernard, Patricia 23

Sheldon, Dyan 162

Sidman, Joyce 1956- 167

Smith, Jos. A. 1936- 170

Smith, Joseph Arthur
    See Smith, Jos. A. 170

Stewart, Amber 175

Svendsen, Mark 1962- 175

Svendsen, Mark Nestor
    See Svendsen, Mark 175

V

Verniero, Joan C. 1949- 178

von Schmidt, Eric 1931-2007
    Obituary Notice 180

W

Waite, Judy Bernard
    See Bernard, Patricia 23

Washburn, Bradford 1910-2007
    Obituary Notice 180

Washburn, Henry Bradford, Jr.
    See Washburn, Bradford 180

Weatherford, Carole Boston 1956- 181

Weissberger, Ela 1930- 185

Weissberger, Ela Stein
    See Weissberger, Ela 185

Wiesner, David 1956- 186

Wilson, Jonathan 1950- 192

Wilson, Phil 1948- 194

Wintz-Litty, Julie
    See Litty, Julie 108

Y

Yerxa, Leo 1947- 195

Yoshikawa, Sachiko 196

Authors in Forthcoming Volumes

Below are some of the authors and illustrators that will be featured in upcoming volumes of *SATA*. These include new entries on the swiftly rising stars of the field, as well as completely revised and updated entries (indicated with *) on some of the most notable and best-loved creators of books for children.

Tiki Barber ∎ Barber, a former National Football League star with the New York Giants, and his identical twin brother Ronde Barber, an All-Pro cornerback with the Tampa Bay Buccaneers, are the coauthors of several illustrated books for children. Their picture books *By My Brother's Side, Game Day,* and *Teammates,* which feature illustrations by Barry Root, are one part of the brothers' off-field activities on behalf of literacy, a cornerstone of their many volunteer efforts.

*Jane Cabrera ∎ Based in London, England, Cabrera is a children's book author and illustrator who focuses on animal characters and environmental topics in her many picture books. In addition to illustrating books for authors such as Joyce Dunbar and Sally Crabtree, she has also created a number of original, self-illustrated tales that feature her brightly-colored, energetic art. Her stories for children include *Cat's Colors, The Lonesome Polar Bear,* and *Mommy, Carry Me Please!,* each of which reflect Cabrera's love of nature, family, and friends.

*Lynne Avril Cravath ∎ Cravath is a popular illustrator of books for children who finds inspiration for her lighthearted cartoon-style art in the everyday things happening all around her. Her work has appeared in a wide variety of picture books, from Stuart J. Murphy's *The Penny Pot* to Barbara Abercrombie's *The Show-and-Tell Lion* and Gail Saltz's humorous nonfiction title *Amazing You!: Getting Smart about Your Private Parts.* Gloria Whelan, Kathleen Leverich, Patricia Reilly Giff, Mary Ann Hoberman, Craig Kee Strete, and Teresa Bateman are some of the other authors whose texts are brought to life in Cravath's art.

Carmen Lomas Garza ∎ Texas-born artist Garza is committed to celebrating the history and culture of the Mexican-American community of the southern United States. She taught herself the tenets of art and drawing at a young age, heavily influenced by the artwork of her mother and grandmother. As an artist, Garza is well celebrated in the Mexican-American community in addition to being known nationally; her self-illustrated books for children include *In My Family/En mi familia, Magic Windows/Ventanas magicas,* and *Family Pictures/Cuadros de familia.*

*Uma Krishnaswami ∎ Drawing on her Asian-Indian heritage, Krishnaswami writes in a variety of genres and gears her work for many age levels. In *Stories of the Flood, The Broken Tusk: Stories of the Hindu God Ganesha,* and *Shower of Gold: Girls and Women in the Stories of India* she honed her storytelling skills in retelling traditional tales from around the world. She has also won critical praise for original picture books that focus on the merge between Indian and American cultural traditions, among them *Chachaji's Cup, The Happiest Tree: A Yoga Story,* and *Bringing Asha Home.*

Ethan Long ∎ Long is an animator, cartoonist, and educator who has also earned a following among young readers. His quirky cartoon illustrations, which have graced the pages of such humorous books as Mary Amato's *Drooling and Dangerous: The Riot Brothers Return!,* Karen M. Stegman-Bourgeois's *Trollerella,* and Jan Carr's *Greedy Apostrophe: A Cautionary Tale,* also take center stage in several original picture books. In *Tickle the Duck!* and *Stop Kissing Me!* Long introduces readers to a somewhat confrontational fowl whose constant demands and determination echo those of a demanding child.

Angela McAllister ∎ British picture-book author McAllister saw her first story, *The King Who Sneezed,* published in the late 1980s, and she has produced, on average, three books a year ever since. Paired with illustrations by a wide variety of artists, McAllister's entertaining tales include the picture books *The Wind Garden, Harry's Box,* and *The Whales' Tale,* and she moves into fantasy with the middle-grade novel *Digory the Dragon Slayer.*

Peter McCarty ∎ Noted for his evocative pencil illustrations, illustrator and author McCarty has gained critical acclaim for his award-winning picture books *Moon Plane, T Is for Terrible,* and the Caldecott Honor book *Hondo and Fabian.* From rabbits to cats and dogs and dinosaurs, MCarty's original stories feature characters whose childlike personalities endear them to young children. In *T Is for Terrible,* for instance, a Tyrannosaurus Rex bemoans his status as a much-feared carnivore with few close friends; meanwhile, a pair of household pets stray into gentle adventures in McCarty's twin picture books *Hondo and Fabian* and *Fabian Escapes.*

*Joann Sfar ∎ One of France's most popular cartoon writers, Sfar made his comic debut in 1994 and has gone on to win accolades for numerous comic-book series that have also been collected in graphic-novel format. Often working in collaboration with Emmanual Guibert, Lewis Trondheim, and others, Sfar's tales have been translated into several languages. English-language installments in his award-winning "Sardine in Outer Space" and "Little Vampire" series have won Sfar a particularly devoted readership among preteens who enjoy his quirky art and humorous wordplay.

Susan Winter ∎ Winter is best known for her collaborations with author Richard Edwards in the "Copycub" books, which include *Copy Me, Copycub, Always Copycub,* and *Good Night, Copycub.* She worked as a social worker in her native South Africa, and made her career switch while raising her family after a move to England. Although she works primarily as an illustrator, Winter also explores sibling rivalry in the original self-illustrated picture book *A Baby Just like Me.*

Introduction

Something about the Author (*SATA*) is an ongoing reference series that examines the lives and works of authors and illustrators of books for children. *SATA* includes not only well-known writers and artists but also less prominent individuals whose works are just coming to be recognized. This series is often the only readily available information source on emerging authors and illustrators. You'll find *SATA* informative and entertaining, whether you are a student, a librarian, an English teacher, a parent, or simply an adult who enjoys children's literature.

What's Inside *SATA*

SATA provides detailed information about authors and illustrators who span the full time range of children's literature, from early figures like John Newbery and L. Frank Baum to contemporary figures like Judy Blume and Richard Peck. Authors in the series represent primarily English-speaking countries, particularly the United States, Canada, and the United Kingdom. Also included, however, are authors from around the world whose works are available in English translation. The writings represented in *SATA* include those created intentionally for children and young adults as well as those written for a general audience and known to interest younger readers. These writings cover the entire spectrum of children's literature, including picture books, humor, folk and fairy tales, animal stories, mystery and adventure, science fiction and fantasy, historical fiction, poetry and nonsense verse, drama, biography, and nonfiction. Obituaries are also included in *SATA* and are intended not only as death notices but also as concise overviews of people's lives and work. Additionally, each edition features newly revised and updated entries for a selection of *SATA* listees who remain of interest to today's readers and who have been active enough to require extensive revisions of their earlier biographies.

Autobiography Feature

Beginning with Volume 103, many volumes of *SATA* feature one or more specially commissioned autobiographical essays. These unique essays, averaging about ten thousand words in length and illustrated with an abundance of personal photos, present an entertaining and informative first-person perspective on the lives and careers of prominent authors and illustrators profiled in *SATA*.

Two Convenient Indexes

In response to suggestions from librarians, *SATA* indexes no longer appear in every volume but are included in alternate (odd-numbered) volumes of the series, beginning with Volume 57.

SATA continues to include two indexes that cumulate with each alternate volume: the Illustrations Index, arranged by the name of the illustrator, gives the number of the volume and page where the illustrator's work appears in the current volume as well as all preceding volumes in the series; the Author Index gives the number of the volume in which a person's biographical sketch, autobiographical essay, or obituary appears in the current volume as well as all preceding volumes in the series.

These indexes also include references to authors and illustrators who appear in *Gale's Yesterday's Authors of Books for Children, Children's Literature Review,* and *Something about the Author Autobiography Series.*

Easy-to-Use Entry Format

Whether you're already familiar with the *SATA* series or just getting acquainted, you will want to be aware of the kind of information that an entry provides. In every *SATA* entry the editors attempt to give as complete a picture of the person's life and work as possible. A typical entry in *SATA* includes the following clearly labeled information sections:

PERSONAL: date and place of birth and death, parents' names and occupations, name of spouse, date of marriage, names of children, educational institutions attended, degrees received, religious and political affiliations, hobbies and other interests.

ADDRESSES: complete home, office, electronic mail, and agent addresses, whenever available.

CAREER: name of employer, position, and dates for each career post; art exhibitions; military service; memberships and offices held in professional and civic organizations.

MEMBER: professional, civic, and other association memberships and any official posts held.

AWARDS, HONORS: literary and professional awards received.

WRITINGS: title-by-title chronological bibliography of books written and/or illustrated, listed by genre when known; lists of other notable publications, such as plays, screenplays, and periodical contributions.

ADAPTATIONS: a list of films, television programs, plays, CD-ROMs, recordings, and other media presentations that have been adapted from the author's work.

WORK IN PROGRESS: description of projects in progress.

SIDELIGHTS: a biographical portrait of the author or illustrator's development, either directly from the biographee—and often written specifically for the *SATA* entry—or gathered from diaries, letters, interviews, or other published sources.

BIOGRAPHICAL AND CRITICAL SOURCES: cites sources quoted in "Sidelights" along with references for further reading.

EXTENSIVE ILLUSTRATIONS: photographs, movie stills, book illustrations, and other interesting visual materials supplement the text.

How a *SATA* Entry Is Compiled

SATA editors examine a wide variety of published sources to gather information for an entry. Biographical and bibliographic sources are consulted, as are book reviews, feature articles, published interviews, and material sometimes obtained from the biographee's family, publishers, agent, or other associates. Whenever possible, the author or illustrator is sent a copy of the entry to check for accuracy and completeness.

Entries that have not been verified by the biographees or their representatives are marked with an asterisk (*).

Contact the Editor

We encourage our readers to examine the entire *SATA* series. Please write and tell us if we can make *SATA* even more helpful to you. Give your comments and suggestions to the editor:

Editor
Something about the Author
The Gale Group
27500 Drake Rd.
Farmington Hills MI 48331-3535

Toll-free: 800-877-GALE
Fax: 248-699-8070

Something about the Author Product Advisory Board

The editors of *Something about the Author* are dedicated to maintaining a high standard of excellence by publishing comprehensive, accurate, and highly readable entries on a wide array of writers for children and young adults. In addition to the quality of the content, the editors take pride in the graphic design of the series, which is intended to be orderly yet inviting, allowing readers to utilize the pages of *SATA* easily and with efficiency. Despite the longevity of the *SATA* print series, and the success of its format, we are mindful that the vitality of a literary reference product is dependent on its ability to serve its users over time. As literature, and attitudes about literature, constantly evolve, so do the reference needs of students, teachers, scholars, journalists, researchers, and book club members. To be certain that we continue to keep pace with the expectations of our customers, the editors of *SATA* listen carefully to their comments regarding the value, utility, and quality of the series. Librarians, who have firsthand knowledge of the needs of library users, are a valuable resource for us. The *Something about the Author* Product Advisory Board, made up of school, public, and academic librarians, is a forum to promote focused feedback about *SATA* on a regular basis. The nine-member advisory board includes the following individuals, whom the editors wish to thank for sharing their expertise:

Eva M. Davis
Youth Department Manager,
Ann Arbor District Library,
Ann Arbor, Michigan

Joan B. Eisenberg
Lower School Librarian,
Milton Academy,
Milton, Massachusetts

Francisca Goldsmith
Teen Services Librarian,
Berkeley Public Library,
Berkeley, California

Susan Dove Lempke
Children's Services Supervisor,
Niles Public Library District,
Niles, Illinois

Robyn Lupa
Head of Children's Services,
Jefferson County Public Library,
Lakewood, Colorado

Victor L. Schill
Assistant Branch Librarian/Children's Librarian,
Harris County Public Library/Fairbanks Branch,
Houston, Texas

Caryn Sipos
Community Librarian,
Three Creeks Community Library,
Vancouver, Washington

Steven Weiner
Director,
Maynard Public Library,
Maynard, Massachusetts

something ABOUT the AUThOR

ADA, Alma Flor 1938-

Personal

Born January 3, 1938, in Camagüey, Cuba; daughter of Modesto A. (a professor) and Alma (a teacher and certified public accountant) Ada; married Armando Zubizarreta, 1961 (divorced 1971); married Jörgen Voss, 1984 (divorced 1995); children: (first marriage) Rosalma, Alfonso, Miguel, Gabriel. *Education:* Universidad Complutense de Madrid, received diploma, 1959; Pontificia Universidad Católica del Perú, M.A., 1963, Ph.D., 1965; Harvard University, postdoctoral study, 1965-67.

Addresses

Home—1459 18th St., No. 138, San Francisco, CA 94107-2801. *Office*—School of Education, University of San Francisco, 2130 Fulton St., San Francisco, CA 94117-1071.

Career

Educator and author. Colegio A. von Humboldt, Lima, Perú, head of Spanish department, 1963-65, 1967-69; Emory University, Atlanta, GA, associate professor of Romance languages, 1970-72; Mercy College of Detroit, Detroit, MI, professor, 1973-75; University of San Francisco, San Francisco, CA, professor of education, 1976—, and director of Center for Multicultural Literature for Children and Young Adults. University of Guam, Agaña, visiting professor, 1978; University of Texas, El Paso, visiting professor, 1979, 1991; Universidad Complutense, Madrid, Spain, visiting professor, 1989, 1990, 1991; St. Thomas University, Houston, TX, visiting professor, 1992, 1993; Fundación José Ortega y Gassett, Madrid, 1996, 1997, 1998. Member of selection committee, Fulbright Overseas Fellowship Program, 1968-69, 1977-78; chairperson, National Seminar on Bilingual Education, 1974, National Policy Conference on Bilingualism in Higher Education, 1978, and International Congress of Children's Literature in Spanish, 1978, 1979, 1981; publishing consultant, 1975-95; member of the board, Books for Youth and Children's Television Workshop's *Sesame Street* (Spanish edition), *Loose Leaf, Between the Lions,* and *Journal of Latinos in Education. Journal of the National Association for Bilingual Education,* founder and first editor-in-chief, University of San Francisco Reading the World annual conference, faculty advisor.

Member

International Reading Association, International Board on Books for Young People, National Association for Bilingual Education (founding member of Michigan and Illinois branches), California Association for Bilingual Education.

Awards, Honors

Fulbright scholar, 1965-67; grants from Institute for International Education, 1965-67, Emory University, 1971, and Michigan Endowment for the Arts, 1974; University of San Francisco Distinguished Research Award from School of Education, 1984; Marta Salotti

Alma Flor Ada (Reproduced by permission.)

gold medal (Argentina), 1989, for *Encaje de piedra;* University of San Francisco Outstanding Teacher Award, 1985; Christopher Award (ages eight-ten), 1992, and Notable Children's Trade Book in the Field of Social Studies, National Council for the Social Studies/ Children's Book Council, both for *The Gold Coin;* Parents' Choice Honor Book, 1995, for *Dear Peter Rabbit;* Aesop Accolade, American Folklore Association, and American Booksellers Pick-of-the-List designation, both 1995, both for *Mediopollito/Half-Chicken;* Simon Wiesenthal Museum of Tolerance Award, 1998, for *Gathering the Sun;* Gold Medal, *Parenting* magazine, 1998, for *The Lizard and the Sun;* California PTA Association Yearly Award; Latina Writers' Award, José Martí World Award (Costa Rica), and named San Francisco Public Library laureate, all 2000; Purá Belpré Award, American Library Association, 2000, for *Under the Royal Palms.*

Writings

FOR CHILDREN

(With Maria del Pilar de Olave) *El enanito de la pared y otras historias* (title means "The Wall's Dwarf and Other Tales"), Editorial Arica (Lima, Peru), 1974.

(With Maria del Pilar de Olave) *Las pintas de la mariquitas* (title means "The Ladybug's Dots"), Editorial Arica (Lima, Peru), 1974.

(With Maria del Pilar de Olave) *Saltarín y sus dos amigas y otras historias* (title means "Springy and His Two Friends, and Other Stories"), Editorial Arica (Lima, Peru), 1974.

(With Maria del Pilar de Olave) *La gallinita costurera y otras historias* (title means "The Little Hen Who Enjoyed Sewing, and Other Stories"), Editorial Arica (Lima, Peru), 1974.

Amigos/Friends, illustrated by Barry Koch, Santillana USA (Miami, FL), 1989.

¿Quién nacera aquí?/Who's Hatching Here?, illustrated by Viví Escrivá, Santillana USA (Miami, FL), 1989.

Me gustaría tener/How Happy I Would Be, Santillana USA (Miami, FL), 1989.

El canto del mosquito/The Song of the Teeny-Tiny Mosquito, Santillana USA (Miami, FL), 1989.

Una extraña visita/Strange Visitors, Santillana USA (Miami, FL), 1989.

The Gold Coin, translated from the Spanish by Bernice Randall, illustrated by Neil Waldman, Atheneum (New York, NY), 1991.

(With daughter, Rosalma Zubizarreta) *Despues de la tormenta/After the Storm,* illustrated by Viví Escrivá, Santillana USA (Compton, CA), 1991.

(With Rosalma Zubizarreta) *La piñata vacia/The Empty Piñata,* illustrated by Viví Escrivá, Santillana USA (Compton, CA), 1991.

(With Rosalma Zubizarreta) *La jaula dorada/The Golden Cage,* illustrated by Viví Escrivá, Santillana USA (Compton, CA), 1991.

(With Rosalma Zubizarreta) *Como nació el arco iris/How the Rainbow Came to Be,* illustrated by Viví Escrivá, Santillana USA (Compton, CA), 1991.

(With Rosalma Zubizarreta) *No quiero derretirme/I Don't Want to Melt,* illustrated by Viví Escrivá, Santillana USA (Compton, CA), 1991.

(With Rosalma Zubizarreta) *La hamaca de la vaca, o, Un amigo mas/In the Cow's Backyard,* illustrated by Viví Escrivá, Santillana USA (Compton, CA), 1991.

(With Rosalma Zubizarreta) *No fui yo . . ./It Wasn't Me,* illustrated by Viví Escrivá, Santillana USA (Compton, CA), 1991.

(With Rosalma Zubizarreta) *Rosa alada/A Rose with Wings,* illustrated by Viví Escrivá, Santillana USA (Compton, CA), 1991.

(With Rosalma Zubizarreta) *La sorpresa de Mamá Coneja/A Surprise for Mother Rabbit,* illustrated by Viví Escrivá, Santillana USA (Compton, CA), 1991.

(With Rosalma Zubizarreta) *¿Pavo para la Cena de Gracias? ¡No, gracias!/Turkey for Thanksgiving? No Thanks!,* illustrated by Viví Escrivá, Santillana USA (Compton, CA), 1991.

(With Rosalma Zubizarreta) *¿El susto de los fantasmas?/ What Are Ghosts Afraid Of?,* illustrated by Viví Escrivá, Santillana USA (Compton, CA), 1991.

Los seis deseos de la jirafa, illustrated by Doug Roy, Hampton-Brown (Carmel, CA), 1992, translated by Shirleyann Costigan as *Giraffe's Sad Tale (with a Happy Ending),* 1992.

Una semilla nada más, illustrated by Frank Remkiewicz, Hampton-Brown (Carmel, CA), 1992, translated by Shirleyann Costigan as *Just One Seed,* 1992.

Serafina's Birthday, illustrated by Louise Bates Satterfield, translated from the Spanish by Ana M. Cerro, Atheneum (New York, NY), 1992.

(With Rosalma Zubizarreta) *El papalote/The Kite,* illustrated by Viví Escrivá, Santillana USA (Compton, CA), 1992.

(With Rosalma Zubizarreta) *Olmo y la mariposa azul,* illustrated by Viví Escrivá, Laredo Publishing (Torrance, CA), 1992, translation by Rosalma Zubizarreta published as *Olmo and the Blue Butterfly,* Laredo Publishing (Beverly Hills, CA), 1995.

(With Janet Thorne and Philip Wingeier-Rayo) *Choices, and Other Stories from the Caribbean,* illustrated by Maria Antonia Ordonez, Friendship Press (New York, NY), 1993.

Barquitos de papel/Paper Boats, illustrated by Pablo Torrecilla, Laredo Publishing (Beverly Hills, CA), 1993.

Barriletes/Kites, illustrated by Pablo Torrecilla, Laredo Publishing (Beverly Hills, CA), 1993.

Canción de todos los niños del mundo (title means "Song of All Children of the World"), Houghton Mifflin (Boston, MA), 1993.

Días de circo, Laredo Publishing (Beverly Hills, CA), 1993, translation by Rosalma Zubizarreta published as *Circus Time,* Laredo Publishing (Beverly Hills, CA), 1993.

La tataranieta de cucarachita Martina/The Great-great-granddaughter of La Cucarachita Martina, illustrated by Ana López Escrivá, Scholastic (New York, NY), 1993.

Me gusta . . . (title means, "I Like. . ."), illustrated by Denise y Fernando, Houghton Mifflin (Boston, MA), 1993.

¡Me gusta jugar! (title means, "I Like to Play!"), illustrated by Jon Godell, McGraw Hill (New York, NY), 1993.

El pañuelo de seda, illustrated by Viví Escrivá, Laredo Publishing (Torrance, CA), 1993, translation by Rosalma Zubizarreta published as *The Silk Scarf,* Laredo Publishing (Beverly Hills, CA), 1995.

Pin, pin, sarabín, illustrated by Pablo Torrecilla, Laredo Publishing (Beverly Hills, CA), 1993.

Pregones, illustrated by Pablo Torrecilla, Laredo Publishing (Torrance, CA), 1993, translation by Rosalma Zubizarreta published as *Vendor's Calls,* Laredo Publishing (Beverly Hills, CA), 1995.

El reino de la geometría, illustrated by José Ramón Sánchez, Laredo Publishing (Torrance, CA), 1993, translation by Rosalma Zubizarreta published as *The Kingdom of Geometry,* Laredo Publishing (Beverly Hills, CA), 1995.

(Reteller) *The Rooster Who Went to His Uncle's Wedding: A Latin-American Folktale,* illustrated by Kathleen Kuchera, Putnam (New York, NY), 1993, published as *El gallo que fue a la boda de su tio,* PaperStar (New York, NY), 1998.

(With Rosalma Zubizarreta) *Dear Peter Rabbit,* illustrated by Leslie Tryon, Atheneum (New York, NY), 1994, reprinted, Aladdin (New York, NY), 2006.

En el barrio/In the Barrio, illustrated by Liliana Wilson Grez, Scholastic (New York, NY), 1994.

(With Rosalma Zubizarreta) *El unicornio del oeste/The Unicorn of the West,* illustrated by Abigail Pizer, Atheneum (New York, NY), 1994.

Me encantan los sabados . . . and Saturdays too, illustrated by Michael Bryant, Atheneum (New York, NY), 1994, English translation published as *I Love Saturdays y Domingos,* illustrated by Elivia Savadier, Atheneum (New York, NY), 1998.

El ratón de la ciudad y el ratón del campo, Grosset & Dunlap (New York, NY), 1994.

Los tres gatitos, Grosset & Dunlap (New York, NY), 1994.

Y colorín colorado, Turtleback Books (Madison, WI), 1995.

(With Pam Schiller) *A Chance for Esperanza/La oportunidad de Esperanza,* McGraw Hill (New York, NY), 1995.

Bernice the Barnacle/Más poderoso que yo, illustrated by Viví Escrivá, McGraw Hill (New York, NY), 1995.

(With Rosalma Zubizarreta) *Mediopollito/Half-Chicken: A New Version of a Traditional Story* (bilingual edition), illustrated by Kim Howard, Doubleday (New York, NY), 1995.

Mi mamá siembra fresas/My Mother Plants Strawberries, illustrated by Larry Ramond, McGraw Hill (New York, NY), 1995.

El vuelo de los colibríes (title means "The Hummingbirds' Flight"), illustrated by Judith Jacobson, Laredo Publishing (Beverly Hills, CA), 1995.

Jordi's Star, illustrated by Susan Gaber, Putnam (New York, NY), 1996.

(With Rosalma Zubizarreta) *The Lizard and the Sun/La lagartija y el sol: A Folktale in English and Spanish,* illustrated by Felipe Dávalos, Doubleday (New York, NY), 1997.

El árbol de Navidad/The Christmas Tree (bilingual edition), illustrated by Viví Escrivá, Santillana USA (Miami, FL), 1997, new edition, illustrated by Terry Ybanez, Hyperion (New York, NY), 1997.

The Malachite Palace, illustrated by Leonid Gore, translation by Rosalma Zubizarreta, Atheneum (New York, NY), 1998.

Yours Truly, Goldilocks, illustrated by Leslie Tryon, Atheneum (New York, NY), 1998.

En la playa (title means "At the Beach"), illustrated by Roberta Ludlow, Harcourt (Orlando, FL), 1999.

Three Golden Oranges, illustrated by Reg Cartwright, Atheneum (New York, NY), 1999.

Daniel's Mystery Egg, illustrated by G. Brian Karas, Harcourt (San Diego, CA), 2000, bilingual edition, 2007.

Friend Frog, illustrated by Lori Lohstoeter, Harcourt (San Diego, CA), 2000.

Daniel's Pet, illustrated by G. Brian Karas, Harcourt, (San Diego, CA), 2001, bilingual edition, 2007.

En el mar (title means "In the Ocean"), illustrated by Richard Bernal, Harcourt (Orlando, FL), 2001.

With Love, Little Red Hen, illustrated by Leslie Tryon, Atheneum (New York, NY), 2001.

(With Douglas Hill) *Brujas y magos,* Santillana USA (Miami, FL), 2002.

One More Friend, illustrated by Sophie Fatus, Harcourt (Orlando, FL), 2007.

Extra! Extra! Fairy-Tale News from Hidden Forest, illustrated by Leslie Tryon, Atheneum (New York, NY), 2007.

Also author of *Así pasaron muchos años; Canción y alegría;* and (with F. Isabel Campoy) *Cieto abierto, En un lugar muy lejano, Erase que se era, Letters, ¿Quieres que te cuente?, The New Hamster, Villacuentos,* and *Y fueron felices.*

POETRY

Una vez en el madio del mar (title means "Once upon a Time in the Middle of the Sea"), illustrated by Ulises Wensell, Escuela Española (Madrid, Spain), 1987.
A la sombra de un ala (title means "Under the Shade of a Wing"), illustrated by Ulises Wensell, Escuela Española (Madrid, Spain), 1988.
Abecedario de los animales (title means "An Animal ABC"), illustrated by Viví Escrivá, Espasa-Calpe (Madrid, Spain), 1990.
(With Rosalma Zubizarreta) *Gathering the Sun: An ABC in Spanish and English,* illustrated by Simón Silva, English Lothrop (New York, NY), 1997.
Coral y espuma (title means "Coral and Foam"), illustrated by Viví Escrivá, Espasa-Calpe (Madrid, Spain), 2003.

CHAPTER BOOKS

Encaje de piedra (title means "Stone Lace"), illustrated by Kitty Lorefice de Passalia, Editorial Guadalupe (Buenos Aires, Argentina), 1989.
El manto de pluma y otros cuentos (title means "The Feather Cloak and Other Stories"), illustrated by Viví Escrivá, Alfaguara (Compton, CA), 1990.
My Name Is María Isabel, translated from the Spanish by Ana M. Cerro, illustrated by K. Dyble Thompson, Atheneum (New York, NY), 1993.
¿Quién cuida al cocodrilo? (title means "Who Will Keep the Crocodile?"), illustrated by Viví Escrivá, Espasa-Calpe (Madrid, Spain), 1994.
(With F. Isabel Campoy) *Ecos del pasado* (title means "Echoes from the Past"), Harcourt Brace (Orlando, FL), 1996.

PLAYS; WITH F. ISABEL CAMPOY

Primer acto, Harcourt School Publishers (Orlando, FL), 1996.
Risas y aplausos, Harcourt School Publishers (Orlando, FL), 1996.
Escenas y alegrías, Harcourt School Publishers (Orlando, FL), 1996.
Actores y flores, Harcourt School Publishers (Orlando, FL), 1996.
Saludos al público, Harcourt School Publishers (Orlando, FL), 1996.
Ensayo general, Harcourt School Publishers (Orlando, FL), 1996.

Acto final, Harcourt School Publishers (Orlando, FL), 1996.
Top Hat, Alfaguara (Miami, FL), 2000.
Curtains Up!, Alfaguara (Miami, FL), 2000.
Rat-a-Tat, Alfaguara (Miami, FL), 2002, published as *Rat-a-Tat Cat,* Santillana USA (Miami, FL), 2002.
Roll 'n' Roll, Alfaguara (Miami, FL), 2002, published as *Roll 'n' Role,* Santillana USA (Miami, FL), 2002.

FOR CHILDREN; WITH F. ISABEL CAMPOY

Sigue la palabra, Harcourt School Publishers (Orlando, FL), 1995.
Imágenes del pasado, Harcourt School Publishers (Orlando, FL), 1995.
Música amiga (anthology of Hispanic folklore; includes tapes and teacher's guide), ten volumes, Del Sol (Westlake, OH), 1996–98.
Una semilla de luz (title means "A Seed of Light"), illustrated by Felipe Dávalos, Alfaguara (Madrid, Spain), 2000.
Tablado de Doña Rosita/Curtain's Up, Santillana USA (Miami, FL), 2001.
¡Feliz cumpleaños, Caperucita Roja!/Happy Birthday, Little Red Riding Hood!, illustrated by Ana López Escrivá, Alfaguara (Miami, FL), 2002.
El nuevo hogar de los siete cabritos/The New Home of the Seven Billy Goats, illustrated by Viví Escrivá, Alfaguara (Miami, FL), 2002.
Ratoncito Perex, Mailman/Ratoncito Perez, cartero, illustrated by Sandra López Escrivá, Alfaguara (Miami, FL), 2002.
One, Two, Three, Who Can It Be?/Uno, dos, tres: ¿Dime quién es?, illustrated by Viví Escrivá, Alfaguara (Miami, FL), 2002.
On the Wings of the Condor/En alas del condor, Alfaguara (Miami, FL), 2002.
Eyes of the Jaguar/Ojos del jaguar, Alfaguara (Miami, FL), 2002.
The Quetzal's Journey/Vuelo del quetzal, illustrated by Felipe Davalos, Santillana USA (Miami, FL), 2002.
(With F. Isabel Campoy) *Tales Our Abuelitas Told: An Hispanic Folktale Collection,* illustrated by Felipe Dávalos, Atheneum (New York, NY), 2004.
Mama Goose: A Latino Nursery Treasury/Un tesor de rimas infantiles, illustrated by Maribel Suárez, Hyperion (New York, NY), 2004.
Cuentos que contaban nuestras abuelitas, Atheneum (New York, NY), 2006.

"MÚSICA AMIGA" SERIES; WITH F. ISABEL CAMPOY

Gorrión, Gorrión, Harcourt School Publishers (Orlando, FL), 1996.
El verde limón, Harcourt School Publishers (Orlando, FL), 1996.
La rama azul, Harcourt School Publishers (Orlando, FL), 1996.
Nuevo día, Harcourt School Publishers (Orlando, FL), 1996.

Huertos de coral, Harcourt School Publishers (Orlando, FL), 1996.

Ríos de lava, Harcourt School Publishers (Orlando, FL), 1996.

Dulce es la sal, Harcourt School Publishers (Orlando, FL), 1996.

Canta la letra, illustrated by Ulises Wensell, Del Sol (Westlake, OH), 1998, with music by Suni Paz, 2003.

Caracolí, illustrated by Ulises Wensell, Del Sol (Westlake, OH), 1998, with music by Suni Paz, 2003.

Con ton y son, illustrated by Ulises Wensell, Del Sol (Westlake, OH), 1998, with music by Suni Paz, 2003.

Corre al coro, illustrated by Ulises Wensell, Del Sol (Westlake, OH), 1998, with music by Suni Paz, 2003.

¡Do, re, mi, sí, sí!, illustrated by Ulises Wensell, Del Sol (Westlake, OH), 1998, with music by Suni Paz, 2003.

El camino de tu risa, illustrated by Ulises Wensell, Del Sol (Westlake, OH), 1998, with music by Suni Paz, 2003.

El son de sol, illustrated by Ulises Wensell, Del Sol (Westlake, OH), 1998, with music by Suni Paz, 2003.

¡Qué rica la ronda!, illustrated by Ulises Wensell, Del Sol (Westlake, OH), 1998, with music by Suni Paz, 2003.

Sigue la música, illustrated by Ulises Wensell, Del Sol (Westlake, OH), 1998, with music by Suni Paz, 2003.

"HAGAMOS CAMINOS" SERIES; WITH MARIA DEL PILAR DE OLAVE

Partimos (title means "We Start"), illustrated by Ulises Wensell, Addison-Wesley (Reading, MA), 1986.

Andamos (title means "We Walk"), illustrated by Ulises Wensell, Addison-Wesley (Reading, MA), 1986.

Corremos (title means "We Run"), illustrated by Ulises Wensell, Addison-Wesley (Reading, MA), 1986.

Volamos (title means "We Fly"), illustrated by Ulises Wensell, Addison-Wesley (Reading, MA), 1986.

Navegamos (title means "We Sail"), illustrated by Ulises Wensell, Addison-Wesley (Reading, MA), 1986.

Exploramos (title means "We Explore"), illustrated by Ulises Wensell, Addison-Wesley (Reading, MA), 1986.

"GATEWAYS TO THE SUN" SERIES; WITH F. ISABEL CAMPOY

Smiles/Sonrisas (biographies of Pablo Picasso, Gabriela Mistral, and Benito Juarez), Alfaguara (Miami, FL), 1998.

Steps/Pasos (biographies of Rita Moreno, Fernando Botero, and Evelyn Cisneros), Alfaguara (Miami, FL), 1998.

Voices/Voces (biographies of Luis Valdez, Judith F. Baca, and Carlos J. Finlay), Alfaguara (Miami, FL), 1998.

Paths/Caminos (biographies of José Marti, Frida Kahlo, and Cesar Chavez), Alfaguara (Miami, FL), 1998.

Yo/I Am, Santillana USA (Miami, FL), 1999.

Rimas/Rhymes, Santillana USA (Miami, FL), 1999.

Poemas/Poems, Santillana USA (Miami, FL), 1999.

Palabras, Santillana USA (Miami, FL), 1999.

Mis relatos/My Stories, Santillana USA (Miami, FL), 1999.

Mis recuerdos, Santillana USA (Miami, FL), 1999.

Mambru, Santillana USA (Miami, FL), 1999.

Letras, Santillana USA (Miami, FL), 1999.

Lapices/Pencils, Santillana USA (Miami, FL), 1999.

Crayones/Crayons, Santillana USA (Miami, FL), 1999.

Colores/Colors, Santillana USA (Miami, FL), 1999.

Así soy/This Is Me, Santillana USA (Miami, FL), 1999.

Acuarela, Santillana USA (Miami, FL), 1999.

Blue and Green/Azul y verde, Alfaguara (Miami, FL), 2000.

Brush and Paint/Brocha y pinchel, Alfaguara (Miami, FL), 2000.

Artist's Easel/Caballete, Alfaguara (Miami, FL), 2000.

Canvas and Paper/Lienzo y papel, Alfaguara (Miami, FL), 2000.

(Selector) *Dreaming Fish/Pimpón* (poetry), Alfaguara (Miami, FL), 2000.

(Selector) *Laughing Crocodiles/Antón Pirulero* (poetry), Alfaguara (Miami, FL), 2000.

(Selector) *Singing Horse/Mambrú* (poetry), Alfaguara (Miami, FL), 2000.

(Selector and contributor) *Flying Dragon,* Alfaguara (Miami, FL), 2000.

Series published in Spanish translation as 'Colleccion Puertas al Sol."

"STORIES TO CELEBRATE" SERIES; WITH F. ISABEL CAMPOY

Celebrate Thanksgiving Day with Beto and Gaby, illustrated by Claudia Rueda, Santillana USA (Miami, FL), 2006.

Celebrate St. Patrick's Day with Samantha and Lola, illustrated by Sandra Lavandeira, Santillana USA (Miami, FL), 2006.

Celebrate Martin Luther King, Jr. Day with Mrs. Park's Class/Celebra ed día de Martin Luther King, Jr. con la clase de la Sra. Park, illustrated by Monica Weiss, Santillana USA (Miami, FL), 2006.

Celebrate Mardi Gras with Joaquin, Harlequin/Celebra el Mardi Gras con Joaquìn, arlequìn, illustrated by Eugenia Nobati, Santillana USA (Miami, FL), 2006.

Celebrate Hannukah with Bubbe's Tales/Celebra Hannukah con un cuento de Bubbe, illustrated by Mariano Epelbaum, Santillana USA (Miami, FL), 2006.

Celebrate Fourth of July with Champ, the Scamp/Celebra el cuatro de julio con Campeón, el glotón, illustrated by Gustavo Mazali, Santillana USA (Miami, FL), 2006.

Celebrate Christmas and Three Kings' Day with Pablo and Carlitos/Celebra la navidad y el día de los reyes magos con Pablo y Carlitos, illustrated by Walter Torres, Santillana USA (Miami, FL), 2006.

Celebrate Kwanzaa with Boots and Her Kittens/Celebra Kwanzaa con Botitas y sus gatitos, illustrated by Valeria Docampo, Santillana USA (Miami, FL), 2006.

Celebrate Halloween and the Day of the Dead with Cristina and Her Blue Bunny/Celebra el Halloween y el día de muertos con Cristina y su conejito azul, illustrated by Ivanova Martinez, Santillana USA (Miami, FL), 2006.

Celebrate Cinco de Mayo with the Mexican Hat Dance/Celebra el Cinco de Mayo con un jarabe tapatio, illustrated by Marcela Gomez and David Silva, Santillana USA (Miami, FL), 2006.

Celebrate Chinese New Year with the Fong Family/Celebra el año nuevo chino con la familia Fong, illustrated by Mima Castro, Santillana USA (Miami, FL), 2006.

Celebrate a Powwow with Sandy Starbright/Celebra un powwow con Sandy Starbright, illustrated by Maria Jesus Alvarez, Santillana USA (Miami, FL), 2006.

TEXTBOOKS AND EDUCATIONAL PUBLICATIONS

Sale el oso ("Big Book, Rimas y Risas Green" series), illustrated by Amy Myers, Hampton-Brown (Carmel, CA), 1988.

¡Manzano, Manzano!, illustrated by Sandra C. Kalthoff, Hampton-Brown (Carmel, CA), 1989.

El oso mas elegante, illustrated by Sandra C. Kalthoff, Hampton-Brown (Carmel, CA), 1989.

Cassette Guide: Culture through Literature and Music (Spanish Elementary series), illustrated by Jan Mayer, Addison-Wesley (Reading, MA), 1989.

Sol Kit, Addison-Wesley (Reading, MA), 1989.

Whole Language and Literature: A Practical Guide, Addison-Wesley (Reading, MA), 1990.

Cinco pollitos y otras poesías favoritas: Tan Small Book Set ("Días y días de poesía" series), Hampton-Brown (Carmel, CA), 1991.

Classroom Set: Tan Set ("Días y Días de Poesía" series), Hampton-Brown (Carmel, CA), 1991.

El patio de mi casa ("Early Learning Packs" series), illustrated by Liz Callen, Hampton-Brown (Carmel, CA), 1991.

Caballito blanco y otras poesías favoritas: Green Small Book Set ("Días y días de poesía" series), Hampton-Brown (Carmel, CA), 1992.

Chart Set: Green Set ("Días y Días de Poesía" series), Hampton-Brown (Carmel, CA), 1992.

Classroom Set: Green Set ("Días y días de poesía" series), Hampton-Brown (Carmel, CA), 1992.

Días y días de poesía: Complete Program (available with small books or tapes), Hampton-Brown (Carmel, CA), 1992.

Bear's Walk ("ESL Theme Links" series), illustrated by Jan Myers, Hampton-Brown (Carmel, CA), 1993.

(With Violet J. Harris and Lee Bennett Hopkins) *A Chorus of Cultures: Developing Literacy through Multicultural Poetry* (anthology), illustrated by Morissa Lipstein, Hampton-Brown (Carmel, CA), 1993.

Hampton-Brown Pre-K Program, Hampton-Brown (Carmel, CA), 1993.

(Editor, with Josefina Villamil Tinajero) *The Power of Two Languages: Literacy and Biliteracy for Spanish-speaking Students,* Macmillan/McGraw-Hill (New York, NY), 1993.

A Magical Encounter: Latino Children's Literature in the Classroom, Santillana USA (Compton, CA), 1994, 2nd edition, Allyn & Bacon (Boston, MA), 2003.

(With Pam Schiller) *DLM Pre-Kindergarten and Kindergarten Early Childhood Programs,* McGraw-Hill (New York, NY), 1995.

Actividades para el hogar, Santillana USA (Miami, FL), 2001.

Teatro del gato garabato, Santillana USA (Miami, FL), 2001.

Teatrín de Don Crispin, Santillana USA (Miami, FL), 2001.

Stories the Year 'Round/Cuentos para todo el año, Santillana USA (Miami, FL), 2001.

Stories for the Telling/Libros para contar, Santillana USA (Miami, FL), 2001.

Guía del Maestro, Santillana USA (Miami, FL), 2001.

Escenario de Polichinela, Santillana USA (Miami, FL), 2001.

(With Colin Baker) *Guía para padres y maestros de niños bilingües,* Multilingual Matters (Clevedon, England), 2002.

Also author of *Transformative Family Literacy: Engaging in Meaningful Dialogue with Spanish-speaking Parents.*

COMPILER

Poesía menuda (anthology; title means "Tiny Poetry"), Editorial Arica (Lima, Peru), 1970.

Poesía pequeña (anthology; title means "Little Poetry"), Editorial Arica (Lima, Peru), 1973.

Poesía niña (anthology; title means "Child Poetry"), Editorial Arica (Lima, Peru), 1973.

Poesía infantil (anthology; title means "Poetry for Children"), Editorial Arica (Lima, Peru), 1974.

Fabulas de siempre (title means "Everlasting Fables"), Editorial Arica (Lima, Peru), 1974.

Cuentos en verso (title means "Stories in Verse"), Editorial Arica (Lima, Peru), 1974.

Vamos a leer (title means "Let's Read"), Editorial Arica (Lima, Peru), 1974.

Adivina adivinador (title means "A Collection of Traditional Riddles"), Editorial Arica (Lima, Peru), 1974.

El nacimiento del imperio Incaico (history; title means "The Origins of the Inca Empire"), Editorial Arica (Lima, Peru), 1974.

El descubrimiento de America (history; title means "The Discovery of the New World"), Editorial Arica (Lima, Peru), 1974.

El sueño de San Martín (history; title means "San Martin's Dream"), Editorial Arica (Lima, Peru), 1974.

Las aceitunas y la cuchara (plays; title means "The Olives and the Wooden Spoon"), Editorial Arica (Lima, Peru), 1974.

La condesita peregrina y La desposada del rey (plays; title means "The Wandering Countess and The King's Bride"), Editorial Arica (Lima, Peru), 1974.

El cuento del gato y otras poesías favoritas, Hampton-Brown (Carmel, CA), 1992.

(With F. Isabel Campoy) *¡Pío peep!: Traditional Spanish Nursery Rhymes* (bilingual edition), illustrated by Viví Escrivá, English adaptations by Alice Schertle, HarperCollins (New York, NY), 2003.

(With F. Isabel Campoy) *Merry Navidad!: Christmas Carols in Spanish and English,* illustrated by Vivi Escrivá, Rayo (New York, NY), 2007.

TRANSLATOR

Lucille Clifton, *El niño que no creía en la primavera* (translation of *The Boy Who Didn't Believe in Spring*), illustrated by Brinton Turkle, Dutton (New York, NY), 1975.

Evaline Ness, *¿Tienes tiempo, Lidia?,* (translation of *Do You Have Time, Lydia?*), Dutton (New York, NY), 1975.

Norma Simon, *Cuando me enojo* (translation of *When I Get Mad*), illustrated by Dora Leder, A. Whitman (Chicago, IL), 1976.

Judith Vigna, *Gregorio y sus puntos* (translation of *Gregory's Stitches*), A. Whitman (Chicago, IL), 1977.

Barbara Williams, *El dolor de muelas de Alberto* (translation of *Albert's Toothache*), illustrated by Kay Chorao, Dutton (New York, NY), 1977.

Barbara Brenner, *Caras* (translation of *Faces*), photographs by George Ancona, Dutton (New York, NY), 1977.

Mary Garcia, *The Adventures of Connie and Diego/Las aventuras de Connie y Diego,* illustrated by Malaquis Montoya, Children's Book Press (San Francisco, CA), 1978.

Lila Perl, *Piñatas and Paper Flowers/Piñatas y flores de papel: Holidays of the Americas in English and Spanish,* illustrated by Victori de Larrea, Clarion Books (New York, NY), 1982.

Harriet Rohmer, *The Legend of Food Mountain/La leyenda de la montaña del alimento,* illustrated by Graciella Carrillo, Children's Book Press (San Francisco, CA), 1982.

Judy Blume, *¿Estás ahí, Dios? Soy yo, Margaret* (translation of *Are You There, God? It's Me, Margaret*), Bradbury Press (Scarsdale, NY), 1983.

Judy Blume, *La ballena* (translation of *Blubber*), Bradbury Press (Scarsdale, NY), 1983.

Donald Charles, *El año de gato Galano* (translation of *Calico Cat's Year*), Children's Book Press (San Francisco, CA), 1985.

Judith Viorst, *Alexander y el día terrible, horrible, espantoso, horroso* (translation of *Alexander and the Terrible, Horrible, No Good, Very Bad Day*), illustrated by Ray Cruz, Macmillan (New York, NY), 1989.

Judith Viorst, *Alexander, que era rico el domingo pasado* (translation of *Alexander, Who Was Rich Last Sunday*), illustrated by Ray Cruz, Macmillan (New York, NY), 1989.

Robert Baden, *Y domingo, siete,* edited by Judith Mathews, illustrated by Michelle Edwards, Albert Whitman (Chicago, IL), 1990.

Watty Piper, *La pequeña locomotora que si pudo* (translation of *The Little Engine That Could*), illustrated by Doris Hauman, Putnam (New York, NY), 1992.

Ruth Heller, *Las gallinas no son las unicas* (translation of *Chickens Aren't the Only Ones*), Grosset & Dunlap (New York, NY), 1992.

Val Willis, *El secreto en la caja de fosforos* (translation of *The Secret in the Matchbox*), illustrated by John Shelley, Farrar, Straus (New York, NY), 1993.

(With Rosalma Zubizarreta) Harriet Rohmer, *Uncle Nacho's Hat/El sombrero del tío Nacho,* illustrated by Mira Reisberg, Children's Book Press (San Francisco, CA), 1993.

Karen Ackerman, *Al amanecer* (translation of *By the Dawn's Early Light*), illustrated by Catherine Stock, Atheneum (New York, NY), 1994.

Keith Baker, *¿Quíen es la bestia?* (translation of *Who Is the Beast?*), Harcourt (San Diego, CA), 1994.

Kristine L. Franklin, *El niño pastor* (translation of *The Shepherd Boy*), illustrated by Jill Kastner, Macmillan (New York, NY), 1994.

James Howe, *Hay un dragón en mi bolsa de dormir* (translation of *There's a Dragon in My Sleeping Bag*), illustrated by David S. Rose, Atheneum (New York, NY), 1994.

Lynne Cherry, *El gran capoquero* (translation of *The Great Kapok Tree*), Harcourt (San Diego, CA), 1994.

Nancy Luenn, *El cuento de Nessa* (translation of *Nessa's Story*), illustrated by Neil Waldman, Atheneum (New York, NY), 1994.

Barbara Shook Hazen, *Fue el gorila* (translation of *The Gorilla Did It*), illustrated by Ray Cruz, Atheneum (New York, NY), 1994.

Barbara Shook Hazen, *¡Adiós! Hola!* (translation of *Goodbye! Hello!*), illustrated by Michael Bryant, Atheneum (New York, NY), 1995.

Nancy Luenn, *La pesca de Nessa* (translation of *Nessa's Fish*), illustrated by Neil Waldman, Atheneum (New York, NY), 1995.

Carolyn S. Bailey, *El conejito que queria tener alas rojas* (translation of *The Little Rabbit That Wanted to Have Red Wings*), illustrated by Jacqueline Rogers, Putnam (New York, NY), 1995.

Margery Williams, *El conejito de pana* (translation of *The Velveteen Rabbit*), illustrated by Florence Graham, Putnam (New York, NY), 1995.

Ann Hayes, *Te presento a la orquesta* (translation of *Meet the Orchestra*), illustrated by Karmen Thompson, Harcourt (San Diego, CA), 1995.

Carol Snyder, *Uno arriba, uno abajo* (translation of *One Up, One Down*), illustrated by Maxie Chambliss, Atheneum (New York, NY), 1995.

Judith Viorst, *Alexander que de ninguna manera—¿le oyen?—¡lo dice en serio!—se va a mudar* (translation of *Alexander Who Is Not—Do You Hear Me?—Going—I Mean It!—to Move*), illustrated by Robin Preiss Glasser, Libros Colibri (New York, NY), 1995.

Judith Viorst, *Alexander se muda* (translation of *Alexander Moves*), Atheneum (New York, NY), 1995.

Audrey Wood, *La casa adormecida* (translation of *The Napping House*), illustrated by Don Wood, Harcourt (San Diego, CA), 1995.

Julie Vivas, *La Natividad* (translation of *The Nativity*), Harcourt (San Diego, CA), 1995.

Sue Williams, *Sali de paseo* (translation of *I Went Walking*), Harcourt (San Diego, CA), 1995.

Jane Yolen, *Encuentro* (translation of *Encounter*), illustrated by David Shannon, Harcourt (San Diego, CA), 1996.

Cynthia Rylant, *Henry y Mudge: el primer libro de sus aventuras* (translation of *Henry and Mudge*), illustrated by Suçie Stevenson, Aladdin (New York, NY), 1996.

Cynthia Rylant, *Henry y Mudge con barro hasta el rabo: segundo libro de sus aventuras* (translation of *Henry*

and Mudge in Puddle Trouble), illustrated by Suçie Stevenson, Aladdin (New York, NY), 1996.

Cynthia Rylant, *Henry y Mudge y el mejor día del año* (translation of *Henry and Mudge and the Best Day of All*), illustrated by Suçie Stevenson, Aladdin (New York, NY), 1997.

Pat Hutchins, *El paseo de Rosie* (translation of *Rosie's Walk*), Aladdin (New York, NY), 1997.

TRANSLATOR; WITH F. ISABEL CAMPOY

Lois Ehlert, *Plumas para almorzar* (translation of *Feathers for Lunch*), Harcourt (San Diego, CA), 1996.

Lois Ehlert, *A sembrar sopa de verduras* (translation of *Growing Vegetable Soup*), Harcourt (San Diego, CA), 1996.

Gary Soto, *¡Que montón de tamales!*, (translation of *Too Many Tamales*), illustrated by Ed Martinez, PaperStar (New York, NY), 1996.

Ellen Stoll Walsh, *Salta y brinca* (translation of *Hop Jump*), Harcourt (San Diego, CA), 1996.

Henry Horenstein, *Béisobol en los barrios,* Harcourt (New York, NY), 1997.

Mem Fox, *Quienquiera que seas* (translation of *Whoever You Are*), illustrated by Leslie Staub, Harcourt (San Diego, CA), 2002.

Gerald McDermott, *Zomo el conejo: un cuento de Africa occidental* (translation of *Zomo the Rabbit*), Harcourt (San Diego, CA), 2002.

Peter Golenbock, *Compañeros de equipo* (translation of *Teammates*), illustrated by Paul Bacon, Harcourt (San Diego, CA), 2002.

Lois Ehlert, *Día de mercado* (translation of *Market Day*), Harcourt (San Diego, CA), 2003.

George Ancona, *Mis bailes/My Dances,* photographs by Ancona, Children's Press (New York, NY), 2004.

George Ancona, *Mis amigos/My Friends,* photographs by Ancona, Children's Press (New York, NY), 2004.

George Ancona, *Mi familia/My Family,* photographs by Ancona, Children's Press (New York, NY), 2004.

George Ancona, *Mi escuela/My School,* photographs by Ancona, Children's Press (New York, NY), 2004.

George Ancona, *Mi casa/My House,* photographs by Ancona, Children's Press (New York, NY), 2004.

George Ancona, *Mi barrio/My Neighborhood,* photographs by Ancona, Children's Press (New York, NY), 2004.

George Ancona, *Mis quehaceres/My Chores,* photographs by Ancona, Children's Press (New York, NY), 2005.

George Ancona, *Mis juegos/My Games,* photographs by Ancona, Children's Press (New York, NY), 2005.

George Ancona, *Mis fiestas/My Celebrations,* photographs by Ancona, Children's Press (New York, NY), 2005.

George Ancona, *Mis comidas/My Foods,* photographs by Ancona, Children's Press (New York, NY), 2005.

George Ancona, *Mi musica/My Music,* photographs by Ancona, Children's Press (New York, NY), 2005.

FOR ADULTS; WITH F. ISABEL CAMPOY

Home School Interaction with Culturally or Language-diverse Families, Del Sol (Westlake, OH), 1998.

Ayudando a nuestros hijos (title means "Helping Our Children"), Del Sol (Westlake, OH), 1998.

Comprehensive Language Arts, Del Sol (Westlake, OH), 1998.

Effective English Acquisition for Academic Success, Del Sol (Westlake, OH), 1998.

(With F. Isabel Campoy and Rosalma Zubizarreta) *Authors in the Classroom: A Transformative Education Process,* Allyn & Bacon (Boston, MA), 2004.

OTHER

(Author of introduction) Mayra Fernandez, *Barrio Teacher,* Sandcastle Publishing, 1992.

Where the Flame Trees Bloom (memoir), illustrated by Antonio Martorell, Atheneum (New York, NY), 1994.

Escribiendo desde el corazón/Writing from the Heart (video), Del Sol (Westlake, OH), 1996.

Meeting an Author (video), Del Sol (Westlake, OH), 1996.

Under the Royal Palms: A Childhood in Cuba (autobiography), Atheneum (New York, NY), 1998.

Aprender cantando I y II (sound recording; title means "Learning through Songs"), voice and music by Suni Paz, Del Sol (Westlake, OH), 1998.

Como una flor (sound recording; title means "Like a Flower"), voice and music by Suni Paz, Del Sol (Westlake, OH), 1998.

A pesar del amor (novel for adults; title means "Love Notwithstanding"), Alfaguara (Miami, FL), 2003.

Alma Flor Ada and You, foreword by Janet Hill and Anthony L. Manna, Libraries Unlimited (Westport, CT), 2006.

Also author of *Pedro Salinal: el diálogo creador,* and *Aserrin Aserran.* Coauthor of "Cuentamundos" literature-based reading series, Macmillan/McGraw-Hill, 1993. Contributor to *In Grandmothers' House: Award-winning Authors Tell Stories about Their Grandmothers,* edited by Bonnie Christiensen, HarperCollins, 2003.

Adaptations

Andamos, Corremos, Exploramos, Navegamos, Partimos, and *Volamos* were adapted for audiocassette by Addison-Wesley, 1987; *Gathering the Sun, Coral y espuma,* and *Abecedario de los animales/An Animal ABC* were voiced by Suni Paz for audio recording and produced by Del Sol (Westlake, OH), 1998; many of the author's books were adapted for audiocassette by Santillana USA, 1999-2000.

Sidelights

Alma Flor Ada is a prolific storyteller as well as a prime mover in the bilingual education movement. As an educator, she promotes the use of literature as an integral part of the curriculum and emphasizes that everyone— teachers, students, and students' families—has important stories, life experiences, and thoughts that deserve to be written and shared. Through her many books, Ada

also serves as a cultural liaison by retelling traditional Latin-American tales, presenting stories set in Latin America, and giving voice to children confronting new cultures and learning to take pride in their Hispanic heritage. Her materials are often used in classrooms where both English and Spanish are taught, and she has done much to give Hispanic culture a wider representation through her nonfiction children's books. At the same time, her children's books, which are available in both English and bilingual versions, have garnered a devoted following among English-speaking children, and Ada expanded into adult fiction in 2003 with the novel *A pesar del amor.*

Ada was born in Camagüey, Cuba, in 1938, and spent her childhood in a region rich with stories. The eleven vignettes in her book *Where the Flame Trees Bloom* contain Ada's memories of growing up in Cuba. In the evenings, family members would reminisce, telling the stories on which Ada has based many of her bilingual tales for children. One of the short stories in *Where the Flame Trees Bloom* offers a portrait of Ada's grandfather, who was confronted at the same time with his wife's imminent death and the collapse of the Cuban economy. Another story recounts how Ada's blind great-grandmother crafted dolls for poor children. Ada also recalls the time when her uncle, a schoolteacher, feared for his students' lives when the school was struck by lightning, an experience that helped him realize the significance of his job as a teacher. According to a critic in the *Bulletin of the Center for Children's Books,* Ada's writing "evokes the warmth and character of her family," and *School Library Journal* contributor Marilyn Long Graham described Ada's writing as "elegant."

More memories of growing up in Cuba during the 1940s fill the pages of Ada's *Under the Royal Palms: A Childhood in Cuba* and *Tales Our Abuelitas Told: An Hispanic Folktale Collection* contains remembered tales as well as an introduction in which Ada and collaborator Campoy "explain . . . how stories develop and change over time," according to *School Library Journal* critic Kirsten Cutler. While in *Where the Flame Trees Bloom* Ada recounts stories she was told as a young girl, the narrative of *Under the Royal Palms* presents her own childhood experiences. "At the core of the collection, there is a heartfelt portrayal of a quickly disappearing culture and a vastly beautiful land," observed a contributor to *Publishers Weekly. Under the Royal Palms* received the Purá Belpré Award of the American Library Association in 2000.

Leaving Cuba as a young woman, Ada enrolled at the Universidad Complutense in Madrid, Spain, and then earned her doctorate in Peru. Postdoctoral studies at Harvard University and at the Radcliffe Institute led Ada to a teaching position at Emory University. She has spent the major part of her career at the University of San Francisco, as both a professor of education and the director for the Center for Multicultural Literature for Children and Young Adults. Her work as a scholar

of Romance languages—she is the author of a major study on Spanish poet Pedro Salinas—has been a strong influence on her writing. Another major influence has been her active promotion of bilingualism and multiculturalism. The author also credits her children as a "constant source of inspiration." She once told *SATA,* "I was brought back to my childhood calling, when, in the midst of writing a very scholarly work, my daughter, who was three years old at the time, complained that I was writing very ugly books." Ada's daughter, Rosalma Zubizarreta, has become an author in her own right and has translated many of her mother's books, her role as inspiration taken over by Ada's grandchildren.

In *The Rooster Who Went to His Uncle's Wedding,* a retelling of a traditional Latin-American folktale, Ada creates an "unusually appealing readaloud," according to a *Kirkus Reviews* writer. In this humorous cumulative tale, a rooster spends so much time grooming himself in preparation for his uncle's wedding that he forgets to eat breakfast. On the way to the wedding, he cannot resist pecking at a kernel of corn he finds in a mud puddle. The rooster asks the grass to clean his muddy beak, but the grass will not help. A lamb refuses to eat the grass, and a dog refuses to bite the lamb . . . but at last the sun, who has always enjoyed the rooster's sunrise song, agrees to help the rooster. *School Library Journal* critic Lauralyn Persson recommended *The Rooster Who Went to His Uncle's Wedding* as a "solid addition to folklore collections."

Ada retells a Spanish folktale in *The Three Golden Oranges,* as three brothers who wish to marry are instructed by a wise old woman to travel to a distant castle and return with three golden oranges. The two foolish older brothers refuse to follow instructions, but the faithfulness of the kind younger son is ultimately rewarded by marriage to the beautiful princess Blancaflor, who helps the young man rescue his brothers. In addition to detecting a feminist twist in the story's ending, in which Blancaflor's sisters refuse to marry the foolish brothers, reviewers praised Ada's simplified rendition of a fairly complex traditional tale. Moving her focus to Mexico, Ada's bilingual picture book *The Lizard and the Sun/La lagartija y el sol* includes an English translation by Zubizarreta. In the story, the Sun has disappeared, and everyone has gone out to search for him. Long after others have given up, Lizard continues to search, eventually finding the Sun curled up inside a rock. "Readers will cheer Lizard as she find the Earth's source of light and warmth," observed Vianela Rivas in *School Library Journal.*

Set in colonial Mexico, *Mediopollito/Half-Chicken: A New Version of a Traditional Story* tells the story of how the weathervane came to be. The story begins with the birth of Half-Chicken, whose unusual appearance—he was born with only one wing and one leg—makes him something of a celebrity in his small village. Desiring more fame, Half-Chicken travels to Mexico City to meet the Spanish viceroy. Along his journey, he

befriends a stream, fire, and wind, all of whom end up coming to his aid when the viceroy's cook decides that Half-Chicken would make a tasty soup. *Mediopollito* is "brimming with silliness and the simple repetition that children savor," remarked Annie Ayres in *Booklist*.

In addition to folk-tale adaptations, Ada has created numerous original picture-book stories. Featuring a fairy-tale theme, *The Malachite Palace* features a lonely young princess who captures a songbird to be her friend. When the songbird ceases to sing, the princess realizes she needs to release him. Once free, the bird helps the girl learn to venture out of her own cage and make friends with children her own age, regardless of their social differences. "Although the story is not highly original, youngsters will enjoy its gentle familiarity," remarked Denise E. Agosto in *School Library Journal*. Another lonely character is at the center of *Jordi's Star,* another original picture book by Ada. Here Jordi tends a herd of goats on a barren hillside. In his loneliness, he comes to believe that a star's reflection in a pool of water is a fallen star which has come to befriend him. Jordi tends the star with care, decorating the place where it dwells until the barren landscape is transformed by his love. "Written with strong emotion and a sense of wonder, this story has the tone and resonance of a folktale," noted Joy Fleishhacker in *School Library Journal,* while *Booklist* critic Susan Dove Lempke called the book a "touching, lyrically told story."

Ada received a Parents' Choice Honor Award for *Dear Peter Rabbit,* a fantasy illustrated by Leslie Tryon that weaves together the tales of storybook characters such as the Three Little Pigs, the Big Bad Wolf, Little Red Riding Hood, Peter Rabbit, Goldilocks, and Baby Bear. Goldilocks is recast as the daughter of Mr. McGregor, the farmer who almost catches Peter Rabbit in the beloved stories by Beatrix Potter. Through the letters the two send to one another, readers learn about the pair's various adventures and misadventures. "Children will be enchanted by this opportunity to meet familiar faces in new settings," commented *School Library Journal* reviewer Joy Fleishhacker. Pointing out that Ada's book belongs to the genre of fairy-tale parodies, Roger Sutton asserted in the *Bulletin of the Center for Children's Books* that *Dear Peter Rabbit* "is as clever as most in the genre."

Ada and Tryon present a sequel to *Dear Peter Rabbit* in *Yours Truly, Goldilocks,* which finds the fairy-tale characters continuing to corresponding in preparation for a housewarming party at the Three Little Pigs' new, wolf-proof home. "This is fairy-tale fun at its best," wrote Beth Tegart in *School Library Journal*. Another sequel, *With Love, Little Red Hen,* covers the arrival of Little Red Hen in the Hidden Forest, the enchanted wood that provided the setting for the first two books. "Lovers of fractured fairy tales will be amused by this further peek into the personal letters of familiar characters," predicted a contributor to *Kirkus Reviews,* while Bina Wil-

Ada's warmhearted picture book **With Love, Little Red Hen** *is brought to life in warm-toned paintings by Leslie Tryon.* (Illustration © 2001 by Leslie Tryon. Reprinted by permission of Atheneum Books for Young Readers, an imprint of Simon & Schuster Children's Publishing Division.)

liams wrote in *School Library Journal* that *With Love, Little Red Hen* and its prequels combine to present readers with a "fun look at nursery rhymes and at letter writing."

In Ada's award-winning picture book *The Gold Coin* a greedy thief named Juan watches through the window, Doña Josefa admires a gold coin and tells herself aloud that she must be the richest woman in the world. Hoping to steal the elderly woman's wealth, Joan lies in wait until she departs. He finds no treasure when he ransacks the home, so Joan begins to pursue the elderly Doña Josefa, intending to force her to give him her gold. When he asks around for her, everyone assumes he must be her friend, and Juan is gradually transformed as he encounters the friendship and goodwill of all the people Doña Josefa has helped. As Ann Welton remarked in *School Library Journal, The Gold Coin* "makes an important point" about the nature of true wealth and the consequences of greed. A critic for *Publishers Weekly* described Ada's story as "unusual" and "rewarding," concluding that it is "worthy of repeated readings."

Raising the self-esteem of Spanish-speaking children and children of Hispanic origin living in a society where Anglo culture dominates is the unstated goal of most of Ada's work. In *My Name Is María Isabel,* María Isabel's family has moved, and she must attend a new school. There are already two Marías in her class, so the teacher decides to give the new girl the name "Mary

Lopez" instead of María Isabel Salazar López. María Isabel has difficulty identifying herself as "Mary," which leads to some unhappy situations. Yet when María Isabel describes her difficulties in an essay she has been assigned, the teacher realizes her mistake and finds a way to remedy the situation. As Irvy Gilbertson wrote in *Five Owls,* the "link of María Isabel's name with her heritage is an important theme in this story," and various Spanish words are used to "expose the reader to a different culture."

I Love Saturdays y Domingos makes "a strong statement about cultural diversity and the universality of love," remarked Ann Welton in *School Library Journal.* In this book, a little girl recounts with joy the pleasures she experiences on the Saturdays she spends with her grandma and grandpa, as well as the Sundays (*domingos*) she spends with her abuelito and abuelita. Both sets of grandparents join together in a celebration of the girl's birthday, illustrating the blessing of belonging to two worlds. Reviewers noted that Ada's bilingual format encourages young readers to understand Spanish-language terms, and a contributor to *Kirkus Reviews* remarked of *I Love Saturdays y Domingos* that "children eager to explore their own heritage will enjoy watching as the heroine embraces all the diversity in her life."

Ada's bilingual picture books, such as *Gathering the Sun: An ABC in Spanish and English* and *¡Pío Peep!: Traditional Spanish Nursery Rhymes,* are often credited as proof that bilingual education can be attractive and motivating for children while offering high aesthetic, literary, and human values. The books in her "Gateways to the Sun" series, coauthored with Campoy, incorporate poetry, theater, art, and biographies of cultural leaders. This collection offers children the opportunity to enjoy the various contributions that have shaped Hispanic culture. "Nothing can surpass the inherent musicality of the [Spanish] language, the deep cultural values incorporated in it," she noted in her publicity release. "Yet [Spanish-speaking] children also need to read the literature that their peers are reading in English, so that their introduction to American culture occurs through the best medium the culture has to offer."

Biographical and Critical Sources

BOOKS

Children's Literature Review, Volume 62, Thomson Gale (Detroit, MI), 2000.
Notable Hispanic American Women, Book II, Thomson Gale (Detroit, MI), 1998.
Zipes, Jack, editor, *The Oxford Companion to Fairy Tales,* Oxford University Press (New York, NY), 2000.

PERIODICALS

American Book Review, November-December, 1997, George R. Bodmer, review of *Gathering the Sun: An ABC in Spanish and English,* pp. 12-13.

Booklist, March 1, 1991, review of *The Gold Coin,* pp. 1395-1396; March 1, 1993, Graciela Italiano, review of *The Rooster Who Went to His Uncle's Wedding,* p. 1231; June 1, 1993, Ilene Cooper, review of *My Name Is María Isabel,* p. 1828; May 1, 1994, Ilene Cooper, review of *Dear Peter Rabbit,* p. 1606; February 1, 1995, Isabel Schon, review of *La pesca de Nessa,* p. 1012; September 15, 1995, Annie Ayres, review of *Mediopollito/Half-Chicken: A New Version of a Traditional Story,* p. 165; December 1, 1996, Susan Dove Lempke, review of *Jordi's Star,* p. 652; April 15, 1997, Annie Ayers, review of *Gathering the Sun,* p. 1431; December 15, 1997, Julie Corsaro, review of *The Lizard and the Sun/La lagartija el sol: A Folktale in English and Spanish,* p. 698; May 1, 1998, Ilene Cooper, review of *Yours Truly, Goldilocks,* p. 1520; May 15, 1998, Hazel Rochman, review of *The Malachite Palace,* p. 1629; November 15, 1998, Hazel Rochman, review of *Under the Royal Palms,* p. 582; May 15, 1999, Hazel Rochman, review of *The Three Golden Oranges,* p. 1698; September 15, 1999, review of *Under the Royal Palms,* p. 254; August, 2000, Isabel Schon, review of *Antón Pirulero,* p. 2154; July, 2001, Carolyn Phelan, review of *Daniel's Mystery Egg,* p. 2022; September 15, 2001, Lauren Peterson, review of *With Love, Little Red Hen,* p. 229; February 1, 2002, Annie Ayres, review of *I Love Saturdays y Domingos,* p. 944; February 15, 2002, Isabel Schon, reviews of *Ratoncito Perez, Mailman, The New Home of the Seven Billy Goats,* and *Happy Birthday, Little Red Riding Hood!,* p. 1022; March 15, 2005, Jennifer Mattson, review of *Mama Goose: A Latino Nursery Treasury/Un tesoro de rimas infantiles,* p. 1296; September 1, 2006, Hazel Rochman, review of *Tales Our Abuelitas Told: An Hispanic Folktale Collection,* p. 124.

Book Report, May-June, 1995, Sherry York, review of *Where the Flame Trees Bloom,* p. 45.

Bulletin of the Center for Children's Books, April, 1994, Roger Sutton, review of *Dear Peter Rabbit,* p. 249; February, 1995, Susan Dove Lempke, review of *Where the Flame Trees Bloom,* p. 190; December, 1996, Amy E. Brandt, review of *Jordi's Star,* p. 126; June, 1997, Janice M. Del Negro, review of *Gathering the Sun,* pp. 348-349; October, 1997, Janice M. Del Negro, review of *The Lizard and the Sun,* p. 40; March, 1998, Pat Matthews, review of *The Malachite Palace,* pp. 234-235; May, 2005, review of *Mama Goose,* p. 370; March, 2007, Hope Morrison, review of *Tales Our Abuelitas Told,* p. 282.

Five Owls, September-October, 1993, Irvy Gilbertson, review of *My Name Is María Isabel,* p. 14.

Horn Book, January-February, 1988, Laurie Sale, review of *The Adventures of Connie and Diego/Las aventuras de Connie y Diego,* p. 89; March-April, 1995, Martha V. Parravano, review of *Where the Flame Trees Bloom,* p. 218; November-December, 1995, Martha V. Parravano, review of *Mediopollito,* p. 749; January-February, 2002, Kitty Flynn, review of *I Love Saturdays y Domingos,* p. 65.

Kirkus Reviews, January 1, 1991, review of *The Gold Coin,* p. 42; May 1, 1993, review of *The Rooster Who Went*

to His Uncle's Wedding, p. 591; March 1, 1994, review of *Dear Peter Rabbit,* p. 297; July 15, 1995, review of *Mediopollito,* p. 1020; July 1, 1997, review of *The Lizard and the Sun,* p. 1026; December 15, 1997, review of *El arbol de Navidad/The Christmas Tree,* p. 1832; May 1, 1998, review of *The Malachite Palace,* p. 654; May 1, 1999, review of *The Three Golden Oranges,* p. 718; September 1, 2001, review of *Daniel's Mystery Egg,* p. 1284; October 1, 2001, review of *With Love, Little Red Hen,* p. 1418; December 1, 2001, review of *I Love Saturdays y Domingos,* p. 1680; March 1, 2003, review of *In My Grandmother's House: Award-winning Authors Tell Stories about Their Grandmothers,* p. 380; April 15, 2003, review of *¡Pío Peep!: Traditional Spanish Nursery Rhymes,* p. 603; March 1, 2005, review of *Mama Goose,* p. 283; August 15, 2006, review of *Tales Our Abuelitas Told,* p. 837.

Language Arts, November, 1995, Miriam Martinez and Marcia F. Nash, review of *Where the Flame Trees Bloom,* pp. 542-543; March, 1996, review of *Me llamo María Isabel,* p. 207.

Library Journal, August, 2001, Lucia M. Gonzalez, review of *Abecedario de los animales-Animal ABC,* p. S26.

Publishers Weekly, April 22, 1983, review of *Piñatas and Paper Flowers,* p. 126; June-July, 1987, review of *The Adventures of Connie and Diego,* p. 82; January 11, 1991, review of *The Gold Coin,* p. 103; February, 1991, review of *Y domingo, siete* and *Amigos,* p. 102; April 19, 1993, review of *My Name Is María Isabel,* p. 62; April 26, 1993, review of *The Rooster Who Went to His Uncle's Wedding,* p. 76; February 21, 1994, review of *Dear Peter Rabbit,* p. 253; November 4, 1996, review of *Jordi's Star,* p. 75; March 31, 1997, review of *Gathering the Sun,* p. 76; October 6, 1997, review of *The Christmas Tree,* p. 54; May 4, 1998, Jennifer M. Brown, review of *The Malachite Palace,* p. 212; May 25, 1998, review of *Yours Truly, Goldilocks,* p. 89; December 7, 1998, review of *Under the Royal Palms,* p. 61; May 31, 1999, review of *Three Golden Oranges,* p. 93; December 10, 2001, review of *I Love Saturdays y Domingos,* p. 69.

Reading Teacher, September, 1993, Kathy G. Short and Kathryn Mitchell Pierce, review of *The Gold Coin,* p. 46; September, 1998, review of *The Lizard and the Sun,* p. 58.

School Library Journal, January, 1981, L. Michael Espinosa, review of *El niño que no creía en la primavera, Caras,* and *El dolor de muelas de Alberto,* p. 33; February, 1988, Louise Yarian Zwick, review of *Volamos, Partimos, Exploramos, Corremos, Andamos,* and *¡Manzano, Manzano!,* p. 92; February, 1990, review of *Alexander y el día terrible, horrible, espantoso, horroso* and *Alexander, que era rico el domingo pasado,* p. 120; August, 1990, Louise Yarian Zwick and Mark Zwick, review of *¿Quién nacera aquí?, Me gustaría tener . . . , Una extraña visita, El canto del mosquito,* and *Abecedario de los animales-Animal ABC,* p. 172; April, 1991, Ann Welton, review of *The Gold Coin,* p. 88; September, 1992, Alexandra Marris, review of *Serafina's Birthday,* p. 196; November,

1992, Rose Zertuche Trevino, review of *Olmo y la mariposa azul,* p. 133; April, 1993, Ann Welton, review of *My Name Is María Isabel,* p. 117; May, 1993, Lauralyn Persson, review of *The Rooster Who Went to His Uncle's Wedding,* p. 92; August, 1993, Rose Zertuche Trevino, review of *El secreto en la caja de fosforos,* p. 204; June, 1994, Jane Marino, review of *The Unicorn of the West,* p. 94; July, 1994, Joy Fleishhacker, review of *Dear Peter Rabbit,* p. 73; August, 1994, Rose Zertuche Trevino, review of *El unicornio del oeste,* p. 181; November, 1994, Rose Zertuche Trevino, review of *¿Quién es la bestia?* and *Querido Pedrin,* p. 130, and review of *La Natividad,* p. 131; February, 1995, Marilyn Long Graham, review of *Where the Flame Trees Bloom,* p. 96, and Rose Zertuche Trevino, review of *Hay un dragón en mi bolsa de dormir, Fue el gorila, Me llamo María Isabel,* and *Al amanecer,* p. 126; August, 1995, Rose Zertuche Trevino, review of *One Up, One Down* and *Good-Bye! Hello!,* p. 167; November, 1995, Graciela Italiano, review of *Mediopollito,* p. 87; February, 1996, Rose Zertuche Trevino, review of *Sali de paseo* and *Te presento a la orquesta,* pp. 128, 130; June, 1996, Cynthia R. Richey and Doreen S. Hurley, review of *The Gold Coin,* p. 54; August, 1996, Rose Zertuche Trevino, review of *Alexander que de ninguna manera—¡le oyen?—¡lo dice en serio!—se va a mudar,* p. 179; December, 1996, Joy Fleishhacker, review of *Jordi's Star,* p. 84; March, 1997, Ann Welton, review of *Gathering the Sun,* pp. 169-170; August, 1997, Vianela Rivas, review of *The Lizard and the Sun/La lagartija y el sol,* p. 180; October, 1997, Jane Marino, review of *The Christmas Tree,* p. 40; May, 1998, Denise E. Agosto, review of *The Malachite Palace,* p. 106; July, 1998, Beth Tegart, review of *Yours Truly, Goldilocks,* p. 64; December, 1998, Sylvia V. Meisner, review of *Under the Royal Palms,* p. 132; July, 1999, Sally Bates Goodroe, review of *Three Golden Oranges,* p. 83; October, 2001, Bina Williams, review of *With Love, Little Red Hen,* p. 104; January, 2002, Ann Welton, review of *I Love Saturdays y Domingos,* p. 89; February, 2002, Kathleen Simonetta, review of *Daniel's Mystery Egg,* p. 96; June, 2003, "The Dynamic Duo of Alma Flor Ada and F. Isabel Campoy," p. 60; July, 2003, Ann Welton, review of *¡Pio Peep!,* p. 121; May, 2005, Ann Welton, review of *Mama Goose,* p. 118.

ONLINE

Alma Flor Ada Home Page, http://www.almaada.com (July 18, 2007).

Houghton Mifflin Reading Web site, http://www.eduplace.com/kids/ (July 18, 2007).

University of San Francisco Web site, http://www.soe.usfca.edu/childlit/ (April 8, 2002), "Alma Flor Ada."

OTHER

Ada, Alma Flor, "Alma Flor Ada" (publicity release), Atheneum (New York, NY), 1994.*

AKIB, Jamel

Personal

Male.

Addresses

Home and office—Leigh-on-Sea, Essex, England.
Agent—Illustration Ltd., 2 Brooks Court, Cringle St.,
London SW8 5BX, England.

Career

Illustrator.

Awards, Honors

Marion Vannett Ridgway Honor Book, 2004, for *Monsoon* by Uma Krishnaswami.

Illustrator

Uma Krishnaswami, *Monsoon,* Farrar, Straus & Giroux
(New York, NY), 2003.
Uma Krishnaswami, *Bringing Asha Home,* Lee & Low
Books (New York, NY), 2006.

"CLASSIC STARTS" SERIES

Martin Woodside, reteller, *Gulliver's Travels* (based on the
story by Jonathan Swift), Sterling Publishing (New
York, NY), 2006.
Kathleen Olmstead, reteller, *The Strange Case of Dr. Jekyll
and Mr. Hyde* (based on the story by Robert Louis
Stevenson), Sterling Publishing (New York, NY),
2006.
Deanna McFadden, reteller, *Frankenstein* (based on the
story by Mary Shelley), Sterling Publishing (New
York, NY), 2006.
Tania Zamorsky, reteller, *Dracula* (based on the story by
Bram Stoker), Sterling Publishing (New York, NY),
2006.
Deanna McFadden, reteller, *Robinson Crusoe* (based on
the story by Daniel Defoe), Sterling Publishing (New
York, NY), 2006.
Oliver Ho, reteller, *The Red Badge of Courage* (based on
the story by Steven Crane), Sterling Publishing (New
York, NY), 2006.
Deanna McFadden, reteller, *Around the World in 80 Days*
(based on the story by Jules Verne), Sterling Publishing (New York, NY), 2007.
Deanna McFadden, reteller, *Rebecca of Sunnybrook Farm,*
Sterling Publishing (New York, NY), 2007.
Kathleen Olmstead, reteller, *Pollyanna* (based on the story
by Eleanor Hodgman Porter), Sterling Publishing
(New York, NY), 2007.
Kathleen Olmstead, reteller, *The Prince and the Pauper*
(based on the story by Mark Twain), Sterling Publishing (New York, NY), 2007.
Oliver Ho, reteller, *The Three Musketeers* (based on the
story by Alexandre Dumas, père), Sterling Publishing
(New York, NY), 2007.

Chris Sasaki, reteller, *The War of the Worlds* (based on the
story by H.G. Wells), Sterling Publishing (New York,
NY), 2007.
Chris Tait, reteller, *The Swiss Family Robinson* (based on
the story by Johann Wyss), Sterling Publishing (New
York, NY), 2007.
Martin Woodside, reteller, *The Wind in the Willows* (based
on the story by Kenneth Grahame), Sterling Publishing (New York, NY), 2007.
Lisa Church, reteller, *Heidi* (based on the story by Johanna
Spyri), Sterling Publishing (New York, NY), 2007.

Sidelights

Jamel Akib uses chalk pastels in the majority of his illustrations for children's books and his art has been recognized by critics for its dramatic hues. Akib's striking color combinations grace the pages of several children's titles, including Sterling Publishing's "Classic Starts" series, which adapts well-known literary classics into simplified illustrated stories for children. Akib's artwork also appears in *Bringing Asha Home* and *Monsoon,* two children's books by Uma Krishnaswami.

Monsoon captures a family's anticipation as members look forward t the upcoming monsoon season and the relief it will bring from the sweltering heat of India. In portraying India's torrid weather, Akib uses opaque color patterns, a technique critics noted pairs well with

Jamel Akib highlights the joy of an adoptive family in his illustrations for Uma Krishnaswami's picture book Bringing Asha Home. (Illustration

Krishnawami's lilting text. A reviewer for *Publishers Weekly* wrote that the illustrator "suggests the heaviness of the air" with "almost dreamlike" images created using "thick strokes and [a] hazy palette." In *Kirkus Reviews* a contributor commented on Akib's use of "saturated colors" that "fill every bit of every page." In addition to his use of bold colors, critics have also remarked on Akib's ability to capture the emotional dimensions of the characters he illustrates. In *School Library Journal,* Liza Graybill observed that Akib's illustrations for *Monsoon* "make stunning use of extreme perspectives" as the characters progress from awaiting the monsoon, to fearing the weather's powerful force, to celebrating the rainy season's passing.

Biographical and Critical Sources

PERIODICALS

Booklist, September 1, 2003, Abby Nolan, review of *Monsoon,* p. 129; February 15, 2006, Hazel Rochman, review of *Robinson Crusoe,* p. 99; October 15, 2006, Linda Perkins, review of *Bringing Asha Home,* p. 54.

Bulletin of the Center for Children's Books, January, 2004, Deborah Stevenson, review of *Monsoon,* p. 196.

Kirkus Reviews, October 1, 2003, review of *Monsoon,* p. 1226; August 15, 2006, review of *Bringing Asha Home,* p. 845.

Publishers Weekly, November 24, 2003, review of *Monsoon,* p. 63.

School Library Journal, December, 2003, Liza Graybill, review of *Monsoon,* p. 118; Julie R. Ranelli, March, 2005, review of *Bringing Asha Home,* p. 98; Kathleen T. Isaacs, review of *Monsoon,* p. 67; April, 2006, Elizabeth Fernandez, review of *Frankenstein,* p. 144; November, 2006, Julie R. Ranelli, review of *Bringing Asha Home,* p. 98.

Tribune Books (Chicago, IL), October 19, 2003, review of *Monsoon,* p. 3.

ONLINE

Lee & Low Web site, http://www.leeandlow.com/ (July 1, 2007), "Jamel Akib."*

*   *   *

AVENI, Anthony 1938-
(Anthony Francis Aveni)

Personal

Born March 5, 1938, in New Haven, CT; son of Anthony M. (a restaurateur) and Frances Aveni; married Lorraine Reiner (an artist), September 5, 1959; children: Patricia, Anthony F., Jr. *Education:* Boston University, A.B., 1960; University of Arizona, Ph.D., 1963.

Anthony Aveni (Courtesy of Anthony Aveni.)

Addresses

Home—Hamilton, NY. *Agent*—Faith Hamlin, Sanford J. Greenburger, 55 5th Ave., New York, NY 10003. *E-mail*—aaveni@mail.colgate.edu.

Career

Colgate University, Hamilton, NY, instructor in astronomy, 1963-65, assistant professor, 1965-69, associate professor, 1969-75, head of department, 1971-73, professor of astronomy, 1975-81, professor of astronomy and anthropology, 1981-82, C.A. Dana professor of astronomy and anthropology, 1982-88, Russell B. Colgate professor of astronomy and anthropology, 1987—. Visiting professor and acting director of observatory at University of South Florida, 1973-74; visiting scholar, University of Padua, 1985, 1989; resident scholar, Centro Internazionale A. Beltrame di Storio dello Spazio et Tempo, Padua, 1985. Conducted field studies in Mexico, Guatemala, Honduras, and Peru; organized international gatherings of scientists; lecturer on astronomy-related subjects for Learning Channel. Appeared on National Public Radio (NPR), Cable News Network (CNN), and television programs *Larry King Show, Today Show,* and *Unsolved Mysteries.*

Member

American Astronomical Society, American Association for the Advancement of Science, American Association

of University Professors, New York Academy of Sciences, Astronomical Society of New York State, Explorers Club.

Awards, Honors

National Science Foundation grants, 1963, 1965, 1968, 1969, 1971, 1973-75, 1975-76, 1977-78; Sigma Xi grant, 1971, to Mexico; OSCO Foundation grants, 1973, 1977; Educational Expeditions International grants to Latin America, 1976, 1977; American Association for the Advancement of Science fellow, 1980; National Professor of the Year award, Council for the Advancement and Support of Education, 1982; Distinguished Teaching Award, Phi Eta Sigma National Honors Society, 1990; Colgate Alumni Award for excellence in teaching, 1997; National Geographic Society grants; H.B. Nicholson Award for Excellence in Mesoamerican Studies, Peabody Museum/Moses Mesoamerican Archive of Harvard University, 2004.

Writings

NONFICTION

(With A.B. Meinel and M.W. Stockton) *Catalog of Emission Lines in Astrophysical Objects,* University of Arizona Press (Tucson, AZ), 1968.

(With B.A. Collea) *A Selected Bibliography on Native American Astronomy,* Colgate University (Hamilton, NY), 1978.

(Author of introduction) Travis Hudson and Ernest Underhay, *Crystals in the Sky: An Intellectual Odyssey Involving Chumash Astronomy, Cosmology, and Rock Art,* Ballena (Socorro, NM), 1978.

Sky Watchers of Ancient America, University of Texas Press (Austin, TX), 1979.

Skywatchers of Ancient Mexico, University of Texas Press (Austin, TX), 1980, revised as *Skywatchers,* 2001.

Maya City Planning and the Calendar, American Philosophical Society (Philadelphia, PA), 1986.

Empires of Time: Calendars, Clocks, and Cultures, Basic Books (New York, NY), 1989.

Conversing with the Planets: How Science and Myth Invented the Cosmos, Times Books (New York, NY), 1989.

Ancient Astronomers (for young adults), Smithsonian Books (Washington, DC), 1993.

Behind the Crystal Ball: Magic, Science, and the Occult from Antiquity through the New Age, Times Books (New York, NY), 1996.

Stairways to the Stars: Skywatching in Three Great Ancient Cultures, John Wiley (New York, NY), 1997.

Between the Lines: The Mystery of the Giant Ground Drawings of Ancient Nasca, Peru, University of Texas Press (Austin, TX), 2000.

Nasca: Eighth Wonder of the World?, British Museum (London, England), 2000.

The Book of the Year: A Brief History of Our Seasonal Holidays, Oxford University Press (New York, NY), 2003.

The First Americans: The Story of Where They Came from and Who They Became (for children), illustrated by S.D. Nelson, Scholastic (New York, NY), 2005.

Uncommon Sense: Understanding Nature's Truths across Time, University Press of Colorado (Boulder, CO), 2006.

Contributor to *In Search of Ancient Astronomies,* edited by Edwin Krupp, Doubleday, 1978. Also contributor of numerous research publications to periodicals including *Science, American Scientist, Sciences, American Antiquity,* and other anthropology, archaeology, and scientific journals.

EDITOR

(And contributor) *Archaeoastronomy in Pre-Columbian America,* University of Texas Press (Austin, TX), 1975.

(And contributor) *Native American Astronomy,* University of Texas Press (Austin, TX), 1977.

Archaeoastronomy in the New World: American Primitive Astronomy (conference proceedings), Cambridge University Press (New York, NY), 1982.

(With Gary Urton) *Ethnoastronomy and Archaeoastronomy in the American Tropics,* New York Academy of Sciences (New York, NY), 1982.

New Directions in American Archaeoastronomy (conference proceedings), B.A.R. (Oxford, England), 1988.

World Archaeoastronomy (conference proceedings), Cambridge University Press (New York, NY), 1989.

The Lines of Nazca, American Philosophical Society (Philadelphia, PA), 1990.

The Sky in Mayan Literature, Oxford University Press (New York, NY), 1992.

(With Gabrielle Vail) *The Madrid Codex: New Approaches to Understanding an Ancient Maya Manuscript,* University Press of Colorado (Boulder, CO), 2004.

Sidelights

Anthony Aveni, a professor of astronomy and anthropology, is considered one of the leading experts on archaeoastronomy, a field of scientific study that examines the sky's influence on the thoughts, beliefs, and understanding of the universe among ancient culture. He combines astronomy, anthropology, sociology, history, and theology in numerous books, among them *Skywatchers of Ancient Mexico, Stairways to the Stars: Skywatching in Three Great Ancient Cultures,* and *Behind the Crystal Ball: Magic, Science, and the Occult from Antiquity through the New Age.* Turning to a younger audience, *Ancient Astronomers* is geared for teen readers and presents a discussion of mankind's eternal fascination with the heavens. Older elementary-grade readers are Aveni's intended audience in *The First Americans: The Story of Where They Came from and Who They Became,* which focuses on the Iroquois, Tinglit, Anasazi, and four other ancient cultures. According to Aveni's hypothesis, these seven peoples all had roots in a migration from Asia to North America

Cover of Aveni's provocative nonfiction work Empires of Time, *featuring a painting by Herbert Bayer.* (University Press of Colorado, 2002. Reproduced by permission.)

along the land bridge known as Beringia, which some scientists have postulated extended from Siberia to Alaska over 20,000 years ago. In *School Library Journal* Nancy Palmer praised *The First Americans* as an "intriguing account" that benefits from Aveni's "style and enthusiasm."

"When writing I try to fuse my traditional background and training in the field of astronomy with a knowledge of ancient native American cultures acquired since I began climbing the fence between physical science and cultural anthropology," Aveni once noted. "By perching on the fencepost between these two disparate fields, perhaps one can see a wider horizon." The many ancient cultures Aveni has studied include the Maya, the Nasca of Peru, the Stonehenge builders, and the Greeks and Romans. In addition to researching ancient manuscripts and other scholarship, he has also traveled around the globe, and his expeditions and field trips have often let him to archaeological ruins in Mexico, Guatemala, Honduras, and Peru.

Aveni's book *Skywatchers of Ancient Mexico* is considered a foundational work in the field of archaeoastronomy. Gordon Brotherston, writing in *Isis,* remarked

that here the author has "gathered between two covers the main advances in Western understanding of Mesoamerican accounts of the sky." In 2001, the book was revised and updated as *Skywatchers.* In five chapters, Aveni explains how experts study archaeoastronomy and take into account historical records including Mexican documents, calendar systems, and observations about the sky. Brotherston praised Aveni for his "excellent, clear, and professional writing" and his ability to "engage the reader directly," concluding that *Skywatchers* "is readable and very well informed and will constantly serve anyone at all concerned with that subject."

In *Conversing with the Planets: How Science and Myth Invented the Cosmos* Aveni explores how ancient astronomers related the movement of planets and stars in the sky to changes on Earth. He discusses how these observations influenced, among other things, cropplanting cycles and goddess stories from the Mayans, Babylonians, and others. *The Book of the Year: A Brief History of Our Seasonal Holidays* explores the origins of holiday traditions such as the Easter bunny and shows the relationship between many holidays and celestial events such as a solstice or equinox, while *Empires of Time: Calendars, Clocks, and Cultures* focuses on man's effort to measure Earth's changes. Aveni tracks the history of science through its magical elements—alchemy, astrology, numerology (the study of the significance of numbers), UFO sightings, alien abductions, and near-death experiences—in *Behind the Crystal Ball* and turns to the heavens as seen and interpreted by the Mayas, the Incas, and the builders of Stonehenge in *Stairways to the Stars.* In addition to the ancient Mayan cult of Venus, this work focuses on the Peruvian city of Cuzco, built by the Incas as an enormous observatory, and England's Stonehenge. Aveni supplements his history with a chapter on skywatching, teaching readers to look at the sky in the same manner as did ancient cultures. He expands his focus on Peru in *Between the Lines: The Mystery of the Giant Ground Drawings of Ancient Nasca, Peru,* which focuses on the giant earth drawings that cover the plateau region near the city of Nasca. In addition to presenting the history of the famous Nasca (or Nazca) lines, including some interesting ideas as to why the lines were created (from roads to alien landing maps), Aveni also gives readers background on ancient Andean culture. In *Booklist,* Gilbert Taylor called *Behind the Crystal Ball* "engaging," while a *Publishers Weekly* critic described it as a "delightful little book" that provides "entertaining glimpses into the cultural evolution of holidays, and explores our human desire to make time work in our favor." *Astronomy* contributor Carol Ryback noted that *Between the Lines* "takes a common-sense look at these giant drawings . . . and sheds light on an ancient mystery," and Patricia Monaghan wrote in her *Booklist* review of the book that "Aveni tells an altogether gripping story that is rather like a mystery novel."

Aveni told *SATA:* "I am never more excited than when I take my students to the ancient ruins left behind by the

first Americans. Whether we walk on the back of an earth serpent in Ohio, stand on the edge of the mesa in Chaco Canyon, climb the steps to the top of Monks Mound, or enter the tomb of a Maya king in the rain forests of Central America—nothing can surpass the experience of seeing things for ourselves. I remember our first visit to Palenque, the ancient Maya ruins buried in the jungle of southeastern Mexico, to see the tomb of the ruler Pacal. We climbed down sixty slimy steps accessed from a trapdoor at the top of a pyramid. Then we entered the chamber of a dead king that had been sealed for more than a thousand years. There he lay, jade face mask intact, showered with obsidian and shell jewelry—unmoved since his subjects first laid him there. What an important person he must have been in his day!

"In our field studies, my students and I measure and map ruins with surveying equipment. We're especially interested in the way ancient astronomers and architects aligned their pyramids with celestial bodies that represented the gods they worshiped. I study fragments of ancient documents to decipher the numbers, words, and pictures that tell why they aligned buildings and temples as they did.

Cover of Aveni's **Behind the Crystal Ball**, *which focuses on the interplay between magic, science, and superstition throughout human history.* (University Press of Colorado, 2002. Reproduced by permission.)

"Though I originally studied astronomy, my interest in people later made me into an anthropologist as well. I try to reflect my combined interest in what I write. In *Empires of Time* I explore why clocks and calendars were invented. *Conversing with the Planets* explores what the universe means to us and what it means to us and what it meant to our ancestors. *Stairways to the Stars* is about archaeoastronomy, the study of how people in different cultures acquired knowledge from the sky. *Ancient Astronomers* is an easily readable book for teens that tells why people all over the world—from China to Polynesia to ancient America—have been fascinated by the sky and how their knowledge of the constellation patterns and the movements of the planets changed their cultures. In *Behind the Crystal Ball* I take readers on a tour through time and space as I try to unveil the many ways people have used magic over the millennia in hopes of improving their lives.

"Studying cultures other than our own is a lot like looking in a mirror. Learning about them is a great way to learn about ourselves."

Biographical and Critical Sources

PERIODICALS

American Antiquity, January, 1982, review of *Skywatchers of Ancient Mexico,* p. 238; January, 1989, Wendy Ashmore, review of *Maya City Planning and the Calendar,* p. 219; July, 1990, Sylvia Meluzin, review of *New Directions in American Archaeoastronomy,* p. 643.

Antiquity, June, 1991, Timothy Taylor, review of *The Lines of Nazca,* p. 407; March, 2001, David Browne, review of *Between the Lines: The Mystery of the Giant Ground Drawings of Ancient Nasca, Peru,* p. 223; December, 2001, N. James and Simon Stoddart, review of *Skywatchers,* p. 886.

Archaeology, March, 1982, review of *Skywatchers of Ancient Mexico,* p. 82; November, 2001, review of *Skywatchers,* p. 57.

Astronomy, March, 1982, review of *Skywatchers of Ancient Mexico,* p. 76; November, 1993, review of *Conversing with the Planets: How Science and Myth Invented the Cosmos,* p. 108, review of *The Sky in Mayan Literature,* p. 108; October, 1997, review of *Stairways to the Stars: Skywatching in Three Great Ancient Cultures,* p. 104; March, 2001, Carol Ryback, review of *Between the Lines,* p. 96.

Booklist, October 1, 1989, review of *Empires of Time: Calendars, Clocks, and Cultures,* p. 247; September 15, 1992, Virginia Dwyer, review of *Conversing with the Planets,* p. 103; August, 1996, Gilbert Taylor, review of *Behind the Crystal Ball: Magic, Science, and the Occult from Antiquity through the New Age,* p. 1858, review of *Behind the Crystal Ball,* p. 1890; June 1, 2000, Patricia Monaghan, review of *Between the Lines,* p. 1840.

Choice, May, 1981, review of *Skywatchers of Ancient Mexico,* p. 1286; September, 1981, review of *Archaeoastronomy in Pre-Columbian America,* p. 40, review of *Native American Astronomy,* p. 81; July, 1990, review of *Empires of Time,* p. 1841; October, 1992, review of *Skywatchers of Ancient Mexico,* p. 253; March, 1993, A.R. Upgren, Jr., review of *Conversing with the Planets,* p. 1178; October, 1997, V.V. Raman, review of *Stairways to the Stars,* p. 316; May, 2001, J.B. Richardson, III, review of *Between the Lines,* p. 1663.

Hispanic American Historical Review, May, 1982, review of *Skywatchers of Ancient Mexico,* p. 275; February, 1994, Michael Edmondson, review of *The Sky in Mayan Literature,* p. 127.

Isis, June, 1991, Olaf Pedersen, review of *Empires of Time,* p. 346; March, 1997, Steven J. Dick, review of *Ancient Astronomers,* p. 131; December, 1999, review of *Stairways to the Stars,* p. 797; December, 2002, Gordon Brotherston, review of *Skywatchers,* p. 679.

Kirkus Reviews, August 15, 1989, review of *Empires of Time,* p. 1209; July 1, 1992, review of *Conversing with the Planets,* p. 819; June 15, 1996, review of *Behind the Crystal Ball,* p. 867; November 15, 2002, review of *The Book of the Year: A Brief History of Our Seasonal Holidays,* p. 1665.

Library Journal, September 15, 1989, Jack W. Weigel, review of *Empires of Time,* p. 132; November 1, 1992, Jack W. Weigel, review of *Conversing with the Planets,* p. 94; August, 1996, James Olson, review of *Behind the Crystal Ball,* p. 106; May 15, 1997, Gloria Maxwell, review of *Stairways to the Stars,* p. 97.

Nature, December 21, 1989, Owen Gingerich, review of *Empires of Time,* p. 871; January 30, 1997, Martin Gardner, review of *Behind the Crystal Ball,* p. 405.

New Scientist, November 16, 1996, review of *Behind the Crystal Ball,* p. 45; January 25, 1998, review of *Stairways to the Stars,* p. 44.

New Statesman and Society, August 10, 1990, Jenny Diski, review of *Empires of Time,* p. 37.

New York Times, July 7, 1981, Richard Severo, review of *Skywatchers of Ancient Mexico,* p. 15; March 25, 1986, William Stockton, "Ancient Astronomy Points to New Views on Mayan Life," p. 15.

New York Times Book Review, December 13, 1992, Marcia Bartusiak, review of *Conversing with the Planets,* p.
11; November 17, 1996, Ed Regis, review of *Behind the Crystal Ball,* p. 32.

Publishers Weekly, August 4, 1989, Genevieve Stuttaford, review of *Empires of Time,* p. 78; July 13, 1992, review of *Conversing with the Planets,* p. 40; July 1, 1996, review of *Behind the Crystal Ball,* p. 52; November 25, 2002, review of *The Book of the Year,* p. 61.

School Library Journal, April, 2006, Nancy Palmer, review of *The First Americans: The Story of Where They Came from and Who They Became,* p. 150.

Science Books and Films, November, 1981, review of *Skywatchers of Ancient Mexico,* p. 72; May, 1990, review of *Empires of Time,* p. 243; January, 1998, review of *Stairways to the Stars,* p. 14; December, 1998, review of *Stairways to the Stars,* p. 264.

Scientific American, October, 1981, Philip Morrison, review of *Skywatchers of Ancient Mexico,* p. 42; August, 1993, Philip Morrison, review of *Conversing with the Planets,* p. 127.

Science News, July 15, 2006, review of *Uncommon Sense: Understanding Nature's Truths across Time and Culture,* p. 47.

Times Literary Supplement, August 23, 1991, John D. North, review of *Empires of Time,* p. 24; December 27, 1996, Keith R. Hutchinson, review of *Behind the Crystal Ball,* p. 30.

Village Voice Literary Supplement, November, 1989, review of *Empires of Time,* p. 5.

Voice of Youth Advocates, October, 1998, review of *Behind the Crystal Ball,* p. 251; February, 2006, review of *The First Americans,* p. 507.

Washington Post Book World, July 16, 1995, review of *Empires of Time,* p. 12.

ONLINE

Anthony Aveni Home Page, http://anthonyfaveni.com (July 8, 2007).

*   *   *

AVENI, Anthony Francis
See AVENI, Anthony

B

BANTA, Susan

Personal
Born in Washington, DC; married; husband a retired librarian; children. *Education:* Syracuse University School of Art, graduate. *Hobbies and other interests:* Reading, quilting, gardening, snowshoeing, cross-country skiing, and yoga.

Addresses
Home and office—133 Apple St., Brookfield, VT 05036. *Agent*—BookMakers, Ltd., P.O. Box 1086, Taos, NM 87571.

Career
Illustrator.

Illustrator

PICTURE BOOKS

William P. Nestor, *Into Winter: Discovering a Season,* Houghton Mifflin (Boston, MA), 1982.

Hello, Hello!, Western Pub. Co. (Racine, WI), 1993.

Shapes/Opposites/Animals/Colors (board books), 4 volumes, McClanahan Books (New York, NY), 1993.

What Can I Give Him? (from a poem by Christina Rosetti), Standard Publishing (Cincinnati, OH), 1994.

Bananas, Western Pub. Co. (Racine, WI), 1994.

Apple, Western Pub. Co. (Racine, WI), 1994.

Grapes, Western Pub. Co. (Racine, WI), 1994.

The Wheels on the Bus, Western Pub. Co. (Racine, WI), 1994.

Orange, Western Pub. Co. (Racine, WI), 1994.

My Little Lambs, Western Pub. Co. (Racine, WI), 1995.

My Little Ducklings, Western Pub. Co. (Racine, WI), 1995.

My Little Chicks, Western Pub. Co. (Racine, WI), 1995.

My Little Bunnies, Western Pub. Co. (Racine, WI), 1995.

E.K. Davis, *My Golden Books Alphabet,* Western Pub. Co. (Racine, WI), 1996.

E.K. Davis, *My Golden Books Alphabet,* Golden Books Pub. Co. (New York, NY), 1999.

Joe Troiano, *The Legend of Spookley the Square Pumpkin,* Backpack Books, 2001.

Did You Ever See a Duckie?, Publications International (Lincolnwood, IL), 2001.

Helen Haidle, *Thank You, Dear God!,* Zonderkidz (Grand Rapids, MI), 2001.

Helen Haidle, *God Bless Me,* Zonderkidz (Grand Rapids, MI), 2001.

Joe Troiano, *Beacon, the Bright Little Firefly,* Sweetwater Press (Birmingham, AL), 2002.

Kathleen Long Bostrom, *Mary's Happy Christmas Day,* Zonderkidz (Grand Rapids, MI), 2003.

Lourdes M. Alvarez, *Pardon My Spanish: La Leyenda del Coquí,* Mi Casa (Puerto Rico), 2003.

Matt Mitter, *Once upon a Rhyme: Story Rhymes,* Gareth Stevens Pub. (Milwaukee, WI), 2004.

Mary Packard, *Same and Different: Comparison Rhymes,* Gareth Stevens Pub. (Milwaukee, WI), 2004.

Charlotte Cowan, *Peeper Has a Fever,* Hippocratic Press (Concord, MA), 2005.

Carol J. Votaw, *Good Morning, Little Polar Bear,* North-Word Books for Young Readers (Minnetonka, MN), 2005.

Joe Troiano, *Halloween Fun with Spookley the Square Pumpkin,* Sterling Publishing Co. (New York, NY), 2006.

Louise Bonnett-Rampersaud, *Bubble and Squeak,* Marshall Cavendish (New York, NY), 2006.

Carol J. Votaw, *Waking up Down Under,* NorthWord Books for Young Readers (Minnetonka, MN), 2007.

Biographical and Critical Sources

PERIODICALS

Library Media Connection, February, 2006, Susanne Johnson, review of *Good Morning, Little Polar Bear,* p. 64.

Publishers Weekly, September 22, 2003, review of *Mary's Happy Christmas Day,* p. 73.

School Library Journal, August, 2004, Robyn Walker, review of *Once upon a Rhyme: Story Rhymes,* p. 11; November, 2005, Angela J. Reynolds, review of *Good Morning, Little Polar Bear,* p. 122; October, 2006, Jayne Damron, review of *Bubble and Squeak,* p. 102.

ONLINE

Bookmakers Ltd. Web site, http://www.bookmakersltd.com/ (July 17, 2007), "Susan Banta."

*　　*　　*

BARDOE, Cheryl

Personal

Married; children: one son, one daughter. *Education:* Attended Northwestern University (journalism).

Addresses

Home and office—Chicago, IL. *E-mail*—cb@cherylbardoe.com.

Career

Writer. Field Museum, Chicago, IL, project manager.

Awards, Honors

Orbis Pictus Honor Book, National Council of Teachers of English, International Reading Association Notable Book designation, and American Library Association Notable Book designation, all 2007, all for *Gregor Mendel: The Friar Who Grew Peas.*

Writings

Gregor Mendel: The Friar Who Grew Peas, illustrated by Jos A. Smith, Abrams Books for Young Readers (New York, NY), 2006.

Sidelights

Gregor Mendel: The Friar Who Grew Peas is Cheryl Bardoe's first contribution to the children's nonfiction bookshelf. A biographical picture book, the work profiles the nineteenth-century friar who made important contributions to modern genetics. A *Kirkus Reviews* critic deemed the book a "lovely tribute" to Mendel that effectively flows from "hard science . . . to the vicissitudes of scholarship" in describing the accomplishments of a man who never received recognition for his contributions to the field of genetics during his lifetime. Stephanie Zvirin, writing in *Booklist,* commented on the visual appeal of the book, adding that Mendel's

"theories, are clearly explained" by the author. Likewise, *School Library Journal* contributor Patricia Manning acknowledged Bardoe's "readable text" and remarked that *Gregor Mendel* "is as much a treat for the eye as it is for the curious mind." Bardoe concludes her picture-book biography by adding an author's note that provides additional information for more science-minded readers.

Prior to writing for young readers, Bardoe used her writing skills in scripting marketing slogans, magazine articles, press kits, and newsletters for various industries. As part of her work at Chicago's Field Museum, she has also written texts for exhibitions and worked with colleagues to tell scientific and cultural stories in three-dimensional space. Having accomplished her goal of becoming a published writer, Bardoe noted on her home page that she views herself as "an 'emerging author.'" "I can't offer the wisdom of someone who has written a library's worth of books but I have learned a few things so far," she added. "Grab any precious moment that you can," she noted, explaining that "eventually those rare gems will add up."

Biographical and Critical Sources

PERIODICALS

Booklinks, November, 2006, Gillian Engberg, review of *Gregor Mendel: The Friar Who Grew Peas,* p. 51.

Booklist, July 1, 2006, Stephanie Zvirin, review of *Gregor Mendel,* p. 62.

Books, December 3, 2006, Mary Harris Russell, review of *Gregor Mendel,* p. 7.

Kirkus Reviews, August 15, 2006, review of *Gregor Mendel,* p. 835.

School Library Journal, September, 2006, Patricia Manning, review of *Gregor Mendel,* p. 188.

ONLINE

Cheryl Bardoe Home Page, http://www.cherylbardoe.com (July 4, 2007).

Children's Bookwatch, http://www.midwestbookreview.com/ (December, 2006), review of *Gregor Mendel.*

*　　*　　*

BENNETT, Holly 1957-

Personal

Born January 3, 1957, in Montréal, Quebec, Canada; daughter of Norman Jack (a pharmacist) and Betty Jane (a homemaker) Bennett; married John Hoffman (a journalist and musician), March 13, 1982; children: Riley, Jesse, Aaron. *Education:* Trent University, B.A. (En-

glish and Native studies; with honors), 1979; Ontario Institute for Studies in Education, M.A. (adult education), 1984. *Politics:* "Lefty." *Religion:* Unitarian.

Addresses

Home—Peterborough, Ontario, Canada. *Agent*—Lynn Bennett, Transatlantic Literary Agency, 72 Glengowan Rd., Toronto, Ontario M4N 1G4, Canada. *E-mail*—hbennett27@cogeco.ca.

Career

Editor and novelist. *Today's Parent* (magazine), Toronto, Ontario, Canada, editorial trainee, 1986, now editor-in-chief of special editions. Program developer for aboriginal organizations and youth counseling agencies.

Member

PEN Canada, Humane Society.

Awards, Honors

New York Public Library Books for the Teen Age inclusion, and International Reading Association Notable Children's Book designation, both 2006, and White Pine Award honor designation, 2007, all for *The Bonemender.*

Writings

YOUNG-ADULT FANTASY NOVELS

The Bonemender, Orca Book Publishers (Custer, WA), 2005.
The Bonemender's Oath (sequel to *The Bonemender*), Orca Book Publishers (Custer, WA), 2006.
The Warrior's Daughter, Orca Book Publishers (Custer, WA), 2007.
The Bonemender's Choice (sequel to *The Bonemender's Oath*), Orca Book Publisher (Custer, WA), 2007.

"OTHER

Also author, with Teresa Pitman, of "Today's Parent Steps and Stages" nonfiction series.

Sidelights

Holly Bennett told *SATA:* "I don't know what switch got thrown that made me, at nearly 45, sit down to write my first novel. I had been editing and writing nonfiction for most of my adult life, and hiding the dirty little secret that, although I loved working on magazines, I didn't love reading them. That what I *read* was—and is—fiction.

"I do know how lucky I am that my first novel, *The Bonemender,* was not only published but well received! But I'm pretty sure I would have kept on writing even

if it had been firmly rejected—I already had a sequel drafted before the first book sold. Writing fiction was pretty much an instant addiction and I really don't feel 'right' now if I don't have a book on the go.

"One of the things I love (and sometimes feel) about fiction writing is the way it can take on a life of its own. When I began writing *The Bonemender* I had most of the plot already planned out. Then one day I looked at the computer screen and saw that I had just sent a main character over the mountains into enemy territory. Or maybe he just up and went there by himself—it certainly felt that way. My first thought was, 'Oh, crap!' Suddenly I had huge problems. I had to invent and describe a whole new country, and I had to somehow find a way to get him back safely. But I also knew that sending him there was the right thing to do—that it perked up a long, boring stretch in the story and gave this character a chance to reveal himself to the readers.

"When my first novel came out, I had to fill out a bio sheet for the publisher and one of the questions was, 'What is your best qualification for writing this book?' I didn't really think I had any qualifications for writing a book, but made a dutiful attempt to answer and said, 'all the fantasy I have read aloud to my kids.' That phrase shows up all over the place now and sounds more lame and embarrassing each time I read it! However, there is a real truth here for aspiring writers: reading widely is an important element of learning to write. And reading out loud is really valuable—it trains you to pay attention to the way words sound and fill together, not just their meaning. I remember reading *The Secret Garden* and marveling at how easily those long Victorian sentences came off the tongue. The book had obviously been written to be read aloud, with rhythm and fluidity, and it was a real pleasure to do so. I read my own writing out loud all the time (or at least mutter it under my breath), and find it is the very best way to discover awkwardness, poor phrasing, clunky dialogue, and a host of other problems.

"I'm really thrilled that kids enjoy reading these books—my favourite review was by a girl who confessed she stayed up until 4 a.m. on a school night reading *The Bonemender's Oath* cover to cover. That kind of reading is one of life's great pleasures. Creating it is another."

Biographical and Critical Sources

PERIODICALS

Booklist, November 1, 2005, Krista Hutley, review of *The Bonemender,* p. 36.
Bulletin of the Center for Children's Books, November, 2005, April Spisak, review of *The Bonemaker,* p. 130.
Canadian Children's Book News, fall, 2005, Ming Wong, review of *The Bonemender,* p. 32.

Kirkus Reviews, October 1, 2005, review of *The Bone-mender,* p. 1076.

Kliatt, November, 2005, Stephanie Squicciarini, review of *The Bonemender,* p. 19; November, 2006, Stephanie Squicciarini, review of *The Bonemender's Oath,* p. 26.

Resource Links, October, 2005, Myra Junyk, review of *The Bonemender,* p. 30; October, 2006, Angela Thompson, review of *The Bonemender's Oath,* p. 29; Margaret Mackey, review of *The Warrior's Daughter,* p. 40.

School Library Journal, December, 2005, Saleena L. Davidson, review of *The Bonemender,* p. 140; February, 2007, Carly B. Wiskoff, review of *The Bonemender's Oath,* p. 115; June, 2007, Nancy Kunz, review of *The Warrior's Daughter,* p. 138.

Voice of Youth Advocates, December, 2006, Michele Winship, review of *The Bonemender's Oath,* p. 438.

ONLINE

Transatlantic Literary Agency Web site, http://www.tla1.com/ (July 16, 2007), "Holly Bennett."

*   *   *

BERGLIN, Ruth Marie 1970-

Ruth Marie Berglin (Courtesy of Ruth Marie Berglin.)

Personal

Born February 28, 1970, in LaPorte, IN; daughter of Robert (a blue-collar worker) and Emily (a teacher) Armstrong; married Joel Berglin (a nurse), December 28, 1993; children: Janinya, Katriana. *Education:* Bethany Lutheran College, A.A., 1991; Mankato State University, B.S. (elementary education), B.S. (Spanish), both 1993; Minnesota State University, Moorhead, M.A. (reading), 1999. *Religion:* Lutheran.

Addresses

Home—Mankato, MN.

Career

Homemaker and writer. English-as-a-Second-Language teacher and Title I communications educator, 1994-99.

Awards, Honors

Minnesota Book Award finalist, 2006, for *Dear Big, Mean, Ugly Monster.*

Writings

Dear Big, Mean, Ugly Monster, illustrated by Carl Di-Rocco, Child & Family Press (Washington, DC), 2005.

Contributor to books, including *Chapel Talks for Christian Children,* Northwestern Publishing House.

Sidelights

Although Ruth Marie Berglin devotes much of her time to raising and home-schooling her two children, the former teacher also became a published writer in 2005. As she explained to *SATA,* her book *Dear Big, Mean, Ugly Monster* "had very humble beginnings. I first told the story in our minivan during a long trip. Both of my daughters are impatient and restless travelers. I've spent many hours reading wonderful books to make the miles go by much faster than the speed limits allow. On this particular trip, I finished our book before the girls were done hearing stories, so I made up my own. Thus were born characters Joe and SAM and the letters that make up their story.

"I thought the story was done when we reached our destination, but the girls kept asking to hear it again. During quiet moments, I found myself tweaking the story; it was begging to be written on paper. My husband Joel said I should mail the story off to a publisher. My sister, Rachel, nagged me until I did it. I mailed it to Child & Family Press, but really did not expect to hear from them. So many people mail off stories, but so few are chosen. The day the call came, I hugged my husband and daughters as I laughed in disbelief and cried with joy.

"I have always loved to write, but this was the first time someone I had never met decided one of my stories was worth the time, effort, and expense of turning

Berglin's first book for young readers, **Dear Big, Mean, Ugly Monster,** *features humorous artwork by Carl DiRocco.* (Child & Family Press, 2005. Illustration © 2005 by Carl DiRocco. All rights reserved. Reproduced by permission.)

it into a book. It has been such a joy to take my story to children in stores, libraries, and schools. They are so eager to listen to stories, ask questions, and tell me about the writing that they have done.

"As I continue to write, my daughters hear the stories first. Sometimes, I am just entertaining them. Other times, the story is a non-threatening way to teach them about something bigger: dealing with sibling rivalry, overcoming fears, controlling tempers. I hope to share these stories, too, with other children. We will see what God has in mind for me!"

Biographical and Critical Sources

PERIODICALS

Children's Bookwatch, November, 2005, review of *Dear Big, Mean, Ugly Monster.*

Kirkus Reviews, November 15, 2005, review of *Dear Big, Mean, Ugly Monster,* p. 1229.

*   *   *

BERNARD, Patricia 1942-
(Trisha Bernard, P. Scot-Bernard, Judy Bernard Waite)

Personal

Born July 6, 1942, in Melbourne, Victoria, Australia; daughter of Robert and Edith Lack; married Kenneth Bernard, 1964; children: Marcelle, Shona, S'Haila, Tyru. *Education:* Attended Australian state schools. *Hobbies and other interests:* Travelling, reading, bike riding.

Addresses

Home—Sydney, New South Wales, Australia. *E-mail*—patriciabernard@iinet.net.au.

Patricia Bernard (Reproduced by permission.)

Career

Writer and lecturer. Worked variously as a kindergarten teacher in the United Kingdom, a pavement artist, nightclub waitress, fine-arts painter, grape picker, and au pair.

Member

Australian Authors Association.

Awards, Honors

Multicultural Award for *Monkey Hill Gold;* Aurealis Award shortlist for *The Outcast.*

Writings

FOR CHILDREN

We Are Tam, Ashton Scholastic (Sydney, New South Wales, Australia), 1983.

Aida's Ghost, Corgi Books (Neutral Bay, New South Wales, Australia), 1988.

(Under name Judy Bernard Waite) *Riddle of the Trumpalar,* Scholastic (Gosford, New South Wales, Australia), 1990.

Challenge of the Trumpalar, Scholastic (Gosford, New South Wales, Australia), 1990.

Monkey Hill Gold, Omnibus Books (Norwood, South Australia, Australia), 1992.

The Outer Space Spy, illustrated by Mike Spoor, Jacaranda Press (Milton, New South Wales, Australia), 1992.

Dream Door of Shinar, illustrated by Garry Fleming, Harcourt (Sydney, New South Wales, Australia), 1992.

Kangaroo Kids, Bantam (Neutral Bay, New South Wales, Australia), 1992.

Jacaranda Shadow, Hodder & Stoughton (Sydney, New South Wales, Australia), 1993.

JB and the Worry Dolls, Hodder Headline (Rydalmere, New South Wales, Australia), 1994.

Outerspace Spy, Transworld, 1994.

Monster Builder, illustrated by Laurie McIntyre, Cool Dude Books (Paddington, New South Wales, Australia), 1996.

Spook Bus, HarperCollins (Pymble, New South Wales, Australia), 1997.

No Sooks on the Starship, Macmillan (Chippendale, New South Wales, Australia), 1998.

Duffy: Everyone's Dog (picture book), illustrated by Cathy Netherwood, Random House (Milsons Point, New South Wales, Australia), 1998.

Wolf-Man, Addison Wesley Longman (Melbourne, Victoria, Australia), 1999.

The Pizza Caper, Addison Wesley Longman (Melbourne, Victoria, Australia), 1999.

Jumping Dogs and Jellyfish, illustrated by Gus Gordon, Addison Wesley Longman (Melbourne, Victoria, Australia), 1999.

The Stolen Giant Cheesecake, Pearson Education (South Melbourne, Victoria, Australia), 2000.

Marcus the Mighty, illustrated by Penny Azar, Blake Educational (Glebe, New South Wales, Australia), 2001.

Cool Dude and Honey Magnet, Pearson Education (South Melbourne, Victoria, Australia), 2002.

Basil Big Boots, illustrated by Nancy Beiman, Cool Dude Books, 2003.

Duffy and the Invisible Crocodile, illustrated by Nancy Beiman, Cool Dude Books, 2003.

Fords and Flying Machines: The Diary of Jack McLaren, Longreach, 1919-1921, Scholastic (Linfield, New South Wales, Australia), 2003.

Stegosaur Stone, Scholastic (Linfield, New South Wales, Australia), 2004.

The Mask, Scholastic (Linfield, New South Wales, Australia), 2005.

Also author of *Into the Future, Temple of Apis,* and *Slap, Dash, Splash.* Contributor of short fiction to educational anthologies, including *Techno Terror,* Addison Wesley Longman, 1999; *Greening the Earth,* edited by Paul Collins and Meredith Costain, Pearson Educational; and *Sparklers 5,* Blake Education, 2001.

"OUTCAST" TRILOGY; FOR YOUNG ADULTS

The Outcast, HarperCollins (Pymble, New South Wales, Australia), 1997.

The Punisher, HarperCollins (Pymble, New South Wales, Australia), 1997.

The Rule Changer, HarperCollins (Pymble, New South Wales, Australia), 1998.

FOR ADULTS

(Under name P. Scot-Bernard) *Sex Is a Deadly Exercise,* Transworld, 1987, published as *Sex Is a Deadly Weapon,* 1990.

Deadly Sister Love, HarperCollins (Pymble, New South Wales, Australia), 1998.

(Under name Trisha Bernard) *With the Kama Sutra under My Arm: An Indian Journey,* East Street Publications (Bowden, South Australia, Australia), 2006.

Also author of novel *Not My Sister's Keeper,* under pseudonym P. Scot-Bernard. Author of scripts for television and film. Author, under name Trisha Bernard, of travel books, including *With a Maasai under My Arm.*

Sidelights

Patricia Bernard left her native Australia at age nineteen to see the world, and has been working, traveling, and finding adventures and romance around the globe ever since. From sailing the Nile river to working as a pavement painter in Berlin, to driving across Alaska in a sports car, she was one of the first Australians allowed into China during the 1970s. Able to speak five languages, Bernard has visited over seventy countries and actually lived in twenty of them. An artist, she worked as a painter of landscapes and portraits for fifteen years, and turned to writing in the 1980s. "I started writing . . . when a friend asked me to write down the stories I was telling at a kindergarten," Bernard once told *SATA.* "Since then, every children's/teenage book I have written has been published." In addition to publishing children's books that include *Jacaranda Shadow, The Mask,* and the "Outcast" science-fiction trilogy, Bernard has also written three novels for adults under a pen name, and also written for film and television.

Discussing her career as a writer, Bernard once told *SATA:* "I hope to achieve racial and national harmony between children and parents in the linguistically diverse Australian schools, and to teach 'even the smallest thing' to the reader while they have a good time reading my books. I work from nine to nine, six days a week when writing, and longer when editing because I hate editing so much. My motto is 'if it is not fun, don't do it,' so when the sun shines I spend three hour lunches at the beach, editing and swimming, and I can be taken away from my computer by any simple excuse given by any friend who drops in and suggests a coffee, a champagne, or a swim. I also lecture in schools and to writers, librarians, and women's literary groups, mostly about myself, my books, and the benefits of turning off the television and reading.

"The purpose behind writing the 'Outcast' trilogy was to invent an entire world with the same tensions as our own, and through a hero and a group of heroes, fix it up. I don't know who has influenced my work, but my favorite authors are Isabelle Allende, Margaret Atwood, and Charles Dickens. The advice I would give to aspiring writers in Australia is 'don't give up your day job. Our population is too small.'"

Biographical and Critical Sources

PERIODICALS

Magpies, May, 1993, pp. 29-30; March, 1994, review of *Jacaranda Shadow,* p. 32; May, 1997, reviews of *Duffy: Everyone's Dog,* p. 28, and *The Outcast,* p. 37; March, 1998, review of *The Punisher,* p. 37.

Publishers Weekly, January 20, 1992, review of *Kangaroo Kids,* p. 66.

ONLINE

Patricia Bernard Home Page, http://www.geocities.com/patriciabernard2001/ (July 20, 2007).

* * *

BERNARD, Trisha
See BERNARD, Patricia

* * *

BLANKENSHIP, LeeAnn 1944-

Personal

Born November 11, 1944, in Huntington, WV; daughter of Ed Bennett (a mechanical engineer) and Jewel A. Bennett Ward (an office nurse); married G. Barry Blan-

LeAnn Blankenship (Courtesy of J. Michael Photography.)

kenship (a fire chief), March 4, 1967; children: Tracy Luna, Todd, Teri Engelmann. *Education:* West Virginia Wesleyan College, B.A. (education); University of Maryland. *Religion:* Jehovah's Witness. *Hobbies and other interests:* Travel, gardening, reading, sewing, Apache history and culture.

Addresses

Home—Kent, OH. *E-mail*—littlecabbage@juno.com.

Career

Social worker, author, and educator. Licensed clinical social worker in Wayne County, WV, 1967-71, and Portage County, OH, 1973-76; Family and Community Services, OH, director of adoption program, 1982-87. Teacher in Cabell County, WV, and Portage County, OH; former realtor.

Member

International Board on Books for Young People, Society of Children's Book Writers and Illustrators (Northern Ohio chapter; former volunteer coordinator).

Awards, Honors

International Reading Association Notable Book of the Year designation, and New Hampshire Ladybug Award nomination, both 2006, both for *Mr. Tuggle's Trouble.*

Writings

Mr. Tuggle's Troubles, illustrated by Karen Dugan, Boyds Mills Press (Honesdale, PA), 2005.

Contributor to periodicals, including *Cricket, Appleseeds, Cobblestone,* and *Highlights for Children.*

Sidelights

LeeAnn Blankenship told *SATA:* "I often encourage other aspiring writers by telling them, 'Don't give up on your dreams.' I first began writing for children shortly after the birth of my son in 1973. That picture book was never accepted for publication, but a complimentary response I received from an editor helped keep my dream alive. For the next twenty years, raising my family and working at a 'regular' job occupied my time. Finally, when my youngest child was almost grown, I decided it was time to take my dream of being a children's author off the back burner and move it to the front of the stovetop!

"I enrolled in a writing course with the Institute of Children's Literature and began writing more regularly. Eventually my nonfiction history articles were published in the magazine market. I wrote the first draft of my humorous picture book, *Mr. Tuggle's Troubles,* in 1995. For the next seven and a half years, I continued

In **Mr. Tuggle's Troubles** *Blankenship joins with illustrator Karen Dugan to capture the life of a busy man during a particularly discombobulated day.* (Illustration © 2005 by Karen Dugan. All rights reserved. Reproduced by permission of Boyd Mills Press.)

to revise and polish the text while submitting it to various publishing companies. Encouraging rejection letters kept my hopes high and in 2003 I got an exciting phone call from Kent Brown with Boyds Mills Press telling me that his company would like to purchase my manuscript for publication. I was sixty years old when my dream of writing a children's book became a reality. I tell others that you're never too old to work for your dreams.

"With my writing, I hope to foster a love for books and reading in youngsters. I love history and with my historical pieces I try to make history fun, exciting, and interesting."

Biographical and Critical Sources

PERIODICALS

Kirkus Reviews, September 15, 2005, review of *Mr. Tuggle's Troubles,* p. 1021.

School Library Journal, October, 2005, Linda Staskus, review of *Mr. Tuggle's Troubles,* p. 103.

ONLINE

Boyds Mills Press Web site, http://www.boydsmillspress. com/ (July 20, 2007), "LeeAnn Blankenship."

* * *

BOYNE, John 1971-

Personal

Born April 30, 1971, in Dublin, Ireland. *Education:* Trinity College Dublin, B.A.; University of East Anglia, M.A. (creative writing).

Addresses

Agent—Simon Trewin, PFD, Drury House, 34-43 Russell St., London WC2B 5HA, England. *E-mail*—info@ johnboyne.com.

Career

Novelist. University of East Anglia writing fellow, 2005.

Awards, Honors

Hennessy Literary Award shortlist, for "The Entertainments Jar"; Curtis Brown Prize, University of East Anglia, 1994-95; *Irish Times* Literature Award longlist, 2000, for *Thief of Time;* Hughes & Hughes Irish Novel of the Year Award shortlist, 2005, for *Crippen;* Berkshire Book Award, Irish Book Award Novel of the Year shortlist, Prix Farmiente (Belgium) shortlist, British Book Award Children's Book of the Year shortlist, Lancashire Book Award shortlist, Sheffield Book Award shortlist, Borders Original Voices Award shortlist, Paolo Ungari award (Italy) shortlist, and Ottakar's Children's Book Prize shortlist, all 2006-07, and Irish Book Awards People's Choice Award and Children's Book of the Year honor, CBI Bisto Book of the Year award, and Carnegie Medal longlist, all 2007, all for *The Boy in the Striped Pyjamas.*

Writings

The Thief of Time, Weidenfeld & Nicolson (London, England), 2000, Thomas Dunne (New York, NY), 2006.
The Congress of Rough Riders, Weidenfeld & Nicolson (London, England), 2001.
Crippen: A Novel of Murder, Penguin UK (London, England), 2004, Thomas Dunne (New York, NY), 2006.
The Boy in the Striped Pyjamas, David Fickling (Oxford, England), 2006, published as *The Boy in the Striped Pajamas: A Fable,* David Fickling (New York, NY), 2006.

Next of Kin, Penguin (London, England), 2006, Thomas Dunne (New York, NY), 2008.

Author of weekly short-story column for Irish *Sunday Tribune.* Contributor to periodicals, including *Cuirt Annual, Image, Irish Times, RTE Sunday Miscellany, Wake, RTE Storylane, Books Ireland, Harlequinned, Concrete, Expo, Cobweb IX,* and *Sunday Tribune New Irish Writing.* Book reviewer for *Irish Times, Sunday Tribune, Sunday Business Post, W,* and *Irish Review of Books.*

Boyne's works have been translated into thirty languages, including Dutch, Russian, Spanish, Danish, French, German, Greek, Hungarian, Italian, Slovenian, Japanese, Korean, Norwegian, Polish, Portuguese, Swedish, and Turkish.

Adaptations

Boyne's short stories have been adapted as television productions, student films, and broadcasts on RTE Radio and BBC Radio 4. *The Boy in the Striped Pyjamas* was adapted as a feature film by Miramax/Heyday Films, 2007.

Sidelights

Inspired by a childhood love of reading, Irish novelist John Boyne never wanted to be anything but a writer. During college, he was shortlisted for the Hennessy Literary Award for a work he published in Ireland's *Sunday Tribune* newspaper, and in the years since he has earned critical praise for the novels *Crippen: A Novel of Murder, The Congress of Rough Riders,* and *The Boy in the Striped Pajamas: A Fable.* Based on a true story about a British physician who murdered his wife and set sail for Canada with his younger mistress during the early twentieth century, *Crippen* was dubbed "gripping historical fare" by *Booklist* contributor Kristine Huntley. Also noted for their compelling characters, imaginative plots, and Boyne's skill as a storyteller, *The Congress of Rough Riders* recounts the life of Buffalo Bill Cody, while *The Thief of Time* follows Matthieu Zela, who, born in 1743, cannot die and looks, to all appearances, as a man in his late forties. While caretaking successive generations of his brother's family, Mattieu finds his life intersecting with characters ranging from Pope Pius IX and Robespierre to Charlie Chaplin in a "lively historical saga" that *Booklist* critic Michael Gannon noted possesses "a touch of the fantastic."

The Boy in the Striped Pajamas presents a tale of an unlikely friendship during World War II and focuses on nine-year-old Bruno. When Bruno moves with his family from Berlin, Germany, to a new location after his father receives a new military assignment, his world is suddenly divided in two by a large fence: on one side lives his family and on the other live the only other children he can see who are his own age. All of them, including Bruno's new friend, Shmuel, wear gray-striped pajamas. While Bruno remains ignorant of the

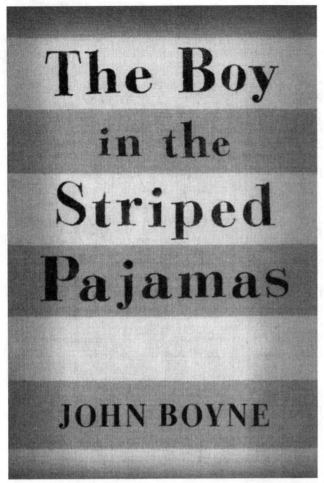

Cover of John Boyne's evocative novel The Boy in the Striped Pajamas, *which received acclaim both in America and the United Kingdom.* (David Fickling Books, 2006. Reproduced by permission of David Fickling Books, an imprint of Random House Children's Books, a division of Random House, Inc.)

true implications of his world, readers quickly realize that the boy resides near the Auschwitz concentration camp, and his father is commandant at the notorious prison.

Described by a *Publishers Weekly* reviewer as a "simple, thought provoking story," *The Boy in the Striped Pajamas* sparked a certain degree of controversy: while many critics felt that the work effectively conveys the horror of its true subject, some expressed concern that the novel diminishes the reality of the Holocaust for younger readers. "Boyne carries the story so effectively, particular in the ending, that few readers will avoid tears," concluded Benedicte Page in a review for *Bookseller,* and Hazel Rochman noted in *Booklist* that, "as the story builds to a horrifying climax, the innocent's experience brings home the unimaginable horror." A *School Library Journal* reviewer concluded that Boyne's "combination of strong characterization and simple, honest narrative make this powerful and memorable tale a unique addition" to Holocaust fiction.

The Boy in the Striped Pajamas marked a change for Boyne. "I tend to plot out my novels quite densely in

advance, but this one was completely different," he explained to Page in *Bookseller.* In this case, the two young characters who figure in the story came to Boyne one evening. He began writing the next day, and completed the first draft of the novel in less than a week.

Biographical and Critical Sources

PERIODICALS

Booklist, March 15, 2006, Kristine Huntley, review of *Crippen: A Novel of Murder,* p. 30; July 1, 2006, Hazel Rochman, review of *The Boy in the Striped Pajamas: A Fable,* p. 48; February 1, 2007, Michael Gannon, review of *The Thief of Time,* p. 29.

Bookseller, October 7, 2005, Benedicte Page, "Books by the Shelf-full: Sitting at His Desk to Write Each Day Is Former Bookseller John Boyne's Definition of the Good Life," p. 25.

Bulletin of the Center for Children's Books, October, 2006, Loretta Gaffney, review of *The Boy in the Striped Pajamas,* p. 60.

Horn Book, September-October, 2006, Roger Sutton, review of *The Boy in the Striped Pajamas,* p. 575.

Kirkus Reviews, January 1, 2006, review of *Crippen,* p. 3; August 15, 2006, review of *The Boy in the Striped Pajamas,* p. 836.

Kliatt, September, 2006, Myrna Marler, review of *The Boy in the Striped Pajamas,* p. 8.

New York Times Book Review, November 12, 2006, A.O. Scott, "Something Is Happening," p. 41.

Publishers Weekly, January 2, 2006, review of *Crippen,* p. 34; July 17, 2006, review of *The Boy in the Striped Pajamas,* p. 158; November 20, 2006, review of *The Thief of Time,* p. 33.

School Library Journal, September, 2006, Susan Scheps, review of *The Boy in the Striped Pajamas,* p. 202.

Sunday Times (London, England), October 1, 2006, Rose Costello, review of *The Boy in the Striped Pajamas,* p. 14.

Voice of Youth Advocates, December, 2006, C.J. Bott, review of *The Boy in the Striped Pajamas,* p. 420; February, 2007, review of *The Boy in the Striped Pajamas,* p. 486.

ONLINE

Irish Writers Centre Web site, http://www.writerscentre.ie/ (June 22, 2007), "John Boyne."

Irish Writers Online, http://www.irishwriters-online.com/ (June 22, 2007), "John Boyne."

John Boyne Home Page, http://www.johnboyne.com (June 22, 2007).

Meet the Author Web site, http://www.meettheauthor.co.uk/ (June 22, 2007), video interview with Boyne.

BROWN, Charlotte Lewis

Personal

Female. *Education:* Ph.D. (paleontology).

Addresses

Home and office—Seattle, WA.

Career

Author. Former instructor in paleontology.

Writings

After the Dinosaurs: Mammoths and Fossil Mammals, illustrated by Phil Wilson, HarperCollins (New York, NY), 2006.

The Day the Dinosaurs Died, illustrated by Phil Wilson, HarperCollins (New York, NY), 2006.

Beyond the Dinosaurs: Monsters of the Air and Sea, illustrated by Phil Wilson, HarperCollins (New York, NY), 2007.

Cover of Charlotte Lewis Brown's beginning reader The Day the Dinosaurs Died, *featuring artwork by Phil Wilson.* (Illustration © 2006 by Phil Wilson. All rights reserved. Reproduced by permission of HarperCollins Children's Books, a division of HarperCollins Publishers.)

Sidelights

Trained as a paleontologist, Charlotte Lewis Brown provides young readers with a factual and scientific look at the prehistoric age and its creatures in her books *After the Dinosaurs: Mammoths and Fossil Mammals, The Day the Dinosaurs Died,* and *Beyond the Dinosaurs: Monsters of the Air and Sea.* In *After the Dinosaurs* she introduces ten creatures that survived the dinosaurs, including the wooly mammoth, saber tooth tiger, and homo sapiens. Brown makes prehistoric information understandable to young children by associating the antiquated animals to the creature which has evolved from it and lives on Earth today. In one example, she compares an extinct creature to a modern species: a small dog. A *Kirkus Reviews* critic praised Brown for presenting "straightforward information" on mammals and fossil animals "in an interesting and accessible package for developing readers."

In *The Day the Dinosaurs Died* Brown takes a more-graphic approach in educating children on how Earth's dinosaur population actually became extinct. She describes how the giant asteroid crashed into the planet, altering Earth's environment and ultimately extinguishing the giant creatures. Danielle J. Ford, writing in *Horn Book,* cautioned that *The Day the Dinosaurs Died* "may not be for the squeamish," but noted that Brown's take on prehistory is "gruesome—yet factually accurate and realistic." In addition to the realistic graphics and details, Brown includes a pronunciation guide to aid readers in tackling dinosaurs names as well as an appended author's note.

Biographical and Critical Sources

PERIODICALS

Horn Book, July-August, 2006, Danielle J. Ford, review of *The Day the Dinosaurs Died,* p. 460.

Kirkus Reviews, May 15, 2006, review of *The Day the Dinosaurs Died,* p. 514; August 15, 2006, review of *After the Dinosaurs: Mammoths and Fossil Mammals,* p. 836.

School Library Journal, June, 2006, Lynda Ritterman, review of *The Day the Dinosaurs Died,* p. 132; February, 2007, Christine Markley, review of *After the Dinosaurs,* p. 105.

ONLINE

HarperCollins Web site, http://www.harpercollinschildrens. com/ (July 7, 2007), "Charlotte Lewis Brown."*

*   *   *

BRUCHAC, Margaret M.
See BRUCHAC, Marge

Marge Bruchac (Courtesy of Marge Bruchac.)

*   *   *

BRUCHAC, Marge
(Margaret M. Bruchac)

Personal

Married Justin Kennick. *Ethnicity:* "Abenaki." *Education:* B.A. (history and theater); M.A. (anthropology); Ph.D. (anthropology).

Addresses

Home and office—63 Franklin St., Northampton, MA 01060. *E-mail*—maligeet@earthlink.net.

Career

Historical consultant, teacher, author, and performer. Freelance museum consultant for Native American programming and exhibitions at Historic Deerfield, Old Sturbridge Village, Plimoth Plantation, and Pocumtuck Valley Memorial Association. Visiting faculty for college courses at Amherst College, Keene State College, Smith College, University of Massachusetts Amherst, and State University of New York at Plattsburgh; artist-in-residence at Mashantucket Pequot Museum and Research Center, 2001; Visiting Indigenous Fellow at Harvard College, 2006-07; McLellan Distinguished Visiting Professor in North Country History, State University of New York, Plattsburgh, 2007. Musician; has recorded stories and folk music. Member, Five-College Native

American Indian Studies Curriculum Committee, Indigenous Archaeology advisory board. Member of boards of trustees for Historic Northampton, Fort Ticonderoga, and Plimoth Plantation. Member, Five College Native American Indian Studies Curriculum Committee, National Caucus of Wordcraft Circle of Native American Writers and Storytellers, and Indigenous Archaeology advisory board.

Awards, Honors

Bay State Historical League scholar-in-residence award, Pocumtuck Valley Memorial Association, 1998; Smith College Women's History Award, 1998, for "Mohegan Women and Cultural Expression"; Five College Theater Departments Playwright Award, 1998, for *Staging the Indian,* 1999, for *molly has her say;* University of Massachusetts Amherst European studies grant, 2000; Storyteller of the Year awards, Wordcraft Circle of Native American Writers and Storytellers, 2000, for performance, 2002 for history, 2004 for academic writing; Aesop Prize, American Folklore Society, 2006, and *Skipping Stones* Honor Award for Multicultural & International Awareness, 2007, both for *Malian's Song;* Distinguished Teaching Award finalist, University of Massachusetts Amherst 2007.

Writings

(With Catherine O'Neill Grace and others) *1621: A New Look at Thanksgiving,* photographs by Sisse Brimberg and Cotton Coulson, National Geographic Society (Washington, DC), 2001.
(With Frederique Apffel-Marglin) *Exorcising Anthropology's Demons,* Multiversity and Citizens International (Penang, Malaysia), 2004.
Malian's Song, illustrated by William Maughan, Vermont Folklife Center (Middlebury, VT), 2006.

Play anthologized in *Keepers of the Morning Star: Native American Women Playwrights,* University of California Press (Los Angeles, CA), 2001. Contributor of essays to books, including *The Abenaki of Vermont: A Living Culture, Teacher's Guide,* Vermont Folklife Center (Middlebury, VT), 2002; *A Place Called Paradise: Culture and Community in Northampton, Massachusetts, 1654-2004,* University of Massachusetts Press (Amherst, MA), 2004; *Indigenous Archaeologies: Politics and Practice,* 2005; *Captive Histories: Captivity Narratives, French Relations, and Native Stories of the 1704 Deerfield Raid,* 2006; and *Where the Mountain Stands Alone: Stories of Place in the Monadnock Region,* University Press of New England, University Press of New England (Hanover, NH), 2006.

Sidelights

As a Native American author, historian, scholar, and performer, Marge Bruchac works to educate the public on the culture and history of native peoples by present-

In his illustrations for **Malian's Song,** *William Maughan brings to life Bruchac's story of a Native American family living in what is now New England.* (The Vermont Folklife Center, 2005. Reproduced by permission.)

ing accurate historical information and reexamining stereotypes. Bruchac—the sister of noted writer Joseph Bruchac—shares her knowledge of northeastern Abenaki and Algonkian Indian history through historical lectures, musical renderings, and story tellings that she presents and performs in such diverse venues as schools, historical societies, and world music festivals. As a scholar, she has designed and taught college courses on colonial history, decolonizing methodologies, indigenous archaeologies, oral tradition, and cultural performance, and has contributed writings to academic publications that focus on Native American histories. Her book *Malian's Song* introduces young children to the lifeways of eighteenth-century Abenaki people and the impact of colonial trade and conflict on Native survival.

Malian's Song illustrates the personal experience of two young Abenaki Indian girls—Malian and Maliazonis—who survived the October 4, 1759 attack by Major Robert Rogers on the St. Francis Abenaki village of Odanak. This account, based on the oral history of the Abenaki as corroborated by the French Jesuit records, counters the impression left by Rogers and later historians who reported that there were few survivors left after the burning of the village. This story is based on Abenaki family traditions, as recorded by Elvine Obomsawin and her granddaughter Jeanne Brink, during the mid-late 20th century. Bruchac's intent was to render some of the lifeways and traditions of the Abenaki people visible, while also demonstrating the incredible complexity of relations along the Native, British, American, and French colonial frontiers. Authentic representa-

tions of Abenaki families can be seen in the evocative illustrations, and their voices can be heard in the Abenaki words scattered throughout the text. In the historical essay at the end of the story (an expanded version can be found on the Vermont Folklife Center Web site), Bruchac notes that Abenaki histories are still poorly understood today, in part because of the impact of Rogers' Raid, as well as the lack of awareness of other historic Abenaki communities situated across Vermont, New Hampshire, and northern Massachusetts.

Cris Reidel, writing in *School Library Journal,* acknowledged that *Malian's Song* details a "a lesser-known piece of history passed down through oral storytelling," and a *Small Press Bookwatch* reviewer deemed the work "more than a children's picturebook" because "it preserves a piece of American and Native American history."

Biographical and Critical Sources

PERIODICALS

Booklist, August 1, 2006, Kathleen Odean, review of *Malian's Song,* p. 80.

Kirkus Reviews, June 15, 2006, review of *Malian's Song,* p. 631.

New York Times Book Review, August 13, 2006, Simon Rodberg, review of *Malian's Song.*

Resource Links, December, 2006, Kathryn McNaughton, review of *Malian's Song,* p. 13.

Small Press Bookwatch, October, 2006, review of *Malian's Song.*

School Library Journal, January, 2007, Cris Riedel, review of *Malian's Song,* p. 113.

ONLINE

Androscoggin Valley Community Network Web site, http://www.avcnet.org/ (July 7, 2007), "Marge Bruchac."

Vermont Folklife Center Web site, http://www.vermontfolklifecenter.org/ (July 23, 2007), "*Malian's Song:* Cultural and Historical Background."

C

CALLAN, Jim 1951-

Personal

Born January 16, 1951, in Nyack, NY; son of John (a builder) and Viola (a homemaker) Callan; married Polly Corman (a psychotherapist), June 26, 1999. *Education:* Fordham University, B.A. (communications); New York University, M.A. (cinema). *Politics:* Democrat.

Addresses

Home and office—Nyack, NY. *E-mail*—jimcallan@optonline.net.

Career

Author; freelance writer and editor; previously worked as senior editor, McGraw-Hill.

Writings

NONFICTION

The New York Public Library Amazing Scientists: A Book of Answers for Kids, J. Wiley (New York, NY), 2001.
America in the 1930s ("Decades of American History" series), Facts on File (New York, NY), 2005.
America in the 1900s and 1910s ("Decades of American History" series), Facts on File (New York, NY), 2006.
America in the 1960s ("Decades of American History" series), Facts on File (New York, NY), 2006.

Biographical and Critical Sources

PERIODICALS

Booklist, January 1, 2006, Ilene Cooper, review of *America in the 1930s,* p. 77.

School Library Journal, August, 2006, John Peters, review of "Decades of American History" series, p. 70.
Voice of Youth Advocates, April, 2006, Stephanie Petruso, review of "Decades of American History" series, p. 82.

*   *   *

CAMPOY, F. Isabel 1946-

Personal

Born June 25, 1946, in Alicante, Spain; daughter of Juan Diego Campoy (a professor of English) and Maria Coronado Guerro (a homemaker). *Ethnicity:* "Hispanic." *Education:* Universidad Complutense (Madrid, Spain), B.A., M.A. (English philology); Reading University, M.A. (dialectology); doctoral studies in applied linguistics at University of California, Los Angeles. *Politics:* "Defender of justice and peace." *Hobbies and other interests:* Painting, sculpting, observing children and nature.

Addresses

Home—San Francisco, CA. *Office*—38 Miller Ave., No. 181, Mill Valley, CA 94941. *E-mail*—fisabelcampoy@yahoo.com.

Career

Poet and playwright. Author and lecturer on educational and multicultural matters. Transformative Education Services, president.

Member

International Reading Association (member of board on social responsibility), CABE, NABE, Association of Spanish Professionals in the USA (president, 1994-96), various national and regional bilingual education associations.

Awards, Honors

Fulbright scholar, 1979-81; Friends and Foundation of San Francisco Public Library Laureate Award, 2003; Reading the World Award, 2004, for *Cuentos que contaban nuestras abuelitas;* Junior Library Guild Premier Selection Award, and American Library Association Notable Book designaton, both 2006, both for *¡Pío Peep!*

Writings

FOR CHILDREN

¿Quieres que to cuente?, Harcourt School Publishers (Orlando, FL), 1995.

En un lugar muy lejano, Harcourt School Publishers (Orlando, FL), 1995.

Erase que se era, Harcourt School Publishers (Orlando, FL), 1995.

Y fueron felices, Harcourt School Publishers (Orlando, FL), 1995.

Y colorín colorado, Harcourt School Publishers (Orlando, FL), 1995.

Así pasaron muchos años, Harcourt School Publishers (Orlando, FL), 1995.

(Adaptor) *Rosa Raposa,* illustrated by Ariane Dewey and Jose Aruego, Harcourt (New York, NY), 2002.

Get up, Rick!, illustrated by Bernard Adnet, Harcourt (Orlando, FL), 2007.

FOR CHILDREN; WITH ALMA FLOR ADA

Sigue la palabra, Harcourt School Publishers (Orlando, FL), 1995.

Imágenes del pasado, Harcourt School Publishers (Orlando, FL), 1995.

Ecos del pasado (chapter book; title means "Echoes from the Past"), Harcourt Brace (Orlando, FL), 1996.

Música amiga (anthology of Hispanic folklore; includes tapes and teacher's guide), ten volumes, Del Sol (Westlake, OH), 1996–98.

Una semilla de luz (title means "A Seed of Light"), illustrated by Felipe Dávalos, Alfaguara (Madrid, Spain), 2000.

Tablado de Doña Rosita/Curtain's Up, Santillana USA (Miami, FL), 2001.

¡Feliz cumpleaños, Caperucita Roja!/Happy Birthday, Little Red Riding Hood!, illustrated by Ana López Escrivá, Alfaguara (Miami, FL), 2002.

El nuevo hogar de los siete cabritos/The New Home of the Seven Billy Goats, illustrated by Viví Escrivá, Alfaguara (Miami, FL), 2002.

Ratoncito Perez, Mailman/Ratoncito Perez, cartero, illustrated by Sandra López Escrivá, Alfaguara (Miami, FL), 2002.

One, Two, Three, Who Can It Be?/Uno, dos, tres: ¿Dime quién es?, illustrated by Viví Escrivá, Alfaguara (Miami, FL), 2002.

On the Wings of the Condor/En alas del condor, Alfaguara (Miami, FL), 2002.

Eyes of the Jaguar/Ojos del jaguar, Alfaguara (Miami, FL), 2002.

The Quetzal's Journey/Vuelo del quetzal, illustrated by Felipe Davalos, Santillana USA (Miami, FL), 2002.

(Compiler) *¡Pío Peep!: Traditional Spanish Nursery Rhymes* (bilingual edition), illustrated by Viví Escrivá, English adaptations by Alice Schertle, HarperCollins (New York, NY), 2003.

Tales Our Abuelitas Told: An Hispanic Folktale Collection, illustrated by Felipe Dávalos, Atheneum (New York, NY), 2004.

Mama Goose: A Latino Nursery Tresury/Un tesor de rimas infantiles, illustrated by Maribel Suárez, Hyperion (New York, NY), 2004.

Cuentos que contaban nuestras abuelitas, Atheneum (New York, NY), 2006.

(Compiler) *Merry Navidad!: Christmas Carols in Spanish and English,* illustrated by Vivi Escrivá, Rayo (New York, NY), 2007.

Also coauthor, with Alma Flor Ada, of Spanish language-arts programs "Cielo abierto," "Vamos de fiesta!," "Villacuentos," and "Trofeos," Harcourt School Publishers (Orlando, FL), 1997, and of English-as-a-second-language programs.

PLAYS; WITH ALMA FLOR ADA

Primer acto, Harcourt School Publishers (Orlando, FL), 1996.

Risas y aplausos, Harcourt School Publishers (Orlando, FL), 1996.

Escenas y alegrías, Harcourt School Publishers (Orlando, FL), 1996.

Actores y flores, Harcourt School Publishers (Orlando, FL), 1996.

Saludos al público, Harcourt School Publishers (Orlando, FL), 1996.

Ensayo general, Harcourt School Publishers (Orlando, FL), 1996.

Acto final, Harcourt School Publishers (Orlando, FL), 1996.

Top Hat, Alfaguara (Miami, FL), 2000.

Curtains Up!, Alfaguara (Miami, FL), 2000.

Rat-a-Tat, Alfaguara (Miami, FL), 2002, published as *Rat-a-Tat Cat,* Santillana USA (Miami, FL), 2002.

Roll 'n' Roll, Alfaguara (Miami, FL), 2002, published as *Roll 'n' Role,* Santillana USA (Miami, FL), 2002.

"MÚSICA AMIGA" SERIES; WITH ALMA FLOR ADA

Gorrión, Gorrión, Harcourt School Publishers (Orlando, FL), 1996.

El verde limón, Harcourt School Publishers (Orlando, FL), 1996.

La rama azul, Harcourt School Publishers (Orlando, FL), 1996.

Nuevo día, Harcourt School Publishers (Orlando, FL), 1996.

Huertos de coral, Harcourt School Publishers (Orlando, FL), 1996.

Ríos de lava, Harcourt School Publishers (Orlando, FL), 1996.

Dulce es la sal, Harcourt School Publishers (Orlando, FL), 1996.

Canta la letra, illustrated by Ulises Wensell, Del Sol (Westlake, OH), 1998, with music by Suni Paz, 2003.

Caracolí, illustrated by Ulises Wensell, Del Sol (Westlake, OH), 1998, with music by Suni Paz, 2003.

Con ton y son, illustrated by Ulises Wensell, Del Sol (Westlake, OH), 1998, with music by Suni Paz, 2003.

Corre al coro, illustrated by Ulises Wensell, Del Sol (Westlake, OH), 1998, with music by Suni Paz, 2003.

¡Do, re, mi, sí, sí!, illustrated by Ulises Wensell, Del Sol (Westlake, OH), 1998, with music by Suni Paz, 2003.

El camino de tu risa, illustrated by Ulises Wensell, Del Sol (Westlake, OH), 1998, with music by Suni Paz, 2003.

El son de sol, illustrated by Ulises Wensell, Del Sol (Westlake, OH), 1998, with music by Suni Paz, 2003.

¡Qué rica la ronda!, illustrated by Ulises Wensell, Del Sol (Westlake, OH), 1998, with music by Suni Paz, 2003.

Sigue la música, illustrated by Ulises Wensell, Del Sol (Westlake, OH), 1998, with music by Suni Paz, 2003.

"GATEWAYS TO THE SUN" SERIES; WITH ALMA FLOR ADA

Smiles/Sonrisas (biographies of Pablo Picasso, Gabriela Mistral, and Benito Juarez), Alfaguara (Miami, FL), 1998.

Steps/Pasos (biographies of Rita Moreno, Fernando Botero, and Evelyn Cisneros), Alfaguara (Miami, FL), 1998.

Voices/Voces (biographies of Luis Valdez, Judith F. Baca, and Carlos J. Finlay), Alfaguara (Miami, FL), 1998.

Paths/Caminos (biographies of José Marti, Frida Kahlo, and Cesar Chavez), Alfaguara (Miami, FL), 1998.

Yo/I Am, Santillana USA (Miami, FL), 1999.

Rimas/Rhymes, Santillana USA (Miami, FL), 1999.

Poemas/Poems, Santillana USA (Miami, FL), 1999.

Palabras, Santillana USA (Miami, FL), 1999.

Mis relatos/My Stories, Santillana USA (Miami, FL), 1999.

Mis recuerdos, Santillana USA (Miami, FL), 1999.

Mambru, Santillana USA (Miami, FL), 1999.

Letras, Santillana USA (Miami, FL), 1999.

Lapices/Pencils, Santillana USA (Miami, FL), 1999.

Crayones/Crayons, Santillana USA (Miami, FL), 1999.

Colores/Colors, Santillana USA (Miami, FL), 1999.

Así soy/This Is Me, Santillana USA (Miami, FL), 1999.

Acuarela, Santillana USA (Miami, FL), 1999.

Blue and Green/Azul y verde, Alfaguara (Miami, FL), 2000.

Brush and Paint/Brocha y pinchel, Alfaguara (Miami, FL), 2000.

Artist's Easel/Caballete, Alfaguara (Miami, FL), 2000.

Canvas and Paper/Lienzo y papel, Alfaguara (Miami, FL), 2000.

(Selector) *Dreaming Fish/Pimpón* (poetry), Alfaguara (Miami, FL), 2000.

(Selector) *Laughing Crocodiles/Antón Pirulero* (poetry), Alfaguara (Miami, FL), 2000.

(Selector) *Singing Horse/Mambrú* (poetry), Alfaguara (Miami, FL), 2000.

(Selector and contributor) *Flying Dragon,* Alfaguara (Miami, FL), 2000.

Series published in Spanish translation as "Colleccion Puertas al Sol."

"STORIES TO CELEBRATE" SERIES; WITH ALMA FLOR ADA

Celebrate Thanksgiving Day with Beto and Gaby, illustrated by Claudia Rueda, Santillana USA (Miami, FL), 2006.

Celebrate St. Patrick's Day with Samantha and Lola, illustrated by Sandra Lavandeira, Santillana USA (Miami, FL), 2006.

Celebrate Martin Luther King, Jr. Day with Mrs. Park's Class/Celebra ed día de Martin Luther King, Jr. con la clase de la Sra. Park, illustrated by Monica Weiss, Santillana USA (Miami, FL), 2006.

Celebrate Mardi Gras with Joaquin, Harlequin/Celebra el Mardi Gras con Joaquìn, arlequìn, illustrated by Eugenia Nobati, Santillana USA (Miami, FL), 2006.

Celebrate Hannukah with Bubbe's Tales/Celebra Hannukah con un cuento de Bubbe, illustrated by Mariano Epelbaum, Santillana USA (Miami, FL), 2006.

Celebrate Fourth of July with Champ, the Scamp/Celebra el cuatro de julio con Campeón, el glotón, illustrated by Gustavo Mazali, Santillana USA (Miami, FL), 2006.

Celebrate Christmas and Three Kings' Day with Pablo and Carlitos/Celebra la navidad y el día de los reyes magos con Pablo y Carlitos, illustrated by Walter Torres, Santillana USA (Miami, FL), 2006.

Celebrate Kwanzaa with Boots and Her Kittens/Celebra Kwanzaa con Botitas y sus gatitos, illustrated by Valeria Docampo, Santillana USA (Miami, FL), 2006.

Celebrate Halloween and the Day of the Dead with Cristina and Her Blue Bunny/Celebra el Halloween y el día de muertos con Cristina y su conejito azul, illustrated by Ivanova Martinez, Santillana USA (Miami, FL), 2006.

Celebrate Cinco de Mayo with the Mexican Hat Dance/Celebra el Cinco de Mayo con un jarabe tapatio, illustrated by Marcela Gomez and David Silva, Santillana USA (Miami, FL), 2006.

Celebrate Chinese New Year with the Fong Family/Celebra el año nuevo chino con la familia Fong, illustrated by Mima Castro, Santillana USA (Miami, FL), 2006.

Celebrate a Powwow with Sandy Starbright/Celebra un powwow con Sandy Starbright, illustrated by Maria Jesus Alvarez, Santillana USA (Miami, FL), 2006.

TRANSLATOR; WITH ALMA FLOR ADA

Lois Ehlert, *Plumas para almorzar* (translation of *Feathers for Lunch*), Harcourt (San Diego, CA), 1996.

Lois Ehlert, *A sembrar sopa de verduras* (translation of *Growing Vegetable Soup*), Harcourt (San Diego, CA), 1996.

Gary Soto, *¡Que montón de tamales!* (translation of *Too Many Tamales*), illustrated by Ed Martinez, PaperStar (New York, NY), 1996.

Ellen Stoll Walsh, *Salta y brinca* (translation of *Hop Jump*), Harcourt (San Diego, CA), 1996.

Henry Horenstein, *Béisobol en los barrios,* Harcourt (New York, NY), 1997.

Mem Fox, *Quienquiera que seas* (translation of *Whoever You Are*), illustrated by Leslie Staub, Harcourt (San Diego, CA), 2002.

Gerald McDermott, *Zomo el conejo: un cuento de Africa occidental* (translation of *Zomo the Rabbit*), Harcourt (San Diego, CA), 2002.

Peter Golenbock, *Compañeros de equipo* (translation of *Teammates*), illustrated by Paul Bacon, Harcourt (San Diego, CA), 2002.

Lois Ehlert, *Día de mercado* (translation of *Market Day*), Harcourt (San Diego, CA), 2003.

George Ancona, *Mis bailes/My Dances,* photographs by Ancona, Children's Press (New York, NY), 2004.

George Ancona, *Mis amigos/My Friends,* photographs by Ancona, Children's Press (New York, NY), 2004.

George Ancona, *Mi familia/My Family,* photographs by Ancona, Children's Press (New York, NY), 2004.

George Ancona, *Mi escuela/My School,* photographs by Ancona, Children's Press (New York, NY), 2004.

George Ancona, *Mi casa/My House,* photographs by Ancona, Children's Press (New York, NY), 2004.

George Ancona, *Mi barrio/My Neighborhood,* photographs by Ancona, Children's Press (New York, NY), 2004.

George Ancona, *Mis quehaceres/My Chores,* photographs by Ancona, Children's Press (New York, NY), 2005.

George Ancona, *Mis juegos/My Games,* photographs by Ancona, Children's Press (New York, NY), 2005.

George Ancona, *Mis fiestas/My Celebrations,* photographs by Ancona, Children's Press (New York, NY), 2005.

George Ancona, *Mis comidas/My Foods,* photographs by Ancona, Children's Press (New York, NY), 2005.

George Ancona, *Mi musica/My Music,* photographs by Ancona, Children's Press (New York, NY), 2005.

FOR ADULTS; WITH ALMA FLOR ADA

Home School Interaction with Culturally or Language-diverse Families, Del Sol (Westlake, OH), 1998.

Ayudando a nuestros hijos (title means "Helping Our Children"), Del Sol (Westlake, OH), 1998.

Comprehensive Language Arts, Del Sol (Westlake, OH), 1998.

Effective English Acquisition for Academic Success, Del Sol (Westlake, OH), 1998.

(With Rosalma Zubizarreta) *Authors in the Classroom: A Transformative Education Process,* Allyn & Bacon (Boston, MA), 2004.

Sidelights

"From my mother I inherited a robust pride in my roots, a wealth of folklore through her storytelling and sayings, and an abundant sense of humor. From my father, the passion for learning and the art of teaching," author and playwright F. Isabel Campoy noted on her home

F. Isabel Campoy's many collaborations with author Alma Flor Ida include the picture-book anthology ¡Pío Peep!, featuring artwork by Viví Escrivá. (Illustration © 2003 by Viví Escrivá. Used by permission of HarperCollins Children's Books, a division of HarperCollins Publishers.)

page. Frequently collaborating with fellow author and educator Alma Flor Ada, Campoy specializes in bilingual materials for children of Hispanic heritage: plays, poems, educational materials, picture books, biographies, and easy-readers. In addition to stand-alone books, the collaborators have produced a number of book series, and several of their works have been included in the "Gateways to the Sun"/"Coleccion puertas al sol" series designed to introduce young readers to Hispanic culture. Their *Música amiga* series, published beginning in 1996, encompasses ten volumes of Hispanic folklore, along with original lyrics by Campoy, while other books, such as *¡Feliz cumpleaños, Caperucita Roja!/Happy Birthday, Little Red Riding Hood!* "combine the charm of traditional tales with the surprise of the unexpected," according to *Booklist* reviewer Isabel Schon. Praising their popular bilingual anthology *¡Pío Peep!: Traditional Spanish Nursery Rhymes, Booklist* contributor Ilene Cooper predicted that the co-authors' text, with its "sweet, rhythmic simplicity, . . . will get children singing, clapping, and perhaps making some forays into a new language."

Books by Campoy and Ada that are part of the "Gateways to the Sun" series include the art books *Blue and Green* and *Brush and Paint,* as well as a four-book series of biographies of notable Hispanic men and woman

titled *Smiles, Steps, Voices,* and *Paths.* Profiling such diverse individuals as artist Frida Kahlo, labor activist Cesar Chavez, and actress Rita Moreno, these books "briefly tell about the lives and achievements" of their subjects, according to *Booklist* reviewer Schon, who praised the entire series as "a very appealing introduction" to Spanish-language culture.

In addition to her works with Ada, Campoy has authored a number of Spanish-language early readers, as well as the picture books *Rosa Raposa* and *Get up, Rick! Rosa Raposa* contains three stories adapted from Spanish trickster tales that take readers to South America and the Amazon rain forest. In "A Cry for Help," "A Strong North Wind," and "The Green Dress" clever little fox Rosa Raposa manages to outwit a hungry and bullying jaguar. A *Publishers Weekly* contributor praised *Rosa Raposa* for its lively watercolor illustrations by Ariane Dewey and Jose Aruego, while Julie Cummins wrote in *Booklist* that Campoy's book features a "well-paced text" that, with the rhyming conclusion to each story, "will make for lively read-alouds." Calling the book "delightful," *School Library Journal* contributor Judith Constantinides added that Campoy's stories do much to promote "the idea that brains are better than brawn."

Campoy once commented: "I was born by the Mediterranean Sea in a town called Alicante, an ideal vacation place in Spain both for national and international tourists, so during my childhood I was always in contact with people coming and going—family and friends from all over the world.

"That, and the fact that my father was a professor of English and wanted his children to become proficient in as many languages as possible, provided me with a great desire to travel and be in touch with other cultures very early on. My favorite books as a child were always full of adventure, from the medieval chivalric romances and the pirates of Sandocán to *Treasure Island, The Adventures of Tom Sawyer,* and *Alice's Adventures in Wonderland.* But perhaps my favorite of all times is *The Little Prince* by Antoine de Sainte-Exupéry.

"My curiosity for all things far and different was nurtured by my father's vast collection of *National Geographic* magazines that covered one side of our hallway from floor to ceiling, with copies that went back as far as 1924. Each picture was a promise of a new adventure, and I started writing about them in a huge accounting book my brother and I shared: on his end, the names of soccer players and winning teams; on mine, the products of my fertile imagination. My first published story was about a snowman. I was eleven, and I had never seen snow.

"At age sixteen, after a hard time convincing my mother and many competitive examinations, I won a scholarship as an exchange student to Trenton, Michigan. Finally, that winter, I saw snow—almost daily! I have the impression that I have been traveling ever since.

"In my twenties I crossed Europe and in Greece I fell in love with mythology. Years later I wrote down many legends of the Hispanic world.

"Morocco, Egypt, and Turkey were countries that fascinated me and inspired my research into the Arabic contributions to the history of Spain and Latin America.

"Names in the Hispanic culture include both last names from parents. My complete name is Francisca Isabel Campoy Coronado and one summer I set up to follow the path of Coronado in the southwest. That encounter with history (my history) opened a new era of discoveries both for my mind and heart. My travels through México, Puerto Rico, Cuba, Colombia, Costa Rica, Guatemala, Chile, and Argentina have provided me with tools I want to put in the hands of Latino children.

"Whether in Asia or Micronesia, Africa or the Middle East, I have always found reason to admire other cultures and reflect on them. Perhaps that is why I write about Hispanic art, artists, theatre, poetry, and folklore: in the process of looking at other cultures, I discovered the beauty and richness of my own."

Biographical and Critical Sources

PERIODICALS

Booklist, August, 2000, p. 2154; February 15, 2002, Isabel Schon, review of *¡Feliz cumpleaños, Caperucita Roja!/Happy Birthday, Little Red Riding Hood!* and *The New Home of the Seven Billy Goats,* p. 1022; September 1, 2002, Julie Cummins, review of *Rosa Raposa,* p. 136; September 1, 2003, Ilene Cooper, review of *¡Pío Peep!: Traditional Spanish Nursery Rhymes,* p. 126.

Kirkus Reviews, August 15, 2002, review of *Rosa Raposa,* p. 1219.

Publishers Weekly, September 9, 2002, review of *Rosa Raposa,* p. 66.

School Library Journal, September, 2002, Judith Constantinides, review of *Rosa Raposa,* p. 181; June, 2003, "The Dynamic Duo of Alma Flor Ada and F. Isabel Campoy," p. 60; July, 2003, Ann Welton, review of *¡Pío Peep!,* p. 121.

ONLINE

F. Isabel Campoy Home Page, http://www.isabelcampoy.com (July 26, 2007).

OTHER

Path to My Word: A Latina Writer's Journey (videotape), Del Sol (Westlake, OH), 1999.

CECCOLI, Nicoletta

Personal

Born in San Marino. *Education:* Attended State Institute of Art (Urbino, Italy).

Addresses

Home—Via 28 Luglio, 184, 47893 Borgo Maggiore, Repubblica di San Marino. *E-mail*—nceccoli@omniway.sm.

Career

Illustrator. *Exhibitions:* Work exhibited at Bologna Children's Book Fair, Bologna, Italy; L'Art a la Page, Paris, France; Ottogallery, Bologna; Storyopolis, Los Angeles, CA; and Daimuru museum, Osaka, Japan.

Awards, Honors

Three-time recipient of Communication Arts award of excellence; Andersen Prize for Best Italian Illustrator, 2001; Society of Illustrators Silver Medal, 2006.

Illustrator

Anna Lavatelle, *La superbarba,* Maresche (Italy), 1996.

Guido Quarzo, *Talpa lumaca pesciolino: tre piccole storie di bambini,* Fatatrac (Florence, Italy), 1997.

Vanna Cercenà, *A immagine e somiglianza,* Fatatrac (Florence, Italy), 1998.

Riccardo Geminiani, *Nuvolando,* Arka (Milan, Italy), 1998.

Paola Pallottini, *Maria Moll Cappero,* Fatatrac (Florence, Italy), 1999.

Gail Gilles, *Il respiro del drago,* Mondadori (Verona, Italy), 1999.

Carmen Martin Gaite, *La torta del diavolo,* Mondadori (Verona, Italy), 1999.

Beatrice Masini, *L'uomo della luna,* Arka (Milan, Italy), 1999.

Vanna Cercenà and Nicoletta Codignola, *Teseo e Arianna,* Fatatrac (Florence, Italy), 1999.

Chiara Carminati, *Il mare in una rima,* Mondadori (Verona, Italy), 2000.

Italo Calvino, *La foresta radice-labririnto,* Mondadori (Verona, Italy), 2000.

Maria Vago, *La bambina bianca,* Arka (Milan, Italy), 2000.

Dacia Mariani, *La pecora Dolly e altre storie per bambini,* Narrativa Fabbri (Milan, Italy), 2001.

Carlo Collodi, *Le Avventure di Pinocchio,* Mondadori (Verona, Italy), 2001.

Bianca Tarozzi, *Storie di Matilde,* Mondadori (Verona, Italy), 2001.

Riccardo Germiniani, *Teresa è nervosa,* San Paolo (Milan, Italy), 2001.

Adriana Merenda, *Il mistero delle luccipietre,* Nuove Edizioni Romane (Italy), 2001.

Charles Perrault, *Fiabe classiche. I racconti di Mamma Oca,* Mondadori (Verona, Italy), 2001.

Sara Boero, *L'estate del non ritorno,* Fatatrac (Florence, Italy), 2001.

Ornella Pozzolo, *Anna senza confini,* Arka (Milan, Italy), 2002.

Stella Blackstone, *An Island in the Sun,* Barefoot Books (Cambridge, MA), 2002.

Francesca Lazzarato, *Sei fiabe di gatti,* Mondadori (Verona, Italy), 2002.

Miguel Ángel Asturias, *L'uomo che Aveva tutto tutto tutto,* Mondadori (Verona, Italy), 2003.

Tanya Robyn Batt, *The Faerie's Gift,* Barefoot Books (Cambridge, MA), 2003.

Josephine Evetts-Secker, reteller, *Little Red Riding Hood,* Barefoot Books (Cambridge, MA), 2004.

Tanya Robyn Batt, reteller, *The Princess and the White Bear King,* Barefoot Books (Cambridge, MA), 2004.

Malachy Doyle, *The Barefoot Book of Fairy Tales,* Barefoot Books (Cambridge, MA), 2005.

Lynda Gene Rymond, *The Village of the Basketeers,* Houghton Mifflin (Boston, MA), 2005.

Joseph Helgerson, *Horns and Wrinkles,* Houghton Mifflin (Boston, MA), 2006.

Dashka Slater, *Firefighters in the Dark,* Houghton Mifflin (Boston, MA), 2006.

Carol Ann Duffy, *The Tear Thief,* Barefoot Books (Cambridge, MA), 2007.

Brian Keaney, *The Hollow People,* Knopf (New York, NY), 2007.

Lynda Gene Rymond, *Oscar and the Mooncats,* Houghton Mifflin (Boston, MA), 2007.

Kate Bernheimer, *The Girl in the Castle inside the Museum,* Schwartz & Wade (New York, NY), 2008.

Also illustrator of *Rapunzel,* Ta Chien (Taiwan); *Der sonne und mond,* Friedrich Reinhardt Verlag (Basel, Switzerland); *Romance Poetry* and *Fruit Gathering,* Grimm Press (Taiwan); and *Gli indagatori del mistero* and *Fiabe ebraiche,* Mondadori.

Sidelights

Illustrator Nicoletta Ceccoli was born and still lives in the Republic of San Marino, a little-known enclave that, surrounded on all sides by Italy, is actually the oldest constitutional republic in the world. Despite her political allegiance, Ceccoli represents Italy in the world of art, where in 2000 she was awarded the prestigious Andersen Prize as the best children's book illustrator in Italy. Although Ceccoli's illustrations have been familiar to Italian readers since she began her book-illustration career in the mid-1990s, for American children they have been a newfound delight. First appearing in the pages of Stella Blackstone's picture book *An Island in the Sun,* Ceccoli's soft-edged, almost surreal art has since been paired with texts by Joseph Helgerson, Carol Ann Duffy, Lynda Gene Rymond, and Malachy Doyle.

Ceccoli trained in illustration at the State Institute of Art in Urbino, Italy, and received her first picture-book project in 1996. Quickly attracting the attention of larger publishers, she soon juggled projects from Verona-based Mondadori, Florence's Fatatrac, and Milan publisher Arka. Her Italian work, which includes creating art for

Italian illustrator Nicoletta Ceccoli's unique artwork can be found in picture books such as Dashka Slater's **Firefighters in the Dark.** (Illustration © 2006 by Nicoletta Ceccoli. All rights reserved. Reproduced by permission of Houghton Mifflin Company.)

Carmen Martin Gaite's *La torta del diavolo,* Italo Calvino's *La foresta radice-labririnto,* and Ornella Pozzolo's *Anna senza confini,* was represented three times at the prestigious and highly selective Bologna Children's Book Fair. In 2006 Cecceci earned the equally coveted silver medal from New York's Society of Illustrators.

Response to Ceccoli's work among English-speaking readers and critics has been enthusiastic. Reviewing her work for Tanya Robyn Batt's version of *The Princess and the White Bear King,* Linda M. Kenton noted in *School Library Journal* that Ceccoli's rich-hued pastel and acrylic paintings "magnify the adventure, offering varied perspectives and highlighting the magic of the northern landscape." Evoking what *Booklist* contributor GraceAnne A. DeCandido described as a "pleasant, dreamy and brightly colored" summer day, her images for *An Island in the Sun* feature "whimsically colored" details, while Laurie Edwards maintained in her *School Library Journal* review of the same book that Ceccoli's "surreal" and "memorable" illustrations are "stronger than the story." A *Kirkus Reviews* writer called her work for Josephine Evetts-Secker's retelling of *Little Red*

Riding Hood "a glowing feast for the eyes," and cited in particular the illustrations' "luminous colors" and "deft combination of visual delicacy and richness." Calling attention to Ceccoli's characteristic "round-faced, folksy" characters, with their oversized heads and large, expressive eyes, Angela Reynolds noted of her art for Rymonds's *The Village of Basketeers* that these characters inhabit a unique world of Ceccoli's creation: "a curved, windblown world full of light and fantasy colors."

Biographical and Critical Sources

PERIODICALS

Booklist, May 1, 2002, GraceAnne A. DeCandido, review of *An Island in the Sun,* p. 1530; March 15, 2004, Hazel Rochman, review of *Little Red Riding Hood,* p. 1307; November 1, 2004, Carolyn Phelan, review of *The Princess and the White Bear King,* p. 486; December 1, 2005, Gillian Engberg, review of *The Barefoot Book of Fairy Tales,* p. 50; September, 2006, Robyn Gioia, review of *Horns and Wrinkles,* p. 208.

Bulletin of the Center for Children's Books, April, 2004, Janice Del Negro, review of *Little Red Riding Hood,* p. 324.

Kirkus Reviews, February 1, 2004, review of *Little Red Riding Hood,* p. 132; May 1, 2005, review of *The Village of Basketeers,* p. 545; August 15, 2006, review of *Horns and Wrinkles,* p. 842; October 1, 2006, review of *Firefighters in the Dark,* p. 1025.

Publishers Weekly, March 4, 2002, review of *An Island in the Sun,* p. 78; December 23, 2002, review of *The Faerie's Gift,* p. 69; February 2, 2004, review of *Little Red Riding Hood,* p. 76; November 8, 2004, review of *The Princess and the White Bear King,* p. 54; September 11, 2006, review of *Horns and Wrinkles,* p. 55; October 9, 2006, review of *Firefighters in the Dark,* p. 54.

School Library Journal, July, 2002, Laurie Edwards, review of *An Island in the Sun,* p. 83; August, 2004, Catherine Threadgill, review of *Little Red Riding Hood,* p. 107; January, 2005, Linda M. Kenton, review of *The Princess and the White Bear King,* p. 86; May, 2005, Angela J. Reynolds, review of *The Village of Basketeers,* p. 96; February, 2006, Miriam Lang Budin, review of *The Barefooot Book of Fairy Tales,* p. 116; October, 2006, Jayne Damron, review of *Firefighters in the Dark,* p. 126.

ONLINE

Nicoletta Ceccoli Home Page, http://www.nicolettaceccoli. com (July 20, 2007).

Barefoot Books Web site, http://www.barefootbooks.com/ (July 20, 2007), "Nicoletta Ceccoli."*

COLE, Henry 1955-

Personal

Born 1955, in VA. *Education:* Virginia Polytechnic and State University, degree (science).

Addresses

Home—FL.

Career

Educator and illustrator. Langley Elementary School, Langley, VA, science teacher, 1984-99. Freelance illustrator.

Awards, Honors

Best Children's Book of the Year designation, Bank Street College of Education, 1996, ABC Children's Booksellers Choices Award, 1997, and California Young Reader Medal, 1999, all for *Livingstone Mouse;* Notable Children's Books in the Language Arts citation, National Council of Teachers of English, 1997, for *Some Smug Slug;* Best Children's Book of the Year designation, Bank Street College of Education, 1997-98, and Nevada Young Readers' Award, 2001, both for *Barefoot: Escape on the Underground Railroad;* International Reading Association (IRA) Children's Choice Award, 1998, for *Moosetache;* Best Children's Book of the Year designation, Bank Street College of Education, 1999, and several state children's choice awards, 2000-01, all for *Honk!;* Best Children's Book of the Year, Bank Street College of Education, and Outstanding Science Trade Book selection, National Science Teachers Association (NSTA), both 1999, both for *I Took a Walk;* IRA Children's Literature and Reading selection, 2001, for *Boston Tea Party* and *Warthogs Paint*; Lambda Literary Award finalist, 2002, for *The Sissy Duckling;* IRA Children's Choice selection, 2003, for *Can You Make a Piggy Giggle?;* Joan G. Sugarman Children's Book Award honorable mention, 2003, for *Muldoon;* Best Children's Book of the Year designation, Bank Street College of Education, 2004, for *Why Do Kittens Purr?;* Bill Martin Jr. Picture Book Award nomination, 2004, for *The Wright Brothers;* Best Children's Book of the Year designation, Bank Street College of Education, and NSTA Outstanding Science Trade Book selection, both 2004, both for *On the Way to the Beach;* numerous state awards and nominations.

Writings

SELF-ILLUSTRATED

Jack's Garden, Greenwillow Press (New York, NY), 1995.
I Took a Walk, Greenwillow Press (New York, NY), 1998.
On the Way to the Beach, Greenwillow Press (New York, NY), 2003.

On Meadowview Street, Greenwillow Press (New York, NY), 2007.

ILLUSTRATOR

Pamela Duncan Edwards, *Four Famished Foxes and Fosdyke,* HarperCollins (New York, NY), 1995.

Ann Earle, *Zipping, Zapping, Zooming Bats,* HarperCollins (New York, NY), 1995.

Pamela Duncan Edwards, *Livingstone Mouse,* HarperCollins (New York, NY), 1996.

Pamela Duncan Edwards, *Some Smug Slug,* HarperCollins (New York, NY), 1996.

Pamela Duncan Edwards, *Barefoot: Escape on the Underground Railroad,* HarperCollins (New York, NY), 1997.

Pamela Duncan Edwards, *Dinorella: A Prehistoric Fairy Tale,* HarperCollins (New York, NY), 1997.

Margie Palatini, *Moosetache,* Hyperion (New York, NY), 1997.

Pamela Duncan Edwards, *Honk!,* HarperCollins (New York, NY), 1998.

Pamela Duncan Edwards, *Warthogs in the Kitchen: A Sloppy Counting Book,* Hyperion (New York, NY), 1998.

Julie Andrews Edwards, *Little Bo: The Story of Bonnie Boadicea,* Hyperion (New York, NY), 1999.

Pamela Duncan Edwards, *Ed and Fred Flea,* Hyperion (New York, NY), 1999.

Pamela Duncan Edwards, *The Worrywarts,* HarperCollins (New York, NY), 1999.

Pamela Duncan Edwards, *Bravo, Livingstone Mouse!,* Hyperion (New York, NY), 2000.

Pamela Duncan Edwards, *Roar: A Noisy Counting Book,* HarperCollins (New York, NY), 2000.

Jonathon London, *Who Bop,* HarperCollins (New York, NY), 2000.

Margie Palatini, *Moosletoe,* Hyperion (New York, NY), 2000.

Rick Walton, *Little Dogs Say "Rough!",* Putnam (New York, NY), 2000.

Susan Saunders, *New Pup on the Block,* Avon (New York, NY), 2001.

Susan Saunders, *On the Scent of Trouble,* Avon (New York, NY), 2001.

Susan Saunders, *Camp Barkalot,* Avon (New York, NY), 2001.

Susan Saunders, *Uptown Poodle, Downtown Pups,* Avon (New York, NY), 2001.

Susan Saunders, *Puppysaurus,* Avon (New York, NY), 2001.

Susan Saunders, *The Bake-off Burglar,* Avon (New York, NY), 2001.

Pamela Duncan Edwards, *Boston Tea Party,* Putnam (New York, NY), 2001.

Pamela Duncan Edwards, *Clara Caterpillar,* Putnam (New York, NY), 2001.

Pamela Duncan Edwards, *Slop Goes the Soup: A Noisy Warthog Word Book,* Hyperion (New York, NY), 2001.

Pamela Duncan Edwards, *Warthogs Paint: A Messy Color Book,* Hyperion (New York, NY), 2001.

Linda Ashman, *Can You Make a Piggy Giggle?,* Dutton (New York, NY), 2002.

Julie Andrews Edwards, *Little Bo in France: The Further Adventures of Bonnie Boadicea,* Hyperion (New York, NY), 2002.

Pamela Duncan Edwards, *Muldoon,* Hyperion (New York, NY), 2002.

Pamela Duncan Edwards, *Wake-up Kisses,* HarperCollins (New York, NY), 2002.

Harvey Fierstein, *The Sissy Duckling,* Simon & Schuster (New York, NY), 2002.

Laura Krauss Melmed, *Fright Night Flight,* HarperCollins (New York, NY), 2002.

Margie Palatini, *Bad Boys,* Katherine Tegen Books (New York, NY), 2003.

Jim Aylesworth, *Naughty Little Monkeys,* Dutton (New York, NY), 2003.

Marion Dane Bauer, *Why Do Kittens Purr?,* Simon & Schuster (New York, NY), 2003.

Arthur Dorros, *City Chicken,* HarperCollins (New York, NY), 2003.

Pamela Duncan Edwards, *Rosie's Roses,* HarperCollins (New York, NY), 2003.

Pamela Duncan Edwards, *The Wright Brothers,* Hyperion (New York, NY), 2003.

Laurie Berkner, *Victor Vito and Freddie Vasco, Two Polar Bears on a Mission to Save the Klondike Café!,* Orchard (New York, NY), 2004.

Pamela Duncan Edwards, *Gigi and Lulu's Gigantic Fight,* Katherine Tegen (New York, NY), 2004.

Pamela Duncan Edwards, *The Leprechaun's Gold,* Katherine Tegen (New York, NY), 2004.

Rhonda Gowler Greene, *Santa's Stuck,* Dutton (New York, NY), 2004.

Margie Palatini, *Moosekitos: A Moose Family Reunion,* Hyperion (New York, NY), 2004.

Pamela Duncan Edwards, *Ms. Bitsy Bat's Kindergarten,* Hyperion (New York, NY), 2005.

Justin Richardson and Peter Parnell, *And Tango Makes Three,* Simon & Schuster (New York, NY), 2005.

Marie and Roland Smith, *Z Is for Zookeeper: A Zoo Alphabet,* Sleeping Bear Press (Chelsea, MI), 2005.

Leslie Helakoski, *Big Chickens,* Dutton (New York, NY), 2006.

Margie Palatini, *Bad Boys Get Cookie!,* Katherine Tegen (New York, NY), 2006.

Margie Palatini, *Oink?,* Simon & Schuster (New York, NY), 2006.

June Sobel, *Shiver Me Letters: A Pirate ABC,* Harcourt (Orlando, FL), 2006.

Paul Tripp, *Tubby the Tuba,* Dutton (New York, NY), 2006.

Pamela Duncan Edwards, *Old House,* Dutton (New York, NY), 2007.

Pamela Duncan Edwards, *Jack's Treehouse,* Katherine Tegen (New York, NY), 2008.

John G. Keller, *The Rubber-legged Duck,* Harcourt (Orlando, FL), 2008.

Sidelights

Before Henry Cole started his career in children's book illustrating, he worked as a science teacher for more than fourteen years. While growing up on a dairy farm

Jim Aylesworth's humorous tale about a group of mischievous imps comes to life via Henry Cole's artwork in **Naughty Little Monkeys.** (Illustration © by Henry Cole, 2003. All rights reserved. Reproduced by permission of Puffin Books, a division of Penguin Putnam Books for Young Readers.)

in Virginia, he gained love of nature that inspired him to study forestry in college. Even as a science teacher, however, Cole's artistic talent stood out. "I really enjoyed using my artwork in the classroom," he recalled to an online interviewer for *Reading Rockets.* "I found that being able to draw something quickly on the board to demonstrate an idea or a concept in science was really terrific, and the kids seemed to like that, too." "As an elementary teacher, I saw many authors and illustrators come to our school and talk about their work," he noted on the HarperCollins Web site. "Each time they came I would say to myself, 'Self, this is just the thing you'd like to do!'"

Cole's move from teacher to illustrator began in 1996, when he and colleague Pamela Duncan Edwards, the librarian at the elementary school where he taught, decided to collaborate on a picture book. Of the many books they have created since, *Boston Tea Party,* includes what a *Publishers Weekly* critic described as "lifelike paintings [that] effectively evoke the period setting on both sides of the Atlantic." Another collaboration, *Warthogs Paint: A Messy Color Book,* features a group of warthogs each trying to paint a masterpiece. As brought to life by Cole, "these creatures are appropriately bumbling and comical," according to *School Library Journal* critic Joy Fleishhacker. Susan Hepler, reviewing Cole and Edwards' *Wake-up Kisses* for *School*

Library Journal, complimented the book's "charming, soft-edged pastel illustrations."

Apart from his work with Edwards, Cole also creates art for other picture-book authors. His work with popular writer Margie Palatini involves a moose or two. *Mooseltoe,* for example, features what a *School Library Journal* critic dubbed "playful pen-and-ink acrylic cartoons [that] convey the same silliness as the text." In *Bad Boys* Cole illustrates Palatini's story about two big bad wolves who hide from an angry Little Red Riding Hood by donning sheep's clothing. "Cole depicts two decidedly doggy predators unsuccessfully trying to hide their delight" as they are surrounded by potential dinners, wrote a contributor to *Kirkus Reviews.* "The ever-waggish Cole . . . advances the plot with his own steady stream of visual humor," noted a *Publishers Weekly* critic. *Bad Boys Get Cookie!* find the wolves once again up to no good. Here a *Kirkus Reviews* contributor commented on "Cole's merry, slapstick art," adding that "never has a runaway cookie been so annoying looking."

Cole teamed up with actor Harvey Fierstein on *The Sissy Duckling,* in which his depiction of the duck Elmer "makes a sympathetic hero of the skinny yellow nonconformist," according to a *Publishers Weekly* contributor. *School Library Journal* critic Lynda S. Poling described Cole's illustrations for Laura Ashman's *Can*

You Make a Piggy Giggle? as "artful, silly cartoons in deep, bold colors," and in award-winning author Marion Dane Bauer's *Why Do Kittens Purr?* he "brings the wild kingdom indoors," according to *Booklist* reviewer Karin Snelson. Veteran writer Jim Aylesworth's *Naughty Little Monkeys* benefits from what a *Kirkus Reviews* contributor described as "full-bleed illustrations in deep, vibrant colors [that] are a riotous activity of monkey mischief," and in *Tubby the Tuba* Cole's illustrations accompany the lyrics of a song from the 1940s. "The colorful cartoons . . . create a retro mood without looking dated," wrote Marilyn Ackerman in her *School Library Journal* review of the nostalgic picture book.

And Tango Makes Three, written by Justin Richardson and Peter Parnell, caused a measure of controversy when it was released. The picture book is based on a true story about two male penguins that raised a penguin chick at New York City's Central Park Zoo. Argu-

Cole serves as both author and illustrator in his wildlife-centered picture book On the Way to the Beach, *which introduces children to the coastal Atlantic ecosystem.* (Illustration © 2003 by Henry Cole. All rights reserved. Reproduced by permission of HarperCollins Children's Books, a division of HarperCollins Publishers.)

ing that the title promotes homosexuality, some librarians elected to remove it from their picture-book sections, placing it instead in nonfiction. Cole's work on the book is notable for its realism, a departure from his often cartoonish style. "Cole's pictures complement the perfectly cadenced text," wrote *Booklist* contributor Jennifer Mattson, and a *Kirkus Reviews* contributor wrote that in *And Tango Makes Three* the illustrator "depicts figures and setting with tidy, appealing accuracy."

In addition to creating art for texts by others, Cole also offers readers several original self-illustrated picture books. In *On the Way to the Beach* he explores the flora and fauna of the mid-Atlantic by following a child's walk through the woods to the beach. Cole's "marvelously detailed and accurate illustrations give readers a peek into the natural world," wrote a *Kirkus Reviews* contributor, and a *Publishers Weekly* critic praised the inclusion of a key to the animals and plants included in the book. Commenting on the work's format, Marlene Gawron wrote in *School Library Journal* that each location the child visits, from forest to marsh to dunes, "is gloriously depicted in a three-page foldout that is entered through a die-cut."

Another original work, *On Meadowview Street*, describes a girl's project to let her yard naturalize into a field of wildflowers. After the lawn mower is put away, the lawn grows free, and Caroline plants a maple tree and digs a pond to invite new wildlife into her yard. According to a *Publishers Weekly* critic, "the growing lushness of the yard—beautifully portrayed in meticulously detailed, velvety acrylics" reflects the girl's sense of accomplishment. As he did in *On the Way to the Beach*, in *On Meadowview Street* Cole closes with a panel of animals readers have seen over the course of the story. According to a *Kirkus Reviews* contributor, readers "will enjoy a final rendering of all the meadow creatures next to their proper names."

When asked by an interviewer for the Reading Is Fundamental Web site whether he prefers working alone or collaborating with another writer on his picture-book projects, Cole replied: "It's very satisfying to create something on your own. The only person who you have to satisfy is yourself, other than the publisher. On the other hand, it's fun to work on collaborations. Getting other people's ideas is great fun. If the chemistry is right, and what you're doing pleases the author, that's a great feeling."

Biographical and Critical Sources

PERIODICALS

Booklist, June 1, 2001, Kay Weisman, review of *Boston Tea Party,* p. 1885, Carolyn Phelan, review of *Warthogs Paint: A Messy Color Book,* p. 1890; July, 2001, Carolyn Phelan, review of *Clara Caterpillar,* p. 2018; October 15, 2001, Gillian Engberg, review of *Slop Goes the Soup: A Noisy Warthog Word Book,* p. 400; February 1, 2002, Carolyn Phelan, review of *Wake-up Kisses,* p. 945; July, 2002, Ilene Cooper, review of *Can You Make a Piggy Giggle?,* p. 1853; September 1, 2002, Gillian Engberg, review of *Fright Night Flight,* p. 140; January 1, 2003, Karin Snelson, review of *Why Do Kittens Purr?,* p. 904; February 15, 2003, Michael Cart, review of *Muldoon,* p. 1073; March 15, 2003, Gillian Engberg, review of *City Chicken,* p. 1331; May 15, 2003, Carolyn Phelan, review of *On the Way to the Beach,* p. 1669; September 1, 2003, Carolyn Phelan, review of *Naughty Little Monkeys,* p. 127; November 15, 2003, GraceAnne A. DeCandido, review of *Bad Boys,* p. 602; January 1, 2004, Lauren Peterson, review of *The Leprechaun's Gold,* p. 874; August, 2004, GraceAnne A. DeCandido, review of *Moosekitos,* p. 1944; September 1, 2004, Ilene Cooper, review of *Gigi and Lulu's Gigantic Fight,* p. 130; May 15, 2005, Jennifer Mattson, review of *And Tango Makes Three,* p. 1657; August, 2005, review of *Ms. Bitsy Bat's Kindergarten,* p. 2038; February 1, 2006, Gillian Engberg, review of *Big Chicken,* p. 55; March 15, 2006, Kathleen Odean, review of *Oink?,* p. 53; June 1, 2006, Julie Cummings, review of *Shiver Me Letters: A Pirate ABC,* p. 89; December 1, 2006, review of *Tubby the Tuba,* p. 55.

Childhood Education, fall, 2004, Sonia Mastrangelo, review of *The Leprechaun's Gold,* p. 46; spring, 2006, Janette Holmes, review of *Bad Boys,* p. 177.

Horn Book, March-April, 2003, Betty Carter, review of *City Chicken,* p. 202.

Kirkus Reviews, September 15, 2001, review of *Slop Goes the Soup,* p. 1356; November 15, 2001, review of *Wake-up Kisses,* p. 1611; April 15, 2002, review of *Can You Make a Piggy Giggle?,* p. 560, review of *The Sissy Duckling,* p. 568; August 15, 2002, review of *Fright Night Flight,* p. 1229; December 1, 2002, review of *City Chicken,* p. 1767; February 15, 2003, review of *Why Do Kittens Purr?,* p. 299; March 1, 2003, review of *Rosie's Roses,* p. 382; June 1, 2003, review of *The Wright Brothers,* p. 802; July 1, 2003, review of *Naughty Little Monkeys,* p. 906; August 1, 2003, review of *Bad Boys,* p. 1021; January 1, 2004, review of *The Leprechaun's Gold,* p. 35; February 1, 2004, review of *Victor Vito and Freddie Vasco,* p. 129; June 1, 2004, review of *Moosekitos,* p. 539; August 15, 2004, review of *Gigi and Lulu's Giant Fight,* p. 805; June 1, 2005, review of *And Tango Makes Three,* p. 642; December 15, 2005, review of *Big Chickens,* p. 1322; March 15, 2006, review of *Oink?,* p. 298; May 1, 2006, review of *Shiver Me Letters,* p. 467; August 15, 2006, review of *Bad Boys Get Cookie!,* p. 849; September 15, 2006, review of *Tubby the Tuba,* p. 969.

Publishers Weekly, February 12, 2001, review of *New Pup on the Block,* p. 212; July 2, 2001, review of *Boston Tea Party,* p. 75; March 25, 2002, review of *The Sissy Duckling,* p. 64; November 25, 2002, review of *City Chicken,* p. 66; December 9, 2002, review of *Why Do Kittens Purr?,* p. 82; March 17, 2003, review of *Rosie's Roses,* p. 75; March 31, 2003, review of *On the*

Way to the Beach, p. 70; June 16, 2003, review of *The Wright Brothers,* p. 70; July 28, 2003, review of *Naughty Little Monkeys,* p. 93; October 6, 2003, review of *Bad Boys,* p. 83; January 5, 2004, review of *The Leprechaun's Gold,* p. 60; March 29, 2004, review of *Victor Vito and Freddie Vasco,* p. 62; September 27, 2004, review of *Santa's Stuck,* p. 61; November 1, 2004, review of *Gigi and Lulu's Gigantic Fight,* p. 60; May 16, 2005, review of *And Tango Makes Three,* p. 61; July 11, 2005, review of *Ms. Bitsy Bat's Kindergarten,* p. 91; June 5, 2006, review of *Shiver Me Letters,* p. 62; May 28, 2007, review of *On Meadowview Street,* p. 61.

School Library Journal, October, 2000, review of *Mooseltoe,* p. 62, Roxanne Burg, review of *Bravo, Livingstone Mouse!,* p. 122; June, 2001, Holly Belli, review of *Clara Caterpillar,* p. 112; July, 2001, Anne Chapman Callaghan, review of *Boston Tea Party,* p. 93; August, 2001, Joy Fleishhacker, review of *Warthogs Paint,* p. 146; December, 2001, Kay Bowes, review of *Slop Goes the Soup,* and Susan Hepler, review of *Wake-up Kisses,* both p. 99; May, 2002, Heather E. Miller, review of *The Sissy Duckling,* p. 112; June, 2002, Lynda S. Poling, review of *Can You Make a Piggy Giggle?,* p. 80; September, 2002, Melinda Piehler, review of *Fright Night Flight,* p. 201; December, 2002, Judith Constantinides, review of *Muldoon,* p. 94; February, 2003, Carol Ann Wilson, review of *City Chicken,* p. 104; March, 2003, Carolyn Janssen, review of *Why Do Kittens Purr?,* p. 176; May, 2003, Marlene Gawron, review of *On the Way to the Beach,* p. 110; August, 2003, Rachel G. Payne, review of *Naughty Little Monkeys,* p. 122; October, 2003, Barbara Buckley, review of *The Wright Brothers,* p. 150; November, 2003, Helen Foster James, review of *Bad Boys,* p. 112; February, 2004, Wendy Lukehart, review of *The Leprechaun's Gold,* p. 111; March, 2004, Marge Loch-Wouters, review of *Victor Vito and Freddie Vasco,* p. 190; July, 2004, Jane Barrer, review of *Moosekitos,* p. 84; November, 2004, Kelley Rae Unger, review of *Gigi and Lulu's Gigantic Fight,* p. 103; July, 2005, Julie Roach, review of *And Tango Makes Three,* p. 81; August, 2005, Blair Christolon, review of *Ms. Bitsy Bat's Kindergarten,* p. 93; September, 2005, Corrina Austin, review of *Z Is for Zookeeper,* p. 196; February, 2006, Lauralyn Persson, review of *Big Chick,* p. 103; March, 2006, Maryann H. Owen, review of *Oink?,* p. 200; June, 2006, Maura Bresnahan, review of *Shiver Me Letters,* p. 127; October, 2006, Piper L. Nyman, review of *Bad Boys Get Cookie!,* p. 122; November, 2006, Marilyn Ackerman, review of *Tubby the Tuba,* p. 114.

ONLINE

Children's Lit Web site, http://www.childrenslit.com/ (July 3, 2007), "Henry Cole."

HarperCollins Web site, http://www.harpercollins.com/ (July 3, 2007), interview with Cole.

Henry Cole Home Page, http://www.henrycole.net (June 25, 2007).

Reading Is Fundamental Web site, http://www.rif.org/ (July 2, 2007), interview with Cole.

Reading Rockets Web site, http://www.readingrockets.org/ (July 3, 2007), interview with Cole.

*   *   *

COONEY, Doug

Personal

Male. *Education:* Attended University of Virginia, University of Florida, and Trinity Repertory Conservatory.

Addresses

Home and office—Los Angeles, CA; south FL. *Agent*—Harden-Curtis Associates, 850 7th Ave., Ste. 903, New York, NY 10019.

Career

Author and playwright.

Member

Dramatists Guild, Writers Guild of America, Society of Children's Book Writers and Illustrators, ASSITEJ International, Circle Rising, Alternate ROOTS.

Awards, Honors

First Look Prize, Tada!, for *The Beloved Dearly* (play).

Writings

FOR YOUNG ADULTS

The Wind That Blew, School Board of Dade County (Miami, FL), 1993.

I Know Who Likes You, Simon & Schuster Books for Young Readers (New York, NY), 2004.

(With Marlee Matlin) *Nobody's Perfect,* Simon & Schuster Books for Young Readers (New York, NY), 2006.

(With Marlee Matlin) *Leading Ladies,* Simon & Schuster Books for Young Readers (New York, NY), 2007.

PLAYS

The Beloved Dearly (play; produced in New York, NY, 2000), adapted as *The Beloved Dearly,* Simon & Schuster Books for Young Readers (New York, NY), 2002.

The Final Tour, produced at Sundance Institute, Beverly Hills, CA, 2003.

The Legend of Alex, produced by in Los Angeles, CA, 2004.

Author of plays produced at Kennedy Center, Alabama Shakespeare Festival, Cincinnati Playhouse in the Park, Cleveland Playhouse, Dance Theater Workshop, International Very-Special-Arts Festival, and Edinburgh Fringe Festival.

Sidelights

Playwright Doug Cooney is also the author of children's books, the most notable of which is an adaptation of his award-winning play *The Beloved Dearly.* Working with actress Marlee Matlin, Cooney has also coauthored the young-adult novels *Nobody's Perfect* and *Leading Ladies,* and has written the teen novel *I Know Who Likes You.* Praising *I Know Who Likes You,* which reprises the characters of *The Beloved Dearly,* Nancy P. Reader wrote in *School Library Journal* that Cooney's novel features a "well-balanced mix of description and realistic dialogue." A *Kirkus Reviews* writer also praised the book, citing the story's "teasing, but never mean-spirited" cast of preteens and predicted that *I Know Who Likes You* "will keep young readers solidly entertained from first page to last."

Originally a play that debuted at New York City's Lincoln Center, *The Beloved Dearly* was adapted into a children's book that features the same cast of characters seen on stage: Ernie Castellan, Dusty, Swimming Pool, and Tony. Ernie is a twelve-year-old opportunist who thinks up moneymaking schemes in order to get rich quick. After being grounded by his parents for trying to make a sales profit at school, Ernie decides to devise a new scheme that can be transacted off school grounds. When he discovers an empty lot near his home, the preteen sees its earning potential and transforms it into a pet cemetery. Supported in his new business by his team of friends-turned-employees, Ernie quickly turns a tidy profit. Things take a turn, however, when the preteen's greed overtakes his better judgment and he becomes increasingly arrogant. The lesson is learned when Ernie's own beloved pet, Mister Doggie, passes away, forcing the boy to understand the emotional component of his scheme and decide for himself what is really valuable in life.

In their assessment of *The Beloved Dearly,* critics often commented on Cooney's ability to integrate aspects of the stage play into his children's-book adaptation. A *Publishers Weekly* reviewer noted that Cooney's playwriting skills "is evident in the tight arc of his plot and in the snappy dialogue" and added that *The Beloved Dearly* is "a likable story with solid appeal." Connie Tyrrell Burns, reviewing the adaptation for *School Library Journal,* regarded the book version of *The Beloved Dearly* as "witty, clever, yet touching" and with "certain kid appeal."

Biographical and Critical Sources

PERIODICALS

Booklist, January 1, 2002, Ilene Cooper, review of *The Beloved Dearly,* p. 858; March 1, 2003, Brian Wilson, review of *The Beloved Dearly,* p. 1214; July 1, 2006, Nancy Kim, review of *Nobody's Perfect,* p. 55.

Center for Children's Books Bulletin, May, 2002, review of *The Beloved Dearly,* p. 315.
Kirkus Reviews, December 1, 2001, review of *The Beloved Dearly,* p. 1683; January 15, 2004, review of *I Know Who Likes You,* p. 81; May 15, 2006, review of *Nobody's Perfect,* p. 520.
Publishers Weekly, December 10, 2001, review of *The Beloved Dearly,* p. 71; September 1, 2003, review of *The Beloved Dearly,* p. 91.
School Library Journal, January, 2002, Connie Tyrrell Burns, review of *The Beloved Dearly,* p. 132; February, 2004, Nancy P. Reeder, review of *I Know Who Likes You,* p. 142; August, 2006, Kathleen Kelly MacMillan, review of *Nobody's Perfect,* p. 124.

ONLINE

Doug Cooney Home Page, http://www.dougcooney.com (July 7, 2007).
Florida Cultural Fairs Division Web site, http://www.florida-arts.org/ (July 8, 2007), "Doug Cooney."
Simon & Schuster Web site, http://www.simonsays.com/ (July 8, 2007), "Doug Cooney."*

*　　*　　*

COOPER, Michael L. 1950-

Personal

Born July 6, 1950. *Education:* University of Kentucky, B.A. (English), 1974; City University of New York, M.A. (history), 1989.

Addresses

Home—Lexington, KY. *E-mail*—MLCooper@michaellcooper.com.

Career

Author.

Member

Authors Guild, Authors League of America, Children's Book Guild of Washington, DC, PEN American Center, Society of Children's Book Writers and Illustrators, Organization of American Historians.

Awards, Honors

Golden Kite Best Nonfiction Book designation, Society of Children's Book Writers and Illustrators, 2004, and Capital Choices inclusion, 2005, both for *Dust to Eat;* Carter G. Woodson Award, National Council of the Social Studies, 2003, for *Remembering Manzanar.*

Writings

Racing Sled Dogs, Clarion (New York, NY), 1988.

Klondike Fever: The Famous Gold Rush of 1898, Clarion (New York, NY), 1989.

Playing America's Game: The Story of Negro League Baseball, Lodestar (New York, NY), 1993.

From Slave to Civil War Hero: The Life and Times of Robert Smalls, Lodestar (New York, NY), 1994.

Bound for the Promised Land: The Great Black Migration, Lodestar (New York, NY), 1995.

Hell Fighters: African-American Soldiers in World War I, Lodestar (New York, NY), 1997.

The Double V Campaign: African Americans and World War II, Lodestar (New York, NY), 1998.

Indian School: Teaching the White Man's Way, Clarion (New York, NY), 1999.

Fighting for Honor: Japanese Americans and World War II, Clarion (New York, NY), 2000.

Slave Spirituals and the Jubilee Singers, Clarion (New York, NY), 2001.

Remembering Manzanar: Life in a Japanese Relocation Camp, Clarion (New York, NY), 2002.

Dust to Eat: Drought and Depression in the 1930s, Clarion (New York, NY), 2004.

Hero of the High Seas: John Paul Jones and the American Revolution, National Geographic (Washington, DC), 2006.

Jamestown, 1607, Holiday House (New York, NY), 2007.

Sidelights

Michael L. Cooper has established a reputation as a writer of insightful nonfiction geared for young adults through books that include *Bound for the Promised Land: The Great Black Migration, Dust to Eat: Drought and Depression in the 1930s,* and *Hero of the High Seas: John Paul Jones and the American Revolution.* Several of Cooper's books, such as *Bound for the Promised Land, Hell Fighters: African American Soldiers in World War I,* and *Slave Spirituals and the Jubilee Singers,* focus on the role played by African Americans, while other books allow the author to pursue his interest in other aspects of the nation's history, from the colonization of Jamestown through the U.S. Civil War era to the Dust Bowl of the 1930s and the treatment of Japanese Americans during World War II. Praising Cooper's colorful biography of one of the nation's best-known Revolutionary-era naval hero, a *Kirkus Reviews* contributor wrote of *Hero of the High Seas* that the author "writes with clear and lively prose, effectively incorporating quotations for dramatic effect." In each of his books Cooper includes numerous photos and other illustrations, and h inserts quotes from contemporary newspapers and other accounts in his clearly written texts. Also reviewing *Hero of the High Seas, School Library Journal* reviewer Michael Santangelo noted that the author's "narrative style will appeal to reluctant readers, for it reads like a chronicle of thrilling naval adventure."

In *Bound for the Promised Land* Cooper examines the era of 1915 to 1930 when more than a million African Americans emigrated from the rural South to urban

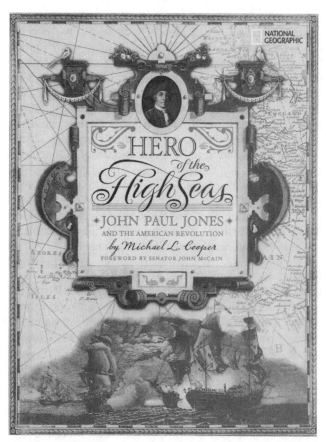

Cover of Michael L. Cooper's nautical history Hero of the High Seas, ***which brings to life the career of eighteenth-century naval captain*** John Paul Jones. (National Geographic, 2006. Front cover © Bettmann/Corbis (portrait, battle); © Stapleton Collection/Corbis. Reproduced by permission.)

Northern and Midwestern states in pursuit of factory work and larger opportunities. Cooper pieces his history together from first-person accounts, newspaper stories, and contemporary photographs, emphasizing living conditions in the South prior to migration, the type of neighborhoods and jobs blacks found in the North, and how this new population influenced urban U.S. culture during the early twentieth century, particularly in the Harlem Renaissance. In *Bulletin of the Center for Children's Books,* Elizabeth Bush dubbed the work a "cogent, eminently readable history," noting that the author achieves a "balanced" presentation of the Great Migration by noting the discrimination and violence blacks met in the North (as well as in the South) and presenting the conflicting voices of African-American leaders on the subject of migration. *Voice of Youth Advocates* reviewer Laura L. Lent, attesting to the scarcity of books on the subject, called *Bound for the Promised Land* "indispensable for its historical value."

Cooper focuses on the participation of American blacks in World War I in *Hell Fighters.* In this account of the Fifteenth New York Voluntary Infantry of the National Guard—formed in Harlem in 1916—and transformed into the 369th Regiment of the U.S. Army during the war, Cooper resurrects an important moment in the early civil rights movement, noted David A. Lindsey in *School*

Library Journal. The company, composed mostly of African Americans, began as poorly equipped and poorly trained volunteers in the National Guard who found little recognition from the U.S. Army for their fighting in the trenches, until the French awarded the regiment the Croix de Guerre in 1918. According to Cooper, although the Harlem press termed them "hell fighters" and they returned to the states to participate in a triumphant ticker-tape parade in New York City, the 369th was nonetheless targeted for discriminatory acts within the military after the end of the conflict in order to make sure that black soldiers would not mistakenly expect the same respect accorded white soldiers. Bush commented in another *Bulletin of the Center for Children's Books* article, "Cooper packs a lot into a little space in this account of the 369th Regiment."

Moving forward in time to World War II, Cooper focuses on the fate of the Japanese immigrants living in the United States during wartime in both *Fighting for Honor: Japanese Americans and World War II* and *Remembering Manzanar: Life in a Japanese Relocation Camp.* Highlighted with numerous photographs, *Fighting for Honor* follows those Japanese Americans who distinguished themselves through their service in the American military as well as the over 100,000 others who were relocated to internment camps. Noting the conflicting policy of the U.S. government in both drafting Japanese-American soldiers and interring the civilian relatives of these draftees, Randy Meyer wrote in *Booklist* that the author's "description of life in the camps is vivid, and the battlefield accounts are graphic and dramatic." "Cooper's awareness of the power of understatement permeates the book," commented *Horn Book* critic Jennifer M. Brabander, "rendering the facts all the more powerful."

In *Remembering Manzanar* Cooper concentrates on the result of U.S. President Franklin Delano Roosevelt's decision to round up Americans of Japanese ancestry following the Japanese bombing of Pearl Harbor. He draws on oral histories, letters, newspapers, and school yearbooks in describing the experiences of the many men, women, and children who were divested of their homes and possessions and relocated to camps such as eastern California's Manzanar between 1942 and the end of the war. Including photographs by noted photojournalists Ansel Adams and Dorothea Lange as well as others, the work was praised by *Booklist* contributor Hazel Rochman as "a moving introduction" to the period. Describing the book as an "incisive companion" to *Fighting for Honor,* a *Publishers Weekly* contributor concluded that in *Remembering Manzanar* Cooper combines "visuals and text [to] resolutely portray a painful chapter in America's past."

Cooper once told *SATA:* "Books were very important to me as a child. I was one of those kids who seemed unable to do anything very well except read. I loved books

of all kinds. I hoarded them the way other boys hoarded baseball cards. Every day when I sit down to work my inspiration my hope is that my writing will nurture a similar love of books among young readers."

Biographical and Critical Sources

PERIODICALS

Booklist, January 1, 2001, Randy Meyer, review of *Fighting for Honor: Japanese Americans and World War II,* p. 930; December 1, 2001, Carolyn Phelan, review of *Slave Spirituals and the Jubilee Singers,* p. 637; January 1, 2003, review of *Remembering Manzanar: Life in a Japanese Relocation Camp,* p. 156; July, 2004, Hazel Rochman, review of *Dust to Eat: Drought and Depression in the 1930s,* p. 1839; June 1, 2006, Carolyn Phelan, review of *Hero of the High Seas: John Paul Jones and the American Revolution,* p. 98; April 15, 2007, Carolyn Phelan, review of *Jamestown, 1607,* p. 36.

Bulletin of the Center for Children's Books, December, 1995, Elizabeth Bush, review of *Bound for the Promised Land,* p. 124; February, 1997, Elizabeth Bush, review of *Hell Fighters,* p. 201; February, 2001, review of *Fighting for Honor,* p. 219; January, 2003, review of *Remembering Manzanar,* p. 194; September, 2004, Elizabeth Bush, review of *Dust to Eat,* p. 11; February, 2007, Elizabeth Bush, review of *Hero of the High Seas,* p. 248.

Horn Book, March, 2001, Jennifer M. Brabander, review of *Fighting for Honor,* p. 226; January-February, 2002, Margaret A. Bush, review of *Slave Spirituals and the Jubilee Singers,* p. 94.

Kansas City Star, March 28, 1993, p. J9.

Kirkus Reviews, November 15, 2002, review of *Remembering Manzanar,* p. 1690; August 15, 2006, review of *Hero of the High Seas,* p. 838; March 1, 2007, review of *Jamestown, 1607,* p. 219.

Publishers Weekly, November 11, 2002, review of *Remembering Manzanar,* p. 66.

School Library Journal, April, 1993; December, 1995, Carol Jones Collins, review of *Bound for the Promised Land,* p. 114; February, 1997, David A. Lindsey, review of *Hell Fighters,* pp. 111-112; February, 2000, Mary B. McCarthy, review of *Indian School: Teaching the White Man's Way,* p. 130; December, 2001, Ginny Gustin, review of *Slave Spirituals and the Jubilee Singers,* p. 156; February, 2003, Ginny Gustin, review of *Remembering Manzanar,* p. 156; September, 2004, Joyce Adam Burner, review of *Dust to Eat,* p. 224; August, 2005, Blair Christolon, review of *Dust to Eat,* p. 50; September, 2006, Michael Santangelo, review of *Hero of the High Seas,* p. 226.

Voice of Youth Advocates, April, 1996, Laura L. Lent, review of *Bound for the Promised Land,* p. 52; February, 2002, review of *Slave Spirituals and the Jubilee*

Singers, p. 453; August, 2003, review of *Remembering Manzanar,* p. 187; October, 2004, Jenny Ingram, review of *Dust to Eat,* p. 323.

ONLINE

Michael L. Cooper Home Page, http://www.michaellcooper.com (July 15, 2007).

D

DARROW, Sharon

Personal
Female. *Education:* Vermont College, M.F.A. (fiction and poetry), 1996.

Addresses
E-mail—SharonDarrow@hotmail.com.

Career
Poet and fiction writer. Vermont College M.F.A. program in creative writing, teacher; previously taught at Columbia College Chicago; leader of writing workshops at College of DuPage, Waubonsee Community College, Off-Campus Writers' Workshop Barrington Area Arts Council, and Society of Children's Book Writers and Illustrators' conferences and retreats in the United States, Spain, and France. Associate editor of magazines, including *Rhino* and *Columbia Poetry Review.*

Member
Society of Children's Book Writers and Illustrators, Authors Guild.

Awards, Honors
Illinois Arts' Council Award nomination; Pushcart Prize nomination; Society of Children's Book Writers and Illustrators work-in-progress grant; Spur Award Storyteller honor finalist, Western Writers of America, 2000, for *Old Thunder and Miss Raney;* Oklahoma Book Award, 2004, for *The Painters of Lexieville;* Oklahoma Book Award finalist, 2006, for *Trash.*

Writings
Old Thunder and Miss Raney, illustrated by Kathryn Brown, Dorling Kindersley (New York, NY), 2000.

Through the Tempests Dark and Wild: A Story of Mary Shelley, Creator of Frankenstein, illustrated by Angela Barrett, Candlewick Press (Cambridge, MA), 2003.
The Painters of Lexieville, Candlewick Press (Cambridge, MA), 2003.
Trash, Candlewick Press (Cambridge, MA), 2006.

Contributor of poetry to *Home to Me: Poems across America,* edited by Lee Bennett Hopkins, Orchard Books (New York, NY), 2002. Contributor of poetry, short fiction, and essays to periodicals, including *Other Voices, Whetstone, Great River Review, Another Chicago Magazine, Columbia Review, Folio,* and *In the Middle of the Middle West.*

Sidelights
Sharon Darrow is the author of both picture books such as *Old Thunder and Miss Raney* and young-adult novels such as *Trash.* Growing up in the Southern United States, Darrow listened to the tales recounted by friends and family, and her love of such stories has inspired much of her work as a writer. "I think I wanted to write to continue to tell stories like those I'd heard, transforming them into the kind of fiction I was reading in my library books," Darrow explained to Ann Jacobus for the Kid Book Pros Web site.

Darrow's first book, *Old Thunder and Miss Raney* finds Miss Raney Cloud busy assembling the ingredients for her soon-to-be prize-winning Sooner Biscuits, only to be swept up into a tornado, along with her horse Old Thunder. The picture book was inspired by a story fragment Darrow recalled hearing from her Great-Aunt Thelma. As the writer told Cynthia Leitich-Smith for *Cynsations* online, Thelma began the story by saying: "'Kids, did I ever tell you about the time my horse and buggy and I got picked up by a tornado and blown all the way to town?' Before she could finish, we were called to the table, then my family had to leave and I never heard the end of the tale." The story Darrow's imagination subsequently fleshed out contains "just the right amount of action, humor and heart," according to

Cover of Sharon Darrow's young-adult novel **Trash,** *featuring artwork by Daniel Natola.* (Jacket background photograph © 2006 by James Weinberg. Reproduced by permission of Candlewick Press, Inc., Cambridge, MA.)

a *Publishers Weekly* critic. In *Horn Book* a critic wrote that the book's "entertaining pace, unpretentious tone, and folksy dialogue make [it] . . . a natural choice for reading aloud." According to *School Library Journal* critic Barbara Buckley, "the pace and timing of the story leave one breathless by the last page."

In *Through the Tempests Dark and Wild: A Story of Mary Shelley, Creator of Frankenstein* Darrow imagines how early nineteenth-century writer Mary Shelley's early life might have helped inspire the monster she would create in her famous novel. As Darrow explained on the *Candlewick Press Web site,* she has always felt a kinship with Shelley, who was married to Romantic poet Percy Bysshe Shelley until her death in 1851. "We share a concern about the effects of new technologies on our hearts, minds, and lives," she wrote. "We are both preoccupied by the complexity of parent-child relationships, and we have both made choices that were difficult but personally necessary." Along with her fictionalized picture-book depiction of Shelley's early life, Darrow provides an afterword to help readers separate fact from fiction. Beth Tegart, reviewing the book for *School Library Journal,* called *Through the Tem-*

pests Dark and Wild "an intriguing and haunting glimpse into the early life" of a fascinating literary figure.

Darrow turns her attention to teen readers with the novels *The Painters of Lexieville* and *Trash,* which introduce the Lexie family from the small town of Lexieville, Arkansas. According to Claire Rosser in *Kliatt,* the novels are based on Darrow's experiences working in the Arkansas County Welfare Office when she was a teenager. *The Painters of Lexieville* finds Pert struggling to finish high school so that she can break the cycle of poverty in her family, although her abusive Uncle Orris threatens her dreams. "Darrow seems to get it all right," wrote Rosser, citing the detail Darrow uses to depict the Lexie family. Frances Bradburn, writing in *Booklist,* called the novel "a harrowing, suspenseful, grudgingly hopeful book that will haunt the reader long after its conclusion."

Sissy and Boy, two of the characters introduced in *The Painters of Lexieville,* find their way into Darrow's verse novel *Trash.* Forced to support themselves after their guardian loses his job, the teens find work at a trash-collection service, but when their employers abuse them, they flee to the city in the hopes that they can find a stable home. Urban life holds a new series of challenges for Sissy and Boy, however, and the pair soon take up the dangerous hobby of graffiti tagging. "The language, though rich, evocative and rhythmic, is bleak, with only glimpses of salvation and light," wrote a *Kirkus Reviews* writer, and Kelly Czarnecki noted in *School Library Journal* that "Sissy's poignant first-person narrative blends staccato verses with free-flowing prose."

Discussing her work as a writer with Cynthia Leitich Smith for *Cynsations* online, Darrow noted that "books aren't the only products of the writing life. We also gain life skills and friendships. We learn new things about the world all the time, we get to travel both in reality and in imagination, and we get the chance to do what we've dreamed because it's what we were meant to do. What joy!"

Biographical and Critical Sources

PERIODICALS

Booklist, November 1, 2000, Carolyn Phelan, review of *Old Thunder and Miss Raney,* p. 547; June 1, 2003, Hazel Rochman, review of *Through the Tempests Dark and Wild: A Story of Mary Shelley, Creator of Frankenstein,* p. 1793; November 15, 2003, Frances Bradburn, review of *The Painters of Lexieville,* p. 606; December 1, 2006, Holly Koelling, review of *Trash,* p. 38.

Bulletin of the Center for Children's Books, November, 2000, review of *Old Thunder and Miss Raney,* p. 101; January, 2004, review of *The Painters of Lexieville,* p. 188; October, 2006, Loretta Gaffney, review of *Trash,* p. 64.

Horn Book, September, 2000, review of *Old Thunder and Miss Raney,* p. 549.

Kirkus Reviews, September 15, 2003, review of *The Painters of Lexieville,* p. 1173; August 15, 2006, review of *Trash,* p. 838.

Kliatt, July, 2003, Claire Rosser, review of *The Painters of Lexieville,* p. 10; September, 2006, Claire Rosser, review of *Trash,* p. 10.

Publishers Weekly, August 21, 2000, review of *Old Thunder and Miss Raney,* p. 72; December 1, 2003, review of *The Painters of Lexieville,* p. 57; October 23, 2006, review of *Trash,* p. 52.

School Library Journal, October, 2000, Barbara Buckley, review of *Old Thunder and Miss Raney,* p. 119; June, 2003, Beth Tegart, review of *Through the Tempests Dark and Wild,* p. 158; March, 2004, Susan Geye, review of *The Painters of Lexieville,* p. 204; October, 2006, Kelly Czarnecki, review of *Trash,* p. 150.

Tribune Books (Chicago, IL), February 23, 2003, review of *Throught the Tempests Dark and Wild,* p. 5.

Times Educational Supplement, review of *Through the Tempests Dark and Wild,* p. 26.

Voice of Youth Advocates, April, 2004, Cass Kvenild, review of *The Painters of Lexieville,* p. 42.

ONLINE

Candlewick Press Web site, http://www.candlewick.com/ (July 2, 2007), "Sharon Darrow."

Cynsations, http://cynthialeitichsmith.blogspot.com/ (June 26, 2006), interview with Darrow.

Kids Book Pros Web site, http://www.kidsbookpros.com/ (July 2, 2007), Ann Jacobus, interview with Darrow.

Sharon Darrow Home Page, http://www.www.sharondarrow.com (June 25, 2007).

Society of Childrens' Book Writers and Illustrators, Illinois Web site, http://www.scbwi-illinois.org/ (June 25, 2007), "Sharon Darrow."

*   *   *

DAY, Larry 1956-

Personal

Born 1956, in IL; married; wife's name Melanie; children: Andrew, Peter. *Education:* Southern Illinois University, A.A. (commercial art), 1978.

Addresses

Home and office—Downers Grove, IL. *E-mail*—larry@dayhere.com.

Career

Illustrator. Storyboard artist for advertising campaigns, beginning 1987, clients including Altria, Circuit City, Hallmark, Maytag, McDonalds, Proctor & Gamble, Starbucks, Tropicana, Walt Disney, and the U.S. Army.

Exhibitions: Watercolor paintings have been exhibited in numerous solo shows, including Society of Illustrators, New York, NY.

Member

Society of Illustrators, Illustrator's Partnership of America, Society of Children's Book Writers and Illustrators.

Awards, Honors

Golden Kite Award, 2006, Kansas Notable Book designation, 2007, and North Carolina Picture Book Award nomination, 2008, all for *Not Afraid of Dogs.*

Illustrator

Emily Costello, *Runaway Wolf Pups,* Avon Books (New York, NY), 1999.

Emily Costello, *Bad Luck Lion,* Avon Books (New York, NY), 1999.

Emily Costello, *Frightened Fawn,* Avon Books (New York, NY), 2000.

Emily Costello, *Pony in Trouble,* Avon Books (New York, NY), 2000.

Stephen Krensky, *Taking Flight: The Story of the Wright Brothers,* Simon & Schuster Books for Young Readers (New York, NY), 2000.

Emily Costello, *Lost Kitten,* Avon Books (New York, NY), 2000.

Emily Costello, *Hit-and-Run-Retriever,* Avon Books (New York, NY), 2000.

Stephen Krensky, *Pearl Harbor,* Simon & Schuster Books for Young Readers (New York, NY), 2001.

Emily Costello, *Lonely Lamb,* Avon Books (New York, NY), 2001.

Ginger Howard, *William's House,* Millbrook Press (Brookfield, CT), 2001.

Stephanie Spinner, *Who Was Annie Oakley?,* Grosset & Dunlap (New York, NY), 2002.

Susan Provost Beller, *Yankee Doodle and the Redcoats: Soldiering in the Revolutionary War,* Twenty-first Century Books (Brookfield, CT), 2003.

Gare Thompson, *The Monitor: The Iron Warship That Changed the World,* Grosset & Dunlap (New York, NY), 2003.

Diane ZuHone Shore, *Rosa Loves to Read,* Children's Press (New York, NY), 2004.

Dennis B. Fradin, *Let It Begin Here!: Lexington and Concord: First Battles of the American Revolution,* Walker & Co. (New York, NY), 2005.

Suzanne Jurmain, *George Did It,* Dutton Children's Books (New York, NY), 2006.

Susanna Pitzer, *Not Afraid of Dogs,* Walker (New York, NY), 2006.

Biographical and Critical Sources

PERIODICALS

Booklinks, July, 2005, Carolyn Phelan, review of *Let It Begin Here!: Lexington and Concord: First Battles of the American Revolution,* p. 8; January-February, 2006, Laura Tillotson, review of *George Did It,* p. 28.

Booklist, June 1, 2006, Carolyn Phelan, review of *Not Afraid of Dogs,* p. 88.

Bulletin of the Center for Children's Books, February, 2006, Elizabeth Bush, review of *George Did It,* p. 270.

Horn Book, July-August, 2006, Jennifer M. Brabander, review of *Not Afraid of Dogs,* p. 429.

Kirkus Reviews, May 15, 2006, review of *Not Afraid of Dogs,* p. 522.

Library Media Connection, October, 2006, Maureen Mooney, review of *George Did It,* p. 83; October, 2006, Marilyn Teicher, review of *Not Afraid of Dogs,* p. 68.

School Library Journal, July, 2006, Kathleen Kelly Mac-Millan, review of *Not Afraid of Dogs,* p. 84.

ONLINE

Larry Day Home Page, http://dayhere.com (July 17, 2007).

Walker Publishing Company Web site, http://www.walkeryoungreaders.com/ (July 17, 2007), "Larry Day."*

*   *   *

DENTON, Kady MacDonald 1942-

Personal

Born 1942, in Winnipeg, Manitoba, Canada; married; husband's name Trevor. *Education:* University of Toronto, B.A. (with honors), and graduate studies (town and regional planning).

Addresses

Home—Peterborough, Ontario, Canada.

Career

Author and illustrator of children's books. Art Gallery of Southwestern Manitoba, Brandon, Manitoba, Canada, teacher, 1978-85, member of board of directors, 1980-85. *Exhibitions:* Work exhibited at galleries in Manitoba, Canada, and included in group shows Canada at Bologna, 1990, Books from Afar, Rome Italy, 1992, and CANSCAIP Annual Exhibition, Canada, 1992, 2001.

Awards, Honors

Amelia Frances Howard Gibbon Award, 1990, for *Till All the Stars Have Fallen,* 1999, for *A Child's Treasury of Nursery Rhyme;* Mr. Christie Book Award, 1991, for *The Story of Little Quack* by Betty Gibson; Governor General's Literary Award (illustration, English), 1998, for *A Child's Treasury of Nursery Rhymes;* Elizabeth Mrazik-Cleaver Award, 1999, for *A Child's Treasury of Nursery Rhyme,* and 2006, for *Snow.*

Writings

SELF-ILLUSTRATED CHILDREN'S BOOKS

The Picnic, Dutton (New York, NY), 1988.

Granny Is a Darling, Margaret K. McElderry Books (New York, NY), 1988.

Dorothy's Dream, Margaret K. McElderry Books (New York, NY), 1989.

The Christmas Boot, Little, Brown (Boston, MA), 1990.

Janet's Horses, Walker (London, England), 1990, Clarion (New York, NY), 1991.

Would They Love a Lion?, Kingfisher (London, England), 1995.

Watch out, William, Kingfisher (London, England), 1997.

(Editor) *A Child's Treasury of Nursery Rhymes,* Kingfisher (Boston, MA), 1998, published with CD, 2004.

My First Year, Kingfisher (Toronto, Ontario, Canada), 2005.

ILLUSTRATOR

Pam Zinnemann-Hope, *Find Your Coat, Ned,* Margaret K. McElderry Books (New York, NY), 1987.

Pam Zinnemann-Hope, *Let's Play Ball, Ned,* Margaret K. McElderry Books (New York, NY), 1987.

Pam Zinnemann-Hope, *Let's Go Shopping, Ned,* Margaret K. McElderry Books (New York, NY), 1987.

Pam Zinnemann-Hope, *Time for Bed, Ned,* Margaret K. McElderry Books (New York, NY), 1987.

David Booth, editor, *Til All the Stars Have Fallen: Canadian Poems for Children,* Kids Can Press (Toronto, Ontario, Canada), 1989, Viking (New York, NY), 1990.

Betty Gibson, *The Story of Little Quack,* Kids Can Press (Toronto, Ontario, Canada), 1990.

Ann Pilling, reteller, *Before I Go to Sleep: A Collection of Bible Stories, Poems, and Prayers for Children,* Crown (New York, NY), 1990, published as *Before I Go to Sleep: A Collection of Bible Stories, Poems, and Prayers for Bedtime,* Kingfisher (New York, NY), 2000.

David Wynn Millward, *Jenny and Bob,* Delacorte (New York, NY), 1991.

P.K. Page, reteller, *The Travelling Musicians of Bremen,* Kids Can Press (Toronto, Ontario, Canada), 1991, Joy Street Books (Boston, NA), 1992.

Ann Pilling, reteller, *The Kingfisher Children's Bible: Stories from the Old and New Testaments,* Kingfisher (Boston, MA), 1993, published as *The Kingfisher Book of Bible Stories,* 2003.

Ann Pilling, reteller, *Realms of Gold: Myths and Legends from around the World,* Kingfisher (Boston, MA), 1993, published as *The Kingfisher Treasury of Myths and Legends,* 2003.

Shen Roddie, *Toes Are to Tickle,* Tricycle Press (Berkeley, CA), 1997.

Janet Lunn, *The Umbrella Party,* Douglas & McIntyre (Vancouver, British Columbia, Canada), 1998.

Mary Ellis, *The Arctic Fox,* Collins (London, England), 1999.

Margaret Park Bridges, *If I Were Your Mother,* Morrow Junior Books (New York, NY), 1999.

Margaret Park Bridges, *If I Were Your Father,* Morrow Junior Books (New York, NY), 1999.

Robert Heidbreder, *I Wished for a Unicorn,* Kids Can Press (Niagara, NY), 2000.

Claire Masurel, *Two Homes,* Candlewick Press (Cambridge, MA), 2001.

Sam McBratney, *In the Light of the Moon, and Other Bedtime Stories,* Kingfisher (New York, NY), 2001, published as *The Kingfisher Mini-Treasury of Bedtime Stories,* 2004.

Nan Gregory, *Amber Waiting,* Red Deer Press (Calgary, Alberta, Canada), 2003.

Jean Little, *I Gave My Mom a Castle: Poems,* Orca Book (Victoria, British Columbia, Canada), 2003.

Hazel Hutchins, *A Second Is a Hiccup: A Child's Book of Time,* North Winds Press (Markham, Ontario, Canada), 2004, Arthur A. Levine (New York, NY), 2007.

Joan Clark, *Snow,* Groundwood Books (Toronto, Ontario, Canada), 2006.

Robert Heidbreder, *A Sea-wishing Day,* Kids Can Press (Toronto, Ontario, Canada), 2007.

Bonny Becker, *A Visitor for Bear,* Candlewick Press (Cambridge, MA), 2008.

Sidelights

Kady MacDonald Denton, the illustrator of a number of picture books for preschool-age readers, has also authored or edited several titles herself. Her art work, which has been paired with texts by Sam McBratney, Hazel Hutchins, and Robert Heidbreder, has won consistent praise for the whimsical, cozy world depicted in her art; "charming" is an oft-repeated adjective used in reviews. Her self-illustrated books, such as *Would They Love a Lion?* and *Watch out, William,* have also earned commendation for their brief but enchanting storylines.

In her reassuring art for Claire Masurel's **Two Homes,** *Kady MacDonald Denton focuses on a little girl who splits time between two parents.* (Illustration © 2001 by Kady MacDonald Denton. All rights reserved. Reproduced by permission of Candlewick Press, Inc., Cambridge, MA, on behalf of Walker Books. Ltd., London.)

DUNBAR, Polly 1980-

Personal

Born 1980, in the Cotswalds, England; daughter of Joyce Dunbar (a writer). *Education:* Attended Norwich Art School; Brighton University, degree, 1999.

Addresses

Home—London, England. *Agent*—Celia Catchpole, 56 Gilpin Ave., London SW14 8QY, England. *E-mail*—polly@pollydunbar.com.

Career

Writer and illustrator. Puppeteer.

Awards, Honors

Cuffie Award for Most Promising New Illustrator, *Publishers Weekly,* for *Flyaway Katie* and *Dog Blue;* NASEN/*Times Educational Supplement* Special Education Needs Children's Book Award, 2006, for *Looking after Louis;* Best Children's Show honor, Brighton Festival, 2006, for puppet-theater adaptation of *Shoe Baby.*

Writings

SELF-ILLUSTRATED

Help! I'm out with the In-Crowd, and Other Saturday Nightmares, Kingfisher (London, England), 1996.

Help! I've Forgotten My Brain, and Other Exam Nightmares, Kingfisher (London, England), 1996.

Scrooge: Hole Story, Scholastic (London, England), 2002.

Henry VIII: Hole Story, Scholastic (London, England), 2002.

Cleopatra: Hole Story, Scholastic (London, England), 2002.

Flyaway Katie, Candlewick (Cambridge, MA), 2004.

Dog Blue, Candlewick (Cambridge, MA), 2004.

Penguin, Candlewick (Cambridge, MA), 2007.

ILLUSTRATOR

Sherry Ashworth, *Fat,* Scholastic (London, England), 1997.

Elizabeth Laird, editor, *Me and My Electric,* Mammoth (London, England), 1998.

Jeanette Baker, *A Survivor's Guide to School,* Wayland (Hove, England), 1999.

Jeanette Baker, *A Survivor's Guide to Love, Etc.,* Wayland (Hove, England), 1999.

Jeanette Baker, *A Survivor's Guide to Friends,* Wayland (Hove, England), 1999.

Jeanette Baker, *A Survivor's Guide to Families,* Wayland (Hove, England), 1999.

Polly Dunbar (Photograph courtesy of Polly Dunbar.)

Myra Barrs and Sue Ellis, editors, *A Saucepan on His Head, and Other Nonsense Poems,* Walker (London, England), 2001.

Sandra Cain and Michelle Maxwell, *The Total Volunteering Book,* A & C Black (London, England), 2001.

Sherry Ashworth, *English Literature: Exam Success without the Stress,* Scholastic (London, England), 2001.

June Crebbin, *The Dragon Test,* Walker (London, England), 2003.

June Crebbin, *Hal the Highwayman,* Walker (London, England), 2003.

Pippa Goodhart, *Ratboy,* Barrington Stoke (Edinburgh, Scotland), 2004.

Lesley Ely, *Looking after Louis,* Albert Whitman (Morton Grove, IL), 2004.

June Crebbin, *Lucy and the Firestone,* Walker (London, England), 2004.

June Crebbin, *Hal the Pirate,* Walker (London, England), 2004.

Joyce Dunbar, *Shoe Baby,* Candlewick (Cambridge, MA), 2005.

Margaret Mahy, *Down the Back of the Chair,* Clarion (New York, NY), 2006.

Jane Yolen and Andrew Fusek Peters, editors, *Here's a Little Poem: A Very First Book of Poetry,* Candlewick (Cambridge, MA), 2007.

OTHER

(Adaptor, with Katherine Morton) *Shoe Baby* (puppet play based on her picture book), produced at Brighton Festival, 2006.

Sidelights

Polly Dunbar has been writing and illustrating books professionally since she was sixteen years old. Her first two books, *Help! I'm out with the In-Crowd, and Other Saturday Nightmares* and *Help! I've Forgotten My Brain, and Other Exam Nightmares,* are "cartoon books inspired by teenage antics," as Dunbar wrote on her home page. Since those debut titles, Dunbar has written and illustrated several books of her own, as well as providing illustrations for other writers, including her mother, prolific children's writer Joyce Dunbar.

Collaborating with author Lesley Ely, Dunbar produced *Looking after Louis,* a story about accepting differences. The story is told from the point of view of a young girl who sits next to Louis, an autistic boy, in her class. "Dunbar's childlike paintings cleverly show how Louis is essentially the same as the other kids," wrote Kathleen Kelly MacMillan in *School Library Journal.* A *Kirkus Reviews* contributor noted the illustrator's use of "sketchy scenes rendered in a childlike, cartoon style." A project of Dunbar and mom Joyce Dunbar, *Shoe Baby* finds a young baby traveling to fantastic locations in a shoe. "The mixed-media artwork is particularly enticing," wrote Ilene Cooper in *Booklist,* and a *Kirkus Reviews* contributor noted that Polly Dunbar's "delightful mixed-media collage illustrations of eccentric creatures great and small burst forth with . . . glee."

Dunbar's whimsical art pairs well with Australian writer Margaret Mahy's humorous story in **Down the Back of the Chair.** (Illustration © 2006 by Polly Dunbar. All rights reserved. Reproduced by permission of Houghton Mifflin Company.)

Dunbar's work with well-known poet Margaret Mahy resulted in *Down the Back of the Chair.* Here Dunbar's "cacophonous, sunny, paint-and-paper collages" pair with Mahy's text, according to *Booklist* critic Gillian Engberg. A *Kirkus Reviews* contributor noted that the "whimsical creatures, juicy colors and . . . motion" of Dunbar's art "match the kinetic energy of the text."

In addition to illustration, Dunbar has also created several self-illustrated books. In *Flyaway Katie* she tells a story about the power of imagination to drive away the doldrums. Katie wakes up feeling gray, quite literally: her world is colorful, but Katie is depicted in gray tones. Trying to make herself feel more cheerful, she dons a bright green hat and yellow tights. As she adds more and more color to her ensemble, the colors begin to whirl and Katie is transformed into a colorful bird. Spending the afternoon flying about, Katie arrives home—happily pink—just in time for her bath. "The magical makeover, a literal flight of fancy, will make readers' spirits soar, too," wrote a *Publishers Weekly* critic, and Cooper predicted that young readers will enjoy the "neatly framed pictures that eventually burst into a mixed-media multihued whirl." Asserting that the picture book is "told at just the right pace," Wanda Meyers-Hines wrote in *School Library Journal* that Dunbar's "whimsical story presents a gentle reminder of the power of a child's imagination," and a *Kirkus Reviews* contributor deemed *Flyaway Katie* "a joyous cure for a case of the doldrums."

Shoe Baby, *a large-format picture book, is one of many mother-daughter collaborations between Polly Dunbar and her mother, Joyce Dunbar.* (Illustration © 2005 by Polly Dunbar. Reproduced by permission of Candlewick Press, Inc., Cambridge, MA, on behalf of Walker Books, Ltd., London.)

Another self-illustrated picture book by Dunbar, *Dog Blue* also focuses on the theme of imagination. Here Bertie wants a dog in his favorite color, blue. Because he does not have a real-life pup, Bertie creates one in his mind, playing with his imaginary dog and fetching his own sticks. When a spotted dog arrives in Bertie's

Although she began her career creating art for books by her mother, Joyce Dunbar, Polly Dunbar's work is now paired with stories by many authors. (Illustration courtesy of Polly Dunbar.)

life, the boy is disappointed that it is not blue, but instead of turning away, he names the dog Blue and now has a friend to play with. "Young Bertie's joy comes through loud and clear" in both the story and the artwork, according to a *Kirkus Reviews* contributor. Although she found the story's resolution gratifying, Jennifer Mattson wrote in *Booklist* that "it's Bertie's ingenious self-sufficiency that truly resonates." A *Publishers Weekly* contributor also praised the picture book, writing that *Dog Blue* features "polished artwork and skilled pacing."

Along with writing and illustrating, Dunbar is also a member of the Long Nose Puppets Theater Company with friends from her university days. She lives and works in London.

Biographical and Critical Sources

PERIODICALS

Booklist, April 15, 2004, Connie Fletcher, review of *Looking after Louis,* p. 1445; June 1, 2004, Ilene Cooper, review of *Flyaway Katie,* p. 1740; July, 2004, Jennifer Mattson, review of *Dog Blue,* p. 1846; June 1, 2005, Ilene Cooper, review of *Shoe Baby,* p. 1821; May 1, 2006, Gillian Engberg, review of *Down the Back of the Chair,* p. 92.

Horn Book, September-October, 2004, Joanna Rudge Long, review of *Dog Blue,* p. 566.

Kirkus Reviews, March 15, 2004, review of *Looking after Louis,* p. 268; June 15, 2004, review of *Flyaway Katie,*

p. 576; July 1, 2004, review of *Dog Blue,* p. 627; July 1, 2005, review of *Shoe Baby,* p. 733; May 15, 2006, review of *Down the Back of the Chair,* p. 520.

Publishers Weekly, July 5, 2004, review of *Flyaway Katie,* p. 54; August 30, 2004, review of *Dog Blue,* p. 53; September 5, 2005, review of *Shoe Baby,* p. 60; April 10, 2006, review of *Down the Back of the Chair,* p. 70.

School Library Journal, April, 2004, Kathleen Kelly MacMillan, review of *Looking after Louis,* p. 109; September, 2004, Janet M. Bair, review of *Dog Blue,* and Wanda Meyers-Hines, review of *Flyaway Katie,* p. 158; August, 2005, Marianne Saccardi, review of *Shoe Baby,* p. 93; June, 2006, Carol L. MacKay, review of *Down the Back of the Chair,* p. 122.

Times Educational Supplement, October 27, 2006, Karen Gold, "All Together Now," p. 30, Jane Doonan, "Art World Is Their Oyster," p. 34.

Tribune Books (Chicago, IL), July 2, 2006, Mary Harris Russell, review of *Down the Back of the Chair,* p. 7.

ONLINE

Houghton Mifflin Web site, http://www.houghton-mifflinbooks.com/ (July 3, 2007), "Polly Dunbar."

Images of Delight Web site, http://www.imagesofdelight.com/ (July 3, 2007), "Polly Dunbar."

Long Nose Puppets Web site, http://www.longnosepuppets.com/ (July 3, 2007), "Polly Dunbar."

Meet the Author Web site, http://www.meettheauthor.co.uk/ (July 3, 2007), video interview with Dunbar.

Polly Dunbar Home Page, http://www.pollydunbar.com (July 3, 2007).

Walker Books Web site, http://www.walkerbooks.co.uk/ (July 3, 2007), "Polly Dunbar."

*   *   *

DUVAL, Kathy 1946-

Personal

Born January 21, 1946, in Enid, OK; daughter of Tom Hall (an electrical engineer) and Gloria (an occupational therapy assistant) Robb; married Glen Duval (a project information manager), December 13, 1974; children: Jon Paul Hamilton, Kara. *Education:* University of Houston, B.S. (art education), 1970, M.A. (behavioral science), 1978. *Hobbies and other interests:* Reading, art, yoga, making jewelry, spending time with grandchildren.

Addresses

Home—TX. *Agent*—Erin Murphy, 2700 Woodlands Village Blvd., Flagstaff, AZ 86001. *E-mail*—kathy@kathy-duval.com.

Career

Art teacher, art therapist, and author of children's books. Art teacher in Houston, TX public schools, 1970-78; art

Kathy Duval (Photograph courtesy of Kathy Duval.)

therapist in Houston, beginning 1981. House of Tiny Treasures, Houston, art therapist for homeless children.

Member

Society of Children's Writers and Illustrators, Author's Guild, American Art Therapy Association.

Writings

FOR CHILDREN

The Three Bears' Christmas, illustrated by Paul Meisel, Holiday House (New York, NY), 2005.
The Three Bears' Halloween, illustrated by Paul Meisel, Holiday House (New York, NY), 2007.

Contributor of poems to periodicals, including *Ladybug* and *Babybug,* and to anthologies, including *"I Invited a Dragon to Dinner," and Other Poems to Make You Laugh out Loud,* Philomel, and *Ladybug, Ladybug, and Other Favorite Poems,* Cricket Magazine Group.

Sidelights

Kathy Duval told *SATA:* "When I was a kid I wanted to be an archaeologist. I read books like *Swiss Family Robinson* and *Treasure Island* and dreamed of explor-

ing. I ended up being an art teacher and art therapist, exploring inner worlds instead of outer. For ten years, I satisfied my itch for the exotic by being a weekend gypsy at the Texas Renaissance festival as a musician in a balalaika orchestra. I also went to art school and exhibited my art.

"I suffered a particularly nasty mid-life crisis, and thought I needed a new career. I seriously investigated horticulture, landscape architecture, medical illustration, art conservation, and at least a half dozen more I can't remember now.

"Then I took a writing course. What an awesome discovery to find out how much I love writing!

"Although I'd identified myself as an artist since I won an art contest in the sixth grade, looking back I see that a writer lurked inside me, too. In high school, I wrote poetry and loved rewriting my poems until the rhythm felt just right. When my husband asked me where I'd like to go on Saturday night, I'd tell him the bookstore. I've taken zillions of books to the Half-Price Bookstore to make more room in my house for new ones. In graduate school, I secretly enjoyed researching and writing papers while other students complained. I bought picture books for myself long after my two children had

Duval's holiday-themed picture book* The Three Bears' Christmas *is enhanced by Paul Meisel's engaging full-color art. (Illustration © 2005 by Paul Meisel. All rights reserved. Reproduced by permission of Holiday House, Inc.)

moved on to sci-fi and historical fiction. And for years before I started writing for publication, I wrote and illustrated my dreams in journals. A while back, I stacked my dream journals, and the stack reached my elbow. I'm only 5'2", but its still an impressive amount of writing for someone who didn't know she was a writer."

Asked to pass along some advice for aspiring young writers," Duval suggested: "Read lots and lots of children's books! Several times a week I go to a bookstore and read with a critical eye. What makes this book good? Publishers receive thousands and thousands of submissions a year. What made someone want to publish this one? You will learn what children today are interested in reading and what types of books are being published. If you want to write picture books, you will get the feel for the rhythm and conciseness of picture books. Writing picture books is very much like writing poetry.

"The most important bit of advice I can give to aspiring writers is to keep writing. A beginning piano student doesn't expect to play on a concert stage right away, but for some reason beginning writers often have unrealistic expectations about how long it takes to get published. I think talent for something is really having passion for it, so that you are willing to spend whatever time it takes to learn to do it well. Without that passion, you give up."

Biographical and Critical Sources

PERIODICALS

Booklist, September 1, 2005, Ilene Cooper, review of *The Three Bears' Christmas,* p. 124.

Horn Book, November-December, 2005, review of *The Three Bears' Christmas,* p. 692.

Houston Chronicle, November 17, 2005, Flori Meeks, "Town and Country Bookstore to Host Writer," p. 6.

Kirkus Reviews, November 1, 2005, review of *The Three Bears' Christmas,* p. 1192.

School Library Journal, October, 2005, review of *The Three Bears' Christmas.*

ONLINE

Kathy Duval Home Page, http://www.kathyduval.com (July 17, 1997).

E-F

ERLBRUCH, Wolf 1948-

Personal
Born 1948, in Wuppertal, Germany. *Education:* Folkwang Hochschule (Essen, Germany), degree (graphic design), 1967.

Addresses
Home—Wuppertal, Germany.

Career
Illustrator, author, and educator. Freelance illustrator, beginning c. 1970; Fachhochschule Düsseldorf, Düsseldorf, Germany, professor of illustration, beginning 1990; Bergischen Universität, Wuppertal, Germany, professor of illustration and design, beginning 1997.

Member
Art Directors Club (New York, NY).

Awards, Honors
Deutscher Jugendliteraturpreis, 1992, for *Das Bärenwunder;* Schnabelsteherpreis, 1996, and Silver Paintbrush award, 1998, both for *Frau Meier, die Amsel;* Luchs des Jahres, 1999, for *Nachts;* Silver Paintbrush award, 1999, for *Loenoard,* and 2004, for *Die große Frage;* Troisdorfer Bilderbuchpreis, 2000, for *Neues ABC Buch für Kinder;* Von der Heydt-Kulturpreis (Wuppertal, Germany); German Children's Literature Award, and Gutenberg prize (Leipzig, Germany), all 2003; Silver Pencil prize, 2004; Bologna Book Fair Ragazzi Award, 2004, for *The Big Question;* Hans Christian Andersen Medal for Illustration, International Board on Books for Young People, 2006.

Writings

SELF-ILLUSTRATED

Die fürchterlichen Fünf (title means "The Terrible Five"), Peter Hammer (Wuppertal, Germany) 1990.

Leonard, Peter Hammer (Wuppertal, Germany), 1991, translation published under same title, Orchard Books (New York, NY), 1995.

Das Bärenwunder, Peter Hammer (Wuppertal, Germany), 1992, translation by Michael Reynolds published as *The Miracle of the Bears,* Europa Editions (New York, NY), 2006.

Ratten, Maro (Augsburg, Germany), 1993.

Zehn grüne Heringe, Hanser (Munich, Germany), 1995.

Frau Meier, die Amstel, Peter Hammer (Wuppertal, Germany), 1995, translation published as *Mrs. Meyer, the Bird,* Orchard Books (New York, NY), 1997.

Engel und anderes Geflügel, 1998.

Nachts (title means "Nighttime"), Peter Hammer (Wuppertal, Germany), 1999.

La grand question, Éditions Être (Paris, France), 2003, German translation published as *Die große Frage,* Peter Hammer (Wuppertal, Germany), 2004, translation by Michael Reynolds published as *The Big Question,* Europa Editions (New York, NY), 2005.

Das Adressbuch, Kunstmann (Munich, Germany), 2006.

Ente, Tod und Tulpe, Kunstmann (Munich, Germany), 2007.

Author's books have been translated into several languages, including Spanish, French, Italian, Swedish, and Danish.

ILLUSTRATOR

James Aggrey, *Der Adler, der nicht fliegen wollte,* Peter Hammer (Wuppertal, Germany), 1985, translation published as *The Eagle That Would Not Fly*), Little Tiger Press, 1985.

Werner Holzwarth, *Vom kleinen Maulwurf, der wissen wollte, wer ihm auf den Kopf gemacht hat,* Peter Hammer Verlag (Wuppertal, Germany), 1991, translation published as *The Story of the Little Mole Who Went in Search of Whodunit,* Stewart, Tabori & Chang (New York, NY), 1993, published as *The Story of the Little Mole, Who Knew It Was None of His Business,* Bennett Books (St. Albans, England), 1994.

John Saxby, *Die Abenteuer von Eduard Speck,* Hanser (Munich, Germany), 1993.

Leo Brawand, *Manager sind auch nur Menschen,* Moskau (Düsseldorf, Germany), 1994.

Rafik Schami, *Das ist kein Papagei!,* Hanser (Munich, Germany), 1994.

Giocanda Belli, *Die Werkstatt der Schmetterlinge,* Peter Hamer (Wuppertal, Germany), 1994, translation published as *The Butterfly Workshop,* Europa Editions (New York, NY), 2006.

Thomas Winding, *Mein kleiner Hund Mister,* Rowohlt (Hamburg, Germany), 1996.

Valérie Dayre, *Die Menschenfresserin,* Peter Hammer (Wuppertal, Germany), 1996.

Thomas Winding, *Mein kleiner Hund Mister in der Nacht,* Carlsen (Hamburg, Germany), 1998.

Johann Wolfgang von Goethe, *Das Hexen-Einmal-Eins,* Hanser (Munich, Germany), 1998.

John Saxby, *Neue Abenteuer von Eduard Speck,* Hanser (Munich, Germany), 1998.

Dolf Verroen, *Der Bär auf dem Spielplatz,* Beltz & Gelberg (Weinheim, Germany), 1998.

Miriam Pressler and Yaakov Shabtai, *Die wundersame Reise des kleinen Kröterichs,* Hanser (Munich, Germany), 1998.

Hermann Schulz, *Auf dem Strom,* Carlsen (Hamburg, Germany), 1999.

Carli Biessels, *Benni und die Wörter: eine Geschichte vom Lesenlernen,* Beltz & Gelberg (Weinheim, Germany), 2000.

Karl Philipp Moritz, *Neues ABC Buch,* Künstmann (Munich, Germany), 2000.

Bart Moeyaert, *Am Anfang,* Peter Hammer (Wuppertal, Germany), 2003.

Dolf Verroen, *Ein Himmel für den kleinen Bären,* Hanser (Munich, Germany), 2003.

Erik Orsenna, *Die Grammatik ist ein sanftes Lied,* Hanser (Munich, Germany), 2004.

Ljudmila Ulitzkaja, *Eiin glücklicher Zufall und andere Kindergeschichten,* Hanser (Munich, Germany), 2005.

Lee Bennett Hopkins, editor, *Oh, No! Where Are My Pants?, and Other Disasters* (poems), HarperCollins (New York, NY), 2005.

Bart Moeyaert, *Olek schoß einen Bärem und nähte sich aus dem Pelz eine Mütze,* Peter Hammer (Wuppertal, Germany), 2006.

Rufus Beck, editor, *Geschichten für und Kinder,* Rowohlt (Berlin, Germany), 2006.

Ein Baum von deiner Größe kann dir keinen Schatten spenden: Weisheiten aus Afrika, Peter Hammer (Wuppertal, Germany), 2006.

Contributor of illustrations to periodicals, including *Playboy, Esquire,* and *Stern.*

Adaptations

Several of Erlbruch's stories have been adapted for the German stage. Book illustrations have been collected and reproduced as calendar art and on notecards.

Sidelights

Considered one of Germany's most beloved illustrators, Wolf Erlbruch has received many prestigious awards for his work, among them the Deutscher Jugendliteraturpreis, the 2003 Gutenberg prize, and the 2006 Hans Christian Andersen Medal for Illustration. In his art for children's picture books, Erlbruch creates a unique mix of collage and drawing, captivating both children and adults alike, and his images have also appeared on calendars and cards. Incorporating humorous, over-the-top characters and imaginative details in his mix of collage and line, Erlbruch also incorporates both wit and emotion. His books, which include the German-language classics *Die fürchterlichen Fünf, Das Bärenwunder, Frau Meier, die Amstel, Nachts,* and *Die große Frage,* have been translated into numerous languages. English-language editions include *The Big Question, The Miracle of the Bears, Leonard,* and *Mrs. Meyer, the Bird.*

Erlbruch's style as an illustrator has developed since his first picture-book project: creating art for Ghanaian author James Aggrey's *Der Adler, der nicht fliegen wollte* (published in English as *The Eagle That Would Not Fly*). As Konrad Heidkamp noted in an essay for the *New Books in German* Web site, "there are a number of ingredients that we've come to associate with Erlbruch: the squared maths-book-style paper, the green kitchen-wall-like paper, the topographical maps, the rubber stamps, the animals cut out of picture encyclopaedias. The material is used so sparingly that there's space and time to see, to take in both content and substance," Heidkamp continued, concluding that "these . . . much-loved Erlbruch recipes . . . have been served up many times." The first book to exhibit the classic Erlbruch "recipe", according to Heidkamp, was *The Story of the Little Mole, Who Knew It Was None of His Business,* a quirky 1989 book by German journalist Werner Holzwarth. Other classics include Erlbruch's own *Die fürchterlichen Fünf* the self-illustrated *Nachts,* about a little boy who cannot sleep, and *Frau Meier, die Amsel,* the last published in English translation as *Mrs Meyer, the Bird.* In addition to being the illustrator's first original story, *Die fürchterlichen Fünf* features "a number of new components . . . [in] Erlbruch's personal mythology," according to Heidkamp: "the ever-present moon that illuminates his dusky drawings, his love of offbeat music, his attention to typography, and the careful design of the end-papers."

In another early self-illustrated picture book, *Leonard,* Erlbruch tells the story of a boy who loves dogs despite his fear of them. Hoping to overcome this fear, the boy wishes that he could become a dog, and his wish is granted. A similar story about overcoming fear is recounted in *Mrs. Meyer, the Bird,* as a woman overlooks her own worries while teaching an abandoned young bird to fly. In *Publishers Weekly* a contributor wrote that in *Leonard* Erlbruch "sketches a telling psychological portrait." Another *Publishers Weekly* reviewer cited

First published in Germany, **The Miracle of the Bears** *is one of Wolf Erlbruch's most beloved stories for children.* (Europa Editions, 2001. Reproduced by permission.)

the "down-to-earth warmth" of *Mrs. Meyer, the Bird,* noting that the author/illustrator "ground[s his] . . . agreeable fantasy in a firm foundation of homey humor."

Erlbruch focuses on the cycle of life in *The Miracle of the Bears.* One spring, waking from a long hibernation, a bear cub goes in search of companionship after realizing that life only has meaning when it is shared. The author/illustrator grapples with another universal theme in the award-winning picture book *The Big Question,* which poses the quandary: "Why am I here?" In presenting a world of answers from a host of creatures, Erlbruch encourages each child to ponder and celebrate his or her own purpose on Earth. Calling *The Big Question* "striking in its simplicity," *Booklist* contributor Ilene Cooper added that the book's "amazing images" and "inventive" text will spark "conversation" and "musings." A *Kirkus Reviews* contributor echoed Cooper's assessment, calling Erlbruch's book "certain to leave even younger readers in a reflective mood." "Existentialists, and those who enjoy the occasional Zen koan, will appreciate this volume's inquisitive spirit and multiplicity of possible answers," concluded a *Publishers Weekly* reviewer of the work.

While noting the range of award-winning artwork Erlbruch has contributed to the texts of authors such as Gioconda Belli, Johann Wolfgang von Goethe, and Karl Philipp Moritz, Heidkamp maintained that the illustrator's original stories, such as *Nacht, Mrs. Meyer, the Bird,* and *The Miracle of the Bears,* are the "most moving. No fantasy adventures, no social problems and no heroes," the critic added." "Just simple, quiet stories. About not being able to sleep at night, about grandpa dying, about wanting to have someone to hug, about

taking care of the bird that can't fly. Or about getting up every day and having to create a bit more world. Just simple stories that become great books."

Biographical and Critical Sources

BOOKS

Wolf Erlbruch, Institut für Buchkunst (Leipzig, Germany), 2005.

PERIODICALS

Booklist, May 1, 1992, p. 1613; April 1, 1997, Ilene Cooper, review of *Mrs. Meyer, the Bird,* p. 74; February 15, 2005, Hazel Rochman, review of *Oh, No! Where Are My Pants?, and Other Disasters,* p. 1082; January 1, 2006, Ilene Cooper, review of *The Big Question,* p. 111.

Bulletin of the Center for Children's Books, October, 1995, review of *Leonard,* p. 51; February, 2005, Deborah Stevenson, review of *Oh, No! Where Are My Pants?, and Other Disasters,* p. 252.

Children's Bookwatch, June, 2007, review of *The Story of the Little Mole Who Went in Search of Whodunit.*

Horn Book, May-June, 2005, Martha V. Parravano, review of *Oh, No! Where Are My Pants?, and Other Disasters,* p. 337.

Kirkus Reviews, January 15, 2005, review of *Oh, No! Where Are My Pants?, and Other Disasters,* p. 121; October 1, 2005, review of *The Big Question,* p. 1079; October 15, 2006, review of *The Miracle of the Bears,* p. 1070.

Publishers Weekly, August 28, 1995, review of *Leonard,* p. 112; January 13, 1997, review of *Mrs. Meyer, the Bird,* p. 74; September 19, 2005, review of *The Big Question,* p. 66; November 27, 2006, review of *The Miracle of the Bears,* p. 50.

School Library Journal, January, 1996, Kate McClelland, review of *Leonard,* p. 83; February, 2005, Lauralyn Persson, review of *Oh, No! Where Are My Pants?, and Other Disasters,* p. 122; November, 2006, Margaret Bush, review of *The Miracle of the Bears,* p. 90.

Times Educational Supplement, April 23, 2004, Geraldine Brennan, review of *The Big Question,* p. A17.

ONLINE

New Books in German Web site, http://www.new-books-in-german.com/ (August 10, 2007), Konrad Heidkamp, "How Simple Stories Become Great Books."*

*   *   *

FINE, Howard 1961-

Personal

Born 1961; married; wife's name Rona; children: three. *Education:* Attended Bucknell University and Philadelphia College of Art.

Addresses

Agent—Linda Pratt, 10 E. 40th St., Ste. 3205, New York, NY 10016. *E-mail*—hfine@howardfineillustration.com.

Career

Dentist and children's book author and illustrator.

Awards, Honors

National Education Association Children's Top 100 Book List, American Library Association (ALA) Notable Book designation, National Council Teachers of English Notable Trade Book in the Language Arts, New York Public Library selection, and several state book awards, all for *Piggie Pie!* by Margie Palatini; Volunteer State Book Award nomination and Wyoming Buckaroo Award nomination, both 2000-01, both for *Zoom Broom* by Palatini; Book Sense 76 Pick, for *Dinosailors* by Deb Lund; Best of the Best Picture Book citation, Chicago Public Library, 2004, Pennsylvania Keystone to Reading Book Award, 2005-06, Michigan Reads! One State, One Preschool Book Award and Missouri Building Block Award nomination, both 2006, and Missouri Show-Me Readers Book Award nomination, 2006-07, all for *Bed Hogs* by Kelly S. Dipucchio; International Reading Association Children's Choice designation, and Irma S. and James H. Black Award, both for *Zak's Lunch* by Palatini.

Howard Fine (Photograph courtesy of Howard Fine.)

Writings

SELF-ILLUSTRATED

A Piggie Christmas, Hyperion (New York, NY), 2000.
Piggie's Twelve Days of Christmas, Hyperion (New York, NY), 2001.

ILLUSTRATOR

Margie Palatini, *Piggie Pie!,* Clarion (New York, NY), 1995.
Karla Kuskin, *The Upstairs Cat,* Clarion (New York, NY), 1997.
Margie Palatini, *Zoom Broom,* Hyperion (New York, NY), 1998.
Margie Palatini, *Zak's Lunch,* Clarion (New York, NY), 1998.
Margie Palatini, *Ding Dong Ding Dong,* Hyperion (New York, NY), 1999.
Catherine E. Wright, *Steamboat Annie and the Thousand-Pound Catfish,* Philomel (New York, NY), 2001.
Nancy Shaw, *Raccoon Tune,* Holt (New York, NY), 2003.
Deb Lund, *Dinosailors,* Harcourt (San Diego, CA), 2003.
Mary Beth Lundgren, *Seven Scary Monsters,* Clarion (New York, NY), 2003.
Margie Palatini, *Broom Mates,* Hyperion (New York, NY), 2003.
Kelly S. DiPucchio, *Bed Hogs,* Hyperion (New York, NY), 2004.
Lilian Moore, *Beware, Take Care: Fun and Spooky Poems,* new edition, Holt (New York, NY), 2006.

Deb Lund, *All aboard the Dinotrain,* Harcourt (Orlando, FL), 2006.

Bruce Hale, *Snoring Beauty,* Harcourt (Orlando, FL), 2007.

Sidelights

As a middle-school student, Howard Fine decided that he would set aside his hobby of drawing in order to become a professional basketball player. After spending more than one season on the bench, he let go of the dream and decided to become a dentist instead. As Fine recalled on his home page, while attending dental school "drawing and I resumed our acquaintance. We've stayed friends ever since. I really discovered how much I loved to draw and that, even better, that I wasn't half bad at it." As an illustrator and a dentist, Fine has the best of both worlds: "Every day, I get to help people smile two ways: I help them have healthy teeth and my books give them a reason to grin."

Fine's first picture book, *Piggie Pie!,* was the first of several collaborations with popular writer Margie Palatini. Here, Fine's "bold, forceful, in-your-face illustrations are . . . absolutely suited to the story," according to *Horn Book* critic Ann A. Flowers, and Stephanie Zvirin cited "Fine's bold, expressive artwork" in her *Booklist* review. Illustrations for another Fine-Palatini collaboration, *Zak's Lunch,* "feature exaggerated close-ups and skewed perspectives, adding a frenzied quality" to the work. In *Zoom Broom,* which features references to famous witches and wizards, "Fine makes his own visual asides to pop-culture sorcery," according to a *Publishers Weekly* critic. Maryann H. Owen, reviewing the companion volume, *Broom Mates,* for *School Library Journal,* wrote that Fine's "paintings offer varying perspectives, close-ups, bright rich colors, and grossly humorous details."

Inspired by his work creating pig characters for his collaborations with Palatini, Fine has also created two

Howard Fine teams up with popular writer Margie Palatini in the humorous picture book **Piggie Pie!** (Clarion Books, 1995. Illustration © 1995 by Howard Fine. All rights reserved. Reproduced by permission of Houghton Mifflin Company.)

original picture-book titles: *A Piggie Christmas* and *Piggie's Twelve Days of Christmas.* The first, described as an "irrepressibly jolly book" by *Booklist* critic Carolyn Phelan, features a number of variations and interpretations of traditional Christmas carols. Elizabeth Devereaux, reviewing the work for *Publishers Weekly,* deemed *A Piggie Christmas* "a little piece of hog heaven."

In addition to his work with Palatini, Fine has also illustrated books for other writers. His "realistic pastel illustrations help maintain the whimsy" in Karla Kuskin's text for *The Upstairs Cat,* according to a *Publishers Weekly* contributor. Zvirin, reviewing the same picture book for *Booklist,* wrote that, through his interesting "use [of] perspective," Fine creates "dynamic" illustrations that "solidly ground the story." The "the larger-than-life characters" Fine creates for Catherine E. Wright's *Steamboat Annie and the Thousand-Pound Catfish* "explode into life thanks to Fine's wonderfully expressive, detailed paintings." Discussing his work for Nancy Shaw's *Raccoon Tune,* a *Kirkus Reviews* writer noted that "Fine's oil paintings . . . are charming, mischievous, and dynamic." Readers of Mary Beth Lundgren's *Seven Scary Monsters* will be mesmerized by "the illustrations alone," predicted Gay Lynn Van Vleck in *School Library Journal,* and the illustrator's "comical, moonlit paintings plunge readers right into the thick of" Kelly S. Di Pucchio's *Bed Hogs,* according to a *Publishers Weekly* contributor. Hazel Rochman, writing in *Booklist,* praised "Fine's new illustrations," which "add deliciously shivery fun" to a new edition of Lilian Moore's poetry collection *Beware, Take Care: Fun and Spooky Poems.*

Working with Deb Lund, Fine introduces readers to fun-loving dinosaurs in both *Dinosailors* and *All aboard the Dinotrain.* In *Dinosailors,* his "dinosaurs are both identifiable, and in high spirits or low, easy to identify with," according to a *Kirkus Reviews* writer. Steven Engelfried, in *School Library Journal,* noted that Fine's art for this book contributes both "humor and appeal." Of *All aboard the Dinotrain,* a *Publishers Weekly* critic found the illustrator's juxtaposition of the goofy and the serious "hilarious," adding that Fine's "painterly brushstrokes and luminous, almost romantic pastel hues make the pictures seem like natural history museum murals as imagined by a daft paleontologist."

Biographical and Critical Sources

PERIODICALS

Booklist, September 1, 1995, Stephanie Zvirin, review of *Piggie Pie!,* p. 74; November 15, 1997, Stephanie Zvirin, review of *The Upstairs Cat,* p. 565; October 1, 1998, Stephanie Zvirin, review of *Zoom Broom,* p. 336; September 1, 2000, Carolyn Phelan, review of *A Piggie Christmas,* p. 132; July, 2001, Gillian Engberg, review of *Steamboat Annie and the Thousand-Pound Catfish,* p. 2015; September 1, 2003, Stephanie Zvirin,

review of *Dinosailors,* p. 129; November 1, 2003, Jennifer Mattson, review of *Broom Mates,* p. 505; April 1, 2006, John Peters, review of *All aboard the Dinotrain,* p. 48; September 1, 2006, Hazel Rochman, review of *Beware, Take Care: Fun and Spooky Poems,* p. 131.

Bulletin of the Center for Children's Books, September, 2001, review of *Steamboat Annie and the Thousand-Pound Catfish,* p. 41; January, 2004, Elizabeth Bush, review of *Dinosailors,* p. 197.

Horn Book, March-April, 1996, Ann A. Flowers, review of *Piggie Pie!,* p. 189.

Kirkus Reviews, September 15, 2001, review of *Steamboat Annie and the Thousand-Pound Catfish,* p. 1372; May 15, 2003, review of *Raccoon Tune,* p. 756; June 15, 2003, review of *Broom Mates,* p. 862; September 15, 2003, review of *Dinosailors,* p. 1177; April 1, 2004, review of *Bed Hogs,* p. 328; March 1, 2006, review of *All aboard the Dinotrain,* p. 235; August 15, 2006, review of *Beware, Take Care,* p. 849.

Publishers Weekly, August 18, 1997, review of *Piggie Pie!,* p. 95; October 13, 1997, review of *The Upstairs Cat,* p. 74; April 27, 1998, review of *Zak's Lunch,* p. 66; November 9, 1998, review of *Zoom Broom,* p. 76; September 13, 1999, review of *Ding Dong Ding Dong,* p. 83; September 25, 2000, Elizabeth Devereaux, review of *A Piggie Christmas,* p. 67; October 29, 2001, review of *Steamboat Annie and the Thousand-Pound Catfish,* p. 63; April 28, 2003, review of *Raccoon Tune,* p. 69; August 4, 2003, review of *Broom Mates,* p. 77, review of *Seven Scary Monsters,* p. 79; September 8, 2003, review of *Dinosailors,* p. 75; May 17, 2004, review of *Bed Hogs,* p. 49; January 30, 2006, review of *All aboard the Dinotrain,* p. 68.

School Library Journal, October, 2000, review of *A Piggie Christmas,* p. 59; October, 2001, Susan Helper, review of *Steamboat Annie and the Thousand-Pound Catfish,* p. 134; July, 2003, Louise L. Sherman, review of *Raccoon Tune,* p. 106; September, 2003, Steven Engelfried, review of *Dinosailors,* p. 184; September, 2003, Gay Lynn Van Vleck, review of *Seven Scary Monsters,* p. 184, Maryann H. Owen, review of *Broom Mates,* p. 186; May, 2004, Carolyn Janssen, review of *Bed Hogs,* p. 109; May, 2006, Robin L. Gibson, review of *All aboard the Dinotrain,* p. 94; October, 2006, Margaret Bush, review of *Beware, Take Care,* p. 140.

ONLINE

Houghton Mifflin Web site, http://www.houghton-mifflinbooks.com/ (July 3, 2007), "Howard Fine."

Howard Fine Home Page, http://www.howardfineillustration.com (July 3, 2007).

* * *

FLETCHER, Susan 1951-
(Susan Clemens Fletcher)

Personal

Born May 28, 1951, in Pasadena, CA; daughter of Leland (an engineer) and Reba (a teacher) Clemens; mar-

Susan Fletcher (Photograph courtesy of Susan Fletcher.)

ried Jerry Fletcher (a marketing consultant), June 4, 1977; children: Kelly. *Education:* University of California, Santa Barbara, B.A. (with highest honors), 1973; University of Michigan, M.A., 1974.

Addresses

Home and office—32475 Armitage Rd., Wilsonville, OR 90707. *Agent*—Emilie Jacobson, Curtis Brown Ltd., 10 Astor Place, New York, NY 10003. *E-mail*—susan-fletcher@centurytel.net.

Career

Writer. Campbell-Mithun (advertising agency), Minneapolis, MN, and Denver, CO, media buyer, 1974-77, advertising copywriter, 1977-79; Portland Community College, Portland, OR, lecturer, 1988-90; Vermont College, Montpelier, instructor in M.F.A. program in writing for children, 2000-04.

Member

Society of Children's Book Writers and Illustrators (Northwest chapter), Authors Guild, Phi Beta Kappa.

Awards, Honors

Oregon Book Award, 1990, Young Adults' Choice, International Reading Association (IRA), 1991, Young Readers' Choice nomination, Pacific Northwest Library Association, 1992, and South Carolina Young-Adult Book Award nomination, 1992-93, all for *Dragon's Milk;* International Youth Library Selection, 1992, for *The Stuttgart Nanny Mafia;* Outstanding Book designation, *World Book Encyclopedia* Annual Supplement, 1993, Oregon Book Award finalist, 1994, Best Books for Young Adults, American Library Association (ALA), and IRA Young Adults' Choice, both 1995, Sequoyah Award nomination, 1995-96, and Texas Lone Star Reading List inclusion, 1996-97, all for *Flight of the Dragon Kyn;* Best Books designation, *School Library Journal,* and Blue Ribbon award, *Bulletin of the Center for Children's Books,* both 1998, Children's Literature Choice listee, 1999, Pennsylvania Young Readers' Choice nomination, and Dorothy Canfield Fisher Award nomination, both 1999-2000, and ALA Notable Books for Older Readers and Best Books for Young Adults designations, and Notable Children's Trade Book in the Field of Social Studies, National Council on the Social Studies/Children's Book Council, all for *Shadow Spinner;* Sequoyah Award nomination, 1998-99, for *Sign of the Dove;* Bank Street College of Education Best Children's Book of the Year designation, Spur Award finalist, Western Writers of America, Willa Literary Award finalist, Women Writing in the West, Children's Literature Choice selection, and Dorothy Canfield Fisher Master List inclusion, all 2002, all for *Walk across the Sea;* New York Public Library Books for the Teen Age designation, CBC Notable Social Studies Trade Book designation, Cooperative Children's Book Center Choice designation, and ALA Best Book for Young Adults designation, all 2007, and Dorothy Canfield Fisher Master List inclusion, all 2007-08, all for *Alphabet of Dreams.*

Writings

NOVELS

The Haunting Possibility (mystery), Crosswinds Press (New York, NY), 1988.
The Stuttgart Nanny Mafia, Atheneum (New York, NY), 1991.
Shadow Spinner, Atheneum (New York, NY), 1998.
Walk across the Sea, Atheneum (New York, NY), 2001.
Alphabet of Dreams, Atheneum (New York, NY), 2006.

"DRAGON CHRONICLES"

Dragon's Milk, Atheneum (New York, NY), 1989.
Flight of the Dragon Kyn (prequel to *Dragon's Milk*), Atheneum (New York, NY), 1993.
Sign of the Dove, Atheneum (New York, NY), 1996.

OTHER

Dadblamed Union Army Cow (picture book), illustrated by Kimberly Bulken Root, Candlewick Press (Cambridge, MA), 2007.

Contributor to periodicals, including *Ms., Woman's Day, Family Circle,* and *Mademoiselle.*

Adaptations

Shadow Spinner and *Walk across the Sea* were adapted as audiobooks by Recorded Books, 1999 and 2002 respectively. *Alphabet of Dreams* was adapted as audiobooks by Listening Library, 2006.

Sidelights

Novelist Susan Fletcher is the author of historical and fantasy fiction for young readers, including a popular trilogy that includes the books *Dragon's Milk, Flight of the Dragon Kyn,* and *Sign of the Dove.* With a medieval setting inspired by pictures of the Welsh countryside from where Fletcher traces her roots, the "Dragon Chronicles" saga features an imaginative, dragon-centered plot that has won the author praise from reviewers and readers alike. Calling *Flight of the Dragon Kyn* "a joy to read," *Booklist* contributor Deborah Abbott added that in the novel "Fletcher pens some of the best yarns around."

Cover of Fletcher's fantasy novel Dragon's Milk, *featuring artwork by Rebecca Guay.* (Aladdin Paperbacks, 1997. Illustration © 1997 by Rebecca Guay. Reproduced by permission.)

In addition to her fantasy trilogy, Fletcher has also produced the award-winning standalone novels *Shadow Spinner* and *Alphabet of Dreams,* two books that contain elements of both historical fiction and magical realism. She has also penned the historical novel *Walk across the Sea,* as well as a picture book titled *Dadblamed Union Army Cow.* Based on a true story in which a Union soldier is followed into war by his family's cow, *Dadblamed Union Army Cow* was praised by *Booklist* critic Debbie Carton as a "well-constructed . . . read aloud." Praising Fletcher's narrative style, a *Kirkus Reviews* writer noted that the homespun tale "engages the reader and captures just the right tone without caricaturizing or sensationalizing" the wartime event.

Born in Pasadena, California, in 1951, Fletcher and her family moved to Ohio when she was seven years old. She had dreamed of being a writer ever since she entered the third grade. "Back then my name was Susan Clemens," she once explained to *SATA.* "One day my teacher told us about a famous author named Mark Twain, whose real name was Samuel Clemens, [and] whose daughter's name was Susan. It was fate, I thought. I decided not to become the daughter of a famous author (which is impossible to arrange), but to become a famous author myself (which is difficult enough)."

Returning to California in sixth grade, Fletcher graduated from high school in 1969, having spent her senior year as fiction editor of her school's literary magazine. She enrolled at the University of California at Santa Barbara and earned her bachelor's degree in English. She then moved to Michigan, where she earned her master's degree in English from the University of Michigan. After a move to Colorado, Fletcher got a job with a local advertising agency and met her soon-to-be husband, Jerry, whom she married in 1977. Moving again, this time to Minneapolis, Minnesota, she put her writing talent to work creating copy for radio advertisements, work she enjoyed and was good at. After her husband's job relocated the couple to Portland, Oregon, Fletcher planned to look for a similar position, but those plans changed when she discovered that she and her husband would soon be having a child. Magazine writing became her new focus—it was something Fletcher could do from home—and from there it was a short step to becoming a children's-book writer.

Fletcher's first novel for young readers, 1988's *The Haunting Possibility,* was inspired by Oregon's Lake Oswego area and the practice of draining the lake each winter to allow dock repairs to be made. Learning the nuances of characterization and plotting as she went, Fletcher completed the manuscript and sent it to almost twenty publishers before it was accepted. She quickly involved herself in a local group of children's writers, meeting several editors and gaining constructive criticism of her work in the process.

"While I was sending out *The Haunting Possibility,* an idea began to tease at the edges of my mind," Fletcher wrote in an essay published in *Something about the Author Autobiography Series* (SAAS), discussing the inspiration for her "Dragon Chronicles" trilogy. As she recalled, her town librarian "directed me to some really fine fantasy novels for children, and I began to be drawn to that genre." Working in the fantasy genre also allowed Fletcher to address the portrayal of female protagonists in typical fairy tales. "The typical fairy-tale heroine would sit around being beautiful, singing nicely, and being kind to birds and animals until her boyfriend—The Prince—came along and solved all her problems for her," the author explained. That type of character was not one Fletcher cared to perpetuate, and in her next novel she "decided to write a story about a girl who had the courage to solve her own problems." Thinking back to her own early teens, Fletcher hit upon the one task that had required extraordinary amounts of courage, fortitude, bravery, patience, and just plain hard work: babysitting the notorious La Rue kids, four unruly boys who lived on Fletcher's street when she was young.

Published in 1989 as the first installment in the "Dragon" trilogy, *Dragon's Milk* is a baby-sitting adventure that takes place in the fantasy kingdom of Elythia. Kaeldra, the protagonist, is an adopted child whose emerald-green eyes identify her as a descendent of the dragon-sayers, humans who are able to communicate with the fire-breathers telepathically. When her younger sister, Lyf, becomes ill with a fever and can only be made well again by drinking dragon's milk, Kaeldra must search for a dragon. She finds one and agrees to babysit for its three offspring, called draclings, in exchange for the milk. The mother dragon goes out to find food, planning to return to her brood in a short while; when she is killed, Kaeldra is left to protect the draclings from men who want to destroy them.

Critics found *Dragon's Milk* entertaining and imaginative. Focusing on the novel's blend of action, suspense, magic, and romance, they also noted Fletcher's clever and convincing portrayal of the young dragons. "The three draclings, each with an individual personality, are endearing in the clumsy way of young animals," noted *School Library Journal* contributor Susan M. Harding, the critic concluding that, "with its satisfying heroine, [*Dragon's Milk*] is a thoroughly enjoyable story."

The saga of the dragons continues in *Sign of the Dove,* as the last of the dragon's eggs begins to hatch. Kaeldra's younger sister Lyf has by now been cured with dragons' milk, and her eyes have turned as green as those of her adopted sister as a result. Other less-visible changes to Lyf have also occurred, and the young teen is now being sought, along with other green-eyes, by those who would use her power to call dragons forth for evil. While taking flight with Kaeldra, Kaeldra's husband Jeorg, and three dragon hatchlings, Lyf soon finds herself alone and in charge of the dra-

clings, which get stronger and more curious with each passing day. Although not enthusiastic about her role as protector as was her sister, Lyf attempts to save the baby dragons from enemies who would kill them for their hearts, which are rumored to possess healing powers. *Booklist* contributor Sally Estes praised *Sign of the Dove* as "a rousing story filled with well-realized dragon lore."

Because of the transformation of its heroine, *Sign of the Dove* served as a personal statement for its author. In 1989 Fletcher had been diagnosed with cancer, and she fought the disease for a year before receiving a clean bill of health. While she found it impossible to write about her feelings as she confronted the possibility of losing the battle against cancer, her feelings found their way into her novel. "During the time when I was writing *Sign of the Dove,*" Fletcher recalled in *SAAS,* "I heard a Jewish couple speaking about the people who helped the German Jews during the Holocaust. . . . Suddenly, I realized that the book I was writing was about rescuers—people who help those who are in trouble, at risk to themselves and with no expectation of gain. On some level, it was about the people who helped *me.*" *Sign of the Dove* "is dedicated to them—my rescuers," the novelist explained.

The background to both *Dragon's Milk* and *Sign of the Dove* is laid out in *Flight of the Dragon Kyn.* In this novel, fifteen-year-old Kara, who has a natural gift for calling birds down from the sky, is called before King Orrik and asked to channel her power into bringing certain dragons to ground. Birds and dragons are rumored to be close relatives, and these particular dragons have been laying waste to the kingdom of Kragland. They are now held responsible for the deaths of both the father and brother of the king's future wife, Princess Signy. Aided by Skava, a wild gyrfalcon, Kara sets out on her quest, realizing too late that she is calling the dragons to their death in an ambush planned by the king. Also, by helping King Orrik, Kara gets on the wrong side of the king's brother Rog, who has designs of his own on the kingdom. Fleeing to the hills, the teen takes refuge with a dragon "kyn," or family, and helps the group find a home far from human unkindness.

Calling *Flight of the Dragon Kyn* "a solid fantasy in a medieval . . . setting," Kathryn Jennings added in a *Bulletin of the Center for Children's Books* review that the novel contains enough "drama, romance, and knavery to keep genre fans happy." Joyce W. Yen agreed in her *Voice of Youth Advocates* appraisal, praising Fletcher's incorporation of "a budding romance, an inner struggle, and a power struggle" into her "intriguing" tale. One of the novel's main characters required Fletcher to do her homework; in preparation for writing *Flight of the Dragon Kyn,* the novelist volunteered at a local zoo and learned the habits of birds of prey: their sleeping patterns, what they eat, their social behaviors.

Cover of Fletcher's fantasy novel Flight of the Dragon Kyn, *part of her "Dragon Chronicles" series, featuring artwork by Rebecca Guay.* (Aladdin Paperbacks, 1997. Illustration © 1997 by Rebecca Guay. Reproduced by permission.)

Thus she was able to fully realize a character that *School Library Journal* contributor Margaret A. Chang cited among the book's "most engaging": the gyrfalcon Skava.

In addition to her "Dragon" fantasy novels, Fletcher has written several other books with teen appeal. In *The Stuttgart Nanny Mafia,* Aurora MacKenzie tries every trick under the sun to get Tanja, her nineteen-year-old au pair, fired and sent packing back to Germany, thus opening the way for Aurora and her mother to spend more quality time together, away from her mother's new husband and new baby. Praised by *Booklist* contributor Deborah Abbott for highlighting the emotions of stepchildren "pushed out by new family members and having to cope with the dynamics of a changed situation," *The Stuttgart Nanny Mafia* is similar to *Dragon's Milk* and *Sign of the Dove* in that its roots are in Fletcher's own experience. As she would later note in *SAAS:* "Bits of [my daughter Kelly's]. . . life sometimes make their way into my books. After reading parts of *The Stuttgart Nanny Mafia,* Kelly protested, 'Mom, you plagiarized my life!'"

In *Shadow Spinner* Fletcher provides an explanation for the amazing wealth of tales amassed by famous Persian storyteller Shahrazad in *1,001 Arabian Nights.* In Fletcher's imaginative novel, a crippled orphan named Marjan, handmaiden to the princess Shahrazad, becomes the source for many of the tales used by the princess to postpone her death. Noting that the story is a fictional take on a traditional tale, *Horn Book* reviewer Mary M. Burns asserted that "Fletcher puts her own spin on the source material, telling a tale in which the pace is consistent, the characters interesting, and the plot impelling." *Booklist* contributor Hazel Rochman had particular praise for Fletcher's preface to each of the book's chapters, "about how we find ourselves in our stories, how sharing stories brings strangers together." Patricia A. Dollisch, writing in *School Library Journal,* declared that "there are no weak spots in the telling of this tale. Even the minor characters make real impressions." While the "voices are clear and the dialogue works beautifully," Dollisch added of *Shadow Spinner* that "it is the structure that really makes this book sing."

Fletcher spins another magical story in *Alphabet of Dreams.* Again setting her story in Persia, she introduces fourteen-year-old Mitra and her five-year-old brother Babak, a boy able to see the future in his dreams. Disguised as beggars, the siblings are actually the children of a king who hope to find their family. When Babak's gift is discovered by Melchoir, a Zoroastrian priest, Mitra and her brother must join with Melchoir and his fellow priests Balthazaar and Gaspar on a journey that leads them from their home in Rhagae to a mysterious destination. Led by the stars and by the predictions of the ever-more-sickly Babak, the rag-tag band ultimately finds itself at the crib of a tiny baby born in a stable in Bethlehem. In *Publishers Weekly* a contributor dubbed *Alphabet of Dreams* a "richly imagined novel" enriched by a "feisty and honorable" heroine and Fletcher's "lush and often poetic language." Acknowledging the story's Biblical origins, GraceAnne A. DeCandido wrote in *School Library Journal* that "the rhythms of desert life form one intriguing dimension" to the author's tale. While *Kliatt* reviewer Donna Scanlon maintained that the author's "elegantly simple language" might challenge some readers, "the story itself," as well as its "well rounded and well drawn" characters, "will draw them in." "A fine weaver of historical fiction," Fletcher "creates a fully realized world for her characters and builds a plot full of suspense and anguish," concluded *School Library Journal* contributor Connie C. Rockman in a review of *Alphabet of Dreams.*

Fletcher turns again to historical fiction by turning back the clock to the 1880s in *Walk across the Sea.* Set in Crescent City, California, and based on a true story, the novel focuses on the treatment of Chinese immigrant laborers, who are shunned due to their religion and eventually run out of town due to fears that they will take scarce jobs away from Caucasian workers. In her novel, Fletcher shows that the bravery of one young teen, fifteen-year-old Eliza Jane McCully, can change

the mood of the prejudiced townspeople of her coastal community when she returns the kindness of a young Chinese artist, Wah Chung, after he saves her from being drowned. Calling *Walk across the Sea* an "emotionally tumultuous novel," a *Kirkus Reviews* writer added that the novel is made especially vivid due to Fletcher's incorporation of "carefully researched detail." In *Publishers Weekly* a reviewer described the novel as an "eye-opening" work in which Eliza's "wryly humorous voice emerges as the novel's greatest strength," and *School Library Journal* contributor William McLoughlin concluded that Fletcher's "deft analysis of racial discrimination makes the book even more powerful."

Although Fletcher writes her books for young readers from an office inside her Oregon home, she has traveled as far away as Iran and flown as high as a dragon to research her stories. As the author once explained, her novels are created in several stages. First comes research, followed by a first, sometimes very rough, draft. "I allow myself to write really badly at first if I need too," the author admitted in *SAAS*. Several other drafts may follow until the words "sound right." Fletcher also benefits from her editor and critique group. However, as she once explained in *SATA*, "my own inner ear is the final test."

Biographical and Critical Sources

BOOKS

Something about the Author Autobiography Series, Volume 25, Thomson Gale (Detroit, MI), 1998, pp. 95-116.

PERIODICALS

Booklist, November 1, 1989, review of *Dragon's Milk,* p. 547; December 15, 1991, Deborah Abbott, review of *The Stuttgart Nanny Mafia,* pp. 764-765; January 15, 1994, Deborah Abbott, review of *Flight of the Dragon Kyn,* p. 931; May 1, 1996, Sally Estes, review of *Sign of the Dove,* p. 1506; June 1, 1998, Hazel Rochman, review of *Shadow Spinner,* p. 1746; November 1, 2001, Hazel Rochman, review of *Walk across the Sea,* p. 476; September 1, 2006, GraceAnne A. DeCandido, review of *Alphabet of Dreams,* p. 109; July 1, 2007, Debbie Carton, review of *Dadblamed Union Army Cow,* p. 64.

Bulletin of the Center for Children's Books, September, 1991, review of *The Stuttgart Nanny Mafia,* p. 10; January, 1994, Kathryn Jennings, review of *Flight of the Dragon Kyn,* p. 153; July, 1998, review of *Shadow Spinner,* p. 394; January, 2007, Laura Baas, review of *Alphabet of Dreams,* p. 212.

Horn Book, September-October, 1996, Ann A. Flowers, review of *Sign of the Dove,* p. 595; July, 1998, Mary M. Burns, review of *Shadow Spinner,* p. 488.

Kirkus Reviews, October 15, 1993, review of *Flight of the Dragon Kyn,* p. 1239; May 1, 1998, review of *Shadow Spinner,* p. 657; October 15, 2001, review of *Walk across the Sea,* p. 1482; August 1, 2006, review of *Alphabet of Dreams,* p. 785; June 15, 2007, review of *Dadblamed Union Army Cow.*

Kliatt, July, 2003, Claire Rosser, review of *Walk across the Sea,* p. 20; September, 2006, Susan Allison, review of *Alphabet of Dreams,* p. 11.

Publishers Weekly, August 16, 1991, review of *The Stuttgart Nanny Mafia,* p. 58; November 5, 2001, review of *Walk across the Sea,* p. 69; October 30, 2006, review of *Alphabet of Dreams,* p. 63.

School Library Journal, November, 1989, Susan M. Harding, review of *Dragon's Milk,* pp. 107-108; November, 1993, Margaret A. Chang, review of *Flight of the Dragon Kyn,* p. 108; May, 1996, review of *Sign of the Dove,* p. 112; June, 1998, Patricia A. Dollisch, review of *Shadow Spinner,* p. 145; November, 2001, William McLoughlin, review of *Walk across the Sea,* p. 154; November, 2006, Connie C. Rockman, review of *Alphabet of Dreams,* p. 135.

Voice of Youth Advocates, February, 1994, Joyce W. Yen, review of *Flight of the Dragon Kyn,* p. 380; August, 1996, review of *Sign of the Dove,* p. 168; June, 2002, review of *Walk across the Sea,* p. 117; February, 2007, Cheryl French, review of *Alphabet of Dreams,* p. 524.

ONLINE

Susan Fletcher Home Page, http://susancfletcher.com (July 28, 2007).*

* * *

FLETCHER, Susan Clemens
See FLETCHER, Susan

* * *

FOX, Helen 1962-

Personal

Born 1962; married. *Education:* Oxford University, graduate.

Addresses

Home—London, England.

Career

Writer. Worked variously as a primary school teacher, marketing executive, tour guide, and actor.

Writings

Eager (middle-grade novel), Hodder Children's (London, England), 2003, Wendy Lamb Books (New York, NY), 2004.

Eager's Nephew (middle-grade novel), Hodder Children's (London, England), 2004, Wendy Lamb Books (New York, NY), 2006.

Eager and the Mermaid (middle-grade novel), Hodder Children's (London, England), 2007.

Sidelights

Helen Fox's first book for young teens, *Eager,* takes place in late-twenty-first-century England. Gavin Bell's parents are middle-class professionals who have a family robot, but Grumps is an older model and is beginning to have problems. Unfortunately, the Bell family is not able to afford the latest BDC4 model, which is produced by LifeCorp, the conglomerate controlling most technology. When a friend and former LifeCorp scientist asks if the Bells would like to try a yet-untested model EGR3 robot, they agree.

The EGR3—nicknamed "Eager"—is designed to learn like a real child; a self-aware robot, it learns by trial and error, and the fact that it is capable of independent thought prompted LifeCorp to pull this particular model from production. Eager soon becomes part of the Bell family, although Gavin's sister Fleur Bell is embarrassed by the robot's unsophisticated appearance, which is not at all like the sleek BDC4 model her friend Marcie has. However, the BDC4's soon begin rebelling against their owners. Eager, who has developed the capacity for love, sadness, and joy, is aware of the danger his family faces, and he exhibits the kind of bravery and growth that makes him wonder if he is actually alive. A *Kirkus Reviews* critic commented that, "while Eager's adventure isn't thrilling, his discoveries about life, formed through amusing conversations with virtual reality Socrates, are thought-provoking." Elizabeth Bush noted in the *Bulletin of the Center for Children's Books* that Fox "shines at times with flashes of humor and tenderness, as when Eager learns that sticky babies cannot be cleaned in a washing machine." *School Library Journal* contributor Sharon Rawlins wrote that Fox "raises thought-provoking questions about what it means to be human, the dangers of technology, and the concept of free will."

The adventures of Eager and the Bell family continue in *Eager's Nephew* and *Eager and the Mermaid.* A dozen years have gone by and self-aware robots can now reproduce. They are also illegal, so Eager has joined his sister Allegra and her shape-shifting robot son Jonquil in hiding. When he disguises himself as a servant-bot on his annual trip to visit the Bells, Eager is joined by Jonquil, and the two find themselves in trouble. Self-aware robots are no longer banned in *Eager and the Mermaid*; in fact, the government is gathering them together to help battle a planet-wide technological crisis. Although Eager enjoys the company of other robots, he worries that things—including his new robot friends—may not be what they seem. Praising *Eager's Nephew,* *Horn Book* contributor Vicky Smith noted Fox's discussion of "questions of morality and

Cover of Helen Fox's middle-grade novel Eager, *featuring artwork by Adam Willis.* (Cover art © 2004 by Adam Willis. All rights reserved. Reproduced by permission of Yearling Books, an imprint of Random House Children's Books, a division of Random House, Inc.)

identity," and dubbed the novel "good fun," while *School Library Journal* critic Walter Minkel commented that the adventure and humor in the story is "both . . . restrained and clever."

Biographical and Critical Sources

PERIODICALS

Booklist, June 1, 2004, Todd Morning, review of *Eager,* p. 1716; October 15, 2006, Todd Morning, review of *Eager's Nephew,* p. 45.

Bulletin of the Center for Children's Books, June, 2004, Elizabeth Bush, review of *Eager,* p. 417.

Horn Book, July-August, 2004, Peter D. Sieruta, review of *Eager,* p. 451; September-October, 2006, Vicky Smith, review of *Eager's Nephew,* p. 582.

Kirkus Reviews, May 15, 2004, review of *Eager,* p. 491; August 1, 2006, review of *Eager's Nephew,* p. 785.

School Library Journal, August, 2004, Sharon Rawlins, review of *Eager,* p. 121; January, 2007, Walter Minkel, review of *Eager's Nephew,* p. 128.*

G

GOODMAN, Susan E. 1952-

Personal

Born 1952; children: Jake; Matthew (stepson). *Education:* Goddard College, M.A. (applied psychology).

Addresses

Office—5 Oakview Terrace, Boston, MA 02130. *E-mail*—sugoodman@aol.com.

Career

Educator, author, and journalist. Tufts University, Boston, MA, professor; Lesley University, Cambridge, MA, professor. Freelance journalist; General Learning Corporation, Northbrook, IL, contributing editor. Formerly workes as a social worker.

Awards, Honors

Washington Post Book World Best Book designation, 2004, for *On This Spot;* Chicago Public Library Best of the Best designation, 2004, for *The Truth about Poop;* Maryland Blue Crab Young Readers Award for Nonfiction, 2004, for *Choppers!; Booklist* Top Ten Sci-Fi Books for Youth designation, 2004, for *Skyscraper.*

Writings

FOR CHILDREN

Amazing Artifacts: The Human Body, Animals, Plants, P. Bedrick Books (New York, NY), 1993.

Amazing Spacefacts: Solar System, Stars, Space Travel, P. Bedrick Books (New York, NY), 1993.

Unseen Rainbows, Silent Songs: The World beyond Human Senses, illustrated by Beverly Duncan, Atheneum Books for Young Readers (New York, NY), 1995.

The Great Antler Auction, photographs by Michael J. Doolittle, Atheneum Books for Young Readers (New York, NY), 1996.

Pilgrims of Plymouth, National Geographic Society (Washington, DC), 1999.

Animal Rescue: The Best Job There Is, Aladdin (New York, NY), 2000.

Chopsticks for My Noodle Soup: Eliza's Life in Malaysia, photographs by Michael J. Doolittle, Millbrook Press (Brookfield, CT), 2000.

Seeds, Stems, and Stamens: The Ways Plants Fit into Their World, photographs by Michael J. Doolittle, Millbrook Press (Brookfield, CT), 2001.

Claws, Coats, and Camouflage: The Ways Animals Fit into Their World, photographs by Michael J. Doolittle, Millbrook Press (Brookfield, CT), 2001.

What Do You Do . . . at the Zoo?, illustrated by Steve Pica, Millbrook Press (Brookfield, CT), 2002.

What Do You Do on a Farm?, illustrated by Steve Pica, Millbrook Press (Brookfield, CT), 2002.

Nature Did It First!, photographs by Dorothy Handelman, Millbrook Press (Brookfield, CT), 2003.

Skyscraper: From the Ground Up, illustrated by Michael J. Doolittle, Knopf (New York, NY), 2004.

On This Spot: An Expedition Back through Time, illustrated by Lee Christiansen, Greenwillow Books (New York, NY), 2004.

The Truth about Poop, illustrated by Elwood H. Smith, Viking (New York, NY), 2004.

Choppers!, photographs by Michael J. Doolittle, Random House (New York, NY), 2004.

Saber-toothed Cats, illustrated by Kerry Maguire, Millbrook Press (Minneapolis, MN), 2006.

Life on the Ice, photographs by Michael J. Doolittle, Millbrook Press (Minneapolis, MN), 2006.

Gee Whiz!: It's all about Pee, illustrated by Elwood H. Smith, Viking (New York, NY), 2006.

All in Just One Cookie, illustrated by Timothy Bush, Greenwillow (New York, NY), 2006.

Motorcycles!, photographs by Michael Doolittle, Random House (New York, NY), 2007.

Saving the Whooping Crane, illustrated by Phyllis V. Saroff, Millbrook Press (Minneapolis, MN), 2008.

Contributor to periodicals, including *National Geographic Traveler, Modern Maturity, Women's Day, National Wildlife, Redbook, Family Circle, Child, Harp-*

er's Bazaar, Glamour, New Woman, Barons, Self, Mademoiselle, Health, Working Woman, Ranger Rick, Outside Kids, Yankee, Woman, Bride's, Modern Bride, Horticulture, Science, Highlights for Children, Old Farmer's Almanac, Current Health, Real Paper, and *Bay State Guardian.*

"ULTIMATE FIELD TRIP" SERIES; FOR CHILDREN

Bats, Bugs, and Biodiversity: Adventures in the Amazonian Rain Forest, photographs by Michael J. Doolittle, Atheneum Books for Young Readers (New York, NY), 1995.

Stones, Bones, and Petroglyphs: Digging into Southwest Archaeology, photographs by Michael J. Doolittle, Atheneum Books for Young Readers (New York, NY), 1998.

Ultimate Field Trip 3: Wading into Marine Biology, photographs by Michael J. Doolittle, Atheneum Books for Young Readers (New York, NY), 1999.

Ultimate Field Trip 4: A Week in the 1800s, photographs by Michael J. Doolittle, Atheneum Books for Young Readers (New York, NY), 2000.

Ultimate Field Trip 5: Blasting off to Space Academy, photographs by Michael J. Doolittle, Millbrook Press (Brookfield, CT), 2001.

"BRAVE KIDS: TRUE STORIES FROM AMERICA'S PAST" SERIES

Cora Frear: A True Story, illustrated by Doris Ettlinger, Aladdin (New York, NY), 2002.

Robert Henry Hendersot, illustrated by Doris Ettlinger, Aladdin (New York, NY), 2003.

Hazelle Boxberg, illustrated by Doris Ettlinger, Aladdin (New York, NY), 2004.

Sidelights

Susan E. Goodman is a journalist as well as a prolific writer of books for children and young adults. Her many contributions to children's fiction and nonfiction include several titles in the "Ultimate Field Trip" series, a wide-ranging group of books that include the titles *Bats, Bugs, and Biodiversity: Adventures in the Amazonian Rain Forest* and *Ultimate Field Trip 5: Blasting off to Space Academy.* Her fact-based stories for the "Brave Kids" series profile young people from various eras of American history, while standalone titles such as *Gee Whiz!: It's All about Pee, Choppers!, On This Spot: An Expedition Back through Time,* and *It's all in One Cookie* showcase Goodman's ability to tantalize even reluctant readers by ferreting out interesting facts about a wide variety of subjects. Many books find the author collaborating with photographer Michael J. Doolittle. Reviewing their basic introduction to Antarctica, published as *Life on the Ice, School Library Journal* reviewer Amelia Jenkins praised the work as an "appealing collaboration" in which the coauthors' "simplifications of a complex subject work."

Cover of Susan E. Goodman's nonfiction picture book Choppers!, *featuring a photograph by Michael J. Doolittle.* (Photograph © 2004 by Michael J. Doolittle. Reproduced by permission of Random House, an imprint of Random House Children's Books, a division of Random House, Inc.)

Ultimate Field Trip 2: Digging into Southwest Archaeology, another of Goodman's contributions to the "Ultimate Field Trip" series, focus on a group of eighth graders participating in an excavation at Mesa Verdi National Park in the Four Corners region of the U.S. southwest. The book recounts the week the students spend digging at the site and discovering new things about the Puebloans, the indigenous people who once lived there. Although *Ultimate Field Trip 2* was described as a "cheerful jumble" by Ilene Cooper in *Booklist, Horn Book* reviewer Margaret A. Bush took issue with the book's "lack of maps and . . . clutter of design elements." Bush went on to note, however, that Goodman takes "a felicitous and ambitious approach" to her subject "that will whet the interest of many readers." *Ultimate Field Trip 5* follows a group of young people undergoing an astronaut training program similar to the regular training program of professional astronauts. *School Library Journal* reviewer Betsy Barnett called the book "an appealing offering for general readers," noting that the artwork as well as the photographs by Doolittle are "artistically appealing as well as informative."

The Great Antler Auction, Chopsticks for My Noodle Soup: Eliza's Life in Malaysia, Claws, Coats, and Camouflage: The Ways Animals Fit into Their Worlds, and *Seeds, Stems, and Stamens: The Ways Plants Fit into Their Worlds* are also the result of Goodman and Doolittle's collaboration. Geared for readers in the upper elementary grades, *The Great Antler Auction* details the annual search by a group of Boy Scouts through the National Elk Refuge, their goal to retrieve discarded antlers that can be auctioned to the public. Money made from their annual auction is used to purchase food for the refuge to help its animals survive the winter. In her book Goodman describes the life of the elk, as well as the history of the auction and the many uses for antlers. *Booklist* critic Susan DeRonne claimed that *The Great Antler Auction* "will spark interest in animal lovers of an even wider age range."

"Creative and inviting" is the way Carolyn Jenks described *Seeds, Stems, and Stamens* in her *School Library Journal* review of the book, which details the ways plants interact within the environment. Questions as well as photographs showing the development of specific plants' progress appear on each page. Jenks wrote that Doolittle and Goodman's "presentation may inspire readers to continue questioning and to go on to other books and resources to satisfy their curiosity."

Also for upper elementary-grade readers, *Claws, Coats, and Camouflage* mirrors the premise of *Seeds, Stems, and Stamens,* applying it this time to animals by describing how various living creatures fit into the environment. *School Library Journal* contributor Sally Bates Goodroe claimed that Doolittle's "bright photographs will draw students to this book," and that Goodman's "sound-bite approach" to her subject-matter may be more appropriate for "browsing than reports."

The titles of *The Truth about Poop* and *Gee Whiz!* are guaranteed to attract readers, and in both works Goodman's text is accented by Elwood H. Smith's "jaunty, sometimes silly cartoon-style illustrations," according to *Booklist* critic Ilene Cooper. In *The Truth about Poop* Goodman discusses how animals process and recycle the many different foods they ingest, and includes the history of human bathroom facilities and sewage systems. The companion volume also begins with the way urine is generated, then reveals the many uses both animals and resourceful humans have found for the substance. In *School Library Journal* Christine Markley praised Goodman's "clever wordplay" and ability to assemble interesting factoids and pee-related stories in *Gee Whiz!,* while a *Kirkus Reviews* writer described the book's text as "redolent with both wisecracks and well-digested research." "Naturally, kids will find all this marvelously gross," wrote Cooper in a review of *The Truth about Poop,* "but along with the yuks, they'll get plenty of information." In *School Library Journal* Rachel G. Payne also praised the book as "chock-full of

intriguing, gross, and bizarre facts about animal and human excrement."

Goodman's first work of historical fiction, *Cora Frear: A True Story,* is also the first installment in the "Brave Kids: True Stories from America's Past" series. Based on an actual diary, the book focuses on a young girl living in the late-nineteenth-century Midwest. One day, as Cora accompanies her father, a doctor, on his house calls, a prairie fire breaks out. Pat Leach, reviewing the book for *School Library Journal,* likened Goodman's "straightforward style" to that of "Little House on the Prairie" author Laura Ingalls Wilder. Leach stated that *Cora Frear* would make "a great stepping stone" for more advanced works of historical fiction.

Other books in the "Brave Kids" chapter-book series include *Robert Henry Hendershot* and *Hazelle Boxberg.* *Robert Henry Hendershot* introduces readers to the twelve-year-old boy who went down in U.S. Civil War history as the "Drummer boy of the Rappahannock," After running away from home to join the Union Army, Hendershot was on the field during the Battle of Fredericksburg in the winter of 1862. Capturing a Confederate soldier, he eventually met President Abraham Lincoln. Noting that in her fictionalization of actual events, Goodman remains "true to the essence of Robert's actual story," a *Kirkus Reviews* writer added that *Robert Henry Hendershot* is "a solid offering for young readers." Moving foreword in time to 1918, *Hazelle Boxberg* introduces an eleven-year-old New York City orphan who joins many other children on an orphan train headed for Texas. In this story, Goodman brings to life the orphan-train system, whereby urban children were sent to rural homes where they sometimes became family members but often were treated like servants or, as in Hazelle's case, trained to care for childless couples in their old age.

From the history of people, Goodman moves to the history of a building in *Skyscraper: From the Ground Up.* In this work, her text follows Doolittle's photo essay about the building of New York City's Random House building. Facts about the building process, as well as a description of the many duties performed by members of the building's construction crew, both figure in her simple text, which "conveys both respect for the builders and awe at the precision and effort" needed to undertake the project, in the opinion of *Horn Book* contributor Betty Carter. In *School Library Journal* Delia Fritz noted in particular the book's appeal to reluctant readers, and added that Goodman and Doolittle's "visual time line" incorporates comments from everyone involved, from the architect and building engineers to masons, signalmen, and others whose labor helped a skyscraper rise from a city lot. Also citing Goodman's inclusion of "moving quotes" from those involved in highrise construction, *Booklist* contributor Gillian Engberg concluded that *Skyscraper* melds a "graceful, clear

Goodman tackles a much-talked-about but little-understood subject in **The Truth about Poop,** *featuring humorous cartoon drawings by Elwood H. Smith.* (Illustration © by Elwood H. Smith, 2004. All rights reserved. Reproduced by permission of Viking, a division of Penguin Putnam Books for Young Readers.)

text and exciting color photos" into a "thoughtful, well-composed offering."

Biographical and Critical Sources

PERIODICALS

Booklist, May 1, 2001, Carolyn Phelan, review of *Ultimate Field Trip 5: Blasting off to Space Academy,* p. 1676; September 1, 1996, Susan DeRonne, review of *The Great Antler Auction,* p. 121; June 1, 1998, Ilene

Cooper, review of *Stones, Bones, and Petroglyphs: Digging into Southwest Archaeology,* p. 1754; May 1, 2003, Carolyn Phelan, review of *Nature Did It First!,* p. 1620; May 15, 2003, Hazel Rochman, review of *Robert Henry Hendershot,* p. 1665; May 15, 2004, Ilene Cooper, review of *The Truth about Poop,* p. 1616; June 1, 2004, Hazel Rochman, review of *On This Spot: An Expedition Back through Time,* p. 1735; December 1, 2004, Gillian Engberg, review of *Skyscraper: From the Ground Up,* p. 668; March 15, 2006, Carolyn Phelan, review of *Life on the Ice,* p. 45; November 1, 2006, Ilene Cooper, review of *Gee Whiz!: It's all about Pee,* p. 47.

Bulletin of the Center for Children's Books, June, 2004, Deborah Stevenson, review of *The Truth about Poop,* p. 418; October, 2006, Deborah Stevenson, review of *Gee Whiz!,* p. 69.

Horn Book, March-April, 1998, Margaret A. Bush, review of *Stones, Bones, and Petroglyphs,* p. 234; January-February, 2005, Betty Carter, review of *Skyscraper,* p. 110.

Kirkus Reviews, February 1, 2003, review of *Robert Henry Hendershot,* p. 229; February 15, 2004, review of *On This Spot,* p. 178; April 15, 2004, review of *The Truth about Poop,* p. 393; May 1, 2006, review of *All in Just One Cookie,* p. 458; August 1, 2006, review of *Gee Whiz!,* p. 786.

Publishers Weekly, April 8, 2002, review of *Cora Frear: A True Story,* p. 228; June 7, 2004, review of *The Truth about Poop,* p. 50.

School Library Journal, June, 2001, Betsy Barnett, review of *Ultimate Field Trip 5,* pp. 171-172; November, 2001, Carolyn Jenks, review of *Seeds, Stems, and Stamens: The Ways Plants Fit into Their World,* p. 146; November, 2001, Sally Bates Goodroe, review of *Claws, Coats, and Camouflage: The Ways Animals Fit into Their World,* p. 156; August, 2002, Pat Leach, review of *Cora Frear,* p. 156; February, 2003, Melinda Piehler, review of *What Do You Do at the Zoo?,* p. 111; October, 2003, Pat Leach, review of *Robert Henry Hendershot,* p. 125; July, 2004, Rachel G. Payne, review of *The Truth about Poop,* p. 93; December, 2004, Jane Barrer, review of *On This Spot,* p. 130; February, 2004, Delia Fritz, review of *Skyscraper,* p. 147; August, 2006, Linda L. Walkins, review of *All in Just One Cookie,* p. 87, and Amelia Jenkins, review of *Life on the Ice,* p. 104; November, 2006, Christine Markley, review of *Gee Whiz!,* p. 120.

ONLINE

Susan E. Goodman Home Page, http://www.susangood-manbooks.com (July 30, 2007).*

*   *   *

GRAY, Serena
See SHELDON, Dyan

*   *   *

GUIBERT, Emmanuel 1964-

Personal

Born 1964, in Paris, France. *Education:* Attended École Hourdé. *Hobbies and other interests:* Prix René Goscinny, and Alph'Art Coup de Coeur, both 1998, both for *La fille du professeur.*

Addresses

Home and office—Paris, France.

Career

Comics artist.

Writings

SELF-ILLUSTRATED COMICS

Brune, Relié (Gordes, France), 1992.
La campagne à la mer: Guibert en Normandie (sketchbook), Ouest-France (Rennes, France), 2002.
Les poixons, Cartonnée (Paris, France), 2003.
Le pavè de Paris, Relié (Gordes, France), 2004.

ILLUSTRATOR; COMICS

(With Joann Sfar) *La fille du professeur* (graphic novel), Dupuis (Marcinelle, Belgium), 1997, translated by Alexis Siegel as *The Professor's Daughter,* First Second (New York, NY), 2007.
(With Guy Deliste) *La guerre d'Alan,* Broché (Paris, France), 2000.
(With B. David) *Le capitaine Écarlate,* Cartonné (Paris, France), 2000.
(With Didier Lefèvre) *Le photographe: Tome 1,* Dupuis (Marcinelle, Belgium), 2003.
(With Didier Lefèvre) *Voyages en Afghanistan: le pays des critons doux et des oranges amères,* Relié (Gordes, France), 2003.
(With Didier Lefèvre) *Le photographe: Tome 2,* Dupuis (Marcinelle, Belgium), 2004.
Va et Vient, Broché (Paris, France), 2005.
(With Bernadette Després, Jacqueline Cohen, and Evelyne Rebert) *Tom-Tom et Nana, Tome 33: Ben ça, Alors!,* Broché (Paris, France), 2005.
(With Christian Rosset, Gilles Clement, and Marie Lallouet) *Monographie prématurée,* Broché (Paris, France), 2006.
(With Gilles Tevessin and Romain Multier) *Un taxi nommé Nadir,* Broché (Paris, France), 2006.
(With Didier Lefèvre) *Le photographe: Tome 3,* Dupuis (Marcinelle, Belgium), 2006.

"LES OLIVES NOIRES" SERIES; COMICS

(With Joann Sfar) *Pourquoi cette nuit est-elle différente des autres nuits?,* Dupuis (Marcinelle, Belgium), 2001.
(With Joann Sfar) *Adam Harishon,* Dupuis (Marcinelle, Belgium), 2002.
(With Joann Sfar) *Tu ne mangeras pas le chevreau dans le lait de sa mère,* Dupuis (Marcinelle, Belgium), 2003.

"SARDINE IN SPACE" GRAPHIC NOVEL SERIES; FOR YOUNG READERS

(With Joann Sfar) *Sardine de l'espace: le doigt dans l'oeil,* Broché (Paris, France), 2000, translated by Sasha Watson as *Sardine in Outer Space: Volume One,* First Second (New York, NY), 2006.
(With Joann Sfar) *Sardine de l'espace 2: le bar des ennemis,* Broché (Paris, France), 2000, translated by Sasha Watson as *Sardine in Outer Space: Volume Two,* First Second (New York, NY), 2006.

(With Joann Sfar) *Sardine de l'espace 3: la machine à laver la cervelle,* Broché (Paris, France), 2001, translated by Sasha Watson as *Sardine in Outer Space: Volume Three,* First Second (New York, NY), 2007.

(With Joann Sfar) *Sardine de l'espace 4: Les voleurs de Yaourt,* Broché (Paris, France), 2001, translated by Sasha Watson as *Sardine in Outer Space: Volume Four,* First Second (New York, NY), 2007.

(With Joann Sfar) *Sardine de l'espace 5: le championnat de Boxe,* Broché (Paris, France), 2002.

(With Joann Sfar) *Sardine de l'espace 6: le capitaine tout rouge,* Broché (Paris, France), 2002.

(With Joann Sfar) *Sardine de l'espace 7: le grande sardine,* Broché (Paris, France), 2003.

(With Joann Sfar) *Sardine de l'espace 8: les tatouages carnivores,* Broché (Paris, France), 2003.

(With Joann Sfar) *Sardine de l'espace 9: les montagne électorale,* Cartonné (Paris, France), 2004.

(With Joann Sfar) *Sardine de l'espace 10: le cyber disc-jockey,* Album, 2005.

"ARIOL" SERIES; COMICS COLLECTIONS; FOR YOUNG READERS

(With Marc Boutavant) *Ariol: Debout!,* Broché (Paris, France), 2002.

(With Marc Boutavant) *Ariol: jeux idiots,* Broché (Paris, France), 2002.

(With Marc Boutavant) *Ariol: Bête comme âne, sale commen un cochon . . . ,* Broché (Paris, France), 2003.

(With Marc Boutavant) *Ariol: le vaccin à réaction,* Broché (Paris, France), 2003.

(With Marc Boutavant) *Ariol: karaté!* Album, 2004.

(With Marc Boutavant) *Ariol: Oh! la mer!* Album, 2005.

(With Marc Boutavant) *Ariol: copain comme cochon,* Broché (Paris, France), 2007.

Sidelights

French comics artist Emmanuel Guibert began drawing as a child, and has admitted that "pencil" was one of the first words in his vocabulary. Now best known for his contributions to comics series such as Joann Sfar's "Sardine de l'espace" ("Sardine in Outer Space") and Marc Boutavant's "Ariol," Guibert started his creative career as a story-board artist for videos and films. In 1992, he published his first original comic, *Brune,* which weaves a tale around the rise of facism in pre-World War II Germany. From 1995 through 1999, Guibert shared a studio in Paris with noted comics artist and writer Joann Sfar. According to the First Second Books Web site, at their studio "stories grew . . . like ragweed," and the resulting works included the 'Sardine in Outer Space" comic series as well as the stand-alone graphic novel *The Professor's Daughter.* A *Publishers Weekly* critic, in a review of the latter title, called Sfar and Guibert "two of France's best graphic novel talents."

Sardine, the titular heroine of "Sardine in Outer Space," is a rebellious space pirate fighting against the evil Chief Executive Dictator of the Universe, Supermus-

cleman, and his henchmen. Sardine's companions include Little Louie, her trusty sidekick, and Uncle Yellow Shoulder, who looks after the crew and the ship, *Huckleberry.* Supermuscleman runs a space orphanage, wherein he requires all the young residents to conform to what he views as appropriate manners. The series plays out over ten volumes, the first of which contains Sardine's first twelve adventures. *Sardine in Outer Space: Volume One* was described by *Booklist* contributor Jesse Karp as "a free-wheeling ride peppered with as much grisly monster-filleting action and bodily fluid humor as a young reader could want." A *Kirkus Reviews* contributor also cited the volume's "nonstop action, humor geared to multiple levels of cultural awareness and the promise of more episodes to come." A *Publishers Weekly* contributor felt that, although the "plots are wispy, . . . the pirate humor and gothic panels . . . provide surprises in every space vignette."

Sardine and company continue to encounter adventures in a similar fashion in further series volumes. In *Sardine in Outer Space: Volume Two,* for example, she joins Louie in sabotaging the machine Supermuscleman uses to brainwash orphans into proper behavior. The volume also includes a rescue of Captain Yellow Shoulder and a high-speed chase along the Milky Way. Though noting that adults might find the tales repetitious, a *Kirkus Reviews* contributor felt that Sfar and Guibert's stories "will keep the younger audiences to whom they're actually addressed chortling." Karp wrote that the low-brow, bathroom jokes "give the book an illicit, forbidden-fruit appeal," while *School Library Journal* critic Dawn Rutherford dubbed the second series installment "delightful and entertaining."

Guibert and Sfar's other notable collaboration, *The Professor's Daughter,* presents a gothic tale of love between the teenaged daughter of a professor and a mummy. Although a *Publishers Weekly* critic found much to enjoy in the graphic novel, "Guibert's work is the real treat," according to the critic.

Biographical and Critical Sources

PERIODICALS

Booklist, March 15, 2006, Jesse Karp, review of *Sardine in Outer Space: Volume One,* p. 56; September 1, 2006, Jesse Karp, review of *Sardine in Outer Space: Volume Two,* p. 128.

Kirkus Reviews, April 15, 2006, review of *Sardine in Outer Space: Volume One,* p. 407; August 15, 2006, review of *Sardine in Outer Space: Volume Two,* p. 841.

Kliatt, January, 2007, George Galuschak, review of *Sardine in Outer Space: Volume One,* p. 31.

Publishers Weekly, June 12, 2006, review of *Sardine in Outer Space: Volume One,* p. 52; November 27, 2006, "And Then What Happened?," p. 53; February 5, 2007, review of *The Professor's Daughter,* p. 46.

School Library Journal, July, 2006, Benjamin Russell, review of *Sardine in Outer Space: Volume One,* p. 125; November, 2006, Dawn Rutherford, review of *Sardine in Outer Space: Volume Two,* p. 166.

ONLINE

First Second Books Web site, http://www.firstsecondbooks. net/ (July 2, 2007), "Emmanuel Guibert."

Lambiek Web site, http://lambiek.net/ (July 2, 2007), "Emmanuel Guibert."

Powells Web site, http://www.powells.com/ (July 2, 2007), interview with Guibert.*

*   *   *

GWALTNEY, Doris 1932-

Personal

Born 1932, in Isle of Wight, VA; married Atwill Gwaltney, 1959; children: three.

Addresses

Home and office—1500 Magruder Rd., Smithfield, VA 23430. *E-mail*—dorisgwaltney@verizon.net.

Career

Writer. Cypress Creek Press, Charlottesville, VA, founder, c. 1995. Christopher Newport University, Newport News, VA, coordinator of writers' conference, until 1995, and teacher in Lifelong Learning Society. Lecturer and instructor at creative writing workshops.

Member

Society of Children's Book Writers and Illustrators (Mid-Atlantic chapter), Authors Guild, Virginia Writers Club, Poetry Society of Virginia.

Writings

Shakespeare's Sister (adult novel), Cypress Creek Press (Charlottesville, VA), 1996.
George Purdie, Merchant of Smithfield (nonfiction), 1996.
Duncan Browdie, Gent (adult novel), Pearl Line Press, 2002.
Homefront, Simon & Schuster (New York, NY), 2006.
A Mirror in Time: History in First Person, Script Works Press, 2007.

Contributor of short fiction to periodicals, including *Greensboro Review* and *Poet's Domain.*

Sidelights

Author and educator Doris Gwaltney first gained critical attention with her adult novel *Shakespeare's Sister,* a work of historical fiction that imagines what life might have been like for a talented sister of noted Elizabethan playwright William Shakespeare. Inspired by a quote from Virginia Woolf's novel *A Room of One's Own* as well as by her own in-depth study of Shakespeare's works, Gwaltney worked on the manuscript for her first novel for two years. Unable to place the book with a publisher, she then decided to establish a small press, Cypress Creek, and publish *Shakespeare's Sister* herself. With the success of her first book, Gwaltney has gone on to write several other books, including the young-adult novel *Homefront.*

Homefront is set during World War II and describes the rivalry between two cousins. Margaret Ann is an American girl who assumed she would finally have her own bedroom once older sister Elizabeth left home for college. However, the room is now given to Courtney, Margaret Ann's cousin and a refugee of the London blitz. Hiding her fear and loneliness by being obnoxious and antagonistic toward her cousin, the newcomer worms her way into the hearts of the people Margaret Ann loves, and it takes both cleverness and a little growing up for Margaret Ann to get herself back in everyone's good graces.

"Gwaltney provides vivid character portrayals," wrote Carolyn Phelan in her *Booklist* review of *Homefront.* Nancy P. Reeder, writing in *School Library Journal,* praised the novelist's "careful characterization," and concluded that her "perceptive novel focuses on how war affects the people who are left at home—their fears, dreams, hardships, and, above all, hopes." Although a *Kirkus Reviews* contributor maintained that the novel's narrative is broken by descriptions of how the war changed life in the United States, the critic nonetheless concluded that Gwaltney's use of "language and dialogue evoke the setting beautifully."

In an interview with Bill Glose for *Grit,* Gwaltney provided her advice for aspiring writers. "If there's any way you can get your life structured so that you write every day then I think that's when success comes to you. Inspiration is real, but it doesn't come to people who haven't worked for it."

Biographical and Critical Sources

PERIODICALS

Booklist, July 1, 2006, Carolyn Phelan, review of *Homefront,* p. 56.
Bulletin of the Center for Children's Books, October, 2006, Elizabeth Bush, review of *Homefront,* p. 71.
Grit, March 16, 2003, Bill Glose, "Woman Published after 27 Years," p. 8.
Kirkus Reviews, June 15, 2006, review of *Homefront,* p. 633.

School Library Journal, July, 2006, Nancy P. Reeder, review of *Homefront,* p. 103.

Virginian-Pilot, January 7, 1996, Bill Ruehlmann, "Knowing the Bard Helps in Creating His Sister," p. J3; February 21, 1996, Allison T. Williams, "Smithfield Writer Creates a Sister for Shakespeare," p. 12; June 18, 2006, Phyllis Speidell, "Did You Know That Local Author Is behind *Homefront*?," p. SU2.

ONLINE

Doris Gwaltney Home Page, http://www.dorisg.com (July 3, 2007).

Society of Children's Book Writers and Illustrators Mid-Atlantic Web site, http://www.scbwi-midatlantic.org/ (July 3, 2007), "Doris Gwaltney."

H

HAMMOND, Andrew 1970-

Personal

Born March 13, 1970, in Dundee, Scotland; son of Leonard (a shop owner and manager) and Isabel Anne (a secretary) Hammond; married Rola Mahmoud Abou-Hashish (an actress and singer), 1980. *Education:* London University, B.A. (history and Arabic).

Addresses

Home—Cairo, Egypt. *Office*—Reuters Saudia Ltd., Box 62422, Riyadh 11585, Saudi Arabia. *E-mail*—andrew-hammond@reuters.com.

Career

Journalist. *Middle East Times,* Egypt, former editor; Reuters (multimedia news agency), senior correspondent in Saudi Arabian bureau. *Cairo Times* (weekly magazine), Cairo, Egypt, cofounder with Hesham Qasem.

Writings

Pop Culture Arab World!: Media, Arts, and Lifestyle, ABC-Clio (Santa Barbara, CA), 2005.
What the Arabs Think of America, Greenwood Press (Westport, CT), 2007.

Sidelights

As senior editor of the Saudi Arabian bureau of Reuters news agency and a resident of the Middle East since his graduation from London University in the mid-1990s, journalist Andrew Hammond is an expert on Middle-Eastern culture. In his book *Pop Culture Arab World!: Media, Arts, and Lifestyle* Hammond shares his wide-ranging insights with American readers. In addition to media, theatre, sports, language, religion, and film,

Hammond also discusses such uniquely Arabian things as belly dancing and the musical genre known as Arab-pop. According to *Library Journal* contributor Stanley P. Hodge, Hammond "blends a serious journalistic style with an academician's affinity for documenting sources in this timely work," which is part of ABC-Clio's "Popular Culture in the Contemporary World" nonfiction series. Valuable because of Hammond's inclusion of an index of Arabic terms and names as well as a list of useful print and Web resources, the work also discusses the cultural shifts underlying the region's pop culture, such as the role of women, the rise of radical Islam, and the influence of Western consumer culture. Hodge went on to cite the work as "a much-needed and timely statement" on the current state of the region, and *School Library Journal* reviewer Diane S. Marton dubbed *Pop Culture Arab World!* an "authoritative" book that is both "fascinating and unbiased" in its approach.

Discussing his motive for writing *Pop Culture Arab World!* with *Asharq Alawsat* online interviewer Najah al Osaymi, Hammond noted: "I wanted to emphasize the bright and distinguished elements in Arab culture, based on my experience, readings, and my journalistic work in Sudan, Iraq, Egypt, Al Sham and the Gulf region." Hammond explained that, in the book, he concentrates his focus on "similarities in the Arab identity" as they exist in the region's music and visual arts because, as he told al Osaymi, "the Arab world is full of charms that many in the western world do not comprehend."

Biographical and Critical Sources

PERIODICALS

Choice, June, 2005, A. Rassam, review of *Pop Culture Arab World!: Media, Arts, and Lifestyle,* p. 1880.
Journal of Popular Culture, April, 2006, Rami Khalaf, review of *Pop Culture Arab World!,* p. 330.

Library Journal, March 15, 2005, Stanley P. Hodge, review of *Pop Culture Arab World!,* p. 102.

School Library Journal, October, 2005, Diane S. Marton, review of *Pop Culture Arab World!,* p. 88.

ONLINE

Asharqu Alawsat Web site, http://www.asharq-e.com/ (September 19, 2006), Najah al Osaymi, interview with Hammond.

* * *

HASLER, Eveline 1933-

Personal

Born March 22, 1933, in Glarus, Switzerland; daughter of Walter (in business) and Lili Schubiger; married Paul Hasler (a professor), October 5, 1962; children: Regula, Paul, Isable. *Education:* Attended University of Paris and University of Fribourg.

Addresses

Home—Lehnhaldenstrasse 46, 9014 St. Gallen, Switzerland.

Career

College instructor in French.

Member

Schweizer Schriftstellerverein.

Awards, Honors

Diploma of Merit, 1968; Hans Christian Andersen Award, International Board on Books for Young People, 1976; Schweizerischer Jugendbuchpreis, 1978; Preis der Schillerstiftung, 1980, for *Novemberinsel;* Ehrengabe (Zurich, Switzerland), 1988; Schubart-Literatpreis, 1989; Zurich book prize, 1991; Droste-Preis (Meersburg), 1994; Kulturpreise (St. Gallen, Switzerland), 1994; Justinus-Kerner-Preis (Weinsberg, Germany), 1999.

Writings

FOR CHILDREN

Stop, Daniela! Sowie, die Eidechse mit den Similisteinen, und andere Erzaehlungen, Rex-Verlag (Lucerne, Switzerland), 1962.

Ferdi und die Angelrute, illustrated by Robert Wyss, Rex-Verlag (Lucerne, Switzerland), 1963.

Komm wieder, Pepino!, illustrated by Esther Emmel, Benziger (Zurich, Switzerland), 1967.

Adieu Paris, Adieu Catherine, Benziger (Zurich, Switzerland), 1969.

Die seltsamen Freunde, Benziger (Zurich, Switzerland), 1970.

Ein Baum für Filippo, Atlantis, 1973.

Der Sonntagsvater, Otto Maier, 1973.

Unterm Neonmond, George Bitter, 1974.

Der Zauberelefant: ein Bilderbuch, illustrated by Antonella Bollinger-Savelli, Benzinger (Zurich, Switzerland), 1974, translated by Elizabeth Shub as *Miranda's Magic,* Macmillan (New York, NY), 1975.

Denk an mich Mauro, Benziger (Zurich, Switzerland), 1976.

Dann kroch Martin durch den Zaun, illustrated by Dorothea Desmarowitz, Maier (Ravensburg, Germany), 1977, translated as *Martin Is Our Friend,* Abingdon (Nashville, TN), 1981.

Der Buchstabenkoenig und die Hexe Lakritze, Benziger (Zurich, Switzerland), 1977.

Novemberinsel, Arche (Zurich, Switzerland), 1979.

Anna Göldin, letzte Hexe (novel), Benziger (Zurich, Switzerland), 1982.

Winter Magic (translation of *Im Winterland*), William Morrow (New York, NY), 1984.

Ibicaba, das Paradies in den Köpfen (novel), Nagel & Kimche (Zurich, Switzerland), 1985.

Das Schweinchen Bobo, illustrated by Maren Briswalter, Nagel & Kimche (Zurich, Switzerland), 1986.

Due Blumenstadt: eine Geschichte, illustrated by Stepán Zavrel, Bohem (Zurich, Switzerland), 1987.

Der Riese im Baum, Nagel & Kimche (Zurich, Switzerland), 1988.

Babas Große Reise, illustrated by Maren Briswalter, Nagel & Kimche (Zurich, Switzerland), 1989.

So ein sausen ist in der Luft: nach einer Sage aus der Südschweiz, illustrated by Käthi Bhend, Ravensburger (Ravensburg, Germany), 1992, translated by Marianne Martens as *A Tale of Two Brothers,* North-South Books (New York, NY), 2006.

Die Wachsflügelfrau: Geschichte der Emily Kempin-Spyri, Nagel & Kimche (Zurich, Switzerland), 1992, translated by Edna McCown as *Flying with Wings of Wax: The Story of Emily Kempin-Spyri,* Fromm, 1993.

Die Schule Fliegt ins Pfefferland, illustrated by Maren Briswalter, Benziger (Zurich, Switzerland), 1993.

Der Zeitreisende: Die Visionen des Henry Dunant, Nagel & Kimche (Zurich, Switzerland), 1994.

Der Buchstabenvogel: eine Geschichte, illustrated by Lio Fromm, Deutscher Taschenbuch (Munich, Germany), 1995, illustrated by Elso Schiavo, Lehrmittelverlag (Zurich, Switzerland), 2005.

Die Riesin, illustrated by Renate Seelig, Ellermann (Munich, Germany), 1996, translated by Laura McKenna as *The Giantess,* Kane/Miller (Brooklyn, NY), 1997.

Die Vogelmacherin: die Geschichte von Hexenkindern (novel), Nagel & Kimche (Zurich, Switzerland), 1997.

Der Jubiläums-Apfel und andere Notizen vom Tage, Deutscher Taschenbuch (Munich, Germany), 1998.

Die namenlose Geliebte: Geshichten und Gedichte, Nagel & Kimche (Zurich, Switzerland), 1999.

Der Buchstabenräber, illustrated by Rolf Rettich, Deutscher Taschenbuch (Munich, Germany), 1999.

Der Buchstabenclown, illustrated by Rolf Rettich, Deutscher Taschenbuch (Munich, Germany), 1999.

Sätzlinge: Gedichte, Nagel & Kimche (Zurich, Switzerland), 2000.

Aline und die Erfindung der Liebe (novel), Nagel & Kimche (Zurich, Switzerland), 2000.

Spaziergänge durch mein Tessin: Landschaft, Kulture und Küche, illustrated by Hannes Binder, Sanssouci (Zurich, Switzerland), 2002.

Die Nacht im Zauberwald: nach einer Sage aus der Südschweiz, illustrated by Käthi Bhend, NordSud (Zurich, Switzerland), 2006.

Stein bedeuten Liebe: Tregina Ullmann und Otto Gross (novel), Nagel & Kimche (Zurich, Switzerland), 2007.

Translator of stories from the French. Author of other works published in Switzerland.

Hasler's books have been translated into numerous languages, including Korean, French, Turkish, and Spanish.

Biographical and Critical Sources

BOOKS

Eveline Hasler, Pendo-Verlag, 1986.

PERIODICALS

Booklist, February 15, 1994, Denise Perry Donavin, review of *Flying with Wings of Wax: The Story of Emily Kempin-Spyri,* p. 1060; December 1, 1997, Ilene Cooper, review of *The Giantess,* p. 640; September 1, 2006, Hazel Rochman, review of *A Tale of Two Brothers,* p. 136.

Bulletin of the Center for Children's Books, December, 1981, review of *Martin Is Our Friend,* p. 68.

Canadian Review of Materials, March, 1990, review of *Winter Magic,* p. 64.

Horn Book, November-December, Hanna B. Zeiger, review of *Winter Magic,* p. 728.

Kirkus Reviews, August 15, 2006, review of *A Tale of Two Brothers,* p. 842.

Library Journal, January, 1994, Dorothy Golden, review of *Flying with Wings of Wax,* p. 160.

Publishers Weekly, December 6, 1993, review of *Flying with Wings of Wax,* p. 63; October 13, 1997, review of *The Giantess,* p. 73.

School Library Journal, November, 1981, Karen Harris, review of *Martin Is Our Friend,* p. 76; November, 1985, Anne E. Mulherkar, review of *Winter Magic,* p. 71; December, 1997, Barbara Chatton, review of *The Giantess,* p. 92.

Vaterland, December 15, 1979.

*   *   *

HEINZ, Brian J. 1946-
(Brian James Heinz)

Personal

Born November 1, 1946, in Brooklyn, NY; son of Howard (a truck driver and dispatcher) and Kathleen (a homemaker) Heinz; married Judy Louise Candelora (a

Brian J. Heinz (Photograph by Judy L. Heinz. Reproduced by permission.)

kindergarten teacher), June 27, 1987. *Education:* Suffolk County Community College, A.A., 1966; State University of New York at Stony Brook, B.A., 1974, M.L.S., 1976. *Hobbies and other interests:* Travel, photography, softball, plank-on-frame ship modeling, cross-country skiing, reading, Native American art, restoring antique furniture, fishing.

Addresses

Home—1 Sylvan Dr., Wading River, NY 11792. *E-mail*—Brian@brianheinz.com.

Career

Author and educator. Middle Country School District, elementary-grade teacher, 1974-78; William Floyd School District, elementary-grade science teacher, beginning 1978. State University of New York at Stony Brook, adjunct instructor at Center for Science, Math, and Technology Education, 1987-92; Hofstra University, adjunct instructor in English. New York State Department of Education, regional elementary science mentor for eastern Long Island, 1985-95. Presenter at professional conferences.

Member

Society of Children's Book Writers and Illustrators, World Wildlife Fund, Natural Resources Defense Council, Defenders of Wildlife, Science Teachers Association

of New York State, New York State Marine Education Association, New York State Outdoor Education Association, Suffolk County Science Teachers Association, East End Children's Book Writers and Illustrators (chairperson; past president).

Awards, Honors

Named Elementary Science Teacher of the Year, Suffolk County Science Teachers Association, 1990; Excellence in Science Teaching Award, Science Teachers Association of New York State, 1991; *Booklist* Editor's Choice designation, for *The Wolves;* Outstanding Children's Science Trade Book designation, National Science Teachers Association/Children's Book Council, for *Butternut Hollow Pond;* International Board on Books for Young People Silver Medal, 2007, for *Cheyenne Medicine Hat; ForeWord* Book of the Year honorable mention, 2007, for *Red Fox at McCloskey's Farm.*

Writings

(And illustrator) *Beachcraft Bonanza,* foreword by Lester J. Paldy, Ballyhoo Books (Shoreham, NY), 1986.

Beachcrafts, Too!, Ballyhoo Books (Shoreham, NY), 1988.

The Alley Cat, illustrated by David Christiana, Doubleday (New York, NY), 1993.

Introduction to Space, Cobblestone (Peterborough, NH), 1994.

The Wolves, illustrated by Bernie Fuchs, Dial Books for Young Readers (New York, NY), 1996.

Kayuktuk: An Arctic Quest, illustrated by Jon van Zyle, Chronicle Books (New York, NY), 1996.

The Monsters' Test, illustrated by Sal Murdocca, Millbrook Press (Brookfield, CT), 1996.

Nanuk, Lord of the Ice, illustrated by Gregory Manchess, Dial (New York, NY), 1998.

Butternut Hollow Pond, illustrated by Bob Marstall, Millbrook Press (Brookfield, CT), 2000.

The Barnyard Cat, illustrated by June H. Blair, Ballyhoo BookWorks (Shoreham, NY), 2000.

The Alley Cat, illustrated by June H. Blair, Ballyhoo BookWorks (Shoreham, NY), 2002.

Cheyenne Medicine Hat, illustrated by Greg Manchess, Creative Editions (Mankato, MN), 2006.

Red Fox at McCloskey's Farm, illustrated by Chris Sheban, Creative Editions (Mankato, MN), 2006.

Nathan of Yesteryear and Michael of Today, illustrated by Joanne Frian, Millbrook Press (Minneapolis, MN), 2007.

Contributor to magazines, including *Instructor, Science and Children,* and *Children's Writer.*

Sidelights

A former science teacher, Brian J. Heinz focuses on the natural world in his many books for young readers. His picture books, which include *The Wolves, Butternut Squash Farm, The Barnyard Cat,* and *Kayuktuk: An*

Arctic Quest, reflect the author's travels to unique habitats and his interest in the interactions and ecological roles played by the magnificent creatures, both large and small, that live there. In his writing, Heinz attempts to capture the essence of animals and their environment, hoping to inspire young readers with a growing appreciation for the natural world and their unique responsibility as human caretakers. Praising *Butternut Hollow Pond* in *Booklist,* Lauren Peterson wrote that Heinz's picture-book study of a pond ecosystem features "action and sensory-loaded language that pulls children in as no science textbook can."

Heinz is perhaps best known for his highly acclaimed book *The Wolves.* Illustrated in evocative paintings by Bernie Fuchs, the work provides historical information about wolves and follows a wolf pack as it hunts an elk herd. A *Kirkus Reviews* contributor called *The Wolves* "an exquisite story of the wild" and described Heinz's language as "poetic without being heavy-handed." Stephanie Zvirin, writing in *Booklist,* noted that the wolf "is powerfully and realistically presented in a picture book that rings with deep understanding and reverence for the natural world," and a *Publishers Weekly* critic cited Heinz's "action-filled, present-tense account and expressive language" for "quicken[ing] the pulse" in his "spellbinding" tale.

The natural world is again the focus of *Nanuk, Lord of the Ice,* which takes readers to the high Arctic, and *Kayuktuk,* which is set in Alaska. Brought to life in oil paintings by Gregory Manchess that a *Publishers Weekly* contributor described as "sculpted as if from ice and light," *Nanuk, Lord of the Ice* finds a giant polar bear hunting for seals and walrus in the frozen north. As Nanuk the bear pursues his quarry in order to stay alive, an Inuit boy and his sled dogs are on the track of the giant creature, moving the story toward a battle between man and nature. *Kayuktuk* is a coming-of-age story about an Inuit boy named Aknik who must discover what or who is robbing his traps in order to prove his worthiness to the older hunters in his village. Calling *Nanuk, Lord of the Ice* "a gripping, edge-of-the-seat" tale, the *Publishers Weekly* critic added that the author's "keen appreciation for the wild lights up his highly descriptive prose," and *Booklist* critic Carolyn Phelan dubbed Heinz's text "vivid and dignified."

Moving to the prairies of the American west, *Cheyenne Medicine Hat* finds a wild mare working to protect her band of wild Medicine Hat mustangs from a predatory cougar and the efforts of Wyoming cowboys to capture and restrain them. In *The Barnyard Cat* and *The Alley Cat* Heinz collaborates with illustrator June H. Blair to introduce more familiar creatures which encounter challenges while living on the fringes of human habitation. In her *School Library Journal* review, Susan E. Murray noted that Heinz's text "enriche[s] . . . the narrative [of *Cheyenne Medicine Hat*] with the vocabulary of the prairie, making readers truly a part of the animal's survival."

Heinz once told *SATA:* "A love of language was fostered in me at an early age by my parents. When I was a child, my mom, who was born in Ireland, would sing to me or recite prayers in Gaelic before I went to bed. Although I didn't understand a word, the music of this ancient language tickled my ear. Other times, she might read to me or tell me stories. On long car trips, my dad would point to signs and ask me, 'What does that say?' or 'Can you read those words?' As a result, I was reading before I started school.

"I was a voracious reader as a child, reading every dog and horse novel written, and devouring biographies of historical figures like Davy Crockett and Crazy Horse. Sometimes my appetite for the printed word caused me trouble. On school nights, after being sent to bed, I'd get under the covers with a flashlight to read. Mom always came to check on me and would see the glow under the blanket. Then she'd yell at me, but I'm sure she was secretly pleased by such a positive late-night activity.

"Through high school and into college, I continued to read and expose myself to new ideas. I loved learning in general, and I loved new experiences. I worked at many jobs before going into the education field as an elementary school teacher. I worked in a supermarket dairy department and in construction; I worked as a truck driver and a road laborer; I worked as a surveyor, shipping clerk, and a guitarist in a rock band. I was always learning something new.

"My travels have taken me camping across Canada and the northern United States. I've been to the Deep South, the California coast, the deserts of the southwest, and the Rockies. I've been to Ireland. I am fascinated by the cultural differences, the wildlife, and the environments.

"As a science teacher, these experiences enrich me and, I hope, motivate my students. I've always loved wild things and wild places. Each year I take my sixth-grade classes on a six-hour canoe trip down the Peconic River on eastern Long Island."

"I am not one of those writers who writes every day, but I *think* about writing every day," Heinz more recently explained to *SATA.* "I'm forever churning up characters (usually animals), events, and settings in my mind's eye, and letting them play out life on my mental stage. When the idea can no longer be carried in my head, it pours out onto paper. I often use poetic devices in my prose and select sensory details that will allow my readers to connect with, and experience, the story first-hand in a sort of 'you are there' way." "I work for carefully selected words, rich use of language, and passion in my writing," he added on his home page. "The revision process is sometimes painstakingly slow, but vital to a final piece that sparkles on the page and echoes in the mind's ear long after it has been read."

Describing his surroundings, Heinz explained that his family's home "is secluded, a sanctuary where we enjoy gardening, watching and feeding our many different wild birds, and sharing companionship with our dogs. I am a native Long Islander and a builder of museum-quality, wooden ship models. I also studied Scottish highland dancing for several years during the 1980s and became a competitive dancer at regional games from Canada to Virginia, winning more than sixty medals and trophies."

Biographical and Critical Sources

PERIODICALS

Booklist, September 15, 1996, Stephanie Zvirin, review of *The Wolves;* January 1, 1999, Carolyn Phelan, review of *Nanuk, Lord of the Ice,* p. 86; January 1, 2001, Lauren Peterson, review of *Butternut Hollow Pond,* p. 951; October 15, 2006, Shelle Rosenfeld, review of *Nathan of Yesteryear and Michael of Today,* p. 42.
Canadian Review of Materials, November 12, 1000, review of *Nanuk, Lord of the Ice.*
Kirkus Reviews, August 15, 1996, review of *The Wolves,* p. 1235; September 15, 1996, p. 1401; August 15, 2006, review of *Red Fox at McCloskey's Farm,* p. 842.
Publishers Weekly, October 28, 1996, review of *The Wolves,* p. 81; November 15, 1998, review of *Nanuk, Lord of the Ice,* p. 74.
School Library Journal, August, 1993, p. 140; October, 1996, Elisabeth Palmer Abarbanel, review of *The Monsters' Test,* p. 96; March, 2001, JoAnn Jonas, review of *Butternut Hollow Pond,* p. 236; November, 2006, Carolyn Janssen, review of *Red Fox at McCloskey's Farm,* p. 96, and Susan E. Murray, review of *Cheyenne Medicine Hat,* p. 161.

ONLINE

Brian J. Heinz Home Page, http://www.brianheinz.com (August 1, 2007).

*   *   *

HEINZ, Brian James
See HEINZ, Brian J.

*   *   *

HELGERSON, Joseph 1950-

Personal

Born 1950; married; children: one daughter, one son. *Education:* University of Minnesota, bachelor's degree (American studies).

Addresses

Home and office—Minneapolis, MN.

Career

Author.

Writings

Horns and Wrinkles, illustrated by Nicoletta Ceccoli, Houghton Mifflin (Boston, MA), 2006.

Sidelights

Joseph Helgerson grew up in Winona, Minnesota, a small town situated close to the Mississippi River. As the author noted in an interview for the Houghton Mifflin Web site, most of his childhood summers were spent "exploring sloughs and backwaters with friends—fishing, lashing rafts together, occasionally filling a corncob pipe with enough rabbit tobacco to turn you a lovely shade of green." The adventures he experienced growing up along the river have inspired the setting of his middle-grade novel *Horns and Wrinkles.* Set in Blue Wing, Minnesota, Helgerson's story finds twelve-year-old Claire setting out on a quest to learn why the residents of her town are turning to stone and why, even more amazingly, her cousin Duke is slowly being transformed into a rhinoceros. Joined on her journey by Duke, Claire soon finds that the answers to her questions lie within magical realms within the Mississippi River, where the mystical River Trolls and Rock Trolls are feuding.

In *Booklist,* Shelle Rosenfeld praised the "folksy charm, inventive fantasy, and diverse characters" found within the pages of Helgerson's fiction debut, which features illustrations by award-winning Italian illustrator Nicoletta Ceccoli. Robyn Gioia, reviewing for *School Library Journal,* wrote that the "tongue-in-cheek humor" in *Horns and Wrinkles* adds "to the playfully inventive storytelling and [Helgerson's] fast-paced plot."

Biographical and Critical Sources

PERIODICALS

Booklist, September 1, 2006, Shelle Rosenfeld, review of *Horns and Wrinkles,* p. 128.

Books, October 22, 2006, Mary Harris Russell, review of *Horns and Wrinkles,* p. 9.

Kirkus Reviews, August 15, 2006, review of *Horns and Wrinkles,* p. 842.

Publishers Weekly, September 11, 2006, review of *Horns and Wrinkles,* p. 55.

School Library Journal, September, 2006, Robyn Gioia, review of *Horns and Wrinkles,* p. 208.

ONLINE

Houghton Mifflin Web site, http://www.houghton-mifflinbooks.com/ (July 8, 2007), "Joseph Helgerson."

Publishers Weekly Online, http://www.publishersweekly.com/ (December 18, 2006), Barry Lyga, "Flying Starts."*

J-K

JANISCH, Heinz 1960-

Personal

Born 1960, in Güssing, Austria. *Education:* University of Vienna, degree (German literature and journalism).

Addresses

Home and office—Mühlgasse 9/14, 1040 Vienna, Austria; Burgenland. *E-mail*—heinz.janisch@orf.at.

Career

Children's book author and journalist. Ö-1 Redakteur (radio station), recording engineer and editor of series "Menschenbilder," beginning 1982.

Member

Grazer Autorenversammlung.

Awards, Honors

Federhasenpreis, 1996, for *Benni und die sieben Löwen,* and 2000, for *Zack Bumm!;* Österreichischer Förderungspreis, 1998; Kinderbuchpreis (Vienna, Austria), 2004, for *Schenk mir Flügel,* 2005, for *Herr Jemineh hat Glück;* Deutschen Jugendliteraturpreis nomination, Bologna Ragazzi Award, Auswahlliste Österreichischer Staatspreis for children's literature, and Buch des Monats prize, Instituts für Jugendliteratur, all 2006, all for *Rote Wangen;* LesePeter August award, 2006, for *Ein Haus am Meer.*

Writings

Vom Untergang der Sonne am frühen Morgen (stories), Umbruch (Mödling, Austria), 1989.

Mario, der Tagmaler, Neuer Breitschopf (Vienna, Austria), 1989.

(Reteller) *Till Eulenspiegel,* illustrated by Lisbeth Zwerger, Neugebauer (Salzburg, Austria), 1990, translated by Anthea Bell as *The Merry Pranks of Till Eulenspiegel,* Picture Book Studio (Saxonville, MA), 1990.

Salbei & Brot: Gerüche der Kindheit, Verlag Austria (Vienna, Austria), 1992.

Gute Reise, Leo, illustrated by Eugen Sopko, St. Gabriel (Vienna, Austria), 1993.

Schon nähert sich das Meer (stories), Bibliothek der Provinz (Vienna, Austria), 1994.

Lobreden auf Dinge (stories), Bibliothek der Provinz (Vienna, Austria), 1994.

Ein Krokodil zuviel, illustrated by Gabriele Kernke, Betz (Vienna, Austria), 1994.

Nach Lissabon (stories), Bibliotek der Provinz (Vienna, Austria), 1994.

(Reteller) *Leben mit der Angst: vom Umgang mit Ängsten und Depressionen,* Ueberreuter (Vienna, Austria), 1995.

Benni und die sieben Löwen, illustrated by Gabriele Kernke, Betz (Vienna, Austria), 1995.

Sarah und der Wundervogel, illustrated by Bernhard Oberdieck, Betz (Vienna, Austria), 1996.

Der rote Pirat und andere Rucksackgeschichten, St. Gabriel (Vienna, Austria), 1996.

Die Arche Noah, illustrated by Lisbeth Zwerger, Neugebauer (Zurich, Germany), 1997, translated by Rosemary Lanning as *Noah's Ark,* North-South Books (New York, NY), 1997.

Josef ist im Büro oder der Weg nach Bethlehem, illustrated by Gabriele Kernke, Betz (Vienna, Austria), 1998.

Der Sonntagsriese, illustrated by Susanne Wechdorn, Jungbrunnen (Vienna, Austria), 1998.

Die Prinzessin auf dem Kürbis (stories), illustrated by Linda Wolfsgruber, Gabriel (Vienna, Austria), 1998.

Ich schenk dir einen Ton aus meinem Saxofon, illustrated by Linda Wolfsgruber, Jungbrunnen (Vienna, Austria), 1999.

Gesang, um den Schalf gefügig zu machen (stories), Bibliothek der Provinz (Vienna, Austria), 1999.

Heut bin ich stark, illustrated by Silke Brix-Henker, Betz (Vienna, Austria), 2000.

Zack Bumm!, illustrated by Helga Bansch, Jungbrunnen (Vienna, Austria), 2000.

Es gibt so Tage . . . , illustrated by Helga Bansch, Jungbrunner (Vienna, Austria), 2001.

Die Reise zu den Fliegenden Inseln, Jungbrunnen (Vienna, Austria), 2001.

Her mit den Prinzen!, illustrated by Birgit Antoni, Betz (Vienna, Austria), 2002.

Venn Anna Angst hat, illustrated by Barbara Jung, Junbrunnen (Vienna, Austria), 2002.

Zu Haus, illustrated by Helga Bansch, Jungbrunnen (Vienna, Austria), 2002.

Bärenhunger, illustrated by Helga Bansch, Jungbrunnen (Vienna, Austria), 2002.

(Reteller) *The Fire: An Ethiopian Folk Tale,* illustrated by Fabricio Vanden Broeck, translated by Shelley Tankaka, Douglas & McIntyre (Berkeley, CA), 2002.

Ich bin noch gar nicht müde, illustrated by Gisela Dürr, Betz (Vienna, Austria), 2003.

Schenk mir Flügel, illustrated by Selda Marlin Soganci, Residenz (St. Pölten, Austria), 2003.

Her mit den Prinzen! (stories), illustrated by Birgit Antoni, Büchergilde Gutenberg (Vienna, Austria), 2003.

Einer für alle! Alle für einem!: eine Hasengeschichte, illustrated by Brigit Antoni, Betz (Vienna, Austria), 2004.

Ein ganz gewöhnlicher Montag, illustrated by Sabine Wiemers, Betz (Vienna, Austria), 2004.

Katzensprung, illustrated by Helga Bansch, Jungbrunnen (Vienna, Austria), 2004.

Der Prinz im Pyjama, illustrated by Birgit Antoni, Betz (Vienna, Austria), 2004.

Herr Jemineh hat Glück, illustrated by Selda Marlin Soganci, NP (Vienna, Austria), 2004.

Bist du morgen auch noch da?, illustrated by Julia Kaergel, Gabriel (Vienna, Austria), 2005.

Cleo in der Klemme, illustrated by Philippe Goossens, Nord-Süd (Zurich, Switzerland), 2005.

Drei Birken, illustrated by Marion Goedelt, NP (Vienna, Austria), 2005.

Heute will ich langsam sein, illustrated by Linda Wolfsgruber, Jungbrunnen (Vienna, Austria), 2005.

Rote Wangen, illustrated by Aljoscha Blau, Aufbau (Berlin, Germany), 2005.

Ho ruck!, illustrated by Carola Holland, Betz (Vienna, Austria), 2005, translation published as *Heave Ho!,* North-South (New York, NY), 2006.

Morgennatz und Ringelstern: Gedichte von Christian Morgenstern und Joachim Ringelnatz, illustrated by Christine Sormann, Betz (Vienna, Austria), 2005.

Die kluge Katze: die schösten Tiermärchen aus aller Welt, illustrated by Marion Goedelt, Betz (Vienna, Austria), 2006.

Ein Haus am Meer, illustrated by Helga Bansch, Jungbrunnen (Vienna, Austria), 2006.

Ich bin Flonx, illustrated by Selda Marlin Soganci, Residenz (Salzburg, Austria), 2006.

Der große Hu und die Farben der Menschen, illustrated by Marion Goedlet, Sauerländer (Düsseldorf, Germany), 2006.

Über die Liebe, illustrated by Silke Leffler, Betz (Vienna, Austria), 2006.

Der Stärske von allen!, illustrated by Daniela Bunge, Betz (Vienna, Austria), 2006.

Krone sucht König, illustrated by Helga Bansch, Jungbrunnen (Vienna, Austria), 2006.

Einfach du, illustrated by Jutta Bauer, Sanssouci (Munich, Germany), 2006.

Der Tod auf Urlaub: Wegen Urlaub geschlossen!, illustrated by Herwig Zens, Kunsthander (Vienna, Austria), 2006.

Rittergeschichten, illustrated by Birgit Antoni, Ravensburger (Ravensburg, Germany), 2007.

Wenn ich nachts nicht schlafen kann, illustrated by Helga Bansch, Jungbrunnen (Vienna, Austria), 2007.

Der Ritt auf dem Seepferd: alte und durch wundersame Zufälle neu entdeckte Schriften über die unglublichen Abenteuer des Carl Friedrich Hieronymus Freiherr von Münchausen, illustrated by Aljoscha Blau, Aufbau (Berlin, Germany), 2007.

Zeppelin: ein Geschichte, illustrated by Heide Stöllinger, Bajazzo (Zurich, Switzerland), 2007.

Schatten, illustrated by Artem, Bajazzo (Zurich, Switzerland), 2007.

Lilli und die Dschunglebande, illustrated by Frauke Weldin, Nord-Süd (Zurich, Switzerland), 2007.

Eine Wolke in meinem Bett, illustrated by Isabel Pin, Aufbau (Berlin, Germany), 2007.

Der große Gustav und die kleinste Frau der Welt, illustrated by Karsten Teich, Terzio (Munich, Germany), 2007.

Ich hab ein kleines Problem, sagt der Bär, illustrated by Silke Leffler, Betz (Vienna, Austria), 2007.

Der kleine Nikolaus, illustrated by Evelyn Daviddi, Betz (Vienna, Austria), 2007.

Author's works have been translated into several languages, including Spanish, French, and Swedish.

Sidelights

Heinz Janisch, the author of books for both children and adults, is known for his skill as a storyteller and the lyricism he brings to his picture-book texts. Many of his stories for young children feature familiar objects made strange; in *Ich schenk dir einen Ton aus meinem Saxofon,* for example, a house with a headache moves to the country, and a frog decides to travel to Africa. *Prinzessin auf dem Kürbis,* he turns the tables on the traditional story about the princess and the pea, while *Zack bumm!* follows a young bird who can only croak a strange, meaningless phrase after a fall from his nest, until he finds help from a wise rabbit. Janisch's books, which have become beloved to many children around the world in translation, have also received awards in the author's native Austria as well as internationally. Among the titles available in English translation are *The Merry Pranks of Till Eulenspiegel, Noah's Ark,* and *Heave Ho!*

Born in Güssing, Austria, in 1960, Janisch studied German literature and journalism at the University of Vienna, then hired on as a program engineer at Ö-1 Redakteur radio. His picture book *Mario, der Tagmaler*

Noah's Ark *is one of several collaborations between German author Heinz Janisch and illustrator Lisbeth Zwerger.* (Illustration © 1997 by Nord Sud Verlag AG, Zurich, Switzerland. Used with permission of North-South Books, Inc., New York.)

was published in 1989, beginning his prolific career as a writer. One of his early works, a retelling of classic German folktales that was published in translation as *The Merry Pranks of Till Eulenspiegel,* was described by a *Publishers Weekly* reviewer as "distinctly quaint and European." The book is also notable for its illustrations by Hans Christian Andersen Medalist Lisbeth Zwerger, and represents one of several collaborations between author and illustrator. Another is *Noah's Ark,* which features Janisch's adaptation of the biblical story. Noting that Janisch's version is "far more ominous" than other retellings for children, *Horn Book* reviewer

Lauren Adams nonetheless concluded that *Noah's Ark* "effectively maintains the awesome and reverential tone of the original." Animals return in *Heave Ho!,* a more humorous outing that features cartoon art by Carola Holland. Within only a dozen sentences, Janisch tells an animated tale about a cat, mouse, and dog that, according to a *Kirkus Reviews* writer, features "a clever concept" which effectively communicates "a subtle message of teamwork."

In *The Fire: An Ethiopian Folk Tale* Janisch joins with noted Mexican illustrator Fabricio vanden Broeck to tell an African story with universal meaning. Author

and illustrator met during an International Board on Books for Young People congress, when Janisch told the story to rapt audiences. Vanden Broeck, attending as an award finalist, agreed to create paintings to illustrate the tale. *The Fire* focuses on a loyal slave who has worked for his master for many years. When the slave finally requests his freedom, the unappreciative master agrees to the request only if the slave performs a seemingly impossible task: climbing to a snow-topped mountain peak and spending the frigid night there, with neither clothing nor shelter. Fortunately, a wise friend comes to the slave's aid, leading readers to a conclusion that Hazel Rochman deemed "elemental" and "powerful" in her *Booklist* review.

Biographical and Critical Sources

PERIODICALS

Booklist, October 1, 1997, Susan Dove Lempke, review of *Noah's Ark,* p. 323; December 15, 2002, Hazel Rochman, review of *The Fire: An Ethiopian Folk Tale,* p. 764.
Bulletin of the Center for Children's Books, December, 1997, review of *Noah's Ark,* p. 115; February, 2003, review of *The Fire,* p. 239.
Canadian Review of Materials, November 15, 2002, Denise Wier, review of *The Fire.*
Horn Book, March-April, 1991, Ethel L. Heins, review of *The Merry Pranks of Till Eulenspiegel,* p. 210; March-April, 1998, Lauren Adams, review of *Noah's Ark,* p. 213.
Kirkus Reviews, August 15, 2006, review of *Heave Ho!,* p. 844.
Publishers Weekly, November 16, 1990, review of *The Merry Pranks of Till Eulenspiegel,* p. 56.
School Library Journal, June, 1991, review of *The Merry Pranks of Till Eulenspiegel,* p. 94; November, 1997, Kathy Piehl, review of *Noah's Ark,* p. 84; February, 2003, Grace Oliff, review of *The Fire,* p. 134; November, 2006, Teresa Pfeifer, review of *Heave Ho!,* p. 97.

ONLINE

Berlin International Literaturfestival Web site, http://www.literaturfestival.com/ (August 10, 2007), "Heinz Janisch."
Heinz Janisch Home Page, http://www.heinz-janisch.com (August 10, 2007).*

*   *   *

JARVIS, Robin 1963-

Personal

Born May 8, 1963, in Liverpool, England. *Education:* Newcastle Polytechnic (now Northumbria University), degree (graphic design).

Addresses
Home—South London, England.

Career
Children's writer, 1989—. Previously worked as a model-maker for television programming.

Awards, Honors
Nestlé Smarties Book Prize shortlist, 1989, and *Booklist* Editors' Choice designation, 2000, both for *The Dark Portal;* Lancashire Libraries Award, for *The Whitby Witches.*

Writings

SELF-ILLUSTRATED

The Thorn Ogres of Hagwood, Puffin (London, England), 1999, Silver Whistle (San Diego, CA), 2002.
Deathscent, Collins (London, England), 2001.
The Dark Waters of Hagwood, Puffin (London, England), 2008.

"DEPTFORD" SERIES; SELF-ILLUSTRATED

The Dark Portal, Purnell (London, England), 1989, SeaStar (New York, NY), 2000.
The Crystal Prison, Purnell (London, England), 1989, SeaStar (New York, NY), 2001.
The Final Reckoning, Simon & Schuster UK (Hemel Hempstead, England), 1990, SeaStar (New York, NY), 2002.
(And illustrator) *The Alchmyst's Cat,* Simon & Schuster UK (Hemel Hempstead, England), 1991 published as *The Alchemist's Cat,* SeaStar (San Francisco, CA), 2004.
The Oaken Throne, Simon & Schuster UK (Hemel Hempstead, England), 1993, SeaStar (San Francisco, CA), 2005.
Thomas, Macdonald Young (Hemel Hempstead, England), 1995, Chronicle (San Francisco, CA), 2006.
The Deptford Mice Almanack (omnibus), Macdonald Young (Hove, England), 1997.
Fleabee's Fortune, Hodder (London, England), 2004.
Whortle's Hope, Hodder (London, England), 2007.
Ogmund's Gift, Hodder (London, England), 2008.

"WHITBY WITCHES TRILOGY"

The Whitby Witches, Simon & Schuster UK (Hemel Hempstead, England), 1991, Chronicle Books (San Francisco, CA), 2006.
A Warlock in Whitby, Simon & Schuster UK (Hemel Hempstead, England), 1992.
The Whitby Child, Simon & Schuster UK (Hemel Hempstead, England), 1994.

"TALES FROM THE WYRD MUSEUM" SERIES; SELF-ILLUSTRATED

The Woven Path, Collins (London, England), 1995.
The Raven's Knot, Collins (London, England), 1996.
The Fatal Strand, Collins (London, England), 1998.

Adaptations

The Dark Portal was recorded as an audiobook.

Sidelights

Robin Jarvis stumbled accidentally into a career as a children's book author when he penned the first of his "Deptford" fantasy novels about a group of mice. "I never intended to write books at all," the British author explained on his home page. "I used to work as a model-maker for television programs, and commercials. The Deptford Mice evolved when I was taking a break from designing a large, furry alien and fancied drawing something small for a change." Jarvis's sketch of the first Deptford mouse launching him on a career that made him well-known in the United Kingdom. More than ten years later he earned new fans when "Deptford" novels such as *The Dark Portal, The Oaken Throne,* and *Thomas* crossed the Atlantic and won over American readers.

The Dark Portal introduces readers to the world of the Deptford Mice, who live in an abandoned old house and follow the traditions and religion of the Green Mouse. When father mouse Albert Brown is drawn into the sewers through magic, the peaceful world of the mice collides with the realm of the villain Jupiter, an enchanter, and the dangerous sewer rats that follow him. "Jarvis provides counterpoint to the heart-racing adventure with scenes of haunting beauty," wrote a contributor to *Publishers Weekly,* and *Kliatt* critic Deirdre B. Root found the novel to be "entertaining and genuinely frightening."

The "Deptford" series continues in *The Crystal Prison,* as Arthur's daughter Audrey Brown undertakes a quest to bring an ancient squirrel mystic back to Deptford. In return for the squirrel's services, Audrey must accompany a rat to the countryside, where she is blamed for a series of murders. To clear her name, she and other city mice work to uncover the identity of the dark figures lurking within the country community. In *The Final Reckoning* the evil Jupiter has returned as the Unbeast, a mystical force of evil. The conclusion of *The Crystal Prison* is "breathtakingly thrilling," noted Eva Mitnick in *School Library Journal,* and a *Kirkus Reviews* contributor called *The Final Reckoning* "a gripping page turner" in which Jarvis builds to "a crescendo of savage horror, relieved only by a few grace notes of tender poignancy." In *Booklist* Sally Estes called the concluding novel "a humdinger of a tale."

The "Deptford" series is comprised of three sub-trilogies, the second which focuses on Jupiter's history. In *The Alchemist's Cat,* set in 1664 London, a boy

Cover of Robin Jarvis's fantasy novel Thomas, *featuring artwork by Leonid Gore.*

named Will Godwin rescues a cat and three kittens from likely death, only to accidentally bring them into contact with an evil alchemist. "Jarvis delivers a vivid tale of treachery, cruelty, and sorcery, leavened only by Will's innate goodness," wrote *Booklist* contributor Sally Estes. Taking up the story, *The Oaken Throne* describes the age-old war between the bats and the squirrels, and *Thomas* reveals the past of a character from the original trilogy: shipmouse Thomas Triton. "Despite these veiled hints of an underlying supernatural conflict, the characters and their dilemmas remain immediate and exquisitely drawn," explained a contributor to *Kirkus Reviews* in an appraisal of *The Oaken Thone.* Jarvis's "heroes are stalwart and true; the villains sadistic and grotesque; and the nonstop action builds," maintained another *Kirkus Reviews* critic in reviewing *Thomas.* The third subtrilogy in the "Depford" saga consists of *Fleabee's Fortune, Whortle's Hope,* and *Ogmund's Gift.*

In addition to the "Deptford" books, Jarvis has also penned two fantasy series about humans. In *The Woven Path,* the first book in his "Tales from the Wyrd Museum" trilogy, young Neil is blackmailed by a time-

Cover of Jarvis's standalone fantasy novel **The Whitby Witches,** *featuring artwork by Jeff Petersen.* (Illustration © 2006 by Jeff Petersen. Reproduced by permission of Chronicle Books, LLC, San Francisco. Visit www.ChronicleBooks.com.)

traveling bear to go into the past to rescue four-year-old Josh. As they journey through London during the *Blitzkrieg*—the bombing Germany inflicted on that city during World War II—Neil meets soldiers as well as demons trying to keep him from returning home. The series continues in *The Raven's Knot* and *The Fatal Strand.* "Time-travel fantasy and family drama are mixed in with horror," Lisa Prolman wrote in her *School Library Journal* review of *The Woven Path.*

The Whitby Witches, which, along with *A Warlock in Whitby* and *The Whitby Child,* comprises another fantasy series, introducing orphans Ben and Jennet. Ben's ability to see ghosts makes people frightened of him, so he and Jennet move to the seaside village of Whitby, where they live with Alice Boston, an elderly woman who is not what she seems. When dangerous enchantments begin affecting Alice's friends, the three must work together to solve the mystery. Kay Weisman, writing in *Booklist,* called *The Whitby Witches* "equal parts mystery and fantasy," comparing Alice to Agatha Christie's famous sleuth Miss Marple. Saleena L. Davidson, reviewing the same novel for *School Library Journal,* deemed the book "a dark but delightful read that involves ghosts, evil magicians (and good ones), and an ancient curse."

Both *The Thorn Ogres of Hagwood* and its sequel, *The Dark Waters of Hagwood,* feature small creatures known as werlings, which are shape changers. Gamaliel Tumpin seems an unlikely hero as he cannot master the basics of shape changing, but when he and others are saved by the Wandering Smith, an exile from the land of Faerie, Gamaliel is drawn into a much larger quest and the fate of all the werlings may depend on him. "Fantasy adventure fans will be grateful for the cliffhanger ending that promises another installment," wrote a contributor to *Kirkus Reviews* in a review of *The Thorn Ogres of Hagwood,* and a *Publishers Weekly* critic concluded that "Jarvis turns up the volume on his trademark suspense blended with whimsy."

Along with writing the novels, Jarvis provides illustrations for many of the covers and interiors. Discussing his decision to write fantasy on his home page, he noted: "My main pleasure . . . is in giving myself and the reader as much variety as possible. I'd hate to have to write about the same old thing all the time."

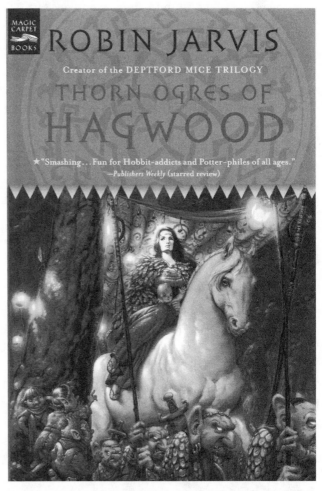

Jarvis's "Hagwood Trilogy" begins with **The Thorn Ogres of Hagwood,** *a book featuring cover artwork by Tim Jessel.* (Illustration © 2002 by Tim Jessell. Reproduced by permission in North America by Harcourt. Reproduced by permission in United Kingdom by Penguin Group UK, Ltd. This material may not be reproduced in any form or by any means without the prior written permission of the publisher.)

Biographical and Critical Sources

PERIODICALS

Booklist, October 15, 2000, Sally Estes, review of *The Dark Portal,* p. 438; April 15, 2001, Sally Estes, review of *The Dark Portal,* p. 1561; August, 2002, Sally Estes, review of *The Final Reckoning,* p. 1949; November 1, 2002, Sally Estes, review of *The Thorn Ogres of Hagwood,* p. 496; April 15, 2003, review of *The Thorn Ogres of Hagwood,* p. 1465; November 1, 2004, Sally Estes, review of *The Alchemist's Cat,* p. 484; September 1, 2005, Sally Estes, review of *The Oaken Throne,* p. 111; October 1, 2006, Kay Weisman, review of *The Whitby Witches,* p. 54; January 1, 2007, Ilene Cooper, review of *Thomas,* p. 81.

Childhood Education, summer, 2003, Aaron Condon, review of *The Thorn Ogres of Hagwood,* p. 245.

Kirkus Reviews, July 15, 2002, review of *The Final Reckoning,* p. 1034; September 1, 2002, review of *The Thorn Ogres of Hagwood,* p. 1311; September 15, 2004, review of *The Alchemist's Cat,* p. 915; October 1, 2005, review of *The Oaken Throne,* p. 1081; August 15, 2006, review of *Thomas,* p. 844; September 1, 2006, review of *The Whitby Witches,* p. 905.

Kliatt, January, 2002, Deirdre B. Root, review of *The Dark Portal,* p. 18.

Publishers Weekly, September 4, 2000, review of *The Dark Portal,* p. 109; August 27, 2001, reviews of *The Crystal Prison,* p. 86, and *The Dark Portal,* p. 87; October 14, 2002, review of *The Thorn Ogres of Hagwood,* p. 84; November 20, 2006, review of *The Whitby Witches,* p. 59.

School Librarian, May, 1992, review of *The Alchmyst's Cat,* p. 71; spring, 2005, Josie Hervey, review of *Fleabee's Fortune,* p. 35.

School Library Journal, December, 2000, Steven Engelfield, review of *The Dark Portal,* p. 145; June, 2001, Lisa Prolman, review of *The Woven Path,* p. 150; November, 2001, Eva Mitnick, review of *The Crystal Prison,* p. 159; September, 2002, Beth Wright, review of *The Final Reckoning,* p. 226; November, 2002, Eva Mitnick, review of *The Thorn Ogres of Hagwood,* p. 169; December, 2004, Christine McGinty, review of *The Alchemist's Cat,* p. 148; February, 2006, Christine McGinty, review of *The Oaken Throne,* p. 132; October, 2006, Saleena L. Davidson, review of *The Whitby Witches,* p. 158.

Times Educational Supplement, March 21, 1997, review of *The Raven's Knot,* p. 14; January 8, 1999, review of *The Fatal Strand,* p. 26.

Voice of Youth Advocates, April, 2001, review of *The Dark Portal,* p. 12; April, 2003, reviews of *The Thorn Ogres of Hagwood,* p. 26, and *The Final Reckoning,* p. 65; February, 2004, review of *The Thorn Ogres of Hagwood,* p. 456; February, 2007, Christine Sanderson, review of *The Whitby Witches,* p. 540.

ONLINE

Robin Jarvis Home Page, http://www.robinjarvis.com (June 25, 2007).*

KLISE, Kate

Personal

Born in Peoria, IL; daughter of Thomas S. (a writer and film producer) and Marjorie A. (president of Thomas S. Klise Co.) Klise. *Education:* Marquette University, graduate.

Addresses

Home and office—P.O. Box 744, Mountain Grove, MO 65711.

Career

Writer and journalist. Correspondent for *People* magazine.

Awards, Honors

Young Adults' Choice Award, Children's Book Council, 1999, for *Regarding the Fountain,* and 2000, for *Letters from Camp;* Juvenile Fiction Award, Friends of American Writers, 2002, for *Trial by Journal.*

Writings

FOR CHILDREN

Deliver Us from Normal, Scholastic Press (New York, NY), 2005.

Far from Normal, Scholastic Press (New York, NY), 2006.

FOR CHILDREN; ILLUSTRATED BY SISTER, M. SARAH KLISE

Regarding the Fountain: A Tale, in Letters, of Liars and Leaks, Avon (New York, NY), 1998.

Letters from Camp, Avon (New York, NY), 1999.

Trial by Journal, HarperCollins (New York, NY), 2001.

Regarding the Sink: Where, Oh Where, Did Waters Go?, Harcourt (Orlando, FL), 2004.

Shall I Knit You a Hat?: A Christmas Yarn, Henry Holt (New York, NY), 2004.

Regarding the Trees: A Splintered Saga Rooted in Secrets, Harcourt (Orlando, FL), 2005.

Why Do You Cry?: Not a Sob Story, Henry Holt (New York, NY), 2006.

Regarding the Bathrooms: A Privy to the Past, Harcourt (San Diego, CA), 2006.

Imagine Harry, Harcourt (Orlando, FL), 2007.

Regarding the Bees: A Lesson, in Letters, on Honey, Dating, and Other Sticky Subjects, Harcourt (Orlando, FL), 2007.

Little Rabbit and the Nightmare, Harcourt (Orlando, FL), 2008.

43 Old Cemetery Road: The First Summer, Harcourt (Orlando, FL), 2008.

Sidelights

Kate Klise writes children's books, many of which are designed and illustrated by her sister, M. Sarah Klise. Called a "comic epistolary novel" by a critic in the *New York Times Book Review,* the duo's first collaboration was *Regarding the Fountain: A Tale, in Letters, of Liars and Leaks.* The sisters' story is told through a series of drawings, letters, newspaper clippings, memos, and school announcements, a story-telling device used in many of the duo's illustrated novels. *Regarding the Fountain* focuses on the need to replace a leaking drinking fountain at the Dry Creek Middle School. When Principal Russ decides to get his school's new fountain from Flowing Waters Fountains, he expects to receive a traditional fountain. To his surprise, and to the delight of the children, owner Florence Waters turns out to be an artist who creates fountains that are individually sculpted pieces of art. Her ideas for the school fountain include an ice-skating rink, a chocolate-milk dispenser, a natural whirlpool, and a flock of exotic birds. A subplot involves the disappearance of the town's water supply, the activities of villainous Dee Eel, president of Dry Creek Water Company, and Sally Mander, head of the Dry Creek Swimming Pool. Clues to the mystery surrounding the missing water are uncovered by a fifth-grade class working on a history project about the town. Writing in *Kirkus Reviews,* a critic dubbed *Regarding the Fountain* "a tale overflowing with imagination and fun," while Rita Soltan noted in *School Library Journal* that Klise "cleverly establishes character traits and motive" and called the book "fresh, funny, and a delight to read." A *Publishers Weekly* contributor called the book a "good-natured story with an irrepressible main character."

Regarding the Sink: Where, Oh Where, Did Waters Go? finds Flo Waters once again taking center stage as the sixth graders of Geyser Creek Middle School ask her to replace a dilapidated cafeteria sink. The only problem is that Flo has vanished while on a trip to China, and now the middle graders are determined to find her. Meanwhile, to further complicate school life, beans have become the staple of school lunches as the result of slimy Senator Sue Ergass's moneymaking scam (which includes feeding cows nothing but beans so they produce more methane gas). A *Kirkus Reviews* contributor called *Regarding the Sink* "an amusing sequel," while in *Horn Book,* Susan P. Bloom commented that, "the Klises provide a satisfying denouement to this utter mayhem." In a review for *School Library Journal,* Jean Gaffney called the illustrated novel "a clever, unconventional reading experience."

In *Regarding the Trees: A Splintered Saga Rooted in Secrets* "the puns fall faster than autumn leaves," according to *Horn Book* contributor Susan P. Bloom. Worried over an upcoming school evaluation, Principal Russ asks Flo to assist in trimming the school trees, thereby sparking student protests, a town uprising, and a cooking face-off between two local chefs. All ends well, however, and romance even blooms. Police reports take their place among letters, newspaper articles, and other communications in *Regarding the Bathrooms: A Privy*

Kate Klise collaborates with sister and artist M. Sarah Klise on **Regarding the Bathrooms,** *one of several books featuring a class of enterprising middle graders.* (Illustration © 2006 by M. Sarah Klise. All rights reserved. Reproduced by permission of Harcourt in North America. Reproduced by permission of Specialty Book Marketing in the United Kingdom. This material may not be reproduced in any form or by any means without the prior written permission of the publisher.)

to the Past as the principal's hope of renovating a basement bathroom during summer session is stalled when several escaped convicts are found hiding in the school, along with a cache of stolen Roman antiquities. The action moves to seventh grade in *Regarding the Bees,* as budding student romances, stresses over standardized tests, and difficulties surrounding the school mascot's appearance at a regional spelling bee culminate in a flurry of humorous visual communications. Describing *Regarding the Trees* as "filled with humor and whimsical characters," Shelle Rosenfeld added in *Booklist* that "kids will enjoy the peppy, multiformat read." In *School Library Journal,* Cheryl Ashton noted that "each page" of the book "is painstakingly laid out in scrapbook form," and a *Kirkus Reviews* writer dubbed *Regarding the Trees* "consistently clever and often hilarious."

Leaving the students of Geyser Middle School behind, Klise has also written stand-alone novels for preteen readers, among them *Deliver Us from Normal* and *Far from Normal.* In *Deliver Us from Normal* Klise tells the story of twelve-year-old Charlie Harrisong, who lives in

Normal, Illinois, but whose poor family is far from the norm. Charlie is teased at school and is embarrassed about his family and their unusual lifestyle. When the family decides to leave Normal and live on a junky houseboat, Charlie is at first distressed that his life will never, ever be normal, but he eventually learns that not being normal has its benefits. When readers rejoin Charlie in *Far from Normal,* two years have passed and the family's circumstances have changed drastically. After Charlie's article about life on the houseboat is published in a national magazine, he and the Harrisong family are strong-armed into becoming the spokesfamily for the discount retailer Bargain Bonanza. Although they are set up in an all-expense-paid home in a luxury apartment with all the Bargain Bonanza merchandise they desire, this glamorous life comes with a cost, and the stress of fame takes its toll on everyone.

In a *Horn Book* review, Susan Dove Lempke wrote that in *Deliver Us from Normal* Klise "shows a gift for getting inside her narrator, [and] delivering his perceptions with immediacy and self-deprecating humor," while *Far from Normal* benefits from a "fast-moving plot" and its author's "grasp of family relationships and her sharp wit." In *Booklist,* Jennifer Hubert compared Klise's humor to that of authors Gordon Korman and David Lubar, noting her arch commentary "on commercialism and the cult of celebrity." Even in the modern world Charlie and his family "remind readers what is really important—honesty, integrity and the loyalty of family," concluded Janis Flint-Ferguson in her *Kliatt* review of *Far from Normal.*

Another standalone novel by Klise, *Letters from Camp,* also features M. Sarah Klise's unique art. The story focuses on Camp Happy Harmony, where brothers and sisters who cannot get along are sent to learn to love and respect each other. The camp's owners, however, are a group of singers turned con artists who are bent on killing each other and who use the children like slaves, to do all the work of maintaining the camp, including cleaning septic lines, building fences, and painting, all the while making them wear strange uniforms and sing bizarre songs. Not-so-happy campers are kept in line through drugged food served in the Wysteria Cafeteria. Despite the circumstances, the children learn to cooperate, and brothers and sisters eventually do learn to care for each other as they solve the mysteries of Camp Happy Harmony. A *Publishers Weekly* contributor found the book a "bit less satisfying" than *Regarding the Fountain,* but also noted that "the humor is obvious but kid-friendly, the mystery simple yet fun to solve." Writing in *Booklist,* Debbie Carton commented that the story is "all in all, an entirely satisfying camp adventure that even those who have never been to camp will relish." Other standalone novels by both sisters include *Trial by Journal.*

The Klise sisters address a younger crowd in their picture book *Shall I Knit You a Hat?: A Christmas Yarn.* Here they tell the story of Mother Rabbit who knits a hat for her son to protect him from an oncoming bliz-

Cover of Klise's middle-grade novel Deliver Us from Normal, *featuring artwork by Joe Zeff.* (Cover art © 2005 by Joe Zeff. Reprinted by permission of Scholastic Inc.)

zard. Little Rabbit loves his hat and never takes it off, but he is concerned for his other animal friends and suggests that he and his mother make hats for all of them as Christmas gifts. Little Rabbit returns in several other picture books, turning five in *Why Do You Cry?* and creating an imaginary friend in *Imagine Harry.* "The Klises consistently sound notes of tenderness and humor," noted a *Publishers Weekly* contributor of *Shall I Knit You a Hat?,* and *School Library Journal* critic Suzanne Myers Harold cited *Imagine Harry* as a picture book that "strikes a balance between humor and understanding." J.D. Biersdorfer, reviewing *Shall I Knit You a Hat?* for the *New York Times Book Review,* described Klise's story as "a nice change of pace" and noted that "the Klise sisters team up to show that the giving is just as important as the gift."

Biographical and Critical Sources

PERIODICALS

Booklist, August, 1998, Susan Dove Lempke, review of *Regarding the Fountain: A Tale, in Letters, of Liars and Leaks,* p. 2006; September 1, 2001, Shelle Rosen-

feld, review of *Trial by Journal,* p. 106; September 1, 2004, Francisca Goldsmith, review of *Regarding the Sink: Where, Oh Where, Did Waters Go?,* p. 124; December 1, 2004, Ilene Cooper, review of *Shall I Knit You a Hat?: A Christmas Yarn,* p. 659; November 1, 2005, Shelle Rosenfeld, review of *Regarding the Trees: A Splintered Saga Rooted in Secrets,* p. 47; May 1, 2006, Kathleen Odean, review of *Why Do You Cry?: Not a Sob Story,* p. 92; September 1, 2006, Shelle Rosenfeld, review of *Regarding the Bathroom: A Privy to the Past,* p. 129; October 15, 2006, Jennifer Hubert, review of *Far from Normal,* p. 45.

Horn Book, May-June, 1998, Nancy Vasilakis, review of *Regarding the Fountain,* p. 345; May-June, 2001, Susan P. Brabander, review of *Trial by Journal,* p. 328; September-October, 2004, Susan P. Bloom, review of *Regarding the Sink,* p. 588; July-August, 2005, Susan Dove Lempke, review of *Deliver Us from Normal,* p. 471; September-October, 2005, Susan P. Bloom, review of *Regarding the Trees,* p. 582; November-December, 2006, Susan Dove Lempke, review of *Far from Normal,* p. 717.

Kirkus Reviews, July 15, 2004, review of *Regarding the Sink,* p. 688; November 1, 2004, review of *Shall I Knit You a Hat?,* p. 1051; July 15, 2005, review of *Regarding the Trees,* p. 792; May 15, 2006, review of *Why Do You Cry?,* p. 519; July 15, 2006, review of *Regarding the Bathrooms,* p. 725; September 15, 2006, review of *Far from Normal,* p. 958; May 15, 2007, review of *Imagine Harry;* July 1, 2007, review of *Regarding the Bees.*

Kliatt, March, 2005, Nola Theiss, review of *Deliver Us from Normal;* November, 2006, Janis Flint-Ferguson, review of *Far from Normal,* p. 45.

New York Times Book Review, September 20, 1998, review of *Regarding the Fountain,* p. 32; December 19, 2004, J.D. Biersdorfer, review of *Shall I Knit You a Hat?,* p. 26.

Publishers Weekly, April 30, 2001, review of *Trial by Journal,* p. 78; September 27, 2004, review of *Shall I Knit You a Hat?,* p. 61; May 1, 2006, review of *Why Do You Cry?,* p. 62.

School Library Journal, June, 1998, Rita Soltan, review of *Regarding the Fountain,* p. 147; June, 1999, Connie Tyrrell Burns, review of *Letters from Camp,* p. 132; June, 2001, Sharon McNeil, review of *Trial by Journal,* p. 152; October, 2004, Jean Gaffney, review of *Regarding the Sink,* p. 170; November, 2005, Cheryl Ashton, review of *Regarding the Trees,* p. 138; July, 2006, Robin L. Gibson, review of *Why Do You Cry?,* p. 80; August, 2006, Wendy Woodfill, review of *Regarding the Bathrooms,* p. 123; December, 2006, Rebecca Stine, review of *Far from Normal,* p. 148; June, 2007, Suzanne Myers Harold, review of *Imagine Harry,* p. 110.

Voice of Youth Advocates, April, 2007, Anita Beaman, review of *Far from Normal,* p. 52.

ONLINE

Flamingnet.com, http://flamingnet.com/ (February 17, 2005), Caroline Devilbiss, review of *Deliver Us from Normal.*

Kate and Sarah Klise Home Page, http://www.kateandsarahklise.com (July 20, 2005).

*   *   *

KROMMES, Beth 1956-

Personal

Born January 6, 1956, in Allentown, PA; daughter of Frederick and Shirley Krommes; married David Rowell (a computer programmer), September 25, 1982; children: Olivia, Marguerite. *Education:* Syracuse University, B.F.A. (painting; magna cum laude), 1977; attended St. Martin's School of Art (London, England), 1976; University of Massachusetts—Amherst, M.A.T. (art education), 1980. *Politics:* Democrat. *Religion:* Lutheran.

Addresses

Home and office—310 Old Street Rd., Peterborough, NH 03458.

Career

Illustrator of children's books. Worked variously as an art director and designer for a computer magazine, manager of a handicraft shop, managing director of an arts organization, and as a junior-and senior-high-school art teacher. Freelance wood engraver and illustrator, 1984—. *Exhibitions:* Works exhibited in Pennsylvania, Massachusetts, and New Hampshire, and in England.

Beth Krommes (Photograph by Dave Rowell. Reproduced by permission of Beth Krommes.)

Member

Society of Children's Book Writers and Illustrators, Society of Wood Engravers.

Awards, Honors

Certificates of Design Excellence, *PRINT's Regional Design Annual,* 1985, 1986, 1987, 1988, 1990, 1991, 1994, 1999; Yankee Print Awards, League of New Hampshire Craftsmen Foundation annual juried exhibit, 1986, 1987; Merit Awards in Printmaking, Sharon, NH, Arts Center annual regional juried exhibitions, 1986, 1989; Bologna Children's Book Fair Illustrator's Exhibit selection for fiction, 2000, for *Grandmother Winter;* Bologna Children's Book Fair Illustrator's Exhibit selection for nonfiction, 2001, and Golden Kite Award for Illustration, 2002, both for *The Lamp, the Ice, and the Boat Called Fish.*

Illustrator

Ruth Adams Bronz, *Miss Ruby's American Cooking,* Harper & Row (New York, NY), 1989.

Marjorie Holmes, *At Christmas the Heart Goes Home,* Doubleday (New York, NY), 1991.

James Villas, *French Country Kitchen,* Bantam (New York, NY), 1992.

Tales of the Grizzly, Homestead Publishing (Moose, WY), 1992.

Down Home Cooking, Reader's Digest (Pleasantville, NY), 1994.

Sandra J. Taylor, editor, *Yankee Magazine's New England Innkeepers Cookbook,* Villard (New York, NY), 1996.

Tales of the Wolf, Homestead Publishing (Moose, WY), 1996.

Ric Lynden Hardman, *Sunshine Rider* (young-adult novel), Bantam (New York, NY), 1998.

Phyllis Root, *Grandmother Winter* (picture book), Houghton (Boston, MA), 1999.

Carrie Young, *Prairie Cooks, Three Day Burns, and Other Reminiscences,* University of Iowa Press (Iowa City, IA), 1999.

Jacqueline Briggs Martin, *The Lamp, the Ice, and the Boat Called Fish* (picture book), Houghton (Boston, MA), 2001.

Judith Nicholls, editor, *The Sun in Me: Poems about the Planet,* Barefoot Books (Bristol, England), 2002, Barefoot Books (Cambridge, MA), 2003.

Lise Lunge-Larsen, *The Hidden Folk: Stories of Fairies, Dwarves, Selkies, and Other Secret Beings* (picture book), Houghton Mifflin (Boston, MA), 2004.

Joyce Sidman, *Butterfly Eyes, and Other Secrets of the Meadow,,* Houghton Mifflin (Boston, MA) 2006.

Sidelights

Known for her engravings, Beth Krommes is an illustrator whose works have appeared in many exhibitions and galleries in New Hampshire, where she makes her home. Since the early 1990s, she has illustrated children's books using a scratchboard-and-watercolor technique, among them the picture books *Grandmother Win-*

ter by Phyllis Root, *The Lamp, the Ice, and the Boat Called Fish* by Jacqueline Briggs Martin, and *The Hidden Folk: Stories of Fairies, Dwarves, Selkies, and Other Secret Beings,* by Lise Lunge-Larsen. Reviewing her work for *The Sun in Me: Poems about the Planet,* a *Kirkus Reviews* writer dubbed Krommes' illustrations "gorgeous," commenting on her "brilliant use of pattern and placement in space along with color that leaps from the page."

For *Grandmother Winter,* a lyrical tale of people's and animals' responses to the coming of winter, Krommes created "delightful scratchboard illustrations, tinted with soft watercolors," according to *Booklist* reviewer Kay Weisman. A contributor to *Horn Book* commented on the bats, worms, frogs, fish, bears, and other creatures Krommes integrates into her images, calling them "carefully observed as well as decorative." The illustrator's work for Joyce Sidman's verse collection *Butterfly Eyes, and Other Secretes of the Meadow* also focuses on nature, in this case a pond ecosystem. "Visual clues complement the poetic suggestions in striking scratchboard scenes . . . saturated with color," wrote Margaret Bush in a *School Library Journal* review of the book. Calling Krommes' stylized art "splendid," *Horn Book* reviewer Joanna Rudge Long added that the pictures "reflect such precise observation that each species is easily recognizable" to young readers.

In *The Lamp, the Ice, and the Boat Called Fish* Martin recounts the true story of an expedition that set out in

In her stylized art, Krommes brings to life Jacqueline Briggs Martin's retelling of a true story in The Lamp, the Ice, and the Boat Called Fish. (Illustration © 2001 by Beth Krommes. Reproduced by permission of Houghton Mifflin Company.)

The fantasy world created by Lise Lunge-Larsen in her book **The Hidden Folk** ***is given a folkloric feel via Krommes' illustrations.*** (Illustration © 2004 by Beth Krommes. All rights reserved. Reproduced by permission of Houghton Mifflin Company.)

1913, led by Arctic explorer Vilhjalmur Stefansson. Hoping to prove that a continent was hidden under the

Arctic ice cap, Stefansson was ultimately forced to abandon his ice-trapped fishing boat, the *Karluk.* Krom-

mes' scratchboard art for the work was deemed "outstanding" by a *Horn Book* writer, the critic adding that "ice, artifacts, and characters are delineated in handsome black, softened with crosshatching and a limited palette." In *School Library Journal* Sue Sherif added that the "evocative scratchboard illustrations show many details of the cultural and physical environment" Krommes brings to life.

More fanciful in its focus, *The Hidden Folk* presents a history of magical creatures as they appear in the European folk tradition, from dwarves and flower fairies to selkies and river sprites. Noting Krommes' use of decorative borders that echo the theme of each interior illustration, *School Library Journal* contributor Harriett Fargnoli wrote that "the vivid hues and interesting textures make an eye-catching combination." John Peters concluded in his *Booklist* review of *The Hidden Folk* that Krommes' creative contribution "give[s] this gathering a suitably folktale feel," and a *Kirkus Reviews* critic wrote that the illustrator's use of "rich and brilliant color [is] at once cozy and majestic."

Biographical and Critical Sources

PERIODICALS

Booklist, November 15, 1999, Kay Weisman, review of *Grandmother Winter*, p. 637; September 1, 2004, John Peters, review of *The Hidden Folk: Stories of Fairies, Dwarves, Selkies, and Other Secret Beings*, p. 117; October 1, 2006, Gillian Engberg, review of *Butterfly Eyes, and Other Secrets of the Meadow*, p. 51.

Horn Book, September, 1999, review of *Grandmother Winter*, p. 599; March, 2001, review of *The Lamp, the Ice, and the Boat Called Fish*, p. 198; September-October, 2006, Joanna Rudge Long, review of *Butterfly Eyes, and Other Secrets of the Meadows*, p. 603.

Kirkus Reviews, January 15, 2003, review of *The Sun in Me: Poems about the Planet*, p. 144; July 15, 2004, review of *The Hidden Folk*, p. 690; August 15, 2006, review of *Butterfly Eyes, and Other Secrets of the Meadow*, p. 852.

Natural History, December, 2002, review of *The Lamp, the Ice, and the Boat Called Fish*, p. 70.

New York Times Book Review, April 15, 2001, Heather Vogel Frederick, review of *The Lamp, the Ice, and the Boat Called Fish*, p. 25.

Publishers Weekly, September 2, 1989, Molly McQuade, review of *Miss Ruby's American Cooking*, p. 54; August 30, 1999, review of *Grandmother Winter*, p. 82.

School Library Journal, July, 2001, Sue Sherif, review of *The Lamp, the Ice, and the Boat Called Fish*, p. 96; March, 2003, Kathleen Whalin, review of *The Sun in Me*, p. 222; December, 2004, Harriett Fargnoli, review of *The Hidden Folk*, p. 134; October, 2006, Margaret Bush, review of *Butterfly Eyes, and Other Secrets of the Meadow*, p. 142.

ONLINE

New Hampshire State Council on the Arts Web site, http://www.nh.gov/ (July 20, 2007), "Beth Krommes."

L

LaREAU, Jenna

Personal
Born in Stratford, CT.

Addresses
Home and office—CT. *E-mail*—info@lareausisters.com.

Career
Illustrator and graphic designer.

Illustrator
Paul B. Janeczko, *Top Secret: A Handbook of Codes, Ciphers, and Secret Writing,* Candlewick Press (Cambridge, MA), 2004.

Kara LaReau, *Rocko and Spanky Go to a Party,* Harcourt (Orlando, FL), 2004.

Kara LaReau, *Rocko and Spanky Have Company,* Harcourt (Orlando, FL), 2006.

Sidelights
For SIDELIGHTS, see entry on Kara LaReau.

Biographical and Critical Sources

PERIODICALS

Booklinks, May, 2006, Terri Ruyter, review of *Top Secret: A Handbook of Codes, Ciphers, and Secret Writing,* p. 61.

Booklist, May 15, 2004, Jennifer Mattson, review of *Top Secret,* p. 1621.

Publishers Weekly, May 31, 2004, review of *Rocko and Spanky Go to a Party,* p. 73; June 7, 2004, "Spy vs. Spy," p. 53; May 22, 2006, review of *Rocko and Spanky Have Company,* p. 54.

School Library Journal, May, 2004, review of *Top Secret,* p. 170; October, 2004, Sheilah Kosco, review of *Rocko and Spanky Go to a Party,* p. 120; July, 2006, Zeilstra Sawyer, review of *Rocko and Spanky Have Company,* p. 81.

Voice of Youth Advocates, August, 2004, review of *Top Secret,* p. 238.

ONLINE

Harcourt Web site, http://www.harcourtbooks.com/ (July 18, 2007), interview with the LaReau sisters.

LaReau Sisters Home Page, http://www.lareausisters.com (July 18, 2007).

Raincoast Books Web site, http://www.raincoast.com/kids/ (July 18, 2007), interview with the LaReau sisters.

*   *   *

LaREAU, Kara

Personal
Born in Stratford, CT.

Addresses
Home and office—RI. *E-mail*—info@lareausisters.com.

Career
Author and editor.

Writings

Rocko and Spanky Go to a Party, illustrated by sister, Jenna LaReau, Harcourt (Orlando, FL), 2004.

Snowbaby Could Not Sleep, illustrated by Jim Ishikawa, Little, Brown (New York, NY), 2005.

Rocko and Spanky Have Company, illustrated by Jenna LaReau, Harcourt (Orlando, FL), 2006.

Ugly Fish, *Kara LaReau's quirky story about a pug-ugly bully with fins, is well-paired with Scott Magoon's humorous art.* (Illustration © 2006 by Scott Magoon. All rights reserved. Reproduced by permission of Harcourt, Inc. This material may not be reproduced in any form or by any means without the prior written permission of the publisher.)

Ugly Fish, illustrated by Scott Magoon, Harcourt (Orlando, FL), 2006.
Rabbit and Squirrel, illustrated by Scott Magoon, Harcourt (Orlando, FL), 2008.

Sidelights

Kara LaReau teams up with her sister, illustrator Jenna LaReau, to create a series of entertaining children's books in which sock monkeys take the leading roles. The sisters' "Rocko and Spanky" series—which includes the books *Rocko and Spanky Go to a Party* and *Rocko and Spanky Have Company*—find the frisky twin monkeys rushing headlong into every adventure that comes their way. In a *Publishers Weekly* review of *Rocko and Spanky Go to a Party,* the critic deemed the work a "kicky debut" and a "fashionable and sweet-natured romp."

In addition to her work with her sister, Kara LaReau has also penned several children's books illustrated by other artists. Featuring cartoon art by Scott Magoon, her picture book *Ugly Fish* presents readers with a les-

son about sharing and bullying. Ugly Fish, an intimidating and aggressive scaly green fish, rules the aquarium and does not like to share his watery "turf." Smaller fish fear him and often fall victim to his bite, and eventually Ugly Fish gets his wish and has the tank all to himself. This does not last long, however; the bully is soon joined by a new fish that is far bigger that Ugly Fish . . . and a bigger bully as well. Julie Roach, reviewing *Ugly Fish* for *School Library Journal,* remarked that while LaReau's story is "not for the faint of heart," young children will "thoroughly enjoy its humor and shock value."

Biographical and Critical Sources

PERIODICALS

Booklist, January 1, 2006, Jennifer Mattson, review of *Snowbaby Could Not Sleep,* p. 117.

Bulletin of the Center for Children's Books, December, 2005, review of *Snowbaby Could Not Sleep,* p. 190; July-August, 2006, Deborah Stevenson, review of *Ugly Fish,* p. 505.

Kirkus Reviews, October 1, 2005, review of *Snowbaby Could Not Sleep,* p. 1082; May 15, 2006, review of *Ugly Fish,* p. 519.

Publishers Weekly, May 31, 2004, review of *Rocko and Spanky Go to a Party,* p. 73; November 28, 2005, review of *Snowbaby Could Not Sleep,* p. 50; May 22, 2006, review of *Rocko and Spanky Have Company,* p. 54; June 26, 2006, review of *Ugly Fish,* p. 50.

School Library Journal, October, 2004, Sheilah Kosco, review of *Rocko and Spanky Go to a Party,* p. 120; January, 2006, Dristine M. Casper, review of *Snowbaby Could Not Sleep,* p. 106; July, 2006, Zeilstra Sawyer, review of *Rocko and Spanky Have Company,* p. 81, and Julie Roach, review of *Ugly Fish,* p. 82.

ONLINE

Cynsations Web site, http://cynthialeitichsmith.blogspot.com/ (July 18, 2007), Cynthia Leitich-Smith, review of *Ugly Fish.*

Harcourt Web site, http://www.harcourtbooks.com/ (July 18, 2007), interview with the LaReau sisters.

LaReau Sisters Home Page, http://www.lareausisters.com/ (July 18, 2007).

Raincoast Books Web site, http://www.raincoast.com/kids/ (July 18, 2007), interview with the LaReau sisters.

*   *   *

LARSON, Kirby 1954-

Personal

Born August 17, 1954, in Seattle, WA; daughter of David Neil (a mechanical contractor) and Donna Marie (a bookkeeper) Miltenberger; married Neil Edwin Larson (a certified public accountant), September 6, 1975; children: Tyler Kenton, Quinn Lois. *Education:* Western Washington State College, B.A., 1976; University of Washington, M.A., 1980. *Hobbies and other interests:* Reading, quilting, traveling, birding.

Addresses

Home and office—Kenmore, WA. *E-mail*—kirby@kirbylarson.com.

Career

Children's book author. Whidbey Island Writers Workshop, Whidbey Island, WA, former member of creative-writing faculty. Northshore Performing Arts Center Foundation, cofounder. Moorlands Elementary PTA, co-president, 1991-94; Northshore School District, member of board of directors, 1994-2001.

Member

Author's Guild, Society of Children's Book Writers and Illustrators, PEN.

Kirby Larson (Photograph by Shawn Jezerinac. Reproduced by permission.)

Awards, Honors

Golden Acorn Award, 1994, for PTA Service; Oppenheim Platinum Award, Cybils Award finalist, *Seattle Times* Best Book designation, Borders Original Voice designation, Montana Book Award, and Book Links Lasting Connections designation, all 2006, and Newbery Honor designation and several children's choice awards, all 2007, all for *Hattie Big Sky.*

Writings

FICTION; FOR CHILDREN

Second-Grade Pig Pals, illustrated by Nancy Poydar, Holiday House (New York, NY), 1994.

Cody and Quinn, Sitting in a Tree, illustrated by Nancy Poydar, Holiday House (New York, NY), 1996.

The Magic Kerchief, illustrated by Rosanne Litzinger, Holiday House (New York, NY), 2000.

Hattie Big Sky (young-adult novel), Delacorte (New York, NY), 2006.

(With Mary Nethery) *The Tale of Two Bobbies: A True Story of Huricane Katrina, Friendship, and Survival,* illustrated by Jean Cassels, Walker (New York, NY), 2008.

"SWEET VALLEY KIDS" CHAPTER-BOOK SERIES

Scaredy-Cat Elizabeth, Bantam Doubleday Dell (New York, NY), 1995.

Elizabeth Hatches an Egg, Bantam Doubleday Dell (New York, NY), 1996.

Adaptations

Hattie Big Sky was adapted as an audiobook narrated by Kirsten Potter, Listening Library, 2007.

Sidelights

Kirby Larson began her writing career penning chapter books while seated at her kitchen table, setting aside her work to serve up her family's meals. Never a prolific writer, she nonetheless gained critical praise for creating good-humored stories that accurately reflect the problems and concerns of children in the early elementary grades. Larson focuses on plot and character development in her chapter books *Second-Grade Pig Pals* and *Cody and Quinn, Sitting in a Tree,* as well as in her picture book *The Magic Kerchief.* Her focus on such details paid off when she turned to older readers in her young-adult novel *Hattie Big Sky.* The sixth book written by Larson over a span of a dozen years, *Hattie Blue Sky* earned the Washington State author a prestigious Newbery Honor designation from the American Library Association following its 2006 publication.

Larson's first two chapter books, *Second-Grade Pig Pals* and *Cody and Quinn, Sitting in a Tree,* introduce a second grader named Quinn. In addition to worries about celebrating a holiday devoted to swine in *Second-Grade Pig Pals,* Quinn finds herself with friend problems when her efforts to befriend Manuela, a new student, are foiled by more-aggressive classmate Annie May. Quinn's solution to her dilemma, which involves the girls working together to compose a limerick about pigs, gives the book a "whole-hoggedly satisfying ending," in the opinion of *School Library Journal* contributor Janet M. Bair. The class bully, with his relentless taunting, tries to ruin Quinn's friendship with a boy in *Cody and Quinn, Sitting in a Tree.* Susan Dove Lempke, reviewing Larson's first book for the *Bulletin of the Center for Children's Books,* predicted that young readers will enjoy following Quinn's "travails as she agonizes, in true-to-life second-grade fashion, over the pigs and Manuela." In *Cody and Quinn, Sitting in a Tree* Quinn and company "act out this typical school story with a generous measure of humor and sensitivity," concluded Pat Mathews in *Bulletin of the Center for Children's Books,* and Kay Weisman declared in *Booklist* that "Larson has an accurate sense of seven-year-olds' preoccupations and a good ear for dialogue."

Turning to younger children in *The Magic Kerchief,* Larson tells the story of a crabby old woman named Griselda, whose terse and insulting remarks win her few friends in her small village. When the sharp-

Cover of Kirby Larsen's young-adult novel **Hattie Big Sky,** *featuring artwork by Jonathan Barkat.* (Illustration © 2006 by Jonathan Barkat. All rights reserved. Reproduced by permission of Delacorte Press, an imprint of Random House Children's Books, a division of Random House, Inc.)

tongued woman's kindness toward a traveling stranger earns her the gift of a magic scarf, however, Griselda gains the ability to speak in a way that matches her generosity of heart. Featuring pastel-toned illustrations by Rozanne Litzinger, *The Magic Kerchief* was praised by *School Library Journal* reviewer Sheilah Kosco for its "simple, humorous prose." In *Publishers Weekly* a critic wrote that Larson's "buoyant original folktale bristles with lively description," and a *Horn Book* critic concluded that the "lighthearted" picture book "offers a humorous take on the theme of kindness being its own reward."

Larson honors the life of her own great-grandmother, Hattie Inez Brooks Wright, in her teen novel *Hattie Blue Sky.* Readers meet Hattie Brooks when she is sixteen years old and an orphan living in Arlington, Iowa. When she receives word that she has inherited a homesteading claim from her Uncle Chester, Hattie makes the journey west to Montana and attempts to improve the claim despite the hardships of wartime between 1917 and 1919 as well as the efforts of a nearby rancher to take over her land. Noting that the young woman's

first year is consumed by her need to survive the harsh conditions and also do the fence-mending, planting, and harvesting required to maintain her claim, *Booklist* reviewer Kathleen Odean wrote that Larson's "richly textured" novel features "figurative language . . . that draws on the "sounds, smells, and sights of the prairie." In *Kliatt,* Claire Rosser predicted that *Hattie Big Sky* would appeal to fans of Laura Ingalls Wilder's "Little House on the Prairie" series, and wrote that the "strength and intelligence, . . . courage and loyal friendship" of Larson's protagonist "make her a real hero." Dubbing the book "heartwarming yet poignant," *School Library Journal* reviewer Sharon Morrison praised the author's ability to paint, for teens, "a masterful picture of the homesteading experience and the people who persevered." A *Kirkus Reviews* writer called *Hattie Big Sky* a "fine offering [that] may well inspire readers to find out more about their own family histories."

Larson once told *SATA:* "Once upon a time, there was a little girl with a funny name and blue cats-eye glasses. Her family moved around a lot; nearly every fall, she was the new kid in school. Sometimes she was lonely but she never worried about making friends—she had two brothers and a sister to play with and hundreds of companions in the books she read. When she wasn't reading, the girl liked to build cushion forts in the living room or put on plays for her parents. She never broke any bones or world records, except maybe for reading. The girl loved to read so much that sometimes even her teachers complained!

"When the little girl grew up, she did many things—went to college, worked at a radio station; she even made those annoying sales calls people hang up on. Along the way, she met a handsome prince (maybe not a prince, but definitely handsome), got married and had two children, a boy and a girl. Those babies loved being read to! Which was good because, even though she was grown up, the girl still loved to read. She especially loved to read about George and Martha, Frog and Toad, dear little Frances and anything by Betsy Byars. The girl loved these children's books so much that she wanted to write one herself. So she did.

"And it was awful. She wrote another one and it was worse. And no fairy godmother showed up to help her, either. She kept writing. Some of it was still bad. But some of it was getting better! The girl didn't give up and, one day, one of her stories was published.

"You've no doubt guessed that this fairy tale is about me. Everything's absolutely true—except for the part about not having a fairy godmother. Actually, I have many! They are fellow children's book writers who tell me when my story needs work and give me good ideas about how to fix it, as well as illustrators and designers who make the books look lovely and publicists and booksellers who tell the world about them. That is why I so treasure all my fairy godmothers.

"Just because your books are published doesn't necessarily mean you've arrived. The truth is writers have to start over again with each new book they write—at least I do. After my third book, *The Magic Kerchief,* debuted, I didn't sell anything for five depressing years. One day I was sitting with my grandmother, who'd been overcome by age and Alzheimers. We were folding kitchen towels and she said the oddest thing: 'The only time Mom was ever afraid was in the winter when the wild horses stampeded.' I had no idea what the remark referred to, nor if it was even true, but I had to find out.

"Despite hating history, I immersed myself in genealogy files, national archives, newspapers, and old photos to learn more about my great grandmother, Hattie Inez Brooks, who had homesteaded by herself in eastern Montana. Eventually her story became the inspiration for what I soon realized was my first novel. I wrote and wrote and wrote—through the bad stuff—until I began to find some good stuff. I kept writing. Three years later, thanks to the encouragement of my family and dear writing friends, I sold *Hattie Big Sky* to Delacorte Press. Even if *Hattie Big Sky* hadn't received a 2007 Newbery Honor award, I would feel successful. I am proud of it not because of any awards or reviews, but because it touches other people just like the books I read as a child and budding writer had touched me.

"Now that I'm hard at work on my next picture book, *A Tale of Two Bobbies,* a true story of the friendship between a dog and cat that survived Hurricane Katrina together, I'm rediscovering the process all over again. That's the best part about being a writer . . . and the most frustrating too! There's no secret formula, no one way to go about it. Each book is a new adventure.

"Recently I was visiting a school and a young girl asked me, 'Do you feel lucky to be writing children's books?' I answered with an enthusiastic, 'Yes, I do!' In fact, as long as I can write children's books, I'll live 'happily ever after.'"

Biographical and Critical Sources

PERIODICALS

Booklist, November 1, 1994, Mary Harris Veeder, review of *Second-Grade Pig Pals,* p. 497; April 1, 1996, Kay Weisman, review of *Cody and Quinn, Sitting in a Tree,* p. 1366; August, 2000, Shelle Rosenfeld, review of *The Magic Kerchief,* p. 2148; September 1, 2006, Kathleen Odean review of *Hattie Big Sky,* p. 126.
Bulletin of the Center for Children's Books, December, 1994, Susan Dove Lempke, review of *Second-Grade Pig Pals,* p. 1334; September, 1996, Pat Mathews, review of *Cody and Quinn, Sitting in a Tree,* p. 19; March, 2007, Elizabeth Bush, review of *Hattie Big Sky,* p. 299.

Horn Book, September, 2000, review of *The Magic Kerchief,* p. 551.

Kirkus Reviews, September 1, 2006, review of *Hattie Big Sky,* p. 906.

Kliatt, September, 2006, Claire Rosser, review of *Hattie Big Sky,* p. 14.

Publishers Weekly, September 18, 2000, review of *The Magic Kerchief,* p. 111.

School Library Journal, November, 1994, Janet M. Bair, review of *Second-Grade Pig Pals,* p. 84; April, 1996, Cheryl Cufari, review of *Cody and Quinn, Sitting in a Tree,* p. 113; November, 2006, Sharon Morrison, review of *Hattie Big Sky,* p. 140; July, 2007, Charli Osborne, review of *Hattie Big Sky,* p. 56.

Seattle Times, January 27, 2007, "A Plucky Legacy," p. C1.

ONLINE

Kirby Larson Home Page, http://www.kirbylarson.com (July 20, 2007).

*   *   *

LITTY, Julie 1971-
(Julie Wintz-Litty)

Personal

Born December 27, 1971, in Annecy, France; married; husband a riding instructor; children: three. *Education:* Kunstakademie Lyon, degree (graphic design); École Emil Cohl (Lyon, France), studied illustration. *Hobbies and other interests:* Horseback riding.

Addresses

Home and office—31, route royale, 73100 Aix-les-Bains, France. *E-mail*—julie.litty@wanadoo.fr.

Career

Illustrator and author.

Writings

SELF-ILLUSTRATED

Tyrano et la Cravache magique, translated by Charise Myngheer as *Chloe and the Magic Baton,* Penguin Young Readers (New York, NY), 2006.

ILLUSTRATOR

(Under name Julie Wintz-Litty) Geraldine Elschner, *Mystère et goutte de lait,* Nord-Sud (Saint-Germain en Laye, France), 1996.

(Under name Julie Wintz-Litty) Brigitte Weninger, *Lumina,* Nord-Sud (Saint-Germain en Laye, France), 1997, translated by Anthea Bell as *Lumina: A Story for the Dark Time of the Year,* North-South Books (New York, NY), 1997.

Jane Goodall, *Dr. White,* North-South Books (New York, NY), 1999.

Ute Blaich, *L'etoile de Noël,* Nord-Sud (Saint-Germain en Laye, France), 2001, translated by Sibylle Kazeroid as *The Star,* North-South Books (New York, NY), 2001.

Sidelights

French-born illustrator Julie Litty studied graphic design at the Kunstakademie Lyon and attended the illustration program at Lyon's École Emil Cohl before embarking on her career as a freelance illustrator. Her first picture-book project was creating art for Geraline Elschener's *Mystère et goutte de lait,* which was published in 1996. Praising Litty's watercolor-and-ink art, a *Publishers Weekly* contributor noted that in her illustrations for Jane Goodall's picture book *Dr. White* her "close-up portraits offer a warm contrast with a full range of human (as well as canine) expressions" Litty's holiday-themed art for both Ute Blaich's *The Star* and Brigitte Weninger's *Lumina: A Story for the Dark Time of the Year* also attracted critical praise, Lauren Peterson writing that Litty's "gorgeous, flowing watercolors . . . nicely complement" Weninger's "happily-ever-after holiday story." The artist's "elegant pen-and-ink and watercolor illustrations effectively portray the stark, chilly landscape" in *The Star,* according to a *School Library Journal* contributor. In *The Star* readers are transported via Litty's art to a winter scene on a cold Christmas Eve, as Owl explains to his hungry animal friends that the meaning of Christmas is grounded in love and kindness. Other books featuring Litty's art include *Dr. White,* an animal-centered tale for young children by noted anthropologist Jane Goodall.

After illustrating several books for other authors, Litty took on the dual role of author/illustrator in *Tyrano et la Cravache magique,* a book that has been translated into English as *Chloe and the Magic Baton. Chloe and the Magic Baton* was inspired by its author's love of horseback riding. In fact, Litty is married to a riding teacher, and horseback riding is a favored activity of the Littys as well as their three children. In *Chloe and the Magic Baton,* a girl credits the luck in the riding crop her uncle brought her from Mexico to her achievement in a series of riding competitions. When the crop disappears prior to the championship event, Chloe must rely on her own talents in curbing the behavior of her temperamental pony.

Biographical and Critical Sources

PERIODICALS

Booklist, October 15, 1997, Lauren Peterson, review of *Lumina: A Story for the Dark Time of the Year,* p.

417; May 1, 1999, Susan Dove Lempke, review of *Dr. White,* p. 1599.

Kirkus Reviews, May 1, 2006, review of *Chloe and the Magic Baton,* p. 462.

Publishers Weekly, March 1, 1999, review of *Dr. White,* p. 69.

School Librarian, spring, 1998, review of *Lumina,* p. 22; winter, 2001, review of *The Star,* p. 222.

School Library Journal, November, 1997, Mary M. Hopf, review of *Lumina,* p. 102; March, 1999, Arwen Marshall, review of *Dr. White,* p. 175; October, 2001, review of *The Star,* p. 62; August, 2006, Alice DiNizo, review of *Chloe and the Magic Baton,* p. 91.

ONLINE

Repertoire Web site, http://www.charte.repertoire.free/fr/ (August 10, 2007), "Julie Wintz-Litty."*

*　　*　　*

LOBEL, Gillian

Personal

Born in Coventry, England; married; children: two daughters. *Education:* University of Manchester, degree (English); University of Leicester, postgraduate certificate (education). *Hobbies and other interests:* Arts and crafts, gardening, walking.

Addresses

Home and office—Leicester, England.

Career

Author and private tutor. Formerly worked as an English teacher at comprehensive schools.

Awards, Honors

Children's Book Award shortlist, Federation of Children's Book Groups, 2001, for *Ellie and the Butterfly Kitten;* Bisto Book of the Year Award shortlist, Children's Book Ireland, 2006, for *Fancy That!*

Writings

Starlight, illustrated by Nic Wickens, Tamarind (Camberley, England), 1999.

Ellie and the Butterfly Kitten, illustrated by Karin Littlewood, Orchard (London, England), 2000.

Does Anybody Love Me?, illustrated by Rosalind Beardshaw, Good Books (Intercourse, PA), 2002.

Midnight Tiger, Oxford University Press (Oxford, England), 2003.

More Precious than Gold, Hodder Children's (London, England), 2003.

Little Bear's Special Wish, illustrated by Gaby Hansen, Tiger Tales (Wilton, CT), 2004.

Hazel, Not a Nut, Orchard (London, England), 2004.

Best Daddy in All the World, illustrated by Vanessa Cabban, Orchard (London, England), 2005.

Fancy That!, illustrated by Adrienne Geoghegan, Frances Lincoln Children's Books (London, England), 2005.

Little Honey Bear and the Smiley Moon, illustrated by Tim Warnes, Good Books (Intercourse, PA), 2006.

Too Small for Honey Cakes, illustrated by Sebastien Braun, Harcourt (Orlando, FL), 2006.

Forever Family, Orchard (London, England), 2007.

Sidelights

English children's book author Gillian Lobel made her U.S. debut in 2002 with *Does Anybody Love Me?* Lobel's story is told from the perspective of a little girl named Charlie who has a creative, yet messy, imagination. The story begins when Charlie is reprimanded by her parents for bringing a pile of dirt into the kitchen in order to create a tidal wave for her toy boats. Things get even messier when Charlie simulates a thunderstorm for her boats in the bathroom sink. When the sink floods over onto the floor, Charlie receives still more scolding from her parents. Feeling as though no one appreciates her, Charlie decides to run away into the "the jungle," a place in her backyard where she can escape her parents' anger. Charlie's grandpa ultimately finds a way to bring the girl out of the jungle and back into the house, where she is lovingly welcomed by her parents. A *Kirkus Reviews* critic acknowledged *Does Anybody Love Me?* as a "tale that poignantly depicts the conflict between a child's languorous fantasy world and her parents' harried reality."

Too Small for Honey Cakes is also written from the perspective of a young child and focuses on the jealousy Little Fox experiences when his new sibling arrives at the fox family's den. Little Fox is disappointed by the arrival of the new family member. Although the tiny one is too little to play games, it captures all the attention of Little Fox's father, Daddy Fox. Tired of being ignored, Little Fox hides in the cupboard underneath the stairs where he sings songs that expresses his jealousy. Lulled out of the cupboard by the smell of the honey cakes Daddy Fox bakes, Little Fox eventually comes to terms with his tiny new sibling.

Biographical and Critical Sources

PERIODICALS

Booklist, September 1, 2006, Connie Fletcher, review of *Too Small for Honey Cakes,* p. 138.

Kirkus Reviews, September 15, 2002, review of *Does Anybody Love Me?,* p. 1394; review of *Little Honey Bear and the Smiley Moon,* p. 960; August 15, 2006, review of *Too Small for Honey Cakes,* p. 847.

Publishers Weekly, October 7, 2002, review of *Does Anybody Love Me?,* p. 72.

School Library Journal, February, 2003, Jody McCoy, review of *Does Anybody Love Me?,* p. 115; November, 2006, Andrea Tarr, review of *Little Honey Bear and the Smiley Moon,* p. 99.

ONLINE

World Book Day Web site, http://www.worldbookday.net/ (July 8, 2007), "Gillian Lobel."*

* * *

LÓPEZ, Lorraine M. 1956-

Personal

Born 1956, in Los Angeles, CA; children: Nicholaus. *Education:* California State University, Northridge, B.A.; University of Georgia, M.A., Ph.D. (English).

Addresses

Home—Nashville, TN. *Office*—Department of English, Vanderbilt University, Box 1654, Station B, Nashville, TN 37235. *E-mail*—lorraine.lopez@vanderbilt.edu.

Career

Educator, poet, and fiction-writer. Former middle-school and high-school teacher; Brenau University, Gainesville, GA, former instructor in English; Vanderbilt University, Nashville, TN, currently assistant professor of English. Institute for Violence Prevention, Athens, GA, cofounder and former education programs director.

Awards, Honors

Miguel Marmól Prize for Fiction, Independent Publishers Book Award for Multicultural Fiction, and Latino Book Award for Short Stories, Latino Literary Hall of Fame, all for *Soy la Avon Lady, and Other Stories.*

Writings

Soy la Avon Lady, and Other Stories, Curbstone Press (Willimantic, CT), 2002.
Call Me Henri (young-adult novel), Curbstone Press (Willimantic, CT), 2006.

Contributor of reviews, poetry, and short fiction to periodicals, including *Southern Review Prairie Schooner, U.S. Latino Review, Crab Orchard Review, Watershed Anthology,* and *New Letters.*

Sidelights

In addition to her work as a teacher of English and creative writing in public schools and, more recently, at the university level, Lorraine M. López is also an award-winning fiction writer and poet. Her short fiction, which focuses on transcending differences in class, culture, and race, has appeared in periodicals such as *New Letters* and *Prairie Schooner,* and eleven of her tales have been collected in *Soy la Avon Lady, and Other Stories.* Focusing on the dynamics of modern Chicano culture, *Soy la Avon Lady, and Other Stories* introduces a variety of predominately southwestern characters whose circumstances range from the comic to the tragic. Noting that López "is brilliant in her depiction of extended families," Mary Margaret Benson called the work "superb" in her *Library Journal* review, while *Booklist* critic Carlos Orellana deemed it "vibrant and memorable."

Dealing with differences and the need to fit in is the subject of López's young-adult novel *Call Me Henri.* In the story, middle-schooler Enrique copes with his abusive alcoholic stepfather at home and danger on the streets of his barrio. For Enrique school is a welcome refuge and the way to a better life, but his difficulty in learning the English language threatens his academic success. While language problems could be easily solved, in Enrique's view, by learning French instead of English (hence the book's title), problems elsewhere do not resolve themselves so neatly. When the gang violence escalates, resulting in the death of a good friend and threats on Enrique's own life, his teachers and a special friend help the preteen survive in a novel *School Library Journal* contributor Carol A. Edwards praised for its "admirably human and resilient protagonist."

Cover of Lorraine M. López's young-adult novel, Call Me Henri, *which focuses on a young man's efforts to assimilate into a new culture.* (Curbstone Press, 2006. Reproduced by permission.)

"Although López writes fiction, she delivers a hard-hitting, accurate description of life" as it is lived by many teens, according to a *Kirkus Reviews* writer.

"I often write about incidents that have happened to me or that I have heard about from family or friends," López noted in an interview for the Curbstone Press Web site, "and I invent characters and events as well. Most often I mix what I know has occurred with what I have invented, and the same is true for characters. I may meet a person who has an interesting quality or habit, and I will form a character with the same trait, while inventing other aspects."

Biographical and Critical Sources

PERIODICALS

Booklist, August, 2002, Carlos Orellana, review of *Soy la Avon Lady, and Other Stories,* p. 1922.

Bulletin of the Center for Children's Books, September, 2006, Maggie Hommel, review of *Call Me Henri,* p. 23.

Choice, January, 2003, R.B. Shuman, review of *Soy la Avon Lady, and Other Stories,* p. 826.

Kirkus Reviews, May 1, 2002, review of *Soy la Avon Lady, and Other Stories,* p. 613; May 15, 2006, review of *Call Me Henri,* p. 520.

Library Journal, June 1, 2002, Mary Margaret Benson, review of *Soy la Avon Lady, and Other Stories,* p. 199.

School Library Journal, August, 2006, Carol A. Edwards, review of *Call Me Henri,* p. 123.

Washington Post Book World, October 1, 2006, Elizabeth Ward, review of *Call Me Henri,* p. 8.

ONLINE

Curbstone Press Web site, http://www.curbstone.org/ (July 20, 2007), interview with López.*

M

MacRAE, Tom 1980-

Personal
Born 1980.

Addresses
Home—West London, England.

Career
Television writer and author of children's fiction. Creator of television program *Mile High*.

Awards, Honors
British Academy of Film and Television Arts Award, 2002, for "Off Limits: School's Out"; Parents Choice Silver Honor Award, 2006, for *The Opposite*.

Writings

The Opposite, illustrated by Elena Odriozola, Peachtree (Atlanta, GA), 2006.

Author of teleplay *Growing up Gay: School's Out,* televised in the United Kingdom, and of television film *Marple: At Bertram's Hotel.* Author of episodes for television programs including *Coming Up, Mayo,* and *Doctor Who.*

Sidelights
Television writer Tom MacRae's work has appeared in a number of popular television series, including the award-winning *School's Out* and the long-running cult favorite *Doctor Who.* In 2006, young readers were introduced to MacRae's writing via his first picture book, *The Opposite.* Brought to life in illustrations by Elena Odriozola, MacRae's tale introduces a young boy

Tom MacRae tells a quirky tale about a man shadowed by a determined alterego in **The Opposite,** *featuring artwork by Elena Odriozola.* (Peachtree, 2006. Illustration © 2006 by Elena Odriozola. All rights reserved. Reproduced by permission.)

named Nate, who wakes up to find a creature he calls the Opposite staring down at him from the bedroom ceiling. Throughout the day, the Opposite is Ned's constant companion, and it always does the opposite of whatever Nate asks it to do, which often gets Nate into trouble.

Noting that MacRae's story "begins in mesmerizing fashion," *Washington Post Book World* critic Jabari Asim called *The Opposite* "a wonderfully off-beat tale."

Amanda Craig, writing in the London *Times,* recommended the book's ability to make young ones giggle, calling it "a little gem of contrariness," and a *Publishers Weekly* critic praised MacRae for creating a "diverting debut." Kate Kellaway, writing for the London *Observer,* called the title "a beguiling, wayward book," and *School Library Journal* reviewer Genevieve Gallagher predicted that *The Opposite* "would make an interesting choice for storytime or a discussion of opposites."

Biographical and Critical Sources

PERIODICALS

Kirkus Reviews, August 15, 2006, review of *The Opposite,* p. 848.

Observer (London, England), April 16, 2006, Kate Kellaway, "The Attraction of Opposite," p. 23.

Publishers Weekly, September 11, 2006, review of *The Opposite,* p. 54.

School Library Journal, October, 2006, Genevieve Gallagher, review of *The Opposite,* p. 118.

Sun (London, England), May 10, 2006, Sara Nathan, "My Cyber Nightmare," p. 23.

Times (London, England), March 4, 2006, Amanda Craig, "From the Mundane to the Magical."

Times Educational Supplement, June 16, 2006, Ted Dewan, "The Main Draw," p. 18.

Washington Post Book World, December 10, 2006, Jabari Asim, "Opposites Attract," p. 8.*

*   *   *

MATLIN, Marlee 1965-

Personal

Born August 24, 1965, in Chicago, IL; daughter of Donald and Libby Matlin; married Kevin Grandalski (a police officer), 1994; children: Sarah Rose, Brandon, Tyler, Isabelle Jane Grandalski. *Religion:* Jewish.

Addresses

Office—12300 Wilshire Blvd., Ste. 200, Los Angeles, CA 90025. *Agent*—Spanky Taylor, 3727 W. Magnolia Blvd., Burbank, CA 91505.

Career

Actor and author. Appeared in films, including *Children of a Lesser God,* 1986; *Walker,* 1988; *Bridge to Silence,* 1989; *The Man in the Golden Mask,* 1990; *The Linguini Incident,* 1991; *The Player,* 1992; *Hear No Evil,* 1993; *Against Her Will: The Carrie Buck Story,* 1994; *It's My Party,* 1995; *Dead Silence,* 1996; *Freak City,* 1998; *Where the Truth Lies,* 1999; *Askari,* 2001; and *What the*

Marlee Matlin (Copyright © UPI/Bettmann/Corbis.)

Bleep Do We Know, 2005. Appeared in television programs, including *Reasonable Doubts,* 1991-93; *Seinfeld,* 1993; *Adventures in Wonderland,* 1993; *Picket Fences,* 1993, 1994-96; *Sweet Justice,* 1995; *People in Motion,* 1996; *The Larry Sanders Show,* 1997; *Spin City,* 1997; *ER,* 1998; *Judging Amy,* 1999; *Blue's Clues,* 2000-03; *The Practice,* 2000; *Gideon's Crossing,* 2001; *The Division,* 2002; *Law and Order: SVU,* 2004-05; *Extreme Makeover: The Home Edition,* 2004, 2006; *Desperate Housewives,* 2005; *The West Wing,* 2000-06; *CSI: NY,* 2006; *My Name Is Earl,* 2006; and *The L Word,* 2007. Executive producer of *Where the Truth Lies,* 1999, and *Eddie's Million Dollar Cook-off,* 2003. Involved in the production of *Baby Einstein* DVD series. American Red Cross, spokesperson, 1992; National Volunteer Week, chairperson, 1994.

Awards, Honors

Academy Award for Best Actress, and Golden Globe Award for Best Actress, Drama, both 1987, both for *Children of a Lesser God;* Golden Globe nomination for Best Actress, and People's Choice Award nomination for Favorite Actress, Drama, both 1992-93, both for *Reasonable Doubts;* CableAce nomination for Best Actress in a Miniseries, 1994, for *Against Her Will;*

Emmy Award nominations for *Seinfeld, Picket Fences, The Practice,* and *Law and Order: SVU.*

Writings

Deaf Child Crossing, Simon & Schuster (New York, NY), 2002.
(With Doug Cooney) *Nobody's Perfect,* Simon & Schuster (New York, NY), 2006.
(With Doug Cooney) *Leading Ladies,* Simon & Schuster (New York, NY), 2007.

Sidelights

Widely known as an award-winning film actress, Marlee Matlin is also the author of *Deaf Child Crossing, Nobody's Perfect,* and *Leading Ladies,* novels that help young readers understand what it is like to be deaf. Matlin has a lot of material to draw on: she herself has been deaf since she was eighteen months old. "I must say that the challenges of motherhood, along with working as an actor in Hollywood with a hearing impair-

Cover of **Nobody's Perfect,** *a sequel to* **Deaf Child Crossing** *that was coauthored by Matlin and Doug Cooney.* (Jacket photograph copyright © 2006 by Plush Studios/Getty Images. Reproduced by permission of Simon & Schuster Books for Young Readers, an imprint of Simon & Schuster Macmillan.)

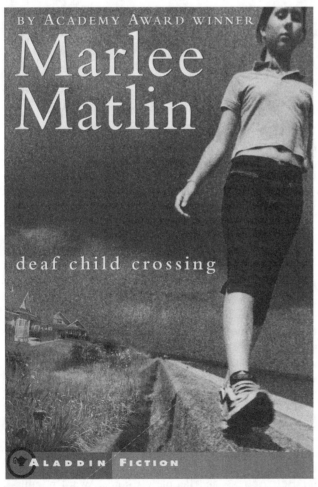

Cover of actress and author Matlin's children's novel **Deaf Child Crossing,** *which finds two girls developing into friends despite their differences.* (Illustration © 2002 by Fran Harper/Photonica. Reproduced by permission of Aladdin Paperbacks, an imprint of Simon & Schuster Macmillan.)

ment, provide food for thought and inspiration for anyone willing to listen to my story," she told Jackie Loohauis of the *Milwaukee Journal Sentinel.* Matlin lives with her husband and four children in Los Angeles, California, where she is actively involved both in her Hollywood career and in various community service organizations.

In *Deaf Child Crossing* readers meet nine-year-old neighbors Megan and Cindy. Megan, who is deaf, is outgoing and enthusiastic while Cindy is shy. Nevertheless, Megan is determined that the two girls will become best friends. A *Kirkus Reviews* contributor found Matlin's first novel to be flawed but promising, and concluded that "Megan's rather unique character begs a sequel . . . for a broader range of readership." "Matlin is at her best when delving into Megan's inner world, such as her heightened sense of smell," commented a *Publishers Weekly* contributor. While noting that the story is loosely based on Matlin's own childhood expe-

riences, Anne O'Malley wrote in *Booklist* that *Deaf Child Crossing* "is as much Cindy's story as Megan's, and readers will identify with both girls' sorrows and successes."

Megan and Cindy's adventures continue in *Nobody's Perfect* and *Leading Ladies,* which Maitlin coauthors with award-winning playwright and novelist Doug Cooney. In the former, Megan tries her hardest to be nice to Alexis, a girl who seems repulsed by Megan's deafness. As she struggles to get to know Alexis, Megan realizes that Alexis has an autistic brother and does not want other students to find out. When Megan teaches Alexis's brother the basics of sign-language, she opens a door to communication for her new friend's family. *Leading Ladies* finds Megan and Cindy vying for the lead role in the school play. "Megan is . . . endearingly sincere," wrote a *Kirkus Reviews* contributor in a review of *Nobody's Perfect,* and Nancy Kim noted in *Booklist* that although audience appeal may be limited, for Matlin's target readers the novel "perfectly captures the intensity of a young girl's life."

Biographical and Critical Sources

PERIODICALS

Booklist, November 15, 2002, Anne O'Malley, review of *Deaf Child Crossing,* p. 598; July 1, 2006, Nancy Kim, review of *Nobody's Perfect,* p. 55.
Bulletin of the Center for Children's Books, November, 2002, review of *Deaf Child Crossing,* p. 116.
Kirkus Reviews, October 1, 2002, review of *Deaf Child Crossing,* p. 1476; May 15, 2006, review of *Nobody's Perfect,* p. 520.
Milwaukee Journal Sentinel, March 29, 1999, Jackie Loohauis, "Marlee Matlin's Courage in Life Paves Way to Success."
Publishers Weekly, September 16, 2002, review of *Deaf Child Crossing,* p. 69; December 22, 2003, John F. Baker, "Actress's YA Series Expands," p. 11.
School Library Journal, August, 2006, Kathleen Kelly MacMillan, review of *Nobody's Perfect,* p. 124.

ONLINE

Celebrity Café Web site, http://thecelebritycafe.com/ (July 5, 2007), Dominick A. Miserandino, interview with Matlin.
iParenting.com, http://iparenting.com/ (July 5, 2007), interview with Matlin.
Marlee Matlin Home Page, http://www.marleematlinsite.com (June 25, 2007).*

*   *   *

McCORMICK, Patricia 1956-

Personal

Born May 23, 1956, in Washington, DC; daughter of A.J. and Ann McCormick; married Paul W. Critchlow (a public-relations specialist), September 11, 1988; children: Meaghan, Matt. *Education:* Rosemont College, B.S., 1978; Columbia University, M.S., 1985; New School for Social Research (now New School University), M.F.A., 1999.

Addresses

Home and office—New York, NY. *E-mail*—Pattymcpushback@aol.com.

Career

Journalist and novelist. *New Brunswick (NJ) I Home News,* crime reporter; *New York Times* children's movie reviewer; *Parents* magazine, children's movie reviewer; freelance writer. Columbia University Graduate School of Journalism, former adjunct professor; New School University, former instructor of creative writing. The Writers Room, New York, NY, board member.

Member

Authors Guild, Society of Children's Book Writers and Illustrators.

Awards, Honors

New York Public Library Books for the Teen Age designation, 2000, Quick Pick for Reluctant Young Adult Readers, American Library Association (ALA), 2001, and Best Book for Young Adults, ALA, 2002, all for *Cut;* New York Public Library Books for the Teen Age designation, 2004, for *My Brother's Keeper;* New York Foundation for the Arts fellowship; Virginia Center for the Creative Arts fellowship; National Book Award finalist in Young People's Literature, National Book Foundation, ALA Best Book of the Year designation, Chicago Public Library Best of the Best listee, New York Public Library Books for the Teen Age designation, Children's Literature Council Choice designation, and *Booklist* Top-Ten Women's History Books for Youth designation, all 2006, all for *Sold.*

Writings

NOVELS

Cut, Front Street Books (New York, NY), 2000.
My Brother's Keeper, Hyperion (New York, NY), 2005.
Sold, Hyperion (New York, NY), 2006.

OTHER

(With Steven Cohen) *Parents' Guide to the Best Family Videos,* St. Martin's Press (New York, NY), 1999.

Contributor of articles to periodicals, including *Ladies' Home Journal, Town & Country, Reader's Digest, More, Mademoiselle, New York Times Book Review,* and *New York Times.* Former contributing editor to *Parents* magazine.

Adaptations

Cut, My Brother's Keeper, and *Sold* were adapted as audiobooks by Listening Library.

Sidelights

In 2000 Patricia McCormick made her entrance into children's literature with her young-adult novel *Cut.* The combination of a *New York Times Magazine* article about young women cutting themselves and the stress then present in her own life sparked in McCormick the idea for a novel about a fifteen-year-old girl in a residential treatment facility who is kept there because she cuts herself in response to the pressures she feels at home. "I kept the article for months, then I finally threw it away," McCormick told Elizabeth Devereaux in *Publishers Weekly.* The author continues her focus on young teens in the novels *My Brother's Keeper* and *Sold,* the latter a finalist for the National Book Award in Young People's Literature.

McCormick wrote *Cut* while working toward her M.F.A. at the New School for Social Research in New York City. "I found myself writing in the voice of a girl, addressing her shrink in a loony bin," the author explained to Devereaux. During the writing process, McCormick resisted the urge to over-research and smother the story and her central character in details. Callie, the protagonist of *Cut,* has chosen to be mute, except to the reader, who is privy to her memories of her family: a severely asthmatic brother, a distracted mother, and a non-coping father. During the course of Callie's narrative, the reader also follows the sequence of events that led to the teen's need to cut herself in order to maintain some semblance of control over her life.

Reviewers found much to praise in *Cut,* particularly its verisimilitude. Writing in *School Library Journal,* Gail Richmond described the novel as "poignant and compelling reading" that avoids pathos and stereotypes." According to a *Publishers Weekly* critic, McCormick does not sensationalize her story, instead presenting a "persuasive view of the teenage experience." "A too-tidy ending notwithstanding, this is an exceptional character study of a young woman," noted *Booklist* reviewer Frances Bradburn. *Horn Book* contributor Lauren Adams also found the story's resolution—and Callie's father's sudden understanding of his daughter's situation—somewhat unrealistic, but nonetheless praised McCormick's "sensitive portrayal of a young girl's illness and her difficult path to recovery." "I'd never understood cutting before I read *Cut,*" wrote Elizabeth Crow in her review of the book for the *New York Times Book Review.* "The story of how Callie and some of the others begin to get well demystifies mental illness, but doesn't oversimplify or sentimentalize it," Crow added. "To McCormick's credit, we care—about the girls and about their clumsy, frightened parents."

"We all do self-destructive or at least self-defeating things—usually at the very times when we need to take

Cover of Patricia McCormick's young-adult novel **Sold**, *which focuses on the resilient spirit of a teen sold into slavery by her family.* (Jacket photograph from back to front: wall texture © Isabelle Rozenbaum/ GettyImages: fabric pattern © Alan Kearney/Getty Images and girl © Philip Reeve/GettyImages. All rights reserved. Reproduced by permission of Hyperion Books for Children.)

the best care of ourselves," McCormick once told *SATA* in discussing her first novel. "Most times, the actions are relatively harmless: locking ourselves out of the house, forgetting an assignment, overdosing on Ben & Jerry's. They hurt us more than they hurt anyone else.

"The challenge in writing Callie's story was to make her experience authentic—to render it as truthfully as I knew how—without rendering her actions in a way that would frighten or offend readers. I hope I've done that. I hope that I've approached her story with empathy and integrity."

Addressing an issue of international scope, *Sold* highlights the sex trade in the villages of India and Nepal through the story of Nepalese teen Lakshmi. To research the novel, McCormick traveled to Kathmandu and interviewed girls, women, and men regarding the system whereby thousands of young women are sold to brothels by family members every year. She tells her story in free verse, which "allowed me to deal with the horror in carefully controlled language," the author explained to *Booklist* interviewer Hazel Rochman. In *Sold*

McCormick's thirteen-year-old heroine is a member of a poor farming family in rural Nepal until her stepfather sells her to a Calcutta brothel called Happiness House in order to make good on a gambling debt. Abused by the brothel's madame, Mumtaz, until she submits to male clients, and living in squalid conditions, Lakshmi narrates her experiences as well as the ironies between her life as a prisoner and the outside world she and her fellow prostitutes see only through television. Noting that McCormick avoids sensationalizing her horrific subject, Rochman praised the author's "beautiful clear prose" and ability to "remain . . . true to the child's viewpoint." *Sold* "is an important story," concluded *Kliatt* contributor Claire Rosser, "and McCormick tells it well." Calling the novel "searing" in her *Horn Book* review, Christine M. Hepperman predicted that "readers will admire Lakshmi's bravery" and cheer as the intervention of American rescuers lifts *Sold* from the realm of tragedy.

McCormick focuses on a male protagonist in *My Brother's Keeper,* which finds baseball fan and high school freshman Toby Malone dealing with his father's abandonment, his distracted mother's love life, and older brother Jake's growing drug-abuse problem. As Toby attempts to keep things from falling further apart by covering for Jake, he also tries to shelter his impressionable younger brother Eli, who is becoming increasingly withdrawn. Toby's first-person narration in *My Brother's Keeper* is "clever and believable," according to *Booklist* contributor Holly Koelling, the critic calling the novel's teen protagonist "a responsible, caring, and appealing kid." "One of the best things in the book is the way McCormick captures Toby's isolation, sadness, [and] desperation," noted Lois Metzger in a review of the book for the *New York Times Book Review,* and a *Publishers Weekly* writer asserted that the storyline "credibly . . . demonstrates why playing the role of enabler ultimately does more harm than good." "McCormick has tackled a tough subject in language teens can grasp," contended Diana Pierce in *School Library Journal,* the critic adding that *My Brother's Keeper* is "written in a realistic and engaging manner and is a good discussion starter."

"When I read stories, I see, or hope to see, aspects of my life reflected in them," McCormick noted to *SATA.* "I'm always looking for answers in the books I read; if not answers, at least somebody who has the same question. I hope a book of mine will be that kind of book for some reader."

Biographical and Critical Sources

PERIODICALS

Booklist, January 1, 2001, Frances Bradburn, review of *Cut,* p. 940; March 15, 2002, review of *Cut,* p. 1228; June 1, 2005, Holly Koelling, review of *My Brother's Keeper,* p. 1786; September 15, 2006, Hazel Rochman, "Daughters for Sale" and review of *Sold,* p. 54.

Bulletin of the Center for Children's Books, January, 2001, review of *Cut,* p. 188; July-August, 2005, review of *My Brother's Keeper,* p. 501; December, 2006, Karen Coats, review of *Sold,* p. 181.

Horn Book, November, 2000, Lauren Adams, review of *Cut,* p. 759; September-October, 2006, Christine M. Heppermann, review of *Sold,* p. 591.

Kirkus Reviews, June 1, 2005, review of *My Brother's Keeper,* p. 640; September 1, 2006, review of *Sold,* p. 908.

Kliatt, May, 2002, Paula Rohrlick, review of *Cut,* p. 20; September, 2006, Claire Rosser, review of *Sold,* p. 15.

New York Times Book Review, November 19, 2000, Elizabeth Crow, "Sounds of Silence," p. 38; October 23, 2005, Lois Metzger, review of *My Brother's Keeper,* p. 20.

Publishers Weekly, October 23, 2000, review of *Cut,* p. 76; December 18, 2000, Elizabeth Devereaux, "Patricia McCormick," p. 26; August 28, 2006, review of *Sold,* p. 55.

School Library Journal, December, 2000, Gail Richmond, review of *Cut,* p. 146; July 11, 2005, review of *My Brother's Keeper,* p. 93; August, 2005, Diana Pierce, review of *My Brother's Keeper,* p. 131; September, 2006, Alexa Sandmann, review of *Sold,* p. 211; April, 2007, review of *Sold,* p. 65.

Voice of Youth Advocates, February, 2001, review of *Cut,* p. 425; February, 2002, review of *Cut,* p. 409; June, 2005, Rollie Welch, review of *My Brother's Keeper,* p. 134; December, 2006, Vikki Terrile, review of *Sold,* p. 428.

ONLINE

Front Street Books Web site, http://www.frontstreetbooks.com/ (February 1, 2002), "Patricia McCormick."

Patricia McCormick Home Page, http://www.pattymccormick.com (July 25, 2007).

*   *   *

MIURA, Taro 1968-

Personal

Born 1968, in Aichi, Japan. *Education:* Osaka University of Arts, degree (silk screen), 1991.

Addresses

Home—Japan. *E-mail*—info@taromira.com.

Career

Illustrator and author of children's books. *Exhibitions:* Works exhibited throughout Japan and at Bologna Illustrators Exhibition, beginning 2001.

Awards, Honors

Exhibition of Japanese Illustration Award, 1990; Nippon Graphic Exhibition Sponsor's Prize, 1990; Chanel Christmas Card Exhibition winner, 1992; Choice award, 2002.

Writings

PICTURE BOOKS

Je Suis . . . , Joie de Lire (Geneva, Switzerland), 2004.

Ton, Edizioni Corraini (Italy), 2004, English translation, Chronicle Books (San Francisco, CA), 2006.

Arnesi/Tools, Edizioni Corraini (Italy), 2005, English translation published as *Tools,* Chronicle Books (San Francisco, CA), 2006.

Kuttuita, Kogumasha (Tokyo, Japan), 2005.

Bokuwamaru, Bronze Publishing (Japan), 2006.

Bokuwasankaku, Bronze Publishing (Japan), 2006.

Des jours pas comme je autres, Joie de Lire (Geneva, Switzerland), 2006.

Erase 21 veces caperucita roja, Media Vaca (Madrid, Spain), 2006.

Tokio, Media Vaca (Madrid, Spain), 2006.

Also illustrator of covers for Japanese text books.

Author's work have been translated into French, Spanish, and Korean.

Biographical and Critical Sources

PERIODICALS

Booklist, November 1, 2006, Carolyn Phelan, review of *Tools,* p. 57.

Kirkus Reviews, May 15, 2006, review of *Ton,* p. 521; August 1, 2006, review of *Tools,* p. 793.

Publishers Weekly, May 15, 2006, review of *Ton,* p. 70.

School Library Journal, September, 2006, Kristine M. Casper, review of *Ton,* p. 194; October, 2006, Martha Simpson, review of *Tools,* p. 120.

ONLINE

Taro Miura Home Page, http://www.taromiura.com (July 17, 2007).*

*   *   *

MONTSERRAT, Pep

Personal

Born in Spain. *Education:* Llotja Art School (Barcelona, Spain), graduated, c. 1988; Eina School (Barcelona), coursework in graphic design.

Addresses

Home—Barcelona, Spain.

Career

Illustrator and author. Edicions de la Magrana (Catalan publisher), art director, 1995-2001; La Massana Arts School, Barcelona, Spain, instructor in illustration, beginning 1998. Creator, with Montse Ganges, of television series *Miniman.*

Awards, Honors

Nacional del Ministerio de Cultura award, 1995; Internacional Catalònia award, 1997; Generalitat de Catalunya award, 1998, for *La mila va a l'escola* by Teresa Durán; Best Illustrated Book for Children Award, 1997, and International Board on Books for Young People Honor List inclusion, 1998, both for *The Gift* by Gabriela Keselman.

Writings

SELF-ILLUSTRATOR

Ms. Rubinstein's Beauty, Sterling (New York, NY), 2006.

ILLUSTRATOR

Gabriela Keselman, *El regalo,* [Barcelona, Spain], 1997, translated by Laura McKenna as *The Gift,* Kane/Miller (Brooklyn, NY), 1999.

Teresa Durán, *La mila va a l'escola* (Catalan), Rústica (Enquadernació, Spain), 1998.

Las tres naranjas de la vida, La Galera (Spain), 1998.

Christine Nostlinger, *Querido señor diablo/Dear Mr. Devil,* Gaviota (Spain), 2001.

Snow White, Circulo de Lectores-Aura, 2003.

Roser Ros, adapter, *The Musicians of Bremen/Los músicos de Bremen,* Chronicle Books (San Francisco, CA), 2005.

Jordi Sierra i Fabra, *Kafka y la muñeca viajera,* Ediciones Siruela (Madrid, Spain), 2006.

Josep Vallverduí, reteller, *Aladdin and the Magic Lamp/ Aladino y la lámpara marvillosa: From The Thousand and One Nights,* Chronicle Books (San Francisco, CA), 2006.

Eric A. Kimmel, *McElderry Book of Greek Myths,* Simon & Schuster (New York, NY), 2007.

Contributor of illustrations to periodicals, including *Avui, La Vanguardia, El País, Chicago Tribune, New York Times, Wall Street Journal, Boston Globe, Woman, Quéleer, Cuerpomente, Ser Padres, New Yorker,* and *Travel & Leisure.*

Sidelights

Pep Montserrat is an illustrator and graphic designer who has also gained an international reputation as a children's book illustrator. A native of Spain, Montserrat attended Barcelona's Llotja Art School and began his career in illustration in the late 1980s. His award-winning artwork, which has appeared in magazines and newspapers both in Europe and North America, is familiar to English-language readers mainly through the pages of children's books such as *The Gift* by Gabriela Keseleman, Eric A. Kimmel's *McElderry Book of Greek Myths,* and the bilingual folk-tale retellings *The Musicians of Bremen/Los músicos de Bremen* and *Aladdin*

Spanish artist Pep Montserrat contributes his stylized folk-art illustrations to Roser Ros's bilingual retelling of The Musicians of Bremen. (Illustrations © 1997 by Pep Montserrat. All rights reserved. Used with permission in North America by Chronicle Books, LLC, San Francisco. Visit www.ChronicleBooks.com. Used with permission in the world by La Gelera Sau Editorial.)

and the Magic Lamp/Aladino y la lámpara marvillosa: From The Thousand and One Nights. In addition to his collaborations with other writers, Montserrat has also gained recognition for the original story he pairs with his unique stylized art in the picture book *Ms. Rubinstein's Beauty.*

A work by Montserrat is immediately recognizable due to its dramatic contrasts, stylized shapes, and modernistic design. Reviewing the artist's work for *The Musicians of Bremen/Los músicos de Bremen* in *School Library Journal,* Ann Welton wrote that the illustrator's "earth-toned acrylics have an almost linocut look and make excellent and arresting use of form and volume"

in bringing to life a classic story about the adventures of four elderly animals. *Booklist* critic Stella Clark had a similar reaction to the work, writing that Montserrat's "simple, elegant" images are "done in vivid yet understated colors, giving the tale a modern feel."

An unusual story that illustrates the adage that "Beauty is in the eye of the beholder" greets readers in *Ms. Rubinstein's Beauty.* In graphic shades of red, black, and tan, Montserrat brings to life the unusual courtship of Mr. Pavlov and Ms. Rubinstein through his stylized art. Although readers never see the characters' full faces until the book's end, they come to know and like both people through their gentle, mannered conversation and

kind actions. Only at story's end do they realize that the growing affection between Mr. Pavlov and Ms. Rubinstein has nothing to do with their physical beauty: Pavlov is a circus elephant man and Ms. Rubinstein is a bearded lady. Children "will find much beauty in these characters, and in their story," concluded *School Library Journal* contributor DeAnn Okamura of the book, which a *Kirkus Reviews* writer dubbed a "valentine [that] celebrates the way true love looks beneath surface irregularities." "Everyone feels like a monster sometimes," Hazel Rochman noted in her *Booklist* review, adding that in *Ms. Rubinstein's Beauty* "even children who begin by laughing" at Montserrat's unusual protagonists will find themselves caught up in "the operatic romance of two outcasts who find each other."

Biographical and Critical Sources

PERIODICALS

Booklist, August, 1997, review of *El regalo,* p. 1913; April 1, 2000, review of *Las tres naranjas de la vida,* p. 1460; November 1, 2005, Stella Clark, review of *The Musicians of Bremen/Los músicos de Bremen,* p. 50; September 1, 2006, Stella Clark, review of *Aladdin and the Magic Lamp/Aladino y la lámpara marvillosa: From The Thousand and One Nights,* p. 124; September 15, 2006, Hazel Rochman, review of *Ms. Rubinstein's Beauty,* p. 71.

Kirkus Reviews, August 15, 2006, review of *Ms. Rubinstein's Beauty,* p. 848.

Publishers Weekly, October 11, 1999, review of *The Gift,* p. 74.

School Library Journal, December, 1999, Ann Welton, review of *The Gift,* p. 100; October, 2005, Ann Welton, review of *The Musicians of Bremen/Los músicos de Bremen,* p. 148; October, 2006, Maria Otero-Boisvert, review of *Aladdin and the Magic Lamp/Aladino y la lámpara marvillosa,* p. 145; January, 2007, DeAnn Okamura, review of *Ms. Rubinstein's Beauty,* p. 100.

ONLINE

Pep Montserrat Home Page, http://www.pepmonsterrat. com (July 15, 2007).*

N

NELSON, Kadir

Personal

Born in Washington, DC; son of Emily-Diane Gunter (a motivational speaker and author); married; children: two daughters. *Education:* Pratt Institute, graduated (with honors).

Addresses

Office—6977 Navajo Rd., Ste. 124, San Diego, CA 92119. *E-mail*—office@kadirnelson.com.

Career

Artist and illustrator. Painter of commissioned works for corporations and publishers, including Dreamworks, Nike, Coca-Cola, and Major League Baseball. Conceptual artist for motion pictures, including *Amistad* and *Spirit: Stallion of the Cimarron. Exhibitions:* Paintings exhibited at galleries and museums, including Simon Wiesenthal Center Museum of Tolerance, Los Angeles, CA; Academy of Motion Pictures and Sciences, Los Angeles; Negro Baseball Museum, Kansas City, MO; Museum of African American History, Detroit, MI; Society of Illustrators, New York, NY; and Center for Culture, Tijuana, Mexico.

Awards, Honors

National Association for the Advancement of Colored People Image Award, 2001, for *Just the Two of Us;* Silver Medal for original art, Society of Illustrators, 2002, for *Under the Christmas Tree;* Coretta Scott King Honor Book designation, American Library Association, 2004, for *Thunder Rose* by Jerdine Nolen; Coretta Scott King Award for Illustration, 2004, and Once upon a World Children's Book Award, Simon Wiesenthal Center, 2005, both for *Ellington Was Not a Street* by Ntozake Shange; Caldecott Honor designation, 2007 for *Moses* by Carole Boston Weatherford.

Kadir Nelson (Photo by David Harrison.)

Illustrator

FOR CHILDREN

Debbie Allen, *Brothers of the Knight,* Dial Books (New York, NY), 1999.

Debbie Allen, *Dancing in the Wings,* Dial Books (New York, NY), 2000.

Deloris Jordan and Roslyn M. Jordan, *Salt in His Shoes: Michael Jordan in Pursuit of a Dream,* Simon & Schuster (New York, NY), 2000.

Jerdine Nolen, *Big Jabe,* HarperCollins (New York, NY), 2000.

Will Smith, *Just the Two of Us,* Scholastic (New York, NY), 2001.

Ann Grifalconi, *The Village That Vanished,* Dial Books (New York, NY), 2002.

Nikki Grimes, *Under the Christmas Tree,* HarperCollins (New York, NY), 2002.

Spike Lee and Tonya Lewis Lee, *Please, Baby, Please,* Simon & Schuster (New York, NY), 2002.

Jerdine Nolen, *Thunder Rose,* Harcourt (San Diego, CA), 2003.

Ntozake Shange, *Ellington Was Not a Street,* Simon & Schuster (New York, NY), 2004.

(With others) Tina Packer, *Tales from Shakespeare,* Scholastic (New York, NY), 2004.

Jerdine Nolen, *Hewitt Anderson's Big Life,* Simon & Schuster (New York, NY), 2005.

Charisse K. Richardson, *The Real Slam Dunk,* Puffin Books (New York, NY), 2005.

Spike Lee and Tonya Lewis Lee, *Please, Puppy, Please,* Simon & Schuster (New York, NY), 2005.

He's Got the Whole World in His Hands, Dial Books for Young Readers (New York, NY), 2005.

Deloris Jordan and Roslyn M. Jordan, *Michael's Golden Rules,* Simon & Schuster (New York, NY), 2006.

Carole Boston Weatherford, *Moses: When Harriet Tubman Led Her People to Freedom,* Hyperion (New York, NY), 2006.

Ellen Levine, *Henry's Freedom Box,* Scholastic Press (New York, NY), 2007.

OTHER

Steven Spielberg, Maya Angelou, and Debbie Allen, *Amistad: "Give Us Free": A Celebration of the Film by Steven Spielberg,* Newmarket Press (New York, NY), 1998.

Illustrations have appeared in *New Yorker, New York Times,* and *Sports Illustrated.*

Sidelights

"Kadir Nelson is an illustrator to watch," declared Janice M. Del Negro in the *Bulletin of the Center for Children's Books.* Nelson, an artist who paints primarily in oils, has seen his work exhibited in galleries and museums throughout the United States and abroad, as well as in publications such as *Sports Illustrated,* the *New York Times,* and the *New Yorker.* Since illustrating his first book, actress and choreographer Debbie Allen's *Brothers of the Knight,* in 1999, he has also gained renown as a children's-book illustrator who often collaborates with celebrity authors, other of whom include actor and rapper Will Smith and film director Spike Lee. In addition to his Caldecott Honor-winning work for Carole Boston Weatherford's *Moses: When Harriet Tubman Led Her People to Freedom,* Nelson has also contributed artwork to such award-winning titles as Nikki Grimes' *Under the Christmas Tree,* Ntozake Shange's *Ellington Was Not a Street,* and Jerdine Nolen's tall-tale picture-book *Thunder Rose.*

Nelson began drawing at the age of three. "I have always been an artist," he remarked on his home page. "It's part of my DNA." At age eleven he spent a summer with his uncle, an artist and art teacher. "He first taught me about perspective, different mediums, color mixing," Nelson explained to *San Diego Union-Tribune* contributor Leigh Fenly. "That was the first time I'd used watercolor with any know-how." At age sixteen he began working in oils, again under the tutelage of his uncle. After graduating from high school, Nelson won an art scholarship to study at the prestigious Pratt Institute in Brooklyn, New York. Immediately upon graduating from Pratt, he garnered job offers from *Sports Illustrated* and the Dreamworks motion-picture studio, and has since received commissions to create images for Nike, Coca-Cola, and Major League Baseball, among others.

Nelson's picture-book debut, *Brothers of the Knight,* is a retelling of the fairy tale "The Twelve Dancing Princesses" that focuses on Reverend Knight, a Harlem preacher with a dozen sons. Each morning, the pastor finds that his sons' shoes are worn to threads. The family's magical housekeeper, Sunday, quickly discovers the boys' secret: they slip out at night to dance at the Big Band Ballroom. *Booklist* critic Ilene Cooper praised *Brothers of the Knight,* remarking that Allen's "snappy text is matched by Nelson's high-energy pictures." According to a *Publishers Weekly* reviewer, Nelson's "sepia-toned illustrations possess the precision of line

Nelson's award-winning art is featured along Ntozake Shange's text in the highly acclaimed picture book **Ellington Was Not a Street.** (Illustration © 2004 by Kadir Nelson. Reprinted with the permission of Simon & Schuster Books for Young Readers, an imprint of Simon & Schuster Children's Publishing Division.)

accorded to pen-and-inks, filled out with a full palette of oil paints." Allen and Nelson collaborated again on *Dancing in the Wings,* in which Sassy dreams of becoming a ballet dancer. Her feelings are hurt, however, by comments about her tall, gangly frame. Finally, with her uncle's encouragement, Sassy auditions for a summer dance festival and impresses the show's director. "Nelson's animated illustrations depict Sassy with a grace that belies her self-image and that effectively foreshadows the accolades to come," stated a contributor to *Publishers Weekly. Booklist* critic Carolyn Phelan observed that Nelson's artwork "clearly shows the characters' attitudes and emotions."

Nelson teamed with Smith for *The Two of Us,* a picture-book adaptation of Smith's hit song "Just the Two of Us." In the work, a father reveals his love, hopes, and dreams for his son. *School Library Journal* reviewer Judith Constantinides complimented the book's "moving pencil-and-oil illustrations," adding that "many of the stunning images are set against a blue sky and conjure up a marvelous atmosphere of spaciousness and freedom." A *Publishers Weekly* contributor wrote that Nelson "effectively conveys the affirming message of the text."

In *Please, Baby, Please,* a book coauthored by Lee and his wife, Tonya Lewis Lee, Nelson's art chronicles a day in the life of a rambunctious two year old whose parents run out of energy long before their child does. A *Kirkus Reviews* critic found much to like in the work, citing Nelson's "richly colored and meticulously detailed paintings" and stating that "the repetitive text, sunny illustrations, and entirely familiar scenarios will make this a favorite of parents and children alike." In an interview with Lynda Jones for *Black Issues Book Review,* coauthor Tanya Lewis Lee commented that Nelson's illustration style is a good match for her text. "In particular, with our book, the baby is so expressive and so alive," Lee stated. "And the colors are so vibrant that you really get a sense of a living, breathing thing. As in his [Nelson's] other work, it's just his fluidity; his subjects just come to life." Nelson rejoins the Lees for *Please, Puppy, Please,* which a *Kirkus Reviews* writer deemed an "exuberant story" in which the artist's "vibrant oil paintings" gain energy from his use of a "wide range of perspectives."

Big Jabe marked the first of several collaborations between Nelson and author Jerdine Nolen. In the work, a young slave named Addy goes to the riverbank and finds a boy floating in a basket. Addy soon realizes that this is no ordinary child: Jabe grows to maturity in a few months, commands fish to jump out of the water, and possesses the strength of fifty men. When several abused slaves disappear from the plantation, Addy suspects Jabe of spiriting them away. "Part magical savior, part tall-tale hero, Big Jabe personifies the triumph of African Americans who . . . escaped from slavery," remarked a *Horn Book* contributor. Reviewing the book for *School Library Journal,* Ellen A. Greever added that "Nelson's watercolor-and-gouache paintings bring the characters fully to life and provide a realistic and his-

torically accurate setting for the fantastic events." A *Publishers Weekly* reviewer held a similar view, observing that the artist's "finely hatched watercolor and gouache illustrations emphasize images of slave life; when he does depict Big Jabe's fantastic feats, his naturalistic style permits him to depict them with an apparent realism, In this way, Nelson supports Nolen in using superhuman elements to distill all-too-human truths."

Nelson and Nolen team up again for *Thunder Rose* and *Hewitt Anderson's Big Life.* In the tall tale *Thunder Rose* an African-American girl born during a thunder storm demonstrates remarkable talents, including the ability to gather lightning into a ball. "Nolen and Nelson offer up a wonderful tale of joy and love, as robust and vivid as the wide West," concluded Andrea Tarr in her review of the book for *School Library Journal.* Nelson's illustrations "capture the Wild West vistas, the textures of grass and homespun cloth, and the character's personalities," wrote *Booklist* critic GraceAnne A. DeCandido. A human-sized boy finds himself living in a family of giants in *Hewitt Anderson's Big Life,* in which Nelson's funny, larger-than-life oil paintings warmly depict [an] . . . African-American family and give readers a real sense of gigantic proportions," according to Mary N. Oluonye in *School Library Journal.*

Nelson's artwork has graced the pages of books by several other authors, as well as bringing to life a traditional American song in *He's Got the Whole World in His Hands.* According to *School Library Journal* contributor Mirian Lang Budin, Nelson's work for Ann Grifalconi's *The Village That Vanished,* about an African village whose residents escape from a band of slave traders, is "wonderfully evocative of place, mood, posture, and expression." Nelson also provided illustrations for *Under the Christmas Tree,* a holiday poetry collection by Nikki Grimes. Winner of the Coretta Scott King Award for Illustration, *Ellington Was Not a Street* is based on author Ntozake Shange's poem "Mood Indigo," and describes her childhood home, where her family was visited by such celebrated figures as Paul Robeson, W.E.B. DuBois, Dizzy Gillespie, and Duke Ellington. Shange's text is "more than matched by Nelson's thrilling, oversize oil paintings," wrote Cooper, describing the book's award-winning art as "a cross between family photo album and stage set." In the words of *San Diego Union-Tribune* contributor Fenly, Nelson's artwork for the book is "most striking in storytelling, composition, and color."

Nelson's art for Weatherford's award-winning *Moses* was inspired by his memories of another strong woman: his own grandmother. The picture-book account of Harriet Tubman's journey from slavery to world-renown abolitionist is highlighted by "Tubman's beautifully furrowed face," which Margaret Bush described as both "expressive and entrancing" in her *School Library Journal* review. The images created by the artist "illuminate both the dire physical and transcendent spiritual journey" Tubman undertook in her work leading hundreds of slaves to freedom prior to the U.S. Civil War, noted a *Kirkus Reviews* contributor. In the *New York Times*

A traditional Negro spiritual comes to life in Nelson's light-filled paintings for **He's Got the Whole World in His Hands.** (Copyright © 2005 by Kadir Nelson. All rights reserved. Reproduced by permission of Dial Books for Young Readers, a division of Penguin Putnam Books for Young Readers.)

Book Review, Rebecca Zerkin wrote that in "panoramic oil paintings [that] evoke the pastoral landscape of 19th-century America," Nelson joins with Weatherford to "push us to feel the scale of [Tubman's] . . . bravery."

Critics often use words like "expressive," "rewarding," and "uplifting" to describe Nelson's art. "My work is all about healing and giving people a sense of hope and nobility," the painter explained on his home page. "I want to show the strength and integrity of the human spirit."

Biographical and Critical Sources

PERIODICALS

Black Issues Book Review, November-December, 2002, Lynda Jones, "The Lees Do the Write Thing," p. 40.

Booklist, November 15, 1999, Ilene Cooper, review of *Brothers of the Knight,* p. 629; November 15, 2000, Carolyn Phelan, review of *Dancing in the Wings,* p. 646; February 1, 2001, Denia Hester, review of *Salt in His Shoes: Michael Jordan in Pursuit of a Dream,* p.

1056; November 1, 2003, GraceAnne A. DeCandido, review of *Thunder Rose,* p. 505; February 15, 2004, Ilene Cooper, review of *Ellington Was Not a Street,* p. 1070; November 1, 2005, Diane Foote, review of *Please, Puppy, Please,* p. 53; October 1, 2005, Carolyn Phelan, review of *He's Got the Whole World in His Hands,* p. 70; February 1, 2007, Ilene Cooper, review of *Henry's Freedom Box,* p. 59, and Candace Smith, review of *He's Got the Whole World in His Hands,* p. 63; March 1, 2007, Julie Cummins, review of *Michael's Golden Rules,* p. 88.

Bulletin of the Center for Children's Books, December, 2000, Janice M. Del Negro, "Rising Star: Kadir Nelson, Illustrator"; February 15, 2004, Ilene Cooper, review of *Ellington Was Not a Street,* p. 1070; March, 2004, Elizabeth Bush, review of *Ellington Was Not a Street,* p. 295; December, 2005, review of *Please, Puppy, Please,* p. 190; November, 2006, Karen Coats, review of *Moses: When Harriet Tubman Led Her People to Freedom,* p. 78; April, 2007, Elizabeth Bush, review of *Henry's Freedom Box,* p. 334.

Childhood Education, September 15, 2001, Jeanie Burnett, review of *Just the Two of Us,* p. 394.

Ebony, September, 1999, review of *Brothers of the Knight,* p. 20.

Horn Book, July, 2000, Joanna Rudge Long, review of *Big Jabe,* p. 440; September-October, 2002, Joanna Rudge Long, review of *The Village That Vanished,* pp. 551-553; November-December, 2006, Michelle H. Martin, review of *Moses,* p. 737; March-April, 2007, Susan Dove Lempke, review of *Henry's Freedom Box,* p. 186.

International Review of African-American Art, Volume 9, number 2, "A Nurturing Romance of Sport."

Kirkus Reviews, October 15, 2002, review of *Please, Baby, Please,* p. 1533; November 1, 2002, review of *Under the Christmas Tree,* p. 1619; September 15, 2003, review of *Thunder Rose,* p. 1180; February 1, 2005, review of *The Real Slam Dunk,* p. 181; August 1, 2005, review of *He's Got the Whole World in His Hands,* p. 855; October 15, 2005, review of *Please, Puppy, Please,* p. 1140; September 1, 2006, review of *Moses,* December 1, 2006, reviews of *Michael's Golden Rules,* p. 1222, and *Henry's Freedom Box,* p. 1223.

New Yorker, November 17, 1997, "Old Wounds."

New York Times Book Review, February 11, 2007, Rebecca Zerkins, review of *Moses,* p. 17.

Publishers Weekly, October 11, 1999, review of *Brothers of the Knight,* p. 76; April 17, 2000, review of *Big Jabe,* p. 79; September 25, 2000, review of *Dancing in the Wings,* p. 116; November 13, 2000, review of *Salt in His Shoes,* p. 103; April 30, 2001, review of *Just the Two of Us,* p. 76; August 26, 2002, review of *The Village That Vanished,* p. 68; October 14, 2002, review of *Please, Baby, Please,* p. 82; December 22, 2003, review of *Ellington Was Not a Street,* p. 59; July 25, 2005, review of *He's Got the Whole World in His Hands,* p. 79; July 31, 2006, review of *Moses,* p. 78; January 1, 2007, review of *Henry's Freedom Box,* p. 49; January 8, 2007, review of *Michael's Golden Rules,* p. 50.

San Diego, October, 2001, Eilene Zimmerman, "Drawing Attention."

School Library Journal, December, 1998, William Byrd, review of *Amistad: "Give Us Free": A Celebration of the Film by Steven Spielberg,* p. 147; October, 1999, Kate McClelland, review of *Brothers of the Knight,* p. 131; June, 2000, Ellen A. Greever, review of *Big Jabe,* p. 122; September, 2000, Kay Bowes, review of *Dancing in the Wings,* p. 184; June, 2001, Jeffrey A. French, review of *Salt in His Shoes,* p. 121, and Judith Constantinides, review of *Just the Two of Us,* p. 129; October, 2002, Maureen Wade, review of *Under the Christmas Tree,* p. 59; December, 2002, Miriam Lang Budin, review of *The Village That Vanished,* p. 97, and Anna DeWind, review of *Please, Baby, Please,* p. 100; September, 2003, Andrea Tarr, review of *Thunder Rose,* p. 186; January, 2004, Mary N. Oluonye, review of *Ellington Was Not a Strett,* p. 122; April, 2005, Nina Lindsay, review of *Ellington Was Not a Street,* p. 56; May, 2005, Mary N. Oluonye, review of *Hewitt Anderson's Great Big Life,* p. 92; September, 2005, Tracy Bell, review of *He's Got the Whole World in His Hands,* p. 193; October, 2006, Margaret Bush, review of *Moses,* March, 2007, Barbara Katz, review of *Michael's Golden Rules,* p. 174, and review of *Henry's Freedom Box,* p. 176.

Sports Illustrated, August 30, 1999, "Leading Off."

ONLINE

Kadir Nelson Home Page, http://kadirnelson.com (July 30, 2007).

HarperTeacher Web site, http://www.harperchildrens.com/ (August 16, 2004), "Kadir Nelson."*

*   *   *

NELSON, S.D.

Personal

Son of a U.S. Army officer. *Ethnicity:* "Norwegian/Lakota." *Education:* Minnesota State University—Moorhead, B.A. (art education), 1972.

Addresses

Home—Flagstaff, AZ.

Career

Artist and children's book writer. Worked as a middle-school art teacher in Flagstaff, AZ. Lecturer to schools on writing and Lakota culture.

Awards, Honors

Oklahoma Book Award finalist, 1998, for *Spider Spins a Story,* by Jill Max; Parent's Choice Gold Award; Spur Story Teller Award, Western Writers of America; American Library Association Notable Book designation; Reading Magic Award, *Parenting* magazine; International Reading Association Notable Book for a Global Society designation.

Writings

SELF-ILLUSTRATED

Gift Horse: A Lakota Story, Harry N. Abrams (New York, NY), 1999.

The Star People: A Lakota Story, Harry N. Abrams (New York, NY), 2003.

Quiet Hero: The Ira Hayes Story, Lee & Low (New York, NY), 2006.

Coyote's Christmas, Harry N. Abrams (New York, NY), 2007.

ILLUSTRATOR

(With others) Jill Max, *Spider Spins a Story: Fourteen Legends from Native America,* Rising Moon (Flagstaff, AZ), 1998.

Joseph Bruchac, *Crazy Horse's Vision,* Lee & Low (New York, NY), 2000.

Joseph Bruchac, *Jim Thorpe's Bright Path,* Lee & Low (New York, NY), 2004.

Anthony F. Aveni, *The First Americans: The Story of Where They Came from and Who They Became,* Scholastic (New York, NY), 2005.

Sidelights

A member of the Standing Rock Sioux tribe of the Dakotas, artist and author S.D. Nelson grew up learning the traditional stories of his Lakota ancestors. "As a boy, my mother told me coyote stories about Iktomi, the Trickster," he recalled on his home page. His career as a children's-book illustrator and author was inspired, in part, by his mother; as Nelson explained, she "taught me at an early age to see the world with both the curious eyes of a child and the wistful eyes of an old man." Books such as *Gift Horse: A Lakota Story* evoke Nelson's childhood memories of summers spent with his family on the Lakota's Standing Rock Reservation, located on the Dakota prairie.

Nelson draws on the stories he learned from his mother for his first self-illustrated picture book, *Gift Horse.* Based on the life of his great-great-grandfather, Flying Cloud, the book follows the efforts of the Lakota warrior to reclaim his horse, Storm, after Storm and several other horses are captured by a Crow raiding party. Nelson's "colorful illustrations fill the pages with striking images of tribal life on the Great Plains," wrote Karen Hutt in a *Booklist* review of *Gift Horse.* Although a *Publishers Weekly* critic noted that Neson's text is spare, the reviewer added that readers "who can adjust to Nelson's quiet approach will find that the story has staying power."

Nelson retells a traditional Lakota story in *The Star People,* as Sister Girl and her brother find themselves caught in a prairie fire. Though they make it to safety, the siblings soon realize that they are lost. Only with the help of the Star People do they ultimately make it home. Nelson's "art enhances the text by blending the supernatural world with that of the children's reality," wrote Linda M. Kenton in *School Library Journal,* while *Booklist* contributor Gillian Engberg praised the author/illustrator's "clear, captivating language."

With *Quiet Hero: The Ira Hayes* story, Nelson moves from traditional story to biography, introducing readers to the Native American Marine who appears in the iconic photograph taken at the World War II battle of Iwo Jima. Portraying Hayes as a hero who never wanted to be celebrated, Nelson begins his biography with Hayes's childhood on a Pima Indian reservation. Moving into the Marine's service in the Pacific theatre through his death at age thirty-two, he parallels his text with illustrations that "obscure . . . the faces of the soldiers in battle, emphasizing their anonymity," according to Jayne Damron in *School Library Journal. Booklist* contributor GraceAnne A. DeCandido wrote that while some of Nelson's images and text seem stiff, "several spreads dynamically capture the fury of war, and the text is readable and informative."

Along with his self-illustrated works, Nelson has illustrated a number of texts by other authors. Collaborating with author Joseph Bruchac, he created *Crazy Horse's Vision,* a picture-book biography of famous Lakota warrior Crazy Horse. "Nelson fills the pages with both action and quiet drama," wrote Karen Hutt in *Booklist.*

S.D. Nelson introduces readers to a Native-American myth in his self-illustrated picture book **The Star People.** (Harry N. Abrams, Inc., 2003. Illustration © 2003 by S.D. Nelson. All rights reserved. Reproduced by permission.)

Cover of Nelson's biographical picture book Quiet Hero, *the story of a Native American who returned from World War II as a national hero.*
(Illustration © 2006 by S.D. Nelson. All rights reserved. Reproduced by permission of Lee & Low Books, Inc.)

According to a *Publishers Weekly* critic, the illustrator "blends contemporary and traditional elements" to create "striking illustrations," and Wendy Lukehart, writing in *School Library Journal,* deemed the collaboration "a fine introduction to a hero long overlooked."

Bruchac and Nelson pair up again to tell the story of Pottowatomie Olympian Jim Thorpe in *Jim Thorpe's Bright Path.* "Nelson switches to a less-stylized, mystical look" in this work, explained a *Kirkus Reviews* contributor, and *Booklist* critic Stephanie Nelson noted that the illustrator's "thickly painted artwork is appropriately muscular and energetic."

When not working on his books, Nelson offers seminars about children's literature and art, as well as about traditional and contemporary Lakota culture. In addition to his illustration work, which appears on book jackets, greeting cards, and CD covers, he also crafts rawhide drums and reproduces traditional beadwork.

Biographical and Critical Sources

PERIODICALS

Black Issues Book Review, September, 2000, Khafre Abif, review of *Crazy Horse's Vision,* p. 79.

Booklist, December 1, 1999, Karen Hutt, review of *Gift Horse: A Lakota Story,* p. 708; May 15, 2000, Karen Hutt, review of *Crazy Horse's Vision,* p. 1747; March 15, 2001, review of *Crazy Horse's Vision,* p. 1378; November 15, 2003, Gillian Engberg, review of *The Star People: A Lakota Story,* p. 602; August, 2004, Stephanie Zvirin, review of *Jim Thorpe's Bright Path,* p. 1938; September 15, 2006, GraceAnne A. DeCandido, review of *Quiet Hero: The Ira Hayes Story,* p. 59.

Bulletin of the Center for Children's Books, September, 2000, review of *Crazy Horse's Vision,* p. 9; December, 2003, Janice Del Negro, review of *The Star People,* p. 160; September, 2004, Elizabeth Bush, review of *Jim Thorpe's Bright Path,* p. 8.

Five Owls, spring, 2004, Michael Levy, review of *The Star People,* p. 83.

Horn Book, July, 2000, review of *Crazy Horse's Vision,* p. 433; September-October, 2006, Betty Carter, review of *Quiet Hero,* p. 608.

Kirkus Reviews, August 15, 2003, review of *The Star People,* p. 1076; April 1, 2004, review of *Jim Thorpe's Bright Path,* p. 325; August 15, 2006, review of *Quiet Hero,* p. 849.

Library Media Connection, April-May, 2006, Rose Kent Solomon, review of *The First Americans,* p. 86.

Publishers Weekly, December 6, 1999, review of *Gift Horse,* p. 76; May 29, 2000, review of *Crazy Horse's Vision,* p. 83.

Reading Teacher, November, 2005, Ally McArdle, review of *Jim Thorpe's Bright Path,* p. 275.

School Librarian, winter, 2003, review of *The Star People,* p. 201.

School Library Journal, July, 2000, Wendy Lukehart, review of *Crazy Horse's Vision,* p. 68; September, 2003, Linda M. Kenton, review of *The Star People,* p. 185; June, 2004, Liza Graybill, review of *Jim Thorpe's Bright Path,* p. 124; September, 2006, Jayne Damron, review of *Quiet Hero,* p. 194.

Voice of Youth Advocates, February, 2006, Beth Gallaway, review of *The First Americans,* p. 507.

ONLINE

Crizmac Art and Cultural Education Materials Web site, http://www.crizmac.com/ (July 5, 2007), "S.D. Nelson."

S.D. Nelson Home Page, http://www.sdnelson.net (July 2, 2007).*

*   *   *

NICKLE, John

Personal

Male. *Education:* University of South Florida, M.F.A., 1983.

Addresses

Home—Brooklyn, NY. *E-mail*—info@johnnickle.net.

Career

Illustrator and author. Curator of art exhibits, beginning 1996. *Exhibitions:* Work exhibited at Society of Illustrators shows, 1987-90, 1998; DFN Gallery, New York, NY, 2002, 2004-05; and Storyopolis, Los Angeles, CA, 2006.

Writings

SELF-ILLUSTRATED

The Ant Bully, Scholastic (New York, NY), 1999.
TV Rex, Scholastic (New York, NY), 2001.
Alphabet Explosion!: Search and Count from Alien to Zebra, Schwartz & Wade (New York, NY), 2006.

ILLUSTRATOR

Judi Barrett, *The Things That Are Most in the World,* Atheneum (New York, NY), 1998.
Judi Barrett, *Never Take a Giraffe to the Movies, and Other Things Not to Do,* Atheneum (New York, NY), 2007.
Kathryn Coombs, adaptor, *Hans-My-Hedgehog* (based on "Hans mein Igel" by the brothers Grimm), Atheneum (New York, NY), 2009.

Adaptations

The Ant Bully was adapted as an animated motion picture by John A. Davis, Warner, c. 2006, and novelized by Benjamin Harper as *The Ant Bully: Revenge of the Ants,* by Quinlan B. Lee as *The Ant Bully: The Great Ant Adventure,* and by Judy Katschke as *The Ant Bully,* all published by Scholastic, 2006.

Sidelights

In addition to creating editorial illustrations for major periodicals, John Nickle has also established a successful career in children's-book publishing. In 1998 his illustrations for his first picture-book project, Judi Barrett's *The Things That Are Most in the World,* prompted a *Publishers Weekly* contributor to praise Nickle's "flamboyant arsenal of colors" and his creation of engaging "oddball critters" to bring to life Barrett's introduction to superlatives. "Nickle adds his own imaginative bits to the mix," wrote Carolyn Phelan in a review of the work for *Booklist,* the critic adding that *The Things That Are Most in the World* would have the greatest appeal among nonsense fans. In addition to collaborating with Barrett on a second book, *Never Take a Giraffe to the Movies, and Other Things Not to Do,* Nickle has also created art for a little-known Grimm brothers fairy tale adapted by Kathryn Coombs.

In addition to illustrations, Nickle also has a talent for writing, and he has created the self-illustrated story *The Ant Bully,* as well as *TV Rex* and *Alphabet Explosion!:*

John Nickle's busy and brightly colored acrylic paintings make learning fun for readers of his picture book Alphabet Explosion! (Illustration © 2006 by John Nickle. All rights reserved. Reproduced by permission of Schwartz & Wade, an imprint of Random House Children's Books, a division of Random House, Inc.)

Search and Count from Alien to Zebra. In addition to being popular with young readers, *The Ant Bully* was adapted as an animated movie starring the voices of well-known actors Julia Roberts and Nicholas Cage. In Nickle's picture-book version, a nerdish-looking boy named Lucas responds to being bullied by a bigger boy named Sid by becoming a bully himself. Left alone to play, he spends his time using a squirt gun to terrorize the ant population in his family's yard. The tiny ants eventually get even, however: shrinking Lucas down to ant size and pulling the boy into an ant hole, they assign him the tasks of a worker ant: finding food, caring for the Queen, and battling predatory spiders. Noting that the author/illustrator "ground[s] his highly imaginative and very funny fantasy in scientific fact—if not always in scientific reality," a *Horn Book* reviewer also cited the inclusion of "wonderfully comic touches" within his brightly colored art. Nickle "credibly anthropomorphizes ant societies, stressing equality and cooperation," according to a reviewer for *Publishers Weekly,* the critic noting the detail in the author/illustrator's "fine-line acrylic illustrations."

Other original works by Nickle include *TV Rex,* in which a sad boy named Rex misses his Grandpa, with whom he used to watch a favorite undersea television drama. Now that the elderly man is gone, Rex watches too much television; so much so that the set ultimately breaks down. Without Grandpa to fix it, Rex realizes that the television is just a useless box; he climbs inside it, crying, and soon his tears have filled the box and

transported him under the sea where a host of amazing adventures await. Comparing Nickle's illustrations to works by popular artist William Joyce, Ilene Cooper added in *Booklist* that the book's "sturdy pictures veer from retro to computer cartoons," and a *Publishers Weekly* contributor dubbed *TV Rex* a "fun flight of fancy" for young television addicts.

In *Alphabet Explosion!* Nickle pairs "fine artwork with a fanciful hunt-and-seek game" that *Booklist* critic Gillian Engberg predicted would appeal to both early and pre-readers. Citing the book's vocabulary-building ability, a *Publishers Weekly* also praised the illustrator's abecedarium, dubbing *Alphabet Explosion!* a "riveting read" that motivates readers to "don their thinking caps without feeling like they are being schooled."

Biographical and Critical Sources

PERIODICALS

Booklist, September 15, 1998, Carolyn Phelan, review of *The Things That Are Most in the World,* p. 234; February 1, 1999, Kathleen Squires, review of *The Ant Bully,* p. 982; January 1, 2001, Ilene Cooper, review of *TV Rex,* p. 970; October 1, 2006, Gillian Engberg, review of *Alphabet Explosion!: Search and Count from Alien to Zebra,* p. 55.

Bulletin of the Center for Children's Books, July, 1998, review of *The Things That Are Most in the World,* p. 387; February, 1999, review of *Things That Are Most in the World,* p. 377; March, 2001, review of *TV Rex,* p. 274.

Horn Book, January, 1999, review of *The Ant Bully,* p. 54.

Kirkus Reviews, August 15, 2006, review of *Alphabet Explosion!,* p. 849.

Publishers Weekly, January 25, 1999, review of *The Ant Bully,* p. 94; February 26, 2001, review of *TV Rex,* p. 86; August 21, 2006, review of *Alphabet Explosion!,* p. 67.

School Library Journal, June, 1998, Anne Knickerbocker, review of *The Things That Are Most in the World,* p. 94; April, 2001, Alicia Eames, review of *TV Rex,* p. 119; September, 2006, Suzanne Myers Harold, review of *Alphabet Explosion!,* p. 194.

ONLINE

John Nickle Home Page, http://johnnickle.net (July 20, 2007).*

P-R

PITZER, Susanna 1958-

Personal

Born October 28, 1958, in KS; father a veterinarian. *Education:* Wichita State University, graduated; attended University of Kansas, School of Visual Arts, and Art Students League. *Hobbies and other interests:* Playing piano and guitar, tap dancing, collecting marbles.

Addresses

Home—New York, NY. *E-mail*—susanna@susannapitzer.com; spitzer@nyc.rr.com.

Career

Author and illustrator of children's books. Actress and playwright with Seem to Be Players (children's theatre company), Lawrence, KS; Visible Theatre, New York, NY, writing mentor and playwright; also worked as a managing editor, copywriter, advertising executive, television production assistant, scriptwriter, and creative-arts therapist. Conducts writing, art, and acting workshops in schools throughout the United States.

Member

Society of Children's Book Writers and Illustrators, Children's Book Illustrators Group, Kansas Center for the Book.

Awards, Honors

Golden Kite Award, 2006, Kansas Notable Book designation, and International Reading Association/Children's Book Council Children's Choice designation, both 2007, and North Carolina Picture Book Award nomination, 2008, all for *Not Afraid of Dogs*.

Writings

PICTURE BOOKS

Grandfather Hurant Lives Forever, illustrated by Kyra Teis, Centering Corporation (Omaha, NE), 2001.

Susanna Pitzer (Photograph courtesy of Susanna Pitzer.)

Not Afraid of Dogs, illustrated by Larry Day, Walker & Co. (New York, NY), 2006.

Also author of plays produced in Lawrence, KS, including *Monsters in the Closet,* 1983; *A Fairy's Tale,* 1994; *The Adventures of Ballerina Bunny,* 1995; *Traveling through Dreams,* 1995; *Grimm Sisters,* 1996, revised, 2007; *Can You Hear the Talking Dog?,* 1997; *Cinderella,* 1997; *The Tale of Jemima Puddleduck* (adaptation), 1997; and *Mystery at Ghastly Hall!*

ILLUSTRATOR

Earl Grollman, *Talking about Divorce and Separation,* Centering Corporation (Omaha, NE), 2005.

Dorothy Ferguson, *A Bunch of Balloons,* Centering Corporation (Omaha, NE), 2006.

Sidelights

Playwright and children's book creator Susanna Pitzer grew up in Kansas, and although she now lives in New York City, she returns to the Midwest frequently, both to visit with friends and family and meet with school groups. In addition to writing and illustrating books for young readers, Pitzer is also a playwright. Her works have been produced by Lawrence, Kansas's children's theatre troupe the Seem to Be Players since the mid-1980s, and she penned the play produced during the troupe's thirty-fifth anniversary season in 2007.

Pitzer's best-known book for children, *Not Afraid of Dogs,* features illustrations by Larry Day and was published in 2006. Winner of the Golden Kite Award, the book was actually inspired by Zzazu, one of the three Shetland sheepdogs that share Pitzer's home. In the story, a young boy named Daniel is fearless when it comes to many things, but dogs make him uncomfortable. Although the boy hides his fear from his older sister by saying that he does not like dogs, the arrival of Bandit, a pup belonging to Daniel's vacationing aunt, forces Daniel into hiding in his bedroom. The boy gets over his fear later that night when, during a loud thunder storm, he emerges from his room to comfort the nervous pup. Calling *Not Afraid of Dogs* an "appealing story [told] with simplicity and restraint," *Booklist* contributor Carolyn Phelan predicted that Pitzer's story will encourage young readers who harbor similar fears of their own. Daniel's nervousness is "sensitively handled," a *Kirkus Reviews* writer concluded, adding

that "a dog's ability to win over the heart of a caring human" is captured in both Pitzer's text and Day's pen-and-ink and watercolor illustrations.

Biographical and Critical Sources

PERIODICALS

Booklist, June 1, 2006, Carolyn Phelan, review of *Not Afraid of Dogs,* p. 88.
Horn Book, July-August, 2006, Jennifer M. Brabander, review of *Not Afraid of Dogs,* p. 429.
Kirkus Reviews, May 15, 2006, review of *Not Afraid of Dogs,* p. 522.
School Library Journal, July, 2006, Kathleen Kelly MacMillan, review of *Not Afraid of Dogs,* p. 84.

ONLINE

Susanna Pitzer Home Page, http://www.susannapitzer.com (July 20, 2007).

*　　*　　*

QUINTANO, D.M.
See SHELDON, Dyan

*　　*　　*

REDLICH, Ben 1977-

Personal

Born May 23, 1977, in Brisbane, Queensland, Australia. *Hobbies and other interests:* Painting, sculpting, puppetry, animation, music, nostalgia.

Addresses

Home and office—Brisbane, Queensland, Australia. *E-mail*—benredlich@froggy.com.au.

Career

Freelance illustrator, cartoonist, and filmmaker. Also works as a church cleaner.

Awards, Honors

Joey's R-2 Kanga Award, 2005, for *The Great Montefiasco.*

Writings

SELF-ILLUSTRATED

Who Flung Dung?, Meadowside (London, England), 2006.

ILLUSTRATOR

Andy Small, *The Shikker Co-La Cows,* privately published (Australia), 2000.

Susanna Pitzer's bold, brightly colored paintings feature simple lines that carry a humorous message. (Illustration courtesy of Susanna Pitzer.)

Damien Broderick, *Jack and the Aliens,* Word Weavers Press (Brisbane, Queensland, Australia), 2002.

Damien Broderick, *Jack and the Skyhook,* Word Weavers Press (Brisbane, Queensland, Australia), 2003.

Mark Svendsen, *Ratface and Snake Eyes,* Lothian Books (Melbourne, Victoria, Australia), 2003.

Mark Svendsen, *Shadow Snake,* Lothian Books (Melbourne, Victoria, Australia), 2004.

Colin Thompson, *The Great Montefiasco,* Lothian Books (Melbourne, Victoria, Australia), 2004, Star Bright Books (New York, NY), 2005.

Rowley Monkfish, *Nicholas and the Chronoporter,* Penguin Australia (Camberwell, Victoria, Australia), 2005.

Mark Svendsen, *Circus Carnivore,* Lothian Books (Melbourne, Victoria, Australia), 2005, Houghton Mifflin (Boston, MA), 2006.

Adrienne Frater, *Pet Palace,* Lothian Books (Melbourne, Victoria, Australia), 2006.

Alan Sunderland, *Octavius O'Malley and the Mystery of the Exploding Cheese,* HarperCollins Australia (Pymble, New South Wales, Australia), 2006.

Mark Svendsen, *Whacko the Chook,* Lothian Books (Melbourne, Victoria, Australia), 2007.

Biographical and Critical Sources

PERIODICALS

Courier-Mail (Brisbane, Queensland, Australia), May 14, 2005, Patrick Watson, "Success Is Absolute Nonsense."

Kirkus Reviews, December 15, 2004, review of *The Great Montefiasco,* p. 1209; August 15, 2006, review of *Circus Carnivore,* p. 853.

Library Media Connection, August-September, 2005, Pam Watts Flavin, review of *The Great Montefiasco,* p. 72.

Publishers Weekly, February 7, 2005, review of *The Great Montefiasco,* p. 60.

School Library Journal, November, 2006, Genevieve Gallagher, review of *Circus Carnivore,* p. 114.

ONLINE

Ben Redlich Home Page, http://www.benredlich.com (July 18, 2007).*

*   *   *

ROSEN, Michael 1946-
(Michael Wayne Rosen)

Personal

Born May 7, 1946, in Harrow, Middlesex, England; son of Harold (a professor) and Connie Ruby (a college lecturer) Rosen; married Elizabeth Susanna Steele, 1976 (divorced, 1987); married Geraldine Clark, 1987 (divorced, 1997); companion of Emma-Louise Williams; children: (first marriage) Joseph Steele, Eddie Steele (deceased); (second marriage) Isaac Louis; (step-daughters) Naomi Imogen Hill, Laura Clark; (with Williams) Elsie Lavender Ruby. *Education:* Attended Middlesex Hospital Medical School, 1964-65, and National Film School, 1973-76; Wadham College, Oxford, B.A. (English language and literature), 1969; University of Reading, M.A. (children's literature; with distinction), 1993; University of North London, Ph.D., 1997. *Politics:* Socialist. *Religion:* Atheist. *Hobbies and other interests:* "Watching Arsenal F.C."

Addresses

Home and office—49 Parkholme Rd., London E8 3AQ, England. *Agent*—Peter, Fraser & Dunlop Group, Ltd., Drury House, 34-43 Russell St., London WC2B 5HA, England. *E-mail*—michael@michaelrosen.co.uk.

Career

Writer, poet, educator, playwright, performer, and broadcaster. Host and guest on British Broadcasting Corporation (BBC) television and radio shows, including *Meridian Books, Treasure Islands,* 1988-89, *Best Worlds,* and *Word of Mouth,* beginning 1998. Writer-in-residence at schools in London, England; lecturer at universities and colleges in the United Kingdom and Canada. Presenter at conferences in the United Kingdom, Australia, United States, Canada, Singapore, and Italy; performer at venues in the United Kingdom, including the Shaw Theatre, National Theatre, Edinburgh Book Festival, and BBC Children's Poetry Festival. Political candidate representing the Respect Coalition, c. 2006.

Member

National Union of Journalists.

Awards, Honors

Best Original Full-Length Play Award, London *Sunday Times* National Union of Students Drama Festival, 1968, for *Backbone; Signal* magazine Poetry Award, 1982, for *You Can't Catch Me!;* Other Award, *Children's Book Bulletin,* 1983, for *Everybody Here;* British Book Award runner-up, 1989; Nestlé Smarties Best Children's Book of the Year Award and *Boston Globe/Horn Book* Award, both 1990, and Japanese Picture Book Award, 1991, all for *We're Going on a Bear Hunt;* Cuffies Award for best anthology, *Publishers Weekly,* 1992, and Best Book Award, National Association of Parenting Publications, 1993, both for *Poems for the Very Young;* Glennfiddich Award for best radio program on the subject of food, 1996, for *"Treasure Islands* Special: Lashings of Ginger Beer";* Eleanor Farjeon Award for distinguished services to children's literature, 1997; Play and Learn Award, *Parent* magazine, 1998, for *Snore;* Talkies Award for best poetry audiotape of the year, 1998, for *You Wait till I'm Older than You;* International Reading Association Teachers' Choice selection, 1999, for *Classic Poetry;* Sony Radio Academy Silver Award, 2000,

for radio feature "Dr. Seuss: Who Put the Cat in the Hat?," and Gold Award, 2003, for "On Saying Goodbye"; English Association Exceptional Award, 2004, and *Boston Globe/Horn Book* Nonfiction Honor Book designation, 2006, both for *Michael Rosen's Sad Book;* honorary doctorate, Open University, 2005; National Literacy WOW Award, 2005, for *Alphabet Poem;* appointed Children's Laureate of Great Britain, 2007-09.

Writings

FOR CHILDREN

Once There Was a King Who Promised He Would Never Chop Anyone's Head Off, illustrated by Kathy Henderson, Deutsch (London, England), 1976.

She Even Called Me Garabaldi, BBC Books (London, England), 1977.

The Bakerloo Flea, illustrated by Quentin Blake, Longman (London, England), 1979.

Nasty!, illustrated by Amanda Macphail, Longman (London, England), 1982, revised edition, Puffin (Harmondsworth, England), 1984.

How to Get out of the Bath, and Other Problems, illustrated by Graham Round, Scholastic (New York, NY), 1984.

Hairy Tales and Nursery Crimes, illustrated by Alan Baker, Deutsch (London, England), 1985.

You're Thinking about Doughnuts, illustrated by Tony Pinchuck, Deutsch (London, England), 1987.

Beep Beep! Here Come—The Horribles!, illustrated by John Watson, Walker (London, England), 1988.

Jokes and Verses, illustrated by Quentin Blake, BBC Books (London, England), 1988.

Norma and the Washing Machine, illustrated by David Hingham, Deutsch (London, England), 1988.

Silly Stories (jokes), illustrated by Mik Brown, Kingfisher (London, England), 1988 revised as *Michael Rosen's Horribly Silly Stories,* 1994, revised as *Off the Wall: A Very Silly Joke Book,* Kingfisher (New York, NY), 1994.

The Class Two Monster, illustrated by Maggie King, Heinemann (London, England), 1989.

The Deadman Tapes, Deutsch (London, England), 1989.

The Royal Huddle and *The Royal Muddle,* illustrated by Colin West, Macmillan (London, England), 1990.

Clever Cakes, illustrated by Caroline Holden, Walker (London, England), 1991.

Burping Bertha, illustrated by Tony Ross, Andersen (London, England), 1993.

Moving, illustrated by Sophy Williams, Viking (New York, NY), 1993.

Songbird Story, illustrated by Jill Down, Frances Lincoln (London, England), 1993.

The Arabian Frights and Other Gories, illustrated by Chris Fisher, Scholastic (London, England), 1994.

Dad, illustrated by Tony Ross, Longman (Harlow, England), 1994, Sundance (Littleton, MA), 1997.

Figgy Roll, illustrated by Tony Ross, Longman (Harlow, England), 1994, published as *Dad's Fig Bar,* Sundance (Littleton, MA), 1997.

Lisa's Letter, illustrated by Tony Ross, Longman (Harlow, England), 1994, Sundance (Littleton, MA), 1997.

Even Stevens, F.C., illustrated by John Rogan, Collins (London, England), 1995.

This Is Our House, illustrated by Bob Graham, Candlewick Press (Cambridge, MA), 1996.

Norma's Notebook, illustrated by Tony Ross, Sundance (Littleton, MA), 1997.

(Author of text) *I Want to Be a Superhero,* score by Robert Kapilow, G. Schirmer (New York, NY), 1998.

Snore!, illustrated by Jonathan Langley, HarperCollins (London, England), 1998.

Mission Ziffoid, illustrated by Arthur Robins, Walker (London, England), Candlewick Press (Cambridge, MA), 1999.

Rover, illustrated by Neal Layton, Bloomsbury (London, England), Random House (New York, NY), 1999.

Lunch Boxes Don't Fly, illustrated by Korky Paul, Puffin (London, England), 1999.

A Thanksgiving Wish, illustrated by John Thompson, Blue Sky Press (New York, NY), 1999.

Lovely Old Roly, illustrated by Pricilla Lamont, Frances Lincoln (London, England), 2002.

One Push, illustrated by Martin Olsson, Storycircus.com, 2002.

Oww!: A Wriggly Piglet with a Prickly Problem, illustrated by Jonathan Langley, HarperCollins (London, England), 2003, Trafalgar, 2005.

Howler, illustrated by Neal Layton, Bloomsbury (London, England), 2003, Bloomsbury (New York, NY), 2004.

Michael Rosen's Sad Book, illustrated by Quentin Blake, Candlewick Press (Cambridge, MA), 2005.

Fantastically Funny Stories, illustrated by Mik Brown, Kingfisher (Boston, MA), 2005.

Totally Wonderful Miss Plumberry, illustrated by Chinlun Lee, Candlewick Press (Cambridge, MA), 2006.

Bear's Day Out, illustrated by Adrian Reynolds, Bloomsbury Children's Books (New York, NY), 2007.

Contributor of short fiction to *Round about Six,* edited by Kaye Webb, Frances Lincoln (London, England, 1993.

Author's works have been translated into numerous languages, including Albanian, Bengali, Gujarati, Somali, and Welsh.

POETRY; FOR CHILDREN

Mind Your Own Business, illustrated by Quentin Blake, Deutsch (London, England), 1974.

Wouldn't You Like to Know, illustrated by Quentin Blake, Deutsch (London, England), 1977, revised edition, Penguin (Harmondsworth, England), 1981.

Bathtime, BBC Books (London, England), 1979.

(With Roger McGough) *You Tell Me,* illustrated by Sara Midda, Kestrel (London, England), 1979.

You Can't Catch Me!, illustrated by Quentin Blake, Deutsch (London, England), 1981, reprinted, 1996.

Quick, Let's Get out of Here, illustrated by Quentin Blake, Deutsch (London, England), 1983.

Smacking My Lips, illustrated by Quentin Blake, Puffin (London, England), 1983.

Don't Put Mustard in the Custard, illustrated by Quentin Blake, Deutsch (London, England), 1985.

Chocolate Cake, illustrated by Amelia Rosato, BBC Books (London, England), 1986.

When Did You Last Wash Your Feet?, illustrated by Tony Pinchuck, Deutsch (London, England), 1986.

The Hypnotiser, illustrated by Andrew Tiffen, Deutsch (London, England), 1988.

We're Going on a Bear Hunt, illustrated by Helen Oxenbury, Walker (London, England), 1989, Aladdin (New York, NY), 1992.

Freckly Feet and Itchy Knees, illustrated by Sami Sweeten, Doubleday (New York, NY), 1990.

Never Mind!, BBC Books (London, England), 1990.

Little Rabbit Foo Foo, illustrated by Arthur Robins, Simon & Schuster (New York, NY), 1990.

Who Drew on the Baby's Head?, Deutsch (London, England), 1991.

Mind the Gap, Scholastic (London, England), 1992.

Nuts about Nuts, illustrated by Sami Sweeten, Collins (London, England), 1993.

The Best of Michael Rosen, illustrated by Quentin Blake, RDR Books (Oakland, CA), 1995.

Michael Rosen's ABC, illustrated by Bee Wiley, Macdonald (London, England), 1996.

You Wait till I'm Older than You, illustrated by Shoo Rainer, Viking (London, England), 1997.

The Michael Rosen Book of Nonsense, illustrated by Clare Mackie, Wayland Macdonald (Brighton, England), 1997.

Tea in the Sugar Bowl, Potato in My Shoe, illustrated by Quentin Blake, Walker (London, England), 1998.

Centrally Heated Knickers, illustrated by Harry Horse, Puffin (London, England), 1999.

Even More Nonsense from Michael Rosen, illustrated by Clare Mackie, Hodder (London, England), 2000.

Views of Notley Green, photographs by Ed Clark, Design Council (London, England), 2000.

Uncle Billy Being Silly, illustrated by Korky Paul, Puffin (London, England), 2001.

No Breathing in Class, illustrated by Korky Paul, Puffin (London, England), 2003.

Alphabet Poem, illustrated by Herve Tullet, Milet (London, England), 2004.

Something's Drastic (collection), illustrated by Tim Archbold, Collins (London, England), 2007.

Also author of *Zoo at Night,* illustrated by Bee Willey, Tradewind Books (Vancouver, British Columbia, Canada). Contributor of poetry to educational materials.

RETELLINGS; FOR CHILDREN

A Cat and Mouse Story, illustrated by William Rushton, Deutsch (London, England), 1982.

The Wicked Tricks of Till Owlyglass, illustrated by Fritz Wegner, Walker (London, England), 1989.

Peter Pan, illustrated by Francesca Rovira, Firefly (Hove, England), 1989.

Aladdin, illustrated by Jose M. Lavarello, Firefly (Hove, England), 1989.

Alice in Wonderland, illustrated by Francesca Rovira, Firefly (Hove, England), 1989.

Cinderella, illustrated by Agusti Ascensio, Firefly (Hove, England), 1989.

The Three Little Pigs, illustrated by Agusti Ascensio, Firefly (Hove, England), 1989.

Goldilocks and the Three Bears, illustrated by Jose M. Lavarello, Firefly (Hove, England), 1989.

Hansel and Gretel, illustrated by Francesca Rovira, Firefly (Hove, England), 1989.

Little Red Riding Hood, illustrated by Jose M. Lavarello, Firefly (Hove, England), 1989.

Snow White, illustrated by Agusti Ascensio, Firefly (Hove, England), 1989.

The Little Tin Soldier, illustrated by Agusti Ascensio, Firefly (Hove, England), 1990.

The Princess and the Pea, illustrated by Francesca Rovira, Firefly (Hove, England), 1990.

Sinbad the Sailor, illustrated by Francesca Rovira, Firefly (Hove, England), 1990.

The Golem of Old Prague, illustrated by Val Biro, Deutsch (London, England), 1990, illustrated by Brian Simons, Five Leaves (Nottingham, England), 1997.

How the Animals Got Their Colours: Animal Myths from around the World, illustrated by John Clementson, Harcourt (New York, NY), 1992.

The First Giraffe, illustrated by John Clementson, Studio Editions (London, England), 1992, published as *How Giraffe Got Such a Long Neck . . . and Why Rhino Is So Grumpy,* Dial (New York, NY), 1993.

The Old Woman and the Pumpkin, illustrated by Bob Hewis, Learning by Design (London, England), 1994.

The Man with No Shadow (based on a story by Adelbert von Chamisso), illustrated by Reg Cartwright, Longmans (London, England), 1994, published as *The Man Who Sold His Shadow,* 1998.

Crow and Hawk: A Traditional Pueblo Indian Story, illustrated by John Clementson, Harcourt (New York, NY), 1995.

Two European Tales, illustrated by Barry Wilkinson and Gwen Touret, Pearson Education (Harlow, England), 2001.

A Jewish Tale, Longman (Harlow, England), 2002.

Shakespeare's Romeo and Juliet, illustrated by Jane Ray, Candlewick Press (Cambridge, MA), 2004.

"SCRAPBOOK" SERIES; POETRY AND PROSE COLLECTIONS; FOR CHILDREN

Smelly Jelly Smelly Fish, illustrated by Quentin Blake, Prentice-Hall (New York, NY), 1986.

Under the Bed, illustrated by Quentin Blake, Prentice-Hall (New York, NY), 1986.

Hard-Boiled Legs, illustrated by Quentin Blake, Prentice-Hall (New York, NY), 1987.

Spollyollydiddilytiddlyitis, illustrated by Quentin Blake, Walker (London, England), 1987, published as *Down at the Doctor's: The Sick Book,* Simon & Schuster (New York, NY), 1987.

NONFICTION; ADAPTED FROM SPANISH; FOR CHILDREN

Fear, the Attic, illustrated by Agusti Ascensio, Firefly (Hove, England), 1989.

Friendship, the Oar, illustrated by H. Elena, Firefly (Hove, England), 1989.

Imagination, the Tree, illustrated by Conxita Rodriguez, Firefly (Hove, England), 1989.

Intelligence, the Formula, illustrated by Carme Peris, Firefly (Hove, England), 1989.

Shyness, Isabel, illustrated by F. Infante, Firefly (Hove, England), 1989.

Lying, the Nose, illustrated by Carme Peris, Firefly (Hove, England), 1989.

"ZOOMABABY" SERIES; FOR CHILDREN

Zoomababy and the Great Dog Chase, illustrated by Caroline Holden, Longman (Harlow, England), 2002.

Zoomababy and the Locked Cage, illustrated by Caroline Holden, Longman (Harlow, England), 2002.

Zoomababy and the Mission to Mars, illustrated by Caroline Holden, Longman (Harlow, England), 2002.

Zoomababy and the Rescue, illustrated by Caroline Holden, Longman (Harlow, England), 2002.

Zoomababy and the Search for the Lost Mummy, illustrated by Caroline Holden, Longman (Harlow, England), 2002.

Zoomababy at the World Cup, illustrated by Caroline Holden, Longman (Harlow, England), 2002.

EDITOR; FOR CHILDREN

Everybody Here, (miscellany), Bodley Head (London, England), 1982.

(With Susanna Steele) *Inky Pinky Ponky: Children's Playground Rhymes,* illustrated by Dan Jones, Granada (London, England), 1982.

(With David Jackson) *Speaking to You,* Macmillan (London, England), 1984.

(With Joan Griffiths), *That'd Be Telling,* Cambridge University Press (Cambridge, England), 1985.

The Kingfisher Book of Children's Poetry, illustrated by Alice Englander, Kingfisher (London, England), 1985.

A Spider Bought a Bicycle, and Other Poems for Young Children, illustrated by Inga Moore, Kingfisher (Boston, MA), 1986.

The Kingfisher Book of Funny Stories, illustrated by Tony Blundell, Kingfisher (London, England), 1988.

Culture Shock, Viking (London, England), 1990.

Stories from Overseas/Histoires d'Outre-Mer, Ges-editions (Paris, France), 1990.

Give Me Shelter, Bodley Head (London, England), 1991.

A World of Poetry, Kingfisher (London, England), 1991.

Minibeasties, illustrated by Alan Baker, Firefly (Hove, England), 1991, published as *Itsy-Bitsy Beasties: Poems from around the World,* Carolrhoda Books (Minneapolis, MN), 1992.

Sonsense Nongs, illustrated by Shoo Rayner, A & C Black (London, England), 1992.

South and North, East and West: The Oxfam Book of Children's Stories, Candlewick (Cambridge, MA), 1992.

Action Replay, Anecdotal Poems, illustrated by Andrzej Krauze, Viking (London, England), 1993.

Poems for the Very Young, illustrated by Bob Graham, Kingfisher (London, England), 1993, Kingfisher (Boston, MA), 1994.

Rude Rhymes II, Signet (New York, NY), 1994.

Pilly Soems, illustrated by Shoo Rayner, A & C Black (London, England), 1994.

A Different Story: Poems from the Past, English and Media Centre (London, England), 1994.

Rap with Rosen, Longmans (London, England), 1995.

Walking the Bridge of Your Nose, illustrated by Chloe Cheese, Kingfisher (London, England), 1996.

The Secret Life of Schools, Channel 4 Learning (London, England), 1997.

Classic Poetry: An Illustrated Collection, illustrated by Paul Howard, Candlewick Press (Cambridge, MA), 1998.

Night-Night, Knight, and Other Poems, illustrated by Sue Heap, Walker (London, England), 1998.

Poems Are Crazy, Longman (Harlow, England), 2002.

Poems Are Noisy, Longman (Harlow, England), 2002.

Poems Are Pictures, Longman (Harlow, England), 2002.

Poems Are Private, Longman (Harlow, England), 2002.

Poems Are Public, Longman (Harlow, England), 2002.

Poems Are Quiet, Longman (Harlow, England), 2002.

NONFICTION; FOR ADULTS

Did I Hear You Write?, illustrated by Alan Pinchuck, Deutsch (London, England), 1989.

Goodies and Daddies: An A-Z Guide to Fatherhood, Murray (London, England), 1991.

(Coauthor) *Holocaust Denial: The New Nazi Lie,* Anti-Nazi League (London, England), 1992.

(With Jill Burridge) *Treasure Islands II: An Adult Guide to Children's Writers,* BBC Books (London, England), 1992.

Just Kids: How to Survive the Twos to Tens, illustrated by Caroline Holden, John Murray (London, England), 1995.

(And editor, with Myra Barrs) *A Year with Poetry: Teachers Write about Teaching Poetry,* Centre for Language in Primary Education (London, England), 1997.

(With Simon Elmes) *Word of Mouth,* Oxford University Press (Oxford, England), 2002.

ANTHOLOGIES; FOR ADULTS

Rude Rhymes, illustrated by Riana Duncan, Deutsch (London, England), 1989, revised edition reprinted with *Dirty Ditties* and *Vulgar Verses,* Signet (London, England), 1992.

Dirty Ditties, (also see above), illustrated by Riana Duncan, Deutsch (London, England), 1990.

Vulgar Verses, (also see above), illustrated by Riana Duncan, Deutsch (London, England), 1991.

(With David Widgery) *The Chatto Book of Dissent,* Chatto & Windus (London, England), 1991.

Penguin Book of Childhood, Penguin (New York, NY), 1994.

Rude Rhymes Two, Signet (London, England), 1994.

POETRY; FOR ADULTS

Bloody L.I.A.R.S., illustrated by Alan Gilbey, privately printed, 1984.

You Are, Aren't You?, Jewish Socialist Group and Mushroom Bookshop (Nottingham, England), 1993.

The Skin of Your Back, Five Leaves Press (Nottingham, England), 1996.

Selected Poems, Penguin (Harmondsworth, England), 2007.

OTHER

Stewed Figs (play), produced at Oxford University, 1966.

Backbone (play; produced at Oxford University, 1967; produced on the West End, 1968), Faber (London, England), 1968.

Regis Debray (radio play), BBC-Radio 4, 1971.

I See a Voice (on poetry), Thames Television-Hutchinson (London, England), 1981.

Mordecai Vanunu: A Reconstruction (play), performed at Hackney Empire, October, 1993.

Pinocchio in the Park (play), produced in London, England, 2001.

Shakespeare: His Work and His World (nonfiction), illustrated by Robert Ingpen, Candlewick Press (Cambridge, MA), 2001, revised and abridged as *What's So Special about Shakespeare?,* Walker (London, England), 2007.

Carrying the Elephant: A Memoir of Love and Loss, Penguin (London, England), 2002.

This Is Not My Nose: A Memoir of Illness and Recovery, Penguin (London, England), 2004.

Dickens: His Work and His World (nonfiction), illustrated by Robert Ingpen, Candlewick Press (Cambridge, MA), 2005, revised and abridged as *What's So Special about Dickens?,* Walker (London, England), 2007.

Contributor to books, including *There's a Poet behind You!,* edited by Morag Styles and Helen Cook, A & C Black (London, England), 1988; *After Alice: Exploring Children's Literature,* edited by Morag Styles, Victor Watson, and Eve Bearne, Cassell (London, England), 1992; and *Tales, Tellers, and Texts,* edited by Gabrielle Cliff Hodges, Mary Jane Drummind, and Morag Styles, Cassell, 2000. Contributor to periodicals, including London *Guardian, Books for Keeps,* London *Daily Telegraph, Signal, Times Educational Supplement,* and *Children's Literature in Education.*

Author and presenter of radio programs for BBC Radio 4, BBC Radio 3, BBC World Service, and BBC Schools Radio, 1970—, including "*Treasure Islands* Special: Lashings of Ginger Beer" and "Dr. Seuss: Who Put the Cat in the Hat?" Author of scripts for television series, including *The Juice Job,* Thames TV, 1981, 1984; *You Tell Me,* Thames TV, 1982; *Everybody Here,* BBC Channel 4, 1982; *Black and White and Read All Over,* BBC Channel 4, 1984; and *Talk Write Read,* Central TV, 1986. Editor of video scripts, including *Why Poetry, Mike Rosen, Count to Five and Say I'm Alive, Poetry Workshop,* and *A Poet's Life.* Author of five plays about grandparenting for British Social Action Unit, BBC Radio, 2000.

Adaptations

Many of Rosen's books were adapted for audiocassette, read by the author, including *The Bakerloo Flea, You Can't Catch Me, Quick, Let's Get out of Here, Hairy Tales and Nursery Crimes, Don't Put Mustard in the Custard, Sonsense Nongs, The Wicked Tricks of Till Owlyglass, You Wait till I'm Older than You,* and *Centrally Heated Knickers.*

Sidelights

As *School Librarian* critic Margaret Meek proclaimed, anyone "who has seen Michael Rosen on TV, at work with children in school," or reading to children "testifies to his Pied Piper magic with words." Rosen's love of words, his talent for combining them in fresh and exciting ways, and his delightful ability to speak words the way a child would speak them has made him one of England's most popular children's storytellers and poets. It also contributed to his appointment as child's laureate in his native Great Britain in 2007. Describing *The Best of Michael Rosen,* a collection of over sixty poems from Rosen's work, *Booklist* contributor Carolyn Phelan praised the author for his "excellent descriptions of childhood experiences, sharp insights into people, and . . . humor." Citing his picture books and other writings as well, an essayist in the *St. James Guide to Children's Writers* asserted that "Rosen's poetry ha[d] become almost a school institution" in Great Britain by the late twentieth century. The "humor, accessibility, and child's-eye view" of Rosen's verse "has not only brought children into its spell but has enabled them to enter the world of poetry more widely," the essayist concluded. "That poetry's profile is now higher in schools than in the past, despite the odds currently stacked against it, is due in no small measure to him."

Rosen's love of words is reflected in his enthusiasm for compiling or creating anecdotes, jokes, songs, folk tales, fairytales, vignettes, and nonsense verse in books such as *Action Replay, Anecdotal Poems* and *That'd Be Telling.* Rosen's habit of collecting stories—or parts of them—is also apparent in his prose works, such as *You're Thinking about Doughnuts* and *The Deadman Tapes,* each of which contain several stories within the larger plot. As Rosen once told *SATA,* some "people are worried about whether what I write is 'poetry.' If they are worried, let them call it something else, for example, 'stuff.'"

Rosen realized the importance of following his own muse after reading twentieth-century Irish author James Joyce's unconventional novel *Portrait of the Artist as a*

Young Man as a teenager. "That book really came home to me," he told an interviewer for *Language Matters.* "It was really quite extraordinary, because for the first time I realized that you could actually play around with different ways of saying something. So, for example, you could do a stream of consciousness or you could write about things that happened to you when you were six, and you could do it in the voice of a child of six. So I became absolutely fascinated by this idea and I started to write a few things of that sort."

In college, Rosen developed an interest in drama, and one of his plays was performed at London's Royal Court theatre. A study of the poems his mother selected for a British Broadcasting Corporation (BBC) program she helped produce inspired him to combine his interests in drama and verse and write poems for radio and television programs. Although his poems quickly made the air waves, it took longer for them to find a home on the printed page. As Rosen recalled in *Language Matters,* publishers rejected his submissions, "saying that 'Children don't like poems written from the child's point of view.'" That dictum would be proved wrong in 1974 when an editor at Deutsch paired Rosen's verse with quirky drawing by illustrator Quentin Blake and *Mind Your Own Business* was published.

Since publication of *Mind Your Own Business,* Rosen's reputation for writing nonsense verse and humorous dialogue has steadily grown. According to *Times Educational Supplement* critic Edward Blishen, reviewing the early collections *You Can't Catch Me!* and *Wouldn't You Like to Know,* Rosen's talent lies in his ability to show "how far from being ordinary are the most ordinary of events." Such events are the subjects of the humorous *You Can't Catch Me!,* as one poem finds a father and child teasing one another, another ponders the joy of sailing, and still another focuses on the fear of the dark. Like *You Can't Catch Me!, Wouldn't You Like to Know* focus on relationships, fears, and simple joys. Noting the compatibility of the Blake/Rosen collaboration, a reviewer for *Junior Bookshelf* concluded that *You Can't Catch Me!* is a "gorgeous book," and a *Junior Bookshelf* contributor wrote of *Wouldn't You Like to Know* that Rosen's verse gives young teens "comforting insights into the problems that can make adults so troublesome."

The free-verse poems in *Quick, Let's Get out of Here* recall the events, episodes, and special moments of childhood: fights, birthday parties, tricks and schemes, and the like. As Helen Gregory related in *School Library Journal,* Rosen evokes emotions ranging from the "hysteria of silly joking" to "the agony of breaking a friend's toy." *Horn Book* contributor Ann A. Flowers remarked that, with its "irrepressible" and "outrageous" poems, *Quick, Let's Get out of Here* is a "far cry" from more traditional childhood classics. *You Wait till I'm Older than You* continues Rosen's poetic take on childhood with his characteristic "originality, authenticity, wit and affection," in the opinion of a *Books for Keeps*

contributor. Noting that the collection "fully lives up to expectations," *School Librarian* reviewer Diane Broughton also had praise for the "moments of poignancy" provided by a series of verses recalling Rosen's own childhood, as well as for Shoo Rayner's "appealing" pen-and-ink illustrations. While the compilation volume *Tea in the Sugar Bowl, Potato in My Shoe* was considered too brief at only twenty-two pages of text and illustrations, *New Statesman* reviewer Michael Glover nonetheless dubbed the volume "a beautiful piece of work and an exemplary piece of publishing."

Rosen's ability to bring smiles to the faces of his young readers through rhyme also manifests itself in collections of silly verses and songs. *Freckly Feet and Itchy Knees* presents a list of body parts, describes their owners, and explains their functions in rhythmic verse. Before the end of the book, children are encouraged to wiggle and jiggle their own body parts. In the opinion of a *Publishers Weekly* reviewer, *Freckly Feet and Itchy Knees* is "always lighthearted" and "ideal for reading aloud." *Nuts about Nuts* contains another list set to rhyme, but this time the focus is on food: sweets like ice cream, cake, and honey as well as staples like bread, eggs, nuts, and rice are, as a *Junior Bookshelf* critic noted, "celebrated and examined." The English alphabet also comes in for a humorous reworking by Rosen in *Michael Rosen's ABC,* as easily recognizable characters like Goldilocks, Rudolph the Red-nosed Reindeer, Humpty Dumpty, King Kong, and actor Charlie Chaplin team with well-known objects beginning with various letters of the alphabet to parade before readers in what *School Library Journal* contributor Tania Elias characterized as "tongue-twisting" fashion. Describing the text as a "glorious glut of alliterative nonsense," Jill Bennett noted in her *Books for Keeps* review of *Michael Rosen's ABC* that the collection is "peppered with wondrous words."

The works in *Sonsense Nongs*—eight ballads, parodies, and silly songs written by Rosen with contributions from children—are meant to be sung out loud. According to a *Junior Bookshelf* reviewer, *Sonsense Nongs* may help children gain a "deeper understanding of language as well as much fun and laughter." Children may also sing the words to Rosen's *Little Rabbit Foo Foo,* which is based on a children's finger-play song in which Little Rabbit Foo Foo bops his helpless victims on the head. Judith Sharman testified in *Books for Keeps* that her son found *Little Rabbit Foo Foo* so charming that she had to "sneak" the book away from him while he slept in order to write her review of it.

In addition to original verses, Rosen has also edited several volumes of poetry for young listeners. *Walking the Bridge of Your Nose* includes traditional and composed poems that "play with words, their sounds and their spellings, [and] their punctuations," according to *Junior Bookshelf* contributor Marcus Crouch. Readers will relish the puns, tongue twisters, chants, and quips Rosen serves up while "demonstrating the peculiarities

and foolishness of the English language," Judith Constantinides noted in a *School Library Journal* review of the work. Other edited anthologies include *The Kingfisher Book of Children's Poetry,* which contains 250 poems, the multi-volume "Poems Are" books, and *Classic Poetry: An Illustrated Collection,* in which Rosen couples brief biographies of noted English-language poets from William Shakespeare to Langston Hughes with selections from their works. Containing over eighty poems, *Classic Poetry* "reaffirms the English poetry canon familiar to students throughout the English-speaking world since the 1940s," explained a *Magpies* contributor of the historic overview.

In addition to verse, Rosen is well known for his picture-book texts for pre-and beginning readers. In

This Is Our House, a cardboard box takes on a new life to a group of playground friends and a young boy learns an important lesson about acceptance, resulting in what a *Kirkus Reviews* critic dubbed "a persuasive and entertaining morality play" that reflects the way children think and learn. Praising the "clear and engaging manner" in which Rosen evokes the insecurity and other feelings at the root of discrimination, *School Library Journal* reviewer Steven Engelfried added that the author includes "no lectures in the text," leaving the young protagonists to "work out the problem on their own using actions rather than speeches." "Rosen has an instinctive feel for the way children confront one another, ponder, negotiate and form alliances," concluded a *Publishers Weekly* contributor, the critic adding that "every word" of Rosen's text "rings true."

Michael Rosen captures the relationship between a young girl and her inspiring teacher in **Totally Wonderful Miss Plumberry,** *a book featuring Chinlun Lee's engaging cartoon art.* (Illustration © 2006 by Chinlun Lee. All rights reserved. Reproduced by permission of the publisher Candlewick Press, Inc., Cambridge, MA on behalf of Walker Books Ltd., London.)

Other picture books by Rosen include *Rover* and its sequel, *Howler,* as well as *Mission Ziffoid, We're Going on a Bear Hunt, Michael Rosen's Sad Book,* and *Totally Wonderful Miss Plumberry.* Featuring entertaining art by Neal Layton, both *Rover* and its follow-up overturn the usual perspective on children and their pets as the dog narrates the accounts of life with his pet humans. *Rover* finds the customs of his human pets Rex and Cindy odd: at the seashore, for example, they run around and then lay down and play dead, while at home they stare for hours at a loud box rather than playing with toys. In *Howler,* when Cindy grows visibly larger, Rover is concerned; when she leaves home and then returns several days later with a small, loud, and prune-like creature the dog quickly names Howler, the pup goes from concerned to dismayed. However, a friendship with a neighborhood dog named Ruff Ruff results in a litter of puppies and ultimately Rover rebuilds his relationship with his human family. Barbara James praised *Rover* as "bright and breezy" in tone in her review for *Magpies,* adding that young children "will enjoy the leap of imagination of seeing humans from a dog's point of view." In *Kirkus Reviews,* a contributor described *Howler* as a "lively, equally droll follow-up to *Rover.*"

Rosen spins an offbeat story in *Mission Ziffoid,* as a boy builds a faulty spaceship and winds up in the center of a football game played by small, greenish alien beings . . . at least, according to the ship-builder's little brother. Praising the text as "laconic and hilarious," a *Magpies* reviewer noted that the story's "imaginative flights of fancy" result from Rosen's care in listening "to young children telling cumulative yarns." Calling *Mission Ziffoid* "a natural readaloud with a generous dose of kid-pleasing hilarity," Janice M. Del Negro added in her review for the *Bulletin of the Center for Children's Books* that "the text zips right along," fueled by Arthur Robins' over-the-top, neon-colored illustrations.

Many children will recognize the story in Rosen's multi-award-winning picture book *We're Going on a Bear Hunt,* which is based on a traditional British children's song. Eager to find a bear, a young family wades through mud, water, grass, and snow and braves the dangers of a forest, a river, and a cave. As they meet each obstacle, they make their way through the muck with joyful chants. When the family finally finds the bear, the creature scares them so much that they turn around and hurry back through each obstacle. As Elizabeth S. Watson commented in *Horn Book,* Rosen's text has "a driving rhythm" and "new sounds" that give the familiar tale added "sparkle." Another joyous experience is at the heart of *Totally Wonderful Miss Plumberry,* which focuses on Molly and the teacher who, even in a bustling classroom, takes the time to share the girl's enthusiasm for a special treasure. Calling Rosen "spot-on in addressing emotions," a *Kirkus Reviews* contributor noted his ability to transform quicksilver mood changes into metaphors children will immediately relate to.

While the characters in *We're Going on a Bear Hunt* and *Totally Wonderful Miss Plumberry* are optimistic and upbeat, *Michael Rosen's Sad Book* focuses on the other end of the emotional spectrum. Featuring a spare text and scribbly pen-and-wash illustrations by Blake, the book is an intensely personal one—it was inspired by the author's depression following the death of his teenaged son, Eddie. Reviewing *Michael Rosen's Sad Book* in *Booklist,* Ilene Cooper addressed the question of whether the work was appropriate for children. "To think that [it is not] would be to dismiss the truth we all try to hide from," Cooper hastened to add. "Sadness is part of the human condition. Children know this as well as adults and perhaps feel it even more keenly since they haven't had as much time to develop defenses." "Rosen's poetic revelation of his conflicting emotions and coping strategies will resonate with—and help—anyone mourning a loss or dealing with an indefinable sadness," added a *Publishers Weekly* of the work, while *Horn Book* reviewer Joanna Rudge Long found the conclusion to be "upbeat but not jarringly so." Noting the value of *Michael Rosen's Sad Book* for anyone "who's seriously depressed or grieving," Long described Rosen and Blake's collaboration "a beautiful, solacing book."

Rosen's ability to capture, in few words, a range of emotion pairs with Quentin Blake's line art in the highly acclaimed **Michael Rosen's Sad Book.** (Illustration © 2004 by Quentin Blake. All rights reserved. Reproduced by permission of the publisher Candlewick Press, Inc., Cambridge, MA on behalf of Walker Books Ltd., London.)

Robert Ingpen contributes his artistic talents to Rosen's detailed profile of one of the most popular English writers of all time in **Shakespeare: His Work and His World.** (Illustration © 2001 by Robert Ingpen. All rights reserved. Reproduced by permission of the publisher Candlewick Press, Inc., Cambridge, MA on behalf of Walker Books Ltd., London.)

Rosen's treatment of folktales is tempered by his respect for their origins. Described by *School Library Journal* contributor Lee Bock as "lively" and "bright," *How Giraffe Got Such a Long Neck . . . and Why Rhino*

Is So Grumpy is his version of an Eastern and Southern African *porquoi* tale that tells how Giraffe—originally a small beast—and the much larger Rhino implore Man to help them survive the drought. Although Man in-

structs Giraffe and Rhino to visit him the next day for help reaching the leaves high in the trees, Rhino does not arrive on time, and Giraffe eats his portion of Man's remedy as well as her own. As a result, Giraffe's neck grows long. Rhino, who feels cheated, only grows grumpy.

The Golem of Old Prague collects stories concerning the legendary Rabbi Loeb of Prague and tell how the rabbi creates a golem—a huge, strong, but mindless creature—out of clay and gives him life. With the help of the powerful and loyal golem, Rabbi Loeb ensures the Jewish community's survival when they are persecuted by the monk Thaddeus. Writing in *Books for Your Children,* S. Williams concluded that *The Golem of Old Prague* "gives insight to Jewish thinking, customs, and way of life" in sixteenth-century Prague.

South and North, East and West: The Oxfam Anthology of Children's Stories, which Rosen edited, is a collection of twenty-five stories that includes tales from Cyprus, Korea, the Dominican Republic, Bangladesh, China, Jamaica, Malta, Vietnam, and England. Betsy Hearne, writing in the *Bulletin of the Center for Children's Books,* found these retellings to be "fresh and colloquial." The royalties from *South and North, East and West* benefit Oxfam, the international organization that establishes self-help development programs in countries disrupted by natural or man-made disasters.

Rosen's work for older children and teenagers frequently addresses serious issues. His poetry collection *When Did You Last Wash Your Feet?,* for example, deals with topics from racism to terminal illness. *Mind the Gap,* a collection of poems Sue Rogers described in *School Librarian* as "brilliant," features "comic, sad," and "controversial" all at once, including one verse that recalls the past as the narrator's mother is dying. *Books for Keeps* critic Adrian Jackson advised librarians to buy many copies, predicting that "teenagers will love it." In *Culture Shock,* a collection of poems Rosen selected from around the world, racism, sexism, love, and hate are also addressed.

Like Rosen's more serious poetry, several of Rosen's novels contain serious undertones. *The Deadman Tapes* presents a series of stories within a larger plot. When Paul Deadman plays some tapes he has found in the attic of his new house, he is introduced to the voices and stories of eight troubled teens. With occasional interruptions from Paul, these stories make up the novel's text. The short novel *You're Thinking about Doughnuts* also contains several stories, in this case told from strange perspectives. Frank, who is just eight years old, must wait in the dark halls of the museum where his mother works every Friday night. One night, the exhibits, including a skeleton, a space suit, several Greek statues, and a stuffed tiger, come alive. As these exhibits tell Frank about their lives before they were taken to the quiet museum, Rosen also injects questions about the

"honesty and integrity of an institutional building like a museum," according to *School Librarian* contributor Tom Lewis.

Like his poetry, Rosen's prose for older children often develops around episodes and anecdotes, calls upon his performer's love of dialogue, and insightfully expresses the perspectives of his protagonist. In one example, the story collection *Nasty!* is narrated by a talkative Cockney cleaning woman known as the Bakerloo Flea Woman. She tells the story of the giant Bakerloo flea, recalls how wasps plagued the residents of London's East End one winter, and remembers how they dealt with the mice that invaded their homes. Rosen's love of drama, as well as his appreciation for literature, are also apparent in his biographies of two literary giants. Featuring highly detailed paintings by Robert Ingpen, both *Shakespeare: His Work and His World* and *Dickens: His Work and His World* put two influential English writers into a cultural context that makes each man come alive for readers, while also retelling several major works by each man. Reviewing *Dickens* in *Booklist,* Cooper called Rosen's retelling of the nineteenth-century novelist's life "a tale as gripping as any of his [Charles Dickens'] stories," and a *Kirkus Reviews* writer dubbed *Shakespeare* "beautiful and engaging."

Rosen enjoys sharing the techniques that have made him a successful children's writer. He has published books on writing such as *Did I Hear You Write?,* and also visits schools and libraries. He revealed one of the secrets of his unique style to *Language Matters:* "What I try to do in my mind is to go back and write about my feelings when I was ten. . . . I write about my experience using the voice of a ten year old. I write in that voice, using what I know as a performer will work, knowing, that is, what children can take off a page." Discussing the opportunities that the position as children's laureate would provide, he told *Bookseller* interviewer Caroline Horn: "I have been doing performance poetry for 30 years and I know how children respond to it. You look at their faces when you start and it's like an infection—it spreads across their face, through their bodies, around them. They move, they light up. Wouldn't it be lovely to see more and more of that?"

Biographical and Critical Sources

BOOKS

Children's Literature Review, Volume 45, Thomson Gale (Detroit, MI), 1997, pp. 127-152.

Language Matters, Centre for Language in Primary Education (London, England), 1983.

Nettell, Stephanie, editor, *Meet the Authors,* Scholastic (New York, NY), 1994.

Powling, Chris, *What It's Like to Be Michael Rosen,* Ginn (Oxford, England), 1990.

St. James Guide to Children's Writers, 5th edition, St. James Press (Detroit, MI), 1999.

Styles, Morag, and Helen Cook, editors, *There's a Poet behind You,* A & C Black (London, England), 1988.

PERIODICALS

Booklist, December 1, 1993, Elizabeth Bush, review of *How Giraffe Got Such a Long Neck . . . and Why Rhino Is So Grumpy,* p. 695; December 15, 1993, Julie Corsaro, review of *Moving,* p. 766; January 1, 1994, Carolyn Phelan, review of *Poems for the Very Young,* p. 821; April 15, 1995, Karen Hutt, review of *Crow and Hawk: A Traditional Pueblo Indian Story,* p. 1503; February 1, 1996, Carolyn Phelan, review of *The Best of Michael Rosen,* p. 929; November 1, 1996, Carolyn Phelan, review of *This Is Our House,* p. 510; June 1, 1997, Kathleen Squires, review of *Michael Rosen's ABC,* p. 1712; January 1, 1999, Carolyn Phelan, review of *Classic Poetry: An Illustrated Collection,* p. 862; July, 1999, Stephanie Zvirin, review of *Rover,* p. 1953; November 1, 2001, John Peters, review of *Shakespeare: His Work and His World,* p. 477; December 1, 2003, Hazel Rochman, review of *Shakespeare's Romeo and Juliet,* p. 659; May 15, 2005, Ilene Cooper, review of *Michael Rosen's Sad Book,* p. 1658; September 15, 2005, Ilene Cooper, review of *Dickens: His Work and His World,* p. 62; August 1, 2006, Ilene Cooper, review of *Totally Wonderful Miss Plumberry,* p. 96.

Bookseller, June 15, 2007, Caroline Horn, interview with Rosen.

Books for Keeps, May, 1992, Judith Sharman, review of *Little Rabbit Foo Foo,* p. 11; September, 1992, Adrian Jackson, review of *Mind the Gap,* p. 13; March, 1996, Jill Bennett, review of *Michael Rosen's ABC,* p. 28; January, 1997, review of *You Wait till I'm Older than You,* p. 25; September, 1999, review of *Rover,* p. 21.

Books for Your Children, spring, 1991, S. Williams, review of *The Golem of Old Prague,* p. 24.

Bulletin of the Center for Children's Books, December, 1992, Betsy Hearne, review of *South and North, East and West,* pp. 121-122; June, 1999, Deborah Stevenson, review of *Rover,* p. 363; November, 1999, Janice M. Del Negro, review of *Mission Ziffoid,* pp. 104-105; April, 2005, Deborah Stevenson, review of *Michael Rosen's Sad Book,* p. 355; March, 2006, April Spisak, review of *Dickens,* p. 325.

Horn Book, June, 1984, Anne A. Flowers, review of *Quick, Let's Get out of Here,* p. 345; December, 1989, Elizabeth S. Watson, review of *We're Going on a Bear Hunt,* p. 765; September-October, 1993, Maeve Visser Knoth, review of *How Giraffe Got Such a Long Neck . . . and Why Rhino Is So Grumpy,* p. 611; July-August, 1996, Margaret A. Bush, review of *This Is Our House,* p. 454; May-June, 2005, Joanna Rudge Long, review of *Michael Rosen's Sad Book,* p. 313.

Junior Bookshelf, February, 1982, review of *You Can't Catch Me!,* p. 22; October, 1992, review of *Sonsense Nongs,* p. 201; June, 1993, review of *Nuts about Nuts,* p. 100; June, 1995, pp. 93-94; April, 1996, Marcus Crouch, review of *Walking the Bridge of Your Nose,* p. 71; October, 1996, review of *You Can't Catch Me,* p. 194; December, 1996, review of *Wouldn't You Like to Know,* pp. 259-260.

Kirkus Reviews, June 1, 1996, review of *This Is Our House,* p. 829; October 15, 2001, review of *Shakespeare,* p. 149; November 15, 2003, review of *Shakespeare's Romeo and Juliet,* p. 1363; April 15, 2004, review of *Howler,* p. 400; January 15, 2005, review of *Michael Rosen's Sad Book,* p. 125; April 1, 2005, review of *Oww!: A Wriggly Piglet with a Prickly Problem,* p. 423; September 15, 2005, review of *Dickens,* p. 1033; August 15, 2006, review of *Totally Wonderful Miss Plumberry,* p. 850.

Magpies, March, 1996, review of *Crow and Hawk,* p. 29; November, 1998, review of *Classic Poetry,* pp. 18-19; July, 1999, review of *Mission Ziffoid,* pp. 26-27; November, 1999, review of *Rover,* p. 28.

New Statesman, December 5, 1997, review of *Tea in the Sugar Bowl, Potato in My Shoe,* p. 63.

Observer (London, England), May 30, 1999, review of *The Kingfisher Book of Children's Poetry,* p. 13.

Publishers Weekly, June 30, 1989, review of *We're Going on a Bear Hunt,* p. 104; June 8, 1990, review of *Freckly Feet and Itchy Knees,* p. 54; September 21, 1992, review of *South and North, East and West,* p. 94; July 26, 1993, review of *How Giraffe Got Such a Long Neck . . . and Why Rhino Is So Grumpy,* p. 71; February 27, 1995, review of *Crow and Hawk,* p. 102; October 16, 1995, review of *Walking the Bridge of Your Nose,* p. 61; December 18, 1995, review of *The Best of Michael Rosen,* p. 54; June 24, 1996, review of *This Is Our House,* p. 58; March 3, 1997, review of *Michael Rosen's ABC,* p. 77; December 14, 1998, review of *Classic Poetry,* p. 77; April 26, 1999, review of *Walking the Bridge of Your Nose,* p. 85; June 7, 1999, review of *Rover,* p. 83; December 3, 2001, review of *Shakespeare,* p. 61; April 4, 2005, review of *Michael Rosen's Sad Book,* p. 58.

School Librarian, March, 1985, Colin Walter, review of *Hairy Tales and Nursery Crimes,* p. 40; May, 1988, Tom Lewis, review of *You're Thinking about Doughnuts,* p. 59; August, 1989, Margaret Meek, review of *Did I Hear You Write?,* p. 128; November, 1992, Sue Rogers, review of *Mind the Gap,* p. 156; February, 1997, Diane Broughton, review of *You Wait till I'm Older than You!,* p. 43; winter, 1999, Anne Rowe, review of *Lunch Boxes Don't Fly,* p. 208.

School Library Journal, May, 1982, review of *You Can't Catch Me,* p. 56; November, 1983, Margaret L. Chatham, review of *A Cat and Mouse Story,* p. 69; October, 1984, Helen Gregory, review of *Quick, Let's Get out of Here,* p. 161; January, 1987, Barbara McGinn, review of *Don't Put Mustard in the Custard,* p. 78; May, 1989, Lucy Young Clem, review of *Down at the Doctor's,* p. 101; February, 1991, JoAnn Rees, review of *Little Rabbit Foo Foo,* p. 74; December, 1992, Karen Wehner, review of *Itsy-Bitsy Beasties,* p. 127; October, 1993, Lee Bock, review of *How Giraffe Got Such a Long Neck . . . and Why Rhino Is So Grumpy,* pp. 121-22; March, 1994, Carolyn Noah, review of *Moving,* p. 208; July, 1995, Lisa Dennis, review of *Crow and Hawk,* p. 74; January, 1996, Judith

Constantinides, review of *Walking the Bridge of Your Nose,* p. 105; July, 1996, Steven Engelfried, review of *This Is Our House,* p. 71; March, 1997, Tana Elias, review of *Michael Rosen's ABC,* p. 165; June, 1999, Carol Ann Wilson, review of *Rover,* p. 106; December, 1999, Sally R. Dow, review of *Mission Ziffoid,* p. 112; November, 2001, Patricia Lothrop-Green, review of *Shakespeare,* p. 184; February, 2004, Nancy Menaldi-Scanlan, review of *Shakespeare's Romeo and Juliet,* p. 168; August, 2004, Wendy Woodfill, review of *Howler,* p. 93; March, 2005, Maryann H. Owen, review of *Michael Rosen's Sad Book,* p. 218; November, 2005, Nancy Menaldi-Scanlan, review of *Dickens,* p. 170; September, 2006, Piper L. Nyman, review of *Totally Wonderful Miss Plumberry,* p. 183.

Times Educational Supplement, November 20, 1981, Edward Blishen, "Nonsense Not Nauseous," p. 34; October 31, 1997, review of *Tea in the Sugarbowl, Potato in My Shoe,* p. 244; October 19, 2001, John Mole, review of *Shakespeare,* p. B22.

Times Higher Education Supplement, May 6, 1994, Colwyn Williamson, review of *The Chatto Book of Dissent,* p. 28.

Times Literary Supplement, March 8, 1985, George Szirtes, review of *Hairy Tales and Nursery Crimes,* p. 270; April 7, 1989, Carol Ann Duffy, review of *Didn't I Hear You Write?,* p. 381; November 24, 1989, D.J. Enright, review of *Rude Rhymes,* p. 1310.

Voice of Youth Advocates, August, 2004, review of *Shakespeare's Romeo and Juliet,* p. 241; February, 2007, Jonatha Masters, review of *Shakespeare,* p. 556.

ONLINE

Michel Rosen Home Page, http://www.michaelrosen.co.uk (August 10, 2007).

WriteWords Writers' Community Web site, http://www.writewords.org/ (February, 2006), interview with Rosen.*

*   *   *

ROSEN, Michael Wayne
See ROSEN, Michael

*   *   *

ROTH, Susan L.

Personal

Born in New York, NY; married; children: three children. *Education:* Mills College, B.A. (art), 1965, M.A. (printmaking and art history), 1968. *Hobbies and other interests:* Art, music, theater, travel, dogs.

Addresses

Home and office—New York, NY. *E-mail*—slr@susanlroth.com.

Career

Collage artist and author. Formerly worked as a teacher. *Exhibitions:* Work exhibited at Les Cloîtres, Tarascon, France; Elizabeth Stone Gallery, Bloomfield Hills, MI; Society of Illustrators Original Art Show, New York, NY, 1989, 1991, 1993; and Berkeley Store Gallery, 1996.

Member

Children's Book Guild of Washington, DC.

Awards, Honors

Cooperative Children's Book Center (CCBC) Choice designation, 1984, for *Patchwork Tales; New York Times* Best Illustrated Book designation, 1988, and 1996, for *Fire Came to the Earth People;* National Council for the Social Studies (NCSS) Notable Social Studies Trade Book designation, and American Booksellers Association (ABA) Pick of the Lists inclusion, and Maryland Black-eyed Susan Picture-Book Award, all 1990, all for *The Story of Light;* ABA Pick of the Lists inclusion, and Aesop Accolade, American Folklore Society, both 1992, both for *Ishi's Tale of the Lizard* by Leanne Hinton; NCSS Notable Social Studies Trade Book designation, Maryland Black-eyed Susan Picture-Book Award, and Child Study Children's Book Committee Children's Book of the Year designation, all 1994, all for *The Great Ball Game* by Joseph Bruchac; CCBC Choice designation, 1995, for *How Thunder and Lightning Came to Be;* Kentucky Bluegrass Award, and Aesop Accolade, American Folklore Society, both 1998, both for *The Biggest Frog in Australia;* YALSA Best Book for Young Adults designation, Bank Street College of Education Best Children's Book of the Year, Capitol Choices selection, NCSS Notable Social Studies Trade Book designation, and *Riverbank Review* and *Smithsonian* Notable Book designations, all 1997, and Woodson Elementary Award, American Library Association Notable Book designation, International Reading Association Teachers' Choice, *Boston Globe/Horn Book* Award for Nonfiction, and Jefferson Cup Award, all 1998, and several state literature awards, all for *Leon's Story* by Leon Walter Tillage; New York Public Library 100 Titles for Reading and Sharing designation, 1998, for *Cinnamon's Day Out;* NCSS Notable Social Studies Trade Book designation, and National Parenting Publications Gold Award, both 2001, both for *Made in Mexico* by Peter Laufer; NCSS Notable Social Studies Trade Book designation, 2002, and Art Director's Club of Metropolitan Washington Certificate of Merit, 2001, for *Happy Birthday Mr. Kang;* Bank Street College of Education Children's Book of the Year, and Children's Book Council Notable Social Studies Trade Book designation, both 2004, both for *Hard Hat Area.*

Writings

SELF-ILLUSTRATED

(With Ruth Phang) *Patchwork Tales,* Atheneum (New York, NY), 1984.

(With Ruth Phang) *We Build a Climber,* Atheneum (New York, NY), 1986.

Fire Came to the Earth People: A Dahomean Folktale, St. Martin's Press (New York, NY), 1988.

Kanahena: A Cherokee Story, St. Martin's Press (New York, NY), 1988.

We'll Ride Elephants through Brooklyn, Farrar, Straus & Giroux (New York, NY), 1989.

Marco Polo: His Notebook, Doubleday (New York, NY), 1990.

The Story of Light, Morrow Junior Books (New York, NY), 1990.

Gypsy Bird Song, Farrar, Straus & Giroux (New York, NY), 1991.

Another Christmas, Morrow Junior Books (New York, NY), 1992.

Princess, Hyperion Books for Children (New York, NY), 1993.

Buddha, Delacorte Press (New York, NY), 1994.

Creak, Thump, Bump!: A Very Spooky Mystery, Simon & Schuster (New York, NY), 1995.

The Biggest Frog in Australia, Simon & Schuster (New York, NY), 1996.

Brave Martha and the Dragon, Dial Books for Young Readers (New York, NY), 1996.

My Love for You, Dial Books for Young Readers (New York, NY), 1997, bilingual edition published as *Mi amor por ti = My Love for You,* 2003.

Cinnamon's Day Out: A Gerbil Adventure, Dial Books for Young Readers (New York, NY), 1998.

Night-Time Numbers: A Scary Counting Book, Barefoot Books (Cambridge, MA), 1999.

Happy Birthday Mr. Kang, National Geographic Society (Washington, DC), 2001.

It's a Dog's New York, National Geographic Society (Washington, DC), 2001.

Grandpa Blows His Penny Whistle until the Angels Sing, Barefoot Books (Cambridge, MA), 2001.

My Love for You All Year Round, Dial Books for Young Readers (New York, NY), 2003.

Hard Hat Area, Bloomsbury Children's Books (New York, NY), 2004.

Hanukkah, Oh Hanukkah, Dial Books for Young Readers (New York, NY), 2004.

(With Angelo Mafucci) *Do Re Mi: If You Can Read Music, Thank Guido d'Arezzo,* Houghton Mifflin (Boston, MA), 2006.

Great Big Guinea Pigs, Bloomsbury Children's Books (New York, NY), 2006.

(With Nancy Patz) *Babies Can't Eat Kimchee!,* Bloomsbury Children's Books (New York, NY), 2007.

ILLUSTRATOR

Ishi, *Ishi's Tale of Lizard,* translated by Leanne Hinton, Farrar, Straus & Giroux (New York, NY), 1992.

Cheryl Chapman, *Pass the Fritters, Critters,* Four Winds Press (New York, NY), 1993.

Joseph Bruchac, *The Great Ball Game: A Muskogee Story,* Dial (New York, NY), 1994.

Beatrice Orcutt Harrell, *How Thunder and Lightning Came to Be,* Dial Books for Young Readers (New York, NY), 1995.

Patricia Hooper, *How the Sky's Housekeeper Wore Her Scarves,* Little, Brown (Boston, MA), 1995.

Leon Walter Tillage, *Leon's Story,* Farrar, Straus & Giroux (New York, NY), 1997.

Peter Laufer, *Made in Mexico,* National Geographic Society (Washington, DC), 2000.

Walt Whitman, *Nothing but Miracles: From Leaves of Grass,* National Geographic (Washington, DC), 2003.

Adaptations

Nothing but Miracles: From Leaves of Grass and *Do Re Mi: If You Can Read Music, Thank Guido d'Arezzo* were both adapted as choral productions by Victoria Bond and produced, respectively, in Baltimore, MD, 2004, and Arezzo, Italy, 2006.

Sidelights

Armed with only a camera, scissors, paste, tape, and tweezers, Susan L. Roth has gained reknown as an artist specializing in cut-and torn-paper collages as well as woodcuts. Combining her highly textured, mixed-media art with detailed research and original stories, she has created a niche for herself, captivating young children with both nonfiction and fictional books that include the popular counting book *My Love for You* as well as *Cinnamon's Day Out: A Gerbil Adventure, Hanukkah, Oh Hanukkah, Happy Birthday Mr. Kang, Hard Hat Area,* and *Do Re Mi: If You Can Read Music, Thank Guido d'Arezzo.* Praising *My Love for You,* Ilene Cooper cited in particular Roth's characteristic use of a "pithy yet endearing text and eye-catching illustrations," while a *Kirkus Reviews* writer dubbed *Do Re Mi* "a sublime blend of education and entertainment." As an illustrator, Roth frequently collaborates on texts by other writers. Among these titles is the award-winning *Leon's Story,* the autobiography of school custodian Leon Walter Tillage, who Roth was introduced to by her twelve-year-old daughter. A quiet but direct account of a black man whose life experiences included growing up amid racism and the predations of the Ku Klux Klan as the son of poor Southern sharecroppers, *Leon's Story* was transcribed by Roth and illustrated with what a *Publishers Weekly* contributor described as "dramatic black and-white collages [that] pay homage to the power of Leon's story."

Roth's first self-illustrated picture books were written in collaboration with Ruth Phang. The first of these, *Patchwork Tales,* features woodcut art shaded in tones of red, yellow, blue, and green that brings to life the stories Grandma tells her young granddaughter at bedtime. The book includes instructions on how to make a quilt, augmenting what *School Library Journal* reviewer Nancy Kewish called a "charming and thoughtfully put together" work. In *The Story of Light* Roth retells a porquoi tale based on a Cherokee myth. The story describes

how, when the larger creatures Possum and Buzzard fail to bring light to Earth, it is up to tiny Spider—called "too small," "too old," and "a woman"—to complete the job. Mary Harris Veeder, reviewing the work for the *Chicago Tribune,* dubbed the unity of story and pictures in Roth's picture book "remarkable."

Roth brings to life traditional folk tales in several other books, among them *The Biggest Frog in Australia,* in which she retells a tall tale about a frog that drinks all the water on the continent. In *How Thunder and Lightning Came to Be: A Choctaw Legend* she illustrates a story from Native American mythology, while *How the Sky's Housekeeper Wore Her Scarves* explains, in mythical terms, how a rainbow forms. Roth's illustrations for *The Great Ball Game: A Muskogee Story* bring to life a stickball game between animals with wings and animals with teeth. Drawing from the Christian faith, *Brave Martha and the Dragon* depicts how St. Martha, after seeing her brother Lazarus rise from the dead, voyages to France to tame a dragon that is frightening villagers.

From tall tales, Roth turns to tall buildings in *Hard Hat Area,* and uses torn-photo collages to "take . . . readers into the clouds," according to *Horn Book* reviewer Bridget T. McCaffrey. Here she focuses on Kristen, a female ironworker-in-training, as she arrives on the construction site and assists the more-experienced workers construct a skyscraper's iron skeleton. Drawing on research that included climbing into the scaffolding of a

Susan L. Roth contributes her highly acclaimed collage art to Abenaki storyteller Joseph Bruchac's retelling of a Native-American folk tale in **The Great Ball Game.** (Illustration © 1994 by Susan L. Roth. Reproduced by permission of Dial Books for Young Readers, an imprint of Penguin Putnam Books for Young Readers, a division of Penguin Putnam Inc. All rights reserved.)

New York City construction site, Roth "brings alive the ironworkers' sense of community, and how they embrace anyone willing to start at the bottom and work their way up," noted a *Publishers Weekly* contributor. A *Kirkus Reviews* critic predicted that "kids who are intrigued by construction sites and equipment will find this unusually structured book a solid hit."

Roth turns her attention to slightly older children in her fictionalized picture-book biographies *Marco Polo: His Notebooks, Buddha,* and *Do Re Mi.* Formatted as a series of fictional journal entries dictated by the explorer to a writer, the book follows Polo's trek through Jerusalem, Iran, and Afghanistan. According to *Five Owls* critic Mary Lou Burket, the work presents children with "a tantalizing peek at distant places that currently dominate world affairs" and serves "as a visually unified and lively introduction to a large subject." In a review for the *Bulletin of the Center for Children's Books,* a critic noted the omission of captions and other explanatory notes but went on to write that the story "has a romantic allure . . . and Roth is good about providing the details that give evidence to the wonder." In *Buddha* Roth recounts the transformation of Siddhartha into Buddha, while *Do Re Mi* focuses on the medieval Italian monk who developed the first musical notation system. *Booklist* reviewer Ilene Cooper called *Buddha* an "ambitious offering" and praised Roth's handmade, torn-paper collage illustrations as "extraordinary." Noting that the story of Guido d'Arezzo "is certain to capture the imagination of any budding musician," a *Publishers Weekly* critic praised *Do Re Mi* for its "carefully researched prose" and "marvelous" collage accompaniment. The book, written in collaboration with Maestro Angelo Mafucci, was a special labor of love for Roth. In addition to being adapted as a musical composition by Victoria Bond and staged by Mafucci's Children's Choir of Arezzo, Italy, in 2006, *Do Re Mi* was presented by Roth to Pope Benedict XVI at the Vatican the following year.

While many of Roth's books include factual information, some keep all the focus on fun. *Break, Thump, Bump!: A Very Spooky Mystery* finds three children and a dog bumping around in the dark while attempting to discover the sources of some odd sounds, while *Cinnamon's Day Out* finds a frisky gerbil taking a holiday in the house. Far more weighty rodents take to the pages of *Great Big Guinea Pigs,* which couches facts about the rampages of prehistoric Venezuelan guinea pigs within a fictional bedtime story. "Who can resist a title like this?," queried Ilene Cooper in *Booklist,* the critic adding that in "typically super" torn-paper collages the author/illustrator "make[s] her guinea pigs look equally adorable (in the present) and ferocious (in the past)."

Early on in her career, Roth adopted a rule she has only veered from once: "No pencils, pens nor paints." Each book project is a unique work in which she adapts her collages to suit the needs of the particular story. For example, in *Cinnamon's Day Out,* wood shavings, fluff,

Roth brings to life the world of the Italian monk who created musical notation in both text and textured collage art in **Do Re Me.** (Illustration © 2006 by Susan L. Roth. All rights reserved. Reproduced by permission of Houghton Mifflin Company.)

and corrugated paper can all be found in the mixed-media collages that accompany the text, providing children with "an engaging but safely vicarious adventure," according to Carol Ann Wilson in *School Library Journal.* In *Hanukkah, Oh Hanukkah* she incorporates the lace and nuts evocative of a special holiday, and a close look at the illustrations of *Do Re Mi* reveal sheet music, foil, and handmade papers from throughout the world. Asked where she gets her ideas, Roth explained on her home page: "World, universe, *New York Times,* friends, family, sky, head, dogs, traveling, museums, libraries, walks, good coffee, cooking, looking out the window, listening. . . ."

Biographical and Critical Sources

BOOKS

Morgan, Margaret, *Susan L. Roth,* Harcourt (Sydney, New South Wales, Australia), 2007.

PERIODICALS

Booklist, June 1, 1988, review of *Kanahena: A Cherokee Story,* p. 83; September 15, 1988, Ilene Cooper, review of *Fire Came to the Earth People: A Dahomean Folktale,* p. 165; December, 1991, review of *Gypsy Bird Song,* p. 768; September, 1992, review of *Another Christmas,* pp. 156-157; June, 1993, review of *Pass the Fritters, Critters,* pp. 1852-1853; October 1, 1997, Hazel Rochman, review of *Leon's Story,* p. 332; April 1, 2001, Ilene Cooper, review of *Grandpa Blows His Penny Whistle until the Angels Sing,* p. 1479; December 1, 2003, Ilene Cooper, review of *My Love for You All Year Round,* p. 584; September 1, 2004, Ilene Cooper, review of *Sing the Season,* p. 130; November 1, 2004, Karin Snelson, review of *Hard Hat Area,* p. October 15, 2006, Ilene Cooper, review of *Great Big Guinea Pigs,* p. 47; December 1, 2006, Gillian Engberg, review of *Do Re Mi: If You Can Read Music, Thank Guido d'Arezzo,* p. 55.

Bulletin of the Center for Children's Books, January, 1985, review of *Patchwork Tales,* pp. 93-94; October, 1988, review of *Kanahena,* pp. 51-52; February, 1991, review of *Marco Polo: His Notebook,* pp. 153-154; September, 1998, Elizabeth Bush, review of *Cinnamon's Day Out: A Gerbil Adventure,* pp. 28-29; April, 2001, review of *Happy Birthday Mr. Kang,* p. 314; January, 2005, Elizabeth Bush, review of *Hard Hat Area,* p. 225.

Chicago Tribune, November 11, 1990, Mary Harris Veeder, review of *The Story of Light,* pp. 6-7.

Five Owls, March-April, 1991, review of *Marco Polo,* pp 78-80; September-October, 1991, Susan Stan, review of *Marco Polo,* p. 5.

Horn Book, March, 1990, Ethel Twichell, review of *We'll Ride Elephants through Brooklyn,* p. 194; November, 1990, Ellen Fader, review of *The Story of Light,* p. 754; November, 1992, Ellen Fader, review of *Another Christmas,* p. 713; fall, 1996, Nancy Vasilakis, review of *The Biggest Frog in Australia,* p. 273; November-December, 1997, Nancy Vasilakis, review of *Leon's Story,* p. 699; January, 1999, Susan L. Roth, transcript of *Boston Globe/Horn Book* Awards speech, p. 46; October 1, 2001, review of *Grandpa Blows His Penny Whistle until the Angels Sing;* November-December, 2004, Bridget T. McCaffrey, review of *Hanukkah, Oh Hanukkah,* p. 663; January-February, 2005, Betty Careter, review of *Hard Hat Area,* p. 110.

Kirkus Reviews, December 1, 1989, review of *We'll Ride Elephants through Brooklyn,* p. 1753; June 15, 1990, review of *The Story of Light,* p. 884; June 1, 1994, review of *Buddha,* p. 781; September 15, 1995, review of *Creak, Thump, Bonk!,* p. 1357; May 15, 1996, review of *The Biggest Frog in Australia,* p. 750; June 1, 1996, review of *Brave Martha and the Dragon,* p. 829; December 15, 1996, review of *My Love for You,* p. 1808; October 1, 1999, review of *Night-Time Numbers: A Scary Counting Book,* p. 1586; April 1, 2001, review of *Grandpa Blows His Penny Whistle until the Angels Sing;* November 15, 2003, review of *My Love for You All Year Round,* p. 1363; August 15, 2004, review of *Hanukkah, Oh Hanukkah,* p. 1053; November 15, 2006, review of *Do Re Mi,* p. 177; December 1, 2006, review of *Babies Can't Eat Kimchee!,* p. 1224.

New York Times Book Review, December 23, 1984, review of *Patchwork Tales,* p. 20; December 6, 1992, review of *Another Christmas,* p. 91; April 18, 1993, review

of *Ishi's Tale of Lizard,* p. 25; September 8, 1997, review of *Leon's Story,* p. 77; February 15, 1998, review of *Leon's Story,* p. 25; March 11, 2001, review of *Happy Birthday Mr. Kang,* p. 26; May 19, 2002, Beth Gutcheon, review of *It's a Dog's New York,* p. 27.

Publishers Weekly, September 28, 1984, review of *Patchwork Tales,* p. 112; June 24, 1988, Kimberly Fakih, review of *Kanahena,* p. 113; November 24, 1989, review of *We'll Ride Elephants through Brooklyn,* p. 70; November 15, 1999, review of *Night-Time Numbers,* p. 64; May 28, 2001, review of *Grandpa Blows His Penny Whistle until the Angels Sing,* p. 85; November 3, 2003, review of *Nothing but Miracles,* p. 72; December 15, 2003, review of *My Love for You All Year Round,* p. 75; September 27, 2004, review of *Hanukkah, Oh Hanukkah,* p. 59; November 1, 2004, review of *Hard Hat Area,* p. 61; December 11, 2006, review of *Do Re Mi,* p. 69.

School Librarian, spring, 2000, Rebecca Taylor, review of *Night-Time Numbers,* p. 20.

School Library Journal, January, 1985, Nancy Kewish, review of *Patchwork Tales,* p. 68; October, 1986, Constance Mellon, review of *We Build a Climber,* p. 165; December, 1988, Karen Litton, review of *Fire Came to the Earth People,* p. 101; February, 1990, Leda Schubert, review of *We'll Ride Elephants through Brooklyn,* p. 78; February, 1991, Carolyn Polese, review of *The Story of Light,* p. 80, Jean McGrath, review of *Marco Polo,* p. 91; December, 1991, Anna Biagion Hart, review of *Gypsy Bird Song,* p. 100; June, 1993, Christian Moesch, review of *Pass the Fritters, Critters,* p. 72; January, 1994, Bambi Williams, review of *Princess,* p. 97; June, 1994, Jane Gardner Connor, review of *Buddha,* p. 141; June, 1995, Lauralyn Persson, review of *How the Sky's Housekeeper Wore Her Scarves,* p. 87; August, 1995, Donna Scanlon, review of *How Thunder and Lightning Came to Be,* p. 134; December, 1995, Lauralyn Persson, review of *Creak, Thump, Bonk!,* p. 90; June, 1996, Ellen Fader, review of *The Biggest Frog in Australia,* p. 108; August, 1996, Wendy Lukehart, review of *Brave Martha and the Dragon,* p. 141; February, 1997, Patricia Pearl Dole, review of *My Love for You,* p. 84; December, 1997, Marie Wright, review of *Leon's Story,* p. 148; July, 1998, Carol Ann Wilson, review of *Cinnamon's Day Out,* p. 81; October, 1999, Sarah O'Neal, review of *Night-Time Numbers,* p. 124; February, 2000, Selene Vasquez, review of *Made in Mexico,* p. 141; May 1, 2001, Linda M. Kenton, review of *Grandpa Blows His Penny Whistle until the Angels Sing,* p. 133.

Voice of Youth Advocates, April, 1998, review of *Leon's Story,* p. 39.

Wilson Library Bulletin, April, 1995, Donnarae McCann and Olga Richard, review of *The Great Ball Game: A Muskogee Story,* p. 111.

ONLINE

Children's Book Guild of Washington, DC Web site, http://www.childrensbookguild.org/ (July 13, 2007), "Susan L. Roth."

Childrenslit.com, http://www.childrenslit.com/ (August 10, 2007), Marilyn Courtot, interview with Roth.*

Susan L. Roth Web site, http://www.susanlroth.com/ (September 10, 2007).

* * *

RUBEL, Nicole 1953-

Personal

Born April 29, 1953, in Miami, FL; daughter of Theodore (an importer) and Janice (an importer) Rubel; married Richard C. Langsen (a family therapist), May 25, 1987. *Education:* Tufts University and Boston Museum School of Fine Arts, B.S. (joint degree), 1975. *Hobbies and other interests:* "My Siamese cat, Corgi dog, two saddlebred horses, and my plum farm."

Addresses

Home and office—Aurora, OR. *E-mail*—nicole@nicolerubel.com.

Career

Painter, illustrator, and writer. Designer of toys and greeting cards. *Exhibitions:* Works included in exhibitions at Boston Public Library, 1977; Boston Museum of Fine Arts, 1979; Belmont Library, 1979; Brookline Public Library, 1979; American Illustrators Graphic Association Traveling Show, 1979; Master Eagle Gallery, New York, NY, 1981, 1984; Justin Schiller Gallery, New York, NY, 1981; Key Biscayne Library, 1990; Gresham City Hall, 1995; and Wilsonville Library, 2002.

Awards, Honors

Children's Books Showcase Award for Outstanding Graphic Design, 1977, for *Rotten Ralph;* American Book Association (ABA) award and American Institute of Graphic Arts award, both 1979; American Bookseller Association (ABA) Pick of the Lists, 1984, for *Rotten Ralph,* and 1992, for *It Came from the Swamp* and *Grizzly Riddles;* ABA Pick of the Lists, 2001, for *A Cowboy Named Ernestine;* Oppenheim Toy Portfolio Platinum Book Award, 2005, for *Twice as Nice.*

Writings

FOR CHILDREN; SELF-ILLUSTRATED

Bruno Brontosaurus, Avon (New York, NY), 1983, published as *Pete Apatosaurus,* Bantam (New York, NY), 1991.

Me and My Kitty, Macmillan (New York, NY), 1983.

I Can Get Dressed, Macmillan (New York, NY), 1984.

Bernie the Bulldog, Scholastic (New York, NY), 1984.

Nicole Rubel (Photograph by Richard Langsen. Reproduced by permission of Nicole Rubel.)

Pirate Jupiter and the Moondogs, Dial (New York, NY), 1985.

Uncle Henry and Aunt Henrietta's Honeymoon, Dial (New York, NY), 1986.

It Came from the Swamp, Dial (New York, NY), 1988.

Goldie, Harper (New York, NY), 1989.

Goldie's Nap, HarperCollins (New York, NY), 1991.

The Ghost Family Meets Its Match, Dial (New York, NY), 1992.

Conga Crocodile, Houghton (Boston, MA), 1993.

Cyrano the Bear, Dial (New York, NY), 1995.

No School for Penelope Pig, Troll (Mahwah, NJ), 1997.

A Cowboy Named Ernestine, Dial (New York, NY), 2001.

No More Vegetables, Farrar, Straus & Giroux (New York, NY), 2002.

Grody's Not-So-Golden Rules, Harcourt (San Diego, CA), 2003.

It's Hot and Cold in Miami, Farrar, Straus & Giroux (New York, NY), 2006.

Ham and Pickles: First Day of School, Harcourt (Orlando, FL), 2006.

"SAM AND VIOLET" SERIES; SELF-ILLUSTRATED; FOR CHILDREN

Sam and Violet Are Twins, Avon (New York, NY), 1981.

Sam and Violet Go Camping, Avon (New York, NY), 1981.

Sam and Violet's Christmas Story, Avon (New York, NY), 1981.

Sam and Violet's Birthday Book, Avon (New York, NY), 1982.

Sam and Violet's Get Well Story, Avon (New York, NY), 1985.

Sam and Violet's Bedtime Mystery, Avon (New York, NY), 1985.

ILLUSTRATOR; FOR CHILDREN

Jack Gantos, *Sleepy Ronald,* Houghton (Boston, MA), 1976.

Jack Gantos, *Aunt Bernice,* Houghton (Boston, MA), 1978.

Jack Gantos, *Fairweather Friends,* Houghton (Boston, MA), 1978.

Jack Gantos, *Willy's Raiders,* Parents Magazine Press (New York, NY), 1978.

Jack Gantos, *The Perfect Pal,* Houghton (Boston, MA), 1979.

Jack Gantos, *Greedy Greeny,* Doubleday (New York, NY), 1979.

Jack Gantos, *The Werewolf Family,* Houghton (Boston, MA), 1980.

Jack Gantos, *Swamp Alligator,* Simon & Schuster (New York, NY), 1980.

Steven Kroll, *Woof! Woof!,* Dial (New York, NY), 1982.

Michaela Muntean, *The House That Bear Built,* Dial (New York, NY), 1984.

Michaela Muntean, *Alligator's Garden,* Dial (New York, NY), 1984.

Michaela Muntean, *Little Lamb Bakes a Cake,* Dial (New York, NY), 1984.

Michaela Muntean, *Monkey's Marching Band,* Dial (New York, NY), 1984.

Patty Wolcott, *This Is Weird,* Scholastic (New York, NY), 1986.

Richard C. Langsen, *When Someone in the Family Drinks Too Much: A Guide for Children,* Dial (New York, NY), 1996.

Marilyn Singer, *The One and Only Me,* HarperFestival (New York, NY), 2000.

"ROTTEN RALPH" SERIES; ILLUSTRATOR; FOR CHILDREN

Jack Gantos, *Rotten Ralph,* Houghton (Boston, MA), 1975.

Jack Gantos, *Worse than Rotten Ralph,* Houghton (Boston, MA), 1979.

Jack Gantos, *Rotten Ralph's Rotten Christmas,* Houghton (Boston, MA), 1984.

Jack Gantos, *Rotten Ralph's Trick or Treat,* Houghton (Boston, MA), 1986.

Jack Gantos, *Rotten Ralph's Show and Tell,* Houghton (Boston, MA), 1989.

Jack Gantos, *Happy Birthday Rotten Ralph,* Houghton (Boston, MA), 1990.

Jack Gantos, *Not So Rotten Ralph,* Houghton (Boston, MA), 1994.

Jack Gantos, *Rotten Ralph's Rotten Romance,* Houghton (Boston, MA), 1997.

Jack Gantos, *Rotten Ralph's Halloween Howl,* HarperFestival (New York, NY), 1998.

Jack Gantos, *Back to School for Rotten Ralph,* HarperCollins (New York, NY), 1998.

Jack Gantos, *The Christmas Spirit Strikes Rotten Ralph,* HarperFestival (New York, NY), 1998.

Jack Gantos, *Rotten Ralph's Thanksgiving Wish,* HarperFestival (New York, NY), 1999.

Jack Gantos, *Wedding Bells for Rotten Ralph,* HarperCollins (New York, NY), 1999.

Jack Gantos, *Rotten Ralph Helps Out,* (chapter book), Farrar, Straus & Giroux (New York, NY), 2001.

Jack Gantos, *Practice Makes Perfect for Rotten Ralph,* Farrar, Straus & Giroux (New York, NY), 2002.

Jack Gantos, *Rotten Ralph Feels Rotten,* Farrar, Straus & Giroux (New York, NY), 2004.

Jack Gantos, *Best in Show for Rotten Ralph,* Farrar, Straus & Giroux (New York, NY), 2005.

"RIDDLES" SERIES; ILLUSTRATOR; FOR CHILDREN

Katy Hall and Lisa Eisenberg, *Grizzly Riddles,* Dial (New York, NY), 1989.

Katy Hall and Lisa Eisenberg, *Batty Riddles,* Dial (New York, NY), 1993.

Katy Hall and Lisa Eisenberg, *Bunny Riddles,* Dial (New York, NY), 1997.

Katy Hall and Lisa Eisenberg, *Mummy Riddles,* Dial (New York, NY), 1997.

Katy Hall and Lisa Eisenberg, *Dino Riddles,* Dial (New York, NY), 2002.

OTHER

Getting Married: A Guide for the Bride to Be (for adults), St. Martin's Press (New York, NY), 1988.

Twice as Nice: What It's Like to Be a Twin, Farrar, Straus & Giroux (New York, NY), 2004.

Contributor of illustrations to periodicals, including *Boston, Instructor, Redbook, Spider,* and *Scholastic Pre-K.*

Adaptations

Rotten Ralph was adapted for audio cassette, 1988, and for television for the Fox Family channel, 1999; *It Came from the Swamp, Pirate Jupiter and the Moondogs,* and *Goldie* were all adapted for CD-ROM, 1995-96.

Sidelights

Bringing to life a brightly colored world filled with zany cats, argumentative alligators, overly artful bears, and brazen bull dogs, illustrator and author Nicole Rubel is inspired by the paintings of Henri Matisse and by the art deco architecture of Miami, Florida, where she grew up. As an illustrator, Rubel is perhaps best known for bringing to life the antics of Rotten Ralph, a motley, ill-tempered feline that terrorizes his young owner, Sarah, throughout the popular easy-reader series by author Jack Gantos. In other collaborative projects, she has created artwork for the "Riddle" book series by Katy Hall and Lisa Eisenberg. A prolific illustrator, Rubel has also proved to be a talented author, creating dozens of self-illustrated picture books, among them *A Cowboy Named Ernestine, No More Vegetables!,* and the popular "Sam and Violet" books about twin kittens.

In an autobiographical vein, she focuses on her experiences as a twin in both the elementary-grade novel *It's Hot and Cold in Miami* and the award-winning picture book *Twice as Nice: What It's Like to Be a Twin.* Described by *Booklist* reviewer Ilene Cooper as a "sprightly" compendium of facts, jokes, anecdotes, advice, and profiles of famous twins throughout world history, *Twice as Nice* features twin guides Bonnie and Ronnie along with "child-friendly illustrations, photographs, and [an] engaging, witty text," according to a *Kirkus Reviews* contributor.

Rubel was born and raised in Florida, and although she now makes her home in Oregon, her illustrations draw on the vivid palette of the sunshine state. Being born an identical twin has also affected Rubel's chosen career: her "Sam and Violet" books are inspired by her relationship with her twin sister Bonnie. As she recalled on her home page, Rubel was a shy child and let her sister speak for her. Finally, through the encouragement of a teacher, she found her own voice, learning to speak and write for herself. Because of this early experience, finding one's true self and learning to express thoughts and feelings are characteristic themes in Rubel's books for children.

Rubel attended school in Coral Gables, Florida, and started drawing and painting at an early age. An early inspiration was her view of the colorful houses across the street from her family home that were built in the Chinese style. She loved to draw these buildings as well as the vibrant flowering bushes and trees growing in and around Miami. At age fourteen she stopped drawing for a time and began experimenting with papier-maché monsters, which she painted with bright colors.

Attending art school in Boston, Rubel further experimented with ceramics and silk screen, until a series of drawings featuring goldfish set her on the path to book illustration. When Jack Gantos, an up-and-coming children's-book author, offered to create a story around one series of her pictures, it was the start of a creative collaboration that has produced the "Rotten Ralph" books as well as several others. Inspired by an ill-tempered feline that was then sharing Rubel's home, the "Rotten Ralph" the series takes Ralph through holidays, birthdays, romance, and show and tell, among other adventures.

In *Rotten Ralph's Trick or Treat* the ever-patient Sarah and Ralph attend a Halloween costume party dressed as each other. When Ralph performs as usual—stealing all the candy and pouring the goldfish bowl into the punch—all the party-goers blame Sarah, and the two are asked to leave. Another excursion is the focus of *Rotten Ralph's Show and Tell,* as Sarah takes Ralph to school for show and tell after he ruins her other plans—breaking the strings on her violin and decorating himself with her stamp collection. At school, Ralph continues his antics by ringing the dismissal bell early. Ralph shows some remorse in *Happy Birthday Rotten Ralph,*

Rubel's brightly colored cartoon art showcases a young hamster's fears about an important life step in **Ham and Pickles: First Day of School.** (Illustration © 2006 by Nicole Rubel. All rights reserved. Reproduced by permission of Harcourt in North America. Reproduced by permission of the Jennifer De Chiara Literary Agency in the United Kingdom.)

after Sarah tricks him with a surprise party. In *Not So Rotten Ralph* the disobedient feline is banished to finishing school, but Sarah is unhappy with his ensuing polite behavior and happy when Ralph once again returns to his mischievous ways. By Valentine's Day he is back to his old tricks, and in *Rotten Ralph's Rotten Romance* the antisocial puss rubs himself in garbage in hopes that he will be left alone at a party Sarah drags him to.

From the outset of the series, Rubel captured the essence of the naughty cat in her illustrations. As a *Horn Book* critic noted of the third title in the series, *Rotten Ralph's Rotten Christmas,* Rubel's "energetic illustrations are a marvel." Ellen Fader, also writing in *Horn Book,* commented that in *Rotten Ralph's Show and Tell* "Rubel's trademark illustrations, bright and flat in a cartoonlike style, supply the humorous details that make Ralph's unrepentant antics all the more outrageous." Reviewing the same book, a reviewer for *Publishers Weekly* predicted that "readers will be cheered by the

cat's awful antics," while *Booklist* reviewer Ilene Cooper noted that Rubel's "wildly colored pictures capture all of the naughty goings-on with sizzle and snap." Reviewing *Happy Birthday Rotten Ralph* in *Booklist,* Stephanie Zvirin wrote that the "busy, brightly colored paintings . . . are a perfect match for the text," while a *Publishers Weekly* contributor concluded: "Thanks to this talented author and illustrator, Ralph more than lives up to his reputation in his latest captivating caper."

Rubel's illustrations for *Rotten Ralph's Rotten Romance* "invest the obstreperous cat with more than enough personality to make him memorable," noted Zvirin, while a *Publishers Weekly* reviewer maintained that the book's "wildly colorful illustrations, loaded with comic details, busy with floral motifs and tiny hearts, gleefully convey the sentimentality Ralph despises and his vain attempts to avoid it." Reviewing *Back to School for Rotten Ralph,* *Horn Book* contributor Elizabeth S. Watson praised Rubel for her ability to make the cantankerous cartoon

kitty "believable whether worried and abandoned or loved and purring."

In addition to picture books, Rotten Ralph and friend Sarah have also made appearances in several chapter books in the "Rotten Ralph" series. *Rotten Ralph Helps Out* finds Sarah working on a school project on ancient Egypt. Wanting to be included, Ralph accompanies her to the library and constructs a pyramid out of books while Sarah does her research; then he practices drawing hieroglyphics on the library walls. Back at home, the cat floods the bathroom when Sarah attempts to build a model of an Egyptian boat and fills the living room with sand to recreate a desert oasis. Ultimately, the troublesome cat comes to the rescue, when he dresses up as a sphinx and adds zest to Sarah's presentation. In *Practice Makes Perfect for Rotten Ralph*, Sarah and Ralph go to a carnival and are joined by an over-achieving tabby cat named Percy. Percy hopes to shine at the carnival, and has been practicing the baseball throw as well as tossing darts. Jealousy rears its ugly head when Percy wins all the prizes for Sarah. When Ralph suddenly begins to win all sorts of toys—by cheating, of course—Sarah becomes suspicious and the contrite Ralph returns all the prizes unfairly won.

According to a *Horn Book* critic, Rubel's illustrations in *Rotten Ralph Helps Out* "not only parallel the story but also reflect the underlying frenzy through contrasting colors, busy detail, and diagonal lines." Gillian Engberg noted in her *Booklist* review of *Practice Makes Perfect for Rotten Ralph* that Rubel's "bright, clear illustrations . . . nicely extend all the fun."

In her work for the "Riddle" series of books, she creates a different animal character for each title, and matches her art to the riddles collected in each book, from the silly to the sophisticated. In a *Booklist* review of *Bunny Riddles*, Zvirin noted that while Rubel's cartoons do not necessarily provide clues to the solution of the riddles, they are a "strong, colorful complement to the goofy conundrums and are loaded with clever details." In another *Booklist* review, Hazel Rochman maintained that the "bright, detailed illustrations" in *Mummy Riddles* "are as deadpan and silly as the words." Discussing *Dino Riddles*, which presents silly puzzlers about dinosaurs in an easy-reader format, Rubel's "colorful cartoons" contribute to what Patricia Manning deemed a "winning title" in her *School Library Journal* review.

Another multi-book collaboration—this time between Rubel and writer Michaela Muntean—has produced such lighthearted works as *The House That Bear Built, Alligator's Garden, Little Lamb Bakes a Cake,* and *Monkey's Marching Band.* Teaming up with Marilyn Singer, she illustrated *The One and Only Me,* in which a little girl describes how she is similar to various members of her extended family. Both drawings and rhymes indicate that while parts of her anatomy resemble other

family members, the child is still unique. "The simple, childlike cartoons are brightly colored and have lots of action and changes of scenery," wrote Shanla Brookshire in a *School Library Journal* review of *The One and Only Me.*

Rubel produced her first original self-illustrated picture book, *Sam and Violet Are Twins,* in 1981, and continues to write and illustrate issue-oriented titles that attract fans of her whimsical humor and colorful style. Nancy Palmer, reviewing *Sam and Violet's Birthday Book* for *School Library Journal,* commented on Rubel's "original, attention-holding pictures" with their "wonderfully patterned interiors." Another pair of siblings stars in the picture book *Ham and Pickles: First Day of School,* which finds round-eyed hamster Pickles heading off for that all-important big day, under the care of older brother Ham. Noting that Ham's wisecrack efforts to put a rest to his little sister's worries might be confusing to "literal-minded" toddlers, a *Publishers Weekly* contributor recommended the book to older readers, noting that "Rubel's mixed-media illustrations complement the book's off-the-wall flavor."

Familiar household pets pop up again in *Me and My Kitty, No More Vegetables!,* and *Grody's Not So Golden Rules,* the last about a dirty dog with an unusual code of conduct. With *Bruno Brontosaurus,* however, Rubel finds animal inspiration far from home. A takeoff on the ugly duckling story, *Bruno Brontosaurus* features "bright and simple pictures" with "high child appeal," according to Lauralyn Levesque in *School Library Journal.* Going even further afield, the space-age counting book *Pirate Jupiter and the Moondogs* follows a tough bulldog and his crew of moondogs as they search the galaxies for treasure. According to *School Library Journal* reviewer Jean Hammond Zimmerman, in *Pirate Jupiter and the Moondogs* the author/illustrator's "use of black ink and colored markers is well suited to the text." With "trenchant wit and mad cartoony types . . . Rubel has attracted an army of boys and girls who will embrace this blastoff into space," concluded a *Publishers Weekly* contributor of the book, while a critic for the same periodical wrote that in *No More Vegetables!* Rubel's "irreverent visuals turn a familiar tale into a piquant little offering" about a poetic picky eater.

Uncle Henry and Aunt Henrietta's Honeymoon is a bedtime reminiscence about the honeymoon of two green crocodiles, while Alfie the alligator stars in *It Came from the Swamp.* The story of a baseball-playing critter who gets hit by a line drive and subsequently suffers from amnesia, *It Came from the Swamp* will "tickle funny bones," predicted a *Kirkus Reviews* writer. With the drum-playing crocodile in *Conga Crocodile,* Rubel "introduces yet another obstreperous fellow—and again displays her wry sense of humor," according to a *Publishers Weekly* reviewer.

A feisty cowgirl takes center stage in *A Cowboy Named Ernestine.* Here mail-order bride Ernestine O'Reilly makes the long trek from Ireland to Lizard Lick, Texas,

only to discover that her intended is, in fact, a rather rotten human. Unwilling to live with a boor, the feisty Irish lass disguises herself as a man, runs off, and becomes a cattle herder under the name of Ernest T. O'Reilly. While her initial plan is to earn the funds needed to return to Ireland, Ernestine discovers that she loves the cowboy life. After she begins competing in rodeos, her hat inevitably falls off and reveals her true identity, opening the door to true love with cowboy buddy Texas Teeth. "Rubel's words and pictures work together to bring this Wild West romp to life," wrote *School Library Journal* critic Steven Engelfried of *A Cowboy Named Ernestine,* the critic adding that the book's "bold ink-and-marker drawings capture the humor perfectly." Reviewing the title in *Booklist,* Shelle Rosenfeld noted that Rubel's "delightful western tale" features a "folksy, droll narrative; plenty of action; and an admirably resourceful heroine." A *Publishers Weekly* contributor also had positive words for Rubel's artwork, writing that amid "clapboard saloons, cactus and critters galore" the author/illustrator spins a "humdinger of a campfire story."

With *It's Hot and Cold in Miami* Rubel brings her storytelling talent to an older audience through her tale of fifth-grade twin sisters living in Miami during the summer of 1964. Rachel and Rebecca Ringwood may look identical, but in fact they are very different. While Rebecca follows the correct path and pleases her teachers and parents with good grades and appropriate behavior, Rachel has a more unconventional world view as well as a more vivid imagination. As they follow Rachel's engaging narrative, readers learn that there is much to value in her unique perspective, even when it causes her to be looked down on by her ever-critical parents. Calling Rachel an "empathetic underdog in a voice filled with matter-of-fact resignation and some deserved angst," a *Kirkus Reviews* writer explained that, with a teacher's help, she discovers her "artistic flair and subsequent self-confidence." Despite their many differences, the sisters share "lively adventures" during the course of the summer, according to *Horn Book* critic Joanna Rudge Long, the reviewer adding that Rachel's eventual insight into her creative nature and her acceptance of her family's problems are "perfectly reflected in Rubel's astute drawings." "In her *Booklist* review of *It's Hot and Cold in Miami,* Nancy Kim also praised the author's pen-and-ink art, writing that Rubel's "distinctive illustrations capture the details that make Rachel's daily adventures so appealing."

Biographical and Critical Sources

BOOKS

Silvey, Anita, editor, *Children's Books and Their Creators,* Houghton (Boston, MA), 1995.

PERIODICALS

Booklist, May 1, 1986, Denise M. Wilms, review of *Uncle Henry and Aunt Henrietta's Honeymoon,* p. 1317; October 15, 1988, Phillis Wilson, review of *It Came from the Swamp,* p. 414; October 1, 1989, Ilene Cooper, review of *Rotten Ralph's Show and Tell,* p. 348; October 1, 1990, Stephanie Zvirin, review of *Happy Birthday Rotten Ralph,* pp. 338-339; March 1, 1994, Stephanie Zvirin, review of *Not So Rotten Ralph,* p. 1269; June 1, 1995, Denia Hester, review of *Cyrano the Bear,* pp. 1788-1789; November 15, 1996, Stephanie Zvirin, review of *Rotten Ralph's Rotten Romance,* p. 593; November 15, 1996, Stephanie Zvirin, review of *Bunny Riddles,* p. 596; August, 1997, Hazel Rochman, review of *Mummy Riddles,* p. 1909; August, 1998, Michael Cart, review of *Back to School for Rotten Ralph,* p. 2014; June 1, 1999, Ilene Cooper, review of *Wedding Bells for Rotten Ralph,* p. 1841; April 1, 2001, Shelle Rosenfeld, review of *A Cowboy Named Ernestine,* p. 1480; May 1, 2001, Gillian Engberg, review of *Wedding Bells for Rotten Ralph,* p. 1689; March 1, 2002, Gillian Engberg, review of *Practice Makes Perfect for Rotten Ralph,* p. 1136; December 15, 2002, Shelle Rosenfeld, review of *No More Vegetables,* p. 769; March 1, 2003, Tim Arnold, review of *Grody's Not So Golden Rules,* p. 1203; November 15, 2004, Ilene Cooper, review of *Twice as Nice: What It's Like to Be a Twin,* p. 578; April 15, 2006, Nancy Kim, review of *It's Hot and Cold in Miami,* p. 48; August 1, 2006, Jennifer Mattson, review of *Ham and Pickles: The First Day of School,* p. 96.

Bulletin of the Center for Children's Books, May, 1985, review of *Pirate Jupiter and the Moondogs,* p. 127; June, 2003, review of *Grody's Not So Golden Rules,* p. 420.

Horn Book, November-December, 1984, review of *Rotten Ralph's Rotten Christmas,* p. 279; November-December, 1989, Ellen Fader, review of *Rotten Ralph's Show and Tell,* p. 759; January-February, 1991, Hanna B. Zeiger, review of *Happy Birthday Rotten Ralph,* p. 94; January-February, 1993, Mary M. Burns, review of *The Ghost Family Meets Its Match,* pp. 77-78; September-October, 1998, Elizabeth S. Watson, review of *Back to School for Rotten Ralph,* p. 598; September-October, 2001, review of *Rotten Ralph Helps Out,* p. 582; May-June, 2006, Joanna Rudge Long, review of *It's Hot and Cold in Miami,* p. 329.

Kirkus Reviews, September 1, 1984, review of *Rotten Ralph's Rotten Christmas,* p. 60; February 15, 1986, review of *Uncle Henry and Aunt Henrietta's Honeymoon,* p. 306; June 15, 2002, review of *No More Vegetables!,* p. 887; October 1, 2004, review of *Twice as Nice,* p. 967; April 1, 2006, review of *It's Hot and Cold in Miami,* p. 356.

Publishers Weekly, May 24, 1985, review of *Pirate Jupiter and the Moondogs,* p. 70; August 22, 1986, review of *Rotten Ralph's Trick or Treat,* p. 95; August 11, 1989, review of *Rotten Ralph's Show and Tell,* pp. 457-458; June 29, 1990, review of *Happy Birthday Rotten Ralph,* pp. 100-101; July 27, 1992, review of *The Ghost Family Meets Its Match,* pp. 61-62; July 5, 1993, review of *Conga Crocodile,* p. 71; January 10, 1994, review of *Not So Rotten Ralph,* pp. 61-62; May 29, 1995, review of *Cyrano the Bear,* p. 84; June 17, 1996, review of *When Someone in the Family Drinks Too Much,* pp. 64-65; November 25, 1996, review of

Rotten Ralph's Rotten Romance, pp. 75-76; July 26, 1999, review of *Bunny Riddles,* p. 93; January 22, 2001, review of *A Cowboy Named Ernestine,* p. 323; July 2, 2001, review of *Rotten Ralph Helps Out,* p. 76; July 1, 2002, review of *No More Vegetables!,* p. 78; April 15, 2003, review of *Grody's Not So Golden Rules,* p. 70; June 12, 2006, review of *Ham and Pickles,* p. 50.

School Library Journal, November, 1981, George Shannon, review of *Sam and Violet Are Twins* and *Sam and Violet Go Camping,* p. 81; May, 1982, Nancy Palmer, review of *Sam and Violet's Birthday Book,* p. 80; February, 1984, Lauralyn Levesque, review of *Bruno Brontosaurus,* pp. 63-64; October, 1985, Jean Hammond Zimmerman, review of *Pirate Jupiter and the Moondogs,* pp. 161-162; January, 1989, review of *It Came from the Swamp,* p. 66; November, 1992, Anna Biagioni, review of *The Ghost Family Meets Its Match,* p. 77; July, 1996, Marsha McGrath, review of *When Someone in the Family Drinks Too Much,* p. 79; November, 1997, Eunice Weech, review of *Mummy Riddles,* p. 107; June, 1999, Jane Marino, review of *Wedding Bells for Rotten Ralph,* pp. 94-95; July, 2000, Shanla Brookshire, review of *The One and Only Me,* p. 87; March, 2001, Steven Engelfried, review of *A Cowboy Named Ernestine,* p. 219; February, 2002, Patricia Manning, review of *Dino Riddles,* p. 120; August, 2002, Linda M. Kenton, review of *No More Vegetables!,* p. 155; July, 2003, Kathleen Kelly MacMillan, review of *Grody's Not So Golden Rules,* p 105; November, 2004, Joy Fleishhacker, review of *Twice as Nice,* p. 130; May, 2006, Miriam Lang Budin, review of *It's Hot and Cold in Miami,* p. 136; July, 2006, Lisa Gangemi Kropp, review of *Ham and Pickles,* p. 86.

ONLINE

Nicole Rubel Home Page, http://www.nicolerubel.com (July 14, 2007).

*   *   *

RUBY, Laura

Personal

Married; children: two step daughters.

Addresses

Home—Chicago, IL. *E-mail*—lauraruby@lauraruby.com.

Career

Writer.

Awards, Honors

Parent's Choice Silver Honor for Fiction, 2003, and Edgar Allan Poe Award nomination for best juvenile mystery, Mystery Writers of America, 2004, both for *Lily's Ghosts.*

Writings

Lily's Ghosts (children's novel), HarperCollins (New York, NY), 2003.
The Wall and the Wing (children's novel), Eos (New York, NY), 2006.
Good Girls (young-adult novel), HarperTempest (New York, NY), 2006.
I'm Not Julia Roberts (short fiction; for adults), Warner Books (New York, NY), 2007.
The Chaos King (sequel to *The Wall and the Wing*), Eos (New York, NY), 2007.

Contributor of short fiction to periodicals, including *Other Voices, Florida Review, Literal Latte, Sycamore Review,* and *Nimrod.* Contributor of essay to anthology *Everything I Needed to Know about Being a Girl I Learned from Judy Blume,* Pocket Books, 2007.

Sidelights

Beginning her writing career as the author of middle-grade novels, Laura Ruby has also written short fiction for adult readers and a contemporary-themed novel for young adults. Considered controversial due to its focus on teen sexuality, *Good Girls* finds the reputation of high school senior and Audrey blackened when a camera-phone video of her engaged in compromising behavior with arrogant boyfriend Luke is posted on the Web for all to see. Shunned by her friends and condemned by her disappointed parents, honor student Audrey must now reexamine her choices and learn how her present behavior will impact her future. As a *Publishers Weekly* writer noted, in Audrey's narration Ruby "offers plenty of frank, sisterly insight about teen sexuality" and "leaves readers with plenty to ponder."

In *Lily's Ghosts* Ruby focuses on a thirteen-year-old girl who is being haunted by ghosts. Lily Crabtree and her mother have recently moved to an old Victorian house in Cape May, New Jersey, that belongs to a very distant family relative. Upon entering the house, Lily discovers a creepy portrait of her great uncle, which she decides to put in a closet. From that point on, strange occurrences plague the teen, such as finding jam in her shoes and seeing objects moving about mysteriously. When Lily decides that she is being haunted by ghosts, she calls on a friend to help her discover what is actually going on in her house. A reviewer for *Publishers Weekly* commended Ruby for her "sharp-witted narrative and lively characterizations," while Renee Steinberg, reviewing *Lily's Ghosts* for *School Library Journal,* predicted that "readers will be hooked right up to the surprising ending."

Ruby turns from ghosts to fantasy in the middle-grade novel *The Wall and the Wing* and its sequel, *The Chaos King.* In *The Wall and the Wing* readers are transported to a large, dazzling metropolis where magic is commonplace and many inhabitants have the power of flight. Much to her dismay, twelve-year-old orphaned

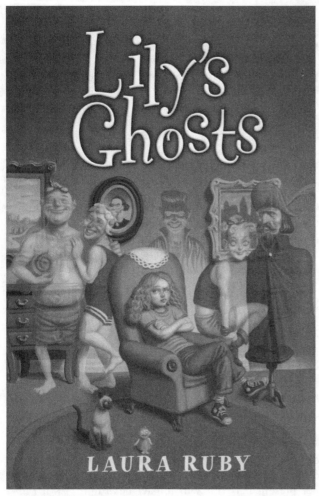

Cover of Laura Ruby's children's novel Lily's Ghosts, *featuring artwork by Peter Ferguson.* (Cover art © 2003 by Peter Ferguson. Reproduced by permission of HarperCollins Publishers.)

Gurl is one of the flightless living in this Manhattan of the future. However, she has another skill, one that is highly coveted: she has the ability to make herself invisible by fading into shadow. Taken advantage of by the matron of the orphanage where she lives, Gurl escapes with fellow orphan Bug. The two soon find themselves on the run from a series of surreal pursuers, among them giant red-eyed rat men, a creature with a zipper face, and a professor who has grass atop his head where hair should be. Noting that "it takes time to sort out the large cast" in *The Wall and the Wing,* Kay Weisman nonetheless deemed the novel "intriguing" in her *Booklist* review. Ruby's "fast-paced wackiness is told with humor, often black, that will have young readers giggling," concluded Connie Tyrrell Burn in her *School Library Journal* review of *The Wall and the Wing.*

A year older and orphaned no more, Gurl is known as Georgie when readers meet up with her again in *The Chaos King.* Still able to disappear at will, she is also phenomenally wealthy, but when her parents enroll her at an exclusive high-school prep school Georgie realizes that money does not always buy happiness. When best friend Bug—now a local celebrity—is briefly abducted by a huge octopus, the occurrence marks the first in a series of unusual events, many linked to Georgie's mysterious but absent-minded new friend, the Professor. After the Professor disappears, Georgie and Bug express concern, but school and social squabbles take top priority until something dire threatens their entire magical world. Citing Ruby's "off-the-wall writing style and infinite imagination," *Kliatt* contributor Cara Chancellor called *The Chaos King* "a wonderful story about . . . being different." Also praising the novel, a *Kirkus Reviews* writer remarked that Ruby's "zany adventure unfolds in a startlingly odd alternate universe" that is brought to vivid life through the author's "humorous narration."

Apart from her novel-length works, Ruby focuses on adult themes in the short fiction she has published in various periodicals. Ten of these stories are collected in *I'm Not Julia Roberts,* and their interconnected storylines feature three women and the blended families they are part of. As Joanne Wilkinson noted in *Booklist,* Ruby's collection comprises a "smart take on fractured families" that "captures both warring emotions and fleeting moments of connection" among its compelling characters. Despite the praise her adult fiction has received, Ruby has no intention of abandoning her teen and pre-teen readership. "The reason I write for kids is because it's fun . . . ," the author told Cynthia Letitch-Smith in *Cynsations* online. "Kids and teens are the most passionate readers there are; I know, because I was one of those passionate readers. And I'll never apologize for writing for kids or teens and I can't imagine I'll ever stop."

Biographical and Critical Sources

PERIODICALS

Booklist, February 1, 2006, Kay Weisman, review of *The Wall and the Wing,* p. 51; October 1, 2006, Joanne Wilkinson, review of *I'm Not Julia Roberts,* p. 38.

Bulletin of the Center for Children's Books, September, 2003, Janice Del Negro, review of *Lily's Ghosts,* p. 31; April, 2006, April Spisak, review of *The Wall and the Wing,* p. 371.

Kirkus Reviews, July 1, 2003, review of *Lily's Ghosts,* p. 914; January 15, 2006, review of *The Wall and the Wing,* p. 89; August 15, 2006, review of *Good Girls,* p. 851; September 1, 2006, review of *I'm Not Julia Roberts,* p. 871; May 1, 2007, review of *The Chaos King.*

Kliatt, May, 2007, Cara Chancellor, review of *The Chaos King,* p. 18.

Library Journal, January 1, 2007, Beth Gibbs, review of *I'm Not Julia Roberts,* p. 98.

Publishers Weekly, August 11, 2003, review of *Lily's Ghosts,* p. 281; March 13, 2006, review of *The Wall and the Wing,* p. 66; September 4, 2006, review of *I'm Not Julia Roberts,* p. 35; September 11, 2006, review of *Good Girls,* p. 57.

School Library Journal, December, 2003, Renee Steinberg, review of *Lily's Ghosts,* p. 160; February, 2006, Connie Tyrrell Burns, review of *The Wall and the Wing,* p. 136; November, 2006, Jane Cronkhite, review of *Good Girls,* p. 148.

Voice of Youth Advocates, June, 2004, Deborah Dubois, review of *Lily's Ghosts,* p. 146; February, 2006, Michele Winship, review of *The Wall and the Wing,* p. 504; December, 2006, Caitlin Augusta, review of *Good Girls,* p. 432.

ONLINE

Cynsations, http://www.cynthialeitichsmith.blogspot.com/ (May 25, 2006), Cynthia Leitich-Smith, interview with Ruby.

Kidsreads.com, http://www.kidsreads.com/ (September, 2003), "Laura Ruby."

Laura Ruby Home Page, http://www.lauraruby.com (July 20, 2007).

S

SAPERGIA, Barbara 1943-

Personal
Born 1943, in Moose Jaw, Saskatchewan, Canada; married Geoffrey Ursell. *Education:* University of Saskatchewan, B.A. (English), 1964; University of Manitoba, M.A., 1966.

Addresses
Home and office—Saskatoon, Saskatchewan, Canada.

Career
Fiction writer and dramatist for stage, radio, and television. Instructor in English at University of Victoria and University of British Columbia. Coteau Books, Regina, Saskatchewan, Canada, co-founder, children's editor, and member of board of directors, beginning 1975. Playwright-in-residence, Persephone Theatre, 1985-86.

Awards, Honors
Saskatchewan Writers Guild Long Manuscript Award for Drama, 1989, for *Double Take,* 1985, for *Roundup;* Saskatchewan Book Award nomination, 1999, for *Secrets in Water,* 2005, and John W. Campbell Award nomination for best science-fiction novel, 2007, both for *Dry;* John V. Hicks Long Manuscript Award, Saskatchewan Writers Guild, 2006, for play *Nell.*

Writings

Dirt Hills Mirage (poetry), Thistledown Press (Saskatoon, Saskatchewan, Canada), 1980.
Foreigners (novel), Douteau Books (Regina, Saskatchewan, Canada), 1984.
South Hill Girls (short fiction), Fifth House Publishers (Calgary, Alberta, Canada), 1998.
Secrets in Water (novel), Coteau Books (Regina, Saskatchewan, Canada), 1999.
Dry (novel), Coteau Books (Regina, Saskatchewan, Canada), 2006.

PLAYS

Lokkinen (produced 1982), Playwrights Canada (Toronto, Ontario, Canada), 1984.
Blizzard and the Christmas Spirit, produced 1985.
The Great Orlando, produced 1985.
Matty and Rose, produced 1985.
The Skipping Show, produced 1986.
Roundup (produced 1990), Coteau Books (Regina, Saskatchewan, Canada), 1992.
(With husband, Geoffrey Ursell) *Winning the Prairie Gamble,* produced 2005.

Also author of television and radio plays. Co-creator and writer for children's television series *Prairie Berry Pie,* Global Television/Aboriginal People's Television Network; writer for *Mythquest,* Canadian Broadcasting Corporation.

Sidelights
Barbara Sapergia, well known in her native Canada for her fiction and for drama for stage, radio, and television. For many years she was also the children's editor of Coteau Books, a Saskatchewan-based publishing company she cofounded in the mid-1970s. Her plays include *Matty and Rose,* which focuses on the lives of Canadian railway porters working during the 1940s, and *Roundup,* a published play that focuses on the effects of prairie drought among the Saskatchewan farming community.

A more recent work by Sapergia, the novel *Dry,* is a bit of a departure for the writer, whose focus has predominately been on the lives of people living in small prairie towns. *Dry* takes place in the near future, as the effects of global warming have caused a severe, decade-long drought and resulted in the overuse of chemicals and other drastic land-use measures on the prairie's large-

scale commercial farms. While many in the region have left or resorted to living underground to avoid the relentless sun, [;amt scoemtosts Tomas Nilsson and his sister, Signy Nilsson, hope to find a way to grow wheat under drought conditions. The siblings' challenges increase when Magnus Dragland, a ruthless, land-grabbing neighbor, begins aggressive efforts to acquire the Nilsson's farm, which has been family land since it was settled by Swedish immigrants in the 1930s. As tensions grow and secrets between the neighboring farmers are revealed, Signy's deaf, twelve-year-old son David reveals an unusual ability that affects the story's tragic outcome. Praising *Dry,* Ann Hart wrote in *Kliatt* that Sapergia's novel presents "a serious look at our kinship with the earth and each other." In the Toronto *Globe and Mail* Carol Giangrande wrote that Sapergia's "writing is crisp and the story has the fascination of a well-told futuristic tale." Because of its focus and compelling story, *Dry* has also been studied in schools in Nova Scotia, Canada.

Biographical and Critical Sources

BOOKS

Hillis, Doris, editor, *Plainspeaking: Interviews with Saskatchewan Writers,* Coteau Books (Regina, Saskatchewan, Canada), 2004.

PERIODICALS

Books in Canada, January, 1982, review of *Dirt Hills Mirage,* p. 8; June, 1985, review of *Foreigners,* p. 21; May, 1992, review of *South Hill Girls,* p. 54; November, 2005, Antony Di Nardo, review of *Dry,* p. 17.
Canadian Book Review Annual, 2000, review of *Secrets in Water,* p. 161.
Canadian Review of Materials, September, 1992, review of *South Hill Girls,* p. 223.
Globe and Mail (Toronto, Ontario, Canada), October 15, 2005, Carol Giangrande, review of *Dry.*
Kliatt, May, 2006, Ann Hart, review of *Dry,* p. 24.
Maclean's, February, 25, 1985, Michelle Heinemann, review of *Foreigners,* p. 72.
Prairie Fire, Summer, 1993, review of *200 Percent Cracked Wheat,* p. 119.
Quill and Quire, May, 1992, review of *South Hill Girls,* p. 20; November, 1999, review of *Secrets in Water,* p. 34.
Voice of Youth Advocates, April, 2006, Kathleen Beck, review of *Dry,* p. 65.

ONLINE

Coteau Books Web site, http://www.coteaubooks.com/ (July 17, 2007), "Barbara Sapergia."
Encyclopedia of Saskatchewan Online, http://esask.uregina.ca/ (July 17, 2007), Justin Messner, "Barbara Sapergia."

SCHLESINGER, Arthur Meier, Jr.
See SCHLESINGER, Arthur M., Jr.

*   *   *

SCHLESINGER, Arthur M., Jr. 1917-2007
(Arthur Meier Schlesinger, Jr.)

OBITUARY NOTICE— See index for *SATA* sketch: Born October 15, 1917, in Columbus, OH; died of heart failure February 28, 2007, in New York, NY. Historian, educator, and author. Schlesinger was a Pulitzer prize-winning historian who was most noted for his writings on the Andrew Jackson, Franklin D. Roosevelt, and John F. Kennedy administrations. He held a B.A. from Harvard University, earned in 1938, and was a fellow there when his first book was published. As a young man, Schlesinger entertained thoughts of becoming a theater critic, but his father convinced him of his potential as an historian, based on his senior thesis. This thesis was published as *Orestes A. Brownson: A Pilgrim's Progress* (1939) and was a Catholic Book Club selection. With the start of World War II, Schlesinger worked for the Office of War Information in Washington, DC, and then for the Office of Strategic Services in Washington, London, and Paris; he was briefly a corporal in the army in 1945. He freelanced after the war, publishing *The Age of Jackson* (1945), which earned him his first Pulitzer prize. On the strength of this work, he was offered an assistant professorship at Harvard University, an accomplishment fairly unprecedented for someone with only an undergraduate degree to his credit. Schlesinger was made a full professor in 1954, and released his acclaimed three-volume work, *The Age of Roosevelt* (1957, 1959, 1960). By the 1950s, he was becoming involved in politics. He campaigned for Adlai E. Stevenson in the 1952 and 1956 U.S presidential elections, and though he was disappointed with Stevenson's failures, he once commented that he felt Stevenson helped pave the way for Kennedy's later success. When Kennedy was elected in 1960, the new president chose Schlesinger for the rather unique position of special assistant to the White House. The historian took a leave from Harvard to work for Kennedy. His job was sometimes described as that of "court philosopher," and he served as an intermediary between the president and disgruntled liberals as well as other White House critics. Perhaps his most noted act was writing a pair of memos that warned of the potentially disastrous consequences of the Bay of Pigs invasion of Cuba. Schlesinger also tried to protect the president in the aftermath by telling Kennedy he should lay the blame on his subordinates, although the president ultimately accepted responsibility himself. After Kennedy's assassination in 1963, Schlesinger remained on the White House staff briefly under President Lyndon B. Johnson, but soon quit to return to teaching. Instead of going back to Harvard, however, he joined the City University of New York as Albert Schweitzer Professor in the Hu-

manities in 1966. In 1965 he released his *A Thousand Days: John F. Kennedy in the White House*, which earned the historian his second Pulitzer Prize. The book conveys the author's high opinion of Kennedy, just as several of his later works were extremely critical of the Johnson and Nixon administrations. For a time, Schlesinger continued to be involved in political campaigns, assisting with Robert F. Kennedy's bid for the presidency before Robert, too, was assassinated. Later, Schlesinger would write *Robert Kennedy and His Times* (1978), which won the National Book Award. The two Kennedy assassinations made Schlesinger rather bitter about the state of the world. His *The Imperial Presidency* (1973) was critical of President Richard M. Nixon, whom he felt abused his power in office. In later works he continued to show his willingness to critique American politics and society, including *The Disuniting of America: Reflections on a Multicultural Society* (1991; revised edition, 1997) and *War and the American Presidency* (2004). Retired from teaching in 1995, Schlesinger was awarded the National Humanities Medal in 1998. As a scholar, he is remembered for his contributions to the understanding of the evolution of American democracy during the eras of three important U.S. presidents.

OBITUARIES AND OTHER SOURCES:

PERIODICALS

Los Angeles Times, March 1, 2007, pp. A1, A22.
New York Times, March 2, 2007, p. A18; March 2, 2007, p. A2; March 8, 2007, p. A2.
Washington Post, March 2, 2007, pp. A1, A8.

*   *   *

SCHNEIDER, Howie 1930-2007

Personal

Born 1930, in New York, NY; died from complications due to heart surgery, June 28, 2007, in MA; married Susan Seligson (a writer), 1992; children: Peter, Evan. *Hobbies and other interests:* Travel, community activism.

Career

Editorial cartoonist and sculptor. *Providence Banner,* Providence, RI, editorial cartoonist, beginning 2000. Cofounder of Yearrounders Festival, Provincetown, MA. Member of board, Newspapers Features Council and National Cartoonists Society.

Awards, Honors

Two New England Press Association Awards for Best Editorial Cartoon, for work on *Provincetown Banner.*

Writings

FOR CHILDREN; SELF-ILLUSTRATED

(With wife, Susan Seligson) *Amos: The Story of an Old Dog and His Couch,* Joy Street Books (Boston, MA), 1987.
(With Susan Seligson) *The Amazing Amos and the Greatest Couch on Earth,* Joy Street Books (Boston, MA), 1989.
(With Susan Seligson) *Amos, Ahoy!: A Couch Adventure on Land and Sea,* Joy Street Books (Boston, MA), 1990.
(With Susan Seligson) *Amos Camps Out: A Couch Adventure in the Woods,* Joy Street Books (Boston, MA), 1992.
Uncle Lester's Hat, Putnam (New York, NY), 1993.
No Dogs Allowed, Putnam's (New York, NY), 1995.
Chewy Louie, Rising Moon (Flagstaff, AZ), 2000.
Wilky the White House Cockroach, Putnam (New York, NY), 2006.

SELF-ILLUSTRATED

The World Is No Place for Children, Doubleday (Garden City, NY), 1960.
The Deceivers, Doubleday (Garden City, NY), 1961.
Mom's the Word: Some Unlikely Admonitions from Mothers of Famous People to Their Offspring, World Publishing (Cleveland, OH), 1968.

Creator of comic strips "Eek and Meek," 1965-2000, "The Sunshine Club: Life in Generation Rx," 2003-06, "Unshucked," "Percy's World," and "Bimbo's Circus."

ILLUSTRATOR

Olga Cossi, *Gus the Bus,* Scholastic (New York, NY), 1989.
Jean Davies Okimoto, *Blumpoe the Grumpoe Meets Arnold the Cat,* Joy Street Books (Boston, MA), 1990.

Cartoons appeared in numerous periodicals, including *New Yorker, Esquire, Redbook, Playboy,* and *McCall's.*

Sidelights

Although Howie Schneider spent much of his career as an editorial cartoonist and creator of the long-running comic strip "Eek and Meek," he led something of a dual life as the author and illustrator of humorous books for children. His first three picture books, written between 1987 and 1990 and beginning with *Amos: The Story of an Old Dog and His Couch,* were coauthored with his wife, writer Susan Seligson and feature the adventures of a sedentary Irish setter. Schneider's subsequent self-illustrated books for children included *Uncle Lester's Hat, Chewy Louie,* and *Wilky the White House Cockroach.* He occasionally collaborated with other writers, producing illustrations for Olga Cossi's *Gus the*

Bus and Jean Davies Okimoto's *Blumpoe the Grumpoe Meets Arnold the Cat,* the latter book a humorous tale about a curmudgeonly man and a persistent pussycat that is enlivened by what a *Publishers Weekly* reviewer described as "winsome, nostalgic illustrations."

Born in 1930, Schneider started his "Eek and Meek" comic, about a pair of darkly philosophical mice, in 1965. Picked up by United Media, the strip grew in popularity, appearing in syndication in over 400 newspapers before its author decided to call it quits in 2000. Three years later, Schneider returned to newspapers via "The Sunshine Club: Life in Generation Rx," a strip geared for ageing baby boomers. Highlighting a host of senior moments via its cast of ageing animal characters—including Uncle Bunty, George, Edna, Willard, unhappily widowed Fran, the happily married Bovines, the television-addicted Badgers, and elder statesman Professor Noodle—"The Sunshine Club" was syndicated in dozens of newspapers before ending shortly before Schneider's death in 2007. Making his home on Cape Cod, Massachusetts, Schneider also worked as an editorial cartoonist for the *Provincetown Banner.* In a 2004 interview with *Editor & Publisher* contributor Dave Astor, Schneider noted of his return to comics following the end of his "Eek and Meek" series: "You get in the habit of looking at the world through these little droplets of humor. If you don't have characters' mouths to put observations in, you feel frustrated. It's like taking away a ventriloquist's dummy."

Schneider's picture books often included dog characters. In *Chewy Louie,* for example, a growing puppy finds that his opportunities to chew expand as he grows, and from his toys and food bowl his nibble radius ex-

A tiny, misguided bug accidentally infiltrates the Oval Office and stirs up trouble in Schneider's humorous **Wilky the White House Cockroach.**

pands to his family's furniture, the family car, and even the family house. Try as they might, obedience trainers cannot break the fuzzy black pup of his destructive habit, so all must wait until he matures into a full-grown dog. Noting Schneider's upbeat cartoon drawings for the book, *Booklist* reviewer Todd Morning praised *Chewy Louie* as "a goofy tale with a lot of kid appeal." Also noting the book's lighthearted humor, Maryann H. Owen wrote in *School Library Journal* that "Chewy Louie's exuberance is almost palpable and his teeth marks are everywhere" in Schneider's "entertaining tale." *No Dogs Allowed,* another book by Schneider, also spins a silly story, this time focusing on a family's efforts to thwart a hotel's rule against pets by dressing their dog Mercer as an erudite Frenchman.

Schneider presented readers with a witty play on everything from high-tech security systems to bug behavior in *Wilky the White House Cockroach.* Illustrated with Schneider's characteristic spare cartoon drawings, a little cockroach named Willy hides in a pizza box leaving his family's pizza parlor home and winds up hitching a ride into the Oval Office, where the president and his staff are looking forward to lunch. When Wilky is spotted scuttling across the presidential desk and across the floor into the War Room in an effort to escape, he becomes the object of a hunt that spins out of control and eventually includes the Minister of Creepy Crawlies and the Exterminator General, as well as a representative of every national media outlet. Fortunately, recalling the advice of his wise and long-lived Uncle

Howie Schneider's love of dogs, despite their bad habits, shines through in his illustrations for his original picture book **Chewy Louie.**

Julius, Wilky manages to survive his short stint as a national security threat. In *Booklist* Carolyn Phelan remarked on the book's appeal for both children and adults, and called *Wilky the White House Cockroach* "broadly comical in effect," and a *Publishers Weekly* writer noted that the author/illustrator's "clear drawings enable beginning readers to easily grasp the plot" of a "mischievous twist on a familiar story." While calling Schneider's tale "slight," Wendy Woodfill concluded in *School Library Journal* that *Wilky the White House Cockroach* contains "zany illustrations [that] are filled with sophisticated humor."

Biographical and Critical Sources

PERIODICALS

Booklist, September 1, 1992, Ellen Mandel, review of *Amos Camps Out: A Couch Adventure in the Woods,* p. 69; July, 1995, Ilene Cooper, review of *No Dogs Allowed,* p. 1884; August, 2000, Todd Morning, review of *Chewy Louie,* p. 2149; October 15, 2006, Carolyn Phelan, review of *Wilky the White House Cockroach,* p. 55.

Bulletin of the Center for Children's Books, January, 2007, Elizabeth Bush, review of *Wilky the White House Cockroach,* p. 229.

Editor & Publisher, April 15, 2004, Dave Astor, interview with Schneider.

Horn Book, January-February, 1988, Ann A. Flowers review of *Amos: The Story of an Old Dog and His Couch,* p. 56; May, 1989, review of *The Amazing Amos and the Greatest Couch on Earth,* p. 391; July-August, 1990, Martha V. Parravano, review of *Blumpoe the Grumpoe Meets Arnold the Cat,* p. 447.

Kirkus Reviews, August 15, 2006, review of *Wilky the White House Cockroach,* p. 85.

Publishers Weekly, September 25, 1987, review of *Amos,* p. 108; December 9, 1988, review of *Gus the Bus,* p. 64; February 10, 1989, review of *The Amazing Amos and the Greatest Couch on Earth,* p. 70; May 11, 1990, review of *Blumpoe the Grumpoe Meets Arnold the Cat,* p. 259; August 9, 1993, review of *Uncle Lester's Hat,* p. 477; June 19, 1995, review of *No Dogs Allowed,* p. 59.

School Library Journal, December, 1987, Susan Scheps, review of *Amos,* p. 76; April, 1989, Mary Lou Budd, review of *The Amazing Amos and the Greatest Couch on Earth,* p. 91; July, 1989, John Philborok, review of *Gus the Bus,* p. 63; July, 1990, John Peters, review of *Blumpoe the Grumpoe Meets Arnold the Cat,* p. 63; October, 1990, Luann Toth, review of *Amos Ahoy!,* p. 201; September, 1992, Anna Biagioni Hart, review of *Amos Camps Out,* p. 210; November, 1993, Mary Lou Budd, review of *Uncle Lester's Hat,* p. 90; August, 1995, Christina Dorr, review of *No Dogs Allowed,* p. 1289; November, 2000, Maryann H. Owen, review of *Chewy Louie,* p. 132; September, 2006, Wendy Woodfill, review of *Wilky the White House Cockroach,* p. 184.

OBITUARIES

PERIODICALS

Editor and Publisher, June 19, 2007.

ONLINE

Boston Globe Online, http://www.boston.com/ (July 1, 2007).

Provincetown Banner Online, http://www.provincetownbanner.com/ (June 28, 2007).*

*   *   *

SCHUBERT, Leda 1945-

Personal

Born 1945, in Washington, DC; father an academic, mother a business owner; married Bob Rosenfeld. *Education:* Brandeis, B.A.; Harvard University, M.A.T. (English); Vermont College, M.F.A. (writing for children and young adults).

Addresses

Home—Plainfield, VT. *Agent*—Steven Chudney, Chudney Agency, 72 N. State Rd., Ste. 501, Briarcliff Manor, NY 10510. *E-mail*—leda@ledaschubert.com.

Career

Author and educator. Cabot School, Cabot, VT, librarian, beginning 1980; also librarian at Kellogg-Hubbard Library, Montpelier, VT, and Uniondale, NY, public schools; formerly worked as a teacher, librarian, and preschool director. Vermont Department of Education, school library consultant, 1986-2003. Former member of award committees for Caldecott, Arbuthnot, *Boston Globe/Horn Book,* and Vermont state book awards.

Member

Society of Children's Book Writers and Illustrators, Authors Guild, American Library Association, Association of Library Services for Children.

Awards, Honors

Book Sense Winter Pick, 2005, for *Here Comes Darrell;* New York Public Library 100 Titles for Reading and Sharing designation, and *New York Times* Editors' Choice title, both 2006, both for *Ballet of the Elephants.*

Writings

FOR CHILDREN

Winnie All Day Long, illustrated by William Benedict, Candlewick Press (Cambridge, MA), 2000.

Winnie Plays Ball, illustrated by William Benedict, Candlewick Press (Cambridge, MA), 2000.

Here Comes Darrell, illustrated by Mary Azarian, Houghton Mifflin (Boston, MA), 2005.

Ballet of the Elephants, illustrated by Robert Andrew Parker, Roaring Brook Press (New Milford, CT), 2006.

Donna and the Robbers, illustrated by Ken Stewart, Vermont Folklife Center (Middlebury, VT), 2007.

Feeding the Sheep, illustrated by Andrea U'Ren, Farrar, Straus & Giroux (New York, NY), 2008.

Also author of six-part serialized novel *Nathan's Song* published in *Boston Globe Online* as part of spring, 2007, Newspapers in Education project. Contributor to periodicals, including *Horn Book* and *School Library Journal.*

Sidelights

Children's book author Leda Schubert lives in Vermont, and her stories for young children are inspired by her personal curiosity as well as by her colorful New England surroundings. Although she has enjoyed writing since childhood, Schubert viewed it as a hobby for many years while working as a teacher, librarian, and library consultant. Working as a librarian allowed Schubert to learn what kinds of books her young patrons liked, and her subsequent job as a library consultant for the Vermont Department of Education gave her a familiarity with almost every book published for children. With this background, it is not surprising that Schubert's picture books, which include *Here Comes Darrell, Ballet of the Elephants,* and the beginning readers *Winnie All Day Long* and *Winnie Plays Ball,* have received critical accolades as well as awards.

"I was lucky that all of my jobs involved reading to children," Schubert explained of her background to *Seven Days Vermont* online interviewer Margot Harrison. "I started writing a little bit, but I had no idea what I was doing. I never gave up this dream." Her "Winnie" books, which were written while Schubert worked as a library consultant, were designed to fill what she saw as a specific need: "more trade books for kids that they could buy at the bookstore that would encourage reading, but that were funny and not didactic." Based on Schubert's own dog, *Winnie All Day Long* introduces large, rambunctious Winnie and her human playmate Annie, and follows the interaction between the two as Winnie's high spirits, napping, mealtimes, and desire for attention affect Annie and her family throughout the day. The oversized pooch celebrates a birthday in *Winnie Plays Ball,* and the toy balls she receives generate several games with Annie. After her "Winnie" stories were accepted for publication by Candlewick Press as part of the publisher's "Brand New Readers" series, Schubert "got more and more convinced that [writing for children] . . . was what I had to do." She left her job in education and turned to writing.

Leda Schubert joins with illustrator and fellow Vermonter Mary Azarian to create the picture book **Here Comes Darrell.** (Illustration © 2005 by Mary Azarian. All rights reserved. Reproduced by permission of Houghton Mifflin Company.)

Schubert's collaboration with Caldecott Medal-winning illustrator Mary Azarian on *Here Comes Darrell* is also based on the author's life: in this case a generous neighbor who plowed driveways in her town so that local working folk could be on the job on time following snowstorms. Set amid the northern New England seasons that both author and illustrator know so well, the story focuses on a man who takes time to help out neighbors with backhoe work and snowplowing, and shares his supply of wood, instead of spending all his time on his own property. When a severe storm hits the area and destroys the roof of his barn, Darrell's kindness is returned, "celebrat[ing] . . . a way of life in a rural community where neighbors help each other through the year," according to a *Publishers Weekly* contributor. Calling the collaboration between author and illustrator "delightful," *School Library Journal* contributor Teresa Pfeifer cited Azarian's "distinguished, detailed woodcuts and concluded that *Here Comes Darrell* "will be a pleasure to pair with many other books on the seasons, neighbors, and communities" during story hours.

Inspired by a television special Schubert watched about the life of renowned twentieth-century ballet choreographer George Balanchine, *Ballet of the Elephants* was written after the author completed her M.F.A. degree in writing for children and young adults at Vermont Col-

lege. The book follows the efforts of Balanchine and circus promoter John Ringling North to stage North's dream of a "Circus Polka," a dance involving fifty elephants and fifty ballerinas. Set to music by Russian composer Igor Stravinsky, the mammoth undertaking premiered in 1942 as part of the famous Ringling Brothers and Barnum & Bailey Circus. It starred the famous elephant Modoc and prima ballerina Vera Zorina. In her fact-filled text, Schubert brings to life the international proportions of the undertaking, as well as the daunting task of costuming fifty rotund pachyderms in fluffy pink tutus and glittering tiaras. Another true story involving animals is brought to life in her book *Donna and the Robbers,* which transports readers to turn-of-the-twentieth-century Maine and the horse who foiled the robbery of a small town during a blizzard. In *Booklist,* Hazel Rochman praised Schubert's "simple and lyrical" text in *Ballet of the Elephants,* as well as her inclusion of an afterword that answers the questions of more curious readers. Robert Andrew Parker's ink and water color images "capture the movement and vitality of this creative undertaking," added Carol Schene in her *School Library Journal* review of the same book, the critic concluding that Schubert's "clearly written" story "provides a unique introduction to . . . a curious moment in musical history." "Schubert's deft, incisive way of telling the incredible story will set young minds spinning," announced Jed Perl, hailing the picture-book history in the *New York Times Book Review.* "Woven through this casually opulent volume is an inspiriting idea," Perl added: "that boys and girls will be tantalized by the works . . . of geniuses like Balanchine and Stravinsky, men whose achievements our dumb-it-down era sometimes regards as too demanding even for adults."

Biographical and Critical Sources

PERIODICALS

Booklist, October 1, 2005, Ilene Cooper, review of *Here Comes Darrell,* p. 66; April 1, 2006, Hazel Rochman, review of *Ballet of the Elephants,* p. 46.
Bulletin of the Center for Children's Books, November, 2005, Elizabeth Bush, review of *Here Comes Darrell,* p. 155; May, 2006, Deborah Stevenson, review of *Ballet of the Elephants,* p. 421.
Horn Book, July-August, 2006, Betty Carter, review of *Ballet of the Elephants,* p. 469.
Kirkus Reviews, October 15, 2005, review of *Here Comes Darrell,* p. 1146; March 15, 2006, review of *Ballet of the Elephants,* p. 299.
New York Times Book Review, May 14, 2006, Jed Perl, "The Big Dance," p. 20.
Publishers Weekly, October 31, 2005, review of *Here Comes Darrell,* p. 55; April 10, 2006, review of *Ballet of the Elephants,* p. 70.
School Library Journal, November, 2005, Teresa Pfeifer, review of *Here Comes Darrell,* p. 107; April, 2006, Carol Schene, review of *Ballet of the Elephants,* p. 132.

ONLINE

Cynsations, http://cynthialeitichsmith.blogspot.com/ (February 22, 2006), Cynthia Leitich-Smith, interview with Schubert.
Leda Schubert Home Page, http://www.ledaschubert.com (August 15, 2007).
Seven Days Vermont Online, http://www.sevendaysvt.com/ (September 13, 2006), Margot Harrison, interview with Schubert.

* * *

SCOT-BERNARD, P.
See BERNARD, Patricia

* * *

SHELDON, Dyan
(Serena Gray, D.M. Quintano)

Personal

Born in Brooklyn, NY; children: one daughter.

Addresses

Home—England. *E-mail*—dyan@dyansheldon.co.uk.

Career

Novelist, humorist, and author of children's books.

Awards, Honors

American Library Association Recommended Book for Reluctant Young-Adult Readers designation and New York Public Library Book for the Teen Age designation, both 1999, both for *Confessions of a Teenage Drama Queen.*

Writings

FOR CHILDREN

A Witch Got on at Paddington Station, illustrated by Wendy Smith, Dutton (New York, NY), 1987.
Alison and the Prince, illustrated by Helen Cusack, Methuen (London, England), 1988.
I Forgot, illustrated by John Rogan, Four Winds Press (New York, NY), 1988.
Jack and Alice, illustrated by Alice Garcia De Lynam, Hutchinson (London, England), 1990.
The Whales' Song, illustrated by Gary Blythe, Hutchinson (London, England), 1990, Dial (New York, NY), 1991.
Harry and Chicken, illustrated by Sue Heap, Walker (London, England), 1990, Candlewick Press (Cambridge, MA), 1992.

Harry the Explorer, illustrated by Sue Heap, Walker Books (London, England), 1991, Candlewick Press (Cambridge, MA), 1992.

Seymour Finds a Home, illustrated by Nigel McMullen, Simon & Schuster (New York, NY), 1991.

Lilah's Monster, illustrated by Wendy Smith, Young Piper (London, England), 1992.

My Brother Is a Visitor from Another Planet, illustrated by Derek Brazell, Viking (London, England), 1992, Candlewick Press (Cambridge, MA), 1993.

Sky Watching, illustrated by Graham Percy, Walker (London, England), 1992.

Harry's Holiday, illustrated by Sue Heap, Walker (London, England), 1992, published as *Harry on Vacation,* Candlewick Press, 1993.

The Garden, illustrated by Gary Blythe, Hutchinson (London, England), 1993, published as *Under the Moon,* Dial (New York, NY), 1994.

A Night to Remember, illustrated by Robert Crowther, Walker (London, England), 1993.

Only Binky, illustrated by Honey de Lacey, Methuen (London, England), 1993.

Counting Cows, illustrated by Wendy Smith, Hutchinson (London, England), 1994.

Ride On, Sister Vincent, Walker (London, England), 1994.

Love, Your Bear, Pete, illustrated by Tania Hurt-Newton, Candlewick Press (Cambridge, MA), 1994.

A Bad Place for a Bus Stop, Pan Macmillan (London, England), 1994.

My Brother Is a Superhero, illustrated by Derek Brazell, Viking (London, England), 1994, Candlewick Press (Cambridge, MA), 1996.

Elena the Frog, illustrated by Sue Heap, Walker (London, England), 1997.

Unicorn Dreams, illustrated by Neil Reed, Dial (New York, NY), 1997.

Lizzie and Charley Go Shopping, Walker (London, England), 1999.

Leon Loves Bugs, illustrated by Scoular Anderson, Walker (London, England), 2000.

Undercover Angel, Walker (London, England), 2000.

Undercover Angel Strikes Again, Walker (London, England), 2000.

Clara and Buster Go Moondancing, illustrated by Caroline Anstey, Dorling Kindersley (New York, NY), 2001.

Lizzie and Charley Go to the Movies, Walker (London, England), 2001.

He's Not My Dog, illustrated by Kate Sheppard, Walker (London, England), 2001.

Lizzie and Charley Go away for the Weekend, Walker (London, England), 2002.

The Last Angel, illustrated by Sophy Williams, Macmillan (London, England), 2003.

Vampire across the Way, Walker (London, England), 2004.

Whatever Mona Wants, Mona Gets, illustrated by Ella Okstad, Walker (London, England), 2005.

Contributor to anthologies, including *Funny Stories,* Walker (London, England), 1995; *The Second Storybook Collection,* Macdonald Young (Hemel Hempstead, England), 1995; and *Stories for Six Year Olds,* Walker, 1995.

Author's works have been translated into several languages, including Arabic, Bengali, Chinese, Spanish, Vietnamese, and Urdu.

FOR YOUNG ADULTS

Tall, Thin, and Blonde, Candlewick Press (Cambridge, MA), 1993.

You Can Never Go Home Anymore ("Hauntings" series), Bantam (London, England), 1993.

Save the Last Dance for Me ("Hauntings" series), Bantam (New York, NY), 1993.

The Boy of My Dreams, Candlewick Press (Boston, MA), 1997.

Confessions of a Teenage Drama Queen, Candlewick Press (Cambridge, MA), 1999.

And Baby Makes Two, Walker (London, England), 2000.

My Perfect Life, Candlewick Press (Cambridge, MA), 2002.

Planet Janet (also see below), Walker (London, England), 2002, Candlewick Press (Cambridge, MA), 2003.

Sophie Pitt-Turnbull Discovers America, Walker (London, England), 2003, Candlewick Press (Cambridge, MA), 2005.

Planet Janet in Orbit (also see below), Candlewick Press (Cambridge, MA), 2004.

(Under name D.M. Quintano) *Perfect,* Macmillan (London, England), 2005.

Confessions of a Hollywood Star, Walker (London, England), 2005, Candlewick Press (Cambridge, MA), 2006.

I Conquer Britain, Walker (London, England), 2006, Candlewick Press (Cambridge, MA), 2007.

Deep and Meaningful Diaries from Planet Janet (contains *Planet Janet* and *Planet Janet in Orbit*), Candlewick Press (Cambridge, MA), 2007.

FOR ADULTS

Victim of Love, Heinemann (London, England), 1982, Viking (New York, NY), 1993.

The Dreams of an Average Man, Heinemann (London, England), 1985, Crown (New York, NY), 1986.

My Life as a Whale, Villard (New York, NY), 1992.

On the Road Reluctantly, Little, Brown (London, England), 1995, published as *Dream Catching: A Wander 'round the Americas,* Abacus (London, England), 1995.

Also author of books under pseudonym Serena Gray.

Adaptations

Confessions of a Teenage Drama Queen was adapted by Gail Parent as a feature film, directed by Sara Sugarman, 2004.

Sidelights

After finding success writing two novels for adults, Dyan Sheldon expanded her audience to children and, a decade later, to young adults. A prolific writer, she has

penned over thirty books for children as well as over a dozen books for teen readers since beginning her career in children's literature in the late 1980s, and has even seen one of her teen novels, *Confessions of a Teenage Drama Queen,* adapted as a feature film starring actress Lindsay Lohan. Among Sheldon's other books for teens are *Tall, Thin, and Blonde, My Perfect Life,* and *Sophie Pitt-Turnbull Discovers America,* while her books *Harry and Chicken* and *My Brother Is a Superhero* appeal to elementary-grade readers.

Although Sheldon now makes England her home, she was born in Brooklyn, New York. At age six, she and her family moved to Long Island, where Sheldon's parents hoped that the young girl could experience the benefits of fresh air, sunshine, and the freedom to roam the countryside. Although Sheldon never warmed to her rural surroundings, the move made her more adaptable to change, and after leaving home after high school she spent time in upstate New York, New England, Mississippi, New Jersey, and several New York City boroughs before leaving the United States altogether. As an American in London, Sheldon quickly realized that she had many things to learn about culture and language. These experiences helped inspire her young-adult novels *I Conquer Britain* and *Sophie Pitt-Turnbull Discovers America.*

In *Sophie Pitt-Turnbull Discovers America* a London teen from an affluent family spends the summer in New York City, where things prove far less exciting than she had hoped. Trading places with the daughter of her mother's friend from art school, Sophie finds herself taking care of two children and sharing the family's small, chaotic Brooklyn home with a dog, an iguana, and a pig. After learning to accept the differences between British and American culture, the teen makes some new close friends and learns to be more accepting of others in a novel that *Kliatt* reviewer Claire Rosser dubbed "lighthearted fun."

Sixteen-year-old British teen Janet Bandry is the star of *Planet Janet* and *Planet Janet in Orbit,* two novels that unfold in diary form. Janet is frustrated with typical teen issues: annoying parents, unreasonably demanding school teachers, and worries over her place in the world. Responding to their intellectual interests, in *Planet Janet* Janet and her best friend Disha decide to enter a "Dark Phase" by adopting pseudo-Bohemian posturing that finds them dressing in black, dying their hair purple, piercing their noses, adopting vegetarianism, drowning their melancholy with jazz, and struggling through a challenging literary novel. Janet's self-absorbed journalings reveal other facts that give the novel a poignancy, and also lead readers to the sequel. The teen's summer job, her parents' failing marriage, and Disha's all-consuming romance fill the pages of *Planet Janet in Orbit,* which finds Janet taking a break from the seriousness of the Dark Side. Praising Janet's "hilarious misadventures" in *Planet Janet in Orbit, School Library Journal* reviewer Jane Cronkhite recommended Janet's saga for fans of writers Meg Cabot and Louise Rennison, while Gillian Engberg predicted in *Booklist* that Sheldon's "fast-paced, clever writing . . . will keep teens eagerly reading." Calling Janet "an incredibly witty teen," a *Kirkus Reviews* writer concluded that *Planet Janet in Orbit* showcases it author's "deft ability with funny dialogue and a wacky setting, while still delivering a smart story."

Confessions of a Teenage Drama Queen takes readers to Woodford, the upper-crust New Jersey suburb Manhattan teen Mary Elizabeth Cep calls home after her parents relocate the family there. Disappointed by the lack of excitement in her new town, Mary soon sees an opportunity: she decided that being the new girl in school is the perfect opportunity to transform herself into sassy fashionista Lola. Hoping to inject excitement into her school, Lola makes a new best friend in Ella, crashes a celebrity concert, and then winds up as a heroine in her own teen drama when she runs afowl of the snobby budding socialite Carla Santini. Calling *Confessions of a Teenage Drama Queen* "hilarious," *Booklist*

Cover of Dyan Sheldon's teen novel **Sophie Pitt-Turnbull Discovers America,** *featuring artwork by Phil Hankinson.* (Candlewick Press, 2003. Jacket illustration copyright © 2005 by Phil Hankinson. Reproduced by permission of the publisher Candlewick Press, Inc., Cambridge, MA.)

Cover of Sheldon's popular teen novel Confessions of a Teenage Drama Queen, *featuring artwork by Thomas Hart.* (Cover illustration copyright © 1999 by Thomas Hart. Reproduced by permission of the publisher Candlewick Press, Inc., Cambridge, MA on behalf of Walker Books Ltd., London.)

contributor Frances Bradburn added that in Lola Sheldon creates "a real teenager—warped judgment, mercurial moods, and all." The novel's humorous plot pits a "deliciously despicable villainess against an irresistible heroine glittering with wit and charm," noted a *Publishers Weekly* contributor in another positive review of the novel. In *Kliatt,* Paula Rohrlick praised the book as "a fast and funny read, narrated by the lively Lola and peopled by realistic characters."

Lola returns in *My Perfect Life* and *Confessions of a Hollywood Star. My Perfect Life* finds the outspoken teen planning campaign strategy for Ella, who is running for student council president against the ultra popular Carla. Lola pursues her own dream—becoming a famous stage actress—in *My Perfect Life.* Lola and Ella are graduate from high school in *Confessions of a Hollywood Star,* and the larger-than-Woodford world now beckons. Thwarted by her mom from attending London's Royal Academy of Dramatic Art, the teen decides to track down a film director shooting his new film in town. Reviewing *My Perfect Life, Booklist* contributor Anne Malley described the novel as "a delightfully zany spoof of high school, politics, and affluent subur-

bia, capturing teen angst with wit and poignancy." Featuring what Engberg described as "over-the-top high jinks and unlikely, entertaining adventures," *Confessions of a Hollywood Star* rewards readers expecting the same level of humor generated by Sheldon's previous novels. "Lola's expressive wit and wholesomeness make her an appealing heroine," concluded Erin Schirota in her *School Library Journal* of the series.

Sheldon's stories for the upper-elementary grades are *My Brother Is a Visitor from Another Planet* and *My Brother Is a Superhero.* The two novels focus on Adam, who finds it frustrating to unsuccessfully measure up to the standards set by his perfect older brother, Keith. Trying to distance himself from Keith, Adam joins his own friends on several adventures and sometimes winds up needing the help Keith is willing to provide. Noting the book's value to reluctant readers, Janice Del Negro wrote in *Booklist* that the humor in *My Brother Is a Superhero* "lightens the text, and the plot moves quickly to a satisfactory conclusion."

Geared for younger elementary-grade readers, Sheldon's "Harry" series focuses on a cat-like creature from outer space who, with a human girl named Chicken, has many adventures after landing on Earth. The two meet in *Harry and Chicken* as Chicken adopts the creature her parents believe is a cat and Harry quickly begins getting into a series of humorous scrapes. The adventures continue in *Harry on Vacation* where the two share a camping vacation, and *Harry the Explorer.* Sheldon's "short, fast-moving story abounds with humorous exaggeration and snappy dialogue," noted a *Publishers Weekly* in a review of *Harry and Chicken.*

While Sheldon has become well known for her teen novels in recent years, one of her early works is considered something of a childhood classic. First published in 1991, *The Whales' Song* describes a young girl's visit to her grandmother's home on the coast. Lilly listens to the stories her grandmother tells about growing up with the whales, recalling that when she left the whales a small gift such as a shell or pretty stone, they rewarded her in return. When the girl leaves her own gift for the whales, she is rewarded later that night when she hears her name in the creatures' song. Brought to life in "haunting, evocative" realistic paintings by Gary Blythe, "Sheldon's poetic text manages to overlay a homespun practicality with an ethereal, fairy-tale magic," according to a *Publishers Weekly* reviewer.

"Being a writer is like being a spy (but without the guns and stuff like that)," Sheldon noted on the Walker Books Web site. "You look like just a regular person, staggering onto the bus with your shopping, but you're not. You're always watching and listening. You take notes. You take stories or lines people told you and you use them shamelessly. You never think 'Wow, I wish I'd said that!' You think, 'I'll be saying that soon.'"

Sheldon's beloved picture book The Whales' Song *features evocative paintings by Gary Blythe.* (Illustration © 1990 by Gary Blythe. All rights reserved. Reproduced by permission of Puffin Pied Piper Books, a division of Penguin Putnam Books for Young Readers.)

Biographical and Critical Sources

PERIODICALS

Booklist, May 1, 1992, Donna Seaman, review of *My Life as a Whale,* p. 1585; October 15, 1992, Ilene Cooper, review of *Harry the Explorer,* p. 431; June 1, 1993, Ellen Mandel, review of *Harry on Vacation,* p. 1836; August, 1993, Chris Sherman, review of *My Brother Is a Visitor from Another Planet,* p. 2036; November 1, 1993, Susan DeRonne, review of *Tall, Thin, and Blonde,* p. 515; June 1, 1994, Mary Harris Veeder, review of *Under the Moon,* p. 1845; June 1, 1994, Kathryn Broderick, review of *Love, Your Bear Pete,* p. 1845; May 1, 1996, Janice Del Negro, review of *My Brother Is a Superhero,* p. 1508; November 1, 1997, Anne O'Malley, review of *The Boy of My Dreams,* p. 462; February 1, 1998, Helen Rosenberg, review of *Unicorn Dreams,* p. 924; November 1, 1999, Frances Bradburn, review of *Confessions of a Teenage Drama Queen,* p. 526; July, 2002, Anne O'Malley, review of *My Perfect Life,* p. 1847; March 15, 2003, Gillian Engberg, review of *Planet Janet,* p. 1319; April 1, 2005, Hazel Rochman, review of *Sophie Pitt-Turnbull Discovers America,* p. 1355; October 1, 2005, Cindy Dobrez, review of *Planet Janet in Orbit,* p. 50; June 1, 2006, Gillian Engberg, review of *Confessions of a Hollywood Star,* p. 64.

Bulletin of the Center for Children's Books, May, 1988, review of *I Forgot,* p. 188; July, 1988, review of *Alison and the Prince,* p. 238; May, 1991, review of *The*

Whales' Song, p. 226; May, 1994, review of *Under the Moon,* p. 302; September, 1997, review of *The Boy of My Dreams,* p. 26; December, 1999, review of *Confessions of a Teenage Drama Queen,* p. 149; March, 2003, review of *Planet Janet,* p. 289; May, 2005, review of *Sophie Pitt-Turnbull Discovers America,* p. 402.

Horn Book, July-August, 2006, Anita L. Burkam, review of *Confessions of a Hollywood Star,* p. 451.

Kirkus Reviews, January 15, 2003, review of *Planet Janet,* p. 146; May 1, 2005, review of *Sophie Pitt-Turnbull Discovers America,* p. 546; October 1, 2005, review of *Planet Janet in Orbit,* p. 1089; June 15, 2006, review of *Confessions of a Hollywood Star,* p. 637.

Kliatt, July, 2002, Paula Rohrlick, review of *Confessions of a Teenage Drama Queen,* p. 24; September, 2002, Paula Rohrlick, review of *My Perfect Life,* p. 13; May, 2005, Claire Rosser, review of *Sophie Pitt-Turnbull Discovers America,* p. 18.

Library Journal, February 15, 1983, review of *Victim of Love,* p. 414; May 1, 1992, Rosellen Brewer, review of *My Life as a Whale,* p 120.

Publishers Weekly, February 18, 1983, review of *Victim of Love,* p. 114; May 9, 1986, review of *Dreams of an Average Man,* p. 246; May 20, 1988, review of *Alison and the Prince,* p. 90; May 10, 1991, review of *The Whales' Song,* p. 281; March 9, 1992, review of *My Life as a Whale,* p. 45; May 4, 1992, review of *Harry and Chicken,* p. 56; November 8, 1993, review of *Tall, Thin, and Blonde,* p. 78; December, 1993, review of *Love, Your Bear Pete,* p. 70; March 21, 1994, re-

view of *Under the Moon,* p. 71; July 14, 1997, review of *The Boy of My Dreams,* p. 84; October 27, 1997, review of *Unicorn Dreams,* p. 75; April 27, 1998, review of *My Brother Is a Superhero,* p. 69; August 9, 1999, review of *Confessions of a Teenage Drama Queen,* p. 353; January 6, 2003, review of *Planet Janet,* p. 61.

School Library Journal, July, 1991, Shirley Wilton, review of *The Whales' Song,* p. 64; September, 1992, Carolyn Jenks, review of *Harry the Explorer,* p. 211; June, 1993, Margaret C. Howell, review of *Harry on Vacation,* p. 110; November, 1993, Sharon Korbeck, review of *Tall, Thin, and Blonde,* p. 125; June, 1994, Patricia Dooley, review of *Under the Moon,* p. 113; April, 1996, Christina Door, review of *My Brother Is a Superhero,* p. 142; October, 1997, Connie Tyrell Burns, review of *The Boy of My Dreams,* p. 139; January, 1998, Jeanne Clancy Watkins, review of *Unicorn Dreams,* p. 92; October, 1999, Jane Halsall, review of *Confessions of a Teenage Drama Queen,* p. 158; August, 2002, Susan Geye, review of *My Perfect Life,* p. 197; May, 2003, Susan Riley, review of *Planet Janet,* p. 160; June, 2005, Zusanne Gordon, review of *Sophie Pitt-Turnbull Discovers America,* p. 169; November, 2005, Jane Cronkhite, review of *Planet Janet in Orbit,* p. 148; October, 2006, Erin Schirota, review of *Confessions of a Hollywood Star,* p. 171.

Voice of Youth Advocates, February, 1994, review of *Tall, Thin, and Blonde,* p. 373; February, 1998, review of *The Boy of My Dreams,* p. 391; February, 2000, review of *Confessions of a Teenage Drama Queen,* p. 409; December, 2002, review of *My Perfect Life,* p. 392.

ONLINE

Dyan Sheldon Home Page, http://www.dyansheldon.com (August 15, 2007).

Walker Books Web site, http://www.walkerbooks.co.uk/ (August 15, 2007), "Dyan Sheldon."

*　　*　　*

SIDMAN, Joyce 1956-

Personal

Born June 4, 1956, in Hartford, CT; daughter of Robert J. Von Dohlen (an architect); married a doctor, May 31, 1981; children: two sons. *Ethnicity:* "Caucasian." *Education:* Wesleyan University, B.A. (German), 1978; Macalester College, teacher's license, 1983. *Hobbies and other interests:* Gardening, bird watching, environmental issues.

Addresses

E-mail—mailbox@joycesidman.com.

Career

Journalist and author. *St. Paul Pioneer Press,* St. Paul, MN, columnist, 1996-2000; freelance columnist, 2000—. COMPAS Writers & Artists in the Schools, St.

Joyce Sidman (Photograph by James Sidman. Reproduced by permission.)

Paul, writer-in-residence, 1997—. Volunteer in public schools and at Children's Hospital, Minneapolis, MN. Member, Loft Literary Center, Minneapolis.

Member

Society of Children's Book Writers and Illustrators, Children's Literature Network, Cooperative Children's Book Center (CCBC)-Net.

Awards, Honors

New Women's Voices Award, Finishing Line Press, 1999, for *Like the Air;* Showcase Book citation, Children's Book Council, Best Book of the Year citation, Infolink, 2000, and Children's Literature Choice List citation, 2001, all for *Just Us Two;* Best Book of the Year citation, Bank Street College, and nonfiction honor list citation, *Voice of Youth Advocates,* 2002, both for *Eureka!;* ASPCA Henry Bergh Children's Book Award, Minnesota Book Award finalist, and Best Books for Young Adults selection, American Library Association (ALA), all 2003, all for *The World according to Dog;* *Booklist* Editor's Choice designation, 2005, and Lee Bennet Hopkins Poetry Award, and National Science Teachers Association (NSTA) Outstanding Science Trade Book designation, both 2006, all for *Song of the Water Boatman, and Other Pond Poems;* CCBC Choice designation, 2006, for *Meow Ruff;* ALA Notable Book designation, Cybils Award for Poetry, NSTA Outstanding Science Trade Book designation, and New York Public Library 100 Titles for Reading and Sharing inclusion, all 2006, all for *Butterfly Eyes, and Other Secrets of the Meadow.*

Writings

FOR CHILDREN

Just Us Two: Poems about Animal Dads, illustrated by Susan Swan, Millbrook Press (Brookfield, CT), 2000.

Eureka!: Poems about Inventors, illustrated by K. Bennett Chavez, Millbrook Press (Brookfield, CT), 2002.

(With others) *The World according to Dog: Poems and Teen Voices,* illustrated by Doug Mindel, Houghton Mifflin (Boston, MA), 2003.

Song of the Water Boatman, and Other Pond Poems, illustrated by Beckie Prange, Houghton Mifflin (Boston, MA), 2005.

Butterfly Eyes, and Other Secrets of the Meadow, illustrated by Beth Krommes, Houghton Mifflin (Boston, MA), 2006.

Meow Ruff: A Story in Concrete Poetry, illustrated by Michelle Berg, Houghton Mifflin (Boston, MA), 2006.

This Is Just to Say: Poems of Apology and Forgiveness, illustrated by Pamela Zagarensky, Houghton Mifflin (Boston, MA), 2007.

OTHER

Like the Air (poetry chapbook), Finishing Line Press (Georgetown, KY), 1999.

(Editor) *Good Morning Tulip* (anthology of student writing), illustrated by Dhan Polnau, COMPAS Books (St. Paul, MN), 2002.

Contributor of essays and poems to books, including *Gifts from Our Grandmothers,* edited by Carol Dovi, Crown (New York, NY), 2000; *Stories from Where We Live: The Great North American Prairie,* edited by Sara St. Antoine, Milkweed Press (Minneapolis, MN), 2001; and *Line Drives: 100 Contemporary Baseball Poems,* edited by Brooke Horvath and Time Wiles, Southern Illinois University Press (Carbondale, IL), 2002. Contributor of numerous poems and stories to *Cricket* and *Cicada;* of occasional columns and reviews to *Riverbank Review;* and of poems for adults to journals, including *Christian Science Monitor, Cream City Review, ArtWorld Quarterly,* and *North Coast Review.*

Sidelights

Poet Joyce Sidman has written several books of verse for children and teenagers, including *Just Us Two: Poems about Animal Dads, Eureka!: Poems about Inventors, The World according to Dog: Poems and Teen Voices,* and *This Is Just to Day: Poems of Apology and Forgiveness.* Characteristic of the reception her work has received, *Just Us Two* was praised by *Christian Science Monitor* contributor Karen Carden for the way that Sidman's eleven poems about animal families "capture the tenderness evident in the father-child relationship." The poems are also scientifically accurate: Sidman did extensive research into animal behavior before writing *Just Us Two,* and in the poems she lists some facts about her subjects, which range from wolves to penguins and frogs, in prose form at the back of the book. Nature also takes center stage in *Song of the Water Boatman, and Other Pond Poems,* a Caldecott Honor title in which Sidman's award-winning collection about life in a northern pond is paired with art by Beckie Prange. In praise of the eleven poems in the collection,

Joanna Rudge Long noted in *Horn Book* that, "with a humor born of skillful observation," Sidman and Prange "capture the essence of this environment in all its fascinating particularity."

Eureka! "celebrat[es] that combination of creative insight and steadfastness that characterizes the successful inventor," John Peters explained in his *Booklist* review of Sidman's middle-grade verse collection. Each of the collection's sixteen poems "invites readers inside the head of an individual who, through imagining, laboring, investigating, testing, and persevering, in some way transformed the world for generations to come," as Martha Davis Beck wrote in a review for the *Riverbank Review.* The individuals profiled cover a range of time, from the prehistoric woman who first used clay to make a bowl to Tim Berners-Lee, the father of the World Wide Web, and a range of fields, from science (Marie Curie, the discoverer of radiation) to recreation (Walter Frederick Morrison, the inventor of the Frisbee).

In *The World according to Dog* Sidman combines original poems about life with her own dog with essays by teen writers that focus on their own pets. The combination, which was awarded the Henry Bergh Children's Book Award by the American Society for the Prevention of Cruelty to Animals, is "sure to engage dog fanciers," Margaret Bush predicted in *School Library Jour-*

In Just Us Two: Poems about Animal Dads, *Sidman's verses about the many different families in the animal kingdom are paired with Susan Swan's stylized art.* (Illustration © 2000 by Susan Swan. Reproduced by Millbrook Press, a division of Lerner Publishing Group.)

Sidman's award-winning verse collection **Song of the Water Boatman, and Other Pond Poems** *features artwork by Beckie Prange.* (Illustration © 2005 by Beckie Prange. All rights reserved. Reproduced by permission of Houghton Mifflin Company.)

nal. In her review of the collection, Gillian Engberg hastened to assure *Booklist* readers that "even teens who prefer cats will appreciate Sidman's tight lines, sincere emotion, and clever humor." Cats and dogs are joined by other creatures in *Meow Ruff: A Story in Concrete Poetry,* which features artwork by Michelle Berg. Here Sidman plays with font and the shape of her texts, combining "smooth curvy lines, chunky letters and friendly animal personalities" into a poetic story that a *Publishers Weekly* reviewer dubbed a "springy treat." *Meow Ruff* was praised by *Booklist* reviewer Jennifer Mattson as "a novel entree to concrete poetry" in which readers are "offer[ed].. a glimpse of the world as a poet sees it."

Sidman once told *SATA:* "I was a verbal kid who loved school but ended up being sent out in the hallway a lot, because I couldn't help talking to my neighbor. The temptation for whispered, smart-aleck comments was just too great. I loved to draw, too, and remember creating a series of illustrated comic books with a friend about four girls from different countries (the character representing me was from Egypt, for some reason or other). My attitude toward writing was transformed by a sixth-grade teacher who brought different, wacky pictures each week as story-starters. She liked what I wrote, often reading my work aloud. (My favorite books at about this period were British-style mysteries: *The Diamond in the Window,* by Jane Langton, and the

books of Joan Aiken—*The Wolves of Willoughby Chase,* etc.). As an adolescent, I gravitated toward poetry, which has remained my favorite mode of expression—I love its vivid, metaphorical, condensed language.

"I was blessed with a top-notch education that exposed me to all kinds of literature, and teachers who expected first-rate writing out of me. A long-suffering high school English teacher was an ongoing mentor, reading my poems and kindly commenting on them. At Wesleyan University, I was lucky enough to study with poets Richard Wilbur and F.D. Reeve, and became a total snob about hanging out with exciting 'creative' people vs. boring 'pre-med' people. Fate had the last laugh, however: I married a doctor (a former Peace Corps worker) and have come to find his work fascinating. My husband is an avid reader and often helps me with my work.

"My children have had a profound influence on my writing life. Their personalities and interests have both broadened and inspired me. Seeing the world through their eyes was what drew me once more into children's literature. I loved those days when we would write and draw our own books together!

"The teaching I do—week-long poetry-writing residences in local K-8 schools—definitely informs my work. Turning kids on to poetry and its power is a thrill. Watching them respond to the written word—and see-

ing what they write about themselves—constantly reminds me of their depths and emotions. My students help me see the world in a new way, every single day I teach.

"The natural world remains central to my life, and I continue to find out more about its workings. After writing for several hours in the morning, I walk in the woods daily with my dog, Watson, watching the seasons progress. For me, nature and creativity are firmly entwined. With my books I hope to help young readers delve into the world outside their four cozy walls."

Biographical and Critical Sources

PERIODICALS

Booklist, October 15, 2002, John Peters, review of *Eureka!: Poems about Inventors,* pp. 403-404; April 1, 2003, Gillian Engberg, review of *The World according to Dog: Poems and Teen Voices,* pp. 1405-1406; May 15, 2006, Jennifer Mattson, review of *Meow Ruff: A Story in Concrete Poetry,* p. 49; October 1, 2006, Gillian Engberg, review of *Butterfly Eyes, and Other Secrets of the Meadow,* p. 51; May 15, 2007, Randall Enos, review of *This Is Just to Say: Poems of Apology and Forgiveness,* p. 45.

Bulletin of the Center for Children's Books, March, 2003, review of *The World according to Dog,* p. 290; July-August, 2005, review of *Song of the Water Boatman, and Other Pond Poems,* p. 511; May, 2006, Deborah Stevenson, review of *Meow Ruff,* p. 422; October, 2006, Deborah Stevenson, review of *Butterfly Eyes, and Other Secrets of the Meadow,* p. 94.

Children's Book Review Service, November, 2000, review of *Just Us Two: Poems about Animal Dads.*

Christian Science Monitor, October 26, 2000, Karen Carden, review of *Just Us Two,* p. 21.

Horn Book, May-June, 2005, Joanna Rudge Long, review of *Song of the Water Boatman, and Other Pond Poems,* p. 341; May-June, 2006, Joanna Rudge Long, review of *Meow Ruff,* p. 338; September-October, 2006, Joanna Rudge Long, review of *Butterfly Eyes, and Other Secrets of the Meadow,* p. 603.

Kirkus Reviews, February 1, 2003, review of *The World according to Dog,* p. 239; April 1, 2005, review of *Song of the Water Boatman, and Other Pond Poems,* p. 424; March 1, 2006, review of *Meow Ruff,* p. 239; August 15, 2006, review of *Butterfly Eyes, and Other Secrets of the Meadow,* p. 852.

Publishers Weekly, March 28, 2005, review of *Song of the Water Boatman, and Other Pond Poems,* p. 79; March 20, 2006, review of *Meow Ruff,* p. 55; March 5, 2007, review of *This Is Just to Say,* p. 61.

Reading Teacher, March, 2003, Cyndi Giorgis and Nancy J. Johnson, review of *Eureka!,* pp. 582-590.

Riverbank Review, winter, 2000-2001, Christine Alfano, review of *Just Us Two,* p. 55; spring, 2002, Joyce Sidman, "Touching the World," pp. 25-27; winter, 2002-2003, Martha Davis Beck, review of *Eureka!,* pp. 56-57.

School Library Journal, December, 2000, Carolyn Angus, review of *Just Us Two,* p. 136; January, 2003, Susan Oliver, review of *Eureka!;* May, 2003, John Peters, review of *Eureka!,* p. 103, and Margaret Bush, review of *The World according to Dog,* p. 177; July, 2005, Shawn Brommer, review of *Song of the Water Boatman,* p. 92; July, 2006, Susan Scheps, review of *Meow Ruff,* p. 94; October, 2006, Margaret Bush, review of review of *Butterfly Eyes, and Other Secrets of the Meadow,* p. 142; May, 2007, Lee Bock, review of *This Is Just to Say,* p. 162.

ONLINE

Joyce Sidman Home Page, http://www.joycesidman.com (August 10, 2007).

Children's Literature Network Web site, http://www.childrensliteraturenetwork.com/ (June 30, 2003).

*   *   *

SMITH, Jos. A. 1936-
(Joseph Arthur Smith)

Personal

Born September 5, 1936, in Bellefonte, PA; son of George Leonard (a barber) and Frieda Regina (a beautician) Smith; married Nancy Clare Hutchison (a social worker/family counselor), August 11, 1959 (divorced); married Charlotte Mutsua Honda (a dancer), July, 1972 (divorced); married Charissa Irene Baker (a massage therapist and artist), February 21, 1994; children: (first marriage) Kathryn (Kari) Anne, Joseph A., Emily Christian. *Education:* Attended Pennsylvania State University, 1955-60; attended New York University, New School for Social Research (now New School University), Roscoe Center, and Wainwright Center for Human Resources; Pratt Institute, B.F.A.; graduate study at Pennsylvania State University, 1960-61, and Pratt Institute, 1961-62. *Politics:* Democrat. *Religion:* Buddhist.

Addresses

Home—Easton, PA. *Office*—Pratt Institute, School of Art and Design, 200 Willoughby Ave., Brooklyn, NY 11205.

Career

Fine artist, illustrator, and educator. Pratt Institute School of Art and Design, Brooklyn, NY, member of graduate and undergraduate Fine Arts faculty, beginning 1962. Art instructor at Staten Island Museum, 1964, Wagner College, 1965-66, Art Alliance of Central Pennsylvania, 1969-71, Wainwright Center for Human Resources, 1975, Stockton State College Artist's and Teacher's Institute, 1987-92; Visiting professor of fine arts at Richmond College, London, 1984; visiting artist at Art Institute of Chicago, Oxbow, MI, 1990, and Mis-

sissippi Art Colony, 1992, 1993. Freelance editorial illustrator and political cartoonist, then children's book illustrator. *Exhibitions:* Work included in over twenty solo exhibitions, including at Samuel S. Fleisher Art Memorial, Philadelphia, PA, 1961; Pratt Institute, Brooklyn, NY, 1962; Janet Nessler Gallery, New York, NY, 1963; Lehigh University, Bethlehem, PA, 1964; Staten Island Museum, Staten Island, NY, 1966; Bloomsburg State College, Bloomsburg, PA, 1968; Parsons School of Design, New York, NY, 1971; Chambers Gallery, Pennsylvania State University, University Park, 1972; Bethel Gallery, Bethel, CT, 1978; Newhouse Gallery, Snug Harbor Cultural Center, Staten Island, 1982; Visual Arts Gallery, Adirondack Community College, Glens Falls, NY, 1988; Pratt Institute, Brooklyn, NY, 1997; Esther Allen Greer Museum, University of Rio Grande, Rio Grande, OH, 2000; Art Institute of Chicago, 2001; Sewickley Library, Sewickley, PA, 2001; Gallery 20, New York, NY, 2001; Ohr-O'Keefe Museum, Biloxi, MS, 2002; Kingsborough Community College CUNY, Brooklyn, 2003; University of Connecticut, Storrs, 2004, Muhlenberg College, Allentown, PA, 2005; and Huntington Museum of Art, Huntington, WV, 2007. Work included in numerous group exhibitions, including Pennsylvania State University, 1955-60; City Museum of St. Louis, St. Louis, MO, 1961; American Watercolor Society exhibitions, 1965, 1967, 1969; New York Society of Illustrators exhibit, 1972, 1973, 1975, 1979; National Portrait Gallery, Washington, DC, 1976; Museum of the Surreal and Art Fantastique, New York, NY, 1981; Carlyle Gallery, New York, NY, 1982-83; Circlework Visions Gallery, New York, NY, 1986; Allen Stone Gallery, New York, NY, 1989; Society of Illustrators Museum of American Illustration, New York, NY, 1991; Staemphli Gallery, New York, NY, 1991; University of Mississippi at Oxford, 1991; Trenton City Museum, Trenton, NJ, 1992; Museum of Americah Illustration, New York, NY, 1995, 1996, 1998, 2005; University of Connecticut, Storrsy, 1996; and Muhlenberg College, 2003. Represented in public collections in United States, Cyprus, Germany, Japan, and Mexico, including at Pennsylvania Academy of the Fine Arts, New York Stock Exchange, Lauren Rogers Museum, Library of Congress, Print Club at University of Mississippi, Huntington Museum of Art, Rutgers University, Kassel Documenta Archive, Cöln Ludwig Museum, and Stuttgart Staatsgalerie Grafische Sammlung. *Military service:* U.S. Army, became specialist 4.

Awards, Honors

Mary S. Litt Award, American Watercolor Society, 1967; Juror's Choice Award, Pennsylvania State University, 1971; merit award, National Art Director's Club, 1971, New York Society of Illustrators, 1972, 1973, and 1975, American Institute of Graphic Arts, 1975, Bicentennial in Print, 1976, Art Directors Club of Metropolitan Washington, 1976, and Federal Design Council, 1976; first prize award in professional category, Pennsylvania State University, 1972; Staten Island Advance Award, Staten Island Museum, 1974; Purchase Prize in invita-

tional section, Rutgers University, 1974; Andy Award of Merit, Advertising Club of New York, 1979; Print Club Purchase Award and merit award, University of Mississippi, 1991; *Parents' Choice* Award, Parents' Choice Foundation, 1992, for *Jim Ugly;* Orbis Pictus Award, 2007, for *Gregor Mendel.*

Writings

SELF ILLUSTRATED

The Pen and Ink Book: Materials and Techniques for Today's Artist, Watson-Guptill, 1992.
Circus Train, Harry N. Abrams (New York, NY), 2001.

Also contributor to periodicals, including *Watercolor.*

ILLUSTRATOR; FOR CHILDREN

Stan Steiner, *The Last Horse,* Henry Holt (New York, NY), 1961.
Walter S. Carpenter and Philip Bluehouse, *Two Knots on a Counting Rope: A Navaho Counting Book,* Henry Holt (New York, NY), 1964.
Katharine Carter, reteller, *Tales from Hans Christian Andersen,* Albert Whitman Publishing (Morton Grove, IL), 1965.
Edward William Lane, reteller, *Tales from Arabian Nights,* Albert Whitman Publishing (Morton Grove, IL), 1966.
Norman Borisoff, *Lily, The Lovable Lion,* Scholastic (New York, NY), 1975.
Bernard Evslin, *Hercules,* Morrow (New York, NY), 1984.
Deborah Hautzig, reteller, *The Wizard of Oz,* Random House (New York, NY), 1984.
Robin McKinley, reteller, *Tales from the Jungle Book,* Random House (New York, NY), 1985.
George MacDonald, *The Princess and the Goblin,* Grosset & Dunlap (New York, NY), 1985.
Elizabeth Segel, selector, *Short Takes: A Short-Story Collection for Young Readers,* 1986.
Jenny Overton, *Thirteen Days of Christmas,* 1987.
Barbara Ann Brennan, *Hands of Light,* Pleiades Books, 1987.
Susan Cooper, *Matthew's Dragon,* Margaret K. McElderry Books (New York, NY), 1991.
Helen V. Griffith, *"Mine Will," Said John,* Greenwillow (New York, NY), 1992.
Sid Fleischman, *Jim Ugly,* Greenwillow (New York, NY), 1992.
Lynne Reid Banks, *The Adventures of King Midas,* Morrow (New York, NY), 1992.
Diana Wynne Jones, *Stopping for a Spell: Three Fantasies,* Greenwillow (New York, NY), 1993.
Jessie Haas, *Chipmunk!,* Greenwillow (New York, NY), 1993.
Mary Serfozo, *Benjamin Bigfoot,* Margaret K. McElderry Books (New York, NY), 1993.
Susan Cooper, *Danny and the Kings,* Margaret K. McElderry Books (New York, NY), 1993.

Diane Wolkstein, *Step by Step,* Morrow (New York, NY), 1993.

Jessie Haas, *Mowing,* Greenwillow (New York, NY), 1994.

Betty Levin, *Starshine and Sunglow,* Greenwillow (New York, NY), 1994.

Marc Gellman and Thomas Hartman, *How Do You Spell God?: Answers to the Big Questions from around the World,* foreword by His Holiness the Dalai Lama, Morrow Junior Books (New York, NY), 1995.

Jessie Haas, *A Blue for Beware,* Greenwillow (New York, NY), 1995.

Jessie Haas, *No Foal Yet,* Greenwillow (New York, NY), 1995.

Nicholas Heller, *Goblins in Green,* Greenwillow (New York, NY), 1995.

Jessie Haas, *Sugaring,* Greenwillow (New York, NY), 1996.

Nancy Farmer, *Runnery Granary,* Greenwillow (New York, NY), 1996.

Jessie Haas, *Be Well, Beware,* Greenwillow (New York, NY), 1996.

Betty Levin, *Gift Horse,* Greenwillow (New York, NY), 1996.

Mirra Ginsburg, *Clay Boy,* Greenwillow (New York, NY), 1997.

Nicholas Heller, *The Giant,* Greenwillow (New York, NY), 1997.

Sid Fleischman, *Bandit's Moon,* Greenwillow (New York, NY), 1998.

Charlotte S. Huck, *A Creepy Countdown,* Greenwillow (New York, NY), 1998.

Nicholas Heller, *Ogres! Ogres! Ogres!: A Feasting Frenzy from A to Z,* Greenwillow (New York, NY), 1999.

Betty Levin, *Creature Crossing,* Greenwillow (New York, NY), 1999.

Jessie Haas, *Hurry!,* Greenwillow (New York, NY), 2000.

Nicholas Heller, *Elwood and the Witch,* Greenwillow (New York, NY), 2000.

Susan Goldman Rubin, *The Yellow House: Vincent Van Gogh and Paul Gaughin Side by Side,* Harry N. Abrams (New York, NY), 2001.

Rhonda Gowler Greene, *Eek! Creak! Snicker, Sneak,* Atheneum Books for Young Readers (New York, NY), 2002.

Jennifer Armstrong, *Audubon: Painter of Birds in the Wild Frontier,* Harry N. Abrams (New York, NY), 2003.

Cheryl Bardoe, *Gregor Mendel: The Friar Who Grew Peas,* Harry N. Abrams (New York, NY), 2006.

Arthur Yorinks, *The Witch's Child,* Abrams Books for Young Readers (New York, NY), 2007.

ILLUSTRATOR; FOR ADULTS

Sam Epstein and Beryl Epstein, *European Folk Festivals,* 1968.

The Sierra Club Survival Songbook, collected by Jim Morse and Nancy Mathews, Sierra Club, 1971.

MacKinlay Kantor, *Andersonville,* Franklin Library, 1976.

Erica Jong, *Witches,* Harry N. Abrams (New York, NY), 1981.

Joseph Conrad, *Heart of Darkness, and Other Tales,* Franklin Library, 1982.

Contributor of editorial illustrations and political cartoons to periodicals, including *Time, Newsweek, New York Times, Harper's, Der Spiegel,* and *New Times.*

Sidelights

Apart from his long career as an educator, Jos. A. Smith worked as an editorial illustrator and political cartoonist for well-known periodicals such as the *New York Times, Time, Harper's,* and *Newsweek*—where Smith was the courtroom artist during the historic Watergate trial—before moving into children's book illustration. In addition to contributing art to stories by Mirra Ginsburg, Rhonda Gowler Greene, Nicholas Heller, Jessie Haas, and others, Smith has also been inspired to write his own self-illustrated story for children. *Circus Train,* published in 2001, follows a young boy who, left alone for the day at his family's new rural home, discovers a stranded train full of exotic animals, acrobats, and other performers. Timothy helps the train make it to town in time for the circus's evening show, an adventure that *School Library Journal* reviewer Barbara Buckley praised as "pure fantasy" and "the perfect daydream for a lonely and apprehensive child." Buckley described the book's art as "full of whimsy and color," and GraceAnne A. DeCandido predicted that, with its "shining colors and brilliant detail," Smith's "fanciful wish-fulfillment story . . . is sure to be a hit."

Smith's love of nature is revealed in his finely detailed, realistic illustrations for picture books such as Betsy Lewin's *Creature Crossing* as well as *Chipmunk!,* by Jessie Haas. Smith's "neatly framed color paintings" for *Chipmunk!* "capture the actions and emotions extraordinarily well," declared Deborah Abbott in her *Booklist* review. Also by Haas, *Mowing* focuses on Nora and Gramps, who are out cutting hay. Nora walks ahead of the horse-drawn mower, warning Gramps when a tiny, meadow-living creature is threatened by the sharp blade. In *No Foal Yet,* Nora and her grandparents endure the long wait for a new foal to be born in the stable. In *Mowing* Smith takes as his frame of reference the eye-level of the field animals, allowing "readers [to] see the humans and the horses as peripheral guests in the world," according to Mary Harris Veeder in *Booklist.* His watercolor and colored-pencil illustrations for *No Foal Yet* "are touched with gentle, golden light, like the light of a springtime twilight," Veeder exclaimed. Smith conveys the emotion underlying Haas's *Sugaring,* which details the many steps required to render maple syrup from tree sap. "This fictionalized portrayal allows Nora to take center stage in the sugaring process," observed Kay Weisman in *Booklist,* the critic adding that the process is depicted in minute detail to the benefit of interested young readers.

Special praise has been accorded Smith for his contribution to Jennifer Armstrong's picture-book biography *Audubon: Painter of Birds in the Wild Frontier.* In this large-format work Smith's "watercolor art, embellished with pencil, watercolor pencil, and pen and ink," mixes

Jos A. Smith brings to life a young boy's childhood saga in his paintings for Susan Cooper's **Danny and the Kings.**

with original images by nineteenth-century naturalist painter John James Audubon to provide a "dramatic" and "perfect complement to the vivid prose," according to a *Kirkus Reviews* writer. Praising *Audubon* as a "stunning picture book" *School Library Journal* contributor Robyn Walker added that "Smith's watercolor illustrations are so lifelike that one can virtually feel the beat of . . . swans' wings," while Carolyn Phelan wrote in *Booklist* that the illustrator's use of "varied layouts" results in "scenes that are pleasing in composition and color and often dramatic in content." Another biographical work, Cheryl Bardoe's *Gregor Mendel: The Friar Who Grew Peas,* also benefits from Smith's love of nature. Here he tracks Mendel's life from his decision to join monastic orders to his work in genetics. Stephanie Zvirin, writing in *Booklist,* deemed *Gregor Mendel* a "visually pleasing book," while in *School Library Journal* Patricia Manning called the work "a treat for the eye" due to "Smith's crisp, realistic paintings."

Smith's penchant for whimsy is given free rein in many of his book-illustration projects. In his work for Susan Cooper's *Matthew's Dragon* he brings to life the story of a boy who befriends a dragon that springs from the page of a picture book. Shrunk down to book size, Matthew and the dragon enjoy a snack together and do battle with a neighborhood cat before growing large and flying off into the sky to frolic with the other dragons created in the pages of fantasy fiction. In one of several collaborations with Heller, Smith conjures up a

panoply of goblins to bring to life the alphabet book *Goblins in Green.* He mixes a troupe of hungry monsters with the same letters in *Ogres! Ogres! Ogres!* His illustrations for Charlotte Huck's *A Creepy Countdown* create similar humor, this time seasoning a basic counting book with a Halloween theme, and he follows the mischievous antics of two nocturnal hobgoblins in the pages of Rhonda Gowler Greene's *Eek! Creak! Snicker, Sneak.* Goblin antics are also the subject of Nancy Farmer's *Runnery Granary,* in which no one can figure who is stealing the grain from the family granary until Granny Runnery decides it must be goblins, and recites an old recipe for catching the tricky creatures.

In *Matthew's Dragon* "Smith's paintings of the dragon-crowded sky are truly breathtaking," commented a reviewer for *Publishers Weekly,* while another critic for the same periodical dubbed *Goblins in Green* a "true treasure" in which Smith's inclusion of visual spoofs of famous paintings and films casts the work in a "zany" light. "The vibrant, detailed pictures" in *Ogres! Ogres! Ogres!* "portray the ogres caught in hilarious acts of bad manners as they play inappropriately with food," wrote *Booklist* critic Shelle Rosenfeld. Smith's scratchboard illustrations for *A Creepy Countdown* "capture the eerie holiday mood without being overly frightening." remarked Zvirin in *Booklist,* and a *Publishers Weekly* contributor concluded of *Runnery Granary* that "Smith's depiction of the greedy gnomes is just right: They're a wee bit scary, but not too much."

From the fantastic, Smith moves to the traditional in his work for Mirra Ginsburg's *Clay Boy.* Based on a Russian fable, the book introduces a creature who is cousin to the fabled Gingerbread Boy. Clay Boy is created by a lonely old couple. Perpetually hungry, he eats everything in sight and grows larger and larger, eventually gobbling up the old man and woman as well as a horse-drawn wagon. A wily goat saves the day, however, when it butts Clay Boy in his tummy, breaking the creature into brittle pieces and allowing all the people the boy has eaten to regain their freedom. "In their play with scale, the illustrations express a wonderful combination of the monstrous and the cozy," observed Hazel Rochman in a review of *Clay Boy* for *Booklist.*

Smith once told *SATA:* "I grew up in the town of State College, Pennsylvania. Pennsylvania State University is located there. Although neither of my parents had had the opportunity to complete even grade school, they raised my brother and me to regard learning as the most important thing in our lives. It didn't matter what we wanted to do, they encouraged us. My brother is now retired chair of the industrial engineering department at Ohio State University, and I am a professor of fine art in the graduate fine art department and the undergraduate painting and drawing department at Pratt Institute in addition to my career as an artist.

"I was also fortunate to be asked by painter/illustrator Richard Lindner to be his studio assistant while I was a student at Pratt Institute. As a result of this I had a rare

opportunity to meet and listen to his friends when they visited him in his studio. These included painter Marcel Duchamp, actress Greta Garbo, artist Adja Yunkers, and cartoonist Saul Steinberg. Lindner was one of the most sensitive people I have ever known. He would stop work in the studio and we would go off for hours riding on all the elevated subway lines we could find in search of a certain red chimney that he had seen once years before, or we might go to Central Park Zoo and look at the eyes of the gorilla because of a wise expression he had. Lindner and Hobson Pittman (a painter on the faculty of the Pennsylvania Academy of the Fine Arts in Philadelphia who I studied with every summer at Pennsylvania State University until he retired and turned his studio workshops over to me) had a profound influence on my life as an artist.

"Other important influences are related to my lifelong interest in drawing imagery from my unconscious for my drawings, sculptures, and paintings. I studied with Jean Houston of the Institute for Mind Research to learn non-drug techniques for inducing altered states. I joined the Princeton Zen Society to learn Zen meditation, and studied Jain meditation with Mouni Sri Chitrabanu, traditional shamanic trance techniques from the anthropologist Michael Harner and joined the Nyingmapa Lineage of the Tibetan Buddhists to learn their elaborate visualization techniques. I also studied biofeedback therapy and own and have used an electroencephalogram (EEG) to record brainwave states evoked by these various methods, to understand them better. I use adaptations of all of these techniques to evoke imagery for my art, and occasionally incorporate some of the simpler forms in my art classes to enable other artists to be able to take advantage of them.

"Another of my lifelong interests is nature and the environment, and I have contributed my art to many environmental causes. One of the high points of my life in this area was spending one summer walking cross-country in East Africa, drawing people and photographing and filming wildlife. I have always had one or more pets, which usually included some snakes. For twenty years I shared my studio/loft in New York City with a boa constrictor and a ball python. Now I am living in Easton, Pennsylvania. My forested property abounds with birds and animals and snakes. My house, which includes my studio and my wife's printing studio, is shared by a Siamese cat named Suki and an aquarium full of local fish from the Delaware River."

Biographical and Critical Sources

PERIODICALS

American Artist, July, 1981, Jane Cottingham, "The Imaginary Drawings of Joseph A. Smith."

Booklist, October 15, 1993, Deborah Abbott, review of *Danny and the Kings*, p. 451, review of *Chipmunk!*, p. 452; March 15, 1994, Mary Harris Veeder, review of *Step by Step*, p. 1376; June 1, 1994, Mary Harris Veeder, review of *Mowing*, p. 1838; June 1, 1995, Mary Harris Veeder, review of *No Foal Yet*, p. 1785; September 1, 1995, Mary Harris Veeder, review of *Goblins in Green*, p. 86; June 1, 1996, Carolyn Phelan, review of *Runnery Granary*, p. 1731; November 15, 1996, Kay Weisman, review of *Sugaring*, p. 594; April 15, 1997, Hazel Rochman, review of *Clay Boy*, p. 1422; September 1, 1998, Stephanie Zvirin, review of *A Creepy Countdown*, p. 133; March 1, 1999, Sally Estes, review of *Jim Ugly*, p. 1212; October 15, 1999, Shelle Rosenfeld, review of *Ogres! Ogres! Ogres!: A Feasting Frenzy from A to Z*, p. 452; May 15, 2000, Gillian Engberg, review of *Hurry!*, p. 1748; August, 2000, Ilene Cooper, review of *Elwood and the Witch*, p. 2146; April 1, 2001, GraceAnne A. DeCandido, review of *Circus Train*, p. 1480; November 15, 2001, Gillian Engberg, review of *The Yellow House: Vincent Van Gogh and Paul Gauguin Side by Side*, p. 1366; April 1, 2003, Carolyn Phelan, review of *Audubon*, p. 1391; July 1, 2006, Stephanie Zvirin, review of *Gregor Mendel: The Friar Who Grew Peas*, p. 62.

Horn Book, November-December, 1993, Ann A. Flowers, review of *Danny and the Kings*, p. 722; May-June, 1994, Elizabeth S. Watson, review of *Mowing*, p. 315; September-October, 1996, Lolly Robinson, review of *Runnery Granary*, p. 575; March-April, 1997, Ann A. Flowers, review of *Clay Boy*, p. 206; May, 1999, review of *Creature Crossing*, p. 331; July, 2000, Martha V. Parravano, review of *Hurry!*, p. 435.

Kirkus Reviews, September 15, 2001, review of *The Yellow House*, p. 1366; January 15, 2002, review of *Eek! Creak! Snicker, Sneak*, p. 104; March 15, 2003, review of *Audubon*, p. 458; August 15, 2006, review of *Gregor Mendel*, p. 835.

Publishers Weekly, August 28, 1981, p. 386; July 12, 1991, review of *Matthew's Dragon*, p. 65; September 20, 1993, Elizabeth Devereaux and Kit Alderdice, review of *Danny and the Kings*, p. 39; March 14, 1994, review of *Step by Step*, p. 72; October 9, 1995, review of *Goblins in Green*, p. 86; May 20, 1996, review of *Runnery Granary*, p. 259; May 5, 1997, review of *Clay Boy*, p. 209; October 27, 1997, review of *The Giant*, p. 75; March 27, 2000, review of *Bandit's Moon*, p. 83; September 3, 2001, review of *The Yellow House*, p. 87; December 3, 2001, review of *Eek! Creak! Snicker, Sneak*, p. 59.

School Library Journal, September, 1984, p. 114; April, 1992, p. 113; February, 1994, Nancy A. Gifford, review of *Chipmunk!*, p. 84; June, 2000, Lee Bock, review of *Hurry!*, p. 114; September, 2000, Joy Fleishhacker, review of *Elwood and the Witch*, p. 199; April, 2001, Barbara Buckley, review of *Circus Train*, p. 122; January, 2002, Robin L. Gibson, review of *The Yellow House*, p. 124; February, 2002, Carol Ann Wilson, review of *Eek! Creak! Snicker, Sneak*, p. 101; May, 2003, Robyn Walker, review of *Audubon*, p. 134; September, 2006, Patricia Manning, review of *Gregor Mendel*, p. 188.

Teacher Librarian, September, 1998, Shirley Lewis, review of *A Creepy Countdown*, p. 47.

ONLINE

Drawger Web site, http://www.drawger.com/jos/ (July 24, 2007), "Jos. A. Smith."
Jos A. Smith Home Page, http://josasmith.com (July 24, 2007).

*　　*　　*

SMITH, Joseph Arthur
See SMITH, Jos. A.

*　　*　　*

STEWART, Amber

Personal

Born in England; married; children: one daughter. *Hobbies and other interests:* Riding horses, running.

Addresses

Home and office—London, England.

Career

Book editor and author.

Writings

How Many Sleeps?, illustrated by Layn Marlow, Oxford University Press (Oxford, England), 2005.
Rabbit Ears, illustrated by Laura Rankin, Bloomsbury Children's Books (New York, NY), 2006.
I'm Big Enough, illustrated by Layn Marlow, Orchard Books (New York, NY), 2007.
Birthday Countdown, illustrated by Layn Marlow, Orchard Books (New York, NY), 2007.

Author's works have been translated into Spanish.

Biographical and Critical Sources

PERIODICALS

Booklist, February 1, 2006, Ilene Cooper, review of *Rabbit Ears,* p. 58; January 1, 2007, Carolyn Phelan, review of *I'm Big Enough,* p. 118.
Bulletin of the Center for Children's Books, May, 2006, Hope Morrison, review of *Rabbit Ears,* p. 425.
Kirkus Reviews, January 15, 2006, review of *Rabbit Ears,* p. 90; February 1, 2007, review of *I'm Big Enough,* p. 129.
Publishers Weekly, February 13, 2006, review of *Rabbit Ears,* p. 88.

School Library Journal, April, 2006, Susan Weitz, review of *Rabbit Ears,* p. 119.*

*　　*　　*

SVENDSEN, Mark 1962-
(Mark Nestor Svendsen)

Personal

Born August 7, 1962, in Yeppoon, Queensland, Australia; son of Nestor (a farmer) and Dell (a farmer) Svendsen; married Rosamunde Anne Kneeshaw (a musician and composer), September 22, 1984; children: Thyri, Hannah. *Education:* University of Queensland, B.A. (English literature), 1983; Queensland University of Technology, graduate diploma (arts administration), 1991, M.A. (creative writing), 2004.

Addresses

Office—P.O. Box 61, Emu Park, Queensland 4702, Australia.

Career

Poet, fiction writer, lyricist, and arts administrator. Regional Centre of the Arts, Rockhampton, Australia, graduate administrative officer, 1991-92, administrator, 1992-95. Presenter at workshops and poetry readings throughout Queensland and New South Wales, Australia, 1995—. Queensland Writers Centre, member; consultant to Regional Arts Development Fund, Livingstone Shire Council, and Gracemere Shire Council.

Member

Australia Council, Children's Book Council of Australia.

Awards, Honors

Writing grants, 1995, 1996, 1997, and 1998; Australia Council grant, 2000; Children's Book Council Notable Book designation, 2000, for *Snigger James on Grey,* 2002, for *Poison under Their Lips,* and 2004, for *Ratface and Snake-eyes.*

Writings

FOR CHILDREN

(Under name Mark Nestor Svendsen) *The Bunyip and the Night* (poems), illustrated by Annmarie Scott, University of Queensland Press (St. Lucia, Queensland, Australia), 1994.
Three Moon Lagoon (novella), illustrated by Wendy Kneen, Greater Glider Productions (Maleny, Queensland, Australia), 1996.

Snigger James on Grey (young-adult novel), Lothian (South Melbourne, Victoria, Australia), 2000.

Poison under Their Lips (young-adult novel), Lothian (South Melbourne, Victoria, Australia), 2001.

Captain Me, illustrated by David Cox, Lothian (South Melbourne, Victoria, Australia), 2002.

Ratface and Snake-eyes (middle-grade novel), Lothian (South Melbourne, Victoria, Australia), 2003.

Shadowsnake (elementary-grade novel), Lothian (South Melbourne, Victoria, Australia), 2004.

Circus Carnivore (picture book), illustrated by Ben Redlich, Lothian (South Melbourne, Victoria, Australia), 2005, Houghton Mifflin (Boston, MA), 2006.

The Kestrel (picture book), illustrated by Steven Woolman and Laura Peterson, Lothian (South Melbourne, Victoria, Australia), 2006.

Wacko the Chook (picture book), illustrated by Ben Redlich, Lothian (Sydney, New South Wales, Australia), 2007.

Short fiction represented in anthologies, including *Sounds Spooky,* Greater Glider Productions, 1994; *The Girl Who Married a Fly,* Australian Association for the Teaching of English, 1997; and *Let's Jabberwocky,* edited by Jenny Poulter, Currency Press, 2001.

FOR ADULTS

The Turtle Damns the Pursuit of Happiness (poems), Metro Arts Press (Brisbane, Queensland, Australia), 1994.

(Editor) *Songs of the East Coast,* Central Queensland University Press (Rockhampton, Queensland, Australia), 1997.

(Editor) Glenda Gabrielle and Meredyth Curlie, *True Blue Christmas,* Literacy Land, 1997.

(Editor) *Dust Road Coming,* Central Queensland University Press (Rockhampton, Queensland, Australia), 1998.

(Editor with Barbara Damska) *Local Miracle, and Other Real-Life Stories of Survival, Benevolence, Hope, and Inclusion by South-east Queensland Women,* MECDA (Salisbury, Queensland, Australia), 2004.

Contributor to magazines, including *Northern Perspectives, Imago, Social Alternatives, Idiom 23,* and *Educating Young Children;* contributor of book reviews to *Courier Mail.*

Sidelights

Mark Svendsen is an Australian poet and author who writes for children, teens, and adults. His novels for young adults include *Snigger James on Grey,* a coming-of-age story of teen friendships that draws on both past and present. Also for teen readers, his historical novel *Poison under Their Lips* focuses on a young, idealistic Christian teen who leaves his comfortable home in South Australia to travel to colonial Queensland and help control the region's indigenous populations. One of several collaborations with illustrator Ben Redlich, *Circus Carnivore* is a picture book in which the non-

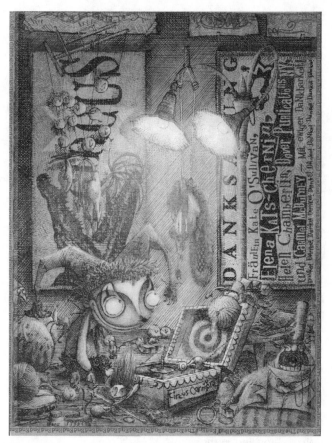

Mark Svendsen's quirky picture book **Circus Carnivore** *is given a surreal edge via Ben Redlich's engrossing illustrations.* (Illustration © 2006 by Ben Redlich. All rights reserved. Reproduced by permission of Houghton Mifflin Company.)

sense rhymes by Svendsen are paired with illustrations that *School Library Journal* contributor Genevieve Gallagher described as "an explosion of oils, ink, and collage."

"In the past I have written about bunyips, those mythic creatures said to inhabit the creeks, water holes, and billabongs of Australia," Svendsen once told *SATA.* "Embodied in those mythical beings is the essence of fear with which characters, through their love and acceptance, can grapple and ultimately overcome. *The Bunyip and the Night* is a picture book of six poems on the bunyip theme. Illustrated by six different illustrators, the book is not for little children but works very well for older children. Fear of the dark, adults, lonely places, and ourselves are all topics which have been raised by children when reading this book with me.

"*Three Moon Lagoon* (the euphonic name is of a real place near where I live) is a novella for nine to twelve year olds. It deals with the notion that our dreams, or our love for the future, *are* our future, and if we cannot dream we are stuck in the rut of today, now being what we fear most. Of course, the two children in this nightmare work out a riddle to overcome their fears and claim the future to be their own.

"*Snigger James on Grey* deals with the overcoming of fear as the growth which the adolescent must undertake

to become fully adult. The child must die, and the adult must begin to grow. My second young-adult novel, *Poison under Their Lips,* traces the life of an adolescent cadet officer with Queensland's infamous Native Police Force, whose sole job was the 'dispersal of troublesome blacks.' This phrase became a euphemism for murder on sight, a directive followed with all too brutal efficiency. This force, whose activities ceased in 1901, charts the period of one of the most barbarous and callous periods of official Australian colonial history."

Biographical and Critical Sources

PERIODICALS

Kirkus Reviews, August 15, 2006, review of *Circus Carnivore,* p. 853.

School Library Journal, November, 2006, Genevieve Gallagher, review of *Circus Carnivore,* p. 114.

ONLINE

Booked Out Web site, http://www.bookedout.com.au/ (July 29, 2007), "Mark Svendsen."

Brisbane Writers Festival Web site, http://www.brisbanewritersfestival.com.au/ (July 31, 2007), "Mark Svendsen."*

*   *   *

SVENDSEN, Mark Nestor
See SVENDSEN, Mark

V-Y

VERNIERO, Joan C. 1949-

Personal

Born 1949, in Nutley, NJ. *Education:* Seton Hall University, B.A.; Bank Street College of Education, M.A.; attended Vassar Institute of Children's Literature. *Hobbies and other interests:* Ballet.

Addresses

Home—Monroe, CT. *E-mail*—jvstory@aol.com.

Career

Children's book author and educator. Founder of two experimental education programs in New York, NY. Naugatuck Valley Community Technical College, adjunct instructor; Masuk High School, Monroe, CT, language-arts and reading teacher; University of Bridgeport, Bridgeport, CT, graduate-level instructor in education. Member, Bank Street College Writers Lab; member, Project Dream; consultant to Wonder Tots.

Member

Society of Children's Book Writers and Illustrators, Authors Guild, National League of American Pen Women.

Awards, Honors

You Can Call Me Willy included in *Good Morning America* Millenium Time Capsule, 1995.

Writings

You Can Call Me Willy: A Story for Children about AIDS, illustrated by Verdon Flory, Magination Press (New York, NY), 1995.

One-hundred-and-one Read-aloud Bible Stories: From the Old and New Testament, Black Dog (New York, NY), 1998.

(With Robin Fitzsimmons) *One-hundred-and-one Read-aloud Myths and Legends,* Black Dog (New York, NY), 1999.

One-hundred-and-one Read-aloud Celtic Myths and Legends: Ten-Minute Readings from the World's Best-loved Literature, Black Dog (New York, NY), 2000.

One-hundred-and-one Asian Read-aloud Myths and Legends: Ten-Minute Readings from the World's Best-loved Asian Literature, Black Dog (New York, NY), 2001.

(With Doreen Rappaport) *Victory or Death!: Stories of the American Revolution,* illustrated by Greg Call, HarperCollins (New York, NY), 2003.

(With Robin Fitzsimmons) *An Illustrated Treasury of Read-aloud Myths and Legends: The World's Best-loved Myths and Legends for Parent and Child to Share,* Black Dog (New York, NY), 2004.

(With Doreen Rappaport) *United No More!: Stories of the Civil War,* illustrated by Rick Reeves, HarperCollins (New York, NY), 2006.

Contributor to periodicals, including *Education Week* and *Psychological Perspectives.*

Sidelights

As a child, Joan C. Verniero read everything she could get her hands on. "Just as much fun was taking pretend trips from the overgrown garden in front of my apartment building to faraway, imaginary places," the author and educator added on her home page. "I still love those faraway, imaginary places and, now as a writer, I get to take my readers along." Verniero's love of story has inspired her to collect myths and legends from throughout the world in books such as *One-hundred-and-one Asian Read-aloud Myths and Legends: Ten-Minute Readings from the World's Best-loved Asian Literature* and other titles in the "One-hundred-and-one Read-aloud" series.

Verniero began her writing career with the picture book *You Can Call Me Willy: A Story for Children about AIDS.* The book introduces Wilhelmina Jones, an eight

year old who loves baseball. Willy also has AIDS, and through her narration Verniero helps young readers understand what AIDS patients experience because of others' fear and discrimination. Although the details of the disease are never discussed, Willy's courage is clearly shown in the story. "The simple text, focusing on the ordinary events in a little girl's life, will invite compassion," predicted Virginia E. Jeschlnig in her *School Library Journal* review of *You Can Call Me Willy.*

In collaboration with fellow author Doreen Rappaport, Verniero introduces young readers to U.S. history in *Victory or Death!: Stories of the American Revolution.* In the book's eight tales, readers meet both well-known and lesser-known historical figures, among them James Armistead, a slave who became a spy, and Deborah Samson, a woman who disguised herself as a man in order to fight. "What is often a dry memorizing of facts in history class is given vigorous and original treatment here," wrote a contributor to *Kirkus Reviews,* noting the book's multicultural focus. Jean Gaffney, reviewing *Victory or Death!* in *School Library Journal,* wrote that "historical detail, much of which is drawn from primary resources, is seamlessly integrated" in the coauthors' text.

Verniero and Rappaport continue their focus on U.S. history with *United No More!: Stories of the Civil War.* Using the same multicultural viewpoint they adopted in *Victory or Death!,* the coauthors include tales reflecting

Verniero collaborates with Doreen Rappaport on the story collection **United No More!: Stories of the Civil War,** *which features illustrations by Rick Reeves.* (Illustration © 2006 by Rick Reeves. All rights reserved. Reproduced by permission of HarperCollins Children's Books, a division of HarperCollins Publishers.)

Cover of **An Illustrated Treasury of Read-Aloud Myths and Legends,** *a work coedited by Joan Verniero and Robin Fitzsimmons.* (Black Dog & Leventhal Publishers, 2004. Jacket illustration Mary Evans Picture Library. Reproduced by permission.)

the perspectives of North and South, women and men, and various racial backgrounds. "These accounts could be used for read-alouds or to entice students to do further research," wrote Mary Mueller in her *School Library Journal* review, while a *Kirkus Reviews* contributor dubbed *United No More!* "a terrific history for the intended audience." Betty Carter noted in *Horn Book* that, although the coauthors fictionalize the tales, they do so clearly, "giving fair warning to readers to be critical and thoughtful as they approach these histories."

Biographical and Critical Sources

PERIODICALS

Archives of Pediatrics and Adolescent Medicine, December, 1995, review of *You Can Call Me Willy: A Story for Children about AIDS,* p. 1404.

Booklist, June 1, 2003, GraceAnne A. DeCandido, review of *Victory or Death!: Stories of the American Revolution,* p. 1770.

Bulletin of the Center for Children's Books, February, 2006, Elizabeth Bush, review of *United No More!: Stories of the Civil War,* p. 282.

Horn Book, March-April, 2006, Betty Carter, review of *United No More!,* p. 208.

Kirkus Reviews, April 1, 2003, review of *Victory or Death!,* p. 539; December 1, 2005, review of *United No More!,* p. 1279.

School Library Journal, September, 1995, Virginia E. Je-schelnig, review of *You Can Call Me Willy,* p. 197; August, 1999, Cheri Estes, review of *One-hundred-and-one Read-aloud Myths and Legends,* p. 180; June, 2003, Jean Gaffney, review of *Victory or Death!,* p. 168; February, 2006, Mary Mueller, review of *United No More!,* p. 152.

ONLINE

HarperCollins Web site, http://www.harpercollins.com/ (July 5, 2007), "Joan C. Verniero."

Joan C. Verniero Home Page, http://www.jvstory.com (July 2, 2007).

Pen Women Web site, http://www.penwomen.org/ (July 5, 2007), "Joan C. Verniero."*

*   *   *

von SCHMIDT, Eric 1931-2007

OBITUARY NOTICE— See index for *SATA* sketch: Born May 28, 1931, in Bridgeport, CT; died February 2, 2007, in Fairfield, CT. Artist, musician, and author. Von Schmidt was a folk musician and composer who influenced such legends as Bob Dylan and Joan Baez. The son of a painter, he learned to be an artist from his father. Instead of going to college, he continued his education in Florence, Italy, on a Fulbright scholarship and then served two years in the U.S. Army. Von Schmidt settled in Cambridge, Massachusetts, in 1957, and gained a following of students from Harvard University and elsewhere who were interested in his upbeat and energetic interpretations of blues and folk songs; among these disciples were Baez, Dylan, and Tom Rush. Dylan was perhaps his most ardent pupil. The legendary folk-rock artist learned many songs from von Schmidt, and did not forget to credit his mentor's influence. Though not as famous as Dylan or Baez, von Schmidt had a successful music career, too, with thirty copyrighted songs to his credit. He released albums such as *The Folk Blues of Eric von Schmidt* (1964) and *Who Knocked the Brains out of the Sky?* (1969). He was also a graphic artist and author and illustrator of children's books. He illustrated over fifty juvenile titles by such writers as Eve Bunting and Sid Fleischman, and also wrote and illustrated several of his own books. Among these are *Come for to Sing* (1963), *The Ballad of Bad Ben Bilge* (1965), and *Feeling Circus* (1970). Music, however, was von Schmidt's primary passion, and he faced difficulties when throat cancer, diagnosed in 2000, robbed him of his ability to sing. Because he was also ill with Lyme disease, he was unable to play music, so he consoled himself with painting a series of works titled "Giants of the Blues." In 2007, von Schmidt also suffered from a stroke, which may have been in a factor in his death.

OBITUARIES AND OTHER SOURCES:

PERIODICALS

Chicago Tribune, February 8, 2007, section 3, p. 9.

New York Times, February 3, 2007, p. A13; February 7, 2007, p. A2.

Times (London, England), February 6, 2007, p. 48.

Washington Post, February 5, 2007, p. B5.

*   *   *

WAITE, Judy Bernard
See BERNARD, Patricia

*   *   *

WASHBURN, Bradford 1910-2007
(Henry Bradford Washburn, Jr.)

OBITUARY NOTICE— See index for *SATA* sketch: Born June 7, 1910, in Cambridge, MA; died of heart failure January 10, 2007, in Lexington, MA. Cartographer, photographer, mountaineer, museum director, and author. A former director of the Boston Museum of Science, Washburn was a noted photographer and cartographer who contributed to the accurate mapping of the Grand Canyon. He was a Harvard University graduate, earning a B.A. in 1933 and a master's degree in 1960. His became interested in mountains at an early age, and as a teenager he climbed the Matterhorn and Mont Blanc in Europe. In America, Washburn was an instructor at the Institute of Geographical Explorations from 1935 until 1942, and he led expeditions to the Yukon and Mount McKinley for the National Geographic Society throughout the 1930s. He was named director of the New England Museum of Natural History in Boston (now the Museum of Science) in 1939. During World War II, Washburn was a cold-climate equipment consultant for the U.S. Army Air Forces and he directed Alaskan test projects. His military work reduced frostbite in soldiers by ninety percent. Through the 1940s, 1950s, and 1960s, he led a number of expeditions to Alaskan mountains, often traveling with his wife, who was the first woman to ascend Mt. McKinley. He wrote articles about his travels and submitted photographs to such magazines as *National Geographic, Look, Scientific American, Polar Record, Sports Illustrated,* and *Life.* Washburn was most often recognized, however, for his groundbreaking work in the early 1970s in mapping the Grand Canyon, which he completed using the most advanced technology available, including lasers. He and his team created new maps in 1974 and 1978 that were highly detailed and accurate. Although Washburn never climbed Mt. Everest, he was noted, for using global positioning devices in 1999 to accurately measure the peak at 29,035 feet. As director of the Mu-

seum of Science, Washburn was credited with turning an old-fashioned facility into a leading center for science and research that now attracts 1.4 million visitors a year. He retired from his position in 1980, but continued to work at the museum as chair of the corporation until 1985; he retained an office there as honorary director until 2000. The author of such books as *Bradford on Mt. Fairweather* (1930) and *A Tourist Guide to Mount McKinley* (1971), he received numerous awards for his accomplishments, including the Gold Medal from the Harvard Travellers Club in 1959, the Gold Research Medal of the Royal Scottish Geographical Society in 1979 and the Cherry Kearton Medal in 1988 from the Royal Geographical Society. The Bradford Washburn Gold Medal and Award was named in his honor by the Museum of Science in 1964.

OBITUARIES AND OTHER SOURCES:

BOOKS

Science and Its Times, Volume 6: *1900-1949,* Thomson Gale (Detroit, MI), 2000.

PERIODICALS

Chicago Tribune, January 14, 2007, section 4, p. 6.
New York Times, January 16, 2007, p. A29.
Times (London, England), January 22, 2007, p. 48.

* * *

WASHBURN, Henry Bradford, Jr.
See WASHBURN, Bradford

* * *

WEATHERFORD, Carole Boston 1956-

Personal

Born February 13, 1956, in Baltimore, MD; daughter of Joseph Alexander and Carolyn Virginia Boston; married Ronald Jeffrey Weatherford (a writer), February 2, 1985; children: one daughter, one son. *Education:* American University, B.A., 1977; University of Baltimore, M.A. (publication design), 1982; University of North Carolina—Greensboro, M.F.A. *Politics:* Democrat. *Religion:* Methodist.

Addresses

Home and office—3313 Sparrowhawk Dr., High Point, NC 27265-9350. *E-mail*—weathfd@earthlink.net.

Career

Educator and author. English teacher at public schools in Baltimore, MD, 1978; American Red Cross, Baltimore, MD, field representative in Blood Services De-

partment, 1978-79; *Black Arts Review* (radio talk show), creator, producer, and host, 1979; Art Litho Co., Baltimore, account executive, 1981; National Bar Association, Washington, DC, director of communications, 1981-85; B & C Associates, Inc., High Point, NC, vice president and creative director, 1985-88; freelance writer and publicist, beginning 1988; Fayetteville State University, Fayetteville, NC, professor, 2002—. Publicist and consultant to Black Classic Press, 1985—, and *Chronicle,* 1990—; consultant to Dudley Products Co. and local schools.

Member

North Carolina Writers Network (vice president, 1996-97), Phi Kappa Phi, Delta Sigma Theta, Alpha Kappa Alpha.

Awards, Honors

North Carolina Writers Network Black Writers Speak Competition winner, 1991, and Harperprints Chapbook Competition winner, 1995, both for *The Tan Chanteuse;* North Carolina Arts Council fellowship, 1995; Carter G. Woodson Book Award in elementary category, National Council for the Social Studies, 2001, for *The Sound That Jazz Makes;* AAUW-North Carolina Juvenile Literature Award, 2002, for *Remember the Bridge;* North Carolina Children's Book Award finalist, Bank Street College Best Children's Book designation, and North Carolina Juvenile Literature Award, all 2002, all for *Freedom on the Menu;* Bank Street College Best Children's Book designation, 2003, for *Sidewalk Chalk;* Furious Flower Poetry Prize, James Madison University; International Reading Association (IRA) Notable Book for a Global Society designation, 2005, for *A Negro League Scrapbook;* Golden Kite Honor designation, Society of Children's Book Writers and Illustrators, and National Association for the Advancement of Colored People Image Award nomination, both 2006, both for *Dear Mr. Rosenwald;* IRA/Children's Book Council (CBC) Teachers' Choice designation; National Council on the Social Studies Notable Children's Trade Book designation, American Library Association Notable Book designation, IRA Notable Book for a Global Society designation, and New York Public Library 100 Books for Reading and Sharing designation, all 2006, all for *Moses.*

Writings

FOR CHILDREN

My Favorite Toy, Writers and Readers Publishing (New York, NY), 1994.
Juneteenth Jamboree, illustrated by Yvonne Buchanan, Lee & Low Books (New York, NY), 1995.
Me and My Family Tree, illustrated by Michelle Mills, Black Butterfly (New York, NY), 1996.

Grandma and Me, illustrated by Michelle Mills, Black Butterfly (New York, NY), 1996.

Mighty Menfolk, illustrated by Michelle Mills, Black Butterfly (New York, NY), 1996.

The Sound That Jazz Makes (poetry), illustrated by Eric Velasquez, Walker (New York, NY), 2000.

The African-American Struggle for Legal Equality in American History, Enslow Publishers (Berkeley Heights, NJ), 2000.

Princeville: The 500-Year Flood, illustrated by Douglas Alvord, Coastal Carolina Press (Wilmington, NC), 2001.

Sidewalk Chalk: Poems of the City, illustrated by Dimitrea Tokunbo, Wordsong/Boyds Mills Press (Honesdale, PA), 2001.

Jazz Baby, illustrated by Laura Freeman, Lee & Low Books (New York, NY), 2002.

Remember the Bridge: Poems of a People, Philomel Books (New York, NY), 2002.

Great African-American Lawyers: Raising the Bar of Freedom, Enslow Publishers (Berkeley Heights, NJ), 2003.

Freedom on the Menu: The Greensboro Sit-Ins, illustrated by Jerome Lagarrigue, Dial Books for Young Readers (New York, NY), 2005.

A Negro League Scrapbook, Boyds Mills Press (Honesdale, PA), 2005.

Jesse Owens: The Fastest Man Alive, illustrated by Eric Valasquez, Walker & Co. (New York, NY), 2006.

Dear Mr. Rosenwald, illustrated by R. Gregory Christie, Scholastic Press (New York, NY), 2006.

Birmingham, 1963, Wordsong (Honesdale, PA), 2007.

Champions on the Bench: The 1955 Cannon Street YMCA All-Stars, illustrated by Leonard Jenkins, Dial Books for Young Readers (New York, NY), 2007.

Before John Was a Jazz Giant: A Song of John Coltrane, illustrated by Sean Qualls, Henry Holt (New York, NY), 2008.

I, Matthew Henson, illustrated by Eric Velasquez, Walker (New York, NY), 2008.

OTHER

The Tan Chanteuse (poetry; for adults), 1995.

Sink or Swim: African-American Lifesavers of the Outer Banks (audiobook), Coastal Carolina Press (Wilmington, NC), 1999.

(With husband, Ronald Jeffrey Weatherford) *Somebody's Knocking at Your Door: AIDS and the African-American Church,* Haworth Pastoral Press (Binghamton, NY), 1999.

The Tar Baby on the Soapbox, Longleaf Press at Methodist College, 1999.

The Carolina Parakeet: America's Lost Parrot in Art and Memory (nonfiction), Avian Publications, 2005.

Contributor of articles and poetry to magazines and newspapers, including *Essence, Christian Science Monitor,* and *Washington Post.*

Sidelights

The writings of North Carolina writer Carole Boston Weatherford, which include both fiction and nonfiction, were described as "remarkably forthright celebrations" and "a colorful assembly of African American tradition, pride, and love" by Heather Ross Miller in her *African American Review* appraisal of Weatherford's picture book *Juneteenth Jamboree. Juneteenth Jamboree,* a story that revolves around the traditional celebration of that day in 1865 when Texas slaves finally got word of their emancipation, is characteristic of much of Weatherford's writing in its focus on revisiting important moments in African-American history and grounding such moments in perseverance, family ties, and closely held tradition. Among her award-winning titles for younger children are the picture books *The Sound That Jazz Makes, A Negro League Scrapbook, Freedom on the Menu: The Greensboro Sit-ins, Remember the Bridge: Poems of a People,* and *Dear Mr. Rosenwald.* Weatherford's inspiring picture book *Moses: When Harriet Tubman Led Her People to Freedom,* in addition to receiving numerous accolades for its text, earned a Caldecott Honor designation and a Coretta Scott King Award for Illustration for the contributions of noted artist Kadir Nelson.

In one of her early books for children, *Juneteenth Jamboree,* Weatherford introduces readers to Cassandra, a young girl who has recently moved to Texas and has never heard of "Juneteenth," despite the fact that it became a legal holiday in that state in 1980. She witnesses the elaborate preparations with the eyes of a newcomer and feels the excitement rising in her community without understanding, at first, what it means. Gradually, Cassandra and the reader learn the significance of this historic celebration, its importance amplified by the jubilant crowds, the parades and dances, and the picnic that all bring the community together. "Weatherford does an excellent job" of introducing the reader to an unusual regional holiday, commented Carol Jones Collins in *School Library Journal,* while in *Publishers Weekly* a contributor remarked that the "enthusiastic text allows readers to discover—and celebrate—the holiday along with Cassandra."

Featuring illustrations by Dimitrea Tokunbo, *Sidewalk Chalk: Poems of the City* is an expression of pride, according to a reviewer for the *Bulletin of the Center for Children's Books.* In twenty vignettes, Weatherford celebrates the city as a child might experience it. Her poems evoke the spirit of the neighborhood and the daily activities of the people who live there: jumping rope on a sidewalk, getting a haircut, or going to the Laundromat or to church. "The overall tone of the collection is upbeat and positive," remarked *Booklist* contributor Kathy Broderick, and the *Bulletin of the Center for Children's Books* critic dubbed the author's verses "vivid snapshots of city life."

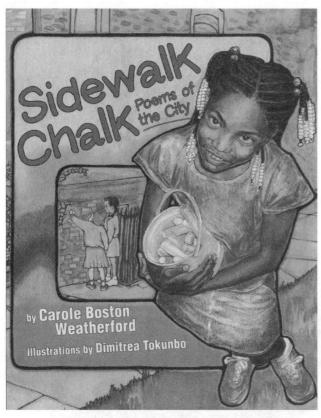

Cover of Carole Boston Weatherford's **Sidewalk Chalk,** *a poetry collection featuring artwork by Dimitrea Tokunbo.* (Wordsong/Boyds Mills Press, Inc., 2001. Illustration © 2001 by Dimitrea Tokunbo. All rights reserved. Reproduced by permission.)

Weatherford focuses on black musicians in the books *Jazz Baby, The Sound That Jazz Makes* and *Before John Was a Jazz Giant: A Song of John Coltrane.* A celebration in rhyme of American music, *The Sound That Jazz Makes* follows the uniquely American musical form's roots into African-American history. Weatherford's short poems pair with paintings by award-winning artist Eric Velasquez to depict a musical journey from the drumbeats of Africa to the sound of rap music that can be heard in the streets of the city. Poet and illustrator lead the reader from the work-chants of the cotton fields to the plaintive laments of the blues echoing through the Mississippi delta, to the celebrations of gospel, the sweet rhythms of the swing era, and the bold harmonies of the nightclubs of Harlem. According to *Booklist* contributor Bill Ott, Weatherford's poems "possess a flowing rhythm that younger readers [in particular] will respond to eagerly." Although a *Publishers Weekly* reviewer found the book's rhymes to be "at odds with" the rhythms of jazz music, in *Black Issues Book Review* Khafre Abif described *The Sounds That Jazz Makes* as "a soft poetic journey of rhythm" in which the "words are as seamless as the rhythm's growth" from primitive drumbeats into one of the most far-reaching musical movements of modern times.

Black athletes teach readers important lessons about determination and personal growth in books such as *Jesse Owens: Fastest Man Alive, Champions on the Bench: The 1955 Cannon Street YMCA All-Stars,* and *A Negro League Scrapbook.* In *Champions on the Bench,* readers meet a young baseball player whose talented team is in the running for the 1955 Little League World Series playoff until their white opponents refuse to meet them on the playing field. Praised by *School Library Journal* critic Marilyn Taniguchi as "an engaging overview, richly augmented by archival photographs," *A Negro League Scrapbook* provides a visual history of the Negro Leagues from 1887 to 1947, when Jackie Robinson became the first black player to sign with the majors. Weatherford moves from the baseball diamond to the 1936 Olympic Games in Berlin, Germany for *Jesse Owens,* which a *Publishers Weekly* praised as a "poetic tribute" to the American athlete's "remarkable performance" during wartime. *Booklist* reviewer GraceAnne A. DeCandido, noting that Weatherford "lightly fictionalizes" the true story that inspired *Champions on the Bench,* added that Leonard Jenkins' "dramatic paintings . . . capture the joy of baseball and the boys' frustration," while Mary Hazelton concluded in *School Library Journal* that the book presents "a powerful story, well told."

Weatherford moves from black culture to history in books such as *Freedom on the Menu, Moses,* and *Dear Mr. Rosenwald.* Segregation and the civil-rights movement is the subject of *Freedom on the Menu,* a picture book based on a true story that took place near where Weatherford grew up. The book's story follows eight-year-old Connie as she experiences segregation at a downtown Greensboro lunch counter, then watches as her older siblings band with other blacks and take the seats at the counter that have been denied to them as a result of the town's Jim Crow laws. Former slave turned abolitionist Harriet Tubman is the focus of *Moses,* which profile's Tuman's courageous work helping escaped slaves travel north on the Underground Railway in the years leading up to the U.S. Civil War. Reviewing *Freedom on the Menu* in *Publishers Weekly,* a critic described the book as "a fresh and affecting interpretation of a pivotal event in the civil rights movement," while another reviewer in the same periodical likened Weatherford's three-tier narrative in *Moses* to "a wholly engrossing dramatic play."

A collaboration with artist R. Gregory Christie, *Dear Mr. Rosenwald* was inspired by the memories of Weatherford's mother, who attended one of the many "Rosenwald" schools that were established throughout the rural south during the 1920s, thanks to the donations of Sears, Roebuck & Company president Julius Rosenwald and the hard work of many small towns. In the story, ten-year-old Ovella, whose father works as a sharecropper, watches as the residents of her poor community work together to earn matching funds and invest time and hard work in a new town school. Reviewing the book in *Publishers Weekly,* a contributor dubbed

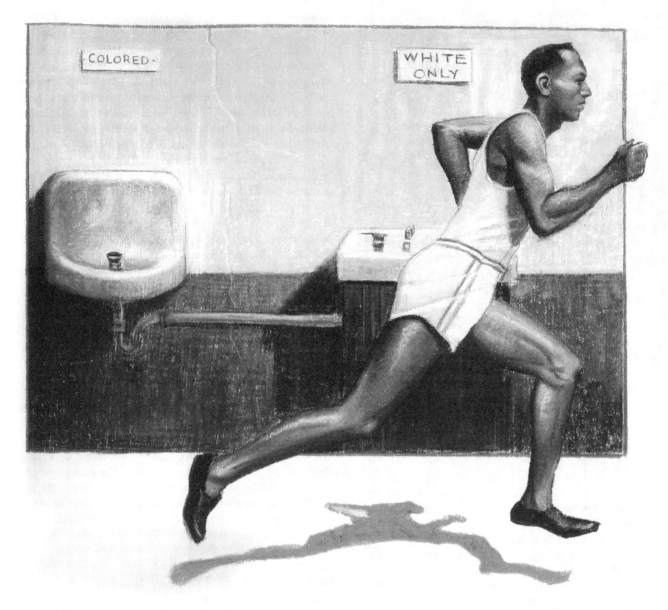

Weatherford recounts the story of one of the most famous black athletes of all time in **Jesse Owens, Fastest Man Alive,** *featuring artwork by Eric Velasquez.* (Walker & Company, 2007. Illustration © 2007 by Eric Velasquez. All rights reserved. Reproduced by permission.)

Dear Mr. Rosenwald "a heartening sliver of American history," while in *Booklist* Hazel Rochman cited Weatherford's "clear free verse" and Christie's "exuberant gouache and colored-pencil illustrations."

Weatherford views African-American history on a broad scale in *Remember the Bridge,* a poetic celebration of men and women from America's earliest days through to the twentieth century. Weatherford writes of the great and the not so great: the leaders whose names are familiar to everyone and the people whose names were never known. For these latter people she creates fictional profiles, exploring in her poetry how it must have felt to be sold into slavery and showcasing the diversity of African Americans in a wide array of occupations. Critical response was mixed. A *Publishers Weekly* reviewer appreciated the free-verse poems but was less satisfied with the metered rhymes, calling the chrono-

logical narrative somewhat "confusing." In contrast, a contributor to *Kirkus Reviews* claimed that Weatherford "brilliantly summarizes . . . a complete timeline" of history. The last poem in *Remember the Bridge,* titled "I Am the Bridge," reflects the belief that every individual can be a part of what the *Kirkus Reviews* writer called "a bridge toward understanding and acceptance."

Biographical and Critical Sources

PERIODICALS

African American Review, spring, 1998, Heather Ross Miller, review of *The Tan Chanteuse* and *Juneteenth Jamboree,* pp. 169-171.

American Visions, December-January, 1995, Yolanda Robinson Coles, review of *Juneteenth Jamboree,* p. 37.

Black Issues Book Review, September, 2000, Khafre Abif, review of *The Sound That Jazz Makes,* p. 81.

Booklist, December 15, 1999, Carolyn Phelan, review of *Sink or Swim: African-American Lifesavers of the Outer Banks,* pp. 783-784; August, 2000, Bill Ott, review of *The Sound That Jazz Makes,* p. 2133; September 15, 2001, Kathy Broderick, review of *Sidewalk Chalk: Poems of the City,* p. 224; February 15, 2002, Kay Weisman, review of *Princeville: The 500-Year Flood,* p. 1014, and Gillian Engberg, review of *Remember the Bridge: Poems of a People,* p. 1030; February 15, 2003, Gillian Engberg, review of *Great African-American Lawyers: Raising the Bar of Freedom,* p. 1080; February 1, 2005, GraceAnne A. DeCandido, review of *A Negro League Scrapbook,* p. 976, and Carolyn Phelan, review of *Freedom on the Menu: The Greensboro Sit-ins,* p. 980; October 1, 2006, Hazel Rochman, review of *Dear Mr. Rosenwald,* p. 61; February 1, 2007, GraceAnne A. DeCandido, review of *Champions on the Bench: The Cannon Street YMCA All-Stars,* p. 61.

Bulletin of the Center for Children's Books, October, 2001, review of *Sidewalk Chalk,* p. 81; May, 2002, review of *Remember the Bridge,* p. 344; February, 2005, Karen Coats, review of *Freedom on the Menu,* p. 268; October, 2006, Deborah Stevenson, review of *Dear Mr. Rosenwald,* p. 53; November, 2006, Karen Coats, review of *Moses: When Harriet Tubman Led Her People to Freedom,* p. 148; January, 2007, Elizabeth Bush, review of *Champions on the Bench,* p. 233.

Canadian Review of Materials, March, 2001, AnnMarie Hamar, review of *The Sound That Jazz Makes,* p. 23.

Georgia Review, summer, 1997, Ted Kooser, review of *The Tan Chanteuse,* p. 375.

Horn Book, January-February, 2005, Joanna Rudge Long, review of *Freedom on the Menu,* p. 87; November-December, 2006, Michelle H. Martin, review of *Moses,* p. 737.

Kirkus Reviews, December 1, 2001, review of *Remember the Bridge,* p. 1691; December 15, 2004, review of *Freedom on the Menu,* p. 1211; March 1, 2005, review of *A Negro League Scrapbook,* p. 297; August 15, 2006, review of *Dear Mr. Rosenwald,* p. 853; September 1, 2006, review of *Moses,* p. 914; December 1, 2006, review of *Jesse Owens,* p. 1226.

New York Times Book Review, February 11, 2007, Rebecca Zerkin, review of *Moses,* p. 17.

Publishers Weekly, October 30, 1995, review of *Juneteenth Jamboree,* p. 61; May 15, 2000, review of *The Sound That Jazz Makes,* p. 115; September 17, 2001, review of *Sidewalk Chalk,* p. 82; December 24, 2001, review of *Remember the Bridge,* p. 62; January 3, 2005, review of *Freedom on the Menu,* p. 55; July 31, 2006, review of *Moses,* p. 78; October 23, 2006, review of *Dear Mr. Rosenwald,* p. 51; December 11, 2006, review of *Champions on the Bench,* p. 69; January 1, 2007, review of *Jesse Owens: Fastest Man Alive,* p. 49.

School Library Journal, January, 1996, Carol Jones Collins, review of *Juneteenth Jamboree,* p. 97; July, 2000, Ginny Gustin, review of *The Sound That Jazz Makes,* p. 99; January, 2002, review of *Sidewalk Chalk,* p. 127; June, 2002, Marge Loch-Woulters, review of *Jazz Baby,* p. 114; March, 2005, Marilyn Taniguchi, review of *A Negro League Scrapbook,* p. 236; April, 2005, Mary N. Oluonye, review of *Freedom on the Menu,* p. 115; August, 2005, Blair Christolon, review of *Freedom on the Menu,* p. 50; October, 2006, Margaret Bush, review of *Moses,* and Catherine Threadgill, review of *Dear Mr. Rosenwald,* both p. 129; January, 2007, Mary Hazelton, review of *Champions of the Bench,* p. 110; March, 2007, Suzanne Myers Harold, review of *Jesse Owens,* p. 236.

Voice of Youth Advocates, August, 2002, review of *Remember the Bridge,* p. 213.

ONLINE

Carole Boston Weatherford Home Page, http://www.caroleweatherford.com (August 1, 2007).

*   *   *

WEISSBERGER, Ela 1930- (Ela Stein Weissberger)

Personal

Born June 30, 1930, in Czechoslovakia; daughter of Max and Marketa Stein; married Leopold Weissberger. *Education:* Attended art school. *Religion:* Jewish.

Addresses

Home and office—Tappan, NY.

Career

Author. *Military service:* Israeli Army; became sergeant.

Writings

(With Susan Goldman Rubin) *The Cat with the Yellow Star: Coming of Age in Terezin,* Holiday House (New York, NY), 2006.

Sidelights

As a Holocaust survivor, it has been Ela Weissberger's goal to share her stories of life within the concentration camps with younger generations. Weissberger was born in Czechoslovakia in 1930, and her world changed when the German Nazis invaded her country in the fall of 1938. Weissberger and her family were Jews, and three years later, at age eleven, she and her family were transported from her home to the Terezin concentration camp, located outside the city of Prague. Of the 15,000

children held in Terezin throughout the duration of World War II, only one hundred survived, Weissberger being one of them. Weissberger shares her story of survival through speaking engagements as well as in her autobiography *The Cat with the Yellow Star: Coming of Age in Terezin,* coauthored with Susan Goldman Rubin. In an interview for the *Cincinnati Enquirer,* Weissberger remarked of her experiences: "It is by a miracle that I can talk about it. I was saved. I think I speak in the voices of those that couldn't make it."

The Cat with the Yellow Star describes the arrival of Weissberger and her family at Terezin and includes Weissberger's recollections of performing in the opera *Brundibar,* a work composed by Czech composer and prison-camp inmate Hans Krása as part of a 1944 Nazi propaganda film. Weissberger played the part of the Cat and appeared in all fifty-five performances that were staged within the camp. In addition to telling Weissberger's story, *The Cat with the Yellow Star* features examples of art work Weissberger created while in Terezin, and also includes photographs of the children who became her friends. Teri Markson, writing in *School Library Journal,* regarded Weissberger's story as a "finely tuned collaboration [that] weaves together narrative and memories into one cohesive story of trauma, friendship, and survival." In *Kirkus Reviews* a critic also commented on the poignancy of the work, calling Weissberger's tale an "intense, brisk and plainspoken" work that "makes for irresistible reading." Hazel Rochman, in her review of *The Cat with the Yellow Star* for *Booklist,* called the work a "poignant biography of a Holocaust survivor" that details events "without concealment or exploitation."

Biographical and Critical Sources

PERIODICALS

Booklist, June 1, 2006, Hazel Rochman, review of *The Cat with the Yellow Star: Coming of Age in Terezin,* p. 100.
Horn Book, July-August, 2006, Joanna Rudge Long, review of *The Cat with the Yellow Star,* p. 468.
Kirkus Reviews, May 15, 2006, review of *The Cat with the Yellow Star,* p. 522.
Publishers Weekly, March 20, 2006, review of *The Cat with the Yellow Star,* p. 57.
School Library Journal, June, 2006, Teri Markson, review of *The Cat with the Yellow Star,* p. 184.

ONLINE

Cincinnati Enquirer Online, http://news.enquirer.com/ (October 19, 2000), Janelle Gelfand, interview with Weissberger.
Colorado Springs Independent Online, http://www.csindy. com/ (January 13, 2000), Owen Perkins, "Songs of Resistance: Ela Stein Weissberger Recalls Her Role in *Brundibar,* a Children's Opera Staged in the Terezin Concentration Camp."

Music of Remembrance Web site, http://www. musicofremembrance.org/ (July 8, 2007), "Ela Stein Weissberger."
Time Online, http://www.time.com/ (May 25, 2003), Heather Won Tesoriero, "Where Young Things Are."

*   *   *

WEISSBERGER, Ela Stein
See WEISSBERGER, Ela

*   *   *

WIESNER, David 1956-

Personal

Surname pronounced "*weez*-ner"; born February 5, 1956, in Bridgewater, NJ; son of George (a research manager at a chemical plant) and Julia (a homemaker) Wiesner; married Kim Kahng (a surgeon), May 21, 1983; children: Kevin, Jaime. *Education:* Rhode Island School of Design, B.F.A., 1978.

Career

Author and illustrator of children's books. *Exhibitions:* Works displayed at Metropolitan Museum of Art, New York, NY, 1982, and at galleries, including Master Eagle Gallery, New York, NY, 1980-89, Academy of Natural Sciences, Philadelphia, PA; Rhode Island School of Design Museum of Art, Providence; Brooklyn Public Library, Brooklyn, NY; Muscarele Museum of Art; College of William and Mary, Society of Illustrators, New York, NY; and Greenwich Public Library, Greenwich, CT.

Awards, Honors

Children's Picturebook Award, *Redbook* magazine, 1987, for *The Loathsome Dragon;* Caldecott Honor designation, American Library Association (ALA), 1989, for *Free Fall;* Pick of the Lists citation, American Booksellers Association (ABA), 1990, for *Hurricane;* Notable Children's Book citation, ALA, Ten Best Books of the year citation, *Parenting* magazine, and ABA Pick of the Lists citation, all 1991, and Caldecott Medal, 1992, all for *Tuesday;* Parent's Choice citation, 1992, for *June 29, 1999;* Bank Street College of Education Best Book designation, Carolyn W. Field Award Honor designation, and New York Public Library 100 Titles for Reading and Sharing designation, all 1994, all for *Night of the Gargoyles* by Eve Bunting; Caldecott Medal, 2002, for *The Three Pigs,* and 2007, for *Flotsam;* Caldecott Honor designation, ALA Notable Book designation, Bank Street College of Education Best Books designation, New York Public Library Best Book for Reading and Sharing designation, and ABA Choice designation, all 2000, all for *Sector 7.*

Writings

SELF-ILLUSTRATED PICTURE BOOKS

(Reteller, with wife, Kim Kahng) *The Loathsome Dragon,* Putnam (New York, NY), 1987, revised edition, Clarion Books (New York, NY), 2005.

Free Fall, Lothrop (New York, NY), 1988.

Hurricane, Clarion Books (New York, NY), 1990.

Tuesday, Clarion Books (New York, NY, 1991.

June 29, 1999, Clarion Books (New York, NY), 1992.

Sector 7, Clarion Books (New York, NY), 1999.

The Three Pigs, Clarion Books (New York, NY), 2001.

Flotsam, Clarion Books (New York, NY), 2006.

ILLUSTRATOR

Gloria Skurzynski, *Honest Andrew,* Harcourt (New York, NY), 1980.

Avi, *Man from the Sky,* Knopf (New York, NY), 1980.

Nancy Luenn, *The Ugly Princess,* Little, Brown (Boston, MA), 1981.

David R. Collins, *The One Bad Thing about Birthdays,* Harcourt (New York, NY), 1981.

Jane Yolen, *The Boy Who Spoke Chimp,* Knopf (New York, NY), 1981.

Jane Yolen, *Neptune Rising: Songs and Tales of the Undersea Folk,* Philomel (New York, NY), 1982.

Mike Thaler, *Owly,* Harper (New York, NY), 1982.

Vera Chapman, *Miranty and the Alchemist,* Avon (New York, NY), 1983.

Allan W. Eckert, *The Dark Green Tunnel,* Little, Brown (Boston, MA), 1984.

William Kotzwinkle, *E.T.: The Storybook of the Green Planet* (based on a story by Steven Spielberg), Putnam (New York, NY), 1985.

Allan W. Eckert, *The Wand: The Return to Mesmeria,* Little, Brown (Boston, MA), 1985.

Dennis Haseley, *Kite Flier,* Four Winds Press (New York, NY), 1986.

Nancy Willard, *Firebrat,* Knopf (New York, NY), 1988.

Marianna Mayer, reteller, *The Sorcerer's Apprentice: A Greek Fable,* Bantam (New York, NY), 1989.

Laurence Yep, *The Rainbow People,* HarperCollins (New York, NY), 1989.

Laurence Yep, reteller, *Tongues of Jade* (Chinese-American folk tales), HarperCollins (New York, NY), 1991.

Eve Bunting, *Night of the Gargoyles,* Houghton (Boston, MA), 1994.

Adaptations

Free Fall was adapted for videocassette with teacher's guide, American School Publications, 1990. *Tuesday* was adapted for videocassette, American School Publications, 1992. *The Three Pigs* was optioned for film by Disney Feature Animation, 2002.

Sidelights

"I create books I think I would have liked to have seen when I was a kid," award-winning author and illustrator David Wiesner once remarked in an interview for *SATA.*

"I loved being able to get lost in paintings and to get involved in all the details." Winner of the prestigious Caldecott Medal for his picture books *Tuesday, The Three Pigs,* and *Flotsam,* Wiesner has also produced other highly praised original works, among them *Free Fall, Hurricane,* and *Sector 7.*

Born in 1956, Wiesner grew up in a creatively inclined family—art and music number among his sibling's interests—and an environment that encouraged his own flair for drawing. "I never had the sense that I had to rebel at home so my parents would let me be an artist," he recalled in his interview. The diverse landscape surrounding the Wiesner family's Bridgewater, New Jersey, hometown encouraged his active imagination: making use of the local cemetery, a nearby river, woods, and the town dump, Wiesner and his friends concocted various games, "army" being a particular favorite.

Even though neighborhood companions in Bridgewater were in abundance, Wiesner enjoyed spending long stretches of time by himself, often drawing. His interest in art was fueled further by the television *You Are an Artist,* which was hosted by artist Jon Gnagy and which aired in reruns when Wiesner was about six or seven years old. Fascinated with Gnagy's attention to perspective, light, and scale, the budding illustrator bought Gnagy's instruction books and earnestly practiced drawing all the pictures first in charcoal, then in color. "The books and program probably provided my first formal exposure to techniques and ideas about drawing," Wiesner recalled in his *SATA* interview. "I still keep a framed picture of him [Gnagy] on my wall."

In junior high school Wiesner discovered the Renaissance and surrealism, particularly the works of Renaissance artists Michelangelo, Leonardo da Vinci, Albrecht Dürer, and Pieter Brueghel the Elder. He also developed a love of the fantastic, especially horror and science-fiction films such as Stanley Kubrick's *2001: A Space Odyssey.* High school provided Wiesner with another creative influence in the person of art teacher Robert Bernabe. "In Mr. Bernabe I finally found someone I could talk to about art," Wiesner revealed in his *SATA* interview. "He essentially encouraged me to follow whatever inclinations I had and was willing to do what he could to facilitate that."

Accepted at the prestigious Rhode Island School of Design (RISD) after high school, Wiesner experienced what he later described in his interview as a "pretty intense first year" during which he unlearned many old habits and absorbed new ideas and ways of thinking about art. "I remember going to my life-drawing class and noticing that while the teacher didn't really respond to my work, he would look at another student's work and say, 'this is really terrific,' or something like that. I would look at the same work and wonder, 'why is he saying that? He doesn't understand.' Yet by the end of the year I was able to look at that same work and real-

ize 'that's great stuff.' RISD helped me reorient myself and helped me get rid of some of my preconceived notions."

The thought of expanding the painting into a narrative—either with words or without—fascinated Wiesner, and his work at RISD began to reflect this interest. At first he directed his talent toward adult fantasy, short, wordless sequences done in oils. As he gained experience, he began developing his own style, primarily using watercolors, and experimenting with characters, settings, and story lines of a lengthier nature. As graduation loomed, Wiesner considered working as an illustrator for adult fantasy magazines; a career in children's literature hardly crossed his mind. "If you looked at the work I was doing, though," the artist later admitted, "it was obvious I should be going into children's books." Fortunately, RISD instructor Lester Abrams encouraged Wiesner to show his art portfolio to noted children's author and illustrator Trina Schart Hyman during Hyman's visit to the RISD campus. Hyman, then art director for *Cricket* children's magazine, promptly offered the young artist the opportunity to create art for a magazine cover.

Children's literature has proved to be a fertile artistic niche for Wiesner. Beginning as a textbook illustrator after graduation, he compiled a professional portfolio. By the 1980s he was living in New York City with partner Kim Kahng and developing a distinctive style as a picture-book illustrator. Despite a personal setback in 1983—the apartment building where Wiesner and Kahng lived burned to the ground, destroying everything the newly married couple owned—during the 1980s he illustrated such works as William Kotzwinkle's *E.T.: The Storybook of the Green Planet,* Allan W. Eckert's *Wand: The Return to Mesmeria,* and Dennis Haseley's *Kite Flier.*

In 1987 Wiesner and Kanhg collaborated on *The Loathsome Dragon,* a work based on the English fairy tale "The Laidly Worm of Spindleston Huegh" that was re-released in 2005 with a revised text, new cover, and reformatted artwork. The narrative relates the story of the beautiful Princess Margaret, who becomes trapped inside the body of an enormous dragon through the sorcery of her evil, jealous stepmother. Only three kisses from Margaret's brother, Childe Wynd, who is traveling in a far-off land, will free the princess from the spell. Wiesner's detailed watercolor paintings for the original edition of *The Loathsome Dragon* feature medieval-styled landscapes and seascapes, sprawling castles, elaborate robes, jewelry, and armor, drew praise from reviewers. Responding to this version, Caldecott Medalist and RISD department head David Macaulay wrote in *Horn Book:* "Take a look at the watercolor landscapes [*The Loathsome Dragon*] contains and tell me you don't see a little Da Vinci in there." Describing the 2005 revision, *School Library Journal* reviewer Marie Orlando called the images "more vivid," adding that

Wiesner's "softly colored and patterned frames have been replaced with white borders that make the pictures less remote."

The product of several years' work, Wiesner's 1988 work, *Free Fall,* is a wordless picture book that follows a young boy on a fantastic journey he experiences during a dream. The narrative opens as the youngster falls asleep while studying a book of maps. Reality fades as his bedspread transforms into a landscape, and he is transported, along with exotic companions, onto a chessboard with live game pieces, then to a medieval castle housing knights and a dragon, to rocky cliffs that merge into a city skyline, and then to a larger-than-life breakfast table. Finally the boy floats among swans, fishes, and leaves and arrives back at his starting place. Many events and characters the young boy encounters during his dream correspond to objects in the youngster's bedroom, from the bowl of goldfish next to his bed to the chess pieces stashed in his nightstand, the pigeons hovering near his window, and the leaves sketched on his wallpaper.

Critical reaction to *Free Fall* was mixed. While a *Bulletin of the Center for Children's Books* critic deemed it "an excellent replication of a dream," some commentators found the book too complex to be readily understood by a young audience. "The nameless protagonist's . . . adventures are confusing, complicated, and illogical," Julie Corsaro maintained in *School Library Journal.* This divided reaction did not extend to the committee selecting the 1989 Caldecott Honor books, which awarded Wiesner's work an Honor Book designation. As the artist later recalled, "having *Free Fall* named a Caldecott Honor Book was a wonderful confirmation that 'yes, this does seem to be the way to go.' It felt really, really satisfying because all along I had the feeling I had been going in the right direction with the pieces I had done and conceived on my own."

Based on an incident from Wiesner's childhood, *Hurricane* opens with "detailed, exquisitely rendered paintings [that] draw the reader into his story of a hurricane's progress," as a *Publishers Weekly* reviewer described it. After the storm, two boys create exotic imaginative landscapes using a tree that was downed by the hurricane. "The child-focused, low perspective gives even ordinary scenes an extra measure of drama," Patricia Dooley observed in *School Library Journal,* the critic adding that Wiesner's "fantasy spreads are detailed delights."

Wiesner's first Caldecott Medal-winning picture book, *Tuesday,* is a whimsical tale about a night when a crowd of frogs ascend skyward on lily pads and soar over the surrounding neighborhood. Zooming past startled birds and an incredulous resident indulging in a late-night snack, the frogs speed through a clothesline (causing some minor entanglements), and spook Rusty, a sizable dog. They even sneak into a living room housing a sleepy elderly lady and watch some television (one

In **Tuesday,** *illustrator and author David Wiesner places himself in his own surreal story.* (Clarion Books, 1991. Illustrations © 1991 by David Wiesner. Reproduced by permission of Houghton Mifflin Company.)

member of the assemblage operates the remote control with his spindly tongue). A *Publishers Weekly* critic termed the book's illustrations "stunning . . . and executed with a seeming flawless command of palette and perspective." "What saves this book from simply being a gorgeous gallery of paintings," Roger Sutton explained in the *Bulletin of the Center for Children's Books,* "is its warmth and humor: these frogs are having a lot of fun." Carolyn Phelan likewise noted the humor of the illustrations, writing in *Booklist* that "the narrative artwork tells a simple, pleasant story with a consistency and authenticity that make the fantasy convincing." *School Library Journal* contributor Patricia Dooley also praised Wiesner's use of color and perspective, predicting of *Tuesday* that "kids will love its lighthearted, meticulously imagined, fun-without-a-moral fantasy."

Wiesner followed up *Tuesday* with *June 29, 1999.* This amusing and innovative picture book revolves around young Holly Evans, who sends an assortment of vegetable seedlings into the atmosphere as part of a science experiment for school. A little more than a month later, on June 29, 1999—a Tuesday, of course—gigantic rutabagas, avocados, lima beans, artichokes, cucumbers, peas, and all sorts of other vegetables begin falling to earth. Amazement, anxiety, and confusion overcome citizens. In addition, rumors spread ("4,000 lb. Radish Has Face of ELVIS!" screams one tabloid headline); business opportunities in real estate flourish ("Gourd Estates" quickly sprouts in North Carolina); and at least one Iowa farmer is ecstatic ("At last, the blue ribbon at the state fair is mine!" he announces upon finding a gargantuan head of cabbage on his property).

In *June 29, 1999* Wiesner's story matches the wit of his art, according to critical consensus. Linda Perkins, for example, commenting in the *New York Times Book Review,* wrote that "the succinct story . . . provides just

enough background with perfect deadpan wit and even a few alliterative flourishes, and packs a final punch of its own." It was Wiesner's artwork in *June 29, 1999* that garnered the bulk of the praise, however. "The exquisite watercolors are truly out of this world," Luann Toth remarked in *School Library Journal,* pointing out the artist's use of "unusual perspective" and "clever detail." As Perkins explained, "Wiesner's real strength is vivid, innovative illustration," and his "sly details" add greatly to the book's humor. Dubbing *June 29, 1999* "a visual and literary feast," a *Publishers Weekly* reviewer concluded: "Spectacular to look at, great fun to read—it is, in sum, executed with consummate skill."

Odd metamorphoses are again evident in *Sector 7,* a wordless book in which an imaginative young boy is transported during a visit to the Empire State Building and winds up on a tour of the celestial cloud factory known as Sector 7. A *Horn Book* reviewer wrote that Wiesner's illustrations "are startlingly and powerfully conceived, the fanciful cloud-shapes both funny and el-

egant." In *Publishers Weekly,* a contributor lauded the book for providing a glimpse into "an ingenious world of nearly unlimited possibilities" via paintings that "contain such a wealth of details that they reveal new discoveries even after repeated examinations."

Wiesner earned his second Caldecott Medal for *The Three Pigs,* which brings such visual inventiveness to the classic tale that *Booklist* critic Gillian Engberg described it as a "post-modern fantasy" that "deliciously reinvents the pigs' tale [and] invites readers to step beyond the boundaries of story and picture book altogether." Instead of adhering to the traditional narrative in which the wolf blows down the pig's straw house, Wiesner's wolf blows the pig right out of the picture; the two other pigs escape in a similar fashion, capering through flying pages of text and discovering other storybook "planets." Finally, the pigs put the pages of their own story back together and return to their world to outwit the still-waiting wolf. "Wiesner has created a funny, wildly imagined tale that encourages kids to leap

Wiesner's ability to conjure magic from everyday things results in picture books such as the award-winning **Flotsam.** (Clarion Books, 2006. Copyright © 2006 by David Wiesner. All rights reserved. Reproduced by permission of Houghton Mifflin Company.)

beyond the familiar," wrote Engberg, "to think critically about conventional stories and illustration, and perhaps to flex their imaginations and create wonderfully subversive versions of their own stories."

Yet another Caldecott Medal came Wiesner's way with *Flotsam,* a captivating wordless picture book that uses the passage of years and a sea-tossed underwater camera to transcend both time and the reader's perception about the underwater world. During a day at the beach, a boy discovers a black box camera washed up by the tide. Exposing the reel of film inside, he discovers that the camera has captured amazing images of undersea life, including fantastic fishes and other sea creatures whose actions seem surreal and oddly human-like. Some developed pictures reveal images of other children who have also encountered the camera during the many years it has floated and bobbed through the world's waterways. In each snapshot, a child holds a photo from the camera that depicts another child holding a photo of still other child, creating a visual time tunnel into the camera's past. Praising the "clue-and-fancy-strewn" images in *Flotsam,* Sutton concluded in *Horn Book* that "the meticulous and rich detail of Wiesner's watercolors makes the fantasy involving and convincing." "Masterfully altering the pace with panel sequences and full-bleed spreads, [Wiesner] . . . fills every inch of the pages with intricate, imaginative watercolor details," a *Publishers Weekly* reviewer noted. In *School Library Journal,* Joy Fleishhacker noted of *Flotsam* that, "filled with inventive details and delightful twists, each snapshot is a tale waiting to be told," and all combine in "a mind-bending journey of imagination."

In addition to his original picture books, Wiesner continued to create art for texts by other writers through the mid-1990s. One of his most notable collaborations was with Eve Bunting on *Night of the Gargoyles.* Bunting's oddly macabre tale of stone gargoyles at play while the city sleeps is interpreted by Wiesner with a surreal sense of whimsy. The illustrator's charcoal pictures "capture the huge heaviness of the stone figures and their gloomy malevolence," according to *Booklist* contributor Hazel Rochman. Claiming that "if anyone could bring gargoyles to life pictorially, it's Wiesner," *School Library Journal* contributor Julie Cummins applauded the artist's work on this book, adding that the illustrations combine to create "a deliciously eerie, spooky scenario."

"I'm hoping kids have fun when they read my books," Wiesner noted in his *SATA* interview. "I have found that wordless picture books are as enriching and as involving as a book with words in it." "In a wordless book, each reader really completes the story," he also explained; "There is no author's voice narrating the story. In books like *Free Fall* or *Tuesday,* there is a lot going on there, and you really need to *read* the picture. A reader can't just flip through the book; all the details add up to more fully tell the story. It's exciting to me to develop that visual literacy."

Biographical and Critical Sources

BOOKS

Authors of Books for Young People, edited by Martha E. Ward, third edition, Scarecrow Press (Metuchen, NJ), 1990.

Children's Book Illustration and Design, edited by Julie Cummins, Library of Applied Design, PBC International (New York, NY), 1992.

Children's Books and Their Creators, edited by Anita Silvey, Houghton Mifflin (Boston, MA), 1995, pp. 679-680.

Children's Literature Review, Volume 43, Thomson Gale (Detroit, MI), 1997, pp. 196-217.

St. James Guide to Children's Writers, 5th edition, St. James Press (Detroit, MI), 1999, pp. 1118-1119.

Wiesner, David, *June 29, 1999,* Clarion Books (New York, NY), 1992.

PERIODICALS

Booklist, May 1, 1991, Carolyn Phelan, review of *Tuesday,* p. 1723; October 1, 1994, Hazel Rochman, review of *Night of the Gargoyles,* p. 331; September 15, 1999, Stephanie Zvirin, review of *Sector 7,* p. 270; May 15, 2001, Gillian Engberg, review of *The Three Pigs,* p. 1761; February 15, 2005, Gillian Engberg, review of *The Loathsome Dragon,* p. 1082; August 1, 2006, Gillian Engberg, review of *Flotsam,* p. 76.

Bulletin of the Center for Children's Books, May, 1988, review of *Free Fall,* p. 193; November, 1990, p. 74; May, 1991, Roger Sutton, review of *Tuesday,* p. 231; November, 1992, pp. 93-94; September, 2006, Deborah Stevenson, review of *Flotsam,* p. 44.

Horn Book, January-February, 1991, pp. 61-62; January-February, 1992, p. 84; July-August, 1992, David Macaulay, "David Wiesner," pp. 423-428; July-August, 1992, David Wiesner, "Caldecott Acceptance Speech," pp. 416-422; September, 1999, review of *Sector 7,* p. 603; May, 2001, review of *The Three Pigs,* p. 341; July-August, 2002, David Wiesner, "Caldecott Medal Acceptance," p. 393; July-August, 2002, Anita Silvey, "David Wiesner," p. 401; September-October, 2006, Roger Sutton, review of *Flotsam,* p. 571.

Kirkus Reviews, October 1, 1992, review of *June 29, 1999,* p. 1262; August 1, 2006, review of *Flotsam,* p. 798.

New York Times Book Review, August, 1988, p. 99; September 25, 1988, p. 51; November 8, 1992, Linda Perkins, "Hocus-Pocus in Ho-Ho-Kus," p. 31; November 21, 1999, Andrew Leonard, review of *Sector 7,* p. 36; May 20, 2001, Sean Kelly, review of *The Three Pigs,* p. 20.

Publishers Weekly, July 25, 1986, pp. 187-188; October 30, 1987, review of *The Loathsome Dragon,* p. 70; May 12, 1989, p. 294; August 31, 1990, review of *Hurricane,* p. 66; March 1, 1991, review of *Tuesday,* p. 73; September 20, 1991, p. 134; October 26, 1992, review of *June 29, 1999,* p. 69; August 8, 1994, p. 436; August 31, 1999, review of *Sector 7,* p. 83; No-

vember 1, 1999, review of *Sector 7*, p. 57; November 22, 1999, Cindi Di Marzo, interview with Wiesner, p. 22; February 26, 2001, review of *The Three Pigs*, p. 86; February 21, 2005, review of *The Loathsome Dragon*, p. 175; July 24, 2006, review of *Flotsam*, p. 56.

School Library Journal, January, 1986, p. 66; November, 1986, p. 78; March, 1988, Constance A. Mellon, review of *The Loathsome Dragon*, p. 178; June-July, 1988, Julie Corsaro, review of *Free Fall*, p. 95; August, 1988, p. 99; May, 1990, pp. 107-108; October, 1990, Patricia Dooley, review of *Hurricane*, p. 104; December, 1990, p. 25; January, 1991, p. 56; May, 1991, Patricia Dooley, review of *Tuesday*, p. 86; December, 1991, p. 132; November, 1992, Luann Toth, review of *June 29, 1999*, p. 81; October, 1994, Julie Cummins, review of *Night of the Gargoyles*, p. 86; September, 1999, Julie Cummins, review of *Sector 7*, p. 209; April, 2001, Wendy Lukehart, review of *The Three Pigs*, p. 26; April, 2005, Marie Orlando, review of *The Loathsome Dragon*, p. 116' September, 2006, Joy Fleishhacker, review of *Flotsam*, p. 186.

ONLINE

BookPage Web site, http://www.bookpage.com/ (September, 1999), Miriam Drennan, interview with Wiesner.
Houghton Mifflin Web site, http://www. houghtonmifflinbooks.com/ (August 27, 2007).

*   *   *

WILSON, Jonathan 1950-

Personal

Born February 26, 1950, in London, England; immigrated to United States, c. 1981; naturalized citizen; son of Lewis and Doris Wilson; married Sharon Kaitz (an artist), August 30, 1960; children: Adam, Gabriel. *Education*: University of Essex, B.A. (with honors), 1968; Hebrew University of Jerusalem, Ph.D., 1974. *Religion*: Jewish. *Hobbies and other interests*: Soccer.

Addresses

Office—Department of English, Tufts University, 209 East Hall, Medford, MA, 02155. *Agent*—Gail Hochman, Brandt-Hochman, 1501 Broadway, New York, NY 10036. *E-mail*—jonathan.wilson@tufts.edu.

Career

Educator and author. Tufts University, Medford, MA, professor of English, beginning 1982, then director of creative writing, currently Fletcher Professor of rhetoric and debate and director of Humanities Institute.

Awards, Honors

Guggenheim fellowship, 1994; National Jewish Book Award finalist, 2004, for *A Palestine Affair*.

Writings

FICTION

The Hiding Room, Viking (New York, NY), 1995.
Schoom (short fiction), Penguin (New York, NY), 1995.
A Palestine Affair, Pantheon (New York, NY), 2003.
An Ambulance Is on the Way: Stories of Men in Trouble, Pantheon (New York, NY), 2005.

OTHER

On Bellow's Planet: Reading from the Dark Side, Associated University Presses (Cranbury, NJ), 1985.
Herzog: The Limits of Ideas, Twayne Publishers (Boston, MA), 1990.
Marc Chagall, Nextbook-Schocken (New York, NY), 2007.

Contributor to periodicals, including *New Yorker*.

Sidelights

Jonathan Wilson is a fiction writer as well as an educator and literary critic. In the novels and short fiction for which he is best known—the novels *The Hiding Room* and *A Palestine Affair*, as well as short-story collections *Schoon* and *An Ambulance Is on the Way: Stories of Men in Trouble*—he explores the nature of identity. "I'm Jewish. I'm an American citizen. I lived in Israel for four years," Wilson told *Boston Globe* interviewer David Mehegan. "The issues of blurring identity fascinate me, and that's why my imagination takes me to places where all those things are blurred and challenged."

The youngest of three brothers, Wilson grew up in an observant Jewish family in the Willesden section of London. At Oxford University he was one of the first graduate students to begin a D.Phil. exclusively in American literature. During a visit to New York City in 1976 to research American novelist Saul Bellow, Wilson discovered a new and welcome freedom from the anti-Semitism that often surfaced in London. As he recalled to Mehegan: "I absolutely fell in love with New York. I had never seen Jewish people have so much fun before, and I loved it. It was the first time I didn't feel like a self-effacing minority." After teaching and finishing his doctorate at Hebrew University, where he met his Boston-born wife, artist Sharon Kaitz, Wilson returned to the United States and made his permanent residence there. He began his academic career at Tufts University in the early 1980s, where he taught contemporary American literature and creative writing and was eventually honored with the appointment as Fletcher Professor of rhetoric and debate. He is presently director of the Humanities Institute.

Schoom, published in 1993, focuses on Jewish dislocation. The characters in the book's stories are inevitably victims: individuals trapped in situations or circum-

stances that they cannot control. In the title tale, for example, a patient is intimidated into stealing by his psychoanalyst. In "Migrants" an American family immigrates to Israel and befriends a family of Russian immigrants who eventually rob them. "Wilson's people tend to stray where they don't belong," commented David Gates in the *New York Times Book Review*. "To some of these characters, the very idea of belonging anywhere seems alien."

Wilson's second collection of short fiction, *An Ambulance Is on the Way,* contains eleven tales that a *Publishers Weekly* reviewer dubbed "lightly comic" and "contemplative." The stories move in setting from Boston to such exotic locations as Israel, Jamaica, and Ireland. In one tale, "Dead Ringers," approaching death and guilt prompt a middle-aged man to visit the grave site of a brother who died in infancy, and "Fundamentals" follows a trusting American Jewish woman who get caught up in a terrorist scheme. "Wilson is a deft, subtle writer who often neatly turns the tables on his protagonists to reveal the surprising inside the mundane," concluded the *Publishers Weekly* writer, while *Library Journal* contributor Jim Coan deemed Wilson's collection "elegantly written with humor and grit." Recommending *An Ambulance Is on the Way* for teen readers, *Kliatt* reviewer Daniel Levinson noted that Wilson's "funny, insightful" stories in *An Ambulance Is on the Way* contain "some (probably) quite recognizable aspects of family life today."

The Hiding Room echoes Wilson's characteristic theme of the wandering Jew as it follows a beleaguered film editor as he travels to Jerusalem to bury his deceased mother and learn more about his father, who met his mother while working as a British intelligence officer during World War II. *The Hiding Room* contains two narratives, one devoted to the hero's search and the other concerning the actual relationship between the editor's parents decades earlier. "History has its nodes where two just causes intersect and each becomes the other's unjust cause," Richard Eder noted of the work in his *Los Angeles Times* review. Eder described *The Hiding Room* as "a love story shattered at one such intersection," while in *Publishers Weekly* a reviewer wrote that, in his book, Wilson exhibits "a convincing grasp of both the physical and emotional terrain he describes."

Published in 2003 and a finalist for the National Jewish Book Award, *A Palestine Affair* is based on a true story: the murder of a Dutch Orthodox Jew named Yaakov De Haan in Jerusalem in 1924, when the Zionist movement was achieving momentum. Wilson's story straddles genres, combining mystery with political thriller. The plot of the novel revolves around the efforts of British-born painter Mark Bloomberg, a recent arrival in Jerusalem, to solve the mystery of an Arab man murdered on his doorstep. In *Publishers Weekly* a contributor cited the author's ability to paint a "vivid picture of Jerusalem" in the 1920s, while Gershom Gorenberg wrote in the *Washington Post* that the novelist "has down the irritating macho tone of the old-fashioned detective genre." Richard Eder reviewed *A Palestine Affair* for the *New York Times Book Review* and praised the author's narrative skills, writing that "Wilson has devised a story that tautens the sinuous strands of this period into a lethal knot. The strengths of his novel are the tension and pace of its plot." While Frank Caso noticed that the tale's secondary plot lines "fizzle out," he judged the novel to be "well written" in his *Booklist* review, as did a *Kirkus Reviews* contributor who wrote that *A Palestine Affair* contains "just the right mix of psychological incisiveness and historical drama." In *Library Journal*, Molly Abramowitz dubbed the book "a fascinating read" that illuminates, for readers, the history behind ongoing conflicts in the Middle East."

In addition to writing fiction, Wilson has published two volumes of literary criticism devoted to the works of Jewish-American writer Saul Bellow, as well as a biography of Jewish painter Marc Chagall. Born in Vitebsk, Belorussia in 1887, Chagall was inspired to incorporate the broad strokes and dramatic colors of Matisse in his folkloric works. Eventually making his home in Paris, he returned temporarily to Vitebsk where he founded an art school, and fled to New York City while the Nazi-friendly Vicky government ruled France during World War II. Although maintaining that Wilson's profile draws heavily on other biographies of the painter, a *Publishers Weekly* contributor nonetheless praised Wilson as an "incisive, lively writer." The novelist's "inventive way with words perfectly matches his subject's topsy-turvy visual lexicon," noted Donna Seaman in her *Booklist* review of *Marc Chagall*, the critic adding that the biography reveals in "fresh and penetrating ways the mysteries and sorrows inherent in Chagall's complex work."

Biographical and Critical Sources

PERIODICALS

Booklist, September 1, 1985, review of *On Bellow's Planet: Reading from the Dark Side,* p. 20; May 15, 2003, Frank Caso, review of *A Palestine Affair,* p. 1641; May 15, 2007, Donna Seaman, review of *Marc Chagall,* p. 13.

Boston Globe, August 20, 2003, David Mehegan, review of *A Palestine Affair,* p. D1.

Choice, May, 1986, review of *On Bellow's Planet,* pp. 1395-1396; June, 1990, p. 6682.

Christian Science Monitor, November 13, 1995, Merle Rubin, review of *The Hiding Room,* p. 13.

Kirkus Reviews, April 15, 2003, review of *A Palestine Affair,* pp. 569-570; February 1, 2007, review of *Marc Chagall,* p. 118.

Kliatt, May, 2006, Daniel Levinson, review of *An Ambulance Is on the Way: Stories of Men in Trouble,* p. 28.

Library Journal, July, 1995, Molly Abramowitz, reviews of *The Hiding Room* and *Schoom,* p. 125; May 1, 2003, Molly Abramowitz, review of *A Palestine Affair,* p. 158; January 1, 2005, Jim Coan, review of *An Ambulance Is on the Way,* p. 104.

New Yorker, February 12, 1996, review of *The Hiding Room,* p. 82.

New York Times Book Review, September 3, 1995, David Gates, reviews of *Schoom* and *The Hiding Room,* p. 10; June 22, 2003, Richard Eder, "Trouble in Balfourland," p. 7; December 7, 2003, review of *A Palestine Affair,* p. 69.

Publishers Weekly, May 22, 1995, review of *The Hiding Room,* pp. 45-46; June 26, 1995, review of *Schoom,* p. 104; May 12, 2003, review of *A Palestine Affair,* p. 44; January 15, 2005, review of *An Ambulance Is on the Way,* p. 34; January 15, 2007, review of *Marc Chagall,* p. 44.

Times Literary Supplement, August 6, 1993, Bryan Cheyette, review of *Schoom,* p. 20; November 17, 1995, Peter Sherwood, review of *The Hiding Room,* p. 27.

Tribune Books (Chicago, IL), March 25, 2007, Jonathan Kirsch, "Illuminating Biography Offers Insight into the Life and Art of Marc Chagall," p. 9.

Washington Post, June 8, 2003, Gershom Gorenberg, review of *A Palestine Affair,* p. T6.

ONLINE

Barnes & Noble Web site, http://www.barnesandnoble. com/ (summer, 2004), interview with Wilson.

Random House Web site, http:// www.randomhouse.com/ (August 15, 2007), "Jonathan Wilson."

*   *   *

WILSON, Phil 1948-

Personal

Born 1948, in PA. *Education:* Art Institute of Pittsburgh, graduated, 1968. *Hobbies and other interests:* Science fiction, photography, model building, Sherlock Holmes mysteries, playing guitar, the Beatles, paleontology, Disney.

Addresses

Agent—Cliff Knecht, 309 Walnut Rd., Pittsburgh, PA 15202.

Career

Illustrator. Co-owner and operator of an animation studio for over fifteen years, producing animation for television specials, feature films, a Tom Petty music video, and numerous television commercials. Illustrator of Disney collector plates for The Bradford Exchange.

Member

Pittsburgh Society of Illustrators.

Illustrator

FOR CHILDREN

Willabel L. Tong, *A Three-Dimensional Victorian Doll House,* Piggy Toes Press (Santa Monica, CA), 1998.

Bruce Hopkins, *Dinosaur Discovery 3-D: Construct Your Own Velociraptor,* Piggy Toes Press (Santa Monica, CA), 2000.

Louise Gikow, *Pandora's Box,* Golden Books (New York, NY), 2001.

Brian Conway, *My First Big Book of Questions and Answers,* Publications International (Lincolnwood, IL), 2002.

Don Lessem, *Dinosaurs,* Publications International (Lincolnwood, IL), 2004.

Ruth Ashby, *Pteranodon: The Life Story of a Pterosaur,* Harry N. Abrams (New York, NY), 2005.

Charlotte Lewis Brown, *The Day the Dinosaurs Died,* HarperCollins (New York, NY), 2006.

Charlotte Lewis Brown, *After the Dinosaurs: Mammoths, and Fossil Mammals,* HarperCollins (New York, NY), 2006.

Susan Ring, *Dinosaurs: An Adventure Back in Time,* Innovative Kids (Norwalk, CT), 2006.

Charlotte Lewis Brown, *Beyond the Dinosaurs: Monsters of the Air and Sea,* HarperCollins (New York, NY), 2007.

Illustrator of dozens of other picture books.

OTHER

Southwestern Pennsylvania, Treasures Map, District (Pittsburgh, PA), 1988.

Biographical and Critical Sources

PERIODICALS

Horn Book, July-August, 2006, Danielle J. Ford, review of *The Day the Dinosaurs Died,* p. 460.

Kirkus Reviews, June 1, 2005, review of *The Life Story of a Pterosaur,* p. 632; May 15, 2006, review of *The Day the Dinosaurs Died,* p. 514; August 15, 2006, review of *After the Dinosaurs: Mammoths and Fossil Mammals,* p. 836.

Publishers Weekly, October 27, 1997, "A Three-Dimensional Medieval Castle," p. 79; October 30, 2000, review of *The Scientific Method,* p. 78; August 4, 2003, review of *Disney's Build Your Own Haunted Mansion,* p. 82.

School Library Journal, February, 1995, Steven Engelfried, review of *Disney's Beauty and the Best Teacup Mix-Up,* p. 92; July, 2005, Patricia Manning, review of *The Life Story of a Pterosaur,* p. 86; June, 2006, Lynda Ritterman, review of *The Day the Dinosaurs Died,* p. 132; February, 2007, Christine Markley, review of *After the Dinosaurs: Mammoths and Fossil Mammals,* p. 105.

ONLINE

Cliff Knecht Artist Representative Web site, http://www. artrep1.com/ (July 16 2007), "Phil Wilson."

Derrick & News Herald Online, http://www.the derrick. com/ (July 16 2007), Michael Molitoris, "You Can Make a Living in Art."

Pittsburgh Society of Illustrators Web site, http://www. pittsburghillustrators.org/ (July 16 2007), "Phil Wilson."

*   *   *

WINTZ-LITTY, Julie
See LITTY, Julie

*   *   *

YERXA, Leo 1947-

Personal

Born 1947, on Little Eagle Reserve, Ontario, Canada; son of Ojibwa parents. *Ethnicity:* "Ojibwa." *Education:* Algonquin College, degree (graphic arts); University of Waterloo, degree (fine arts).

Addresses

Home and office—Ottawa, Ontario, Canada.

Career

Author and illustrator.

Awards, Honors

Mr. Christie's Book Award, Christie Brown & Co., Elizabeth Mrazik-Cleaver Canadian Picture Book Award, International Board on Books for Young People, and Amelia Frances Howard-Gibbon Illustrator's Award, Canadian Library Association, all 1994, all for *Last Leaf First Snowflake to Fall*; Governor General's Literary Awards in Children's Literature—Illustration, Canada Council for the Arts, 2006, for *Ancient Thunder.*

Writings

Renegade: The Art of Leo Yerxa: March 16-May 6, 1984, The Centre (Thunder Bay, Ontario, Canada), 1984.
Last Leaf First Snowflake to Fall, Orchard Books (New York, NY), 1994.
A Fish Tale; or, The Little One That Got Away, Douglas & McIntyre (Vancouver, British Columbia, Canada), 1995.
Tomson Highway, *Johnny National, Super Hero,* Health Canada (Ottawa, Ontario, Canada), 2001.
Ancient Thunder, Groundwood Books (Toronto, Ontario, Canada), 2006.

Sidelights

Native American author and illustrator Leo Yerxa infuses simple poetry with vibrant illustrations in order to depict the natural world. In his 2006 self-illustrated title, *Ancient Thunder,* Yerxa portrays how wild horses are interconnected to North America's native peoples through a series of short poems. His illustrations in the book feature backdrops composed of traditional textiles against which are set images of wild horses roaming the Great Plains. *School Library Journal* reviewer Carol Schene remarked that in *Ancient Thunder* Yerxa incorporates beautiful images with a sparse "but poetically perceptive text," the critic adding that the illustrator and poet artfully blends these elements "to create a unique vision of the mystical allure of horses." While some critics noted that the book lacks a linear story, a reviewer for *Publishers Weekly* maintained nonetheless that "older readers . . . may well find much to linger over."

In *Last Leaf First Snowflake to Fall* Yerxa again highlights elements of the natural world, this time following the changes that occur as season shift and autumn moves into winter. In her review for *Booklist,* Karen Hutt called *Last Leaf First Snowflake* "a lovely, poetic introduction to winter" and remarked on Yerxa's "beautifully constructed collages." Also praising the work, *Publishers Weekly* critic acknowledged the author/illustrator for his ability to fashion verses that "mirror nature's own repetitive cycles."

Canadian artist Leo Yerxa draws from his Native-American heritage in the picture book **Ancient Thunder.** (Illustration © 2006 by Leo Yerxa. Reproduced by permission of Groundwood Books/Douglas & McIntyre.)

Biographical and Critical Sources

PERIODICALS

Books, November 19, 2006, review of *Ancient Thunder,* p. 7.

Books in Canada, November, 1993, review of *Last Leaf First Snowflake to Fall,* p. 58.

Booklist, October 1, 1994, Karen Hutt, review of *Last Leaf First Snowflake to Fall,* p. 335.

Bulletin of the Center for Children's Books, September, 1996, review of *A Fish Tale,* p. 39.

Canadian Review Annual, 1994, review of *Last Leaf First Snowflake to Fall,* p. 514; 1995, review of *A Fish Tale,* p. 491.

Emergency Librarian, November, 1994, review of *Last Leaf First Snowflake to Fall,* p. 45; March, 1995, review of *Last Leaf First Snowflake to Fall,* p. 18.

Kirkus Reviews, August 15, 2006, review of *Ancient Thunder,* p. 855.

Publishers Weekly, September 19, 1994, review of *Last Leaf First Snowflake to Fall,* p. 70; April 29, 1996, review of *A Fish Tale,* p. 72; October 23, 2006, review of *Ancient Thunder,* p. 48.

Quill & Quire, September, 1993, review of *Last Leaf First Snowflake to Fall,* p. 66; September, 1995, review of *A Fish Tale,* p. 72.

Resource Links, February, 1997, review of *Last Leaf First Snowflake to Fall,* p. 142.

School Librarian, May, 1996, review of *A Fish Tale,* p. 58; November, 1997, review of *Last Leaf First Snowflake to Fall,* p. 202.

School Library Journal, December, 1994, Cynthia K. Richey, review of *Last Leaf First Snowflake to Fall,* p. 92; November, 2006, Carol Schene, review of *Ancient Thunder,* p. 126.

Times Educational Supplement, December 8, 1995, review of *A Fish Tale,* p. 12.

ONLINE

Canada Council for the Arts Web site, http://www.canadacouncil.ca/ (July 8, 2007), "Winners of the 2006 Governor General's Literary Awards."*

*   *   *

YOSHIKAWA, Sachiko

Personal

Born in Japan; married; husband's name Wayne; children: Kinu. *Education:* Studied art.

Addresses

Home and office—Seattle, WA. *Agent*—HK Portfolio, 10 E. 29th St., Ste. 40G, New York, NY 10016.

Sachiko Yoshikawa's child-friendly art pairs with Rebecca Kai Dotlich's nonfiction text in **What Is Science?** (Illustration © 2006 by Sachiko Yoshikawa. Reprinted by permission of Henry Holt and Company.)

Career

Illustrator.

Awards, Honors

Finalist for Excellence in Science Books Award, *Science Books & Films,* 2007, for *What Is Science?* by Rebecca Kai Dotlich.

Illustrator

L.B. Manz, *Noshi's Special Gift,* All About Kids Publishing (San Jose, CA), 2003.

Steve Tomecek, *Stars,* National Geographic (Washington, DC), 2003.

Pat Brisson, *Beach Is to Fun: A Book of Relationships,* Henry Holt (New York, NY), 2004.

Virgina Kroll, *Boy, You're Amazing!,* Albert Whitman (Morton Grove, IL), 2004.

Linda Walvoord, *Razzamadaddy,* Marshall Cavendish (New York, NY), 2004.

Dayle Ann Dodds, *Hello, Sun!,* Dial Books for Young Readers (New York, NY), 2005.

Rebecca Kai Dotlich, *What Is Science?,* Henry Holt (New York, NY), 2006.

Toni Buzzeo, *Our Librarian Won't Tell Us Anything!,* Upstart Books, 2006.

Brod Bagert, *Shout!: Little Poems That Roar,* Dial Books for Young Readers (New York, NY), 2007.

Elizabeth Wojtusik, *Kitty Up!,* Dial Books for Young Readers (New York, NY), 2008.

Sidelights

Sachiko Yoshikawa grew up in Tokyo, Japan, then came to the United States to study art in San Francisco. Originally interested in designing jewelry, she developed a

Yoshikawa uses bright, summery colors to bring to life Pat Brisson's concept picture book **Beach Is to Fun.** (Henry Holt and Co., 2004. Illustration © 2004 by Sachiko Yoshikawa. Reprinted by permission of Henry Holt and Company.)

knack for graphic design that would eventually lead to narrative illustration. As an artist, Yoshikawa enjoys combining several media in her images, among them collage and acrylics. A seasoned traveler, she incorporates into her works the inspirations and experiences she gleans from those travels. Yoshikawa has contributed illustrations to a variety of children's titles, among them *Beach Is to Fun: A Book of Relationships* by Pat Brisson, *Hello, Sun!* by Dale Ann Dodds, and *What Is Science?* by Rebecca Kai Dotlich. Praising *Hello, Sun!*, *Booklist* contributor Carolyn Phelan noted that Yoshikawa's "cheerful" images "amplify the energy and comic spirit" of Dodds' text, while a *Kirkus Reviews* writer dubbed her work for *Beach Is to Fun* as "brightly colored as a beach ball." Also reviewing Brisson's book, Phelan highlighted a characteristic of Yoshikawa's art, writing that the illustrator's "jaunty" images "are energized by bold color combinations."

What Is Science? presents an introduction to the sciences geared for young readers, introducing such fields as geology, oceanography, meteorology, and zoology. Dotlich's text, written in verse, is balanced by Yoshikawa's colorful and engaging illustrations. A *Kirkus Reviews* critic remarked of the work that "Yoshikawa's artwork truly makes science come alive for young readers" by integrating "books, tools, maps and notebooks" so that readers can learn more about the topics under discussion. The illustrator also adds humorous details to her work, keeping young readers engaged. Carolyn Phelan, writing in *Booklist,* acknowledged *What Is Science?* as a "vividly illustrated" work and noted that Yoshikawa's "well-composed" images effectively utilize repetition "to create a sense of visual rhythm that suits the rhyming text well."

Biographical and Critical Sources

PERIODICALS

Booklist, April 15, 2004, Terry Glover, review of *Boy, You're Amazing!,* p. 1446; August, 2004, Carolyn Phelan, review of *Beach Is to Fun: A Book of Relationships,* p. 1940; June 1, 2005, Carolyn Phelan, review of *Hello Sun!,* p. 1820; September 15, 2006, Carolyn Phelan, review of *What Is Science?,* p. 63; February 1, 2007, Hazel Rochman, review of *Shout!: Little Poems That Roar,* p. 48.

Bulletin of the Center for Children's Books, July-August, 2004, Elizabeth Bush, review of *Beach Is to Fun,* p. 456.

Kirkus Reviews, February 15, 2004, review of *Boy, You're Amazing!,* p. 181; May 15, 2004, review of *Beach Is to Fun,* p. 488; August 15, 2006, review of *What Is Science?,* p. 839.

School Library Journal, May, 2003, Dona Ratterree, review of *Stars,* p. 143; May, 2004, Terry Glover, review of *Boy, You're Amazing!,* p. 116; July, 2004, Linda L. Walkins, review of *Beach Is to Fun,* p. 68, Sheilah Kosco, review of *Razzamadaddy,* p. 89; June, 2005, Kathleen Simonetta, review of *Hello Sun!,* p. 108; November, 2006, Lynda Ritterman, review of *What Is Science?,* p. 119; February, 2007, Gloria Koster, review of *Our Librarian Won't Tell Us Anything!,* p. 85, and Sally R. Dow, review of *Shout!,* p. 99.

ONLINE

HK Portfolio Web site, http://www.hkportfolio.com/ (July 8, 2007), "Sachiko Yoshikawa."*

Illustrations Index

(In the following index, the number of the *volume* in which an illustrator's work appears is given *before* the colon, and the *page number* on which it appears is given *after* the colon. For example, a drawing by Adams, Adrienne appears in Volume 2 on page 6, another drawing by her appears in Volume 3 on page 80, another drawing in Volume 8 on page 1, and so on and so on. . . .)

YABC

Index references to *YABC* refer to listings appearing in the two-volume *Yesterday's Authors of Books for Children,* also published by The Gale Group. *YABC* covers prominent authors and illustrators who died prior to 1960.

A

Aas, Ulf *5:* 174
Abbe, S. van
  See van Abbe, S.
Abel, Raymond *6:* 122; *7:* 195; *12:* 3; *21:* 86; *25:* 119
Abelliera, Aldo *71:* 120
Abolafia, Yossi *60:* 2; *93:* 163; *152:* 202
Abrahams, Hilary *26:* 205; *29:* 24, 25; *53:* 61
Abrams, Kathie *36:* 170
Abrams, Lester *49:* 26
Abulafia, Yossi *154:* 67; *177:* 3
Accorsi, William *11:* 198
Acs, Laszlo *14:* 156; *42:* 22
Adams, Adrienne *2:* 6; *3:* 80; *8:* 1; *15:* 107; *16:* 180; *20:* 65; *22:* 134, 135; *33:* 75; *36:* 103, 112; *39:* 74; *86:* 54; *90:* 2, 3
Adams, Connie J. *129:* 68
Adams, John Wolcott *17:* 162
Adams, Lynn *96:* 44
Adams, Norman *55:* 82
Adams, Pam *112:* 1, 2
Adams, Sarah *98:* 126; *164:* 180
Adamson, George *30:* 23, 24; *69:* 64
Addams, Charles *55:* 5
Addy, Sean *180:* 8
Ade, Rene *76:* 198
Adinolfi, JoAnn *115:* 42; *176:* 2
Adkins, Alta *22:* 250
Adkins, Jan *8:* 3; *69:* 4; *144:* 2, 3, 4
Adler, Peggy *22:* 6; *29:* 31
Adler, Ruth *29:* 29
Adlerman, Daniel *163:* 2
Adragna, Robert *47:* 145
Agard, Nadema *18:* 1
Agee, Jon *116:* 8, 9, 10; *157:* 4
Agre, Patricia *47:* 195
Aguirre, Alfredo *152:* 218
Ahl, Anna Maria *32:* 24
Ahlberg, Allan *68:* 6, 7, 9; *165:* 5
Ahlberg, Janet *68:* 6, 7, 9
Aicher-Scholl, Inge *63:* 127
Aichinger, Helga *4:* 5, 45
Aitken, Amy *31:* 34
Akaba, Suekichi *46:* 23; *53:* 127
Akasaka, Miyoshi *YABC 2:* 261
Akib, Jamel *181:* 13
Akino, Fuku *6:* 144
Alain *40:* 41

Alajalov *2:* 226
Alborough, Jez *86:* 1, 2, 3; *149:* 3
Albrecht, Jan *37:* 176
Albright, Donn *1:* 91
Alcala, Alfredo *91:* 128
Alcantará, Felipe Ugalde *171:* 186
Alcorn, John *3:* 159; *7:* 165; *31:* 22; *44:* 127; *46:* 23, 170
Alcorn, Stephen *110:* 4; *125:* 106; *128:* 172; *150:* 97; *160:* 188; *165:* 48
Alcott, May *100:* 3
Alda, Arlene *44:* 24; *158:* 2
Alden, Albert *11:* 103
Aldridge, Andy *27:* 131
Aldridge, George *105:* 125
Alejandro, Cliff *176:* 75
Alex, Ben *45:* 25, 26
Alexander, Ellen *91:* 3
Alexander, Lloyd *49:* 34
Alexander, Martha *3:* 206; *11:* 103; *13:* 109; *25:* 100; *36:* 131; *70:* 6, 7; *136:* 3, 4, 5; *169:* 120
Alexander, Paul *85:* 57; *90:* 9
Alexeieff, Alexander *14:* 6; *26:* 199
Alfano, Wayne *80:* 69
Aliki
  See Brandenberg, Aliki
Allamand, Pascale *12:* 9
Allan, Judith *38:* 166
Alland, Alexandra *16:* 255
Allen, Gertrude *9:* 6
Allen, Graham *31:* 145
Allen, Jonathan *131:* 3, 4; *177:* 8, 9, 10
Allen, Joy *168:* 185
Allen, Pamela *50:* 25, 26, 27, 28; *81:* 9, 10; *123:* 4, 5
Allen, Rowena *47:* 75
Allen, Thomas B. *81:* 101; *82:* 248; *89:* 37; *104:* 9
Allen, Tom *85:* 176
Allender, David *73:* 223
Alley, R.W. *80:* 183; *95:* 187; *156:* 100, 153; *169:* 4, 5; *179:* 17
Allison, Linda *43:* 27
Allon, Jeffrey *119:* 174
Allport, Mike *71:* 55
Almquist, Don *11:* 8; *12:* 128; *17:* 46; *22:* 110
Aloise, Frank *5:* 38; *10:* 133; *30:* 92
Althea
  See Braithwaite, Althea

Altschuler, Franz *11:* 185; *23:* 141; *40:* 48; *45:* 29; *57:* 181
Alvin, John *117:* 5
Ambrus, Victor G. *1:* 6, 7, 194; *3:* 69; *5:* 15; *6:* 44; *7:* 36; *8:* 210; *12:* 227; *14:* 213; *15:* 213; *22:* 209; *24:* 36; *28:* 179; *30:* 178; *32:* 44, 46; *38:* 143; *41:* 25, 26, 27, 28, 29, 30, 31, 32; *42:* 87; *44:* 190; *55:* 172; *62:* 30, 144, 145, 148; *86:* 99, 100, 101; *87:* 66, 137; *89:* 162; *134:* 160
Ames, Lee J. *3:* 12; *9:* 130; *10:* 69; *17:* 214; *22:* 124; *151:* 13
Amon, Aline *9:* 9
Amoss, Berthe *5:* 5
Amstutz, Andre *152:* 102
Amundsen, Dick *7:* 77
Amundsen, Richard E. *5:* 10; *24:* 122
Ancona, George *12:* 11; *55:* 144; *145:* 7
Anderson, Alasdair *18:* 122
Andersen, Bethanne *116:* 167; *162:* 189; *175:* 17
Anderson, Bob *139:* 16
Anderson, Brad *33:* 28
Anderson, C.W. *11:* 10
Anderson, Carl *7:* 4
Anderson, Catherine Corley *72:* 2
Anderson, Cecil *127:* 152
Anderson, David Lee *118:* 176
Anderson, Derek *169:* 9; *174:* 180
Anderson, Doug *40:* 111
Anderson, Erica *23:* 65
Anderson, Laurie *12:* 153, 155
Anderson, Lena *99:* 26
Anderson, Peggy Perry *179:* 2
Anderson, Sara *173:* 3
Anderson, Scoular *138:* 13
Anderson, Susan *90:* 12
Anderson, Wayne *23:* 119; *41:* 239; *56:* 7; *62:* 26; *147:* 6
Andreasen, Daniel *86:* 157; *87:* 104; *103:* 201, 202; *159:* 75; *167:* 106, 107; *168:* 184; *180:* 247
Andrew, Ian *111:* 37; *116:* 12; *166:* 2
Andrew, John *22:* 4
Andrews, Benny *14:* 251; *31:* 24; *57:* 6, 7
Andrews, Vaughn *166:* 28
Anelay, Henry *57:* 173
Angel, Marie *47:* 22
Angelo, Valenti *14:* 8; *18:* 100; *20:* 232; *32:* 70

Anglund, Joan Walsh *2:* 7, 250, 251; *37:* 198, 199, 200
Anholt, Catherine *74:* 8; *131:* 7; *141:* 5
Anholt, Laurence *141:* 4
Anno, Mitsumasa *5:* 7; *38:* 25, 26, 27, 28, 29, 30, 31, 32; *77:* 3, 4; *157:* 10, 11
Antal, Andrew *1:* 124; *30:* 145
Antram, David *152:* 133
Apostolou, Christy Hale
  See Hale, Christy
Apple, Margot *33:* 25; *35:* 206; *46:* 81; *53:* 8; *61:* 109; *64:* 21, 22, 24, 25, 27; *71:* 176; *77:* 53; *82:* 245; *92:* 39; *94:* 180; *96:* 107; *152:* 4, 5; *162:* 192, 194; *173:* 44
Appleyard, Dev *2:* 192
Aragones, Sergio *48:* 23, 24, 25, 26, 27
Araneus *40:* 29
Arbo, Cris *103:* 4
Archambault, Matt *85:* 173; *138:* 19, 20; *143:* 33; *145:* 144; *179:* 103
Archer, Janet *16:* 69; *178:* 156
Ardizzone, Edward *1:* 11, 12; *2:* 105; *3:* 258; *4:* 78; *7:* 79; *10:* 100; *15:* 232; *20:* 69, 178; *23:* 223; *24:* 125; *28:* 25, 26, 27, 28, 29, 30, 31, 33, 34, 35, 36, 37; *31:* 192, 193; *34:* 215, 217; *60:* 173; *64:* 145; *87:* 176; *YABC 2:* 25
Arena, Jill *176:* 49
Arenella, Roy *14:* 9
Argent, Kerry *103:* 56; *138:* 17; *158:* 134
Arisman, Marshall *162:* 50
Armer, Austin *13:* 3
Armer, Laura Adams *13:* 3
Armer, Sidney *13:* 3
Armitage, David *47:* 23; *99:* 5; *155:* 4
Armitage, Eileen *4:* 16
Armstrong, George *10:* 6; *21:* 72
Armstrong, Shelagh *102:* 114
Arno, Enrico *1:* 217; *2:* 22, 210; *4:* 9; *5:* 43; *6:* 52; *29:* 217, 219; *33:* 152; *35:* 99; *43:* 31, 32, 33; *45:* 212, 213, 214; *72:* 72; *74:* 166; *100:* 169
Arnold, Caroline *174:* 5
Arnold, Emily *76:* 7, 9, 10
Arnold, Katya *115:* 11; *168:* 2, 3
Arnold, Tedd *116:* 14; *133:* 152; *160:* 5
Arnosky, James Edward *22:* 20; *70:* 9, 10, 11; *118:* 3, 5; *160:* 8, 10
Arnsteen, Katy Keck *105:* 97; *116:* 145
Arrowood, Clinton *12:* 193; *19:* 11; *65:* 210
Artell, Mike *89:* 8
Arting, Fred J. *41:* 63
Artzybasheff, Boris *13:* 143; *14:* 15; *40:* 152, 155
Aruego, Ariane *6:* 4
Aruego, José *4:* 140; *6:* 4; *7:* 64; *33:* 195; *35:* 208; *68:* 16, 17; *75:* 46; *93:* 91, 92; *94:* 197; *109:* 65, 67; *125:* 2, 3, 4, 5; *127:* 188; *143:* 25; *178:* 17, 19, 74
Arzoumanian, Alik *177:* 12
Asare, Meshack *86:* 9; *139:* 19
Ascensios, Natalie *105:* 139
Asch, Frank *5:* 9; *66:* 2, 4, 6, 7, 9, 10; *102:* 18, 19, 21; *154:* 12
Ashby, Gail *11:* 135
Ashby, Gil *146:* 4
Ashby, Gwynneth *44:* 26
Ashley, C.W. *19:* 197
Ashmead, Hal *8:* 70
Aska, Warabe *56:* 10
Assel, Steven *44:* 153; *77:* 22, 97
Astrop, John *32:* 56
Atene, Ann *12:* 18
Atherton, Lisa *38:* 198
Atkinson, Allen *60:* 5
Atkinson, J. Priestman *17:* 275
Atkinson, Janet *86:* 147; *103:* 138
Atkinson, Mike *127:* 74
Atkinson, Wayne *40:* 46
Attebery, Charles *38:* 170
Atwell, Debby *150:* 6

Atwood, Ann *7:* 9
Aubrey, Meg Kelleher *77:* 159
Auch, Herm *173:* 7, 8
Auch, Mary Jane *173:* 7
Augarde, Steve *25:* 22; *159:* 7
Austerman, Miriam *23:* 107
Austin, Margot *11:* 16
Austin, Robert *3:* 44
Austin, Virginia *81:* 205; *127:* 221
Auth, Tony *51:* 5
Avendano, Dolores *158:* 74
Avedon, Richard *57:* 140
Averill, Esther *1:* 17; *28:* 39, 40, 41
Axeman, Lois *2:* 32; *11:* 84; *13:* 165; *22:* 8; *23:* 49; *61:* 116; *101:* 124
Axtel, David *155:* 110
Ayer, Jacqueline *13:* 7
Ayer, Margaret *15:* 12; *50:* 120
Ayers, Alan *91:* 58; *107:* 169
Ayliffe, Alex *95:* 164
Ayto, Russell *111:* 5; *112:* 54
Azarian, Mary *112:* 9, 10; *114:* 129; *117:* 171; *137:* 163; *171:* 4, 5; *181:* 161

B

B.T.B.
  See Blackwell, Basil T.
Babbitt, Bradford *33:* 158
Babbitt, Natalie *6:* 6; *8:* 220; *68:* 20; *70:* 242, 243
Baca, Maria *104:* 5
Bacchus, Andy *94:* 87
Bacha, Andy *109:* 169
Bachem, Paul *48:* 180; *67:* 65; *144:* 206
Back, Adam *63:* 125
Back, George *31:* 161
Backhouse, Colin *78:* 142
Bacon, Bruce *4:* 74
Bacon, Paul *7:* 155; *8:* 121; *31:* 55; *50:* 42; *56:* 175; *62:* 82, 84
Bacon, Peggy *2:* 11, 228; *46:* 44
Baek, Matthew J. *169:* 95
Baer, Julie *161:* 2
Baicker-McKee, Carol *177:* 15; *180:* 215
Bailey, Peter *58:* 174; *87:* 221
Bailey, Sheila *155:* 11
Baker, Alan *22:* 22; *61:* 134; *93:* 11, 12; *146:* 6, 7, 10
Baker, Charlotte *2:* 12
vBaker, Garin *89:* 65
Baker, Jeannie *23:* 4; *88:* 18, 19, 20
Baker, Jim *22:* 24
Baker, Joe *82:* 188; *111:* 55; *124:* 70
Baker, Keith *179:* 6, 7
Baker, Leslie *112:* 214; *132:* 103, 246; *180:* 74, 246
Baldridge, Cyrus LeRoy *19:* 69; *44:* 50
Baldus, Zachary *152:* 231
Balet, Jan *11:* 22
Balian, Lorna *9:* 16; *91:* 16
Balit, Christina *102:* 24; *159:* 9; *162:* 118, 119
Ballantyne, R.M. *24:* 34
Ballis, George *14:* 199
Balouch, Kristen *176:* 11
Baltzer, Hans *40:* 30
Banbery, Fred *58:* 15
Banfill, A. Scott *98:* 7; *112:* 59
Bang, Molly Garrett *24:* 37, 38; *69:* 8, 9, 10; *111:* 7, 9, 10, 11; *140:* 11; *158:* 37, 38, 39
Banik, Yvette Santiago *21:* 136
Banner, Angela
  See Maddison, Angela Mary
Bannerman, Helen *19:* 13, 14
Bannon, Laura *6:* 10; *23:* 8
Bantock, Nick *74:* 229; *95:* 6
Baptist, Michael *37:* 208
Baracca, Sal *135:* 206
Barasch, Lynne *126:* 16

Barbarin, Lucien C., Jr. *89:* 88
Barbour, Karen *96:* 5; *74:* 209; *170:* 16
Bare, Arnold Edwin *16:* 31
Bare, Colleen Stanley *32:* 33
Barger, Jan *147:* 11
Bargery, Geoffrey *14:* 258
Barkat, Jonathan *149:* 177; *164:* 254; *181:* 106
Barker, Carol *31:* 27
Barker, Cicely Mary *49:* 50, 51
Barkley, James *4:* 13; *6:* 11; *13:* 112
Barks, Carl *37:* 27, 28, 29, 30, 31, 32, 33, 34
Barling, Joy *62:* 148
Barling, Tom *9:* 23
Barlow, Gillian *62:* 20
Barlow, Perry *35:* 28
Barlowe, Dot *30:* 223
Barlowe, Wayne *37:* 72; *84:* 43; *105:* 5
Barnard, Bryn *88:* 53; *13:* 55; *169:* 13
Barner, Bob *29:* 37; *128:* 33; *136:* 19, 20; *177:* 21
Barnes, Hiram P. *20:* 28
Barnes, Tim *137:* 28
Barnes-Murphy, Rowan *88:* 22
Barnett, Charles II *175:* 150
Barnett, Ivan *70:* 14
Barnett, Moneta *16:* 89; *19:* 142; *31:* 102; *33:* 30, 31, 32; *41:* 153; *61:* 94, 97
Barney, Maginel Wright *39:* 32, 33, 34; *YABC 2:* 306
Barnum, Jay Hyde *11:* 224; *20:* 5; *37:* 189, 190
Baron, Alan *80:* 3; *89:* 123
Barr, George *60:* 74; *69:* 64
Barragan, Paula S. *134:* 116
Barrall, Tim *115:* 152
Barrauds *33:* 114
Barrer-Russell, Gertrude *9:* 65; *27:* 31
Barret, Robert *85:* 134
Barrett, Angela *40:* 136, 137; *62:* 74; *75:* 10; *76:* 142; *144:* 137; *145:* 14
Barrett, Jennifer *58:* 149
Barrett, John E. *43:* 119
Barrett, Moneta *74:* 10
Barrett, Peter *55:* 169; *86:* 111
Barrett, Robert *62:* 145; *77:* 146; *82:* 35
Barrett, Ron *14:* 24; *26:* 35
Barron, John N. *3:* 261; *5:* 101; *14:* 220
Barrow, Ann *136:* 27
Barrows, Walter *14:* 268
Barry, Ethelred B. *37:* 79; *YABC 1:* 229
Barry, James *14:* 25
Barry, Katharina *2:* 159; *4:* 22
Barry, Robert E. *6:* 12
Barry, Scott *32:* 35
Bartenbach, Jean *40:* 31
Barth, Ernest Kurt *2:* 172; *3:* 160; *8:* 26; *10:* 31
Bartlett, Alison *101:* 88; *165:* 93
Barton, Byron *8:* 207; *9:* 18; *23:* 66; *80:* 181; *90:* 18, 19, 20, 21; *126:* 29, 30
Barton, Harriett *30:* 71
Barton, Jill *129:* 108; *135:* 120; *145:* 185, 189
Bartram, Robert *10:* 42
Bartsch, Jochen *8:* 105; *39:* 38
Bascove, Barbara *45:* 73
Base, Graeme *101:* 15, 16, 17, 18; *162:* 8, 10, 12
Baseman, Gary *174:* 12
Bash, Barbara *132:* 9
Bash, Norman *5:* 16
Bates, Leo *24:* 35
Batet, Carmen *39:* 134
Batherman, Muriel *31:* 79; *45:* 185
Battaglia, Aurelius *50:* 44
Batten, John D. *25:* 161, 162

Batten, Mary *162:* 14, 15
Battles, Asa *32:* 94, 95
Bauer, Jutta *150:* 32
Bauernschmidt, Marjorie *15:* 15
Baum, Allyn *20:* 10
Baum, Willi *4:* 24, 25; *7:* 173
Bauman, Leslie *61:* 121
Baumann, Jill *34:* 170
Baumhauer, Hans *11:* 218; *15:* 163, 165, 167
Baxter, Glen *57:* 100
Baxter, Leon *59:* 102
Baxter, Robert *87:* 129
Bayer, Herbert *181:* 16
Bayley, Dorothy *37:* 195
Bayley, Nicola *40:* 104; *41:* 34, 35; *69:* 15; *129:* 33, 34, 35
Baylin, Mark *158:* 233
Baynes, Pauline *2:* 244; *3:* 149; *13:* 133, 135, 137, 141; *19:* 18, 19, 20; *32:* 208, 213, 214; *36:* 105, 108; *59:* 12, 13, 14, 16, 17, 18, 20; *100:* 158, 159, 243; *133:* 3, 4
Beach, Lou *150:* 150
Beame, Rona *12:* 40
Bear's Heart *73:* 215
Beard, Dan *22:* 31, 32
Beard, J.H. *YABC 1:* 158
Bearden, Romare *9:* 7; *22:* 35
Beardshaw, Rosalind *169:* 22
Beardsley, Aubrey *17:* 14; *23:* 181; *59:* 130, 131
Bearman, Jane *29:* 38
Beaton, Cecil *24:* 208
Beaton, Clare *125:* 28
Beauce, J.A. *18:* 103
Beaujard, Sophie *81:* 54
Beck, Charles *11:* 169; *51:* 173
Beck, Ian *138:* 27
Beck, Ruth *13:* 11
Becker, Harriet *12:* 211
Beckett, Sheilah *25:* 5; *33:* 37, 38
Beckhoff, Harry *1:* 78; *5:* 163
Beckman, Kaj *45:* 38, 39, 40, 41
Beckman, Per *45:* 42, 43
Beddows, Eric *72:* 70
Bedford, F.D. *20:* 118, 122; *33:* 170; *41:* 220, 221, 230, 233
Bee, Joyce *19:* 62
Beeby, Betty *25:* 36
Beech, Carol *9:* 149
Beek *25:* 51, 55, 59
Beeke, Tiphanie *177:* 127
Beekman, Doug *125:* 146, 148
Beerbohm, Max *24:* 208
Beeson, Bob *108:* 57
Begin, Maryjane *82:* 13
Beha, Philippe *172:* 85
Behr, Joyce *15:* 15; *21:* 132; *23:* 161
Behrens, Hans *5:* 97
Beier, Ellen *135:* 170; *139:* 47
Beinicke, Steve *69:* 18
Beisner, Monika *46:* 128, 131; *112:* 127
Belden, Charles J. *12:* 182
Belina, Renate *39:* 132
Bell, Corydon *3:* 20
Bell, Graham *54:* 48
Bell, Julia *151:* 214
Bell, Julie *172:* 165; *165:* 18
Bell, Thomas P. *76:* 182
Bellamy, Glen *127:* 15
Beltran, Alberto *43:* 37
Bemelmans, Ludwig *15:* 19, 21; *100:* 27
Ben-Ami, Doron *75:* 96; *84:* 107; *108:* 132; *110:* 63; *159:* 157
Bendall-Brunello, John *150:* 4; *157:* 163
Benda, Wladyslaw T. *15:* 256; *30:* 76, 77; *44:* 182
Bender, Robert *77:* 162; *79:* 13; *160:* 23
Bendick, Jeanne *2:* 24; *68:* 27, 28
Benioff, Carol *121:* 42; *175:* 23
Benner, Cheryl *80:* 11
Bennett, Charles H. *64:* 6

Bennett, Erin Susanne *165:* 216
Bennett, F.I. *YABC 1:* 134
Bennett, James *146:* 240
Bennett, Jill *26:* 61; *41:* 38, 39; *45:* 54
Bennett, Rainey *15:* 26; *23:* 53
Bennett, Richard *15:* 45; *21:* 11, 12, 13; *25:* 175
Bennett, Susan *5:* 55
Benny, Mike *142:* 78
Benoit, Elise *77:* 74
Benson, Linda *60:* 130; *62:* 91; *75:* 101; *79:* 156; *134:* 129
Benson, Patrick *68:* 162; *147:* 17, 18, 19, 20
Bentley, Carolyn *46:* 153
Bentley, James *149:* 30
Bentley, Roy *30:* 162
Benton, Jim *172:* 22
Benton, Thomas Hart *2:* 99
Berelson, Howard *5:* 20; *16:* 58; *31:* 50
Berenstain, Jan *12:* 47; *64:* 33, 34, 36, 37, 38, 40, 42, 44; *135:* 25, 28, 31, 35
Berenstain, Stan *12:* 47; *64:* 33, 34, 36, 37, 38, 40, 42, 44; *135:* 25, 28, 31, 35
Berenzy, Alix *65:* 13; *73:* 6; *78:* 115
Berg, Joan *1:* 115; *3:* 156; *6:* 26, 58
Berg, Ron *36:* 48, 49; *48:* 37, 38; *67:* 72
Bergen, David *115:* 44
Berger, Barbara *77:* 14
Berger, William M. *14:* 143; *YABC 1:* 204
Bergherr, Mary *74:* 170; *151:* 123
Bergin, Mark *114:* 8, 9; *143:* 95; *160:* 26, 27
Bergstreser, Douglas *69:* 76
Bergum, Constance R. *121:* 14, 15
Bering, Claus *13:* 14
Berkeley, Jon *139:* 218
Berkowitz, Jeanette *3:* 249
Berman, Paul *66:* 14
Bernal, Richard *154:* 176
Bernadette
    See Watts, Bernadette
Bernardin, James *112:* 24; *167:* 94
Bernath, Stefen *32:* 76
Bernhard, Durga *80:* 13
Bernstein, Michel J. *51:* 71
Bernstein, Ted *38:* 183; *50:* 131
Bernstein, Zena *23:* 46
Berridge, Celia *86:* 63
Berrill, Jacquelyn *12:* 50
Berry, Erick
    See Best, Allena
Berry, William D. *14:* 29; *19:* 48
Berry, William A. *6:* 219
Berson, Harold *2:* 17, 18; *4:* 28, 29, 220; *9:* 10; *12:* 19; *17:* 45; *18:* 193; *22:* 85; *34:* 172; *44:* 120; *46:* 42; *80:* 240
Berton, Patsy *99:* 16
Bertschmann, Harry *16:* 1
Besco, Don *70:* 99
Beskow, Elsa *20:* 13, 14, 15
Bess, Clayton *63:* 94
Best, Allena *2:* 26; *34:* 76
Betera, Carol *74:* 68
Bethell, Thomas N. *61:* 169
Bethers, Ray *6:* 22
Bettina
    See Ehrlich, Bettina
Betts, Ethel Franklin *17:* 161, 164, 165; *YABC 2:* 47
Betz, Rudolf *59:* 161
Bewick, Thomas *16:* 40, 41, 43, 44, 45, 47; *54:* 150; *YABC 1:* 107
Beyer, Paul J. III *74:* 24
Bezencon, Jacqueline *48:* 40
Biamonte, Daniel *40:* 90
Bianchi, John *91:* 19
Bianco, Pamela *15:* 31; *28:* 44, 45, 46
Bible, Charles *13:* 15
Bice, Clare *22:* 40
Bierman, Don *57:* 184
Biggers, John *2:* 123
Bileck, Marvin *3:* 102; *40:* 36, 37

Bilibin, Ivan *61:* 8, 9, 12, 13, 14, 15, 151, 152, 154, 162
Billington, Patrick *98:* 71
Billout, Guy *144:* 38, 39
Bimen, Levent *5:* 179
Binch, Caroline *81:* 18; *140:* 15, 16; *144:* 115
Binder, Hannes *169:* 163
Bing, Christopher *126:* 34
Binger, Bill *121:* 46
Binks, Robert *25:* 150
Binzen, Bill *24:* 47
Birch, Reginald *15:* 150; *19:* 33, 34, 35, 36, 37; *37:* 196, 197; *44:* 182; *46:* 176; *YABC 1:* 84; *2:* 34, 39
Birchall, Mark *123:* 188
Bird, Esther Brock *1:* 36; *25:* 66
Birdsong, Keith *167:* 85
Birkett, Rachel *78:* 206
Birling, Paul *109:* 30
Birmingham, Christian *132:* 243; *143:* 114
Birmingham, Lloyd P. *12:* 51; *83:* 13
Biro, Val *1:* 26; *41:* 42; *60:* 178; *67:* 23, 24; *84:* 242, 243
Bischoff, Ilse *44:* 51
Bishop, Gavin *97:* 17, 18; *144:* 42, 44
Bishop, Kathleen Wong *115:* 67
Bishop, Rich *56:* 43
Bite, I. *60:* 14
Bittinger, Ned *93:* 117
Bjorklund, Lorence *3:* 188, 252; *7:* 100; *9:* 113; *10:* 66; *19:* 178; *33:* 122, 123; *35:* 36, 37, 38, 39, 41, 42, 43; *36:* 185; *38:* 93; *47:* 106; *66:* 194; *YABC 1:* 242
Bjorkman, Steve *91:* 199; *160:* 110
Black Sheep *164:* 100
Blackburn, Loren H. *63:* 10
Blackford, John *137:* 105; *180:* 36
Blackwell, Basil T. *YABC 1:* 68, 69
Blackwood, Gary L. *118:* 17
Blades, Ann *16:* 52; *37:* 213; *50:* 41; *69:* 21; *99:* 215
Blair, Jay *45:* 46; *46:* 155
Blaisdell, Elinore *1:* 121; *3:* 134; *35:* 63
Blake, Quentin *3:* 170; *10:* 48; *13:* 38; *21:* 180; *26:* 60; *28:* 228; *30:* 29, 31; *40:* 108; *45:* 219; *46:* 165, 168; *48:* 196; *52:* 10, 11, 12, 13, 14, 15, 16, 17; *73:* 41, 43; *78:* 84, 86; *80:* 250, 251; *84:* 210, 211, 212; *87:* 177; *96:* 24, 26, 28; *124:* 79; *125:* 32, 34; *181:* 139
Blake, Robert J. *37:* 90; *53:* 67; *54:* 23; *160:* 28, 29
Blake, William *30:* 54, 56, 57, 58, 59, 60
Blanchard, N. Taylor *82:* 140
Blass, Jacqueline *8:* 215
Blazek, Scott R. *91:* 71
Bleck, Cathie *118:* 116
Blegvad, Erik *2:* 59; *3:* 98; *5:* 117; *7:* 131; *11:* 149; *14:* 34, 35; *18:* 237; *32:* 219; *60:* 106; *66:* 16, 17, 18, 19; *70:* 233; *76:* 18; *82:* 106; *87:* 45; *100:* 188; *129:* 125; *132:* 17, 18, 19, 20; *176:* 14; *YABC 1:* 201
Blessen, Karen *93:* 126
Bliss, Corinne Demas *37:* 38
Blitt, Barry *179:* 199
Bloch, Lucienne *10:* 12
Blondon, Herve *129:* 48
Bloom, Lloyd *35:* 180; *36:* 149; *47:* 99; *62:* 117; *68:* 231; *72:* 136; *75:* 185; *83:* 99; *108:* 19
Bloom, Suzanne *172:* 23, 24
Blossom, Dave *34:* 29
Blumenschein, E.L. *YABC 1:* 113, 115
Blumer, Patt *29:* 214
Blundell, Kim *29:* 36
Bluthenthal, Diana Cain *93:* 32; *104:* 106; *177:* 26
Blythe, Benjamin *128:* 7
Blythe, Gary *112:* 52; *181:* 166
Boake, Kathy *176:* 185
Board, Perry *171:* 99

Boardman, Gwenn *12:* 60
Bober, Richard *125:* 145; *132:* 40
Bobri *30:* 138; *47:* 27
Bock, Vera *1:* 187; *21:* 41
Bock, William Sauts *8:* 7; *14:* 37; *16:* 120; *21:* 141; *36:* 177; *62:* 203
Bodecker, N(iels) M(ogens) *8:* 13; *14:* 2; *17:* 55, 56, 57; *73:* 22, 23, 24
Boehm, Linda *40:* 31
Bogacki, Tomek *138:* 31, 32; *144:* 123
Bogdan, Florentina *107:* 43
Bohdal, Susi *22:* 44; *101:* 20
Bohlen, Nina *58:* 13
Boies, Alex *96:* 53
Bolam, Emily *101:* 216; *159:* 12
Bolian, Polly *3:* 270; *4:* 30; *13:* 77; *29:* 197
Bolle, Frank *87:* 100
Bollen, Roger *79:* 186; *83:* 16
Bolling, Vickey *114:* 44
Bollinger, Peter *101:* 7; *128:* 198; *172:* 26
Bolognese, Don *2:* 147, 231; *4:* 176; *7:* 146; *17:* 43; *23:* 192; *24:* 50; *34:* 108; *36:* 133; *71:* 24, 25; *103:* 131; *129:* 39, 40
Bolton, A.T. *57:* 158
Bond, Arnold *18:* 116
Bond, Barbara Higgins *21:* 102
Bond, Bruce *52:* 97
Bond, Felicia *38:* 197; *49:* 55, 56; *89:* 170; *90:* 171; *126:* 37
Bond, Higgins *177:* 22, 23
Bonn, Pat *43:* 40
Bonners, Susan *41:* 40; *85:* 36; *94:* 99, 100; *151:* 105, 106
Bonsall, Crosby *23:* 6
Boon, Debbie *103:* 6; *144:* 188
Boon, Emilie *86:* 23, 24
Boone, Debbie *165:* 77
Boore, Sara *60:* 73
Bootman, Colin *155:* 13; *159:* 35; *174:* 192
Booth, Franklin *YABC 2:* 76
Booth, Graham *32:* 193; *37:* 41, 42
Borda, Juliette *102:* 188
Bordier, Georgette *16:* 54
Boren, Tinka *27:* 128
Borges, Jose Francisco *119:* 62
Borja, Robert *22:* 48
Born, Adolf *49:* 63
Bornstein, Ruth *14:* 44; *88:* 45, 46; *107:* 30
Borten, Helen *3:* 54; *5:* 24
Bosin, Blackbear *69:* 104
Bossom, Naomi *35:* 48
Bostock, Mike *83:* 221; *114:* 14
Boston, Peter *19:* 42
Bosustow, Stephen *34:* 202
Boszko, Ron *75:* 47
Bottner, Barbara *14:* 46
Boucher, Joelle *41:* 138
Boulat, Pierre *44:* 40
Boulet, Susan Seddon *50:* 47
Bouma, Paddy *118:* 25; *128:* 16
Bour, Daniele *66:* 145
Bourke-White, Margaret *15:* 286, 287; *57:* 102
Boutet de Monvel, M. *30:* 61, 62, 63, 65
Bowen, Betsy *105:* 222
Bowen, Richard *42:* 134
Bowen, Ruth *31:* 188
Bower, Ron *29:* 33
Bowers, David *95:* 38; *115:* 20; *127:* 169, 170; *165:* 57
Bowman, Claire *174:* 177
Bowman, Eric *151:* 24
Bowman, Leslie *85:* 203; *105:* 108; *116:* 76; *128:* 234
Bowman, Peter *146:* 214, 215; *150:* 115
Bowser, Carolyn Ewing *22:* 253
Boxall, Ed *178:* 28
Boyd, Aaron *158:* 242
Boyd, Patti *45:* 31
Boyle, Eleanor Vere *28:* 50, 51
Boynton, Sandra *57:* 13, 14, 15; *107:* 36, 37; *152:* 12, 13, 14

Bozzo, Frank *4:* 154
Brabbs, Derry *55:* 170
Brace, Eric *132:* 193, 194; *152:* 71
Brackers de Hugo, Pierre *115:* 21
Bradford, June *158:* 138
Bradford, Ron *7:* 157
Bradley, David P. *69:* 105
Bradley, Richard D. *26:* 182
Bradley, William *5:* 164
Brady, Irene *4:* 31; *42:* 37; *68:* 191
Bragg, Michael *32:* 78; *46:* 31
Bragg, Ruth Gembicki *77:* 18
Brainerd, John W. *65:* 19
Braithwaite, Althea *23:* 12, 13; *119:* 16
Brak, Syd *146:* 187
Bralds, Braldt *90:* 28; *91:* 151
Bram, Elizabeth *30:* 67
Bramley, Peter *4:* 3
Brandenberg, Aliki *2:* 36, 37; *24:* 222; *35:* 49, 50, 51, 52, 53, 54, 56, 57; *75:* 15, 17; *92:* 205; *113:* 18, 19, 20; *157:* 28; *156:* 111
Brandenburg, Alexa *75:* 19
Brandenburg, Jim *47:* 58; *150:* 212
Brandi, Lillian *31:* 158
Brandon, Brumsic, Jr. *9:* 25
Bransom, Paul *17:* 121; *43:* 44
Braren, Loretta Trezzo *87:* 193
Braun, Wendy *80:* 17, 18
Brautigam, Don *115:* 175, 176
Brazell, Derek *75:* 105; *79:* 9
Breathed, Berkeley *86:* 27, 28, 29; *161:* 13, 14
Brennan, Steve *83:* 230; *101:* 184
Brenner, Fred *22:* 85; *36:* 34; *42:* 34
Brett, Bernard *22:* 54
Brett, Harold M. *26:* 98, 99, 100
Brett, Jan *30:* 135; *42:* 39; *71:* 31, 32; *130:* 23, 24, 25, 26, 27; *171:* 15, 16
Brewer, Paul *106:* 115; *145:* 202
Brewer, Sally King *33:* 44
Brewster, Patience *40:* 68; *45:* 22, 183; *51:* 20; *66:* 144; *89:* 4; *97:* 30, 31
Brick, John *10:* 15
Brickman, Robin D. *131:* 88; *142:* 150; *155:* 18; *178:* 109
Bridge, David R. *45:* 28
Bridgman, L.J. *37:* 77
Bridwell, Norman *4:* 37; *138:* 36, 37, 40
Brierley, Louise *91:* 22; *96:* 165
Briggs, Harry *172:* 187
Briggs, Raymond *10:* 168; *23:* 20, 21; *66:* 29, 31, 32; *131:* 28, 29
Brigham, Grace A. *37:* 148
Bright, Robert *24:* 55
Brighton, Catherine *107:* 39
Brinckloe, Julie *13:* 18; *24:* 79, 115; *29:* 35; *63:* 140; *81:* 131
Brion *47:* 116
Brisley, Joyce L. *22:* 57
Brisson, James F. *110:* 60
Brittingham, Geoffrey *88:* 37
Brix-Henker, Silke *81:* 194
Brock, Charles E. *15:* 97; *19:* 247, 249; *23:* 224, 225; *36:* 88; *42:* 41, 42, 43, 44, 45; *100:* 189; *YABC 1:* 194, 196, 203
Brock, Emma *7:* 21
Brock, Henry Matthew *15:* 81; *16:* 141; *19:* 71; *34:* 115; *40:* 164; *42:* 47, 48, 49; *49:* 66
Brocksopp, Arthur *57:* 157
Broda, Ron *136:* 180; *174:* 123
Brodkin, Gwen *34:* 135
Brodovitch, Alexi *52:* 22
Bromhall, Winifred *5:* 11; *26:* 38
Bromley, Lizzy *159:* 179
Bronson, Linda *150:* 210; *174:* 133
Brooke, L. Leslie *16:* 181, 182, 183, 186; *17:* 15, 16, 17; *18:* 194
Brooker, Christopher *15:* 251
Brooker, Krysten *111:* 94; *140:* 28; *162:* 111; *175:* 108
Brooks, Erik *166:* 52
Brooks, Maya Itzna *92:* 153

Brooks, Ron *94:* 15
Brooks, S.G. *178:* 127
Broomfield, Maurice *40:* 141
Brotman, Adolph E. *5:* 21
Brown, Buck *45:* 48
Brown, Calef *179:* 18
Brown, Christopher *62:* 124, 125, 127, 128
Brown, Craig McFarland *73:* 28; *84:* 65
Brown, Dan *61:* 167; *115:* 183, 184; *116:* 28, 29
Brown, David *7:* 47; *48:* 52
Brown, Denise *11:* 213
Brown, Don *172:* 29
Brown, Ford Madox *48:* 74
Brown, Judith Gwyn *1:* 45; *7:* 5; *8:* 167; *9:* 182, 190; *20:* 16, 17, 18; *23:* 142; *29:* 117; *33:* 97; *36:* 23, 26; *43:* 184; *48:* 201, 223; *49:* 69; *86:* 227; *110:* 188; *153:* 7
Brown, Kathryn *98:* 26
Brown, Laurie Krasny *99:* 30
Brown, Marc (Tolon) *10:* 17, 197; *14:* 263; *51:* 18; *53:* 11, 12, 13, 15, 16, 17; *75:* 58; *80:* 24, 25, 26; *82:* 261; *99:* 29; *145:* 22, 23, 25, 27; *162:* 198
Brown, Marcia *7:* 30; *25:* 203; *47:* 31, 32, 33, 34, 35, 36, 37, 38, 39, 40, 42, 43, 44; *YABC 1:* 27
Brown, Margery W. *5:* 32, 33; *10:* 3
Brown, Martin *101:* 43
Brown, Mary Barrett *97:* 74
Brown, Palmer *36:* 40
Brown, Paul *25:* 26; *26:* 107
Brown, Richard *61:* 18; *67:* 30
Brown, Rick *78:* 71; *150:* 154
Brown, Robert S. *85:* 33
Brown, Rod *157:* 142
Brown, Ruth *55:* 165; *86:* 112, 113; *105:* 16, 17, 18; *171:* 178
Brown, Trevor *99:* 160; *139:* 247
Browne, Anthony *45:* 50, 51, 52; *61:* 21, 22, 23, 24, 25; *105:* 21, 22, 23, 25
Browne, Dik *8:* 212; *67:* 32, 33, 35, 37, 39
Browne, Gordon *16:* 97; *64:* 114, 116, 117, 119, 121
Browne, Hablot K. *15:* 65, 80; *21:* 14, 15, 16, 17, 18, 19, 20; *24:* 25
Browne, Jane *165:* 222
Browning, Coleen *4:* 132
Browning, Mary Eleanor *24:* 84
Bruce, Robert *23:* 23
Brude, Dick *48:* 215
Bruel, Nick *166:* 41
Brule, Al *3:* 135
Brumbeau, Jeff *157:* 29
Bruna, Dick *43:* 48, 49, 50; *76:* 27, 28
Brundage, Frances *19:* 244
Brunhoff, Jean de *24:* 57, 58
Brunhoff, Laurent de *24:* 60; *71:* 35, 36, 37
Brunkus, Denise *84:* 50; *123:* 117; *178:* 209
Brunson, Bob *43:* 135
Bryan, Ashley *31:* 44; *72:* 27, 28, 29; *107:* 92; *116:* 192; *132:* 24; *178:* 33, 34, 35
Bryant, Laura J. *176:* 36
Bryant, Michael *93:* 74
Brychta, Alex *21:* 21
Bryer, Diana *107:* 121
Bryson, Bernarda *3:* 88, 146; *39:* 26; *44:* 185; *131:* 40
Buba, Joy *12:* 83; *30:* 226; *44:* 56
Buchanan, George *166:* 198
Buchanan, Lilian *13:* 16
Buchanan, Rachel *171:* 71
Bucholtz-Ross, Linda *44:* 137
Buchs, Thomas *40:* 38
Buck, Margaret Waring *3:* 30
Buckhardt, Marc *172:* 59
Buckley, Mike *166:* 180
Budwine, Greg *175:* 172
Buehner, Mark *104:* 12, 15; *105:* 160; *119:* 98; *157:* 188; *159:* 39, 40, 43
Buehr, Walter *3:* 31

Buff, Conrad *19:* 52, 53, 54
Buff, Mary *19:* 52, 53
Bull, Charles Livingston *18:* 207; *88:* 175, 176
Bullen, Anne *3:* 166, 167
Bullock, Kathleen *77:* 24
Bumgarner-Kirby, Claudia *77:* 194
Burbank, Addison *37:* 43
Burchard, Peter Duncan *3:* 197; *5:* 35; *6:* 158, 218; *143:* 17
Burckhardt, Marc *94:* 48; *110:* 89
Burger, Carl *3:* 33; *45:* 160, 162
Burgeson, Marjorie *19:* 31
Burgess, Anne *76:* 252
Burgess, Gelett *32:* 39, 42
Burgess, Mark *157:* 31
Burke, Jim *179:* 19
Burke, Phillip *95:* 117
Burkert, Nancy Ekholm *18:* 186; *22:* 140; *24:* 62, 63, 64, 65; *26:* 53; *29:* 60, 61; *46:* 171; *YABC 1:* 46
Burkhardt, Bruce *142:* 86
Burkhardt, Melissa A. *142:* 86
Burleson, Joe *104:* 35; *172:* 139
Burn, Doris *6:* 172
Burn, Jeffrey *89:* 125; *152:* 132
Burn, Ted
　See Burn, Thomas E.
Burn, Thomas E. *151:* 41
Burnard, Damon *115:* 23
Burnett, Virgil *44:* 42
Burningham, John *9:* 68; *16:* 60, 61; *59:* 28, 29, 30, 31, 32, 33, 35; *111:* 18, 19, 21; *160:* 37
Burns, Howard M. *12:* 173
Burns, Jim *47:* 70; *86:* 32; *91:* 197; *123:* 16
Burns, M.F. *26:* 69
Burns, Raymond *9:* 29
Burns, Robert *24:* 106
Burr, Dan *65:* 28; *108:* 134; *164:* 203
Burr, Dane *12:* 2
Burra, Edward *YABC 2:* 68
Burrell, Galen *56:* 76
Burri, Rene *41:* 143; *54:* 166
Burridge, Marge Opitz *14:* 42
Burris, Burmah *4:* 81
Burroughs, John Coleman *41:* 64
Burroughs, Studley O. *41:* 65
Burton, Marilee Robin *46:* 33
Burton, Virginia Lee *2:* 43; *44:* 49, 51; *100:* 46, 47; *YABC 1:* 24; *147:* 56
Busoni, Rafaello *1:* 186; *3:* 224; *6:* 126; *14:* 5; *16:* 62, 63
Butchkes, Sidney *50:* 58
Butler, Geoff *94:* 20
Butler, Ralph *116:* 212
Butterfield, Ned *1:* 153; *27:* 128; *79:* 63
Butterworth, Nick *106:* 43, 44; *149:* 34
Buxton, John *123:* 12
Buzelli, Christopher *105:* 149
Buzonas, Gail *29:* 88
Buzzell, Russ W. *12:* 177
Byard, Carole *39:* 44; *57:* 18, 19, 20; *60:* 60; *61:* 93, 96; *69:* 210; *78:* 246; *79:* 227
Byars, Betsy *46:* 35
Byfield, Barbara Ninde *8:* 18
Byfield, Graham *32:* 29
Bynum, Janie *176:* 50
Byrd, Robert *13:* 218; *33:* 46; *158:* 70
Byrd, Samuel *123:* 104

C

Cabat, Erni *74:* 38
Cabban, Vanessa *138:* 73; *176:* 39
Cabrera, Jane *103:* 24; *152:* 27
Caddy, Alice *6:* 41
Cady, Harrison *17:* 21, 23; *19:* 57, 58
Caffrey, Aileen *72:* 223; *141:* 154
Cairns, Julia *177:* 37

Caldecott, Randolph *16:* 98, 103; *17:* 32, 33, 36, 38, 39; *26:* 90; *100:* 49, 50; *YABC 2:* 172
Calder, Alexander *18:* 168
Calderón, Gloria *179:* 5
Calderon, W. Frank *25:* 160
Caldwell, Ben *105:* 75; *149:* 60
Caldwell, Clyde *98:* 100; *116:* 39
Caldwell, Doreen *23:* 77; *71:* 41
Caldwell, John *46:* 225
Call, Greg *126:* 135; *165:* 49
Callahan, Kevin *22:* 42
Callahan, Philip S. *25:* 77
Callan, Jamie *59:* 37
Calvin, James *61:* 92
Camburn-Bracalente, Carol A. *118:* 22
Cameron, Julia Margaret *19:* 203
Cameron, Scott *99:* 18
Camm, Martin *140:* 208, 209, 210
Campbell, Ann *11:* 43; *123:* 182
Campbell, Bill *89:* 39
Campbell, Ken *126:* 143
Campbell, Robert *55:* 120
Campbell, Rod *51:* 27; *98:* 34
Campbell, Walter M. *YABC 2:* 158
Camps, Luis *28:* 120, 121; *66:* 35
Cann, Helen *124:* 50; *141:* 78; *170:* 138; *179:* 22, 23
Cannon, Janell *78:* 25; *128:* 40
Canright, David *36:* 162
Canty, Thomas *85:* 161; *92:* 47; *113:* 192; *134:* 60
Canyon, Christopher *150:* 44; *151:* 112
Caporale, Wende *70:* 42
Capp, Al *61:* 28, 30, 31, 40, 41, 43, 44
Cappon, Manuela *154:* 64
Caras, Peter *36:* 64
Caraway, Caren *57:* 22
Caraway, James *3:* 200, 201
Carbe, Nino *29:* 183
Cares, Linda *67:* 176
Carigiet, Alois *24:* 67
Carle, Eric *4:* 42; *11:* 121; *12:* 29; *65:* 32, 33, 34, 36; *73:* 63, 65; *163:* 55, 56
Carling, Amelia Lau *164:* 46
Carlino, Angela *168:* 43
Carlson, Nancy L. *41:* 116; *56:* 25; *90:* 45; *144:* 48, 50
Carlluccio, Maria *175:* 129
Carmi, Giora *79:* 35; *149:* 40
Carpenter, Nancy *76:* 128; *86:* 173; *89:* 171; *131:* 186; *134:* 8; *138:* 215; *153:* 204; *159:* 93; *165:* 232
Carr, Archie *37:* 225
Carrick, Donald *5:* 194; *39:* 97; *49:* 70; *53:* 156; *63:* 15, 16, 17, 18, 19, 21; *80:* 131; *86:* 151; *118:* 24
Carrick, Malcolm *28:* 59, 60
Carrick, Paul *118:* 26
Carrick, Valery *21:* 47
Carrier, Lark *71:* 43
Carroll, Jim *88:* 211; *140:* 177; *153:* 99
Carroll, Lewis
　See Dodgson, Charles L.
Carroll, Michael *72:* 5
Carroll, Pamela *84:* 68; *128:* 214
Carroll, Ruth *7:* 41; *10:* 68
Carter, Abby *81:* 32; *97:* 121; *102:* 61; *163:* 139; *164:* 125
Carter, Barbara *47:* 167, 169
Carter, David A. *114:* 24, 25; *170:* 42, 43
Carter, Don *124:* 54
Carter, Harry *22:* 179
Carter, Helene *15:* 38; *22:* 202, 203; *YABC 2:* 220, 221
Carter, Penny *173:* 91
Cartlidge, Michelle *49:* 65; *96:* 50, 51
Cartwright, Reg *63:* 61, 62; *78:* 26; *143:* 4
Cartwright, Shannon *176:* 81
Carty, Leo *4:* 196; *7:* 163; *58:* 131
Cary *4:* 133; *9:* 32; *20:* 2; *21:* 143

Cary, Page *12:* 41
Casale, Paul *71:* 63; *109:* 122; *136:* 28
Case, Sandra E. *16:* 2
Caseley, Judith *87:* 36; *159:* 47, 48, 49
Casilla, Robert *78:* 7; *167:* 124
Casino, Steve *85:* 193
Cassel, Lili
　See Wronker, Lili Cassel
Cassel-Wronker, Lili
　See Wronker, Lili Cassel
Cassels, Jean *8:* 50; *150:* 119; *173:* 37
Cassen, Melody *140:* 51
Cassity, Don *104:* 24
Cassler, Carl *75:* 137, 138; *82:* 162
Casson, Hugh *65:* 38, 40, 42, 43
Castellon, Federico *48:* 45, 46, 47, 48
Castle, Jane *4:* 80
Castro, Antonio *84:* 71
Catalano, Dominic *94:* 79; *163:* 60, 61; *162:* 54
Catalanotto, Peter *63:* 170; *70:* 23; *71:* 182; *72:* 96; *74:* 114; *76:* 194, 195; *77:* 7; *79:* 157; *80:* 28, 67; *83:* 157; *85:* 27; *108:* 11; *113:* 30, 31, 33, 34, 36; *114:* 27, 28, 29; *117:* 53; *124:* 168; *159:* 54, 55
Catania, Tom *68:* 82
Cather, Carolyn *3:* 83; *15:* 203; *34:* 216
Catrow, David *117:* 179; *152:* 31, 33; *173:* 24
Cauley, Lorinda Bryan *44:* 135; *46:* 49
Cayard, Bruce *38:* 67
Cazet, Denys *52:* 27; *99:* 39, 40; *163:* 65, 66
Ceccoli, Nicoletta *181:* 39
Cecil, Randy *127:* 132, 133
Cellini, Joseph *2:* 73; *3:* 35; *16:* 116; *47:* 103
Cepeda, Joe *90:* 62; *109:* 91; *134:* 172; *159:* 57, 58, 164
Chabrian, Debbi *45:* 55
Chabrian, Deborah *51:* 182; *53:* 124; *63:* 107; *75:* 84; *79:* 85; *82:* 247; *89:* 93; *101:* 197
Chagnon, Mary *37:* 158
Chalmers, Mary *3:* 145; *13:* 148; *33:* 125; *66:* 214
Chamberlain, Christopher *45:* 57
Chamberlain, Margaret *46:* 51; *106:* 89
Chamberlain, Nigel *78:* 140
Chambers, C.E. *17:* 230
Chambers, Dave *12:* 151
Chambers, Jill *134:* 110
Chambers, Mary *4:* 188
Chambliss, Maxie *42:* 186; *56:* 159; *93:* 163, 164; *103:* 178
Champlin, Dale *136:* 124
Chan, Harvey *96:* 236; *99:* 153; *143:* 218; *179:* 144
Chandler, David P. *28:* 62
Chaney, Howard *139:* 27
Chang, Warren *101:* 209
Chapel, Jody *68:* 20
Chapman, C.H. *13:* 83, 85, 87
Chapman, Frederick T. *6:* 27; *44:* 28
Chapman, Gaynor *32:* 52, 53
Chapman, Jane *145:* 186; *150:* 56; *166:* 220; *174:* 202; *176:* 43, 44; *179:* 131
Chapman, Lynne *175:* 31
Chappell, Warren *3:* 172; *21:* 56; *27:* 125
Charles, Donald *30:* 154, 155
Charlip, Remy *4:* 48; *34:* 138; *68:* 53, 54; *119:* 29, 30
Charlot, Jean *1:* 137, 138; *8:* 23; *14:* 31; *48:* 151; *56:* 21
Charlot, Martin *64:* 72
Charlton, Michael *34:* 50; *37:* 39
Charmatz, Bill *7:* 45
Chartier, Normand *9:* 36; *52:* 49; *66:* 40; *74:* 220; *145:* 169; *168:* 91; *177:* 108
Chase, Lynwood M. *14:* 4
Chast, Roz *97:* 39, 40
Chastain, Madye Lee *4:* 50
Chateron, Ann *152:* 19
Chatterton, Martin *68:* 102; *152:* 19
Chau, Tungwai *140:* 35

Chauncy, Francis *24:* 158
Chayka, Doug *145:* 97; *177:* 150
Chee, Cheng-Khee *79:* 42; *81:* 224; *180:* 245
Chen, Chih-sien *90:* 226
Chen, Tony *6:* 45; *19:* 131; *29:* 126; *34:* 160
Cheney, T.A. *11:* 47
Cheng, Judith *36:* 45; *51:* 16
Chermayeff, Ivan *47:* 53
Cherry, David *93:* 40
Cherry, Lynne *34:* 52; *65:* 184; *87:* 111; *99:* 46, 47
Chesak, Lina *135:* 118
Chess, Victoria *12:* 6; *33:* 42, 48, 49; *40:* 194; *41:* 145; *69:* 80; *72:* 100; *92:* 33, 34; *104:* 167
Chessare, Michele *41:* 50; *56:* 48; *69:* 145
Chesterton, G.K. *27:* 43, 44, 45, 47
Chestnutt, David *47:* 217
Chesworth, Michael *75:* 24, 152; *88:* 136; *94:* 25; *98:* 155; *160:* 42
Chetham, Celia *134:* 34
Chetwin, Grace *86:* 40
Cheung, Irving *158:* 96
Chevalier, Christa *35:* 66
Chew, Ruth *7:* 46; *132:* 147
Chewning, Randy *92:* 206
Chichester Clark, Emma *72:* 121; *77:* 212; *78:* 209; *87:* 143; *117:* 37, 39, 40; *144:* 138; *156:* 24, 25
Chifflart *47:* 113, 127
Child, Lauren *119:* 32
Chin, Alex *28:* 54
Chitwood, Susan Tanner *163:* 16
Cho, Shinta *8:* 126
Chodos-Irvine, Margaret *52:* 102, 103, 107; *152:* 44
Choi, Yangsook *171:* 134; *173:* 135; *178:* 38, 39, 40
Chollat, Emilie *170:* 203
Chollick, Jay *25:* 175
Choma, Christina *99:* 169
Chorao, Kay *7:* 200, 201; *8:* 25; *11:* 234; *33:* 187; *35:* 239; *69:* 35; *70:* 235; *123:* 174
Chowdhury, Subrata *62:* 130; *162:* 22, 23
Christelow, Eileen *38:* 44; *83:* 198, 199; *90:* 57, 58
Christensen, Bonnie *93:* 100; *153:* 67
Christensen, Gardell Dano *1:* 57
Christensen, James C. *140:* 226
Christiana, David *90:* 64; *135:* 13; *171:* 7
Christiansen, Per *40:* 24
Christie, R. Gregory *116:* 107; *127:* 20, 21; *162:* 179; *164:* 114; *165:* 137; *174:* 157; *179:* 172
Christy, Howard Chandler *17:* 163, 164, 165, 168, 169; *19:* 186, 187; *21:* 22, 23, 24, 25
Chronister, Robert *23:* 138; *63:* 27; *69:* 167
Church, Caroline Jayne *179:* 27
Church, Frederick *YABC 1:* 155
Chute, Marchette *1:* 59
Chwast, Jacqueline *1:* 63; *2:* 275; *6:* 46, 47; *11:* 125; *12:* 202; *14:* 235
Chwast, Seymour *3:* 128, 129; *18:* 43; *27:* 152; *92:* 79; *96:* 56, 57, 58; *146:* 32, 33
Cieslawksi, Steve *101:* 142; *127:* 116; *158:* 169, 171
Cinelli, Lisa *146:* 253
Cirlin, Edgard *2:* 168
Clairin, Georges *53:* 109
Clapp, John *105:* 66; *109:* 58; *126:* 7; *129:* 148; *130:* 165
Clark, Brenda *119:* 85; *153:* 55
Clark, David *77:* 164; *134:* 144, 145
Clark, Emma Chichester
    See Chichester Clark, Emma
Clark, Victoria *35:* 159
Clarke, Greg *169:* 134
Clarke, Gus *72:* 226; *134:* 31
Clarke, Harry *23:* 172, 173
Clarke, Peter *75:* 102
Claverie, Jean *38:* 46; *88:* 29

Clayton, Elaine *159:* 60
Clayton, Robert *9:* 181
Cleaver, Elizabeth *8:* 204; *23:* 36
Cleland, T.M. *26:* 92
Clemens, Peter *61:* 125
Clement, Charles *20:* 38
Clement, Rod *97:* 42
Clement, Stephen *88:* 3
Clementson, John *84:* 213
Clevin, Jorgen *7:* 50
Clifford, Judy *34:* 163; *45:* 198
Clokey, Art *59:* 44
Clouse, James *84:* 15
Clouse, Nancy L. *78:* 31; *114:* 90
Clover, Peter *152:* 45
Cneut, Carll *156:* 166; *165:* 67
Coalson, Glo *9:* 72, 85; *25:* 155; *26:* 42; *35:* 212; *53:* 31; *56:* 154; *94:* 37, 38, 193
Cober, Alan E. *17:* 158; *32:* 77; *49:* 127
Cober-Gentry, Leslie *92:* 111
Cocca-Leffler, Maryann *80:* 46; *136:* 60; *139:* 193
Cochran, Bobbye *11:* 52
CoConis, Ted *4:* 41; *46:* 41; *51:* 104
Cocozza, Chris *87:* 18; *110:* 173; *111:* 149
Cockroft, Jason *152:* 20
Coerr, Eleanor *1:* 64; *67:* 52
Coes, Peter *35:* 172
Cogancherry, Helen *52:* 143; *69:* 131; *77:* 93; *78:* 220; *109:* 204; *110:* 129
Coggins, Jack *2:* 69
Cohen, Alix *7:* 53
Cohen, Miriam *155:* 23, 24
Cohen, Nancy R. *165:* 35
Cohen, Santiago *164:* 26
Cohen, Sheldon *105:* 33, 34; *166:* 46, 47
Cohen, Vincent O. *19:* 243
Cohen, Vivien *11:* 112
Coker, Paul *51:* 172
Colbert, Anthony *15:* 41; *20:* 193
Colby, C.B. *3:* 47
Cole, Babette *58:* 172; *96:* 63, 64; *155:* 29
Cole, Brock *68:* 223; *72:* 36, 37, 38, 192; *127:* 23; *136:* 64, 65
Cole, Gwen *87:* 185
Cole, Henry *178:* 36; *181:* 42, 43
Cole, Herbert *28:* 104
Cole, Michael *59:* 46
Cole, Olivia H.H. *1:* 134; *3:* 223; *9:* 111; *38:* 104
Colin, Paul *102:* 59; *123:* 118; *126:* 152
Collicott, Sharleen *98:* 39; *143:* 29, 30
Collier, Bryan *126:* 54; *151:* 166; *174:* 16, 17, 18
Collier, David *13:* 127
Collier, John *27:* 179
Collier, Steven *50:* 52
Collier-Morales, Roberta *168:* 61
Collins, Heather *66:* 84; *67:* 68; *81:* 40; *98:* 192, 193; *129:* 95, 96, 98
Collins, Matt *167:* 90
Collins, Ross *140:* 23, 24
Colman, Audrey *146:* 161
Colón, Raul *108:* 112; *113:* 5; *117:* 167; *134:* 112; *146:* 23; *159:* 92; *166:* 73; *180:* 107
Colonna, Bernard *21:* 50; *28:* 103; *34:* 140; *43:* 180; *78:* 150
Comport, Sally Wern *117:* 169; *169:* 104
Conde, J.M. *100:* 120
Condon, Grattan *54:* 85 Condon, Ken *161:* 44
Cone, Ferne Geller *39:* 49
Cone, J. Morton *39:* 49
Conklin, Paul *43:* 62
Connolly, Howard *67:* 88
Connolly, Jerome P. *4:* 128; *28:* 52
Connolly, Peter *47:* 60
Conoly, Walle *110:* 224
Conover, Chris *31:* 52; *40:* 184; *41:* 51; *44:* 79
Contreras, Gerry *72:* 9
Converse, James *38:* 70
Conway *62:* 62

Conway, Michael *69:* 12; *81:* 3; *92:* 108
Cook, G.R. *29:* 165
Cook, Joel *108:* 160
Cookburn, W.V. *29:* 204
Cooke, Donald E. *2:* 77
Cooke, Tom *52:* 118
Coomaraswamy, A.K. *50:* 100
Coombs, Charles *43:* 65
Coombs, Deborah *139:* 175
Coombs, Patricia *2:* 82; *3:* 52; *22:* 119; *51:* 32, 33, 34, 35, 36, 37, 38, 39, 40, 42, 43
Cooney, Barbara *6:* 16, 17, 50; *12:* 42; *13:* 92; *15:* 145; *16:* 74, 111; *18:* 189; *23:* 38, 89, 93; *32:* 138; *38:* 105; *59:* 48, 49, 51, 52, 53; *74:* 222; *81:* 100; *91:* 25; *96:* 71, 72, 74; *100:* 149; *YABC 2:* 10
Cooper, Elisha *157:* 38, 39
Cooper, Floyd *79:* 95; *81:* 45; *84:* 82; *85:* 74; *91:* 118; *96:* 77, 78; *103:* 149; *144:* 54; *145:* 151; *159:* 198; *176:* 133, 134
Cooper, Heather *50:* 39
Cooper, Helen *102:* 42, 43, 44
Cooper, Mario *24:* 107
Cooper, Marjorie *7:* 112
Cope, Jane *61:* 201; *108:* 52
Copeland, Mark *180:* 12
Copelman, Evelyn *8:* 61; *18:* 25
Copley, Heather *30:* 86; *45:* 57
Corbett, Grahame *30:* 114; *43:* 67
Corbino, John *19:* 248
Corcos, Lucille *2:* 223; *10:* 27; *34:* 66
Corey, Robert *9:* 34
Corlass, Heather *10:* 7
Cornell, James *27:* 60
Cornell, Jeff *11:* 58
Cornell, Laura *94:* 179; *95:* 25
Corrigan, Barbara *8:* 37
Corrigan, Patrick *145:* 149
Corwin, Judith Hoffman *10:* 28
Cory, Fanny Y. *20:* 113; *48:* 29
Cosentino, Ralph *169:* 32
Cosgrove, Margaret *3:* 100; *47:* 63; *82:* 133
Costabel, Eva Deutsch *45:* 66, 67
Costanza, John *58:* 7, 8, 9
Costello, Chris *86:* 78
Costello, David F. *23:* 55
Cote, Nancy *126:* 139; *156:* 101; *174:* 101
Couch, Greg *94:* 124; *110:* 13; *162:* 31; *168:* 149
Councell, Ruth Tietjen *79:* 29
Courtney, Cathy *58:* 69, 144; *59:* 15; *61:* 20, 87
Courtney, R. *35:* 110
Counihan, Claire *133:* 106
Cousineau, Normand *89:* 180; *112:* 76
Cousins, Lucy *172:* 53, 54
Couture, Christin *41:* 209
Covarrubias, Miguel *35:* 118, 119, 123, 124, 125
Coville, Katherine *32:* 57; *36:* 167; *92:* 38
Covington, Neverne *113:* 87
Cowdrey, Richard *169:* 170; *178:* 205
Cowell, Cressida *140:* 39
Cowell, Lucinda *77:* 54
Cox *43:* 93
Cox, Charles *8:* 20
Cox, David *56:* 37; *90:* 63; *119:* 38
Cox, Palmer *24:* 76, 77
Cox, Steve *140:* 96
Coxe, Molly *69:* 44
Coxon, Michele *158:* 80
Crabb, Gordon *70:* 39
Crabtree, Judith *98:* 42
Craft, Kinuko *22:* 182; *36:* 220; *53:* 122, 123, 148, 149; *74:* 12; *81:* 129; *86:* 31; *89:* 139; *127:* 27, 28, 29; *132:* 142; *139:* 38
Craig, Daniel *177:* 67; *180:* 11
Craig, David *136:* 198
Craig, Helen *49:* 76; *62:* 70, 71, 72; *69:* 141; *94:* 42, 43, 44; *112:* 53; *135:* 101, 102
Crane, Alan H. *1:* 217

Crane, H.M. *13:* 111
Crane, Jack *43:* 183
Crane, Jordan *174:* 21
Crane, Walter *18:* 46, 47, 48, 49, 53, 54, 56, 57, 59, 60, 61; *22:* 128; *24:* 210, 217; *100:* 70, 71
Cravath, Lynne W. *98:* 45
Crawford, Denise *137:* 213
Crawford, Will *43:* 77
Credle, Ellis *1:* 69
Czernecki, Stefan *154:* 104; *178:* 68, 69
Crespi, Francesca *87:* 90
Cressy, Michael *124:* 55
Crews, Donald *32:* 59, 60; *76:* 42, 43, 44
Crews, Nina *97:* 49
Crichlow, Ernest *74:* 88; *83:* 203
Croft, James *150:* 57
Crofut, Bob *80:* 87; *81:* 47
Crofut, Susan *23:* 61
Croll, Carolyn *80:* 137; *102:* 52
Cross, Peter *56:* 78; *63:* 60, 65
Crowe, Elizabeth *88:* 144
Crowell, Pers *3:* 125
Cruikshank, George *15:* 76, 83; *22:* 74, 75, 76, 77, 78, 79, 80, 81, 82, 84, 137; *24:* 22, 23
Crump, Fred H. *11:* 62
Cruz, Ray *6:* 55; *70:* 234; *123:* 173; *172:* 192
Csatari, Joe *44:* 82; *55:* 152; *63:* 25, 28; *102:* 58
Cuetara, Mittie *158:* 85
Cuffari, Richard *4:* 75; *5:* 98; *6:* 56; *7:* 13, 84, 153; *8:* 148, 155; *9:* 89; *11:* 19; *12:* 55, 96, 114; *15:* 51, 202; *18:* 5; *20:* 139; *21:* 197; *22:* 14, 192; *23:* 15, 106; *25:* 97; *27:* 133; *28:* 196; *29:* 54; *30:* 85; *31:* 35; *36:* 101; *38:* 171; *42:* 97; *44:* 92, 192; *45:* 212, 213; *46:* 36, 198; *50:* 164; *54:* 80, 136, 137, 145; *56:* 17; *60:* 63; *66:* 49, 50; *70:* 41; *71:* 132; *77:* 157; *78:* 58, 149; *79:* 120; *85:* 2, 152
Cugat, Xavier *19:* 120
Cumings, Art *35:* 160
Cummings, Chris *29:* 167
Cummings, Michael *159:* 142
Cummings, Pat *42:* 61; *61:* 99; *69:* 205; *71:* 57, 58; *78:* 24, 25; *93:* 75; *107:* 49, 50; *164:* 259
Cummings, Richard *24:* 119
Cunette, Lou *20:* 93; *22:* 125
Cunningham, Aline *25:* 180
Cunningham, David *11:* 13
Cunningham, Imogene *16:* 122, 127
Cunningham, Kelley *176:* 159
Cupples, Pat *107:* 12; *126:* 109
Curlee, Lynn *98:* 48; *141:* 39
Curry, John Steuart *2:* 5; *19:* 84; *34:* 36; *144:* 126
Curry, Tom *127:* 131
Curtis, Bruce *23:* 96; *30:* 88; *36:* 22
Curtis, Neil *167:* 30
Cusack, Margaret *58:* 49, 50, 51
Cushman, Doug *65:* 57; *101:* 39, 40; *133:* 179; *157:* 45
Cyrus, Kurt *132:* 39; *179:* 36, 37
Czechowski, Alicia *95:* 21; *171:* 37
Czernecki, Stefan *117:* 173

D

Dabcovich, Lydia *25:* 105; *40:* 114; *99:* 75, 76
Dacey, Bob *82:* 175; *152:* 65
d'Achille, Gino *127:* 175, 176
Dailey, Don *78:* 197
Dain, Martin J. *35:* 75
Dale, Penny *127:* 224; *151:* 57; *160:* 89
Dale, Rae *72:* 197
Daley, Joann *50:* 22
Dalton, Anne *40:* 62; *63:* 119
Daly, Deborah M. *74:* 213
Daly, Jim *103:* 60; *150:* 48

Daly, Jude *138:* 118, 119
Daly, Nicholas *37:* 53; *76:* 48, 49
Daly, Niki *107:* 15; *114:* 38, 39, 40; *164:* 86
Daly, Paul *97:* 205
Dalziel, Brothers *33:* 113
D'Amato, Alex *9:* 48; *20:* 25
D'Amato, Janet *9:* 48; *20:* 25; *26:* 118
D'Amico, Steve *170:* 52
Danalis, Johnny *167:* 27
Daniel, Alan *23:* 59; *29:* 110; *76:* 50, 53, 55, 56; *153:* 76 *115:* 74; *134:* 70
Daniel, Lea *76:* 53, 55; *153:* 76
Daniel, Lewis C. *20:* 216
Daniels, Beau *73:* 4
Daniels, Steve *22:* 16
Daniels, Stewart *56:* 12
Dann, Bonnie *31:* 83
Dann, Penny *82:* 128
Danska, Herbert *24:* 219
Danyell, Alice *21:* 27
Darley, F.O.C. *16:* 145; *19:* 79, 86, 88, 185; *21:* 28, 36; *35:* 76, 77, 78, 79, 80, 81; *YABC 2:* 175
Darling, Lois *3:* 59; *23:* 30, 31
Darling, Louis *1:* 40, 41; *2:* 63; *3:* 59; *23:* 30, 31; *43:* 54, 57, 59; *121:* 53
Darrow, David R. *84:* 101
Darrow, Whitney, Jr. *13:* 25; *38:* 220, 221
Darwin, Beatrice *43:* 54
Darwin, Len *24:* 82
Dastolfo, Frank *33:* 179
Dauber, Liz *1:* 22; *3:* 266; *30:* 49
Daugherty, James *3:* 66; *8:* 178; *13:* 27, 28, 161; *18:* 101; *19:* 72; *29:* 108; *32:* 156; *42:* 84; *YABC 1:* 256; *2:* 174
d'Aulaire, Edgar Parin *5:* 51; *66:* 53
d'Aulaire, Ingri Parin *5:* 51; *66:* 53
Davalos, Felipe *99:* 197; *159:* 66; *174:* 163
Davenier, Christine *125:* 88; *127:* 32; *128:* 152; *179:* 39, 40
Davick, Linda *151:* 124
David, Jonathan *19:* 37
Davidson, Kevin *28:* 154
Davidson, Raymond *32:* 61
Davie, Helen K. *77:* 48, 49
Davis, Allen *20:* 11; *22:* 45; *27:* 222; *29:* 157; *41:* 99; *47:* 99; *50:* 84; *52:* 105
Davis, Bette J. *15:* 53; *23:* 95
Davis, Dimitris *45:* 95
Davis, Hendon *151:* 122
Davis, Jack E. *145:* 139; *175:* 84, 85
Davis, Jim *32:* 63, 64
Davis, Katie *152:* 52, 53, 54
Davis, Lambert *110:* 23, 24; *176:* 58
Davis, Marguerite *31:* 38; *34:* 69, 70; *100:* 34; *YABC 1:* 126, 230
Davis, Nelle *69:* 191
Davis, Paul *78:* 214
Davis, Yvonne LeBrun *94:* 144
Davisson, Virginia H. *44:* 178
DaVolls, Andy *85:* 53
Dawson, Diane *24:* 127; *42:* 126; *52:* 130; *68:* 104
Day, Alexandra *67:* 59; *97:* 54; *166:* 65; *169:* 40
Day, Larry *169:* 88
Day, Rob *94:* 110; *127:* 24
Dean, Bob *19:* 211
de Angeli, Marguerite *1:* 77; *27:* 62, 65, 66, 67, 69, 70, 72; *100:* 75, 76; *YABC 1:* 166
DeArmond, Dale *70:* 47
Deas, Michael *27:* 219, 221; *30:* 156; *67:* 134; *72:* 24; *75:* 155; *84:* 206; *88:* 124
Debon, Nicolas *151:* 60; *177:* 46
de Bosschere, Jean *19:* 252; *21:* 4
De Bruyn, M(onica) G. *13:* 30, 31
Decker, C.B. *172:* 120
De Cuir, John F. *1:* 28, 29
Deeter, Catherine *74:* 110; *103:* 150; *137:* 50

Degen, Bruce *40:* 227, 229; *57:* 28, 29; *56:* 156; *75:* 229; *76:* 19; *81:* 36, 37; *92:* 26; *93:* 199; *97:* 56, 58, 59; *124:* 40; *147:* 39, 40, 41; *168:* 23
De Grazia *14:* 59; *39:* 56, 57
DeGrazio, George *88:* 40
deGroat, Diane *9:* 39; *18:* 7; *23:* 123; *28:* 200, 201; *31:* 58, 59; *34:* 151; *41:* 152; *43:* 88; *46:* 40, 200; *49:* 163; *50:* 89; *52:* 30, 34; *54:* 43; *63:* 70; *136:* 71; *99:* 73; *117:* 156; *77:* 34; *85:* 48; *86:* 201; *87:* 142; *90:* 72, 73, 143; *95:* 182; *111:* 123; *118:* 160; *126:* 8; *130:* 130; *138:* 93, 94; *169:* 46, 47
de Groot, Lee *6:* 21
Deines, Brian *110:* 139
DeJohn, Marie *89:* 78
Dekhteryov, B. *61:* 158
de Kiefte, Kees *94:* 107
Delacre, Lulu *36:* 66; *156:* 35
Delaney, A. *21:* 78
Delaney, Michael *180:* 16
Delaney, Molly *80:* 43
Delaney, Ned *28:* 68; *56:* 80; *102:* 11
DeLange, Alex Pardo *179:* 128
DeLapine, Jim *79:* 21
De La Roche Saint Andre, Anne *75:* 37
de Larrea, Victoria *6:* 119, 204; *29:* 103; *72:* 203; *87:* 199
Delessert, Étienne *7:* 140; *46:* 61, 62, 63, 65, 67, 68; *130:* 38, 39, 40, 41, 42; *179:* 46, 47, 48, 49; *YABC 2:* 209
DeLorenzo, Christopher *154:* 149
Delulio, John *15:* 54
DeLuna, Tony *88:* 95
Demarest, Chris L. *45:* 68, 69, 70; *73:* 172, 173, 176; *78:* 106; *82:* 48, 49; *89:* 212; *92:* 86; *128:* 57, 58; *175:* 46, 48
De Mejo, Oscar *40:* 67
Demi *11:* 135; *15:* 245; *66:* 129, 130; *89:* 216; *102:* 66, 67, 68
Denetsosie, Hoke *13:* 126; *82:* 34
Denise, Christopher *147:* 43, 44; *176:* 101
Dennis, Morgan *18:* 68, 69; *64:* 89
Dennis, Wesley *2:* 87; *3:* 111; *11:* 132; *18:* 71, 72, 73, 74; *22:* 9; *24:* 196, 200; *46:* 178; *69:* 94, 96; *129:* 62
Denslow, W.W. *16:* 84, 85, 86, 87; *18:* 19, 20, 24; *29:* 211; *100:* 21
Denton, Kady MacDonald *110:* 82; *130:* 70; *181:* 54, 55, 56
Denton, Terry *72:* 163; *174:* 26
DePalma, Mary Newell *132:* 114; *139:* 75
de Paola, Tomie *8:* 95; *9:* 93; *11:* 69; 25; *103:* 28: 157; *29:* 80; *39:* 52, 53; *40:* 226; *46:* 187; *59:* 61, 62, 63, 64, 65, 66, 67, 68, 69, 71, 72, 74; *62:* 19; *108:* 63, 67, 68, 70; *155:* 62, 64, 66; *180:* 105
Deraney, Michael J. *77:* 35; *78:* 148
deRosa, Dee *70:* 48; *71:* 210; *91:* 78
Dervaux, Isabelle *111:* 117
DeSaix, Deborah *180:* 15
De Saulles, Tony *119:* 39
de Seve, Peter *146:* 261
Deshaprabhu, Meera Dayal *86:* 192
Desimini, Lisa *86:* 68; *94:* 47; *96:* 7; *104:* 107; *125:* 194; *131:* 180; *172:* 56
de St. Menin, Charles *70:* 17
Detmold, Edward J. *22:* 104, 105, 106, 107; *35:* 120; *64:* 5; *YABC 2:* 203
Detrich, Susan *20:* 133
Deutermann, Diana *77:* 175
DeVelasco, Joseph E. *21:* 51
de Veyrac, Robert *YABC 2:* 19
DeVille, Edward A. *4:* 235
de Visser, John *55:* 119
Devito, Bert *12:* 164
Devlin, Harry *11:* 74; *74:* 63, 65; *136:* 77, 78
Dewan, Ted *108:* 73; *157:* 55; *165:* 129
Dewar, Nick *133:* 122

Dewey, Ariane *7:* 64; *33:* 195; *35:* 208; *68:* 16, 17; *75:* 46; *93:* 91; *94:* 197; *109:* 65, 66, 67; *125:* 2, 3, 4, 5; *127:* 188; *143:* 25; *178:* 17, 19, 74
Dewey, Jennifer (Owings) *58:* 54; *64:* 214; *65:* 207; *88:* 169; *103:* 45
Dewey, Kenneth *39:* 62; *51:* 23; *56:* 163
de Zanger, Arie *30:* 40
Diakité, Baba Wagué *174:* 28
Diamond, Donna *21:* 200; *23:* 63; *26:* 142; *35:* 83, 84, 85, 86, 87, 88, 89; *38:* 78; *40:* 147; *44:* 152; *50:* 144; *53:* 126; *69:* 46, 47, 48, 201; *71:* 133; *123:* 19
Dias, Ron *71:* 67
Diaz, David *80:* 213; *96:* 83, 84; *108:* 228; *110:* 29; *149:* 106; *150:* 63; *179:* 160
Dibley, Glin *138:* 83; *141:* 128
DiCesare, Joe *70:* 38; *71:* 63, 106; *79:* 214; *93:* 147; *116:* 217; *143:* 111; *166:* 57
Dick, John Henry *8:* 181
Dickens, Frank *34:* 131
Dickey, Robert L. *15:* 279
Dickson, Mora *84:* 21
Didier, Sam *166:* 114
Dietz, James *128:* 223
di Fate, Vincent *37:* 70; *90:* 11; *93:* 60; *109:* 219, 220
Di Fiori, Lawrence *10:* 51; *12:* 190; *27:* 97; *40:* 219; *93:* 57; *130:* 45
Digby, Desmond *97:* 180
Di Grazia, Thomas *32:* 66; *35:* 241
Dillard, Annie *10:* 32
Dillard, Sarah *136:* 186
Dillon, Corinne B. *1:* 139
Dillon, Diane *4:* 104, 167; *6:* 23; *13:* 29; *15:* 99; *26:* 148; *27:* 136, 201; *51:* 29, 48, 51, 52, 53, 54, 55, 56, 57, 58, 59, 60, 61, 62; *54:* 155; *56:* 69; *58:* 127, 128; *61:* 95; *62:* 27; *64:* 46; *68:* 3; *69:* 209; *74:* 89; *79:* 92; *86:* 89; *92:* 28, 177; *93:* 7, 210; *94:* 239, 240; *97:* 167; *106:* 58, 59, 61, 64; *107:* 3; *139:* 246; *167:* 77
Dillon, Leo *4:* 104, 167; *6:* 23; *13:* 29; *15:* 99; *26:* 148; *27:* 136, 201; *51:* 29, 48, 51, 52, 53, 54, 55, 56, 57, 58, 59, 60, 61, 62; *54:* 155; *56:* 69; *58:* 127, 128; *61:* 95; *62:* 27; *64:* 46; *68:* 3; *69:* 209; *74:* 89; *79:* 92; *86:* 89; *92:* 28, 177; *93:* 7, 210; *94:* 239, 240; *97:* 167; *106:* 58, 59, 61, 64; *107:* 3; *139:* 246; *167:* 77
Dillon, Sharon Saseen *59:* 179, 188
DiMaccio, Gerald *121:* 80
DiMaggio, Joe *36:* 22
DiMassi, Gina *169:* 17
Dinan, Carol *25:* 169; *59:* 75
Dines, Glen *7:* 66, 67
Dinesen, Thomas *44:* 37
Dinh, Pham Viet *167:* 184
Dinnerstein, Harvey *42:* 63, 64, 65, 66, 67, 68; *50:* 146
Dinsdale, Mary *10:* 65; *11:* 171
Dinyer, Eric *86:* 148; *109:* 163; *110:* 239; *124:* 11; *150:* 69; *170:* 4; *171:* 30
Dion, Nathalie *170:* 124
DiRocco, Carl *181:* 23
DiSalvo-Ryan, DyAnne *59:* 77; *62:* 185; *117:* 46; *144:* 64; *150:* 153
Disney, Walt *28:* 71, 72, 73, 76, 77, 78, 79, 80, 81, 87, 88, 89, 90, 91, 94
DiTerlizzi, Tony *105:* 7; *147:* 22; *154:* 31, 32, 33
Divito, Anna *83:* 159
Dixon, Don *74:* 17; *109:* 196
Dixon, Larry *127:* 125
Dixon, Maynard *20:* 165
Doares, Robert G. *20:* 39
Dobias, Frank *22:* 162
Dobrin, Arnold *4:* 68
Dobson, Steven Gaston *102:* 103
Dockray, Tracy *139:* 77
Docktor, Irv *43:* 70

Dodd, Ed *4:* 69
Dodd, Julie *74:* 73
Dodd, Lynley *35:* 92; *86:* 71; *132:* 45, 46, 47
Dodge, Bill *96:* 36; *118:* 7, 8, 9; *133:* 135
Dodgson, Charles L. *20:* 148; *33:* 146; *YABC 2:* 98
Dodson, Bert *9:* 138; *14:* 195; *42:* 55; *54:* 8; *60:* 49; *101:* 125
Dodson, Liz Brenner *105:* 117; *111:* 15
Dohanos, Stevan *16:* 10
Dolce, J. Ellen *74:* 147; *75:* 41
Dolch, Marguerite P. *50:* 64
Dolesch, Susanne *34:* 49
Dollar, Diane *57:* 32
Dolobowsky, Mena *81:* 54
Dolson, Hildegarde *5:* 57
Domanska, Janina *6:* 66, 67; *YABC 1:* 166
Domi *134:* 113
Dominguez, El *53:* 94
Domjan, Joseph *25:* 93
Domm, Jeffrey C. *84:* 69; *135:* 70
Donahey, William *68:* 209
Donahue, Dorothy *76:* 170
Donahue, Vic *2:* 93; *3:* 190; *9:* 44
Donald, Elizabeth *4:* 18
Donalty, Alison *149:* 195, 196, 197
Donato *85:* 59; *149:* 204
Doney, Todd L.W. *87:* 12; *93:* 112; *98:* 135; *101:* 57; *104:* 40; *118:* 163; *135:* 162, 163; *151:* 18
Donna, Natalie *9:* 52
Donohue, Dorothy *95:* 2; *132:* 30; *176:* 54, 55; *178:* 77, 78, 79
Dooling, Michael *82:* 19; *105:* 55; *106:* 224; *125:* 135; *171:* 46; *172:* 12; *176:* 120
Doran, Ben-Ami *128:* 189
Dore, Gustave *18:* 169, 172, 175; *19:* 93, 94, 95, 96, 97, 98, 99, 100, 101, 102, 103, 104, 105; *23:* 188; *25:* 197, 199
Doremus, Robert *6:* 62; *13:* 90; *30:* 95, 96, 97; *38:* 97
Dorfman, Ronald *11:* 128
Doriau *86:* 59; *91:* 152
Dorros, Arthur *78:* 42, 43; *91:* 28
Doruyter, Karel *165:* 105
dos Santos, Joyce Audy *57:* 187, 189
Doty, Roy *28:* 98; *31:* 32; *32:* 224; *46:* 157; *82:* 71; *142:* 7
Doucet, Bob *132:* 238; *169:* 159
Dougherty, Charles *16:* 204; *18:* 74
Doughty, Rebecca *177:* 174
Doughty, Thomas *118:* 31; *140:* 60
Douglas, Aaron *31:* 103
Douglas, Carole Nelson *73:* 48
Douglas, Goray *13:* 151
Dow, Brian *150:* 92
Dowd, Jason *132:* 51, 52; *164:* 244
Dowd, Vic *3:* 244; *10:* 97
Dowden, Anne Ophelia *7:* 70, 71; *13:* 120
Dowdy, Mrs. Regera *29:* 100
Downes, Belinda *180:* 29
Downing, Julie *60:* 140; *81:* 50; *86:* 200; *99:* 129
Doyle, Janet *56:* 31
Doyle, Richard *21:* 31, 32, 33; *23:* 231; *24:* 177; *31:* 87
Draper, Angie *43:* 84
Drath, Bill *26:* 34
Drawson, Blair *17:* 53; *126:* 65
Dray, Matt *177:* 47
Drescher, Henrik *105:* 60, 62, 63; *172:* 72
Drescher, Joan *30:* 100, 101; *35:* 245; *52:* 168; *137:* 52
Drew, Patricia *15:* 100
Drummond, V.H. *6:* 70
Drury, Christian Potter *105:* 97
Dubanevich, Arlene *56:* 44
Ducak, Danilo *99:* 130; *108:* 214
Duchesne, Janet *6:* 162; *79:* 8
Duda, Jana *102:* 155
Dudash, Michael *32:* 122; *77:* 134; *82:* 149

Duer, Douglas *34:* 177
Duffy, Daniel Mark *76:* 37; *101:* 196; *108:* 147, 148
Duffy, Joseph *38:* 203
Duffy, Pat *28:* 153
Dugan, Karen *181:* 26
Dugin, Andrej *77:* 60
Dugina, Olga *77:* 60
Duke, Chris *8:* 195; *139:* 164
Duke, Kate *87:* 186; *90:* 78, 79, 80, 81
Duke, Marion *165:* 87
Dulac, Edmund *19:* 108, 109, 110, 111, 112, 113, 114, 115, 117; *23:* 187; *25:* 152; *YABC 1:* 37; *2:* 147
Dulac, Jean *13:* 64
Dumas, Philippe *52:* 36, 37, 38, 39, 40, 41, 42, 43, 45; *119:* 40, 41, 42
Dunaway, Nancy *108:* 161
Dunbar, James *76:* 63
Dunbar, Polly *181:* 60, 61
Duncan, Beverly *72:* 92
Duncan, John *116:* 94
Dunn, H.T. *62:* 196
Dunn, Harvey *34:* 78, 79, 80, 81
Dunn, Iris *5:* 175
Dunn, Phoebe *5:* 175
Dunne, Jeanette *72:* 57, 173, 222
Dunnick, Regan *176:* 51; *178:* 83, 84
Dunnington, Tom *3:* 36; *18:* 281; *25:* 61; *31:* 159; *35:* 168; *48:* 195; *79:* 144; *82:* 230
Dunn-Ramsey, Marcy *117:* 131
Dunrea, Olivier *59:* 81; *118:* 53, 54; *124:* 43
Duntze, Dorothee *88:* 28; *160:* 76
Dupasquier, Philippe *86:* 75; *104:* 76; *151:* 63
DuQuette, Keith *90:* 83; *155:* 73, 74
Duroussy, Nathalie *146:* 150
Durrell, Julie *82:* 62; *94:* 62
Dutz *6:* 59
Duvoisin, Roger *2:* 95; *6:* 76, 77; *7:* 197; *28:* 125; *30:* 101, 102, 103, 104, 105, 107; *47:* 205; *84:* 254
Dyer, Dale *141:* 71
Dyer, Jane *75:* 219; *129:* 28; *147:* 49, 50, 51; *168:* 121
Dypold, Pat *15:* 37

E

E.V.B.
See Boyle, Eleanor Vere (Gordon)
Eachus, Jennifer *29:* 74; *82:* 201; *164:* 153
Eadie, Bob *63:* 36
Eagle, Bruce *95:* 119
Eagle, Ellen *82:* 121; *89:* 3
Eagle, Jeremy *141:* 71
Eagle, Michael *11:* 86; *20:* 9; *23:* 18; *27:* 122; *28:* 57; *34:* 201; *44:* 189; *73:* 9; *78:* 235; *85:* 43
Earl-Bridges, Michele *159:* 128
Earle, Edwin *56:* 27
Earle, Olive L. *7:* 75
Earle, Vana *27:* 99
Early, Lori *132:* 2
Early, Margaret *72:* 59
East, Stella *131:* 223
Eastman, P.D. *33:* 57
Easton, Reginald *29:* 181
Eaton, Tom *4:* 62; *6:* 64; *22:* 99; *24:* 124
Ebel, Alex *11:* 89
Ebert, Len *9:* 191; *44:* 47
Echevarria, Abe *37:* 69
Eckersley, Maureen *48:* 62
Eckert, Horst *72:* 62
Ede, Janina *33:* 59
Edens, Cooper *49:* 81, 82, 83, 84, 85; *112:* 58
Edens, John *109:* 115
Edgar, Sarah E. *41:* 97
Edliq, Emily S. *131:* 107
Edrien *11:* 53

Edwards, Freya *45:* 102
Edwards, George Wharton *31:* 155
Edwards, Gunvor *2:* 71; *25:* 47; *32:* 71; *54:* 106
Edwards, Jeanne *29:* 257
Edwards, Linda Strauss *21:* 134; *39:* 123; *49:* 88, 89
Edwards, Michelle *152:* 62, 63
Edwards, Wallace *170:* 55
Egan, Tim *155:* 76, 77, 78
Egge, David *102:* 71
Eggenhofer, Nicholas *2:* 81
Eggleton, Bob *74:* 40; *81:* 190, 191; *105:* 6; *121:* 183; *149:* 203; *166:* 215
Egielski, Richard *11:* 90; *16:* 208; *33:* 236; *38:* 35; *49:* 91, 92, 93, 95, 212, 213, 214, 216; *79:* 122; *106:* 67, 68, 69; *134:* 135; *144:* 244; *163:* 82, 84
Ehlert, Lois *35:* 97; *69:* 51; *112:* 7; *113:* 208; *128:* 63, 64, 65; *172:* 77, 79, 80
Ehrlich, Bettina *1:* 83
Eitan, Ora *160:* 165
Eichenberg, Fritz *1:* 79; *9:* 54; *19:* 248; *23:* 170; *24:* 200; *26:* 208; *50:* 67, 68, 69, 70, 71, 72, 73, 74, 75, 77, 79, 80, 81; *60:* 165; *100:* 137; *YABC 1:* 104, 105; *2:* 213
Einsel, Naiad *10:* 35; *29:* 136
Einsel, Walter *10:* 37
Einzig, Susan *3:* 77; *43:* 78; *67:* 155; *129:* 154
Eisner, Will *165:* 82, 83
Eitzen, Allan *9:* 56; *12:* 212; *14:* 226; *21:* 194; *38:* 162; *76:* 218
Eldridge, H. *54:* 109
Eldridge, Harold *43:* 83
Elgaard, Greta *19:* 241
Elgin, Kathleen *9:* 188; *39:* 69
Ellacott, S.E. *19:* 118
Elliott, Mark *93:* 69; *105:* 108; *107:* 123; *140:* 53; *165:* 189; *173:* 67
Elliott, Sarah M. *14:* 58
Ellis, Dianne *130:* 208
Ellis, Jan Davey *88:* 50; *115:* 80
Ellis, Richard *130:* 47, 48
Ellison, Pauline *55:* 21
Elmer, Richard *78:* 5
Elmore, Larry *90:* 8
Elwell, Tristan *110:* 39; *121:* 182; *127:* 46; *137:* 144; *141:* 173; *151:* 236; *158:* 264; *167:* 119, 120, 121; *169:* 20
Elzbieta *88:* 80, 81
Emberley, Ed *8:* 53; *70:* 53, 54; *146:* 65, 69, 70
Emberley, Michael *34:* 83; *80:* 72; *119:* 47, 48; *147:* 100; *158:* 115
Emerling, Dorothy *104:* 27
Emery, Leslie *49:* 187
Emmett, Bruce *49:* 147; *80:* 175; *101:* 206
Emry-Perrott, Jennifer *61:* 57
Emshwiller, Ed *174:* 45
Engel, Diana *70:* 57
Engle, Mort *38:* 64
Englebert, Victor *8:* 54
English, Mark *101:* 207
Enik, Ted *142:* 39
Enos, Randall *20:* 183
Enright, Maginel Wright *19:* 240, 243; *39:* 31, 35, 36
Enrique, Romeo *34:* 135
Ensor, Barbara *180:* 30
Epstein, Stephen *50:* 142, 148
Erdogan, Buket *174:* 179
Erdrich, Louise *141:* 62
Erhard, Walter *1:* 152
Erickson, Phoebe *11:* 83; *59:* 85
Erikson, Mel *31:* 69
Eriksson, Eva *63:* 88, 90, 92, 93
Ering, Timothy Basil *131:* 100; *176:* 63, 64
Erlbruch, Wolf *181:* 66
Ernst, Lisa Campbell *47:* 147; *95:* 47; *154:* 46, 47, 48; *164:* 88
Esco, Jo *61:* 103

Escourido, Joseph *4:* 81
Escrivá, Viví *119:* 51; *181:* 36
Este, Kirk *33:* 111
Estep, David *73:* 57
Estes, Eleanor *91:* 66
Estoril, Jean *32:* 27
Estrada, Pau *74:* 76
Estrada, Ric *5:* 52, 146; *13:* 174
Etchemendy, Teje *38:* 68
Etheredges, the *73:* 12
Etienne, Kirk-Albert *145:* 184
Ets, Marie Hall *2:* 102
Ettlinger, Doris *171:* 98
Eulalie *YABC 2:* 315
Evans, Greg *73:* 54, 55, 56; *143:* 40, 41
Evans, Katherine *5:* 64
Evans, Leslie *144:* 227
Evans, Shane W. *159:* 142; *160:* 190; *168:* 39
Everitt, Betsy *151:* 110
Ewart, Claire *76:* 69; *145:* 59, 60
Ewing, Carolyn *66:* 143; *79:* 52
Ewing, Juliana Horatia *16:* 92
Eyolfson, Norman *98:* 154

F

Fabian, Limbert *136:* 114
Facklam, Paul *132:* 62
Falconer, Ian *125:* 66; *179:* 59
Falconer, Pearl *34:* 23
Falkenstern, Lisa *70:* 34; *76:* 133; *78:* 171; *127:* 16
Falls, C.B. *1:* 19; *38:* 71, 72, 73, 74
Falter, John *40:* 169, 170
Falwell, Cathryn *118:* 77; *137:* 185
Fancher, Lou *138:* 219; *141:* 64; *144:* 199; *177:* 51
Fanelli, Sara *89:* 63; *126:* 69
Faria, Rosana *150:* 143
Farmer, Andrew *49:* 102
Farmer, Peter *24:* 108; *38:* 75
Farnsworth, Bill *93:* 189; *116:* 147; *124:* 8; *135:* 52; *146:* 242, 243, 244
Farquharson, Alexander *46:* 75
Farrell, David *40:* 135
Farris, David *74:* 42
Fasolino, Teresa *118:* 145
Fatigati, Evelyn *24:* 112
Faul-Jansen, Regina *22:* 117
Faulkner, Jack *6:* 169
Faulkner, Matt *161:* 174; *167:* 75
Fava, Rita *2:* 29
Fax, Elton C. *1:* 101; *4:* 2; *12:* 77; *25:* 107
Fay *43:* 93
Fearnley, Jan *153:* 82, 83
Fearrington, Ann *146:* 80
Federspiel, Marian *33:* 51
Fedorov, Nickolai Ivanovich *110:* 102
Feelings, Tom *5:* 22; *8:* 56; *12:* 153; *16:* 105; *30:* 196; *49:* 37; *61:* 101; *69:* 56, 57; *93:* 74; *105:* 88
Fehr, Terrence *21:* 87
Feiffer, Jules *3:* 91; *8:* 58; *61:* 66, 67, 70, 74, 76, 77, 78; *111:* 47, 48, 49, 50; *132:* 122; *157:* 62
Feigeles, Neil *41:* 242
Feldman, Elyse *86:* 7
Feller, Gene *33:* 130
Fellows, Muriel H. *10:* 42
Felstead, Cathie *116:* 85
Felts, Shirley *33:* 71; *48:* 59
Fennell, Tracy *171:* 69
Fennelli, Maureen *38:* 181
Fenton, Carroll Lane *5:* 66; *21:* 39
Fenton, Mildred Adams *5:* 66; *21:* 39
Ferguson, Peter *177:* 30, 31; *181:* 154
Ferguson, Walter W. *34:* 86
Fernandes, Eugenie *77:* 67
Fernandes, Stanislaw *70:* 28

Fernandez, Fernando *77:* 57
Fernandez, Laura *77:* 153; *101:* 117; *131:* 222; *170:* 119; *175:* 182
Ferrington, Susan *172:* 22
Fetz, Ingrid *11:* 67; *12:* 52; *16:* 205; *17:* 59; *29:* 105; *30:* 108, 109; *32:* 149; *43:* 142; *56:* 29; *60:* 34; *85:* 48; *87:* 146
Fiammenghi, Gioia *9:* 66; *11:* 44; *12:* 206; *13:* 57, 59; *52:* 126, 129; *66:* 64; *85:* 83; *91:* 161; *166:* 169
Fiedler, Joseph Daniel *96:* 42; *113:* 173; *129:* 164; *146:* 17; *159:* 68; *162:* 104
Field, Rachel *15:* 113
Fielding, David *70:* 124
Fieser, Stephen *152:* 36
Fine, Howard *145:* 159; *159:* 64; *165:* 134; *174:* 129; *181:* 68
Fine, Peter K. *43:* 210
Finger, Helen *42:* 81
Fink, Sam *18:* 119
Finlay, Winifred *23:* 72
Finney, Pat *79:* 215
Fiore, Peter *99:* 196; *125:* 139; *144:* 225; *160:* 169; *180:* 72
Fiorentino, Al *3:* 240
Firehammer, Karla *174:* 202
Firmin, Charlotte *29:* 75; *48:* 70
Firmin, Peter *58:* 63, 64, 65, 67, 68, 70, 71
Firth, Barbara *81:* 208; *127:* 218; *179:* 62
Fischel, Lillian *40:* 204
Fischer, Hans *25:* 202
Fischer-Nagel, Andreas *56:* 50
Fischer-Nagel, Heiderose *56:* 50
Fisher, Carolyn *154:* 50
Fisher, Chris *79:* 62; *158:* 248
Fisher, Cynthia *117:* 45; *137:* 118
Fisher, Jeffrey *142:* 80
Fisher, Leonard Everett *3:* 6; *4:* 72, 86; *6:* 197; *9:* 59; *16:* 151, 153; *23:* 44; *27:* 134; *29:* 26; *34:* 87, 89, 90, 91, 93, 94, 95, 96; *40:* 30; *50:* 150; *60:* 158; *73:* 68, 70, 71, 72, 73; *176:* 71, 72, 73; *YABC 2:* 169
Fisher, Lois *20:* 62; *21:* 7
Fisher, Valorie *177:* 55
Fisk, Nicholas *25:* 112
Fitschen, Marilyn *2:* 20, 21; *20:* 48
Fitz-Maurice, Jeff *175:* 2
Fitzgerald, F.A. *15:* 116; *25:* 86, 87
Fitzhugh, Louise *1:* 94; *9:* 163; *45:* 75, 78
Fitzgerald, Joanne *157:* 153, 154
Fitzhugh, Susie *11:* 117
Fitzpatrick, Jim *109:* 130
Fitzpatrick, Marie-Louise *125:* 69, 70
Fitzsimmons, Arthur *14:* 128
Fix, Philippe *26:* 102
Flack, Marjorie *21:* 67; *100:* 93; *YABC 2:* 122
Flagg, James Montgomery *17:* 227
Flavin, Teresa *132:* 115
Flax, Zeona *2:* 245
Fleetwood, Tony *171:* 51
Fleishman, Seymour *14:* 232; *24:* 87
Fleming, Denise *71:* 179; *81:* 58; *126:* 71, 72, 73; *173:* 52, 53
Fleming, Guy *18:* 41
Flesher, Vivienne *85:* 55
Fletcher, Claire *80:* 106; *157:* 159
Flint, Russ *74:* 80
Floate, Helen *111:* 163
Floca, Brian *155:* 88, 89
Floethe, Richard *3:* 131; *4:* 90
Floherty, John J., Jr. *5:* 68
Flook, Helen *160:* 81
Flora, James *1:* 96; *30:* 111, 112
Florczak, Robert *166:* 51
Florian, Douglas *19:* 122; *83:* 64, 65; *125:* 71, 72, 74, 76; *128:* 130; *177:* 58, 60
Flory, Jane *22:* 111
Flower, Renee *125:* 109
Floyd, Gareth *1:* 74; *17:* 245; *48:* 63; *62:* 35, 36, 37, 39, 40, 41; *74:* 245; *79:* 56
Fluchere, Henri A. *40:* 79

Flynn, Barbara 7: 31; 9: 70
Fogarty, Thomas 15: 89
Folger, Joseph 9: 100
Folkard, Charles 22: 132; 29: 128, 257, 258
Foott, Jeff 42: 202
Forberg, Ati 12: 71, 205; 14: 1; 22: 113; 26: 22; 48: 64, 65
Ford, George 24: 120; 31: 70, 177; 58: 126; 81: 103; 107: 91; 136: 100
Ford, H.J. 16: 185, 186
Ford, Jason 174: 119
Ford, Pamela Baldwin 27: 104
Fordham, John 168: 160, 161
Foreman, Michael 2: 110, 111; 67: 99; 73: 78, 79, 80, 81, 82; 93: 146; 135: 55, 56, 57
Forrester, Victoria 40: 83
Forsey, Chris 140: 210
Fortnum, Peggy 6: 29; 20: 179; 24: 211; 26: 76, 77, 78; 39: 78; 58: 19, 21, 23, 27; YABC 1: 148
Foster, Brad W. 34: 99
Foster, Genevieve 2: 112
Foster, Gerald 7: 78
Foster, Jon 146: 18
Foster, Laura Louise 6: 79
Foster, Marian Curtis 23: 74; 40: 42
Foster, Sally 58: 73, 74
Foucher, Adele 47: 118
Foust, Mitch 168: 50
Fowler, Mel 36: 127
Fowler, Richard 87: 219
Fowles, Selley 165: 127
Fox, Charles Phillip 12: 84
Fox, Jim 6: 187
Fox-Davies, Sarah 76: 150
Frace, Charles 15: 118
Frailey, Joy 72: 108
Frame, Paul 2: 45, 145; 9: 153; 10: 124; 21: 71; 23: 62; 24: 123; 27: 106; 31: 48; 32: 159; 34: 195; 38: 136; 42: 55; 44: 139; 60: 39, 40, 41, 42, 44, 46; 73: 183
Frampton, David 85: 72; 102: 33; 139: 182; 152: 37
Francois, Andre 25: 117
Francoise
    See Seignobosc, Francoise
Frank, Lola Edick 2: 199
Frank, Mary 4: 54; 34: 100
Franke, Phil 45: 91
Frankel, Alona 66: 70
Frankel, Julie 40: 84, 85, 202
Frankenberg, Robert 22: 116; 30: 50; 38: 92, 94, 95; 68: 111
Frankfeldt, Gwen 84: 223; 110: 92
Frankland, David 169: 137
Franklin, Ashton 165: 144
Franklin, John 24: 22
Franson, Leanne R. 111: 57, 58; 151: 7
Frascino, Edward 9: 133; 29: 229; 33: 190; 48: 80, 81, 82, 83, 84, 85, 86
Frasconi, Antonio 6: 80; 27: 208; 53: 41, 43, 45, 47, 48; 68: 145; 73: 226; 131: 68
Fraser, Betty 2: 212; 6: 185; 8: 103; 31: 72, 73; 43: 136; 111: 76
Fraser, Eric 38: 78; 41: 149, 151
Fraser, F.A. 22: 234
Fraser, James 171: 68
Fraser, Mary Ann 137: 63
Frasier, Debra 69: 60; 112: 67
Fraustino, Lisa Rowe 146: 87
Frazee, Marla 72: 98; 105: 79, 80; 151: 67, 68; 164: 165; 171: 190, 191
Frazetta, Frank 41: 72; 58: 77, 78, 79, 80, 81, 82, 83
Frazier, Craig 177: 63
Freas, John 25: 207
Fredrickson, Mark 103: 33
Freeland, Michael J. 118: 115
Freeman, Don 2: 15; 13: 249; 17: 62, 63, 65, 67, 68; 18: 243; 20: 195; 23: 213, 217; 32: 155; 55: 129

Freeman, Irving 67: 150
Freeman, Laura 144: 111
Freeman, Pietri 140: 223
Freeman, Tom 167: 118
Freeman, Tor 164: 93
Fregosi, Claudia 24: 117
Fremaux, Charlotte Murray 138: 29; 141: 95
French, Fiona 6: 82, 83; 75: 61; 109: 170; 132: 79, 80, 81, 82
French, Martin 163: 4
Frendak, Rodney 126: 97, 98
Freschet, Gina 175: 73
Freynet, Gilbert 72: 221
Friedman, Judith 43: 197; 131: 221
Friedman, Marvin 19: 59; 42: 86
Frinta, Dagmar 36: 42
Frith, Michael K. 15: 138; 18: 120
Fritz, Ronald 46: 73; 82: 124
Fromm, Lilo 29: 85; 40: 197
Frost, A.B. 17: 6, 7; 19: 123, 124, 125, 126, 127, 128, 129, 130; 100: 119; YABC 1: 156, 157, 160; 2: 107
Frost, Kristi 118: 113
Frost, Michael 151: 209
Froud, Brian 150: 82, 83
Froud, Wendy 151: 237
Fry, Guy 2: 224
Fry, Rosalie 3: 72; YABC 2: 180, 181
Fry, Rosalind 21: 153, 168
Fryer, Elmer 34: 115
Fuchs, Bernie 110: 10; 162: 46
Fuchs, Erich 6: 84
Fuchshuber, Annegert 43: 96
Fufuka, Mahiri 32: 146
Fuge, Charles 144: 91, 93
Fujikawa, Gyo 39: 75, 76; 76: 72, 73, 74
Fulford, Deborah 23: 159
Fuller, Margaret 25: 189
Fulweiler, John 93: 99
Funai, Mamoru 38: 105
Funk, Tom 7: 17, 99
Furchgott, Terry 29: 86
Furness, William Henry, Jr. 94: 18
Furukawa, Mel 25: 42
Fusari, Erika 164: 227

G

Gaadt, David 78: 212; 121: 166
Gaadt, George 71: 9
Gaber, Susan 99: 33; 115: 57, 58; 164: 195; 169: 61, 62, 63
Gaberell, J. 19: 236
Gabler, Mirko 99: 71
Gackenbach, Dick 19: 168; 41: 81; 48: 89, 90, 91, 92, 93, 94; 54: 105; 79: 75, 76, 77
Gad, Victor 87: 161
Gaetano, Nicholas 23: 209
Gaffney-Kessell, Walter 94: 219; 174: 188
Gag, Flavia 17: 49, 52
Gag, Wanda 100: 101, 102; YABC 1: 135, 137, 138, 141, 143
Gagnon, Cecile 11: 77; 58: 87
Gal, Laszlo 14: 127; 52: 54, 55, 56; 65: 142; 68: 150; 81: 185; 96: 104, 105
Galazinski, Tom 55: 13
Galdone, Paul 1: 156, 181, 206; 2: 40, 241; 3: 42, 144; 4: 141; 10: 109, 158; 11: 21; 12: 118, 210; 14: 12; 16: 36, 37; 17: 70, 71, 72, 73, 74; 18: 111, 230; 19: 183; 21: 154; 22: 150, 245; 33: 126; 39: 136, 137; 42: 57; 51: 169; 55: 110; 66: 80, 82, 139; 72: 73; 100: 84
Gale, Cathy 140: 22; 143: 52
Gall, Chris 176: 79, 80
Gallagher, S. Saelig 105: 154
Gallagher, Sears 20: 112
Galloway, Ewing 51: 154
Galouchko, Annouchka Gravel 95: 55

Galster, Robert 1: 66
Galsworthy, Gay John 35: 232
Galvez, Daniel 125: 182
Gamble, Kim 112: 64, 65; 124: 77
Gammell, Stephen 7: 48; 13: 149; 29: 82; 33: 209; 41: 88; 50: 185, 186, 187; 53: 51, 52, 53, 54, 55, 56, 57, 58; 54: 24, 25; 56: 147, 148, 150; 57: 27, 66; 81: 62, 63; 87: 88; 89: 10; 106: 223; 126: 2; 128: 71, 73, 74, 77; 154: 34
Gamper, Ruth 84: 198
Gampert, John 58: 94
Ganly, Helen 56: 56
Gannett, Ruth Chrisman 3: 74; 18: 254; 33: 77, 78
Gantschev, Ivan 45: 32
Garafano, Marie 73: 33
Garbot, Dave 131: 106
Garbutt, Bernard 23: 68
Garcia 37: 71
Garcia, Manuel 74: 145
Garcia-Franco, Rebecca 173: 46
Gardiner, Lindsey 178: 128
Gardner, Earle 45: 167
Gardner, Joan 40: 87
Gardner, Joel 40: 87, 92
Gardner, John 40: 87
Gardner, Lucy 40: 87
Gardner, Richard
    See Cummings, Richard
Gardner, Sally 171: 177; 177: 66, 68
Gargiulo, Frank 84: 158
Garland, Michael 36: 29; 38: 83; 44: 168; 48: 78, 221, 222; 49: 161; 60: 139; 71: 6, 11; 72: 229; 74: 142; 89: 187; 93: 183; 104: 110; 131: 55; 139: 209; 168: 56
Garland, Peggy 60: 139
Garland, Sarah 62: 45; 135: 67, 68; 171: 118
Garn, Aimee 75: 47
Garner, Joan 128: 170
Garneray, Ambroise Louis 59: 140
Garnett, Eve 3: 75
Garnett, Gary 39: 184
Garns, Allen 80: 125; 84: 39; 165: 231
Garraty, Gail 4: 142; 52: 106
Garrett, Agnes 46: 110; 47: 157
Garrett, Edmund H. 20: 29
Garrett, Tom 107: 194
Garrick, Jacqueline 67: 42, 43; 77: 94
Garrison, Barbara 19: 133; 104: 146; 109: 87
Garro, Mark 108: 131; 128: 210
Garvey, Robert 98: 222
Garza, Carmen Lomas 80: 211
Gates, Frieda 26: 80
Gaughan, Jack 26: 79; 43: 185
Gaver, Becky 20: 61
Gawing, Toby 72: 52
Gay, Marie-Louise 68: 76, 77, 78; 102: 136; 126: 76, 78, 81, 83; 127: 55, 56; 179: 70, 72, 73, 74
Gay, Zhenya 19: 135, 136
Gaydos, Tim 62: 201
Gazsi, Ed 80: 48
Gazso, Gabriel 73: 85
Geary, Clifford N. 1: 122; 9: 104; 51: 74
Geary, Rick 142: 44, 46
Gee, Frank 33: 26
Geehan, Wayne 157: 181
Geerinck, Manuel 173: 128
Gehm, Charlie 36: 65; 57: 117; 62: 60, 138
Geisel, Theodor Seuss 1: 104, 105, 106; 28: 108, 109, 110, 111, 112, 113; 75: 67, 68, 69, 70, 71; 89: 127, 128; 100: 106, 107, 108
Geisert, Arthur 92: 67, 68; 133: 72, 73, 74; 165: 97, 98; 171: 64, 65
Geldart, William 15: 121; 21: 202
Genia 4: 84

Gentry, Cyrille R. *12:* 66
Genzo, John Paul *136:* 74
George, Jean *2:* 113
George, Lindsay Barrett *95:* 57; *155:* 97, 98
Geraghty, Paul *130:* 60, 61
Gerard, Jean Ignace *45:* 80
Gerard, Rolf *27:* 147, 150
Gerber, Mark *61:* 105
Gerber, Mary Jane *112:* 124; *171:* 56
Gerber, Stephanie *71:* 195
Gerdstein, Mordecai *169:* 105
Gergely, Tibor *54:* 15, 16
Geritz, Franz *17:* 135
Gerlach, Geff *42:* 58
Gerrard, Roy *47:* 78; *90:* 96, 97, 98, 99
Gerritsen, Paula *177:* 69
Gershinowitz, George *36:* 27
Gerstein, Mordicai *31:* 117; *47:* 80, 81, 82, 83, 84, 85, 86; *51:* 173; *69:* 134; *107:* 122; *142:* 49, 52; *165:* 209; *176:* 119; *178:* 95, 97, 99
Gervase *12:* 27
Geter, Tyrone *146:* 249; *150:* 86
Getz, Arthur *32:* 148
Gewirtz, Bina *61:* 81
Giancola, Donato *95:* 146; *164:* 226
Gibbons, Gail *23:* 78; *72:* 77, 78, 79; *82:* 182; *104:* 65; *160:* 99, 100
Gibbs, Tony *40:* 95
Gibran, Kahlil *32:* 116
Gider, Iskender *81:* 193
Giebfried, Rosemary *170:* 135
Giesen, Rosemary *34:* 192, 193
Giffard, Hannah *83:* 70
Giguere, George *20:* 111
Gilbert, John *19:* 184; *54:* 115; *YABC 2:* 287
Gilbert, W.S. *36:* 83, 85, 96
Gilbert, Yvonne *116:* 70; *128:* 84; *149:* 119
Gilchrist, Jan Spivey *72:* 82, 83, 84, 85, 87; *77:* 90; *105:* 89, 91; *130:* 63, 64; *155:* 105, 107
Giles, Will *41:* 218
Gili, Phillida *70:* 73
Gill, Margery *4:* 57; *7:* 7; *22:* 122; *25:* 166; *26:* 146, 147
Gillen, Denver *28:* 216
Gillette, Henry J. *23:* 237
Gilliam, Stan *39:* 64, 81
Gillies, Chuck *62:* 31
Gilliland, Jillian *87:* 58
Gillman, Alec *98:* 105
Gilman, Esther *15:* 124
Gilman, Phoebe *104:* 70, 71
Ginsberg, Sari *111:* 184
Ginsburg, Max *62:* 59; *68:* 194 *Girard, Roge 161:* 30
Girouard, Patrick *155:* 100
Giovanopoulos, Paul *7:* 104; *60:* 36
Giovine, Sergio *79:* 12; *93:* 118; *139:* 118
Githens, Elizabeth M. *5:* 47
Gladden, Scott *99:* 108; *103:* 160
Gladstone, Gary *12:* 89; *13:* 190
Gladstone, Lise *15:* 273
Glanzman, Louis S. *2:* 177; *3:* 182; *36:* 97, 98; *38:* 120, 122; *52:* 141, 144; *71:* 191; *91:* 54, 56
Glaser, Byron *154:* 59, 60
Glaser, Milton *3:* 5; *5:* 156; *11:* 107; *30:* 26; *36:* 112; *54:* 141; *151:* 70
Glass, Andrew *36:* 38; *44:* 133; *48:* 205; *65:* 3; *68:* 43, 45; *90:* 104, 105; *150:* 89
Glass, Marvin *9:* 174
Glasser, Judy *41:* 156; *56:* 140; *69:* 79; *72:* 101
Glattauer, Ned *5:* 84; *13:* 224; *14:* 26
Glauber, Uta *17:* 76
Gleeson, J.M. *YABC 2:* 207
Glegg, Creina *36:* 100
Glienke, Amelie *63:* 150
Gliewe, Unada *3:* 78, 79; *21:* 73; *30:* 220
Gliori, Debi *72:* 91; *138:* 82; *162:* 37
Glovach, Linda *7:* 105

Gobbato, Imero *3:* 180, 181; *6:* 213; *7:* 58; *9:* 150; *18:* 39; *21:* 167; *39:* 82, 83; *41:* 137, 251; *59:* 177
Goble, Paul *25:* 121; *26:* 86; *33:* 65; *69:* 68, 69; *131:* 79, 80
Goble, Warwick *46:* 78, 79
Godal, Eric *36:* 93
Godkin, Celia *145:* 84, 86
Godfrey, Michael *17:* 279
Godon, Ingrid *166:* 163
Goembel, Ponder *42:* 124
Goffe, Toni *61:* 83, 84, 85; *89:* 11; *90:* 124; *178:* 118
Goffstein, M.B. *8:* 71; *70:* 75, 76, 77
Golbin, Andre *15:* 125
Gold, Robert *166:* 151, 152
Goldfeder, Cheryl *11:* 191
Goldsborough, June *5:* 154, 155; *8:* 92, *14:* 226; *19:* 139; *54:* 165
Goldsmith, Robert *110:* 77
Goldstein, Leslie *5:* 8; *6:* 60; *10:* 106
Goldstein, Nathan *1:* 175; *2:* 79; *11:* 41, 232; *16:* 55
Goldstrom, Robert *98:* 36; *145:* 51, 52
Golembe, Carla *79:* 80, 81; *136:* 91; *144:* 113
Golin, Carlo *74:* 112
Gomez, Elizabeth *127:* 70; *133:* 76
Gomi, Taro *64:* 102; *103:* 74, 76
Gon, Adriano *101:* 112
Gonsalve, Ron *178:* 213
Gonzalez, Maya Christina *104:* 3; *136:* 92
Goodall, John S. *4:* 92, 93; *10:* 132; *66:* 92, 93; *YABC 1:* 198
Goode, Diane *15:* 126; *50:* 183; *52:* 114, 115; *76:* 195; *84:* 94; *99:* 141; *114:* 76, 77, 78; *170:* 99, 101
Goodelman, Aaron *40:* 203
Goodenow, Earle *40:* 97
Goodfellow, Peter *62:* 95; *94:* 202
Goodman, Joan Elizabeth *50:* 86
Goodman, Vivienne *82:* 251; *146:* 181, 182
Goodnow, Patti *117:* 33
Goodwin, Harold *13:* 74
Goodwin, Philip R. *18:* 206
Goor, Nancy *39:* 85, 86
Goor, Ron *39:* 85, 86
Gorbachev, Valeri *89:* 96; *112:* 97; *143:* 63, 64
Gordon, Gwen *12:* 151
Gordon, Margaret *4:* 147; *5:* 48, 49; *9:* 79
Gordon, Mike *101:* 62, 63, 64
Gordon, Russell *204:* *137:* 214
Gordon, Walter *138:* 9
Gore, Leonid *89:* 51; *94:* 74; *136:* 8; *158:* 117; *166:* 136; *168:* 36; *170:* 107; *181:* 94
Gorecka-Egan, Erica *18:* 35
Gorey, Edward *1:* 60, 61; *13:* 169; *18:* 192; *20:* 201; *29:* 90, 91, 92, 93, 94, 95, 96, 97, 98, 99, 100; *30:* 129; *32:* 90; *34:* 200, 65: 48; *68:* 24, 25; *69:* 79; *70:* 80, 82, 83, 84, 85; *136:* *127:* 62
Gorsline, Douglas *1:* 98; *6:* 13; *11:* 113; *13:* 104; *15:* 14; *28:* 117, 118; *YABC 1:* 15
Gorton, Julia *108:* 94; *178:* 81, 82
Gosfield, Josh *118:* 165, 166; *149:* 67
Gosner, Kenneth *5:* 135
Gosney, Joy *167:* 142
Gotlieb, Jules *6:* 127
Goto, Scott *115:* 86; *136:* 69
Gottlieb, Dale *67:* 162; *107:* 16; *149:* 6
Goudey, Ray *97:* 86
Gough, Alan *91:* 57
Gough, Philip *23:* 47; *45:* 90
Gould, Chester *49:* 112, 113, 114, 116, 117, 118
Gould, Jason *151:* 232
Gourbault, Martine *177:* 159
Govern, Elaine R. *26:* 94
Gower, Teri *102:* 184
Gowing, Toby *60:* 25; *63:* 33; *78:* 70, 252; *83:* 228; *86:* 187; *93:* 145; *108:* 133; *110:* 217
Grabianski *20:* 144

Grabianski, Janusz *39:* 92, 93, 94, 95
Graboff, Abner *35:* 103, 104
Graef, Renee *61:* 188; *72:* 207
Grafe, Max *156:* 173; *178:* 237
Graham, A.B. *11:* 61
Graham, Bob *101:* 66, 67, 68; *151:* 74, 75
Graham, L. *7:* 108
Graham, Margaret Bloy *11:* 120; *18:* 305, 307
Graham, Mark *88:* 208; *159:* 153
Grahame-Johnstone, Janet *13:* 61
Grahame-Johnstone, Anne *13:* 61
Grainger, Sam *42:* 95
Gralley, Jean *166:* 86
Gramatky, Hardie *1:* 107; *30:* 116, 119, 120, 122, 123
Gran, Julie *168:* 118
Granahan, Julie *84:* 84
GrandPré, Mary *84:* 131; *109:* 199; *118:* 76; *180:* 65
Grandström, Brita *176:* 139
Grandville, J.J. *45:* 81, 82, 83, 84, 85, 86, 87, 88; *47:* 125; *64:* 10
Granger, Paul *39:* 153
Granström, Brita *162:* 35; *167:* 46
Grant, (Alice) Leigh *10:* 52; *15:* 131; *20:* 20; *26:* 119; *48:* 202
Grant, Gordon *17:* 230, 234; *25:* 123, 124, 125, 126; *52:* 69; *YABC 1:* 164
Grant, Melvyn *159:* 186, 187; *170:* 48, 49
Grant, Renee *77:* 40
Grant, Shirley *109:* 45
Graves, Elizabeth *45:* 101
Graves, Keith *167:* 89
Gray, Harold *33:* 87, 88
Gray, Les *82:* 76; *83:* 232
Gray, Reginald *6:* 69
Greder, Armin *76:* 235
Green, Ann Canevari *62:* 48
Green, Eileen *6:* 97
Green, Elizabeth Shippen *139:* 109
Green, Jonathan *86:* 135; *105:* 109
Green, Ken *111:* 68
Green, Michael *32:* 216
Green, Robina *87:* 138
Green, Jonathan *157:* 105
Greene, Jeffrey *117:* 93
Greenaway, Kate *17:* 275; *24:* 180; *26:* 107; *41:* 222, 232; *100:* 115, 116; *YABC 1:* 88, 89; *2:* 131, 133, 136, 138, 139, 141
Greenberg, Melanie Hope *72:* 93; *80:* 125; *101:* 174; *133:* 180
Greenseid, Diane *178:* 106, 107
Greenstein, Elaine *150:* 100
Greenwald, Sheila *1:* 34; *3:* 99; *8:* 72
Greger, Carol *76:* 86
Gregorian, Joyce Ballou *30:* 125
Gregory, Emilian *177:* 146
Gregory, Fran *130:* 4; *140:* 93
Gregory, Frank M. *29:* 107
Greiffenhagen, Maurice *16:* 137; *27:* 57; *YABC 2:* 288
Greiner, Robert *6:* 86
Gretter, J. Clemens *31:* 134
Gretz, Susanna *7:* 114
Gretzer, John *1:* 54; *3:* 26; *4:* 162; *7:* 125; *16:* 247; *18:* 117; *28:* 66; *30:* 85, 211; *33:* 235; *56:* 16
Grey, Mini *166:* 90
Grey Owl *24:* 41
Gri *25:* 90
Grieder, Walter *9:* 84
Griesbach/Martucci *59:* 3
Grifalconi, Ann *2:* 126; *3:* 248; *11:* 18; *13:* 182; *46:* 38; *50:* 145; *66:* 99, 100, 101, 104, 106; *69:* 38; *70:* 64; *87:* 128; *90:* 53; *93:* 49; *128:* 48; *133:* 79, 81
Griffin, Gillett Good *26:* 96
Griffin, James *30:* 166
Griffin, John Howard *59:* 186
Griffin, Rachel *131:* 23
Griffith, Gershom *94:* 214

Griffiths, Dave 29: 76
Griffiths, Dean 168: 180; 169: 182
Grimsdell, Jeremy 83: 75
Grimwood, Brian 82: 89
Gringhuis, Dirk 6: 98; 9: 196
Gripe, Harald 2: 127; 74: 98
Grisha 3: 71
Grohmann, Susan 84: 97
Gropper, William 27: 93; 37: 193
Gros 60: 199
Grose, Helen Mason YABC 1: 260; 2: 150
Grossman, Nancy 24: 130; 29: 101
Grossman, Robert 11: 124; 46: 39
Groth, John 15: 79; 21: 53, 54; 83: 230
Grover, Lorie Ann 168: 59
Grubb, Lisa 160: 116
Gruelle, Johnny 35: 107
Gschwind, William 11: 72
Guay-Mitchell, Rebecca 110: 95, 96; 135: 240;
  180: 76; 181: 71, 73
Guback, Georgia 88: 102
Guerguerion, Claudine 105: 73
Guevara, Susan 97: 87; 167: 49
Guggenheim, Hans 2: 10; 3: 37; 8: 136
Guida, Lisa Chauncy 172: 188
Guilbeau, Honore 22: 69
Guillette, Joseph 137: 37
Guisewite, Cathy 57: 52, 53, 54, 56, 57
Gukova, Julia 95: 104; 154: 103; 168: 195
Gundersheimer, Karen 35: 240; 82: 100
Gunderson, Nick 57: 120
Gurney, James 76: 97; 86: 32
Gurney, John Steven 75: 39, 82; 110: 175;
  143: 67, 68; 169: 172
Gusman, Annie 38: 62
Gustafson, Scott 34: 111; 43: 40
Gustavson, Adam 104: 10; 171: 183; 176: 87
Guthridge, Bettina 108: 79
Guthrie, R. Dale 64: 143
Guthrie, Robin 20: 122
Gutierrez, Akemi 172: 87
Gutierrez, Alan 136: 31, 32
Gutierrez, Rudy 97: 162
Gutmann, Bessie Pease 73: 93, 94
Gwynne, Fred 41: 94, 95
Gyberg, Bo-Erik 38: 131

H

Haas, Irene 17: 77; 87: 46; 96: 117
Hack, Konrad 51: 127
Hader, Berta H. 16: 126
Hader, Elmer S. 16: 126
Haeffele, Deborah 76: 99
Haemer, Alan 62: 109
Hafner, Marylin 22: 196, 216; 24: 44; 30: 51;
  35: 95; 51: 25, 160, 164; 86: 16; 105: 196;
  121: 93, 94; 149: 208, 209; 179: 82, 83, 84,
  115
Hagerty, Sean 62: 181
Hague, Michael 32: 128; 48: 98, 99, 100, 101,
  103, 105, 106, 107, 108, 109, 110; 49: 121;
  51: 105; 64: 14, 15; 79: 134; 80: 91, 92; 83:
  135; 100: 241; 102: 29; 129: 101, 103, 104
Hair, Jonathan 115: 135
Halas, John 29: 41, 47, 48
Haldane, Roger 13: 76; 14: 202
Hale, Christy 79: 124; 84: 200; 114: 201; 128:
  2, 3; 146: 203; 158: 243; 167: 99; 179: 87
Hale, Irina 26: 97
Hale, James Graham 88: 207
Hale, Kathleen 17: 79; 66: 114, 116, 118
Haley, Gail E. 43: 102, 103, 104, 105; 78: 65,
  67; 136: 106, 107
Hall, Amanda 96: 110
Hall, Chuck 30: 189
Hall, Douglas 15: 184; 43: 106, 107; 86: 100;
  87: 82; 129: 72
Hall, H. Tom 1: 227; 30: 210

Hall, Melanie 116: 48, 49; 169: 77, 78
Hall, Sydney P. 31: 89
Hall, Tim 164: 196
Hall, Vicki 20: 24
Hallinan, P.K. 39: 98
Hallman, Tom 98: 166
Hally, Greg 101: 200; 151: 224
Halperin, Wendy Anderson 96: 151; 125: 96,
  97, 98, 99; 139: 22; 140: 84
Halpern, Joan 10: 25
Halpern, Shari 174: 172
Halsey, Megan 96: 172; 114: 185; 180: 8
Halstead, Virginia 125: 105
Halverson, Janet 49: 38, 42, 44
Hallensleben, Georg 134: 5, 6; 172: 17
Hamanaka, Sheila 71: 100
Hamann, Brad 78: 151
Hamann, Sigune 104: 115
Hamberger, John 6: 8; 8: 32; 14: 79; 34: 136;
  88: 78
Hamil, Tom 14: 80; 43: 163
Hamilton, Bill and Associates 26: 215
Hamilton, Helen S. 2: 238
Hamilton, J. 19: 83, 85, 87
Hamilton, Laurie 116: 210
Hamilton, Todd Cameron 84: 15
Hamlin, Janet 97: 136; 124: 90; 137: 157
Hamlin, Louise 71: 135
Hammond, Chris 21: 37
Hammond, Elizabeth 5: 36, 203
Hampshire, Michael 5: 187; 7: 110, 111; 48:
  150; 51: 129
Hampson, Denman 10: 155; 15: 130
Hampton, Blake 41: 244
Handford, Martin 64: 105, 106, 107, 109
Handforth, Thomas 42: 100, 101, 102, 103,
  104, 105, 107
Handville, Robert 1: 89; 38: 76; 45: 108, 109
Hane, Roger 17: 239; 44: 54
Haney, Elizabeth Mathieu 34: 84
Hanke, Ted 71: 10
Hankinson, Phil 181: 164
Hanley, Catherine 8: 161
Hann, Jacquie 19: 144
Hanna, Cheryl 91: 133
Hanna, Wayne A. 67: 145
Hannon, Mark 38: 37
Hansen, Gabby 159: 11
Hansen, Mia 149: 76
Hanson, Joan 8: 76; 11: 139
Hanson, Peter E. 52: 47; 54: 99, 100; 73: 21;
  84: 79; 116: 144
Hansson, Gunilla 64: 111, 112
Hardcastle, Nick 121: 82; 175: 185
Hardy, David A. 9: 96; 119: 74
Hardy, Paul YABC 2: 245 Haring, Keith 145:
  65
Harlan, Jerry 3: 96
Harlin, Greg 89: 194; 103: 82; 118: 161; 121:
  167
Harness, Cheryl 106: 80; 131: 87; 178: 111
Harnischfeger 18: 121
Harper, Arthur YABC 2: 121
Harper, Betty 126: 90
Harper, Jamie 174: 71
Harper, Piers 79: 27; 105: 102; 161: 67
Harrington, Glenn 82: 18; 94: 66, 68
Harrington, Jack 83: 162
Harrington, Richard 5: 81
Harris, Jim 127: 130
Harris, John 83: 25
Harris, Nick 86: 177
Harris, Susan Yard 42: 121
Harrison, Florence 20: 150, 152
Harrison, Harry 4: 103
Harrison, Jack 28: 149
Harrison, Mark 105: 157; 165: 190
Harrison, Ted 56: 73
Harsh, Fred 72: 107
Harston, Jerry 105: 143
Hart, Lewis 98: 115

Hart, Thomas 181: 165
Hart, William 13: 72
Hartland, Jessie 171: 80, 81
Hartung, Susan Kathleen 150: 107, 108; 173:
  106; 175: 106
Hartelius, Margaret 10: 24
Hartshorn, Ruth 5: 115; 11: 129
Harvey, Amanda 145: 44
Harvey, Bob 48: 219
Harvey, Gerry 7: 180
Harvey, Lisa 97: 21
Harvey, Paul 88: 74
Harvey, Roland 71: 88; 123: 63; 179: 94
Hassall, Joan 43: 108, 109
Hassall, Hilton YABC 1: 187
Hassett, John 162: 59
Hasselriis, Else 18: 87; YABC 1: 96
Hastings, Glenn 89: 183
Hastings, Ian 62: 67
Hauman, Doris 2: 184; 29: 58, 59; 32: 85, 86,
  87
Hauman, George 2: 184; 29: 58, 59; 32: 85,
  86, 87
Hausherr, Rosmarie 15: 29
Hawkes, Kevin 78: 72; 104: 198; 105: 197;
  112: 109; 126: 87; 144: 88; 149: 210; 150:
  110, 135; 156: 94; 164: 35
Hawkins, Jacqui 112: 86; 162: 64
Hawkinson, John 4: 109; 7: 83; 21: 64
Hawkinson, Lucy 21: 64
Hawthorne, Mike 140: 228
Haxton, Elaine 28: 131
Haydock, Robert 4: 95
Hayes, Geoffrey 26: 111; 44: 133; 91: 85
Haynes, Max 72: 107
Hays, Michael 73: 207; 83: 93; 139: 197; 146:
  202, 250
Haywood, Carolyn 1: 112; 29: 104
Heale, Jonathan 104: 117
Healy, Daty 12: 143
Healy, Deborah 58: 181, 182; 101: 111
Heap, Sue 102: 207; 150: 113, 114
Hearn, Diane Dawson 79: 99; 113: 13
Hearon, Dorothy 34: 69
Heaslip, William 57: 24, 25
Hechtkopf, H. 11: 110
Heck, Ed 173: 81
Hedderwick, Mairi 30: 127; 32: 47; 36: 104;
  77: 86; 145: 91, 93, 95
Hefferman, Phil 146: 197
Hefter, Richard 28: 170; 31: 81, 82; 33: 183
Hehenberger, Shelly 126: 91
Heigh, James 22: 98
Heighway, Richard 25: 160; 64: 4
Heighway-Bury, Robin 159: 89
Heine, Helme 67: 86; 135: 91, 92
Heinly, John 45: 113
Hellard, Susan 81: 21
Hellebrand, Nancy 26: 57
Heller, Linda 46: 86
Heller, Ruth M. 66: 125; 77: 30, 32
Hellmuth, Jim 38: 164
Helms, Georgeann 33: 62
Helquist, Brett 142: 203; 146: 133, 134; 156:
  10; 173: 25; 180: 106
Helweg, Hans 41: 118; 50: 93; 58: 22, 26
Hemphill, Helen 179: 95
Henba, Bobbie 90: 195
Henderson, Dave 73: 76; 75: 191, 192, 193,
  194; 82: 4
Henderson, Douglas 103: 68
Henderson, Kathy 55: 32; 155: 118
Henderson, Keith 35: 122
Henderson, Meryl 127: 58, 60; 169: 81
Hendry, Linda 80: 104; 83: 83; 164: 216
Hengeveld, Dennis 142: 86
Henkes, Kevin 43: 111; 108: 106, 107, 108
Henneberger, Robert 1: 42; 2: 237; 25: 83
Henriksen, Harold 35: 26; 48: 68
Henriquez, Celeste 103: 137
Henriquez, Elsa 82: 260

Henriquez, Emile F. *89:* 88
Henry, Everett *29:* 191
Henry, Matthew *117:* 58
Henry, Paul *93:* 121
Henry, Thomas *5:* 102
Hensel *27:* 119
Henshaw, Jacqui *141:* 127
Henstra, Friso *8:* 80; *36:* 70; *40:* 222; *41:* 250; *73:* 100, 101
Henterly, Jamichael *93:* 4
Heo, Yumi *89:* 85, 86; *94:* 89, 90; *146:* 40, 137, 138; *163:* 227
Hepple, Norman *28:* 198
Herbert, Helen *57:* 70
Herbert, Wally *23:* 101
Herbster, Mary Lee *9:* 33
Herge
    See Remi, Georges
Hermansen, Pal *133:* 113
Hermanson, Dennis *10:* 55
Hermes, Gertrude *54:* 161
Herr, Margo *57:* 191
Herr, Susan *83:* 163
Herriman, George *140:* 74, 75, 76, 77, 78
Herriman, Lisa *87:* 190
Herring, Michael *121:* 76
Herrington, Roger *3:* 161
Herscovici, C. *165:* 240
Hescox, Richard *85:* 86; *90:* 30; *139:* 35
Heslop, Mike *38:* 60; *40:* 130
Hess, Lydia J. *85:* 17
Hess, Mark *111:* 146; *113:* 207
Hess, Paul *134:* 47; *166:* 133
Hess, Richard *42:* 31
Hester, Ronnie *37:* 85
Heuser, Olga J. *121:* 116
Heusser, Sibylle *168:* 195
Heustis, Louise L. *20:* 28
Hewitson, Jennifer *74:* 119; *124:* 167
Hewitt, Kathryn *80:* 126; *149:* 105
Hewitt, Margaret *84:* 112
Heyduck-Huth, Hilde *8:* 82
Heyer, Carol *74:* 122; *130:* 72, 73
Heyer, Hermann *20:* 114, 115
Heyer, Marilee *102:* 108
Heyman, Ken *8:* 33; *34:* 113
Heyne, Ulrike *146:* 151
Heywood, Karen *48:* 114
Hickling, P.B. *40:* 165
Hickman, Stephen *85:* 58; *136:* 33; *171:* 128
Hierstein, Judy *56:* 40; *162:* 168
Higashi, Sandra *154:* 59, 60
Higginbottom, J. Winslow *8:* 170; *29:* 105, 106
Higgins, Chester *101:* 79
Higham, David *50:* 104
Hilb, Nora *176:* 8
Hildebrandt, Greg *8:* 191; *55:* 35, 36, 38, 39, 40, 42, 46; *172:* 110
Hildebrandt, Tim *8:* 191; *55:* 44, 45, 46
Hilder, Rowland *19:* 207
Hill, Eric *66:* 127, 128; *133:* 91
Hill, Gregory *35:* 190
Hill, Pat *49:* 120
Hillenbrand, Will *84:* 115; *92:* 76, 80; *93:* 131; *104:* 168; *128:* 137; *145:* 187; *146:* 184; *147:* 105, 106, 107; *152:* 59
Hillier, Matthew *45:* 205
Hillman, Priscilla *48:* 115
Hills, Tad *113:* 4; *137:* 147; *173:* 83
Himler, Ronald *6:* 114; *7:* 162; *8:* 17, 84, 125; *14:* 76; *19:* 145; *26:* 160; *31:* 43; *38:* 116; *41:* 44, 79; *43:* 52; *45:* 120; *46:* 43; *54:* 44, 83; *58:* 180; *59:* 38; *68:* 146; *69:* 231; *70:* 98; *71:* 177, 178; *77:* 219; *79:* 212; *83:* 62; *89:* 5; *91:* 160; *92:* 91, 92, 93; *94:* 93; *95:* 69, 174, 194; *99:* 99, 112; *113:* 92; *118:* 114; *137:* 73, 74, 77, 167; *163:* 99; *165:* 138; *178:* 9, 220
Himmelman, John *47:* 109; *65:* 87; *94:* 96, 97; *159:* 85

Hinds, Bill *37:* 127, 130
Hines, Anna Grossnickle *51:* 90; *74:* 124; *95:* 78, 79, 80, 81
Hines, Bob *135:* 149, 150
Hiroko *99:* 61
Hiroshige *25:* 71
Hirsh, Marilyn *7:* 126
Hiscock, Bruce *137:* 80, 81
Hissey, Jane *103:* 90; *130:* 81
Hitch, Jeff *99:* 206; *128:* 86
Hitz, Demi *11:* 135; *15:* 245; *66:* 129, 130; *152:* 94, 95
Hnizdovsky, Jacques *32:* 96; *76:* 187
Ho, Kwoncjan *15:* 132
Hoban, Lillian *1:* 114; *22:* 157; *26:* 72; *29:* 53; *40:* 105, 107, 195; *41:* 80; *69:* 107, 108; *71:* 98; *77:* 168; *106:* 50; *113:* 86; *136:* 118
Hoban, Tana *22:* 159; *104:* 82, 83, 85
Hobbs, Leigh *166:* 95
Hoberman, Norman *5:* 82
Hobson, Sally *77:* 185
Hockerman, Dennis *39:* 22; *56:* 23
Hodgell, P.C. *42:* 114
Hodges, C. Walter *2:* 139; *11:* 15; *12:* 25; *23:* 34; *25:* 96; *38:* 165; *44:* 197; *45:* 95; *100:* 57; *YABC 2:* 62, 63
Hodges, David *9:* 98
Hodgetts, Victoria *43:* 132
Hofbauer, Imre *2:* 162
Hoff, Syd *9:* 107; *10:* 128; *33:* 94; *72:* 115, 116, 117, 118; *138:* 114, 115
Hoffman, Rosekrans *15:* 133; *50:* 219; *63:* 97
Hoffman, Sanford *38:* 208; *76:* 174; *88:* 160, 161; *151:* 156
Hoffmann, Felix *9:* 109
Hoffnung, Gerard *66:* 76, 77
Hofsinde, Robert *21:* 70
Hogan, Inez *2:* 141
Hogarth, Burne *41:* 58; *63:* 46, 48, 49, 50, 52, 53, 54, 55, 56
Hogarth, Paul *41:* 102, 103, 104; *YABC 1:* 16
Hogarth, William *42:* 33
Hogenbyl, Jan *1:* 35
Hogner, Nils *4:* 122; *25:* 144
Hogrogian, Nonny *3:* 221; *4:* 106, 107; *5:* 166; *7:* 129; *15:* 2; *16:* 176; *20:* 154; *22:* 146; *25:* 217; *27:* 206; *74:* 127, 128, 129, 149, 152; *127:* 99; *YABC 2:* 84, 94
Hokanson, Lars *93:* 111; *172:* 137
Hokusai *25:* 71
Hol, Colby *126:* 96
Holberg, Richard *2:* 51
Holbrook, Kathy *107:* 114
Holdcroft, Tina *38:* 109
Holden, Caroline *55:* 159
Holder, Heidi *36:* 99; *64:* 9
Holder, Jimmy *151:* 224
Holiday, Henry *YABC 2:* 107
Holl, F. *36:* 91
Holland, Brad *45:* 59, 159
Holland, Gay W. *128:* 105
Holland, Janice *18:* 118
Holland, Marion *6:* 116
Holldobler, Turid *26:* 120
Holliday, Keaf *144:* 236
Holling, Holling C. *15:* 136, 137
Hollinger, Deanne *12:* 116
Holm, Sharon Lane *114:* 84; *115:* 52
Holmes, B. *3:* 82
Holmes, Bea *7:* 74; *24:* 156; *31:* 93
Holmes, Dave *54:* 22
Holmes, Lesley *135:* 96
Holmgren, George Ellen *45:* 112
Holmlund, Heather D. *150:* 140
Holt, Norma *44:* 106
Holt, Pater *151:* 188
Holtan, Gene *32:* 192
Holub, Joan *149:* 72
Holyfield, John *149:* 231
Holz, Loretta *17:* 81
Hom, Nancy *79:* 195

Homar, Lorenzo *6:* 2
Homer, Winslow *128:* 8; *YABC 2:* 87
Honey, Elizabeth *112:* 95, 96; *137:* 93, 94
Honeywood, Varnette P. *110:* 68, 70
Hong, Lily Toy *76:* 104
Honigman, Marian *3:* 2
Honore, Paul *42:* 77, 79, 81, 82
Hood, Alun *69:* 145, 218; *72:* 41; *80:* 226; *87:* 4; *95:* 139
Hood, Susan *12:* 43
Hook, Christian *104:* 103
Hook, Frances *26:* 188; *27:* 127
Hook, Jeff *14:* 137; *103:* 105
Hook, Richard *26:* 188
Hooks *63:* 30
Hooper, Hadley *177:* 145
Hoover, Carol A. *21:* 77
Hoover, Russell *12:* 95; *17:* 2; *34:* 156
Hope, James *141:* 116
Hopkins, Chris *99:* 127
Hopman, Philip *178:* 184
Hoppin, Augustus *34:* 66
Horacek, Petr *163:* 117
Horder, Margaret *2:* 108; *73:* 75
Horne, Daniel *73:* 106; *91:* 153; *109:* 127; *110:* 232; *164:* 176
Horne, Richard *111:* 80
Horse, Harry *128:* 195; *169:* 86
Horvat, Laurel *12:* 201
Horvath, Ferdinand Kusati *24:* 176
Horvath, Maria *57:* 171
Horwitz, Richard *57:* 174
Hotchkiss, De Wolfe *20:* 49
Hough, Charlotte *9:* 112; *13:* 98; *17:* 83; *24:* 195
Houlihan, Ray *11:* 214
Housman, Laurence *25:* 146, 147
Houston, James *13:* 107; *74:* 132, 134, 135
Hovland, Gary *88:* 172; *171:* 148
Hoyt, Eleanor *158:* 231
How, W.E. *20:* 47
Howard, Alan *16:* 80; *34:* 58; *45:* 114
Howard, Arthur *165:* 111, 112
Howard, J.N. *15:* 234
Howard, John *33:* 179
Howard, Kim *116:* 71
Howard, Paul *142:* 126, 129; *144:* 187
Howard, Rob *40:* 161
Howarth, Daniel *170:* 34
Howe, John *115:* 47; *176:* 106
Howe, John F. *79:* 101; *80:* 150
Howe, Phillip *79:* 117; *175:* 115
Howe, Stephen *1:* 232
Howell, Karen *119:* 123
Howell, Pat *15:* 139
Howell, Troy *23:* 24; *31:* 61; *36:* 158; *37:* 184; *41:* 76, 235; *48:* 112; *56:* 13; *57:* 3; *59:* 174; *63:* 5; *74:* 46; *89:* 188; *90:* 231; *95:* 97; *98:* 130; *99:* 189; *153:* 156, 157, 158; *176:* 104
Howes, Charles *22:* 17
Hoyt, Ard *145:* 141
Hranilovich, Barbara *127:* 51
Hu, Ying-Hwa *116:* 107; *152:* 236; *173:* 171
Huang, Benrei *137:* 55
Huang, Zhong-Yang *117:* 30, 32
Hubbard, Woodleigh Marx *98:* 67; *115:* 79; *160:* 138
Hubley, Faith *48:* 120, 121, 125, 130, 131, 132, 134
Hubley, John *48:* 125, 130, 131, 132, 134
Hudak, Michal *143:* 74
Hudnut, Robin *14:* 62
Huerta, Catherine *76:* 178; *77:* 44, 45; *90:* 182
Huffaker, Sandy *10:* 56
Huffman, Joan *13:* 33
Huffman, Tom *13:* 180; *17:* 212; *21:* 116; *24:* 132; *33:* 154; *38:* 59; *42:* 147
Hughes, Arthur *20:* 148, 149, 150; *33:* 114, 148, 149

Hughes, Darren *95:* 44
Hughes, David *36:* 197
Hughes, Shirley *1:* 20, 21; *7:* 3; *12:* 217; *16:* 163; *29:* 154; *63:* 118; *70:* 102, 103, 104; *73:* 169; *88:* 70; *110:* 118, 119; *159:* 103
Hugo, Victor *47:* 112
Hull, Cathy *78:* 29
Hull, Richard *95:* 120; *123:* 175; *172:* 195
Hulsmann, Eva *16:* 166
Hummel, Berta *43:* 137, 138, 139
Hummel, Lisl *29:* 109; *YABC 2:* 333, 334
Humphrey, Henry *16:* 167
Humphreys, Graham *25:* 168
Humphries, Tudor *76:* 66; *80:* 4; *124:* 4, 5
Hunt, James *2:* 143
Hunt, Jonathan *84:* 120
Hunt, Paul *119:* 104; *129:* 135; *139:* 160; *173:* 112
Hunt, Robert *110:* 206, 235; *147:* 136, 137; *170:* 3
Hunter, Anne *133:* 190; *178:* 150
Huntington, Amy *180:* 99
Hurd, Clement *2:* 148, 149; *64:* 127, 128, 129, 131, 133, 134, 135, 136; *100:* 37, 38
Hurd, Peter *24:* 30, 31,; *YABC 2:* 56
Hurd, Thacher *46:* 88, 89; *94:* 114, 115, 116; *123:* 81, 82, 84
Hurlimann, Ruth *32:* 99
Hussar, Michael *114:* 113; *117:* 159
Hustler, Tom *6:* 105
Hutchins, Laurence *55:* 22
Hutchins, Pat *15:* 142; *70:* 106, 107, 108; *178:* 131, 132
Hutchinson, Sascha *95:* 211
Hutchinson, William M. *6:* 3, 138; *46:* 70
Hutchison, Paula *23:* 10
Hutton, Clarke *YABC 2:* 335
Hutton, Kathryn *35:* 155; *89:* 91
Hutton, Warwick *20:* 91
Huyette, Marcia *29:* 188
Hyatt, John *54:* 7
Hyatt, Mitch *178:* 162
Hyde, Maureen *82:* 17; *121:* 145, 146
Hyman, David *117:* 64
Hyman, Trina Schart *1:* 204; *2:* 194; *5:* 153; *6:* 106; *7:* 138, 145; *8:* 22; *10:* 196; *13:* 96; *14:* 114; *15:* 204; *16:* 234; *20:* 82; *22:* 133; *24:* 151; *25:* 79, 82; *26:* 82; *29:* 83; *31:* 37, 39; *34:* 104; *38:* 84, 100, 128; *41:* 49; *43:* 146; *46:* 91, 92, 93, 95, 96, 97, 98, 99, 100, 101, 102, 103, 104, 105, 108, 109, 111, 197; *48:* 60, 61; *52:* 32; *60:* 168; *66:* 38; *67:* 214; *72:* 74; *75:* 92; *79:* 57; *82:* 95, 238; *89:* 46; *95:* 91, 92, 93; *100:* 33, 199; *132:* 12; *147:* 33, 35, 36; *167:* 58, 60; *177:* 189, 190

I

Ibarra, Rosa *147:* 91
Ibatoulline, Bagram *156:* 48; *174:* 33, 82
Ichikawa, Satomi *29:* 152; *41:* 52; *47:* 133, 134, 135, 136; *78:* 93, 94; *80:* 81; *146:* 143, 145, 146
Ide, Jacqueline *YABC 1:* 39
Ilsley, Velma *3:* 1; *7:* 55; *12:* 109; *37:* 62; *38:* 184
in den Bosch, Nicole *150:* 204
Inga *1:* 142
Ingman, Bruce *134:* 50
Ingpen, Robert *109:* 103, 104; *132:* 138; *137:* 177; *166:* 103; *181:* 140
Ingraham, Erick *21:* 177; *84:* 256; *103:* 66
Inkpen, Mick *99:* 104, 105; *106:* 44
Innerst, Stacy *149:* 104
Innocenti, Roberto *21:* 123; *96:* 122; *159:* 111, 197
Inoue, Yosuke *24:* 118
Iofin, Michael *97:* 157
Iosa, Ann *63:* 189

Ipcar, Dahlov *1:* 124, 125; *49:* 137, 138, 139, 140, 141, 142, 143, 144, 145; *147:* 122, 124, 126
Irvin, Fred *13:* 166; *15:* 143, 144; *27:* 175
Irving, Jay *45:* 72
Irving, Laurence *27:* 50
Isaac, Joanne *21:* 76
Isaacs, Gary *170:* 188
Isadora, Rachel *43:* 159, 160; *54:* 31; *79:* 106, 107, 108; *121:* 100, 102; *165:* 116, 117
Ishmael, Woodi *24:* 111; *31:* 99
Ives, Ruth *15:* 257
Iwai, Melissa *149:* 233

J

Jabar, Cynthia *101:* 201
Jackness, Andrew *94:* 237
Jackson, Julian *91:* 104, 106
Jackson, Michael *43:* 42
Jackson, Shelley *79:* 71; *99:* 109
Jacob, Murv *89:* 30
Jacobi, Kathy *62:* 118
Jacobs, Barbara *9:* 136
Jacobs, Lou, Jr. *9:* 136; *15:* 128
Jacobsen, Laura *176:* 98; *177:* 85, 86
Jacobson, Rick *131:* 222; *170:* 119
Jacobus, Tim *79:* 140; *109:* 126; *129:* 180
Jacques, Robin *1:* 70; *2:* 1; *8:* 46; *9:* 20; *15:* 187; *19:* 253; *32:* 102, 103, 104; *43:* 184; *73:* 135; *YABC 1:* 42
Jaffee, Al *66:* 131, 132
Jagr, Miloslav *13:* 197
Jahn-Clough, Lisa *88:* 114; *152:* 104
Jahnke, Robert *84:* 24
Jainschigg, Nicholas *80:* 64; *91:* 138; *95:* 63; *99:* 25; *108:* 50; *171:* 41
Jakesavic, Nenad *85:* 102
Jakobsen, Kathy *116:* 83
Jakubowski, Charles *14:* 192
Jambor, Louis *YABC 1:* 11
James, Ann *73:* 50; *82:* 113; *158:* 61
James, Brian *140:* 91
James, Derek *35:* 187; *44:* 91; *61:* 133; *74:* 2; *80:* 57; *86:* 88; *130:* 30; *179:* 29
James, Gilbert *YABC 1:* 43
James, Harold *2:* 151; *3:* 62; *8:* 79; *29:* 113; *51:* 195; *74:* 90
James, Kennon *126:* 211
James, Robin *50:* 106; *53:* 32, 34, 35
James, Will *19:* 150, 152, 153, 155, 163
Janosch
   See Eckert, Horst
Janovitch, Marilyn *68:* 168
Janovitz, Marilyn *87:* 187; *130:* 198
Jansons, Inese *48:* 117
Jansson, Tove *3:* 90; *41:* 106, 108, 109, 110, 111, 113, 114
Jaques, Faith *7:* 11, 132, 133; *21:* 83, 84; *69:* 114, 116; *73:* 170
Jaques, Frances Lee *29:* 224
Jauss, Anne Marie *1:* 139; *3:* 34; *10:* 57, 119; *11:* 205; *23:* 194
Jay, Alison *158:* 97, 98
Jeffers, Oliver *175:* 111
Jeffers, Susan *17:* 86, 87; *25:* 164, 165; *26:* 112; *50:* 132, 134, 135; *70:* 111, 112, 113; *137:* 107, 108, 109, 110, 111
Jefferson, Louise E. *4:* 160
Jenkin-Pearce, Susie *78:* 16
Jenkins, Debra Reid *85:* 202; *114:* 89; *173:* 134
Jenkins, Jean *98:* 79, 102
Jenkins, Leonard *157:* 169; *167:* 128
Jenkins, Patrick *72:* 126
Jenkins, Steve *124:* 177; *154:* 90, 91, 92, 93
Jenks, Aleta *73:* 117; *124:* 225
Jenkyns, Chris *51:* 97
Jensen, Bruce *95:* 39

Jensinius, Kirsten *56:* 58
Jeram, Anita *89:* 135; *102:* 122, 123; *129:* 112; *154:* 96, 97, 98; *164:* 154
Jernigan, E. Wesley *85:* 92
Jerome, Karen A. *72:* 194
Jeruchim, Simon *6:* 173; *15:* 250
Jeschke, Susan *20:* 89; *39:* 161; *41:* 84; *42:* 120
Jessel, Camilla *29:* 115
Jessell, Tim *159:* 3; *177:* 87; *181:* 95
Jiang, Cheng An *109:* 108
Jiang, Wei *109:* 108
Jimenez, Maria *77:* 158; *93:* 127
Jobling, Curtis *138:* 74
Jocelyn, Marthe *118:* 83; *137:* 219; *163:* 119, 120
Joerns, Consuelo *38:* 36; *44:* 94
John, Diana *12:* 209
John, Helen *1:* 215; *28:* 204
Johns, Elizabeth *127:* 33
Johns, Jasper *61:* 172
Johns, Jeanne *24:* 114
Johnson, Adrian *143:* 50
Johnson, Bruce *9:* 47
Johnson, Cathy *92:* 136
Johnson, Crockett
   See Leisk, David
Johnson, D. William *23:* 104
Johnson, David *175:* 18
Johnson, Gillian *119:* 175; *164:* 217
Johnson, Harper *1:* 27; *2:* 33; *18:* 302; *19:* 61; *31:* 181; *44:* 46, 50, 95
Johnson, Ingrid *37:* 118
Johnson, James Ralph *1:* 23, 127
Johnson, James David *12:* 195
Johnson, Jane *48:* 136
Johnson, Joel Peter *98:* 18; *128:* 111
Johnson, John E. *34:* 133
Johnson, Kevin *72:* 44
Johnson, Kevin Eugene *109:* 215
Johnson, Larry *47:* 56; *123:* 107; *159:* 203
Johnson, Margaret S. *35:* 131
Johnson, Meredith Merrell *71:* 181; *83:* 158; *89:* 103; *104:* 88
Johnson, Milton *1:* 67; *2:* 71; *26:* 45; *31:* 107; *60:* 112; *68:* 96
Johnson, Pamela *16:* 174; *52:* 145; *62:* 140; *73:* 116; *85:* 64
Johnson, Paul Brett *83:* 95; *132:* 119
Johnson, Stephen T. *80:* 15; *131:* 35; *141:* 96; *145:* 40; *164:* 187; *175:* 32
Johnson, Steve *138:* 219; *141:* 64; *144:* 199; *177:* 51
Johnson, William R. *38:* 91
Johnson-Petrov, Arden *115:* 206
Johnston, David McCall *50:* 131, 133
Johnston, Lynne *118:* 85, 87, 89
Johnstone, Anne *8:* 120; *36:* 89
Johnstone, Janet Grahame *8:* 120; *36:* 89
Jonas, Ann *50:* 107, 108, 109; *135:* 113
Jones, Bob *71:* 5; *77:* 199
Jones, Carol *5:* 131; *72:* 185, 186; *153:* 111, 112
Jones, Chuck *53:* 70, 71
Jones, Davy *89:* 176
Jones, Elizabeth Orton *18:* 124, 126, 128, 129
Jones, Harold *14:* 88; *52:* 50
Jones, Holly *127:* 3
Jones, Jeff *41:* 64
Jones, Laurian *25:* 24, 27
Jones, Margaret *74:* 57
Jones, Randy *131:* 104
Jones, Richard *127:* 222
Jones, Robert *25:* 67
Jones, Wilfred *35:* 115; *YABC 1:* 163
Jordan, Charles *89:* 58
Jordan, Jess *158:* 136
Jordan, Martin George *84:* 127
Jordan, Richard *84:* 36
Jorgenson, Andrea *91:* 111

Jorisch, Stéphane *153:* 56, 193; *177:* 29; *178:* 138, 139
Joseph, James *53:* 88
Joudrey, Ken *64:* 145; *78:* 6
Joyce, William *72:* 131, 132, 133, 134; *73:* 227; *145:* 37
Joyner, Jerry *34:* 138
Juan, Ana *175:* 38; *179:* 111, 112
Jucker, Sita *5:* 93
Judkis, Jim *37:* 38
Juhasz, Victor *31:* 67
Jullian, Philippe *24:* 206; *25:* 203
Jung, Tom *91:* 217
Junge, Walter *67:* 150
Jupo, Frank *7:* 148, 149
Jurisch, Stephane *154:* 105
Justice, Martin *34:* 72

K

Kabatova-Taborska, Zdenka *107:* 153
Kachik, John *165:* 230
Kaczman, James *156:* 98
Kahl, David *74:* 95; *97:* 35; *109:* 174; *110:* 213
Kahl, M.P. *37:* 83
Kahl, Virginia *48:* 138
Kahn, Katherine Janus *90:* 135
Kakimoo, Kozo *11:* 148
Kalett, Jim *48:* 159, 160, 161
Kalin, Victor *39:* 186
Kalman, Maira *96:* 131, 132; *137:* 115
Kalmenoff, Matthew *22:* 191
Kalow, Gisela *32:* 105
Kamen, Gloria *1:* 41; *9:* 119; *10:* 178; *35:* 157; *78:* 236; *98:* 82
Kaminsky, Jef *102:* 153
Kandell, Alice *35:* 133
Kane, Henry B. *14:* 90; *18:* 219, 220
Kane, Robert *18:* 131
Kanfer, Larry *66:* 141
Karalus, Bob *41:* 157
Karas, G. Brian *80:* 60; *99:* 179; *115:* 41; *118:* 50; *136:* 168; *145:* 166; *149:* 245; *159:* 65; *171:* 192; *178:* 142, 143
Karasz, Ilonka *128:* 163
Karlin, Eugene *10:* 63; *20:* 131
Karlin, Nurit *63:* 78; *103:* 110
Karpinski, Tony *134:* 160
Kasamatsu, Shiro *139:* 155
Kasparavicius, Kestutis *139:* 210
Kassian, Olena *64:* 94
Kastner, Jill *79:* 135; *117:* 84, 85
Kasuya, Masahiro *41:* 206, 207; *51:* 100
Katona, Robert *21:* 85; *24:* 126
Katz, Karen *158:* 123
Kauffer, E. McKnight *33:* 103; *35:* 127; *63:* 67
Kaufman, Angelika *15:* 156
Kaufman, Joe *33:* 119
Kaufman, John *13:* 158
Kaufman, Stuart *62:* 64; *68:* 226; *137:* 44
Kaufmann, John *1:* 174; *4:* 159; *8:* 43, 1; *10:* 102; *18:* 133, 134; *22:* 251
Kaye, Graham *1:* 9; *67:* 7, 8
Kaye, M.M. *62:* 95
Kazalovski, Nata *40:* 205
Keane, Bil *4:* 135
Kearney, David *72:* 47; *121:* 83
Keating, Pamel T. *77:* 37
Keats, Ezra Jack *3:* 18, 105, 257; *14:* 101, 102; *33:* 129; *57:* 79, 80, 82, 83, 84, 87
Keegan, Charles *166:* 211
Keegan, Marcia *9:* 122; *32:* 93
Keeler, Patricia A. *81:* 56
Keely, Jack *119:* 95
Keely, John *26:* 104; *48:* 214
Keen, Eliot *25:* 213
Keep, Richard C. *170:* 122

Keeping, Charles *9:* 124, 185; *15:* 28, 134; *18:* 115; *44:* 194, 196; *47:* 25; *52:* 3; *54:* 156; *69:* 123, 124; *74:* 56; *155:* 9
Keeter, Susan *168:* 46
Keith, Eros *4:* 98; *5:* 138; *31:* 29; *43:* 220; *52:* 91, 92, 93, 94; *56:* 64, 66; *60:* 37; *79:* 93
Keleinikov, Andrei *65:* 101, 102
Kelen, Emery *13:* 115
Keller, A.J. *62:* 198
Keller, Arthur I. *26:* 106
Keller, Dick *36:* 123, 125
Keller, Holly *45:* 79; *76:* 118, 119, 120, 121; *108:* 137, 138, 140; *157:* 117, 118, 119
Keller, Katie *79:* 222; *93:* 108
Keller, Ronald *45:* 208
Kelley, True *41:* 114, 115; *42:* 137; *75:* 35; *92:* 104, 105; *124:* 62; *130:* 100, 101; *179:* 120, 121, 122
Kellogg, Steven *8:* 96; *11:* 207; *14:* 130; *20:* 58; *29:* 140, 141; *30:* 35; *41:* 141; *57:* 89, 90, 92, 93, 94, 96; *59:* 182; *73:* 141; *77:* 129; *130:* 105, 106; *177:* 94, 95, 96, 97; *YABC 1:* 65, 73
Kelly, Billy *158:* 143
Kelly, Geoff *97:* 196; *112:* 25
Kelly, Irene *147:* 134
Kelly, Joseph *174:* 94
Kelly, Kathleen M. *71:* 109
Kelly, Laura *89:* 217
Kelly, True *163:* 87
Kelly, Walt *18:* 136, 137, 138, 139, 140, 141, 144, 145, 146, 148, 149
Kemble, E.W. *34:* 75; *44:* 178; *YABC 2:* 54, 59
Kemp-Welsh, Lucy *24:* 197; *100:* 214
Kendall, Jane *150:* 105
Kendall, Peter *152:* 85
Kendrick, Dennis *79:* 213
Kennaway, Adrienne *60:* 55, 56; *171:* 88, 89
Kennedy, Paul Edward *6:* 190; *8:* 132; *33:* 120
Kennedy, Richard *3:* 93; *12:* 179; *44:* 193; *100:* 15; *YABC 1:* 57
Kent, Jack *24:* 136; *37:* 37; *40:* 81; *84:* 89; *86:* 150; *88:* 77
Kent, Rockwell *5:* 166; *6:* 129; *20:* 225, 226, 227, 229; *59:* 144
Kenyon, Tony *81:* 201; *127:* 74
Kepes, Juliet *13:* 119
Kerins, Anthony *76:* 84
Kerr, Judity *24:* 137
Kerr, Phyllis Forbes *72:* 141
Kessler, Leonard *1:* 108; *7:* 139; *14:* 107, 227; *22:* 101; *44:* 96; *67:* 79; *82:* 123
Kest, Kristin *168:* 99; *173:* 23
Kesteven, Peter *35:* 189
Ketcham, Hank *28:* 140, 141, 142
Kettelkamp, Larry *2:* 164
Key, Alexander *8:* 99
Khalsa, Dayal Kaur *62:* 99
Kiakshuk *8:* 59
Kidd, Chip *94:* 23
Kidd, Richard *152:* 110
Kidd, Tom *64:* 199; *81:* 189
Kiddell-Monroe, Joan *19:* 201; *55:* 59, 60; *87:* 174; *121:* 112
Kidder, Harvey *9:* 105; *80:* 41
Kidwell, Carl *43:* 145
Kieffer, Christa *41:* 89
Kiesler, Kate *110:* 105; *136:* 142
Kiff, Ken *40:* 45
Kilbride, Robert *37:* 100
Kilby, Don *141:* 144
Kim, Glenn *99:* 82
Kimball, Anton *78:* 114; *119:* 105
Kimball, Yeffe *23:* 116; *37:* 88
Kimber, Murray *171:* 91
Kimmel, Warren *176:* 112
Kincade, Orin *34:* 116
Kindersley, Barnabas *96:* 110
Kindred, Wendy *7:* 151
King, Colin *53:* 3

King, Robin *10:* 164, 165
King, Stephen Michael *141:* 31
King, Tara Calahan *139:* 172
King, Tony *39:* 121
Kingman, Dong *16:* 287; *44:* 100, 102, 104
Kingsley, Charles *YABC 2:* 182
Kingston, Julie *147:* 14
Kingston, Maxine Hong *53:* 92
Kipling, John Lockwood *YABC 2:* 198
Kipling, Rudyard *YABC 2:* 196
Kipniss, Robert *29:* 59
Kirchherr, Astrid *55:* 23
Kirchhoff, Art *28:* 136
Kirk, Daniel *153:* 115, 116, 117; *173:* 101
Kirk, David *117:* 88, 89; *161:* 97, 98
Kirk, Ruth *5:* 96
Kirk, Steve *170:* 37
Kirk, Tim *32:* 209, 211; *72:* 89; *83:* 49
Kirmse, Marguerite *15:* 283; *18:* 153
Kirsch, Vincent X. *124:* 207
Kirschner, Ruth *22:* 154
Kish, Ely *73:* 119; *79:* 2
Kitamura, Satoshi *62:* 102; *98:* 91; *101:* 147; *138:* 2; *143:* 83, 85, 86
Kiss, Andrew *168:* 115
Kitchel, JoAnn E. *133:* 32
Kitchen, Herbert Thomas *70:* 126
Kittelsen, Theodor *62:* 14
Kiuchi, Tatsuro *114:* 71
Kiwak, Barbara *172:* 135
Klahr, Susan *176:* 196
Klapholz, Mel *13:* 35
Klein, Bill *89:* 105
Klein, Robert *55:* 77
Klein, Suzanna *63:* 104
Kleinman, Zalman *28:* 143
Kleven, Elisa *173:* 96, 97
Kliban, B. *35:* 137, 138
Kline, Michael *127:* 66
Klise, M. Sarah *180:* 117, 118; *181:* 97
Knabel, Lonnie *73:* 103; *75:* 187, 228
Kneen, Maggie *140:* 139
Knight, Ann *34:* 143
Knight, Christopher *13:* 125
Knight, Hilary *1:* 233; *3:* 21; *15:* 92, 158, 159; *16:* 258, 259, 260; *18:* 235; *19:* 169; *35:* 242; *46:* 167; *52:* 116; *69:* 126, 127; *132:* 129; *YABC 1:* 168, 169, 172
Knorr, Peter *126:* 92, 93
Knotts, Howard *20:* 4; *25:* 170; *36:* 163
Knutson, Barbara *112:* 134
Knutson, Kimberley *115:* 90
Kobayashi, Ann *39:* 58
Kocsis, J.C.
    See Paul, James
Koehler, Hanne Lore *176:* 203
Koehn, Ilse *34:* 198; *79:* 123
Koelsch, Michael *99:* 182; *107:* 164; *109:* 239; *138:* 142; *150:* 94; *176:* 105
Koering, Ursula *3:* 28; *4:* 14; *44:* 5; *64:* 140, 141; *85:* 46
Koerner, Henry
    See Koerner, W.H.D.
Koerner, W.H.D. *14:* 216; *21:* 88, 89, 90, 91; *23:* 211
Koetsch, Mike *166:* 68
Koffler, Camilla *36:* 113
Kogan, Deborah Ray *161:* 101, 102
Koide, Yasuko *50:* 114
Kolado, Karen *102:* 228
Komoda, Kiyo *9:* 128; *13:* 214
Kompaneyets, Marc *169:* 92
Konashevich, Vladimir *61:* 160
Konashevicha, V. *YABC 1:* 26
Konigsburg, E.L. *4:* 138; *48:* 141, 142, 144, 145; *94:* 129, 130; *126:* 129, 130, 131
Kono, Erin Eitter *177:* 99
Kooiker, Leonie *48:* 148
Koonook, Simon *65:* 157
Koontz, Robin Michal *136:* 155
Koopmans, Loek *101:* 121

Kopelke, Lisa *154:* 107
Kopper, Lisa *72:* 152, 153; *105:* 135, 136
Korach, Mimi *1:* 128, 129; *2:* 52; *4:* 39; *5:* 159; *9:* 129; *10:* 21; *24:* 69
Koren, Edward *5:* 100; *65:* 65, 67
Kosaka, Fumi *164:* 130
Koscielniak, Bruce *99:* 122; *153:* 120, 121, 122
Koshkin, Alexander *92:* 180
Kossin, Sandy *10:* 71; *23:* 105
Kostin, Andrej *26:* 204
Kosturko, Bob *164:* 56
Kotzky, Brian *68:* 184
Kovacevic, Zivojin *13:* 247
Kovalski, Maryann *58:* 120; *84:* 88; *97:* 124, 125, 126; *158:* 3
Krahn, Fernando *2:* 257; *34:* 206; *49:* 152
Kramer, Anthony *33:* 81
Kramer, David *96:* 162; *109:* 132; *150:* 220
Kramer, Frank *6:* 121
Krantz, Kathy *35:* 83
Kratter, Paul *139:* 65
Kraus, Robert *13:* 217; *65:* 113; *93:* 93, 94
Krause, Jon *176:* 62
Krauss, Trisha *174:* 10
Kredel, Fritz *6:* 35; *17:* 93, 94, 95, 96; *22:* 147; *24:* 175; *29:* 130; *35:* 77; *YABC 2:* 166, 300
Krementz, Jill *17:* 98; *49:* 41
Krenina, Katya *117:* 106; *125:* 133; *176:* 117
Kresin, Robert *23:* 19
Krieger, Salem *54:* 164
Kriegler, Lyn *73:* 29
Krommes, Beth *128:* 141; *149:* 136; *181:* 100, 101
Krone, Mike *101:* 71
Kronheimer, Ann *135:* 119
Krosoczka, Jarrett J. *155:* 142
Kruck, Gerald *88:* 181
Krupinski, Loretta *67:* 104; *102:* 131; *161:* 105, 106
Krupp, Robin Rector *53:* 96, 98
Krush, Beth *1:* 51, 85; *2:* 233; *4:* 115; *9:* 61; *10:* 191; *11:* 196; *18:* 164, 165; *32:* 72; *37:* 203; *43:* 57; *60:* 102, 103, 107, 108, 109
Krush, Joe *2:* 233; *4:* 115; *9:* 61; *10:* 191; *11:* 196; *18:* 164, 165; *32:* 72, 91; *37:* 203; *43:* 57; *60:* 102, 103, 107, 108, 109
Krych, Duane *91:* 43
Krykorka, Vladyana *96:* 147; *143:* 90, 91; *168:* 14
Kubick, Dana *165:* 91
Kubinyi, Laszlo *4:* 116; *6:* 113; *16:* 118; *17:* 100; *28:* 227; *30:* 172; *49:* 24, 28; *54:* 23; *167:* 149
Kubricht, Mary *73:* 118
Kucharik, Elena *139:* 31
Kuchera, Kathleen *84:* 5
Kuhn, Bob *17:* 91; *35:* 235
Kulikov, Boris *163:* 185
Kukalis, Romas *90:* 27; *139:* 37
Kuklin, Susan *63:* 82, 83, 84
Kunhardt, Dorothy *53:* 101
Kunhardt, Edith *67:* 105, 106
Kunstler, Mort *10:* 73; *32:* 143
Kurchevsky, V. *34:* 61
Kurczok, Belinda *121:* 118
Kurelek, William *8:* 107
Kuriloff, Ron *13:* 19
Kurisu, Jane *160:* 120
Kuskin, Karla *2:* 170; *68:* 115, 116; *111:* 116
Kutzer, Ernst *19:* 249
Kuzma, Steve *57:* 8; *62:* 93
Kuznetsova, Berta *74:* 45
Kvasnosky, Laura McGee *93:* 103; *142:* 83
Kwas, Susan Estelle *179:* 116
Kyong, Yunmee *165:* 139

L

LaBlanc, Andre *24:* 146
Laboccetta, Mario *27:* 120
LaBrose, Darcie *157:* 134
Labrosse, Darcia *58:* 88; *108:* 77; *178:* 89
LaCava, Vince *95:* 118
Laceky, Adam *32:* 121
Lacis, Astra *85:* 117
Lacome, Julie *174:* 96, 97
La Croix *YABC 2:* 4
Ladwig, Tim *98:* 212; *117:* 76
La Farge, Margaret *47:* 141
LaFave, Kim *64:* 177; *72:* 39; *97:* 146; *99:* 172; *106:* 123; *149:* 126
Lafontaine, Roger *167:* 158
Lagarrigue, Jerome *136:* 102
Laimgruber, Monika *11:* 153
Laite, Gordon *1:* 130, 131; *8:* 209; *31:* 113; *40:* 63; *46:* 117
Laliberté, Louise-Andrée *169:* 98
LaMarche, Jim *46:* 204; *61:* 56; *94:* 69; *114:* 22; *129:* 163; *162:* 78, 80
Lamb, Jim *10:* 117
Lambase, Barbara *101:* 185; *150:* 221; *166:* 234
Lambert, J.K. *38:* 129; *39:* 24
Lambert, Sally Anne *133:* 191
Lambert, Saul *23:* 112; *33:* 107; *54:* 136
Lambert, Stephen *109:* 33; *174:* 99
Lambo, Don *6:* 156; *35:* 115; *36:* 146
Lamontagne, Jacques *166:* 227
Lamut, Sonja *57:* 193
Lamut, Sonya *85:* 102
Landa, Peter *11:* 95; *13:* 177; *53:* 119
Landau, Jacob *38:* 111
Landis, Joan *104:* 23
Landon, Lucinda *79:* 31
Landshoff, Ursula *13:* 124
Landström, Lena *146:* 165, 166
Landström, Olof *146:* 166, 168; *170:* 22
Lane, Daniel *112:* 60
Lane, John R. *8:* 145
Lane, John *15:* 176, 177; *30:* 146
Lane, Nancy *166:* 74
Lang, G.D. *48:* 56
Lang, Gary *73:* 75
Lang, Jerry *18:* 295
Lange, Dorothea *50:* 141
Langley, Jonathan *162:* 128
Langner, Nola *8:* 110; *42:* 36
Lanino, Deborah *105:* 148
Lantz, Paul *1:* 82, 102; *27:* 88; *34:* 102; *45:* 123
Larkin, Bob *84:* 225
Laroche, Giles *126:* 140; *146:* 81
LaRochelle, David *171:* 97
Larrecq, John *44:* 108; *68:* 56
Larsen, Suzanne *1:* 13
Larson, Gary *57:* 121, 122, 123, 124, 125, 126, 127
Larsson, Carl *35:* 144, 145, 146, 147, 148, 149, 150, 152, 153, 154
Larsson, Karl *19:* 177
Lartitegui, Ana G. *105:* 167
LaRue, Jenna *167:* 20
La Rue, Michael D. *13:* 215
Lasker, Joe *7:* 186, 187; *14:* 55; *38:* 115; *39:* 47; *83:* 113, 114, 115
Latham, Barbara *16:* 188, 189; *43:* 71
Lathrop, Dorothy *14:* 117, 118, 119; *15:* 109; *16:* 78, 79, 81; *32:* 201, 203; *33:* 112; *YABC 2:* 301
Lattimore, Eleanor Frances *7:* 156
Lauden, Claire *16:* 173
Lauden, George, Jr. *16:* 173
Laune, Paul *2:* 235; *34:* 31
Laure, Jason *49:* 53; *50:* 122
Lauter, Richard *63:* 29; *67:* 111; *77:* 198

Lavallee, Barbara *74:* 157; *92:* 154; *96:* 126; *145:* 193; *166:* 125, 126
Lave, Fitz Hugh *59:* 139
Lavis, Stephen *43:* 143; *87:* 137, 164, 165
Layton, Neal *152:* 120, 121
Lawrason, June *168:* 30
Lawrence, John *25:* 131; *30:* 141; *44:* 198, 200
Lawrence, Stephen *20:* 195
Lawson, Carol *6:* 38; *42:* 93, 131; *174:* 56
Lawson, George *17:* 280
Lawson, Robert *5:* 26; *6:* 94; *13:* 39; *16:* 11; *20:* 100, 102, 103; *54:* 3; *66:* 12; *100:* 144, 145; *YABC 2:* 222, 224, 225, 227, 228, 229, 230, 231, 232, 233, 234, 235, 237, 238, 239, 240, 241
Layfield, Kathie *60:* 194
Lazare, Jerry *44:* 109; *74:* 28
Lazarevich, Mila *17:* 118
Lazarus, Claire *103:* 30
Lazarus, Keo Felker *21:* 94
Lazzaro, Victor *11:* 126
Lea, Bob *166:* 208
Lea, Tom *43:* 72, 74
Leacroft, Richard *6:* 140
Leaf, Munro *20:* 99
Leake, Donald *70:* 41
Leander, Patricia *23:* 27
Lear, Edward *18:* 183, 184, 185
Lear, Rebecca *149:* 46
Lebenson, Richard *6:* 209; *7:* 76; *23:* 145; *44:* 191; *87:* 153
Le Cain, Errol *6:* 141; *9:* 3; *22:* 142; *25:* 198; *28:* 173; *68:* 128, 129; *86:* 49
Lechon, Daniel *113:* 211
Leder, Dora *129:* 172
Ledger, Bill *181:* 58
Leduc, Bernard *102:* 36
Lee, Alan *62:* 25, 28
Lee, Bryce *99:* 60; *101:* 195
Lee, Chinlun *181:* 138
Lee, Dom *83:* 118, 120; *93:* 123; *121:* 121, 126; *146:* 174, 175, 206, 207; *174:* 204
Lee, Doris *13:* 246; *32:* 183; *44:* 111
Lee, Hector Viveros *115:* 96
Lee, Jeanne M. *158:* 56
Lee, Jared *93:* 200; *157:* 229
Lee, Jody *81:* 121; *82:* 225; *91:* 155; *100:* 182
Lee, Jody A. *127:* 124, 126, 127
See also Lee, Jody
Lee, Manning de V. *2:* 200; *17:* 12; *27:* 87; *37:* 102, 103, 104; *YABC 2:* 304
Lee, Marie G. *138:* 157
Lee, Paul *97:* 100; *105:* 72, 209; *109:* 177; *128:* 113
Lee, Robert J. *3:* 97; *67:* 124
Lee, Victor *96:* 228; *105:* 182; *140:* 196
Leech, Dorothy *98:* 76
Leech, John *15:* 59
Leedy, Loreen *84:* 142; *128:* 144, 145, 146; *175:* 125, 126, 127
Leeman, Michael *44:* 157
Leeming, Catherine *87:* 39
Lees, Harry *6:* 112
LeFever, Bill *88:* 220, 221
Legenisel *47:* 111
Legrand, Edy *18:* 89, 93
Lehman, Barbara *73:* 123; *170:* 130
Lehrman, Rosalie *2:* 180
Leichman, Seymour *5:* 107
Leighton, Clare *25:* 130; *33:* 168; *37:* 105, 106, 108, 109
Leisk, David *1:* 140, 141; *11:* 54; *30:* 137, 142, 143, 144
Leister, Brian *89:* 45; *106:* 37; *114:* 67; *149:* 236
Leloir, Maurice *18:* 77, 80, 83, 99
Lematire, Pascal *144:* 175; *176:* 130
Lemieux, Michele *100:* 148; *139:* 153
Lemke, Horst *14:* 98; *38:* 117, 118, 119
Lemke, R.W. *42:* 162

Lemon, David Gwynne 9: 1
LeMoult, Adolph 82: 116
Lenn, Michael 136: 89
Lennon, John 114: 100
Lennox, Elsie 95: 163; 143: 160
Lenski, Lois 1: 144; 26: 135, 137, 139, 141; 100: 153, 154
Lent, Blair 1: 116, 117; 2: 174; 3: 206, 207; 7: 168, 169; 34: 62; 68: 217; 133: 101
Leonard, Richard 91: 128
Leone, Leonard 49: 190
Lerner, Carol 86: 140, 141, 142
Lerner, Judith 116: 138
Lerner, Sharon 11: 157; 22: 56
Leroux-Hugon, Helene 132: 139
Leslie, Cecil 19: 244
Lessac, Frane 80: 182, 207; 96: 182
Lessing, Erich 167: 52; 173: 60
Lester, Alison 50: 124; 90: 147, 148; 129: 130
Le Tord, Bijou 49: 156; 95: 112
Leutz, Emanuel 165: 27
Levai, Blaise 39: 130
Levin, Ted 12: 148
Levine, David 43: 147, 149, 150, 151, 152; 64: 11
Levine, Joe 71: 88
Levine, Marge 81: 127
Levinson, David 178: 232
Levit, Herschel 24: 223
Levstek, Ljuba 131: 192; 134: 216; 149: 65; 168: 180
Levy, Jessica Ann 19: 225; 39: 191
Levy, Lina 117: 126
Lewin, Betsy 32: 114; 48: 177; 90: 151; 91: 125; 92: 85; 115: 105; 169: 110, 111; 178: 47
Lewin, Ted 4: 77; 8: 168; 20: 110; 21: 99, 100; 27: 110; 28: 96, 97; 31: 49; 45: 55; 48: 223; 60: 20, 119, 120; 62: 139; 66: 108; 71: 12; 72: 21; 74: 226; 76: 139, 140; 77: 82; 79: 87; 85: 49, 177; 86: 55; 88: 182; 93: 28, 29; 94: 34, 182, 194; 99: 156; 104: 8; 115: 123; 118: 74; 119: 114, 116; 131: 54; 145: 99; 165: 151; 177: 75; 178: 42
Lewis, Allen 15: 112
Lewis, E.B. 88: 143; 93: 109; 119: 79; 124: 113; 128: 49; 151: 167; 168: 110; 173: 121; 174: 66; 176: 7
Lewis, H.B. 170: 124
Lewis, J. Patrick 162: 83
Lewis, Jan 81: 22
Lewis, Kim 136: 165
Lewis, Richard W. 52: 25
Lewis, Robin Baird 98: 193
Leydon, Rita Floden 21: 101
Lichtenheld, Tom 152: 125, 126
Lieblich, Irene 22: 173; 27: 209, 214
Lieder, Rick 108: 197
Lies, Brian 92: 40; 141: 101; 150: 138
Liese, Charles 4: 222
Life, Kay 79: 49
Lifton, Robert Jay 66: 154
Lightburn, Ron 86: 153; 91: 122
Lightfoot, Norman R. 45: 47
Lignell, Lois 37: 114
Lill, Debra 121: 70
Lilly, Charles 8: 73; 20: 127; 48: 53; 72: 9, 16; 77: 98; 102: 94
Lilly, Ken 37: 224
Lim, John 43: 153
Limona, Mercedes 51: 183
Lin, Grace 143: 217; 162: 86, 87; 174: 185
Lincoln, Patricia Henderson 27: 27; 78: 127
Lindahn, Ron 84: 17
Lindahn, Val 84: 17
Lindberg, Howard 10: 123; 16: 190
Lindberg, Jeffrey 64: 77; 77: 71; 79: 54; 80: 149; 174: 109; 179: 52
Linden, Seymour 18: 200, 201; 43: 140
Lindenbaum, Pija 144: 143
Linder, Richard 27: 119

Lindman, Maj 43: 154
Lindsay, Norman 67: 114
Lindsay, Vachel 40: 118
Lindstrom, Jack 145: 118
Line, Les 27: 143
Linell
    See Smith, Linell
Lionni, Leo 8: 115; 72: 159, 160, 161
Lipinsky, Lino 2: 156; 22: 175
Lippincott, Gary A. 70: 35; 119: 118
Lippman, Peter 8: 31; 31: 119, 120, 160
Lisi, Victoria 89: 145
Lisker, Emily 169: 114
Lisker, Sonia O. 16: 274; 31: 31; 44: 113, 114
Lisowski, Gabriel 47: 144; 49: 157
Lissim, Simon 17: 138
Little, Ed 89: 145; 151: 53
Little, Harold 16: 72
Little, Mary E. 28: 146
Littlewood, Karen 165: 126
Litty, Julie 111: 63
Litzinger, Rosanne 151: 101; 176: 118
Liu, Lesley 143: 72
Lively, Lorna 19: 216
Livingston, Susan 95: 22
Liwska, Renata 164: 113
Ljungkvist, Laura 180: 120
Llerena, Carlos Antonio 19: 181
Lloyd, Errol 11: 39; 22: 178
Lloyd, Megan 77: 118; 80: 113; 97: 75; 117: 94, 95
Lo, Beth 165: 154
Lo, Koon-chiu 7: 134
Loates, Glen 63: 76
Lobel, Anita 6: 87; 9: 141; 18: 248; 55: 85, 86, 87, 88, 93, 104; 60: 67; 78: 263; 82: 110; 96: 157, 159; 101: 84; 132: 35; 162: 93, 94
Lobel, Arnold 1: 188, 189; 5: 12; 6: 147; 7: 167, 209; 18: 190, 191; 25: 39, 43; 27: 40; 29: 174; 52: 127; 55: 89, 91, 94, 95, 97, 98, 99, 100, 101, 102, 103, 105, 106; 60: 18, 31; 66: 181, 183; 75: 57; 82: 246; 136: 146
Locker, Thomas 109: 134
Lodge, Bernard 107: 125, 126; 153: 93
Lodge, Jeph 153: 177
Lodge, Jo 112: 119
Loefgren, Ulf 3: 108
Loescher, Ann 20: 108
Loescher, Gil 20: 108
Loew, David 93: 184; 171: 120
Lofting, Hugh 15: 182, 183; 100: 161, 162
Lofts, Pamela 60: 188
Loh, George 38: 88
Lomberg, Jon 58: 160
Lonette, Reisie 11: 211; 12: 168; 13: 56; 36: 122; 43: 155
Long, Ethan 168: 146; 178: 12
Long, Laurel 162: 135
Long, Loren 99: 176; 172: 65
Long, Melinda 152: 128
Long, Miles 115: 174
Long, Sally 42: 184
Long, Sylvia 74: 168; 132: 63; 179: 134
Longoni, Eduardo 73: 85
Longtemps, Ken 17: 123; 29: 221; 69: 82
Looser, Heinz YABC 2: 208
Lopshire, Robert 6: 149; 21: 117; 34: 166; 73: 13
Lord, John Vernon 21: 104; 23: 25; 51: 22
Lorenz, Albert 40: 146; 115: 127
Loretta, Sister Mary 33: 73
Lorraine, Walter H. 3: 110; 4: 123; 16: 192; 103: 119
Los, Marek 146: 22
Loss, Joan 11: 163
Louderback, Walt YABC 1: 164
Lousada, Sandra 40: 138
Louth, Jack 149: 252; 151: 191, 192
Love, Judy 173: 43

Low, Joseph 14: 124, 125; 18: 68; 19: 194; 31: 166; 80: 239
Low, William 62: 175; 80: 147; 112: 194; 150: 202; 169: 175; 177: 110
Lowe, Vicky 177: 130
Lowenheim, Alfred 13: 65, 66
Lowenstein, Sallie 116: 90, 91
Lowitz, Anson 17: 124; 18: 215
Lowrey, Jo 8: 133
Lubach, Vanessa 142: 152
Lubell, Winifred 1: 207; 3: 15; 6: 151
Lubin, Leonard B. 19: 224; 36: 79, 80; 45: 128, 129, 131, 132, 133, 134, 135, 136, 137, 139, 140, 141; 70: 95; YABC 2: 96
Lucht, Irmgard 82: 145
Ludwig, Helen 33: 144, 145
Lufkin, Raymond 38: 138; 44: 48
Luhrs, Henry 7: 123; 11: 120
Lujan, Tonita 82: 33
Lupo, Dom 4: 204
Lustig, Loretta 30: 186; 46: 134, 135, 136, 137
Luthardt, Kevin 172: 125, 126
Luxbacher, Irene 153: 145
Luzak, Dennis 52: 121; 99: 142
Lydbury, Jane 82: 98
Lydecker, Laura 21: 113; 42: 53
Lynch, Charles 16: 33
Lynch, Marietta 29: 137; 30: 171
Lynch, P.J. 126: 228; 129: 110; 132: 247
Lyon, Carol 102: 26
Lyon, Elinor 6: 154
Lyon, Fred 14: 16
Lyon, Tammie 175: 170
Lyons, Oren 8: 193
Lyster, Michael 26: 41

M

Maas, Dorothy 6: 175
Maas, Julie 47: 61
Macaulay, David 46: 139, 140, 141, 142, 143, 144, 145, 147, 149, 150; 72: 167, 168, 169; 137: 129, 130, 131, 132
MacCarthy, Patricia 69: 141
Macdonald, Alister 21: 55
Macdonald, Roberta 19: 237; 52: 164
MacDonald, Norman 13: 99
MacDonald, Suse 54: 41; 109 138; 130: 156
Mace, Varian 49: 159
Macguire, Robert Reid 18: 67
Machetanz, Fredrick 34: 147, 148
MacInnes, Ian 35: 59
MacIntyre, Elisabeth 17: 127, 128
Mack, Jeff 161: 128
Mack, Stan 17: 129; 96: 33
Mackay, Donald 17: 60
MacKaye, Arvia 32: 119
Mackenzie, Stuart 73: 213
MacKenzie, Garry 33: 159
Mackie, Clare 87: 134
Mackinlay, Miguel 27: 22
MacKinstry, Elizabeth 15: 110; 42: 139, 140, 141, 142, 143, 144, 145
MacLeod, Lee 91: 167
Maclise, Daniel YABC 2: 257
MacRae, Tom 181: 112
Madden, Don 3: 112, 113; 4: 33, 108, 155; 7: 193; 78: 12; YABC 2: 211
Maddison, Angela Mary 10: 83
Madsen, Jim 146: 259; 152: 237
Maestro, Giulio 8: 124; 12: 17; 13: 108; 25: 182; 54: 147; 59: 114, 115, 116, 117, 118, 121, 123, 124, 125, 126, 127; 68: 37, 38; 106: 129, 130, 131, 136, 137, 138
Maffia, Daniel 60: 200
Maggio, Viqui 58: 136, 181; 74: 150; 75: 90; 85: 159; 90: 158; 109: 184
Magnus, Erica 77: 123

Magnuson, Diana *28:* 102; *34:* 190; *41:* 175
Magoon, Scott *181:* 104
Magovern, Peg *103:* 123
Maguire, Sheila *41:* 100
Magurn, Susan *91:* 30
Mahony, Will *37:* 120
Mahony, Will *85:* 116
Mahood, Kenneth *24:* 141
Mahurin, Matt *164:* 225; *175:* 95
Maik, Henri *9:* 102
Maione, Heather Harms *106:* 5; *178:* 8
Maisto, Carol *29:* 87
Maitland, Antony *1:* 100, 176; *8:* 41; *17:* 246;
    24: 46; *25:* 177, 178; *32:* 74; *60:* 65, 195;
    67: 156; *87:* 131; *101:* 110
Majewski, Dawn W. *169:* 95
Mak, Kam *72:* 25; *75:* 43; *87:* 186; *97:* 24;
    102: 154; *149:* 195
Makie, Pam *37:* 117
Maktima, Joe *116:* 191
Maland, Nick *99:* 77
Male, Alan *132:* 64
Malone, James Hiram *84:* 161
Malone, Nola Langner *82:* 239
Malsberg, Edward *51:* 175
Malvern, Corinne *2:* 13; *34:* 148, 149
Manchess, Gregory *165:* 241
Mancusi, Stephen *63:* 198, 199
Mandelbaum, Ira *31:* 115
Manders, John *138:* 152, 155
Manet, Edouard *23:* 170
Mangiat, Jeff *173:* 127
Mangurian, David *14:* 133
Manham, Allan *42:* 109; *77:* 180; *80:* 227
Manley, Matt *103:* 167; *117:* 98; *172:* 49
Manna, Giovanni *178:* 44
Manniche, Lise *31:* 121
Manning, Jane *96:* 203
Manning, Jo *63:* 154
Manning, Mick *176:* 139
Manning, Samuel F. *5:* 75
Mantel, Richard *57:* 73; *63:* 106; *82:* 255
Maraja *15:* 86; *YABC 1:* 28; *2:* 115
Marcellino, Fred *20:* 125; *34:* 222; *53:* 125;
    58: 205; *61:* 64, 121, 122; *68:* 154, 156,
    157, 158, 159; *72:* 25; *86:* 184; *98:* 181;
    118: 129, 130, 131; *149:* 218
Marchesi, Stephen *34:* 140; *46:* 72; *50:* 147;
    66: 239; *70:* 33; *73:* 18, 114, 163; *77:* 47,
    76, 147; *78:* 79; *80:* 30; *81:* 6; *89:* 66; *93:*
    21, 130; *94:* 94; *97:* 66; *98:* 96; *114:* 115,
    116
Marchiori, Carlos *14:* 60
Marciano, John Bemelmans *118:* 133; *167:*
    110, 111, 112
Marcus, Barry David *139:* 248; *145:* 18
Margules, Gabriele *21:* 120
Mariana
    See Foster, Marian Curtis
Mariano, Michael *52:* 108
Marino, Dorothy *6:* 37; *14:* 135
Mario, Heide Stetson *101:* 202
Maris, Ron *71:* 123
Maritz, Nicolaas *85:* 123
Mark, Mona *65:* 105; *68:* 205; *116:* 213
Markham, R.L. *17:* 240
Marks, Alan *104:* 104; *109:* 182; *164:* 92
Marks, Cara *54:* 9
Marokvia, Artur *31:* 122
Marquez, Susan *108:* 121
Marrella, Maria Pia *62:* 116
Marriott, Pat *30:* 30; *34:* 39; *35:* 164, 165,
    166; *44:* 170; *48:* 186, 187, 188, 189, 191,
    192, 193; *91:* 92
Mars, W.T. *1:* 161; *3:* 115; *4:* 208, 225; *5:* 92,
    105, 186; *8:* 214; *9:* 12; *13:* 121; *27:* 151;
    31: 180; *38:* 102; *48:* 66; *62:* 164, 165; *64:*
    62; *68:* 229; *79:* 55
Marschall, Ken *85:* 29
Marsh, Christine *3:* 164
Marsh, James *73:* 137

Marsh, Reginald *17:* 5; *19:* 89; *22:* 90, 96
Marshall, Anthony D. *18:* 216
Marshall, Felicia *170:* 190
Marshall, James *6:* 160; *40:* 221; *42:* 24, 25,
    29; *51:* 111, 112, 113, 114, 115, 116, 117,
    118, 119, 120, 121; *64:* 13; *75:* 126, 127,
    128, 129; *102:* 10, 12
Marshall, Janet *97:* 154
Marstall, Bob *55:* 145; *84:* 153, 170; *104:* 145;
    154: 166, 167, 168
Martchenko, Michael *50:* 129, 153, 155, 156,
    157; *83:* 144, 145; *154:* 137, 138, 139
Marten, Ruth *129:* 52
Martin, Charles E. *70:* 144
Martin, David Stone *24:* 232; *62:* 4
Martin, Fletcher *18:* 213; *23:* 151
Martin, Rene *7:* 144; *42:* 148, 149, 150
Martin, Richard E. *51:* 157; *131:* 203
Martin, Ron *32:* 81
Martin, Stefan *8:* 68; *32:* 124, 126; *56:* 33
Martin, Whitney *166:* 137
Martinez, Ed *58:* 192; *72:* 231; *77:* 33; *80:*
    214; *167:* 123
Martinez, John *6:* 113; *118:* 13; *139:* 143
Martinez, Sergio *158:* 190
Martiniere, Stephan *171:* 130
Marton, Jirina *95:* 127, 128; *144:* 145
Martorell, Antonio *84:* 6; *97:* 161
Martucci, Griesbach *52:* 106
Marvin, Frederic *83:* 86
Marx, Robert F. *24:* 143
Masefield, Judith *19:* 208, 209
Masheris, Robert *78:* 51
Mason, George F. *14:* 139
Mason, Robert *84:* 96
Massey, Barbara *68:* 142
Massie, Diane Redfield *16:* 194
Massie, Kim *31:* 43
Mataya, David *121:* 66
Mathers, Petra *119:* 135; *163:* 104; *176:* 143,
    144
Mathewuse, James *51:* 143
Mathieu, Joseph *14:* 33; *39:* 206; *43:* 167; *56:*
    180; *79:* 126; *94:* 147
Matje, Martin *169:* 177, 178; *172:* 180
Matsubara, Naoko *12:* 121
Matsuda, Shizu *13:* 167
Matte, L'Enc *22:* 183
Mattelson, Marvin *36:* 50, 51
Mattheson, Jenny *180:* 132
Matthews, F. Leslie *4:* 216
Mattingly, David *71:* 76, 77; *82:* 64; *91:* 216,
    217; *109:* 25
Matulay, Laszlo *5:* 18; *43:* 168
Matus, Greta *12:* 142
Maughan, William *181:* 31
Mauldin, Bill *27:* 23
Mauterer, Erin Marie *119:* 5
Mawicke, Tran *9:* 137; *15:* 191; *47:* 100
Mawson, Matt *74:* 115
Max, Peter *45:* 146, 147, 148, 149, 150
Maxie, Betty *40:* 135
Maxwell, John Alan *1:* 148
Mayan, Earl *7:* 193
Mayer, Danuta *117:* 103
Mayer, Marianna *32:* 132
Mayer, Mercer *11:* 192; *16:* 195, 196; *20:* 55,
    57; *32:* 129, 130, 132, 133, 134; *41:* 144,
    248, 252; *58:* 186; *73:* 140, 142, 143; *137:*
    137, 138
Mayforth, Hal *166:* 77
Mayhew, James *85:* 121; *138:* 187; *149:* 140
Mayhew, Richard *3:* 106
Mayo, Gretchen Will *38:* 81; *84:* 166
Mays, Victor *5:* 127; *8:* 45, 153; *14:* 245; *23:*
    50; *34:* 155; *40:* 79; *45:* 158; *54:* 91; *66:*
    240
Mazal, Chanan *49:* 104
Maze, Deborah *71:* 83
Mazellan, Ron *75:* 97, 98
Mazetti, Alan *112:* 72

Mazille, Capucine *96:* 168
Mazza, Adriana Saviozzi *19:* 215
Mazzella, Mary Jo *82:* 165
Mazzetti, Alan *45:* 210
McAfee, Steve *135:* 146; *167:* 176
McAlinden, Paul *112:* 128
McBride, Angus *28:* 49; *103:* 40
McBride, Will *30:* 110
McCaffery, Janet *38:* 145
McCallum, Graham *78:* 78
McCallum, Stephen *141:* 143; *156:* 5; *166:*
    228
McCann, Gerald *3:* 50; *4:* 94; *7:* 54; *41:* 121
McCarthy, Dan *174:* 74
McCarthy, Linda *177:* 128
McCarthy, Meghan *168:* 134
McCauley, Adam *157:* 36
McCay, Winsor *41:* 124, 126, 128, 129, 130,
    131; *134:* 77, 79
McClary, Nelson *1:* 111
McClintock, Barbara *57:* 135; *95:* 130; *146:*
    190
McClintock, Theodore *14:* 141
McCloskey, Robert *1:* 184, 185; *2:* 186, 187;
    17: 209; *39:* 139, 140, 141, 142, 143, 146,
    147, 148; *85:* 150, 151; *100:* 172, 173, 174
McClung, Robert *2:* 189; *68:* 166, 167
McClure, Gillian *31:* 132; *150:* 53
McConnel, Jerry *31:* 75, 187
McConnell, Mary *102:* 49
McCord, Kathleen Garry *78:* 236
McCormack, John *66:* 193
McCormick, A.D. *35:* 119
McCormick, Dell J. *19:* 216
McCrady, Lady *16:* 198; *39:* 127
McCrea, James *3:* 122; *33:* 216
McCrea, Ruth *3:* 122; *27:* 102; *33:* 216
McCue, Lisa *65:* 148, 149; *77:* 54; *80:* 132;
    175: 33; *177:* 133, 135
McCully, Emily Arnold *2:* 89; *4:* 120, 121,
    146, 197; *5:* 2, 129; *7:* 191; *11:* 122; *15:*
    210; *33:* 23; *35:* 244; *37:* 122; *39:* 88; *40:*
    103; *50:* 30, 31, 32, 33, 34, 35, 36, 37; *52:*
    89, 90; *57:* 6; *62:* 3; *70:* 195; *86:* 82; *96:*
    192; *97:* 93; *110:* 143, 144; *117:* 47; *167:* 96
McCurdy, Michael *13:* 153; *24:* 85; *81:* 160;
    82: 157, 158; *86:* 125; *97:* 92; *117:* 178;
    132: 6; *147:* 159, 160
McCusker, Paul *99:* 19
McDaniel, Jerry *132:* 135
McDaniel, Preston *160:* 206; *170:* 139
McDermott, Beverly Brodsky *11:* 180
McDermott, Gerald *16:* 201; *74:* 174, 175;
    163: 150, 151
McDermott, Mike *96:* 187
McDonald, Jill *13:* 155; *26:* 128
McDonald, Mercedes *169:* 118
McDonald, Ralph J. *5:* 123, 195
McDonnell, Flora *146:* 199, 200
McDonnell, Patrick *179:* 153, 154
McDonough, Don *10:* 163
McElmurry, Jill *137:* 148; *163:* 141
McElrath-Eslick, Lori *129:* 145; *142:* 21; *173:*
    123
McEntee, Dorothy *37:* 124
McEwan, Keith *88:* 116; *165:* 122, 123
McEwen, Katharine *169:* 34
McFall, Christie *12:* 144
McFeely, Daniel *160:* 213
McGee, Barbara *6:* 165
McGee, Marni *163:* 153
McGillvray, Kim *158:* 171; *165:* 213
McGinley-Nally, Sharon *131:* 19
McGinnis, Robert *110:* 113; *177:* 80
McGovern, Tara *98:* 171
McGraw, Sheila *83:* 146
McGregor, Malcolm *23:* 27
McGuirk, Leslie *152:* 159
McHale, John *138:* 190
McHugh, Tom *23:* 64

McIntosh, Jon *42:* 56
McKay, Donald *2:* 118; *32:* 157; *45:* 151, 152
McKean, Dave *150:* 71; *174:* 156
McKeating, Eileen *44:* 58
McKee, David *10:* 48; *21:* 9; *70:* 154, 155; *107:* 139, 140, 141; *134:* 218; *158:* 148, 149, 150, 151
McKee, Diana *109:* 185
McKelvey, Patrick *164:* 141
McKendry, Joe *170:* 136
McKeveny, Tom *164:* 60; *173:* 79
McKie, Roy *7:* 44
McKillip, Kathy *30:* 153
McKinney, Ena *26:* 39
McKinnon, James *136:* 75
McKowen, Scott *172:* 63
McLachlan, Edward *5:* 89
McLaren, Chesley *133:* 53
McLaren, Kirsty *123:* 99; *124:* 226
Mclean, Andrew *113:* 117, 118, 120, 121; *172:* 130, 131
Mclean, Janet *172:* 130
McLean, Meg *94:* 196
McLean, Sammis *32:* 197
McLean, Wilson *90:* 29; *113:* 195
McLoughlin, John C. *47:* 149
McLoughlin, Wayne *102:* 230; *134:* 178
McMahon, Robert *36:* 155; *69:* 169
McManus, Shawn *85:* 71
McMenemy, Sarah *156:* 139
McMillan, Bruce *22:* 184
McMullan, James *40:* 33; *67:* 172; *87:* 142; *99:* 63, 64
McMullen, Nigel *146:* 177
McNeely, Tom *162:* 55
McNaught, Harry *12:* 80; *32:* 136
McNaughton, Colin *39:* 149; *40:* 108; *92:* 144, 145, 146; *134:* 104, 106
McNicholas, Maureen *38:* 148
McNicholas, Shelagh *173:* 61
McPhail, David *14:* 105; *23:* 135; *37:* 217, 218, 220, 221; *47:* 151, 152, 153, 154, 155, 156, 158, 159, 160, 162, 163, 164; *71:* 211; *81:* 139, 140, 142; *86:* 123; *132:* 150; *140:* 129, 131, 132
McPhee, Richard B. *41:* 133
McPheeters, Neal *78:* 132; *86:* 90; *99:* 162; *111:* 141; *142:* 162
McQuade, Jacqueline *124:* 223
McQueen, Lucinda *28:* 149; *41:* 249; *46:* 206; *53:* 103
McQuillan, Mary *153:* 97
McVay, Tracy *11:* 68
McVicker, Charles *39:* 150
Mead, Ben Carlton *43:* 75
Meade, Holly *90:* 102; *94:* 101; *149:* 8; *151:* 107
Mecray, John *33:* 62
Meddaugh, Susan *20:* 42; *29:* 143; *41:* 241; *77:* 50; *84:* 173, 174, 175, 176, 177, 178; *125:* 160, 161, 162; *176:* 148, 149, 150, 151
Meehan, Dennis B. *56:* 144
Meents, Len W. *73:* 147, 150
Meers, Tony *99:* 113
Meisel, Paul *98:* 137; *124:* 18; *162:* 180; *179:* 16; *181:* 62
Melanson, Luc *149:* 229
Melendez, Francisco *72:* 180
Melnychuk, Monika *153:* 65
Melo, John *16:* 285; *58:* 203
Meloni, Maria Teresa *98:* 62
Meltzer, Ericka
    See O'Rourke, Ericka
Menasco, Milton *43:* 85
Mendelson, Steven T. *86:* 154
Mendelssohn, Felix *19:* 170
Mendola, Christopher *88:* 223
Meng, Heinz *13:* 158
Merian, Maria Sibylla *140:* 88
Mero, Lee *34:* 68

Merrill, Frank T. *16:* 147; *19:* 71; *YABC 1:* 226, 229, 273
Merriman, Rachel *98:* 108; *114:* 122; *149:* 142
Meryman, Hope *27:* 41
Meryweather, Jack *10:* 179
Meseldzija, Petar *168:* 97
Messick, Dale *64:* 150, 151, 152
Meth, Harold *24:* 203
Meyer, Herbert *19:* 189
Meyer, Renate *6:* 170
Meyers, Bob *11:* 136
Meyers, Nancy *172:* 124
Meynell, Louis *37:* 76
Micale, Albert *2:* 65; *22:* 185
Miccuci, Charles *82:* 163; *144:* 150
Micich, Paul *164:* 163
Middleton, Jeffrey *177:* 173
Middleton-Sandford, Betty *2:* 125
Mieke, Anne *45:* 74
Mighell, Patricia *43:* 134
Miglio, Paige *101:* 203; *151:* 223
Mikolaycak, Charles *9:* 144; *12:* 101; *13:* 212; *21:* 121; *22:* 168; *30:* 187; *34:* 103, 150; *37:* 183; *43:* 179; *44:* 90; *46:* 115, 118, 119; *49:* 25; *78:* 121, 122, 205, 207; *81:* 4
Milelli, Pascal *129:* 66; *135:* 153
Miles, Elizabeth *117:* 77
Miles, Jennifer *17:* 278
Milgrim, David *158:* 157
Milhous, Katherine *15:* 193; *17:* 51
Millais, John E. *22:* 230, 231
Millar, H.R. *YABC 1:* 194, 195, 203
Millard, C.E. *28:* 186
Millard, Kerry *105:* 124
Miller, Don *15:* 195; *16:* 71; *20:* 106; *31:* 178
Miller, Edna *29:* 148
Miller, Edward *115:* 64
Miller, Frank J. *25:* 94
Miller, Grambs *18:* 38; *23:* 16
Miller, Ian *99:* 128
Miller, Jane *15:* 196
Miller, Marcia *13:* 233
Miller, Marilyn *1:* 87; *31:* 69; *33:* 157
Miller, Mitchell *28:* 183; *34:* 207
Miller, Phil *175:* 150
Miller, Shane *5:* 140
Miller, Virginia *81:* 206
Millman, Isaac *172:* 18
Mills, Elaine *72:* 181
Mills, Judith Christine *130:* 168, 169
Mills, Lauren *92:* 170
Mills, Yaroslava Surmach *35:* 169, 170; *46:* 114
Millsap, Darrel *51:* 102
Milone, Karen *89:* 169
Milord, Susan *147:* 163, 164
Milton, Debbie *162:* 161
Mims, Ashley *170:* 51
Miner, Julia *98:* 69
Minor, Wendell *39:* 188; *52:* 87; *56:* 171; *58:* 116; *62:* 56; *66:* 109; *74:* 93; *78:* 129; *94:* 67; *117:* 12, 13; *124:* 84, 86; *136:* 121; *164:* 168, 169; *170:* 71
Minter, Daniel *176:* 154; *179:* 177
Mirocha, Paul *81:* 133
Mitchell, Judith *109:* 117
Mitchell, Mark *91:* 208
Mitgutsch, Ali *76:* 161
Mitsuhashi, Yoko *45:* 153
Miyake, Yoshi *38:* 141
Mizumura, Kazue *10:* 143; *18:* 223; *36:* 159
Mochi, Ugo *8:* 122; *38:* 150
Mock, Paul *55:* 83; *123:* 32
Modarressi, Mitra *90:* 236; *126:* 168; *173:* 165, 166
Modell, Frank *39:* 152
Mogenson, Jan *74:* 183
Mohn, Susan *89:* 224
Mohr, Mark *133:* 201
Mohr, Nicholasa *8:* 139; *113:* 127
Molan, Christine *60:* 177; *84:* 183

Moldon, Peter L. *49:* 168
Molk, Laurel *92:* 150
Momaday, N. Scott *48:* 159
Mombourquette, Paul *112:* 91; *126:* 142
Monks, Julie *165:* 231
Montgomery, Lucy *150:* 126
Montgomery-Higham, Amanda *169:* 131
Montiel, David *69:* 106; *84:* 145
Montresor, Beni *2:* 91; *3:* 138; *38:* 152, 153, 154, 155, 156, 157, 158, 159, 160; *68:* 63
Montserrat, Pep *128:* 135; *181:* 119
Moon, Carl *25:* 183, 184, 185
Moon, Eliza *14:* 40
Moon, Ivan *22:* 39; *38:* 140
Moore, Adrienne *67:* 147
Moore, Agnes Kay Randall *43:* 187
Moore, Cyd *117:* 107, 108; *159:* 137, 138
Moore, Gustav *127:* 181, 182; *170:* 162, 163
Moore, Jackie *128:* 79
Moore, Janet *63:* 153
Moore, Margie *176:* 156
Moore, Mary *29:* 160
Moore, Yvette *101:* 11, 12; *154:* 141
Mora, Giovanni *179:* 127
Mora, Raul Mina *20:* 41
Moraes, Odilon *102:* 144
Morales, Yuyi *154:* 144
Moran, Rosslyn *111:* 26
Moran, Tom *60:* 100
Mordvinoff, Nicolas *15:* 179
Moreno, René King *169:* 59
Morgan, Barbara *169:* 116
Morgan, Jacqui *58:* 57
Morgan, Mary *114:* 133, 134, 135; *123:* 11
Morgan, Tom *42:* 157
Morgan, Pierr *173:* 148
Morgenstern, Michael *158:* 7, 57; *171:* 103; *174:* 60
Morice, Dave *93:* 142
Morin, Paul *73:* 132; *79:* 130; *88:* 140; *137:* 143
Moriuchi, Mique *177:* 203
Morozumi, Atsuko *110:* 155
Morrill, Leslie *18:* 218; *29:* 177; *33:* 84; *38:* 147; *42:* 127; *44:* 93; *48:* 164, 165, 167, 168, 169, 170, 171; *49:* 162; *63:* 136, 180; *70:* 72; *71:* 70, 91, 92; *72:* 228; *80:* 163, 164, 165; *90:* 121; *121:* 88; *178:* 117
Morrill, Rowena A. *84:* 16; *98:* 163
Morris, *47:* 91
Morris, Frank *55:* 133; *60:* 28; *76:* 2
Morris, Harry O. *119:* 138
Morris, Jackie *128:* 194; *144:* 119; *151:* 146
Morris, Jennifer E. *179:* 157
Morris, Oradel Nolen *128:* 180
Morris, Tony *62:* 146; *70:* 97
Morrison, Bill *42:* 116; *66:* 170; *69:* 40
Morrison, Gordon *87:* 150; *113:* 93; *128:* 181, 182
Morrison, Frank *169:* 162
Morrison, Taylor *159:* 144, 145
Morrow, Gray *2:* 64; *5:* 200; *10:* 103, 114; *14:* 175
Morton, Lee Jack *32:* 140
Morton, Marian *3:* 185
Mosberg, Hilary *117:* 195; *118:* 164; *149:* 55
Moser, Barry *56:* 68, 117, 118, 119, 120, 121, 122, 123, 124; *59:* 141; *60:* 160; *79:* 91, 147, 149, 151, 152; *82:* 81; *90:* 118; *91:* 35; *95:* 210; *97:* 91, 93; *102:* 152; *126:* 4; *128:* 175; *133:* 141; *138:* 167, 171, 174; *153:* 205; *174:* 130
Moser, Cara *90:* 118; *138:* 167
Moses, Grandma *18:* 228
Moses, Will *178:* 170, 171
Moskof, Martin Stephen *27:* 152
Mosley, Francis *57:* 144
Moss, Donald *11:* 184
Moss, Geoffrey *32:* 198
Moss, Marissa *71:* 130; *104:* 127; *163:* 156
Most, Bernard *48:* 173; *91:* 142, 143; *134:* 120

Mowry, Carmen *50:* 62
Moxley, Sheila *96:* 174; *169:* 26
Moyers, William *21:* 65
Moyler, Alan *36:* 142
Mozley, Charles *9:* 87; *20:* 176, 192, 193; *22:* 228; *25:* 205; *33:* 150; *43:* 170, 171, 172, 173, 174; *YABC 2:* 89
Mueller, Hans Alexander *26:* 64; *27:* 52, 53
Mugnaini, Joseph *11:* 35; *27:* 52, 53; *35:* 62
Mujica, Rick *72:* 67; *88:* 95; *111:* 53; *180:* 185
Mullen, Douglas *180:* 178
Muller, Robin *86:* 161
Muller, Steven *32:* 167
Muller, Jorg *35:* 215; *67:* 138, 139
Mulock, Julie *163:* 112
Mullins, Edward S. *10:* 101
Mullins, Patricia *51:* 68
Multer, Scott *80:* 108
Munari, Bruno *15:* 200
Munch, Edvard *140:* 143
Munowitz, Ken *14:* 148; *72:* 178, 179
Munro, Roxie *58:* 134; *136:* 177; *137:* 218
Munsinger, Lynn *33:* 161; *46:* 126; *71:* 92; *82:* 80; *89:* 218; *92:* 125; *94:* 157, 158, 159, 160; *98:* 196; *103:* 198; *142:* 143; *145:* 133, 134, 136; *153:* 203; *176:* 162; *177:* 140, 141, 142
Munson, Russell *13:* 9
Munster, Sebastian *166:* 107
Munoz, William *42:* 160
Munzar, Barbara *149:* 75
Murdocca, Salvatore *73:* 212; *98:* 132; *111:* 168; *157:* 228; *164:* 257
Murphy, Bill *5:* 138; *130:* 170
Murphy, Jill *37:* 142; *70:* 166; *142:* 132, 134
Murphy, Kelly *130:* 212; *143:* 119; *176:* 158
Murr, Karl *20:* 62
Murray, Joe *175:* 37
Murray, Ossie *43:* 176
Mussino, Attilio *29:* 131; *100:* 164
Mutchler, Dwight *1:* 25
Myers, Bernice *9:* 147; *36:* 75; *81:* 146, 147, 148
Muth, Jon J. *165:* 169; *167:* 109
Myers, Duane O. *99:* 145
Myers, Tim *147:* 168
Myers, V.G. *142:* 41
Myers, Lou *11:* 2

N

Nachreiner, Tom *29:* 182
Nacht, Merle *65:* 49
Nadler, Ellis *88:* 91
Nagle, Shane *180:* 223
Najaka, Marlies *62:* 101
Nakai, Michael *30:* 217; *54:* 29
Nakata, Hiroe *157:* 156; *162:* 30
Nakatani, Chiyoko *12:* 124
Narahashi, Keiko *77:* 188; *82:* 213; *115:* 142, 143, 144
Nascimbene, Yan *133:* 128; *173:* 132, 133
Nash, Lesa *87:* 135
Nash, Linell *46:* 175
Nash, Scott *130:* 36
Naso, John *33:* 183
Nason, Thomas W. *14:* 68
Nasser, Muriel *48:* 74
Nast, Thomas *21:* 29; *28:* 23; *51:* 132, 133, 134, 135, 136, 137, 138, 139, 141
Nasta, Vincent *78:* 185
Natale, Vincent *76:* 3; *78:* 125; *112:* 47; *166:* 81; *174:* 189
Natchev, Alexi *96:* 177
Nathan, Charlott *125:* 151
Nathan, Cheryl *150:* 104
Natti, Susanna *20:* 146; *32:* 141, 142; *35:* 178; *37:* 143; *71:* 49; *93:* 98; *125:* 166, 168; *126:* 228; *151:* 6; *178:* 8

Navarra, Celeste Scala *8:* 142
Naylor, Penelope *10:* 104
Nazz, James *72:* 8
Nebel, M. *45:* 154
Neebe, William *7:* 93
Needler, Jerry *12:* 93
Neel, Alice *31:* 23
Neely, Beth *119:* 184
Neely, Keith R. *46:* 124
Neff, Leland *78:* 74
Negri, Rocco *3:* 213; *5:* 67; *6:* 91, 108; *12:* 159
Negrin, Fabian *174:* 125; *175:* 15
Neidigh, Sherry *128:* 53
Neilan, Eujin Kim *180:* 241
Neill, John R. *18:* 8, 10, 11, 21, 30; *100:* 22
Neilsen, Cliff *158:* 131; *177:* 112, 121
Neilsen, Terese *116:* 74
Nelson, Craig *62:* 151; 153
Nelson, Gail White *68:* 140
Nelson, Jennifer *129:* 152
Nelson, Kadir *151:* 185; *154:* 146, 147; *157:* 189, 222; *181:* 122, 124
Nelson, S.D. *131:* 34; *181:* 126, 127
Ness, Evaline *1:* 164, 165; *2:* 39; *3:* 8; *10:* 147; *12:* 53; *26:* 150, 151, 152, 153; *49:* 30, 31, 32; *56:* 30; *60:* 113
Neubecker, Robert *170:* 143
Neville, Vera *2:* 182
Nevwirth, Allan *79:* 168
Newberry, Clare Turlay *1:* 170
Newbold, Greg *108:* 125; *145:* 199; *151:* 23
Newfeld, Frank *14:* 121; *26:* 154
Newman, Andy *149:* 61
Newman, Ann *43:* 90
Newsham, Ian *143:* 162
Newsom, Carol *40:* 159; *44:* 60; *47:* 189; *65:* 29; *70:* 192; *80:* 36; *85:* 137, 138; *92:* 167
Newsom, Tom *49:* 149; *71:* 13, 62; *75:* 156; *91:* 113
Newton, Jill *83:* 105
Ng, Michael *29:* 171
Ng, Simon *167:* 7
Nicholson, William *15:* 33, 34; *16:* 48
Nickens, Bessie *104:* 153
Nicklaus, Carol *45:* 194; *62:* 132, 133
Nickle, John *181:* 128
Nickless, Will *16:* 139
Nicholas, Corasue *154:* 20
Nicolas *17:* 130, 132, 133; *YABC 2:* 215
Niebrugge, Jane *6:* 118
Nielsen, Jon *6:* 100; *24:* 202
Nielsen, Kay *15:* 7; *16:* 211, 212, 213, 215, 217; *22:* 143; *YABC 1:* 32, 33
Nielson, Cliff *95:* 207, 208; *105:* 58; *114:* 112; *124:* 12; *125:* 91, 92; *132:* 224; *135:* 187; *136:* 40; *137:* 168; *145:* 54; *149:* 28; *158:* 129; *165:* 64, 158; *168:* 169; *170:* 6; *175:* 114, 116
Nikola-Lisa, W. *180:* 180
Niland, Deborah *25:* 191; *27:* 156; *135:* 50; *172:* 143
Niland, Kilmeny *25:* 191; *75:* 143
Nino, Alex *59:* 145
Ninon *1:* 5; *38:* 101, 103, 108
Nissen, Rie *44:* 35
Nithael, Mark *158:* 237
Nivola, Claire A. *78:* 126; *140:* 147
Nixon, K. *14:* 152
Noble, Louise *61:* 170
Noble, Marty *97:* 168; *125:* 171
Noble, Trinka Hakes *39:* 162; *84:* 157
Noda, Takayo *168:* 143
Noguchi, Yoshie *30:* 99
Nolan, Dennis *42:* 163; *67:* 163; *78:* 189; *82:* 225; *83:* 26; *92:* 169, 170; *103:* 166; *111:* 35; *112:* 213; *127:* 171; *166:* 161
Noll, Sally *82:* 171
Nolte, Larry *121:* 63, 65
Nones, Eric Jon *61:* 111; *76:* 38; *77:* 177
Noonan, Daniel *100:* 224

Noonan, Julia *4:* 163; *7:* 207; *25:* 151; *91:* 29; *95:* 149
Norcia, Ernie *108:* 155; *140:* 47
Nordenskjold, Birgitta *2:* 208
Noreika, Robert *173:* 20
Norling, Beth *149:* 153, 154
Norman, Elaine *77:* 72, 176; *94:* 35; *136:* 63; *178:* 42
Norman, Mary *36:* 138, 147
Norman, Michael *12:* 117; *27:* 168
Northway, Jennifer *85:* 96
Nostlinger, Christiana *162:* 131
Novak, Linda *166:* 205
Novak, Matt *104:* 132, 133; *165:* 173, 174
Novelli, Luca *61:* 137
Nugent, Cynthia *106:* 189
Numeroff, Laura Joffe *28:* 161; *30:* 177
Nurse, Chris *164:* 91
Nussbaumer, Paul *16:* 219; *39:* 117
Nutt, Ken *72:* 69; *97:* 170
Nyce, Helene *19:* 219
Nygren, Tord *30:* 148; *127:* 164

O

Oakley, Graham *8:* 112; *30:* 164, 165; *84:* 188, 189, 190, 191, 192
Oakley, Thornton *YABC 2:* 189
Oberheide, Heide *118:* 37
Obligado, Lilian *2:* 28, 66, 67; *6:* 30; *14:* 179; *15:* 103; *25:* 84; *61:* 138, 139, 140, 141, 143
Obrant, Susan *11:* 186
O'Brien, Anne Sibley *53:* 116, 117; *155:* 115
O'Brien, John *41:* 253; *72:* 12; *89:* 59, 60; *98:* 16; *161:* 185; *169:* 16; *180:* 196
O'Brien, Teresa *87:* 89
O'Brien, Tim *93:* 25; *136:* 94; *164:* 57; *169:* 57; *173:* 55; *175:* 86
O'Clair, Dennis *127:* 25
Odell, Carole *35:* 47
Odem, Mel *99:* 164; *167:* 84, 87
O'Donohue, Thomas *40:* 89
Oechsli, Kelly *5:* 144, 145; *7:* 115; *8:* 83, 183; *13:* 117; *20:* 94; *81:* 199
Offen, Hilda *42:* 207
Ogden, Bill *42:* 59; *47:* 55
Ogg, Oscar *33:* 34
Ogle, Nancy Gray *163:* 144
Ohi, Ruth *90:* 175, 177; *131:* 63; *135:* 106; *175:* 107; *179:* 55
Ohlsson, Ib *4:* 152; *7:* 57; *10:* 20; *11:* 90; *19:* 217; *41:* 246; *82:* 106; *92:* 213
Ohtomo, Yasuo *37:* 146; *39:* 212, 213
O'Keefe, Jennifer *136:* 184
O'Kelley, Mattie Lou *36:* 150
Olbinski, Rafal *149:* 27; *158:* 77
Oliver, Isaac *171:* 182
Oliver, Jenni *23:* 121; *35:* 112
Oliver, Narelle *152:* 192
Oller, Erika *128:* 186; *134:* 126
Olschewski, Alfred *7:* 172
Olsen, Ib Spang *6:* 178, 179; *81:* 164
Olson, Alan *77:* 229
Olugebefola, Ademola *15:* 205
O'Malley, Kevin *94:* 180; *106:* 8; *113:* 108; *136:* 70; *157:* 193
O'Neil, Dan IV *7:* 176
O'Neill, Catharine *72:* 113; *84:* 78; *134:* 153
O'Neill, Jean *22:* 146
O'Neill, Michael J. *54:* 172
O'Neill, Rose *48:* 30, 31
O'Neill, Steve *21:* 118
Ono, Chiyo *7:* 97
Orbaan, Albert *2:* 31; *5:* 65, 171; *9:* 8; *14:* 241; *20:* 109
Orbach, Ruth *21:* 112
Orfe, Joan *20:* 81
Org, Ed *119:* 93
Ormai, Stella *72:* 129

Ormerod, Jan *55:* 124; *70:* 170, 171; *90:* 39; *132:* 172, 173, 174; *147:* 98

Ormsby, Virginia H. *11:* 187

O'Rourke, Ericka *108:* 216; *117:* 194; *111:* 142; *119:* 194; *137:* 152; *150:* 134; *167:* 64; *172:* 164

O'Rourke, Ericka Meltzer
See O'Rourke, Ericka

Orozco, Jose Clemente *9:* 177

Orr, Forrest W. *23:* 9

Orr, N. *19:* 70

Ortiz, Vilma *88:* 158

Osborn, Cathy *152:* 232

Osborn, Robert *65:* 49

Osborne, Billie Jean *35:* 209

Osmond, Edward *10:* 111

O'Sullivan, Tom *3:* 176; *4:* 55; *78:* 195

Otani, June *124:* 42; *156:* 53

Ottley, Matt *147:* 221; *171:* 133

Otto, Svend *22:* 130, 141; *67:* 188, 189

Oudry, J.B. *18:* 167

Oughton, Taylor *5:* 23; *104:* 136

Overeng, Johannes *44:* 36

Overlie, George *11:* 156

Owens, Carl *2:* 35; *23:* 521

Owens, Gail *10:* 170; *12:* 157; *19:* 16; *22:* 70; *25:* 81; *28:* 203, 205; *32:* 221, 222; *36:* 132; *46:* 40; *47:* 57; *54:* 66, 67, 68, 69, 70, 71, 72, 73; *71:* 100; *73:* 64; *77:* 157; *80:* 32; *82:* 3; *99:* 226

Owens, Mary Beth *113:* 202, 203

Owens, Nubia *84:* 74

Oxenbury, Helen *3:* 150, 151; *24:* 81; *68:* 174, 175, 176; *81:* 209; *84:* 213, 245; *129:* 56; *149:* 159

Oz, Robin *88:* 167

P

Padgett, Jim *12:* 165

Page, Homer *14:* 145

Page, Mark *162:* 70

Paget, Sidney *24:* 90, 91, 93, 95, 97

Paget, Walter *64:* 122

Paillot, Jim *173:* 89

Pajouhesh, Noushin *160:* 121

Pak *12:* 76

Pak, Yu Cha *86:* 174

Paladino, Lance *134:* 30

Palazzo, Tony *3:* 152, 153

Palecek, Josef *56:* 136; *89:* 158

Palen, Debbie *135:* 88

Palencar, John Jude *84:* 12, 45; *85:* 87; *92:* 187; *99:* 128; *110:* 204; *150:* 122; *171:* 86

Palin, Nicki *81:* 201; *89:* 161

Palladini, David *4:* 113; *40:* 176, 177, 178, 179, 181, 224, 225; *50:* 138; *78:* 186

Pallarito, Don *43:* 36

Palmer, Carol *158:* 230

Palmer, Heidi *15:* 207; *29:* 102

Palmer, Jan *42:* 153; *82:* 161

Palmer, Judd *153:* 160, 161

Palmer, Juliette *6:* 89; *15:* 208

Palmer, Kate Salley *104:* 143; *154:* 169

Palmer, Lemuel *17:* 25, 29

Palmisciano, Diane *110:* 62; *162:* 26

Palmquist, Eric *38:* 133

Panesis, Nicholas *3:* 127

Panton, Doug *52:* 99

Paparone, Pamela *129:* 174

Papas, William *11:* 223; *50:* 160

Papin, Joseph *26:* 113

Papish, Robin Lloyd *10:* 80

Paradis, Susan *40:* 216

Paraquin, Charles H. *18:* 166

Paris, Peter *31:* 127

Parisi, Elizabeth B. *141:* 82; *164:* 57

Park, Nick *113:* 143

Park, Seho *39:* 110

Park, W.B. *22:* 189

Parker, Ant *82:* 87, 88; *104:* 121

Parker, Lewis *2:* 179

Parker, Nancy Winslow *10:* 113; *22:* 164; *28:* 47, 144; *52:* 7; *69:* 153; *91:* 171, 174; *132:* 175

Parker, Robert *4:* 161; *5:* 74; *9:* 136; *29:* 39

Parker, Robert Andrew *11:* 81; *29:* 186; *39:* 165; *40:* 25; *41:* 78; *42:* 123; *43:* 144; *48:* 182; *54:* 140; *74:* 141; *91:* 24; *111:* 115; *151:* 201; *154:* 156

Parker-Rees, Guy *149:* 145

Parkin, Trevor *140:* 151

Parkins, David *114:* 123; *146:* 176; *176:* 168

Parkinson, Kathy *71:* 143; *144:* 234

Parkinson, Keith *70:* 66

Parks, Gordon, Jr. *33:* 228

Parnall, Peter *5:* 137; *16:* 221; *24:* 70; *40:* 78; *51:* 130; *69:* 17, 155; *136:* 22, 23, 24

Parnall, Virginia *40:* 78

Parow, Lorraine *158:* 127

Parr, Todd *134:* 139, 140; *179:* 163, 164, 165

Parrish, Anne *27:* 159, 160

Parrish, Dillwyn *27:* 159

Parrish, Maxfield *14:* 160, 161, 164, 165; *16:* 109; *18:* 12, 13; *YABC 1:* 149, 152, 267; *2:* 146, 149

Parry, David *26:* 156

Parry, Marian *13:* 176; *19:* 179

Partch, Virgil *45:* 163, 165

Pascal, David *14:* 174

Paschkis, Julie *177:* 153, 154

Pasquier, J.A. *16:* 91

Pasternak, Robert *119:* 53

Paterson, Diane *13:* 116; *39:* 163; *59:* 164, 165, 166, 167; *72:* 51, 53; *129:* 175; *177:* 156, 157

Paterson, Helen *16:* 93

Patkau, Karen *112:* 123

Paton, Jane *15:* 271; *35:* 176

Patrick, John *139:* 190

Patrick, Pamela *90:* 160; *93:* 211; *105:* 12

Patterson, Geoffrey *54:* 75

Patterson, Robert *25:* 118

Patz, Nancy *111:* 40; *154:* 161

Paul, James *4:* 130; *23:* 161

Paul, Korky *102:* 85

Paull, Grace *24:* 157; *87:* 127

Paulsen, Ruth Wright *79:* 160, 164

Pavlov, Elena *80:* 49

Payne, Adam S. *135:* 166

Payne, C.F. *145:* 138, 140; *179:* 168

Payne, Joan Balfour *1:* 118

Payne, Tom *170:* 27

Payson, Dale *7:* 34; *9:* 151; *20:* 140; *37:* 22

Payzant, Charles *21:* 147

Peacock, Ralph *64:* 118

Peake, Mervyn *22:* 136, 149; *23:* 162, 163, 164; *YABC 2:* 307

Pearson, Larry *38:* 225

Pearson, Tracey Campbell *64:* 163, 164, 167, 168, 169; *118:* 51; *156:* 169, 171, 172; *163:* 140

Peat, Fern B. *16:* 115

Peck, Anne Merriman *18:* 241; *24:* 155

Peck, Beth *66:* 242; *79:* 166; *80:* 136; *91:* 34; *95:* 9; *101:* 77; *164:* 197

Pedersen, Judy *66:* 217; *121:* 36; *172:* 67

Pedersen, Vilhelm *YABC 1:* 40

Pederson, Sharleen *12:* 92

Pedlar, Elaine *161:* 45

Peek, Merle *39:* 168

Peet, Bill *2:* 203; *41:* 159, 160, 161, 162, 163; *78:* 158, 159, 160, 161

Peguero, Adrian *116:* 133

Peguero, Gerard *116:* 133

Pels, Winslow Pinney *55:* 126

Peltier, Leslie C. *13:* 178

Penberthy, Mark *171:* 78

Pendle, Alexy *7:* 159; *13:* 34; *29:* 161; *33:* 215; *86:* 62

Pendola, Joanne *76:* 203; *81:* 125; *105:* 181; *178:* 152, 153

Pene du Bois, William *4:* 70; *10:* 122; *26:* 61; *27:* 145, 211; *35:* 243; *41:* 216; *68:* 180, 181; *73:* 45

Penfound, David *102:* 185

Pennington, Eunice *27:* 162

Peppe, Mark *28:* 142

Peppe, Rodney *4:* 164, 165; *74:* 187, 188, 189

Pepper, Hubert *64:* 143

Percy, Graham *63:* 2

Pericoli, Matteo *178:* 177

Perini, Ben *173:* 77

Perkins, David *60:* 68

Perkins, Lucy Fitch *72:* 199

Perkins, Lynne Rae *172:* 146

Perl, Susan *2:* 98; *4:* 231; *5:* 44, 45, 118; *6:* 199; *8:* 137; *12:* 88; *22:* 193; *34:* 54, 55; *52:* 128; *YABC 1:* 176

Perrone, Donna *78:* 166

Perry, Marie Fritz *165:* 180

Perry, Patricia *29:* 137; *30:* 171

Perry, Roger *27:* 163

Perske, Martha *46:* 83; *51:* 108, 147

Persson, Stina *175:* 166

Pesek, Ludek *15:* 237

Petach, Heidi *149:* 166

Peters, David *72:* 205

Petersen, Jeff *181:* 95

Petersham, Maud *17:* 108, 147, 148, 149, 150, 151, 152, 153

Petersham, Miska *17:* 108, 147, 148, 149, 150, 151, 152, 153

Peterson, Eric *109:* 125

Peterson, Nisse *99:* 27

Peterson, R.F. *7:* 101

Peterson, Russell *7:* 130

Petie, Haris *2:* 3; *10:* 41, 118; *11:* 227; *12:* 70

Petricic, Dusan *153:* 75, 76, 77; *170:* 12; *172:* 13; *176:* 170; *179:* 56

Petrides, Heidrun *19:* 223

Petrone, Valeria *159:* 160; *171:* 92

Petrosino, Tamara *177:* 40

Petruccio, Steven James *67:* 159; *127:* 5

Pettingill, Ondre *64:* 181; *70:* 64

Peyo *40:* 56, 57

Peyton, K.M. *15:* 212

Pfeifer, Herman *15:* 262

Pfister, Marcus *83:* 165, 166, 167; *146:* 152; *150:* 160

Pfloog, Jan *124:* 60

Pham, LeUyen *160:* 48; *175:* 154, 156; *179:* 149

Phillips, Craig *70:* 151

Phillips, Douglas *1:* 19

Phillips, F.D. *6:* 202

Phillips, Louise *133:* 67

Phillips, Thomas *30:* 55

Philpot, Glyn *54:* 46

Phiz
See Browne, Hablot K.

Piatti, Celestino *16:* 223

Pica, Steve *115:* 181

Picarella, Joseph *13:* 147

Picart, Gabriel *121:* 165

Pichon, Liz *174:* 139

Pickard, Charles *12:* 38; *18:* 203; *36:* 152

Picken, George A. *23:* 150

Pickens, David *22:* 156

Pienkowski, Jan *6:* 183; *30:* 32; *58:* 140, 141, 142, 143, 146, 147; *73:* 3; *87:* 156, 157; *131:* 189

Pignataro, Anna *163:* 220 Pileggi, Steve *145:* 122

Pilkey, Dav *68:* 186; *115:* 164, 166; *166:* 173, 174, 175

Pimlott, John *10:* 205

Pincus, Harriet *4:* 186; *8:* 179; *22:* 148; *27:* 164, 165; *66:* 202

Pini, Wendy *89:* 166

Pinkett, Neil *60:* 8

Pinkney, Brian *81:* 184, 185; *94:* 107; *113:*
  146, 147; *117:* 121, 166; *132:* 145; *158:* 108,
  191; *160:* 189
Pinkney, Jerry *8:* 218; *10:* 40; *15:* 276; *20:* 66;
  24: 121; *33:* 109; *36:* 222; *38:* 200; *41:* 165,
  166, 167, 168, 169, 170, 171, 173, 174; *44:*
  198; *48:* 51; *53:* 20; *56:* 61, 68; *58:* 184; *60:*
  59; *61:* 91; *71:* 146, 148, 149; *72:* 17; *73:*
  149; *74:* 159, 192; *75:* 45; *80:* 206; *81:* 44;
  85: 144; *95:* 50; *107:* 158, 159, 160; *108:*
  164; *112:* 114, 115; *133:* 58
Pinkwater, Daniel Manus *46:* 180, 181, 182,
  185, 188, 189, 190; *151:* 161 *76:* 178, 179,
  180
Pinkwater, Manus *8:* 156; *46:* 180
  See also Pinkwater, Daniel Manus
Pinkwater, Jill *114:* 160, 161; *158:* 179
Pinto, Ralph *10:* 131; *45:* 93
Pinon, Mark *74:* 22
Piven, Hanoch *173:* 142
Pistolesi *73:* 211
Pittman, Helena Clare *71:* 151
Pitz, Henry C. *4:* 168; *19:* 165; *35:* 128; *42:*
  80; *YABC 2:* 95, 176
Pitzenberger, Lawrence J. *26:* 94
Pitzer, Susanna *181:* 131
Player, Stephen *82:* 190
Plecas, Jennifer *84:* 201; *106:* 124; *149:* 168
Ploog, Mike *180:* 19
Plowden, David *52:* 135, 136
Plume, Ilse *170:* 149
Plummer, William *32:* 31
Podwal, Mark *56:* 170, 173; *101:* 154, 155,
  157; *149:* 176; *160:* 194
Pogany, Willy *15:* 46, 49; *19:* 222, 256; *25:*
  214; *44:* 142, 143, 144, 145, 146, 147, 148
Pohrt, Tom *67:* 116; *104:* 80; *152:* 199
Poirson, V.A. *26:* 89
Polacco, Patricia *74:* 195, 196, 197, 198; *123:*
  121, 122, 123; *180:* 189, 190, 191, 193, 194
Polgreen, John *21:* 44
Politi, Leo *1:* 178; *4:* 53; *21:* 48; *47:* 173, 174,
  176, 178, 179, 180, 181
Pollema-Cahill, Phyllis *123:* 126
Pollen, Samson *64:* 80
Polonsky, Arthur *34:* 168
Polseno, Jo *1:* 53; *3:* 117; *5:* 114; *17:* 154; *20:*
  87; *32:* 49; *41:* 245
Pomaska, Anna *117:* 148
Ponter, James *5:* 204
Poole, Colin *111:* 27
Poortvliet, Rien *6:* 212; *65:* 165, 166, 167
Popp, Wendy *72:* 122; *158:* 68
Poppel, Hans *71:* 154, 155
Porfirio, Guy *76:* 134
Portal, Colette *6:* 186; *11:* 203
Porter, George *7:* 181
Porter, Janice Lee *136:* 175; *164:* 37
Porter, John *113:* 47
Porter, Pat Grant *84:* 112; *125:* 101
Porter, Sue *146:* 246, 247
Porter, Walter *124:* 175
Posen, Michael *175:* 82
Posthuma, Sieb *150:* 163
Postma, Lidia *79:* 17
Potter, Beatrix *100:* 194, 195; *132:* 179, 180,
  181, 182; *YABC 1:* 208, 209, 210, 212, 213
Potter, Giselle *117:* 123; *143:* 44; *144:* 170,
  197; *149:* 7; *150:* 165
Potter, Katherine *104:* 147; *171:* 135; *173:* 136
Potter, Miriam Clark *3:* 162
Poulin, Stephane *98:* 140, 141
Poullis, Nick *146:* 210
Powell, Constance Buffington *174:* 141
Powell, Gary *151:* 208
Powell, Ivan *67:* 219
Power, Margaret *105:* 122
Powers, Daniel *161:* 173
Powers, Richard M. *1:* 230; *3:* 218; *7:* 194;
  26: 186
Powledge, Fred *37:* 154

Powzyk, Joyce *74:* 214
Poydar, Nancy *96:* 149
Pracher, Richard *91:* 166
Prachaticka, Marketa *126:* 126
Prange, Beckie *181:* 169
Prap, Lila *177:* 165
Prater, John *103:* 142, 143, 144; *149:* 172
Pratt, Charles *23:* 29
Pratt, George *116:* 208
Pratt, Pierre *150:* 73; *166:* 183; *168:* 172
Prebenna, David *73:* 174
Preiss-Glasser, Robin *123:* 176; *152:* 40; *172:*
  194
Press, Jenny *116:* 95
Preston, Mark *152:* 162
Pretro, Korinna *91:* 126
Price, Christine *2:* 247; *3:* 163, 253; *8:* 166
Price, Cynthia *118:* 156
Price, Edward *33:* 34
Price, Garrett *1:* 76; *2:* 42
Price, Hattie Longstreet *17:* 13
Price, Norman *YABC 1:* 129
Price, Willard *48:* 184
Priceman, Marjorie *81:* 171; *136:* 169; *156:*
  200; *168:* 153, 154
Priestley, Alice *168:* 33
Primavera, Elise *26:* 95; *58:* 151; *73:* 37; *80:*
  79; *86:* 156; *105:* 161
Primrose, Jean *36:* 109
Prince, Alison *86:* 188, 189
Prince, Leonora E. *7:* 170
Pritchett, Shelley *116:* 148
Prittie, Edwin J. *YABC 1:* 120
Proimos, James *176:* 4
Proimos, John *173:* 144
Prosmitsky, Jenya *132:* 33
Provensen, Alice *37:* 204, 215, 222; *70:* 176,
  177, 178, 180; *71:* 213; *147:* 184
Provensen, Martin *37:* 204, 215, 222; *70:* 176,
  177, 178, 180; *71:* 213
Pucci, Albert John *44:* 154
Pudlo *8:* 59
Pulver, Harry, Jr. *129:* 159
Pulver, Robin *160:* 4
Punchatz, Don *99:* 57
Purdy, Susan *8:* 162
Pursell, Weimer *55:* 18
Purtscher, Alfons *97:* 6
Puskas, James *5:* 141
Pyk, Jan *7:* 26; *38:* 123
Pyle, Chuck *99:* 149
Pyle, Howard *16:* 225, 226, 227, 228, 230,
  231, 232, 235; *24:* 27; *34:* 124, 125, 127,
  128; *59:* 132; *100:* 198

Q

Quackenbush, Robert *4:* 190; *6:* 166; *7:* 175,
  178; *9:* 86; *11:* 65, 221; *41:* 154; *43:* 157;
  70: 185, 186; *71:* 137; *85:* 47; *92:* 148; *133:*
  154, 164, 169
Qualls, Sean *177:* 167, 168
Quennell, Marjorie (Courtney) *29:* 163, 164
Quidor, John *19:* 82
Quirk, John *62:* 170
Quirk, Thomas *12:* 81

R

Rackham, Arthur *15:* 32, 78, 214-227; *17:* 105,
  115; *18:* 233; *19:* 254; *20:* 151; *22:* 129,
  131, 132, 133; *23:* 175; *24:* 161, 181; *26:*
  91; *32:* 118; *64:* 18; *100:* 9, 16, 203, 204;
  YABC 1: 25, 45, 55, 147; *2:* 103, 142, 173,
  210
Racz, Michael *56:* 134

Radcliffe, Andrew *82:* 215
Rader, Laura *101:* 219
Radunsky, Vladimir *177:* 170
Rafilson, Sidney *11:* 172
Raglin, Tim *125:* 24
Raible, Alton *1:* 202, 203; *28:* 193; *35:* 181;
  110: 207
Raine, Patricia *82:* 74; *88:* 154
Rama, Sue *173:* 45
Ramhorst, John *117:* 11
Ramirez, Gladys *177:* 19
Ramsey, James *16:* 41
Ramsey, Marcy Dunn *82:* 11; *180:* 186
Ramus, Michael *51:* 171
Rand, Paul *6:* 188
Rand, Ted *67:* 9, 10, 121, 123; *74:* 190; *84:*
  170; *103:* 170; *112:* 6; *114:* 73; *139:* 168;
  143: 194; *156:* 154; *161:* 9, 10
Randazzo, Tony *81:* 98
Randell, William *55:* 54
Rane, Walter *93:* 144; *143:* 109
Rankin, Joan *163:* 40
Rankin, Laura *176:* 173, 174; *179:* 150
Ransome, Arthur *22:* 201
Ransome, James E. *74:* 137; *75:* 80; *84:* 181;
  94: 108; *117:* 115; *123:* 128, 129, 130; *158:*
  101, 102; *159:* 205; *178:* 188, 189, 190
Rantz, Don *119:* 184
Rao, Anthony *28:* 126
Raphael, Elaine *23:* 192; *71:* 24, 25
Rappaport, Eva *6:* 190
Raschka, Chris *80:* 187, 189, 190; *97:* 211;
  115: 210; *117:* 151, 152, 153, 154; *143:* 195;
  145: 153; *166:* 190, 191; *170:* 114
Rash, Andy *158:* 178; *162:* 172
Raskin, Ellen *2:* 208, 209; *4:* 142; *13:* 183;
  22: 68; *29:* 139; *36:* 134; *38:* 173, 174, 175,
  176, 177, 178, 179, 180, 181; *60:* 163; *86:*
  81
Rathmann, Peggy *93:* 32; *94:* 168; *157:* 212,
  214
Ratkus, Tony *77:* 133
Ratzkin, Lawrence *40:* 143
Rau, Margaret *9:* 157
Raverat, Gwen *YABC 1:* 152
Ravid, Joyce *61:* 73
Ravielli, Anthony *1:* 198; *3:* 168; *11:* 143
Ravilious, Robin *77:* 169
Rawlins, Donna *72:* 198; *73:* 15, 129
Rawlins, Janet *76:* 79
Rawlings, Steve *143:* 139; *151:* 54
Rawlinson, Debbie *75:* 132
Ray, Deborah Kogan *8:* 164; *29:* 238; *50:* 112,
  113; *62:* 119; *78:* 191
Ray, Jane *96:* 166; *97:* 104; *152:* 208
Ray, Ralph *2:* 239; *5:* 73
Rayann, Omar *162:* 205
Rayevsky, Robert *64:* 17; *70:* 173; *80:* 204;
  117: 79
Raymond, Larry *31:* 108; *97:* 109
Rayner, Hugh *151:* 170
Rayner, Mary *22:* 207; *47:* 140; *72:* 191; *87:*
  171, 172
Rayner, Shoo
  See Rayner, Hugh
Raynes, John *71:* 19
Raynor, Dorka *28:* 168
Raynor, Paul *24:* 73
Rayyan, Omar *110:* 222; *112:* 17; *125:* 131
Razzi, James *10:* 127
Read, Alexander D. *20:* 45
Reader, Dennis *71:* 157
Reasoner, Charles *53:* 33, 36, 37
Reczuch, Karen *115:* 132; *145:* 131
Redlich, Ben *163:* 221
Reed, Joseph *116:* 139
Reed, Lynn Rowe *115:* 173; *171:* 146
Reed, Tom *34:* 171
Reeder, Colin *74:* 202; *77:* 113
Rees, Mary *134:* 219
Reese, Bob *60:* 135

Reeve, Philip *171:* 50
Reeves, Eira B. *130:* 173, 174; *141:* 151
Reeves, Rick *181:* 179
Regan, Dana *117:* 116
Regan, Laura *103:* 198; *153:* 206
Reichert, Renée *169:* 127
Reid, Barbara *82:* 178; *92:* 17; *93:* 169, 170
Reid, Stephen *19:* 213; *22:* 89
Reim, Melanie *104:* 151; *150:* 98
Reinert, Kirk *89:* 138
Reinertson, Barbara *44:* 150; *62:* 103
Reiniger, Lotte *40:* 185
Reisberg, Mira *119:* 2
Reisch, Jesse *158:* 130
Reiser, Lynn *81:* 175; *138:* 184; *180:* 200
Reiss, John J. *23:* 193
Relf, Douglas *3:* 63
Relyea, C.M. *16:* 29; *31:* 153
Remi, Georges *13:* 184
Remington, Frederic *19:* 188; *41:* 178, 179, 180, 181, 183, 184, 185, 186, 187, 188; *62:* 197
Remkiewicz, Frank *67:* 102; *77:* 171; *80:* 130; *113:* 107; *152:* 116; *152:* 211, 212; *157:* 148
Rendon, Maria *116:* 141; 192; *134:* 152
Renfro, Ed *79:* 176
Renlie, Frank *11:* 200
Reschofsky, Jean *7:* 118
Rethi *60:* 181
Rethi, Lili *2:* 153; *36:* 156
Reusswig, William *3:* 267
Rex, Adam *156:* 172; *169:* 91
Rex, Michael *157:* 147
Rey, H.A. *1:* 182; *26:* 163, 164, 166, 167, 169; *69:* 172, 173, 174, 175; *86:* 195, 196, 197; *100:* 211; *YABC 2:* 17
Reynolds, Doris *5:* 71; *31:* 77
Reynolds, Peter H. *142:* 12; *179:* 175, 176
Rhead, Louis *31:* 91; *100:* 228
Rhodes, Andrew *38:* 204; *50:* 163; *54:* 76; *61:* 123, 124; *87:* 200
Ribbons, Ian *3:* 10; *37:* 161; *40:* 76
Ricci, Regolo *93:* 22; *164:* 148
Rice, Elizabeth *2:* 53, 214
Rice, Eve *34:* 174, 175; *91:* 172
Rice, James *22:* 210; *93:* 173
Richards, Chuck *170:* 154
Richards, George *40:* 116, 119, 121; *44:* 179
Richards, Henry *YABC 1:* 228, 231
Richardson, Ernest *2:* 144
Richardson, Frederick *18:* 27, 31
Richardson, John *110:* 88
Richman, Hilda *26:* 132
Richmond, George *24:* 179
Riddell, Chris *114:* 170, 195; *166:* 179
Riddle, Tohby *74:* 204; *151:* 179
Riding, Peter *63:* 195
Rieniets, Judy King *14:* 28
Riger, Bob *2:* 166
Riggio, Anita *73:* 191; *85:* 63; *137:* 184; *172:* 165
Riley, Jon *74:* 70
Riley, Kenneth *22:* 230
Riley-Webb, Charlotte *153:* 143
Rinaldi, Angelo *165:* 60, 69
Ringgold, Faith *71:* 162; *114:* 173, 174, 176
Ringi, Kjell *12:* 171
Rios, Tere
    See Versace, Marie
Ripper, Charles L. *3:* 175
Ripplinger, Henry *117:* 31
Ritchie, William *74:* 183
Ritter, John *175:* 14
Ritz, Karen *41:* 117; *72:* 239; *87:* 125; *102:* 7; *106:* 6
Rivers, Ruth *178:* 193
Rivkin, Jay *15:* 230
Rivoche, Paul *45:* 125
Roach, Marilynne *9:* 158
Robbin, Jodi *44:* 156, 159
Robbins, Frank *42:* 167

Robbins, Ken *147:* 191, 192
Robbins, Ruth *52:* 102
Roberts, Cliff *4:* 126
Roberts, David *154:* 4, 6
Roberts, Doreen *4:* 230; *28:* 105
Roberts, Jim *22:* 166; *23:* 69; *31:* 110
Roberts, Tony *109:* 195, 214
Roberts, W. *22:* 2, 3
Robins, Arthur *137:* 172; *151:* 225
Robinson, Aminah Brenda Lynn *86:* 205; *103:* 55; *159:* 175
Robinson, Charles [1870-1937] *17:* 157, 171, 172, 173, 175, 176; *24:* 207; *25:* 204; *YABC 2:* 308, 309, 310, 331
Robinson, Charles *3:* 53; *5:* 14; *6:* 193; *7:* 150; *7:* 183; *8:* 38; *9:* 81; *13:* 188; *14:* 248, 249; *23:* 149; *26:* 115; *27:* 48; *28:* 191; *32:* 28; *35:* 210; *36:* 37; *48:* 96; *52:* 33; *53:* 157; *56:* 15; *62:* 142; *77:* 41; *111:* 148
Robinson, Jerry *3:* 262
Robinson, Joan G. *7:* 184
Robinson, Lolly *90:* 227
Robinson, T.H. *17:* 179, 181, 182, 183; *29:* 254
Robinson, W. Heath *17:* 185, 187, 189, 191, 193, 195, 197, 199, 202; *23:* 167; *25:* 194; *29:* 150; *YABC 1:* 44; *2:* 183
Roche, Christine *41:* 98
Roche, Denis *99:* 184; *180:* 32
Roche, P.K. *57:* 151, 152
Rocker, Fermin *7:* 34; *13:* 21; *31:* 40; *40:* 190, 191
Rocklen, Margot *101:* 181
Rockwell, Anne *5:* 147; *33:* 171, 173; *71:* 166, 167, 168; *114:* 183, 184
Rockwell, Gail *2:* 186
Rockwell, Harlow *33:* 171, 173, 175
Rockwell, Lizzy *114:* 182; *162:* 182
Rockwell, Norman *23:* 39, 196, 197, 199, 200, 203, 204, 207; *41:* 140, 143; *123:* 47; *YABC 2:* 60
Rockwood, Richard *119:* 75
Rodanas, Kristina *156:* 183, 184
Rodegast, Roland *43:* 100
Rodgers, Frank *69:* 177
Rodriguez, Joel *16:* 65
Rodriguez, Robert *145:* 145
Rodriguez-Howard, Pauline *177:* 18
Roeckelein, Katrina *134:* 223
Roennfeldt, Robert *66:* 243
Roever, J.M. *4:* 119; *26:* 170
Roffey, Maureen *33:* 142, 176, 177
Rogasky, Barbara *46:* 90
Rogé *173:* 160
Rogers, Carol *2:* 262; *6:* 164; *26:* 129
Rogers, Chris M. *150:* 59
Rogers, Forest *87:* 160; *101:* 76
Rogers, Frances *10:* 130
Rogers, Gregory *104:* 76; *126:* 57; *171:* 26
Rogers, Jacqueline *78:* 249; *80:* 34; *86:* 54 *103:* 70; *115:* 72; *129:* 173; *131:* 57, 225; *143:* 211; *153:* 100
Rogers, Walter S. *31:* 135, 138; *67:* 65, 168; *100:* 81
Rogers, William A. *15:* 151, 153, 154; *33:* 35
Rogoff, Barbara *95:* 20
Rohmann, Eric *103:* 152
Rojankovsky, Feodor *6:* 134, 136; *10:* 183; *21:* 128, 129, 130; *25:* 110; *28:* 42; *68:* 120
Rolfsen, Alf *62:* 15
Romain, Trevor *134:* 157
Roman, Barbara J. *103:* 171
Romas *114:* 111; *165:* 63
Romano, Robert *64:* 68
Roos, Maryn *168:* 198
Root, Barry *80:* 212; *90:* 196; *146:* 78; *156:* 165; *159:* 161
Root, Kimberly Bulcken *86:* 72; *98:* 21; *108:* 111; *127:* 114; *159:* 162; *176:* 134
Roper, Bob *65:* 153
Roraback, Robin *111:* 156

Rorer, Abigail *43:* 222; *85:* 155
Rosales, Melodye *80:* 35
Rosamilia, Patricia *36:* 120
Rose, Carl *5:* 62
Rose, David S. *29:* 109; *70:* 120
Rose, Gerald *68:* 200, 201; *86:* 48
Rose, Ted *93:* 178
Rosenbaum, Jonathan *50:* 46
Rosenberg, Amye *74:* 207, 208
Rosenberry, Vera *87:* 22, 26; *144:* 212, 213; *158:* 120
Rosenblum, Richard *11:* 202; *18:* 18
Rosier, Lydia *16:* 236; *20:* 104; *21:* 109; *22:* 125; *30:* 151, 158; *42:* 128; *45:* 214; *77:* 227, 228
Rosing, Jens *85:* 142
Ross
    See Thomson, Ross
Ross, Christine *83:* 172, 173
Ross, Clare Romano *3:* 123; *21:* 45; *48:* 199
Ross, Dave *32:* 152; *57:* 108
Ross, Herbert *37:* 78
Ross, John *3:* 123; *21:* 45
Ross, Johnny *32:* 190
Ross, Larry *47:* 168; *60:* 62
Ross, Ruth *109:* 233
Ross, Tony *17:* 204; *56:* 132; *65:* 176, 177, 179; *90:* 123; *123:* 186, 187, 190; *130:* 188, 190, 191, 192; *132:* 242; *174:* 159; *176:* 181, 182, 183
Rossetti, Dante Gabriel *20:* 151, 153
Rostant, Larry *180:* 221
Roth, Arnold *4:* 238; *21:* 133
Roth, Julie Jersild *180:* 206
Roth, Marci *135:* 223
Roth, Rob *105:* 98; *146:* 41
Roth, Robert *176:* 159
Roth, Roger *61:* 128
Roth, Stephanie *136:* 171, 172
Roth, Susan L. *80:* 38; *93:* 78; *134:* 165, 166; *181:* 145, 146
Rothenberg, Joani Keller *162:* 190, 191
Rothman, Michael *139:* 62 Rotman, Jeffrey L. *145:* 30
Rotondo, Pat *32:* 158
Roughsey, Dick *35:* 186
Rouille, M. *11:* 96
Rounds, Glen *8:* 173; *9:* 171; *12:* 56; *32:* 194; *40:* 230; *51:* 161, 162, 166; *56:* 149; *70:* 198, 199; *YABC 1:* 1, 2, 3; *112:* 163
Roundtree, Katherine *114:* 88; *168:* 102
Rowan, Evadne *52:* 51
Rowe, Eric *111:* 161
Rowe, Gavin *27:* 144; *72:* 47; *88:* 201
Rowe, John *132:* 70, 71; *180:* 126
Rowell, Kenneth *40:* 72
Rowen, Amy *52:* 143
Rowena *116:* 101
Rowland, Andrew *164:* 136
Rowland, Jada *83:* 73
Rowles, Daphne *58:* 24
Roy, Jeroo *27:* 229; *36:* 110
Royo *118:* 32; *144:* 105, 106, 108; *165:* 19; *166:* 166
Rubel, Nicole *18:* 255; *20:* 59; *81:* 66, 67; *95:* 169, 170; *119:* 60; *135:* 177, 179, 180; *169:* 68; *181:* 150
Rubel, Reina *33:* 217
Rud, Borghild *6:* 15
Ruddell, Gary *110:* 238; *116:* 207
Rudolph, Norman Guthrie *17:* 13
Rue, Leonard Lee III *37:* 164
Ruelle, Karen Gray *126:* 193
Ruff, Donna *50:* 173; *72:* 203; *78:* 49; *80:* 120, 121; *93:* 162; *164:* 121
Ruffins, Reynold *10:* 134, 135; *41:* 191, 192, 193, 194, 195, 196; *125:* 187, 188, 189; *162:* 197
Ruhlin, Roger *34:* 44
Ruiz, Art *95:* 154; *110:* 91
Runnerstroem, Bengt Arne *75:* 161

Ruse, Margaret *24:* 155
Rush, Ken *98:* 74
Rush, Peter *42:* 75
Russell, Charles M. *167:* 171
Russell, E.B. *18:* 177, 182
Russell, Jim *53:* 134
Russell, P. Craig *80:* 196; *146:* 102; *162:* 186
Russo, Marisabina *84:* 51; *106:* 164; *151:* 183
Russo, Susan *30:* 182; *36:* 144
Russon, Mary *87:* 145
Ruth, Rod *9:* 161
Rutherford, Alexa *110:* 108
Rutherford, Jenny *78:* 5
Rutherford, Meg *25:* 174; *34:* 178, 179; *69:* 73; *72:* 31
Rutland, Jonathan *31:* 126
Ruurs, Margriet *147:* 195
Ruzzier, Sergio *159:* 176, 177; *163:* 184
Ryan, Will *86:* 134
Ryden, Hope *8:* 176
Rylant, Cynthia *112:* 170, 172
Rymer, Alta M. *34:* 181
Ryniak, Christopher *178:* 11
Rystedt, Rex *49:* 80

S

Saaf, Chuck *49:* 179
Saaf, Donald *101:* 220; *124:* 180
Sabaka, Donna R. *21:* 172
Sabin, Robert *45:* 35; *60:* 30; *99:* 161
Sabuda, Robert *170:* 166, 167, 168
Sacker, Amy *16:* 100
Saelig, S.M. *129:* 73; *173:* 59
Saffioti, Lino *36:* 176; *48:* 60
Saflund, Birgitta *94:* 2
Sagsoorian, Paul *12:* 183; *22:* 154; *33:* 106; *87:* 152
Sahara, Tony *168:* 106; *177:* 181; *178:* 228
Sahlberg, Myron *57:* 165
Saidens, Amy *145:* 162
Saint Exupery, Antoine de *20:* 157
Saint James, Synthia *152:* 220
Saldutti, Denise *39:* 186; *57:* 178
Sale, Morton *YABC 2:* 31
Sale, Tim *153:* 177
Salerno, Steven *150:* 79; *176:* 188
Salter, George *72:* 128, 130
Saltzberg, Barney *135:* 184, 185
Saltzman, David *86:* 209
Salwowski, Mark *71:* 54
Salzman, Yuri *86:* 12
Sambourne, Linley *YABC 2:* 181
Sampson, Katherine *9:* 197
Samson, Anne S. *2:* 216
San Souci, Daniel *40:* 200; *96:* 199, 200; *113:* 171; *157:* 149; *170:* 69
Sancha, Sheila *38:* 185
Sanchez, Enrique O. *155:* 84
Sand, George X. *45:* 182
Sandberg, Lasse *15:* 239, 241
Sanders, Beryl *39:* 173
Sanderson, Ruth *21:* 126; *24:* 53; *28:* 63; *33:* 67; *41:* 48, 198, 199, 200, 201, 202, 203; *43:* 79; *46:* 36, 44; *47:* 102; *49:* 58; *62:* 121, 122; *85:* 3; *109:* 207, 208, 209, 210; *172:* 157, 158
Sandia *119:* 74
Sandin, Joan *4:* 36; *6:* 194; *7:* 177; *12:* 145, 185; *20:* 43; *21:* 74; *26:* 144; *27:* 142; *28:* 224, 225; *38:* 86; *41:* 46; *42:* 35; *59:* 6; *80:* 136; *94:* 188; *140:* 116; *153:* 179, 180
Sandland, Reg *39:* 215
Sandoz, Edouard *26:* 45, 47
Sanford, John *66:* 96, 97
Sankey, Tom *72:* 103
sano, Kazuhiko *153:* 208
Santore, Charles *54:* 139
Santoro, Christopher *74:* 215

Santos, Jesse J. *99:* 24
Sapieha, Christine *1:* 180
Saport, Linda *123:* 137, 138
Sara
    See De La Roche Saint Andre, Anne
Sardinha, Rick *175:* 151
Sarg, Tony *YABC 2:* 236
Sargent, Claudia *64:* 181
Sargent, Robert *2:* 217
Saris *1:* 33
Sarony *YABC 2:* 170
Sasaki, Goro *170:* 46
Sasek, Miroslav *16:* 239, 240, 241, 242
Sassman, David *9:* 79
Satty *29:* 203, 205
Sauber, Robert *40:* 183; *76:* 256; *78:* 154; *87:* 92
Saunders, Dave *85:* 163, 164, 165
Savadier, Elivia *84:* 50; *145:* 45; *164:* 206
Savage, Naomi *56:* 172
Savage, Steele *10:* 203; *20:* 77; *35:* 28
Savage, Stephen *174:* 182
Savio *76:* 4
Savitt, Sam *8:* 66, 182; *15:* 278; *20:* 96; *24:* 192; *28:* 98
Sawyer, Kem Knapp *84:* 228, 229
Say, Allen *28:* 178; *69:* 182, 183, 232; *110:* 194, 195, 196; *161:* 154, 155
Sayles, Elizabeth *82:* 93; *105:* 155; *109:* 116; *180:* 64
Scabrini, Janet *13:* 191; *44:* 128
Scanlan, Peter *83:* 27; *153:* 165
Scanlon, Paul *83:* 87
Scannell, Reece *105:* 105
Scarry, Huck *35:* 204, 205
Scarry, Richard *2:* 220, 221; *18:* 20; *35:* 193, 194, 195, 196, 197, 198, 199, 200, 201, 202; *75:* 165, 167, 168
Schachner, Judith Byron *88:* 180; *92:* 163; *93:* 102; *142:* 82; *178:* 199, 200
Schaeffer, Mead *18:* 81, 94; *21:* 137, 138, 139; *47:* 128
Schaffer, Amanda *90:* 206
Schanzer, Rosalyn *138:* 192, 193
Scharl, Josef *20:* 132; *22:* 128
Scheel, Lita *11:* 230
Scheffler, Axel *180:* 23, 24
Scheib, Ida *29:* 28
Schermer, Judith *30:* 184
Schick, Eleanor *82:* 210, 211; *144:* 222
Schick, Joel *16:* 160; *17:* 167; *22:* 12; *27:* 176; *31:* 147, 148; *36:* 23; *38:* 64; *45:* 116, 117; *52:* 5, 85; *104:* 159
Schields, Gretchen *75:* 171, 203
Schindelman, Joseph *1:* 74; *4:* 101; *12:* 49; *26:* 51; *40:* 146; *56:* 158; *73:* 40
Schindler, Edith *7:* 22
Schindler, S.D. *38:* 107; *46:* 196; *74:* 162; *75:* 172, 173; *99:* 133; *112:* 177; *118:* 185, 186; *121:* 71; *136:* 159; *143:* 45; *149:* 120; *156:* 30; *169:* 135; *171:* 161, 162, 163; *172:* 9
Schlesinger, Bret *7:* 77
Schmid, Eleanore *12:* 188; *126:* 196, 197
Schmiderer, Dorothy *19:* 224
Schmidt, Bill *73:* 34; *76:* 220, 222, 224
Schmidt, Elizabeth *15:* 242
Schmidt, George Paul *132:* 122
Schmidt, Karen Lee *54:* 12; *71:* 174; *92:* 56; *94:* 190, 191; *127:* 103
Schmidt, Lynette *76:* 205
Schneider, Christine M. *171:* 165
Schneider, Howie *181:* 159
Schneider, Rex *29:* 64; *44:* 171
Schnurr, Edward *170:* 62
Schoberle, Cecile *80:* 200; *92:* 134
Schoenherr, Ian *32:* 83; *173:* 41
Schoenherr, John *1:* 146, 147, 173; *3:* 39, 139; *17:* 75; *29:* 72; *32:* 83; *37:* 168, 169, 170; *43:* 164, 165; *45:* 160, 162; *51:* 127; *66:* 196, 197, 198; *68:* 83; *72:* 240; *75:* 225; *88:* 176

Scholder, Fritz *69:* 103
Schomburg, Alex *13:* 23
Schongut, Emanuel *4:* 102; *15:* 186; *47:* 218, 219; *52:* 147, 148, 149, 150
Schoonover, Frank *17:* 107; *19:* 81, 190, 233; *22:* 88, 129; *24:* 189; *31:* 88; *41:* 69; *YABC 2:* 282, 316
Schories, Pat *164:* 210
Schottland, Miriam *22:* 172
Schramm, Ulrik *2:* 16; *14:* 112
Schreiber, Elizabeth Anne *13:* 193
Schreiber, Ralph W. *13:* 193
Schreiter, Rick *14:* 97; *23:* 171; *41:* 247; *49:* 131
Schroeder, Binette *56:* 128, 129
Schroeder, E. Peter *12:* 112
Schroeder, Ted *11:* 160; *15:* 189; *30:* 91; *34:* 43
Schrotter, Gustav *22:* 212; *30:* 225
Schubert, Dieter *101:* 167, 168
Schubert-Gabrys, Ingrid *101:* 167, 168
Schucker, James *31:* 163
Schuett, Stacey *72:* 137
Schulder, Lili *146:* 29
Schulke, Debra *57:* 167
Schulke, Flip *57:* 167
Schulz, Barbara *167:* 24
Schulz, Charles M. *10:* 137, 138, 139, 140, 141, 142; *118:* 192, 193, 194, 196, 199
Schutzer, Dena *109:* 32
Schwark, Mary Beth *51:* 155; *72:* 175
Schwartz, Amy *47:* 191; *82:* 100; *83:* 178, 179, 180, 181; *129:* 107; *131:* 197, 198
Schwartz, Carol *124:* 41; *130:* 199
Schwartz, Charles *8:* 184
Schwartz, Daniel *46:* 37
Schwartz, Joanie *124:* 170
Schwartzberg, Joan *3:* 208
Schweitzer, Iris *2:* 137; *6:* 207
Schweninger, Ann *29:* 172; *82:* 246; *159:* 202; *168:* 166
Schwinger, Laurence *84:* 44; *91:* 61
Scofield, Penrod *61:* 107; *62:* 160
Scott, Anita Walker *7:* 38
Scott, Art *39:* 41
Scott, Frances Gruse *38:* 43
Scott, Julian *34:* 126
Scott, Roszel *33:* 238
Scott, Sally *87:* 27
Scott, Steve *166:* 230, 231; *171:* 93
Scott, Trudy *27:* 172
Scrace, Carolyn *143:* 95, 96
Scribner, Joanne *14:* 236; *29:* 78; *33:* 185; *34:* 208; *78:* 75; *164:* 237
Scrofani, Joseph *31:* 65; *74:* 225
Seaman, Mary Lott *34:* 64
Searle, Ronald *24:* 98; *42:* 172, 173, 174, 176, 177, 179; *66:* 73, 74; *70:* 205, 206, 207
Searle, Townley *36:* 85
Sebree, Charles *18:* 65
Sedacca, Joseph M. *11:* 25; *22:* 36
Seder, Jason *108:* 102
Seeger, Laura Vaccaro *172:* 162
Seegmiller, Don *174:* 57
Seely, David *164:* 173
Seeley, Laura L. *97:* 105
Segal, John *178:* 202
Segar, E.C. *61:* 179, 181
Segur, Adrienne *27:* 121
Seibold, J. Otto *83:* 188, 190, 191; *149:* 212, 214, 215, 216
Seignobosc, Francoise *21:* 145, 146
Sejima, Yoshimasa *8:* 187
Selig, Sylvie *13:* 199
Seltzer, Isadore *6:* 18; *133:* 59
Seltzer, Meyer *17:* 214
Selven, Maniam *144:* 133
Selway, Martina *169:* 157
Selznick, Brian *79:* 192; *104:* 25; *117:* 175; *126:* 156; *134:* 171; *158:* 76, 78; *169:* 70; *171:* 172, 173

Sempe, Jean-Jacques *47:* 92; *YABC 2:* 109
Sendak, Maurice *1:* 135, 190; *3:* 204; *7:* 142; *15:* 199; *17:* 210; *27:* 181, 182, 183, 185, 186, 187, 189, 190, 191, 192, 193, 194, 195, 197, 198, 199, 203; *28:* 181, 182; *32:* 108; *33:* 148, 149; *35:* 238; *44:* 180, 181; *45:* 97, 99; *46:* 174; *73:* 225; *91:* 10, 11 *YABC 1:* 167; *113:* 163, 165, 167, 168; *118:* 153; *127:* 161
Senders, Marci *180:* 79
Sengler, Johanna *18:* 256
Senn, Steve *60:* 145
Seredy, Kate *1:* 192; *14:* 20, 21; *17:* 210
Sergeant, John *6:* 74
Servello, Joe *10:* 144; *24:* 139; *40:* 91; *70:* 130, 131; *146:* 159
Seton, Ernest Thompson *18:* 260-269, 271
Seuss, Dr.
    See Geisel, Theodor
Severin, John Powers *7:* 62
Sewall, Marcia *15:* 8; *22:* 170; *37:* 171, 172, 173; *39:* 73; *45:* 209; *62:* 117; *69:* 185, 186; *71:* 212; *90:* 232; *96:* 127; *102:* 101; *107:* 129; *119:* 176, 177, 178, 180
Seward, James *70:* 35
Seward, Prudence *16:* 243
Sewell, Helen *3:* 186; *15:* 308; *33:* 102; *38:* 189, 190, 191, 192
Seymour, Stephen *54:* 21
Shachat, Andrew *82:* 179
Shahn, Ben *39:* 178; *46:* 193
Shalansky, Len *38:* 167
Shanks, Anne Zane *10:* 149
Shannon, David *57:* 137; *107:* 184; *112:* 216; *135:* 12; *152:* 223, 224, 225; *158:* 192
Sharp, Paul *52:* 60
Sharp, William *6:* 131; *19:* 241; *20:* 112; *25:* 141
Sharratt, Nick *102:* 207, 208; *104:* 163; *153:* 198; *175:* 176
Shaw, Barclay *74:* 14, 16; *118:* 138
Shaw, Charles *21:* 135; *38:* 187; *47:* 124; *126:* 219
Shaw, Charles G. *13:* 200
Shaw-Smith, Emma *144:* 117
Shea, Edmund *56:* 19
Shearer, Ted *43:* 193, 194, 195, 196
Shecter, Ben *16:* 244; *25:* 109; *33:* 188, 191; *41:* 77
Shed, Greg *74:* 94; *84:* 204; *129:* 149, *167:* 91; *179:* 192
Sheeban, Chris *144:* 190; *158:* 163
Shefcik, James *48:* 221, 222; *60:* 141
Shefelman, Karl *58:* 168
Shefts, Joelle *48:* 210
Shein, Bob *139:* 189
Shekerjian, Haig *16:* 245
Shekerjian, Regina *16:* 245; *25:* 73
Shemie, Bonnie *96:* 207
Shenton, Edward *45:* 187, 188, 189; *YABC 1:* 218, 219, 221
Shepard, Ernest H. *3:* 193; *4:* 74; *16:* 101; *17:* 109; *25:* 148; *33:* 152, 199, 200, 201, 202, 203, 204, 205, 206, 207; *46:* 194; *98:* 114; *100:* 111, 178, 179, 217, 219, 220, 221; *YABC 1:* 148, 153, 174, 176, 180, 181
Shepard, Mary *4:* 210; *22:* 205; *30:* 132, 133; *54:* 150, 152, 153, 157, 158; *59:* 108, 109, 111; *100:* 246
Shepherd, Irana *171:* 112
Shepperson, Rob *96:* 153; *177:* 163; *178:* 204
Sherman, Theresa *27:* 167
Sherwan, Earl *3:* 196
Shields, Charles *10:* 150; *36:* 63
Shields, Leonard *13:* 83, 85, 87
Shiffman, Lena *139:* 167; *168:* 136
Shigley, Neil K. *66:* 219
Shillabeer, Mary *35:* 74
Shilston, Arthur *49:* 61; *62:* 58

Shimin, Symeon *1:* 93; *2:* 128, 129; *3:* 202; *7:* 85; *11:* 177; *12:* 139; *13:* 202, 203; *27:* 138; *28:* 65; *35:* 129; *36:* 130; *48:* 151; *49:* 59; *56:* 63, 65, 153
Shine, Andrea *104:* 165; *128:* 34
Shinn, Everett *16:* 148; *18:* 229; *21:* 149, 150, 151; *24:* 218
Shinn, Florence Scovel *63:* 133, 135
Shore, Robert *27:* 54; *39:* 192, 193; *YABC 2:* 200
Shortall, Leonard *4:* 144; *8:* 196; *10:* 166; *19:* 227, 228, 229, 230; *25:* 78; *28:* 66, 167; *33:* 127; *52:* 125; *73:* 12, 212
Shortt, T.M. *27:* 36
Shpitalnik, Vladimir *83:* 194
Shropshire, Sandy *170:* 191
Shtainments, Leon *32:* 161
Shulevitz, Uri *3:* 198, 199; *17:* 85; *22:* 204; *27:* 212; *28:* 184; *50:* 190, 191, 192, 193, 194, 195, 196, 197, 198, 199, 201; *106:* 181, 182, 183; *165:* 203, 205; *166:* 138
Shulman, Dee *180:* 140
Shupe, Bobbi *139:* 80, 81
Shute, A.B. *67:* 196
Shute, Linda *46:* 59; *74:* 118
Siberell, Anne *29:* 193
Sibley, Don *1:* 39; *12:* 196; *31:* 47
Sibthorp, Fletcher *94:* 111, 112
Sidjakov, Nicolas *18:* 274
Siebel, Fritz *3:* 120; *17:* 145
Siebold, J. Otto *158:* 227
Siegel, Hal *74:* 246
Siegl, Helen *12:* 166; *23:* 216; *34:* 185, 186
Sill, John *140:* 194; *141:* 157
Sills, Joyce *5:* 199
Silva, Simon *108:* 122
Silver, Maggie *85:* 210
Silveria, Gordon *96:* 44
Silverstein, Alvin *8:* 189
Silverstein, Shel *33:* 211; *92:* 209, 210
Silverstein, Virginia *8:* 189
Silvey, Joe *135:* 203
Simard, Remy *95:* 156
Simmons, Elly *110:* 2; *127:* 69; *134:* 181
Simon, Eric M. *7:* 82
Simon, Hilda *28:* 189
Simon, Howard *2:* 175; *5:* 132; *19:* 199; *32:* 163, 164, 165
Simont, Marc *2:* 119; *4:* 213; *9:* 168; *13:* 238, 240; *14:* 262; *16:* 179; *18:* 221; *26:* 210; *33:* 189, 194; *44:* 132; *58:* 122; *68:* 117; *73:* 204, 205, 206; *74:* 221; *126:* 199, 200; *133:* 195; *164:* 128
Sims, Agnes *54:* 152
Sims, Blanche *44:* 116; *57:* 129; *75:* 179, 180; *77:* 92; *104:* 192; *152:* 117; *156:* 160; *160:* 70; *168:* 174, 175
Singer, Edith G. *2:* 30
Singer, Gloria *34:* 56; *36:* 43
Singer, Julia *28:* 190
Singh, Jen *178:* 146
Siomades, Lorianne *134:* 45
Simont, Marc *163:* 40
Siracusa, Catherine *68:* 135; *82:* 218
Sis, Peter *67:* 179, 181, 183, 184, 185; *96:* 96, 98; *106:* 193, 194, 195; *149:* 224, 226; *180:* 177
Sivard, Robert *26:* 124
Sivertson, Liz *116:* 84
Skardinski, Stanley *23:* 144; *32:* 84; *66:* 122; *84:* 108
Slackman, Charles B. *12:* 201
Slade, Paul *61:* 170
Slark, Albert *99:* 212
Slater, Rod *25:* 167
Sloan, Joseph *16:* 68
Sloane, Eric *21:* 3; *52:* 153, 154, 155, 156, 157, 158, 160
Sloat, Teri *164:* 231

Slobodkin, Louis *1:* 200; *3:* 232; *5:* 168; *13:* 251; *15:* 13, 88; *26:* 173, 174, 175, 176, 178, 179; *60:* 180
Slobodkina, Esphyr *1:* 201
Slonim, David *166:* 167, 168
Small, David *50:* 204, 205; *79:* 44; *95:* 189, 190, 191; *126:* 203, 204; *136:* 119; *143:* 201, 202, 203; *144:* 246; *150:* 5; *161:* 176
Small, W. *33:* 113
Smalley, Janet *1:* 154
Smedley, William T. *34:* 129
Smee, David *14:* 78; *62:* 30
Smee, Nicola *167:* 156
Smith, A.G., Jr. *35:* 182
Smith, Alvin *1:* 31, 229; *13:* 187; *27:* 216; *28:* 226; *48:* 149; *49:* 60
Smith, Anne Warren *41:* 212
Smith, Barry *75:* 183
Smith, Carl *36:* 41
Smith, Cat Bowman *146:* 39; *164:* 219
Smith, Craig *97:* 197; *172:* 175
Smith, Donald A. *178:* 7
Smith, Doris Susan *41:* 139
Smith, Duane *171:* 152
Smith, E. Boyd *19:* 70; *22:* 89; *26:* 63; *YABC 1:* 4, 5, 240, 248, 249
Smith, Edward J. *4:* 224
Smith, Elwood H. *157:* 231; *181:* 79
Smith, Eunice Young *5:* 170
Smith, Gary *113:* 216
Smith, George *102:* 169
Smith, Howard *19:* 196
Smith, J. Gerard *95:* 42
Smith, Jacqueline Bardner *27:* 108; *39:* 197
Smith, Jay J. *61:* 119
Smith, Jeff *93:* 191
Smith, Jessie Willcox *15:* 91; *16:* 95; *18:* 231; *19:* 57, 242; *21:* 29, 156, 157, 158, 159, 160, 161; *34:* 65; *100:* 223; *YABC 1:* 6; *2:* 180, 185, 191, 311, 325
Smith, Jos. A. *52:* 131; *72:* 120; *74:* 151; *84:* 147, 148; *85:* 146; *87:* 96; *94:* 219; *96:* 97; *104:* 33; *108:* 126, 127, 128; *111:* 140; *136:* 145; *181:* 173
Smith, Kenneth R. *47:* 182
Smith, Kevin Warren *89:* 112
Smith, L.H. *35:* 174
Smith, Lane *76:* 211, 213; *88:* 115; *105:* 202, 203, 204, 205; *131:* 207; *160:* 217, 221; *179:* 183, 184, 185, 186
Smith, Lee *29:* 32
Smith, Linell Nash *2:* 195
Smith, Maggie Kaufman *13:* 205; *35:* 191; *110:* 158; *178:* 226
Smith, Mavis *101:* 219
Smith, Moishe *33:* 155
Smith, Philip *44:* 134; *46:* 203
Smith, Ralph Crosby *2:* 267; *49:* 203
Smith, Robert D. *5:* 63
Smith, Sally J. *84:* 55
Smith, Susan Carlton *12:* 208
Smith, Terry *12:* 106; *33:* 158
Smith, Virginia *3:* 157; *33:* 72
Smith, William A. *1:* 36; *10:* 154; *25:* 65
Smith-Moore, J.J. *98:* 147
Smolinski, Dick *84:* 217
Smoljan, Joe *112:* 201
Smollin, Mike *39:* 203
Smyth, Iain *105:* 207
Smyth, M. Jane *12:* 15
Smythe, Fiona *151:* 213
Smythe, Theresa *141:* 37
Snair, Andy *176:* 4
Sneed, Brad *125:* 25
Snyder, Andrew A. *30:* 212
Snyder, Jerome *13:* 207; *30:* 173
Snyder, Joel *28:* 163
So, Meilo *162:* 201
Soentpiet, Chris K. *97:* 208; *110:* 33; *159:* 184; *161:* 10; *163:* 130
Sofia *1:* 62; *5:* 90; *32:* 166; *86:* 43

Sofilas, Mark *93:* 157
Sokol, Bill *37:* 178; *49:* 23
Sokolov, Kirill *34:* 188
Solbert, Ronni *1:* 159; *2:* 232; *5:* 121; *6:* 34; *17:* 249
Solomon, Michael *174:* 115
Solonevich, George *15:* 246; *17:* 47
Soma, Liana *81:* 118
Soman, David *90:* 122; *102:* 126; *140:* 120; 93
Sommer, Robert *12:* 211
Sorel, Edward *4:* 61; *36:* 82; *65:* 191, 193; *126:* 214
Sorensen, Henrik *62:* 16
Sorensen, Svend Otto *22:* 130, 141; *67:* 188, 189
Sorra, Kristin *155:* 80
Sotomayor, Antonio *11:* 215
Souhami, Jessica *112:* 128; *176:* 193
Souza, Diana *71:* 139
Sovak, Jan *115:* 190
Soyer, Moses *20:* 177
Spaenkuch, August *16:* 28
Spafford, Suzy *160:* 228
Spain, Valerie *105:* 76
Spain, Sunday Sahara *133:* 204
Spalenka, Greg *149:* 69; *151:* 228
Spanfeller, James *1:* 72, 149; *2:* 183; *19:* 230, 231, 232; *22:* 66; *36:* 160, 161; *40:* 75; *52:* 166; *76:* 37
Sparks, Mary Walker *15:* 247
Speidel, Sandra *78:* 233; *94:* 178; *134:* 180
Speirs, John *67:* 178
Spence, Geraldine *21:* 163; *47:* 196
Spence, Jim *38:* 89; *50:* 102
Spencer, Laurie *113:* 12
Spencer, Mark *57:* 170
Spengler, Kenneth J. *146:* 256
Sperling, Andrea *133:* 182
Spiegel, Doris *29:* 111
Spiegelman, Art *109:* 227
Spier, Jo *10:* 30
Spier, Peter *3:* 155; *4:* 200; *7:* 61; *11:* 78; *38:* 106; *54:* 120, 121, 122, 123, 124, 125, 126, 127, 128, 129, 130, 131, 132, 133, 134
Spilka, Arnold *5:* 120; *6:* 204; *8:* 131
Spirin, Gennady *95:* 196, 197; *113:* 172; *128:* 9; *129:* 49; *134:* 210; *153:* 9
Spivak, I. Howard *8:* 10; *13:* 172
Spohn, David *72:* 233
Spohn, Kate *87:* 195; *147:* 201, 202
Spollen, Christopher J. *12:* 214
Spooner, Malcolm *40:* 142
Spowart, Robin *82:* 228; *92:* 149; *133:* 131; *176:* 163; *177:* 183, 184
Sprague, Kevin *150:* 60
Sprattler, Rob *12:* 176
Spring, Bob *5:* 60
Spring, Ira *5:* 60
Springer, Harriet *31:* 92
Spudvilas, Anne *110:* 74
Spurll, Barbara *78:* 199; *88:* 141, 142; *99:* 215
Spurrier, Steven *28:* 198
Spuvilas, Anne *85:* 114
Spy
 See Ward, Leslie
Squires, Stuart *127:* 74
St. Aubin, Bruno *179:* 54
St. John, J. Allen *41:* 62
Stabin, Victor *101:* 131; *164:* 158
Stadler, John *62:* 33
Staffan, Alvin E. *11:* 56; *12:* 187
Stahl, Ben *5:* 181; *12:* 91; *49:* 122; *71:* 128; *87:* 206; *112:* 107
Stair, Gobin *35:* 214
Stallwood, Karen *73:* 126
Stamaty, Mark Alan *12:* 215
Stammen, JoEllen McAllister *113:* 14
Stampnick, Ken *51:* 142
Stanbridge, Joanne *150:* 91
Stanley, Diane *3:* 45; *37:* 180; *80:* 217, 219
Stanley, Sanna *145:* 228

Starcke, Helmut *86:* 217
Starr, Branka *73:* 25
Stasiak, Krystyna *49:* 181; *64:* 194
Staub, Leslie *103:* 54
Staunton, Ted *112:* 192
Stawicki, Matt *164:* 250
Stead, L. *55:* 51, 56
Steadman, Broeck *97:* 185, 186; *99:* 56; *121:* 48
Steadman, Ralph *32:* 180; *123:* 143, 145
Steckler, June *90:* 178
Steele, Robert Gantt *169:* 174
Steichen, Edward *30:* 79
Steig, William *18:* 275, 276; *70:* 215, 216, 217, 218; *111:* 173, 174, 175, 176, 177
Stein, Harve *1:* 109
Steinberg, Saul *47:* 193
Steinel, William *23:* 146
Steiner, Charlotte *45:* 196
Steiner, Joan *110:* 219
Steirnagel, Michael *80:* 56
Stemp, Eric *60:* 184
Stephens, Alice Barber *66:* 208, 209
Stephens, Charles H. *YABC 2:* 279
Stephens, Pat *126:* 110; *128:* 101
Stephens, William M. *21:* 165
Steptoe, Javaka *151:* 203, 204
Steptoe, John *8:* 197; *57:* 9; *63:* 158, 159, 160, 161, 163, 164, 165, 166, 167; *96:* 4; *105:* 87
Stern, Simon *15:* 249, 250; *17:* 58; *34:* 192, 193
Sterret, Jane *53:* 27
Stetsios, Debbie *165:* 108, 109
Steven, Kat *158:* 237
Stevens, David *62:* 44
Stevens, Janet *40:* 126; *57:* 10, 11; *80:* 112; *90:* 221, 222; *109:* 156; *130:* 34; *166:* 202; *176:* 53, 116
Stevens, Mary *11:* 193; *13:* 129; *43:* 95
Stevenson, Harvey *66:* 143; *80:* 201, 221; *153:* 60
Stevenson, James *42:* 182, 183; *51:* 163; *66:* 184; *71:* 185, 187, 188; *78:* 262; *87:* 97; *113:* 182, 183, 184, 185; *161:* 182, 183
Stevenson, Sucie *92:* 27; *104:* 194, 195; *112:* 168; *160:* 202
Stewart, April Blair *75:* 210
Stewart, Arvis *33:* 98; *36:* 69; *60:* 118; *75:* 91; *127:* 4
Stewart, Charles *2:* 205
Stewart, Joel *151:* 205
Stieg, William *172:* 58
Stiles, Fran *26:* 85; *78:* 56; *82:* 150
Stillman, Susan *44:* 130; *76:* 83
Stimpson, Tom *49:* 171
Stinemetz, Morgan *40:* 151
Stinson, Paul *110:* 86
Stirnweis, Shannon *10:* 164
Stites, Joe *86:* 96
Stobbs, William *1:* 48, 49; *3:* 68; *6:* 20; *17:* 117, 217; *24:* 150; *29:* 250; *60:* 179; *87:* 204, 205, 206
Stock, Catherine *37:* 55; *65:* 198; *72:* 7; *99:* 225; *114:* 197, 198, 199; *126:* 3; *145:* 161; *161:* 82; *173:* 149
Stockman, Jack *113:* 24
Stoeke, Janet Morgan *90:* 225; *136:* 196
Stoerrle, Tom *55:* 147
Stolp, Jaap *49:* 98
Stolp, Todd *89:* 195
Stone, David L. *87:* 154
Stone, David *9:* 173
Stone, David K. *4:* 38; *6:* 124; *9:* 180; *43:* 182; *60:* 70
Stone, Helen V. *6:* 209
Stone, Helen *44:* 121, 122, 126
Stone, Kazuko G. *134:* 43
Stone, Phoebe *86:* 212; *134:* 213; *162:* 188
Stone, Steve *166:* 213
Stone, Tony *150:* 34, 35
Stoud, Virginia A. *89:* 31

Stover, Jill *82:* 234
Stratton, Helen *33:* 151
Stratton-Porter, Gene *15:* 254, 259, 263, 264, 268, 269
Streano, Vince *20:* 173
Street, Janet Travell *84:* 235
Streeter, Clive *121:* 2
Stringer, Lauren *129:* 187; *154:* 172, 173; *161:* 127
Strodl, Daniel *47:* 95
Strogart, Alexander *63:* 139
Stromoski, Rick *111:* 179; *124:* 161, 190
Strong, Joseph D., Jr. *YABC 2:* 330
Stroyer, Poul *13:* 221
Strugnell, Ann *27:* 38
Struzan, Drew *117:* 6
Stubbs, William *73:* 196
Stubis, Talivaldis *5:* 182, 183; *10:* 45; *11:* 9; *18:* 304; *20:* 127
Stubley, Trevor *14:* 43; *22:* 219; *23:* 37; *28:* 61; *87:* 26
Stuck, Marion *104:* 44
Stuecklen, Karl W. *8:* 34, 65; *23:* 103
Stull, Betty *11:* 46
Stutzman, Mark *119:* 99
Stutzmann, Laura *73:* 185
Suarez, Maribel *162:* 208
Suba, Susanne *4:* 202, 203; *14:* 261; *23:* 134; *29:* 222; *32:* 30
Sueling, Barbara *98:* 185
Sueling, Gwenn *98:* 186
Sugarman, Tracy *3:* 76; *8:* 199; *37:* 181, 182
Sugimoto, Yugo *170:* 144
Sugita, Yutaka *36:* 180, 181
Suh, John *80:* 157
Sullivan, Dorothy *89:* 113
Sullivan, Edmund J. *31:* 86
Sullivan, James F. *19:* 280; *20:* 192
Sully, Tom *104:* 199, 200
Sumichrast, Jozef *14:* 253; *29:* 168, 213
Sumiko *46:* 57
Summers, Leo *1:* 177; *2:* 273; *13:* 22
Summers, Mark *118:* 144
Sutton, Judith *94:* 164
Svarez, Juan *56:* 113
Svendsen, Mark *181:* 176
Svolinsky, Karel *17:* 104
Swain, Carol *172:* 182
Swain, Su Zan Noguchi *21:* 170
Swan, Susan *22:* 220, 221; *37:* 66; *60:* 146; *145:* 205; *181:* 168
Swann, Susan *86:* 55
Swanson, Karl *79:* 65; *89:* 186
Swayne, Sam *53:* 143, 145
Swayne, Zoa *53:* 143, 145
Swearingen, Greg *152:* 56; *165:* 135; *173:* 2
Sweat, Lynn *25:* 206; *57:* 176; *73:* 184; *168:* 178
Sweet, Darrell K. *60:* 9; *69:* 86; *74:* 15; *75:* 215; *76:* 130, 131; *81:* 96, 122; *82:* 253; *83:* 11; *84:* 14; *85:* 37; *89:* 140; *90:* 6; *91:* 137, 139; *95:* 160, 161; *126:* 25
Sweet, Darrell K. *1:* 163; *4:* 136; *164:* 175
Sweet, Melissa *71:* 94; *72:* 172; *111:* 82; *139:* 53, 58; *141:* 88; *142:* 231; *155:* 121; *159:* 121, 122; *172:* 185
Sweet, Ozzie *31:* 149, 151, 152
Sweetland, Robert *12:* 194
Swiatkowska, Gabi *132:* 43; *175:* 139; *180:* 218
Swope, Martha *43:* 160; *56:* 86, 87, 89
Sylvada, Peter *154:* 174
Sylvester, Natalie G. *22:* 222
Szafran, Gene *24:* 144
Szasz, Susanne *13:* 55, 226; *14:* 48
Szekeres, Cyndy *2:* 218; *5:* 185; *8:* 85; *11:* 166; *14:* 19; *16:* 57, 159; *26:* 49, 214; *34:* 205; *60:* 150, 151, 152, 153, 154; *73:* 224; *74:* 218; *131:* 213, 215
Szpura, Beata *81:* 68; *119:* 65; *168:* 201

T

Taback, Simms *40:* 207; *52:* 120; *57:* 34; *80:* 241; *104:* 202, 203; *170:* 176, 177
Taber, Patricia *75:* 124
Tabor, Nancy Maria Grande *89:* 210; *161:* 188
Taddei, Richard *112:* 13, 14
Tadgell, Nicole *150:* 77; *161:* 20; *177:* 186
Tadiello, Ed *133:* 200
Tafuri, Nancy *39:* 210; *75:* 199, 200; *92:* 75; *130:* 215, 216, 217
Tailfeathers, Gerald *86:* 85
Tait, Douglas *12:* 220; *74:* 105, 106
Takabayashi, Mari *113:* 112; *130:* 22; *156:* 169
Takahashi, Hideko *136:* 160
Takakjian, Portia *15:* 274
Takashima, Shizuye *13:* 228
Talarczyk, June *4:* 173
Talbott, Hudson *84:* 240; *163:* 100
Tallarico, Tony *116:* 197
Tallon, Robert *2:* 228; *43:* 200, 201, 202, 203, 204, 205, 206, 207, 209
Tamas, Szecsko *29:* 135
Tamburine, Jean *12:* 222
Tandy, H.R. *13:* 69
Tandy, Russell H. *65:* 9; *100:* 30, 131
Tang, Charles *81:* 202; *90:* 192
Tang, Susan *80:* 174; *108:* 158
Tang, You-shan *63:* 100
Tankersley, Paul *69:* 206; *133:* 219
Tannenbaum, Robert *48:* 181
Tanner, Jane *87:* 13; *97:* 37
Tanner, Tim *72:* 192; *84:* 35
Tanobe, Miyuki *23:* 221
Tarabay, Sharif *110:* 149; *113:* 123; *169:* 83
Tarkington, Booth *17:* 224, 225
Tarlow, Phyllis *61:* 198
Tate, Don *159:* 141, 191
Tauss, Herbert *95:* 179
Tauss, Marc *117:* 160; *126:* 155; *178:* 221
Tavares, Matt *159:* 192, 193
Taylor, Ann *41:* 226
Taylor, Dahl *129:* 157
Taylor, Geoff *93:* 156
Taylor, Isaac *41:* 228
Taylor, Mike *143:* 99, 100
Teague, Mark *83:* 6; *139:* 241; *170:* 180, 181
Teale, Edwin Way *7:* 196
Teason, James *1:* 14
Teeple, Lyn *33:* 147
Tee-Van, Helen Damrosch *10:* 176; *11:* 182
Teicher, Dick *50:* 211
Teichman, Mary *77:* 220; *124:* 208; *127:* 22
Temertey, Ludmilla *96:* 232; *104:* 43, 45; *109:* 244
Tempest, Margaret *3:* 237, 238; *88:* 200
Temple, Frances *85:* 185, 186, 187
Temple, Herbert *45:* 201
Templeton, Owen *11:* 77
Tenggren, Gustaf *18:* 277, 278, 279; *19:* 15; *28:* 86; *YABC 2:* 145
Tennent, Julie *81:* 105
Tenneson, Joyce *153:* 166
Tenney, Gordon *24:* 204
Tenniel, John *74:* 234, 235; *100:* 89; *YABC 2:* 99; *153:* 63
Tepper, Matt *116:* 80
Terkel, Ari *103:* 162
Terry, Michael *180:* 209
Terry, Will *131:* 73
Teskey, Donald *71:* 51
Thacher, Mary M. *30:* 72
Thackeray, William Makepeace *23:* 224, 228
Thamer, Katie *42:* 187
Tharlet, Eve *146:* 149
Thelwell, Norman *14:* 201
Theobalds, Prue *40:* 23
Theurer, Marilyn Churchill *39:* 195
Thiesing, Lisa *89:* 134; *95:* 202; *156:* 190; *159:* 195

Thiewes, Sam *133:* 114
Thistlethwaite, Miles *12:* 224
Thollander, Earl *11:* 47; *18:* 112; *22:* 224
Thomas, Allan *22:* 13
Thomas, Art *48:* 217
Thomas, Eric *28:* 49
Thomas, Harold *20:* 98
Thomas, Jacqui *125:* 95
Thomas, Mark *42:* 136
Thomas, Martin *14:* 255
Thomas, Middy *177:* 114
Thompson, Arthur *34:* 107
Thompson, Carol *85:* 189; *95:* 75; *102:* 86; *147:* 166
Thompson, Colin *95:* 204
Thompson, Ellen *51:* 88, 151; *60:* 33; *67:* 42; *77:* 148; *78:* 75, 219; *79:* 122, 170; *84:* 219; *85:* 97; *87:* 37; *88:* 192, 194; *89:* 80; *93:* 37; *98:* 59; *132:* 14
Thompson, George W. *22:* 18; *28:* 150; *33:* 135
Thompson, John *58:* 201; *102:* 226; *124:* 154; *128:* 228; *129:* 157; *150:* 49
Thompson, Julie *44:* 158
Thompson, Katherine *132:* 146
Thompson, K. Dyble *84:* 6
Thompson, Miles *152:* 77
Thompson, Sharon *74:* 113; *158:* 60; *165:* 87
Thomson, Arline K. *3:* 264
Thomson, Hugh *26:* 88
Thomson, Ross *36:* 179
Thorkelson, Gregg *95:* 183, 184; *98:* 58; *165:* 30, 31
Thornberg, Dan *104:* 125
Thornburgh, Rebecca McKillip *143:* 37
Thorne, Diana *25:* 212
Thornhill, Jan *77:* 213
Thorpe, Peter *58:* 109
Thorvall, Kerstin *13:* 235
Threadgall, Colin *77:* 215
Thurber, James *13:* 239, 242, 243, 245, 248, 249
Thurman, Mark *63:* 173; *168:* 116
Tibbles, Jean-Paul *115:* 200
Tibbles, Paul *45:* 23
Tibo, Gilles *67:* 207; *107:* 199, 201
Tichenor, Tom *14:* 207
Tichnor, Richard *90:* 218
Tiegreen, Alan *36:* 143; *43:* 55, 56, 58; *77:* 200; *94:* 216, 217; *121:* 54, 59
Tierney, Tom *113:* 198, 200, 201
Tilley, Debbie *102:* 134; *133:* 226; *137:* 101; *159:* 96
Tilney, F.C. *22:* 231
Timbs, Gloria *36:* 90
Timmins, Harry *2:* 171
Tinkelman, Murray *12:* 225; *35:* 44
Titherington, Jeanne *39:* 90; *58:* 138; *75:* 79; *135:* 161
Tobin, Nancy *145:* 197
Toddy, Irving *172:* 144
Tokunbo, Dimitrea *181:* 183
Tolbert, Jeff *128:* 69
Tolford, Joshua *1:* 221
Tolkien, J.R.R. *2:* 243; *32:* 215
Tolmie, Ken *15:* 292
Tomei, Lorna *47:* 168, 171
Tomes, Jacqueline *2:* 117; *12:* 139
Tomes, Margot *1:* 224; *2:* 120, 121; *16:* 207; *18:* 250; *20:* 7; *25:* 62; *27:* 78, 79; *29:* 81, 199; *33:* 82; *36:* 186, 187, 188, 189, 190; *46:* 129; *56:* 71; *58:* 183; *70:* 228; *75:* 73, 75; *80:* 80; *83:* 97; *90:* 205
Toner, Raymond John *10:* 179
Tong, Gary *66:* 215
Tongier, Stephen *82:* 32
Tooke, Susan *173:* 162
Toothill, Harry *6:* 54; *7:* 49; *25:* 219; *42:* 192
Toothill, Ilse *6:* 54
Topolski, Feliks *44:* 48
Torbert, Floyd James *22:* 226

Torgersen, Don *55:* 157
Torline, Kevin *169:* 171
Tormey, Bertram M. *75:* 3, 4
Torrecilla, Pablo *176:* 207
Torres, Leyla *156:* 199, 201
Torrey, Helen *87:* 41
Torrey, Marjorie *34:* 105
Toschik, Larry *6:* 102
Totten, Bob *13:* 93
Toy, Julie *128:* 112
Trachok, Cathy *131:* 16
Tracy, Libba *82:* 24
Trago, Keith *158:* 253
Trail, Lee *55:* 157
Trang, To Ngoc *167:* 180
Trang, Winson *89:* 151
Trapani, Iza *116:* 202
Travers, Bob *49:* 100; *63:* 145
Treatner, Meryl *95:* 180
Tremain, Ruthven *17:* 238
Tresilian, Stuart *25:* 53; *40:* 212
Trez, Alain *17:* 236
Trezzo, Loretta *86:* 45
Trier, Walter *14:* 96
Trimby, Elisa *47:* 199
Trinkle, Sally *53:* 27
Tripp, F.J. *24:* 167
Tripp, Wallace *2:* 48; *7:* 28; *8:* 94; *10:* 54, 76; *11:* 92; *31:* 170, 171; *34:* 203; *42:* 57; *60:* 157; *73:* 182
Trivas, Irene *53:* 4; *54:* 168; *82:* 46, 101
Trnka, Jiri *22:* 151; *43:* 212, 213, 214, 215; *YABC 1:* 30, 31
Troughton, Joanna *37:* 186; *48:* 72
Troyer, Johannes *3:* 16; *7:* 18
Trudeau, G.B. *35:* 220, 221, 222; *48:* 119, 123, 126, 127, 128, 129, 133; *168:* 189
Trueman, Matthew *165:* 208
Truesdell, Sue *55:* 142; *108:* 219, 220
Tryon, Leslie *84:* 7; *139:* 214; *143:* 10; *181:* 10
Tseng, Jean *72:* 195; *94:* 102; *119:* 126; *151:* 106; *173:* 138, 139
Tseng, Mou-sien *72:* 195; *94:* 102; *119:* 126; *151:* 106; *173:* 138, 139
Tsinajinie, Andy *2:* 62
Tsinganos, Jim *180:* 142
Tsugami, Kyuzo *18:* 198, 199
Tucker, Ezra *156:* 31
Tuckwell, Jennifer *17:* 205
Tudor, Bethany *7:* 103
Tudor, Tasha *18:* 227; *20:* 185, 186, 187; *36:* 111; *69:* 196, 198; *100:* 44; *YABC 2:* 46, 314; *160:* 234
Tuerk, Hanne *71:* 201
Tulloch, Maurice *24:* 79
Tunis, Edwin *1:* 218, 219; *28:* 209, 210, 211, 212
Tunnicliffe, C.F. *62:* 176; *177, 178, 179; *181
Turkle, Brinton *1:* 211, 213; *2:* 249; *3:* 226; *11:* 3; *16:* 209; *20:* 22; *50:* 23; *67:* 50; *68:* 65; *79:* 205, 206, 207; *128:* 47; *YABC 1:* 79
Turnbull, Christopher J. *143:* 99, 100
Turner, Gwenda *59:* 195
Turska, Krystyna *12:* 103; *31:* 173, 174, 175; *56:* 32, 34; *100:* 66
Tusa, Tricia *72:* 242; *111:* 180, 181; *157:* 165; *164:* 186
Tusan, Stan *6:* 58; *22:* 236, 237
Tworkov, Jack *47:* 207
Tyers, Jenny *89:* 220
Tylden-Wright, Jenny *114:* 119
Tyrol, Adelaide Murphy *103:* 27
Tyrrell, Frances *107:* 204
Tzimoulis, Paul *12:* 104

U

Uchida, Yoshiko *1:* 220
Uderzo *47:* 88
Ueno, Noriko *59:* 155
Ulm, Robert *17:* 238
Ulrich, George *73:* 15; *75:* 136, 139; *99:* 150
Ulriksen, Mark *101:* 58
Unada *84:* 67
    See Gliewe, Unada
Underhill, Liz *53:* 159
Underwood, Clarence *40:* 166
Unger, Jim *67:* 208
Ungerer, Tomi *5:* 188; *9:* 40; *18:* 188; *29:* 175; *33:* 221, 222, 223, 225; *71:* 48; *106:* 209, 210, 211, 212
Unwin, Nora S. *3:* 65, 234, 235; *4:* 237; *44:* 173, 174; *YABC 1:* 59; *2:* 301
Upitis, Alvis *145:* 179
Urban, Helle *149:* 243
Urbanovic, Jackie *86:* 86
Uris, Jill *49:* 188, 197
Ursell, Martin *50:* 51
Utpatel, Frank *18:* 114
Utz, Lois *5:* 190

V

Vagin, Vladimir *66:* 10; *142:* 215
Vaillancourt, Francois *107:* 199
Vainio, Pirkko *123:* 157, 158
Valério, Geraldo *180:* 225
Vallejo, Boris *62:* 130; *72:* 212; *91:* 38; *93:* 61
Van Abbe, S. *16:* 142; *18:* 282; *31:* 90; *YABC 2:* 157, 161
Van Allsburg, Chris *37:* 205, 206; *53:* 161, 162, 163, 165, 166, 167, 168, 169, 170, 171; *105:* 215, 216, 217, 218; *156:* 176, 177, 178
Vance, James *65:* 28
Van Der Linde, Henry *99:* 17
van der Meer, Ron *98:* 204, 205
van der Meer, Atie *98:* 204, 205
Vandivert, William *21:* 175
Van Dongen, H.R. *81:* 97
Van Dusen, Chris W. *173:* 169
Van Everen, Jay *13:* 160; *YABC 1:* 121
Van Fleet, John *165:* 12, 13
Van Frankenhuyzen, Gijsbert *145:* 230; *149:* 164
van Genechten, Guido *165:* 226
Van Horn, William *43:* 218
van Lawick, Hugo *62:* 76, 79
Van Loon, Hendrik Willem *18:* 285, 289, 291
Van Munching, Paul *83:* 85
Van Rynbach, Iris *102:* 192
Van Sciver, Ruth *37:* 162
VanSeveren, Joe *63:* 182
Van Stockum, Hilda *5:* 193
Van Wely, Babs *16:* 50; *79:* 16
Van Wright, Cornelius *72:* 18; *102:* 208; *116:* 107; *152:* 236; *173:* 170, 171
Van Zyle, Jon *103:* 125; *160:* 181, 182; *176:* 199, 200
Vardzigulyants, Ruben *90:* 54
Varga, Judy *29:* 196
Vargo, Kurt *79:* 224
Varley, Susan *61:* 199; *63:* 176, 177; *101:* 148; *134:* 220
Vasconcellos, Daniel *80:* 42
Vasiliu, Mircea *2:* 166, 253; *9:* 166; *13:* 58; *68:* 42
Vaughn, Frank *34:* 157
Vavra, Robert *8:* 206
Vawter, Will *17:* 163
Vayas, Diana *71:* 61
Vazquez, Carlos *125:* 184
Veeder, Larry *18:* 4

Velasquez, Eric *45:* 217; *61:* 45; *63:* 110, 111; *88:* 162; *90:* 34, 144; *94:* 213; *107:* 147; *132:* 192; *138:* 213; *159:* 126; *181:* 184
Velasquez, Jose A. *63:* 73
Velez, Walter *71:* 75; *91:* 154; *121:* 181; *168:* 49
Velthuijs, Max *110:* 228, 229
Vendrell, Carme Sole *42:* 205
Venezia, Mike *54:* 17
Venti, Anthony Bacon *124:* 103; *126:* 26
Venturo, Piero *61:* 194, 195
Ver Beck, Frank *18:* 16, 17
Verkaaik, Ben *110:* 209
Verling, John *71:* 27
Verney, John *14:* 225; *75:* 8
Verrier, Suzanne *5:* 20; *23:* 212
Versace, Marie *2:* 255
Verstraete, Randy *108:* 193
Vestal, H.B. *9:* 134; *11:* 101; *27:* 25; *34:* 158
Vicatan *59:* 146
Vickrey, Robert *45:* 59, 64
Victor, Joan Berg *30:* 193
Viereck, Ellen *3:* 242; *14:* 229
Vigna, Judith *15:* 293; *102:* 194, 195, 196, 197
Vilato, Gaspar E. *5:* 41
Villiard, Paul *51:* 178
Vimnera, A. *23:* 154
Vincent, Eric *34:* 98
Vincent, Felix *41:* 237
Vincent, Gabrielle *121:* 175
Vip *45:* 164
Viskupic, Gary *83:* 48
Vitale, Stefano *109:* 71, 107; *114:* 219, 220; *123:* 106; *138:* 232; *180:* 228, 229
Vivas, Julie *51:* 67, 69; *96:* 225
Voake, Charlotte *114:* 221, 222; *180:* 232
Vo-Dinh, Mai *16:* 272; *60:* 191
Vogel, Ilse-Margret *14:* 230
Voigt, Erna *35:* 228
Vojnar, Kamil *95:* 31; *114:* 4; *115:* 62; *121:* 90; *124:* 72; *130:* 31; *141:* 81; *146:* 196; *150:* 123; *158:* 5, 6; *158:* 154; *171:* 119, 188; *179:* 15; *180:* 112
Vojtech, Anna *42:* 190; *108:* 222, 223; *150:* 203; *174:* 173
von Buhler, Cynthia *149:* 237; *162:* 177; *177:* 205; *180:* 77
von Roehl, Angela *126:* 191
von Schmidt, Eric *8:* 62; *50:* 209, 210
von Schmidt, Harold *30:* 80
Vosburgh, Leonard *1:* 161; *7:* 32; *15:* 295, 296; *23:* 110; *30:* 214; *43:* 181
Voss, Tom *127:* 104
Voter, Thomas W. *19:* 3, 9
Vroman, Tom *10:* 29
Vulliamy, Clara *72:* 65

W

Waber, Bernard *47:* 209, 210, 211, 212, 213, 214; *95:* 215, 216, 217; *156:* 203, 205, 206, 207
Wack, Jeff *95:* 140; *110:* 90
Wagner, John *8:* 200; *52:* 104
Wagner, Ken *2:* 59
Waide, Jan *29:* 225; *36:* 139
Wainwright, Jerry *14:* 85
Waites, Joan C. *171:* 2
Wakeen, Sandra *47:* 97
Wakiyama, Hanako *171:* 96
Waldherr, Kris *81:* 186
Waldman, Bruce *15:* 297; *43:* 178
Waldman, Neil *35:* 141; *50:* 163; *51:* 180; *54:* 78; *77:* 112; *79:* 162; *82:* 174; *84:* 5, 56, 106; *94:* 232, 233, 234; *96:* 41; *111:* 139; *113:* 9; *118:* 30; *142:* 220, 223
Waldrep, Richard *111:* 147
Walker, Brian *144:* 128

Walker, Charles *1:* 46; *4:* 59; *5:* 177; *11:* 115; *19:* 45; *34:* 74; *62:* 168; *72:* 218
Walker, Dugald Stewart *15:* 47; *32:* 202; *33:* 112
Walker, Gil *8:* 49; *23:* 132; *34:* 42
Walker, Jeff *55:* 154; *123:* 116
Walker, Jim *10:* 94
Walker, Mort *8:* 213
Walker, Norman *41:* 37; *45:* 58
Walker, Stephen *12:* 229; *21:* 174
Wallace, Beverly Dobrin *19:* 259
Wallace, Cly *87:* 93
Wallace, Ian *53:* 176, 177; *56:* 165, 166; *58:* 4; *98:* 4; *101:* 191; *112:* 124; *141:* 197, 198, 199, 200; *151:* 212
Wallace, John *105:* 228
Wallace, Nancy Elizabeth *141:* 204
Wallenta, Adam *123:* 180
Waller, S.E. *24:* 36
Wallner, Alexandra *15:* 120; *156:* 183
Wallner, John C. *9:* 77; *10:* 188; *11:* 28; *14:* 209; *31:* 56, 118; *37:* 64; *51:* 186, 187, 188, 189, 190, 191, 192, 193, 194, 195; *52:* 96; *53:* 23, 26; *71:* 99; *73:* 158; *89:* 215; *141:* 9
Wallner, John *162:* 17
Wallower, Lucille *11:* 226
Walotsky, Ron *93:* 87
Walsh, Ellen Stoll *99:* 209; *147:* 219
Walsh, Rebecca *158:* 193
Walsh, Vivian *149:* 215; *158:* 227
Walters, Audrey *18:* 294
Walther, Tom *31:* 179
Walton, Garry *69:* 149
Walton, Tony *11:* 164; *24:* 209; *153:* 8; *177:* 73
Waltrip, Lela *9:* 195
Waltrip, Mildred *3:* 209; *37:* 211
Waltrip, Rufus *9:* 195
Wan *12:* 76
Warburton, Sarah *154:* 187
Wappers, G. *121:* 40
Ward, Fred *52:* 19
Ward, Helen *72:* 244; *144:* 240, 242
Ward, John *42:* 191; *96:* 54; *97:* 110; *123:* 105; *124:* 71; *173:* 66
Ward, Keith *2:* 107; *132:* 69
Ward, Leslie *34:* 126; *36:* 87
Ward, Lynd *1:* 99, 132, 133, 150; *2:* 108, 158, 196, 259; *18:* 86; *27:* 56; *29:* 79, 187, 253, 255; *36:* 199, 200, 201, 202, 203, 204, 205, 206, 207, 209; *43:* 34; *56:* 28; *60:* 116; *100:* 65
Ward, Peter *37:* 116
Waring, Geoff *172:* 84
Warhola, James *92:* 5; *115:* 85, 87; *118:* 174, 175, 177; *176:* 84
Warner, Ben *159:* 171
Warner, Peter *14:* 87
Warnes, Tim *175:* 159
Warnick, Elsa *113:* 223
Warren, Betsy *2:* 101
Warren, Jim *85:* 81
Warren, Marion Cray *14:* 215
Warshaw, Jerry *30:* 197, 198; *42:* 165
Wasden, Kevin *102:* 162
Washington, Nevin *20:* 123
Washington, Phyllis *20:* 123
Wasserman, Amy L. *92:* 110
Waterman, Stan *11:* 76
Watkins-Pitchford, D.J. *6:* 215, 217
Watling, James *67:* 210; *78:* 112; *101:* 81; *117:* 189, 190; *127:* 119, 120
Watson, Aldren A. *2:* 267; *5:* 94; *13:* 71; *19:* 253; *32:* 220; *42:* 193, 194, 195, 196, 197, 198, 199, 200, 201; *YABC 2:* 202
Watson, G. *83:* 162
Watson, Gary *19:* 147; *36:* 68; *41:* 122; *47:* 139
Watson, J.D. *22:* 86
Watson, Karen *11:* 26
Watson, Mary *117:* 193

Watson, Richard Jesse *62:* 188, 189
Watson, Wendy *5:* 197; *13:* 101; *33:* 116; *46:* 163; *64:* 12; *74:* 242, 243; *91:* 21; *142:* 228
Watt, Melanie *136:* 206
Wattenberg, Jane *174:* 200
Watterson, Bill *66:* 223, 225, 226
Watts, Bernadette *4:* 227; *103:* 182, 183
Watts, James *59:* 197; *74:* 145; *86:* 124
Watts, John *37:* 149
Watts, Leslie Elizabeth *150:* 207; *165:* 106
Watts, Stan *116:* 205
Weatherby, Mark Alan *77:* 141
Webb, Jennifer *110:* 79
Webb, Lanny *142:* 175
Webb, Sophie *135:* 214
Webber, Helen *3:* 141
Webber, Irma E. *14:* 238
Weber, Erik *56:* 19, 20
Weber, Florence *40:* 153
Weber, Jill *127:* 227, 228
Weber, Roland *61:* 204
Weber, William J. *14:* 239
Webster, Jean *17:* 241
Weeks, Sarah *162:* 39
Wegman, William *78:* 243
Wegner, Fritz *14:* 250; *20:* 189; *44:* 165; *86:* 62
Weidenear, Reynold H. *21:* 122
Weigel, Jeff *170:* 193
Weihs, Erika *4:* 21; *15:* 299; *72:* 201; *107:* 207, 208
Weil, Lisl *7:* 203; *10:* 58; *21:* 95; *22:* 188, 217; *33:* 193
Weiman, Jon *50:* 162, 165; *52:* 103; *54:* 78, 79, 81; *78:* 80; *82:* 107; *93:* 82; *97:* 69; *105:* 179
Weiner, Sandra *14:* 240
Weiner, Scott *55:* 27
Weinhaus, Karen Ann *53:* 90; *71:* 50; *86:* 124
Weisgard, Leonard *1:* 65; *2:* 191, 197, 204, 264, 265; *5:* 108; *21:* 42; *30:* 200, 201, 203, 204; *41:* 47; *44:* 125; *53:* 25; *85:* 196, 198, 200, 201; *100:* 139, 207; *YABC 2:* 13
Weisman, David *173:* 47
Weiss, Ellen *44:* 202
Weiss, Emil *1:* 168; *7:* 60
Weiss, Harvey *1:* 145, 223; *27:* 224, 227; *68:* 214; *76:* 245, 246, 247
Weiss, Nicki *33:* 229
Weissman, Bari *49:* 72; *90:* 125; *139:* 142
Weitzman, David L. *172:* 199
Welch, Sheila Kelly *130:* 221
Welkes, Allen *68:* 218
Wellington, Monica *99:* 223; *157:* 259, 260, 261
Welliver, Norma *76:* 94
Wellner, Fred *127:* 53
Wells, Frances *1:* 183
Wells, H.G. *20:* 194, 200
Wells, Haru *53:* 120, 121
Wells, Rosemary *6:* 49; *18:* 297; *60:* 32; *66:* 203; *69:* 215, 216; *114:* 227; *118:* 149, 150; *156:* 188, 189, 190, 191
Wells, Rufus III *56:* 111, 113
Wells, Susan *22:* 43
Wendelin, Rudolph *23:* 234
Wengenroth, Stow *37:* 47
Werenskiold, Erik *15:* 6; *62:* 17
Werner, Honi *24:* 110; *33:* 41; *88:* 122
Werth, Kurt *7:* 122; *14:* 157; *20:* 214; *39:* 128
West, Harry A. *124:* 38
Westcott, Nadine Bernard *68:* 46; *84:* 49; *86:* 133; *106:* 199; *111:* 78; *113:* 111; *130:* 224; *139:* 54; *158:* 256
Westerberg, Christine *29:* 226
Westerduin, Anne *105:* 229
Westerman, Johanna *162:* 206
Weston, Martha *29:* 116; *30:* 213; *33:* 85, 100; *53:* 181, 182, 183, 184; *77:* 95; *80:* 152; *119:* 196, 197, 198, 199; *127:* 189; *133:* 196
Wetherbee, Margaret *5:* 3

Wexler, Jerome *49:* 73; *150:* 129
Whalley, Peter *50:* 49
Wheatley, Arabelle *11:* 231; *16:* 276
Wheeler, Cindy *49:* 205
Wheeler, Dora *44:* 179
Wheelright, Rowland *15:* 81; *YABC 2:* 286
Whelan, Michael *56:* 108; *70:* 27, 29, 67, 68, 148; *74:* 18; *84:* 14; *91:* 195, 196; *95:* 147; *98:* 150, 151; *106:* 157; *113:* 218, 220; *116:* 99, 100
Whelan, Patrick *135:* 145
Whistler, Rex *16:* 75; *30:* 207, 208
White, Craig *110:* 130; *119:* 193; *130:* 33; *179:* 31
White, David Omar *5:* 56; *18:* 6
White, Joan *83:* 225
White, Martin *51:* 197; *85:* 127
Whitear *32:* 26
Whitehead, Beck *86:* 171
Whitehead, S.B. *154:* 132
Whithorne, H.S. *7:* 49
Whitney, George Gillett *3:* 24
Whitney, Jean *99:* 53
Whitson, Paul *102:* 161
Whittam, Geoffrey *30:* 191
Whyte, Mary *96:* 127
Wiberg, Harald *38:* 127; *93:* 215
Wick, Walter *77:* 128
Wickstrom, Sylvie *106:* 87; *169:* 180
Widener, Terry *105:* 230; *106:* 7; *163:* 23
Wiese, Kurt *3:* 255; *4:* 206; *14:* 17; *17:* 18, 19; *19:* 47; *24:* 152; *25:* 212; *32:* 184; *36:* 211, 213, 214, 215, 216, 217, 218; *45:* 161; *100:* 92
Wiesner, David *33:* 47; *51:* 106; *57:* 67; *58:* 55; *64:* 78, 79, 81; *69:* 233; *72:* 247, 248, 249, 251, 252, 253, 254; *83:* 134; *104:* 31; *117:* 197, 199, 200, 202; *139:* 223, 224; *151:* 51; *181:* 189, 190
Wiesner, William *4:* 100; *5:* 200, 201; *14:* 262
Wiggins, George *6:* 133
Wijngaard, Juan *111:* 36; *114:* 124
Wikkelsoe, Otto *45:* 25, 26
Wikland, Ilon *5:* 113; *8:* 150; *38:* 124, 125, 130; *127:* 162
Wikler, Madeline *114:* 233
Wilbur, C. Keith, M.D. *27:* 228
Wilburn, Kathy *53:* 102; *68:* 234
Wilcox, Cathy *105:* 123
Wilcox, J.A.J. *34:* 122
Wilcox, R. Turner *36:* 219
Wild, Jocelyn *46:* 220, 221, 222; *80:* 117
Wilde, George *7:* 139
Wildsmith, Brian *16:* 281, 282; *18:* 170, 171; *66:* 25; *69:* 224, 225, 227; *77:* 103; *83:* 218; *124:* 214, 217, 219
Wildsmith, Mike *140:* 229
Wilhelm, Hans *58:* 189, 191; *73:* 157; *77:* 127; *135:* 229, 230, 233, 234
Wilkin, Eloise *36:* 173; *49:* 208, 209, 210
Wilkinson, Barry *50:* 213
Wilkinson, Gerald *3:* 40
Wilkon, Jozef *31:* 183, 184; *71:* 206, 207, 209; *133:* 222
Wilks, Mike *34:* 24; *44:* 203
Willems, Mo *154:* 245, 246, 247; *180:* 236, 237, 239
Willey, Bee *103:* 129; *139:* 159; *173:* 115
Willhoite, Michael A. *71:* 214
William, Maria *168:* 51
Williams, Berkeley, Jr. *64:* 75
Williams, Ferelith Eccles *22:* 238
Williams, Garth *1:* 197; *2:* 49, 270; *4:* 205; *15:* 198, 302, 304, 307; *16:* 34; *18:* 283, 298, 299, 300, 301; *29:* 177, 178, 179, 232, 233, 241, 242, 243, 244, 245, 248; *40:* 106; *66:* 229, 230, 231, 233, 234; *71:* 192; *73:* 218, 219, 220; *78:* 261; *100:* 251, 252, 255; *136:* 117; *YABC 2:* 15, 16, 19
Williams, J. Scott *48:* 28
Williams, Jennifer *102:* 201

Williams, Jenny *60:* 202; *81:* 21; *88:* 71
Williams, Kent *180:* 18
Williams, Kit *44:* 206, 207, 208, 209, 211, 212
Williams, Marcia *97:* 214; *159:* 208, 209
Williams, Maureen *12:* 238
Williams, Patrick *14:* 218
Williams, Richard *44:* 93; *72:* 229; *74:* 133; *78:* 155, 237; *91:* 178; *110:* 212; *136:* 201, 202, 203; *152:* 115
Williams, Sam *124:* 222; *153:* 11; *177:* 201, 202; *180:* 34
Williams, Sophy *135:* 236
Williams, Vera B. *53:* 186, 187, 188, 189; *102:* 201, 202, 203
Williamson, Alex *177:* 180
Williamson, Mel *60:* 9
Willingham, Fred *104:* 206; *154:* 157
Willis, Adam *181:* 75
Willmore, J.T. *54:* 113, 114
Wilsdorf, Anne *180:* 122
Wilson, Anne *160:* 114
Wilson, Charles Banks *17:* 92; *43:* 73
Wilson, Connie *113:* 179
Wilson, Dagmar *10:* 47
Wilson, Dawn *67:* 161; *81:* 120; *113:* 158
Wilson, Edward A. *6:* 24; *16:* 149; *20:* 220, 221; *22:* 87; *26:* 67; *38:* 212, 214, 215, 216, 217
Wilson, Forrest *27:* 231
Wilson, Gahan *35:* 234; *41:* 136
Wilson, George *76:* 87
Wilson, Helen Miranda *140:* 61
Wilson, Jack *17:* 139
Wilson, Janet *77:* 154; *96:* 114; *99:* 219, 220; *153:* 64 *106:* 122; *130:* 210; *145:* 178; *173:* 64
Wilson, John *22:* 240
Wilson, Maurice *46:* 224
Wilson, Patten *35:* 61
Wilson, Peggy *15:* 4; *84:* 20
Wilson, Phil *181:* 29
Wilson, Rowland B. *30:* 170
Wilson, Sarah *50:* 215
Wilson, Tom *33:* 232
Wilson, W.N. *22:* 26
Wilson-Max, Ken *170:* 196; *180:* 181
Wilton, Nicholas *103:* 52
Wilwerding, Walter J. *9:* 202
Wimmer, Mike *63:* 6; *70:* 121; *75:* 186; *76:* 21, 22, 23; *91:* 114; *97:* 45, 46; *98:* 28; *107:* 130; *146:* 21; *149:* 47; *173:* 126
Winborn, Marsha *78:* 34; *99:* 70
Winch, John *165:* 233
Winchester, Linda *13:* 231
Wind, Betty *28:* 158
Windham, Kathryn Tucker *14:* 260
Winfield, Alison *115:* 78
Winfield, Wayne *72:* 23
Wing, Gary *64:* 147
Wing, Ron *50:* 85
Wingerter, Linda S. *132:* 199; *174:* 181
Winick, Judd *124:* 227, 228, 229
Winslow, Will *21:* 124
Winstead, Rosie *180:* 243
Winsten, Melanie Willa *41:* 41
Winter, Jeanette *151:* 240, 241, 242
Winter, Milo *15:* 97; *19:* 221; *21:* 181, 203, 204, 205; *64:* 19; *YABC 2:* 144
Winter, Paula *48:* 227
Winter, Susan *163:* 177
Winters, Greg *70:* 117
Winters, Nina *62:* 194
Wise, Louis *13:* 68
Wiseman, Ann *31:* 187
Wiseman, B. *4:* 233
Wishnefsky, Phillip *3:* 14
Wiskur, Darrell *5:* 72; *10:* 50; *18:* 246
Wisniewski, David *95:* 220, 221
Wisniewski, Robert *95:* 10; *119:* 192
Witschonke, Alan *153:* 149, 150
Witt, Dick *80:* 244

Wittmann, Patrick *162:* 204
Wittman, Sally *30:* 219
Wittner, Dale *99:* 43
Wittwer, Hala *158:* 267
Woehr, Lois *12:* 5
Wohlberg, Meg *12:* 100; *14:* 197; *41:* 255
Wohnoutka, Mike *137:* 68
Wojtowycz, David *167:* 168
Woldin, Beth Weiner *34:* 211
Wolf, Elizabeth *133:* 151
Wolf, J. *16:* 91
Wolf, Janet *78:* 254
Wolf, Linda *33:* 163
Wolfe, Corey *72:* 213
Wolff, Ashley *50:* 217; *81:* 216; *156:* 216, 217; *170:* 57; *174:* 174
Wolff, Glenn *178:* 230
Wolfsgruber, Linda *166:* 61
Wondriska, William *6:* 220
Wong, Janet S. *98:* 225; *152:* 43
Wong, Nicole *174:* 13
Wonsetler, John C. *5:* 168
Wood, Audrey *50:* 221, 222, 223; *81:* 219, 221
Wood, Don *50:* 220, 225, 226, 228, 229; *81:* 218, 220; *139:* 239, 240
Wood, Grant *19:* 198
Wood, Heather *133:* 108
Wood, Ivor *58:* 17
Wood, Muriel *36:* 119; *77:* 167; *171:* 55
Wood, Myron *6:* 220
Wood, Owen *18:* 187; *64:* 202, 204, 205, 206, 208, 210
Wood, Ruth *8:* 11
Woodbridge, Curtis *133:* 138
Wooding, Sharon L. *66:* 237
Woodruff, Liza *132:* 239
Woodruff, Thomas *171:* 73
Woods, John, Jr. *109:* 142
Woodson, Jack *10:* 201
Woodson, Jacqueline *94:* 242
Woodward, Alice *26:* 89; *36:* 81
Wool, David *26:* 27
Woolley, Janet *112:* 75
Woolman, Steven *106:* 47; *163:* 73
Wooten, Vernon *23:* 70; *51:* 170
Worboys, Evelyn *1:* 166, 167
Word, Reagan *103:* 204
Wormell, Christopher *154:* 251
Worth, Jo *34:* 143
Worth, Wendy *4:* 133
Wosmek, Frances *29:* 251
Wrenn, Charles L. *38:* 96; *YABC 1:* 20, 21
Wright, Barbara Mullarney *98:* 161
Wright, Cliff *168:* 203
Wright, Dare *21:* 206
Wright-Frierson, Virginia *58:* 194; *110:* 246
Wright, George *YABC 1:* 268
Wright, Joseph *30:* 160
Wronker, Lili Cassel *3:* 247; *10:* 204; *21:* 10
Wummer, Amy *154:* 181; *168:* 150; *176:* 85
Wyant, Alexander Helwig *110:* 19
Wyatt, David *97:* 9; *101:* 44; *114:* 194; *140:* 20; *167:* 13

Wyatt, Stanley *46:* 210
Wyeth, Andrew *13:* 40; *YABC 1:* 133, 134
Wyeth, Jamie *41:* 257
Wyeth, N.C. *13:* 41; *17:* 252, 253, 254, 255, 256, 257, 258, 259, 264, 265, 266, 267, 268; *18:* 181; *19:* 80, 191, 200; *21:* 57, 183; *22:* 91; *23:* 152; *24:* 28, 99; *35:* 61; *41:* 65; *100:* 206; *YABC 1:* 133, 223; *2:* 53, 75, 171, 187, 317
Wyman, Cherie R. *91:* 42

X

Xuan, YongSheng *119:* 202, 207, 208; *140:* 36

Y

Yaccarino, Dan *141:* 208, 209; *147:* 171
Yakovetic, Joe *59:* 202; *75:* 85
Yalowitz, Paul *93:* 33
Yamaguchi, Marianne *85:* 118
Yamasaki, James *167:* 93
Yang, Belle *170:* 198
Yang, Jay *1:* 8; *12:* 239
Yap, Weda *6:* 176
Yaroslava
    See Mills, Yaroslava Surmach
Yashima, Taro *14:* 84
Yates, John *74:* 249, 250
Yayo *178:* 88
Yee, Cora *166:* 233
Yee, Wong Herbert *115:* 216, 217; *172:* 204, 205
Yeo, Brad *135:* 121
Yerxa, Leo *181:* 195
Yezerski, Thomas F. *162:* 29
Ylla
    See Koffler, Camilla
Yohn, F.C. *23:* 128; *YABC 1:* 269
Yorinks, Adrienne *144:* 248
Yorke, David *80:* 178
Yoshida, Toshi *77:* 231
Yoshikawa, Sachiko *168:* 104; *177:* 28; *181:* 196, 197
Youll, Paul *91:* 218
Youll, Stephen *92:* 227; *118:* 136, 137; *164:* 248
Young, Cybéle *167:* 9
Young, Ed *7:* 205; *10:* 206; *40:* 124; *63:* 142; *74:* 250, 251, 252, 253; *75:* 227; *81:* 159; *83:* 98; *94:* 154; *115:* 160; *137:* 162; *YABC 2:* 242; *173:* 174, 175, 176
Young, Mary O'Keefe *77:* 95; *80:* 247; *134:* 214; *140:* 213
Young, Noela *8:* 221; *89:* 231; *97:* 195
Young, Selina *153:* 12
Yun, Cheng Mung *60:* 143

Z

Zacharow, Christopher *88:* 98
Zacks, Lewis *10:* 161
Zadig *50:* 58
Zaffo, George *42:* 208
Zagwyn, Deborah Turney *138:* 227
Zaid, Barry *50:* 127; *51:* 201
Zaidenberg, Arthur *34:* 218, 219, 220
Zalben, Jane Breskin *7:* 211; *79:* 230, 231, 233; *170:* 202
Zallinger, Jean *4:* 192; *8:* 8, 129; *14:* 273; *68:* 36; *80:* 254; *115:* 219, 220, 222
Zallinger, Rudolph F. *3:* 245
Zakrajsek, Molly *177:* 146
Zappa, Ahmet *180:* 250
Zebot, George *83:* 214
Zeck, Gerry *40:* 232
Zeff, Joe *181:* 98
Zeifert, Harriet *154:* 265, 267
Zeiring, Bob *42:* 130
Zeldich, Arieh *49:* 124; *62:* 120
Zeldis, Malcah *86:* 239; *94:* 198; *146:* 265, 266
Zelinsky, Paul O. *14:* 269; *43:* 56; *49:* 218-223; *53:* 111; *68:* 195; *102:* 219, 222, 221, 222; *154:* 255, 256, 257; *171:* 141
Zelvin, Diana *72:* 190; *76:* 101; *93:* 207
Zemach, Kaethe *149:* 250
Zemach, Margot *3:* 270; *8:* 201; *21:* 210, 211; *27:* 204, 205, 210; *28:* 185; *49:* 22, 183, 224; *53:* 151; *56:* 146; *70:* 245, 246; *92:* 74
Zeman, Ludmila *153:* 212
Zemsky, Jessica *10:* 62
Zepelinsky, Paul *35:* 93
Zerbetz, Evon *127:* 34; *158:* 109
Zhang, Ange *101:* 190; *172:* 41
Zhang, Son Nang *163:* 113; *170:* 206
Ziegler, Jack *84:* 134
Zimdars, Berta *129:* 155
Zimet, Jay *147:* 94; *152:* 74
Zimic, Tricia *72:* 95
Zimmer, Dirk *38:* 195; *49:* 71; *56:* 151; *65:* 214; *84:* 159; *89:* 26; *147:* 224
Zimmer, Tracie Vaughn *169:* 183
Zimmermann, H. Werner *101:* 223; *112:* 197
Zimnik, Reiner *36:* 224
Zingone, Robin *180:* 134
Zinkeisen, Anna *13:* 106
Zinn, David *97:* 97
Zoellick, Scott *33:* 231
Zonia, Dhimitri *20:* 234, 235
Zorn, Peter A., Jr. *142:* 157
Zudeck, Darryl *58:* 129; *63:* 98; *80:* 52
Zug, Mark *88:* 131
Zulewski, Tim *164:* 95
Zuma *99:* 36
Zvorykin, Boris *61:* 155
Zweifel, Francis *14:* 274; *28:* 187
Zwerger, Lisbeth *54:* 176, 178; *66:* 246, 247, 248; *130:* 230, 231, 232, 233; *181:* 92
Zwinger, Herman H. *46:* 227
Zwolak, Paul *67:* 69, 71, 73, 74

Author Index

The following index gives the number of the volume in which an author's biographical sketch, Autobiography Feature, Brief Entry, or Obituary appears.

This index includes references to all entries in the following series, which are also published by The Gale Group.

YABC—*Yesterday's Authors of Books for Children: Facts and Pictures about Authors and Illustrators of Books for Young People from Early Times to 1960*
CLR—*Children's Literature Review: Excerpts from Reviews, Criticism, and Commentary on Books for Children*
SAAS—*Something about the Author Autobiography Series*

A

Aaron, Chester 1923- 74
  Earlier sketch in SATA 9
  See also SAAS 12
Aaseng, Nate
  See Aaseng, Nathan
Aaseng, Nathan 1953- 172
  Brief entry 38
  Earlier sketches in SATA 51, 88
  See also CLR 54
  See also SAAS 12
Abbas, Jailan 1952- 91
Abbey, Lynn
  See Abbey, Marilyn Lorraine
Abbey, Marilyn Lorraine 1948- 156
Abbott, Alice
  See Borland, Kathryn Kilby
  and Speicher, Helen Ross S(mith)
Abbott, Jacob 1803-1879 22
Abbott, Manager Henry
  See Stratemeyer, Edward L.
Abbott, R(obert) Tucker 1919-1995 61
  Obituary 87
Abbott, Sarah
  See Zolotow, Charlotte (Gertrude) S(hapiro)
Abbott, Tony 1952- 159
Abdelsayed, Cindy 1962- 123
Abdul, Raoul 1929- 12
Abel, Raymond 1911- 12
Abell, Kathleen 1938- 9
Abelove, Joan 110
Abels, Harriette S(heffer) 1926- 50
Abercrombie, Barbara (Mattes) 1939- 16
Abercrombie, Lynn
  See Sorrells, Walter
Abernethy, Robert G(ordon) 1927- 5
Abisch, Roslyn Kroop 1927- 9
Abisch, Roz
  See Abisch, Roslyn Kroop
Abodaher, David J. (Naiph) 1919- 17
Abolafia, Yossi 1944-
  See Abulafia, Yossi
Abouzeid, Chris 175
Abrahall, Clare Hoskyns
  See Hoskyns-Abrahall, Clare (Constance Drury)
Abrahams, Hilary (Ruth) 1938- 29
Abrahams, Robert David 1905-1998 4

Abrams, Joy 1941- 16
Abrams, Lawrence F. 58
  Brief entry 47
Abrashkin, Raymond 1911-1960 50
Abulafia, Yossi 1944- 177
  Brief entry 46
  Earlier sketch in SATA 60
Acampora, Paul 175
Achebe, Albert Chinualumogu
  See Achebe, Chinua
Achebe, Chinua 1930- 40
  Brief entry 38
  Earlier sketch in SATA 38
  See also CLR 20
Ackerman, Diane 1948- 102
Ackerman, Eugene (Francis) 1888-1974 10
Ackerman, Karen 1951- 126
Ackerman, Susan Yoder 1945- 92
Ackison, Wendy Wassink 1956- 103
Ackley, Peggy Jo 1955- 58
Ackroyd, Peter 1949- 153
Acorn, John (Harrison) 1958- 79
Acredolo, Linda (Potter) 1947- 159
Acs, Laszlo (Bela) 1931- 42
  Brief entry 32
Acuff, Selma Boyd 1924- 45
Ada, Alma Flor 1938- 181
  Earlier sketches in SATA 43, 84, 143
  See also CLR 62
Adair, Gilbert 1944- 98
Adair, Ian 1942- 53
Adair, Margaret Weeks (?)-1971 10
Adam, Cornel
  See Lengyel, Cornel Adam
Adam, Mark
  See Alexander, Marc
Adam, Robert 1948- 93
Adams, Adrienne 1906- 90
  Earlier sketch in SATA 8
  See also CLR 73
Adams, Andy 1859-1935
  See YABC 1
Adams, Barbara Johnston 1943- 60
Adams, Bruin
  See Ellis, Edward S(ylvester)
Adams, Captain Bruin
  See Ellis, Edward S(ylvester)
Adams, Captain J. F. C.
  See Ellis, Edward S(ylvester)

Adams, Dale
  See Quinn, Elisabeth
Adams, Daniel
  See Nicole, Christopher (Robin)
Adams, Debra
  See Speregen, Devra Newberger
Adams, Douglas 1952-2001 116
  Obituary 128
Adams, Douglas Noel
  See Adams, Douglas
Adams, Edith
  See Shine, Deborah
Adams, Florence 1932- 61
Adams, Harriet S(tratemeyer) 1892(?)-1982 . 1
  Obituary 29
Adams, Harrison
  See Rathborne, St. George (Henry)
  and Stratemeyer, Edward L.
Adams, Hazard 1926- 6
Adams, Hazard Simeon
  See Adams, Hazard
Adams, John Anthony 1944- 67
Adams, Laurie 1941- 33
Adams, Lowell
  See Joseph, James (Herz)
Adams, Nicholas
  See Pine, Nicholas
Adams, Nicholas
  See Smith, Sherwood
Adams, Nicholas
  See Doyle, Debra
  and Macdonald, James D.
Adams, Pam 1919- 112
Adams, Pamela
  See Adams, Pam
Adams, Richard (George) 1920- 69
  Earlier sketch in SATA 7
  See also CLR 121
Adams, Ruth Joyce 14
Adams, William Taylor 1822-1897 28
Adam Smith, Janet (Buchanan) 1905-1999
  63
Adamson, Gareth 1925-1982(?) 46
  Obituary 30
Adamson, George (Worsley) 1913-2005 30
Adamson, Graham
  See Groom, Arthur William

Adamson, Joy(-Friederike Victoria) 1910-1980
...... *11*
  Obituary *22*
Adamson, Wendy Writson 1942- *22*
Addona, Angelo F. 1925- *14*
Addy, Sharon Hart 1943- *108*
Addy, Ted
  See Winterbotham, R(ussell) R(obert)
Adelberg, Doris
  See Orgel, Doris
Adelson, Leone 1908- *11*
Adinolfi, JoAnn *176*
Adkins, Jan 1944- *144*
  Earlier sketches in SATA *8, 69*
  See also CLR *77*
  See also SAAS *19*
Adler, C(arole) S(chwerdtfeger) 1932- *126*
  Earlier sketches in SATA *26, 63, 102*
  See also CLR *78*
  See also SAAS *15*
Adler, David A. 1947- *178*
  Earlier sketches in SATA *14, 70, 106, 151*
  See also CLR *108*
Adler, Irene
  See Penzler, Otto
  and Storr, Catherine (Cole)
Adler, Irving 1913- *29*
  Autobiography Feature *164*
  Earlier sketch in SATA *1*
  See also CLR *27*
  See also SAAS *15*
Adler, Larry 1939- *36*
Adler, Peggy *22*
Adler, Ruth 1915-1968 ...... *1*
Adlerman, Daniel (Ezra) 1963- *163*
  Earlier sketch in SATA *96*
Adlerman, Kim
  See Adlerman, Kimberly M(arie)
Adlerman, Kimberly M(arie) 1964- *163*
  Earlier sketch in SATA *96*
Adoff, Arnold 1935- *96*
  Earlier sketches in SATA *5, 57*
  See also CLR *7*
  See also SAAS *15*
Adoff, Jaime (Levi) *163*
Adorjan, Carol (Madden) 1934- *71*
  Earlier sketch in SATA *10*
Adrian, Frances
  See Polland, Madeleine A(ngela Cahill)
Adrian, Mary
  See Jorgensen, Mary Venn
Adshead, Gladys L(ucy) 1896-1985 ...... *3*
Aesop 620(?)B.C.-560(?)B.C. *64*
  See also CLR *14*
Aesop, Abraham
  See Newbery, John
Affabee, Eric
  See Stine, R.L.
Agapida, Fray Antonio
  See Irving, Washington
Agard, John 1949- *138*
Agard, Nadema 1948- *18*
Agarwal, Deepa 1947- *141*
Agee, Jon 1960- *157*
  Earlier sketch in SATA *116*
Agell, Charlotte 1959- *150*
  Earlier sketch in SATA *99*
Agent Orange
  See Moseley, James W(illett)
Aghill, Gordon
  See Garrett, (Gordon) Randall (Phillip)
  and Silverberg, Robert
Agle, Nan Hayden 1905- *3*
  See also SAAS *10*
Agnew, Edith J(osephine) 1897-1988 ...... *11*
Agonito, Joseph *177*
Agonito, Rosemary 1937- *177*
Ahern, Margaret McCrohan 1921- *10*
Ahl, Anna Maria 1926- *32*

Ahlberg, Allan 1938- *165*
  Brief entry *35*
  Earlier sketches in SATA *68, 120*
  See also CLR *18*
Ahlberg, Janet 1944-1994 ...... *120*
  Brief entry *32*
  Obituary *83*
  Earlier sketch in SATA *68*
  See also CLR *18*
Aichinger, Helga 1937- *4*
Aiken, Clarissa (M.) Lorenz 1899-1992 ...... *12*
  Obituary *109*
Aiken, Conrad (Potter) 1889-1973 ...... *30*
  Earlier sketch in SATA *3*
Aiken, Joan (Delano) 1924-2004 ...... *73*
  Autobiography Feature *109*
  Obituary *152*
  Earlier sketches in SATA *2, 30*
  See also CLR *90*
  See also SAAS *1*
Ainsley, Alix
  See Steiner, Barbara A(nnette)
Ainsworth, Catherine Harris 1910- *56*
Ainsworth, Norma 1911-1987 ...... *9*
Ainsworth, Ruth (Gallard) 1908- *73*
  Earlier sketch in SATA *7*
Ainsworth, William Harrison 1805-1882 ...... *24*
Aistrop, Jack 1916- *14*
Aitken, Amy 1952- *54*
  Brief entry *40*
Aitken, Dorothy 1916- *10*
Aitmatov, Chingiz (Torekulovich) 1928- *56*
  See Aytmatov, Chingiz
Akaba, Suekichi 1910- *46*
Akers, Floyd
  See Baum, L(yman) Frank
Akib, Jamel *181*
Aks, Patricia 1926-1994 ...... *68*
Alagoa, Ebiegberi Joe 1933- *108*
Alain
  See Brustlein, Daniel
Alan, David
  See Horsfield, Alan
Alan, Robert
  See Silverstein, Robert Alan
Alarcon, Francisco X(avier) 1954- *104*
Albert, Burton 1936- *22*
Albert, Louise 1928- *157*
Albert, Richard E. 1909-1999 ...... *82*
Albert, Susan Wittig 1940- *107*
Alberts, Frances Jacobs 1907-1989 ...... *14*
Albertson, Susan
  See Wojciechowski, Susan
Albion, Lee Smith *29*
Alborough, Jez 1959- *149*
  Earlier sketch in SATA *86*
Albrecht, Lillie (Vanderveer H.) 1894-1985
...... *12*
Albyn, Carole Lisa 1955- *83*
Alchemy, Jack
  See Gershator, David
Alcock, Gudrun 1908- *56*
  Brief entry *33*
Alcock, Vivien (Dolores) 1924-2003 ...... *76*
  Brief entry *38*
  Obituary *148*
  Earlier sketch in SATA *45*
  See also CLR *26*
Alcorn, John 1935- *31*
  Brief entry *30*
Alcorn, Stephen 1958- *110*
Alcott, Louisa May 1832-1888 ...... *100*
  See also YABC *1*
  See also CLR *109*
Alda, Arlene 1933- *158*
  Brief entry *36*
  Earlier sketches in SATA *44, 106*
  See also CLR *93*
Alden, Isabella (Macdonald) 1841-1930 ...... *115*
  See also YABC *2*

Alden, Sue
  See Francis, Dorothy Brenner
Alderman, Clifford Lindsey 1902-1988 ...... *3*
Alderson, Sue Ann 1940- *59*
  Brief entry *48*
Alding, Peter
  See Jeffries, Roderic
Aldis, Dorothy (Keeley) 1896-1966 ...... *2*
Aldiss, Brian W. 1925- *34*
Aldiss, Brian Wilson
  See Aldiss, Brian W.
Aldon, Adair
  See Meigs, Cornelia Lynde
Aldous, Allan (Charles) 1911- *27*
Aldrich, Ann
  See Meaker, Marijane
Aldrich, Bess Streeter 1881-1954
  See CLR *70*
Aldrich, Thomas (Bailey) 1836-1907 ...... *114*
  Earlier sketch in SATA *17*
Aldridge, (Harold Edward) James 1918- *87*
Aldridge, Josephine Haskell *14*
Alegria, Ricardo E(nrique) 1921- *6*
Aleksin, Anatolii Georgievich 1924- *36*
Alenov, Lydia 1948- *61*
Alex, Ben (a pseudonym) 1946- *45*
Alex, Marlee (a pseudonym) 1948- *45*
Alexander, Anna B(arbara Cooke) 1913- *1*
Alexander, Anne
  See Alexander, Anna B(arbara Cooke)
Alexander, Ellen 1938- *91*
Alexander, Frances (Laura) 1888-1979 ...... *4*
Alexander, Jocelyn Anne Arundel 1930- *22*
Alexander, Linda 1935- *2*
Alexander, Lloyd 1924-2007 ...... *135*
  Earlier sketches in SATA *3, 49, 81, 129*
  See also CLR *48*
  See also SAAS *19*
Alexander, Lloyd Chudley
  See Alexander, Lloyd
Alexander, Marc 1929- *117*
Alexander, Martha 1920- *136*
  Earlier sketches in SATA *11, 70*
Alexander, Rae Pace
  See Alexander, Raymond Pace
Alexander, Raymond Pace 1898-1974 ...... *22*
Alexander, Rod
  See Pellowski, Michael (Joseph)
Alexander, Sally Hobart 1943- *84*
Alexander, Sue 1933- *136*
  Earlier sketches in SATA *12, 89*
  See also SAAS *15*
Alexeieff, Alexandre A. 1901-1979 ...... *14*
Alger, Horatio, Jr.
  See Stratemeyer, Edward L.
Alger, Horatio, Jr. 1832-1899 ...... *16*
  See also CLR *87*
Alger, Leclaire (Gowans) 1898-1969 ...... *15*
Aliki
  See CLR *71*
  See Brandenberg, Aliki (Liacouras)
Alkema, Chester Jay 1932- *12*
Al-Khalili, Jim 1962- *124*
Alkiviades, Alkis 1953- *105*
Allaby, John Michael
  See Allaby, Michael
Allaby, Michael 1933- *167*
Allamand, Pascale 1942- *12*
Allan, Mabel Esther 1915-1998 ...... *75*
  Earlier sketches in SATA *5, 32*
  See also CLR *43*
  See also SAAS *11*
Allan, Nicholas 1956- *123*
  Earlier sketch in SATA *79*
Allan-Meyer, Kathleen 1918- *51*
  Brief entry *46*
Allard, Harry
  See Allard, Harry G(rover), Jr.
Allard, Harry G(rover), Jr. 1928- *102*
  Earlier sketch in SATA *42*
  See also CLR *85*

Allee, Marjorie Hill 1890-1945 .... *17*
Allen, Adam
　See Epstein, Beryl (M. Williams)
　and Epstein, Samuel
Allen, Alex B.
　See Heide, Florence Parry
Allen, Allyn
　See Eberle, Irmengarde
Allen, Betsy
　See Harrison, Elizabeth (Allen) Cavanna
Allen, Bob 1961- *76*
Allen, Gertrude E(lizabeth) 1888-1984 .... *9*
Allen, Grace
　See Hogarth, Grace (Weston Allen)
Allen, Jeffrey (Yale) 1948- *42*
Allen, John
　See Perry, Ritchie (John Allen)
Allen, Jonathan 1957- *177*
　Earlier sketch in SATA *131*
Allen, Jonathan Dean
　See Allen, Jonathan
Allen, Judy (Christina) 1941- *124*
　Earlier sketch in SATA *80*
Allen, Kenneth S. 1913-1981 .... *56*
Allen, Leroy 1912- *11*
Allen, Linda 1925- *33*
Allen, Marjorie 1931- *22*
Allen, Maury 1932- *26*
Allen, Merritt Parmelee 1892-1954 .... *22*
Allen, Nancy Kelly 1949- *171*
　Earlier sketch in SATA *127*
Allen, Nina (Stroemgren) 1935- *22*
Allen, Pamela (Kay) 1934- *123*
　Earlier sketches in SATA *50, 81*
　See also CLR *44*
Allen, Rodney F. 1938-1999 .... *27*
Allen, Roger MacBride 1957- *105*
Allen, Ruth
　See Peterson, Esther (Allen)
Allen, Samuel W(ashington) 1917- *9*
Allen, T. D.
　See Allen, Terril Diener
Allen, Terril Diener 1908- *35*
　See Allen, T. D.
Allen, Terry D.
　See Allen, Terril Diener
Allen, Thomas B(enton) 1929- *140*
　Earlier sketch in SATA *45*
Allen, Tom
　See Allen, Thomas B(enton)
Allende, Isabel 1942- *163*
　See also CLR *99*
Allerton, Mary
　See Govan, (Mary) Christine Noble
Alley, Robert W.
　See Alley, R.W.
Alley, R.W. *169*
Alleyn, Ellen
　See Rossetti, Christina
Allington, Richard L(loyd) 1947- *39*
　Brief entry *35*
Allison, Amy 1956- *138*
Allison, Bob *14*
Allison, Diane Worfolk *78*
Allison, Jennifer *173*
Allison, Linda 1948- *43*
Allman, Barbara 1950- *137*
Allmendinger, David F(rederick), Jr. 1938-
　... *35*
Allred, Alexandra Powe 1965- *144*
Allred, Gordon T(hatcher) 1930- *10*
Allsop, Kenneth 1920-1973 .... *17*
Almedingen, E. M. *3*
　See Almedingen, Martha Edith von
Almon, Russell
　See Clevenger, William R.
　and Downing, David A(lmon)
Almond, David 1951- *158*
　Earlier sketch in SATA *114*
　See also CLR *85*
Almquist, Don 1929- *11*

Alphin, Elaine Marie 1955- *139*
　Autobiography Feature *139*
　Earlier sketches in SATA *80, 130*
Alsop, Mary O'Hara 1885-1980 .... *34*
　Obituary *24*
　Earlier sketch in SATA *2*
　See O'Hara, Mary
Alter, Anna 1974- *135*
Alter, Judith (MacBain) 1938- *101*
　Earlier sketch in SATA *52*
Alter, Judy
　See Alter, Judith (MacBain)
Alter, Robert Edmond 1925-1965 .... *9*
Althea
　See Braithwaite, Althea
Altman, Linda Jacobs 1943- *21*
Altman, Suzanne
　See Orgel, Doris
　and Schecter, Ellen
Alton, Steve *169*
Altschuler, Franz 1923- *45*
Altsheler, Joseph A(lexander) 1862-1919
　See YABC *1*
Alvarez, John
　See del Rey, Lester
Alvarez, Joseph A. 1930- *18*
Alvarez, Julia 1950- *129*
al-Windawi, Thura
　See Windawi, Thura al-
Alyer, Philip A.
　See Stratemeyer, Edward L.
Amann, Janet 1951- *79*
Amato, Carol A. 1942- *92*
Amato, Mary 1961- *178*
　Earlier sketch in SATA *140*
Ambrose, Stephen E. 1936-2002 .... *138*
　Earlier sketch in SATA *40*
Ambrose, Stephen Edward
　See Ambrose, Stephen E.
Ambrus, Gyozo Laszlo 1935- *41*
　See Ambrus, Victor G.
Ambrus, Victor G. *1*
　See also SAAS *4*
　See Ambrus, Gyozo Laszlo
Amend, Bill 1962- *147*
Amerman, Lockhart 1911-1969 .... *3*
Ames, Evelyn 1908-1990 .... *13*
　Obituary *64*
Ames, Gerald 1906-1993 .... *11*
　Obituary *74*
Ames, Lee J(udah) 1921- *151*
　Earlier sketch in SATA *3*
Ames, Mildred 1919-1994 .... *85*
　Earlier sketches in SATA *22, 81*
Amico, Tom 1960(?)- *176*
Ammon, Richard 1942- *124*
Amon, Aline 1928- *9*
Amoss, Berthe 1925- *112*
　Earlier sketch in SATA *5*
Anastasio, Dina 1941- *94*
　Brief entry *30*
　Earlier sketch in SATA *37*
Anckarsvard, Karin Inez Maria 1915-1969 ... *6*
Ancona, George 1929- *145*
　Earlier sketches in SATA *12, 85*
　See also SAAS *18*
Anders, C. J.
　See Bennett, Cherie
Anders, Isabel 1946- *101*
Anders, Lou *176*
Andersdatter, Karla M(argaret) 1938- *34*
Andersen, Hans Christian 1805-1875 .... *100*
　See also YABC *1*
　See also CLR *113*
Andersen, Ted
　See Boyd, Waldo T.
Andersen, Yvonne 1932- *27*
Anderson, Bernice G(oudy) 1894-1997 .... *33*
Anderson, Bob 1944- *139*
　Earlier sketch in SATA *136*

Anderson, Brad(ley Jay) 1924- *33*
　Brief entry *31*
Anderson, C. C.
　See Anderson, Catherine Corley
Anderson, C(larence) W(illiam) 1891-1971
　... *11*
Anderson, Catherine C.
　See Anderson, Catherine Corley
Anderson, Catherine Corley 1909-2001 ...... *72*
Anderson, Clifford
　See Gardner, Richard (M.)
Anderson, Daryl Shon 1963- *93*
Anderson, Dave
　See Anderson, David (Poole)
Anderson, David (Poole) 1929- *60*
Anderson, Derek 1969- *169*
Anderson, Eloise Adell 1927- *9*
Anderson, George
　See Groom, Arthur William
Anderson, Grace Fox 1932- *43*
Anderson, J(ohn) R(ichard) L(ane) 1911-1981
　... *15*
　Obituary *27*
Anderson, Joy 1928- *1*
Anderson, Kevin J. 1962- *117*
　Earlier sketch in SATA *74*
Anderson, Kevin James
　See Anderson, Kevin J.
Anderson, Kirsty 1978- *108*
Anderson, Laurie Halse 1961- *132*
　Earlier sketch in SATA *95*
Anderson, LaVere Francis Shoenfelt 1907-1998
　... *27*
Anderson, Leone Castell 1923- *53*
　Brief entry *49*
Anderson, Lisa G. 1963- *108*
Anderson, Lonzo *2*
　See Anderson, John L(onzo)
Anderson, Lucia (Lewis) 1922- *10*
Anderson, Madelyn Klein 1926-2005 .... *28*
Anderson, Margaret J(ean) 1931- *27*
　See also SAAS *8*
Anderson, Marilyn D. 1943- *144*
Anderson, Mary 1939- *82*
　Earlier sketch in SATA *7*
　See also SAAS *23*
Anderson, Matthew Tobin
　See Anderson, M.T.
Anderson, Mona 1910-2004 .... *40*
Anderson, Mrs. Melvin
　See Anderson, Catherine Corley
Anderson, M.T. 1968- *146*
　Earlier sketch in SATA *97*
Anderson, Norman Dean 1928- *22*
Anderson, Peggy Perry 1953- *179*
　Earlier sketch in SATA *84*
Anderson, Poul 1926-2001 .... *90*
　Autobiography Feature *106*
　Brief entry *39*
　See also CLR *58*
Anderson, Poul William
　See Anderson, Poul
Anderson, Rachel 1943- *86*
　Earlier sketch in SATA *34*
　See also SAAS *18*
Anderson, Richard
　See Anderson, J(ohn) R(ichard) L(ane)
Anderson, Sara *173*
Anderson, (Tom) Scoular *138*
Anderson, Susan 1952- *90*
Anderson, W. B.
　See Schultz, James Willard
Anderson, Wayne 1946- *147*
　Earlier sketch in SATA *56*
Andre, Evelyn M(arie) 1924- *27*
Andreassen, Karl
　See Boyd, Waldo T.
Andreassi, K. Robert
　See DeCandido, Keith R.A.
Andrew, Ian 1962- *166*
　Earlier sketch in SATA *116*

Andrew, Ian Peter
    See Andrew, Ian
Andrew, Prudence (Hastings) 1924- 87
Andrews, Benny 1930-2006 31
    Obituary 178
Andrews, Eleanor Lattimore
    See Lattimore, Eleanor Frances
Andrews, Elton V.
    See Pohl, Frederik
Andrews, F(rank) Emerson 1902-1978 22
Andrews, J(ames) S(ydney) 1934- 4
Andrews, Jan 1942- 167
    Brief entry 49
    Earlier sketches in SATA *58, 98*
Andrews, Julie 1935- 153
    Earlier sketch in SATA *7*
    See also CLR *85*
Andrews, Roy Chapman 1884-1960 19
Andrews, Tamra 1959- 129
Andrews, Wendy
    See Sharmat, Marjorie Weinman
Andrews, William G(eorge) 1930- 74
Andrezel, Pierre
    See Blixen, Karen (Christentze Dinesen)
Andriani, Renee
    See Williams-Andriani, Renee
Andrist, Ralph K. 1914-2004 45
Andryszewski, Tricia 1956- 148
    Earlier sketch in SATA *88*
Angel, Carl 178
Angel, Marie 1923- 47
Angeles, Peter A. 1931- 40
Angeletti, Roberta 1964- 124
Angeli, Marguerite (Lofft) de
    See de Angeli, Marguerite (Lofft)
Angell, Madeline 1919- 18
Angelo, Valenti 1897- 14
Angelou, Maya 1928- 136
    Earlier sketch in SATA *49*
    See also CLR *53*
Angier, Bradford -1997 12
Anglund, Joan Walsh 1926- 2
    See also CLR *94*
Ango, Fan D.
    See Longyear, Barry B(rookes)
Angrist, Stanley W(olff) 1933- 4
Anholt, Catherine 1958- 131
    Earlier sketch in SATA *74*
Anholt, Laurence 1959- 141
    Earlier sketch in SATA *74*
Anita
    See Daniel, Anita
Anmar, Frank
    See Nolan, William F(rancis)
Annett, Cora
    See Scott, Cora Annett (Pipitone)
Annie-Jo
    See Blanchard, Patricia
    and Suhr, Joanne
Annixter, Jane
    See Sturtzel, Jane Levington
Annixter, Paul
    See Sturtzel, Howard A(llison)
Anno, Mitsumasa 1926- 157
    Earlier sketches in SATA *5, 38, 77*
    See also CLR *122*
Anrooy, Francine Van
    See Van Anrooy, Francine
Ansary, Mir Tamim 1948- 140
Anstey, Caroline 1958- 81
Antell, Will D. 1935- 31
Anthony, Barbara
    See Barber, Antonia
Anthony, C. L.
    See Smith, Dorothy Gladys
Anthony, Edward 1895-1971 21
Anthony, John
    See Beckett, Ronald Brymer
    and Ciardi, John (Anthony)
    and Sabini, John Anthony
Anthony, Joseph Patrick 1964- 103

Anthony, Patricia 1947- 109
Anthony, Piers 1934- 129
    Autobiography Feature 129
    Earlier sketch in SATA *84*
    See also CLR *118*
    See also SAAS *22*
Anthony, Susan C(arol) 1953- 87
Anticaglia, Elizabeth 1939- 12
Antle, Nancy 1955- 102
Anton, Michael J(ames) 1940- 12
Antonacci, Robert J(oseph) 1916- 45
    Brief entry 37
Anvil, Christopher
    See Crosby, Harry C., Jr.
Aoki, Hisako 1942- 45
Apfel, Necia H(alpern) 1930- 51
    Brief entry 41
Aphrodite, J.
    See Livingston, Carole
Apikuni
    See Schultz, James Willard
Apostolou, Christine Hale 1955- 128
    Earlier sketch in SATA *82*
    See also Hale, Christy
Appel, Allen (R.) 1945- 115
Appel, Benjamin 1907-1977 39
    Obituary 21
Appel, Martin E(liot) 1948- 45
Appel, Marty
    See Appel, Martin E(liot)
Applebaum, Diana Muir Karter 1953- 132
Appelt, Kathi 1954- 129
    Earlier sketch in SATA *83*
Apperley, Dawn 1969- 135
Appiah, Peggy 1921-2006 84
    Earlier sketch in SATA *15*
    See also SAAS *19*
Apple, Margot 152
    Brief entry 42
    Earlier sketch in SATA *64*
Applebaum, Stan 1922- 45
Applegate, K. A.
    See CLR *90*
    See Applegate, Katherine (Alice)
Applegate, Katherine (Alice) 1956- 162
    Earlier sketch in SATA *109*
    See Applegate, K. A.
Appleton, Victor 67
    Earlier sketch in SATA *1*
    See Barrett, Neal, Jr.
    and Doyle, Debra
    and Macdonald, James D.
    and Stratemeyer, Edward L.
    and Vardeman, Robert E(dward)
Appleton, Victor II 67
    Earlier sketch in SATA *1*
    See Goulart, Ron(ald Joseph)
Apsler, Alfred 1907-1982 10
Aragones, Sergio 1937- 48
    Brief entry 39
Araujo, Frank P. 1937- 86
Arbo, Cris 1950- 103
Arbuthnot, May Hill 1884-1969 2
Archambault, John 163
    Earlier sketches in SATA *67, 112*
Archbold, Rick 1950- 97
Archer, Colleen Rutherford 1949- 164
Archer, Jules 1915- 85
    Earlier sketch in SATA *4*
    See also SAAS *5*
Archer, Marion Fuller 1917- 11
Archer, Nathan
    See Evans, Lawrence Watt
Archibald, Joe
    See Archibald, Joseph S(topford)
Archibald, Joseph S(topford) 1898-1986 3
    Obituary 47
Ardagh, Philip 1961- 154
Ardai, Charles 1969- 85
Arden, Barbi
    See Stoutenburg, Adrien (Pearl)

Arden, William
    See Lynds, Dennis
Ardizzone, Edward (Jeffrey Irving) 1900-1979
    28
    Obituary 21
    Earlier sketch in SATA *1*
    See also CLR *3*
Ardley, Neil (Richard) 1937- 121
    Earlier sketch in SATA *43*
Arehart-Treichel, Joan 1942- 22
Arena, Felice 1968- 151
Arenella, Roy 1939- 14
Argent, Kerry 1960- 138
Argueta, Jorge 179
Arkin, Alan 1934- 59
    Brief entry 32
Arkin, Alan Wolf
    See Arkin, Alan
Arksey, Neil 158
Arlen, Leslie
    See Nicole, Christopher (Robin)
Arley, Robert
    See Jackson, Mike
Armer, Alberta (Roller) 1904-1986 9
Armer, Laura Adams 1874-1963 13
Armistead, John 1941- 130
Armitage, David 1943- 155
    Brief entry 38
    Earlier sketch in SATA *99*
Armitage, Frank
    See Carpenter, John (Howard)
Armitage, Ronda (Jacqueline) 1943- 155
    Brief entry 38
    Earlier sketches in SATA *47, 99*
Armour, Richard (Willard) 1906-1989 14
    Obituary 61
Armstrong, Alan 1939- 172
Armstrong, Alan W.
    See Armstrong, Alan
Armstrong, George D. 1927- 10
Armstrong, Gerry (Breen) 1929- 10
Armstrong, Jeannette (C.) 1948- 102
Armstrong, Jennifer 1961- 165
    Autobiography Feature 120
    Earlier sketches in SATA *77, 111*
    See also CLR *66*
    See also SAAS *24*
Armstrong, Louise 43
    Brief entry 33
Armstrong, Martin Donisthorpe 1882-1974
    115
Armstrong, Ralph Richard
    See Armstrong, Richard
Armstrong, Richard 1903-1986 11
Armstrong, William H(oward) 1914-1999 4
    Obituary 111
    See also CLR *117*
    See also SAAS *7*
Armstrong-Ellis, Carey (Fraser) 1956- 145
Arndt, Ursula (Martha H.) 56
    Brief entry 39
Arneson, D(on) J(on) 1935- 37
Arnett, Caroline
    See Cole, Lois Dwight
Arnett, Jack
    See Goulart, Ron(ald Joseph)
Arnette, Robert
    See Silverberg, Robert
Arno, Enrico 1913-1981 43
    Obituary 28
Arnold, Caroline 1944- 174
    Brief entry 34
    Earlier sketches in SATA *36, 85, 131*
    See also CLR *61*
    See also SAAS *23*
Arnold, Elizabeth 1944- 164
Arnold, Elliott 1912-1980 5
    Obituary 22
Arnold, Emily 1939- 76
    Earlier sketch in SATA *50*
    See McCully, Emily Arnold

Arnold, Katya 1947- *168*
  Earlier sketches in SATA 82, *115*
Arnold, Louise *175*
Arnold, Marsha Diane 1948- *147*
  Earlier sketch in SATA *93*
Arnold, Nick 1961- *113*
Arnold, Oren 1900-1980 .... *4*
Arnold, Susan (Riser) 1951- *58*
Arnold, Tedd 1949- *160*
  Earlier sketches in SATA 69, *116*
Arnoldy, Julie
  See Bischoff, Julia Bristol
Arnosky, James Edward 1946- *160*
  Earlier sketch in SATA *22*
  See also CLR *93*
  See Arnosky, Jim
Arnosky, Jim *118*
  Earlier sketch in SATA *70*
  See also CLR *93*
  See Arnosky, James Edward
Arnott, Kathleen 1914- *20*
Arnov, Boris, Jr. 1926- *12*
Arnow, Harriette (Louisa) Simpson 1908-1986
  .... *42*
  Obituary *47*
Arnsteen, Katy Keck 1934- *68*
Arnstein, Helene S(olomon) 1915- *12*
Arntson, Herbert E(dward) 1911-1982 .... *12*
Aroner, Miriam *82*
Aronson, Marc 1950- *175*
  Earlier sketch in SATA *126*
Aronson, Virginia 1954- *122*
Arora, Shirley (Lease) 1930- *2*
Arrasmith, Patrick *176*
Arrigan, Mary 1943- *142*
Arrington, Stephen L. 1948- *97*
Arrington, Stephen Lee
  See Arrington, Stephen L.
Arrley, Richmond
  See Delany, Samuel R., Jr.
Arrowood, (McKendrick Lee) Clinton 1939-
  .... *19*
Artell, Mike 1948- *134*
  Earlier sketch in SATA *89*
Arthur, Robert, (Jr.) 1909-1969 .... *118*
  See Arthur, Robert (Andrew)
Arthur, Robert (Andrew) 1909-1969
  See Arthur, Robert, (Jr.)
Arthur, Ruth M(abel) 1905-1979 .... *26*
  Earlier sketch in SATA *7*
Artis, Vicki Kimmel 1945- *12*
Artzybasheff, Boris (Miklailovich) 1899-1965
  .... *14*
Aruego, Ariane
  See Dewey, Ariane
Aruego, Jose 1932- *178*
  Earlier sketches in SATA 6, 68, *125*
  See also CLR *5*
Aruego, Jose Espiritu
  See Aruego, Jose
Arundel, Honor (Morfydd) 1919-1973 .... *4*
  Obituary *24*
  See also CLR *35*
Arundel, Jocelyn
  See Alexander, Jocelyn Anne Arundel
Arvey, Michael 1948- *79*
Arzoumanian, Alik *177*
Asare, Meshack (Yaw) 1945- *139*
  Earlier sketch in SATA *86*
Asaro, Catherine 1955- *165*
  Earlier sketch in SATA *101*
  See Asaro, Catherine Ann
Asaro, Catherine Ann 1955-
  See Asaro, Catherine
Asay, Donna Day 1945- *127*
Asbjornsen, Peter Christen 1812-1885 .... *15*
  See also CLR *104*
  See Asbjornsen and Moe
Asch, Frank 1946- *154*
  Earlier sketches in SATA 5, 66, *102*
Ash, Jutta 1942- *38*

Ashabranner, Brent 1921- *166*
  Earlier sketches in SATA 1, 67, *130*
  See also CLR *28*
  See also SAAS *14*
Ashabranner, Brent Kenneth
  See Ashabranner, Brent
Ashbless, William
  See Blaylock, James P.
  and Powers, Tim
Ashby, Gil 1958- *146*
Ashby, Gwynneth 1922- *44*
Ashby, Ruth *170*
Ashby, Yvonne 1955- *121*
Ashe, Arthur (Robert, Jr.) 1943-1993 .... *65*
  Obituary *87*
Ashe, Geoffrey (Thomas) 1923- *17*
  Autobiography Feature *125*
Ashe, Mary Ann
  See Lewis, Mary (Christianna)
Asher, Sandra Fenichel *71*
  Brief entry *34*
  Earlier sketch in SATA *36*
  See also SAAS *13*
  See Asher, Sandy
Asher, Sandy 1942- *158*
  Autobiography Feature *158*
  Earlier sketch in SATA *118*
  See Asher, Sandra Fenichel
Asheron, Sara
  See Moore, Lilian
Ashey, Bella
  See Breinburg, Petronella
Ashford, Daisy
  See Ashford, Margaret Mary
Ashford, Jeffrey
  See Jeffries, Roderic
Ashford, Margaret Mary 1881-1972 .... *10*
Ashley, Bernard (John) 1935- *155*
  Brief entry *39*
  Earlier sketches in SATA 47, *79*
  See also CLR *4*
Ashley, Elizabeth
  See Salmon, Annie Elizabeth
Ashley, Ray
  See Abrashkin, Raymond
Ashman, Linda 1960- *150*
Ashton, Lorayne
  See Gottfried, Theodore Mark
Ashton, Warren T.
  See Adams, William Taylor
Asimov, Isaac 1920-1992 .... *74*
  Earlier sketches in SATA 1, *26*
  See also CLR *79*
Asinof, Eliot 1919- *6*
Aska, Warabe *56*
  See Masuda, Takeshi
Asprin, Robert L(ynn) 1946- *92*
Asquith, Cynthia Mary Evelyn (Charteris)
  1887-1960 .... *107*
Asquith, Ros *153*
Astley, Juliet
  See Lofts, Norah (Robinson)
Aston, Dianna Hutts 1964- *176*
Aston, James
  See White, T(erence) H(anbury)
Ata, Te 1895-1995 .... *119*
Atene, Ann
  See Atene, (Rita) Anna
Atene, (Rita) Anna 1922- *12*
Atheling, William, Jr.
  See Blish, James (Benjamin)
Atkins, Catherine *160*
Atkins, Jeannine 1953- *172*
  Earlier sketch in SATA *113*
Atkinson, Allen G. 1953(?)-1987 .... *60*
  Brief entry *46*
  Obituary *55*
Atkinson, M. E.
  See Frankau, Mary Evelyn Atkinson
Atkinson, Margaret Fleming *14*

Attema, Martha 1949- *156*
  Earlier sketch in SATA *94*
Atticus
  See Davies, Hunter
  and Fleming, Ian
  and Pawle, Gerald Strachan
  and Wilson, (Thomas) Woodrow
Atwater, Florence (Hasseltine Carroll)
  1896-1979 .... *66*
  Earlier sketch in SATA *16*
  See also CLR *19*
Atwater, Montgomery Meigs 1904-1976 .... *15*
Atwater, Richard (Tupper) 1892-1948 .... *66*
  Brief entry *27*
  Earlier sketch in SATA *54*
  See also CLR *19*
Atwater-Rhodes, Amelia 1984- *170*
  Earlier sketch in SATA *124*
Atwell, Debby 1953- *150*
  Earlier sketch in SATA *87*
Atwood, Ann (Margaret) 1913-1992 .... *7*
Atwood, Margaret 1939- *170*
  Earlier sketch in SATA *50*
Atwood, Margaret Eleanor
  See Atwood, Margaret
Aubrey, Meg Kelleher 1963- *83*
Aubry, Claude B. 1914-1984 .... *29*
  Obituary *40*
Auch, Herm *173*
Auch, Mary Jane *173*
  Earlier sketch in SATA *138*
Auch, M.J.
  See Auch, Mary Jane
Auch, M.J.
  See Auch, Mary Jane
Auclair, Joan 1960- *68*
Auel, Jean M(arie) 1936- *91*
Auer, Martin 1951- *77*
Augarde, Steve 1950- *159*
  Earlier sketch in SATA *25*
Augelli, John P(at) 1921- *46*
Augustine, Mildred
  See Benson, Mildred (Augustine Wirt)
Ault, Phil
  See Ault, Phillip H(alliday)
Ault, Phillip H(alliday) 1914- *23*
Ault, Rosalie Sain 1942- *38*
Ault, Roz
  See Ault, Rosalie Sain
Aung, (Maung) Htin 1909- *21*
Aunt Weedy
  See Alcott, Louisa May
Auseon, Andrew 1976- *166*
Austen, Carrie
  See Bennett, Cherie
Austin, Carrie
  See Seuling, Barbara
Austin, Elizabeth S. 1907-1977 .... *5*
Austin, Harry
  See McInerny, Ralph
Austin, Margot 1909(?)-1990 .... *11*
  Obituary *66*
Austin, Michael *178*
Austin, Oliver L(uther), Jr. 1903-1988 .... *7*
  Obituary *59*
Austin, Patricia 1950- *137*
Austin, R. G.
  See Gelman, Rita Golden
  and Lamb, Nancy
Austin, Virginia 1951- *152*
  Earlier sketch in SATA *80*
Auteur, Hillary
  See Gottfried, Theodore Mark
Auth, Tony
  See Auth, William Anthony, Jr.
Auth, William Anthony, Jr. 1942- *51*
Autry, Gloria Diener
  See Allen, Terril Diener
Auvil, Peggy A 1954- *122*
Auvil, Peggy Appleby
  See Auvil, Peggy A

Aveni, Anthony F. 1938- *181*
Aveni, Anthony Francis
  See Aveni, Anthony F.
Averill, Esther (Holden) 1902-1992 .... *28*
  Obituary *72*
  Earlier sketch in SATA *1*
Avery, A. A.
  See Montgomery, Rutherford George
Avery, Al
  See Montgomery, Rutherford George
Avery, Gillian (Elise) 1926- *137*
  Autobiography Feature *137*
  Earlier sketches in SATA *7, 75*
  See also SAAS *6*
Avery, Kay 1908- *5*
Avery, Lorraine
  See Older, Effin
  and Older, Jules
Avery, Lynn
  See Cole, Lois Dwight
Avi *108*
  Earlier sketch in SATA *71*
  See also CLR *68*
  See also Wortis, Avi
Avishai, Susan 1949- *82*
Awdry, Christopher Vere 1940- *67*
Awdry, Wilbert Vere 1911-1997 .... *94*
  See also CLR *23*
Axelrod, Amy *131*
Axelsen, Stephen 1953- *165*
Axton, David
  See Koontz, Dean R.
Ayars, James S(terling) 1898-1986 .... *4*
Aye, A. K.
  See Edwards, Hazel (Eileen)
Ayer, Eleanor H. 1947-1998 .... *121*
  Earlier sketch in SATA *78*
Ayer, Jacqueline 1930- *13*
Ayer, Margaret (?)-1981 .... *15*
Aylesworth, Jim 1943- *139*
  Earlier sketches in SATA *38, 89*
  See also CLR *89*
Aylesworth, Thomas G(ibbons) 1927-1995 . *88*
  Earlier sketch in SATA *4*
  See also CLR *6*
  See also SAAS *17*
Aylward, Marcus
  See Alexander, Marc
Aymar, Brandt 1911- *22*
Ayme, Marcel (Andre) 1902-1967 .... *91*
  See also CLR *25*
Ayres, Becky
  See Hickox, Rebecca (Ayres)
Ayres, Pam 1947- *90*
Aytmatov, Chingiz
  See Aitmatov, Chingiz (Torekulovich)
Ayto, Russell 1960- *166*
  Earlier sketch in SATA *111*
Azaid
  See Zaidenberg, Arthur
Azar, Penny 1952- *121*
Azarian, Mary 1940- *171*
  Earlier sketch in SATA *112*

B

Baastad, Babbis Friis
  See Friis-Baastad, Babbis Ellinor
Bab
  See Gilbert, W(illiam) S(chwenck)
Babbis, Eleanor
  See Friis-Baastad, Babbis Ellinor
Babbitt, Lucy Cullyford 1960- *85*
Babbitt, Natalie (Zane Moore) 1932- *106*
  Earlier sketches in SATA *6, 68*
  See also CLR *53*
  See also SAAS *5*
Babcock, Chris 1963- *83*
Babcock, Dennis Arthur 1948- *22*

Baber, Carolyn Stonnell 1936- *96*
Baca, Maria 1951- *104*
Bach, Alice (Hendricks) 1942- *93*
  Brief entry *27*
  Earlier sketch in SATA *30*
Bach, Bellamy
  See Windling, Terri
Bach, Mary 1960- *125*
Bach, Richard 1936- *13*
Bach, Richard David
  See Bach, Richard
Bache, Ellyn 1942- *124*
Bachel, Beverly K. 1957- *142*
Bachman, Fred 1949- *12*
Bachman, Richard
  See King, Stephen
Bachrach, Deborah *80*
Bacmeister, Rhoda W(arner) 1893-1991 ..... *11*
Bacon, Betty
  See Bacon, Elizabeth
Bacon, Elizabeth 1914-2001 .... *3*
  Obituary *131*
Bacon, Joan Chase
  See Bowden, Joan Chase
Bacon, Josephine Dodge (Daskam) 1876-1961
  .... *48*
Bacon, Margaret Frances
  Obituary *50*
  See Bacon, Peggy
Bacon, Margaret Hope 1921- *6*
Bacon, Martha Sherman 1917-1981 .... *18*
  Obituary *27*
  See also CLR *3*
Bacon, Melvin 1950- *93*
Bacon, Melvin L.
  See Bacon, Melvin
Bacon, Peggy 1895-1987 .... *2*
  See Bacon, Margaret Frances
Bacon, R(onald) L(eonard) 1924- *84*
  Earlier sketch in SATA *26*
Baden, Robert 1936- *70*
Baden-Powell, Robert (Stephenson Smyth)
  1857-1941 .... *16*
Badt, Karin L(uisa) 1963- *91*
Baehr, Kingsley M. 1937- *89*
Baehr, Patricia 1952- *65*
Baehr, Patricia Goehner
  See Baehr, Patricia
Baer, Jill
  See Gilbert, (Agnes) Joan (Sewell)
Baer, Judy 1951- *71*
Baer, Julie 1960- *161*
Baer-Block, Roxanna *172*
Baerg, Harry J(ohn) 1909-1996 .... *12*
Baeten, Lieve 1954- *83*
Bagert, Brod 1947- *80*
Baggette, Susan K. 1942- *126*
Bagnold, Enid 1889-1981 .... *25*
  Earlier sketch in SATA *1*
Bahlke, Valerie Worth 1933-1994 .... *81*
  See Worth, Valerie
Bahous, Sally 1939- *86*
Bahr, Mary (Madelyn) 1946- *95*
Bahr, Robert 1940- *38*
Bahti, Tom 1926-1972 .... *57*
  Brief entry *31*
Baicker-McKee, Carol 1958- *177*
Bailey, Alice Cooper 1890-1978 .... *12*
Bailey, Anne 1958- *71*
Bailey, Bernadine (Freeman) 1901-1995 ..... *14*
Bailey, Carolyn Sherwin 1875-1961 .... *14*
Bailey, Debbie 1954- *123*
Bailey, Donna (Veronica Anne) 1938- *68*
Bailey, Jane H(orton) 1916- *12*
Bailey, John (Robert) 1940- *52*
Bailey, Linda 1948- *107*
Bailey, Maralyn Collins (Harrison) 1941- ... *12*
Bailey, Matilda
  See Radford, Ruby L(orraine)
Bailey, Maurice Charles 1932- *12*
Bailey, Pearl (Mae) 1918-1990 .... *81*

Bailey, Ralph Edgar 1893-1982 .... *11*
Bailey, Sheila (Lucas) 1960- *155*
Baillie, Allan 1943- *151*
  Earlier sketch in SATA *87*
  See also CLR *49*
  See also SAAS *21*
Baillie, Allan Stuart
  See Baillie, Allan
Baines, John (David) 1943- *71*
Bains, Larry
  See Sabin, Louis
Baird, Alison 1963- *138*
Baird, Bil 1904-1987 .... *30*
  Obituary *52*
Baird, Thomas (P.) 1923-1990 .... *45*
  Brief entry *39*
  Obituary *64*
Baird, William Britton
  See Baird, Bil
Baity, Elizabeth Chesley 1907-1989 .... *1*
Baiul, Oksana 1977- *108*
Bakeless, John (Edwin) 1894-1978 .... *9*
Bakeless, Katherine Little 1895-1992 .... *9*
Baker, Alan 1951- *146*
  Earlier sketches in SATA *22, 93*
Baker, Augusta 1911-1998 .... *3*
Baker, Betty Lou 1928-1987 .... *73*
  Obituary *54*
  Earlier sketch in SATA *5*
Baker, Carin Greenberg 1959- *79*
Baker, Charlotte 1910- *2*
Baker, Christopher W. 1952- *144*
Baker, (Mary) Elizabeth (Gillette) 1923- *7*
Baker, Gayle Cunningham 1950- *39*
Baker, James W. 1924- *65*
  Earlier sketch in SATA *22*
Baker, James W. 1926- *122*
Baker, Janice E(dla) 1941- *22*
Baker, Jeanette *178*
Baker, Jeannie 1950- *156*
  Earlier sketches in SATA *23, 88*
  See also CLR *28*
Baker, Jeffrey J(ohn) W(heeler) 1931- *5*
Baker, Jim
  See Baker, James W.
Baker, Keith 1953- *179*
Baker, Ken 1962- *133*
Baker, Laura Nelson 1911- *3*
Baker, Margaret 1890-1965 .... *4*
Baker, Margaret J(oyce) 1918- *12*
  See also SAAS *8*
Baker, Mary Gladys Steel 1892-1974 .... *12*
Baker, (Robert) Michael (Graham) 1938- *4*
Baker, Nina (Brown) 1888-1957 .... *15*
Baker, Pamela J. 1947- *66*
Baker, Rachel 1904-1978 .... *2*
  Obituary *26*
Baker, Rosalie F. 1945- *166*
Baker, Samm Sinclair 1909-1997 .... *12*
  Obituary *96*
Baker, Susan (Catherine) 1942-1991 .... *29*
Balaam
  See Lamb, G(eoffrey) F(rederick)
Balan, Bruce 1959- *113*
Balcavage, Dynise 1965- *137*
Balch, Glenn 1902-1989 .... *3*
  Obituary *83*
  See also SAAS *11*
Balderose, Nancy Ward 1952- *93*
Balderson, Margaret 1935- *151*
Baldry, Cherith 1947- *167*
  Earlier sketch in SATA *72*
Balducci, Carolyn (Feleppa) 1946- *5*
Baldwin, Alex
  See Griffin, W.E.B.
Baldwin, Anne Norris 1938- *5*
Baldwin, Clara *11*
Baldwin, Gordo
  See Baldwin, Gordon C(ortis)
Baldwin, Gordon C(ortis) 1908-1983 .... *12*
Baldwin, James 1841-1925 .... *24*

Baldwin, James 1924-1987 9
  Obituary 54
Baldwin, Louis 1919- 110
Baldwin, Margaret
  See Weis, Margaret
Baldwin, Stan(ley C.) 1929- 62
  Brief entry 28
Bales, Carol Ann 1940- 57
  Brief entry 29
Balet, Jan (Bernard) 1913- 11
Balgassi, Haemi 1971- 131
Balian, Lorna 1929- 91
  Earlier sketch in SATA 9
Balit, Christina 1961- 159
  Earlier sketch in SATA 102
Ball, Duncan 1941- 73
Ball, Zachary
  See Janas, Frankie-Lee
  and Masters, Kelly R(ay)
Ballantine, Lesley Frost
  See Frost, Lesley
Ballantyne, R(obert) M(ichael) 1825-1894 . 24
Ballard, James Graham
  See Ballard, J.G.
Ballard, Jane
  See Gorman, Carol
Ballard, J.G. 1930- 93
Ballard, John 1945- 110
Ballard, Lowell C(lyne) 1904-1986 12
  Obituary 49
Ballard, (Charles) Martin 1929- 1
Ballard, Mignon F(ranklin) 1934- 64
  Brief entry 49
Ballard, Robert D(uane) 1942- 85
  See also CLR 60
Ballard, Robin 1965- 126
Balliett, Blue 1955- 156
Ballinger, Bryan 1968- 161
Ballouhey, Pierre 1944- 90
Balogh, Penelope 1916-1975 1
  Obituary 34
Balouch, Kristen 176
Balow, Tom 1931- 12
Baltazzi, Evan S(erge) 1921- 90
Baltimore, J.
  See Catherall, Arthur
Baltzer, Hans (Adolf) 1900- 40
Bambara, Toni Cade 1939-1995 112
Bamfylde, Walter
  See Bevan, Tom
Bamman, Henry A. 1918- 12
Banat, D. R.
  See Bradbury, Ray
Bancroft, Griffing 1907-1999 6
Bancroft, Laura
  See Baum, L(yman) Frank
Bandel, Betty 1912- 47
Baner, Skulda Vanadis 1897-1964 10
Banerjee, Anjali 174
Banfill, A. Scott 1956- 98
Bang, Betsy 1912- 48
  Brief entry 37
Bang, Garrett
  See Bang, Molly
Bang, Molly 1943- 158
  Earlier sketches in SATA 24, 69, 111
  See also CLR 8
Bang, Molly Garrett
  See Bang, Molly
Bang-Campbell, Monika 140
Banjo, The
  See Paterson, A(ndrew) B(arton)
Banke, Cecile de
  See de Banke, Cecile
Banks, Kate 1960- 172
  Earlier sketch in SATA 134
Banks, Lynne Reid
  See CLR 86
  See Reid Banks, Lynne
Banks, Michael A. 1951- 101
Banks, Paul 1952- 174

Banks, Sara (Jeanne Gordon Harrell) 26
  See Harrell, Sara (Jeanne) Gordon
Bannatyne-Cugnet, Elizabeth Jo-Anne
  See Bannatyne-Cugnet, Jo
Bannatyne-Cugnet, Jo 1951- 101
Banner, Angela
  See CLR 24
  See Maddison, Angela Mary
Bannerman, Helen (Brodie Cowan Watson)
  1862(?)-1946 19
  See also CLR 21
Banning, Evelyn I. 1903-1993 36
Bannon, Laura (?)-1963 6
Bannor, Brett 1959- 143
Banta, Susan 181
Bantock, Nick 1950(?)- 95
Barasch, Lynne 1939- 126
  Earlier sketch in SATA 74
Barbalet, Margaret 1949- 77
Barbary, James
  See Beeching, Jack
Barbash, Shepard 1957- 84
Barbe, Walter Burke 1926- 45
Barber, Antonia 1932- 163
  Earlier sketch in SATA 29
Barber, Lynda
  See Graham-Barber, Lynda
Barber, Lynda Graham
  See Graham-Barber, Lynda
Barber, Richard (William) 1941- 35
Barbera, Joe 1911-2006 51
  Obituary 179
Barbera, Joseph
  See Barbera, Joe
Barbera, Joseph Roland
  See Barbera, Joe
Barberis, Juan C(arlos) 1920- 61
Barbour, Karen 1956- 170
  Earlier sketches in SATA 63, 121
Barbour, Ralph Henry 1870-1944 16
Barclay, Bill
  See Moorcock, Michael
Barclay, Isabel
  See Dobell, I(sabel) M(arian) B(arclay)
Barclay, William Ewert
  See Moorcock, Michael
Bardhan-Quallen, Sudipta 168
Bardoe, Cheryl 181
Bare, Arnold Edwin 1920- 16
Bare, Colleen Stanley 32
Bargar, Gary W. 1947-1985 63
Barger, Jan 1948- 147
Barish, Matthew 1907-2000 12
Barkan, Joanne 127
  Earlier sketch in SATA 77
Barker, Albert W. 1900- 8
Barker, Carol (Minturn) 1938- 31
Barker, Cicely Mary 1895-1973 49
  Brief entry 39
  See also CLR 88
Barker, Melvern 1907-1989 11
Barker, S(quire) Omar 1894-1985 10
Barker, Will 1913-1983 8
Barkin, Carol 1944- 52
  Earlier sketch in SATA 42
Barklem, Jill 1951- 96
  See also CLR 31
Barkley, Brad 178
Barkley, James Edward 1941- 6
Barks, Carl 1901-2000 37
Barley, Janet Crane 1934- 95
Barnaby, Ralph S(tanton) 1893-1986 9
Barnard, A. M.
  See Alcott, Louisa May
Barnard, Bryn 1956- 169
  Earlier sketch in SATA 115
Barne, Kitty
  See Barne, Marion Catherine
Barne, Marion Catherine 1883-1957 97
  See Barne, Kitty

Barner, Bob 1947- 136
  Earlier sketch in SATA 29
Barnes, Dawn 1957- 175
Barnes, (Frank) Eric Wollencott 1907-1962
  22
Barnes, Joyce Annette 1958- 85
Barnes, Laura T. 1958- 119
Barnes, Loutricia
  See Barnes-Svarney, Patricia L(ou)
Barnes, Michael 1934- 55
Barnes-Murphy, Frances 1951- 88
Barnes-Murphy, Rowan 1952- 88
Barnes-Svarney, Patricia L(ou) 1953- 67
Barnet, Nancy 1954- 84
Barnett, Ivan 1947- 70
Barnett, Lincoln (Kinnear) 1909-1979 36
Barnett, Moneta 1922-1976 33
Barnett, Naomi 1927- 40
Barney, Maginel Wright 1881(?)-1966 39
  Brief entry 32
Barnhart, Clarence L(ewis) 1900-1993 48
  Obituary 78
Barnouw, Victor 1915-1989 43
  Brief entry 28
Barnstone, Willis 1927- 20
Barnum, Jay Hyde 1888(?)-1962 20
Barnum, P. T., Jr.
  See Stratemeyer, Edward L.
Barnum, Richard 67
  Earlier sketch in SATA 1
Barnum, Theodore
  See Stratemeyer, Edward L.
Baron, Kathy 1954- 90
Baron, Virginia Olsen 1931- 46
  Brief entry 28
Barr, Donald 1921-2004 20
  Obituary 152
Barr, George 1907-1992 2
Barr, Jene 1922-1985 16
  Obituary 42
  See Cohen, Jene Barr
Barr, Nevada 1952- 126
  Earlier sketch in SATA 115
Barrer, Gertrude
  See Barrer-Russell, Gertrude
Barrer-Russell, Gertrude 1921- 27
Barrett, Angela (Jane) 1955- 145
  Earlier sketch in SATA 75
Barrett, Ethel 87
  Brief entry 44
Barrett, Joyce Durham 1943- 138
Barrett, Judi
  See Barrett, Judith
Barrett, Judith 1941- 26
  See also CLR 98
Barrett, Robert T(heodore) 1949- 92
Barrett, Ron 1937- 14
Barrett, Susan (Mary) 1938- 113
Barrett, Tracy 1955- 156
  Earlier sketches in SATA 84, 115
Barretta, Gene 176
Barrie, J(ames) M(atthew) 1860-1937 100
  See also YABC 1
  See also CLR 16
Barringer, William 1940-1996 153
Barrington, Michael
  See Moorcock, Michael
Barris, George 1925- 47
Barrol, Grady
  See Bograd, Larry
Barron, Rex 1951- 84
Barron, T(homas) A(rchibald) 1952- 126
  Earlier sketch in SATA 83
  See also CLR 86
Barron, Tom
  See Barron, T(homas) A(rchibald)
Barrow, Lloyd H. 1942- 73
Barrows, Annie 1962- 180
Barry, Dan 1958- 177
Barry, Dana (Marie Malloy) 1949- 139
Barry, James P(otvin) 1918- 14

Barry, Katharina Watjen 1936- *4*
Barry, Robert (Everett) 1931- *6*
Barry, Scott 1952- *32*
Barry, Sheila Anne -2003 .... *91*
Bartell, Susan S. *175*
Bartenbach, Jean 1918- *40*
Barth, Edna 1914-1980 .... *7*
    Obituary *24*
Barth, Kelly L. 1964- *152*
Barthelme, Donald 1931-1989 .... *7*
    Obituary *62*
Bartholomew, Barbara 1941- *86*
    Brief entry *42*
Bartholomew, Jean
    See Beatty, Patricia (Robbins)
Bartlett, Alison *153*
Bartlett, Philip A. *1*
Bartlett, Robert Merrill 1899-1995 .... *12*
Bartoletti, Susan Campbell 1958- *173*
    Earlier sketches in SATA *88, 129, 135*
Barton, Byron 1930- *126*
    Earlier sketches in SATA *9, 90*
Barton, Jill(ian) 1940- *75*
Barton, May Hollis *67*
    Earlier sketch in SATA *1*
Barton, Pat *59*
    See Arrowsmith, Pat
Bartos-Hoeppner, Barbara 1923- *5*
Bartram, Simon *156*
Bartsch, Jochen 1906- *39*
Baruch, Dorothy W(alter) 1899-1962 .... *21*
Barunga, Albert 1912(?)-1977 .... *120*
Bas, Rutger
    See Rutgers van der Loeff-Basenau, An(na)
    Maria Margaretha
Base, Graeme (Rowland) 1958- *162*
    Earlier sketches in SATA *67, 101*
    See also CLR *22*
Baseman, Gary 1960- *174*
Bash, Barbara 1948- *132*
Bashevis, Isaac
    See Singer, Isaac Bashevis
Bashevis, Yitskhok
    See Singer, Isaac Bashevis
Baskin, Leonard 1922-2000 .... *120*
    Brief entry *27*
    Earlier sketch in SATA *30*
Baskin, Nora Raleigh 1961- *129*
Bason, Lillian 1913- *20*
Bass, L. G.
    See Geringer, Laura
Bassett, Jeni 1959- *64*
    Brief entry *43*
Bassett, John Keith
    See Keating, Lawrence A.
Bassett, Lisa 1958- *61*
Bassil, Andrea
    See Nilsen, Anna
Bastyra, Judy *108*
Bat-Ami, Miriam 1950- *150*
    Autobiography Feature *150*
    Earlier sketches in SATA *82, 122*
Bate, Lucy 1939-1993 .... *18*
Bate, Norman (Arthur) 1916- *5*
Bateman, Colin 1962- *172*
Bateman, Teresa 1957- *168*
    Earlier sketch in SATA *112*
Bates, Barbara S(nedeker) 1919- *12*
Bates, Betty *19*
    See Bates, Elizabeth
Bates, Dianne 1948- *147*
Bates, Ivan *175*
Bates, Katharine Lee 1859-1929 .... *113*
    See Lincoln, James
Bates, Martine
    See Leavitt, Martine
Bateson, Catherine 1960- *157*
Batey, Tom 1946- *52*
    Brief entry *41*
Bath, Kevin P.
    See Bath, K.P.

Bath, K.P. *171*
Batherman, Muriel
    See Sheldon, Muriel
Batson, Larry 1930- *35*
Batt, Tanya Robyn 1970- *131*
Battaglia, Aurelius 1910- *50*
    Brief entry *33*
Batten, H(arry) Mortimer 1888-1958 .... *25*
Batten, Mary 1937- *162*
    Earlier sketches in SATA *5, 102*
Batterberry, Ariane Ruskin 1935- *13*
Batterberry, Michael Carver 1932- *32*
Battle-Lavert, Gwendolyn 1951- *155*
    Earlier sketch in SATA *85*
    See Lavert, Gwendolyn Battle
Battles, (Roxy) Edith 1921- *7*
Baudouy, Michel-Aime 1909- *7*
Bauer, Caroline Feller 1935- *98*
    Brief entry *46*
    Earlier sketch in SATA *52*
    See also SAAS *24*
Bauer, Fred 1934- *36*
Bauer, Helen 1900-1988 .... *2*
Bauer, Joan 1951- *160*
    Earlier sketch in SATA *117*
Bauer, Jutta 1955- *150*
Bauer, Marion Dane 1938- *144*
    Autobiography Feature *144*
    Earlier sketches in SATA *20, 69, 113*
    See also SAAS *9*
Bauer, Michael Gerard 1955(?)- *167*
Bauer, Steven 1948- *125*
Bauerschmidt, Marjorie 1926- *15*
Baughman, Dorothy 1940- *61*
Baum, Allyn Z(elton) 1924-1997 .... *98*
    Earlier sketch in SATA *20*
Baum, L. Frank
    See Thompson, Ruth Plumly
Baum, L(yman) Frank 1856-1919 .... *100*
    Earlier sketch in SATA *18*
    See also CLR *107*
Baum, Louis 1948- *64*
    Brief entry *52*
Baum, Louis F.
    See Baum, L(yman) Frank
Baum, Willi 1931- *4*
Baumann, Amy (Brown) Beeching 1922- ... *10*
Baumann, Hans 1914- *2*
    See also CLR *35*
Baumann, Kurt 1935- *21*
Baumgartner, Barbara 1939- *86*
Baurys, Flo(rence) 1938- *122*
Bausum, Ann *173*
Bawden, Nina (Mary Mabey) 1925- *72*
    Earlier sketch in SATA *4*
    See also CLR *51*
    See also SAAS *16*
    See Kark, Nina Mary
Bay, Jeanette Graham 1928- *88*
Bayer, Harold
    See Gregg, Andrew K.
Bayley, Nicola 1949- *129*
    Earlier sketches in SATA *41, 69*
Baylor, Byrd 1924- *136*
    Earlier sketches in SATA *16, 69*
    See also CLR *3*
Baynes, Pauline (Diana) 1922- *133*
    Earlier sketches in SATA *19, 59*
BB
    See Watkins-Pitchford, Denys James
Beach, Charles
    See Reid, (Thomas) Mayne
Beach, Charles Amory *1*
Beach, Edward L. 1918-2002 .... *12*
    Obituary *140*
Beach, Edward Latimer
    See Beach, Edward L.
Beach, Lisa 1957- *111*
Beach, Lynn
    See Lance, Kathryn
Beach, Stewart T(aft) 1899-1979 .... *23*

Beachcroft, Nina 1931- *18*
Beagle, Peter S. 1939- *130*
    Earlier sketch in SATA *60*
Beagle, Peter Soyer
    See Beagle, Peter S.
Beaglehole, Helen 1946- *117*
Beale, Fleur *107*
Bealer, Alex W(inkler III) 1921-1980 .... *8*
    Obituary *22*
Beales, Valerie 1915- *74*
Beals, Carleton 1893-1979 .... *12*
Beame, Rona 1934- *12*
Beamer, (George) Charles (Jr.) 1942- *43*
Bean, Normal
    See Burroughs, Edgar Rice
Bean, Carolyn
    See Udall, Jan Beaney
Beaney, Jan
    See Udall, Jan Beaney
Beaney, Jane
    See Udall, Jan Beaney
Bear, Carolyn
    See Rayban, Chloe
Bear, Greg(ory Dale) 1951- *105*
    Earlier sketch in SATA *65*
Bearanger, Marie
    See Messier, Claire
Beard, Charles A(ustin) 1874-1948 .... *18*
Beard, Dan(iel Carter) 1850-1941 .... *22*
Beard, Darleen Bailey 1961- *96*
Bearden, Romare (Howard) 1914(?)-1988 .. *22*
    Obituary *56*
Beardmore, Cedric
    See Beardmore, George
Beardmore, George 1908-1979 .... *20*
Beardsley, Martyn R. 1957- *150*
Bearman, Jane (Ruth) 1917- *29*
Beaton, Clare 1947- *125*
Beatty, Elizabeth
    See Holloway, Teresa (Bragunier)
Beatty, Hetty Burlingame 1907-1971 .... *5*
Beatty, Jerome, Jr. 1918- *5*
Beatty, John (Louis) 1922-1975 .... *6*
    Obituary *25*
Beatty, Patricia (Robbins) 1922-1991 .... *73*
    Obituary *68*
    Earlier sketches in SATA *1, 30*
    See also SAAS *4*
Beaty, Mary (T.) 1947- *146*
Bechard, Margaret 1953- *164*
    Earlier sketch in SATA *85*
Bechtel, Louise Seaman 1894-1985 .... *4*
    Obituary *43*
Beck, Barbara L. 1927- *12*
Beck, Ian (Archibald) 1947- *138*
Beck, Peggy 1949- *171*
Becker, Beril 1901-1999 .... *11*
Becker, Deborah Zimmett 1955- *138*
Becker, Helaine 1961- *142*
Becker, John (Leonard) 1901- *12*
Becker, John E(mil) 1942- *148*
Becker, Joyce 1936- *39*
Becker, May Lamberton 1873-1958 .... *33*
Becker, Neesa 1951- *123*
Becker, Shari *174*
Beckett, Sheilah 1913- *33*
Beckman, Delores 1914-1994 .... *51*
Beckman, Gunnel 1910- *6*
    See also CLR *25*
    See also SAAS *9*
Beckman, Kaj
    See Beckman, Karin
Beckman, Karin 1913- *45*
Beckman, Per (Frithiof) 1913- *45*
Bedard, Michael 1949- *154*
    Earlier sketch in SATA *93*
    See also CLR *35*
Beddows, Eric
    See Nutt, Ken
Bedford, A. N.
    See Watson, Jane Werner
Bedford, Annie North
    See Watson, Jane Werner

Bedford, David 159
Bedoukian, Kerop 1907-1981 53
Bee, Jay
　See Brainerd, John W(hiting)
Beebe, B(urdetta) F(aye) 1
　See Johnson, B(urdetta) F(aye)
Beebe, (Charles) William 1877-1962 19
Beeby, Betty 1923- 25
Beech, Webb
　See Griffin, W.E.B.
Beecham, Jahnna 161
Beechcroft, William
　See Hallstead, William F(inn III)
Beeching, Jack 1922- 14
Beeke, Tiphanie 163
Beeler, Janet
　See Shaw, Janet
Beeler, Nelson F(rederick) 1910-1978 13
Beere, Peter 1951- 97
Beers, Dorothy Sands 1917- 9
Beers, Lorna 1897-1989 14
Beers, V(ictor) Gilbert 1928- 130
　Earlier sketch in SATA 9
Beeton, Max
　See Redding, Robert Hull
Begay, Shonto 1954- 137
Begaye, Lisa Shook
　See Beach, Lisa
Begin, Maryjane 1963- 82
Begin-Callanan, Maryjane
　See Begin, Maryjane
Begley, Kathleen A(nne) 1948- 21
Behan, Leslie
　See Gottfried, Theodore Mark
Behler, Deborah A. 1947- 145
Behler, John L. 1943-2006 145
　Obituary 173
Behler, John Luther
　See Behler, John L.
Behn, Harry 1898-1973 2
　Obituary 34
Behnke, Frances L. 8
Behr, Joyce 1929- 15
Behrens, June York 1925- 19
Behrman, Carol H(elen) 1925- 144
　Earlier sketch in SATA 14
Beifuss, John, (Jr.) 1959- 92
Beil, Karen Magnuson 1950- 124
Beiler, Edna 1923- 61
Beinicke, Steve 1956- 69
Beirne, Barbara 1933- 71
Beiser, Arthur 1931- 22
Beiser, Germaine 1931- 11
Belair, Richard L. 1934- 45
Belaney, Archibald Stansfeld 1888-1938 24
　See Grey Owl
Belbin, David 1958- 164
　Earlier sketch in SATA 106
Belden, Wilanne Schneider 1925- 56
Belfrage, Sally 1936-1994 65
　Obituary 79
Belknap, B. H.
　See Ellis, Edward S(ylvester)
Belknap, Boynton
　See Ellis, Edward S(ylvester)
Belknap, Boynton M.D.
　See Ellis, Edward S(ylvester)
Bell, Anthea 1936- 148
　Earlier sketch in SATA 88
Bell, Clare (Louise) 1952- 99
Bell, Corydon Whitten 1894-1980 3
Bell, David Owen 1949- 99
Bell, Emerson
　See Stratemeyer, Edward L.
Bell, Emily Mary
　See Cason, Mabel Earp
Bell, Frank
　See Benson, Mildred (Augustine Wirt)
Bell, Gertrude (Wood) 1911-1987 12
Bell, Hilari 1958- 151

Bell, Jadrien
　See Golden, Christie
Bell, Janet
　See Clymer, Eleanor
Bell, Janet Cheatham 1937- 127
Bell, Krista (Anne Blakeney) 1950- 126
Bell, Margaret E(lizabeth) 1898-1990 2
Bell, Mary Reeves 1946- 88
Bell, Norman (Edward) 1899- 11
Bell, Raymond Martin 1907-1999 13
Bell, Siobhan 177
Bell, Thelma Harrington 1896-1985 3
Bell, William 1945- 90
　See also CLR 91
Bellairs, John (Anthony) 1938-1991 160
　Obituary 66
　Earlier sketches in SATA 2, 68
　See also CLR 37
Beller, Susan Provost 1949- 128
　Earlier sketch in SATA 84
　See also CLR 106
Bellingham, Brenda 1931- 99
　Brief entry 51
Bello, Rosario de
　See De Bello, Rosario
Belloc, (Joseph) Hilaire (Pierre Sebastien Rene
　Swanton) 1870-1953 112
　See also YABC 1
　See also CLR 102
Belloc, Joseph Peter Rene Hilaire
　See Belloc, (Joseph) Hilaire (Pierre Sebastien
　Rene Swanton)
Belloc, Joseph Pierre Hilaire
　See Belloc, (Joseph) Hilaire (Pierre Sebastien
　Rene Swanton)
Belloli, Andrea P. A. 1947- 86
Bellville, Cheryl Walsh 1944- 54
　Brief entry 49
Belpre, Pura 1899-1982 16
　Obituary 30
Belting, Natalia Maree 1915-1997 6
Belton, John Raynor 1931- 22
Belton, Sandra (Yvonne) 1939- 134
　Earlier sketch in SATA 85
Beltran, Alberto 1923- 43
Beltran-Hernandez, Irene 1945- 74
Belvedere, Lee
　See Grayland, Valerie (Merle Spanner)
Bemelmans, Ludwig 1898-1962 100
　Earlier sketch in SATA 15
　See also CLR 93
Benander, Carl D. 1941- 74
Benary, Margot
　See Benary-Isbert, Margot
Benary-Isbert, Margot 1889-1979 2
　Obituary 21
　See also CLR 12
Benasutti, Marion 1908-1992 6
Benatar, Raquel 1955- 167
Benchley, Nathaniel (Goddard) 1915-1981 . 25
　Obituary 28
　Earlier sketch in SATA 3
Benchley, Peter 1940-2006 164
　Earlier sketches in SATA 3, 89
Benchley, Peter Bradford
　See Benchley, Peter
Bender, Edna 1941- 92
Bender, Esther 1942- 88
Bender, Lucy Ellen 1942- 22
Bender, Robert 1962- 160
　Earlier sketch in SATA 79
Bendick, Jeanne 1919- 135
　Earlier sketches in SATA 2, 68
　See also CLR 5
　See also SAAS 4
Bendick, Robert L(ouis) 1917- 11
Benedetto, William R. 1928- 180
Benedetto, William Ralph
　See Benedetto, William R.
Benedict, Andrew
　See Arthur, Robert, (Jr.)

Benedict, Dorothy Potter 1889-1979 11
　Obituary 23
Benedict, Lois Trimble 1902-1967 12
Benedict, Rex 1920-1995 8
Benedict, Stewart H(urd) 1924- 26
Beneduce, Ann Keay 128
Benet, Laura 1884-1979 3
　Obituary 23
Benet, Stephen Vincent 1898-1943
　See YABC 1
Benet, Sula 1906-1982 21
　Obituary 33
Ben-Ezer, Ehud 1936- 122
Benezra, Barbara (Beardsley) 1921- 10
Benham, Leslie 1922- 48
Benham, Lois (Dakin) 1924- 48
Benham, Mary Lile 1914-1991 55
Benjamin, E. M. J.
　See Bache, Ellyn
Benjamin, Nora
　See Kubie, Nora Gottheil Benjamin
Benjamin, Saragail Katzman 1953- 86
Benner, Cheryl 1962- 80
Benner, Judith Ann 1942- 94
Bennett, Alice
　See Ziner, Florence
Bennett, Cherie 1960- 158
　Earlier sketch in SATA 97
Bennett, Dorothea
　See Young, Dorothea Bennett
Bennett, Holly 1957- 181
Bennett, James (W.) 1942- 153
　Autobiography Feature 153
　Earlier sketches in SATA 93, 148
Bennett, Jay 1912- 87
　Brief entry 27
　Earlier sketch in SATA 41
　See also SAAS 4
Bennett, Jill (Crawford) 1934- 41
Bennett, John 1865-1956
　See YABC 1
Bennett, Penelope (Agnes) 1938- 94
Bennett, Rachel
　See Hill, Margaret (Ohler)
Bennett, Rainey 1907-1998 15
　Obituary 111
Bennett, Richard 1899- 21
Bennett, Russell H(oradley) 1896- 25
Bennett, Veronica 1953- 178
Bennett, William (John) 1943- 102
Benning, Elizabeth
　See Rice, Bebe Faas
Benson, Elizabeth P(olk) 1924- 65
Benson, Kathleen 1947- 111
　Earlier sketch in SATA 62
Benson, Linda M(aria) 1959- 84
Benson, Mildred (Augustine Wirt) 1905-2002
　.............................. 100
　Obituary 135
　Earlier sketch in SATA 65
　See Keene, Carolyn
Benson, Mildred Wirt
　See Benson, Mildred (Augustine Wirt)
Benson, Millie
　See Benson, Mildred (Augustine Wirt)
Benson, Patrick 1956- 147
Benson, Sally 1900-1972 35
　Obituary 27
　Earlier sketch in SATA 1
Bentley, Judith (McBride) 1945- 89
　Earlier sketch in SATA 40
Bentley, Nancy (L.) 1946- 78
Bentley, Phyllis Eleanor 1894-1977 6
　Obituary 25
Bentley, Roy 1947- 46
Bentley, William (George) 1916- 84
Benton, Jim 1963- 172
ben Uzair, Salem
　See Horne, Richard Henry Hengist
Bercaw, Edna Coe 1961- 124
Berck, Judith 1960- 75

Berelson, Howard 1940- 5
Berends, Polly Berrien 1939- 50
    Brief entry 38
Berenstain, Jan 1923- 135
    Earlier sketches in SATA *12, 64, 129*
    See also CLR *19*
    See also SAAS *20*
Berenstain, Janice
    See Berenstain, Jan
Berenstain, Michael 1951- 45
Berenstain, Stan 1923-2005 135
    Obituary 169
    Earlier sketches in SATA *12, 64, 129*
    See also CLR *19*
    See also SAAS *20*
Berenstain, Stanley
    See Berenstain, Stan
Berenzy, Alix 1957- 168
    Earlier sketch in SATA *65*
Beresford, Elisabeth 1928- 141
    Earlier sketches in SATA *25, 86*
    See also SAAS *20*
Berg, Adriane G(ilda) 1948- 152
Berg, Dave
    See Berg, David
Berg, David 1920-2002 27
    Obituary 137
Berg, Elizabeth 1948- 104
Berg, Jean Horton 1913-1995 6
Berg, Joan
    See Victor, Joan Berg
Berg, Ron 1952- 48
Bergaust, Erik 1925-1978 20
Bergel, Colin J. 1963- 137
Bergen, Joyce 1949- 95
Berger, Barbara (Helen) 1945- 77
Berger, Gilda 1935- 88
    Brief entry 42
Berger, Josef 1903-1971 36
Berger, Melvin H. 1927- 158
    Autobiography Feature 124
    Earlier sketches in SATA *5, 88*
    See also CLR *32*
    See also SAAS *2*
Berger, Phil 1942-2001 62
Berger, Samantha (Allison) 1969- 140
Berger, Terry 1933- 8
Bergey, Alyce (Mae) 1934- 45
Bergin, Mark 1961- 160
    Earlier sketch in SATA *114*
Berglin, Ruth Marie 1970- 181
Bergman, Donna 1934- 73
Bergman, Tamar 1939- 95
Bergsma, Jody Lynn 163
Bergum, Constance R. 1952- 121
Berkes, Marianne 173
Berkey, Barry Robert 1935- 24
Berkowitz, Freda Pastor 1908-1994 12
Berkus, Clara Widess 1909- 78
Berlan, Kathryn Hook 1946- 78
Berlfein, Judy Reiss 1958- 79
Berliner, Don 1930- 33
Berliner, Franz 1930- 13
Berlitz, Charles (L. Frambach) 1914-2003 . 32
    Obituary 151
Berman, Linda 1948- 38
Berman, Paul (Lawrence) 1949- 66
Berna, Paul 1910-1994 15
    Obituary 78
    See also CLR *19*
Bernadette
    See Watts, (Anna) Bernadette
Bernard, Bruce 1928-2000 78
    Obituary 124
Bernard, George I. 1949- 39
Bernard, Jacquelyn (de Sieyes) 1921-1983 .. 8
    Obituary 45
Bernard, Patricia 1942- 181
    Earlier sketch in SATA *106*
Bernard, Trish
    See Bernard, Patricia

Bernardin, James (B.) 1966- 112
Bernards, Neal 1963- 71
Bernays, Anne 1930- 32
Bernhard, Durga T. 1961- 80
Bernhard, Emery 1950- 80
Bernstein, Daryl (Evan) 1976- 81
Bernstein, Joanne E(ckstein) 1943- 15
Bernstein, Margery 1933- 114
Bernstein, Nina 180
Bernstein, Theodore M(enline) 1904-1979 . 12
    Obituary 27
Berrien, Edith Heal
    See Heal, Edith
Berrill, Jacquelyn (Batsel) 1905- 12
Berrington, John
    See Brownjohn, Alan
Berry, B. J.
    See Berry, Barbara J.
Berry, Barbara J. 1937- 7
Berry, Erick
    See Best, (Evangel) Allena Champlin
Berry, James 1925- 110
    Earlier sketch in SATA *67*
    See also CLR *22*
Berry, Joy
    See Berry, Joy Wilt
Berry, Joy Wilt 1944- 58
    Brief entry 46
Berry, William D(avid) 1926- 14
Bersani, Shennen 1961- 164
Berson, Harold 1926- 4
Bertagna, Julie 1962- 151
Bertin, Charles-Francois
    See Berlitz, Charles (L. Frambach)
Bertolet, Paul
    See McLaughlin, Frank
Berton, Pierre (Francis de Marigny) 1920-2004
    99
    Obituary 158
Bertrand, Cecile 1953- 76
Bertrand, Diane Gonzales 1956- 177
    Earlier sketch in SATA *106*
Bertrand, Lynne 1963- 164
    Earlier sketch in SATA *81*
Beskow, Elsa (Maartman) 1874-1953 20
    See also CLR *17*
Bess, Clayton
    See CLR *39*
    See Locke, Robert
Best, (Evangel) Allena Champlin 1892-1974
    2
    Obituary 25
Best, Cari 1951- 149
    Earlier sketch in SATA *107*
Best, (Oswald) Herbert 1894-1980 2
Bestall, A(lfred) E(dmeades) 1892-1986 97
    Obituary 48
Betancourt, Jeanne 1941- 148
    Brief entry 43
    Earlier sketches in SATA *55, 96*
Beth, Mary
    See Miller, Mary Beth
Bethancourt, T. Ernesto 11
    See also CLR *3*
    See Paisley, Tom
Bethel, Dell 1929- 52
Bethell, Jean (Frankenberry) 1922- 8
Bethers, Ray 1902-1973 6
Bethke, Bruce Raymond 1955- 114
Bethlen, T. D.
    See Silverberg, Robert
Bethune, J. G.
    See Ellis, Edward S(ylvester)
Bethune, J. H.
    See Ellis, Edward S(ylvester)
Betteridge, Anne
    See Potter, Margaret (Newman)
Bettina
    See Ehrlich, Bettina Bauer
Bettmann, Otto Ludwig 1903-1998 46

Betts, James
    See Haynes, Betsy
Betz, Eva Kelly 1897-1968 10
Bevan, Tom 1868-1930(?)
    See YABC *2*
Bewick, Thomas 1753-1828 16
Beyer, Audrey White 1916- 9
Beyer, Paul J. III 1950- 74
Beynon, John
    See Harris, John (Wyndham Parkes Lucas)
    Beynon
Bezencon, Jacqueline (Buxcel) 1924- 48
Bial, Morrison David 1917- 62
Bial, Raymond 1948- 165
    Earlier sketches in SATA *76, 116*
Biala
    See Brustlein, Janice Tworkov
Biale, Rachel 1952- 99
Bialk, Elisa
    See Krautter, Elisa (Bialk)
Bianchi, John 1947- 91
Bianchi, Robert S(teven) 1943- 92
Bianco, Margery
    See Bianco, Margery Williams
Bianco, Margery Williams 1881-1944 15
    See also CLR *19*
Bianco, Pamela 1906- 28
Bibby, Violet 1908- 24
Bible, Charles 1937- 13
Bibo, Bobette
    See Gugliotta, Bobette
Bice, Clare 1909-1976 22
Bickerstaff, Isaac
    See Swift, Jonathan
Biegel, Paul 1925- 79
    Earlier sketch in SATA *16*
    See also CLR *27*
    See also SAAS *18*
Biemiller, Carl L(udwig), Jr.) 1912-1979 40
    Obituary 21
Bienenfeld, Florence L(ucille) 1929- 39
Bierhorst, John (William) 1936- 149
    Autobiography Feature 149
    Earlier sketches in SATA *6, 91*
    See also SAAS *10*
Biggar, Joan R(awlins) 1936- 120
Biggle, Lloyd, Jr. 1923-2002 65
Bilal, Abdel W(ahab) 1970- 92
Bilbrough, Norman 1941- 111
Bildner, Phil 173
Bileck, Marvin 1920- 40
Bilibin, Ivan (Iakolevich) 1876-1942 61
Bill, Alfred Hoyt 1879-1964 44
Billam, Rosemary 1952- 61
Billings, Charlene W(interer) 1941- 41
Billingsley, Franny 1954- 132
Billington, Elizabeth T(hain) 50
    Brief entry 43
Billout, Guy (Rene) 1941- 144
    Earlier sketch in SATA *10*
    See also CLR *33*
Bilson, Geoffrey 1938-1987 99
Binch, Caroline (Lesley) 1947- 140
    Earlier sketch in SATA *81*
Bing, Christopher (H.) 126
Bingham, Caroline 1962- 158
Bingham, Jane M. 1941- 163
Bingham, Jane Marie
    See Bingham, Jane M.
Bingham, Sam(uel A.) 1944- 96
Bingley, Margaret (Jane Kirby) 1947- 72
Binkley, Anne
    See Rand, Ann (Binkley)
Binzen, Bill 24
    See Binzen, William
Birch, David (W.) 1913-1996 89
Birch, Reginald B(athurst) 1856-1943 19
Birchman, David 1949- 72
Birchmore, Daniel A. 1951- 92
Bird, Carmel 1940- 124
Bird, E(lzy) J(ay) 1911- 58

Birdsall, Jeanne 1952(?)- *170*
Birdseye, Tom 1951- *148*
   Earlier sketches in SATA *66, 98*
Birenbaum, Barbara 1941- *65*
Birmingham, Lloyd P(aul) 1924- *83*
   Earlier sketch in SATA *12*
Birmingham, Ruth
   See Sorrells, Walter
Birney, Betty G. 1947- *169*
   Earlier sketch in SATA *98*
Biro, B.
   See Biro, B(alint) S(tephen)
Biro, B(alint) S(tephen) 1921- *67*
   See Biro, Val
Biro, Val *1*
   See also CLR *28*
   See also SAAS *13*
   See Biro, B(alint) S(tephen)
Bischoff, Julia Bristol 1899-1970 .... *12*
Bishop, Bonnie 1943- *37*
Bishop, Claire Huchet 1899(?)-1993 .... *14*
   Obituary *74*
   See also CLR *80*
Bishop, Courtney
   See Ruemmler, John D(avid)
Bishop, Curtis (Kent) 1912-1967 .... *6*
Bishop, Gavin 1946- *144*
   Earlier sketch in SATA *97*
Bishop, Kathleen Wong 1954- *120*
Bishop, Kathy
   See Bishop, Kathleen Wong
Bishop, Nic 1955- *161*
   Earlier sketch in SATA *107*
Bisset, Donald 1910-1995 .... *86*
   Earlier sketch in SATA *7*
Bisson, Terry 1942- *99*
Bisson, Terry Ballantine
   See Bisson, Terry
Bitter, Gary G(len) 1940- *22*
Bixby, William (Courtney) 1920-1986 .... *6*
   Obituary *47*
Bjoerk, Christina 1938- *99*
   Earlier sketch in SATA *67*
   See also CLR *22*
Bjork, Christina
   See Bjoerk, Christina
Bjorklund, Lorence F. 1913-1978 .... *35*
   Brief entry *32*
Bjorkman, Steve *163*
Black, Algernon David 1900-1993 .... *12*
   Obituary *76*
Black, Holly 1971- *147*
Black, Irma Simonton 1906-1972 .... *2*
   Obituary *25*
Black, Mansell
   See Trevor, Elleston
Black, MaryAnn
   See Easley, MaryAnn
Black, Susan Adams 1953- *40*
Blackall, Bernie 1956- *126*
Blackburn, Claire
   See Altman, Linda Jacobs
Blackburn, John(ny) Brewton 1952- *15*
Blackburn, Joyce Knight 1920- *29*
Blackett, Veronica Heath 1927- *12*
Blackie, Jean Cutler 1943- *79*
Blacklin, Malcolm
   See Chambers, Aidan
Blacklock, Dyan 1951- *112*
Blackman, Malorie 1962- *128*
   Earlier sketch in SATA *83*
Blackton, Peter
   See Wilson, Lionel
Blackwood, Alan 1932- *70*
Blackwood, Gary L. 1945- *169*
   Earlier sketches in SATA *72, 118*
Blade, Alexander
   See Garrett, (Gordon) Randall (Phillip)
   and Hamilton, Edmond
   and Silverberg, Robert

Blades, Ann (Sager) 1947- *69*
   Earlier sketch in SATA *16*
   See also CLR *15*
Bladow, Suzanne Wilson 1937- *14*
Blaine, John
   See Goodwin, Harold L(eland)
Blaine, Marge
   See Blaine, Margery Kay
Blaine, Margery Kay 1937- *11*
Blair, Alison
   See Lerangis, Peter
Blair, Anne Denton 1914-1993 .... *46*
Blair, David Nelson 1954- *80*
Blair, Eric (Arthur) 1903-1950 .... *29*
   See Orwell, George
Blair, Jay 1953- *45*
Blair, Lucile
   See Yeakley, Marjory Hall
Blair, Margaret Whitman 1951- *124*
Blair, Pauline Hunter
   See Clarke, Pauline
Blair, Ruth Van Ness 1912-1999 .... *12*
Blair, Shannon
   See Kaye, Marilyn
Blair, Walter 1900-1992 .... *12*
   Obituary *72*
Blaisdell, Bob
   See Blaisdell, Robert
Blaisdell, Robert 1959- *105*
Blake, Bronwyn 1940- *149*
Blake, Jon 1954- *171*
   Earlier sketch in SATA *78*
Blake, Olive
   See Supraner, Robyn
Blake, Quentin (Saxby) 1932- *125*
   Earlier sketches in SATA *9, 52, 96*
   See also CLR *31*
Blake, Robert 1949- *42*
Blake, Robert J. *160*
Blake, Walker E.
   See Griffin, W.E.B.
Blake, William 1757-1827 .... *30*
   See also CLR *52*
Blakely, Gloria 1950- *139*
Blakely, Roger K. 1922- *82*
Blakeney, Jay D.
   See Chester, Deborah
Blakey, Nancy 1955- *94*
Blanc, Esther S. 1913-1997 .... *66*
Blanchard, Patricia *125*
Blanchet, M(uriel) Wylie 1891-1961 .... *106*
Blanco, Richard L(idio) 1926- *63*
Bland, E.
   See Nesbit, E.
Bland, Edith Nesbit
   See Nesbit, E.
Bland, Fabian
   See Nesbit, E.
Blank, Clarissa Mabel 1915-1965 .... *62*
Blankenship, LeeAnn 1944- *181*
Blassingame, Wyatt Rainey 1909-1985 .... *34*
   Obituary *41*
   Earlier sketch in SATA *1*
Blatchford, Claire H. 1944- *94*
Blauer, Ettagale 1940- *49*
Bledsoe, Glen L. 1951- *108*
Bledsoe, Glen Leonard
   See Bledsoe, Glen L.
Bledsoe, Karen E. 1962- *167*
   Earlier sketch in SATA *108*
Bledsoe, Karen Elizabeth
   See Bledsoe, Karen E.
Bledsoe, Lucy Jane 1957- *162*
   Earlier sketch in SATA *97*
Bleeker, Sonia *2*
   Obituary *26*
   See Zim, Sonia Bleeker
Blegen, Daniel M. 1950- *92*
Blegvad, Erik 1923- *132*
   Earlier sketches in SATA *14, 66*

Blegvad, Lenore 1926- *176*
   Earlier sketches in SATA *14, 66*
Blish, James (Benjamin) 1921-1975 .... *66*
Blishen, Edward (William) 1920-1996 .... *66*
   Obituary *93*
   Earlier sketch in SATA *8*
Bliss, Corinne Demas 1947- *37*
   See Demas, Corinne
Bliss, Frederick
   See Card, Orson Scott
Bliss, Gillian
   See Paton Walsh, Jill
Bliss, Harry 1964- *156*
Bliss, Reginald
   See Wells, H(erbert) G(eorge)
Bliss, Ronald G(ene) 1942- *12*
Bliven, Bruce, Jr. 1916-2002 .... *2*
Blixen, Karen (Christentze Dinesen)
   1885-1962 .... *44*
   See Dinesen, Isak
Blizzard, Gladys S. (?)-1992 .... *79*
Blobaum, Cindy 1966- *123*
Bloch, Lucienne 1909-1999 .... *10*
Bloch, Marie Halun 1910-1998 .... *6*
   See also SAAS *9*
Bloch, Robert (Albert) 1917-1994 .... *12*
   Obituary *82*
Blochman, Lawrence G(oldtree) 1900-1975
   .... *22*
Block, Francesca Lia 1962- *158*
   Earlier sketches in SATA *80, 116*
   See also CLR *116*
   See also SAAS *21*
Block, Irvin 1917- *12*
Blomgren, Jennifer (Alice) 1954- *136*
Blood, Charles Lewis 1929- *28*
Bloom, Barbara Lee 1943- *146*
Bloom, Freddy 1914-2000 .... *37*
   Obituary *121*
Bloom, Lloyd 1947- *108*
   Brief entry *43*
Bloom, Suzanne 1950- *172*
Bloomfield, Michaela 1966- *70*
Bloor, Edward (William) 1950- *155*
   Earlier sketch in SATA *98*
Blos, Joan W(insor) 1928- *153*
   Autobiography Feature *153*
   Brief entry *27*
   Earlier sketches in SATA *33, 69, 109*
   See also CLR *18*
   See also SAAS *11*
Blough, Glenn O(rlando) 1907-1995 .... *1*
Blue, Rose 1931- *166*
   Autobiography Feature *117*
   Earlier sketches in SATA *5, 91, 93*
   See also SAAS *24*
Blue, Zachary
   See Stine, R.L.
Bluggage, Oranthy
   See Alcott, Louisa May
Blumberg, Leda 1956- *59*
Blumberg, Rhoda 1917- *123*
   Earlier sketches in SATA *35, 70*
   See also CLR *21*
Blume, Judy (Sussman) 1938- *142*
   Earlier sketches in SATA *2, 31, 79*
   See also CLR *69*
Blume, Lesley M.M. 1975- *180*
Blumenthal, Deborah *161*
Blumenthal, Shirley 1943- *46*
Blutig, Eduard
   See Gorey, Edward (St. John)
Bly, Janet (Chester) 1945- *43*
Bly, Stephen A(rthur) 1944- *116*
   Earlier sketch in SATA *43*
Blyler, Allison Lee 1966- *74*
Blyton, Carey 1932-2002 .... *9*
   Obituary *138*
Blyton, Enid (Mary) 1897-1968 .... *25*
   See also CLR *31*
Boardman, Fon Wyman, Jr. 1911-2000 .... *6*

Boardman, Gwenn R. *12*
  See Petersen, Gwenn Boardman
Boase, Wendy 1944-1999 .... *28*
  Obituary *110*
Boatner, Mark Mayo III 1921- *29*
Bobbe, Dorothie de Bear 1905-1975 .... *1*
  Obituary *25*
Bober, Natalie S. 1930- *134*
  Earlier sketch in SATA *87*
  See also SAAS *23*
Bobette, Bibo
  See Gugliotta, Bobette
Bobritsky, Vladimir *47*
  Brief entry *32*
  See Bobri, Vladimir V.
Bochak, Grayce 1956- *76*
Bock, Hal
  See Bock, Harold I.
Bock, Harold I. 1939- *10*
Bock, William Sauts Netamux'we 1939- *14*
Bodanis, David *179*
Bode, Janet 1943-1999 .... *96*
  Obituary *118*
  Earlier sketch in SATA *60*
Bodecker, N(iels) M(ogens) 1922-1988 ...... *73*
  Obituary *54*
  Earlier sketch in SATA *8*
Boden, Hilda
  See Bodenham, Hilda Morris
Bodenham, Hilda Morris 1901- *13*
Bodett, Tom *70*
  See Bodett, Thomas Edward
Bodie, Idella F(allaw) 1925- *89*
  Earlier sketch in SATA *12*
Bodker, Cecil 1927- *133*
  Earlier sketch in SATA *14*
  See also CLR *23*
Bodker, Cecil 1927-
  See Bodker, Cecil
Bodsworth, (Charles) Fred(erick) 1918- *27*
Boeckman, Charles 1920- *12*
Boelts, Maribeth 1964- *163*
  Earlier sketch in SATA *78*
Boerst, William J. 1939- *170*
  Earlier sketch in SATA *121*
Boesch, Mark J(oseph) 1917- *12*
Boesen, Victor 1908- *16*
Bogacki, Tomek 1950- *138*
Bogaerts, Gert 1965- *80*
Bogan, Paulette 1960- *129*
Bogart, Jo Ellen 1945- *92*
  See also CLR *59*
Boggs, Ralph Steele 1901-1994 .... *7*
Bograd, Larry 1953- *89*
  Earlier sketch in SATA *33*
  See also SAAS *21*
Bohdal, Susi 1951- *101*
  Earlier sketch in SATA *22*
Bohlen, Nina 1931- *58*
Bohlmeijer, Arno 1956- *94*
Bohner, Charles (Henry) 1927- *62*
Bohnhoff, Maya Kaathryn 1954- *88*
Boiger, Alexandra *178*
Boissard, Janine 1932- *59*
Bojunga, Lygia
  See Nunes, Lygia Bojunga
Bojunga-Nunes, Lygia
  See Nunes, Lygia Bojunga
Boland, Janice *98*
Bolden, Tonya 1959- *138*
  Earlier sketch in SATA *79*
Bolden, Tonya Wilyce
  See Bolden, Tonya
Boles, Paul Darcy 1916-1984 .... *9*
  Obituary *38*
Bolian, Polly 1925- *4*
Bollen, Roger 1941(?)- *83*
  Brief entry *29*
Bolliger, Max 1929- *7*
Bollinger, Max 1929- *167*
Bollinger, Peter *172*

Bolognese, Don(ald Alan) 1934- *129*
  Earlier sketches in SATA *24, 71*
Bolotin, Norman (Phillip) 1951- *93*
Bolton, Carole 1926- *6*
Bolton, Elizabeth
  See St. John, Nicole
Bolton, Evelyn
  See Bunting, (Anne) Eve(lyn)
Bonar, Veronica
  See Bailey, Donna (Veronica Anne)
Bond, B. J.
  See Heneghan, James
Bond, Bruce 1939- *61*
Bond, Felicia 1954- *126*
  Earlier sketch in SATA *49*
Bond, Gladys Baker 1912- *14*
Bond, Higgins 1951- *177*
  Earlier sketch in SATA *83*
Bond, J. Harvey
  See Winterbotham, R(ussell) R(obert)
Bond, (Thomas) Michael 1926- *157*
  Earlier sketches in SATA *6, 58*
  See also CLR *95*
  See also SAAS *3*
Bond, Nancy 1945- *159*
  Autobiography Feature *159*
  Earlier sketches in SATA *22, 82*
  See also CLR *11*
  See also SAAS *13*
Bond, Nancy Barbara
  See Bond, Nancy
Bond, Rebecca 1972- *130*
Bond, Ruskin 1934- *87*
  Earlier sketch in SATA *14*
Bondie, J. D.
  See Cunningham, Chet
Bondoux, Anne-Laure 1971- *175*
Bone, Ian 1956- *158*
  Earlier sketch in SATA *117*
Bonehill, Captain Ralph
  See Stratemeyer, Edward L.
Bonham, Barbara Thomas 1926- *7*
Bonham, Frank 1914-1989 .... *49*
  Obituary *62*
  Earlier sketch in SATA *1*
  See also SAAS *3*
Boniface, William 1963- *102*
Bonn, Pat
  See Bonn, Patricia Carolyn
Bonn, Patricia Carolyn 1948- *43*
Bonner, Mary Graham 1890-1974 .... *19*
Bonner, Mike 1951- *121*
Bonners, Susan 1947- *85*
  Brief entry *48*
Bonnett-Rampersaud, Louise *173*
Bonning, Tony 1948- *169*
Bonsall, Crosby Barbara (Newell) 1921-1995
  .... *23*
  Obituary *84*
Bonsall, Joseph S. 1948- *119*
Bonsignore, Joan 1959- *140*
Bontemps, Arna(ud Wendell) 1902-1973 .... *44*
  Obituary *24*
  Earlier sketch in SATA *2*
  See also CLR *6*
Bonzon, Paul-Jacques 1908-1978 .... *22*
Boock, Paula 1964- *134*
Booher, Dianna Daniels 1948- *33*
Book, Rick 1949- *119*
Book, Rita
  See Holub, Joan
Bookman, Charlotte
  See Zolotow, Charlotte (Gertrude) S(hapiro)
Boon, Debbie 1960- *103*
Boon, Emilie (Laetitia) 1958- *86*
Boone, Charles Eugene
  See Boone, Pat
Boone, Pat 1934- *7*
Boorman, Linda (Kay) 1940- *46*
Boorstin, Daniel J(oseph) 1914-2004 .... *52*
Booth, Ernest Sheldon 1915-1984 .... *43*

Booth, Graham (Charles) 1935- *37*
Bootman, Colin *159*
Borden, Louise (Walker) 1949- *141*
  Autobiography Feature *141*
  Earlier sketches in SATA *68, 104*
Bordier, Georgette 1924- *16*
Borgman, James
  See Borgman, Jim
Borgman, James Mark
  See Borgman, Jim
Borgman, Jim 1954- *122*
  See Borgman, James Mark
Boring, Mel 1939- *168*
  Earlier sketch in SATA *35*
Borja, Corinne 1929- *22*
Borja, Robert 1923- *22*
Borland, Hal *5*
  Obituary *24*
  See Borland, Harold Glen
Borland, Kathryn Kilby 1916- *16*
Borlenghi, Patricia 1951- *79*
Born, Adolf 1930- *49*
Bornstein, Ruth Lercher
  Autobiography Feature *107*
  See Bornstein-Lercher, Ruth
Bornstein-Lercher, Ruth 1927- *88*
  Earlier sketch in SATA *14*
  See Bornstein, Ruth Lercher
Borski, Lucia Merecka *18*
Borten, Helen Jacobson 1930- *5*
Bortolotti, Dan 1969- *157*
Borton, Elizabeth
  See Trevino, Elizabeth B(orton) de
Borton, Lady 1942- *98*
Borton de Trevino, Elizabeth
  See Trevino, Elizabeth B(orton) de
Bortstein, Larry 1942- *16*
Bortz, Alfred B(enjamin) 1944- *139*
  Earlier sketch in SATA *74*
Bortz, Fred
  See Bortz, Alfred B(enjamin)
Bosco, Jack
  See Holliday, Joseph
Boshell, Gordon 1908- *15*
Boshinski, Blanche 1922- *10*
Bosman, Paul 1929- *107*
Bosse, Malcolm (Joseph, Jr.) 1926-2002 .. *136*
  Earlier sketch in SATA *35*
Bosserman, (Charles) Phillip 1931- *84*
Bossom, Naomi 1933- *35*
Bostock, Mike 1962- *114*
Boston, L(ucy) M(aria Wood) 1892-1990 ... *19*
  Obituary *64*
  See also CLR *3*
Bostrom, Kathleen (Susan) Long 1954- *139*
Bostrom, Kathy
  See Bostrom, Kathleen (Susan) Long
Bosworth, J. Allan 1925- *19*
Bothwell, Jean (?)-1977 .... *2*
Botkin, B(enjamin) A(lbert) 1901-1975 ...... *40*
Botsford, Ward 1927-2004 .... *66*
Botting, Douglas (Scott) 1934- *43*
Bottner, Barbara 1943- *170*
  Autobiography Feature *121*
  Earlier sketches in SATA *14, 93*
  See also SAAS *26*
Bottone, Frank G., Jr. 1969- *141*
Bouchard, David 1952- *117*
Boucher, (Clarence) Carter 1954- *129*
Boudelang, Bob
  See Pell, Ed(ward)
Boughton, Richard 1954- *75*
Boulet, Susan Seddon 1941- *50*
Boulle, Pierre (Francois Marie-Louis)
  1912-1994 .... *22*
  Obituary *78*
Boulton, Jane 1921- *91*
Bouma, Paddy 1947- *128*
Bour, Daniele 1939- *62*
Bourdon, David 1934-1998 .... *46*
Bourgeois, Paulette 1951- *153*

Bourne, Lesley
   See Marshall, Evelyn
Bourne, Miriam Anne 1931-1989 .... *16*
   Obituary *63*
Boutet de Monvel, (Louis) M(aurice)
   1850(?)-1913 .... *30*
   See also CLR *32*
Bova, Ben 1932- *133*
   Earlier sketches in SATA *6, 68*
   See also CLR *96*
Bova, Benjamin William
   See Bova, Ben
Bovaird, Anne E(lizabeth) 1960- *90*
Bow, Patricia 1946- *168*
Bowden, Joan Chase 1925- *51*
   Brief entry *38*
Bowen, Alexandria Russell *97*
Bowen, Andy Russell
   See Bowen, Alexandria Russell
Bowen, Anne 1952- *170*
Bowen, Betty Morgan
   See West, Betty
Bowen, Catherine (Shober) Drinker 1897-1973
   .... *7*
Bowen, David
   See Bowen, Joshua David
Bowen, Fred 1953- *136*
Bowen, Joshua David 1930- *22*
Bowen, Rhys
   See Quin-Harkin, Janet
Bowen, Robert Sydney 1900-1977 .... *52*
   Obituary *21*
Bowermaster, Jon 1954- *135*
   Earlier sketch in SATA *77*
Bowers, Terrell L. 1945- *101*
Bowers, Terry
   See Bowers, Terrell L.
Bowie, C. W.
   See Old, Wendie C(orbin)
   and Wirths, Claudine (Turner) G(ibson)
Bowie, Jim
   See Norwood, Victor G(eorge) C(harles)
   and Stratemeyer, Edward L.
Bowkett, Stephen 1953- *67*
Bowler, Jan Brett
   See Brett, Jan
Bowler, Tim 1953- *149*
Bowman, Crystal 1951- *105*
Bowman, James Cloyd 1880-1961 .... *23*
Bowman, John S(tewart) 1931- *16*
Bowman, Kathleen (Gill) 1942- *52*
   Brief entry *40*
Boxall, Ed *178*
Boyce, George A(rthur) 1898- *19*
Boyd, Candy Dawson 1946- *72*
   See also CLR *50*
Boyd, Pauline
   See Schock, Pauline
Boyd, Selma
   See Acuff, Selma Boyd
Boyd, Waldo T. 1918- *18*
Boyden, Linda 1948- *143*
Boyer, Allen B. 1963- *153*
Boyer, Robert E(rnst) 1929- *22*
Boyes, Vivien 1952- *106*
Boyes, Vivien Elizabeth
   See Boyes, Vivien
Boyle, Ann (Peters) 1916- *10*
Boyle, Eleanor Vere (Gordon) 1825-1916 .. *28*
Boyle, Robert H. 1928- *65*
Boylston, Helen Dore 1895-1984 .... *23*
   Obituary *39*
Boyne, John 1971- *181*
Boynton, Sandra (Keith) 1953- *152*
   Brief entry *38*
   Earlier sketches in SATA *57, 107*
   See also CLR *105*
Boz
   See Dickens, Charles (John Huffam)
Bracken, Charles
   See Pellowski, Michael (Joseph)

Brackers de Hugo, Pierre 1960- *115*
Brackett, Dolli Tingle 1911-1993 .... *137*
Brackett, Virginia 1950- *166*
   Earlier sketch in SATA *121*
Brackett, Virginia Roberts Meredith
   See Brackett, Virginia
Bradbury, Bianca (Ryley) 1908-1982 .... *56*
   Earlier sketch in SATA *3*
Bradbury, Edward P.
   See Moorcock, Michael
Bradbury, Ray 1920- *123*
   Earlier sketches in SATA *11, 64*
Bradbury, Ray Douglas
   See Bradbury, Ray
Bradby, Marie *161*
Bradfield, Carl 1942- *91*
Bradford, Ann (Liddell) 1917- *56*
   Brief entry *38*
Bradford, Barbara Taylor 1933- *66*
Bradford, Karleen 1936- *96*
   Earlier sketch in SATA *48*
Bradford, Lois J(ean) 1936- *36*
Bradford, Richard (Roark) 1932-2002 .... *59*
   Obituary *135*
Bradley, Duane
   See Sanborn, Duane
Bradley, Kimberly Brubaker 1967- *179*
Bradley, Marion Zimmer 1930-1999 .... *139*
   Obituary *116*
   Earlier sketch in SATA *90*
   See Chapman, Lee
   and Dexter, John
   and Gardner, Miriam
   and Ives, Morgan
   and Rivers, Elfrida
Bradley, Virginia 1912- *23*
Bradley, Will
   See Strickland, (William) Brad(ley)
Bradman, Tony 1954- *152*
   Earlier sketch in SATA *81*
Bradshaw, Gillian (Joan) 1949- *118*
Bradshaw, Gillian 1956- *127*
Bradshaw, Gillian Marucha
   See Bradshaw, Gillian
Bradstreet, T. J.
   See Thesman, Jean
Brady, Esther Wood 1905-1987 .... *31*
   Obituary *53*
Brady, Irene 1943- *4*
Brady, Kimberley S. 1953- *101*
Brady, Kimberley Smith
   See Brady, Kimberley S.
Brady, Lillian 1902- *28*
Bragdon, Elspeth MacDuffie 1897-1980 .... *6*
Bragdon, Lillian Jacot *24*
Brager, Bruce L. 1949- *146*
Bragg, Mabel Caroline 1870-1945 .... *24*
Bragg, Michael 1948- *46*
Bragg, Ruth Gembicki 1943- *77*
Brahm, Sumishta 1954- *58*
Brailsford, Frances
   See Wosmek, Frances
Brainerd, John W(hiting) 1918- *65*
Braithwaite, Althea 1940- *23*
   Autobiography Feature *119*
   See also SAAS *24*
Bram, Elizabeth 1948- *30*
Brancato, Robin F(idler) 1936- *97*
   See also CLR *32*
   See also SAAS *9*
Branch, Muriel Miller 1943- *152*
   Earlier sketch in SATA *94*
Brand, Christianna
   See Lewis, Mary (Christianna)
Brand, Rebecca
   See Charnas, Suzy McKee
Brandel, Marc 1919- *71*
Brandenberg, Alexa (Demetria) 1966- *97*
Brandenberg, Aliki (Liacouras) 1929- *157*
   Earlier sketches in SATA *2, 35, 75, 113*
   See Aliki

Brandenberg, Franz 1932- *75*
   Earlier sketches in SATA *8, 35*
Brandenburg, Jim 1945- *87*
Brandhorst, Carl T(heodore) 1898-1988 .... *23*
Brandis, Marianne 1938- *149*
   Earlier sketches in SATA *59, 96*
Brandon, Brumsic, Jr. 1927- *9*
Brandon, Curt
   See Bishop, Curtis (Kent)
Brandreth, Gyles 1948- *28*
   See Brandreth, Gyles Daubeney
Brandreth, Gyles Daubeney 1948-
   See Brandreth, Gyles
Brandt, Catharine 1905-1997 .... *40*
Brandt, Keith
   See Sabin, Louis
Brandt, Sue R(eading) 1916- *59*
Branfield, John (Charles) 1931- *11*
Branford, Henrietta 1946-1999 .... *106*
Branley, Franklyn M(ansfield) 1915-2002
   .... *136*
   Earlier sketches in SATA *4, 68*
   See also CLR *13*
   See also SAAS *16*
Branscum, Robbie (Tilley) 1937-1997 .... *72*
   Obituary *96*
   Earlier sketch in SATA *23*
   See also SAAS *17*
Bransom, (John) Paul 1885-1979 .... *43*
Brashares, Ann 1967- *145*
   See also CLR *113*
Braswell, E.J.
   See Lynn, Tracy
Braswell, Elizabeth J.
   See Lynn, Tracy
Braswell, Liz
   See Lynn, Tracy
Bratton, Helen 1899-1986 .... *4*
Bratun, Katy 1950- *160*
   Earlier sketch in SATA *83*
Braude, Michael 1936- *23*
Braun, Lilian Jackson 1916(?)- *109*
Brautigan, Richard (Gary) 1935-1984 .... *56*
Bray, Libba *159*
Braymer, Marjorie Elizabeth 1911-1988 .... *6*
Breathed, Berke 1957- *161*
   Earlier sketch in SATA *86*
Breathed, Guy Berkeley
   See Breathed, Berke
Brecht, Edith 1895-1975 .... *6*
   Obituary *25*
Breck, Vivian
   See Breckenfeld, Vivian Gurney
Breckenfeld, Vivian Gurney 1895-1992 ..... *1*
Breda, Tjalmar
   See DeJong, David C(ornel)
Bredeson, Carmen 1944- *163*
   Earlier sketch in SATA *98*
Breinburg, Petronella 1927- *11*
   See also CLR *31*
Breisky, William J(ohn) 1928- *22*
Brenaman, Miriam *172*
Brennan, Gale (Patrick) 1927- *64*
   Brief entry *53*
Brennan, Herbie
   See Brennan, J(ames) H(erbert)
Brennan, J(ames) H(erbert) 1940- *140*
Brennan, Jan
   See Brennan, J(ames) H(erbert)
Brennan, Joseph Lomas 1903-2000 .... *6*
Brennan, Linda Crotta 1952- *130*
Brenner, Anita 1905-1974 .... *56*
Brenner, Barbara (Johnes) 1925- *124*
   Earlier sketches in SATA *4, 42, 76*
   See also SAAS *14*
Brenner, Fred 1920- *36*
   Brief entry *34*
Brent, Stuart *14*
Breslin, Theresa *128*
   Autobiography Feature *128*
   Earlier sketch in SATA *70*

Breslow, Maurice 1935- *72*
Breslow, Maurice A
  See Breslow, Maurice
Breslow, Susan 1951- *69*
Brett, Bernard 1925- *22*
Brett, Grace N(eff) 1900-1975 .... *23*
Brett, Jan 1949- *171*
  Earlier sketches in SATA *42, 71, 130*
  See also CLR *27*
Brett, Jan Churchill
  See Brett, Jan
Brett Bowler, Jan
  See Brett, Jan
Brewer, James D. 1951- *108*
Brewer, Sally King 1947- *33*
Brewster, Benjamin
  See Folsom, Franklin (Brewster)
Brewster, Hugh 1950- *95*
Brewster, Patience 1952- *97*
Brewton, John E(dmund) 1898-1982 .... *5*
Brian, Janeen (Paulette) 1948- *141*
Briant, Ed *180*
Brick, John 1922-1973 .... *10*
Brickman, Robin D. 1954- *155*
Bride, Nadja
  See Nobisso, Josephine
Bridgers, Sue Ellen 1942- *90*
  Autobiography Feature *109*
  Earlier sketch in SATA *22*
  See also CLR *18*
  See also SAAS *1*
Bridges, Laurie
  See Bruck, Lorraine
Bridges, Ruby (Nell) 1954- *131*
Bridges, William (Andrew) 1901-1984 .... *5*
Bridwell, Norman (Ray) 1928- *138*
  Earlier sketches in SATA *4, 68*
  See also CLR *96*
Brier, Howard M(axwell) 1903-1969 .... *8*
Brierley, (Louise) 1958- *59*
Briggs, Katharine Mary 1898-1980 .... *101*
  Obituary *25*
Briggs, Peter 1921-1975 .... *39*
  Obituary *31*
Briggs, Raymond 1934- *131*
  Earlier sketches in SATA *23, 66*
  See also CLR *10*
Briggs, Raymond Redvers
  See Briggs, Raymond
Bright, Robert (Douglas Sr.) 1902-1988 ..... *63*
  Obituary *60*
  Earlier sketch in SATA *24*
Bright, Sarah
  See Shine, Deborah
Brightfield, Richard 1927- *65*
  Brief entry *53*
Brightfield, Rick
  See Brightfield, Richard
Brighton, Catherine 1943- *107*
  Earlier sketch in SATA *65*
Brill, Marlene Targ 1945- *124*
  Earlier sketch in SATA *77*
Brimberg, Stanlee 1947- *9*
Brimner, Larry Dane 1949- *170*
  Autobiography Feature *112*
  Earlier sketch in SATA *79*
Brin, David 1950- *65*
Brin, Ruth Firestone 1921- *22*
Brinckloe, Julie (Lorraine) 1950- *13*
Brindel, June (Rachuy) 1919- *7*
Brindle, Max
  See Fleischman, Sid
Brindze, Ruth 1903-1984 .... *23*
Brink, Carol Ryrie 1895-1981 .... *100*
  Obituary *27*
  Earlier sketches in SATA *1, 31*
  See also CLR *30*
Brinsmead, H. F(ay)
  See Brinsmead, H(esba) F(ay)
Brinsmead, H. F.
  See Brinsmead, H(esba) F(ay)

Brinsmead, H(esba) F(ay) 1922- *78*
  Earlier sketch in SATA *18*
  See also CLR *47*
  See also SAAS *5*
Briquebec, John
  See Rowland-Entwistle, (Arthur) Theodore
  (Henry)
Brisbane, Henry R.
  See Ellis, Edward S(ylvester)
Brisco, P. A.
  See Matthews, Patricia
Brisco, Patty
  See Matthews, Patricia
  and Matthews, Clayton (Hartley)
Briscoe, Jill (Pauline) 1935- *56*
  Brief entry *47*
Brisley, Joyce Lankester 1896-1978 .... *22*
  Obituary *84*
Brissenden, Connie
  See Brissenden, Constance
Brissenden, Constance 1947- *150*
Brisson, Pat 1951- *177*
  Autobiography Feature *133*
  Earlier sketches in SATA *67, 128, 133*
Britt, Dell 1934- *1*
Brittain, Bill
  See SAAS *7*
  See Brittain, William (E.)
Brittain, C. Dale 1948- *82*
Brittain, William (E.) 1930- *76*
  Earlier sketch in SATA *36*
  See Brittain, Bill
Brittingham, Geoffrey (Hugh) 1959- *76*
Britton, Kate *49*
  See Stegeman, Janet Allais
Britton, Louisa
  See McGuire, Leslie (Sarah)
Britton, Rick 1952- *82*
Bro, Margueritte (Harmon) 1894-1977 .... *19*
  Obituary *27*
Broach, Elise 1963- *173*
Broadhead, Helen Cross 1913- *25*
Brochmann, Elizabeth 1938- *41*
Brock, Betty (Carter) 1923-2003 .... *4*
  Obituary *150*
Brock, C(harles) E(dmund) 1870-1938 ...... *42*
  Brief entry *32*
Brock, Delia
  See Ephron, Delia
Brock, Emma L(illian) 1886-1974 .... *8*
Brock, H(enry) M(atthew) 1875-1960 .... *42*
Brockett, Eleanor Hall 1913-1967 .... *10*
Brockman, C(hristian) Frank 1902-1985 ..... *26*
Brockmeier, Kevin 1972- *176*
Broderick, Dorothy M. 1929- *5*
Brodeur, Ruth Wallace
  See Wallace-Brodeur, Ruth
Brodie, Sally
  See Cavin, Ruth (Brodie)
Brodsky, Beverly
  See McDermott, Beverly Brodsky
Brody, Wendy
  See Staub, Wendy Corsi
Broeger, Achim 1944- *31*
Broekel, Rainer Lothar 1923- *38*
Broekel, Ray
  See Broekel, Rainer Lothar
Broekstra, Lorette 1964- *124*
Broger, Achim
  See Broeger, Achim
Broida, Marian *154*
Brokamp, Marilyn 1920- *10*
Broman, Fred
  See Moseley, James W(illett)
Bromhall, Winifred *26*
Brommer, Gerald F(rederick) 1927- *28*
Brondfield, Jerome 1913-1998 .... *22*
Brondfield, Jerry
  See Brondfield, Jerome
Bronner, Stephen Eric 1949- *101*
Bronowski, Jacob 1908-1974 .... *55*

Bronson, Lynn
  See Lampman, Evelyn Sibley
Brook, Judith (Penelope) 1926- *59*
  Brief entry *51*
Brook, Judy
  See Brook, Judith (Penelope)
Brooke, L(eonard) Leslie 1862-1940 .... *17*
  See also CLR *20*
Brooke, William J. 1946- *139*
Brooke-Haven, P.
  See Wodehouse, P(elham) G(renville)
Brookins, Dana 1931- *28*
Brooks, Anita *5*
  See Abramovitz, Anita (Zeltner Brooks)
Brooks, Bill 1939- *59*
Brooks, Bruce 1950- *112*
  Brief entry *53*
  Earlier sketch in SATA *72*
  See also CLR *25*
Brooks, Caryl 1924- *84*
Brooks, Charlotte K(endrick) 1918-1998 .... *24*
  Obituary *112*
Brooks, Erik 1972- *152*
Brooks, George
  See Baum, L(yman) Frank
Brooks, Gwendolyn 1917-2000 .... *6*
  Obituary *123*
  See also CLR *27*
Brooks, Gwendolyn Elizabeth
  See Brooks, Gwendolyn
Brooks, Jerome 1931- *23*
Brooks, Kevin M. 1959- *150*
Brooks, Lester 1924- *7*
Brooks, Martha 1944- *134*
  Autobiography Feature *134*
  Earlier sketches in SATA *68, 121*
Brooks, Maurice (Graham) 1900- *45*
Brooks, Polly Schoyer 1912- *12*
Brooks, Ron(ald George) 1948- *94*
  Brief entry *33*
Brooks, Terry 1944- *60*
Brooks, Walter R(ollin) 1886-1958 .... *17*
Brooks-Hill, Helen (Mason) 1908-1994 ...... *59*
Broome, Errol 1937- *158*
  Earlier sketch in SATA *105*
Brophy, Nannette 1963- *73*
Brosnan, James Patrick 1929- *14*
Brosnan, Jim
  See Brosnan, James Patrick
Brostoff, Anita 1931- *132*
Brothers Grimm
  See Grimm, Jacob Ludwig Karl
  and Grimm, Wilhelm Karl
Brothers Hildebrandt, The
  See Hildebrandt, Greg
  and Hildebrandt, Tim
Broun, Emily
  See Sterne, Emma Gelders
Brouwer, S. W.
  See Brouwer, Sigmund (W.)
Brouwer, Sigmund (W.) 1959- *109*
Brow, Thea 1934- *60*
Brower, Millicent *8*
Brower, Pauline 1929- *22*
Browin, Frances Williams 1898-1986 .... *5*
Brown, Alexis
  See Baumann, Amy (Brown) Beeching
Brown, Anne Ensign 1937- *61*
Brown, Beverly Swerdlow *97*
Brown, Bill
  See Brown, William L(ouis)
Brown, Billye Walker
  See Cutchen, Billye Walker
Brown, Bob
  See Brown, Robert Joseph
Brown, Buck 1936- *45*
Brown, Calef *179*
Brown, Cassie 1919-1986 .... *55*
Brown, Charlotte Lewis *181*
Brown, Conrad 1922- *31*
Brown, Craig McFarland 1947- *73*

Brown, David
  See Brown, David A(lan)
  and Myller, Rolf
Brown, Dee 1908-2002 .... *110*
  Obituary *141*
  Earlier sketch in SATA *5*
Brown, Dee Alexander
  See Brown, Dee
Brown, Don 1949- *172*
Brown, Drew T. III 1955- *83*
Brown, Drollene P. 1939- *53*
Brown, Eleanor Frances 1908-1987 .... *3*
Brown, Elizabeth Ferguson 1937- *153*
Brown, Elizabeth M(yers) 1915- *43*
Brown, Fern G. 1918- *34*
Brown, (Robert) Fletch 1923- *42*
Brown, Fornan 1901-1996 .... *71*
  Obituary *88*
Brown, George Earl 1883-1964 .... *11*
Brown, George Mackay 1921-1996 .... *35*
Brown, Irene Bennett 1932- *3*
Brown, Irving
  See Adams, William Taylor
Brown, Ivor (John Carnegie) 1891-1974 ...... *5*
  Obituary *26*
Brown, Jane Clark 1930- *81*
Brown, Janet Mitsui *87*
Brown, Jo 1964- *170*
Brown, Joanne 1933- *147*
Brown, Joe David 1915-1976 .... *44*
Brown, Joseph E(dward) 1929- *59*
  Brief entry *51*
Brown, Judith Gwyn 1933- *20*
Brown, Kathryn 1955- *168*
  Earlier sketch in SATA *98*
Brown, Kathy
  See Brown, Kathryn
Brown, Ken (James) *129*
Brown, Kevin 1960- *101*
Brown, Laurene Krasny 1945- *99*
  Earlier sketch in SATA *54*
Brown, Laurie Krasny
  See Brown, Laurene Krasny
Brown, Lloyd Arnold 1907-1966 .... *36*
Brown, Mahlon A.
  See Ellis, Edward S(ylvester)
Brown, Marc (Tolon) 1946- *145*
  Earlier sketches in SATA *10, 53, 80*
  See also CLR *29*
Brown, Marcia (Joan) 1918- *47*
  Earlier sketch in SATA *7*
  See also CLR *12*
Brown, Margaret Wise 1910-1952 .... *100*
  See also YABC *2*
  See also CLR *107*
Brown, Margery (Wheeler) *78*
  Earlier sketch in SATA *5*
Brown, Marion Marsh 1908-2001 .... *6*
Brown, Myra Berry 1918- *6*
Brown, Palmer 1919- *36*
Brown, Pamela (Beatrice) 1924-1989 .... *5*
  Obituary *61*
Brown, Peter 1979- *178*
Brown, Reeve Lindbergh
  See Lindbergh, Reeve
Brown, Richard E. 1946- *61*
Brown, Robert Joseph 1907-1989 .... *14*
Brown, Roderick (Langmere) Haig-
  See Haig-Brown, Roderick (Langmere)
Brown, Rosalie *9*
  See Moore, Rosalie (Gertrude)
Brown, Roswell
  See Webb, Jean Francis (III)
Brown, Roy (Frederick) 1921-1982 .... *51*
  Obituary *39*
Brown, Ruth 1941- *170*
  Earlier sketch in SATA *105*
Brown, Scott 1971- *134*
Brown, Sue Ellen 1954- *81*
Brown, Tricia 1954- *114*
Brown, Vinson 1912-1991 .... *19*

Brown, Walter R(eed) 1929- *19*
Brown, Will
  See Ainsworth, William Harrison
Brown, William L(ouis) 1910-1964 .... *5*
Browne, Anthony 1946- *163*
  Brief entry *44*
  Earlier sketches in SATA *45, 61, 105*
  See also CLR *19*
Browne, Anthony Edward Tudor
  See Browne, Anthony
Browne, Dik
  See Browne, Richard Arthur Allen
Browne, Hablot Knight 1815-1882 .... *21*
Browne, Matthew
  See Rands, William Brighty
Browne, Nicky Matthews
  See Browne, N.M.
Browne, N.M. 1960- *167*
Browne, Richard Arthur Allen 1917-1989 .. *67*
  Brief entry *38*
  See Browne, Dik
Browne, Vee F(rances) 1956- *90*
Browning, Robert 1812-1889
  See YABC *1*
  See also CLR *97*
Brownjohn, Alan 1931- *6*
Brownlee, Walter 1930- *62*
Brownlie, Betty 1946- *159*
Brownlow, Kevin 1938- *65*
Brownridge, William R(oy) 1932- *94*
Bruce, (William) Harry 1934- *77*
Bruce, Mary 1927- *1*
Bruchac, Joseph III
  See Bruchac, Joseph
Bruchac, Joseph 1942- *176*
  Autobiography Feature *176*
  Earlier sketches in SATA *42, 89, 131*
  See also CLR *46*
Bruchac, Margaret M.
  See Bruchac, Marge
Bruchac, Marge *181*
Bruck, Lorraine 1921- *55*
  Brief entry *46*
  See Bridges, Laurie
Bruel, Nick *166*
Bruemmer, Fred 1929- *47*
Brugman, Alyssa (F.) 1974- *152*
Brumbeau, Jeff 1955- *157*
Bruna, Dick 1927- *76*
  Brief entry *30*
  Earlier sketch in SATA *43*
  See also CLR *7*
Brunhoff, Jean de 1899-1937 .... *24*
  See also CLR *116*
Brunhoff, Laurent de 1925- *150*
  Earlier sketches in SATA *24, 71*
  See also CLR *116*
Brunskill, Elizabeth Ann Flatt 1966- *88*
Brush, Karen A(lexandra) 1960- *85*
Brussel-Smith, Bernard 1914- *58*
Brust, Steven K. 1955- *121*
  Earlier sketch in SATA *86*
Brust, Steven K. Zoltan
  See Brust, Steven K.
Brustlein, Daniel 1904- *40*
Brustlein, Janice Tworkov -2000 .... *40*
  Obituary *126*
Brutschy, Jennifer 1960- *84*
Bryan, Ashley 1923- *178*
  Earlier sketches in SATA *31, 72, 132*
  See also CLR *66*
Bryan, Ashley F.
  See Bryan, Ashley
Bryant, Bernice (Morgan) 1908-1976 .... *11*
Bryant, Jen 1949- *175*
  Earlier sketch in SATA *94*
Bryant, Jennifer Fisher
  See Bryant, Jen
Bryant, Laura J. *176*
Brychta, Alex 1956- *21*
Brynie, Faith H. 1946- *113*

Brynie, Faith Hickman
  See Brynie, Faith H.
Bryson, Bernarda 1903-2004 .... *9*
  See Shahn, Bernarda Bryson
Buba, Joy Flinsch 1904- *44*
Buchan, Bryan 1945- *36*
Buchan, John 1875-1940
  See YABC *2*
Buchanan, Debby 1952- *82*
Buchanan, Deborah Leevonne
  See Buchanan, Debby
Buchanan, Jane 1956- *160*
Buchanan, Paul 1959- *116*
Buchanan, Sue 1939- *139*
Buchheimer, Naomi Barnett
  See Barnett, Naomi
Buchignani, Walter 1965- *84*
Buchwald, Art 1925-2007 .... *10*
Buchwald, Arthur
  See Buchwald, Art
Buchwald, Emilie 1935- *7*
Buck, Gisela 1941- *101*
Buck, Lewis 1925- *18*
Buck, Margaret Waring 1905-1997 .... *3*
Buck, Nola
  See Godwin, Laura
Buck, Pearl S(ydenstricker) 1892-1973 .... *25*
  Earlier sketch in SATA *1*
Buck, Siegfried 1941- *101*
Buckeridge, Anthony (Malcolm) 1912-2004 .... *85*
  Earlier sketch in SATA *6*
Buckholtz, Eileen (Garber) 1949- *54*
  Brief entry *47*
Buckler, Ernest 1908-1984 .... *47*
Buckless, Andrea K. 1968- *117*
Buckley, Helen E(lizabeth) 1918- *90*
  Earlier sketch in SATA *2*
Buckley, James, Jr. 1963- *166*
  Earlier sketch in SATA *114*
Buckley, Michael *177*
Buckmaster, Henrietta *6*
  See Stephens, Henrietta Henkle
Bucks, Brad
  See Holub, Joan
Budd, E. S.
  See Sirimarco, Elizabeth
Budd, Lillian (Peterson) 1897-1989 .... *7*
Budhos, Marina *173*
Buehler, Stephanie Jona 1956- *83*
Buehner, Caralyn (M.) 1963- *159*
  Earlier sketch in SATA *104*
Buehner, Mark 1959- *159*
  Earlier sketch in SATA *104*
Buehr, Walter Franklin 1897-1971 .... *3*
Buell, Janet 1952- *106*
Buergel, Paul-Hermann H. 1949- *83*
Buettner, Dan 1960- *95*
Buff, Conrad 1886-1975 .... *19*
Buff, Mary (E. Marsh) 1890-1970 .... *19*
Buffett, Jimmy 1946- *110*
  Earlier sketch in SATA *76*
Buffie, Margaret 1945- *161*
  Earlier sketches in SATA *71, 107*
  See also CLR *39*
Bugni, Alice 1951- *122*
Buhhos, Marina Tamar
  See Budhos, Marina
Buhhos, Marina Tamar
  See Budhos, Marina
Bujold, Lois McMaster 1949- *136*
Bulfinch, Thomas 1796-1867 .... *35*
Bulion, Leslie 1958- *161*
Bull, Angela (Mary) 1936- *45*
Bull, Emma 1954- *99*
  Autobiography Feature *103*
Bull, Norman John 1916- *41*
Bull, Schuyler M. 1974- *138*
Bulla, Clyde R. 1914-2007 .... *139*
  Earlier sketches in SATA *2, 41, 91*
  See also SAAS *6*

Bullard, Lisa 1961- *142*
Bullock, Kathleen (Mary) 1946- *77*
Bullock, Robert (D.) 1947- *92*
Bulpin, (Barbara) Vicki *92*
Bumstead, Kathleen Mary 1918-1987 .... *53*
Bundles, A'Lelia Perry 1952- *76*
Bunin, Catherine 1967- *30*
Bunin, Sherry 1925- *30*
Bunkers, Suzanne L. 1950- *136*
Bunting, A. E.
  See Bunting, (Anne) Eve(lyn)
Bunting, Eve
  See Bunting, (Anne) Eve(lyn)
Bunting, (Anne) Eve(lyn) 1928- *158*
  Earlier sketches in SATA *18, 64, 110*
  See also CLR *82*
  See Bunting, Eve
Bunting, Glenn (Davison) 1957- *22*
Burack, Sylvia K. 1916-2003 .... *35*
  Obituary *143*
Burbank, Addison (Buswell) 1895-1961 ..... *37*
Burch, Joann J(ohansen) *75*
Burch, Robert J(oseph) 1925- *74*
  Earlier sketch in SATA *1*
  See also CLR *63*
Burchard, Peter Duncan 1921- *143*
  Earlier sketches in SATA *5, 74*
  See also SAAS *13*
Burchard, S. H.
  See Burchard, Sue
Burchard, Sue 1937- *22*
Burchardt, Nellie 1921- *7*
Burdett, Lois *117*
Burdick, Eugene (Leonard) 1918-1965 .... *22*
Burford, Eleanor
  See Hibbert, Eleanor Alice Burford
Burgan, Michael 1960- *167*
  Earlier sketch in SATA *118*
Burger, Carl 1888-1967 .... *9*
Burgess, Ann Marie
  See Gerson, Noel Bertram
Burgess, Barbara Hood 1926- *69*
Burgess, Em
  See Burgess, Mary Wyche
Burgess, (Frank) Gelett 1866-1951 .... *32*
  Brief entry *30*
Burgess, Mark *157*
Burgess, Mary Wyche 1916- *18*
Burgess, Melvin 1954- *146*
  Earlier sketch in SATA *96*
Burgess, Michael
  See Gerson, Noel Bertram
Burgess, Robert F(orrest) 1927- *4*
Burgess, Thornton Waldo 1874-1965 .... *17*
Burgess, Trevor
  See Trevor, Elleston
Burgwyn, Mebane Holoman 1914-1992 .... *7*
Burke, David 1927- *46*
Burke, Diana G.
  See Gallagher, Diana G.
Burke, Diana Gallagher
  See Gallagher, Diana G.
Burke, Dianne O'Quinn 1940- *89*
Burke, Janine 1952- *139*
Burke, Jim 1973- *179*
Burke, Katie 1953- *168*
Burke, Patrick 1958- *114*
Burke, Ralph
  See Garrett, (Gordon) Randall (Phillip)
  and Silverberg, Robert
Burkert, Nancy Ekholm 1933- *24*
  See also SAAS *14*
Burke-Weiner, Kimberly 1962- *95*
Burks, Brian 1955- *95*
Burland, Brian (Berkeley) 1931- *34*
Burland, C. A.
  See Burland, Cottie (Arthur)
Burland, Cottie (Arthur) 1905-1983 .... *5*
Burleigh, Robert 1936- *146*
  Earlier sketches in SATA *55, 98*
Burlingame, (William) Roger 1889-1967 ...... *2*

Burman, Ben Lucien 1896-1984 .... *6*
  Obituary *40*
Burn, Doris 1923- *1*
Burn, Ted
  See Burn, Thomas E.
Burn, Thomas E. 1940- *150*
Burnard, Damon 1963- *115*
Burnett, Constance Buel 1893-1975 .... *36*
Burnett, Frances (Eliza) Hodgson 1849-1924
  .... *100*
  See also YABC *2*
  See also CLR *122*
Burnford, Sheila (Philip Cochrane Every)
  1918-1984 .... *3*
  Obituary *38*
  See also CLR *2*
Burnham, Gretchen
  See Sprague, Gretchen
Burnham, Nicole 1970- *161*
Burnham, Niki
  See Burnham, Nicole
Burnham, Sophy 1936- *65*
Burningham, John (Mackintosh) 1936- *160*
  Earlier sketches in SATA *16, 59, 111*
  See also CLR *9*
Burns, Diane L. 1950- *81*
  See also SAAS *24*
Burns, Eloise Wilkin
  See Wilkin, Eloise
Burns, Florence M. 1905-1988 .... *61*
Burns, Khephra 1950- *92*
Burns, Marilyn 1941- *96*
  Brief entry *33*
Burns, Olive Ann 1924-1990 .... *65*
Burns, Paul C. *5*
Burns, Ray
  See Burns, Raymond (Howard)
Burns, Raymond (Howard) 1924- *9*
Burns, Theresa 1961- *84*
Burns, William A. 1909-1999 .... *5*
Burr, Dan 1951- *65*
Burr, Lonnie 1943- *47*
Burrell, Roy E(ric) C(harles) 1923- *72*
Burroughs, Edgar Rice 1875-1950 .... *41*
Burroughs, Jean Mitchell 1908- *28*
Burroughs, Polly 1925- *2*
Burroway, Janet (Gay) 1936- *23*
Burstein, Chaya M(alamud) 1923- *64*
Burstein, Fred 1950- *83*
Burstein, John 1949- *54*
  Brief entry *40*
Burstein, Stanley M.
  See Burstein, Stanley Mayer
Burstein, Stanley Mayer 1941- *175*
Bursztynski, Sue 1953- *114*
Burt, Jesse Clifton 1921-1976 .... *46*
  Obituary *20*
Burt, Olive Woolley 1894-1981 .... *4*
Burton, Gennett 1945- *95*
Burton, Hester (Wood-Hill) 1913-2000 .... *74*
  Earlier sketch in SATA *7*
  See also CLR *1*
  See also SAAS *8*
Burton, Leslie
  See McGuire, Leslie (Sarah)
Burton, Marilee Robin 1950- *82*
  Earlier sketch in SATA *46*
Burton, Maurice 1898-1992 .... *23*
Burton, Robert (Wellesley) 1941- *22*
Burton, Virginia Lee 1909-1968 .... *100*
  Earlier sketch in SATA *2*
  See also CLR *11*
Burton, William H(enry) 1890-1964 .... *11*
Busby, Cylin 1970- *118*
Buscaglia, (Felice) Leo(nardo) 1924-1998 .. *65*
  See Buscaglia, Leo F.
Buscaglia, Leo F.
  See Buscaglia, (Felice) Leo(nardo)
Busch, Phyllis S. 1909- *30*
Bush, Anne Kelleher
  See Kelleher, Anne

Bush, Catherine 1961- *128*
Bushnell, Jack 1952- *86*
Busoni, Rafaello 1900-1962 .... *16*
Buss, Helen M.
  See Clarke, Margaret
Busselle, Rebecca 1941- *80*
Bustard, Anne 1951- *173*
Butcher, Kristin 1951- *140*
Butenko, Bohdan 1931- *90*
Butler, Beverly Kathleen 1932- *7*
Butler, Bill
  See Butler, William (Arthur) Vivian
  and Butler, Ernest Alton
  and Butler, William Huxford
Butler, Charles 1963- *175*
  Earlier sketch in SATA *121*
Butler, Charles Cadman
  See Butler, Charles
Butler, Dori Hillestad 1965- *164*
Butler, Dorothy 1925- *73*
Butler, Geoff 1945- *94*
Butler, M. Christina 1934- *170*
  Earlier sketch in SATA *72*
Butler, Octavia E. 1947-2006 .... *84*
  See also CLR *65*
Butler, Octavia Estelle
  See Butler, Octavia E.
Butler, Vivian
  See Butler, William (Arthur) Vivian
Butler, William
  See Butler, William (Arthur) Vivian
Butler, William (Arthur) Vivian 1927-1987
  .... *79*
  See Marric, J. J.
Butters, Dorothy Gilman *5*
  See Gilman, Dorothy
Butterworth, Emma Macalik 1928- *43*
Butterworth, Nick 1946- *149*
  Earlier sketch in SATA *106*
Butterworth, Oliver 1915-1990 .... *1*
  Obituary *66*
Butterworth, W.E.
  See Griffin, W.E.B.
Butterworth, William E.
  See Griffin, W.E.B.
Butterworth, William Edmund III
  See Griffin, W.E.B.
Butts, Ed 1951- *177*
Butts, Edward P.
  See Butts, Ed
Butts, Ellen R(ubinstein) 1942- *93*
Buxton, Ralph
  See Silverstein, Alvin
  and Silverstein, Virginia B(arbara Opshelor)
Buzzeo, Toni 1951- *135*
Byalick, Marcia 1947- *141*
  Earlier sketch in SATA *97*
Byard, Carole (Marie) 1941- *57*
Byars, Betsy 1928- *163*
  Autobiography Feature *108*
  Earlier sketches in SATA *4, 46, 80*
  See also CLR *72*
  See also SAAS *1*
Byars, Betsy Cromer
  See Byars, Betsy
Byfield, Barbara Ninde 1930- *8*
Byman, Jeremy 1944- *129*
Bynum, Janie *133*
Byrd, Elizabeth 1912-1989 .... *34*
Byrd, Nicole
  See Zach, Cheryl (Byrd)
Byrd, Robert (John) 1942- *158*
  Earlier sketches in SATA *33, 112*
Byrne, Mary Gregg 1951- *162*

C

C. 3. 3.
See Wilde, Oscar (Fingal O'Flahertie Wills)
Cabaniss, J(ames) Allen 1911-1997 5
Cabat, Erni 1914- 74
Cabban, Vanessa 1971- 176
Cable, Mary 1920- 9
Cabot, Meg 1967- 175
  Earlier sketch in SATA 127
  See also CLR 85
Cabot, Meggin
  See Cabot, Meg
Cabot, Meggin Patricia
  See Cabot, Meg
Cabot, Patricia
  See Cabot, Meg
Cabral, O. M.
  See Cabral, Olga
Cabral, Olga 1909- 46
Cabrera, Cozbi A. 1963- 177
Cabrera, Jane 1968- 152
  Earlier sketch in SATA 103
Cabrera, Marcela 1966- 90
Cade, Toni
  See Bambara, Toni Cade
Cadmus and Harmonia
  See Buchan, John
Cadnum, Michael 1949- 165
  Earlier sketches in SATA 87, 121
  See also CLR 78
Caduto, Michael J. 1955- 103
Cadwallader, Sharon 1936- 7
Cady, (Walter) Harrison 1877(?)-1970 19
Caffey, Donna (J.) 1954- 110
Cagle, Malcolm W(infield) 1918- 32
Cahn, Rhoda 1922- 37
Cahn, William 1912-1976 37
Cain, Arthur H(omer) 1913-1981 3
Caine, Geoffrey
  See Walker, Robert W(ayne)
Caines, Jeannette (Franklin) 1938- 78
  Brief entry 43
  See also CLR 24
Cairns, Trevor 1922- 14
Calabro, Marian 1954- 79
Caldecott, Moyra 1927- 22
Caldecott, Randolph (J.) 1846-1886 100
  Earlier sketch in SATA 17
  See also CLR 110
Calder, Charlotte 1952- 125
Calder, David 1932-1997 105
Calder, Lyn
  See Calmenson, Stephanie
Calder, Marie D(onais) 1948- 96
Calderone-Stewart, Lisa
  See Calderone-Stewart, Lisa-Marie
Calderone-Stewart, Lisa-Marie 1958- 123
Caldwell, Doreen (Mary) 1942- 71
Caldwell, John C(ope) 1913-1984 7
Caletti, Deb 1963- 171
Calhoun, B. B. 1961- 98
Calhoun, Chad
  See Barrett, Neal, Jr.
  and Cunningham, Chet
  and Goulart, Ron(ald Joseph)
Calhoun, Dia 1959- 129
Calhoun, Mary 2
  See also CLR 42
  See Wilkins, Mary Huiskamp
Calhoun, T.B.
  See Bisson, Terry
Calif, Ruth 1922- 67
Calkins, Franklin
  See Stratemeyer, Edward L.
Call, Hughie Florence 1890-1969 1
Callahan, Dorothy M(onahan) 1934- 39
  Brief entry 35
Callahan, Philip Serna 1923- 25
Callan, Jamie 1954- 59
Callan, Jim 1951- 181

Callaway, Bernice (Anne) 1923- 48
Callaway, Kathy 1943- 36
Callen, Larry
  See Callen, Lawrence Willard, Jr.
Callen, Lawrence Willard, Jr. 1927- 19
Calley, Karin 1965- 92
Calmenson, Stephanie 1952- 139
  Brief entry 37
  Earlier sketches in SATA 51, 84
Calvert, Elinor H.
  See Lasell, Elinor H.
Calvert, John
  See Leaf, (Wilbur) Munro
Calvert, Patricia 1931- 132
  Earlier sketches in SATA 45, 69
  See also SAAS 17
Camburn, Carol A.
  See Camburn-Bracalente, Carol A.
Camburn-Bracalente, Carol A. 1962- 118
Cameron, Ann 1943- 129
  Earlier sketches in SATA 27, 89
  See also SAAS 20
Cameron, Edna M. 1905-1999 3
Cameron, Eleanor (Frances) 1912-1996 25
  Obituary 93
  Earlier sketch in SATA 1
  See also CLR 72
  See also SAAS 10
Cameron, Elizabeth
  See Nowell, Elizabeth Cameron
Cameron, Elizabeth Jane 1910-1976 32
  Obituary 30
Cameron, Ian
  See Payne, Donald Gordon
Cameron, M(alcolm) G(ordon) Graham
  See Graham-Cameron, M(alcolm) G(ordon)
Cameron, M. Graham
  See Graham-Cameron, M(alcolm) G(ordon)
Cameron, Mike Graham
  See Graham-Cameron, M(alcolm) G(ordon)
Cameron, Polly 1928- 2
Cameron, Scott 1962- 84
Camp, Lindsay 1957- 133
Camp, Walter (Chauncey) 1859-1925
  See YABC 1
Campbell, (Elizabeth) Andrea 1963- 50
Campbell, Ann R. 1925- 11
Campbell, Bill 1960- 89
Campbell, Bruce
  See Epstein, Samuel
Campbell, Camilla 1905-1992 26
Campbell, Carole R. 1939- 125
Campbell, Hope 1925- 20
Campbell, Hugh 1930- 90
Campbell, Jane
  See Edwards, Jane Campbell
Campbell, Julie
  See Tatham, Julie Campbell
Campbell, Patricia J(ean) 1930- 45
Campbell, Patty
  See Campbell, Patricia J(ean)
Campbell, Peter A. 1948- 99
Campbell, R. W.
  See Campbell, Rosemae Wells
Campbell, Robin
  See Strachan, Ian
Campbell, Rod 1945- 98
  Brief entry 44
  Earlier sketch in SATA 51
Campbell, Rosemae Wells 1909- 1
Camper, Cathy 1956- 170
Campion, Nardi Reeder 1917- 22
Campling, Elizabeth 1948- 53
Campoy, F. Isabel 1946- 181
  Earlier sketch in SATA 143
Camps, Luis 1928- 66
Canales, Viola 1957- 141
Canfield, Dorothea F.
  See Fisher, Dorothy (Frances) Canfield
Canfield, Dorothea Frances
  See Fisher, Dorothy (Frances) Canfield

Canfield, Dorothy
  See Fisher, Dorothy (Frances) Canfield
Canfield, Jack 1944- 164
Canfield, Jane White 1897-1984 32
  Obituary 38
Canfield, Muriel 1935- 94
Cann, Helen 1969- 179
  Earlier sketch in SATA 124
Cann, Kate 1954- 152
  Earlier sketch in SATA 103
Cannan, Joanna 82
  See Pullein-Thompson, Joanna Maxwell
Cannon, A(nn) E(dwards) 163
  Earlier sketch in SATA 93
Cannon, Bettie (Waddell) 1922- 59
Cannon, Curt
  See Hunter, Evan
Cannon, Eileen E(mily) 1948- 119
Cannon, Frank
  See Mayhar, Ardath
Cannon, Janell 1957- 128
  Earlier sketch in SATA 78
  See also CLR 120
Cannon, Marian G. 1923- 85
Cannon, Taffy
  See Cannon, Eileen E(mily)
Canusi, Jose
  See Barker, S(quire) Omar
Canyon, Christopher 1966- 150
  Earlier sketch in SATA 104
Capek, Michael 1947- 142
  Earlier sketch in SATA 96
Capes, Bernard (Edward Joseph) 1854-1918
  116
Caponigro, John Paul 1965- 84
Capote, Truman 1924-1984 91
Capp, Al 61
  See Caplin, Alfred Gerald
Cappel, Constance 1936- 22
Cappetta, Cynthia 1949- 125
Cappo, Nan Willard 1955- 143
Capps, Benjamin (Franklin) 1922- 9
Captain Kangaroo
  See Keeshan, Robert J.
Captain Wheeler
  See Ellis, Edward S(ylvester)
Captain Young of Yale
  See Stratemeyer, Edward L.
Capucilli, Alyssa Satin 1957- 163
  Earlier sketch in SATA 115
Capucine
  See Mazille, Capucine
Caraher, Kim(berley Elizabeth) 1961- 105
Caraker, Mary 1929- 74
Caras, Roger A(ndrew) 1928-2001 12
  Obituary 127
Caravantes, Peggy 1935- 140
Caraway, Caren 1939- 57
Carbone, Elisa 1954- 137
  Earlier sketch in SATA 81
  See Carbone, Elisa Lynn
Carbone, Elisa Lynn 173
  See Carbone, Elisa
Carbonnier, Jeanne 1894-1974 3
  Obituary 34
Card, Orson Scott 1951- 127
  Earlier sketch in SATA 83
  See also CLR 116
Carew, Jan (Rynveld) 1925- 51
  Brief entry 40
Carey, Bonnie
  See Marshall, Bonnie C.
Carey, Charles W., Jr. 1951- 170
Carey, Ernestine Gilbreth 1908-2006 2
  Obituary 177
Carey, Lisa 110
Carey, M. V.
  See Carey, Mary V(irginia)
Carey, Mary V(irginia) 1925-1994 44
  Brief entry 39
Carey, Peter 1943- 94

Carey, Valerie Scho 1949- 60
Carheden, Goorel Kristina
    See Naaslund, Goorel Kristina
Carigiet, Alois 1902-1985 24
    Obituary 47
    See also CLR 38
Carini, Edward 1923- 9
Carkeet, David 1946- 75
Carle, Eric 1929- 163
    Earlier sketches in SATA *4, 65, 120*
    See also CLR 72
    See also SAAS 6
Carleton, Captain L. C.
    See Ellis, Edward S(ylvester)
Carleton, Captain Latham C.
    See Ellis, Edward S(ylvester)
Carleton, Latham C.
    See Ellis, Edward S(ylvester)
Carling, Amelia Lau 1949- 164
    Earlier sketch in SATA *119*
Carlisle, Carolyn
    See Hawes, Louise
Carlisle, Clark
    See Holding, James (Clark Carlisle, Jr.)
Carlisle, Olga Andreyev 1930- 35
Carlsen, G(eorge) Robert 1917- 30
Carlsen, Ruth C(hristoffer) 1918- 2
Carlson, Bernice Wells 1910- 8
Carlson, Dale (Bick) 1935- 1
Carlson, Daniel (Bick) 1960- 27
Carlson, Laurie 1952- 173
    Earlier sketch in SATA *101*
Carlson, Laurie Winn
    See Carlson, Laurie
Carlson, Melody 1956- 171
    Earlier sketch in SATA *113*
Carlson, Nancy L.
    See Carlson, Nancy L(ee)
Carlson, Nancy L(ee) 1953- 144
    Brief entry 45
    Earlier sketches in SATA *56, 90*
Carlson, Natalie Savage 1906-1997 68
    Earlier sketch in SATA *2*
    See also SAAS 4
Carlson, Susan Johnston 1953- 88
Carlson, Vada F. 1897- 16
Carlstrom, Nancy White 1948- 156
    Brief entry 48
    Earlier sketches in SATA *53, 92*
Carlton, Keith
    See Robertson, Keith (Carlton)
Carlyon, Richard 55
Carman, Patrick 161
Carmer, Carl (Lamson) 1893-1976 37
    Obituary 30
Carmer, Elizabeth Black 1904- 24
Carmi, Giora 1944- 149
    Earlier sketch in SATA *79*
Carmichael, Carrie 40
    See Carmichael, Harriet
Carmody, Isobelle 1958- 161
Carmody, Isobelle Jane
    See Carmody, Isobelle
Carney, Mary Lou 1949- 170
Carol, Bill J.
    See Knott, William C(ecil, Jr.)
Caron, Romi
    See Caron-Kyselkova', Romana
Caron-Kyselkova', Romana 1967- 94
Caroselli, Remus F(rancis) 1916- 36
Carpelan, Bo (Gustaf Bertelsson) 1926- 8
Carpenter, (John) Allan 1917- 81
    Earlier sketch in SATA *3*
Carpenter, Angelica Shirley 1945- 153
    Earlier sketch in SATA *71*
Carpenter, Frances 1890-1972 3
    Obituary 27
Carpenter, John (Howard) 1948- 58
Carpenter, Johnny
    See Carpenter, John (Howard)
Carpenter, Patricia (Healy Evans) 1920- 11

Carr, Glyn
    See Styles, (Frank) Showell
Carr, Harriett H(elen) 1899-1977 3
Carr, Jan 1953- 132
    Earlier sketch in SATA *89*
Carr, M. J.
    See Carr, Jan
Carr, Mary Jane 1899-1988 2
    Obituary 55
Carr, Philippa
    See Hibbert, Eleanor Alice Burford
Carr, Roger Vaughan 1937- 95
Carrel, Annette Felder 1929- 90
Carrick, Carol (Hatfield) 1935- 118
    Earlier sketches in SATA *7, 63*
    See also SAAS 18
Carrick, Donald (F.) 1929-1989 63
    Earlier sketch in SATA *7*
Carrick, Malcolm 1945- 28
Carrier, Lark 1947- 71
    Brief entry 50
Carrier, Roch 1937- 166
    Earlier sketch in SATA *105*
Carrighar, Sally 1898-1985 24
Carrington, G. A.
    See Cunningham, Chet
Carrington, Marsha Gray 1954- 168
    Earlier sketch in SATA *111*
Carris, Joan Davenport 1938- 44
    Brief entry 42
Carroll, Curt
    See Bishop, Curtis (Kent)
Carroll, Elizabeth
    See Barkin, Carol
    and James, Elizabeth
Carroll, Jenny
    See Cabot, Meg
Carroll, (Archer) Latrobe 1894-1996 7
Carroll, Laura
    See Parr, Lucy
Carroll, Lewis
    See CLR 108
    See Dodgson, Charles L(utwidge)
Carroll, Raymond 1924- 86
    Brief entry 47
Carruth, Hayden 1921- 47
Carryl, Charles E. 1841-1920 114
Carryl, Charles Edward
    See Carryl, Charles E.
Carse, Robert 1902-1971 5
Carson, J(ohn) Franklin 1920-1981 1
    Obituary 107
Carson, Mary Kay 1964- 150
Carson, Rachel
    See Carson, Rachel Louise
Carson, Rachel Louise 1907-1964 23
    See Carson, Rachel
Carson, Rosalind
    See Chittenden, Margaret
Carson, S. M.
    See Gorsline, (Sally) Marie
Carson, William C. 1928- 154
Carter, Alden R 1947- 137
    Earlier sketch in SATA *67*
    See also CLR 22
    See also SAAS 18
Carter, Alden Richardson
    See Carter, Alden R
Carter, Andy 1948- 134
Carter, Angela 1940-1992 66
    Obituary 70
Carter, Angela Olive
    See Carter, Angela
Carter, Anne Laurel 1953- 135
Carter, Asa Earl
    See Carter, Forrest
Carter, Avis Murton
    See Allen, Kenneth S.
Carter, Bruce
    See Hough, Richard (Alexander)
Carter, Carol S(hadis) 1948- 124

Carter, David A. 1957- 170
    Earlier sketch in SATA *114*
Carter, Don 1958- 124
Carter, Dorothy Sharp 1921- 8
Carter, Forrest 1927(?)-1979 32
Carter, Helene 1887-1960 15
Carter, (William) Hodding, Jr. 1907-1972 2
    Obituary 27
Carter, James Earl, Jr.
    See Carter, Jimmy
Carter, Jimmy 1924- 79
Carter, Katharine J(ones) 1905-1984 2
Carter, Lin(wood Vrooman) 1930-1988 91
Carter, Mike 1936- 138
Carter, Nick
    See Avallone, Michael (Angelo, Jr.)
    and Ballard, (Willis) Todhunter
    and Crider, Bill
    and Cassiday, Bruce (Bingham)
    and Chastain, Thomas
    and Dey, Frederic (Merrill) Van Rensselaer
    and Garside, (Clifford) Jack
    and Hayes, Ralph E(ugene)
    and Henderson, M(arilyn) R(uth)
    and Lynds, Dennis
    and Lynds, Gayle (Hallenbeck)
    and Randisi, Robert J.
    and Rasof, Henry
    and Stratemeyer, Edward L.
    and Smith, Martin Cruz
    and Swain, Dwight V(reeland)
    and Vardeman, Robert E(dward)
    and Wallmann, Jeffrey M(iner)
    and White, Lionel
Carter, Peter 1929- 57
Carter, Phyllis Ann
    See Eberle, Irmengarde
Carter, Samuel (Thomson) III 1904-1988 37
    Obituary 60
Carter, William E. 1926-1983 1
    Obituary 35
Cartlidge, Michelle 1950- 96
    Brief entry 37
    Earlier sketch in SATA *49*
Cartner, William Carruthers 1910- 11
Cartwright, Ann 1940- 78
Cartwright, Reg(inald Ainsley) 1938- 64
Cartwright, Sally 1923- 9
Carusone, Al 1949- 89
Carvell, Marlene 172
Carver, John
    See Gardner, Richard (M.)
Carwell, L'Ann
    See McKissack, Patricia C.
Cary
    See Cary, Louis F(avreau)
Cary, Kate 1967(?)- 174
Cary, Louis F(avreau) 1915- 9
Caryl, Jean
    See Kaplan, Jean Caryl Korn
Casanova, Mary 1957- 136
    Earlier sketch in SATA *94*
Cascone, A.G.
    See Cascone, Annette
    and Cascone, Gina
Cascone, Annette 1960- 103
Cascone, Gina 1955- 103
Case, Marshal T(aylor) 1941- 9
Case, Michael
    See Howard, Robert West
Caseley, Judith 1951- 159
    Brief entry 53
    Earlier sketch in SATA *87*
Casewit, Curtis W(erner) 1922-2002 4
Casey, Barbara (Louise) 1944- 147
    Earlier sketch in SATA *79*
Casey, Brigid 1950- 9
Casey, Tina 1959- 141
Cash, Megan Montague 160
Casilla, Robert 1959- 146
    Earlier sketch in SATA *75*

Cason, Mabel Earp 1892-1965 .... *10*
Cass, Joan E(velyn) *1*
Cass-Beggs, Barbara 1904- *62*
Cassedy, Patrice (Rinaldo) 1953- *149*
Cassedy, Sylvia 1930-1989 .... *77*
  Obituary *61*
  Earlier sketch in SATA 27
  See also CLR 26
Cassel, Lili
  See Wronker, Lili Cassel
Cassels, Jean *173*
Cassidy, Anne 1952- *166*
Casson, Hugh Maxwell 1910-1999 .... *65*
  Obituary *115*
Cassutt, Michael 1954- *78*
Cassutt, Michael Joseph
  See Cassutt, Michael
Castaldo, Nancy Fusco 1962- *151*
  Earlier sketch in SATA 93
Castaneda, Omar S. 1954- *71*
Castell, Megan
  See Williams, Jeanne
Castellanos, Jane Mollie Robinson 1913-2001
  .... *9*
Castellon, Federico 1914-1971 .... *48*
Castellucci, Cecil 1969- *176*
Castillo, Edmund L. 1924-2005 .... *1*
  Obituary *167*
Castle, Lee
  See Ogan, George F.
  and Ogan, Margaret E. (Nettles)
Castle, Paul
  See Howard, Vernon (Linwood)
Castle, Robert
  See Hamilton, Edmond
Caswell, Brian 1954- *171*
  Earlier sketch in SATA 97
Caswell, Helen (Rayburn) 1923- *12*
Catalano, Dominic 1956- *163*
  Earlier sketch in SATA 76
Catalano, Grace (A.) 1961- *99*
Catalanotto, Peter 1959- *159*
  Autobiography Feature *113*
  Earlier sketches in SATA 70, 114
  See also CLR 68
  See also SAAS 25
Catanese, P.W. 1961- *179*
Cate, Dick
  See Cate, Richard Edward Nelson
Cate, Richard Edward Nelson 1932- *28*
Cather, Willa (Sibert) 1873-1947 .... *30*
  See also CLR 98
Catherall, Arthur 1906-1980 .... *74*
  Earlier sketch in SATA 3
  See Ruthin, Margaret
Cathon, Laura E(lizabeth) 1908-1991 .... *27*
Catlett, Elizabeth 1919(?)- *82*
Catlin, Wynelle 1930- *13*
Cato, Heather *105*
Cato, Sheila *114*
Catrow, David
  See Catrow, David J. III
Catrow, David J. III *152*
Catt, Louis
  See French, Vivian
Cattell, James 1954- *123*
Catton, (Charles) Bruce 1899-1978 .... *2*
  Obituary *24*
Catz, Max
  See Glaser, Milton
Caudell, Marian 1930- *52*
Caudill, Rebecca 1899-1985 .... *1*
  Obituary *44*
Cauley, Lorinda Bryan 1951- *46*
  Brief entry *43*
Cauman, Samuel 1910-1971 .... *48*
Causley, Charles (Stanley) 1917-2003 .... *66*
  Obituary *149*
  Earlier sketch in SATA 3
  See also CLR 30
Cavallaro, Ann (Abelson) 1918- *62*

Cavallo, Diana 1931- *7*
Cavanagh, Helen (Carol) 1939- *98*
  Brief entry *37*
  Earlier sketch in SATA 48
Cavanah, Frances 1899-1982 .... *31*
  Earlier sketch in SATA 1
Cavanna, Betty *30*
  Earlier sketch in SATA 1
  See also SAAS 4
  See Harrison, Elizabeth (Allen) Cavanna
Cavanna, Elizabeth
  See Harrison, Elizabeth (Allen) Cavanna
Cave, Kathryn 1948- *123*
  Earlier sketch in SATA 76
Cavendish, Peter
  See Horler, Sydney
Cavin, Ruth (Brodie) 1918- *38*
Cavoukian, Raffi 1948- *68*
Cawley, Winifred 1915- *13*
Caxton, Pisistratus
  See Lytton, Edward G(eorge) E(arle) L(ytton)
  Bulwer-Lytton Baron
Cazeau, Charles J(ay) 1931- *65*
Cazet, Denys 1938- *163*
  Brief entry *41*
  Earlier sketches in SATA 52, 99
Cazzola, Gus 1934- *73*
Cebulash, Mel 1937- *91*
  Earlier sketch in SATA 10
Ceccoli, Nicoletta *181*
Ceder, Georgiana Dorcas -1985 .... *10*
Celenza, Anna Harwell *133*
Celestino, Martha Laing 1951- *39*
Cepeda, Joe *159*
Cerf, Bennett (Alfred) 1898-1971 .... *7*
Cerf, Christopher (Bennett) 1941- *2*
Cerullo, Mary M. 1949- *145*
  Earlier sketch in SATA 86
Cervon, Jacqueline
  See Moussard, Jacqueline
Cetin, Frank Stanley 1921- *2*
Chabon, Michael 1963- *145*
Chaconas, D.J.
  See Chaconas, Dori
Chaconas, Dori 1938- *175*
  Earlier sketch in SATA 145
Chaconas, Doris J.
  See Chaconas, Dori
Chadwick, Lester *67*
  Earlier sketch in SATA 1
Chaffee, Allen *3*
Chaffin, Lillie D(orton) 1925- *4*
Chaikin, Miriam 1924- *152*
  Earlier sketches in SATA 24, 102
Chall, Marsha Wilson *150*
Challand, Helen J(ean) 1921- *64*
Challans, Mary 1905-1983 .... *23*
  Obituary *36*
  See Renault, Mary
Chalmers, Mary (Eileen) 1927- *6*
  See also SAAS 14
Chamberlain, Margaret 1954- *46*
Chamberlin, Kate 1945- *105*
Chamberlin, Mary 1960- *177*
Chamberlin, Rich *177*
Chamberlin, Richard
  See Chamberlin, Rich
Chambers, Aidan 1934- *171*
  Earlier sketches in SATA 1, 69, 108
  See also SAAS 12
Chambers, Catherine E.
  See St. John, Nicole
Chambers, John W. 1933- *57*
  Brief entry *46*
Chambers, Kate
  See St. John, Nicole
Chambers, Margaret Ada Eastwood 1911- *2*
Chambers, Peggy
  See Chambers, Margaret Ada Eastwood
Chambers, Robert W(illiam) 1865-1933 ... *107*

Chan, Gillian 1954- *147*
  Earlier sketch in SATA 102
Chance, James T.
  See Carpenter, John (Howard)
Chance, John T.
  See Carpenter, John (Howard)
Chance, Stephen
  See Turner, Philip (William)
Chandler, Caroline A(ugusta) 1906-1979 .... *22*
  Obituary *24*
Chandler, David P(orter) 1933- *28*
Chandler, Edna Walker 1908-1982 .... *11*
  Obituary *31*
Chandler, Jennifer
  See Westwood, Jennifer
Chandler, Karen 1959- *122*
Chandler, Linda S(mith) 1929- *39*
Chandler, Pauline *175*
Chandler, Robert 1953- *40*
Chandler, Ruth Forbes 1894-1978 .... *2*
  Obituary *26*
Chandonnet, Ann F. 1943- *92*
Chaney, Jill 1932- *87*
Chang, Chih-Wei 1966- *111*
Chang, Cindy 1968- *90*
Chang, Margaret 1941- *71*
Chang, Margaret Scrogin
  See Chang, Margaret
Chang, Raymond 1939- *142*
  Earlier sketches in SATA 71, 142 PEN
Chanin, Michael 1952- *84*
Channel, A. R.
  See Catherall, Arthur
Chapian, Marie 1938- *29*
Chapin, Tom 1945- *83*
Chapman, Allen *67*
  Earlier sketch in SATA 1
Chapman, Cheryl O(rth) 1948- *80*
Chapman, (Constance) Elizabeth (Mann) 1919-
  .... *10*
Chapman, Gaynor 1935- *32*
Chapman, Gillian 1955- *120*
Chapman, Jane 1970- *176*
  Earlier sketch in SATA 122
Chapman, Jean *104*
  Earlier sketch in SATA 34
  See also CLR 65
Chapman, Lee
  See Bradley, Marion Zimmer
Chapman, Lynne F(erguson) 1963- *150*
  Earlier sketch in SATA 94
Chapman, Vera (Ivy May) 1898-1996 .... *33*
Chapman, Walker
  See Silverberg, Robert
Chappell, Audrey 1954- *72*
Chappell, Warren 1904-1991 .... *68*
  Obituary *67*
  Earlier sketch in SATA 6
  See also SAAS 10
Charbonneau, Eileen 1951- *118*
  Earlier sketch in SATA 84
Charbonnet, Gabrielle 1961- *81*
Chardiet, Bernice (Kroll) 1927(?)- *27*
Charles, Donald
  See Meighan, Donald Charles
Charles, Louis
  See Stratemeyer, Edward L.
Charles, Nicholas J.
  See Kuskin, Karla
Charles, Norma *153*
Charlip, Remy 1929- *119*
  Earlier sketches in SATA 4, 68
  See also CLR 8
Charlot, Jean 1898-1979 .... *8*
  Obituary *31*
Charlot, Martin (Day) 1944- *64*
Charlton, Michael (Alan) 1923- *34*
Charmatz, Bill 1925-2005 .... *7*
Charnas, Suzy McKee 1939- *110*
  Earlier sketch in SATA 61
Charosh, Mannis 1906- *5*

Chartier, Normand L. 1945- 66
Chase, Alice
  See McHargue, Georgess
Chase, Alyssa 1965- 92
Chase, Andra 1942- 91
Chase, Emily
  See Aks, Patricia
  and Garwood, Julie
  and Sachs, Judith
  and White, Carol
Chase, Mary (Coyle) 1907-1981 17
  Obituary 29
Chase, Mary Ellen 1887-1973 10
Chase, Richard 1904-1988 64
  Obituary 56
Chase, Samantha
  See Glick, Ruth (Burtnick)
Chast, Roz 1954- 97
Chastain, Madye Lee 1908-1989 4
Chataway, Carol 1955- 140
Chatterjee, Debjani 1952- 83
Chauncy, Nan(cen Beryl Masterman)
  1900-1970 6
  See also CLR 6
Chaundler, Christine 1887-1972 1
  Obituary 25
Chbosky, Stephen 1972- 164
Chee, Cheng-Khee 1934- 79
Cheese, Chloe 1952- 118
Chekhonte, Antosha
  See Chekhov, Anton (Pavlovich)
Chekhov, Anton (Pavlovich) 1860-1904 90
Chen, Anthony 1929- 6
Chen, Chih-Yuan 1975- 155
Chen, Ju-Hong 1941- 78
Chen, Sara
  See Odgers, Sally Farrell
Chen, Tony
  See Chen, Anthony
Chen, Yuan-tsung 1932- 65
Chenault, Nell
  See Smith, Linell Nash
Chenery, Janet (Dai) 1923- 25
Cheney, Cora 1916-1999 3
  Obituary 110
Cheney, Glenn (Alan) 1951- 99
Cheney, Lynne V. 1941- 152
Cheney, Ted
  See Cheney, Theodore Albert
Cheney, Theodore A. Rees
  See Cheney, Theodore Albert
Cheney, Theodore Albert 1928- 11
Cheng, Andrea 1957- 172
  Earlier sketch in SATA 128
Cheng, Christopher 1959- 173
  Earlier sketch in SATA 106
Cheng, Judith 1955- 36
Cheng, Shan
  See Jiang, Cheng An
Cheripko, Jan 1951- 155
  Earlier sketch in SATA 83
Chermayeff, Ivan 1932- 47
Chernoff, Dorothy A.
  See Ernst, (Lyman) John
Chernoff, Goldie Taub 1909- 10
Cherry, Carolyn Janice 93
  See Cherryh, C.J.
Cherry, Lynne 1952- 99
  Earlier sketch in SATA 34
Cherryh, C.J. 1942- 172
  See Cherry, Carolyn Janice
Cherryholmes, Anne
  See Price, Olive
Cheshire, Simon 172
Chesler, Bernice 1932-2002 59
Chess, Victoria (Dickerson) 1939- 92
  Earlier sketch in SATA 33
Chester, Deborah 1957- 85
Chester, Kate
  See Guccione, Leslie Davis
Chesterton, G(ilbert) K(eith) 1874-1936 27

Chesworth, Michael 160
Chetin, Helen 1922- 6
Chetwin, Grace 86
  Brief entry 50
Chevalier, Christa 1937- 35
Chevalier, Tracy 1962- 128
Chew, Ruth 1920- 7
Chichester Clark, Emma 1955- 156
  Earlier sketch in SATA 117
  See Clark, Emma Chichester
Chidsey, Donald Barr 1902-1981 3
  Obituary 27
Chiefari, Janet D. 1942- 58
Chien-min, Lin
  See Rumford, James
Child, L. Maria
  See Child, Lydia Maria
Child, Lauren 1965- 160
  Earlier sketch in SATA 119
Child, Lincoln 1957- 113
Child, Lincoln B.
  See Child, Lincoln
Child, Lydia Maria 1802-1880 67
Child, Mrs.
  See Child, Lydia Maria
Child, Philip 1898-1978 47
Children's Shepherd, The
  See Westphal, Arnold Carl
Childress, Alice 1920-1994 81
  Earlier sketches in SATA 7, 48
  See also CLR 14
Childs, H(alla) Fay (Cochrane) 1890-1971 ... 1
  Obituary 25
Chilton, Charles (Frederick William) 1917-
  102
Chimaera
  See Farjeon, Eleanor
Chin, Richard (M.) 1946- 52
Chinery, Michael 1938- 26
Chin-Lee, Cynthia 1958- 102
Chin-Lee D., Cynthia
  See Chin-Lee, Cynthia
Chippendale, Lisa A. 158
Chipperfield, Joseph Eugene 1912-1980(?) . 87
  Earlier sketch in SATA 2
Chisholm, P. F.
  See Finney, Patricia
Chislett, Gail (Elaine) 1948- 58
Chittenden, Elizabeth F. 1903-1999 9
Chittenden, Margaret 1935- 28
Chittum, Ida 1918- 7
Chitwood, Suzanne Tanner 1958- 160
Chmielarz, Sharon Lee 1940- 72
Choate, Judith (Newkirk) 1940- 30
Chocolate, Debbi 1954- 96
Chocolate, Deborah M. Newton
  See Chocolate, Debbi
Chodos-Irvine, Margaret 152
Choi, Sook Nyul 1937- 73
  Autobiography Feature 126
  See also CLR 53
Choi, Yangsook 178
Choldenko, Gennifer 1957- 135
Chorao, (Ann Mc)Kay (Sproat) 1936- 162
  Earlier sketches in SATA 8, 69
Choron, Sandra (Zena Samelson) 1950- ... 146
Chown, Marcus 1959- 137
Choyce, Lesley 1951- 165
  Earlier sketch in SATA 94
Chrisman, Arthur Bowie 1889-1953 124
  See also YABC 1
Christelow, Eileen 1943- 90
  Autobiography Feature 120
  Brief entry 35
  Earlier sketch in SATA 38
Christensen, Bonnie 1951- 157
  Earlier sketch in SATA 110
Christensen, Gardell Dano 1907-1991 1
Christensen, Laurie
  See Steding, Laurie
Christesen, Barbara 1940- 40

Christgau, Alice Erickson 1902-1977 13
Christian, Mary Blount 1933- 9
Christie, Agatha (Mary Clarissa) 1890-1976
  36
Christie, Gregory
  See Christie, R. Gregory
Christie, Philippa 129
  Earlier sketches in SATA 1, 67
  See also CLR 9
  See Pearce, Philippa
Christie, R. Gregory 1971- 127
Christopher, John
  See CLR 2
  See Youd, (Christopher) Samuel
Christopher, Louise
  See Hale, Arlene
Christopher, Matt(hew Frederick) 1917-1997
  80
  Obituary 99
  Earlier sketches in SATA 2, 47
  See also CLR 119
  See also SAAS 9
Christopher, Milbourne 1914(?)-1984 46
Christy, Howard Chandler 1873-1952 21
Chrustowski, Rick 176
Chrystie, Frances N(icholson) 1904-1986 ... 60
Chu, Daniel 1933- 11
Chukovsky, Kornei (Ivanovich) 1882-1969
  34
  Earlier sketch in SATA 5
Church, Caroline Jayne 179
Church, Richard 1893-1972 3
Churchill, E(lmer) Richard 1937- 11
Churchill, Elizabeth
  See Hough, Richard (Alexander)
Chute, B(eatrice) J(oy) 1913-1987 2
  Obituary 53
Chute, Marchette (Gaylord) 1909-1994 1
Chwast, Jacqueline 1932- 6
Chwast, Seymour 1931- 146
  Earlier sketches in SATA 18, 96
Ciardi, John (Anthony) 1916-1986 65
  Obituary 46
  Earlier sketch in SATA 1
  See also CLR 19
  See also SAAS 26
Ciccone, Madonna Louise Veronica
  See Madonna
Ciment, James D. 1958- 140
Cisneros, Sandra 1954-
  See CLR 123
Citra, Becky 1954- 137
Clair, Andree 19
Clampett, Robert 44
  See Clampett, Bob
Clapp, John 1968- 109
Clapp, Patricia 1912- 74
  Earlier sketch in SATA 4
  See also SAAS 4
Clare, Ellen
  See Sinclair, Olga
Clare, Helen
  See Clarke, Pauline
Claremont, Chris 1950- 87
Claremont, Christopher Simon
  See Claremont, Chris
Clark, Ann Nolan 1896-1995 82
  Obituary 87
  Earlier sketch in SATA 4
  See also CLR 16
  See also SAAS 16
Clark, Champ 1923-2002 47
Clark, Christopher (Anthony) Stuart
  See Stuart-Clark, Christopher (Anthony)
Clark, Clara Gillow 1951- 154
  Earlier sketch in SATA 84
Clark, David
  See Hardcastle, Michael
Clark, David Allen
  See Ernst, (Lyman) John

Clark, Emma Chichester 69
　See Chichester Clark, Emma
Clark, Frank J(ames) 1922- 18
Clark, Garel
　See Garelick, May
Clark, Halsey
　See Deming, Richard
Clark, Joan
　See Benson, Mildred (Augustine Wirt)
Clark, Joan 1934- 96
　Earlier sketch in SATA 59
Clark, Leonard 1905-1981 30
　Obituary 29
Clark, M. R.
　See Clark, Mavis Thorpe
Clark, Margaret (D.) 1943- 126
Clark, Margaret Goff 1913- 82
　Earlier sketch in SATA 8
Clark, Mary Higgins 1929- 46
Clark, Mavis Thorpe 1909-1999 74
　Earlier sketch in SATA 8
　See also CLR 30
　See also SAAS 5
Clark, Merle
　See Gessner, Lynne
Clark, Patricia Denise 1921- 117
　See Lorrimer, Claire
Clark, Patricia Finrow 1929- 11
Clark, Ronald William 1916-1987 2
　Obituary 52
Clark, Sherryl 1956- 149
Clark, Van D(eusen) 1909-1974 2
Clark, Virginia
　See Gray, Patricia (Clark)
Clark, Walter Van Tilburg 1909-1971 8
Clarke, Arthur C. 1917- 115
　Earlier sketches in SATA 13, 70
　See also CLR 119
Clarke, Arthur Charles
　See Clarke, Arthur C.
Clarke, Clorinda 1917- 7
Clarke, Gus 1948- 134
Clarke, J.
　See Clarke, Judith
Clarke, James Hall
　See Rowland-Entwistle, (Arthur) Theodore
　(Henry)
Clarke, Joan B. 1921- 42
　Brief entry 27
Clarke, John
　See Laklan, Carli
　and Sontup, Dan(iel)
Clarke, Judith 1943- 164
　Earlier sketches in SATA 75, 110
　See also CLR 61
Clarke, Julia 1950- 138
Clarke, Kenneth 1957- 107
Clarke, Lea
　See Rowland-Entwistle, (Arthur) Theodore
　(Henry)
Clarke, Margaret 1941-
　See CLR 99
Clarke, Mary Stetson 1911-1994 5
Clarke, Michael
　See Newlon, (Frank) Clarke
Clarke, Pauline 1921- 131
　See also CLR 28
　See Clare, Helen
　and Hunter Blair, Pauline
Clarke-Rich, Elizabeth L. 1934- 103
Clarkson, E(dith) Margaret 1915- 37
Clarkson, Ewan 1929- 9
Claudia, Susan
　See Goulart, Ron(ald Joseph)
　and Johnston, William
Claverie, Jean 1946- 38
Clay, Patrice 1947- 47
Claypool, Jane 103
　See Miner, Jane Claypool
Clayton, Elaine 1961- 159
　Earlier sketch in SATA 94

Clayton, Lawrence (Otto, Jr.) 1945- 75
Clayton, Sandra 1951- 110
Cleary, Beverly 1916- 121
　Earlier sketches in SATA 2, 43, 79
　See also CLR 72
　See also SAAS 20
Cleary, Beverly Atlee Bunn
　See Cleary, Beverly
Cleary, Brian P. 1959- 132
　Earlier sketch in SATA 93
Cleaver, Bill 22
　Obituary 27
　See also CLR 6
　See Cleaver, William J(oseph)
Cleaver, Carole 1934- 6
Cleaver, Elizabeth (Ann Mrazik) 1939-1985
　.. 23
　Obituary 43
　See also CLR 13
Cleaver, Hylton Reginald 1891-1961 49
Cleaver, Vera (Allen) 1919-1993 76
　Earlier sketch in SATA 22
　See also CLR 6
Cleishbotham, Jebediah
　See Scott, Sir Walter
Cleland, Mabel
　See Widdemer, Mabel Cleland
Clem, Margaret H(ollingsworth) 1923- 90
Clemens, Samuel Langhorne 1835-1910 ... 100
　See also YABC 2
　See Twain, Mark
Clemens, Virginia Phelps 1941- 35
Clement, Priscilla Ferguson 1942- 171
Clement, Rod 97
Clements, Andrew 1949- 158
　Earlier sketch in SATA 104
Clements, Bruce 1931- 178
　Earlier sketches in SATA 27, 94
Clemons, Elizabeth
　See Nowell, Elizabeth Cameron
Clerk, N. W.
　See Lewis, C.S.
Cleveland-Peck, Patricia 80
Cleven, Cathrine
　See Cleven, Kathryn Seward
Cleven, Kathryn Seward 2
Clevenger, William R. 1954- 84
Clevenger, William Russell
　See Clevenger, William R.
Clevin, Joergen 1920- 7
Clevin, Jorgen
　See Clevin, Joergen
Clewes, Dorothy (Mary) 1907-2003 86
　Obituary 138
　Earlier sketch in SATA 1
Clifford, David
　See Rosenberg, Eth(el) Clifford
Clifford, Eth 92
　See also SAAS 22
　See Rosenberg, Eth(el) Clifford
Clifford, Harold B(urton) 1893-1988 10
Clifford, Margaret Cort 1929- 1
Clifford, Martin
　See Hamilton, Charles (Harold St. John)
Clifford, Mary Louise Beneway 1926- 23
Clifford, Peggy
　See Clifford, Margaret Cort
Clifford, Rachel Mark
　See Lewis, Brenda Ralph
Clifton, Lucille 1936- 128
　Earlier sketches in SATA 20, 69
　See also CLR 5
Clifton, Thelma Lucille
　See Clifton, Lucille
Climo, Shirley 1928- 166
　Autobiography Feature 110
　Brief entry 35
　Earlier sketches in SATA 39, 77
　See also CLR 69
Clinton, Cathryn 1957- 136

Clinton, Dirk
　See Silverberg, Robert
Clinton, Jon
　See Prince, J(ack) H(arvey)
Clish, (Lee) Marian 1946- 43
Clive, Clifford
　See Hamilton, Charles (Harold St. John)
Clokey, Art 1921- 59
Cloudsley-Thompson, J(ohn) L(eonard) 1921-
　.. 19
Clouse, Nancy L. 1938- 78
Clover, Peter 1952- 152
Clutha, Janet Paterson Frame 1924-2004 .. 119
　See Frame, Janet
Clymer, Eleanor 1906-2001 85
　Obituary 126
　Earlier sketch in SATA 9
　See also SAAS 17
Clyne, Patricia (Edwards) 31
Coalson, Glo 1946- 94
　Earlier sketch in SATA 26
Coates, Anna 1958- 73
Coates, Belle 1896-1986 2
Coates, Ruth Allison 1915- 11
Coats, Alice M(argaret) 1905-1976 11
Coatsworth, Elizabeth (Jane) 1893-1986 ... 100
　Obituary 49
　Earlier sketches in SATA 2, 56
　See also CLR 2
Cobalt, Martin
　See Mayne, William (James Carter)
Cobb, Mary 1931- 88
Cobb, Vicki 1938- 136
　Autobiography Feature 136
　Earlier sketches in SATA 8, 69, 131
　See also CLR 2
　See also SAAS 6
Cobbett, Richard
　See Pluckrose, Henry (Arthur)
Cober, Alan E(dwin) 1935-1998 7
　Obituary 101
Cobham, Sir Alan
　See Hamilton, Charles (Harold St. John)
Coburn, Jake 1978- 155
Cocagnac, Augustin Maurice(-Jean) 1924- ... 7
Cocca-Leffler, Maryann 1958- 136
　Earlier sketch in SATA 80
Cochran, Bobbye A. 1949- 11
Cockett, Mary 3
Coddell, Esme Raji
　See Codell, Esme Raji
Codell, Esme Raji 1968- 160
Cody, C. S.
　See Waller, Leslie
Cody, Jess
　See Cunningham, Chet
Coe, Anne (E.) 1949- 95
Coe, Douglas
　See Epstein, Beryl (M. Williams)
　and Epstein, Samuel
Coen, Rena Neumann 1925- 20
Coerr, Eleanor (Beatrice) 1922- 67
　Earlier sketch in SATA 1
Cofer, Judith Ortiz 1952- 164
　Earlier sketch in SATA 110
　See Ortiz Cofer, Judith
Coffey, Brian
　See Koontz, Dean R.
Coffin, Geoffrey
　See Mason, F(rancis) van Wyck
Coffin, M. T.
　See Stanley, George Edward
Coffman, Ramon Peyton 1896-1989 4
Cogan, Karen 1954- 125
Coggins, Jack (Banham) 1911-2006 2
Cohen, Barbara 1932-1992 77
　Obituary 74
　Earlier sketch in SATA 10
　See also SAAS 7

Cohen, Daniel (E.) 1936- 70
    Earlier sketch in SATA 8
    See also CLR 43
    See also SAAS 4
Cohen, Deborah Bodin 1968- 180
Cohen, Jan Barger
    See Barger, Jan
Cohen, Jene Barr
    See Barr, Jene
Cohen, Joan Lebold 1932- 4
Cohen, Judith Love 1933- 78
Cohen, Miriam 1926-1955 155
    Earlier sketches in SATA 29, 106
    See also SAAS 11
Cohen, Nora 75
Cohen, Paul S. 1945- 58
Cohen, Peter Zachary 1931- 150
    Earlier sketch in SATA 4
Cohen, Robert Carl 1930- 8
Cohen, Sholom 1951- 94
Cohn, Angelo 1914-1997 19
Cohn, Rachel 1968- 161
Coit, Margaret Louise 1922-2003 2
    Obituary 142
Colato Lainez, Rene 1970- 176
Colbert, Anthony 1934- 15
Colbert, Nancy A. 1936- 139
Colby, C(arroll) B(urleigh) 1904-1977 35
    Earlier sketch in SATA 3
Colby, Jean Poindexter 1909-1993 23
Cole, Annette
    See Steiner, Barbara A(nnette)
Cole, Babette 1949- 155
    Earlier sketches in SATA 61, 96
Cole, Betsy 1940- 83
Cole, Brock 1938- 136
    Earlier sketch in SATA 72
    See also CLR 18
Cole, Davis
    See Elting, Mary
Cole, Hannah 1954- 74
Cole, Henry 1955- 181
Cole, Jack -1974
    See Stewart, John (William)
Cole, Jackson
    See Curry, Thomas Albert
    and Germano, Peter B.
    and Heckelmann, Charles N(ewman)
    and Newton, D(wight) B(ennett)
    and Schisgall, Oscar
Cole, Jennifer
    See Zach, Cheryl (Byrd)
Cole, Joanna 1944- 168
    Brief entry 37
    Earlier sketches in SATA 49, 81, 120
    See also CLR 40
Cole, Lois Dwight 1903-1979 10
    Obituary 26
Cole, Michael 1947- 59
Cole, Sheila R. 1939- 171
    Earlier sketches in SATA 24, 95
Cole, Sheila Rotenberg
    See Cole, Sheila R.
Cole, Stephen 1971- 161
Cole, William (Rossa) 1919-2000 71
    Earlier sketch in SATA 9
    See also SAAS 9
Coleman, Andrew
    See Pine, Nicholas
Coleman, Clare
    See Bell, Clare (Louise)
    and Easton, M(alcolm) Coleman
Coleman, Loren 1947- 164
Coleman, Loren Elwood, Jr.
    See Coleman, Loren
Coleman, Mary Ann 1928- 83
Coleman, Michael (Lee) 1946- 133
    Autobiography Feature 133
    Earlier sketch in SATA 108
Coleman, William L(eRoy) 1938- 49
    Brief entry 34

Coles, Robert (Martin) 1929- 23
Colfer, Eoin 1965- 148
    See also CLR 112
Colin, Ann
    See Ure, Jean
Collard, Sneed B. III 1959- 139
    Earlier sketch in SATA 84
Colledge, Anne 1939- 142
Collicott, Sharleen 1937- 143
    Earlier sketch in SATA 98
Collier, Bryan 174
    Earlier sketch in SATA 126
Collier, Christopher 1930- 70
    Earlier sketch in SATA 16
Collier, Ethel 1903-1999 22
Collier, James Lincoln 1928- 166
    Earlier sketches in SATA 8, 70
    See also CLR 3
    See also SAAS 21
Collier, Jane
    See Collier, Zena
Collier, Steven 1942- 61
Collier, Zena 1926- 23
    See Collier, Jane
Collings, Gillian 1939- 102
Collington, Peter 1948- 99
    Earlier sketch in SATA 59
Collins, Ace 1953- 82
Collins, Andrew J.
    See Collins, Ace
Collins, David R(aymond) 1940-2001 121
    Earlier sketch in SATA 7
Collins, Heather 1946- 81
Collins, Hunt
    See Hunter, Evan
Collins, Michael
    See Lynds, Dennis
Collins, Michael 1930- 58
Collins, Pat(ricia) Lowery 1932- 151
    Earlier sketch in SATA 31
Collins, Paul 1954- 126
Collins, Suzanne 180
Collinson, A. S.
    See Collinson, Alan S.
Collinson, Alan S. 1934- 80
Collinson, Roger (Alfred) 1936- 133
Collodi, Carlo
    See CLR 120
    See Lorenzini, Carlo
Colloms, Brenda 1919- 40
Colman, Hila 53
    Earlier sketch in SATA 1
    See also SAAS 14
Colman, Penny (Morgan) 1944- 160
    Autobiography Feature 160
    Earlier sketches in SATA 77, 114
Colman, Warren (David) 1944- 67
Colombo, John Robert 1936- 50
Colon, Raul 156
Colonius, Lillian 1911-1992 3
Colorado, Antonio J.
    See Colorado (Capella), Antonio J(ulio)
Colorado (Capella), Antonio J(ulio) 1903-1994
    23
    Obituary 79
Colquhoun, Glenn 1964- 165
Colston, Fifi E. 1960- 150
Colt, Martin
    See Epstein, Beryl (M. Williams)
    and Epstein, Samuel
Colum, Padraic 1881-1972 15
    See also CLR 36
Columbus, Chris 1959- 97
Columbus, Christopher
    See Columbus, Chris
Columella
    See Moore, Clement Clarke
Colver, Anne 1908- 7
Colvin, James
    See Moorcock, Michael
Colwell, Eileen (Hilda) 1904-2002 2

Coman, Carolyn 127
Combs, Lisa M.
    See McCourt, Lisa
Combs, Robert
    See Murray, John
Comfort, Jane Levington
    See Sturtzel, Jane Levington
Comfort, Mildred Houghton 1886-1976 3
Comins, Ethel M(ae) 11
Comins, Jeremy 1933- 28
Commager, Henry Steele 1902-1998 23
    Obituary 102
Compere, Mickie
    See Davidson, Margaret
Compestine, Ying Chang 1963- 140
Compton, Patricia A. 1936- 75
Comte, The Great
    See Hawkesworth, Eric
Comus
    See Ballantyne, R(obert) M(ichael)
Comyns, Nance
    See Comyns-Toohey, Nantz
Comyns-Toohey, Nantz 1956- 86
Conan Doyle, Arthur
    See Doyle, Sir Arthur Conan
Condit, Martha Olson 1913- 28
Condon, Bill 1949- 142
Condon, Judith 83
Condy, Roy 1942- 96
Cone, Ferne Geller 1921- 39
Cone, Molly (Lamken) 1918- 151
    Autobiography Feature 151
    Earlier sketches in SATA 1, 28, 115
    See also SAAS 11
Cone, Patrick 1954- 89
Coney, Michael G. 1932-2005 61
    Obituary 170
Coney, Michael Greatrex
    See Coney, Michael G.
Coney, Mike
    See Coney, Michael G.
Conford, Ellen 1942- 162
    Earlier sketches in SATA 6, 68, 110
    See also CLR 71
Conger, Lesley
    See Suttles, Shirley (Smith)
Conklin, Gladys Plemon 1903- 2
Conklin, Paul S. 1929(?)-2003 43
    Brief entry 33
    Obituary 147
Conkling, Hilda 1910-1986 23
Conlan, Kathleen Elizabeth 1950- 145
Conlan, Kathy
    See Conlan, Kathleen Elizabeth
Conley-Weaver, Robyn 1963- 125
Conlon-McKenna, Marita 1956- 71
Conly, Jane Leslie 1948- 164
    Earlier sketches in SATA 80, 112
Conly, Robert Leslie 1918(?)-1973 23
    See O'Brien, Robert C.
Connolly, Jerome P(atrick) 1931- 8
Connolly, Pat 1943- 74
Connolly, Peter 1935- 105
    Earlier sketch in SATA 47
Conover, Chris 1950- 31
Conquest, Owen
    See Hamilton, Charles (Harold St. John)
Conrad, Joseph 1857-1924 27
Conrad, Pam 1947-1996 133
    Brief entry 49
    Obituary 90
    Earlier sketches in SATA 52, 80
    See also CLR 18
    See also SAAS 19
Conroy, Jack 19
    See Conroy, John Wesley
Conroy, Robert
    See Goldston, Robert (Conroy)
Constable, Kate 1966- 172
Constant, Alberta Wilson 1908-1981 22
    Obituary 28

Conway, Diana C(ohen) 1943- 91
Conway, Gordon
  See Hamilton, Charles (Harold St. John)
Cook, Bernadine 1924- 11
Cook, Fred J(ames) 1911-2003 2
  Obituary 145
Cook, Glen 1944- 171
  Earlier sketch in SATA 108
Cook, Glen Charles
  See Cook, Glen
Cook, Hugh 1956- 85
Cook, Hugh, Walter Gilbert
  See Cook, Hugh
Cook, Jean Thor 1930- 94
Cook, Joel 1934- 79
Cook, Joseph Jay 1924- 8
Cook, Lisa Broadie 157
Cook, Lyn
  See Waddell, Evelyn Margaret
Cook, Roy
  See Silverberg, Robert
Cook, Trish 175
Cooke, Ann
  See Cole, Joanna
Cooke, Arthur
  See Lowndes, Robert A(ugustine) W(ard)
Cooke, Barbara
  See Alexander, Anna B(arbara Cooke)
Cooke, David Coxe 1917- 2
Cooke, Donald Ewin 1916-1985 2
  Obituary 45
Cooke, Frank E. 1920- 87
Cooke, Jean (Isobel Esther) 1929- 74
Cooke, John Estes
  See Baum, L(yman) Frank
Cooke, Trish 1962- 129
Cookson, Catherine (McMullen) 1906-1998 . 9
  Obituary 116
Cooley, Regina Francoise 1940- 177
Coolidge, Olivia E(nsor) 1908- 26
  Earlier sketch in SATA 1
Cooling, Wendy 169
  Earlier sketch in SATA 111
Coombs, Charles I(ra) 1914-1994 43
  Earlier sketch in SATA 3
  See also SAAS 15
Coombs, Chick
  See Coombs, Charles I(ra)
Coombs, Patricia 1926- 51
  Earlier sketch in SATA 3
  See also SAAS 22
Cooney, Barbara 1917-2000 96
  Obituary 123
  Earlier sketches in SATA 6, 59
  See also CLR 23
Cooney, Caroline B. 1947- 179
  Brief entry 41
  Earlier sketches in SATA 48, 80, 113, 130
Cooney, Doug 181
Cooney, Nancy Evans 1932- 42
Coontz, Otto 1946- 33
Cooper, Ann (Catharine) 1939- 104
Cooper, Dutch
  See Kuyper, Sjoerd
Cooper, Elisha 1971- 157
  Earlier sketch in SATA 99
Cooper, Elizabeth Keyser -1992 47
Cooper, Floyd 144
  Earlier sketch in SATA 96
  See also CLR 60
Cooper, Gordon 1932- 23
Cooper, Helen 1963- 169
  Earlier sketch in SATA 102
Cooper, Henry S(potswood) F(enimore), Jr.
  1933- 65
Cooper, Ilene 1948- 145
  Earlier sketches in SATA 66, 97
Cooper, James Fenimore 1789-1851 _Volume_ 19
  See also CLR 105
Cooper, John R. 1
Cooper, Kay 1941- 11

Cooper, Lee Pelham 1926- 5
Cooper, Lester (Irving) 1919-1985 32
  Obituary 43
Cooper, Lettice (Ulpha) 1897-1994 35
  Obituary 82
Cooper, Louise 1952- 152
Cooper, M.E.
  See Lerangis, Peter
Cooper, M.E.
  See Davis, Maggie S.
Cooper, Melrose
  See Kroll, Virginia L.
Cooper, Michael L. 1950- 181
  Earlier sketches in SATA 79, 117
Cooper, Patrick 1949- 134
Cooper, Susan 1935- 151
  Earlier sketches in SATA 4, 64, 104
  See also CLR 67
  See also SAAS 6
Cooper, Susan Mary
  See Cooper, Susan
Cope, Jane U(rsula) 1949- 108
Copeland, Helen 1920- 4
Copeland, Mark 1956- 180
Copeland, Paul W. 23
Coplans, Peta 1951- 84
Copley (Diana) Heather Pickering 1918- 45
Coppard, A(lfred) E(dgar) 1878-1957
  See YABC 1
Copper, Melinda 1952- 172
Copper, Melinda McConnaughey
  See Copper, Melinda
Coralie
  See Anderson, Catherine Corley
Corbett, Grahame 43
  Brief entry 36
Corbett, Scott 1913- 42
  Earlier sketch in SATA 2
  See also CLR 1
  See also SAAS 2
Corbett, Sue 174
Corbett, W(illiam) J(esse) 1938- 102
  Brief entry 44
  Earlier sketch in SATA 50
  See also CLR 19
Corbin, Sabra Lee
  See Malvern, Gladys
Corbin, William
  See McGraw, William Corbin
Corbman, Marjorie 1987- 179
Corby, Dan
  See Catherall, Arthur
Corcoran, Barbara (Asenath) 1911- 77
  Autobiography Feature 125
  Earlier sketch in SATA 3
  See also CLR 50
  See also SAAS 20
Corcos, Lucille 1908-1973 10
Cordell, Alexander
  See Graber, Alexander
Cordell, Alexander
  See Graber, (George) Alexander
Corder, Zizou
  See Young, Louisa
Corella, Joseph
  See Odgers, Sally Farrell
Coren, Alan 1938- 32
Corey, Dorothy 23
Corey, Shana 1974- 133
Corfe, Thomas Howell 1928- 27
Corfe, Tom
  See Corfe, Thomas Howell
Corfield, Robin Bell 1952- 74
Corlett, William 1938-2005 46
  Brief entry 39
Cormack, M(argaret) Grant 1913- 11
Cormack, Maribelle B. 1902-1984 39
Cormier, Robert 1925-2000 83
  Obituary 122
  Earlier sketches in SATA 10, 45
  See also CLR 55

Cormier, Robert Edmund
  See Cormier, Robert
Cornelius, Carol 1942- 40
Cornelius, Kay 1933- 157
Cornell, J.
  See Cornell, Jeffrey
Cornell, James (Clayton, Jr.) 1938- 27
Cornell, Jean Gay 1920- 23
Cornell, Jeffrey 1945- 11
Cornish, Sam(uel James) 1935- 23
Cornwall, Nellie
  See Sloggett, Nellie
Correy, Lee
  See Stine, G(eorge) Harry
Corrick, James A. 1945- 76
Corrigan, (Helen) Adeline 1909- 23
Corrigan, Barbara 1922- 8
Corrigan, Eireann 1977- 163
Corrin, Sara 1918- 86
  Brief entry 48
Corrin, Stephen 86
  Brief entry 48
Cort, M. C.
  See Clifford, Margaret Cort
Cort, Margaret
  See Clifford, Margaret Cort
Corwin, Judith H(offman) 1946- 10
Cory, Rowena
  See Lindquist, Rowena Cory
Cosby, Bill
  See Cosby, William Henry, Jr.
Cosby, William Henry, Jr. 1937- 110
  Earlier sketch in SATA 66
  See Cosby, Bill
Cosentino, Ralph 169
Cosgrove, Margaret (Leota) 1926- 47
Cosgrove, Stephen E(dward) 1945- 53
  Brief entry 40
Coskey, Evelyn 1932- 7
Cosner, Shaaron 1940- 43
Cossi, Olga 1921- 102
  Earlier sketch in SATA 67
Costabel, Eva Deutsch 1924- 45
Costabel-Deutsch, Eva
  See Costabel, Eva Deutsch
Costello, David 174
Costello, David F(rancis) 1904-1990 23
Cott, Jonathan 1942- 23
Cottam, Clarence 1899-1974 25
Cottle, Joan 1960- 135
Cottler, Joseph 1899-1996 22
Cottonwood, Joe 1947- 92
Cottrell, Leonard 1913-1974 24
Cottringer, Anne 1952- 150
  Earlier sketch in SATA 97
Coulman, Valerie 1969- 161
Couloumbis, Audrey 173
Counsel, June 1926- 70
Countryman, The
  See Whitlock, Ralph
Courlander, Harold 1908-1996 6
  Obituary 88
Coursen, Valerie 1965(?)- 102
Courtney, Dayle
  See Goldsmith, Howard
Cousins, Linda 1946- 90
Cousins, Lucy 1964- 172
Cousins, Margaret 1905-1996 2
  Obituary 92
Cousteau, Jacques-Yves 1910-1997 98
  Earlier sketch in SATA 38
Couture, Christin 1951- 73
Coville, Bruce 1950- 155
  Autobiography Feature 155
  Earlier sketches in SATA 32, 77, 118
Covington, Dennis 109
Covington, Linda
  See Windsor, Linda
Cowan, Catherine 121
Coward, Fiona 1963- 178
Cowell, Cressida 1966- 140

Cowen, Eve
  See Werner, Herma
Cowen, Ida 1898-1993 .... *64*
Cowie, Leonard W(allace) 1919- *4*
Cowles, Kathleen
  See Krull, Kathleen
Cowley, Cassia Joy
  See Cowley, Joy
Cowley, Joy 1936- *164*
Cowley, (Cassia) Joy 1936- *90*
  Autobiography Feature *118*
  Earlier sketch in SATA *4*
  See also CLR *55*
  See also SAAS *26*
Cowley, Marjorie 1925- *111*
Cox, (Christopher) Barry 1931- *62*
Cox, Clinton 1934- *108*
  Earlier sketch in SATA *74*
Cox, David (Dundas) 1933- *56*
Cox, Donald William 1921- *23*
Cox, Jack
  See Cox, John Roberts
Cox, John Roberts 1915-1981 .... *9*
Cox, Judy 1954- *160*
  Earlier sketch in SATA *117*
Cox, Palmer 1840-1924 .... *24*
  See also CLR *24*
Cox, Vic 1942- *88*
Cox, Vicki 1945- *158*
Cox, Victoria
  See Garretson, Victoria Diane
Cox, Wally *25*
  See Cox, Wallace (Maynard)
Cox, William R(obert) 1901-1988 .... *46*
  Brief entry *31*
  Obituary *57*
  See Ward, Jonas
Coxe, Molly 1959- *101*
  Earlier sketch in SATA *69*
Coxon, Michele 1950- *158*
  Earlier sketch in SATA *76*
Coy, Harold 1902-1986 .... *3*
Coy, John 1958- *171*
  Earlier sketch in SATA *120*
Craats, Rennay 1973- *131*
Crabtree, Judith 1928- *98*
  Earlier sketch in SATA *63*
Cracker, Edward E.B.
  See Odgers, Sally Farrell
Craft, K. Y.
  See Craft, Kinuko Y(amabe)
Craft, Kinuko
  See Craft, Kinuko Y(amabe)
Craft, Kinuko Y(amabe) 1940- *127*
  Earlier sketch in SATA *65*
Craft, Ruth 1935- *87*
  Brief entry *31*
Craig, A. A.
  See Anderson, Poul
Craig, Alisa
  See MacLeod, Charlotte (Matilda)
Craig, Helen 1934- *94*
  Earlier sketches in SATA *46, 49*
Craig, John Eland
  See Chipperfield, Joseph Eugene
Craig, John Ernest 1921- *23*
Craig, Kit
  See Reed, Kit
Craig, M. F.
  See Craig, Mary (Francis) Shura
Craig, M. Jean *17*
Craig, M. S.
  See Craig, Mary (Francis) Shura
Craig, Margaret (Maze) 1911-1964 .... *9*
Craig, Mary
  See Craig, Mary (Francis) Shura
Craig, Mary Shura
  See Craig, Mary (Francis) Shura

Craig, Mary (Francis) Shura 1923-1991 ..... *86*
  Obituary *65*
  Earlier sketch in SATA *6*
  See also SAAS *7*
Craig, Ruth 1922- *95*
Craik, Mrs.
  See Craik, Dinah Maria (Mulock)
Craik, Dinah Maria (Mulock) 1826-1887 ... *34*
  See Craik, Mrs.
  and Mulock, Dinah Maria
Crandall, Court 1965- *175*
Crandell, Rachel 1943- *152*
Crane, Barbara (Joyce) 1934- *31*
Crane, Caroline 1930- *11*
Crane, Jordan 1973- *174*
Crane, M. A.
  See Wartski, Maureen (Ann Crane)
Crane, Stephen (Townley) 1871-1900
  See YABC *2*
Crane, Walter 1845-1915 .... *100*
  Earlier sketch in SATA *18*
  See also CLR *56*
Crane, William D(wight) 1892-1976 .... *1*
Cranfield, Ingrid 1945- *74*
Cranshaw, Stanley
  See Fisher, Dorothy (Frances) Canfield
Crary, Elizabeth (Ann) 1942- *99*
  Brief entry *43*
Crary, Margaret (Coleman) 1906-1986 .... *9*
Cravath, Lynne W(oodcock) 1951- *148*
  Earlier sketch in SATA *98*
Craven, Thomas 1889-1969 .... *22*
Crawford, Charles P. 1945- *28*
Crawford, Deborah 1922- *6*
Crawford, John E(dmund) 1904-1971 .... *3*
Crawford, K(aren) Michael 1959- *155*
Crawford, Mel 1925- *44*
  Brief entry *33*
Crawford, Phyllis 1899- *3*
Crawley, Dave *177*
Cray, Roberta
  See Emerson, Ru
Crayder, Dorothy *7*
Crayder, Teresa
  See Colman, Hila
Crayon, Geoffrey
  See Irving, Washington
Craz, Albert G. 1926- *24*
Crebbin, June 1938- *169*
  Earlier sketch in SATA *80*
Crecy, Jeanne
  See Williams, Jeanne
Credle, Ellis 1902-1998 .... *1*
Creech, Sharon 1945- *172*
  Earlier sketches in SATA *94, 139*
  See also CLR *89*
Creeden, Sharon 1938- *91*
Creighton, Jill 1949- *96*
Crenson, Victoria 1952- *159*
  Earlier sketch in SATA *88*
Cresp, Gael 1954- *119*
Crespo, George 1962- *82*
Cresswell, Helen 1934-2005 .... *79*
  Obituary *168*
  Earlier sketches in SATA *1, 48*
  See also CLR *18*
  See also SAAS *20*
Cressy, Michael 1955- *124*
Cressy, Mike
  See Cressy, Michael
Cretan, Gladys (Yessayan) 1921- *2*
Cretzmeyer, Stacy (Megan) 1959- *124*
Crew, Gary 1947- *163*
  Earlier sketches in SATA *75, 110*
  See also CLR *42*
Crew, Helen (Cecilia) Coale 1866-1941
  See YABC *2*
Crew, Linda (Jean) 1951- *137*
  Earlier sketch in SATA *71*

Crews, Donald 1938- *76*
  Brief entry *30*
  Earlier sketch in SATA *32*
  See also CLR *7*
Crews, Nina 1963- *158*
  Earlier sketch in SATA *97*
Crichton, John Michael
  See Crichton, Michael
Crichton, Michael 1942- *88*
  Earlier sketch in SATA *9*
Crider, Allen Billy
  See Crider, Bill
Crider, Bill 1941- *99*
Crilley, Mark 1966- *148*
  Autobiography Feature *148*
  Earlier sketch in SATA *120*
Crimi, Carolyn 1959- *176*
Cripps, Enid Margaret
  See Appiah, Peggy
Crisman, Ruth 1914- *73*
Crisp, Marta Marie 1947- *128*
Crisp, Marty
  See Crisp, Marta Marie
Crispin, A(nn) C(arol) 1950- *86*
Crist, James J. *168*
Cristall, Barbara *79*
Crist-Evans, Craig 1954- *153*
Crofford, Emily (Ardell) 1927- *61*
Crofut, William E. III 1934- *23*
Croll, Carolyn 1945- *102*
  Brief entry *52*
  Earlier sketch in SATA *56*
Croman, Dorothy Young
  See Rosenberg, Dorothy
Cromie, Alice Hamilton 1914-2000 .... *24*
Cromie, William J(oseph) 1930- *4*
Crompton, Anne Eliot 1930- *73*
  Earlier sketch in SATA *23*
Crompton, Richmal
  See Lamburn, Richmal Crompton
Cronbach, Abraham 1882-1965 .... *11*
Crone, Ruth 1919-2003 .... *4*
Cronin, A(rchibald) J(oseph) 1896-1981 ..... *47*
  Obituary *25*
Cronin, Doreen (A.) *125*
  See also CLR *105*
Cronin, Doreen 1966(?)- *178*
Cronin, Doreen A.
  See Cronin, Doreen
Crook, Beverly Courtney *38*
  Brief entry *35*
Crook, Connie Brummel 1930- *168*
  Earlier sketch in SATA *98*
Crook, Constance
  See Crook, Connie Brummel
Crosby, Alexander L. 1906-1980 .... *2*
  Obituary *23*
Crosby, Harry C., Jr. *102*
Crosby, Margaret
  See CLR *77*
  See Rathmann, Peggy
Crosher, G. R. *14*
Cross, Gilbert B. 1939- *60*
  Brief entry *51*
Cross, Gillian 1945- *178*
  Autobiography Feature *178*
  Earlier sketches in SATA *38, 71, 110, 165*
  See also CLR *28*
Cross, Gillian Clare
  See Cross, Gillian
Cross, Helen Reeder
  See Broadhead, Helen Cross
Cross, Peter 1951- *95*
Cross, Tom 1954- *146*
Cross, Verda 1914- *75*
Cross, Wilbur Lucius III 1918- *2*
Crossland, Caroline 1964- *83*
Crossley-Holland, Kevin 1941- *165*
  Earlier sketches in SATA *5, 74, 120*
  See also CLR *84*
  See also SAAS *20*

Crossley-Holland, Kevin John William
  See Crossley-Holland, Kevin
Crouch, Marcus 1913-1996 4
Crout, George C(lement) 1917- 11
Crow, Donna Fletcher 1941- 40
Crowe, Andrew 111
Crowe, John
  See Lynds, Dennis
Crowe, (Bettina) Peter Lum 1911- 6
Crowell, Grace Noll 1877-1969 34
Crowell, Pers 1910-1990 2
Crowell, Robert Leland 1909-2001 63
Crowfield, Christopher
  See Stowe, Harriet (Elizabeth) Beecher
Crowley, Arthur McBlair 1945- 38
Crowley, John 1942- 140
  Earlier sketch in SATA 65
Crownfield, Gertrude 1867-1945
  See YABC 1
Crowther, James Gerald 1899-1983 14
Crowther, Robert 1948- 163
Cruikshank, George 1792-1878 22
  See also CLR 63
Cruise, Robin 1951- 179
Crum, Shutta 134
Crummel, Susan Stevens 1949- 176
  Earlier sketch in SATA 130
Crump, Fred H., Jr. 1931- 76
  Earlier sketch in SATA 11
Crump, J(ames) Irving 1887-1979 57
  Obituary 21
Crump, William D(rake) 1949- 138
Crunden, Reginald
  See Cleaver, Hylton Reginald
Crunk, T.
  See Crunk, Tony
Crunk, Tony 1956- 130
Crutcher, Chris 1946- 153
  Earlier sketches in SATA 52, 99
  See also CLR 28
Crutcher, Christopher C.
  See Crutcher, Chris
Cruz, Ray(mond) 1933- 6
Cruz Martinez, Alejandro (?)-1987 74
Crystal, Billy 1947- 154
Cuetara, Mittie 1957- 158
  Earlier sketch in SATA 106
Cuffari, Richard 1925-1978 66
  Obituary 25
  Earlier sketch in SATA 6
Cullen, Countee 1903-1946 18
Culliford, Pierre 1928-1992 40
  Obituary 74
Cullinan, Bernice E(llinger) 1926- 135
Culp, Louanna McNary 1901-1965 2
Culper, Felix
  See McCaughrean, Geraldine
Cumbaa, Stephen 1947- 72
Cumming, Peter 1951- 168
Cumming, Primrose Amy 1915- 24
Cumming, Robert 1945- 65
Cummings, Betty Sue 1918- 15
  See also SAAS 9
Cummings, Parke 1902-1987 2
  Obituary 53
Cummings, Pat (Marie) 1950- 107
  Earlier sketches in SATA 42, 71
  See also CLR 48
  See also SAAS 13
Cummings, Phil 1957- 123
  Earlier sketch in SATA 74
Cummings, Priscilla 1951- 170
  Earlier sketch in SATA 129
Cummings, Richard
  See Gardner, Richard (M.)
Cummins, Maria Susanna 1827-1866
  See YABC 1
Cuneo, Mary Louise -2001 85
Cunliffe, John Arthur 1933- 86
  Earlier sketch in SATA 11

Cunliffe, Marcus (Falkner) 1922-1990 37
  Obituary 66
Cunnane, Kelly 175
Cunningham, Bob
  See May, Julian
Cunningham, Captain Frank
  See Glick, Carl (Cannon)
Cunningham, Cathy
  See Cunningham, Chet
Cunningham, Chet 1928- 23
Cunningham, Dale S(peers) 1932- 11
Cunningham, Dru 91
Cunningham, E. V.
  See Fast, Howard
Cunningham, Julia (Woolfolk) 1916- 132
  Earlier sketches in SATA 1, 26
  See also SAAS 2
Cunningham, Lawrence J. 1943- 125
Cunningham, Virginia
  See Holmgren, Virginia C(unningham)
Curiae, Amicus
  See Fuller, Edmund (Maybank)
Curie, Eve 1904- 1
Curlee, Lynn 1947- 141
  Earlier sketch in SATA 98
Curley, Daniel 1918-1988 23
  Obituary 61
Curley, Marianne 1959- 175
  Earlier sketch in SATA 131
Currie, Robin 1948- 120
Currie, Stephen 1960- 132
  Earlier sketch in SATA 82
Curry, Ann (Gabrielle) 1934- 72
Curry, Jane L(ouise) 1932- 138
  Autobiography Feature 138
  Earlier sketches in SATA 1, 52, 90
  See also CLR 31
  See also SAAS 6
Curry, Peggy Simson 1911-1987 8
  Obituary 50
Curtis, Bruce (Richard) 1944- 30
Curtis, Chara M(ahar) 1950- 78
Curtis, Christopher Paul 1954(?)- 140
  Earlier sketch in SATA 93
  See also CLR 68
Curtis, Gavin 1965- 107
Curtis, Jamie Lee 1958- 144
  Earlier sketch in SATA 95
  See also CLR 88
Curtis, Marci 160
Curtis, Patricia 1921- 101
  Earlier sketch in SATA 23
Curtis, Peter
  See Lofts, Norah (Robinson)
Curtis, Philip (Delacourt) 1920- 62
Curtis, Richard (Alan) 1937- 29
Curtis, Richard Hale
  See Deming, Richard
  and Levinson, Leonard
  and Rothweiler, Paul Roger
Curtis, Wade
  See Pournelle, Jerry (Eugene)
Curtiss, A(rlene) B. 1934- 90
Cusack, Margaret 1945- 58
Cushman, Doug 1953- 157
  Earlier sketches in SATA 65, 101
Cushman, Jerome 2
Cushman, Karen 1941- 147
  Earlier sketch in SATA 89
  See also CLR 55
Cusick, Richie Tankersley 1952- 140
  Earlier sketch in SATA 67
Cutchen, Billye Walker 1930- 15
Cutchins, Judy 1947- 59
Cutler, Daniel S(olomon) 1951- 78
Cutler, Ebbitt 1923- 9
Cutler, Ivor 1923-2006 24
  Obituary 174
Cutler, Jane 1936- 162
  Earlier sketches in SATA 75, 118

Cutler, May Ebbitt
  See Cutler, Ebbitt
Cutler, Samuel
  See Folsom, Franklin (Brewster)
Cutlip, Kimbra L(eigh-Ann) 1964- 128
Cutrate, Joe
  See Spiegelman, Art
Cutt, W(illiam) Towrie 1898-1981 16
  Obituary 85
Cuyler, Margery S(tuyvesant) 1948- 156
  Earlier sketches in SATA 39, 99
Cuyler, Stephen
  See Bates, Barbara S(nedeker)
Cyrus, Kurt 1954- 179
  Earlier sketch in SATA 132
Czernecki, Stefan 1946- 178

D

Dabba Smith, Frank 174
Dabcovich, Lydia 99
  Brief entry 47
  Earlier sketch in SATA 58
Dace, Dolores B(oelens) 1929- 89
Dadey, Debbie 1959- 136
  Earlier sketch in SATA 73
Dahl, Borghild (Margarethe) 1890-1984 7
  Obituary 37
Dahl, Roald 1916-1990 73
  Obituary 65
  Earlier sketches in SATA 1, 26
  See also CLR 111
Dahlberg, Maurine F. 1951- 171
Dahlstedt, Marden (Stewart) 1921-1983 8
  Obituary 110
Dain, Martin J. 1924-2000 35
Dakos, Kalli 1950- 115
  Earlier sketch in SATA 80
Dale, Anna 1971- 170
Dale, Gary
  See Reece, Colleen L.
Dale, George E.
  See Asimov, Isaac
Dale, Jack
  See Holliday, Joseph
Dale, Kim 1957- 123
Dale, Margaret J(essy) Miller 1911- 39
Dale, Mitzi
  See Hemstock, Gillian
Dale, Norman
  See Denny, Norman (George)
Dale, Penny 1954- 151
  Earlier sketch in SATA 70
Daley, Michael J. 170
Dalgliesh, Alice 1893-1979 17
  Obituary 21
  See also CLR 62
Dalkey, Kara 1953- 132
Dalkey, Kara Mia
  See Dalkey, Kara
Dallas, Ruth
  See Mumford, Ruth
Dalmas, John
  See Jones, John R(obert)
Dalton, Annie 1948- 140
  Earlier sketch in SATA 40
Dalton, Kit
  See Cunningham, Chet
Dalton, Pamela
  See Johnson, Pamela
Dalton, Sean
  See Chester, Deborah
Dalton, Sheila 1949- 108
Daly, Jim
  See Stratemeyer, Edward L.
Daly, Jude 1951- 177
Daly, Kathleen N(orah) 124
  Brief entry 37

Daly, Maureen 1921-2006 .... *129*
  Obituary *176*
  Earlier sketch in SATA *2*
  See also CLR *96*
  See also SAAS *1*
Daly, Nicholas 1946- *164*
  Earlier sketches in SATA *37, 76, 114*
  See also CLR *41*
  See Daly, Niki
Daly, Niki
  See SAAS *21*
  See Daly, Nicholas
D'Amato, Alex 1919- *20*
D'Amato, Janet (Potter) 1925- *9*
Damerow, Gail 1944- *83*
Damerow, Gail Jane
  See Damerow, Gail
D'Amico, Carmela *170*
D'Amico, Steve *170*
Damrell, Liz 1956- *77*
Damrosch, Helen
  See Tee-Van, Helen Damrosch
Dana, Barbara 1940- *22*
Dana, Richard Henry, Jr. 1815-1882 .... *26*
Danachair, Caoimhin O
  See Danaher, Kevin
Danaher, Kevin 1913-2002 .... *22*
Danakas, John 1963- *94*
Dandi
  See Mackall, Dandi Daley
D'Andrea, Kate
  See Steiner, Barbara A(nnette)
Dangerfield, Balfour
  See McCloskey, (John) Robert
Daniel, Alan 1939- *76*
  Brief entry *53*
Daniel, Anita 1893(?)-1978 .... *23*
  Obituary *24*
Daniel, Anne
  See Steiner, Barbara A(nnette)
Daniel, Becky 1947- *56*
Daniel, Claire 1949- *164*
Daniel, Colin
  See Windsor, Patricia
Daniel, Hawthorne 1890- *8*
Daniel, (Donna) Lee 1944- *76*
Daniel, Rebecca
  See Daniel, Becky
Daniels, Guy 1919-1989 .... *11*
  Obituary *62*
Daniels, Lucy
  See Oldfield, Jenny
Daniels, Max
  See Gellis, Roberta
Daniels, Olga
  See Sinclair, Olga
Daniels, Patricia 1955- *93*
Daniels, Zoe
  See Laux, Constance
Dank, Gloria Rand 1955- *56*
  Brief entry *46*
Dank, Leonard D(ewey) 1929- *44*
Dank, Milton 1920- *31*
Dann, Max 1955- *62*
Danneberg, Julie 1958- *173*
Dantz, William R.
  See Philbrick, Rodman
Danziger, Paula 1944-2004 .... *149*
  Brief entry *30*
  Obituary *155*
  Earlier sketches in SATA *36, 63, 102*
  See also CLR *20*
Darby, Gene Kegley
  See Darby, Jean (Kegley)
Darby, J. N.
  See Govan, (Mary) Christine Noble
Darby, Jean (Kegley) 1921- *68*
Darby, Patricia (Paulsen) *14*
Darby, Ray(mond) 1912-1982 .... *7*
d'Arcy, Willard
  See Cox, William R(obert)

Dare, Geena
  See McNicoll, Sylvia (Marilyn)
Darian, Shea 1959- *97*
Daringer, Helen Fern 1892-1986 .... *1*
Darke, Marjorie 1929- *87*
  Earlier sketch in SATA *16*
Darley, F(elix) O(ctavius) C(arr) 1822-1888
  .... *35*
Darling, David J. 1953- *60*
  Brief entry *44*
Darling, Kathy
  See Darling, Mary Kathleen
Darling, Lois (MacIntyre) 1917-1989 .... *3*
  Obituary *64*
Darling, Louis, (Jr.) 1916-1970 .... *3*
  Obituary *23*
Darling, Mary Kathleen 1943- *124*
  Earlier sketches in SATA *9, 79*
Darling, Sandra Louise Woodward
  See Day, Alexandra
Darnell, K(athryn) L(ynne) 1955- *150*
Darroll, Sally
  See Odgers, Sally Farrell
Darrow, Sharon *181*
Darrow, Whitney, (Jr.) 1909-1999 .... *13*
  Obituary *115*
Darwin, Len
  See Darwin, Leonard
Darwin, Leonard 1916- *24*
Dasent, Sir George Webbe 1817-1896 .... *62*
  Brief entry *29*
Dash, Joan 1925- *142*
Daskam, Josephine Dodge
  See Bacon, Josephine Dodge (Daskam)
D'ath, Justin 1953- *174*
  Earlier sketch in SATA *106*
Dauer, Rosamond 1934- *23*
Daugherty, Charles Michael 1914- *16*
Daugherty, James (Henry) 1889-1974 .... *13*
  See also CLR *78*
Daugherty, Richard D(eo) 1922- *35*
d'Aulaire, Edgar Parin 1898-1986 .... *66*
  Obituary *47*
  Earlier sketch in SATA *5*
  See also CLR *21*
d'Aulaire, Ingri (Mortenson Parin) 1904-1980
  .... *66*
  Obituary *24*
  Earlier sketch in SATA *5*
  See also CLR *21*
Dave, Dave
  See Berg, David
Daveluy, Paule Cloutier 1919- *11*
Davenier, Christine 1961- *179*
  Earlier sketch in SATA *127*
Davenport, John 1960- *156*
Daves, Michael 1938- *40*
David, A. R.
  See David, A(nn) Rosalie
David, A(nn) Rosalie 1946- *103*
David, Jonathan
  See Ames, Lee J(udah)
David, Lawrence 1963- *165*
  Earlier sketch in SATA *111*
David, Rosalie
  See David, A(nn) Rosalie
Davidson, Alice Joyce 1932- *54*
  Brief entry *45*
Davidson, Basil 1914- *13*
Davidson, (Marie) Diane 1924- *91*
Davidson, Hugh
  See Hamilton, Edmond
Davidson, Jessica 1915-1986 .... *5*
Davidson, Judith 1953- *40*
Davidson, Lionel 1922- *87*
Davidson, Margaret 1936- *5*
Davidson, Marion
  See Garis, Howard R(oger)
Davidson, Mary R. 1885-1973 .... *9*
Davidson, Mary S. 1940- *61*

Davidson, Mickie
  See Davidson, Margaret
Davidson, Nicole
  See Jensen, Kathryn
Davidson, R.
  See Davidson, Raymond
Davidson, Raymond 1926- *32*
Davidson, Rosalie 1921- *23*
Davie, Helen K(ay) 1952- *148*
  Earlier sketch in SATA *77*
Davies, Andrew (Wynford) 1936- *27*
Davies, Bettilu D(onna) 1942- *33*
Davies, Hunter 1936- *55*
  Brief entry *45*
Davies, Jacqueline 1962- *155*
Davies, Joan 1934- *50*
  Brief entry *47*
Davies, Nicola 1958- *150*
  Earlier sketch in SATA *99*
Davies, Peter J(oseph) 1937- *52*
Davies, Sumiko 1942- *46*
Davis, (A.) Aubrey 1949- *153*
Davis, Barbara Steincrohn
  See Davis, Maggie S.
Davis, Bette J. 1923- *15*
Davis, Burke 1913- *4*
Davis, Christopher 1928- *6*
Davis, D(elbert) Dwight 1908-1965 .... *33*
Davis, Daniel S(heldon) 1936- *12*
Davis, David R. 1948- *106*
Davis, Donald 1944- *169*
  Earlier sketch in SATA *93*
Davis, Donald D.
  See Davis, Donald
Davis, Emma
  See Davis, Maggie S.
Davis, Gibbs 1953- *102*
  Brief entry *41*
  Earlier sketch in SATA *46*
Davis, Grania 1943- *88*
  Brief entry *50*
Davis, H(arold) L(enoir) 1896-1960 .... *114*
Davis, Hubert J(ackson) 1904-1997 .... *31*
Davis, James Robert 1945- *32*
  See Davis, Jim
Davis, Jenny 1953- *74*
Davis, Jim
  See Davis, James Robert
Davis, Julia 1900(?)-1993 .... *6*
  Obituary *75*
Davis, Karen (Elizabeth) 1944- *109*
Davis, Katie 1959(?)- *152*
Davis, Lambert *176*
Davis, Leslie
  See Guccione, Leslie Davis
Davis, Louise Littleton 1921- *25*
Davis, Maggie S. 1943- *57*
Davis, Marguerite 1889- *34*
Davis, Mary L(ee) 1935- *9*
Davis, Mary Octavia 1901-1976 .... *6*
Davis, Nelle 1958- *73*
Davis, Ossie 1917-2005 .... *81*
  See also CLR *56*
Davis, Paxton 1925-1994 .... *16*
Davis, Robert 1881-1949
  See YABC *1*
Davis, Robin W(orks) 1962- *87*
Davis, Russell Gerard 1922- *3*
Davis, Tim(othy N.) 1957- *94*
Davis, Verne Theodore 1889-1973 .... *6*
Davis, Yvonne 1927- *115*
Davol, Marguerite W. 1928- *146*
  Earlier sketch in SATA *82*
DaVolls, Andy (P.) 1967- *85*
DaVolls, Linda 1966- *85*
Davys, Sarah
  See Manning, Rosemary (Joy)
Dawes, Claiborne 1935- *111*
Dawson, Elmer A. *67*
  Earlier sketch in SATA *1*

Dawson, Imogen (Zoe) 1948- *126*
　Earlier sketch in SATA *90*
Dawson, Mary 1919- *11*
Day, A(rthur) Grove 1904-1994 .... *59*
Day, Alexandra 1941- *169*
　Earlier sketches in SATA *67, 97*
　See also CLR *22*
　See also SAAS *19*
Day, Beth (Feagles) 1924- *33*
Day, Donna
　See Asay, Donna Day
Day, Edward C. 1932- *72*
Day, Jon 1936(?)- *79*
Day, Larry 1956- *181*
Day, Nancy 1953- *140*
Day, Nancy Raines 1951- *148*
　Earlier sketch in SATA *93*
Day, Shirley 1962- *94*
Day, Thomas 1748-1789
　See YABC *1*
Day, Trevor 1955- *124*
Dazey, Agnes J(ohnston) *2*
Dazey, Frank M. *2*
Deacon, Alexis 1978- *139*
Deacon, Eileen
　See Geipel, Eileen
Deacon, Richard
　See McCormick, (George) Donald (King)
Deak, Erzsi 1959- *152*
Dean, Anabel 1915- *12*
Dean, Carolee 1962- *148*
Dean, Karen Strickler 1923- *49*
Dean, Ruth (Brigham) 1947- *145*
Dean, Zoey
　See Bennett, Cherie
de Angeli, Marguerite (Lofft) 1889-1987 .. *100*
　Obituary *51*
　Earlier sketches in SATA *1, 27*
　See also CLR *1*
Deans, Sis Boulos 1955- *136*
　Earlier sketch in SATA *78*
DeArmand, Frances Ullmann 1904(?)-1984
　.. *10*
　Obituary *38*
DeArmond, Dale 1914- *70*
DeArmond, Dale Burlison
　See DeArmond, Dale
Deary, Terry 1946- *171*
　Brief entry *41*
　Earlier sketches in SATA *51, 101*
Deaver, Julie Reece 1953- *68*
de Banke, Cecile 1889-1965 .... *11*
De Bello, Rosario 1923- *89*
Debon, Nicolas *151*
de Bono, Edward 1933- *66*
de Brissac, Malcolm
　See Dickinson, Peter (Malcolm de Brissac)
de Brunhoff, Jean
　See Brunhoff, Jean de
De Brunhoff, Laurent
　See Brunhoff, Laurent de
De Bruyn, Monica G. 1952- *13*
De Bruyn, Monica Jean Grembowicz
　See De Bruyn, Monica G.
DeBry, Roger K. 1942- *91*
de Camp, Catherine Crook 1907-2000 ...... *83*
　Earlier sketch in SATA *12*
de Camp, L(yon) Sprague 1907-2000 ...... *83*
　Earlier sketch in SATA *9*
DeCandido, Keith R.A. *112*
Dechausay, Sonia E. *94*
Decker, C.B. *172*
Decker, Cynthia B.
　See Decker, C.B.
Decker, Duane 1910-1964 .... *5*
DeClements, Barthe (Faith) 1920- *131*
　Earlier sketches in SATA *35, 71*
　See also CLR *23*
de Conte, Sieur Louis
　See Clemens, Samuel Langhorne
Dedman, Stephen *108*

Dee, Catherine 1964- *138*
Dee, Ruby *77*
　See Wallace, Ruby Ann
Deedy, John 1923- *24*
Deegan, Paul Joseph 1937- *48*
　Brief entry *38*
Deem, James M. 1950- *134*
　Earlier sketch in SATA *75*
Deem, James Morgan
　See Deem, James M.
Deeter, Catherine 1947- *137*
DeFelice, Cynthia 1951- *165*
　Earlier sketches in SATA *79, 121*
DeFelice, Cynthia C.
　See DeFelice, Cynthia
Defoe, Daniel 1660(?)-1731 .... *22*
　See also CLR *61*
DeFord, Deborah H. *123*
deFrance, Anthony
　See DiFranco, Anthony (Mario)
Degen, Bruce 1945- *147*
　Brief entry *47*
　Earlier sketches in SATA *57, 97*
DeGering, Etta (Belle) Fowler 1898-1996 .... *7*
De Goldi, Kate
　See De Goldi, Kathleen Domenica
De Goldi, Kathleen Domenica 1959- *123*
De Grazia, Ted *39*
　See De Grazia, Ettore
deGroat, Diane 1947- *169*
　Earlier sketches in SATA *31, 90*
deGros, J. H.
　See Villiard, Paul
de Grummond, Lena Young *62*
　Earlier sketch in SATA *6*
de Hamel, Joan Littledale 1924- *86*
De Haven, Tom 1949- *72*
de Hugo, Pierre
　See Brackers de Hugo, Pierre
Deiss, Joseph Jay 1915- *12*
de Jenkins, Lyll Becerra 1925-1997 .... *102*
DeJong, David C(ornel) 1905-1967 .... *10*
de Jong, Dola 1911-2003 .... *7*
　Obituary *149*
　See de Jong, Dorothea Rosalie
DeJong, Meindert 1906-1991 .... *2*
　Obituary *68*
　See also CLR *73*
DeJonge, Joanne E. 1943- *56*
Deka, Connie
　See Laux, Constance
de Kay, Ormonde (Jr.) 1923-1998 .... *7*
　Obituary *106*
de Kiriline, Louise
　See Lawrence, Louise de Kiriline
Dekker, Carl
　See Laffin, John (Alfred Charles)
　and Lynds, Dennis
deKruif, Paul (Henry) 1890-1971 .... *50*
　Earlier sketch in SATA *5*
Delacre, Lulu 1957- *156*
　Earlier sketch in SATA *36*
DeLaCroix, Alice 1940- *75*
de la Cruz, Melissa 1971- *179*
De la Garza, Phyllis 1942- *169*
De Lage, Ida 1918- *11*
de la Mare, Walter (John) 1873-1956 ...... *16*
　See also CLR *23*
Delaney, Harry 1932- *3*
Delaney, Joseph 1945- *172*
Delaney, M.C.
　See Delaney, Michael
Delaney, Michael 1955- *180*
　Earlier sketch in SATA *96*
Delaney, Michael Clark
　See Delaney, Michael
Delaney, Ned *28*
　See Delaney, Thomas Nicholas III
Delano, Hugh 1933- *20*
Delany, Samuel R., Jr. 1942- *92*

Delany, Samuel Ray
　See Delany, Samuel R., Jr.
De La Ramee, Marie Louise 1839-1908 ..... *20*
　See Ouida
de la Roche, Mazo 1879-1961 .... *64*
De La Roche Saint Andre, Anne 1950- *75*
Delaune, (Jewel) Lynn (de Grummond) *7*
DeLaurentis, Louise Budde 1920- *12*
Delderfield, Eric R(aymond) 1909-1995 ..... *14*
Delderfield, Ronald Frederick 1912-1972 ... *20*
DeLeeuw, Adele (Louise) 1899-1988 .... *30*
　Obituary *56*
　Earlier sketch in SATA *1*
De Leon, Nephtali 1945- *97*
Delessert, Etienne 1941- *179*
　Brief entry *27*
　Earlier sketches in SATA *46, 130*
　See also CLR *81*
Delgado, James P. 1958- *122*
de Lint, Charles 1951- *157*
　Earlier sketch in SATA *115*
de Lint, Charles Henri Diederick Hofsmit
　See de Lint, Charles
Delmar, Roy
　See Wexler, Jerome (LeRoy)
Deloria, Vine, Jr. 1933-2005 .... *21*
　Obituary *171*
Deloria, Vine Victor, Jr.
　See Deloria, Vine, Jr.
del Rey, Lester 1915-1993 .... *22*
　Obituary *76*
Delrio, Martin
　See Doyle, Debra
　and Macdonald, James D.
Delton, Judy 1931-2001 .... *77*
　Obituary *130*
　Earlier sketch in SATA *14*
　See also SAAS *9*
Delulio, John 1938- *15*
Delving, Michael
　See Williams, Jay
Demarest, Chris L. 1951- *175*
　Brief entry *44*
　Earlier sketches in SATA *45, 82, 128*
Demarest, Christopher Lynn
　See Demarest, Chris L.
Demarest, Doug
　See Barker, Will
Demas, Corinne *131*
　See Bliss, Corinne Demas
Demas, Vida 1927- *9*
DeMatteis, J.M. 1953- *180*
DeMatteis, John Marc
　See DeMatteis, J.M.
De Mejo, Oscar 1911-1992 .... *40*
Demers, Dominique 1956- *177*
de Messieres, Nicole 1930- *39*
Demi
　See Hitz, Demi
Demijohn, Thom
　See Disch, Thomas M.
　and Sladek, John
Deming, Richard 1915-1983 .... *24*
　See Queen, Ellery
Demuth, Patricia Brennan 1948- *84*
　Brief entry *51*
Dendinger, Roger E. 1952- *158*
Denenberg, Barry *175*
Dengler, Marianna (Herron) 1935- *103*
Dengler, Sandy 1939- *54*
　Brief entry *40*
Denim, Sue
　See Pilkey, Dav
Denise, Christopher 1968- *147*
Denmark, Harrison
　See Zelazny, Roger
Dennard, Deborah 1953- *136*
　Earlier sketch in SATA *78*
Denney, Diana 1910-2000 .... *25*
　Obituary *120*
Dennis, Morgan 1891(?)-1960 .... *18*

Dennis, Wesley 1903-1966 .... *18*
Denny, Norman (George) 1901-1982 .... *43*
Denslow, Sharon Phillips 1947- *142*
Earlier sketch in SATA *68*
Denslow, W(illiam) W(allace) 1856-1915 .. *16*
See also CLR *15*
Denton, Kady MacDonald *181*
Earlier sketches in SATA *66, 110*
See also CLR *71*
Denver, Walt
See Redding, Robert Hull
and Sherman, Jory (Tecumseh)
Denzel, Justin F(rancis) 1917-1999 .... *46*
Brief entry *38*
Denzer, Ann Wiseman
See Wiseman, Ann (Sayre)
DePalma, Mary Newell 1961- *139*
dePaola, Thomas Anthony 1934- *155*
Earlier sketches in SATA *11, 59, 108*
See dePaola, Tomie
dePaola, Tomie
See CLR *81*
See also SAAS *15*
See dePaola, Thomas Anthony
deParrie, Paul 1949- *74*
DePauw, Linda Grant 1940- *24*
DeRan, David 1946- *76*
Derby, Ken 1956- *181*
Derby, Kenneth R.
See Derby, Ken
Derby, Pat 1942- *172*
Derby, Sally 1934- *132*
Earlier sketch in SATA *89*
de Regniers, Beatrice Schenk (Freedman)
1914-2000 .... *68*
Obituary *123*
Earlier sketch in SATA *2*
See also SAAS *6*
Dereske, Jo 1947- *72*
Derleth, August (William) 1909-1971 .... *5*
Derman, Martha (Winn) *74*
Derman, Sarah Audrey 1915- *11*
DeRoberts, Lyndon
See Silverstein, Robert Alan
de Roo, Anne Louise 1931-1997 .... *84*
Earlier sketch in SATA *25*
See also CLR *63*
deRosa, Dee *70*
Derrick, Lionel
See Cunningham, Chet
Derrickson, Jim 1959- *141*
Derry Down Derry
See Lear, Edward
Dervaux, Isabelle 1961- *106*
Derwent, Lavinia *14*
Desai, Anita 1937- *126*
Earlier sketch in SATA *63*
De Saulles, Tony 1958- *119*
Desbarats, Peter 1933- *39*
de Selincourt, Aubrey 1894-1962 .... *14*
Deshpande, Chris 1950- *69*
Desimini, Lisa 1964- *148*
Earlier sketch in SATA *86*
Desjarlais, John 1953- *71*
Desjarlais, John J.
See Desjarlais, John
Desmoinaux, Christel 1967- *149*
Earlier sketch in SATA *103*
Desmond, Adrian J(ohn) 1947- *51*
Desmond, Alice Curtis 1897-1990 .... *8*
DeSpain, Pleasant 1943- *87*
Desputeaux, Helene 1959- *95*
Dessen, Sarah 1970- *172*
Earlier sketch in SATA *120*
Detine, Padre
See Olsen, Ib Spang
de Trevino, Elizabeth B.
See Trevino, Elizabeth B(orton) de
de Trevino, Elizabeth Borton
See Trevino, Elizabeth B(orton) de
Detwiler, Susan Dill 1956- *58*

Deuker, Carl 1950- *150*
Earlier sketch in SATA *82*
Deutsch, Babette 1895-1982 .... *1*
Obituary *33*
Deutsch, Eva Costabel
See Costabel, Eva Deutsch
Deutsch, Helen 1906-1992 .... *76*
Deutsch, Kurt
See Singer, Kurt D.
Devaney, John 1926-1994 .... *12*
de Varennes, Monique 1947- *168*
de Varona, Frank J. 1943- *83*
Devereux, Frederick L(eonard), Jr. 1914-1993
.... *9*
Devi, Nila
See Woody, Regina Jones
deVinck, Christopher 1951- *85*
DeVito, Cara 1956- *80*
Devlin, Dorothy Wende
See Devlin, Wende
Devlin, Harry 1918-2001 .... *136*
Earlier sketches in SATA *11, 74*
Devlin, Wende 1918-2002 .... *74*
Earlier sketch in SATA *11*
Devon, Paddie 1953- *92*
Devons, Sonia 1974- *72*
Devorah-Leah *111*
de Vos, Gail 1949- *122*
DeVries, Douglas 1933- *122*
De Waard, E(lliott) John 1935- *7*
Dewan, Ted 1961- *157*
Earlier sketch in SATA *108*
Dewdney, Selwyn (Hanington) 1909-1979 . *64*
DeWeese, Gene
See DeWeese, Thomas Eugene
DeWeese, Jean
See DeWeese, Thomas Eugene
DeWeese, Thomas Eugene 1934- *46*
Brief entry *45*
Dewey, Ariane 1937- *178*
Earlier sketches in SATA *7, 109*
Dewey, Jennifer (Owings) 1941- *103*
Brief entry *48*
Earlier sketch in SATA *58*
Dewey, Kenneth Francis 1940- *39*
De Wire, Elinor 1953- *180*
deWit, Dorothy (May Knowles) 1916-1980
.... *39*
Obituary *28*
Dexter, Alison 1966- *125*
Dexter, John
See Bradley, Marion Zimmer
Deyneka, Anita 1943- *24*
Deyrup, Astrith Johnson 1923- *24*
Dhami, Narinder 1958- *152*
Dhondy, Farrukh 1944- *152*
Earlier sketch in SATA *65*
See also CLR *41*
Diakite, Baba Wague 1961- *174*
Diakite, Penda 1993(?)- *174*
Diamond, Arthur 1957- *76*
Diamond, Donna 1950- *69*
Brief entry *30*
Earlier sketch in SATA *35*
Diamond, Petra
See Sachs, Judith
Diamond, Rebecca
See Sachs, Judith
Dias, Earl Joseph 1916- *41*
Dias, Ron 1937- *71*
Diaz, David 1959(?)- *150*
Earlier sketch in SATA *96*
See also CLR *65*
DiCamillo, Kate 1964- *163*
Earlier sketch in SATA *121*
See also CLR *117*
Di Certo, J(oseph) J(ohn) 1933- *60*
DiCianni, Ron 1952- *107*
Dick, Trella Lamson 1889-1974 .... *9*

Dickens, Charles (John Huffam) 1812-1870
.... *15*
See also CLR *95*
Dickens, Frank
See Huline-Dickens, Frank William
Dickens, Monica (Enid) 1915-1992 .... *4*
Obituary *74*
Dickinson, Emily (Elizabeth) 1830-1886 .... *29*
Dickinson, Mary 1949- *48*
Brief entry *41*
Dickinson, Mary-Anne
See Rodda, Emily
Dickinson, Peter (Malcolm de Brissac) 1927-
.... *150*
Earlier sketches in SATA *5, 62, 95*
See also CLR *29*
Dickinson, Susan 1931- *8*
Dickinson, Terence 1943- *102*
Dickinson, W(illiam) Croft 1897-1963 .... *13*
Dickson, Gordon R(upert) 1923-2001 .... *77*
Dickson, Naida 1916- *8*
Diehn, Gwen 1943- *80*
Dieterich, Michele M. 1962- *78*
Dietz, David H(enry) 1897-1984 .... *10*
Obituary *41*
Dietz, Lew 1907-1997 .... *11*
Obituary *95*
Diffily, Deborah *159*
Di Fiori, Larry
See Di Fiori, Lawrence
Di Fiori, Lawrence 1934- *130*
DiFranco, Anthony (Mario) 1945- *42*
Digby, Anne 1935- *72*
Digges, Jeremiah
See Berger, Josef
Digman, Kristina 1959- *176*
D'Ignazio, Fred(erick) 1949- *39*
Brief entry *35*
Di Grazia, Thomas (?)-1983 .... *32*
Dikty, Julian May
See May, Julian
Dillard, Annie 1945- *140*
Earlier sketch in SATA *10*
Dillard, Kristine 1964- *113*
Dillard, Polly Hargis 1916- *24*
Diller, Harriett 1953- *78*
Dillon, Barbara 1927- *44*
Brief entry *39*
Dillon, Diane (Claire) 1933- *106*
Earlier sketches in SATA *15, 51*
See also CLR *44*
Dillon, Eilis 1920-1994 .... *74*
Autobiography Feature *105*
Obituary *83*
Earlier sketch in SATA *2*
See also CLR *26*
Dillon, Jana (a pseudonym) 1952- *117*
Dillon, Leo 1933- *106*
Earlier sketches in SATA *15, 51*
See also CLR *44*
Dillon, Sharon Saseen
See Saseen, Sharon (Dillon)
Dils, Tracey E. 1958- *83*
Dilson, Jesse 1914-1988 .... *24*
Dinan, Carolyn *59*
Brief entry *47*
Dines, Carol 1956- *175*
Dines, (Harry) Glen 1925-1996 .... *7*
Dinesen, Isak
See Blixen, Karen (Christentze Dinesen)
Dinessi, Alex
See Schembri, Jim
Dinneen, Betty 1929- *61*
Dinnerstein, Harvey 1928- *42*
Dinsdale, Tim(othy Kay) 1924-1987 .... *11*
Diouf, Sylviane A. 1952- *168*
Diouf, Sylviane Anna
See Diouf, Sylviane A.
DiPucchio, Kelly *159*
Dirk
See Gringhuis, Richard H.

Dirks, Wilhelmina 1916- 59
Dirks, Willy
  See Dirks, Wilhelmina
Dirtmeister
  See Tomecek, Steve
DiSalvo, DyAnne 1960- 144
  Earlier sketch in SATA 59
DiSalvo-Ryan, DyAnne
  See DiSalvo, DyAnne
Disch, Thomas M. 1940- 92
  See also CLR 18
  See also SAAS 15
  See Disch, Tom
Disch, Thomas Michael
  See Disch, Thomas M.
Disch, Tom
  See Disch, Thomas M.
Disher, Garry 1949- 125
  Earlier sketch in SATA 81
Disney, Walt(er Elias) 1901-1966 28
  Brief entry 27
DiTerlizzi, Tony 1969- 154
Divakaruni, Chitra Banerjee 1956- 160
Di Valentin, Maria (Amelia) Messuri
  1911-1985 7
Dixon, Ann R(enee) 1954- 127
  Earlier sketch in SATA 77
Dixon, Dougal 1947- 127
  Earlier sketch in SATA 45
Dixon, Franklin W. 100
  Earlier sketches in SATA 1, 67
  See also CLR 61
  See Barrett, Neal, Jr.
  and Goulart, Ron(ald Joseph)
  and Lantz, Francess L(in)
  and Lerangis, Peter
  and McFarlane, Leslie (Charles)
  and Stanley, George Edward
  and Stratemeyer, Edward L.
Dixon, Jeanne 1936- 31
Dixon, Paige
  See Corcoran, Barbara (Asenath)
Dixon, Peter L(ee) 1931- 6
Dixon, Rachel 1952- 74
Djoleto, (Solomon Alexander) Amu 1929- . 80
d'lacey, Chris 1949- 165
Doak, Annie
  See Dillard, Annie
Doane, Pelagie 1906-1966 7
Dobell, I(sabel) M(arian) B(arclay) 1909-1998
  11
Dobie, J(ames) Frank 1888-1964 43
Dobler, Lavinia G. 1910- 6
Dobrin, Arnold 1928- 4
Dobson, Jill 1969- 140
Dobson, Julia 1941- 48
Dobson, Mary 1954- 117
Dockery, Wallene T. 1941- 27
Dockray, Tracy 1962- 139
Dockrey, Karen 1955- 103
Doctor, Bernard
  See Doctor, Bernard Aquina
Doctor, Bernard Aquina 1950- 81
Doctor X
  See Nourse, Alan E(dward)
Dodd, Ed(ward Benton) 1902-1991 4
  Obituary 68
Dodd, Lynley (Stuart) 1941- 132
  Earlier sketches in SATA 35, 86
  See also CLR 62
Dodd, Marty 1921- 142
Dodd, Quentin 1972- 137
Dodds, Bill 1952- 78
Dodds, Dayle Ann 1952- 150
  Earlier sketch in SATA 75
Dodge, Bertha S(anford) 1902-1995 8
Dodge, Fremont
  See Grimes, Lee
Dodge, Gil
  See Hano, Arnold

Dodge, Mary (Elizabeth) Mapes 1831(?)-1905
  100
  Earlier sketch in SATA 21
  See also CLR 62
Dodgson, Charles L(utwidge) 1832-1898 . 100
  See also YABC 2
  See also CLR 2
  See Carroll, Lewis
Dodson, Kenneth MacKenzie 1907-1999 11
Dodson, Susan 1941- 50
  Brief entry 40
Dogyear, Drew
  See Gorey, Edward (St. John)
Doherty, Berlie 1943- 111
  Earlier sketch in SATA 72
  See also CLR 21
  See also SAAS 16
Doherty, Charles Hugh 1913- 6
Doherty, Craig A. 1951- 169
  Earlier sketch in SATA 83
Doherty, Katherine M(ann) 1951- 83
Doherty, Kieran 1945- 164
Dokey, Cameron 1956- 97
Dolan, Edward F(rancis), Jr. 1924- 94
  Brief entry 31
  Earlier sketch in SATA 45
Dolan, Ellen M(eara) 1929-1998 88
Dolan, Sean J. 1958- 74
Dolce, J. Ellen 1948- 75
Dolch, Edward William 1889-1961 50
Dolch, Marguerite Pierce 1891-1978 50
Dollar, Diane (Hills) 1933- 57
Dolson, Hildegarde 5
  See Lockridge, Hildegarde (Dolson)
Domanska, Janina 1913(?)-1995 68
  Obituary 84
  Earlier sketch in SATA 6
  See also CLR 40
  See also SAAS 18
Dominguez, Angel 1953- 76
Domino, John
  See Averill, Esther (Holden)
Domjan, Joseph (Spiri) 1907-1992 25
Domm, Jeffrey C. 1958- 84
Donahue, Dorothy 178
Donald, Rhonda Lucas 1962- 147
Donalds, Gordon
  See Shirreffs, Gordon D(onald)
Donaldson, Bryna
  See Stevens, Bryna
Donaldson, Gordon 1913-1993 64
  Obituary 76
Donaldson, Joan 1953- 78
Donaldson, Julia 1948- 180
  Earlier sketches in SATA 82, 132
Donaldson, Stephen R(eeder) 1947- 121
Doner, Kim 1955- 91
Doney, Todd L. W. 1959- 104
Donkin, Nance (Clare) 1915- 95
Donna, Natalie 1934-1979 9
Donnelly, Elfie 1950-
  See CLR 104
Donnelly, Jennifer 1963- 154
Donnelly, Matt 1972- 148
Donoghue, Emma 1969- 101
Donoughue, Carol 1935- 139
Donovan, John 1928-1992 72
  Brief entry 29
  See also CLR 3
Donovan, Mary Lee 1961- 86
Donze, Mary Terese 1911- 89
Doob, Leonard W(illiam) 1909-2000 8
Dooley, Norah 1953- 74
Dooling, Michael 1958- 105
Dor, Ana
  See Ceder, Georgiana Dorcas
Dore, (Louis Christophe Paul) Gustave
  1832-1883 19
Doremus, Robert 1913- 30
Doren, Marion (Walker) 1928- 57
Dorenkamp, Michelle 1957- 89

Dorflinger, Carolyn 1953- 91
Dorfman, Joaquin 1979- 180
Dorfman, Joaquin Emiliano
  See Dorfman, Joaquin
Dorian, Edith M(cEwen) 1900-1983 5
Dorian, Harry
  See Hamilton, Charles (Harold St. John)
Dorian, Marguerite 7
Dorin, Patrick C(arberry) 1939- 59
  Brief entry 52
Dorman, Michael 1932- 7
Dorman, N. B. 1927- 39
Dorris, Michael 1945-1997 75
  Obituary 94
  See also CLR 58
Dorris, Michael A.
  See Dorris, Michael
Dorris, Michael Anthony
  See Dorris, Michael
Dorritt, Susan
  See Schlein, Miriam
Dorros, Arthur 1950- 168
  Earlier sketches in SATA 78, 122
  See also CLR 42
  See also SAAS 20
Dorros, Arthur M.
  See Dorros, Arthur
Dorson, Richard M(ercer) 1916-1981 30
Doss, Helen (Grigsby) 1918- 20
Doss, Margot Patterson 6
Dothers, Anne
  See Chess, Victoria (Dickerson)
Dottig
  See Grider, Dorothy
Dotts, Maryann J. 1933- 35
Doty, Jean Slaughter 1929- 28
Doty, Roy 1922- 28
Doubtfire, Dianne (Abrams) 1918- 29
Doucet, Sharon Arms 1951- 144
  Autobiography Feature 144
  Earlier sketch in SATA 125
Dougherty, Charles 1922- 18
Dougherty, Terri (L.) 1964- 146
Doughty, Rebecca 1955- 174
Douglas, Blaise 1960- 101
Douglas, Carole Nelson 1944- 73
Douglas, Garry
  See Kilworth, Garry
Douglas, James McM.
  See Griffin, W.E.B.
Douglas, Kathryn
  See Ewing, Kathryn
Douglas, Leonard
  See Bradbury, Ray
Douglas, Marjory Stoneman 1890-1998 10
Douglas, Michael
  See Crichton, Michael
Douglas, Michael
  See Bright, Robert (Douglas Sr.)
Douglass, Barbara 1930- 40
Douglass, Frederick 1817(?)-1895 29
Douglass, Keith
  See Cunningham, Chet
Douty, Esther M(orris) 1909-1978 8
  Obituary 23
Dow, Emily R. 1904-1987 10
Dow, Vicki
  See McVey, Vicki
Dowd, John David 1945- 78
Dowdell, Dorothy (Florence) Karns 1910- . 12
Dowden, Anne Ophelia Todd 1907-2007 7
  Obituary 180
  See also SAAS 10
Dowdey, Landon Gerald 1923- 11
Dowdy, Mrs. Regera
  See Gorey, Edward (St. John)
Dowell, Frances O'Roark 157
Dowling, Terry 1947- 101
Downer, Ann 1960- 155
Downer, Marion 1892(?)-1971 25
Downes, Belinda 1962- 180

Downey, Fairfax D(avis) 1893-1990 .... *3*
  Obituary *66*
Downie, John 1931- *87*
Downie, Mary Alice 1934- *171*
  Earlier sketches in SATA *13, 87*
Downie, Mary Alice Dawe
  See Downie, Mary Alice
Downing, David A(lmon) 1958- *84*
Downing, Julie 1956- *148*
  Earlier sketch in SATA *81*
Downing, Paula E. 1951- *80*
Downing, Warwick 1931- *138*
Downing, Wick
  See Downing, Warwick
Doyle, A. Conan
  See Doyle, Sir Arthur Conan
Doyle, Sir Arthur Conan 1859-1930 .... *24*
  See also CLR *106*
  See Conan Doyle, Arthur
Doyle, Brian 1935- *156*
  Earlier sketches in SATA *67, 104*
  See also CLR *22*
  See also SAAS *16*
Doyle, Charlotte 1937- *178*
  Earlier sketch in SATA *94*
Doyle, Charlotte Lackner
  See Doyle, Charlotte
Doyle, Conan
  See Doyle, Sir Arthur Conan
Doyle, Debra 1952- *165*
  Earlier sketch in SATA *105*
  See Appleton, Victor
Doyle, John
  See Graves, Robert
Doyle, Malachy 1954- *165*
  Earlier sketch in SATA *120*
  See also CLR *83*
Doyle, Richard 1824-1883 .... *21*
Doyle, Sir A. Conan
  See Doyle, Sir Arthur Conan
Dr. A
  See Asimov, Isaac
  and Silverstein, Alvin
  and Silverstein, Virginia B(arbara Opshelor)
Dr. Alphabet
  See Morice, Dave
Dr. Fred
  See Bortz, Alfred B(enjamin)
Dr. Laura
  See Schlessinger, Laura (Catherine)
Dr. Seuss
  See CLR *100*
  See Geisel, Theodor Seuss
  and LeSieg, Theo.
  and Seuss, Dr.
  and Stone, Rosetta
Dr. Zed
  See Penrose, Gordon
Drabble, Margaret 1939- *48*
Drackett, Phil(ip Arthur) 1922- *53*
Draco, F.
  See Davis, Julia
Dracup, Angela 1943- *74*
Dragisic, Patricia *116*
Dragonwagon, Crescent 1952- *133*
  Earlier sketches in SATA *11, 41, 75*
  See also SAAS *14*
Drake, David 1945- *85*
Drake, David Allen
  See Drake, David
Drake, Frank
  See Hamilton, Charles (Harold St. John)
Drake, Jane 1954- *82*
Drakeford, Dale B 1952- *113*
Drakeford, Dale Benjamin
  See Drakeford, Dale B
Draper, Hastings
  See Jeffries, Roderic

Draper, Sharon M. *146*
  Autobiography Feature *146*
  Earlier sketch in SATA *98*
  See also CLR *57*
Draper, Sharon Mills
  See Draper, Sharon M.
Drapier, M. B.
  See Swift, Jonathan
Drawson, Blair 1943- *126*
  Earlier sketch in SATA *17*
Dray, Matt 1967- *177*
Dray, Matthew Frederick
  See Dray, Matt
Dresang, Eliza (Carolyn Timberlake) 1941-
  .... *19*
Drescher, Henrik 1955- *172*
  Earlier sketches in SATA *67, 105*
  See also CLR *20*
Drescher, Joan E(lizabeth) 1939- *137*
  Earlier sketch in SATA *30*
Drew, Patricia (Mary) 1938- *15*
Drewery, Mary 1918- *6*
Drewery, Melanie 1970- *165*
Drewry, Henry N(athaniel) 1924- *138*
Dreyer, Ellen *177*
Drial, J. E.
  See Laird, Jean E(louise)
Drimmer, Frederick 1916-2000 .... *60*
  Obituary *124*
Driskill, J. Lawrence 1920- *90*
Driskill, Larry
  See Driskill, J. Lawrence
Driving Hawk, Virginia
  See Sneve, Virginia Driving Hawk
Drucker, Malka 1945- *111*
  Brief entry *29*
  Earlier sketch in SATA *39*
Drucker, Olga Levy 1927- *79*
Drummond, V(iolet) H(ilda) 1911-2000 .... *6*
Drummond, Walter
  See Silverberg, Robert
Drury, Clare Marie
  See Hoskyns-Abrahall, Clare (Constance Drury)
Drury, Roger W(olcott) 1914-1996 .... *15*
Druse, Eleanor
  See King, Stephen
Dryden, Pamela
  See St. John, Nicole
D.T., Hughes
  See Hughes, Dean
Duane, Diane (Elizabeth) 1952- *145*
  Brief entry *46*
  Earlier sketches in SATA *58, 95*
Dubanevich, Arlene 1950- *56*
Dubelaar, Thea 1947- *60*
du Blane, Daphne
  See Groom, Arthur William
Duble, Kathleen Benner 1958- *164*
Du Bois, Shirley Graham 1907(?)-1977 ...... *24*
  See Graham, Shirley
Du Bois, W(illiam) E(dward) B(urghardt) 1868-1963 .... *42*
du Bois, William Pene
  See Pene du Bois, William (Sherman)
Duboise, Novella 1911-1999 .... *88*
Dubosarsky, Ursula (Bridget) 1961- *147*
  Earlier sketch in SATA *107*
DuBose, LaRocque (Russ) 1926- *2*
Dubrovin, Vivian 1931- *139*
  Earlier sketch in SATA *65*
DuBurke, Randy *172*
Ducey, Jean Sparks 1915- *93*
Du Chaillu, Paul (Belloni) 1835(?)-1903 .... *26*
Ducharme, Dede Fox
  See Ducharme, Lilian Fox
Ducharme, Lilian Fox 1950- *122*
Ducornet, Erica 1943- *7*
  See Ducornet, Rikki
Ducornet, Rikki
  See Ducornet, Erica

Duden, Jane 1947- *136*
Duder, Tessa 1940- *117*
  Earlier sketch in SATA *80*
  See also CLR *43*
  See also SAAS *23*
Dudley, Helen
  See Hope Simpson, Jacynth
Dudley, Nancy
  See Cole, Lois Dwight
Dudley, Robert
  See Baldwin, James
Dudley, Ruth H(ubbell) 1905-2001 .... *11*
Dudley-Smith, T.
  See Trevor, Elleston
Due, Linnea A. 1948- *64*
Dueck, Adele 1955- *97*
Dueland, Joy V(ivian) *27*
Duerr, Gisela 1968- *89*
Duey, Kathleen 1950- *132*
Dufault, Joseph Ernest Nephtali
  See James, Will(iam Roderick)
Duff, Maggie
  See Duff, Margaret K(app)
Duff, Margaret K(app) 1916-2003 .... *37*
  Obituary *144*
Duffey, Betsy (Byars) 1953- *131*
  Earlier sketch in SATA *80*
Duffie, Charles 1960- *144*
Duffield, Katy S. 1961- *147*
Duffy, Carol Ann 1955- *165*
  Earlier sketch in SATA *95*
Dugan, Jack
  See Griffin, W.E.B.
Dugan, John Kevin
  See Griffin, W.E.B.
Dugan, Michael (Gray) 1947- *15*
Duggan, Alfred Leo 1903-1964 .... *25*
Duggan, Maurice (Noel) 1922-1974 .... *40*
  Obituary *30*
Duggleby, John 1952- *94*
Dugin, Andrej 1955- *77*
Dugina, Olga 1964- *77*
du Jardin, Rosamond Neal 1902-1963 .... *2*
Duke, Kate 1956- *148*
  Earlier sketch in SATA *90*
  See also CLR *51*
Duke, Will
  See Gault, William Campbell
Dulac, Edmund 1882-1953 .... *19*
Dumas, Alexandre (pere) 1802-1870 .... *18*
Dumas, Jacqueline 1946- *55*
Dumas, Philippe 1940- *119*
  Earlier sketch in SATA *52*
du Maurier, Daphne 1907-1989 .... *27*
  Obituary *60*
Dumbleton, Mike 1948- *124*
  Earlier sketch in SATA *73*
Dunbar, Fiona 1961- *167*
Dunbar, Joyce 1944- *162*
  Earlier sketches in SATA *76, 112*
Dunbar, Paul Laurence 1872-1906 .... *34*
Dunbar, Polly 1980(?)- *181*
Dunbar, Robert E(verett) 1926- *32*
Duncan, Alexandra
  See Moore, Ishbel (Lindsay)
Duncan, Alice Faye 1967- *168*
  Earlier sketch in SATA *95*
Duncan, Gregory
  See McClintock, Marshall
Duncan, Jane
  See Cameron, Elizabeth Jane
Duncan, Julia K. *1*
  See Benson, Mildred (Augustine Wirt)
Duncan, Lois 1934- *141*
  Autobiography Feature *141*
  Earlier sketches in SATA *1, 36, 75, 133*
  See also CLR *29*
  See also SAAS *2*
Duncan, Norman 1871-1916
  See YABC *1*

Duncan, Terence
    See Nolan, William F(rancis)
Duncombe, Frances (Riker) 1900-1994 25
    Obituary 82
Dunham, Montrew 1919- 162
Dunham, Montrew Goetz
    See Dunham, Montrew
Dunkle, Clare B. 1964- 155
Dunlap, Julie 1958- 84
Dunleavy, Deborah 1951- 133
Dunlop, Agnes M. R. (?)-1982 87
    See Kyle, Elisabeth
Dunlop, Eileen (Rhona) 1938- 76
    Earlier sketch in SATA 24
    See also SAAS 12
Dunn, Anne M. 1940- 107
Dunn, Harvey T(homas) 1884-1952 34
Dunn, Herb
    See Gutman, Dan
Dunn, John M. (III) 1949- 93
Dunn, Judy
    See Spangenberg, Judith Dunn
Dunn, Mary Lois 1930- 6
Dunnahoo, Terry Janson 1927- 7
Dunne, Jeanette 1952- 72
Dunne, Kathleen 1933- 126
Dunne, Marie
    See Clark, Ann Nolan
Dunne, Mary Collins 1914- 11
Dunne, Mary Jo
    See Dunne, Mary Collins
Dunnett, Kaitlyn
    See Emerson, Kathy Lynn
Dunnett, Margaret (Rosalind) 1909-1977 ... 42
Dunnick, Regan 178
Dunrea, Olivier 1953- 160
    Brief entry 46
    Earlier sketches in SATA 59, 118
Dunrea, Olivier Jean-Paul Dominique
    See Dunrea, Olivier
Dunton, Dorothy 1912- 92
Dupasquier, Philippe 1955- 151
    Earlier sketch in SATA 86
DuPrau, Jeanne 1944- 144
Dupuy, T(revor) N(evitt) 1916-1995 4
    Obituary 86
DuQuette, Keith 1960- 155
    Earlier sketch in SATA 90
Duran, Gloria 1924- 171
Duran, Gloria Bradley
    See Duran, Gloria
Duranceau, Suzanne 1952- 162
Durango, Julia 1967- 173
Durant, Alan 1958- 165
    Earlier sketch in SATA 121
Durant, John 1902- 27
Durbin, William 1951- 174
    Earlier sketch in SATA 143
Durell, Ann 1930- 66
Durkee, Sarah 173
Durrant, Lynda 1954- 148
    Earlier sketch in SATA 96
Durrell, Gerald (Malcolm) 1925-1995 8
    Obituary 84
Durrell, Julie 1955- 94
Durrett, Deanne 1940- 144
    Earlier sketch in SATA 92
Du Soe, Robert C. 1892-1958
    See YABC 2
Dussling, Jennifer 1970- 143
    Earlier sketch in SATA 96
DuTemple, Lesley A. 1952- 113
Dutz
    See Davis, Mary Octavia
Duval, Katherine
    See James, Elizabeth
Duval, Kathy 1946- 181
Duvall, Aimee
    See Thurlo, Aimee
    and Thurlo, David
Duvall, Evelyn Millis 1906- 9

Duvall, Jill D(onovan) 1932- 102
Duvoisin, Roger (Antoine) 1904-1980 30
    Obituary 23
    Earlier sketch in SATA 2
    See also CLR 23
Dwiggins, Don(ald J.) 1913-1988 4
    Obituary 60
Dwight, Allan
    See Cole, Lois Dwight
Dwyer, Deanna
    See Koontz, Dean R.
Dwyer, K. R.
    See Koontz, Dean R.
Dyck, Peter J. 1914- 75
Dyer, James (Frederick) 1934- 37
Dyer, Jane 147
Dyess, John (Foster) 1939- 76
Dygard, Thomas J. 1931-1996 97
    Obituary 92
    Earlier sketch in SATA 24
    See also SAAS 15
Dyke, John 1935- 35

E

E. V. L.
    See Lucas, E(dward) V(errall)
Eagar, Frances (Elisabeth Stuart) 1940-1978
    11
    Obituary 55
Eager, Edward (McMaken) 1911-1964 17
    See also CLR 43
Eager, George 1921- 56
    See Eager, George B.
Eager, George B.
    See Eager, George
Eagle, Ellen 1953- 61
Eagle, Kin
    See Adlerman, Daniel (Ezra)
    and Adlerman, Kimberly M(arie)
Eagle, Mike 1942- 11
Earle, Olive L(ydia) 1888-1982 7
Earle, William
    See Johns, W(illiam) E(arle)
Earls, Nick 1963- 156
    Earlier sketch in SATA 95
Early, Jack
    See Scoppettone, Sandra
Early, Jon
    See Johns, W(illiam) E(arle)
Early, Margaret 1951- 72
Earnshaw, Brian 1929- 17
Earnshaw, Micky
    See Earnshaw, Spencer Wright
Earnshaw, Spencer Wright 1939- 88
Easley, MaryAnn 94
Eastman, Charles A(lexander) 1858-1939
    See YABC 1
Eastman, P(hilip) D(ey) 1909-1986 33
    Obituary 46
Easton, Kelly 1960- 141
Eastwick, Ivy (Ethel) O(live) 3
Eaton, Anne T(haxter) 1881-1971 32
Eaton, Anthony 1971- 167
Eaton, George L.
    See Verral, Charles Spain
Eaton, Janet
    See Givens, Janet E(aton)
Eaton, Jeanette 1886-1968 24
Eaton, Tom 1940- 22
Ebel, Alex 1927- 11
Eber, Dorothy (Margaret) Harley 1930- 27
Eberle, Irmengarde 1898-1979 2
    Obituary 23
Eble, Diane 1956- 74
Eboch, Chris 113
Echlin, Kim 1955- 166
Eckblad, Edith Berven 1923- 23

Eckert, Allan W. 1931- 91
    Brief entry 27
    Earlier sketch in SATA 29
    See also SAAS 21
Eckert, Horst 1931- 72
    Earlier sketch in SATA 8
    See Janosch
Ecklar, Julia (Marie) 1964- 112
Eddings, David (Carroll) 1931- 91
Ede, Janina 1937- 33
Edell, Celeste 12
Edelman, Lily (Judith) 1915-1981 22
Edelson, Edward 1932- 51
Edens, Cooper 1945- 166
    Earlier sketches in SATA 49, 112
Edens, (Bishop) David 1926- 39
Edey, Maitland A(rmstrong) 1910-1992 25
    Obituary 71
Edgeworth, Maria 1768-1849 21
Edgy, Wardore
    See Gorey, Edward (St. John)
Edison, Theodore
    See Stratemeyer, Edward L.
Edler, Tim(othy) 1948- 56
Edmiston, Jim 1948- 80
Edmonds, I(vy) G(ordon) 1917- 8
Edmonds, Walter D(umaux) 1903-1998 27
    Obituary 99
    Earlier sketch in SATA 1
    See also SAAS 4
Edmund, Sean
    See Pringle, Laurence P.
Edsall, Marian (Stickney) 1920- 8
Edwards, Al
    See Nourse, Alan E(dward)
Edwards, Anne 1927- 35
Edwards, Audrey 1947- 52
    Brief entry 31
Edwards, Becky (Jane) 1966- 125
Edwards, Bertram
    See Edwards, Herbert Charles
Edwards, Bronwen Elizabeth
    See Rose, Wendy
Edwards, Cecile Pepin 1916- 25
Edwards, Dorothy 1914-1982 88
    Obituary 31
    Earlier sketch in SATA 4
Edwards, F. E.
    See Nolan, William F(rancis)
Edwards, Frank B. 1952- 93
Edwards, Gunvor 32
Edwards, Harvey 1929- 5
Edwards, Hazel (Eileen) 1945- 135
Edwards, Herbert Charles 1912- 12
Edwards, Jane Campbell 1932- 10
Edwards, Julia
    See Stratemeyer, Edward L.
Edwards, Julie
    See Andrews, Julie
Edwards, Julie Andrews
    See Andrews, Julie
Edwards, Linda Strauss 1948- 49
    Brief entry 42
Edwards, Michelle 1955- 152
    Earlier sketch in SATA 70
Edwards, Monica le Doux Newton 1912-1998
    12
Edwards, Olwen
    See Gater, Dilys
Edwards, Page (Lawrence, Jr.) 1941-1999 .. 59
Edwards, R. T.
    See Goulart, Ron(ald Joseph)
Edwards, Sally (Cary) 1929- 7
Edwards, Samuel
    See Gerson, Noel Bertram
Edwards, Wallace 1957(?)- 170
Egan, E(dward) W(elstead) 1922- 35
Egan, Kerry 175
Egan, Lorraine Hopping 1960- 134
    Earlier sketch in SATA 91

Egan, Tim 1957- *155*
    Earlier sketch in SATA *89*
Egermeier, Elsie E(milie) 1890-1986 65
Eggenberger, David 1918- 6
Eggleston, Edward 1837-1902 27
Egielski, Richard 1952- *163*
    Earlier sketches in SATA *11, 49, 106*
Egypt, Ophelia Settle 1903-1984 16
    Obituary 38
Ehlert, Lois 1934- *172*
    Earlier sketches in SATA *35, 69, 128*
    See also CLR *28*
Ehlert, Lois Jane
    See Ehlert, Lois
Ehling, Katalin Olah 1941- 93
Ehrenfreund, Norbert 1921- 86
Ehrlich, Amy 1942- *132*
    Earlier sketches in SATA *25, 65, 96*
Ehrlich, Bettina Bauer 1903-1985 .... *1*
Ehrlich, H. M.
    See Ziefert, Harriet
Eichenberg, Fritz 1901-1990 50
    Earlier sketch in SATA *9*
Eichler, Margrit 1942- 35
Eichner, James A. 1927- *4*
Eidson, Thomas 1944- *112*
Eifert, Virginia (Louise) S(nider) 1911-1966
    .... *2*
Eige, (Elizabeth) Lillian 1915- 65
Eiken, J. Melia 1967- *125*
Einsel, Naiad *10*
Einsel, Walter 1926- *10*
Einzig, Susan 1922- 43
Eiseman, Alberta 1925- 15
Eisenberg, Azriel (Louis) 1903-1985 12
Eisenberg, Lisa 1949- *155*
    Brief entry 50
    Earlier sketch in SATA *57*
Eisenberg, Phyllis Rose 1924- 41
Eisner, Vivienne
    See Margolis, Vivienne
Eisner, Will 1917-2005 .... *165*
    Earlier sketch in SATA *31*
Eisner, William Erwin
    See Eisner, Will
Eitzen, Allan 1928- 9
Eitzen, Ruth (Carper) 1924- 9
Ekwensi, C. O. D.
    See Ekwensi, Cyprian (Odiatu Duaka)
Ekwensi, Cyprian (Odiatu Duaka) 1921- 66
Elam, Richard M(ace, Jr.) 1920- 9
Elborn, Andrew
    See Clements, Andrew
    and Clements, Andrew
Elboz, Stephen 1956- *152*
Eldin, Peter 1939- *154*
Eldon, Kathy 1946- *107*
Elfman, Blossom 1925- 8
Elgin, Kathleen 1923- 39
Elia
    See Lamb, Charles
Eliot, A. D.
    See Jewett, (Theodora) Sarah Orne
Eliot, Alice
    See Jewett, (Theodora) Sarah Orne
Eliot, Anne
    See Cole, Lois Dwight
Eliot, Dan
    See Silverberg, Robert
Elish, Dan 1960- *129*
    Earlier sketch in SATA *68*
Elisha, Ron 1951- *104*
Elkin, Benjamin 1911-1995 .... *3*
Elkins, Dov Peretz 1937- 5
Ellacott, S(amuel) E(rnest) 1911- 19
Elleman, Barbara 1934- *147*
Ellen, Jaye
    See Nixon, Joan Lowery
Eller, Scott
    See Holinger, William (Jacques)
    and Shepard, Jim

Ellestad, Myrvin
    See Ellestad, Myrvin H.
Ellestad, Myrvin H. 1921- *120*
Elliot, David 1952- *122*
Elliott, Bruce
    See Field, Edward
Elliott, David 1952- *163*
Elliott, Don
    See Silverberg, Robert
Elliott, Elizabeth Shippen Green
    See Green, Elizabeth Shippen
Elliott, Janice 1931-1995 .... *119*
Elliott, Joey
    See Houk, Randy
Elliott, Louise *111*
Elliott, Odette 1939- 75
Elliott, Patricia 1946- *176*
Elliott, Sarah M(cCarn) 1930- 14
Elliott, (Robert) Scott 1970- *153*
Elliott, William
    See Bradbury, Ray
Ellis, (Mary) Amabel (Nassau Strachey)
    Williams
    See Williams-Ellis, (Mary) Amabel (Nassau
    Strachey)
Ellis, Anyon
    See Rowland-Entwistle, (Arthur) Theodore
    (Henry)
Ellis, Deborah 1960- *129*
Ellis, E. S.
    See Ellis, Edward S(ylvester)
Ellis, Edward S(ylvester) 1840-1916
    See YABC *1*
Ellis, Ella Thorp 1928- *127*
    Earlier sketch in SATA *7*
    See also SAAS *9*
Ellis, Harry Bearse 1921-2004 9
Ellis, Herbert
    See Wilson, Lionel
Ellis, Mel(vin Richard) 1912-1984 7
    Obituary 39
Ellis, Richard 1938- *130*
Ellis, Sarah 1952- *179*
    Earlier sketches in SATA *68, 131*
    See also CLR *42*
Ellison, Emily *114*
Ellison, Lucile Watkins 1907(?)-1979 50
    Obituary 22
Ellison, Virginia H(owell) 1910- 4
Ellsberg, Edward 1891-1983 7
Ellsworth, Mary Ellen (Tressel) 1940- *146*
Elmer, Robert 1958- *154*
    Earlier sketch in SATA *99*
Elmore, (Carolyn) Patricia 1933- 38
    Brief entry 35
El-Moslimany, Ann P(axton) 1937- 90
Elspeth
    See Bragdon, Elspeth MacDuffie
Elster, Jean Alicia 1953- *150*
Elting, Mary 1906- 88
    Earlier sketch in SATA *2*
    See also SAAS *20*
Elvgren, Jennifer Riesmeyer *179*
Elwart, Joan Potter 1927- *2*
Elwood, Ann 1931- 55
    Brief entry 52
Elwood, Roger 1943-2007 58
Elya, Susan M(iddleton) 1955- *159*
    Earlier sketch in SATA *106*
Elzbieta 88
Emberley, Barbara A(nne) 1932- *146*
    Earlier sketches in SATA *8, 70*
    See also CLR *5*
Emberley, Ed(ward Randolph) 1931- *146*
    Earlier sketch in SATA *8, 70*
    See also CLR *81*
Emberley, Michael 1960- *119*
    Earlier sketches in SATA *34, 80*
Embry, Margaret Jacob 1919-1975 5
Emecheta, Buchi 1944- 66

Emecheta, Florence Onye Buchi
    See Emecheta, Buchi
Emerson, Alice B. 67
    Earlier sketch in SATA *1*
    See Benson, Mildred (Augustine Wirt)
Emerson, Kathy Lynn 1947- 63
Emerson, Ru 1944- *107*
    Earlier sketch in SATA *70*
Emerson, Sally 1952- *111*
Emerson, William K(eith) 1925- 25
Emert, Phyllis R(aybin) 1947- 93
Emery, Anne (McGuigan) 1907- 33
    Earlier sketch in SATA *1*
Emmens, Carol Ann 1944- 39
Emmett, Jonathan 1965- *138*
Emory, Jerry 1957- 96
Emrich, Duncan (Black Macdonald)
    1908-1970(?) *11*
Emshwiller, Carol 1921- *174*
    Autobiography Feature *174*
Emshwiller, Carol Fries
    See Emshwiller, Carol
Emslie, M. L.
    See Simpson, Myrtle L(illias)
Ende, Michael (Andreas Helmuth) 1929-1995
    .... *130*
    Brief entry 42
    Obituary 86
    Earlier sketch in SATA *61*
    See also CLR *14*
Enderle, Dotti 1954- *145*
Enderle, Judith (Ann) Ross 1941- 89
    Autobiography Feature *114*
    Earlier sketch in SATA *38*
    See also SAAS *26*
Enell, Trinka (Gochenour) 1951- 79
Enfield, Carrie
    See Smith, Susan Vernon
Engdahl, Sylvia Louise 1933- *4*
    Autobiography Feature *122*
    See also CLR *2*
    See also SAAS *5*
Engel, Diana 1947- 70
Engelbreit, Mary 1952- *169*
Engelhart, Margaret S. 1924- 59
Engelmann, Kim (V.) 1959- 87
England, George Allan 1877-1936 .... *102*
Englart, Mindi Rose 1965- *146*
Engle, Eloise 9
    See Paananen, Eloise (Katherine)
Englebert, Victor 1933- 8
English, James W(ilson) 1915- 37
Engstrom, Elizabeth 1951- *110*
Enright, D(ennis) J(oseph) 1920-2002 25
    Obituary *140*
Enright, Elizabeth (Wright) 1909-1968 9
    See also CLR *4*
Ensor, Barbara *180*
Ensor, Robert (T.) 1922- 93
Entwistle, (Arthur) Theodore (Henry) Rowland
    See Rowland-Entwistle, (Arthur) Theodore
    (Henry)
Enys, Sarah L.
    See Sloggett, Nellie
Epanya, Christian A(rthur Kingue) 1956- ... *91*
Ephraim, Shelly S(chonebaum) 1952- 97
Ephron, Delia 1944- 65
    Brief entry 50
Epler, Doris M. 1928- 73
Epp, Margaret A(gnes) 1913- 20
Epple, Anne Orth 1927- 20
Epstein, Anne Merrick 1931- 20
Epstein, Beryl (M. Williams) 1910- 31
    Earlier sketch in SATA *1*
    See also CLR *26*
    See also SAAS *17*
Epstein, Perle S(herry) 1938- 27
Epstein, Rachel S. 1941- *102*

Epstein, Samuel 1909-2000 .... *31*
  Earlier sketch in SATA *1*
  See also CLR *26*
  See also SAAS *17*
Erdman, Loula Grace 1905(?)-1976 .... *1*
Erdoes, Richard 1912- *33*
  Brief entry *28*
Erdrich, Karen Louise
  See Erdrich, Louise
Erdrich, Louise 1954- *141*
  Earlier sketch in SATA *94*
Erickson, Betty J. 1923- *97*
Erickson, Betty Jean
  See Erickson, Betty J.
Erickson, John R. 1943- *136*
  Earlier sketch in SATA *70*
Erickson, Jon 1948- *141*
Erickson, Phoebe *59*
Erickson, Russell E(verett) 1932- *27*
Erickson, Sabra Rollins 1912-1995 .... *35*
Erickson, Walter
  See Fast, Howard
Ericson, Walter
  See Fast, Howard
Ericsson, Jennifer A. *170*
Erikson, Mel 1937- *31*
Ering, Timothy Basil *176*
Erlanger, Baba
  See Trahey, Jane
Erlbach, Arlene 1948- *160*
  Earlier sketches in SATA *78, 115*
Erlbruch, Wolf 1948- *181*
Erlich, Lillian (Feldman) 1910-1983 .... *10*
Ermatinger, James W. 1959- *170*
Ernst, (Lyman) John 1940- *39*
Ernst, Kathleen 1959- *162*
Ernst, Kathleen A.
  See Ernst, Kathleen
Ernst, Kathryn (Fitzgerald) 1942- *25*
Ernst, Lisa Campbell 1957- *154*
  Brief entry *44*
  Earlier sketches in SATA *55, 95*
Ervin, Janet Halliday 1923- *4*
Erwin, Will
  See Eisner, Will
Esbaum, Jill *174*
Esbensen, Barbara J(uster) 1925-1996 .... *97*
  Brief entry *53*
  Earlier sketch in SATA *62*
Eschbacher, Roger *160*
Eseki, Bruno
  See Mphahlele, Ezekiel
Eshmeyer, R. E. *29*
  See Eschmeyer, R(einhart) E(rnst)
Eskridge, Ann E. 1949- *84*
Espeland, Pamela (Lee) 1951- *128*
  Brief entry *38*
  Earlier sketch in SATA *52*
Espriella, Don Manuel Alvarez
  See Southey, Robert
Espy, Willard R(ichardson) 1910-1999 .... *38*
  Obituary *113*
Essrig, Harry 1912- *66*
Estep, Irene Compton *5*
Esterl, Arnica 1933- *77*
Estes, Eleanor (Ruth) 1906-1988 .... *91*
  Obituary *56*
  Earlier sketch in SATA *7*
  See also CLR *70*
Estoril, Jean
  See Allan, Mabel Esther
Estrada, Pau 1961- *74*
Etchemendy, Nancy 1952- *166*
  Earlier sketch in SATA *38*
Etchemendy, Nancy Elise Howell
  See Etchemendy, Nancy
Etchison, Birdie L(ee) 1937- *38*
Etchison, Craig 1945- *133*
Etherington, Frank 1945- *58*
Ets, Marie Hall 1893-1984 .... *2*
  See also CLR *33*

Ettlinger, Doris 1950- *173*
Eunson, (John) Dale 1904-2002 .... *5*
  Obituary *132*
Evan, Frances Y. 1951- *167*
Evanoff, Vlad 1916- *59*
Evans, Cambria 1981- *178*
Evans, Douglas 1953- *144*
  Earlier sketch in SATA *93*
Evans, Eva (Knox) 1905-1998 .... *27*
Evans, Freddi Williams 1957- *134*
Evans, Greg 1947- *143*
  Earlier sketch in SATA *73*
Evans, Hubert Reginald 1892-1986 .... *118*
  Obituary *48*
Evans, Katherine (Floyd) 1901-1964 .... *5*
Evans, Larry
  See Evans, Laurence Chubb
Evans, Laurence Chubb 1939- *88*
Evans, Lawrence Watt 1954- *121*
Evans, Lezlie *180*
Evans, Mari 1923- *10*
Evans, Mark *19*
Evans, Nancy 1950- *65*
Evans, Patricia Healy
  See Carpenter, Patricia (Healy Evans)
Evans, (Alice) Pearl 1927- *83*
Evans, Shirlee 1931- *58*
Evans, Tabor
  See Cameron, Lou
  and Knott, William C(ecil, Jr.)
  and Wallmann, Jeffrey M(iner)
  and Whittington, Harry (Benjamin)
Evarts, Esther
  See Benson, Sally
Evarts, Hal G., (Jr.) 1915-1989 .... *6*
Everett, Gail
  See Hale, Arlene
Evernden, Margery 1916- *5*
Eversole, Robyn 1971- *74*
Eversole, Robyn H.
  See Eversole, Robyn
Eversole, Robyn Harbert
  See Eversole, Robyn
Evslin, Bernard 1922-1993 .... *83*
  Brief entry *28*
  Obituary *77*
  Earlier sketch in SATA *45*
Ewart, Claire 1958- *145*
  Earlier sketch in SATA *76*
Ewen, David 1907-1985 .... *4*
  Obituary *47*
Ewing, Juliana (Horatia Gatty) 1841-1885 . *16*
  See also CLR *78*
Ewing, Kathryn 1921- *20*
Eyerly, Jeannette (Hyde) 1908- *86*
  Earlier sketch in SATA *4*
  See also SAAS *10*
Eyre, Dorothy
  See McGuire, Leslie (Sarah)
Eyre, Katherine Wigmore 1901-1970 .... *26*
Ezzell, Marilyn 1937- *42*
  Brief entry *38*

F

Fabe, Maxene 1943- *15*
Faber, Doris (Greenberg) 1924- *78*
  Earlier sketch in SATA *3*
Faber, Harold 1919- *5*
Fabre, Jean Henri (Casimir) 1823-1915 ...... *22*
Facklam, Margery (Metz) 1927- *132*
  Earlier sketches in SATA *20, 85*
Fadiman, Clifton (Paul) 1904-1999 .... *11*
  Obituary *115*
Fahs, Sophia Blanche Lyon 1876-1978 ...... *102*
Fair, David 1952- *96*
Fair, Sylvia 1933- *13*

Fairfax-Lucy, Brian (Fulke Cameron-Ramsay)
  1898-1974 .... *6*
  Obituary *26*
Fairfield, Flora
  See Alcott, Louisa May
Fairman, Joan A(lexandra) 1935- *10*
Faithfull, Gail 1936- *8*
Falcone, L(ucy) M. 1951- *155*
Falconer, Ian 1959- *179*
  Earlier sketch in SATA *125*
  See also CLR *90*
Falconer, James
  See Kirkup, James
Falconer, Lee N.
  See May, Julian
Falkner, Leonard 1900-1977 .... *12*
Fall, Andrew
  See Arthur, Robert, (Jr.)
Fall, Thomas
  See Snow, Donald Clifford
Falls, C(harles) B(uckles) 1874-1960 .... *38*
  Brief entry *27*
Falstein, Louis 1909-1995 .... *37*
Fancher, Lou 1960- *177*
Fanelli, Sara 1969- *126*
  Earlier sketch in SATA *89*
Fanning, Leonard M(ulliken) 1888-1967 ...... *5*
Faralla, Dana 1909- *9*
Faralla, Dorothy W.
  See Faralla, Dana
Farb, Peter 1929-1980 .... *12*
  Obituary *22*
Farber, Norma 1909-1984 .... *75*
  Obituary *38*
  Earlier sketch in SATA *25*
Farish, Terry 1947- *146*
  Earlier sketch in SATA *82*
Farjeon, (Eve) Annabel 1919-2004 .... *11*
  Obituary *153*
Farjeon, Eleanor 1881-1965 .... *2*
  See also CLR *34*
Farley, Carol (J.) 1936- *137*
  Earlier sketch in SATA *4*
Farley, Terri *165*
Farley, Walter (Lorimer) 1915-1989 .... *132*
  Earlier sketches in SATA *2, 43*
Farlow, James O(rville, Jr.) 1951- *75*
Farmer, Nancy 1941- *161*
  Earlier sketches in SATA *79, 117*
Farmer, Patti 1948- *79*
Farmer, Penelope (Jane) 1939- *105*
  Brief entry *39*
  Earlier sketch in SATA *40*
  See also CLR *8*
  See also SAAS *22*
Farmer, Peter 1950- *38*
Farmer, Philip Jose 1918- *93*
Farnham, Burt
  See Clifford, Harold B(urton)
Farnsworth, Bill 1958- *135*
  Earlier sketch in SATA *84*
Farquhar, Margaret C(utting) 1905-1988 .... *13*
Farquharson, Alexander 1944- *46*
Farquharson, Martha
  See Finley, Martha
Farr, Diana (Pullein-Thompson) *82*
  See Pullein-Thompson, Diana
Farr, Finis (King) 1904-1982 .... *10*
Farrar, Jill
  See Morris, Jill
Farrar, Susan Clement 1917- *33*
Farrell, Ben
  See Cebulash, Mel
Farrell, Patrick
  See Odgers, Sally Farrell
Farrell, Sally
  See Odgers, Sally Farrell
Farrer, Vashti *167*
Farrington, S(elwyn) Kip, Jr. 1904-1983 .... *20*
Farshtey, Greg(ory T.) 1965- *148*

Farthing, Alison 1936- 45
  Brief entry 36
Farthing-Knight, Catherine 1933- 92
Fassler, Joan (Grace) 1931- 11
Fast, Howard 1914-2003 7
  Autobiography Feature 107
Fast, Howard Melvin
  See Fast, Howard
Fasulo, Michael 1963- 83
Fatchen, Max 1920- 84
  Earlier sketch in SATA 20
  See also SAAS 20
Fate, Marilyn
  See Collins, Paul
Father Goose
  See Ghigna, Charles
Fatigati, (Frances) Evelyn 1948- 24
Fatio, Louise 1904-1993 6
Faulhaber, Martha 1926- 7
Faulkner, Anne Irvin 1906- 23
Faulkner, Frank
  See Ellis, Edward S(ylvester)
Faulkner, Nancy
  See Faulkner, Anne Irvin
Faulknor, Cliff(ord Vernon) 1913- 86
Favole, Robert J(ames) 1950- 125
Fax, Elton Clay 1909-1993 25
Faxon, Lavinia
  See Russ, Lavinia (Faxon)
Feagles, Anita M(acRae) 1927- 9
Feagles, Elizabeth
  See Day, Beth (Feagles)
Feague, Mildred H. 1915- 14
Fearnley, Jan 1965- 153
Fearrington, Ann (Peyton) 1945- 146
Fecher, Constance
  See Heaven, Constance (Christina)
Feder, Chris Welles 1938- 81
Feder, Harriet K. 1928- 73
Feder, Paula (Kurzband) 1935- 26
Federici, Debbie 1965- 175
Federici, Debbie Tanner
  See Federici, Debbie
Feelings, Muriel (Lavita Grey) 1938- 16
  See also CLR 5
  See also SAAS 8
Feelings, Thomas 1933-2003 8
  Obituary 148
  See Feelings, Tom
Feelings, Tom 69
  See also CLR 58
  See also SAAS 19
  See Feelings, Thomas
Fehler, Gene 1940- 74
Fehrenbach, T(heodore) R(eed, Jr.) 1925- .. 33
Feiffer, Jules 1929- 157
  Earlier sketches in SATA 8, 61, 111
Feiffer, Jules Ralph
  See Feiffer, Jules
Feiffer, Kate 1964- 170
Feig, Barbara Krane 1937- 34
Feikema, Feike
  See Manfred, Frederick (Feikema)
Feil, Hila 1942- 12
Feilen, John
  See May, Julian
Feinberg, Barbara Jane 1938- 58
  See Feinberg, Barbara Silberdick
Feinberg, Barbara Silberdick 123
  See Feinberg, Barbara Jane
Feinstein, John 1956- 163
Feldman, Anne (Rodgers) 1939- 19
Feldman, Elane 79
Felix
  See Vincent, Felix
Fell, Derek 1939- 167
Fell, Derek John
  See Fell, Derek
Fellows, Muriel H. 10
Fellows, Stan 1957- 177

Fellows, Stanley
  See Fellows, Stan
Felsen, Henry Gregor 1916-1995 1
  See also SAAS 2
Feltenstein, Arlene (H.) 1934- 119
Felton, Harold William 1902-1991 1
Felton, Ronald Oliver 1909- 3
Felts, Shirley 1934- 33
Fenderson, Lewis H., Jr. 1907-1983 47
  Obituary 37
Fenner, Carol (Elizabeth) 1929-2002 89
  Obituary 132
  Earlier sketch in SATA 7
  See also SAAS 24
Fenner, Phyllis R(eid) 1899-1982 1
  Obituary 29
Fensham, Elizabeth 169
Fenten, Barbara D(oris) 1935- 26
Fenten, D(onald) X. 1932- 4
Fenton, Carroll Lane 1900-1969 5
Fenton, Edward 1917-1995 7
  Obituary 89
Fenton, Mildred Adams 1899-1995 21
Fenwick, Patti
  See Grider, Dorothy
Feravolo, Rocco Vincent 1922- 10
Ferber, Edna 1887-1968 7
Fergus, Charles 114
Ferguson, Alane 1957- 85
Ferguson, Bob
  See Ferguson, Robert Bruce
Ferguson, Cecil 1931- 45
Ferguson, Robert Bruce 1927-2001 13
Ferguson, Sarah 1959- 180
  Earlier sketches in SATA 66, 110
Ferguson, Sarah Margaret
  See Ferguson, Sarah
Ferguson, Walter (W.) 1930- 34
Fergusson, Erna 1888-1964 5
Fermi, Laura 1907-1977 6
  Obituary 28
Fern, Eugene A. 1919-1987 10
  Obituary 54
Fernandes, Eugenie 1943- 139
  Earlier sketch in SATA 77
Fernandez, Laura 1960- 171
Ferrari, Maria 123
Ferreiro, Carmen 1958- 158
Ferrell, Nancy Warren 1932- 70
Ferrier, Lucy
  See Penzler, Otto
Ferris, Helen Josephine 1890-1969 21
Ferris, James Cody 1
  See McFarlane, Leslie (Charles)
Ferris, Jean 1939- 149
  Brief entry 50
  Earlier sketches in SATA 56, 105
Ferris, Jeri Chase 1937- 84
Ferry, Charles 1927- 92
  Earlier sketch in SATA 43
  See also CLR 34
  See also SAAS 20
Fetz, Ingrid 1915- 30
Feydy, Anne Lindbergh
  Brief entry 32
  See Sapieyevski, Anne Lindbergh
Fiammenghi, Gioia 1929- 66
  Earlier sketch in SATA 9
Fiarotta, Noel 15
  See Ficarotta, Noel
Fiarotta, Phyllis 15
  See Ficarotta, Phyllis
Fichter, George S. 1922-1993 7
Fidler, Kathleen (Annie) 1899-1980 87
  Obituary 45
  Earlier sketch in SATA 3
Fiedler, Jean(nette Feldman) 4
Fiedler, Joseph Daniel 159
Field, Dorothy 1944- 97
Field, Edward 1924- 109
  Earlier sketch in SATA 8

Field, Eugene 1850-1895 16
Field, Gans T.
  See Wellman, Manly Wade
Field, James 1959- 113
Field, Peter
  See Drago, Harry Sinclair
  and Dresser, Davis
  and Mann, E(dward) B(everly)
Field, Rachel (Lyman) 1894-1942 15
  See also CLR 21
Fielding, Kate
  See Oldfield, Jenny
Fienberg, Anna 1956- 112
Fife, Dale (Odile Hollerbach) 1901- 18
Fighter Pilot, A
  See Johnston, H(ugh) A(nthony) S(tephen)
Figler, Jeanie 1949- 123
Figley, Marty Rhodes 1948- 158
  Earlier sketch in SATA 88
Figueredo, D(anilo) H. 1951- 155
Figueroa, Pablo 1938- 9
Fijan, Carol 1918- 12
Filderman, Diane E(lizabeth) 1959- 87
Files, Meg 1946- 107
Fillmore, Parker H(oysted) 1878-1944
  See YABC 1
Filstrup, Chris
  See Filstrup, E(dward) Christian
Filstrup, E(dward) Christian 1942- 43
Finchler, Judy 1943- 93
Finder, Martin
  See Salzmann, Siegmund
Findlay, Jamieson 1958- 169
Findon, Joanne 1957- 161
Fine, Anne 1947- 160
  Earlier sketches in SATA 29, 72, 111
  See also CLR 25
  See also SAAS 15
Fine, Edith Hope 169
Fine, Howard 1961- 181
Fine, Jane
  See Ziefert, Harriet
Finger, Charles J(oseph) 1869(?)-1941 42
Fink, William B(ertrand) 1916- 22
Finke, Blythe Foote 1922- 26
Finkel, George (Irvine) 1909-1975 8
Finkelstein, Norman H. 1941- 137
  Earlier sketch in SATA 73
Finlay, Alice Sullivan 1946- 82
Finlay, Winifred Lindsay Crawford
  (McKissack) 1910-1989 23
Finlayson, Ann 1925- 8
Finley, Martha 1828-1909 43
Finley, Mary Peace 1942- 83
Finney, Jack 109
  See Finney, Walter Braden
Finney, Patricia 1958- 163
Finney, Shan 1944- 65
Firer, Ben Zion
  See Firer, Benzion
Firer, Benzion 1914- 64
Fireside, Bryna J. 1932- 73
Firmin, Charlotte 1954- 29
Firmin, Peter 1928- 58
  Earlier sketch in SATA 15
Firth, Barbara 179
Fischbach, Julius 1894-1988 10
Fischer, John
  See Fluke, Joanne
Fischer, R.J.
  See Fluke, Joanne
Fischer-Nagel, Andreas 1951- 56
Fischer-Nagel, Heiderose 1956- 56
Fischler, Shirley (Walton) 66
Fischler, Stan(ley I.) 66
  Brief entry 36
Fisher, Aileen (Lucia) 1906-2002 73
  Obituary 143
  Earlier sketches in SATA 1, 25
  See also CLR 49

Fisher, Barbara 1940- *44*
  Brief entry *34*
Fisher, Carolyn 1968- *154*
Fisher, Catherine 1957- *155*
Fisher, Chris 1958- *80*
Fisher, Clavin C(argill) 1912- *24*
Fisher, Dorothy (Frances) Canfield 1879-1958
  See YABC *1*
  See also CLR *71*
Fisher, Gary L. 1949- *86*
Fisher, John (Oswald Hamilton) 1909- *15*
Fisher, Laura Harrison 1934- *5*
Fisher, Leonard Everett 1924- *176*
  Autobiography Feature *122*
  Earlier sketches in SATA *4, 34, 73, 120*
  See also CLR *18*
  See also SAAS *1*
Fisher, Lois I. 1948- *38*
  Brief entry *35*
Fisher, Margery (Turner) 1913-1992 .... *20*
  Obituary *74*
Fisher, Marshall Jon 1963- *113*
Fisher, Nikki
  See Strachan, Ian
Fisher, Robert (Tempest) 1943- *47*
Fisher, Suzanne
  See Staples, Suzanne Fisher
Fisher, Valorie *177*
Fishman, Cathy Goldberg 1951- *106*
Fisk, Nicholas *25*
  See Higginbottom, David
Fisk, Pauline 1948- *160*
  Earlier sketch in SATA *66*
Fiske, Tarleton
  See Bloch, Robert (Albert)
Fisscher, Catharina G. M. 1958- *142*
Fisscher, Tiny
  See Fisscher, Catharina G. M.
Fitch, Clarke
  See Sinclair, Upton
Fitch, John IV
  See Cormier, Robert
Fitch, Sheree 1956- *178*
  Earlier sketch in SATA *108*
Fitschen, Dale 1937- *20*
Fitzalan, Roger
  See Trevor, Elleston
Fitzgerald, Captain Hugh
  See Baum, L(yman) Frank
Fitzgerald, Dawn *175*
Fitzgerald, Edward Earl 1919-2001 .... *20*
Fitzgerald, F(rancis) A(nthony) 1940- *15*
Fitzgerald, John D(ennis) 1907(?)-1988 .... *20*
  Obituary *56*
  See also CLR *1*
Fitzgerald, Merni Ingrassia 1955- *53*
Fitzgibbon, Terry 1948- *121*
Fitzhardinge, Joan Margaret 1912- *73*
  Earlier sketch in SATA *2*
  See Phipson, Joan
Fitzhugh, Louise (Perkins) 1928-1974 .... *45*
  Obituary *24*
  Earlier sketch in SATA *1*
  See also CLR *72*
Fitzhugh, Percy Keese 1876-1950 .... *65*
Fitzpatrick, Marie-Louise 1962- *125*
FitzRalph, Matthew
  See McInerny, Ralph
Fitz-Randolph, Jane (Currens) 1915- *51*
Fitzsimons, Cecilia 1952- *97*
Fitzsimons, Cecilia A.L.
  See Fitzsimons, Cecilia
Flack, Marjorie 1897-1958 .... *100*
  See also YABC *2*
  See also CLR *28*
Flack, Naomi John White -1999 .... *40*
  Brief entry *35*
Flake, Sharon G. *166*
Flanagan, John 1944- *180*
Flanagan, John Anthony
  See Flanagan, John

Flannery, Kate
  See De Goldi, Kathleen Domenica
Flatt, Lizann
  See Brunskill, Elizabeth Ann Flatt
Fleagle, Gail S(hatto) 1940- *117*
Fleetwood, Jenni 1947- *80*
Fleischer, Jane
  See Oppenheim, Joanne
Fleischhauer-Hardt, Helga 1936- *30*
Fleischman, Albert Sidney
  See Fleischman, Sid
Fleischman, John 1948- *145*
Fleischman, Paul 1952- *156*
  Brief entry *32*
  Earlier sketches in SATA *39, 72, 110*
  See also CLR *66*
  See also SAAS *20*
Fleischman, Sid 1920- *148*
  Earlier sketches in SATA *8, 59, 96*
  See also CLR *15*
Fleischner, Jennifer 1956- *93*
Fleisher, Paul 1948- *132*
  Earlier sketch in SATA *81*
Fleisher, Robbin 1951-1977 .... *52*
  Brief entry *49*
Fleishman, Seymour 1918- *66*
  Brief entry *32*
Fleming, A. A.
  See Arthur, Robert, (Jr.)
Fleming, Alice Mulcahey 1928- *9*
Fleming, Candace 1962- *143*
  Earlier sketch in SATA *94*
Fleming, Denise 1950- *173*
  Earlier sketches in SATA *81, 126*
Fleming, Ian 1908-1964 .... *9*
Fleming, Ian Lancaster
  See Fleming, Ian
Fleming, Ronald Lee 1941- *56*
Fleming, Sally
  See Walker, Sally M(acArt)
Fleming, Stuart
  See Knight, Damon (Francis)
Fleming, Susan 1932- *32*
Fleming, Thomas 1927- *8*
Fleming, Thomas James
  See Fleming, Thomas
Fleming, Virginia (Edwards) 1923- *84*
Flesch, Y.
  See Flesch, Yolande (Catarina)
Flesch, Yolande (Catarina) 1950- *55*
Fletcher, Charlie May Hogue 1897-1977 .... *3*
Fletcher, Colin 1922-2007 .... *28*
Fletcher, Dirk
  See Cunningham, Chet
Fletcher, George U.
  See Pratt, (Murray) Fletcher
Fletcher, Helen Jill 1910- *13*
Fletcher, Ralph (J.) 1953- *149*
  Earlier sketch in SATA *105*
  See also CLR *104*
Fletcher, Susan 1951- *181*
  Earlier sketches in SATA *70, 110*
Fletcher, Susan Clemens
  See Fletcher, Susan
Fleur, Paul
  See Pohl, Frederik
Flexner, James Thomas 1908-2003 .... *9*
Flinn, Alex 1966- *159*
Flint, Helen 1952- *102*
Flint, Russ 1944- *74*
Flitner, David P(erkins), Jr. 1949- *7*
Floca, Brian *155*
Floethe, Louise Lee 1913-1988 .... *4*
Floethe, Richard 1901-1998 .... *4*
Floherty, John Joseph 1882-1964 .... *25*
Flood, Bo
  See Flood, Nancy Bo
Flood, Nancy Bo 1945- *130*
Flood, Pansie Hart 1964- *140*
Flood, William 1942- *129*

Flooglebuckle, Al
  See Spiegelman, Art
Flora, James (Royer) 1914-1998 .... *30*
  Obituary *103*
  Earlier sketch in SATA *1*
  See also SAAS *6*
Florian, Douglas 1950- *177*
  Earlier sketches in SATA *19, 83, 125*
Flory, Jane Trescott 1917- *22*
Flournoy, Valerie 1952- *95*
Flournoy, Valerie Rose
  See Flournoy, Valerie
Flowerdew, Phyllis -1994 .... *33*
Flowers, Pam 1946- *136*
Flowers, Sarah 1952- *98*
Floyd, Gareth 1940- *62*
  Brief entry *31*
Fluchere, Henri 1914-1991 .... *40*
Fluke, Joanne *88*
Flutsztejn-Gruda, Ilona 1930- *170*
Flynn, Barbara 1928- *9*
Flynn, Jackson
  See Bensen, Donald R.
  and Shirreffs, Gordon D(onald)
Flynn, Nicholas
  See Odgers, Sally Farrell
Flynn, Rachel 1953- *171*
  Earlier sketch in SATA *109*
Flynn, Warren (G.) 1950- *154*
Fodor, R(onald) V(ictor) 1944- *25*
Fogelin, Adrian 1951- *175*
  Earlier sketch in SATA *129*
Foley, (Anna) Bernice Williams 1902-1987
  .... *28*
Foley, June 1944- *44*
Foley, (Mary) Louise Munro 1933- *106*
  Brief entry *40*
  Earlier sketch in SATA *54*
Folke, Will
  See Bloch, Robert (Albert)
Folsom, Franklin (Brewster) 1907-1995 .... *5*
  Obituary *88*
Folsom, Michael (Brewster) 1938-1990 ...... *40*
  Obituary *88*
Fontenot, Mary Alice 1910- *91*
  Earlier sketch in SATA *34*
Fontes, Justine *172*
Foon, Dennis 1951- *119*
Fooner, Michael *22*
Foote, Timothy (Gilson) 1926- *52*
Forberg, Ati *22*
  See Forberg, Beate Gropius
Forbes, Anna 1954- *101*
Forbes, Bryan 1926- *37*
Forbes, Cabot L.
  See Hoyt, Edwin P(almer), Jr.
Forbes, Esther 1891-1967 .... *100*
  Earlier sketch in SATA *2*
  See also CLR *27*
Forbes, Graham B. *1*
Forbes, Kathryn
  See McLean, Kathryn (Anderson)
Forbes, Robert
  See Arthur, Robert, (Jr.)
Ford, Albert Lee
  See Stratemeyer, Edward L.
Ford, Barbara *56*
  Brief entry *34*
Ford, Brian J(ohn) 1939- *49*
Ford, Carolyn (Mott) 1938- *98*
Ford, Christine 1953- *176*
Ford, Elbur
  See Hibbert, Eleanor Alice Burford
Ford, Ellen 1949- *89*
Ford, George (Jr.) *31*
Ford, Hilary
  See Youd, (Christopher) Samuel
Ford, Hildegarde
  See Morrison, Velma Ford
Ford, Jerome W. 1949- *78*

Ford, Jerry
See Ford, Jerome W.
Ford, Juwanda G(ertrude) 1967- *102*
Ford, Marcia
See Radford, Ruby L(orraine)
Ford, Peter 1936- *59*
Ford, S. M.
See Uhlig, Susan
Forde, Catherine 1961- *170*
Foreman, Michael 1938- *135*
Earlier sketches in SATA *2, 73, 129*
See also CLR *32*
See also SAAS *21*
Foreman, Wilmoth 1939- *153*
Forest, Dial
See Gault, William Campbell
Forest, Heather 1948- *120*
Forester, C(ecil) S(cott) 1899-1966 .... *13*
Forman, Brenda 1936- *4*
Forman, James
See Forman, James D.
Forman, James D. 1932- *70*
Earlier sketch in SATA *8*
Forman, James Douglas
See Forman, James D.
Forrest, Elizabeth
See Salsitz, Rhondi Vilott
Forrest, Mary
See Pausacker, Jenny
Forrest, Sybil
See Markun, Patricia Maloney
Forrestal, Elaine 1941- *165*
Earlier sketch in SATA *117*
Forrester, Helen *48*
See Bhatia, Jamunadevi
Forrester, Jade
See Pausacker, Jenny
Forrester, Marian
See Schachtel, Roger
Forrester, Sandra 1949- *166*
Earlier sketch in SATA *90*
Forrester, Victoria 1940- *40*
Brief entry *35*
Forsee, (Frances) Aylesa -1986 .... *1*
Forsey, Chris 1950- *59*
Forshay-Lunsford, Cin 1965- *60*
Forster, E(dward) M(organ) 1879-1970 ...... *57*
Forsyth, Kate 1966- *154*
Fort, Paul
See Stockton, Francis Richard
Forte, Maurizio 1961- *110*
Fortey, Richard (Alan) 1946- *109*
Forth, Melissa D(eal) *96*
Fortnum, Peggy *26*
See Nuttall-Smith, Margaret Emily Noel
Forward, Robert L(ull) 1932-2002 .... *82*
Foster, Alan Dean 1946- *70*
Foster, Brad W. 1955- *34*
Foster, Doris Van Liew 1899-1993 .... *10*
Foster, E(lizabeth) C(onnell) 1902- *9*
Foster, Elizabeth 1902- *12*
Foster, Elizabeth 1905-1963 .... *10*
Foster, F. Blanche 1919- *11*
Foster, G(eorge) Allen 1907-1969 .... *26*
Foster, Genevieve (Stump) 1893-1979 .... *2*
Obituary *23*
See also CLR *7*
Foster, Hal
See Foster, Harold (Rudolf)
Foster, Harold (Rudolf) 1892-1982 .... *31*
See Foster, Hal
Foster, Jeanne
See Williams, Jeanne
Foster, John
See Foster, John L(ouis)
and Furcolo, Foster
Foster, John (Thomas) 1925- *8*
Foster, John L(ouis) 1941- *102*
Foster, Laura Louise (James) 1918- *6*
Foster, Leila Merrell 1929- *73*
Foster, Lynne 1937- *74*

Foster, Marian Curtis 1909-1978 .... *23*
Foster, Sally *58*
Foulds, E. V.
See Foulds, Elfrida Vipont
Foulds, Elfrida Vipont 1902-1992 .... *52*
See Vipont, Elfrida
Fountas, Angela Jane *180*
Fourie, Corlia 1944- *91*
Fourth Brother, The
See Aung, (Maung) Htin
Fowke, Edith (Margaret) 1913-1996 .... *14*
Fowles, John 1926-2005 .... *22*
Obituary *171*
Fowles, John Robert
See Fowles, John
Fox, Aileen 1907-2005 .... *58*
Obituary *170*
Fox, Aileen Mary
See Fox, Aileen
Fox, Annie 1950- *175*
Fox, Charles Philip 1913-2003 .... *12*
Obituary *150*
Fox, Eleanor
See St. John, Wylly Folk
Fox, Freeman
See Hamilton, Charles (Harold St. John)
Fox, Geoffrey 1941- *73*
Fox, Grace
See Anderson, Grace Fox
Fox, Helen 1962- *181*
Fox, Larry *30*
Fox, Lorraine 1922-1976 .... *27*
Earlier sketch in SATA *11*
Fox, Louisa
See Kroll, Virginia L.
Fox, Mary Virginia 1919- *152*
Brief entry *39*
Earlier sketches in SATA *44, 88*
Fox, Mem *103*
See also CLR *23*
See Fox, Merrion Frances
Fox, Merrion Frances 1946- *155*
Earlier sketch in SATA *51*
See also CLR *80*
See Fox, Mem
Fox, Michael W(ilson) 1937- *15*
Fox, Paula 1923- *167*
Earlier sketches in SATA *17, 60, 120*
See also CLR *96*
Fox, Robert J. 1927- *33*
Fradin, Dennis
See Fradin, Dennis Brindell
Fradin, Dennis Brindell 1945- *135*
Earlier sketches in SATA *29, 90*
Fradin, Judith (Bernette) Bloom 1945- *152*
Earlier sketch in SATA *90*
Frailey, Paige (Menefee) 1965- *82*
Frame, Janet
See Clutha, Janet Paterson Frame
Frame, Paul 1913-1994 .... *60*
Brief entry *33*
Obituary *83*
Frances, Miss
See Horwich, Frances R(appaport)
Franchere, Ruth *18*
Francis, Charles
See Holme, Bryan
Francis, Dee
See Haas, Dorothy F.
Francis, Dorothy Brenner 1926- *127*
Earlier sketch in SATA *10*
Francis, Jaye
See Pausacker, Jenny
Francis, Pamela (Mary) 1926- *11*
Franck, Eddie
See Cooke, Frank E.
Franco, Betsy *150*
Franco, Eloise (Bauder) 1910- *62*
Franco, Johan (Henri Gustave) 1908-1988 .. *62*
Franco, Marjorie *38*
Francois, Andre 1915-2005 .... *25*

Francoise
See Seignobosc, Francoise
Frank, Anne(lies Marie) 1929-1945 .... *87*
Brief entry *42*
See also CLR *101*
Frank, Daniel B. 1956- *55*
Frank, Emily R.
See Frank, E.R.
Frank, E.R. 1967- *157*
Frank, Helene
See Vautier, Ghislaine
Frank, Hillary 1976- *148*
Frank, Josette 1893-1989 .... *10*
Obituary *63*
Frank, Lucy 1947- *166*
Earlier sketch in SATA *94*
Frank, Mary 1933- *34*
Frank, R., Jr.
See Ross, Frank (Xavier), Jr.
Frankau, Mary Evelyn Atkinson 1899-1974 . *4*
Frankel, Alona 1937- *66*
Frankel, Bernice *9*
Frankel, Edward 1910- *44*
Frankel, Ellen 1951- *78*
Frankel, Julie 1947- *40*
Brief entry *34*
Frankenberg, Robert 1911- *22*
Franklin, Cheryl J. 1955- *70*
Franklin, Harold 1926- *13*
Franklin, Kristine L. 1958- *124*
Earlier sketch in SATA *80*
Franklin, Lance
See Lantz, Francess L(in)
Franklin, Max
See Deming, Richard
Franklin, Steve
See Stevens, Franklin
Franson, Leanne R. 1963- *111*
Franzen, Nils-Olof 1916- *10*
Frascino, Edward *48*
Brief entry *33*
See also SAAS *9*
Frasconi, Antonio 1919- *131*
Earlier sketches in SATA *6, 53*
See also SAAS *11*
Fraser, Betty
See Fraser, Elizabeth Marr
Fraser, Elizabeth Marr 1928- *31*
Fraser, Eric (George) 1902-1983 .... *38*
Fraser, Mary Ann 1959- *137*
Earlier sketch in SATA *76*
See also SAAS *23*
Fraser, Wynnette (McFaddin) 1925- *90*
Frasier, Debra 1953- *112*
Earlier sketch in SATA *69*
Fraustino, Lisa Rowe 1961- *146*
Autobiography Feature *146*
Earlier sketch in SATA *84*
Frazee, Marla 1958- *151*
Earlier sketch in SATA *105*
Frazetta, Frank 1928- *58*
Frazier, Craig 1955- *177*
Frazier, Neta (Osborn) Lohnes 1890-1990 .... *7*
Frederic, Mike
See Cox, William R(obert)
Fredericks, Anthony D. 1947- *113*
Freed, Alvyn M. 1913-1993 .... *22*
Freedman, Benedict 1919- *27*
Freedman, Jeff 1953- *90*
Freedman, Nancy 1920- *27*
Freedman, Russell 1929- *175*
Earlier sketches in SATA *16, 71, 123*
See also CLR *71*
Freedman, Russell Bruce
See Freedman, Russell
Freeman, Barbara C(onstance) 1906- *28*
Freeman, Bill
See Freeman, William Bradford
Freeman, Don 1908-1978 .... *17*
See also CLR *90*
Freeman, Ira Maximilian 1905-1987 .... *21*

Freeman, Lucy (Greenbaum) 1916-2004 24
Freeman, Mae (Blacker) 1907- 25
Freeman, Marcia S. 1937- 102
Freeman, Martha 1956- 152
　Earlier sketch in SATA *101*
Freeman, Nancy 1932- 61
Freeman, Peter J.
　See Calvert, Patricia
Freeman, Sarah (Caroline) 1940- 66
Freeman, Tor 1977- 164
Freeman, VicToria
　See Freeman, Tor
Freeman, William Bradford 1938- 58
　Brief entry 48
Fregosi, Claudia (Anne Marie) 1946- 24
French, Allen 1870-1946
　See YABC *1*
French, Dorothy Kayser 1926- 5
French, Fiona 1944- 132
　Earlier sketches in SATA *6, 75*
　See also CLR *37*
　See also SAAS *21*
French, Jackie 139
　Autobiography Feature 139
　Earlier sketch in SATA *108*
　See French, Jacqueline Anne
French, Kathryn
　See Mosesson, Gloria R(ubin)
French, Martin 176
French, Michael 1944- 49
　Brief entry 38
French, Paul
　See Asimov, Isaac
French, Simon 1957- 147
　Earlier sketch in SATA *86*
French, Vivian 165
Frenette, Liza 126
Freschet, Gina 1960- 175
　Earlier sketch in SATA *139*
Frewer, Glyn (M.) 1931- 11
Frey, Darcy 98
Freymann, Saxton 1958(?)- 178
Freymann-Weyr, (Rhoda) Garret (Michaela)
　1965- 145
Frick, C. H.
　See Irwin, Constance (H.) Frick
Frick, Constance
　See Irwin, Constance (H.) Frick
Fricke, Aaron 1962- 89
Fridell, Ron 1943- 124
Friedlander, Joanne K(ohn) 1930- 9
Friedman, D. Dina 1957- 180
Friedman, Debra 1955- 150
Friedman, Estelle (Ehrenwald) 1920- 7
Friedman, Frieda 1905- 43
Friedman, Ina R(osen) 1926- 136
　Brief entry 41
　Earlier sketch in SATA *49*
Friedman, Jerrold David
　See Gerrold, David
Friedman, Judi 1935- 59
Friedman, Laurie 1964- 179
　Earlier sketch in SATA *138*
Friedman, Marvin 1930- 42
　Brief entry 33
Friedman, Robin 1968- 162
Friedmann, Stan 1953- 80
Friedrich, Otto (Alva) 1929-1995 33
Friedrich, Priscilla 1927- 39
Friendlich, Dick
　See Friendlich, Richard J.
Friendlich, Richard J. 1909- 11
Friermood, Elisabeth Hamilton 1903-1992 ... 5
Friesen, Bernice (Sarah Anne) 1966- 105
Friesen, Gayle 1960- 109
Friesner, Esther M. 1951- 168
　Earlier sketch in SATA *71*
Friis-Baastad, Babbis Ellinor 1921-1970 7
Frimmer, Steven 1928- 31
Frischmuth, Barbara 1941- 114
Friskey, Margaret (Richards) 1901-1995 5

Fritts, Mary Bahr
　See Bahr, Mary (Madelyn)
Fritz, Jean (Guttery) 1915- 163
　Autobiography Feature 122
　Earlier sketches in SATA *1, 29, 72, 119*
　See also CLR *96*
　See also SAAS *2*
Froehlich, Margaret W(alden) 1930- 56
Frois, Jeanne 1953- 73
Froissart, Jean 1338(?)-1410(?) 28
Froman, Elizabeth Hull 1920-1975 10
Froman, Robert (Winslow) 1917- 8
Fromm, Lilo 1928- 29
Frommer, Harvey 1937- 41
Frost, A(rthur) B(urdett) 1851-1928 19
Frost, Elizabeth
　See Frost-Knappman, Elizabeth
Frost, Erica
　See Supraner, Robyn
Frost, Helen 1949- 157
Frost, Lesley 1899-1983 14
　Obituary 34
Frost, Robert 1874-1963 14
　See also CLR *67*
Frost, Robert Lee
　See Frost, Robert
Frost, Shelley 1960- 138
Frost-Knappman, Elizabeth 1943- 179
Froud, Brian 1947- 150
Fry, Annette R(iley) 89
Fry, Christopher 1907-2005 66
Fry, Edward Bernard 1925- 35
Fry, Rosalie Kingsmill 1911-1992 3
　See also SAAS *11*
Fry, Virginia Lynn 1952- 95
Frye, Sally
　See Moore, Elaine
Fuchs, Bernie 1932- 162
　Earlier sketch in SATA *95*
Fuchs, Erich 1916- 6
Fuchshuber, Annegert 1940- 43
Fuerst, Jeffrey B. 1956- 143
Fuertes, Gloria 1918-1998 115
Fuge, Charles 1966- 144
　Earlier sketch in SATA *74*
Fujikawa, Gyo 1908-1998 76
　Brief entry 30
　Obituary 110
　Earlier sketch in SATA *39*
　See also CLR *25*
　See also SAAS *16*
Fujita, Tamao 1905-1999 7
Fujiwara, Kim 1957- 81
Fujiwara, Michiko 1946- 15
Fuller, Catherine Leuthold 1916- 9
Fuller, Edmund (Maybank) 1914- 21
Fuller, Iola
　See McCoy, Iola Fuller
Fuller, John G(rant, Jr.) 1913-1990 65
Fuller, Kathleen
　See Gottfried, Theodore Mark
Fuller, Lois Hamilton 1915- 11
Fuller, Margaret
　See Ossoli, Sarah Margaret (Fuller)
Fuller, Maud
　See Petersham, Maud (Sylvia Fuller)
Fuller, Roy (Broadbent) 1912-1991 87
Fuller, Sarah Margaret
　See Ossoli, Sarah Margaret (Fuller)
Fuller, Sarah Margaret
　See Ossoli, Sarah Margaret (Fuller)
Fults, John Lee 1932- 33
Funk, Thompson 1911- 7
Funk, Tom
　See Funk, Thompson
Funke, Cornelia 1958- 174
　Earlier sketch in SATA *154*
Funke, Cornelia Caroline
　See Funke, Cornelia
Funke, Lewis 1912-1992 11
Fuqua, Jonathon Scott 1966- 141

Furbee, Mary R.
　See Furbee, Mary Rodd
Furbee, Mary Rodd 1954- 138
Furchgott, Terry 1948- 29
Furlong, Monica (Mavis) 1930-2003 86
　Obituary 142
Furman, Gertrude Lerner Kerman 1909- 21
Furniss, Tim 1948- 49
Furrow, Robert 1985- 172
Furukawa, Toshi 1924- 24
Fusillo, Archimede 1962- 137
Futcher, Jane P. 1947- 76
Fyleman, Rose (Amy) 1877-1957 21
Fyson, J(enny) G(race) 1904- 42

G

Gaan, Margaret 1914- 65
Gaber, Susan 1956- 169
　Earlier sketch in SATA *115*
Gaberman, Judie Angell 1937- 78
　Earlier sketch in SATA *22*
　See also CLR *33*
Gabhart, Ann 1947- 75
Gabler, Mirko 1951- 77
Gabriel, Adriana
　See Rojany, Lisa
Gabrys, Ingrid Schubert
　See Schubert-Gabrys, Ingrid
Gackenbach, Dick 1927- 79
　Brief entry 30
　Earlier sketch in SATA *48*
Gadd, Jeremy 1949- 116
Gaddis, Vincent H. 1913-1997 35
Gadler, Steve J. 1905-1985 36
Gaeddert, Lou Ann (Bigge) 1931- 103
　Earlier sketch in SATA *20*
Gaeddert, Louann
　See Gaeddert, Lou Ann (Bigge)
Gaer, Joseph 1897-1969 118
Gaer, Yossef
　See Gaer, Joseph
Gaetz, Dayle Campbell 1947- 138
Gaffney, Timothy R. 1951- 170
　Earlier sketch in SATA *69*
Gaffron, Norma (Bondeson) 1931- 97
Gag, Wanda (Hazel) 1893-1946 100
　See also YABC *1*
　See also CLR *4*
Gage, Brian 162
Gage, Wilson
　See Steele, Mary Q(uintard Govan)
Gagliano, Eugene M. 1946- 150
Gagnon, Cecile 1936- 58
Gaiman, Neil 1960- 146
　Earlier sketch in SATA *85*
　See also CLR *109*
Gaiman, Neil Richard
　See Gaiman, Neil
Gainer, Cindy 1962- 74
Gaines, Ernest J. 1933- 86
　See also CLR *62*
Gaines, Ernest James
　See Gaines, Ernest J.
Gaither, Gloria 1942- 127
Gal, Laszlo 1933- 96
　Brief entry 32
　Earlier sketch in SATA *52*
　See also CLR *61*
Galbraith, Kathryn O(sebold) 1945- 85
Galdone, Paul 1907(?)-1986 66
　Obituary 49
　Earlier sketch in SATA *17*
　See also CLR *16*
Galinsky, Ellen 1942- 23
Gall, Chris 1961- 176
Gallagher, Diana G. 1946- 153
Gallagher, Lurlene Nora
　See McDaniel, Lurlene

Gallant, Roy A(rthur) 1924- 110
  Earlier sketches in SATA *4, 68*
  See also CLR *30*
Gallardo, Evelyn 1948- 78
Gallaz, Christophe 1948- 162
Gallego Garcia, Laura 1977- 173
Gallico, Paul (William) 1897-1976 13
Gallo, Donald R. 1938- 112
  Autobiography Feature 104
Gallo, Donald Robert
  See Gallo, Donald R.
Galloway, Owateka (S.) 1981- 121
Galloway, Priscilla 1930- 112
  Earlier sketch in SATA *66*
Gallup, Joan 1957- 128
Galouchko, Annouchka Gravel 1960- 95
Galt, Thomas Franklin, Jr. 1908-1989 5
Galt, Tom
  See Galt, Thomas Franklin, Jr.
Galvin, Matthew R. 1950- 93
Galvin, Matthew Reppert
  See Galvin, Matthew R.
Gamble, Kim 1952- 124
  Earlier sketch in SATA *81*
Gambrell, Jamey 82
Gamerman, Martha 1941- 15
Gammell, Stephen 1943- 128
  Earlier sketches in SATA *53, 81*
  See also CLR *83*
Ganly, Helen (Mary) 1940- 56
Gannett, Ruth Chrisman (Arens) 1896-1979
  33
Gannett, Ruth Stiles 1923- 3
Gannon, Robert Haines 1931- 8
Gano, Lila 1949- 76
Gans, Roma 1894-1996 45
  Obituary 93
Gant, Matthew
  See Hano, Arnold
Gantner, Susan (Verble) 1939- 63
Gantos, Jack 1951- 169
  Earlier sketches in SATA *20, 81, 119*
  See also CLR *85*
Gantos, John Bryan, Jr.
  See Gantos, Jack
Ganz, Yaffa 1938- 61
  Brief entry 52
Garafano, Marie 1942- 84
Garant, Andre J. 1968- 123
Garbe, Ruth Moore
  See Moore, Ruth (Ellen)
Garcia, Yolanda P. 1952- 113
Garcia, Yolanda Pacheco
  See Garcia, Yolanda P.
Gard, Janice
  See Latham, Jean Lee
Gard, Joyce
  See Reeves, Joyce
Gard, Robert Edward 1910-1992 18
  Obituary 74
Gardam, Jane (Mary) 1928- 130
  Brief entry 28
  Earlier sketches in SATA *39, 76*
  See also CLR *12*
  See also SAAS *9*
Gardella, Tricia 1944- 96
Garden, Nancy 1938- 147
  Autobiography Feature 147
  Earlier sketches in SATA *12, 77, 114*
  See also CLR *51*
  See also SAAS *8*
Gardiner, John Reynolds 1944-2006 64
  Obituary 174
Gardiner, Lindsey 1971- 144
Gardner, Craig Shaw 1949- 99
Gardner, Dic
  See Gardner, Richard (M.)
Gardner, Graham 159
Gardner, Jane Mylum 1946- 83
Gardner, Jeanne LeMonnier 1925- 5

Gardner, John, Jr. 1933-1982 40
  Obituary 31
Gardner, John Champlin, Jr.
  See Gardner, John, Jr.
Gardner, Martin 1914- 142
  Earlier sketch in SATA *16*
Gardner, Miriam
  See Bradley, Marion Zimmer
Gardner, Richard (M.) 1931- 24
Gardner, Richard A(lan) 1931-2003 13
  Obituary 144
Gardner, Sally 177
Gardner, Sandra 1940- 70
Gardner, Scot 1968- 143
Gardner, Sheldon 1934- 33
Gardner, Ted
  See Gardner, Theodore Roosevelt II
Gardner, Theodore Roosevelt II 1934- 84
Garelick, May 1910-1989 19
Garfield, James B. 1881-1984 6
  Obituary 38
Garfield, Leon 1921-1996 76
  Obituary 90
  Earlier sketches in SATA *1, 32*
  See also CLR *21*
Garis, Howard R(oger) 1873-1962 13
Garland, Mark 1953- 79
Garland, Mark A.
  See Garland, Mark
Garland, Michael 1952- 168
Garland, Sarah 1944- 135
  Earlier sketch in SATA *62*
Garland, Sherry 1948- 145
  Autobiography Feature 145
  Earlier sketches in SATA *73, 114*
Garner, Alan 1934- 69
  Autobiography Feature 108
  Earlier sketch in SATA *18*
  See also CLR *20*
Garner, David 1958- 78
Garner, Eleanor Ramrath 1930- 122
Garner, James Finn 1960(?)- 92
Garnet, A. H.
  See Slote, Alfred
Garnett, Eve C. R. 1900-1991 3
  Obituary 70
Garou, Louis P.
  See Bowkett, Stephen
Garraty, John A(rthur) 1920- 23
Garren, Devorah-Leah
  See Devorah-Leah
Garret, Maxwell R. 1917- 39
Garretson, Victoria Diane 1945- 44
Garrett, Helen 1895- 21
Garrett, Richard 1920- 82
Garrigue, Sheila 1931- 21
Garrison, Barbara 1931- 163
  Earlier sketch in SATA *19*
Garrison, Frederick
  See Sinclair, Upton
Garrison, Mary 1952- 146
Garrison, Webb B(lack) 1919-2000 25
Garrity, Jennifer Johnson 1961- 124
Garrity, Linda K. 1947- 128
Garst, Doris Shannon 1894-1981 1
Garst, Shannon
  See Garst, Doris Shannon
Garth, Will
  See Hamilton, Edmond
  and Kuttner, Henry
Garthwaite, Marion H(ook) 1893-1981 7
Garvie, Maureen 1944- 175
Garvie, Maureen McCallum
  See Garvie, Maureen
Gascoigne, Bamber 1935- 62
Gaskins, Pearl Fuyo 1957- 134
Gasperini, Jim 1952- 54
  Brief entry 49
Gater, Dilys 1944- 41

Gates, Doris 1901-1987 34
  Obituary 54
  Earlier sketch in SATA *1*
  See also SAAS *1*
Gates, Frieda 1933- 26
Gates, Susan 1950- 153
Gates, Viola R. 1931- 101
Gathorne-Hardy, Jonathan G. 1933- 124
  Earlier sketch in SATA *26*
Gatti, Anne 1952- 103
Gatty, Juliana Horatia
  See Ewing, Juliana (Horatia Gatty)
Gauch, Patricia Lee 1934- 80
  Earlier sketch in SATA *26*
  See also CLR *56*
  See also SAAS *21*
Gaul, Randy 1959- 63
Gault, Clare 1925- 36
Gault, Frank 1926-1982 36
  Brief entry 30
Gault, William Campbell 1910-1995 8
Gauthier, Gail 1953- 160
  Earlier sketch in SATA *118*
Gaver, Becky
  See Gaver, Rebecca
Gaver, Rebecca 1952- 20
Gavin, Jamila 1941- 125
  Earlier sketch in SATA *96*
Gay, Amelia
  See Hogarth, Grace (Weston Allen)
Gay, Kathlyn 1930- 144
  Earlier sketch in SATA *9*
Gay, Marie-Louise 1952- 179
  Earlier sketches in SATA *68, 126*
  See also CLR *27*
  See also SAAS *21*
Gay, Michel 1947- 162
Gay, Zhenya 1906-1978 19
Gaze, Gillian
  See Barklem, Jill
Gear, Kathleen M. O'Neal
  See Gear, Kathleen O'Neal
Gear, Kathleen O'Neal 1954- 166
  Earlier sketch in SATA *71*
Gear, W. Michael 1955- 166
  Earlier sketch in SATA *71*
Geary, Rick 1946- 142
Geason, Susan 1946- 122
Gedalof, Robin
  See McGrath, Robin
Gedge, Pauline (Alice) 1945- 101
Gee, Maurice 1931- 101
  Earlier sketch in SATA *46*
  See also CLR *56*
Gee, Maurice Gough
  See Gee, Maurice
Geehan, Wayne (E.) 1947- 107
Geer, Charles 1922- 42
  Brief entry 32
Geeslin, Campbell 1925- 163
  Earlier sketch in SATA *107*
Gehman, Mary W. 1923- 86
Gehr, Mary 1910(?)-1997 32
  Obituary 99
Geipel, Eileen 1932- 30
Geis, Darlene Stern 1918(?)-1999 7
  Obituary 111
Geisel, Helen 1898-1967 26
Geisel, Theodor Seuss 1904-1991 100
  Obituary 67
  Earlier sketches in SATA *1, 28, 75*
  See also CLR *100*
  See Dr. Seuss
Geisert, Arthur 1941- 171
  Brief entry 52
  Earlier sketches in SATA *56, 92, 133*
  See also CLR *87*
  See also SAAS *23*
Geisert, Arthur Frederick
  See Geisert, Arthur

Geisert, Bonnie 1942- *165*
　Earlier sketch in SATA *92*
Geldart, William 1936- *15*
Gelinas, Paul J. 1904-1996 .... *10*
Gellis, Roberta 1927- *128*
Gellis, Roberta Leah Jacobs
　See Gellis, Roberta
Gelman, Marc *112*
Gelman, Amy 1961- *72*
Gelman, Jan 1963- *58*
Gelman, Rita Golden 1937- *131*
　Brief entry *51*
　Earlier sketch in SATA *84*
Gelman, Steve 1934- *3*
Gemming, Elizabeth 1932- *11*
Gennaro, Joseph F(rancis), Jr. 1924- *53*
Gentile, Petrina 1969- *91*
Gentle, Mary 1956- *48*
Gentleman, David (William) 1930- *7*
Geoghegan, Adrienne 1962- *143*
George, Barbara
　See Katz, Bobbi
George, Emily
　See Katz, Bobbi
George, Gail
　See Katz, Bobbi
George, Jean
　See George, Jean Craighead
George, Jean Craighead 1919- *170*
　Earlier sketches in SATA *2, 68, 124*
　See also CLR *1, 80*
George, John L(othar) 1916- *2*
George, Kristine O'Connell 1954- *156*
　Earlier sketch in SATA *110*
George, Lindsay Barrett 1952- *155*
　Earlier sketch in SATA *95*
George, S(idney) C(harles) 1898- *11*
George, Sally
　See Orr, Wendy
George, Twig C. 1950- *114*
Georgiou, Constantine 1927- *7*
Georgiou, Theo
　See Odgers, Sally Farrell
Geraghty, Paul 1959- *130*
Gerard, Jean Ignace Isidore 1803-1847 .... *45*
Geras, Adele 1944- *180*
　Autobiography Feature *180*
　Earlier sketches in SATA *23, 87, 129, 173*
　See also SAAS *21*
Geras, Adele Daphne Weston
　See Geras, Adele
Gerber, Merrill Joan 1938- *170*
　Autobiography Feature *170*
　Earlier sketches in SATA *64, 127*
Gerber, Perren 1933- *104*
Gerberg, Mort 1931- *64*
Gergely, Tibor 1900-1978 .... *54*
　Obituary *20*
Geringer, Laura 1948- *164*
　Earlier sketches in SATA *29, 94*
Gerler, William R(obert) 1917-1996 .... *47*
Gerrard, Jean 1933- *51*
Gerrard, Roy 1935-1997 .... *90*
　Brief entry *45*
　Obituary *99*
　Earlier sketch in SATA *47*
　See also CLR *23*
Gerritsen, Paula 1956- *177*
Gerrold, David 1944- *144*
　Earlier sketch in SATA *66*
Gershator, David 1937- *180*
Gershator, Phillis 1942- *158*
　Earlier sketch in SATA *90*
Gerson, Corinne 1927- *37*
Gerson, Mary-Joan *136*
　Earlier sketch in SATA *79*
Gerson, Noel Bertram 1914-1988 .... *22*
　Obituary *60*

Gerstein, Mordicai 1935- *178*
　Brief entry *36*
　Earlier sketches in SATA *47, 81, 142*
　See also CLR *102*
Gertridge, Allison 1967- *132*
Gervais, Bernadette 1959- *80*
Gesner, Clark 1938-2002 .... *40*
　Obituary *143*
Gessner, Lynne 1919- *16*
Geter, Tyrone *150*
Getz, David 1957- *91*
Getzinger, Donna 1968- *128*
Gevirtz, Eliezer 1950- *49*
Gewe, Raddory
　See Gorey, Edward (St. John)
Ghan, Linda (R.) 1947- *77*
Ghent, Natale 1962- *148*
Gherman, Beverly 1934- *123*
　Earlier sketch in SATA *68*
Ghigna, Charles 1946- *153*
　Earlier sketch in SATA *108*
Giacobbe, Beppe 1953- *174*
Giambastiani, Kurt R. A. 1958- *141*
Giannini, Enzo 1946- *68*
Gibbons, Alan 1953- *124*
Gibbons, Faye 1938- *103*
　Earlier sketch in SATA *65*
Gibbons, Gail 1944- *160*
　Earlier sketches in SATA *23, 72, 104*
　See also CLR *8*
　See also SAAS *12*
Gibbons, Gail Gretchen
　See Gibbons, Gail
Gibbons, Kaye 1960- *117*
Gibbs, Adrea 1960- *126*
Gibbs, Alonzo (Lawrence) 1915-1992 .... *5*
Gibbs, Tony
　See Gibbs, Wolcott, Jr.
Gibbs, Wolcott, Jr. 1935- *40*
Giblin, James Cross 1933- *122*
　Earlier sketches in SATA *33, 75*
　See also CLR *29*
　See also SAAS *12*
Gibson, Andrew (William) 1949- *72*
Gibson, Betty 1911- *75*
Gibson, Jo
　See Fluke, Joanne
Gibson, William 1914- *66*
Gibson, William Ford
　See Gibson, William
Gidal, Nachum
　See Gidal, Tim Nachum
Gidal, Sonia (Epstein) 1922- *2*
Gidal, Tim Nachum 1909-1996 .... *2*
Gidalewitsch, Nachum
　See Gidal, Tim Nachum
Gideon, Melanie 1963- *175*
Giegling, John A(llan) 1935- *17*
Gifaldi, David 1950- *76*
Giff, Patricia Reilly 1935- *160*
　Earlier sketches in SATA *33, 70, 121*
Giffard, Hannah 1962- *83*
Gifford, Griselda 1931- *171*
　Earlier sketch in SATA *42*
Gifford, Kerri 1961- *91*
Gilbert, Ann
　See Taylor, Ann
Gilbert, Anne Yvonne 1951- *128*
Gilbert, Barbara Snow 1954- *97*
Gilbert, Frances
　See Collings, Gillian
Gilbert, Harriett 1948- *30*
Gilbert, (Agnes) Joan (Sewell) 1931- *10*
Gilbert, John (Raphael) 1926- *36*
Gilbert, Nan
　See Gilbertson, Mildred Geiger
Gilbert, Roby Goodale 1966- *90*
Gilbert, Ruth Gallard Ainsworth
　See Ainsworth, Ruth (Gallard)
Gilbert, Sara (Dulaney) 1943- *82*
　Earlier sketch in SATA *11*

Gilbert, Sheri L. *157*
Gilbert, Suzie 1956- *97*
Gilbert, W(illiam) S(chwenck) 1836-1911 .. *36*
Gilbert, Yvonne
　See Gilbert, Anne Yvonne
Gilbertson, Mildred Geiger 1908-1988 .... *2*
Gilbreath, Alice 1921- *12*
Gilbreth, Frank B(unker), Jr. 1911-2001 .... *2*
Gilchrist, Jan Spivey 1949- *130*
　Earlier sketch in SATA *72*
Gilden, Mel 1947- *97*
Giles, Gail *152*
Gilfond, Henry *2*
Gilge, Jeanette 1924- *22*
Gili, Phillida 1944- *70*
Gill, Derek (Lewis Theodore) 1919-1997 ..... *9*
Gill, Margery Jean 1925- *22*
Gill, Shelley *176*
Gill, Stephen 1932- *63*
Gillespie, Carol Ann 1951- *158*
Gillett, Mary (Bledsoe) *7*
Gillette, Henry Sampson 1915- *14*
Gillette, J(an) Lynett 1946- *103*
Gilley, Jeremy 1969- *174*
Gillham, Bill
　See Gillham, W(illiam) E(dwin) C(harles)
Gillham, W(illiam) E(dwin) C(harles) 1936-
　.. *42*
Gilliam, Stan 1946- *39*
　Brief entry *35*
Gilliland, Alexis A(rnaldus) 1931- *72*
Gilliland, (Cleburne) Hap 1918- *92*
Gilliland, Judith Heide *180*
Gillmor, Don 1954- *127*
Gilman, Esther 1925- *15*
Gilman, Laura Anne *178*
Gilman, Phoebe 1940-2002 .... *104*
　Obituary *141*
　Earlier sketch in SATA *58*
Gilmore, Iris 1900-1982 .... *22*
Gilmore, Kate 1931- *87*
Gilmore, Mary (Jean Cameron) 1865-1962
　.. *49*
Gilmore, Susan 1954- *59*
Gilpin, Stephen *177*
Gilroy, Beryl (Agatha) 1924- *80*
Gilson, Barbara
　See Gilson, Charles James Louis
Gilson, Charles James Louis 1878-1943
　See YABC *2*
Gilson, Jamie 1933- *176*
　Brief entry *34*
　Earlier sketches in SATA *37, 91*
Ginsburg, Mirra 1909-2000 .... *92*
　Earlier sketch in SATA *6*
　See also CLR *45*
Giovanni, Nikki 1943- *107*
　Earlier sketch in SATA *24*
　See also CLR *73*
Giovanopoulos, Paul (Arthur) 1939- *7*
Gipson, Fred(erick Benjamin) 1908-1973 ..... *2*
　Obituary *24*
Girard, Linda (Walvoord) 1942- *41*
Girion, Barbara 1937- *78*
　Earlier sketch in SATA *26*
　See also SAAS *14*
Girouard, Patrick 1957- *155*
Girzone, Joseph F. 1930- *76*
Girzone, Joseph Francis
　See Girzone, Joseph F.
Gise, Joanne
　See Mattern, Joanne
Gittings, Jo (Grenville) Manton 1919- *3*
Gittings, Robert (William Victor) 1911-1992
　.. *6*
　Obituary *70*
Givens, Janet E(aton) 1932- *60*
Givner, Joan 1936- *171*
Givner, Joan Mary
　See Givner, Joan

Gladstone, Eve
  See Werner, Herma
Gladstone, Gary 1935- *12*
Gladstone, M(yron) J. 1923- *37*
Glanville, Brian (Lester) 1931- *42*
Glanzman, Louis S. 1922- *36*
Glaser, Byron 1954- *154*
Glaser, Dianne E(lizabeth) 1937- *50*
  Brief entry *31*
Glaser, Isabel Joshlin 1929- *94*
Glaser, Milton 1929- *151*
  Earlier sketch in SATA *11*
Glaser, Shirley *151*
Glaspell, Susan 1882(?)-1948
  See YABC *2*
Glass, Andrew 1949- *150*
  Brief entry *46*
  Earlier sketch in SATA *90*
Glass, Linzi *175*
Glass, Linzi Alex
  See Glass, Linzi
Glasscock, Amnesia
  See Steinbeck, John (Ernst)
Glassman, Bruce 1961- *76*
Glauber, Uta (Heil) 1936- *17*
Glazer, Thomas (Zachariah) 1914-2003 .... *9*
Glazer, Tom
  See Glazer, Thomas (Zachariah)
Gleasner, Diana (Cottle) 1936- *29*
Gleason, Judith 1929- *24*
Gleason, Katherine (A.) 1960- *104*
Gleeson, Libby 1950- *142*
  Autobiography Feature *142*
  Earlier sketches in SATA *82, 118*
Gleiter, Jan 1947- *111*
Gleitzman, Morris 1953- *156*
  Earlier sketch in SATA *88*
  See also CLR *88*
Glen, Maggie 1944- *88*
Glendinning, Richard 1917-1988 .... *24*
Glendinning, Sally
  See Glendinning, Sara W(ilson)
Glendinning, Sara W(ilson) 1913-1993 .... *24*
Glenn, Mel 1943- *93*
  Brief entry *45*
  Earlier sketch in SATA *51*
  See also CLR *51*
Glenn, Patricia Brown 1953- *86*
Glenn, Sharlee *159*
Glenn, Sharlee Mullins
  See Glenn, Sharlee
Glennon, Karen M. 1946- *85*
Gles, Margaret Breitmaier 1940- *22*
Glick, Carl (Cannon) 1890-1971 .... *14*
Glick, Ruth (Burtnick) 1942- *125*
Gliewe, Unada (Grace) 1927- *3*
Glimmerveen, Ulco 1958- *85*
Glines, Carroll V(ane), Jr. 1920- *19*
Gliori, Debi 1959- *138*
  Earlier sketch in SATA *72*
Globe, Leah Ain 1900- *41*
Glori Ann
  See Blakely, Gloria
Glovach, Linda 1947- *105*
  Earlier sketch in SATA *7*
Glover, Denis (James Matthews) 1912-1980
  .... *7*
Glubok, Shirley (Astor) *146*
  Autobiography Feature *146*
  Earlier sketches in SATA *6, 68*
  See also CLR *1*
  See also SAAS *7*
Glyman, Caroline A. 1967- *103*
Glynne-Jones, William 1907-1977 .... *11*
Gobbato, Imero 1923- *39*
Gobbletree, Richard
  See Quackenbush, Robert M(ead)
Goble, Dorothy *26*
Goble, Paul 1933- *131*
  Earlier sketches in SATA *25, 69*
  See also CLR *21*

Goble, Warwick (?)-1943 .... *46*
Godden, (Margaret) Rumer 1907-1998 .... *36*
  Obituary *109*
  Earlier sketch in SATA *3*
  See also CLR *20*
  See also SAAS *12*
Gode, Alexander
  See Gode von Aesch, Alexander (Gottfried
  Friedrich)
Gode von Aesch, Alexander (Gottfried
  Friedrich) 1906-1970 .... *14*
Godfrey, Jane
  See Bowden, Joan Chase
Godfrey, Martyn
  See Godfrey, Martyn N.
  and Godfrey, Martyn N.
Godfrey, Martyn N. 1949-2000 .... *95*
  See also CLR *57*
  See Godfrey, Martyn
Godfrey, William
  See Youd, (Christopher) Samuel
Godkin, Celia (Marilyn) 1948- *145*
  Earlier sketch in SATA *66*
Godwin, Laura 1956- *179*
Goedecke, Christopher (John) 1951- *81*
Goekler, Susan
  See Wooley, Susan Frelick
Goertzen, Glenda *172*
Goettel, Elinor 1930- *12*
Goetz, Delia 1898-1996 .... *22*
  Obituary *91*
Goffe, Toni 1936- *61*
Goffstein, Brooke
  See Goffstein, M(arilyn) B(rooke)
Goffstein, M(arilyn) B(rooke) 1940- *70*
  Earlier sketch in SATA *8*
  See also CLR *3*
Goforth, Ellen
  See Francis, Dorothy Brenner
Gogol, Sara 1948-2004 .... *80*
Goh, Chan Hon 1969- *145*
Going, Kelly L.
  See Going, K.L.
Going, K.L. *156*
Golann, Cecil Paige 1921-1995 .... *11*
Golbin, Andree 1923- *15*
Gold, Alison Leslie 1945- *104*
Gold, Bernice *150*
Gold, Phyllis *21*
  See Goldberg, Phyllis
Gold, Robert S(tanley) 1924- *63*
Gold, Sharlya *9*
Gold, Susan
  See Gold, Susan Dudley
Gold, Susan Dudley 1949- *147*
Goldberg, Grace 1956- *78*
Goldberg, Herbert S. 1926- *25*
Goldberg, Jacob 1943- *94*
Goldberg, Jake
  See Goldberg, Jacob
Goldberg, Jan *123*
  See Curran, Jan Goldberg
Goldberg, Stan J. 1939- *26*
Goldberg, Susan 1948- *71*
Goldberg, Whoopi 1955- *119*
Golden, Christie 1963- *167*
  Earlier sketch in SATA *116*
Goldentyer, Debra 1960- *84*
Goldfeder, Cheryl
  See Pahz, Cheryl Suzanne
Goldfeder, James
  See Pahz, James Alon
Goldfeder, Jim
  See Pahz, James Alon
Goldfrank, Helen Colodny 1912- *6*
Goldin, Augusta 1906-1999 .... *13*
Goldin, Barbara Diamond 1946- *129*
  Autobiography Feature *129*
  Earlier sketch in SATA *92*
  See also SAAS *26*
Goldin, David 1963- *101*

Golding, Theresa Martin 1960- *150*
Golding, William 1911-1993
  See CLR *94*
Golding, William Gerald
  See Golding, William
Goldman, Alex J. 1917- *65*
Goldman, E(leanor) M(aureen) 1943- *103*
Goldman, Elizabeth 1949- *90*
Goldring, Ann 1937- *149*
Goldsborough, June 1923- *19*
Goldsmith, Connie 1945- *147*
Goldsmith, Howard 1943- *108*
  Earlier sketch in SATA *24*
Goldsmith, Oliver 1730(?)-1774 .... *26*
Goldsmith, Ruth M. 1919- *62*
Goldstein, Nathan 1927- *47*
Goldstein, Philip 1910-1997 .... *23*
Goldston, Robert (Conroy) 1927- *6*
Goldstone, Lawrence A.
  See Treat, Lawrence
Golembe, Carla 1951- *79*
Golenbock, Peter 1946- *99*
Goll, Reinhold W(eimar) 1897-1993 .... *26*
Gollub, Matthew 1960- *134*
  Earlier sketch in SATA *83*
Gomez, Elizabeth *133*
Gomez-Freer, Elizabeth
  See Gomez, Elizabeth
Gomi, Taro 1945- *103*
  Earlier sketch in SATA *64*
  See also CLR *57*
Gondosch, Linda 1944- *58*
Gonzalez, Catherine Troxell 1917-2000 ...... *87*
Gonzalez, Christina
  See Gonzalez, Maya Christina
Gonzalez, Gloria 1940- *23*
Gonzalez, Julie 1958- *174*
Gonzalez, Maya
  See Gonzalez, Maya Christina
Gonzalez, Maya Christina 1964- *175*
  Earlier sketch in SATA *115*
Gonzalez, Rigoberto 1970- *147*
Goobie, Beth 1959- *128*
Good, Alice 1950- *73*
Goodall, Daphne Machin
  See Machin Goodall, Daphne (Edith)
Goodall, Jane 1934- *111*
Goodall, John S(trickland) 1908-1996 .... *66*
  Obituary *91*
  Earlier sketch in SATA *4*
  See also CLR *25*
Goodbody, Slim
  See Burstein, John
Goode, Diane 1949- *170*
  Earlier sketches in SATA *15, 84, 114*
Goode, Diane Capuozzo
  See Goode, Diane
Goode, Stephen Ray 1943- *55*
  Brief entry *40*
Goodenow, Earle 1913- *40*
Goodhart, Pippa 1958- *153*
Goodhue, Thomas W. 1949- *143*
Goodin, Sallie (Brown) 1953- *74*
Goodman, Alison 1966- *111*
Goodman, Deborah Lerme 1956- *50*
  Brief entry *49*
Goodman, Elaine 1930- *9*
Goodman, Joan Elizabeth 1950- *162*
  Earlier sketches in SATA *50, 94*
Goodman, Susan E. 1952- *181*
Goodman, Walter 1927-2002 .... *9*
Goodrich, Samuel Griswold 1793-1860 ...... *23*
GoodWeather, Harley
  See King, Thomas
Goodwin, Hal
  See Goodwin, Harold L(eland)
Goodwin, Harold L(eland) 1914-1990 .... *51*
  Obituary *65*
  Earlier sketch in SATA *13*
Goodwin, William 1943- *117*

Goor, Nancy (Ruth Miller) 1944- *39*
  Brief entry *34*
Goor, Ron(ald Stephen) 1940- *39*
  Brief entry *34*
Goossen, Agnes
  See Epp, Margaret A(gnes)
Gootman, Marilyn E. 1944- *179*
Gopnik, Adam 1956- *171*
Gorbachev, Valeri 1944- *143*
  Autobiography Feature *143*
  Earlier sketch in SATA *98*
Gordion, Mark
  See Turtledove, Harry
Gordon, Ad
  See Hano, Arnold
Gordon, Amy 1949- *156*
  Earlier sketch in SATA *115*
Gordon, Bernard Ludwig 1931- *27*
Gordon, Colonel H. R.
  See Ellis, Edward S(ylvester)
Gordon, David *180*
  See Garrett, (Gordon) Randall (Phillip)
Gordon, Donald
  See Payne, Donald Gordon
Gordon, Dorothy 1893-1970 .... *20*
Gordon, Esther S(aranga) 1935- *10*
Gordon, Frederick *1*
Gordon, Gaelyn 1939-1997
  See CLR *75*
Gordon, Gary
  See Edmonds, I(vy) G(ordon)
Gordon, Hal
  See Goodwin, Harold L(eland)
Gordon, Jeffie Ross
  See Enderle, Judith (Ann) Ross
  and Gordon, Stephanie Jacob
Gordon, John
  See Gesner, Clark
Gordon, John (William) 1925- *84*
Gordon, Lew
  See Baldwin, Gordon C(ortis)
Gordon, Margaret (Anna) 1939- *9*
Gordon, Mike 1948- *101*
Gordon, Selma
  See Lanes, Selma Gordon
Gordon, Sheila 1927- *88*
  See also CLR *27*
Gordon, Shirley 1921- *48*
  Brief entry *41*
Gordon, Sol 1923- *11*
Gordon, Stephanie Jacob 1940- *89*
  Autobiography Feature *114*
  Earlier sketch in SATA *64*
  See also SAAS *26*
Gordon, Stewart
  See Shirreffs, Gordon D(onald)
Gorelick, Molly C(hernow) 1920-2003 .... *9*
  Obituary *153*
Gorey, Edward (St. John) 1925-2000 .... *70*
  Brief entry *27*
  Obituary *118*
  Earlier sketch in SATA *29*
  See also CLR *36*
Gorham, Charles Orson 1868-1936 .... *36*
Gorham, Michael
  See Folsom, Franklin (Brewster)
Gorman, Carol *150*
Gorman, Jacqueline Laks 1955- *148*
Gormley, Beatrice 1942- *127*
  Brief entry *35*
  Earlier sketch in SATA *39*
Gorog, Judith (Katharine Allen) 1938- *75*
  Earlier sketch in SATA *39*
Gorrell, Gena K. 1946- *170*
Gorrell, Gena Kinton
  See Gorrell, Gena K.
Gorsline, Douglas (Warner) 1913-1985 .... *11*
  Obituary *43*
Gorsline, (Sally) Marie 1928- *28*
Gorsline, S. M.
  See Gorsline, (Sally) Marie

Gorton, Kaitlyn
  See Emerson, Kathy Lynn
Goryan, Sirak
  See Saroyan, William
Goscinny, Rene 1926-1977 .... *47*
  Brief entry *39*
  See also CLR *37*
Goss, Clay(ton E.) 1946- *82*
Goss, Gary 1947- *124*
Gottesman, S. D.
  See Kornbluth, C(yril) M.
  and Lowndes, Robert A(ugustine) W(ard)
  and Pohl, Frederik
Gottfried, Ted
  See Gottfried, Theodore Mark
Gottfried, Theodore Mark 1928- *150*
  Earlier sketch in SATA *85*
Gottlieb, Gerald 1923- *7*
Gottlieb, William P. 1917-2006 .... *24*
Gottlieb, William Paul
  See Gottlieb, William P.
Goudey, Alice E(dwards) 1898-1993 .... *20*
Goudge, Eileen 1950- *88*
Goudge, Elizabeth (de Beauchamp) 1900-1984
  .... *2*
  Obituary *38*
  See also CLR *94*
Gough, Catherine *24*
  See Mulgan, Catherine
Gough, Philip 1908- *45*
Gough, Sue 1940- *106*
Goulart, Ron(ald Joseph) 1933- *138*
  Earlier sketch in SATA *6*
  See Appleton, Victor II
  and Dixon, Franklin W.
  and Hope, Laura Lee
  and Keene, Carolyn
Gould, Alberta 1945- *96*
Gould, Chester 1900-1985 .... *49*
  Obituary *43*
Gould, Jean R(osalind) 1909-1993 .... *11*
  Obituary *77*
Gould, Lilian *6*
Gould, Marilyn 1928- *76*
  Earlier sketch in SATA *15*
Gould, Robert *154*
Gould, Steven 1955- *95*
Gould, Steven Charles
  See Gould, Steven
Gourley, Catherine 1950- *95*
Gourse, (Roberta) Leslie 1939-2004 .... *89*
Govan, (Mary) Christine Noble 1898-1985 .. *9*
Gove, Doris 1944- *72*
Govern, Elaine 1939- *26*
Gowen, L. Kris 1968- *156*
Graaf, Peter
  See Youd, (Christopher) Samuel
Graber, Alexander 1914-1997 .... *98*
  Earlier sketch in SATA *7*
Graber, (George) Alexander 1914-1997 ...... *98*
Graber, Janet 1942- *170*
Graber, Richard (Fredrick) 1927- *26*
Grabianski, Janusz 1928-1976 .... *39*
  Obituary *30*
Graboff, Abner 1919-1986 .... *35*
Grace, Fran(ces Jane) *45*
Grace, Theresa
  See Mattern, Joanne
Gracza, Margaret Young 1928- *56*
Graduate of Oxford, A
  See Ruskin, John
Graeber, Charlotte Towner *106*
  Brief entry *44*
  Earlier sketch in SATA *56*
Graeme, Roderic
  See Jeffries, Roderic
Graf, Michael
  See Graf, Mike
Graf, Mike 1960- *164*
Graff, Polly Anne Colver
  See Colver, Anne

Graff, (S.) Stewart 1908- *9*
Graham, Ada 1931- *11*
Graham, Alastair 1945- *74*
Graham, Arthur Kennon
  See Harrison, David L(ee)
Graham, Bob 1942- *151*
  Earlier sketches in SATA *63, 101*
  See also CLR *31*
Graham, Brenda Knight 1942- *32*
Graham, Charlotte
  See Bowden, Joan Chase
Graham, Eleanor 1896-1984 .... *18*
  Obituary *38*
Graham, Ennis
  See Molesworth, Mary Louisa
Graham, Frank, Jr. 1925- *11*
Graham, Ian 1953- *112*
Graham, John 1926-2007 .... *11*
Graham, Kennon
  See Harrison, David L(ee)
Graham, Larry
  See Graham, Lawrence (Otis)
Graham, Lawrence (Otis) 1962- *63*
Graham, Linda
  See Graham-Barber, Lynda
Graham, Lorenz (Bell) 1902-1989 .... *74*
  Obituary *63*
  Earlier sketch in SATA *2*
  See also CLR *10*
  See also SAAS *5*
Graham, Margaret Bloy 1920- *11*
Graham, Robin Lee 1949- *7*
Graham, Shirley 1896(?)-1977
  See Du Bois, Shirley Graham
Graham-Barber, Lynda 1944- *159*
  Earlier sketch in SATA *42*
Graham-Cameron, M.
  See Graham-Cameron, M(alcolm) G(ordon)
Graham-Cameron, M(alcolm) G(ordon) 1931-
  .... *53*
  Brief entry *45*
Graham-Cameron, Mike
  See Graham-Cameron, M(alcolm) G(ordon)
Grahame, Kenneth 1859-1932 .... *100*
  See also YABC *1*
  See also CLR *5*
Gralley, Jean *166*
Gramatky, Hardie 1907-1979 .... *30*
  Obituary *23*
  Earlier sketch in SATA *1*
  See also CLR *22*
Grambling, Lois G. 1927- *148*
  Earlier sketch in SATA *71*
Grambo, Rebecca L(ynn) 1963- *109*
Grammer, June Amos 1927- *58*
Grand, Samuel 1912-1988 .... *42*
Grandville, J. J.
  See Gerard, Jean Ignace Isidore
Grandville, Jean Ignace Isidore Gerard
  See Gerard, Jean Ignace Isidore
Granfield, Linda 1950- *160*
  Earlier sketch in SATA *96*
Grange, Peter
  See Nicole, Christopher (Robin)
Granger, Michele 1949- *88*
Granowsky, Alvin 1936- *101*
Granstaff, Bill 1925- *10*
Granstrom, Brita 1969- *167*
  Earlier sketch in SATA *111*
Grant, Bruce 1893-1977 .... *5*
  Obituary *25*
Grant, Cynthia D. 1950- *147*
  Earlier sketches in SATA *33, 77*
Grant, Eva 1907-1996 .... *7*
Grant, Gordon 1875-1962 .... *25*
Grant, Gwen(doline Ellen) 1940- *47*
Grant, Katie M.
  See Grant, K.M.
Grant, K.M. *175*
Grant, (Alice) Leigh 1947- *10*

Grant, Matthew G.
See May, Julian
Grant, Maxwell
See Gibson, Walter B(rown)
and Lynds, Dennis
Grant, Myrna (Lois) 1934- 21
Grant, Neil 1938- 154
Earlier sketch in SATA 14
Grant, Nicholas
See Nicole, Christopher (Robin)
Grant, Richard 1948- 80
Grant, Skeeter
See Spiegelman, Art
Grater, Michael 1923- 57
Gravel, Fern
See Hall, James Norman
Gravelle, Karen 1942- 166
Earlier sketch in SATA 78
Graves, Charles Parlin 1911-1972 4
Graves, Keith 156
Graves, Robert 1895-1985 45
Graves, Robert von Ranke
See Graves, Robert
Graves, Valerie
See Bradley, Marion Zimmer
Gray, Betsy
See Poole, Gray Johnson
Gray, Caroline
See Nicole, Christopher (Robin)
Gray, Elizabeth Janet
See Vining, Elizabeth Gray
Gray, Genevieve S(tuck) 1920-1995 4
Gray, Harold (Lincoln) 1894-1968 33
Brief entry 32
Gray, Jenny
See Gray, Genevieve S(tuck)
Gray, John Lee
See Jakes, John
Gray, Judith A. 1949- 93
Gray, Judith Anne
See Gray, Judith A.
Gray, Keith 151
Gray, Kes 1960- 153
Gray, Les 1929- 82
Gray, Libba Moore 1937- 83
Gray, Luli 1945- 149
Earlier sketch in SATA 90
Gray, Marian
See Pierce, Edith Gray
Gray, Nicholas Stuart 1922-1981 4
Obituary 27
Gray, Nigel 1941- 104
Earlier sketch in SATA 33
Gray, (Lucy) Noel (Clervaux) 1898-1983 ... 47
Gray, Patricia (Clark) 7
Gray, Patsey
See Gray, Patricia (Clark)
Graydon, Shari 1958- 158
Grayland, V. Merle
See Grayland, Valerie (Merle Spanner)
Grayland, Valerie (Merle Spanner) 7
Grayson, Devin (Kalile) 1970- 119
Grayson, Kristine
See Rusch, Kristine Kathryn
Grayson, Paul 1946- 79
Graystone, Lynn
See Brennan, Joseph Lomas
Great Comte, The
See Hawkesworth, Eric
Greaves, Margaret 1914-1995 87
Earlier sketch in SATA 7
Greaves, Nick 1955- 77
Gree, Alain 1936- 28
Green, Adam
See Weisgard, Leonard (Joseph)
Green, Anne Canevari 1943- 62
Green, Brian
See Card, Orson Scott
Green, Cliff(ord) 1934- 126
Green, Connie Jordan 1938- 80

Green, D.
See Casewit, Curtis W(erner)
Green, Elizabeth Shippen 1871-1954 139
Green, Hannah
See Greenberg, Joanne (Goldenberg)
Green, Jane 1937- 9
Green, John 1978(?)- 170
Green, Mary Moore 1906- 11
Green, Morton 1937- 8
Green, Norma B(erger) 1925- 11
Green, Phyllis 1932- 20
Green, Roger (Gilbert) Lancelyn 1918-1987
.... 2
Obituary 53
Green, (James Le)Roy 1948- 89
Green, Sheila Ellen 1934- 148
Earlier sketches in SATA 8, 87
Green, Timothy 1953- 91
Greenaway, Kate 1846-1901 100
See also YABC 2
See also CLR 111
Greenbank, Anthony Hunt 1933- 39
Greenberg, David T. 1954- 171
Greenberg, Harvey R. 1935- 5
Greenberg, Jan 1942- 125
Earlier sketch in SATA 61
Greenberg, Joanne (Goldenberg) 1932- 25
Greenberg, Melanie Hope 1954- 72
Greenberg, Polly 1932- 52
Brief entry 43
Greenblat, Rodney Alan 1960- 106
Greenburg, Dan 1936- 175
Earlier sketch in SATA 102
Greene, Bette 1934- 161
Earlier sketches in SATA 8, 102
See also CLR 2
See also SAAS 16
Greene, Carla 1916- 67
Earlier sketch in SATA 1
Greene, Carol 102
Brief entry 44
Earlier sketch in SATA 66
Greene, Constance C(larke) 1924- 72
Earlier sketch in SATA 11
See also CLR 62
See also SAAS 11
Greene, Edgar
See Papademetriou, Lisa
Greene, Ellin 1927- 23
Greene, Graham 1904-1991 20
Greene, Graham Henry
See Greene, Graham
Greene, Jacqueline Dembar 1946- 131
Earlier sketch in SATA 76
Greene, Laura Offenhartz 1935- 38
Greene, Meg
See Malvasi, Meg Greene
Greene, Michele 1962- 178
Greene, Michele Dominguez
See Greene, Michele
Greene, Rhonda Gowler 1955- 160
Earlier sketch in SATA 101
Greene, Stephanie 1953- 173
Earlier sketch in SATA 127
Greene, Wade 1933- 11
Greene, Yvonne
See Flesch, Yolande (Catarina)
Greenfeld, Howard (Scheinman) 1928- 140
Earlier sketch in SATA 19
Greenfeld, Josh(ua Joseph) 1928- 62
Greenfield, Eloise 1929- 155
Earlier sketches in SATA 19, 61, 105
See also CLR 38
See also SAAS 16
Greening, Hamilton
See Hamilton, Charles (Harold St. John)
Greenlaw, M. Jean 1941- 107
Greenleaf, Barbara Kaye 1942- 6
Greenleaf, Peter 1910-1997 33
Greenlee, Sharon 1935- 77
Greeno, Gayle 1949- 81

Greenseid, Diane 1948- 178
Earlier sketch in SATA 93
Greenspun, Adele Aron 1938- 142
Earlier sketch in SATA 76
Greenstein, Elaine 1959- 150
Earlier sketch in SATA 82
Greenwald, Sheila
See Green, Sheila Ellen
Greenwood, Barbara 1940- 129
Earlier sketch in SATA 90
Greenwood, Pamela D. 1944- 115
Greer, Richard
See Garrett, (Gordon) Randall (Phillip)
and Silverberg, Robert
Gregg, Andrew K. 1929- 81
Gregg, Charles T(hornton) 1927- 65
Gregg, Walter H(arold) 1919- 20
Gregor, Arthur 1923- 36
Gregor, Lee
See Pohl, Frederik
Gregori, Leon 1919- 15
Gregorian, Joyce Ballou 1946-1991 30
Obituary 83
Gregorich, Barbara 1943- 66
Gregorowski, Christopher 1940- 30
Gregory, Diana (Jean) 1933- 49
Brief entry 42
Gregory, Harry
See Gottfried, Theodore Mark
Gregory, Jean
See Ure, Jean
Gregory, Kristiana 1951- 136
Earlier sketch in SATA 74
Gregory, Nan 1944- 148
Gregory, Philippa 1954- 122
Gregory, Stephen
See Penzler, Otto
Gregory, Valiska 1940- 82
Greisman, Joan Ruth 1937- 31
Grendon, Stephen
See Derleth, August (William)
Grenville, Pelham
See Wodehouse, P(elham) G(renville)
Gretz, Susanna 1937- 7
Gretzer, John 18
Grewdead, Roy
See Gorey, Edward (St. John)
Grey, Carol
See Lowndes, Robert A(ugustine) W(ard)
Grey, Jerry 1926- 11
Grey, Mini 166
Greybeard the Pirate
See Macintosh, Brownie
Grey Owl
See CLR 32
See Belaney, Archibald Stansfeld
Gri
See Denney, Diana
Gribbin, John 1946- 159
Gribbin, John R.
See Gribbin, John
Grice, Frederick 1910-1983 6
Grider, Dorothy 1915- 31
Gridley, Marion E(leanor) 1906-1974 35
Obituary 26
Grieco-Tiso, Pina 1954- 108
Grieder, Walter 1924- 9
Griego, Tony A. 1955- 77
Griese, Arnold A(lfred) 1921- 9
Griessman, Annette 1962- 170
Earlier sketch in SATA 116
Grieve, James 1934- 146
Grifalconi, Ann 1929- 133
Earlier sketches in SATA 2, 66
See also CLR 35
See also SAAS 16
Griffin, Adele 1970- 153
Earlier sketch in SATA 105
Griffin, Elizabeth May 1985- 89
Griffin, Gillett Good 1928- 26
Griffin, Judith Berry 34

Griffin, Kitty 1951- *137*
Griffin, Peni R(ae Robinson) 1961- *99*
  Earlier sketch in SATA *67*
Griffin, Steven A. 1953- *89*
Griffin, Steven Arthur
  See Griffin, Steven A.
Griffin, W.E.B. 1929- *5*
  See Butterworth, W.E.
Griffith, Connie 1946- *89*
Griffith, Gershom 1960- *85*
Griffith, Helen V(irginia) 1934- *87*
  Autobiography Feature *107*
  Earlier sketch in SATA *39*
Griffith, Jeannette
  See Eyerly, Jeannette (Hyde)
Griffiths, Andy 1961- *152*
Griffiths, Helen 1939- *86*
  Earlier sketch in SATA *5*
  See also CLR *75*
  See also SAAS *5*
Grigson, Jane (McIntire) 1928-1990 .... *63*
Grimes, Lee 1920- *68*
Grimes, Nikki 1950- *174*
  Earlier sketches in SATA *93, 136*
  See also CLR *42*
Grimm, Jacob Ludwig Karl 1785-1863 ...... *22*
  See also CLR *112*
  See Grimm Brothers
Grimm, Wilhelm Karl 1786-1859 .... *22*
  See also CLR *112*
  See Grimm Brothers
Grimm, William C(arey) 1907-1992 .... *14*
Grimm and Grim
  See Grimm, Jacob Ludwig Karl
  and Grimm, Wilhelm Karl
Grimm Brothers
  See CLR *112*
  See Grimm, Jacob Ludwig Karl
  and Grimm, Wilhelm Karl
Grimsdell, Jeremy 1942- *83*
Grimshaw, Nigel (Gilroy) 1925- *23*
Grimsley, Gordon
  See Groom, Arthur William
Grindley, (Jane) Sally 1953- *148*
Gringhuis, Dirk
  See Gringhuis, Richard H.
Gringhuis, Richard H. 1918-1974 .... *6*
  Obituary *25*
Grinnell, George Bird 1849-1938 .... *16*
Grinspoon, David
  See Grinspoon, David H.
Grinspoon, David H. 1959- *156*
Grinspoon, David Harry
  See Grinspoon, David H.
Gripe, Maria 1923- *74*
  Earlier sketch in SATA *2*
  See also CLR *5*
Gripe, Maria Kristina
  See Gripe, Maria
Groch, Judith (Goldstein) 1929- *25*
Grode, Redway
  See Gorey, Edward (St. John)
Groener, Carl
  See Lowndes, Robert A(ugustine) W(ard)
Groening, Matt 1954- *116*
  Earlier sketch in SATA *81*
Grohmann, Susan 1948- *84*
Grohskopf, Bernice *7*
Grol, Lini R(icharda) 1913- *9*
Grollman, Earl A. 1925- *22*
Groom, Arthur William 1898-1964 .... *10*
Grooms, Duffy 1964- *169*
Gross, Alan 1947- *54*
  Brief entry *43*
Gross, Ernie 1913- *67*
Gross, Philip 1952- *164*
  Earlier sketch in SATA *84*
Gross, Philip John
  See Gross, Philip
Gross, Ruth Belov 1929- *33*

Gross, Sarah Chokla 1906-1976 .... *9*
  Obituary *26*
Grosser, Morton 1931- *74*
Grosser, Vicky 1958- *83*
Grossman, Bill 1948- *126*
  Earlier sketch in SATA *72*
Grossman, Nancy 1940- *29*
Grossman, Patricia 1951- *73*
Grossman, Robert 1940- *11*
Grote, JoAnn A. 1951- *113*
Groten, Dallas 1951- *64*
Groth, John (August) 1908-1988 .... *21*
  Obituary *56*
Groth-Fleming, Candace
  See Fleming, Candace
Grove, Vicki 1948- *151*
  Autobiography Feature *151*
  Earlier sketch in SATA *122*
Grover, Lorie Ann 1964- *168*
Grover, Wayne 1934- *69*
Groves, Georgina
  See Symons, (Dorothy) Geraldine
Groves, Maketa 1950- *107*
Groves, Seli *77*
Grubb, Lisa *160*
Gruber, Michael 1940- *173*
Gruber, Terry (deRoy) 1953- *66*
Gruelle, John (Barton) 1880-1938 .... *35*
  Brief entry *32*
  See Gruelle, Johnny
Gruelle, Johnny
  See CLR *34*
  See Gruelle, John (Barton)
Gruenberg, Sidonie Matsner 1881-1974 .... *2*
  Obituary *27*
Gruhzit-Hoyt, Olga (Margaret) 1922- *127*
  Earlier sketch in SATA *16*
Grummer, Arnold E(dward) 1923- *49*
Grunewalt, Pine
  See Kunhardt, Edith
Grunwell, Jeanne Marie 1971- *147*
Grupper, Jonathan *137*
Gryski, Camilla 1948- *72*
Guarino, Dagmar
  See Guarino, Deborah
Guarino, Deborah 1954- *68*
Guay, Georgette (Marie Jeanne) 1952- *54*
Guback, Georgia *88*
Guccione, Leslie Davis 1946- *111*
  Earlier sketch in SATA *72*
Guck, Dorothy 1913-2002 .... *27*
Guerny, Gene
  See Gurney, Gene
Guest, Elissa Haden 1953- *125*
Guest, Jacqueline 1952- *135*
Guevara, Susan *167*
  Earlier sketch in SATA *97*
Gugler, Laurel Dee *95*
Gugliotta, Bobette 1918-1994 .... *7*
Guianan, Eve 1965- *102*
Guiberson, Brenda Z. 1946- *124*
  Earlier sketch in SATA *71*
Guibert, Emmanuel 1964- *181*
Guile, Melanie 1949- *152*
  Earlier sketch in SATA *104*
Guillaume, Jeanette G. Flierl 1899-1990 ...... *8*
Guillot, Rene 1900-1969 .... *7*
  See also CLR *22*
Guisewite, Cathy (Lee) 1950- *57*
Gulbis, Stephen 1959- *142*
Gulley, Judie 1942- *58*
Gump, P. Q.
  See Card, Orson Scott
Gundrey, Elizabeth 1924- *23*
Gunn, James E. 1923- *35*
Gunn, James Edwin
  See Gunn, James E.
Gunn, Robin Jones 1955- *84*
Gunning, Monica Olwen 1930- *161*
Gunston, Bill
  See Gunston, William Tudor

Gunston, William Tudor 1927- *9*
Gunther, John 1901-1970
Guravich, Dan 1918- *74*
Gurko, Leo 1914- *9*
Gurko, Miriam 1910(?)-1988 .... *9*
  Obituary *58*
Gurney, Gene 1924- *65*
Gurney, James 1958- *120*
  Earlier sketch in SATA *76*
Gurney, John Steven 1962- *143*
  Earlier sketch in SATA *75*
Gustafson, Sarah R.
  See Riedman, Sarah R(egal)
Gustafson, Scott 1956- *34*
Gustavson, Adam *176*
Guthrie, A(lfred) B(ertram), Jr. 1901-1991 . *62*
  Obituary *67*
Guthrie, Anne 1890-1979 .... *28*
Guthrie, Donna W. 1946- *105*
  Earlier sketch in SATA *63*
Gutierrez, Akemi *172*
Gutman, Bill *128*
  Brief entry *43*
  Earlier sketch in SATA *67*
Gutman, Dan 1955- *139*
  Earlier sketch in SATA *77*
Gutmann, Bessie Pease 1876-1960 .... *73*
Guy, Geoffrey 1942- *153*
Guy, Ginger Foglesong 1954- *171*
Guy, Rosa (Cuthbert) 1925- *122*
  Earlier sketches in SATA *14, 62*
  See also CLR *13*
Guy, Susan 1948- *149*
Guymer, (Wilhelmina) Mary 1909- *50*
Guzman, Lila 1952- *168*
Guzman, Rick 1957- *168*
Gwaltney, Doris 1932- *181*
Gwynne, Fred(erick Hubbard) 1926-1993 .. *41*
  Brief entry *27*
  Obituary *75*
Gwynne, Oscar A.
  See Ellis, Edward S(ylvester)
Gwynne, Oswald A.
  See Ellis, Edward S(ylvester)

H

Haab, Sherri 1964- *169*
  Earlier sketch in SATA *91*
Haar, Jaap ter
  See CLR *15*
  See ter Haar, Jaap
Haas, Carolyn Buhai 1926- *43*
Haas, Dan 1957- *105*
Haas, Dorothy F. *46*
  Brief entry *43*
  See also SAAS *17*
Haas, Irene 1929- *96*
  Earlier sketch in SATA *17*
Haas, James E(dward) 1943- *40*
Haas, (Katherine) Jessie 1959- *135*
  Autobiography Feature *135*
  Earlier sketch in SATA *98*
Habenstreit, Barbara 1937- *5*
Haber, Karen 1955- *78*
Haber, Louis 1910-1988 .... *12*
Hackett, John Winthrop 1910-1997 .... *65*
Haddix, Margaret Peterson 1964- *125*
  Earlier sketch in SATA *94*
Haddon, Mark 1962- *155*
Hader, Berta (Hoerner) 1891(?)-1976 .... *16*
Hader, Elmer (Stanley) 1889-1973 .... *16*
Hadithi, Mwenye
  See Hobson, Bruce
Hadley, Franklin
  See Winterbotham, R(ussell) R(obert)

Hadley, Lee 1934-1995 89
  Brief entry 38
  Obituary 86
  Earlier sketch in SATA 47
  See also CLR 40
  See Irwin, Hadley
Haeffele, Deborah 1954- 76
Haenel, Wolfram 1956- 89
  See also CLR 64
Hafner, Marylin 1925- 179
  Earlier sketches in SATA 7, 121
Hager, Alan 1940- 176
Hager, Betty 1923- 89
Hager, Sarah 171
Hager, Thomas 1953- 119
Hager, Tom
  See Hager, Thomas
Haggard, H(enry) Rider 1856-1925 16
Haggerty, James J(oseph) 1920- 5
Hagon, Priscilla
  See Allan, Mabel Esther
Hague, (Susan) Kathleen 1949- 49
  Brief entry 45
Hague, Michael R. 1948- 129
  Brief entry 32
  Earlier sketches in SATA 48, 80
Hahn, Emily 1905-1997 3
  Obituary 96
Hahn, Hannelore 8
Hahn, James (Sage) 1947- 9
Hahn, (Mona) Lynn 1949- 9
Hahn, Mary Downing 1937- 157
  Autobiography Feature 157
  Brief entry 44
  Earlier sketches in SATA 50, 81, 138
  See also SAAS 12
Hahn, Michael T. 1953- 92
Haig-Brown, Roderick (Langmere) 1908-1976
  12
  See also CLR 31
Haight, Rip
  See Carpenter, John (Howard)
Haight, Sandy 1949- 79
Haij, Vera
  See Jansson, Tove (Marika)
Haines, Gail Kay 1943- 11
Haines, Margaret Ann Beck
  See Beck, Peggy
Haining, Peter (Alexander) 1940- 14
Hains, Harriet
  See Watson, Carol
Hajdusiewicz, Babs Bell 163
Hakim, Joy 1931- 173
  Earlier sketch in SATA 83
Halacy, D(aniel) S(tephen), Jr. 1919-2002 .. 36
  See Halacy, Dan
Halacy, Dan
  See SAAS 8
  See Halacy, D(aniel) S(tephen), Jr.
Halam, Ann
  See Jones, Gwyneth A(nn)
Haldane, Roger John 1945- 13
Hale, Arlene 1924-1982 49
Hale, Bruce 1957- 123
Hale, Christy 179
  See Apostolou, Christine Hale
Hale, Edward Everett 1822-1909 16
Hale, Glenn
  See Walker, Robert W(ayne)
Hale, Helen
  See Mulcahy, Lucille Burnett
Hale, Irina 1932- 26
Hale, Kathleen 1898-2000 66
  Obituary 121
  Earlier sketch in SATA 17
Hale, Linda (Howe) 1929- 6
Hale, Lucretia P.
  See Hale, Lucretia Peabody
Hale, Lucretia Peabody 1820-1900 26
  See also CLR 105

Hale, Nancy 1908-1988 31
  Obituary 57
Hale, Shannon 158
Haley, Gail E(inhart) 1939- 161
  Autobiography Feature 161
  Brief entry 28
  Earlier sketches in SATA 43, 78, 136
  See also CLR 21
  See also SAAS 13
Haley, Neale 52
Hall, Adam
  See Trevor, Elleston
Hall, Adele 1910- 7
Hall, Anna Gertrude 1882-1967 8
Hall, Barbara 1960- 68
Hall, Beverly B. 1918- 95
Hall, Borden
  See Yates, Raymond F(rancis)
Hall, Brian P(atrick) 1935- 31
Hall, Cameron
  See del Rey, Lester
Hall, Caryl
  See Hansen, Caryl (Hall)
Hall, Donald 1928- 97
  Earlier sketch in SATA 23
Hall, Donald Andrew, Jr.
  See Hall, Donald
Hall, Douglas 1931- 43
Hall, Elizabeth 1929- 77
Hall, Elvajean 1910-1984 6
Hall, Francie 1940- 166
Hall, James Norman 1887-1951 21
Hall, Jesse
  See Boesen, Victor
Hall, Katy
  See McMullan, Kate
Hall, Kirsten Marie 1974- 67
Hall, Lynn 1937- 79
  Earlier sketches in SATA 2, 47
  See also SAAS 4
Hall, Malcolm 1945- 7
Hall, Marjory
  See Yeakley, Marjory Hall
Hall, Melanie W. 1949- 169
  Earlier sketches in SATA 78, 116
Hall, Patricia 1940- 136
Hall, Rosalys Haskell 1914- 7
Hall, Willis 1929-2005 66
Hallard, Peter
  See Catherall, Arthur
Hallas, Richard
  See Knight, Eric
Hall-Clarke, James
  See Rowland-Entwistle, (Arthur) Theodore
    (Henry)
Hallensleben, Georg 1958- 173
Haller, Dorcas Woodbury 1946- 46
Hallett, Mark 1947- 83
Halliburton, Richard 1900-1939(?) 81
Halliburton, Warren J. 1924- 19
Halliday, Brett
  See Dresser, Davis
  and Johnson, (Walter) Ryerson
  and Terrall, Robert
Halliday, William R(oss) 1926- 52
Hallin, Emily Watson 1916-1995 6
Hallinan, P(atrick) K(enneth) 1944- 39
  Brief entry 37
Hallman, Ruth 1929- 43
  Brief entry 28
Hallowell, Tommy
  See Hill, Thomas
Hall-Quest, (Edna) Olga W(ilbourne)
  1899-1986 11
  Obituary 47
Halls, Kelly Milner 1957- 131
Hallstead, William F(inn III) 1924- 11
Hallward, Michael 1889-1982 12
Halperin, Michael 156
Halperin, Wendy Anderson 1952- 125
  Earlier sketch in SATA 80

Halpin, Marlene 1927- 88
Halsell, Grace (Eleanor) 1923-2000 13
Halter, Jon C(harles) 1941- 22
Halvorson, Marilyn 1948- 123
Hamalian, Leo 1920- 41
Hamberger, John 1934- 14
Hamblin, Dora Jane 1920- 36
Hambly, Barbara 1951- 108
Hamer, Martyn
  See Eldin, Peter
Hamerstrom, Frances 1907-1998 24
Hamil, Thomas Arthur 1928- 14
Hamill, Ethel
  See Webb, Jean Francis (III)
Hamilton, (John) Alan 1943- 66
Hamilton, Alice
  See Cromie, Alice Hamilton
Hamilton, Anita 1919- 92
Hamilton, Buzz
  See Hemming, Roy G.
Hamilton, Carol (Jean Barber) 1935- 94
Hamilton, Charles (Harold St. John) 1876-1961
  13
Hamilton, Charles 1913-1996 65
  Obituary 93
Hamilton, Clive
  See Lewis, C.S.
Hamilton, Dorothy (Drumm) 1906-1983 12
  Obituary 35
Hamilton, Edith 1867-1963 20
Hamilton, Edmond 1904-1977 118
Hamilton, (Muriel) Elizabeth (Mollie) 1906-
  23
Hamilton, Emma Walton 1962- 177
Hamilton, Franklin
  See Silverberg, Robert
Hamilton, Gail
  See Corcoran, Barbara (Asenath)
  and Dodge, Mary Abigail
Hamilton, Kersten 1958- 134
Hamilton, Martha 1953- 123
Hamilton, Mary (E.) 1927- 55
Hamilton, Mollie
  See Kaye, M.M.
Hamilton, Morse 1943-1998 101
  Earlier sketch in SATA 35
Hamilton, Peter F. 1960- 109
Hamilton, Priscilla
  See Gellis, Roberta
Hamilton, Ralph
  See Stratemeyer, Edward L.
Hamilton, Virginia 1936-2002 123
  Obituary 132
  Earlier sketches in SATA 4, 56, 79
  See also CLR 40
Hamilton, Virginia Esther
  See Hamilton, Virginia
Hamilton-Paterson, James 1941- 82
Hamlet, Ova
  See Lupoff, Richard A(llen)
Hamley, Dennis 1935- 69
  Earlier sketch in SATA 39
  See also CLR 47
  See also SAAS 22
Hamlin, Peter J. 1970- 84
Hamm, Diane Johnston 1949- 78
Hammer, Charles 1934- 58
Hammer, Richard 1928- 6
Hammerman, Gay M(orenus) 1926- 9
Hammond, Andrew 1970- 181
Hammond, Ralph
  See Hammond Innes, Ralph
Hammond, Winifred G(raham) 1899-1992 . 29
  Obituary 107
Hammond Innes, Ralph 1913-1998 116
  See Innes, (Ralph) Hammond
Hammontree, Marie (Gertrude) 1913- 13
Hample, Zack 1977- 161
Hampshire, Joyce Gregorian
  See Gregorian, Joyce Ballou
Hampshire, Susan 1942- 98

Hampson, (Richard) Denman 1929- *15*
Hampton, Wilborn *156*
Hamre, Leif 1914- *5*
Hamsa, Bobbie 1944- *52*
    Brief entry *38*
Han, Jenny 1981- *175*
Han, Lu
    See Stickler, Soma Han
Han, Soma
    See Stickler, Soma Han
Han, Suzanne Crowder 1953- *89*
Hancock, Mary A. 1923- *31*
Hancock, Sibyl 1940- *9*
Hand, Elizabeth 1957- *167*
    Earlier sketch in SATA *118*
Handford, Martin (John) 1956- *64*
    See also CLR *22*
Handforth, Thomas (Schofield) 1897-1948 . *42*
Handville, Robert (Tompkins) 1924- *45*
Hanel, Wolfram
    See Haenel, Wolfram
Haney, Lynn 1941- *23*
Hanff, Helene 1916-1997 .... *97*
    Earlier sketch in SATA *11*
Hanley, Boniface Francis 1924- *65*
Hanlon, Emily 1945- *15*
Hann, Jacquie 1951- *19*
Hann, Judith 1942- *77*
Hanna, Bill
    See Hanna, William (Denby)
Hanna, Cheryl 1951- *84*
Hanna, Jack (Bushnell) 1947- *74*
Hanna, Nell(ie L.) 1908- *55*
Hanna, Paul R(obert) 1902-1988 .... *9*
Hanna, William (Denby) 1910-2001 .... *51*
    Obituary *126*
Hannam, Charles 1925- *50*
Hannigan, Katherine *170*
Hannon, Ezra
    See Hunter, Evan
Hann-Syme, Marguerite *127*
Hano, Arnold 1922- *12*
Hano, Renee Roth
    See Roth-Hano, Renee
Hanover, Terri
    See Huff, Tanya
Hansen, Ann Larkin 1958- *96*
Hansen, Brooks 1965- *104*
Hansen, Caryl (Hall) 1929- *39*
Hansen, Ian V. 1929- *113*
Hansen, Jennifer 1972- *156*
Hansen, Joyce 1942- *172*
    Autobiography Feature *172*
    Brief entry *39*
    Earlier sketches in SATA *46, 101*
    See also CLR *21*
    See also SAAS *15*
Hansen, Joyce Viola
    See Hansen, Joyce
Hansen, Mark Victor *112*
Hansen, Ron(ald Thomas) 1947- *56*
Hanser, Richard (Frederick) 1909-1981 ...... *13*
Hanson, Joan 1938- *8*
Hanson, Warren 1949- *155*
Hansson, Gunilla 1939- *64*
Harald, Eric
    See Boesen, Victor
Hard, Charlotte (Ann) 1969- *98*
Hardcastle, Michael 1933- *47*
    Brief entry *38*
Harding, Lee 1937- *32*
    Brief entry *31*
Hardt, Helga Fleischhauer
    See Fleischhauer-Hardt, Helga
Hardwick, Richard Holmes, Jr. 1923- *12*
Hardy, Alice Dale *67*
    Earlier sketch in SATA *1*
Hardy, David A(ndrews) 1936- *9*
Hardy, Jon 1958- *53*
Hardy, LeAnne 1951- *154*

Hardy, Stuart
    See Schisgall, Oscar
Hare, Norma Q(uarles) 1924- *46*
    Brief entry *41*
Harel, Nira 1936- *154*
Harford, Henry
    See Hudson, W(illiam) H(enry)
Hargrave, Leonie
    See Disch, Thomas M.
Hargrove, James 1947- *57*
    Brief entry *50*
Hargrove, Jim
    See Hargrove, James
Hariton, Anca I. 1955- *79*
Hark, Mildred
    See McQueen, Mildred Hark
Harkaway, Hal
    See Stratemeyer, Edward L.
Harkins, Philip 1912-1997 .... *6*
    Obituary *129*
Harlan, Elizabeth 1945- *41*
    Brief entry *35*
Harlan, Glen
    See Cebulash, Mel
Harlan, Judith 1949- *135*
    Earlier sketch in SATA *74*
    See also CLR *81*
Harland, Richard 1947- *152*
Harlee, J. V.
    See Leese, Jennifer L.B.
Harler, Ann
    See Van Steenwyk, Elizabeth (Ann)
Harley, Bill 1954- *87*
Harlow, Joan Hiatt 1932- *157*
Harmelink, Barbara (Mary) *9*
Harmer, Mabel 1894-1992 .... *45*
Harmon, Dan
    See Harmon, Daniel E(lton)
Harmon, Daniel E(lton) 1949- *157*
Harmon, Margaret 1906- *20*
Harmon, William (Ruth) 1938- *65*
Harnan, Terry 1920- *12*
Harness, Cheryl 1951- *178*
    Earlier sketch in SATA *131*
Harnett, Cynthia (Mary) 1893-1981 .... *5*
    Obituary *32*
Harper, Anita 1943- *41*
Harper, Betty 1946- *126*
Harper, Charise
    See Harper, Charise Mericle
Harper, Charise Mericle *179*
Harper, Elaine
    See Hallin, Emily Watson
Harper, Ellen
    See Noble, Marty
Harper, Jamie *174*
Harper, Jessica (R.) 1949- *148*
Harper, Jo 1932- *169*
    Earlier sketch in SATA *97*
Harper, Mary Wood
    See Dixon, Jeanne
Harper, Piers 1966- *161*
    Earlier sketch in SATA *105*
Harper, Wilhelmina 1884-1973 .... *4*
    Obituary *26*
Harrah, Madge 1931- *154*
Harrah, Michael 1940- *41*
Harrah, Monique
    See Harrah, Madge
Harrar, George E. 1949- *124*
Harrell, Beatrice Orcutt 1943- *93*
Harrell, Janice 1945- *70*
Harries, Joan 1922- *39*
Harrill, Ronald 1950- *90*
Harrington, Denis J(ames) 1932- *88*
Harrington, Lyn *5*
    See Harrington, Evelyn Davis
Harris, Alan 1944- *71*
Harris, Aurand 1915-1996 .... *37*
    Obituary *91*
Harris, Carol Flynn 1933- *135*

Harris, Catherine
    See Ainsworth, Catherine Harris
Harris, Christie
    See Harris, Christie (Lucy) Irwin
Harris, Christie (Lucy) Irwin 1907-2002 .... *74*
    Autobiography Feature *116*
    Earlier sketch in SATA *6*
    See also CLR *47*
    See also SAAS *10*
Harris, Christine 1955- *105*
Harris, Colver
    See Colver, Anne
Harris, David 1942- *118*
Harris, David William
    See Harris, David
Harris, Dorothy Joan 1931- *153*
    Earlier sketch in SATA *13*
Harris, Geraldine (Rachel) 1951- *54*
Harris, Jacqueline L. 1929- *62*
Harris, Janet 1932-1979 .... *4*
    Obituary *23*
Harris, Jesse
    See Standiford, Natalie
Harris, Joan 1946- *146*
Harris, Joel Chandler 1848-1908 .... *100*
    See also YABC *1*
    See also CLR *49*
Harris, John (Wyndham Parkes Lucas) Beynon
    1903-1969 .... *118*
    See Wyndham, John
Harris, Johnson
    See Harris, John (Wyndham Parkes Lucas)
    Beynon
Harris, Jonathan 1921-1997 .... *52*
Harris, Larry Vincent 1939- *59*
Harris, Lavinia
    See St. John, Nicole
Harris, Leon A., Jr. 1926-2000 .... *4*
Harris, Lorle K(empe) 1912-2001 .... *22*
Harris, Marilyn
    See Springer, Marilyn Harris
Harris, Mark Jonathan 1941- *84*
    Earlier sketch in SATA *32*
Harris, Mary K(athleen) 1905-1966 .... *119*
Harris, Robie H. 1940- *147*
    Brief entry *53*
    Earlier sketch in SATA *90*
Harris, Robin
    See Shine, Deborah
Harris, Rosemary (Jeanne) *82*
    Earlier sketch in SATA *4*
    See also CLR *30*
    See also SAAS *7*
Harris, Ruth Elwin 1935- *164*
Harris, Sherwood 1932- *25*
Harris, Steven Michael 1957- *55*
Harris, Trudy 1949- *128*
Harris-Filderman, Diane
    See Filderman, Diane E(lizabeth)
Harrison, C(hester) William 1913-1994 ...... *35*
Harrison, Carol
    See Harrison, Carol Thompson
Harrison, Carol Thompson *113*
Harrison, David L(ee) 1937- *150*
    Earlier sketches in SATA *26, 92*
Harrison, Deloris 1938- *9*
Harrison, Edward Hardy 1926- *56*
Harrison, Elizabeth (Allen) Cavanna
    1909-2001 .... *142*
    See Cavanna, Betty
Harrison, Harry (Max) 1925- *4*
Harrison, Mette Ivie 1970- *149*
Harrison, Michael 1939- *106*
Harrison, Molly (Hodgett) 1909-2002 .... *41*
Harrison, Sarah 1946- *63*
Harrison, Ted
    See Harrison, Edward Hardy
Harsh, Fred (T.) 1925- *72*
Harshaw, Ruth H(etzel) 1890-1968 .... *27*
Harshman, Marc 1950- *109*
    Earlier sketch in SATA *71*

Hart, Alison
  See Leonhardt, Alice
Hart, Bruce 1938-2006 57
  Brief entry 39
Hart, Carole 1943- 57
  Brief entry 39
Hart, Carolyn 1936- 74
Hart, Carolyn G.
  See Hart, Carolyn
Hart, Carolyn Gimpel
  See Hart, Carolyn
Hart, Jan Siegel 1940- 79
Hart, Joyce 1954- 148
Hart, Lenore 171
Hart, Philip S. 1944- 180
Hart, Virginia 1949- 83
Harte, (Francis) Bret(t) 1836(?)-1902 26
Harter, Debbie 1963- 107
Hartfield, Claire 1957- 147
Hartinger, Brent 1964- 174
  Earlier sketch in SATA *145*
Hartland, Jessie 171
Hartley, Ellen (Raphael) 1915-1980 23
Hartley, Fred Allan III 1953- 41
Hartley, William B(rown) 1913-1980 23
Hartling, Peter
  See CLR *29*
  See Hartling, Peter
Hartling, Peter 1933- 66
  See Hartling, Pete
Hartman, Evert 1937- 38
  Brief entry 35
Hartman, Jane E(vangeline) 1928- 47
Hartman, Louis F(rancis) 1901-1970 22
Hartman, Rachel 174
Hartman, Victoria 1942- 91
Hartnett, Sonya 1968- 176
  Earlier sketches in SATA *93, 130*
Hartshorn, Ruth M. 1928- 11
Hartung, Susan Kathleen 150
Hartwig, Manfred 1950- 81
Harvey, Brett 1936- 61
Harvey, Karen D. 1935- 88
Harvey, Roland 1945- 179
  Earlier sketches in SATA *71, 123*
Harwick, B. L.
  See Keller, Beverly L(ou)
Harwin, Brian
  See Henderson, LeGrand
Harwood, Pearl Augusta (Bragdon) 1903-1998
  9
Haseley, Dennis 1950- 157
  Brief entry 44
  Earlier sketches in SATA *57, 105*
Hashmi, Kerri 1955- 108
Haskell, Arnold L(ionel) 1903-1981(?) 6
Haskins, James
  See Haskins, James S.
Haskins, James S. 1941-2005 132
  Autobiography Feature 132
  Earlier sketches in SATA *9, 69, 105*
  See also CLR *39*
  See Haskins, Jim
Haskins, Jim
  See SAAS *4*
  See Haskins, James S.
Hasler, Eveline 1933- 181
Hasler, Joan 1931- 28
Hass, Robert 1941- 94
Hassall, Joan 1906-1988 43
  Obituary 56
Hassett, Ann 1958- 162
Hassett, John 162
Hassler, Jon 1933- 19
Hassler, Jon Francis
  See Hassler, Jon
Hastings, Beverly
  See Barkin, Carol
  and James, Elizabeth
Hastings, Graham
  See Jeffries, Roderic

Hastings, Ian 1912- 62
Hatch, Lynda S. 1950- 90
Hathaway, Barbara 164
Hathorn, Libby 1943- 156
  Autobiography Feature 156
  Earlier sketches in SATA *74, 120*
  See Hathorn, Elizabeth Helen
Haugaard, Erik Christian 1923- 68
  Earlier sketch in SATA *4*
  See also CLR *11*
  See also SAAS *12*
Haugaard, Kay 117
Haugen, Hayley Mitchell 1968- 172
Haugen, Tormod 1945- 66
Hauman, Doris 1898-1984 32
Hauman, George 1890-1961 32
Hauptly, Denis J(ames) 1945- 57
Hauser, Jill Frankel 1950- 127
Hauser, Margaret L(ouise) 1909- 10
Hausherr, Rosmarie 1943- 86
Hausman, Gerald 1945- 180
  Earlier sketches in SATA *13, 90, 132*
  See also CLR *89*
Hausman, Gerry
  See Hausman, Gerald
Hauth, Katherine B. 1940- 99
Hautman, Pete 1952- 173
  Earlier sketches in SATA *82, 128*
Hautman, Peter Murray
  See Hautman, Pete
Hautzig, Deborah 1956- 106
  Earlier sketch in SATA *31*
Hautzig, Esther Rudomin 1930- 148
  Earlier sketches in SATA *4, 68*
  See also CLR *22*
  See also SAAS *15*
Havel, Geoff 1955- 152
Havel, Jennifer
  See Havill, Juanita
Havelin, Kate 1961- 143
Havighurst, Walter (Edwin) 1901-1994 1
  Obituary 79
Haviland, Virginia 1911-1988 6
  Obituary 54
Havill, Juanita 1949- 155
  Earlier sketch in SATA *74*
Hawes, Judy 1913- 4
Hawes, Louise 1943- 180
  Earlier sketch in SATA *60*
Hawke, Rosanne 1953- 165
  Earlier sketch in SATA *124*
Hawke, Rosanne Joy
  See Hawke, Rosanne
Hawkes, Kevin (Cliff) 1959- 150
  Earlier sketch in SATA *78*
Hawkes, Nigel 1943- 119
Hawkesworth, Eric 1921- 13
Hawkins, Arthur 1903-1985 19
Hawkins, Colin 1945- 162
  Earlier sketch in SATA *112*
Hawkins, Jacqui 162
  Earlier sketch in SATA *112*
Hawkins, Laura 1951- 74
Hawkins, (Helena Ann) Quail 1905-2002 6
  Obituary 141
Hawkinson, John (Samuel) 1912-1994 4
Hawkinson, Lucy (Ozone) 1924-1971 21
Hawks, Robert 1961- 85
Hawley, Mabel C. 67
  Earlier sketch in SATA *1*
Hawthorne, Captain R. M.
  See Ellis, Edward S(ylvester)
Hawthorne, Nathaniel 1804-1864
  See YABC *2*
  See also CLR *103*
Hay, Jeff T. 154
Hay, John 1915- 13
Hay, Timothy
  See Brown, Margaret Wise
Hayashi, Leslie Ann 1954- 115
Hayashi, Nancy 1939- 80

Haycak, Cara 1961- 180
Haycock, Kate 1962- 77
Haycraft, Howard 1905-1991 6
  Obituary 70
Haycraft, Molly Costain 1911- 6
Hayden, Gwendolen Lampshire 1904- 35
Hayden, Robert C(arter), Jr. 1937- 47
  Brief entry 28
Hayden, Robert E(arl) 1913-1980 19
  Obituary 26
Hayden, Torey L. 1951- 163
  Earlier sketch in SATA *65*
Hayden, Torey Lynn
  See Hayden, Torey L.
Hayes, Carlton J(oseph) H(untley) 1882-1964
  11
Hayes, Daniel 1952- 109
  Earlier sketch in SATA *73*
Hayes, Geoffrey 1947- 91
  Earlier sketch in SATA *26*
Hayes, Joe 1945- 131
  Earlier sketch in SATA *88*
Hayes, John F. 1904-1980 11
Hayes, Rosemary 158
Hayes, Sheila 1937- 51
  Brief entry 50
Hayes, Will 7
Hayes, William D(imitt) 1913-1976 8
Haynes, Betsy 1937- 94
  Brief entry 37
  Earlier sketch in SATA *48*
  See also CLR *90*
Haynes, David 1955- 97
Haynes, Linda
  See Swinford, Betty (June Wells)
Haynes, Mary 1938- 65
Haynes, Max 1956- 72
Hays, H(offmann) R(eynolds) 1904-1980 ... 26
Hays, Thomas Anthony 1957- 84
Hays, Tony
  See Hays, Thomas Anthony
Hays, Wilma Pitchford 1909- 28
  Earlier sketch in SATA *1*
  See also CLR *59*
  See also SAAS *3*
Hayward, Linda 1943- 101
  Brief entry 39
Haywood, Carolyn 1898-1990 75
  Obituary 64
  Earlier sketches in SATA *1, 29*
  See also CLR *22*
Hazell, Rebecca (Eileen) 1947- 141
Hazen, Barbara Shook 1930- 178
  Earlier sketches in SATA *27, 90*
Head, Gay
  See Hauser, Margaret L(ouise)
Head, Tom 1978- 167
Headley, Elizabeth
  See Harrison, Elizabeth (Allen) Cavanna
Headley, Justina Chen 1968- 176
Headstrom, (Birger) Richard 1902-1985 8
Heady, Eleanor B(utler) 1917-1979 8
Heagy, William D. 1964- 76
Heal, Edith 1903-1995 7
Heal, Gillian 1934- 89
Heale, Jay (Jeremy Peter Wingfield) 1937-
  84
Healey, Brooks
  See Albert, Burton
Healey, Larry 1927- 44
  Brief entry 42
Heap, Sue 1954- 150
Heaps, Willard A(llison) 1908-1987 26
Hearn, Diane Dawson 1952- 79
Hearn, Emily
  See Valleau, Emily
Hearn, Julie 1958- 152
Hearn, Lian
  See Rubinstein, Gillian
Hearn, Sneed
  See Gregg, Andrew K.

Hearne, Betsy Gould 1942- *146*
  Earlier sketches in SATA *38, 95*
Heath, Charles D(ickinson) 1941- *46*
Heath, Veronica
  See Blackett, Veronica Heath
Heaven, Constance (Christina) 1911- *7*
Hebert-Collins, Sheila 1948- *111*
Hecht, Henri Joseph 1922- *9*
Hechtkopf, Henryk 1910- *17*
Heck, Bessie (Mildred) Holland 1911-1995

.... *26*
Heck, Ed 1963- *173*
Heckert, Connie K(aye Delp) 1948- *82*
Hedderwick, Mairi 1939- *145*
  Earlier sketches in SATA *30, 77*
Hedges, Sid(ney) G(eorge) 1897-1974 .... *28*
Hedrick, Irene Hope 1920- *175*
Heelan, Jamee Riggio 1965- *146*
Heerboth, Sharon
  See Leon, Sharon
Heffernan, John 1949- *168*
  Earlier sketch in SATA *121*
Heffron, Dorris 1944- *68*
Hefter, Richard 1942- *31*
Hegarty, Reginald Beaton 1906-1973 .... *10*
Hehenberger, Shelly 1968- *126*
Heidbreder, Robert K. 1947- *130*
Heide, Florence Parry 1919- *118*
  Earlier sketches in SATA *32, 69*
  See also CLR *60*
  See also SAAS *6*
Heiderstadt, Dorothy 1907-2001 .... *6*
Heidi Louise
  See Erdrich, Louise
Heidler, David S(tephen) 1955- *132*
Heidler, Jeanne T. 1956- *132*
Heilbroner, Joan Knapp 1922- *63*
Heiligman, Deborah 1958- *144*
  Earlier sketch in SATA *90*
Heilman, Joan Rattner *50*
Heimann, Rolf 1940- *164*
  Earlier sketch in SATA *120*
Hein, Lucille Eleanor 1915-1994 .... *20*
Heine, Helme 1941- *135*
  Earlier sketch in SATA *67*
  See also CLR *18*
Heinlein, Robert A. 1907-1988 .... *69*
  Obituary *56*
  Earlier sketch in SATA *9*
  See also CLR *75*
Heinlein, Robert Anson
  See Heinlein, Robert A.
Heins, Ethel L(eah) 1918-1997 .... *101*
Heins, Paul 1909- *13*
Heintze, Carl 1922- *26*
Heinz, Brian J. 1946- *181*
  Earlier sketch in SATA *95*
Heinz, Brian James
  See Heinz, Brian J.
Heinz, W(ilfred) C(harles) 1915- *26*
Heinzen, Mildred
  See Masters, Mildred
Heisel, Sharon E(laine) 1941- *125*
  Earlier sketch in SATA *84*
Heitzmann, William Ray 1948- *73*
Heitzmann, Wm. Ray
  See Heitzmann, William Ray
Helakoski, Leslie *178*
Helberg, Shirley Adelaide Holden 1919- ..*138*
Helfer, Ralph 1937- *177*
Helfman, Elizabeth S(eaver) 1911-2001 .... *3*
Helfman, Harry Carmozin 1910-1995 .... *3*
Helgerson, Joseph 1950- *181*
Hellberg, Hans-Eric 1927- *38*
Heller, Linda 1944- *46*
  Brief entry *40*
Heller, Mike
  See Hano, Arnold
Heller, Ruth M. 1924- *112*
  Earlier sketch in SATA *66*

Hellman, Hal
  See Hellman, Harold
Hellman, Harold 1927- *4*
Helman, Andrea (Jean) 1946- *160*
  Earlier sketch in SATA *107*
Helmer, Diana Star 1962- *86*
Helmer, Marilyn *160*
  Earlier sketch in SATA *112*
Helps, Racey 1913-1971 .... *2*
  Obituary *25*
Helquist, Brett *146*
Helweg, Hans H. 1917- *50*
  Brief entry *33*
Helyar, Jane Penelope Josephine 1933- *138*
  Autobiography Feature *138*
  Earlier sketch in SATA *82*
  See Poole, Josephine
Hemmant, Lynette 1938- *69*
Hemming, Roy G. 1928-1995 .... *11*
  Obituary *86*
Hemphill, Helen 1955- *179*
Hemphill, Kris (Harrison) 1963- *118*
Hemphill, Martha Locke 1904-1973 .... *37*
Hemstock, Gillian 1956- *173*
Henba, Bobbie 1926- *87*
Henbest, Nigel 1951- *55*
  Brief entry *52*
Henderley, Brooks *1*
Henderson, Aileen Kilgore 1921- *178*
Henderson, Aileen Mary
  See Fox, Aileen
Henderson, Gordon 1950- *53*
Henderson, Kathy 1949- *155*
  Brief entry *53*
  Earlier sketches in SATA *55, 95*
Henderson, LeGrand 1901-1965 .... *9*
Henderson, Nancy Wallace 1916- *22*
Henderson, Zenna (Chlarson) 1917-1983 ..... *5*
Hendrickson, Walter Brookfield, Jr. 1936- ... *9*
Hendry, Diana 1941- *106*
  Earlier sketch in SATA *68*
Hendry, Frances Mary 1941- *171*
  Earlier sketch in SATA *110*
Hendry, Linda (Gail) 1961- *83*
Heneghan, James 1930- *160*
  Earlier sketches in SATA *53, 97*
Henkes, Kevin 1960- *154*
  Earlier sketches in SATA *43, 76, 108*
  See also CLR *108*
Hennessy, Barbara G.
  See Hennessy, B.G.
Hennessy, Barbara Gulbrandsen
  See Hennessy, B.G.
Hennessy, B.G. 1951- *175*
Henney, Carolee Wells 1928- *102*
Henriod, Lorraine 1925- *26*
Henriquez, Emile F. 1937- *170*
  Earlier sketch in SATA *89*
Henry, April 1959- *174*
Henry, Ernest 1948- *107*
Henry, Joanne Landers 1927- *6*
Henry, Maeve 1960- *75*
Henry, Marguerite 1902-1997 .... *100*
  Obituary *99*
  See also CLR *4*
  See also SAAS *7*
Henry, Marie H. 1935- *65*
Henry, Marilyn 1939- *117*
Henry, Marion
  See del Rey, Lester
Henry, O.
  See Porter, William Sydney
Henry, Oliver
  See Porter, William Sydney
Henry, T. E.
  See Rowland-Entwistle, (Arthur) Theodore
  (Henry)
Henschel, Elizabeth Georgie *56*
Henson, James Maury
  See Henson, Jim

Henson, Jim 1936-1990 .... *43*
  Obituary *65*
Henstra, Friso 1928- *73*
  Earlier sketch in SATA *8*
  See also SAAS *14*
Hentoff, Nat(han Irving) 1925- *133*
  Brief entry *27*
  Earlier sketches in SATA *42, 69*
  See also CLR *52*
Henty, G(eorge) A(lfred) 1832-1902 .... *64*
  See also CLR *76*
Heo, Yumi 1964- *146*
  Earlier sketch in SATA *94*
Hepler, Heather *177*
Herald, Kathleen
  See Peyton, Kathleen Wendy (Herald)
Herb, Angela M. 1970- *92*
Herbert, Cecil
  See Hamilton, Charles (Harold St. John)
Herbert, Don 1917-2007 .... *2*
Herbert, Donald Jeffrey
  See Herbert, Don
Herbert, Frank 1920-1986 .... *37*
  Obituary *47*
  Earlier sketch in SATA *9*
Herbert, Frank Patrick
  See Herbert, Frank
Herbert, Helen (Jean) 1947- *57*
Herbert, Janis 1956- *139*
Herbert, Wally
  See Herbert, Walter William
Herbert, Walter William 1934-2007 .... *23*
Herbst, Judith 1947- *74*
Herda, D.J. 1948- *80*
Herge
  See CLR *114*
  See Remi, Georges
Heritage, Martin
  See Horler, Sydney
Herkimer, L(awrence) R(ussell) 1925(?)- ... *42*
Herlihy, Dirlie Anne 1935- *73*
Herman, Charlotte 1937- *99*
  Earlier sketch in SATA *20*
Hermanson, Dennis (Everett) 1947- *10*
Hermes, Jules 1962- *92*
Hermes, Patricia (Mary) 1936- *141*
  Earlier sketches in SATA *31, 78*
Hernandez, Natalie Nelson 1929- *123*
Herndon, Ernest *91*
Herold, Ann Bixby 1937- *72*
Herrera, Juan Felipe 1948- *127*
Herrick, Steven 1958- *156*
  Earlier sketch in SATA *103*
Herriman, George (Joseph) 1880-1944 ..... *140*
Herriot, James 1916-1995 .... *135*
  Earlier sketch in SATA *86*
  See also CLR *80*
  See Wight, James Alfred
Herrmanns, Ralph 1933- *11*
Herrold, Tracey
  See Dils, Tracey E.
Herron, Edward A(lbert) 1912- *4*
Herschler, Mildred Barger *130*
Hersey, John 1914-1993 .... *25*
  Obituary *76*
Hersey, John Richard
  See Hersey, John
  and Hersey, John
Hershberger, Priscilla (Gorman) 1951- *81*
Hershenhorn, Esther 1945- *151*
Hershey, Kathleen M. 1934- *80*
Hershey, Mary *173*
Hersom, Kathleen 1911- *73*
Hertz, Grete Janus 1915- *23*
Herzig, Alison Cragin 1935- *87*
Herzog, Brad 1968- *131*
Heslewood, Juliet 1951- *82*
Hess, Lilo 1916- *4*
Hess, Paul 1961- *134*
Hesse, Hermann 1877-1962 .... *50*

Hesse, Karen 1952- *158*
    Autobiography Feature *113*
    Earlier sketches in SATA *74, 103*
    See also CLR *54*
    See also SAAS *25*
Hest, Amy 1950- *129*
    Earlier sketches in SATA *55, 82*
Heuer, Kenneth John 1927- *44*
Heuman, William 1912-1971 .... *21*
Heuston, Kimberley 1960- *167*
Heuston, Kimberley Burton
    See Heuston, Kimberley
Hewes, Agnes Danforth 1874-1963 .... *35*
Hewett, Anita 1918-1989 .... *13*
Hewett, Joan 1930- *140*
    Earlier sketch in SATA *81*
Hewett, Richard 1929- *81*
Hewitson, Jennifer 1961- *97*
Hewitt, Margaret 1961- *84*
Hewitt, Sally 1949- *127*
Hext, Harrington
    See Phillpotts, Eden
Hey, Nigel S(tewart) 1936- *20*
Heyduck-Huth, Hilde 1929- *8*
Heyer, Carol 1950- *130*
    Earlier sketch in SATA *74*
Heyer, Marilee 1942- *102*
    Earlier sketch in SATA *64*
Heyerdahl, Thor 1914-2002 .... *52*
    Earlier sketch in SATA *2*
Heyes, (Nancy) Eileen 1956- *150*
    Earlier sketch in SATA *80*
Heyliger, William 1884-1955
    See YABC *1*
Heyman, Ken(neth Louis) 1930- *114*
    Earlier sketch in SATA *34*
Heyward, (Edwin) DuBose 1885-1940 .... *21*
Heywood, Karen 1946- *48*
Hezlep, William (Earl) 1936- *88*
Hibbert, Christopher 1924- *4*
Hibbert, Eleanor Alice Burford 1906-1993 ... *2*
    Obituary *74*
    See Holt, Victoria
Hickman, Estella (Lee) 1942- *111*
Hickman, Janet 1940- *127*
    Earlier sketch in SATA *12*
Hickman, Martha Whitmore 1925- *26*
Hickman, Pamela M. 1958- *128*
Hickock, Will
    See Harrison, C(hester) William
Hickok, Lorena A. 1893-1968 .... *20*
Hickox, Rebecca (Ayres) *116*
Hicks, Barbara Jean 1953- *165*
Hicks, Clifford B. 1920- *50*
Hicks, Eleanor B.
    See Coerr, Eleanor (Beatrice)
Hicks, Harvey
    See Stratemeyer, Edward L.
Hicks, Peter 1952- *111*
Hicyilmaz, Gaye 1947- *157*
    Earlier sketch in SATA *77*
Hieatt, Constance B(artlett) 1928- *4*
Hiebert, Ray Eldon 1932- *13*
Higdon, Hal 1931- *4*
Higginbottom, David 1923- *87*
    See Fisk, Nicholas
Higginbottom, J(effrey) Winslow 1945- *29*
Higgins, Joanna 1945- *125*
Higgins, Simon (Richard) 1958- *105*
Higginsen, Vy *79*
High, Linda Oatman 1958- *145*
    Earlier sketch in SATA *94*
High, Philip E. 1914- *119*
High, Philip Empson
    See High, Philip E.
Higham, David (Michael) 1949- *50*
Higham, Jon Atlas
    See Higham, Jonathan Huw
Higham, Jonathan Huw 1960- *59*
Highet, Helen
    See MacInnes, Helen (Clark)

Hightower, Florence Cole 1916-1981 .... *4*
    Obituary *27*
Highwater, Jamake (Mamake) 1942(?)-2001
    .... *69*
    Brief entry *30*
    Earlier sketch in SATA *32*
    See also CLR *17*
Hilb, Nora 1953- *178*
Hildebrandt, Greg 1939- *172*
    Brief entry *33*
    Earlier sketch in SATA *55*
Hildebrandt, Tim 1939-2006 .... *55*
    Brief entry *33*
Hildebrandt, Timothy
    See Hildebrandt, Tim
Hildebrandts, The
    See Hildebrandt, Greg
    and Hildebrandt, Tim
Hilder, Rowland 1905-1993 .... *36*
    Obituary *77*
Hildick, E. W.
    See SAAS *6*
    See Hildick, (Edmund) Wallace
Hildick, (Edmund) Wallace 1925-2001 .... *68*
    Earlier sketch in SATA *2*
    See Hildick, E. W.
Hilgartner, Beth 1957- *58*
Hill, Alexis
    See Craig, Mary (Francis) Shura
    and Glick, Ruth (Burtnick)
Hill, Anthony R. 1942- *164*
    Earlier sketch in SATA *91*
Hill, Anthony Robert
    See Hill, Anthony R.
Hill, David 1942- *152*
    Earlier sketch in SATA *103*
Hill, Donna (Marie) 1921- *124*
    Earlier sketch in SATA *24*
Hill, Douglas 1935-2007 .... *78*
    Earlier sketch in SATA *39*
Hill, Douglas Arthur
    See Hill, Douglas
Hill, Elizabeth Starr 1925- *143*
    Earlier sketch in SATA *24*
Hill, Eric 1927- *133*
    Brief entry *53*
    Earlier sketch in SATA *66*
    See also CLR *13*
Hill, Gordon
    See Eldin, Peter
Hill, Grace Brooks *67*
    Earlier sketch in SATA *1*
Hill, Grace Livingston 1865-1947
    See YABC *2*
Hill, Helen M(orey) 1915- *27*
Hill, John
    See Koontz, Dean R.
Hill, Johnson
    See Kunhardt, Edith
Hill, Judy I. R.
    See Roberts, Judy I.
Hill, Kathleen Louise 1917- *4*
Hill, Kay
    See Hill, Kathleen Louise
Hill, Kirkpatrick 1938- *126*
    Earlier sketch in SATA *72*
Hill, Laban Carrick *170*
Hill, Lee Sullivan 1958- *96*
Hill, Lorna 1902-1991 .... *12*
Hill, Margaret (Ohler) 1915- *36*
Hill, Meg
    See Hill, Margaret (Ohler)
Hill, Meredith
    See Craig, Mary (Francis) Shura
Hill, Monica
    See Watson, Jane Werner
Hill, Pamela Smith 1954- *112*
Hill, Ralph Nading 1917-1987 .... *65*
Hill, Robert W(hite) 1919-1982 .... *12*
    Obituary *31*

Hill, Ruth A.
    See Viguers, Ruth Hill
Hill, Ruth Livingston
    See Munce, Ruth Hill
Hill, Thomas 1960- *82*
Hillcourt, William 1900-1992 .... *27*
Hillenbrand, Will 1960- *147*
    Earlier sketch in SATA *84*
Hiller, Ilo (Ann) 1938- *59*
Hillerman, Tony 1925- *6*
Hillert, Margaret 1920- *91*
    Earlier sketch in SATA *8*
Hillman, Elizabeth 1942- *75*
Hillman, John 1952- *120*
Hillman, Martin
    See Hill, Douglas
Hillman, Priscilla 1940- *48*
    Brief entry *39*
Hills, C.A.R. 1955- *39*
Hills, Charles Albert Reis
    See Hills, C.A.R.
Hills, Tad *173*
Hilton, Irene Pothus -1979 .... *7*
Hilton, James 1900-1954 .... *34*
Hilton, Margaret Lynette 1946- *105*
    Earlier sketch in SATA *68*
    See Hilton, Nette
Hilton, Nette
    See CLR *25*
    See also SAAS *21*
    See Hilton, Margaret Lynette
Hilton, Ralph 1907-1982 .... *8*
Hilton, Suzanne 1922- *4*
Hilton-Bruce, Anne
    See Hilton, Margaret Lynette
Himelblau, Linda -2005 .... *179*
Himelstein, Shmuel 1940- *83*
Himler, Ann 1946- *8*
Himler, Ronald (Norbert) 1937- *137*
    Earlier sketches in SATA *6, 92*
Himmelman, John C(arl) 1959- *159*
    Earlier sketches in SATA *47, 94*
Hinckley, Helen
    See Jones, Helen Hinckley
Hind, Dolores (Ellen) 1931- *53*
    Brief entry *49*
Hindin, Nathan
    See Bloch, Robert (Albert)
Hindley, Judy 1940- *179*
    Earlier sketch in SATA *120*
Hinds, P(atricia) Mignon *98*
Hines, Anna Grossnickle 1946- *141*
    Brief entry *45*
    Earlier sketches in SATA *51, 95*
    See also SAAS *16*
Hines, Gary (Roger) 1944- *136*
    Earlier sketch in SATA *74*
Hinojosa, Maria (de Lourdes) 1961- *88*
Hinton, Nigel 1941- *166*
Hinton, Sam 1917- *43*
Hinton, S.E. 1950- *160*
    Earlier sketches in SATA *19, 58, 115*
    See also CLR *23*
Hinton, Susan Eloise
    See Hinton, S.E.
Hintz, Martin 1945- *128*
    Brief entry *39*
    Earlier sketch in SATA *47*
Hintz, Stephen V. 1975- *129*
Hippopotamus, Eugene H.
    See Kraus, (Herman) Robert
Hirano, Cathy 1957- *68*
Hirsch, Karen 1941- *61*
Hirsch, Odo *157*
    Earlier sketch in SATA *111*
Hirsch, Phil 1926- *35*
Hirsch, S. Carl 1913-1990 .... *2*
    See also SAAS *7*
Hirschfelder, Arlene B. 1943- *138*
    Earlier sketch in SATA *80*

Hirschi, Ron 1948- *95*
  Earlier sketch in SATA *56*
Hirschmann, Linda (Ann) 1941- *40*
Hirsh, Marilyn 1944-1988 .... *7*
  Obituary *58*
Hirshberg, Al(bert Simon) 1909-1973 .... *38*
Hiscock, Bruce 1940- *137*
  Earlier sketch in SATA *57*
Hiser, Constance 1950- *71*
Hiser, Iona Seibert -1998 .... *4*
Hislop, Julia Rose Catherine 1962- *74*
Hissey, Jane 1952- *130*
  Autobiography Feature *130*
  Earlier sketches in SATA *58, 103*
Hissey, Jane Elizabeth
  See Hissey, Jane
Hitchcock, Alfred (Joseph) 1899-1980 .... *27*
  Obituary *24*
Hite, Sid 1954- *175*
  Earlier sketches in SATA *75, 136*
Hitte, Kathryn 1919- *16*
Hitz, Demi 1942- *152*
  Earlier sketches in SATA *11, 66, 102*
  See also CLR *58*
  See Demi
Hitzeroth, Deborah L. 1961- *78*
Hnizdovsky, Jacques 1915- *32*
Ho, Minfong 1951- *151*
  Earlier sketches in SATA *15, 94*
  See also CLR *28*
Hoagland, Edward (Morley) 1932- *51*
Hoare, Robert J(ohn) 1921-1975 .... *38*
Hoban, Lillian 1925-1998 .... *69*
  Obituary *104*
  Earlier sketch in SATA *22*
  See also CLR *67*
Hoban, Russell 1925- *136*
  Earlier sketches in SATA *1, 40, 78*
  See also CLR *69*
Hoban, Russell Conwell
  See Hoban, Russell
Hoban, Tana 1917(?)-2006 .... *104*
  Obituary *173*
  Earlier sketches in SATA *22, 70*
  See also CLR *76*
  See also SAAS *12*
Hobart, Lois (Elaine) *7*
Hobbie, Holly 1944- *178*
  See also CLR *88*
Hobbs, Leigh 1953- *166*
Hobbs, Valerie 1941- *145*
  Autobiography Feature *145*
  Earlier sketch in SATA *93*
Hobbs, Will 1947- *177*
  Autobiography Feature *127*
  Earlier sketches in SATA *72, 110*
  See also CLR *59*
Hobbs, William Carl
  See Hobbs, Will
Hoberman, Mary Ann 1930- *158*
  Earlier sketches in SATA *5, 72, 111*
  See also CLR *22*
  See also SAAS *18*
Hobson, Bruce 1950- *62*
Hobson, Burton (Harold) 1933- *28*
Hobson, Laura Z(ametkin) 1900-1986 .... *52*
Hobson, Sally 1967- *172*
  Earlier sketch in SATA *84*
Hoce, Charley E. *174*
Hochschild, Arlie Russell 1940- *11*
Hockaby, Stephen
  See Mitchell, Gladys (Maude Winifred)
Hockenberry, Hope
  See Newell, Hope Hockenberry
Hodge, Deborah 1954- *163*
  Earlier sketch in SATA *122*
Hodge, P. W.
  See Hodge, Paul W(illiam)
Hodge, Paul W(illiam) 1934- *12*
Hodgell, P(atricia) C(hristine) 1951- *42*

Hodges, C. Walter 1909-2004 .... *2*
  Obituary *158*
Hodges, Carl G. 1902-1964 .... *10*
Hodges, Cyril Walter
  See Hodges, C. Walter
Hodges, Elizabeth Jamison *1*
Hodges, Margaret 1911-2005 .... *167*
  Obituary *172*
  Earlier sketches in SATA *1, 33, 75, 117*
  See also SAAS *9*
Hodges, Margaret Moore
  See Hodges, Margaret
Hodgetts, Blake Christopher 1967- *43*
Hodgson, Harriet (W.) 1935- *84*
Hoehne, Marcia 1951- *89*
Hoellwarth, Cathryn Clinton
  See Clinton, Cathryn
Hoestlandt, Jo 1948- *94*
Hoestlandt, Jocelyne
  See Hoestlandt, Jo
Hoexter, Corinne K. 1927- *6*
Hoeye, Michael 1947- *136*
Hoff, Carol 1900-1979 .... *11*
Hoff, Mary (King) 1956- *157*
  Earlier sketch in SATA *74*
Hoff, Syd(ney) 1912-2004 .... *138*
  Obituary *154*
  Earlier sketches in SATA *9, 72*
  See also CLR *83*
  See also SAAS *4*
Hoffman, Edwin D. *49*
Hoffman, Mary (Margaret) 1945- *144*
  Earlier sketches in SATA *59, 97*
  See also SAAS *24*
  See Lassiter, Mary
Hoffman, Mat 1972- *150*
Hoffman, Nina Kiriki 1955- *160*
Hoffman, Phyllis M(iriam) 1944- *4*
Hoffman, Rosekrans 1926- *15*
Hoffmann, E(rnst) T(heodor) A(madeus)
  1776-1822 .... *27*
Hoffmann, Felix 1911-1975 .... *9*
Hoffmann, Heinrich 1809-1894
  See CLR *122*
Hoffmann, Margaret Jones 1910- *48*
Hoffmann, Peggy
  See Hoffmann, Margaret Jones
Hofher, Catherine Baxley 1954- *130*
Hofher, Cathy
  See Hofher, Catherine Baxley
Hofmeyr, Dianne (Louise) *138*
Hofsepian, Sylvia A. 1932- *74*
Hofsinde, Robert 1902-1973 .... *21*
Hogan, Bernice Harris 1929- *12*
Hogan, Inez 1895-1973 .... *2*
Hogan, James P(atrick) 1941- *81*
Hogan, Linda 1947- *132*
Hogarth, Burne 1911-1996 .... *89*
  Earlier sketch in SATA *63*
Hogarth, Grace (Weston Allen) 1905-1995 . *91*
Hogarth, Jr.
  See Kent, Rockwell
Hogarth, (Arthur) Paul 1917-2001 .... *41*
Hogg, Garry 1902-1976 .... *2*
Hogg, Gary 1957- *172*
  Earlier sketch in SATA *105*
Hogner, Dorothy Childs *4*
Hogner, Nils 1893-1970 .... *25*
Hogrogian, Nonny 1932- *74*
  Autobiography Feature *127*
  Earlier sketch in SATA *7*
  See also CLR *95*
  See also SAAS *1*
Hoh, Diane 1937- *102*
  Brief entry *48*
  Earlier sketch in SATA *52*
Hoke, John (Lindsay) 1925- *7*
Hol, Coby 1943- *126*
Holabird, Katharine 1948- *135*
  Earlier sketch in SATA *62*
Holaday, Bobbie 1922- *153*

Holbeach, Henry
  See Rands, William Brighty
Holberg, Ruth L(angland) 1889-1984 .... *1*
Holbrook, Kathy 1963- *107*
Holbrook, Peter
  See Glick, Carl (Cannon)
Holbrook, Sabra
  See Erickson, Sabra Rollins
Holbrook, Sara *131*
Holbrook, Stewart Hall 1893-1964 .... *2*
Holcomb, Jerry (Leona) Kimble 1927- *113*
Holcomb, Nan
  See McPhee, Norma H.
Holden, Elizabeth Rhoda
  See Lawrence, Louise
Holding, James (Clark Carlisle, Jr.) 1907-1997
  .... *3*
Holeman, Linda 1949- *136*
  Autobiography Feature *136*
  Earlier sketch in SATA *102*
Holinger, William (Jacques) 1944- *90*
Holisher, Desider 1901-1972 .... *6*
Holl, Adelaide Hinkle 1910- *8*
Holl, Kristi D(iane) 1951- *51*
Holland, Gay W. 1941- *128*
Holland, Isabelle (Christian) 1920-2002 ..... *70*
  Autobiography Feature *103*
  Obituary *132*
  Earlier sketch in SATA *8*
  See also CLR *57*
Holland, Janice 1913-1962 .... *18*
Holland, John L(ewis) 1919- *20*
Holland, Joyce
  See Morice, Dave
Holland, Julia 1954- *106*
Holland, Lynda (H.) 1959- *77*
Holland, Lys
  See Gater, Dilys
Holland, Marion 1908-1989 .... *6*
  Obituary *61*
Hollander, John 1929- *13*
Hollander, Nicole 1940(?)- *101*
Hollander, Paul
  See Silverberg, Robert
Hollander, Phyllis 1928- *39*
Hollander, Zander 1923- *63*
Holldobler, Turid 1939- *26*
Holliday, Joe
  See Holliday, Joseph
Holliday, Joseph 1910- *11*
Holling, Holling C(lancy) 1900-1973 .... *15*
  Obituary *26*
  See also CLR *50*
Hollingsworth, Alvin C(arl) 1930- *39*
Hollingsworth, Mary 1947- *166*
  Earlier sketch in SATA *91*
Holloway, Teresa (Bragunier) 1906- *26*
Holm, (Else) Anne (Lise) 1922-1998 .... *1*
  See also CLR *75*
  See also SAAS *7*
Holm, Jennifer L. 1968(?)- *163*
  Earlier sketch in SATA *120*
Holm, Matthew 1974- *174*
Holm, Sharon Lane 1955- *114*
  Earlier sketch in SATA *78*
Holman, Felice 1919- *82*
  Earlier sketch in SATA *7*
  See also SAAS *17*
Holm and Hamel
  See Holm, Jennifer L.
Holme, Bryan 1913-1990 .... *26*
  Obituary *66*
Holmes, Barbara Ware 1945- *127*
  Earlier sketch in SATA *65*
Holmes, John
  See Souster, (Holmes) Raymond
Holmes, Marjorie (Rose) 1910-2002 .... *43*
Holmes, Martha 1961- *72*
Holmes, Mary Z(astrow) 1943- *80*
Holmes, Oliver Wendell 1809-1894 .... *34*
Holmes, Peggy 1898- *60*

Holmes, Raymond
    See Souster, (Holmes) Raymond
Holmes, Rick
    See Hardwick, Richard Holmes, Jr.
Holmgren, Helen Jean 1930- 45
Holmgren, Sister George Ellen
    See Holmgren, Helen Jean
Holmgren, Virginia C(unningham) 1909- ... 26
Holmquist, Eve 1921- 11
Holt, Kimberly Willis 1960- 179
    Earlier sketch in SATA 122
Holt, Margaret 1937- 4
Holt, Margaret Van Vechten (Saunders)
    1899-1963 32
Holt, Michael (Paul) 1929- 13
Holt, Rackham
    See Holt, Margaret Van Vechten (Saunders)
Holt, Rochelle L. 41
    See DuBois, Rochelle (Lynn) Holt
Holt, Stephen
    See Thompson, Harlan (Howard)
Holt, Victoria
    See Hibbert, Eleanor Alice Burford
Holton, Leonard
    See Wibberley, Leonard (Patrick O'Connor)
Holtze, Sally Holmes 1952- 64
Holtzman, Jerome 1926- 57
Holub, Joan 1956- 149
    Earlier sketch in SATA 99
Holub, Josef 1926- 175
Holubitsky, Katherine 1955- 165
    Earlier sketch in SATA 121
Holyer, Erna Maria 1925- 22
Holyer, Ernie
    See Holyer, Erna Maria
Holz, Loretta (Marie) 1943- 17
Homel, David 1952- 97
Homze, Alma C. 1932- 17
Honey, Elizabeth 1947- 137
    Autobiography Feature 137
    Earlier sketch in SATA 112
Honeycutt, Natalie 1945- 97
Hong, Lily Toy 1958- 76
Honig, Donald 1931- 18
Honness, Elizabeth H. 1904- 2
Hoobler, Dorothy 1941- 161
    Earlier sketches in SATA 28, 109
Hoobler, Thomas 161
    Earlier sketches in SATA 28, 109
Hood, Joseph F. 1925- 4
Hood, Robert E. 1926- 21
Hood, Sarah
    See Killough, (Karen) Lee
Hook, Brendan 1963- 105
Hook, Frances 1912-1983 27
Hook, Geoffrey R(aynor) 1928- 103
Hook, Jeff
    See Hook, Geoffrey R(aynor)
Hook, Martha 1936- 27
Hooker, Richard
    See Heinz, W(ilfred) C(harles)
Hooker, Ruth 1920-1998 21
hooks, bell 1952(?)- 170
    Earlier sketch in SATA 115
Hooks, William H(arris) 1921- 94
    Earlier sketch in SATA 16
Hoon, Patricia Easterly 1954- 90
Hooper, Mary 1944- 160
Hooper, Maureen Brett 1927- 76
Hooper, Meredith 1939- 159
    Earlier sketches in SATA 28, 101
Hooper, Meredith Jean
    See Hooper, Meredith
Hooper, Patricia 1941- 95
Hoopes, Lyn Littlefield 1953- 49
    Brief entry 44
Hoopes, Ned E(dward) 1932- 21
Hoopes, Roy 1922- 11
Hoose, Phillip M. 1947- 137

Hoover, H(elen) M(ary) 1935- 132
    Brief entry 33
    Earlier sketches in SATA 44, 83
    See also SAAS 8
Hoover, Helen (Drusilla Blackburn) 1910-1984
    12
    Obituary 39
Hope, Christopher (David Tully) 1944- 62
Hope, Laura Lee 67
    Earlier sketch in SATA 1
    See Goulart, Ron(ald Joseph)
    and Stanley, George Edward
Hope Simpson, Jacynth 1930- 12
Hopf, Alice (Martha) L(ightner) 1904-1988 . 5
    Obituary 55
Hopkins, C. M.
    See Hopkins, Cathy
Hopkins, Cathy 1953- 165
Hopkins, Cathy M.
    See Hopkins, Cathy
Hopkins, Ellen L. 1955- 128
Hopkins, Jackie
    See Hopkins, Jackie Mims
Hopkins, Jackie Mims 1952- 178
    Earlier sketch in SATA 92
Hopkins, Joseph G(erard) E(dward) 1909- .. 11
Hopkins, Lee Bennett 1938- 168
    Earlier sketches in SATA 3, 68, 125
    See also CLR 44
    See also SAAS 4
Hopkins, Lyman
    See Folsom, Franklin (Brewster)
Hopkins, Marjorie 1911-1999 9
Hopkins, Mary R(ice) 1956- 97
Hopkinson, Amanda 1948- 84
Hopkinson, Deborah 1952- 180
    Autobiography Feature 180
    Earlier sketches in SATA 76, 108, 159
    See also CLR 118
Hopman, Philip 1961- 177
Hoppe, Joanne 1932- 42
Hoppe, Matthias 1952- 76
Hopper, Nancy J. 1937- 38
    Brief entry 35
Hopping, Lorraine Jean
    See Egan, Lorraine Hopping
Horacek, Petr 163
Horenstein, Henry 1947- 108
Horgan, Paul (George Vincent O'Shaughnessy)
    1903-1995 13
    Obituary 84
Horlak, E. E.
    See Tepper, Sheri S.
Horler, Sydney 1888-1954 102
Horn, Sandra Ann 1944- 154
Hornblow, Arthur, Jr. 1893-1976 15
Hornblow, Leonora 1920-2005 18
    Obituary 171
Hornblow, Leonora Schinasi
    See Hornblow, Leonora
Horne, Constance 1927- 149
Horne, Richard 1960-2007 169
    Obituary 180
    Earlier sketch in SATA 111
Horne, Richard Henry Hengist 1802(?)-1884
    29
Horner, Althea (Jane) 1926- 36
Horner, Dave 1934- 12
Horner, Jack
    See Horner, John R(obert)
Horner, John R(obert) 1946- 106
Hornik, Laurie Miller 159
Horniman, Joanne 1951- 167
    Earlier sketch in SATA 98
Hornos, Axel 1907-1994 20
Hornstein, Reuben Aaron 1912- 64
Horowitz, Anthony 1955- 137
Horowitz, Dave 1973(?)- 172
Horowitz, Ruth 1957- 136
Horrocks, Anita 1958- 169

Horse, Harry
    See Horne, Richard
Horsfield, Alan 1939- 153
Hort, Lenny 179
Horton, James O. 1943- 173
Horton, James Oliver
    See Horton, James O.
Horton, Madelyn (Stacey) 1962- 77
Horvath, Betty 1927- 4
Horvath, Polly 1957- 140
    Earlier sketch in SATA 85
    See also CLR 90
Horwich, Frances R(appaport) 1908-2001 .. 11
    Obituary 130
Horwitz, Elinor Lander 45
    Brief entry 33
Horwood, William 1944- 85
Hosford, Dorothy (Grant) 1900-1952 22
Hosford, Jessie 1892-1990 5
Hoshi, Shin'ichi 1926- 101
Hoskyns-Abrahall, Clare (Constance
    Drury) 13
Hossack, Sylvia 1939- 83
Hossack, Sylvie Adams
    See Hossack, Sylvia
Hosseini, Khaled 1965- 156
Hossell, Karen Price
    See Price, Karen
Hostetler, Marian 1932- 91
Houck, Carter 1924- 22
Hough, (Helen) Charlotte 1924- 9
Hough, Judy Taylor 1932- 63
    Brief entry 51
    Earlier sketch in SATA 56
Hough, Richard (Alexander) 1922-1999 17
Houghton, Eric 1930- 7
Houk, Randy 1944- 97
Houlehen, Robert J. 1918- 18
Household, Geoffrey (Edward West)
    1900-1988 14
    Obituary 59
Housman, Laurence 1865-1959 25
Houston, Dick 1943- 74
Houston, Gloria 138
    Autobiography Feature 138
    Earlier sketch in SATA 81
Houston, James A(rchibald) 1921-2005 74
    Obituary 163
    Earlier sketch in SATA 13
    See also CLR 3
    See also SAAS 17
Houston, James D. 1933- 78
Houston, Jeanne Toyo Wakatsuki
    See Houston, Jeanne Wakatsuki
Houston, Jeanne Wakatsuki 1934- 168
    Autobiography Feature 168
    Earlier sketch in SATA 78
Houston, Juanita C. 1921- 129
Houton, Kathleen
    See Kilgore, Kathleen
Houts, Amy E. 164
Hovey, Kate 158
Howard, Alan 1922- 45
Howard, Alyssa
    See Buckholtz, Eileen (Garber)
    and Glick, Ruth (Burtnick)
    and Titchener, Louise
Howard, Arthur 1948- 165
Howard, Arthur Charles
    See Howard, Arthur
Howard, Elizabeth Fitzgerald 1927- 119
    Earlier sketch in SATA 74
Howard, Ellen 1943- 99
    Earlier sketch in SATA 67
Howard, Jane R(uble) 1924- 87
Howard, Norman Barry 1949- 90
Howard, P. M.
    See Howard, Pauline Rodriguez
Howard, Paul 1967- 118
Howard, Pauline Rodriguez 1951- 124

Howard, Prosper
  See Hamilton, Charles (Harold St. John)
Howard, Robert West 1908-1988 5
Howard, Todd 1964- 135
Howard, Tristan
  See Currie, Stephen
Howard, Vernon (Linwood) 1918-1992 40
  Obituary 73
Howard, Warren F.
  See Pohl, Frederik
Howarth, David (Armine) 1912-1991 6
  Obituary 68
Howarth, Lesley 1952- 94
Howe, Deborah 1946-1978 29
Howe, James 1946- 161
  Earlier sketches in SATA 29, 71, 111
  See also CLR 9
Howe, John F. 1957- 79
Howe, Norma 1930- 126
Howell, Pat 1947- 15
Howell, S.
  See Styles, (Frank) Showell
Howell, Virginia
  See Ellison, Virginia H(owell)
Howes, Barbara 1914-1996 5
Howie, Diana (Melson) 1945- 122
Howker, Janni 1957- 72
  Brief entry 46
  See also CLR 14
  See also SAAS 13
Howland, Ethan 1963- 131
Hoy, Linda 1946- 65
Hoy, Nina
  See Roth, Arthur J(oseph)
Hoyle, Geoffrey 1942- 18
Hoyt, Edwin P(almer), Jr. 1923- 28
Hoyt, Erich 1950- 140
  Earlier sketch in SATA 65
Hoyt, Olga
  See Gruhzit-Hoyt, Olga (Margaret)
Hrdlitschka, Shelley 1956- 167
  Earlier sketch in SATA 111
Hrdlitschka, Shelley Joanne
  See Hrdlitschka, Shelley
Htin Aung, U.
  See Aung, (Maung) Htin
Hu, Ying-Hwa 173
Huang, Benrei 1959- 86
Hubalek, Linda K. 1954- 111
Hubbard, Michelle Calabro 1953- 122
Hubbard, Patricia 1945- 124
Hubbard, Woodleigh Marx 160
  Earlier sketch in SATA 98
Hubbell, Patricia 1928- 132
  Earlier sketch in SATA 8
Hubley, Faith Elliot 1924-2001 48
  Obituary 133
Hubley, John 1914-1977 48
  Obituary 24
Huck, Charlotte S. 1922- 136
  Earlier sketch in SATA 82
Hudak, Michal 1956- 143
Hudson, Cheryl Willis 1948- 160
  Earlier sketch in SATA 81
Hudson, Jan 1954-1990 77
  See also CLR 40
Hudson, Jeffrey
  See Crichton, Michael
Hudson, (Margaret) Kirsty 1947- 32
Hudson, Margaret
  See Shuter, Jane (Margaret)
Hudson, W(illiam) H(enry) 1841-1922 35
Hudson, Wade 1946- 162
  Earlier sketch in SATA 74
Huelsmann, Eva 1928- 16
Huff, Barbara A. 1929- 67
Huff, Tanya 1957- 171
  Earlier sketch in SATA 85
Huff, Tanya Sue
  See Huff, Tanya

Huff, T.S.
  See Huff, Tanya
Huff, Vivian 1948- 59
Huffaker, Sandy 1943- 10
Huffman, Tom 24
Huggins, Nathan Irvin 1927-1989 63
Huggins, Peter 178
Hughes, Carol 1955- 108
Hughes, Dean 1943- 139
  Earlier sketches in SATA 33, 77
  See also CLR 76
Hughes, Eden
  See Griffin, W.E.B.
Hughes, Edward James
  See Hughes, Ted
Hughes, (James Mercer) Langston 1902-1967
  33
  Earlier sketch in SATA 4
  See also CLR 17
Hughes, Libby 71
Hughes, Matilda
  See MacLeod, Charlotte (Matilda)
Hughes, Monica 1925-2003 162
  Earlier sketches in SATA 15, 70, 119
  See also CLR 60
  See also SAAS 11
Hughes, Monica Ince
  See Hughes, Monica
Hughes, Richard (Arthur Warren) 1900-1976
  8
  Obituary 25
Hughes, Sara
  See Saunders, Susan
Hughes, Shirley 1927- 159
  Earlier sketches in SATA 16, 70, 110
  See also CLR 15
Hughes, Ted 1930-1998 49
  Brief entry 27
  Obituary 107
  See also CLR 3
  See Hughes, Edward James
Hughes, Thomas 1822-1896 31
Hughes, Virginia
  See Campbell, Hope
Hughes, Walter (Llewellyn) 1910-1993 26
Hughey, Roberta 1942- 61
Hugo, Pierre Brackers de
  See Brackers de Hugo, Pierre
Hugo, Victor (Marie) 1802-1885 47
Huline-Dickens, Frank William 1931- 34
Huling, Jan 172
Huliska-Beith, Laura 175
Hull, Eleanor (Means) 1913- 21
Hull, Eric Traviss
  See Harnan, Terry
Hull, H. Braxton
  See Jacobs, Helen Hull
Hull, Jesse Redding
  See Hull, Jessie Redding
Hull, Jessie Redding 1932- 51
Hull, Katharine 1921-1977 23
Hull, Lise (E.) 1954- 148
Hull, Maureen 1949- 142
Hulme, Joy N. 1922- 161
  Earlier sketches in SATA 74, 112
Hults, Dorothy Niebrugge 1898-2000 6
Humble, Richard 1945- 60
Hume, Lotta Carswell 7
Hume, Ruth Fox 1922-1980 26
  Obituary 22
Hume, Stephen Eaton 1947- 136
Hummel, Berta 1909-1946 43
Hummel, Sister Maria Innocentia
  See Hummel, Berta
Humphrey, Carol Sue 1956- 167
Humphrey, Henry (III) 1930- 16
Humphrey, Kate
  See Forsyth, Kate
Humphrey, Sandra McLeod 1936- 95
Humphreys, Martha 1943- 71

Humphreys, Susan L.
  See Lowell, Susan
Hundal, Nancy 1957- 128
Huneck, Stephen 1949- 129
Hungerford, Hesba Fay
  See Brinsmead, H(esba) F(ay)
Hungerford, Pixie
  See Brinsmead, H(esba) F(ay)
Hunkin, Timothy Mark Trelawney 1950- ... 53
Hunt, Angela Elwell 1957- 159
  Earlier sketch in SATA 75
Hunt, Francesca
  See Holland, Isabelle (Christian)
Hunt, Irene 1907-2001 91
  Earlier sketch in SATA 2
  See also CLR 1
Hunt, Janie Louise 1963- 102
Hunt, Jonathan 1966- 84
Hunt, Joyce 1927- 31
Hunt, Linda 1940- 39
Hunt, Lisa B(ehnke) 1967- 84
Hunt, Mabel Leigh 1892-1971 1
  Obituary 26
Hunt, Morton M(agill) 1920- 22
Hunt, Nigel
  See Greenbank, Anthony Hunt
Hunt, Peter (Leonard) 1945- 76
Hunter, Anne B. 1966- 118
Hunter, Bernice Thurman 1922-2002 85
  Brief entry 45
Hunter, Bobbi Dooley 1945- 89
Hunter, Captain Marcy
  See Ellis, Edward S(ylvester)
Hunter, Chris
  See Fluke, Joanne
Hunter, Clingham M.D.
  See Adams, William Taylor
Hunter, Edith Fisher 1919- 31
Hunter, Erin
  See Cary, Kate
Hunter, Evan 1926-2005 25
  Obituary 167
  See McBain, Ed
Hunter, George E.
  See Ellis, Edward S(ylvester)
Hunter, Hilda 1921- 7
Hunter, Jim 1939- 65
Hunter, Kristin
  See Lattany, Kristin (Elaine Eggleston) Hunter
Hunter, Leigh
  See Etchison, Birdie L(ee)
Hunter, Lieutenant Ned
  See Ellis, Edward S(ylvester)
Hunter, Mel 1927-2004 39
Hunter, Mollie 1922- 139
  Autobiography Feature 139
  Earlier sketches in SATA 54, 106
  See also CLR 25
  See also SAAS 7
  See McIlwraith, Maureen Mollie Hunter
Hunter, Ned
  See Ellis, Edward S(ylvester)
Hunter, Norman (George Lorimer) 1899-1995
  84
  Earlier sketch in SATA 26
Hunter, Ryan Ann
  See Greenwood, Pamela D.
  and Macalaster, Elizabeth G.
Hunter, Sara Hoagland 1954- 98
Hunter Blair, Pauline 3
  See Clarke, Pauline
Huntington, Amy 1956- 180
  Earlier sketch in SATA 138
Huntington, Geoffrey 145
Huntington, Harriet E(lizabeth) 1909- 1
Huntsberry, William E(mery) 1916- 5
Hurd, Clement (G.) 1908-1988 64
  Obituary 54
  Earlier sketch in SATA 2
  See also CLR 49

Hurd, Edith Thacher 1910-1997 .... *64*
  Obituary *95*
  Earlier sketch in SATA *2*
  See also CLR *49*
  See also SAAS *13*
Hurd, (John) Thacher 1949- *94*
  Autobiography Feature *123*
  Brief entry *45*
  Earlier sketch in SATA *46*
Hurlimann, Bettina *39*
  Obituary *34*
  See Huerlimann, Bettina
Hurlimann, Ruth *32*
  Brief entry *31*
  See Huerlimann, Ruth
Hurmence, Belinda 1921- *77*
  See also CLR *25*
  See also SAAS *20*
Hurst, Carol Otis 1933- *130*
Hurt-Newton, Tania 1968- *84*
Hurwin, Davida Wills 1950- *180*
Hurwitz, Johanna 1937- *175*
  Earlier sketches in SATA *20, 71, 113*
  See also SAAS *18*
Hurwood, Bernhardt J. 1926-1987 .... *12*
  Obituary *50*
Husain, Shahrukh 1950- *108*
Huser, Glen 1943- *151*
Hutchens, Paul 1902-1977 .... *31*
Hutchins, Carleen Maley 1911- *9*
Hutchins, Hazel J. 1952- *175*
  Brief entry *51*
  Earlier sketches in SATA *81, 135*
  See also SAAS *24*
Hutchins, Pat 1942- *178*
  Earlier sketches in SATA *15, 70, 111*
  See also CLR *20*
  See also SAAS *16*
Hutchins, Ross Elliott 1906- *4*
Hutchison, Linda 1942- *152*
Huthmacher, J. Joseph 1929- *5*
Hutto, Nelson (Allen) 1904-1985 .... *20*
Hutton, Kathryn 1915- *89*
Hutton, Warwick 1939-1994 .... *20*
  Obituary *83*
  See also SAAS *17*
Huxley, Aldous (Leonard) 1894-1963 .... *63*
Huxley, Elspeth (Josceline Grant) 1907-1997
  .... *62*
  Obituary *95*
Hyde, Catherine R.
  See Hyde, Catherine Ryan
Hyde, Catherine Ryan 1955- *141*
Hyde, Dayton O(gden) *9*
Hyde, Hawk
  See Hyde, Dayton O(gden)
Hyde, Margaret O(ldroyd) 1917- *139*
  Earlier sketches in SATA *1, 42, 76*
  See also CLR *23*
  See also SAAS *8*
Hyde, Shelley
  See Reed, Kit
Hyde, Wayne Frederick 1922- *7*
Hylander, Clarence J(ohn) 1897-1964 .... *7*
Hyman, Robin P(hilip) 1931- *12*
Hyman, Trina Schart 1939-2004 .... *95*
  Obituary *158*
  Earlier sketches in SATA *7, 46*
  See also CLR *50*
Hymes, Lucia M(anley) 1907-1998 .... *7*
Hyndman, Jane Andrews Lee 1912-1978 ... *46*
  Obituary *23*
  Earlier sketch in SATA *1*
Hyndman, Robert Utley 1906-1973 .... *18*
Hynes, Pat *98*

I

Iannone, Jeanne *7*
  See Balzano, Jeanne (Koppel)
Ibatoulline, Bagram 1965(?)- *174*
Ibbitson, John Perrie 1955- *102*
Ibbotson, Eva 1925- *156*
  Earlier sketches in SATA *13, 103*
Ibbotson, M. C(hristine) 1930- *5*
Icenoggle, Jodi 1967- *168*
Icenoggle, Jodi O.
  See Icenoggle, Jodi
Ichikawa, Satomi 1949- *146*
  Brief entry *36*
  Earlier sketches in SATA *47, 78*
  See also CLR *62*
Ignoffo, Matthew 1945- *92*
Igus, Toyomi 1953- *112*
  Earlier sketch in SATA *76*
Ihimaera, Witi (Tame) 1944- *148*
Ikeda, Daisaku 1928- *77*
Ilowite, Sheldon A. 1931- *27*
Ilsley, Velma (Elizabeth) 1918- *12*
Imai, Miko 1963- *90*
Imershein, Betsy 1953- *62*
Immel, Mary Blair 1930- *28*
Immell, Myra H. 1941- *92*
Impey, Rose 1947- *152*
  Earlier sketch in SATA *69*
Ingelow, Jean 1820-1897 .... *33*
Ingermanson, Randall 1958- *134*
Ingermanson, Randy
  See Ingermanson, Randall
Ingersoll, Norman 1928- *79*
Ingham, Colonel Frederic
  See Hale, Edward Everett
Ingman, Bruce 1963- *134*
Ingman, Nicholas 1948- *52*
Ingold, Jeanette *128*
Ingpen, Robert 1936- *166*
  Earlier sketch in SATA *109*
Ingpen, Robert Roger
  See Ingpen, Robert
Ingraham, Erick 1950- *145*
Ingraham, Leonard W(illiam) 1913-2003 ..... *4*
Ingram, Scott 1948- *167*
  Earlier sketch in SATA *92*
Ingram, W. Scott
  See Ingram, Scott
Ingrams, Doreen 1906-1997 .... *97*
  Earlier sketch in SATA *20*
Ingrid, Charles
  See Salsitz, Rhondi Vilott
Ingves, Gunilla (Anna Maria Folkesdotter)
  1939- *101*
Inkpen, Mick 1952- *154*
  Earlier sketch in SATA *99*
Innes, (Ralph) Hammond
  See Hammond Innes, Ralph
Innes, Ralph Hammond
  See Hammond Innes, Ralph
Innocenti, Roberto 1940- *159*
  Earlier sketch in SATA *96*
  See also CLR *56*
Inyart, Gene *6*
  See Namovicz, Gene Inyart
Ionesco, Eugene 1912-1994 .... *7*
  Obituary *79*
Ipcar, Dahlov (Zorach) 1917- *147*
  Autobiography Feature *147*
  Earlier sketches in SATA *1, 49*
  See also SAAS *8*
Ireland, Karin *151*
  Earlier sketch in SATA *101*
Ironside, Jetske 1940- *60*
Irvin, Fred 1914- *15*
Irvine, Georgeanne 1955- *72*
Irvine, Joan 1951- *80*
Irving, Alexander
  See Hume, Ruth Fox

Irving, Robert
  See Adler, Irving
Irving, Washington 1783-1859
  See YABC *2*
  See also CLR *97*
Irwin, Ann(abelle Bowen) 1915-1998 .... *89*
  Brief entry *38*
  Obituary *106*
  Earlier sketch in SATA *44*
  See also CLR *40*
  See Irwin, Hadley
Irwin, Constance (H.) Frick 1913-1995 .... *6*
Irwin, Hadley
  See CLR *40*
  See also SAAS *14*
  See Hadley, Lee
  and Irwin, Ann(abelle Bowen)
Irwin, Keith Gordon 1885-1964 .... *11*
Isaac, Joanne 1934- *21*
Isaacs, Anne 1949- *90*
Isaacs, Jacob
  See Kranzler, George G(ershon)
Isaacson, Philip M(arshal) 1924- *87*
Isadora, Rachel 1953(?)- *165*
  Brief entry *32*
  Earlier sketches in SATA *54, 79, 121*
  See also CLR *7*
Isbell, Rebecca T(emple) 1942- *125*
Isham, Charlotte H(ickock) 1912- *21*
Ishida, Jui *176*
Ish-Kishor, Judith 1892-1972 .... *11*
Ish-Kishor, Sulamith 1896-1977 .... *17*
Ishmael, Woodi 1914-1995 .... *31*
  Obituary *109*
Isle, Sue 1963- *105*
Israel, Elaine 1945- *12*
Iterson, S(iny) R(ose) Van
  See Van Iterson, S(iny) R(ose)
Ivanko, John D. 1966- *111*
Ivanko, John Duane
  See Ivanko, John D.
Iversen, Jeremy 1980(?)- *174*
Iversen, Jeremy Watt
  See Iversen, Jeremy
Iverson, Carol (L.) 1941- *145*
Iverson, Diane 1950- *122*
Iverson, Eric G.
  See Turtledove, Harry
Ivery, Martha M. 1948- *124*
Ives, David 1951- *173*
Ives, Morgan
  See Bradley, Marion Zimmer
Iwamatsu, Jun Atsushi 1908-1994 .... *81*
  Earlier sketch in SATA *14*
  See Yashima, Taro
Iwasaki (Matsumoto), Chihiro 1918-1974
  See CLR *18*

J

Jac, Lee
  See Morton, Lee Jack, Jr.
Jacka, Martin 1943- *72*
Jackson, Alison 1953- *160*
  Earlier sketches in SATA *73, 108*
Jackson, C(aary) Paul 1902-1991 .... *6*
Jackson, Caary
  See Jackson, C(aary) Paul
Jackson, Dave
  See Jackson, J. David
Jackson, Ellen B. 1943- *167*
  Earlier sketches in SATA *75, 115*
Jackson, Garnet Nelson 1944- *87*
Jackson, Gina
  See Fluke, Joanne
Jackson, Guida M. 1930- *71*
Jackson, J. David 1944- *91*
Jackson, Jacqueline 1928- *65*

Jackson, Jacqueline Dougan
  See Jackson, Jacqueline
Jackson, Jesse 1908-1983 29
  Obituary 48
  Earlier sketch in SATA 2
  See also CLR 28
Jackson, Marjorie 1928- 127
Jackson, Melanie 1956- 141
Jackson, Mike 1946- 91
Jackson, Neta J. 1944- 91
Jackson, O. B.
  See Jackson, C(aary) Paul
Jackson, Rob 1961- 176
Jackson, Robert B(lake) 1926- 8
Jackson, Robert Bradley
  See Jackson, Rob
Jackson, Sally
  See Kellogg, Jean (Defrees)
Jackson, Shirley 1919-1965 2
Jackson, Woody 1948- 92
Jacob, Helen Pierce 1927- 21
Jacobin
  See Bisson, Terry
Jacobs, Flora Gill 1918-2006 5
  Obituary 178
Jacobs, Francine 1935- 150
  Brief entry 42
  Earlier sketch in SATA 43
Jacobs, Frank 1929- 30
Jacobs, Helen Hull 1908-1997 12
Jacobs, Joseph 1854-1916 25
Jacobs, Judy 1952- 69
Jacobs, Laurie A. 1956- 89
Jacobs, Leah
  See Gellis, Roberta
Jacobs, Leland Blair 1907-1992 20
  Obituary 71
Jacobs, Linda
  See Altman, Linda Jacobs
Jacobs, Lou(is), Jr. 1921- 2
Jacobs, Shannon K. 1947- 77
Jacobs, Susan 30
  See Quinn, Susan
Jacobs, William Jay 1933- 89
  Earlier sketch in SATA 28
Jacobsen, Laura 177
Jacobson, Daniel 1923- 12
Jacobson, Jennifer
  See Jacobson, Jennifer Richard
Jacobson, Jennifer Richard 1958- 170
Jacobson, Morris K(arl) 1906- 21
Jacobson, Rick 170
Jacopetti, Alexandra 14
  See Hart, Alexandra
Jacques, Brian 1939- 176
  Earlier sketches in SATA 62, 95, 138
  See also CLR 21
Jacques, Robin 1920-1995 32
  Brief entry 30
  Obituary 86
  See also SAAS 5
Jaekel, Susan M. 1948- 89
Jaffe, Michele 179
Jaffe, Michele Sharon
  See Jaffe, Michele
Jaffee, Al(lan) 1921- 66
  Earlier sketch in SATA 37
Jagendorf, Moritz (Adolf) 1888-1981 2
  Obituary 24
Jahn, Michael
  See Jahn, (Joseph) Michael
Jahn, (Joseph) Michael 1943- 28
Jahn, Mike
  See Jahn, (Joseph) Michael
Jahn-Clough, Lisa 1967- 152
  Earlier sketch in SATA 88
Jahsmann, Allan Hart 1916- 28
Jakes, John 1932- 62
Jakes, John William
  See Jakes, John
  and Jakes, John

James, Andrew
  See Kirkup, James
James, Ann 1952- 168
  Earlier sketches in SATA 82, 117
James, Brian 1976- 140
James, Bronte
  See Nash, Renea Denise
James, Captain Lew
  See Stratemeyer, Edward L.
James, Dynely
  See Mayne, William (James Carter)
James, Edwin
  See Gunn, James E.
James, Elizabeth 1942- 97
  Earlier sketches in SATA 39, 45, 52
James, Emily
  See Standiford, Natalie
James, Harry Clebourne 1896-1978 11
James, J. Alison 1962- 146
  Earlier sketch in SATA 83
James, Josephine
  See Sterne, Emma Gelders
James, Mary
  See Meaker, Marijane
James, Philip
  See del Rey, Lester
  and Moorcock, Michael
James, Robin 1953- 50
James, Robin Irene
  See James, Robin
James, Tegan
  See Odgers, Sally Farrell
James, Will(iam Roderick) 1892-1942 19
Jameson, W. C. 1942- 93
Jamieson, Ian R.
  See Goulart, Ron(ald Joseph)
Jamiolkowski, Raymond M. 1953- 81
Jane, Mary Childs 1909- 6
Jane, Pamela 158
Janeczko, Paul B(ryan) 1945- 155
  Earlier sketches in SATA 53, 98
  See also CLR 47
  See also SAAS 18
Janes, Edward C. 1908- 25
Janes, J(oseph) Robert 1935- 148
  Brief entry 50
  Earlier sketch in SATA 101
Janeway, Elizabeth (Hall) 1913-2005 19
Janger, Kathleen N. 1940- 66
Janice
  See Brustlein, Janice Tworkov
Janisch, Heinz 1960- 181
Janosch
  See CLR 26
  See Eckert, Horst
Janover, Caroline (Davis) 1943- 141
  Earlier sketch in SATA 89
Jansen, Jared
  See Cebulash, Mel
Janson, Dora Jane (Heineberg) 1916- 31
Janson, H(orst) W(oldemar) 1913-1982 9
Jansson, Tove (Marika) 1914-2001 41
  Earlier sketch in SATA 3
  See also CLR 2
Janus, Grete
  See Hertz, Grete Janus
Jaques, Faith 1923-1997 97
  Earlier sketches in SATA 21, 69
Jaquith, Priscilla 1908- 51
Jaramillo, Mari-Luci 1928- 139
Jarman, Julia 1946- 133
Jarman, Rosemary Hawley 1935- 7
Jarrell, Mary Von Schrader 1914- 35
Jarrell, Randall 1914-1965 7
  See also CLR 111
Jarrett, Roxanne
  See Werner, Herma
Jarrow, Gail 1952- 84
Jarvis, E. K.
  See Ellison, Harlan
Jarvis, Robin 1963- 181

Jaskol, Julie 1958- 127
Jasner, W. K.
  See Watson, Jane Werner
Jassem, Kate
  See Oppenheim, Joanne
Jauss, Anne Marie 1902(?)-1991 10
  Obituary 69
Javernick, Ellen 1938- 89
Jayne, Lieutenant R. H.
  See Ellis, Edward S(ylvester)
Jaynes, Clare
  See Mayer, Jane Rothschild
Jeake, Samuel, Jr.
  See Aiken, Conrad (Potter)
Jean-Bart, Leslie 1954- 121
Jeapes, Ben 1965- 174
Jefferds, Vincent H(arris) 1916- 59
  Brief entry 49
Jefferies, (John) Richard 1848-1887 16
Jeffers, Oliver 1977- 175
Jeffers, Susan 1942- 137
  Earlier sketches in SATA 17, 70, 129
  See also CLR 30
Jefferson, Sarah
  See Farjeon, (Eve) Annabel
Jeffries, Roderic 1926- 4
Jeffries, Roderic Graeme
  See Jeffries, Roderic
Jenkin-Pearce, Susie 1943- 80
Jenkins, A.M. 174
Jenkins, Amanda McRaney
  See Jenkins, A.M.
Jenkins, Debra Reid
  See Reid Jenkins, Debra
Jenkins, Emily 1967- 174
  Earlier sketch in SATA 144
Jenkins, Jean 98
Jenkins, Jerry B. 1949- 149
Jenkins, Jerry Bruce
  See Jenkins, Jerry B.
Jenkins, Marie M(agdalen) 1909- 7
Jenkins, Patrick 1955- 72
Jenkins, Steve 1952- 154
Jenkins, William A(twell) 1922-1998 9
Jenkyns, Chris 1924- 51
Jennings, Coleman A(lonzo) 1933- 64
Jennings, Dana Andrew 1957- 93
Jennings, Elizabeth (Joan) 1926-2001 66
Jennings, Gary (Gayne) 1928-1999 9
  Obituary 117
Jennings, Patrick 1962- 160
  Earlier sketch in SATA 96
Jennings, Paul 1943- 165
  Earlier sketch in SATA 88
  See also CLR 40
Jennings, Richard (W.) 1945- 136
Jennings, Robert
  See Hamilton, Charles (Harold St. John)
Jennings, S. M.
  See Meyer, Jerome Sydney
Jennings, Sharon 1954- 95
Jennings, Sharon Elizabeth
  See Jennings, Sharon
Jennison, C. S.
  See Starbird, Kaye
Jennison, Keith Warren 1911-1995 14
Jensen, Kathryn 1949- 81
Jensen, Kristine Mary 1961- 78
Jensen, Niels 1927- 25
Jensen, Vickie (Dee) 1946- 81
Jensen, Virginia Allen 1927- 8
Jenson-Elliott, Cynthia L(ouise) 1962- 143
Jeram, Anita 1965- 154
  Earlier sketches in SATA 71, 102
Jerman, Jerry 1949- 89
Jernigan, E. Wesley 1940- 85
Jernigan, Gisela (Evelyn) 1948- 85
Jeschke, Susan 1942- 42
  Brief entry 27
Jessel, Camilla (Ruth) 1937- 143
  Earlier sketch in SATA 29

Jessell, Tim *177*
Jessey, Cornelia
See Sussman, Cornelia Silver
Jewel
See Kilcher, Jewel
Jewell, Nancy 1940- *109*
Brief entry *41*
Jewett, Eleanore Myers 1890-1967 .... *5*
Jewett, (Theodora) Sarah Orne 1849-1909 . *15*
Jezard, Alison 1919- *57*
Brief entry *34*
Jiang, Cheng An 1943- *109*
Jiang, Ji-li 1954- *101*
Jiang, Zheng An
See Jiang, Cheng An
Jiler, John 1946- *42*
Brief entry *35*
Jimenez, Francisco 1943- *108*
Jinks, Catherine 1963- *155*
Earlier sketch in SATA *94*
Jobb, Jamie 1945- *29*
Jobling, Curtis *131*
Jocelyn, Ann Henning 1948- *92*
Jocelyn, Marthe 1956- *163*
Earlier sketch in SATA *118*
Joerns, Consuelo *44*
Brief entry *33*
Joey D
See Macaulay, Teresa (E.)
Johansen, K(rista) V(ictoria) 1968- *129*
Johansson, Philip *163*
John, Joyce *59*
Johns, Avery
See Cousins, Margaret
Johns, Elizabeth 1943- *88*
Johns, Janetta
See Quin-Harkin, Janet
Johns, Linda 1945- *173*
Johns, W(illiam) E(arle) 1893-1968 .... *55*
Johns, Captain W. E.
See Johns, W(illiam) E(arle)
Johnson, A.
See Johnson, Annabell (Jones)
Johnson, A. E.
See Johnson, Annabell (Jones)
and Johnson, Edgar (Raymond)
Johnson, Angela 1961- *150*
Earlier sketches in SATA *69, 102*
See also CLR *33*
Johnson, Annabel
See Johnson, Annabell (Jones)
Johnson, Annabell (Jones) 1921- *72*
Earlier sketch in SATA *2*
See Johnson, Annabel
Johnson, Art 1946- *123*
Johnson, Benjamin F., of Boone
See Riley, James Whitcomb
Johnson, Bettye 1858-1919
See Rogers, Bettye
Johnson, Caryn
See Goldberg, Whoopi
Johnson, Caryn E.
See Goldberg, Whoopi
Johnson, Charles R. 1925- *11*
Johnson, Charlotte Buel *46*
See von Wodtke, Charlotte Buel Johnson
Johnson, Chuck
See Johnson, Charles R.
Johnson, Crockett
See CLR *98*
See Leisk, David (Johnson)
Johnson, D(onald) B. 1944- *146*
Johnson, D(ana) William 1945- *23*
Johnson, Daniel Shahid 1954- *73*
Johnson, Dinah *130*
See Johnson, Dianne
Johnson, Dolores 1949- *69*
Johnson, Dorothy M(arie) 1905-1984 .... *6*
Obituary *40*
Johnson, E(ugene) Harper *44*

Johnson, Edgar (Raymond) 1912-1990 .... *72*
Earlier sketch in SATA *2*
Johnson, Elizabeth 1911-1984 .... *7*
Obituary *39*
Johnson, Eric W(arner) 1918-1994 ....
Obituary *82*
Earlier sketch in SATA *8*
Johnson, Evelyne 1922- *20*
Johnson, Fred 19(?)-1982 .... *63*
Johnson, Gaylord 1884-1972 .... *7*
Johnson, Gerald White 1890-1980 .... *19*
Obituary *28*
Johnson, Harper
See Johnson, E(ugene) Harper
Johnson, James Ralph 1922- *1*
Johnson, James Weldon 1871-1938 .... *31*
See also CLR *32*
Johnson, Jane 1951- *48*
Johnson, Joan J. 1942- *59*
Johnson, John E(mil) 1929- *34*
Johnson, Johnny 1901-1995
See Johnson, (Walter) Ryerson
Johnson, La Verne B(ravo) 1925- *13*
Johnson, Lee Kaiser 1962- *78*
Johnson, Lissa H(alls) 1955- *65*
Johnson, Lois Smith 1894-1993 .... *6*
Johnson, Lois Walfrid 1936- *130*
Earlier sketches in SATA *22, 91*
Johnson, Margaret S(weet) 1893-1964 .... *35*
Johnson, Marguerite Annie
See Angelou, Maya
Johnson, Meredith Merrell 1952- *104*
Johnson, Milton 1932- *31*
Johnson, Neil 1954- *135*
Earlier sketch in SATA *73*
Johnson, Pamela 1949- *71*
Johnson, Patricia Polin 1956- *84*
Johnson, Paul Brett 1947- *132*
Earlier sketch in SATA *83*
Johnson, Rebecca L. 1956- *147*
Earlier sketch in SATA *67*
Johnson, Rick L. 1954- *79*
Johnson, (Walter) Ryerson 1901-1995 .... *10*
Obituary *106*
See Halliday, Brett
Johnson, Scott 1952- *119*
Earlier sketch in SATA *76*
Johnson, Sherrie 1948- *87*
Johnson, Shirley K(ing) 1927- *10*
Johnson, Spencer 1938- *145*
Brief entry *38*
Johnson, Stephen T. 1964- *141*
Earlier sketch in SATA *84*
Johnson, Steve 1960- *177*
Johnson, Sue Kaiser 1963- *78*
Johnson, Sylvia A. *166*
Brief entry *52*
Earlier sketch in SATA *104*
Johnson, William R. *38*
Johnson, William Weber 1909-1992 .... *7*
Johnston, Agnes Christine
See Dazey, Agnes J(ohnston)
Johnston, Annie Fellows 1863-1931 .... *37*
Johnston, Dorothy Grunbock 1915-1979 .... *54*
Johnston, Ginny 1946- *60*
Johnston, H(ugh) A(nthony) S(tephen)
1913-1967 .... *14*
Johnston, Janet 1944- *71*
Johnston, Johanna 1914(?)-1982 .... *12*
Obituary *33*
Johnston, Julie 1941- *110*
Autobiography Feature *128*
Earlier sketch in SATA *78*
See also CLR *41*
See also SAAS *24*
Johnston, Lynn (Beverley) 1947- *118*
Johnston, Norma *29*
See St. John, Nicole
Johnston, Portia
See Takakjian, Portia

Johnston, Susan Taylor 1942- *128*
Earlier sketch in SATA *83*
See Johnston, Tony
Johnston, Tim(othy Patrick) 1962- *146*
Johnston, Tony *180*
Earlier sketch in SATA *8*
See Johnston, Susan Taylor
Joinson, Carla *160*
Jonas, Ann 1932- *135*
Brief entry *42*
Earlier sketch in SATA *50*
See also CLR *74*
Jonell, Lynne *109*
Jones, Adrienne 1915-2000 .... *82*
Earlier sketch in SATA *7*
See also SAAS *10*
Jones, Annabel
See Lewis, Mary (Christianna)
Jones, Betty Millsaps 1940- *54*
Jones, Carol 1942- *153*
Earlier sketch in SATA *79*
Jones, Charles M(artin) 1912-2002 .... *53*
Obituary *133*
See Jones, Chuck
Jones, Charlotte Foltz 1945- *122*
Earlier sketch in SATA *77*
Jones, Chuck
See Jones, Charles M(artin)
Jones, Constance 1961- *112*
Jones, Diana Wynne 1934- *160*
Earlier sketches in SATA *9, 70, 108*
See also CLR *120*
See also SAAS *7*
Jones, Douglas C(lyde) 1924-1998 .... *52*
Jones, Elizabeth McDavid *155*
Jones, Elizabeth Orton 1910-2005 .... *18*
Obituary *164*
Jones, Evan 1915-1996 .... *3*
Jones, Geraldine
See McCaughrean, Geraldine
Jones, Gillingham
See Hamilton, Charles (Harold St. John)
Jones, Gwyneth A(nn) 1952- *159*
Jones, Harold 1904-1992 .... *14*
Obituary *72*
Jones, Helen Hinckley 1903-1991 .... *26*
Jones, Hettie 1934- *42*
Brief entry *27*
Jones, Hortense P. 1918- *9*
Jones, J. Sydney 1948- *101*
Jones, Jasmine
See Papademetriou, Lisa
Jones, Jennifer (Berry) 1947- *90*
Jones, John R(obert) 1926- *76*
Jones, Jon Sydney
See Jones, J. Sydney
Jones, Marcia Thornton 1958- *115*
Earlier sketch in SATA *73*
Jones, Martha T(annery) 1931- *130*
Jones, Mary Alice 1898(?)-1980 .... *6*
Jones, McClure *34*
Jones, Patrick 1961- *136*
Jones, Penelope 1938- *31*
Jones, Rebecca C(astaldi) 1947- *99*
Earlier sketch in SATA *33*
Jones, Robin D(orothy) 1959- *80*
Jones, Sanford W.
See Thorn, John
Jones, Terence Graham Parry 1942- *127*
See Jones, Terry
and Monty Python
Jones, Terry *67*
Brief entry *51*
See Jones, Terence Graham Parry
Jones, Tim Wynne
See Wynne-Jones, Tim
Jones, V(ictoria) M(ary) 1958- *147*
Jones, Veda Boyd 1948- *119*
Jones, Volcano
See Mitchell, Adrian

Jones, Weyman (B.) 1928- 4
 See also SAAS *11*
Jones, William Glynne
 See Glynne-Jones, William
Jonk, Clarence 1906-1987 10
Jonsberg, Barry 1951- 168
Joos, Francoise 1956- 78
Joos, Frederic 1953- 78
Joosse, Barbara M. 1949- 164
 Earlier sketches in SATA *52, 96*
Joosse, Barbara Monnot
 See Joosse, Barbara M.
Jordan, Alexis Hill
 See Glick, Ruth (Burtnick)
 and Titchener, Louise
Jordan, Anne Devereaux 1943- 80
Jordan, Chris
 See Philbrick, Rodman
Jordan, Don
 See Howard, Vernon (Linwood)
Jordan, Hope Dahle 1905-1995 15
Jordan, Jael (Michal) 1949- 30
Jordan, June 1936-2002 136
 Earlier sketch in SATA *4*
 See also CLR *10*
Jordan, June Meyer
 See Jordan, June
Jordan, Lee
 See Scholefield, Alan
Jordan, Martin George 1944- 84
Jordan, Robert 1948- 95
 See Rigney, James Oliver, Jr.
Jordan, Sherryl 1949- 122
 Earlier sketch in SATA *71*
 See also SAAS *23*
Jordan, Shirley 1930- 154
Jordan, Tanis 1946- 84
Jorgensen, Mary Venn -1995 36
Jorgensen, Norman 1954- 157
Jorgenson, Ivar
 See Silverberg, Robert
Jorisch, Stephane 178
Joseph, Anne
 See Coates, Anna
Joseph, James (Herz) 1924- 53
Joseph, Joan 1939- 34
Joseph, Joseph M(aron) 1903-1979 22
Joseph, Patrick
 See O'Malley, Kevin
Josephs, Rebecca
 See Talbot, Toby
Josh
 See Clemens, Samuel Langhorne
Joshua, Peter
 See Stone, Peter
Joslin, Mary 1953- 176
Joslin, Sesyle 2
 See Hine, Sesyle Joslin
Joyce, Bill
 See Joyce, William
Joyce, J(ames) Avery 1902-1987 11
 Obituary 50
Joyce, Peter 1937- 127
Joyce, William 1957- 118
 Brief entry 46
 Earlier sketch in SATA *72*
 See also CLR *26*
Joyner, Jerry 1938- 34
Juan, Ana 1961- 179
Juby, Susan 1969- 156
Jucker, Sita 1921- 5
Judah, Aaron 1923- 118
Judd, Cyril
 See Kornbluth, C(yril) M.
 and Merril, Judith
 and Pohl, Frederik
Judd, Denis (O'Nan) 1938- 33
Judd, Frances K. 1
 See Benson, Mildred (Augustine Wirt)
Jude, Conny 81

Judson, Clara Ingram 1879-1960 38
 Brief entry 27
Judy, Stephen
 See Tchudi, Stephen N.
Judy, Stephen N.
 See Tchudi, Stephen N.
Juhasz, Victor 1954- 177
Jukes, Mavis 1947- 111
 Brief entry 43
 Earlier sketch in SATA *72*
 See also SAAS *12*
Jules, Jacqueline 1956- 148
Julian, Jane
 See Wiseman, David
Jumpp, Hugo
 See MacPeek, Walter G.
Jungman, Ann 165
Jupo, Frank J. 1904-1981 7
Jurmain, Suzanne 1945- 169
 Earlier sketch in SATA *72*
Jurmain, Suzanne Tripp
 See Jurmain, Suzanne
Juster, Norton 1929- 132
 Earlier sketch in SATA *3*
 See also CLR *112*
Justus, May 1898-1989 1
 Obituary 106
Juvenilia
 See Taylor, Ann

K

Kaaberbol, Lene
 See Kaaberbol, Lene
Kaaberbol, Lene 1960- 159
Kabdebo, Tamas
 See Kabdebo, Thomas
Kabdebo, Thomas 1934- 10
Kabibble, Osh
 See Jobb, Jamie
Kacer, Kathy 1954- 142
Kaczman, James 156
Kadesch, Robert R(udstone) 1922- 31
Kadohata, Cynthia 1956(?)- 180
 Earlier sketch in SATA *155*
 See also CLR *121*
Kaempfert, Wade
 See del Rey, Lester
Kaestner, Erich 1899-1974 14
 See also CLR *4*
 See Kastner, Erich
Kahl, Jonathan (D.) 1959- 77
Kahl, M(arvin) P(hilip) 1934- 37
Kahl, Virginia (Caroline) 1919-2004 48
 Brief entry 38
 Obituary 158
Kahn, Joan 1914-1994 48
 Obituary 82
Kahn, Katherine Janus 1942- 167
 Earlier sketch in SATA *90*
Kahn, Peggy
 See Katz, Bobbi
Kahn, Roger 1927- 37
Kahukiwa, Robyn 1940- 134
Kains, Josephine
 See Goulart, Ron(ald Joseph)
Kaizuki, Kiyonori 1950- 72
Kakimoto, Kozo 1915- 11
Kalashnikoff, Nicholas 1888-1961 16
Kalb, Jonah 1926- 23
Kalbacken, Joan 1925- 96
Kalechofsky, Roberta 1931- 92
Kaler, James Otis 1848-1912 15
Kalish, Claire M. 1947- 92
Kallen, Stuart A(rnold) 1955- 126
 Earlier sketch in SATA *86*
Kallevig, Christine Petrell 1955- 164
Kalman, Bobbie 1947- 63

Kalman, Maira 1949- 137
 Earlier sketch in SATA *96*
 See also CLR *32*
Kalnay, Francis 1899-1992 7
Kaloustian, Rosanne 1955- 93
Kalow, Gisela 1946- 32
Kalstein, Dave 175
Kamen, Gloria 1923- 98
 Earlier sketch in SATA *9*
Kamerman, Sylvia E.
 See Burack, Sylvia K.
Kamm, Josephine (Hart) 1905-1989 24
Kammerman, Sylvia E.
 See Burack, Sylvia K.
Kandel, Michael 1941- 93
Kandell, Alice S. 1938- 35
Kane, Bob 1916-1998 120
Kane, Henry Bugbee 1902-1971 14
Kane, L. A.
 See Mannetti, Lisa
Kane, Robert W. 1910- 18
Kane, Wilson
 See Bloch, Robert (Albert)
Kanefield, Teri 1960- 135
Kaner, Etta 1947- 126
Kanetzke, Howard W(illiam) 1932- 38
Kann, Elizabeth 180
Kann, Victoria 180
Kanoza, Muriel Canfield
 See Canfield, Muriel
Kantner, Seth 1965- 179
Kanzawa, Toshiko
 See Furukawa, Toshi
Kaplan, Andrew 1960- 78
Kaplan, Anne Bernays
 See Bernays, Anne
Kaplan, Bess 1927- 22
Kaplan, Boche 1926- 24
Kaplan, Elizabeth 1956- 83
Kaplan, Elizabeth A.
 See Kaplan, Elizabeth
Kaplan, Irma 1900- 10
Kaplan, Jean Caryl Korn 1926- 10
Kaplow, Robert 1954- 70
Karageorge, Michael
 See Anderson, Poul
Karas, G. Brian 1957- 178
Karas, George Brian
 See Karas, G. Brian
Karen, Ruth 1922-1987 9
 Obituary 54
Kark, Nina Mary 1925- 132
 Earlier sketch in SATA *4*
 See Bawden, Nina (Mary Mabey)
Karl, Herb 1938- 73
Karl, Jean E(dna) 1927-2000 122
 Earlier sketch in SATA *34*
 See also SAAS *10*
Karlin, Bernie 1927- 68
Karlin, Eugene 1918- 10
Karlin, Nurit 103
 Earlier sketch in SATA *63*
Karnes, Frances A. 1937- 110
Karp, Naomi J. 1926- 16
Karpinski, J. Rick
 See Karpinski, John Eric
Karpinski, John Eric 1952- 81
Karpinski, Rick
 See Karpinski, John Eric
Karr, Kathleen 1946- 127
 Earlier sketch in SATA *82*
Karr, Phyllis Ann 1944- 119
Karwoski, Gail 1949- 127
Karwoski, Gail Langer
 See Karwoski, Gail
Kashiwagi, Isami 1925- 10
Kassem, Lou 1931- 62
 Brief entry 51
Kastel, Warren
 See Silverberg, Robert

Kastner, Erich
   See Kaestner, Erich
Kastner, Jill (Marie) 1964- 117
   Earlier sketch in SATA 70
Kasuya, Masahiro 1937- 51
Kasza, Keiko 1951- 124
Kataphusin
   See Ruskin, John
Katchen, Carole 1944- 9
Kathryn
   See Searle, Kathryn Adrienne
Katona, Robert 1949- 21
Katsarakis, Joan Harries
   See Harries, Joan
Katz, Avner 1939- 103
Katz, Bobbi 1933- 179
   Earlier sketch in SATA 12
Katz, Fred(eric Phillip) 1938- 6
Katz, Jane B(resler) 1934- 33
Katz, Karen 1947- 158
Katz, Marjorie P.
   See Weiser, Marjorie P(hillis) K(atz)
Katz, Susan 1945- 156
Katz, Welwyn Wilton 1948- 96
   Autobiography Feature 118
   Earlier sketch in SATA 62
   See also CLR 45
Katz, William 1940- 98
Katz, William Loren 1927- 13
Kaufman, Bel 57
Kaufman, Jeff 1955- 84
Kaufman, Joe 1911-2001 33
Kaufman, Joseph
   See Kaufman, Joe
Kaufman, Mervyn D. 1932- 4
Kaufmann, Angelika 1935- 15
Kaufmann, John 1931- 18
Kaula, Edna Mason 1906-1987 13
Kaur Khalsa, Dayal
   See Khalsa, Dayal Kaur
Kavaler, Lucy 1930- 23
Kavanagh, Jack 1920- 85
Kavanagh, P(atrick) J(oseph Gregory) 1931-
   122
Kavanaugh, Ian
   See Webb, Jean Francis (III)
Kay, Alan N. 1965- 144
Kay, Elizabeth 1949- 165
Kay, Guy Gavriel 1954- 167
   Earlier sketch in SATA 121
Kay, Helen
   See Goldfrank, Helen Colodny
Kay, Jackie 1961- 165
   Earlier sketch in SATA 97
Kay, Jacqueline Margaret
   See Kay, Jackie
Kay, Mara 13
Kay, Verla 1946- 120
Kaye, Geraldine (Hughesdon) 1925- 85
   Earlier sketch in SATA 10
Kaye, Judy
   See Baer, Judy
Kaye, Marilyn 1949- 110
   Earlier sketch in SATA 56
Kaye, Mary Margaret
   See Kaye, M.M.
Kaye, M.M. 1908-2004 62
   Obituary 152
Kaye, Mollie
   See Kaye, M.M.
Kaye, Peggy 1948- 143
Keach, James P. 1950- 125
Keams, Geri 1951- 117
Keane, Bil 1922- 4
Keaney, Brian 1954- 106
Kearney, Meg 1964- 178
Kearny, Jillian
   See Goulart, Ron(ald Joseph)
Keating, Bern
   See Keating, Leo Bernard
Keating, Frank 1944- 143

Keating, Lawrence A. 1903-1966 23
Keating, Leo Bernard 1915- 10
Keats, Emma 1899(?)-1979(?) 68
Keats, Ezra Jack 1916-1983 57
   Obituary 34
   Earlier sketch in SATA 14
   See also CLR 35
Keefer, Catherine
   See Ogan, George F.
   and Ogan, Margaret E. (Nettles)
Keefer, Janice Kulyk 132
   See Kulyk Keefer, Janice
Keegan, Marcia 1943- 104
   Earlier sketch in SATA 9
Keehn, Sally M. 1947- 165
   Earlier sketch in SATA 87
Keel, Frank
   See Keeler, Ronald F(ranklin)
Keeler, Ronald F(ranklin) 1913-1983 47
Keely, Jack 1951- 119
Keen, Martin L. 1913-1992 4
Keenan, Sheila 1953- 95
Keene, Ann T(odd) 1940- 86
Keene, Carolyn 100
   Earlier sketch in SATA 65
   See also CLR 118
   See Benson, Mildred (Augustine Wirt)
   and Goulart, Ron(ald Joseph)
   and Lerangis, Peter
   and McFarlane, Leslie (Charles)
   and Stanley, George Edward
   and Stratemeyer, Edward L.
Keens-Douglas, Richardo 1953- 154
   Earlier sketch in SATA 95
Keep, Linda Lowery
   See Lowery, Linda
Keep, Richard 1949- 170
Keep, Richard Cleminson
   See Keep, Richard
Keeping, Charles (William James) 1924-1988
   69
   Obituary 56
   Earlier sketch in SATA 9
   See also CLR 34
Keeshan, Robert J. 1927-2004 32
   Obituary 151
Kehret, Peg 1936- 149
   Autobiography Feature 149
   Earlier sketches in SATA 73, 108
Keillor, Garrison 1942- 58
Keillor, Gary Edward
   See Keillor, Garrison
Keir, Christine
   See Pullein-Thompson, Christine
Keister, Douglas 1948- 88
Keith, Doug 1952- 81
Keith, Eros 1942- 52
Keith, Hal 1934- 36
Keith, Harold (Verne) 1903-1998 74
   Earlier sketch in SATA 2
Keith, Robert
   See Applebaum, Stan
Keleinikov, Andrei 1924- 65
Kelemen, Julie 1959- 78
Kelen, Emery 1896-1978 13
   Obituary 26
Kelleam, Joseph E(veridge) 1913-1975 31
Kelleher, Anne 1959- 97
Kelleher, Annette 1950- 122
Kelleher, Daria Valerian 1955- 79
Kelleher, Victor (Michael Kitchener) 1939-
   129
   Brief entry 52
   Earlier sketch in SATA 75
   See also CLR 36
Keller, Beverly L(ou) 91
   Earlier sketch in SATA 13
Keller, Charles 1942- 82
   Earlier sketch in SATA 8
Keller, Debra 1958- 94
Keller, Dick 1923- 36

Keller, Emily 96
Keller, Gail Faithfull
   See Faithfull, Gail
Keller, Holly 1942- 157
   Brief entry 42
   Earlier sketches in SATA 76, 108
   See also CLR 45
Keller, Irene (Barron) 1927-2002 36
   Obituary 139
Kelley, Leo P(atrick) 1928- 32
   Brief entry 31
Kelley, Patrick (G.) 1963- 129
Kelley, Patte 1947- 93
Kelley, True 1946- 179
Kelley, True (Adelaide) 1946- 130
   Brief entry 39
   Earlier sketches in SATA 41, 92
Kelley, True Adelaide
   See Kelley, True
Kellin, Sally Moffet 1932- 9
Kelling, Furn L. 1914-2000 37
Kellogg, Gene
   See Kellogg, Jean (Defrees)
Kellogg, Jean (Defrees) 1916-1978 10
Kellogg, Steven 1941- 177
   Earlier sketches in SATA 8, 57, 130
   See also CLR 6
Kellogg, Steven Castle
   See Kellogg, Steven
Kellow, Kathleen
   See Hibbert, Eleanor Alice Burford
Kelly, Clint 1950- 140
Kelly, Eric P(hilbrook) 1884-1960
   See YABC 1
Kelly, Fiona
   See Coleman, Michael (Lee)
   and Hendry, Frances Mary
   and Oldfield, Jenny
   and Welford, Sue
Kelly, Irene 1957- 147
Kelly, Jeff
   See Kelly, Jeffrey
Kelly, Jeffrey 1946- 65
Kelly, Joanne (W.) 1934- 87
Kelly, Kate 1958- 91
Kelly, Kathleen M. 1964- 71
Kelly, Katy 1955- 169
Kelly, Lauren
   See Oates, Joyce Carol
Kelly, Laurene 1954- 123
Kelly, Martha Rose 1914-1983 37
Kelly, Marty
   See Kelly, Martha Rose
Kelly, Mij 166
Kelly, Ralph
   See Geis, Darlene Stern
Kelly, Regina Z(immerman) 1898-1986 5
Kelly, Rosalie (Ruth) 43
Kelly, Walt(er Crawford) 1913-1973 18
Kelsey, Alice Geer 1896-1982 1
Kelsey, Elin 159
Kemnitz, Thomas Milton, Jr. 1984- 152
Kemnitz, Tom, Jr.
   See Kemnitz, Thomas Milton, Jr.
Kemp, Gene 1926- 75
   Earlier sketch in SATA 25
   See also CLR 29
Kempner, Mary Jean 1913-1969 10
Kempton, Jean Welch 1914- 10
Kenda, Margaret 1942- 71
Kendall, Carol (Seeger) 1917- 74
   Earlier sketch in SATA 11
   See also SAAS 7
Kendall, Katherine
   See Applegate, Katherine (Alice)
Kendall, Lace
   See Stoutenburg, Adrien (Pearl)
Kendall, Martha E. 87
Kendall, Russ 1957- 83
Kenealy, James P. 1927- 52
   Brief entry 29

Kenealy, Jim
　See Kenealy, James P.
Kennaway, Adrienne 1945- 171
　Earlier sketch in SATA 60
Kennedy, Brendan 1970- 57
Kennedy, Dana Forrest 1917- 74
Kennedy, Dorothy M(intzlaff) 1931- 53
Kennedy, Doug(las) 1963- 122
Kennedy, John Fitzgerald 1917-1963 11
Kennedy, Joseph Charles 1929- 130
　Autobiography Feature 130
　Earlier sketches in SATA 14, 86
　See Kennedy, X. J.
Kennedy, Pamela (J.) 1946- 87
Kennedy, Paul E(dward) 1929- 113
　Earlier sketch in SATA 33
Kennedy, (Jerome) Richard 1932- 22
Kennedy, Robert 1938- 63
Kennedy, T.A. 1953- 42
　Brief entry 35
Kennedy, Teresa
　See Kennedy, T.A.
Kennedy, Teresa A.
　See Kennedy, T.A.
Kennedy, William 1928- 57
Kennedy, William Joseph
　See Kennedy, William
Kennedy, X. J.
　See CLR 27
　See also SAAS 22
　See Kennedy, Joseph Charles
Kennell, Ruth Epperson 1893-1977 6
　Obituary 25
Kennemore, Tim 1957- 133
Kennett, David 1959- 121
Kenny, Herbert Andrew 1912-2002 13
Kenny, Jude
　See Daly, Jude
Kenny, Kathryn
　See Bowden, Joan Chase
　and Krull, Kathleen
　and Sanderlin, Owenita (Harrah)
　and Stack, Nicolete Meredith
Kenny, Kevin
　See Krull, Kathleen
Kensinger, George
　See Fichter, George S.
Kensington, Kathryn Wesley
　See Rusch, Kristine Kathryn
Kent, Alexander
　See Reeman, Douglas Edward
Kent, David
　See Lambert, David (Compton)
Kent, Deborah Ann 1948- 155
　Brief entry 41
　Earlier sketches in SATA 47, 104
Kent, Jack
　See Kent, John Wellington
Kent, John Wellington 1920-1985 24
　Obituary 45
Kent, Lisa 1942- 90
Kent, Mallory
　See Lowndes, Robert A(ugustine) W(ard)
Kent, Margaret 1894- 2
Kent, Rockwell 1882-1971 6
Kent, Sherman 1903-1986 20
　Obituary 47
Kenward, Jean 1920- 42
Kenworthy, Leonard S. 1912-1991 6
Kenyon, Karen (Smith) 1938- 145
Kenyon, Kate
　See Adorjan, Carol (Madden)
　and Ransom, Candice F.
Kenyon, Ley 1913-1990 6
Keown, Elizabeth 78
Kepes, Juliet A(ppleby) 1919-1999 13
Kerby, Mona 1951- 75
Kerigan, Florence 1896-1984 12
Kerley, Barbara 1960- 138
Kerman, Gertrude
　See Furman, Gertrude Lerner Kerman

Kerns, Thelma 1929- 116
Kerr, Bob 1951- 120
Kerr, Jessica 1901-1991 13
Kerr, (Anne-)Judith 1923-1970 24
Kerr, M. E.
　See CLR 29
　See also SAAS 1
　See Meaker, Marijane
Kerr, P.B.
　See Kerr, Philip
Kerr, Philip 1956- 168
Kerr, Phyllis Forbes 1942- 72
Kerr, Tom 1950- 77
Kerrin, Jessica Scott 174
Kerry, Frances
　See Kerigan, Florence
Kerry, Lois
　See Duncan, Lois
Kershen, (L.) Michael 1982- 82
Kerven, Rosalind 1954- 83
Ker Wilson, Barbara 1929- 121
　Earlier sketches in SATA 20, 70
　See also SAAS 18
Keselman, Gabriela 1953- 128
Kesey, Ken 1935-2001 66
　Obituary 131
Kesey, Ken Elton
　See Kesey, Ken
Kesler, Jay 1935- 65
Kessel, Joyce Karen 1937- 41
Kessler, Ethel 1922- 44
　Brief entry 37
Kessler, Leonard P. 1921- 14
Kest, Kristin 1967- 168
　Earlier sketch in SATA 118
Kesteven, G. R.
　See Crosher, G. R.
Ketcham, Hank
　See Ketcham, Henry King
Ketcham, Henry King 1920-2001 28
　Brief entry 27
　Obituary 128
Ketcham, Sallie 1963- 124
Ketchum, Liza 1946- 132
　See Murrow, Liza Ketchum
Ketner, Mary Grace 1946- 75
Kettelkamp, Larry (Dale) 1933- 2
　See also SAAS 3
Ketteman, Helen 1945- 167
　Earlier sketches in SATA 73, 115
Kettle, Peter
　See Glover, Denis (James Matthews)
Kevles, Bettyann Holtzmann 1938- 23
Key, Alexander (Hill) 1904-1979 8
　Obituary 23
Key, Samuel M.
　See de Lint, Charles
Keyes, Daniel 1927- 37
Keyes, Fenton 1915-1999 34
Keyes, Greg
　See Keyes, J. Gregory
Keyes, J. Gregory 1963- 116
Keyser, Marcia 1933- 42
Keyser, Sarah
　See McGuire, Leslie (Sarah)
Khalsa, Dayal Kaur 1943-1989 62
　See also CLR 30
　See Kaur Khalsa, Dayal
Khan, Rukhsana 1962- 165
　Earlier sketch in SATA 118
Khanshendel, Chiron
　See Rose, Wendy
Kheirabadi, Masoud 1951- 158
Khemir, Sabiha 87
Kherdian, David 1931- 74
　Autobiography Feature 125
　Earlier sketch in SATA 16
　See also CLR 24
Kibbe, Pat (Hosley) 60
Kidd, Diana 1933-2000 150
Kidd, Richard 1952- 152

Kidd, Ronald 1948- 173
　Earlier sketches in SATA 42, 92
Kiddell, John 1922- 3
Kiddell-Monroe, Joan 1908-1972 55
Kidwell, Carl 1910- 43
Kiefer, Irene 1926- 21
Kiefer, Kathleen Balmes 1957- 142
Kierstead, Vera M. 1913- 121
Kiesel, Stanley 1925- 35
Kiesler, Kate (A.) 1971- 152
　Earlier sketch in SATA 90
Kihn, Greg 1952- 110
Kikukawa, Cecily H(arder) 1919- 44
　Brief entry 35
Kilcher, Jewel 1974- 109
Kile, Joan 1940- 78
Kilgore, Kathleen 1946- 42
Kilian, Crawford 1941- 35
Killdeer, John
　See Mayhar, Ardath
Killien, Christi 1956- 73
Killilea, Marie (Lyons) 1913-1991 2
Killingback, Julia 1944- 63
Killough, (Karen) Lee 1942- 64
Kilreon, Beth
　See Walker, Barbara (Jeanne) K(erlin)
Kilworth, Garry 1941- 94
Kilworth, Garry D.
　See Kilworth, Garry
Kilworth, Garry Douglas
　See Kilworth, Garry
Kim, Helen 1899-1970 98
Kimball, Gayle 1943- 90
Kimball, Violet T(ew) 1932- 126
Kimball, Yeffe 1914-1978 37
Kimber, Murray 1964- 171
Kimble, Warren 176
Kimbrough, Emily 1899-1989 2
　Obituary 59
Kimeldorf, Martin 1948- 121
Kimeldorf, Martin R.
　See Kimeldorf, Martin
Kimenye, Barbara 1940(?)- 121
Kimmel, Elizabeth Cody 170
Kimmel, Eric A. 1946- 176
　Earlier sketches in SATA 13, 80, 125
Kimmel, Margaret Mary 1938- 43
　Brief entry 33
Kimmelman, Burt 1947- 180
Kimmelman, Leslie (Grodinsky) 1958- 156
　Earlier sketch in SATA 85
Kincaid, Jamaica 1949-
　See CLR 63
Kincher, Jonni 1949- 79
Kindl, Patrice 1951- 128
　Earlier sketch in SATA 82
Kindred, Wendy (Good) 1937- 7
Kines, Pat Decker 1937- 12
King, Adam
　See Hoare, Robert J(ohn)
King, Alison
　See Martini, Teri
King, (Maria) Anna 1964- 72
King, Billie Jean 1943- 12
King, Christopher (L.) 1945- 84
King, (David) Clive 1924- 144
　Earlier sketch in SATA 28
King, Colin 1943- 76
King, Cynthia 1925- 7
King, Daniel (John) 1963- 130
King, Elizabeth 1953- 83
King, Frank R. 1904-1999 127
King, Jane
　See Currie, Stephen
King, Jeanette (Margaret) 1959- 105
King, Larry L. 1929- 66
King, Laurie R. 1952- 88
King, Marian 1900(?)-1986 23
　Obituary 47
King, Martin Luther, Jr. 1929-1968 14
King, Mary Ellen 1958- 93

King, Paul
  See Drackett, Phil(ip Arthur)
King, Paula
  See Downing, Paula E.
King, Stephen 1947- *161*
  Earlier sketches in SATA *9, 55*
King, Stephen Edwin
  See King, Stephen
King, Stephen Michael *157*
King, Steve
  See King, Stephen
King, Thomas 1943- *96*
King, Tony 1947- *39*
Kingman, Dong (Moy Shu) 1911-2000 .... *44*
Kingman, Lee *67*
  Earlier sketch in SATA *1*
  See also SAAS *3*
  See Natti, (Mary) Lee
Kingsland, Leslie William 1912- *13*
Kingsley, Charles 1819-1875
  See YABC *2*
  See also CLR *77*
Kingsley, Emily Perl 1940- *33*
King-Smith, Dick 1922- *135*
  Brief entry *38*
  Earlier sketches in SATA *47, 80*
  See also CLR *40*
Kingston, Maxine Hong 1940- *53*
Kingston, Maxine Ting Ting Hong
  See Kingston, Maxine Hong
Kinney, C. Cle(land) 1915- *6*
Kinney, Harrison 1921- *13*
Kinney, Jean Stout 1912- *12*
Kinsey, Elizabeth
  See Clymer, Eleanor
Kinsey, Helen 1948- *82*
Kinsey-Warnock, Natalie 1956- *167*
  Earlier sketches in SATA *71, 116*
Kinzel, Dorothy 1950- *57*
Kinzel, Dottie
  See Kinzel, Dorothy
Kipling, (Joseph) Rudyard 1865-1936 ...... *100*
  See also YABC *2*
  See also CLR *65*
Kippax, Frank
  See Needle, Jan
Kirby, David K. 1944- *78*
Kirby, David Kirk
  See Kirby, David K.
Kirby, Margaret
  See Bingley, Margaret (Jane Kirby)
Kirby, Susan E. 1949- *62*
Kirk, Connie Ann 1957- *167*
Kirk, Daniel 1952- *153*
  Earlier sketch in SATA *107*
Kirk, David 1955- *161*
  Earlier sketch in SATA *117*
Kirk, Heather 1949- *166*
Kirk, Ruth (Kratz) 1925- *5*
Kirkham, Dinah
  See Card, Orson Scott
Kirkland, Will
  See Hale, Arlene
Kirkpatrick, Katherine (Anne) 1964- *113*
Kirkup, James 1918- *12*
Kirkwood, Kathryn
  See Fluke, Joanne
Kirshenbaum, Binnie *79*
Kirshner, David S. 1958- *123*
Kish, Eleanor M(ary) 1924- *73*
Kish, Ely
  See Kish, Eleanor M(ary)
Kishida, Eriko 1929- *12*
Kisinger, Grace Gelvin (Maze) 1913-1965 . *10*
Kissin, Eva H. 1923- *10*
Kissinger, Rosemary K.
  See Updyke, Rosemary K.
Kistler, John M. 1967- *160*
Kitamura, Satoshi 1956- *143*
  Earlier sketches in SATA *62, 98*
  See also CLR *60*

Kitchen, Bert
  See Kitchen, Herbert Thomas
Kitchen, Herbert Thomas 1940- *70*
Kite, (L.) Patricia *78*
  See Kite, Pat
Kitt, Tamara
  See de Regniers, Beatrice Schenk (Freedman)
Kittinger, Jo S(usenbach) 1955- *148*
  Earlier sketch in SATA *96*
Kituomba
  See Odaga, Asenath (Bole)
Kitzinger, Sheila 1929- *57*
Kiwak, Barbara 1966- *103*
Kjelgaard, James Arthur 1910-1959 .... *17*
  See also CLR *81*
  See Kjelgaard, Jim
Kjelgaard, Jim
  See Kjelgaard, James Arthur
Kjelle, Marylou Morano 1954- *146*
Klagsbrun, Francine (Lifton) *36*
Klaits, Barrie 1944- *52*
Klaperman, Gilbert 1921- *33*
Klaperman, Libby Mindlin 1921-1982 ...... *33*
  Obituary *31*
Klass, David 1960- *142*
  Earlier sketch in SATA *88*
Klass, Morton 1927-2001 .... *11*
Klass, Sheila Solomon 1927- *99*
  Autobiography Feature *126*
  Earlier sketch in SATA *45*
  See also SAAS *26*
Klause, Annette Curtis 1953- *175*
  Earlier sketch in SATA *79*
  See also CLR *104*
Klaveness, Jan O'Donnell 1939- *86*
Kleberger, Ilse 1921- *5*
Kleeberg, Irene (Flitner) Cumming 1932- *65*
Klein, Aaron E. 1930-1998 .... *45*
  Brief entry *28*
Klein, Bill 1945- *89*
Klein, David 1919-2001 .... *59*
Klein, Frederick C. 1938- *154*
Klein, Gerda Weissmann 1924- *44*
Klein, H(erbert) Arthur *8*
Klein, James 1932- *115*
Klein, Leonore (Glotzer) 1916- *6*
Klein, Mina C(ooper) 1906-1979 .... *8*
Klein, Norma 1938-1989 .... *57*
  Earlier sketch in SATA *7*
  See also CLR *19*
  See also SAAS *1*
Klein, Rachel S. 1953- *105*
Klein, Robin 1936- *164*
  Brief entry *45*
  Earlier sketches in SATA *55, 80*
  See also CLR *21*
Klemin, Diana *65*
Klemm, Barry 1945- *104*
Klemm, Edward G., Jr. 1910-2001 .... *30*
Klemm, Roberta K(ohnhorst) 1884-1975 .... *30*
Kleven, Elisa 1958- *173*
  Earlier sketch in SATA *76*
  See also CLR *85*
Klevin, Jill Ross 1935- *39*
  Brief entry *38*
Kliban, B(ernard) 1935-1990 .... *35*
  Obituary *66*
Klimowicz, Barbara 1927- *10*
Kline, Christina Baker 1964- *101*
Kline, James
  See Klein, James
Kline, Jim
  See Kline, Jim
Kline, Lisa Williams 1954- *143*
Kline, Suzy 1943- *152*
  Brief entry *48*
  Earlier sketches in SATA *67, 99*
Kliros, Thea 1935- *106*
Klise, Kate *181*
Klise, M. Sarah 1961- *180*
  Earlier sketch in SATA *128*

Klug, Ron(ald) 1939- *31*
Knaak, Richard A. 1961- *166*
  Earlier sketch in SATA *86*
Knaak, Richard Allen
  See Knaak, Richard A.
Knapp, Edward
  See Kunhardt, Edith
Knapp, Ron 1952- *34*
Knebel, Fletcher 1911-1993 .... *36*
  Obituary *75*
Kneeland, Linda Clarke 1947- *94*
Knickerbocker, Diedrich
  See Irving, Washington
Knifesmith
  See Cutler, Ivor
Knigge, Robert (R.) 1921(?)-1987 .... *50*
Knight, Anne (Katherine) 1946- *34*
Knight, Brenda *112*
Knight, Christopher G. 1943- *96*
Knight, Damon (Francis) 1922-2002 .... *9*
  Obituary *139*
Knight, David C(arpenter) 1925-1984 .... *14*
  See also CLR *38*
Knight, Eric 1897-1943 .... *18*
Knight, Eric Mowbray
  See Knight, Eric
Knight, Francis Edgar 1905- *14*
Knight, Frank
  See Knight, Francis Edgar
Knight, Hilary 1926- *132*
  Earlier sketches in SATA *15, 69*
Knight, Joan (MacPhail) *159*
  Earlier sketch in SATA *82*
Knight, Joan
  See Knight, Joan (MacPhail)
Knight, Kathryn Lasky
  See Lasky, Kathryn
Knight, Mallory T.
  See Hurwood, Bernhardt J.
Knight, Theodore O. 1946- *77*
Knobloch, Dorothea 1951- *88*
Knoepfle, John (Ignatius) 1923- *66*
Knott, Bill
  See Knott, William C(ecil, Jr.)
Knott, William C(ecil, Jr.) 1927- *3*
  See Knott, Bill
  and Mitchum, Hank
  and Sharpe, Jon
Knotts, Howard (Clayton, Jr.) 1922- *25*
Knowles, Anne 1933- *37*
Knowles, John 1926-2001 .... *89*
  Obituary *134*
  Earlier sketch in SATA *8*
  See also CLR *98*
Knox, Calvin M.
  See Silverberg, Robert
Knox, (Mary) Eleanor Jessie 1909-2000 ..... *59*
  Earlier sketch in SATA *30*
Knox, Elizabeth 1959- *176*
Knox, Elizabeth Fiona
  See Knox, Elizabeth
Knox, James
  See Brittain, William (E.)
Knox, Jolyne 1937- *76*
Knudsen, James 1950- *42*
Knudsen, Michelle *171*
Knudson, R. R.
  See SAAS *18*
  See Knudson, Rozanne
Knudson, Richard L(ewis) 1930- *34*
Knudson, Rozanne 1932- *79*
  Earlier sketch in SATA *7*
  See Knudson, R. R.
Knutson, Barbara 1959-2005 .... *166*
Knutson, Kimberley *115*
Knye, Cassandra
  See Disch, Thomas M.
Koch, Dorothy Clarke 1924- *6*
Koch, Kenneth 1925-2002 .... *65*
Koch, Kenneth Jay
  See Koch, Kenneth

Koch, Phyllis (Mae) McCallum 1911- *10*
Kocsis, J. C.
　See Paul, James
Koda-Callan, Elizabeth 1944- *140*
　Earlier sketch in SATA *67*
Koehler, Phoebe 1955- *85*
Koehler-Pentacoff, Elizabeth 1957- *160*
　Earlier sketch in SATA *96*
Koehn, Ilse
　See Van Zwienen, Ilse Charlotte Koehn
Koenig, Viviane 1950- *80*
Koering, Ursula 1921-1976 .... *64*
Koerner, W(illiam) H(enry) D(avid) 1878-1938
　.. *21*
Koertge, Ronald 1940- *131*
　Earlier sketches in SATA *53, 92*
Koestler-Grack, Rachel A. 1973- *156*
Koff, Richard Myram 1926- *62*
Koffinke, Carol 1949- *82*
Kogan, Deborah *50*
　See Kogan Ray, Deborah
Kogan Ray, Deborah 1940- *161*
　See Kogan, Deborah
　and Ray, Deborah
Kogawa, Joy Nozomi 1935- *99*
Kogler, Jennifer Anne 1982(?)- *174*
Kohl, Herbert 1937- *47*
Kohl, Herbert R.
　See Kohl, Herbert
Kohl, MaryAnn F(aubion) 1947- *144*
　Earlier sketch in SATA *74*
Kohn, Bernice *4*
　See Hunt, Bernice (Kohn)
Kohn, Rita (T.) 1933- *89*
Kohner, Frederick 1905-1986 .... *10*
　Obituary *48*
Koide, Tan 1938-1986 .... *50*
Koike, Kay 1940- *72*
Koja, Kathe 1960- *155*
Kolb, Larry J. 1953- *175*
Kolba, St. Tamara *22*
Kolibalova, Marketa
　See Kolibalova, Marketa
Kolibalova, Marketa 1953- *126*
Koller, Jackie French 1948- *157*
　Earlier sketches in SATA *72, 109*
　See also CLR *68*
Kolodny, Nancy J. 1946- *76*
Komaiko, Leah 1954- *164*
　Earlier sketch in SATA *97*
Komisar, Lucy 1942- *9*
Komoda, Beverly 1939- *25*
Komoda, Kiyo 1937- *9*
Kompaneyets, Marc 1974- *169*
Komroff, Manuel 1890-1974 .... *2*
　Obituary *20*
Konigsburg, E.L. 1930- *126*
　Earlier sketches in SATA *4, 48, 94*
　See also CLR *81*
Konigsburg, Elaine Lobl
　See Konigsburg, E.L.
Koningsberger, Hans *5*
　See Koning, Hans
Konkle, Janet Everest 1917- *12*
Kono, Erin Eitter 1973- *177*
Konzak, Burt 1946- *151*
Koob, Theodora (J. Foth) 1918- *23*
Kooiker, Leonie
　See Kooyker-Romijn, Johanna Maria
Koons, James
　See Pernu, Dennis
Koontz, Dean R. 1945- *165*
　Earlier sketch in SATA *92*
Koontz, Dean Ray
　See Koontz, Dean R.
Koontz, Robin Michal 1954- *136*
　Earlier sketch in SATA *70*
Kooyker, Leonie
　See Kooyker-Romijn, Johanna Maria
Kooyker-Romijn, Johanna Maria 1927- *48*
　See Kooyker, Leonie

Kooyker-Romyn, Johanna Maria
　See Kooyker-Romijn, Johanna Maria
Kopelke, Lisa 1963- *154*
Kopper, Lisa (Esther) 1950- *105*
　Brief entry *51*
Koppes, Steven N. 1957- *169*
Koppes, Steven Nelson
　See Koppes, Steven N.
Korach, Mimi 1922- *9*
Koralek, Jenny 1934- *140*
　Earlier sketch in SATA *71*
Korczak, Janusz *65*
　See Goldszmit, Henryk
Koren, Edward (Benjamin) 1935- *148*
　Earlier sketch in SATA *5*
Korinets, Iurii Iosifovich
　See Korinetz, Yuri (Iosifovich)
Korinetz, Yuri (Iosifovich) 1923- *9*
　See also CLR *4*
Korman, Bernice 1937- *78*
Korman, Gordon 1963- *167*
　Brief entry *41*
　Earlier sketches in SATA *49, 81, 119*
　See also CLR *25*
Korman, Gordon Richard
　See Korman, Gordon
Korman, Justine 1958- *70*
Kornblatt, Marc 1954- *147*
　Earlier sketch in SATA *84*
Kornprobst, Jacques 1937- *177*
Korte, Gene J. 1950- *74*
Korty, Carol 1937- *15*
Koscielniak, Bruce 1947- *153*
　Earlier sketches in SATA *67, 99*
Koshin, Alexander (A.) 1952- *86*
Kositsky, Lynne 1947- *158*
Koskenmaki, Rosalie
　See Maggio, Rosalie
Koss, Amy Goldman 1954- *158*
　Earlier sketch in SATA *115*
Kossin, Sandy (Sanford) 1926- *10*
Kossman, Nina 1959- *84*
Kotzwinkle, William 1938- *146*
　Earlier sketches in SATA *24, 70*
　See also CLR *6*
Kouhi, Elizabeth 1917- *54*
　Brief entry *49*
Kouts, Anne 1945- *8*
Koutsky, Jan Dale 1955- *146*
Kovacs, Deborah 1954- *132*
　Earlier sketch in SATA *79*
Kovalski, Maryann 1951- *175*
　Earlier sketches in SATA *58, 97*
　See also CLR *34*
　See also SAAS *21*
Kowalski, Kathiann M. 1955- *151*
　Earlier sketch in SATA *96*
Kraft, Betsy Harvey 1937- *157*
Krahn, Fernando 1935- *49*
　Brief entry *31*
　See also CLR *3*
Krakauer, Hoong Yee Lee 1955- *86*
Krakauer, Jon 1954- *108*
Kramer, George
　See Heuman, William
Kramer, Nora 1896(?)-1984 .... *26*
　Obituary *39*
Kramer, Remi (Thomas) 1935- *90*
Krantz, Hazel (Newman) *12*
Kranzler, George G(ershon) 1916- *28*
Kranzler, Gershon
　See Kranzler, George G(ershon)
Krasilovsky, Phyllis 1926- *38*
　Earlier sketch in SATA *1*
　See also CLR *83*
　See also SAAS *5*
Krasne, Betty
　See Levine, Betty K(rasne)
Krasner, Steven 1953- *154*
Krasno, Rena 1923- *104*
Kratman, Tom *175*

Kraus, Joanna Halpert 1937- *87*
Kraus, (Herman) Robert 1925-2001 .... *93*
　Obituary *130*
　Earlier sketches in SATA *4, 65*
　See also SAAS *11*
Krauss, Ruth (Ida) 1911-1993 .... *30*
　Obituary *75*
　Earlier sketch in SATA *1*
　See also CLR *42*
Krautter, Elisa (Bialk) 1912(?)-1990 .... *1*
　Obituary *65*
Krautwurst, Terry 1946- *79*
Kray, Robert Clement 1930- *82*
Kredel, Fritz 1900-1973 .... *17*
Kreikemeier, Gregory Scott 1965- *85*
Krementz, Jill 1940- *134*
　Earlier sketches in SATA *17, 71*
　See also CLR *5*
　See also SAAS *8*
Kremer, Marcie
　See Sorenson, Margo
Krenina, Katya 1968- *101*
Krensky, Stephen 1953- *136*
　Brief entry *41*
　Earlier sketches in SATA *47, 93*
Krensky, Stephen Alan
　See Krensky, Stephen
Kresh, Paul 1919-1997 .... *61*
　Obituary *94*
Kress, Nancy 1948- *147*
　Autobiography Feature *147*
　Earlier sketch in SATA *85*
Kricher, John C. 1944- *113*
Krieger, Melanie *96*
Kripke, Dorothy Karp *30*
Krisher, Trudy (B.) 1946- *160*
　Earlier sketch in SATA *86*
Krishnaswami, Uma 1956- *144*
Kristof, Jane 1932- *8*
Kroeber, Theodora (Kracaw) 1897-1979 .... *1*
Kroeger, Mary Kay 1950- *92*
Krohn, Katherine E(lizabeth) 1961- *125*
　Earlier sketch in SATA *84*
Kroll, Francis Lynde 1904-1973 .... *10*
Kroll, Steven 1941- *135*
　Autobiography Feature *135*
　Earlier sketches in SATA *19, 66, 125*
　See also SAAS *7*
Kroll, Virginia L. 1948- *168*
　Earlier sketches in SATA *76, 114*
Kroll, Virginia Louisa
　See Kroll, Virginia L.
Krommes, Beth 1956- *181*
　Earlier sketch in SATA *128*
Kronenwetter, Michael 1943- *62*
Kroniuk, Lisa
　See Berton, Pierre (Francis de Marigny)
Kropp, Paul (Stephan) 1948- *38*
　Brief entry *34*
　See also CLR *96*
Krosoczka, Jarrett J. 1977- *155*
Krovatin, Christopher 1985- *171*
Kruess, James
　See CLR *9*
　See Kruss, James
Krull, Kathleen 1952- *149*
　Autobiography Feature *106*
　Brief entry *39*
　Earlier sketches in SATA *52, 80*
　See also CLR *44*
Krumgold, Joseph (Quincy) 1908-1980 ...... *48*
　Obituary *23*
　Earlier sketch in SATA *1*
Krupinski, Loretta 1940- *161*
　Earlier sketches in SATA *67, 102*
Krupnick, Karen 1947- *89*
Krupp, E(dwin) C(harles) 1944- *123*
　Earlier sketch in SATA *53*
Krupp, Robin Rector 1946- *53*
Krush, Beth 1918- *18*

Krush, Joe 1918- *18*
  See Krush, Joseph P.
Kruss, James 1926-1997 .... *8*
  See Kruess, James
Krykorka, Vladyana 1945- *96*
Kubie, Eleanor Gottheil
  See Kubie, Nora Gottheil Benjamin
Kubie, Nora Benjamin
  See Kubie, Nora Gottheil Benjamin
Kubie, Nora Gottheil Benjamin 1899-1988
  .... *39*
  Obituary *59*
Kubinyi, Laszlo 1937- *94*
  Earlier sketch in SATA *17*
Kudlinski, Kathleen V. 1950- *150*
Kuenstler, Morton 1927- *10*
Kuharski, Janice 1947- *128*
Kuijer, Guus 1942- *179*
Kuklin, Susan 1941- *163*
  Earlier sketches in SATA *63, 95*
  See also CLR *51*
Kulikov, Boris 1966- *170*
Kulling, Monica 1952- *89*
Kullman, Harry 1919-1982 .... *35*
Kumin, Maxine 1925- *12*
Kumin, Maxine Winokur
  See Kumin, Maxine
Kunhardt, Dorothy (Meserve) 1901-1979 ... *53*
  Obituary *22*
Kunhardt, Edith 1937- *67*
Kunjufu, Jawanza 1953- *73*
Kunstler, Morton
  See Kuenstler, Morton
Kuntz, J(ohn) L. 1947- *91*
Kuntz, Jerry 1956- *133*
Kupferberg, Herbert 1918-2001 .... *19*
Kuratomi, Chizuko 1939- *12*
  See also CLR *32*
Kurczok, Belinda 1978- *121*
Kurelek, William 1927-1977 .... *8*
  Obituary *27*
  See also CLR *2*
Kurian, George 1928- *65*
Kurjian, Judi(th M.) 1944- *127*
Kurland, Gerald 1942- *13*
Kurland, Michael 1938- *118*
  Earlier sketch in SATA *48*
Kurland, Michael Joseph
  See Kurland, Michael
Kuroi, Ken 1947- *120*
Kurokawa, Mitsuhiro 1954- *88*
Kurten, Bjorn (Olof) 1924-1988 .... *64*
Kurtz, Jane 1952- *139*
  Earlier sketch in SATA *91*
  See also CLR *123*
Kurtz, Katherine (Irene) 1944- *126*
  Earlier sketch in SATA *76*
Kurz, Rudolf 1952- *95*
Kushner, Donn (J.) 1927- *52*
  See also CLR *55*
Kushner, Ellen 1955- *98*
Kushner, Ellen Ruth
  See Kushner, Ellen
Kushner, Jill Menkes 1951- *62*
Kushner, Lawrence 1943- *169*
  Earlier sketch in SATA *83*
Kushner, Tony 1956- *160*
Kuskin, Karla 1932- *164*
  Earlier sketches in SATA *2, 68, 111*
  See also CLR *4*
  See also SAAS *3*
Kuskin, Karla Seidman
  See Kuskin, Karla
Kusugak, Michael (Arvaaluk) 1948- *143*
Kuttner, Paul 1922- *18*
Kuyper, Sjoerd 1952- *177*
Kuzma, Kay 1941- *39*
Kvale, Velma R(uth) 1898-1979 .... *8*
Kvasnosky, Laura McGee 1951- *142*
  Earlier sketch in SATA *93*
Kwasney, Michelle D. 1960- *162*

Kyle, Benjamin
  See Gottfried, Theodore Mark
Kyle, Elisabeth
  See Dunlop, Agnes M. R.
Kyte, Kathy S. 1946- *50*
  Brief entry *44*

L

L., Barry
  See Longyear, Barry B(rookes)
L., Tommy
  See Lorkowski, Thomas V(incent)
Lace, William W. 1942- *126*
Lachner, Dorothea
  See Knobloch, Dorothea
Lachtman, Ofelia Dumas 1919- *179*
Lackey, Mercedes R. 1950- *127*
  Earlier sketch in SATA *81*
Lackey, Mercedes Ritchie
  See Lackey, Mercedes R.
Lacoe, Addie *78*
Lacome, Julie 1961- *174*
  Earlier sketch in SATA *80*
Lacy, Leslie Alexander 1937- *6*
Ladd, Cheryl (Jean) 1951- *113*
Ladd, Louise 1943- *97*
Ladd, Veronica
  See Miner, Jane Claypool
Laden, Nina 1962- *148*
  Earlier sketch in SATA *85*
Lader, Lawrence 1919-2006 .... *6*
  Obituary *178*
LaDoux, Rita C. 1951- *74*
Lady, A
  See Taylor, Ann
Lady of Quality, A
  See Bagnold, Enid
La Farge, Oliver (Hazard Perry) 1901-1963
  .... *19*
La Farge, Phyllis *14*
LaFaye, A. 1970- *156*
  Earlier sketch in SATA *105*
LaFaye, Alexandria R.T.
  See LaFaye, A.
Laffin, John (Alfred Charles) 1922- *31*
LaFontaine, Bruce 1948- *176*
  Earlier sketch in SATA *114*
La Fontaine, Jean de 1621-1695 .... *18*
Lager, Claude
  See Lapp, Christiane (Germain)
Lager, Marilyn 1939- *52*
Lagercrantz, Rose (Elsa) 1947- *39*
Lagerloef, Selma (Ottiliana Lovisa)
  See Lagerlof, Selma (Ottiliana Lovisa)
Lagerlof, Selma (Ottiliana Lovisa) 1858-1940
  .... *15*
  See also CLR *7*
  See Lagerloef, Selma (Ottiliana Lovisa)
Laguna, Sofie 1968- *158*
LaHaye, Tim F. 1926- *149*
LaHaye, Timothy F.
  See LaHaye, Tim F.
Laiken, Deirdre S(usan) 1948- *48*
  Brief entry *40*
Laimgruber, Monika 1946- *11*
Lain, Anna
  See Lamb, Nancy
Laing, Alexander (Kinnan) 1903-1976 ...... *117*
Laing, Martha
  See Celestino, Martha Laing
Laird, Christa 1944- *108*
  Autobiography Feature *120*
  See also SAAS *26*
Laird, Elizabeth (Mary Risk) 1943- *159*
  Earlier sketches in SATA *77, 114*
  See also CLR *65*
Laird, Jean E(louise) 1930- *38*
Laite, Gordon 1925- *31*

Lake, Harriet
  See Taylor, Paula (Wright)
Laklan, Carli 1907-1988 .... *5*
Laliberte, Louise-Andree 1958- *169*
Lalicki, Barbara *61*
Lally, Soinbhe 1945- *119*
LaMarche, Jim *162*
Lamb, Beatrice Pitney 1904-1997 .... *21*
Lamb, Charles 1775-1834 .... *17*
Lamb, Elizabeth Searle 1917- *31*
Lamb, G(eoffrey) F(rederick) *10*
Lamb, Harold (Albert) 1892-1962 .... *53*
Lamb, Lynton (Harold) 1907-1977 .... *10*
Lamb, Mary Ann 1764-1847 .... *17*
Lamb, Nancy 1939- *80*
Lamb, Robert (Boyden) 1941- *13*
Lambert, David (Compton) 1932- *84*
  Brief entry *49*
Lambert, Janet 1895(?)-1973 .... *25*
Lambert, Martha L. *113*
Lambert, Saul 1928- *23*
Lambert, Stephen *174*
Lamburn, Richmal Crompton 1890-1969 ...... *5*
  See Crompton, Richmal
Lamensdorf, Len
  See Lamensdorf, Leonard
Lamensdorf, Leonard 1930- *120*
Laminack, Lester L. 1956- *163*
  Earlier sketch in SATA *120*
Lamorisse, Albert (Emmanuel) 1922-1970 ... *23*
Lampert, Emily 1951- *52*
  Brief entry *49*
Lamplugh, Lois 1921- *17*
Lampman, Evelyn Sibley 1907-1980 .... *87*
  Obituary *23*
  Earlier sketch in SATA *4*
Lamprey, Louise 1869-1951
  See YABC *2*
Lampton, Chris
  See Lampton, Christopher F.
Lampton, Christopher
  See Lampton, Christopher F.
Lampton, Christopher F. *67*
  Brief entry *47*
Lamstein, Sarah 1943- *174*
  Earlier sketch in SATA *126*
Lamstein, Sarah Marwil
  See Lamstein, Sarah
Lanagan, Margo 1960- *163*
Lancaster, Bruce 1896-1963 .... *9*
Lance, Kathryn 1943- *76*
Land, Barbara (Neblett) 1923- *16*
Land, Jane
  See Borland, Kathryn Kilby
  and Speicher, Helen Ross S(mith)
Land, Myrick (Ebben) 1922-1998 .... *15*
Land, Ross
  See Borland, Kathryn Kilby
  and Speicher, Helen Ross S(mith)
Landau, Elaine 1948- *141*
  Earlier sketches in SATA *10, 94*
Landau, Jacob 1917- *38*
Landeck, Beatrice 1904-1978 .... *15*
Landin, Les 1923- *2*
Landis, J(ames) D(avid) 1942- *60*
  Brief entry *52*
Landis, James D.
  See Landis, J(ames) D(avid)
Landis, Jill Marie 1948- *101*
Landmann, Bimba 1968- *176*
Landon, Dena 1978(?)- *168*
Landon, Lucinda 1950- *56*
  Brief entry *51*
Landon, Margaret (Dorothea Mortenson)
  1903-1993 .... *50*
Landshoff, Ursula 1908-1989 .... *13*
Landstrom, Lena 1943- *146*
Landstrom, Olof 1943- *146*
Lane, Carolyn 1926-1993 .... *10*
Lane, Connie
  See Laux, Constance

Lane, Dakota 1959- *166*
  Earlier sketch in SATA *105*
Lane, Jerry
  See Martin, Patricia Miles
Lane, John (Richard) 1932- *15*
Lane, Margaret 1907-1994 .... *65*
  Brief entry *38*
  Obituary *79*
Lane, Rose Wilder 1887-1968 .... *29*
  Brief entry *28*
Lanes, Selma Gordon 1929- *3*
Lanfredi, Judy 1964- *83*
Lang, Andrew 1844-1912 .... *16*
  See also CLR *101*
Lang, Aubrey *169*
Lang, Paul 1948- *83*
Lang, Susan S. 1950- *68*
Lang, T.T.
  See Taylor, Theodore
Langdo, Bryan 1973- *138*
Lange, John
  See Crichton, Michael
Lange, Suzanne 1945- *5*
Langley, Andrew 1949- *166*
  Earlier sketch in SATA *104*
Langley, Charles P(itman) III 1949- *103*
Langley, Jonathan 1952- *122*
Langley, Wanda *173*
Langner, Nola *8*
  See Malone, Nola Langner
Langone, John (Michael) 1929- *46*
  Brief entry *38*
Langreuter, Jutta 1944- *122*
Langrish, Katherine *177*
Langsen, Richard C. 1953- *95*
Langstaff, John 1920-2005 .... *68*
  Obituary *172*
  Earlier sketch in SATA *6*
  See also CLR *3*
Langstaff, John Meredith
  See Langstaff, John
Langstaff, Launcelot
  See Irving, Washington
Langton, Jane (Gillson) 1922- *140*
  Autobiography Feature *140*
  Earlier sketches in SATA *3, 68, 129*
  See also CLR *33*
  See also SAAS *5*
Lanier, Sidney 1842-1881 .... *18*
Lanier, Sterling E. 1927-2007 .... *109*
Lanier, Sterling Edmund
  See Lanier, Sterling E.
Lanino, Deborah 1964- *123*
Lankford, Mary D. 1932- *112*
  Earlier sketch in SATA *77*
Lannin, Joanne 1951- *121*
Lannin, Joanne A.
  See Lannin, Joanne
Lansdale, Joe R. 1951- *116*
Lansdale, Joe Richard
  See Lansdale, Joe R.
Lansing, Alfred 1921-1975 .... *35*
Lansing, Karen E. 1954- *71*
Lansky, Vicki 1942- *177*
Lantier-Sampon, Patricia 1952- *92*
Lantz, Fran
  See Lantz, Francess L(in)
Lantz, Francess L(in) 1952-2004 .... *153*
  Autobiography Feature *153*
  Obituary *159*
  Earlier sketches in SATA *63, 109*
  See Dixon, Franklin W.
Lantz, Paul 1908- *45*
Lantz, Walter 1900-1994 .... *37*
  Obituary *79*
Lanza, Barbara 1945- *101*
Lapp, Christiane (Germain) 1948- *74*
Lappin, Peter 1911-1999 .... *32*
Larbalestier, Justine *178*
Lardy, Philippe 1963- *168*
LaReau, Jenna *181*

LaReau, Kara *181*
Larios, Julie 1949- *178*
Larios, Julie Hofstrand
  See Larios, Julie
Larkin, Amy
  See Burns, Olive Ann
Larkin, Maia
  See Wojciechowska, Maia (Teresa)
Laroche, Giles 1956- *126*
  Earlier sketch in SATA *71*
LaRochelle, David 1960- *171*
  Earlier sketch in SATA *115*
LaRose, Linda *125*
Larrabee, Lisa 1947- *84*
Larrecq, John M(aurice) 1926-1980 .... *44*
  Obituary *25*
Larrick (Crosby), Nancy 1910-2004 .... *4*
Larsen, Anita 1942- *78*
Larsen, Egon 1904- *14*
Larsen, Rebecca 1944- *54*
Larson, Eve
  See St. John, Wylly Folk
Larson, Gary 1950- *57*
Larson, Ingrid D(ana) 1965- *92*
Larson, Jean Russell 1930- *121*
Larson, Kirby 1954- *181*
  Earlier sketch in SATA *96*
Larson, Norita D(ittberner) 1944- *29*
Larson, William H. 1938- *10*
Larsson, Carl (Olof) 1853-1919 .... *35*
LaSalle, Charles A.
  See Ellis, Edward S(ylvester)
LaSalle, Charles E.
  See Ellis, Edward S(ylvester)
Lasell, Elinor H. 1929- *19*
Lasell, Fen H.
  See Lasell, Elinor H.
Lasenby, Jack 1931- *172*
  Earlier sketches in SATA *65, 103*
Laser, Michael 1954- *117*
Lash, Joseph P. 1909-1987 .... *43*
Lasher, Faith B. 1921- *12*
Lasker, David 1950- *38*
Lasker, Joe *83*
  See also SAAS *17*
  See Lasker, Joseph Leon
Lasker, Joseph Leon 1919- *9*
  See Lasker, Joe
Laski, Marghanita 1915-1988 .... *55*
Laskin, Pamela L. 1954- *75*
Lasky, Kathryn 1944- *157*
  Earlier sketches in SATA *13, 69, 112*
  See also CLR *11*
Lasky Knight, Kathryn
  See Lasky, Kathryn
Lass, Bonnie *131*
Lassalle, C. E.
  See Ellis, Edward S(ylvester)
Lassiter, Mary *59*
  See Hoffman, Mary (Margaret)
Lassiter, Rhiannon 1977- *157*
Latham, Barbara 1896- *16*
Latham, Frank B(rown) 1910-2000 .... *6*
Latham, Jean Lee 1902-1995 .... *68*
  Earlier sketch in SATA *2*
  See also CLR *50*
Latham, Mavis
  See Clark, Mavis Thorpe
Latham, Philip
  See Richardson, Robert S(hirley)
Lathrop, Dorothy P(ulis) 1891-1980 .... *14*
  Obituary *24*
Lathrop, Francis
  See Leiber, Fritz (Reuter, Jr.)
Latimer, Jim 1943- *80*
Latta, Rich
  See Latta, Richard
Latta, Richard 1946- *113*
Latta, Sara L. 1960- *174*
Lattany, Kristin
  See Lattany, Kristin (Elaine Eggleston) Hunter

Lattany, Kristin (Eggleston) Hunter 1931-
  .... *154*
  Autobiography Feature *154*
  Earlier sketch in SATA *132*
Lattany, Kristin (Elaine Eggleston) Hunter
  1931- *132*
  Earlier sketch in SATA *12*
  See also CLR *3*
  See also SAAS *10*
  See Hunter, Kristin
Lattimore, Eleanor Frances 1904-1986 .... *7*
  Obituary *48*
Lattin, Ann
  See Cole, Lois Dwight
Lauber, Patricia (Grace) 1924- *138*
  Earlier sketches in SATA *1, 33, 75*
  See also CLR *16*
Laugesen, Mary E(akin) 1906-1995 .... *5*
Laughbaum, Steve 1945- *12*
Laughlin, Florence Young 1910-2001 .... *3*
Laughlin, Rosemary 1941- *123*
Laure, Ettagale
  See Blauer, Ettagale
Laure, Jason 1940- *50*
  Brief entry *44*
Laurence, Ester Hauser 1935- *7*
Laurie, Rona 1916- *55*
Laurin, Anne
  See McLaurin, Anne
Lauritzen, Jonreed 1902-1979 .... *13*
Lauscher, Hermann
  See Hesse, Hermann
Lauture, Denize 1946- *86*
Laux, Connie
  See Laux, Constance
Laux, Constance 1952- *97*
Laux, Dorothy 1920- *49*
Lavallee, Barbara 1941- *166*
  Earlier sketch in SATA *74*
Lavender, David (Sievert) 1910-2003 .... *97*
  Obituary *145*
  Earlier sketch in SATA *64*
Lavender, William D. 1921- *143*
Laverne, Christine *175*
Lavert, Gwendolyn Battle 1951- *131*
  See Battle-Lavert, Gwendolyn
Laverty, Donald
  See Blish, James (Benjamin)
  and Knight, Damon (Francis)
Lavigne, Louis-Dominique *107*
Lavine, David 1928- *31*
Lavine, Sigmund Arnold 1908-1986 .... *82*
  Earlier sketch in SATA *3*
  See also CLR *35*
Lavond, Paul Dennis
  See Kornbluth, C(yril) M.
  and Lowndes, Robert A(ugustine) W(ard)
  and Pohl, Frederik
Lawhead, Stephen R. 1950- *109*
Lawhead, Steve
  See Lawhead, Stephen R.
Lawlor, Laurie 1953- *137*
  Earlier sketch in SATA *80*
Lawrence, Ann (Margaret) 1942-1987 .... *41*
  Obituary *54*
Lawrence, Iain 1955- *135*
Lawrence, J. T.
  See Rowland-Entwistle, (Arthur) Theodore
  (Henry)
Lawrence, Jerome 1915-2004 .... *65*
Lawrence, John 1933- *30*
Lawrence, Louise 1943- *119*
  Earlier sketches in SATA *38, 78*
Lawrence, Louise de Kiriline 1894-1992 .... *13*
Lawrence, Lynn
  See Garland, Sherry
Lawrence, Margery H. 1889-1969 .... *120*
Lawrence, Michael 1943- *132*
Lawrence, Mildred Elwood 1907-1997 .... *3*
Lawrence, R(onald) D(ouglas) 1921- *55*
Lawrinson, Julia 1969- *141*

Lawson, Amy
    See Gordon, Amy
Lawson, Carol (Antell) 1946- *42*
Lawson, Don(ald Elmer) 1917-1990 .... *9*
Lawson, Joan 1906- *55*
Lawson, Julie 1947- *126*
    Earlier sketch in SATA *79*
    See also CLR *89*
Lawson, Marion Tubbs 1896-1994 .... *22*
Lawson, Robert 1892-1957 .... *100*
    See also YABC *2*
    See also CLR *73*
Lawton, Clive A. 1951- *145*
Laxdal, Vivienne 1962- *112*
Laycock, George (Edwin) 1921- *5*
Layne, Laura
    See Knott, William C(ecil, Jr.)
Layne, Steven L. *171*
Layton, Neal (Andrew) 1971- *152*
Lazare, Gerald John 1927- *44*
Lazare, Jerry
    See Lazare, Gerald John
Lazarevich, Mila 1942- *17*
Lazarus, Keo Felker 1913-1993 .... *21*
    Obituary *129*
Lea, Alec 1907- *19*
Lea, Joan
    See Neufeld, John (Arthur)
Leach, Maria 1892-1977 .... *39*
    Brief entry *28*
Leacock, Elspeth 1946- *131*
Leacroft, Helen (Mabel Beal) 1919- *6*
Leacroft, Richard (Vallance Becher) 1914- ... *6*
Leaf, (Wilbur) Munro 1905-1976 .... *20*
    See also CLR *25*
Leaf, VaDonna Jean 1929- *26*
Leah, Devorah
    See Devorah-Leah
Leakey, Richard E(rskine Frere) 1944- *42*
Leander, Ed
    See Richelson, Geraldine
Lear, Edward 1812-1888 .... *100*
    Earlier sketch in SATA *18*
    See also CLR *75*
Lears, Laurie 1955- *127*
Leasor, (Thomas) James 1923- *54*
Leavitt, Jerome E(dward) 1916- *23*
Leavitt, Martine 1953- *170*
LeBar, Mary E(velyn) 1910-1982 .... *35*
LeBlanc, Annette M. 1965- *68*
LeBlanc, L(ee) 1913- *54*
LeBox, Annette 1943- *145*
Lebrun, Claude 1929- *66*
Le Cain, Errol (John) 1941-1989 .... *68*
    Obituary *60*
    Earlier sketch in SATA *6*
Lecourt, Nancy (Hoyt) 1951- *73*
Ledbetter, Suzann 1953- *119*
Leder, Jane Mersky 1945- *61*
    Brief entry *51*
Lederer, Muriel 1929- *48*
Lederer, William J(ulius) 1912- *62*
Lee, Amanda
    See Baggett, Nancy
    and Buckholtz, Eileen (Garber)
    and Glick, Ruth (Burtnick)
Lee, Benjamin 1921- *27*
Lee, Betsy 1949- *37*
Lee, Carol
    See Fletcher, Helen Jill
Lee, Cora
    See Anderson, Catherine Corley
Lee, Dennis (Beynon) 1939- *102*
    Earlier sketch in SATA *14*
    See also CLR *3*
Lee, Dom 1959- *146*
    Autobiography Feature *121*
    Earlier sketch in SATA *83*
    See also SAAS *26*
Lee, Doris Emrick 1905-1983 .... *44*
    Obituary *35*

Lee, Elizabeth Rogers 1940- *90*
Lee, Harper 1926- *11*
Lee, Hector Viveros 1962- *115*
Lee, Howard N.
    See Goulart, Ron(ald Joseph)
Lee, Huy Voun 1969- *129*
Lee, J(oseph) Edward 1953- *130*
Lee, Jeanne M. 1943- *138*
Lee, John R(obert) 1923-1976 .... *27*
Lee, Jordan
    See Scholefield, Alan
Lee, Julian
    See Latham, Jean Lee
Lee, Liz
    See Lee, Elizabeth Rogers
Lee, Lucy
    See Talbot, Charlene Joy
Lee, Lyn 1953- *128*
Lee, Manning de Villeneuve 1894-1980 ..... *37*
    Obituary *22*
Lee, Marian
    See Clish, (Lee) Marian
Lee, Marie G. 1964- *178*
    Earlier sketches in SATA *81, 130*
Lee, Marie Myung-Ok
    See Lee, Marie G.
Lee, Mary Price 1934- *82*
    Earlier sketch in SATA *8*
Lee, Mildred *6*
    See also SAAS *12*
    See Scudder, Mildred Lee
Lee, Nelle Harper
    See Lee, Harper
Lee, Richard S. 1927- *82*
Lee, Robert C. 1931- *20*
Lee, Robert E(dwin) 1918-1994 .... *65*
    Obituary *82*
Lee, Robert J. 1921- *10*
Lee, Sally 1943- *67*
Lee, Tammie
    See Townsend, Thomas L.
Lee, Tanith 1947- *134*
    Earlier sketches in SATA *8, 88*
Leech, Ben
    See Bowkett, Stephen
Leedy, Loreen 1959- *175*
    Brief entry *50*
    Earlier sketches in SATA *54, 84, 128*
Leedy, Loreen Janelle
    See Leedy, Loreen
Lee-Hostetler, Jeri 1940- *63*
Leekley, Thomas B(riggs) 1910-2001 .... *23*
Leeming, Jo Ann
    See Leeming, Joseph
Leeming, Joseph 1897-1968 .... *26*
Leemis, Ralph B. 1954- *72*
Leese, Jennifer L.B. 1970- *163*
Leeson, Muriel 1920- *54*
Leeson, R. A.
    See Leeson, Robert (Arthur)
Leeson, Robert (Arthur) 1928- *76*
    Earlier sketch in SATA *42*
Leffland, Ella 1931- *65*
Lefler, Irene (Whitney) 1917- *12*
Le Gallienne, Eva 1899-1991 .... *9*
    Obituary *68*
Legg, Gerald 1947- *143*
LeGrand
    See Henderson, LeGrand
Le Guin, Ursula K. 1929- *149*
    Earlier sketches in SATA *4, 52, 99*
    See also CLR *91*
Le Guin, Ursula Kroeber
    See Le Guin, Ursula K.
Legum, Colin 1919-2003 .... *10*
Lehman, Barbara 1963- *170*
    Earlier sketch in SATA *115*
Lehman, Bob *91*
Lehman, Elaine *91*
Lehn, Cornelia 1920- *46*
Lehne, Judith Logan 1947- *93*

Lehr, Delores 1920- *10*
Lehr, Norma 1930- *71*
Leiber, Fritz (Reuter, Jr.) 1910-1992 .... *45*
    Obituary *73*
Leibold, Jay 1957- *57*
    Brief entry *52*
Leichman, Seymour 1933- *5*
Leigh, Nila K. 1981- *81*
Leigh, Tom 1947- *46*
Leigh-Pemberton, John 1911-1997 .... *35*
Leighton, Clare (Veronica Hope) 1899-1989
    .... *37*
Leighton, Margaret (Carver) 1896-1987 .... *1*
    Obituary *52*
Leiner, Al(an) 1938- *83*
Leiner, Katherine 1949- *93*
Leipold, L. Edmond 1902-1983 .... *16*
Leisk, David (Johnson) 1906-1975 .... *30*
    Obituary *26*
    Earlier sketch in SATA *1*
    See also CLR *98*
    See Johnson, Crockett
Leister, Mary 1917- *29*
Leitch, Patricia 1933- *98*
    Earlier sketch in SATA *11*
Leitner, Isabella 1924- *86*
Leland, Bob 1956- *92*
Leland, Robert E.
    See Leland, Bob
Lematre, Pascal 1967- *176*
Lember, Barbara Hirsch 1941- *92*
LeMieux, A.C. 1954- *125*
    Earlier sketch in SATA *90*
    See LeMieux, Anne
LeMieux, Anne
    See LeMieux, A.C.
LeMieux, Anne Connelly
    See LeMieux, A.C.
Lemieux, Michele 1955- *139*
Lemke, Horst 1922- *38*
Lenanton, Carola Mary Anima Oman
    See Oman, Carola (Mary Anima)
L'Engle, Madeleine 1918- *128*
    Earlier sketches in SATA *1, 27, 75*
    See also CLR *57*
    See also SAAS *15*
L'Engle, Madeleine Camp Franklin
    See L'Engle, Madeleine
Lengyel, Cornel Adam 1915- *27*
Lengyel, Emil 1895-1985 .... *3*
    Obituary *42*
Lennon, John (Ono) 1940-1980 .... *114*
Leno, Jay 1950- *154*
LeNoir, Janice 1941- *89*
Lens, Sidney 1912-1986 .... *13*
    Obituary *48*
Lenski, Lois 1893-1974 .... *100*
    Earlier sketches in SATA *1, 26*
    See also CLR *26*
Lent, Blair *133*
    Earlier sketch in SATA *2*
Lent, Henry Bolles 1901-1973 .... *17*
Lent, John 1948- *108*
Leodhas, Sorche Nic
    See Alger, Leclaire (Gowans)
Leokum, Arkady 1916(?)- *45*
Leon, Sharon 1959- *79*
Leonard, Alison 1944- *70*
Leonard, Constance (Brink) 1923- *42*
    Brief entry *40*
Leonard, Elmore 1925- *163*
Leonard, Elmore John, Jr.
    See Leonard, Elmore
Leonard, Jonathan N(orton) 1903-1975 ...... *36*
Leonard, Laura 1923- *75*
Leong, Gor Yun
    See Ellison, Virginia H(owell)
Leonhardt, Alice 1950- *152*

Lerangis, Peter 1955- *171*
  Earlier sketch in SATA 72
  See Dixon, Franklin W.
  and Keene, Carolyn
Lerner, Aaron 1920-2007 .... *35*
  Obituary *179*
Lerner, Aaron Bunsen
  See Lerner, Aaron
Lerner, Carol 1927- *86*
  Earlier sketch in SATA 33
  See also CLR 34
  See also SAAS 12
Lerner, Gerda 1920- *65*
Lerner, Harriet 1944- *101*
Lerner, Marguerite Rush 1924-1987 .... *11*
  Obituary *51*
Lerner, Sharon (Ruth) 1938-1982 .... *11*
  Obituary *29*
Leroe, Ellen W(hitney) 1949- *99*
  Brief entry *51*
  Earlier sketch in SATA 61
Leroux, Gaston 1868-1927 .... *65*
Leroux-Hugon, Helene 1955- *132*
LeRoy, Gen *52*
  Brief entry *36*
LeShan, Eda J(oan) 1922-2002 .... *21*
  See also CLR 6
LeSieg, Theo.
  See Dr. Seuss
  and Geisel, Theodor Seuss
  and Seuss, Dr.
  and Stone, Rosetta
Lesinski, Jeanne M. 1960- *120*
Leslie, Robert Franklin 1911-1990 .... *7*
Leslie, Roger 1961- *168*
Leslie, Roger James
  See Leslie, Roger
Leslie, Sarah
  See McGuire, Leslie (Sarah)
LeSourd, Catherine
  See Marshall, (Sarah) Catherine (Wood)
Lessac, Frane
  See Lessac, Frane
Lessac, Frane 1954- *148*
  Earlier sketch in SATA 61
Lessem, Dino Don
  See Lessem, Don
Lessem, Don 1951- *155*
  Earlier sketch in SATA 97
Lesser, Rika 1953- *53*
Lester, Alison 1952- *129*
  Earlier sketches in SATA 50, 90
Lester, Helen 1936- *145*
  Earlier sketches in SATA 46, 92
Lester, Julius 1939- *157*
  Earlier sketches in SATA 12, 74, 112
  See also CLR 41
Lester, Julius Bernard
  See Lester, Julius
Lester, Mike 1955- *131*
Le Sueur, Meridel 1900-1996 .... *6*
Le Tord, Bijou 1945- *95*
  Earlier sketch in SATA 49
Letts, Billie 1938- *121*
Leuck, Laura 1962- *146*
  Earlier sketch in SATA 85
Leutscher, Alfred (George) 1913- *23*
Levai, Blaise 1919- *39*
Levenkron, Steven 1941- *86*
Leverich, Kathleen 1948- *103*
LeVert, (William) John 1946- *55*
Levete, Sarah 1961- *153*
Levin, Betty 1927- *137*
  Earlier sketches in SATA 19, 84
  See also SAAS 11
Levin, Ira 1929- *66*
Levin, Marcia Obrasky 1918- *13*
Levin, Meyer 1905-1981 .... *21*
  Obituary *27*
Levin, Miriam (Ramsfelder) 1962- *97*

Levine, Abby 1943- *54*
  Brief entry *52*
Levine, Betty K(rasne) 1933- *66*
Levine, David 1926- *43*
  Brief entry *35*
Levine, Edna S(imon) *35*
Levine, Evan 1962- *77*
  Earlier sketch in SATA 74
Levine, Gail Carson 1947- *161*
  Earlier sketch in SATA 98
  See also CLR 85
Levine, I(srael) E. 1923-2003 .... *12*
  Obituary *146*
Levine, Joan Goldman *11*
Levine, Joseph 1910- *33*
Levine, Marge 1934- *81*
Levine, Rhoda *14*
Levine, Sarah 1970- *57*
Levine, Shar 1953- *131*
Levine-Freidus, Gail
  See Provost, Gail Levine
Levinson, Nancy Smiler 1938- *140*
  Earlier sketches in SATA 33, 80
Levinson, Riki *99*
  Brief entry *49*
  Earlier sketch in SATA 52
Levithan, David 1972- *166*
Levitin, Sonia (Wolff) 1934- *131*
  Autobiography Feature *131*
  Earlier sketches in SATA 4, 68, 119
  See also CLR 53
  See also SAAS 2
Levitt, Sidney (Mark) 1947- *68*
Levon, O. U.
  See Kesey, Ken
Levoy, Myron *49*
  Brief entry *37*
Levy, Barrie *112*
Levy, Constance 1931- *140*
  Earlier sketch in SATA 73
  See also SAAS 22
Levy, Elizabeth 1942- *169*
  Earlier sketches in SATA 31, 69, 107
  See also SAAS 18
Levy, Janice *172*
Levy, Marilyn 1937- *67*
Levy, Nathan 1945- *63*
Levy, Robert 1945- *82*
Lewees, John
  See Stockton, Francis Richard
Lewin, Betsy 1937- *169*
  Autobiography Feature *115*
  Earlier sketches in SATA 32, 90
Lewin, Hugh 1939- *72*
  Brief entry *40*
  See also CLR 9
Lewin, Ted 1935- *165*
  Autobiography Feature *115*
  Earlier sketches in SATA 21, 76, 119
Lewis, Alice C. 1936- *46*
Lewis, Amanda 1955- *80*
Lewis, (Joseph) Anthony 1927- *27*
Lewis, Anthony 1966- *120*
Lewis, Barbara A. 1943- *73*
Lewis, Beverly 1949- *80*
Lewis, Brenda Ralph 1932- *72*
Lewis, Brian 1963- *128*
Lewis, Claudia (Louise) 1907-2001 .... *5*
Lewis, Clive Staples
  See Lewis, C.S.
Lewis, C.S. 1898-1963 .... *100*
  Earlier sketch in SATA 13
  See also CLR 109
Lewis, Cynthia Copeland 1960- *111*
Lewis, E. M. *123*
  Earlier sketch in SATA 20
Lewis, Earl Bradley
  See Lewis, E.B.
Lewis, E.B. 1956- *168*
  Earlier sketches in SATA 93, 124

Lewis, Elizabeth Foreman 1892-1958 .... *121*
  See also YABC 2
Lewis, Francine
  See Wells, Helen
Lewis, J. Patrick 1942- *162*
  Earlier sketches in SATA 69, 104
Lewis, Jack P(earl) 1919- *65*
Lewis, Jean 1924- *61*
Lewis, Julinda
  See Lewis-Ferguson, Julinda
Lewis, Kevin *173*
Lewis, Kim 1951- *136*
  Earlier sketch in SATA 84
Lewis, Linda (Joy) 1946- *67*
Lewis, Lucia Z.
  See Anderson, Lucia (Lewis)
Lewis, Marjorie 1929- *40*
  Brief entry *35*
Lewis, Mary (Christianna) 1907(?)-1988 .... *64*
  Obituary *56*
  See Brand, Christianna
Lewis, Mervyn
  See Frewer, Glyn (M.)
Lewis, Michael
  See Untermeyer, Louis
Lewis, Naomi *144*
  Earlier sketch in SATA 76
Lewis, Paeony 1960- *173*
Lewis, Paul
  See Gerson, Noel Bertram
Lewis, Richard 1935- *3*
Lewis, Rob 1962- *72*
Lewis, Roger
  See Zarchy, Harry
Lewis, Shannon
  See Llywelyn, Morgan
Lewis, Shari 1934-1998 .... *35*
  Brief entry *30*
  Obituary *104*
Lewis, Sylvan R.
  See Aronson, Virginia
Lewis, Thomas P(arker) 1936- *27*
Lewis, Wendy A. 1966- *150*
Lewis-Ferguson, Julinda 1955- *85*
Lewison, Wendy Cheyette *177*
Lewiton, Mina 1904-1970 .... *2*
Lexau, Joan M. *130*
  Earlier sketches in SATA 1, 36
Ley, Willy 1906-1969 .... *2*
Leydon, Rita (Floden) 1949- *21*
Leyland, Eric (Arthur) 1911- *37*
Li, Xiao Jun 1952- *86*
Liatsos, Sandra Olson 1942- *103*
Libby, Barbara M. *153*
Libby, Bill
  See Libby, William M.
Libby, William M. 1927-1984 .... *5*
  Obituary *39*
Liberty, Gene 1924- *3*
Lichtenheld, Tom *152*
Liddell, Kenneth 1912-1975 .... *63*
Lidz, Jane *120*
Lieberman, E(dwin) James 1934- *62*
Liebers, Arthur 1913-1984 .... *12*
Lieblich, Irene 1923- *22*
Liers, Emil E(rnest) 1890-1975 .... *37*
Lies, Brian 1963- *131*
Liestman, Vicki 1961- *72*
Lietz, Gerald S. 1918- *11*
Life, Kay (Guinn) 1930- *83*
Lifton, Betty Jean *118*
  Earlier sketch in SATA 6
Lifton, Robert Jay 1926- *66*
Lightburn, Ron 1954- *91*
Lightburn, Sandra 1955- *91*
Lightner, A. M.
  See Hopf, Alice (Martha) L(ightner)
Lightner, Alice
  See Hopf, Alice (Martha) L(ightner)
Lignell, Lois 1911- *37*
Liles, Maurine Walpole 1935- *81*

Lilley, Stephen R. 1950- 97
Lilley, Stephen Ray
    See Lilley, Stephen R.
Lillington, Kenneth (James) 1916-1998 39
Lilly, Ray
    See Curtis, Richard (Alan)
Lim, John 1932- 43
Liman, Ellen (Fogelson) 1936- 22
Limb, Sue 1946- 158
Limburg, Peter R(ichard) 1929- 13
Lin, Grace 1974- 162
    Earlier sketch in SATA *111*
Lincoln, C(harles) Eric 1924-2000 5
Lincoln, James
    See Bates, Katharine Lee
Lindbergh, Anne 81
    See Sapieyevski, Anne Lindbergh
Lindbergh, Anne Morrow 1906-2001 33
    Obituary 125
Lindbergh, Anne Spencer Morrow
    See Lindbergh, Anne Morrow
Lindbergh, Charles A(ugustus, Jr.) 1902-1974
    33
Lindbergh, Reeve 1945- 163
    Earlier sketch in SATA *116*
Lindblom, Steven (Winther) 1946- 94
    Brief entry 39
    Earlier sketch in SATA *42*
Linde, Gunnel 1924- 5
Lindenbaum, Pija 1955- 144
    Earlier sketch in SATA *77*
Lindgren, Astrid (Anna Emilia Ericsson)
    1907-2002 38
    Obituary 128
    Earlier sketch in SATA *2*
    See also CLR *119*
Lindgren, Barbro 1937- 120
    Brief entry 46
    Earlier sketch in SATA *63*
    See also CLR *86*
Lindman, Maj (Jan) 1886-1972 43
Lindop, Edmund 1925- 5
Lindquist, Jennie Dorothea 1899-1977 13
Lindquist, Rowena Cory 1958- 98
Lindquist, Willis 1908-1988 20
Lindsay, Norman Alfred William 1879-1969
    67
    See also CLR *8*
Lindsay, (Nicholas) Vachel 1879-1931 40
Lindsey, Kathleen D(orothy) 1949- 153
Line, David
    See Davidson, Lionel
Line, Les 1935- 27
Linfield, Esther 40
Lingard, Joan (Amelia) 1932- 130
    Autobiography Feature 130
    Earlier sketches in SATA *8, 74, 114*
    See also CLR *89*
    See also SAAS *5*
Link, Martin 1934- 28
Linn, Margot
    See Ziefert, Harriet
Linnea, Sharon 1956- 82
Lion, Melissa 1976- 176
Lionni, Leo(nard) 1910-1999 72
    Obituary 118
    Earlier sketch in SATA *8*
    See also CLR *71*
Lipinsky de Orlov, Lino S. 1908- 22
Lipkind, William 1904-1974 15
Lipman, David 1931- 21
Lipman, Matthew 1923- 14
Lippincott, Gary A. 1953- 119
    Earlier sketch in SATA *73*
Lippincott, Joseph W(harton) 1887-1976 17
Lippincott, Sarah Lee 1920- 22
Lippman, Peter J. 1936- 31
Lipsyte, Robert 1938- 161
    Earlier sketches in SATA *5, 68, 113*
    See also CLR *76*

Lipsyte, Robert Michael
    See Lipsyte, Robert
Lisandrelli, Elaine Slivinski 1951- 94
Lisker, Sonia O. 1933- 44
Lisle, Holly 1960- 98
Lisle, Janet Taylor 1947- 150
    Brief entry 47
    Earlier sketches in SATA *59, 96*
    See also SAAS *14*
Lisle, Rebecca 162
Lisle, Seward D.
    See Ellis, Edward S(ylvester)
Lisowski, Gabriel 1946- 47
    Brief entry 31
Liss, Howard 1922-1995 4
    Obituary 84
Lisson, Deborah 1941- 110
    Earlier sketch in SATA *71*
List, Ilka Katherine 1935- 6
Liston, Robert A. 1927- 5
Litchfield, Ada B(assett) 1916-1999 5
Litchfield, Jo 1973- 116
Lithgow, John (Arthur) 1945- 145
Litowinsky, Olga (Jean) 1936- 26
Littke, Lael J. 1929- 140
    Earlier sketches in SATA *51, 83*
Little, A. Edward
    See Klein, Aaron E.
Little, Douglas 1942- 96
Little, (Flora) Jean 1932- 149
    Earlier sketches in SATA *2, 68, 106*
    See also CLR *4*
    See also SAAS *17*
Little, Lessie Jones 1906-1986 60
    Obituary 50
Little, Mary E. 1912-1999 28
Littlechild, George 1958- 85
Littledale, Freya (Lota) 1929-1992 74
    Earlier sketch in SATA *2*
Littlefield, Bill 1948- 83
Littlefield, Holly 1963- 97
Littlesugar, Amy 1953- 176
    Earlier sketch in SATA *122*
Littleton, Mark R. 1950- 142
    Earlier sketch in SATA *89*
Littman, Sarah Darer 175
Litty, Julie 1971- 181
Lively, Penelope 1933- 164
    Earlier sketches in SATA *7, 60, 101*
    See also CLR *7*
Lively, Penelope Margaret
    See Lively, Penelope
Liverakos, L.A.
    See Gilman, Laura Anne
Liversidge, (Henry) Douglas 1913- 8
Livesey, Claire (Warner) 1927- 127
Livingston, Carole 1941- 42
Livingston, (M.) Irene 1932- 150
Livingston, Myra Cohn 1926-1996 68
    Obituary 92
    Earlier sketch in SATA *5*
    See also CLR *7*
    See also SAAS *1*
Livingston, Richard R(oland) 1922- 8
Livo, Norma J. 1929- 76
Ljungkvist, Laura 180
Llerena Aguirre, Carlos 1952- 19
Llerena Aguirre, Carlos Antonio
    See Llerena Aguirre, Carlos
Llewellyn, Claire 1954- 143
    Earlier sketch in SATA *77*
Llewellyn, Grace 1964- 110
Llewellyn, Grace Katherine
    See Llewellyn, Grace
Llewellyn, Richard
    See Llewellyn Lloyd, Richard Dafydd Vivian
Llewellyn, Sam 1948- 95
Llewellyn Lloyd, Richard Dafydd Vivian
    1906-1983 11
    Obituary 37
    See Llewellyn, Richard

Llewelyn, T. Harcourt
    See Hamilton, Charles (Harold St. John)
Lloyd, Alan
    See Lloyd, A.R.
Lloyd, Alan Richard
    See Lloyd, A.R.
Lloyd, A.R. 1927- 168
    Earlier sketch in SATA *97*
Lloyd, David
    See Lloyd, David T.
Lloyd, David T. 1954- 167
Lloyd, E. James
    See James, Elizabeth
Lloyd, Errol 1943- 22
Lloyd, Hugh
    See Fitzhugh, Percy Keese
Lloyd, James
    See James, Elizabeth
Lloyd, Megan 1958- 117
    Earlier sketch in SATA *77*
Lloyd, (Mary) Norris 1908-1993 10
    Obituary 75
Lloyd-Jones, Sally 1960- 179
Lloyd Webber, Andrew 1948- 56
    See Webber, Andrew Lloyd
Llywelyn, Morgan 1937- 109
Lo, Ginnie 165
Lo, Virginia M.
    See Lo, Ginnie
Lobato, Jose Bento Monteiro 1882-1948 .. 114
Lobel, Anita (Kempler) 1934- 162
    Earlier sketches in SATA *6, 55, 96*
Lobel, Arnold (Stark) 1933-1987 55
    Obituary 54
    Earlier sketch in SATA *6*
    See also CLR *5*
Lobel, Gillian 181
Lobsenz, Amelia 12
Lobsenz, Norman M(itchell) 1919- 6
Lochak, Michele 1936- 39
Lochlons, Colin
    See Jackson, C(aary) Paul
Locke, Clinton W. 1
Locke, Elsie (Violet) 1912-2001 87
Locke, Lucie 1904-1989 10
Locke, Robert 1944- 63
    See Bess, Clayton
Locker, Thomas 1937- 109
    Earlier sketch in SATA *59*
    See also CLR *14*
Lockhart, E.
    See Jenkins, Emily
Lockridge, Hildegarde (Dolson) 1908-1981
    121
    See Dolson, Hildegarde
Lockwood, Mary
    See Spelman, Mary
Lodge, Bernard 1933- 107
    Earlier sketch in SATA *33*
Lodge, Jo 1966- 173
    Earlier sketch in SATA *112*
Loeb, Jeffrey 1946- 57
Loeb, Robert H., Jr. 1917- 21
Loefgren, Ulf 1931- 3
Loehfelm, Bill 1969- 153
Loeper, John J(oseph) 1929- 118
    Earlier sketch in SATA *10*
Loescher, Ann Dull 1942- 20
Loescher, Gil(burt Damian) 1945- 20
Loewer, Jean Jenkins
    See Jenkins, Jean
Loewer, (Henry) Peter 1934- 98
LoFaro, Jerry 1959- 77
Lofo
    See Heimann, Rolf
Lofting, Hugh (John) 1886-1947 100
    Earlier sketch in SATA *15*
    See also CLR *19*
Lofts, Norah (Robinson) 1904-1983 8
    Obituary 36

Logan, Jake
  See Knott, William C(ecil, Jr.)
  and Krepps, Robert W(ilson)
  and Pearl, Jacques Bain
  and Riefe, Alan
  and Rifkin, Shepard
  and Smith, Martin Cruz
Logan, Mark
  See Nicole, Christopher (Robin)
Logan, Rochelle 1954- 169
Logston, Anne 1962- 112
Logue, Christopher 1926- 23
Logue, Mary 1952- 161
  Earlier sketch in SATA *112*
Loh, Morag 1935- 73
Lohans, Alison 1949- 101
Loken, Newton Clayton 1919- 26
Lomas, Steve
  See Brennan, Joseph Lomas
Lomask, Milton (Nachman) 1909-1991 20
Lombard, Jenny 178
Lombino, Salvatore
  See Hunter, Evan
LoMonaco, Palmyra 1932- 102
London, Jack 1876-1916 18
  See also CLR *108*
  See London, John Griffith
London, Jane
  See Geis, Darlene Stern
London, Jonathan (Paul) 1947- 157
  Earlier sketches in SATA *74, 113*
Lonergan, (Pauline) Joy (MacLean) 1909- . 10
Lonette, Reisie (Dominee) 1924- 43
Long, Cathryn J. 1946- 89
Long, Earlene (Roberta) 1938- 50
Long, Emmett
  See Leonard, Elmore
Long, Helen Beecher 1
Long, Judith Elaine 1953- 20
Long, Judy
  See Long, Judith Elaine
Long, Kim 1949- 69
Long, Loren 1966(?)- 151
Long, Melinda 1960- 152
Long, Sylvia 1948- 179
  Earlier sketch in SATA *120*
Longbeard, Frederick
  See Longyear, Barry B(rookes)
Longfellow, Henry Wadsworth 1807-1882 . 19
  See also CLR *99*
Longfellow, Layne (A.) 1937- 102
Longman, Harold S. 1919- 5
Longsworth, Polly 1933- 28
Longtemps, Kenneth 1933- 17
Longway, A. Hugh
  See Lang, Andrew
Longyear, Barry B(rookes) 1942- 117
Look, Lenore 180
Loomans, Diane 1955- 90
Loomis, Christine 160
  Earlier sketch in SATA *113*
Loomis, Jennifer A. 1942- 101
Loomis, Robert D. 5
Lopez, Angelo (Cayas) 1967- 83
Lopez, Barry (Holstun) 1945- 67
Lopez, Jack 1950- 178
Lopez, Lorraine M. 1956- 181
Lopshire, Robert M(artin) 1927- 6
Loraine, Connie
  See Reece, Colleen L.
Lorbiecki, Marybeth 1959- 172
  Earlier sketch in SATA *121*
Lord, Athena V. 1932- 39
Lord, Beman 1924-1991 5
  Obituary 69
Lord, Bette Bao 1938- 58
Lord, (Doreen Mildred) Douglas 1904- 12
Lord, John Vernon 1939- 21
Lord, Nancy
  See Titus, Eve
Lord, Walter 1917-2002 3

Lorde, Diana
  See Reno, Dawn E(laine)
Lorenz, Albert 1941- 115
Lorenzini, Carlo 1826-1890 100
  Earlier sketch in SATA *29*
  See Collodi, Carlo
Lorimer, Janet 1941- 60
Loring, Emilie (Baker) 1864(?)-1951 51
Lorkowski, Thomas V(incent) 1950- 92
Lorkowski, Tom
  See Lorkowski, Thomas V(incent)
Lorraine, Walter (Henry) 1929- 16
Lorrimer, Claire
  See Clark, Patricia Denise
Loss, Joan 1933- 11
Lothrop, Harriet Mulford Stone 1844-1924
  20
Lottridge, Celia Barker 1936- 157
  Earlier sketch in SATA *112*
LoTurco, Laura 1963- 84
Lotz, Wolfgang 1912-1981 65
Louie, Ai-Ling 1949- 40
  Brief entry 34
Louis, Pat
  See Francis, Dorothy Brenner
Louisburgh, Sheila Burnford
  See Burnford, Sheila (Philip Cochrane Every)
Louise, Anita
  See Riggio, Anita
Lourie, Helen
  See Storr, Catherine (Cole)
Lourie, Peter (King) 1952- 142
  Earlier sketch in SATA *82*
Love, Ann 1947- 168
  Earlier sketch in SATA *79*
Love, D. Anne 1949- 180
  Earlier sketches in SATA *96, 145*
Love, Douglas 1967- 92
Love, Katherine (Isabel) 1907- 3
Love, Kathleen Ann
  See Love, Ann
Love, Sandra (Weller) 1940- 26
Lovejoy, Jack 1937- 116
Lovelace, Delos Wheeler 1894-1967 7
Lovelace, Maud Hart 1892-1980 2
  Obituary 23
Lovell, Ingraham
  See Bacon, Josephine Dodge (Daskam)
Loverseed, Amanda (Jane) 1965- 75
Lovett, Margaret (Rose) 1915- 22
Low, Alice 1926- 156
  Earlier sketches in SATA *11, 76*
Low, Elizabeth Hammond 1898-1991 5
Low, Joseph 1911-2007 14
Low, William 177
Lowe, Jay, Jr.
  See Loeper, John J(oseph)
Lowell, Susan 1950- 127
  Earlier sketch in SATA *81*
Lowenstein, Dyno 1914-1996 6
Lowenstein, Sallie 1949- 116
Lowery, Linda 1949- 151
  Earlier sketch in SATA *74*
Lowitz, Anson C. 1901(?)-1978 18
Lowitz, Sadyebeth Heath 1901-1969 17
Lowndes, Robert A(ugustine) W(ard)
  1916-1998 117
Lowrey, Janette Sebring 1892-1986 43
Lowry, Lois 1937- 177
  Autobiography Feature 127
  Earlier sketches in SATA *23, 70, 111*
  See also CLR *72*
  See also SAAS *3*
Lowry, Lois Hammersberg
  See Lowry, Lois
Lowry, Peter 1953- 7
Loyie, Larry 1933- 150
Lozansky, Edward D. 1941- 62
Lozier, Herbert 1915- 26
Lubar, David 1954- 133
Lubell, Cecil 1912-2000 6

Lubell, Winifred (A. Milius) 1914- 6
Lubin, Leonard
  See Lubin, Leonard B.
Lubin, Leonard B. 1943-1994 45
  Brief entry 37
Lubka, S. Ruth 1948- 154
Luby, Thia 1954- 124
Lucado, Max (Lee) 1955- 104
Lucas, Cedric 1962- 101
Lucas, E(dward) V(errall) 1868-1938 20
Lucas, Eileen 1956- 113
  Earlier sketch in SATA *76*
Lucas, George 1944- 56
Lucas, Jerry 1940- 33
Lucas, Victoria
  See Plath, Sylvia
Lucashenko, Melissa 1967- 104
Luccarelli, Vincent 1923- 90
Luce, Celia (Geneva Larsen) 1914- 38
Luce, Willard (Ray) 1914-1990 38
Lucht, Irmgard 1937- 82
Luckett, Dave 1951- 167
  Earlier sketch in SATA *106*
Luckhardt, Mildred Corell 1898-1990 5
Ludel, Jacqueline 1945- 64
Ludlum, Mabel Cleland
  See Widdemer, Mabel Cleland
Ludwig, Helen 33
Ludwig, Lyndell 1923- 63
Ludwig, Trudy 1959- 166
Lueders, Edward (George) 1923- 14
Luenn, Nancy 1954- 79
  Earlier sketch in SATA *51*
Lufkin, Raymond H. 1897- 38
Lugard, Flora Louisa Shaw 1852-1929 21
Luger, Harriett Mandelay 1914- 23
Luhrmann, Winifred B(ruce) 1934- 11
Luis, Earlene W. 1929- 11
Luke, Pauline 178
Luke, Pauline R.
  See Luke, Pauline
Lum, Peter
  See Crowe, (Bettina) Peter Lum
Lumry, Amanda (R.) 159
Lund, Deb 157
Lund, Doris Herold 1919- 12
Lung, Chang
  See Jordan, Robert
Lunge-Larsen, Lise 1955- 138
Lunn, Carolyn (Kowalczyk) 1960- 67
Lunn, Janet (Louise Swoboda) 1928- 110
  Earlier sketches in SATA *4, 68*
  See also CLR *18*
  See also SAAS *12*
Lunsford, Cin Forshay
  See Forshay-Lunsford, Cin
Lupica, Mike 177
  See Lupica, Michael
Lupoff, Dick
  See Lupoff, Richard A(llen)
Lupoff, Richard A(llen) 1935- 60
Lurie, Alison 1926- 112
  Earlier sketch in SATA *46*
Lurie, Morris 1938- 72
Lussert, Anneliese 1929- 101
Lusted, Marcia Amidon 1962- 143
Lustig, Arnost 1926- 56
Lustig, Loretta 1944- 46
Luthardt, Kevin 1973- 172
Luther, Rebekah (Lyn) S(tiles) 1960- 90
Luttmann, Gail
  See Damerow, Gail
Luttrell, Guy L. 1938- 22
Luttrell, Ida (Alleene) 1934- 91
  Brief entry 35
  Earlier sketch in SATA *40*
Luttrell, William (J. III) 1954- 149
Lutz, John 1939- 180
Lutz, John Thomas
  See Lutz, John
Lutz, Norma Jean 1943- 122

Lutzeier, Elizabeth 1952- *72*
Lutzker, Edythe 1904-1991 .... *5*
Luxbacher, Irene M. 1970- *153*
Luzadder, Patrick 1954- *89*
Luzzati, Emanuele 1921-2007 .... *7*
Luzzatto, Paola Caboara 1938- *38*
Lybbert, Tyler 1970- *88*
Lydon, Michael 1942- *11*
Lyfick, Warren
    See Reeves, Lawrence F.
Lyle, Katie Letcher 1938- *8*
Lynch, Chris 1962- *171*
    Earlier sketches in SATA *95, 131*
    See also CLR *58*
Lynch, Lorenzo 1932- *7*
Lynch, Marietta 1947- *29*
Lynch, P(atrick) J(ames) 1962- *122*
    Earlier sketch in SATA *79*
Lynch, Patricia (Nora) 1898-1972 .... *9*
Lynds, Dennis 1924-2005 .... *47*
    Brief entry *37*
Lyngseth, Joan
    See Davies, Joan
Lynn, Elizabeth A(nne) 1946- *99*
Lynn, Mary
    See Brokamp, Marilyn
Lynn, Patricia
    See Watts, Mabel Pizzey
Lynn, Tracy *175*
Lyon, Elinor 1921- *6*
Lyon, George Ella 1949- *148*
    Autobiography Feature *148*
    Earlier sketches in SATA *68, 119*
Lyon, Lyman R.
    See de Camp, L(yon) Sprague
Lyons, Dorothy M(arawee) 1907-1997 .... *3*
Lyons, Grant 1941- *30*
Lyons, Marcus
    See Blish, James (Benjamin)
Lyons, Mary E(velyn) 1947- *142*
    Earlier sketch in SATA *93*
Lystad, Mary (Hanemann) 1928- *11*
Lytle, Elizabeth Stewart 1949- *79*
Lytle, Robert A. 1944- *119*
Lyttle, Richard B(ard) 1927- *23*
Lytton, Edward G(eorge) E(arle) L(ytton)
    Bulwer-Lytton Baron 1803-1873 .... *23*

M

Ma, Wenhai 1954- *84*
Maar, Leonard (Frank, Jr.) 1927- *30*
Maartens, Maretha 1945- *73*
Maas, Selve -1997 .... *14*
Mabie, Grace
    See Mattern, Joanne
Mac
    See MacManus, Seumas
    and Maccari, Ruggero
Macalaster, Elizabeth G. 1951- *115*
MacAlister, Katie *159*
MacAodhagain, Eamon
    See Egan, E(dward) W(elstead)
MacArthur-Onslow, Annette Rosemary 1933-
    .... *26*
Macaulay, David (Alexander) 1946- *137*
    Brief entry *27*
    Earlier sketches in SATA *46, 72*
    See also CLR *14*
Macaulay, Teresa (E.) 1947- *95*
Macavinta, Courtney *176*
MacBeth, George (Mann) 1932-1992 .... *4*
    Obituary *70*
MacBride, Roger Lea 1929-1995 .... *85*
MacCarter, Don 1944- *91*
MacClintock, Dorcas 1932- *8*
MacCullough, Carolyn *174*

MacDonald, Amy 1951- *156*
    Autobiography Feature *156*
    Earlier sketches in SATA *76, 136*
MacDonald, Anne Elizabeth Campbell Bard
    -1958
    See MacDonald, Betty
MacDonald, Anson
    See Heinlein, Robert A.
MacDonald, Betty 1908-1958
    See YABC *1*
    See MacDonald, Anne Elizabeth Campbell
    Bard
Macdonald, Blackie
    See Emrich, Duncan (Black Macdonald)
Macdonald, Caroline 1948- *86*
    Obituary *111*
    See also CLR *60*
Macdonald, Dwight 1906-1982 .... *29*
    Obituary *33*
MacDonald, George 1824-1905 .... *100*
    Earlier sketch in SATA *33*
    See also CLR *67*
MacDonald, Golden
    See Brown, Margaret Wise
Macdonald, James D. 1954- *165*
    Earlier sketches in SATA *81, 114*
    See Appleton, Victor
Macdonald, Marcia
    See Hill, Grace Livingston
MacDonald, Margaret Read 1940- *164*
    Earlier sketch in SATA *94*
Macdonald, Marianne 1934- *113*
Macdonald, Mary
    See Gifford, Griselda
MacDonald, Maryann 1947- *72*
Macdonald, Shelagh 1937- *25*
MacDonald, Suse 1940- *109*
    Brief entry *52*
    Earlier sketch in SATA *54*
Macdonald, Zillah K(atherine) 1885-1979 .. *11*
MacDonnell, Megan
    See Stevens, Serita (Deborah)
MacDougal, John
    See Blish, James (Benjamin)
MacDougal, John
    See Blish, James (Benjamin)
    and Lowndes, Robert A(ugustine) W(ard)
Mace, Elisabeth 1933- *27*
Mace, Varian 1938- *49*
MacEwen, Gwendolyn (Margaret) 1941-1987
    .... *50*
    Obituary *55*
Macfarlan, Allan A. 1892-1982 .... *35*
MacFarlane, Iris 1922- *11*
MacGill-Callahan, Sheila 1926-2000 .... *78*
MacGregor, Carol Lynn *153*
MacGregor, Ellen 1906-1954 .... *39*
    Brief entry *27*
MacGregor-Hastie, Roy (Alasdhair Niall)
    1929- *3*
MacGrory, Yvonne 1948- *142*
Machado, Ana Maria 1941- *150*
MacHale, D.J. 1956- *175*
MacHale, Donald James
    See MacHale, D.J.
Machetanz, Frederick 1908- *34*
Machin Goodall, Daphne (Edith) *37*
Macht, Norman L(ee) 1929- *122*
MacInnes, Helen (Clark) 1907-1985 .... *22*
    Obituary *44*
Macintosh, Brownie 1950- *98*
MacIntyre, Elisabeth 1916- *17*
Mack, L.V.
    See Kimmelman, Burt
Mack, Stan(ley) *17*
Mack, Todd *168*
Mack, Tracy 1968- *128*
Mackall, Dandi D.
    See Mackall, Dandi Daley
Mackall, Dandi Daley 1949- *177*
    Earlier sketch in SATA *118*

Mackay, Claire 1930- *97*
    Autobiography Feature *124*
    Earlier sketch in SATA *40*
    See also CLR *43*
Mackay, Constance D'Arcy (?)-1966 .... *125*
Mackay, Donald 1914-2005 .... *81*
    Obituary *173*
Mackay, Donald Alexander
    See Mackay, Donald
MacKaye, Percy (Wallace) 1875-1956 .... *32*
Mackel, Kathryn 1950- *162*
Mackel, Kathy
    See Mackel, Kathryn
MacKellar, William 1914- *4*
Macken, Walter 1915-1967 .... *36*
MacKenzie, Jill (Kelly) 1947- *75*
Mackey, Ernan
    See McInerny, Ralph
Mackie, Maron
    See McNeely, Jeannette
Mackin, Edward
    See McInerny, Ralph
MacKinnon, Bernie 1957- *69*
MacKinnon Groomer, Vera 1915- *57*
MacKinstry, Elizabeth 1879-1956 .... *42*
Mackler, Carolyn 1973- *156*
MacLachlan, Patricia 1938- *168*
    Brief entry *42*
    Earlier sketches in SATA *62, 107*
    See also CLR *14*
MacLane, Jack
    See Crider, Bill
MacLean, Alistair (Stuart) 1922(?)-1987 .... *23*
    Obituary *50*
Maclean, Art
    See Shirreffs, Gordon D(onald)
MacLean, Christine Kole *177*
MacLean, Glynne 1964- *150*
MacLeod, Beatrice 1910- *162*
    Earlier sketch in SATA *10*
MacLeod, Beatrice Beach
    See MacLeod, Beatrice
MacLeod, Charlotte (Matilda) 1922-2005 ... *28*
    Obituary *160*
MacLeod, Doug 1959- *60*
MacLeod, Elizabeth *158*
MacLeod, Ellen Jane (Anderson) 1916- *14*
MacManus, James
    See MacManus, Seumas
MacManus, Seumas 1869-1960 .... *25*
MacMaster, Eve (Ruth) B(owers) 1942- *46*
MacMillan, Annabelle
    See Quick, Annabelle
MacMillan, Dianne M(arie) 1943- *125*
    Earlier sketch in SATA *84*
Macneill, Janet
    See McNeely, Jeannette
MacPeek, Walter G. 1902-1973 .... *4*
    Obituary *25*
MacPhail, Catherine 1946- *130*
MacPherson, Margaret 1908-2001 .... *9*
    See also SAAS *4*
MacPherson, Winnie 1930- *107*
MacRae, Tom 1980- *181*
Macrae, Travis
    See Feagles, Anita M(acRae)
MacRaois, Cormac 1944- *72*
Macumber, Mari
    See Sandoz, Mari(e Susette)
Macy, Sue 1954- *134*
    Earlier sketch in SATA *88*
Madaras, Lynda 1947- *151*
Madden, Don 1927- *3*
Madden, Kerry 1961- *168*
Madden-Lunsford, Kerry
    See Madden, Kerry
Maddern, Eric 1950- *166*
Maddigan, Beth 1967- *174*
Maddison, Angela Mary 1923- *10*
    See Banner, Angela
Maddock, Reginald (Bertram) 1912-1994 ... *15*

Madenski, Melissa (Ann) 1949- 77
Madian, Jon 1941- 9
Madison, Arnold 1937- 6
Madison, Winifred 5
Madonna 1958- 149
Madsen, Gunnar 171
Madsen, Ross Martin 1946- 82
Madsen, Susan A. 1954- 90
Madsen, Susan Arrington
    See Madsen, Susan A.
Maestro, Betsy (Crippen) 1944- 106
    Brief entry 30
    Earlier sketch in SATA 59
    See also CLR 45
Maestro, Giulio 1942- 106
    Earlier sketches in SATA 8, 59
    See also CLR 45
Maeterlinck, Maurice 1862-1949 66
Magee, Doug 1947- 78
Magee, Wes 1939- 64
Maggio, Rosalie 1943- 69
Magid, Ken(neth Marshall) 65
Magnus, Erica 1946- 77
Magorian, James 1942- 92
    Earlier sketch in SATA 32
Magorian, Michelle 1947- 128
    Earlier sketch in SATA 67
Magorian, Michelle Jane
    See Magorian, Michelle
Magovern, Peg 103
Maguire, Anne
    See Nearing, Penny
Maguire, Gregory 1954- 129
    Earlier sketches in SATA 28, 84
    See also SAAS 22
Maguire, Gregory Peter
    See Maguire, Gregory
Maguire, Jack 1920-2000 74
Maguire, Jesse
    See Smith, Sherwood
Maguire, Jessie
    See Smith, Sherwood
Maher, Ramona 1934- 13
Mahlqvist, (Karl) Stefan 30
    See Maehlqvist, (Karl) Stefan
Mahon, Julia C(unha) 1916- 11
Mahood, Kenneth 1930- 24
Mahy, Margaret 1936- 171
    Earlier sketches in SATA 14, 69, 119
    See also CLR 78
Mahy, Margaret May
    See Mahy, Margaret
Maiden, Cecil (Edward) 1902-1981 52
Maidoff, Ilka
    See List, Ilka Katherine
Maifair, Linda Lee 1947- 83
Maik, Henri
    See Hecht, Henri Joseph
Maillu, David G(ian) 1939- 111
Maine, Trevor
    See Catherall, Arthur
Mains, Randolph P. 1946- 80
Maiorano, Robert 1946- 43
Maisner, Heather 1947- 89
Maison, Della
    See Katz, Bobbi
Maitland, Antony Jasper 1935- 25
Maitland, Barbara 102
Major, Kevin (Gerald) 1949- 134
    Earlier sketches in SATA 32, 82
    See also CLR 11
Majure, Janet 1954- 96
Makie, Pam 1943- 37
Makowski, Silk
    See Makowski, Silvia Ann
Makowski, Silvia Ann 1940- 101
Malam, John 1957- 152
    Earlier sketch in SATA 89
Malcolm, Dan
    See Silverberg, Robert

Malcolm, Jahnna N.
    See Beecham, Jahnna
Malcolmson, Anne
    See von Storch, Anne B.
Malcolmson, David 1899-1978 6
Maletta, Dr. Arlene
    See Feltenstein, Arlene (H.)
Mali, Jane Lawrence 1937-1995 51
    Brief entry 44
    Obituary 86
Malkin, Nina 1959(?)- 179
Mallett, Jerry J. 1939- 76
Mallory, Kenneth 1945- 128
Mallowan, Agatha Christie
    See Christie, Agatha (Mary Clarissa)
Malmberg, Carl 1904-1979 9
Malmgren, Dallin 1949- 65
Malo, John W. 1911-2000 4
Malone, James Hiram 1930- 84
Malone, Patricia 1932- 155
Maloney, Pat
    See Markun, Patricia Maloney
Malory, Sir Thomas 1410(?)-1471(?) 59
    Brief entry 33
Malvasi, Meg Greene 143
Malvern, Corinne 1905-1956 34
Malvern, Gladys (?)-1962 23
Mama G.
    See Davis, Grania
Mammano, Julie (Lynn) 1962- 107
Mamonova, Tatyana 1943- 93
Manchel, Frank 1935- 10
Manchester, William (Raymond) 1922-2004
    65
Mandel, Brett H. 1969- 108
Mandel, Peter (Bevan) 1957-1998 87
Mandel, Sally (Elizabeth) 1944- 64
Mandell, Muriel (Hortense Levin) 1921- 63
Manders, John 1957- 175
Manes, Stephen 1949- 99
    Brief entry 40
    Earlier sketch in SATA 42
Manfred, Frederick (Feikema) 1912-1994 .. 30
Mangin, Marie France 1940- 59
Mangione, Jerre 6
    Obituary 104
    See Mangione, Gerlando
Mango, Karin N. 1936- 52
Mangurian, David 1938- 14
Mania, Cathy 1950- 102
Mania, Robert 1952- 102
Mania, Robert C., Jr.
    See Mania, Robert
Maniatty, Taramesha 1978- 92
Maniscalco, Joseph 1926- 10
Manley, Deborah 1932- 28
Manley, Seon 1921- 15
    See also CLR 3
    See also SAAS 2
Mann, Elizabeth 1948- 153
Mann, Josephine
    See Pullein-Thompson, Josephine (Mary
    Wedderburn)
Mann, Kenny 1946- 91
Mann, Pamela 1946- 91
Mann, Patrick
    See Waller, Leslie
Mann, Peggy 6
    See Houlton, Peggy Mann
Mannetti, Lisa 1953- 57
    Brief entry 51
Mannheim, Grete (Salomon) 1909-1986 10
Manniche, Lise 1943- 31
Manning, Mick 1959- 176
Manning, Rosemary (Joy) 1911-1988 10
    See Davys, Sarah
    and Voyle, Mary
Manning, Sarra 162

Manning-Sanders, Ruth (Vernon) 1895(?)-1988
    73
    Obituary 57
    Earlier sketch in SATA 15
Mannion, Diane
    See Paterson, Diane
Mannis, Celeste Davidson 173
Mansir, A. Richard 1932- 170
Manson, Ainslie Kertland 1938- 115
Manson, Beverlie 1945- 57
    Brief entry 44
Manthorpe, Helen 1958- 122
Mantinband, Gerda (B.) 1917- 74
Manton, Jo
    See Gittings, Jo (Grenville) Manton
Manuel, Lynn 1948- 179
    Earlier sketch in SATA 99
Manushkin, Fran 1942- 166
    Earlier sketches in SATA 7, 54, 93
Manushkin, Frances
    See Manushkin, Fran
Man Without a Spleen, A
    See Chekhov, Anton (Pavlovich)
Manzano, Sonia 1950- 167
Mapes, Mary A.
    See Ellison, Virginia H(owell)
Maple, Marilyn 1931- 80
Mappin, Strephyn 1956- 109
Mara, Barney
    See Roth, Arthur J(oseph)
Mara, Jeanette
    See Cebulash, Mel
Marasmus, Seymour
    See Rivoli, Mario
Marbach, Ethel
    See Pochocki, Ethel (Frances)
Marcal, Annette B.
    See Callaway, Bernice (Anne)
Marcelino
    See Agnew, Edith J(osephine)
Marcellino, Fred 1939-2001 118
    Obituary 127
    Earlier sketch in SATA 68
March, Carl
    See Fleischman, Sid
Marchant, Bessie 1862-1941
    See YABC 2
Marchant, Catherine
    See Cookson, Catherine (McMullen)
Marcher, Marion Walden 1890-1987 10
Marchesi, Stephen 1951- 114
Marchesi, Steve
    See Marchesi, Stephen
    and Older, Effin
    and Older, Jules
Marchetta, Melina 1965- 170
Marciano, John Bemelmans 1970- 167
Marciano, John Bemelmans 1970- 118
    See also CLR 93
Marco, Lou
    See Gottfried, Theodore Mark
Marcus, Leonard S. 1950- 133
Marcus, Paul 1953- 82
Marcus, Rebecca B(rian) 1907- 9
Marcuse, Aida E. 1934- 89
Margaret, Karla
    See Andersdatter, Karla M(argaret)
Margolin, Harriet
    See Ziefert, Harriet
Margolis, Jeffrey A. 1948- 108
Margolis, Richard J(ules) 1929-1991 86
    Obituary 67
    Earlier sketch in SATA 4
Margolis, Vivienne 1922- 46
Mariana
    See Foster, Marian Curtis
Marie, Geraldine 1949- 61
Mariner, Scott
    See Pohl, Frederik
Marino, Dorothy Bronson 1912- 14
Marino, Jan 1936- 114

Marino, Nick
    See Deming, Richard
Marino, Peter 1960- *179*
Mario, Anna
    See Odgers, Sally Farrell
Marion, Henry
    See del Rey, Lester
Maris, Ron *71*
    Brief entry *45*
Mark, Jan 1943-2006 .... *164*
    Obituary *173*
    Earlier sketches in SATA *22, 69, 114*
    See also CLR *11*
Mark, Janet Marjorie
    See Mark, Jan
Mark, Joan T. 1937- *122*
Mark, Pauline (Dahlin) 1913-1997 .... *14*
Mark, Polly
    See Mark, Pauline (Dahlin)
Mark, Ted
    See Gottfried, Theodore Mark
Markel, Michelle *169*
Marker, Sherry 1941- *76*
Markert, Jennifer 1965- *83*
Markert, Jenny
    See Markert, Jennifer
Markham, Lynne 1947- *102*
Markham, Marion M. 1929- *60*
Markins, W. S.
    See Jenkins, Marie M(agdalen)
Markle, Sandra L. 1946- *148*
    Brief entry *41*
    Earlier sketches in SATA *57, 92*
Markle, Sandra Lee
    See Markle, Sandra L.
Marko, Katherine D(olores) *28*
Markoosie
    See Patsauq, Markoosie
Marks, Alan 1957- *151*
    Earlier sketch in SATA *77*
Marks, Burton 1930- *47*
    Brief entry *43*
Marks, Graham *158*
Marks, Hannah K.
    See Trivelpiece, Laurel
Marks, J.
    See Highwater, Jamake (Mamake)
Marks, J(ames) M(acdonald) 1921- *13*
Marks, Laurie J. 1957- *68*
Marks, Mickey Klar -1986 .... *12*
Marks, Peter
    See Smith, Robert Kimmel
Marks, Rita 1938- *47*
Marks, Stan(ley) *14*
Marks-Highwater, J.
    See Highwater, Jamake (Mamake)
Markun, Patricia Maloney 1924- *15*
Markusen, Bruce (Stanley Rodriguez) 1965-
    .... *141*
Marley, Louise 1952- *173*
    Earlier sketch in SATA *120*
Marlin, Hilda
    See Van Stockum, Hilda
Marlow, Max
    See Nicole, Christopher (Robin)
Marlow, Susan K. 1953- *178*
Marlowe, Amy Bell *67*
    Earlier sketch in SATA *1*
Marlowe, Jack
    See Deary, Terry
Marney, Dean 1952- *90*
Marokvia, Artur 1909- *31*
Marokvia, Mireille (Journet) 1918- *5*
Marol, Jean-Claude 1946- *125*
Marr, John S(tuart) 1940- *48*
Marric, J. J.
    See Butler, William (Arthur) Vivian
    and Creasey, John

Marrin, Albert 1936- *126*
    Brief entry *43*
    Earlier sketches in SATA *53, 90*
    See also CLR *53*
Marriott, Alice Lee 1910-1992 .... *31*
    Obituary *71*
Marriott, Janice 1946- *134*
Marriott, Pat(ricia) 1920- *35*
Marroquin, Patricio
    See Markun, Patricia Maloney
Mars, W. T.
    See Mars, Witold Tadeusz J.
Mars, Witold Tadeusz J. 1912-1985 .... *3*
Marsden, Carolyn 1950- *175*
    Earlier sketch in SATA *140*
Marsden, John 1950- *146*
    Earlier sketches in SATA *66, 97*
    See also CLR *34*
    See also SAAS *22*
Marsh, Carole 1946- *127*
Marsh, Dave 1950- *66*
Marsh, J. E.
    See Marshall, Evelyn
Marsh, James 1946- *73*
Marsh, Jean
    See Marshall, Evelyn
Marsh, Joan F. 1923- *83*
Marsh, Valerie 1954- *89*
Marshall, Anthony D(ryden) 1924- *18*
Marshall, Bonnie C. 1941- *141*
    Earlier sketch in SATA *18*
Marshall, Bridget M(ary) 1974- *103*
Marshall, (Sarah) Catherine (Wood) 1914-1983
    .... *2*
    Obituary *34*
Marshall, Douglas
    See McClintock, Marshall
Marshall, Edward
    See Marshall, James
Marshall, Evelyn 1897-1991 .... *11*
Marshall, Felicity 1950- *116*
Marshall, Garry 1934- *60*
Marshall, H. H.
    See Jahn, (Joseph) Michael
Marshall, James 1942-1992 .... *75*
    Earlier sketches in SATA *6, 51*
    See also CLR *21*
Marshall, James Edward
    See Marshall, James
Marshall, James Vance
    See Payne, Donald Gordon
Marshall, Janet (Perry) 1938- *97*
Marshall, Jeff
    See Laycock, George (Edwin)
Marshall, Kim
    See Marshall, Michael (Kimbrough)
Marshall, Michael (Kimbrough) 1948- *37*
Marshall, Percy
    See Young, Percy M(arshall)
Marshall, S(amuel) L(yman) A(twood)
    1900-1977 .... *21*
Marsoli, Lisa Ann 1958- *101*
    Brief entry *53*
Marsten, Richard
    See Hunter, Evan
Marston, Elsa 1933- *156*
Marston, Hope Irvin 1935- *127*
    Earlier sketch in SATA *31*
Marszalek, John F. 1939- *167*
Marszalek, John Francis, Jr.
    See Marszalek, John F.
Marszalek, John Francis 1939-
    See Marszalek, John F.
Martchenko, Michael 1942- *154*
    Earlier sketches in SATA *50, 95*
Martel, Aimee
    See Thurlo, Aimee
    and Thurlo, David
Martel, Suzanne 1924- *99*

Martin, Ann M(atthews) 1955- *126*
    Brief entry *41*
    Earlier sketches in SATA *44, 70*
    See also CLR *32*
Martin, Bill, Jr. *67*
    Brief entry *40*
    See also CLR *97*
    See Martin, William Ivan, Jr.
Martin, Charles E(lmer) *70*
    Earlier sketch in SATA *69*
    See Mastrangelo, Charles E(lmer)
Martin, Christopher
    See Hoyt, Edwin P(almer), Jr.
Martin, Claire 1933- *76*
Martin, David Stone 1913-1992 .... *39*
Martin, Donald
    See Honig, Donald
Martin, Dorothy 1921- *47*
Martin, Eugene *1*
Martin, Eva M. 1939- *65*
Martin, Frances M(cEntee) 1906-1998 .... *36*
Martin, Francesca 1947- *101*
Martin, Fred 1948- *119*
Martin, Fredric
    See Christopher, Matt(hew Frederick)
Martin, George Raymond Richard
    See Martin, George R.R.
Martin, George R.R. 1948- *118*
Martin, J(ohn) P(ercival) 1880(?)-1966 .... *15*
Martin, Jacqueline Briggs 1945- *149*
    Earlier sketch in SATA *98*
Martin, Jane Read 1957- *84*
Martin, Jeremy
    See Levin, Marcia Obrasky
Martin, Les
    See Schulman, L(ester) M(artin)
Martin, Linda 1961- *82*
Martin, Lynne 1923- *21*
Martin, Marcia
    See Levin, Marcia Obrasky
Martin, Marvin 1926- *126*
Martin, Melanie
    See Pellowski, Michael (Joseph)
Martin, Nancy
    See Salmon, Annie Elizabeth
Martin, Patricia Miles 1899-1986 .... *43*
    Obituary *48*
    Earlier sketch in SATA *1*
Martin, Peter
    See Chaundler, Christine
Martin, Rene 1891-1977 .... *42*
    Obituary *20*
Martin, Rupert (Claude) 1905- *31*
Martin, S. R.
    See Mappin, Strephyn
Martin, Stefan 1936- *32*
Martin, Vicky
    See Storey, Victoria Carolyn
Martin, Webber
    See Silverberg, Robert
Martin, Wendy
    See Martini, Teri
Martin, William Ivan, Jr. 1916-2004 .... *145*
    Earlier sketch in SATA *40*
    See Martin, Bill, Jr.
Martineau, Diane 1940- *178*
Martineau, Harriet 1802-1876
    See YABC *2*
Martinet, Jeanne 1958- *80*
Martinez, Agnes *167*
Martinez, Ed(ward) 1954- *98*
Martinez, Elizabeth Coonrod 1954- *85*
Martinez, Victor 1954- *95*
Martini, Teri 1930- *3*
Martini, Therese
    See Martini, Teri
Martino, Alfred C. 1964- *174*
Martinson, Janis
    See Herbert, Janis
Marton, Jirina 1946- *144*
    Earlier sketch in SATA *95*

Marton, Pierre
  See Stone, Peter
Martson, Del
  See Lupoff, Richard A(llen)
Martyr, Paula (Jane) 57
  See Lawford, Paula Jane
Maruki, Toshi 1912-2000 112
  See also CLR 19
Marvin, Isabel R(idout) 1924- 84
Marx, Patricia Windschill 1948- 160
  Earlier sketch in SATA 112
Marx, Robert F(rank) 1936- 24
Marx, Trish
  See Marx, Patricia Windschill
Marzani, Carl (Aldo) 1912-1994 12
Marzollo, Jean 1942- 130
  Earlier sketches in SATA 29, 77
  See also SAAS 15
Masefield, John (Edward) 1878-1967 19
Masoff, Joy 1951- 118
Mason, Adrienne 1962- 163
Mason, Cherie 170
Mason, Ernst
  See Pohl, Frederik
Mason, F(rancis) van Wyck 1901-1978 3
  Obituary 26
Mason, Frank W.
  See Mason, F(rancis) van Wyck
Mason, George Frederick 1904-2000 14
Mason, Miriam E(vangeline) 1900-1973 2
  Obituary 26
Mason, Simon 1962- 178
Mason, Tally
  See Derleth, August (William)
Mason, Van Wyck
  See Mason, F(rancis) van Wyck
Mass, Wendy 1967- 158
Mass, William
  See Gibson, William
Masselman, George 1897-1971 19
Massie, Dianne Redfield 1938- 125
  Earlier sketch in SATA 16
Massie, Elizabeth 108
Masson, Sophie 1959- 179
  Earlier sketch in SATA 133
Masters, Anthony (Richard) 1940-2003 112
  Obituary 145
Masters, Kelly R(ay) 1897-1987 3
Masters, Mildred 1932- 42
Masters, William
  See Cousins, Margaret
Masters, Zeke
  See Bensen, Donald R.
  and Goulart, Ron(ald Joseph)
Matas, Carol 1949- 93
  Autobiography Feature 112
  See also CLR 52
Matchette, Katharine E. 1941- 38
Math, Irwin 1940- 42
Mathabane, Mark 1960- 123
Mather, Kirtley F(letcher) 1888-1978 65
Mathers, Petra 1945- 176
  Earlier sketch in SATA 119
  See also CLR 76
Matheson, Richard (Christian) 1953- 119
Matheson, Shirlee Smith 1942- 155
Mathews, Janet 1914-1992 41
Mathews, Judith 80
  See Goldberger, Judith M.
Mathews, Louise
  See Tooke, Louise Mathews
Mathieu, Joe 1949- 94
  Brief entry 36
  Earlier sketch in SATA 43
Mathieu, Joseph P.
  See Mathieu, Joe
Mathis, Sharon Bell 1937- 58
  Earlier sketch in SATA 7
  See also CLR 3
  See also SAAS 3
Matlin, Marlee 1965- 181

Matlin, Marlee Beth
  See Matlin, Marlee
Matloff, Gregory 1945- 73
Matott, Justin 1961- 109
Matranga, Frances Carfi 1922- 78
Matray, James I. 1948- 161
Matray, James Irving
  See Matray, James I.
Matson, Emerson N(els) 1926- 12
Matsui, Tadashi 1926- 8
Matsuno, Masako 6
  See Kobayashi, Masako Matsuno
Matte, (Encarnacion) L'Enc 1936- 22
Mattern, Joanne 1963- 122
Mattheson, Jenny 180
Matthews, Aline
  See De Wire, Elinor
Matthews, Andrew 1948- 138
Matthews, Caitlin 1952- 122
Matthews, Downs 1925- 71
Matthews, Ellen
  See Bache, Ellyn
Matthews, Ellen 1950- 28
Matthews, Harold Downs
  See Matthews, Downs
Matthews, Jacklyn Meek
  See Meek, Jacklyn O'Hanlon
Matthews, John (Kentigern) 1948- 116
Matthews, Liz
  See Pellowski, Michael (Joseph)
Matthews, Morgan
  See Pellowski, Michael (Joseph)
Matthews, Nicola
  See Browne, N.M.
Matthews, Patricia 1927-2006 28
Matthews, Patricia Anne
  See Matthews, Patricia
Matthews, William Henry III 1919- 45
  Brief entry 28
Matthiessen, Peter 1927- 27
Mattingley, Christobel (Rosemary) 1931- ... 85
  Earlier sketch in SATA 37
  See also CLR 24
  See also SAAS 18
Matulay, Laszlo 1912- 43
Matus, Greta 1938- 12
Maugham, W. S.
  See Maugham, W(illiam) Somerset
Maugham, W(illiam) Somerset 1874-1965 . 54
Maugham, William Somerset
  See Maugham, W(illiam) Somerset
Maurer, Diane Philippoff
  See Maurer-Mathison, Diane V(ogel)
Maurer, Diane Vogel
  See Maurer-Mathison, Diane V(ogel)
Maurer-Mathison, Diane V(ogel) 1944- 89
Mauser, Pat Rhoads
  See McCord, Patricia
Mauser, Patricia Rhoads 37
  See McCord, Patricia
Maves, Mary Carolyn 1916- 10
Maves, Paul B(enjamin) 1913-1994 10
Mavor, Salley 1955- 125
Mawicke, Tran 1911- 15
Max, Peter 1939- 45
Maxon, Anne
  See Best, (Evangel) Allena Champlin
Maxwell, Arthur S. 1896-1970 11
Maxwell, Edith 1923- 7
Maxwell, Gavin 1914-1969 65
Maxwell, Katie
  See MacAlister, Katie
Maxwell-Hyslop, Miranda 1968- 154
May, Charles Paul 1920- 4
May, Elaine Tyler 1947- 120
May, J. C.
  See May, Julian
May, Julian 1931- 11
May, Robert Stephen 1929-1996 46
May, Robin
  See May, Robert Stephen

Mayall, Beth 171
Mayberry, Florence V(irginia) Wilson 10
Maybury, Richard J. 1946- 72
Maybury, Rick
  See Maybury, Richard J.
Mayer, Agatha
  See Maher, Ramona
Mayer, Ann M(argaret) 1938- 14
Mayer, Danuta 1958- 117
Mayer, Jane Rothschild 1903-2001 38
Mayer, Marianna 1945- 132
  Earlier sketches in SATA 32, 83
Mayer, Mercer 1943- 137
  Earlier sketches in SATA 16, 32, 73, 129
  See also CLR 11
Mayerson, Charlotte Leon 36
Mayerson, Evelyn Wilde 1935- 55
Mayfield, Katherine 1958- 118
Mayfield, Sue 1963- 146
  Earlier sketch in SATA 72
Mayhar, Ardath 1930- 38
Mayhew, James (John) 1964- 149
  Earlier sketch in SATA 85
Maynard, Olga 1920- 40
Mayne, William (James Carter) 1928- 122
  Earlier sketches in SATA 6, 68
  See also CLR 123
  See also SAAS 11
Maynes, J. O. Rocky, Jr.
  See Maynes, J. Oscar, Jr.
Maynes, J. Oscar, Jr. 1929- 38
Mayo, Gretchen Will 1936- 163
  Earlier sketch in SATA 84
Mayo, Margaret 1935- 165
  Earlier sketches in SATA 38, 96
Mayo, Margaret Mary
  See Mayo, Margaret
Mays, Lucinda L(a Bella) 1924- 49
Mays, (Lewis) Victor (Jr.) 1927- 5
Mazer, Anne 1953- 105
  Earlier sketch in SATA 67
Mazer, Harry 1925- 167
  Earlier sketches in SATA 31, 67, 105
  See also CLR 16
  See also SAAS 11
Mazer, Norma Fox 1931- 168
  Earlier sketches in SATA 24, 67, 105
  See also CLR 23
  See also SAAS 1
Mazille, Capucine 1953- 96
Mazza, Adriana 1928- 19
Mazzio, Joann 1926- 74
Mbugua, Kioi Wa 1962- 83
McAfee, Carol 1955- 81
McAllister, Amanda
  See Dowdell, Dorothy (Florence) Karns
  and Hager, Jean
  and Meaker, Eloise
McAllister, Margaret I. 1956- 169
  Earlier sketch in SATA 117
McAllister, M.I.
  See McAllister, Margaret I.
McArthur, Nancy 96
McAvoy, Jim 1972- 142
McBain, Ed
  See Hunter, Evan
McBratney, Sam 1943- 164
  Earlier sketch in SATA 89
  See also CLR 44
McBrier, Michael
  See Older, Effin
  and Older, Jules
McCafferty, Jim 1954- 84
McCaffery, Janet 1936- 38
McCaffrey, Anne 1926- 152
  Autobiography Feature 152
  Earlier sketches in SATA 8, 70, 116
  See also CLR 49
  See also SAAS 11
McCaffrey, Anne Inez
  See McCaffrey, Anne

McCaffrey, Mary
  See Szudek, Agnes S(usan) P(hilomena)
McCain, Becky Ray 1954- 138
McCain, Murray (David, Jr.) 1926-1981 7
  Obituary 29
McCall, Edith (Sansom) 1911- 6
McCall, Virginia Nielsen 1909-2000 13
McCall Smith, Alexander 1948- 179
  Earlier sketch in SATA 73
McCall Smith, Alexander Alasdair
  See McCall Smith, Alexander
McCallum, Phyllis
  See Koch, Phyllis (Mae) McCallum
McCallum, Stephen 1960- 91
McCampbell, Darlene Z. 1942- 83
McCann, Edson
  See del Rey, Lester
  and Pohl, Frederik
McCann, Gerald 1916- 41
McCann, Helen 1948- 75
McCannon, Dindga 41
McCants, William D. 1961- 82
McCarter, Neely Dixon 1929- 47
McCarthy, Agnes 1933- 4
McCarthy, Colin (John) 1951- 77
McCarthy, Meghan 168
McCarthy, Ralph F. 1950- 139
McCarthy-Tucker, Sherri N. 1958- 83
McCarty, Rega Kramer 1904-1986 10
McCaslin, Nellie 1914-2005 12
McCaughrean, Geraldine 1951- 173
  Earlier sketches in SATA 87, 139
  See also CLR 38
McCaughren, Tom 1936- 75
McCauley, Adam 1965- 128
McCay, (Zenas) Winsor 1869-1934 134
  Earlier sketch in SATA 41
McClafferty, Carla Killough 1958- 137
McCleery, Patsy R. 1925- 133
  Earlier sketch in SATA 88
McClintock, Barbara 1955- 146
  Earlier sketches in SATA 57, 95
McClintock, Marshall 1906-1967 3
McClintock, May Garelick
  See Garelick, May
McClintock, Mike
  See McClintock, Marshall
McClintock, Norah 178
McClintock, Theodore 1902-1971 14
McClinton, Leon 1933- 11
McCloskey, Kevin 1951- 79
McCloskey, (John) Robert 1914-2003 100
  Obituary 146
  Earlier sketches in SATA 2, 39
  See also CLR 7
McCloy, James F(loyd) 1941- 59
McClung, Robert M(arshall) 1916- 135
  Earlier sketches in SATA 2, 68
  See also CLR 11
  See also SAAS 15
McClure, Gillian Mary 1948- 31
McColley, Kevin 1961- 80
  See also SAAS 23
McConduit, Denise Walter 1950- 89
McConnell, James Douglas Rutherford
  1915-1988 40
  Obituary 56
McCord, Anne 1942- 41
McCord, David (Thompson Watson)
  1897-1997 18
  Obituary 96
  See also CLR 9
McCord, Jean 1924- 34
McCord, Pat Mauser
  See McCord, Patricia
McCord, Patricia 1943- 159
  See Mauser, Patricia Rhoads
McCord, Patricia Sue Rhoads Mauser
  See McCord, Patricia
McCormick, Brooks
  See Adams, William Taylor

McCormick, Dell J. 1892-1949 19
McCormick, (George) Donald (King)
  1911-1998 14
McCormick, Edith (Joan) 1934- 30
McCormick, Kimberly A. 1960- 153
McCormick, Patricia 1956- 181
  Earlier sketch in SATA 128
McCourt, Lisa 1964- 159
  Earlier sketch in SATA 117
McCourt, Malachy 1931- 126
McCoy, Iola Fuller 3
McCoy, J(oseph) J(erome) 1917- 8
McCoy, Karen Kawamoto 1953- 82
McCoy, Lois (Rich) 1941- 38
McCrady, Lady 1951- 16
McCrea, James (Craig, Jr.) 1920- 3
McCrea, Ruth (Pirman) 1921- 3
McCreigh, James
  See Pohl, Frederik
McCrumb, Sharyn 1948- 109
McCue, Lisa 1959- 177
  Earlier sketch in SATA 65
McCue, Lisa Emiline
  See McCue, Lisa
McCullen, Andrew
  See Arthur, Robert, (Jr.)
McCullers, (Lula) Carson (Smith) 1917-1967
  27
McCulloch, John Tyler
  See Burroughs, Edgar Rice
McCulloch, Sarah
  See Ure, Jean
McCullough, David 1933- 62
McCullough, David Gaub
  See McCullough, David
McCullough, Frances Monson 1938- 8
McCullough, Sharon Pierce 1943- 131
McCully, Emily Arnold 134
  Autobiography Feature 134
  Earlier sketches in SATA 5, 110
  See also CLR 46
  See also SAAS 7
  See Arnold, Emily
McCune, Dan
  See Haas, Dorothy F.
McCunn, Ruthanne Lum 1946- 63
McCurdy, Michael (Charles) 1942- 147
  Earlier sketches in SATA 13, 82
McCutcheon, Elsie (Mary Jackson) 1937- 60
McCutcheon, John 1952- 97
McDaniel, Becky Bring 1953- 61
McDaniel, Lurlene 1944- 146
  Earlier sketch in SATA 71
McDaniels, Pellom III 1968- 121
McDearmon, Kay 20
McDermott, Beverly Brodsky 1941- 11
McDermott, Eleni 156
McDermott, Gerald (Edward) 1941- 163
  Earlier sketches in SATA 16, 74
  See also CLR 9
McDermott, Michael 1962- 76
McDevitt, John Charles 155
  Earlier sketch in SATA 94
  See McDevitt, Jack
McDole, Carol
  See Farley, Carol (J.)
McDonald, Collin 1943- 79
McDonald, Gerald D(oan) 1905-1970 3
McDonald, Jamie
  See Heide, Florence Parry
McDonald, Janet 1953- 148
McDonald, Jill (Masefield) 1927-1982 13
  Obituary 29
McDonald, Joyce 1946- 164
  Earlier sketch in SATA 101
McDonald, Lucile Saunders 1898-1992 10
McDonald, Mary Ann 1956- 84
McDonald, Megan 1959- 151
  Autobiography Feature 151
  Earlier sketches in SATA 67, 99, 148
  See also CLR 94

McDonald, Meme 1954- 112
McDonald, Mercedes 1956- 169
  Earlier sketch in SATA 97
McDonell, Chris 1960- 138
McDonnell, Christine 1949- 115
  Earlier sketch in SATA 34
McDonnell, Flora (Mary) 1963- 146
  Earlier sketch in SATA 90
McDonnell, Lois Eddy 1914-2001 10
McDonnell, Patrick 1956- 179
McDonough, Yona Zeldis 1957- 73
McElligott, Matt(hew) 1968- 135
McElmeel, Sharron L. 1942- 128
McElmurry, Jill 159
McElrath, William N. 1932- 65
McElrath-Eslick, Lori 1960- 96
McEntee, Dorothy (Layng) 1902- 37
McFadden, Kevin Christopher 1961(?)- 156
  Earlier sketch in SATA 68
  See also CLR 29
  See Pike, Christopher
McFall, Christie 1918- 12
McFarlan, Donald M(aitland) 1915- 59
McFarland, Henry "Hammer"
  See McFarland, Henry O.
McFarland, Henry O. 1934- 143
McFarland, Kenton D(ean) 1920- 11
McFarland, Martha
  See Smith-Ankrom, M. E.
McFarlane, Leslie (Charles) 1902-1977 31
  See Dixon, Franklin W.
  and Ferris, James Cody
  and Keene, Carolyn
  and Rockwood, Roy
McFarlane, Peter (William) 1940- 95
McFarlane, Sheryl P. 1954- 86
McFarlane, Todd 1961- 117
McGaw, Jessie Brewer 1913-1997 10
McGee, Barbara 1943- 6
McGee, Marni 163
McGiffin, (Lewis) Lee (Shaffer) 1908-1978 1
McGill, Alice 159
McGill, Ormond 1913- 92
McGinley, Jerry 1948- 116
McGinley, Phyllis 1905-1978 44
  Obituary 24
  Earlier sketch in SATA 2
McGinnis, Lila S(prague) 1924- 44
McGinty, Alice B. 1963- 134
McGivern, Justin 1985- 129
McGivern, Maureen Daly
  See Daly, Maureen
McGivern, Maureen Patricia Daly
  See Daly, Maureen
McGough, Elizabeth (Hemmes) 1934- 33
McGovern, Ann 1930- 132
  Earlier sketches in SATA 8, 69, 70
  See also CLR 50
  See also SAAS 17
McGowen, Thomas E. 1927- 109
  Earlier sketch in SATA 2
McGowen, Tom
  See McGowen, Thomas E.
McGrady, Mike 1933- 6
McGrath, Barbara Barbieri 1953- 169
  Earlier sketch in SATA 108
McGrath, Robin 1949- 121
McGrath, Thomas (Matthew) 1916-1990 41
  Obituary 66
McGraw, Eloise Jarvis 1915-2000 67
  Obituary 123
  Earlier sketch in SATA 1
  See also SAAS 6
McGraw, William Corbin 1916-1999 3
McGreal, Elizabeth
  See Yates, Elizabeth
McGregor, Barbara 1959- 82
McGregor, Craig 1933- 8
McGregor, Iona 1929- 25
McGuffey, Alexander Hamilton 1816-1896
  60

McGuigan, Mary Ann 1949- 106
McGuire, Edna 1899- 13
McGuire, Leslie (Sarah) 1945- 94
　Brief entry 45
　Earlier sketch in SATA 52
McGuirk, Leslie (A.) 1960- 152
McGurk, Slater
　See Roth, Arthur J(oseph)
McHargue, Georgess 1941- 77
　Earlier sketch in SATA 4
　See also CLR 2
　See also SAAS 5
McHugh, (Berit) Elisabet 1941- 55
　Brief entry 44
McIlwraith, Maureen Mollie Hunter 2
　See Hunter, Mollie
McInerney, Judith W(hitelock) 1945- 49
　Brief entry 46
McInerny, Ralph 1929- 93
McInerny, Ralph Matthew
　See McInerny, Ralph
McKaughan, Larry (Scott) 1941- 75
McKay, Donald 1895- 45
McKay, Hilary (Jane) 1959- 145
　Earlier sketch in SATA 92
　See also SAAS 23
McKay, Lawrence, Jr. 1948- 114
McKay, Robert W. 1921- 15
McKay, Sharon E. 1954- 165
McKay, Simon
　See Nicole, Christopher (Robin)
McKeating, Eileen 1957- 81
McKee, David (John) 1935- 158
　Earlier sketches in SATA 70, 107
　See also CLR 38
McKee, Tim 1970- 111
McKeever, Marcia
　See Laird, Jean E(louise)
McKelvey, Carole A. 1942- 78
McKelvy, Charles 1950- 124
McKendrick, Melveena (Christine) 1941- ... 55
McKendry, Joe 1972- 170
McKenna, Colleen O'Shaughnessy 1948- . 136
　Earlier sketch in SATA 76
McKenzie, Ellen Kindt 1928- 80
McKernan, Victoria 1957- 171
McKie, Robin 112
McKillip, Patricia A. 1948- 174
　Earlier sketches in SATA 30, 80, 126
McKillip, Patricia Anne
　See McKillip, Patricia A.
McKillip, Patricia Anne
　See McKillip, Patricia A.
McKim, Audrey Margaret 1909-1999 47
McKinley, Jennifer Carolyn Robin
　See McKinley, Robin
McKinley, Robin 1952- 130
　Brief entry 32
　Earlier sketches in SATA 50, 89
　See also CLR 81
McKinney, Barbara Shaw 1951- 116
McKinney, Nadine 1938- 91
McKissack, Fredrick L. 1939- 162
　Brief entry 53
　Earlier sketches in SATA 73, 117
　See also CLR 55
McKissack, Fredrick Lemuel
　See McKissack, Fredrick L.
McKissack, Patricia C. 1944- 162
　Earlier sketches in SATA 51, 73, 117
　See also CLR 55
McKissack, Patricia L'Ann Carwell
　See McKissack, Patricia C.
McKissack and McKissack
　See McKissack, Fredrick L.
　and McKissack, Patricia C.
McKown, Robin (?)-1976 6
McLaren, Clemence 1938- 158
　Earlier sketch in SATA 105
McLaughlin, Frank 1934- 73
McLaurin, Anne 1953- 27

McLean, Andrew 1946- 172
　Earlier sketch in SATA 113
McLean, J. Sloan
　See Gillette, Virginia M(ary)
　and Wunsch, Josephine (McLean)
McLean, Janet 1946- 113
McLean, Kathryn (Anderson) 1909-1966 9
McLean, Virginia Overton 1946- 90
McLean-Carr, Carol 1948- 122
McLeish, Kenneth 1940-1997 35
McLenighan, Valjean 1947- 46
　Brief entry 40
McLennan, Connie 171
McLennan, Will
　See Wisler, G(ary) Clifton
McLeod, Bob 1951- 173
McLeod, Chum 1955- 95
McLeod, Emilie Warren 1926-1982 23
　Obituary 31
McLeod, Kirsty
　See Hudson, (Margaret) Kirsty
McLeod, Margaret Vail
　See Holloway, Teresa (Bragunier)
McLerran, Alice 1933- 137
　Earlier sketch in SATA 68
McLoughlin, John C. 1949- 47
McManus, Patrick F. 1933- 46
McManus, Patrick Francis
　See McManus, Patrick F.
McMeekin, Clark
　See McMeekin, Isabel McLennan
McMeekin, Isabel McLennan 1895-1973 3
McMenemy, Sarah 1965- 156
McMillan, Bruce 1947- 129
　Earlier sketches in SATA 22, 70
　See also CLR 47
McMillan, Naomi
　See Grimes, Nikki
McMorey, James L.
　See Moyer, Terry J.
McMorrow, Annalisa 1969- 104
McMullan, Jim 1934- 150
　Earlier sketch in SATA 87
McMullan, K. H.
　See McMullan, Kate
McMullan, Kate
　See McMullan, Kate
McMullan, Kate 1947- 132
　Brief entry 48
　Earlier sketches in SATA 52, 87
McMullan, Kate Hall
　See McMullan, Kate
McMurtrey, Martin A(loysias) 1921- 21
McNabb, Linda 1963- 147
McNair, Kate 3
McNair, Sylvia 1924-2002 74
McNaught, Harry 32
McNaughton, Colin 1951- 134
　Earlier sketches in SATA 39, 92
　See also CLR 54
McNaughton, Janet 1953- 162
　Earlier sketch in SATA 110
McNeely, Jeannette 1918- 25
McNeer, May (Yonge) 1902-1994 81
　Earlier sketch in SATA 1
McNeese, Tim 1953- 139
McNeill, Janet 97
　Earlier sketch in SATA 1
　See Alexander, Janet
McNicoll, Sylvia (Marilyn) 1954- 113
　See also CLR 99
McNulty, Faith 1918-2005 168
　Earlier sketches in SATA 12, 84, 139
McPhail, David M(ichael) 1940- 140
　Brief entry 32
　Earlier sketches in SATA 47, 81
McPhee, Norma H. 1928- 95
McPhee, Richard B(yron) 1934- 41
McPherson, James M. 1936- 141
　Earlier sketch in SATA 16

McPherson, James Munro
　See McPherson, James M.
McQueen, Lucinda 1950- 58
　Brief entry 48
McQueen, Mildred Hark 1908-1978 12
McRae, Russell (William) 1934- 63
McShean, Gordon 1936- 41
Mc Swigan, Marie 1907-1962 24
McVeity, Jen 148
McVey, Vicki 1946- 80
McVicker, Charles (Taggart) 1930- 39
McVicker, Chuck
　See McVicker, Charles (Taggart)
McWhirter, A(lan) Ross 1925-1975 37
　Obituary 31
McWhirter, Norris (Dewar) 1925-2004 37
McWilliams, Karen 1943- 65
Mdurvwa, Hajara E. 1962- 92
Meacham, Margaret 1952- 95
Meachum, Virginia 1918- 133
　Earlier sketch in SATA 87
Mead, Alice 1952- 146
　Earlier sketch in SATA 94
Mead, Russell (M., Jr.) 1935- 10
Meade, Ellen 5
　See Roddick, Ellen
Meade, Marion 1934- 127
　Earlier sketch in SATA 23
Meader, Stephen W(arren) 1892-1977 1
Meadmore, Susan
　See Sallis, Susan (Diana)
Meadow, Charles T(roub) 1929- 23
Meadowcroft, Enid LaMonte
　See Wright, Enid Meadowcroft (LaMonte)
Meadows, Graham (W.) 1934- 161
Meaker, M. J.
　See Meaker, Marijane
Meaker, Marijane 1927- 160
　Autobiography Feature 111
　Earlier sketches in SATA 20, 61, 99
　See Aldrich, Ann
　and James, Mary
　and Kerr, M. E.
　and Packer, Vin
Meaker, Marijane Agnes
　See Meaker, Marijane
Means, Florence Crannell 1891-1980 1
　Obituary 25
　See also CLR 56
Mearian, Judy Frank 1936- 49
Mecca, Judy Truesdell 1955- 127
Medary, Marjorie 1890-1980 14
Meddaugh, Susan 1944- 176
　Earlier sketches in SATA 29, 84, 125
Medearis, Angela Shelf 1956- 123
　Earlier sketch in SATA 72
Medearis, Mary 1915- 5
Medina, Jane 1953- 167
　Earlier sketch in SATA 122
Medlicott, Mary 1946- 88
Mee, Charles L., Jr. 1938- 72
　Earlier sketch in SATA 8
Meek, Jacklyn O'Hanlon 1933- 51
　Brief entry 34
Meeker, Clare Hodgson 1952- 96
Meeker, Oden 1919(?)-1976 14
Meeker, Richard
　See Brown, Fornan
Meeks, Esther MacBain 1
Meggs, Libby Phillips 1943- 130
Mehdevi, Alexander (Sinclair) 1947- 7
Mehdevi, Anne (Marie) Sinclair 1947- 8
Meidell, Sherry 1951- 73
Meier, Minta 1906- 55
Meighan, Donald Charles 1929- 30
Meigs, Cornelia Lynde 1884-1973 6
　See also CLR 55
Meilach, Dona Z(weigoron) 1926- 34
Meilman, Philip W(arren) 1951- 79
Meinstereifel, Ronald L. 1960- 134
Melcher, Marguerite Fellows 1879-1969 10

Melendez, Francisco 1964- 72
Melin, Grace Hathaway 1892-1973 10
Mellersh, H(arold) E(dward) L(eslie) 1897-
.... 10
Melmoth, Sebastian
  See Wilde, Oscar (Fingal O'Flahertie Wills)
Melnikoff, Pamela (Rita) 97
Meltzer, Milton 1915- 128
  Autobiography Feature 124
  Earlier sketches in SATA *1, 50, 80*
  See also CLR *13*
  See also SAAS *1*
Melville, Anne
  See Potter, Margaret (Newman)
Melville, Herman 1819-1891 59
Melwood, Mary
  See Lewis, E. M.
Melzack, Ronald 1929- 5
Memling, Carl 1918-1969 6
Mendel, Jo
  See Bond, Gladys Baker
  and Gilbertson, Mildred Geiger
Mendelson, Steven T. 1958-1995 86
Mendes, Valerie 1939- 157
Mendez, Raymond A. 1947- 66
Mendonca, Susan
  Brief entry 45
  See Smith, Susan Vernon
Mendoza, George 1934- 41
  Brief entry 39
  See also SAAS *7*
Menendez, Shirley (C.) 1937- 146
Meng, Heinz (Karl) 1924- 13
Mennen, Ingrid 1954- 85
Menotti, Gian Carlo 1911-2007 29
  Obituary 180
Menuhin, Sir Yehudi 1916-1999 40
  Obituary 113
Menville, Douglas 1935- 64
Menzel, Barbara Jean 1946- 63
Mercati, Cynthia 164
Mercati, Cynthia J.
  See Mercati, Cynthia
Mercer, Charles (Edward) 1917-1988 16
  Obituary 61
Meredith, David William
  See Miers, Earl Schenck
Meringoff, Laurene Krasny
  See Brown, Laurene Krasny
Meriwether, Louise 1923- 52
  Brief entry 31
Merlin, Arthur
  See Blish, James (Benjamin)
Merlin, Christina
  See Heaven, Constance (Christina)
Merriam, Eve 1916-1992 73
  Earlier sketches in SATA *3, 40*
  See also CLR *14*
Merrill, Jane 1946- 42
Merrill, Jean (Fairbanks) 1923- 82
  Earlier sketch in SATA *1*
  See also CLR *52*
Merriman, Alex
  See Silverberg, Robert
Merriman, Rachel 1971- 149
  Earlier sketch in SATA *98*
Merrit, Elizabeth
  See Goudge, Eileen
Merski, Patricia K.
  See Merski, P.K.
Merski, P.K. 172
Mertz, Barbara 1927- 49
Mertz, Barbara Gross
  See Mertz, Barbara
Meschel, Susan V. 1936- 83
Messenger, Charles (Rynd Milles) 1942- 59
Messick, Dale 1906-2005 64
  Brief entry 48
Messier, Claire 1956- 103
Messieres, Nicole de
  See de Messieres, Nicole

Messmer, Otto 1892(?)-1983 37
Metcalf, Doris H(unter) 91
Metcalf, Suzanne
  See Baum, L(yman) Frank
Metos, Thomas H(arry) 1932- 37
Metter, Bert(ram Milton) 1927- 56
Metzenthen, David 1958- 167
  Earlier sketch in SATA *106*
Meyer, Barbara 1939- 77
Meyer, Carolyn (Mae) 1935- 142
  Autobiography Feature 142
  Earlier sketches in SATA *9, 70, 118*
  See also SAAS *9*
Meyer, Edith Patterson 1895-1993 5
Meyer, F(ranklyn) E(dward) 1932- 9
Meyer, Jean Shepherd 11
Meyer, Jerome Sydney 1895-1975 3
  Obituary 25
Meyer, June
  See Jordan, June
Meyer, L. A.
  See Meyer, Louis A(lbert), Jr.
Meyer, Louis A(lbert), Jr. 1942- 144
  Earlier sketch in SATA *12*
Meyer, Renate 1930- 6
Meyer, Susan E. 1940- 64
Meyers, Susan 1942- 164
  Earlier sketches in SATA *19, 108*
Meynier, Yvonne (Pollet) 1908- 14
Mezey, Robert 1935- 33
Micale, Albert 1913- 22
Michael, James
  See Scagnetti, Jack
Michael, Livi 1960- 172
Michael, Manfred
  See Winterfeld, Henry
Michael, Olivia
  See Michael, Livi
Michaels, Barbara
  See Mertz, Barbara
Michaels, Joanne Louise
  See Teitelbaum, Michael
Michaels, Kristin
  See Williams, Jeanne
Michaels, Molly
  See Untermeyer, Louis
Michaels, Neal
  See Teitelbaum, Michael
Michaels, Ski
  See Pellowski, Michael (Joseph)
Michaels, Steve 1955- 71
Michaels, William M. 1917- 77
Michel, Anna 1943- 49
  Brief entry 40
Michel, Francois 1948- 82
Michelson, Richard 173
Micich, Paul 74
Micklish, Rita 1931- 12
Micklos, John, Jr. 1956- 173
  Earlier sketch in SATA *129*
Micklos J., John, Jr. 1956-
  See Micklos, John, Jr.
Micucci, Charles (Patrick, Jr.) 1959- 144
  Earlier sketch in SATA *82*
Middleton, Haydn 1955- 152
  Earlier sketch in SATA *85*
Miers, Earl Schenck 1910-1972 1
  Obituary 26
Migdale, Lawrence 1951- 89
Mikaelsen, Ben 1952- 173
  Earlier sketches in SATA *73, 107*
Mikaelsen, Benjamin John
  See Mikaelsen, Ben
Miklowitz, Gloria D. 1927- 129
  Earlier sketches in SATA *4, 68*
  See also SAAS *17*
Mikolaycak, Charles 1937-1993 78
  Obituary 75
  Earlier sketch in SATA *9*
  See also SAAS *4*
Mild, Warren (Paul) 1922- 41

Milelli, Pascal 1965- 135
Miles, Betty 1928- 78
  Earlier sketch in SATA *8*
  See also SAAS *9*
Miles, Miska
  See Martin, Patricia Miles
Miles, (Mary) Patricia 1930- 29
Miles, Patricia A.
  See Martin, Patricia Miles
Milgrim, David 158
Milgrom, Harry 1912-1978 25
Milhous, Katherine 1894-1977 15
Milich, Zoran 174
Milios, Rita 1949- 79
Militant
  See Sandburg, Carl (August)
Millais, Raoul 1901- 77
Millar, Barbara F. 1924- 12
Millar, Margaret (Ellis Sturm) 1915-1994 .. 61
  Obituary 79
Millbank, Captain H. R.
  See Ellis, Edward S(ylvester)
Millen, C(ynthia) M. 1955- 114
Miller, Albert G(riffith) 1905-1982 12
  Obituary 31
Miller, Alice Ann 1958- 150
Miller, Alice P(atricia McCarthy) 22
Miller, Debbie 1951- 160
  Earlier sketch in SATA *103*
Miller, Debbie S.
  See Miller, Debbie
Miller, Deborah Uchill 1944- 61
Miller, Don 1923- 15
Miller, Doris R.
  See Mosesson, Gloria R(ubin)
Miller, Eddie
  See Miller, Edward
Miller, Edna Anita 1920- 29
Miller, Edward 1905-1974 8
Miller, Elizabeth 1933- 41
Miller, Ellanita 1957- 87
Miller, Eugene 1925- 33
Miller, Frances A. 1937- 52
  Brief entry 46
Miller, Helen M(arkley) -1984 5
Miller, Jane (Judith) 1925-1989 15
Miller, Jewel 1956- 73
Miller, John
  See Samachson, Joseph
Miller, Judi 117
Miller, Louise (Rolfe) 1940- 76
Miller, M. L. 85
Miller, Madge 1918- 63
Miller, Margaret J.
  See Dale, Margaret J(essy) Miller
Miller, Marilyn (Jean) 1925- 33
Miller, Marvin 65
Miller, Mary Beth 1942- 9
Miller, Maryann 1943- 73
Miller, Natalie 1917-1976 35
Miller, Robert H. 1944- 91
Miller, Ruth White
  See White, Ruth C.
Miller, Sandra
  See Miller, Sandy
Miller, Sandra Peden
  See Miller, Sandy
Miller, Sandy 1948- 41
  Brief entry 35
Miller, Sarah 1969- 175
Miller, Virginia
  See Austin, Virginia
Miller, William R. 1959- 116
Milligan, Bryce 1953- 170
Milligan, Spike
  See CLR *92*
  See Milligan, Terence Alan
Milligan, Terence Alan 1918-2002 29
  Obituary 134
  See Milligan, Spike

Millington, Ada
　See Deyneka, Anita
Millman, Isaac 1933- *140*
Mills, Adam
　See Stanley, George Edward
Mills, Claudia 1954- *145*
　Brief entry *41*
　Earlier sketches in SATA *44, 89*
Mills, Elaine (Rosemary) 1941- *72*
Mills, Joyce C. 1944- *102*
Mills, Judith Christine 1956- *130*
Mills, Yaroslava Surmach 1925- *35*
Millspaugh, Ben P. 1936- *77*
Millstead, Thomas E. *30*
Milne, A. A. 1882-1956 .... *100*
　See also YABC *1*
　See also CLR *108*
Milne, Alan Alexander
　See Milne, A. A.
Milne, Lorus J. *5*
　See also CLR *22*
　See also SAAS *18*
Milne, Margery *5*
　See also CLR *22*
　See also SAAS *18*
Milne, Terry
　See Milne, Theresa Ann
Milne, Theresa Ann 1964- *84*
Milnes, Irma McDonough 1924- *101*
Milonas, Rolf
　See Myller, Rolf
Milord, Susan 1954- *147*
　Earlier sketch in SATA *74*
Milotte, Alfred G(eorge) 1904-1989 .... *11*
　Obituary *62*
Milstein, Linda 1954- *80*
Milton, Ann *134*
Milton, Hilary (Herbert) 1920- *23*
Milton, John R(onald) 1924- *24*
Milton, Joyce 1946- *101*
　Brief entry *41*
　Earlier sketch in SATA *52*
Milverton, Charles A.
　See Penzler, Otto
Minahan, John A. 1956- *92*
Minar, Barbra (Goodyear) 1940- *79*
Minard, Rosemary 1939- *63*
Minarik, Else Holmelund 1920- *127*
　Earlier sketch in SATA *15*
　See also CLR *33*
Miner, Jane Claypool 1933- *38*
　Brief entry *37*
　See Claypool, Jane
Miner, Lewis S. 1909-1971 .... *11*
Mines, Jeanette 1948- *61*
Mines, Jeanette Marie
　See Mines, Jeanette
Minier, Nelson
　See Stoutenburg, Adrien (Pearl)
Minnitt, Ronda Jacqueline
　See Armitage, David
Minor, Wendell G. 1944- *164*
　Earlier sketches in SATA *78, 109*
Minter, Daniel 1961- *176*
Mintonye, Grace *4*
Miranda, Anne 1954- *109*
　Earlier sketch in SATA *71*
Mirsky, Jeannette 1903-1987 .... *8*
　Obituary *51*
Mirsky, Reba Paeff 1902-1966 .... *1*
Mishica, Clare 1960- *91*
Miskovits, Christine 1939- *10*
Miss Frances
　See Horwich, Frances R(appaport)
Miss Read
　See Saint, Dora Jessie
Mister Rogers
　See Rogers, Fred McFeely
Mitchard, Jacquelyn 1956- *168*
　Earlier sketch in SATA *98*

Mitchell, Adrian 1932- *166*
　Earlier sketch in SATA *104*
Mitchell, Allison
　See Griffin, W.E.B.
Mitchell, Betty Jo
　See Mitchell, B.J.
Mitchell, B.J. 1931- *120*
Mitchell, Clyde
　See Ellison, Harlan
Mitchell, Cynthia 1922- *29*
Mitchell, (Sibyl) Elyne (Keith) 1913- *10*
Mitchell, Gladys (Maude Winifred) 1901-1983
　... *46*
　Obituary *35*
Mitchell, Jay
　See Roberson, Jennifer
Mitchell, Joyce Slayton 1933- *142*
　Brief entry *43*
　Earlier sketch in SATA *46*
Mitchell, K. L.
　See Lamb, Elizabeth Searle
Mitchell, Kathy 1948- *59*
Mitchell, Lori 1961- *128*
Mitchell, Margaree King 1953- *84*
Mitchell, Marianne 1947- *145*
Mitchell, Rhonda *89*
Mitchelson, Mitch
　See Mitchelson, Peter Richard
Mitchelson, Peter Richard 1950- *104*
Mitchison, Naomi (Margaret Haldane)
　1897-1999 .... *24*
　Obituary *112*
Mitchnik, Helen 1901-1982 .... *41*
　Brief entry *35*
Mitchum, Hank
　See Knott, William C(ecil, Jr.)
　and Murray, Stuart A. P.
　and Newton, D(wight) B(ennett)
　and Sherman, Jory (Tecumseh)
Mitgutsch, Ali 1935- *76*
Mitsuhashi, Yoko *45*
　Brief entry *33*
Mitton, Jacqueline 1948- *162*
　Earlier sketches in SATA *66, 115*
Mitton, Simon 1946- *66*
Mitton, Tony 1951- *149*
　Earlier sketch in SATA *104*
Miura, Taro 1968- *181*
Mizner, Elizabeth Howard 1907- *27*
Mizumura, Kazue *18*
Mlynowski, Sarah 1977(?)- *180*
Mobin-Uddin, Asma *172*
Mobley, Joe A. 1945- *91*
Moche, Dinah (Rachel) L(evine) 1936- *44*
　Brief entry *40*
Mochi, Ugo (A.) 1889-1977 .... *38*
Mochizuki, Ken 1954- *146*
　Earlier sketch in SATA *81*
　See also SAAS *22*
Modarressi, Mitra 1967- *126*
Modell, Frank B. 1917- *39*
　Brief entry *36*
Modesitt, Jeanne 1953- *143*
　Earlier sketch in SATA *92*
Modesitt, L.E., Jr. 1943- *164*
　Earlier sketch in SATA *91*
Modesitt, Leland Exton, Jr.
　See Modesitt, L.E., Jr.
Modrell, Dolores 1933- *72*
Moe, Barbara 1937- *20*
Moe, Jorgen (Ingebretsen) 1813-1882
　See CLR *104*
　See Asbjornsen and Moe
Moed-Kass, Pnina *169*
Moerbeek, Kees 1955- *98*
Moeri, Louise 1924- *93*
　Earlier sketch in SATA *24*
　See also SAAS *10*
Moffett, Jami 1952- *84*
Moffett, Martha (Leatherwood) 1934- *8*
Mogensen, Suzanne A(ncher) 1946- *129*

Mohn, Peter B(urnet) 1934- *28*
Mohn, Viola Kohl 1914- *8*
Mohr, Nicholasa 1938- *97*
　Autobiography Feature *113*
　Earlier sketch in SATA *8*
　See also CLR *22*
　See also SAAS *8*
Mok, Esther 1953- *93*
Molan, Christine 1943- *84*
Molarsky, Osmond 1909- *16*
Moldon, Peter L(eonard) 1937- *49*
Mole, John 1941- *103*
　Earlier sketch in SATA *36*
　See also CLR *61*
Molesworth, Mary Louisa 1839-1921 ...... *98*
Molin, Charles
　See Mayne, William (James Carter)
Molina, Silvia 1946- *97*
Molk, Laurel 1957- *162*
　Earlier sketch in SATA *92*
Mollel, Tololwa M. 1952- *88*
Molloy, Anne Baker 1907-1999 .... *32*
Molloy, Michael (John) 1940- *162*
Molloy, Paul (George) 1924- *5*
Moloney, James 1954- *144*
　Autobiography Feature *144*
　Earlier sketch in SATA *94*
Momaday, N. Scott 1934- *48*
　Brief entry *30*
Momaday, Navarre Scott
　See Momaday, N. Scott
Monaco, Octavia 1963- *169*
Monagle, Bernie 1957- *121*
Moncure, Jane Belk 1926- *23*
Monjo, F(erdinand) N(icholas III) 1924-1978
　... *16*
　See also CLR *2*
Monk, Isabell 1952- *136*
Monroe, Lyle
　See Heinlein, Robert A.
Monsell, Helen Albee 1895-1971 .... *24*
Monson-Burton, Marianne 1975- *139*
Montecalvo, Janet *177*
Montenegro, Laura Nyman 1953- *95*
Montero, Gloria 1933- *109*
Montes, Marisa 1951- *144*
Montgomerie, Norah (Mary) 1913- *26*
Montgomery, Constance
　See Cappel, Constance
Montgomery, Elizabeth Rider *34*
　Obituary *41*
　Earlier sketch in SATA *3*
　See Julesberg, Elizabeth Rider Montgomery
Montgomery, Hugh (Edward) 1962- *146*
Montgomery, L(ucy) M(aud) 1874-1942 .. *100*
　See also YABC *1*
　See also CLR *91*
Montgomery, Raymond A. (Jr.) 1936- *39*
Montgomery, Rutherford George 1894-1985
　... *3*
Montgomery, Sy 1958- *132*
　Autobiography Feature *132*
　Earlier sketch in SATA *114*
Montgomery, Vivian *36*
Monthei, Betty *179*
Montijo, Rhode *179*
Montpetit, Charles 1958- *101*
Montresor, Beni 1926-2001 .... *38*
　Earlier sketch in SATA *3*
　See also SAAS *4*
Montserrat, Pep *181*
Monty Python
　See Chapman, Graham
　and Cleese, John (Marwood)
　and Gilliam, Terry
　and Idle, Eric
　and Jones, Terence Graham Parry
　and Palin, Michael (Edward)
Moodie, Craig 1956- *172*
Moodie, Fiona 1952- *133*

Moody, Minerva
   See Alcott, Louisa May
Moody, Ralph Owen 1898-1982 .... *1*
Moon, Carl 1879(?)-1948 .... *25*
Moon, Grace (Purdie) 1877(?)-1947 .... *25*
Moon, Lily
   See Warnes, Tim
Moon, Nicola 1952- *147*
   Earlier sketch in SATA *96*
Moon, Pat 1946- *113*
Moon, Sheila (Elizabeth) 1910-1991 .... *5*
   Obituary *114*
Mooney, Bel 1946- *95*
Mooney, Bill 1936- *122*
   See Mooney, William
Moor, Emily
   See Deming, Richard
Moorcock, Michael 1939- *166*
   Earlier sketch in SATA *93*
   See Bradbury, Edward P.
Moore, Anne Carroll 1871-1961 .... *13*
Moore, Cheri
   See Ladd, Cheryl (Jean)
Moore, Clement Clarke 1779-1863 .... *18*
Moore, Cyd 1957- *133*
   Earlier sketch in SATA *83*
Moore, Elaine 1944- *86*
Moore, Eva 1942- *103*
   Earlier sketch in SATA *20*
Moore, Ishbel (Lindsay) 1954- *140*
Moore, Jack (William) 1941- *46*
   Brief entry *32*
Moore, Janet Gaylord 1905-1992 .... *18*
Moore, Jim 1946- *42*
Moore, John Travers 1908- *12*
Moore, Lilian 1909-2004 .... *137*
   Obituary *155*
   Earlier sketch in SATA *52*
   See also CLR *15*
Moore, Liz
   See Moore, M. Elizabeth
Moore, M. Elizabeth 1959- *156*
Moore, Margaret R(umberger) 1903- *12*
Moore, Margie *176*
Moore, Marianne (Craig) 1887-1972 .... *20*
Moore, Patrick (Alfred Caldwell) 1923- *49*
   Brief entry *39*
   See also SAAS *8*
Moore, Peter 1963- *175*
Moore, Regina
   See Dunne, Mary Collins
Moore, Ruth (Ellen) 1908-1989 .... *23*
Moore, Ruth Nulton 1923- *38*
Moore, S(arah) E. *23*
Moore, Sarah Margaret
   See Hodges, Margaret
Moore, Tara 1950- *61*
Moore, Yvette 1958- *154*
   Earlier sketches in SATA *69, 70*
Mooser, Stephen 1941- *75*
   Earlier sketch in SATA *28*
Mora, Francisco X(avier) 1952- *90*
Mora, Pat 1942- *134*
   Earlier sketch in SATA *92*
   See also CLR *58*
Mora, Patricia
   See Mora, Pat
Morales, Yuyi *180*
   Earlier sketch in SATA *154*
Moran, Tom 1943- *60*
Moranville, Sharelle Byars *152*
Moray Williams, Ursula 1911-2006 .... *142*
   Obituary *177*
   Earlier sketch in SATA *73*
   See also SAAS *9*
   See Williams, Ursula Moray
Mordvinoff, Nicolas 1911-1973 .... *17*
More, Caroline
   See Cone, Molly (Lamken)
   and Strachan, Margaret Pitcairn

Moreton, Andrew Esq.
   See Defoe, Daniel
Morey, Charles
   See Fletcher, Helen Jill
Morey, Walt(er Nelson) 1907-1992 .... *51*
   Obituary *70*
   Earlier sketch in SATA *3*
   See also SAAS *9*
Morgan, Alfred P(owell) 1889-1972 .... *33*
Morgan, Alison (Mary) 1930- *85*
   Earlier sketch in SATA *30*
Morgan, Anne 1954- *121*
Morgan, Douglas
   See Macdonald, James D.
Morgan, Ellen
   See Bumstead, Kathleen Mary
Morgan, Geoffrey 1916- *46*
Morgan, Helen (Gertrude Louise) 1921-1990
   .... *29*
Morgan, Jane
   See Cooper, James Fenimore
   and Franklin, Jane (Morgan)
   and Moren, Sally M(oore)
Morgan, Lenore H. 1908-1976 .... *8*
Morgan, Mary 1957- *114*
   Earlier sketch in SATA *81*
Morgan, Michaela *180*
   See Basile, Gloria Vitanza
Morgan, Nicola 1961- *161*
Morgan, Nina 1953- *110*
Morgan, Pierr 1952- *122*
   Earlier sketch in SATA *77*
Morgan, Robin (Evonne) 1941- *80*
Morgan, Roxanne
   See Gentle, Mary
Morgan, Sarah (Nicola) 1959- *68*
Morgan, Shirley *10*
   See Kiepper, Shirley Morgan
Morgan, Stacy T(owle) 1959- *104*
Morgan, Stevie
   See Davies, Nicola
Morgan, Tom 1942- *42*
Morgan, Wendy
   See Staub, Wendy Corsi
Morgan-Vanroyen, Mary
   See Morgan, Mary
Morgenstern, Susie Hoch 1945- *133*
Mori, Hana 1909-1990(?) *88*
Mori, Kyoko 1957- *122*
   Autobiography Feature *126*
   See also CLR *64*
   See also SAAS *26*
Moriarty, Jaclyn *162*
Moriarty, William J. 1930- *127*
Morice, Dave 1946- *93*
Morin, Isobel V. 1928- *110*
Morley, Wilfred Owen
   See Lowndes, Robert A(ugustine) W(ard)
Morningstar, Mildred (Whaley) 1912-1997
   .... *61*
   Obituary *114*
Morozumi, Atsuko *110*
Morpurgo, Michael 1943- *143*
   Earlier sketch in SATA *93*
   See also CLR *51*
Morrah, Dave
   See Morrah, David Wardlaw, Jr.
Morrah, David Wardlaw, Jr. 1914-1991 ...... *10*
Morreale-de la Garza, Phyllis
   See De la Garza, Phyllis
Morressy, John 1930-2006 .... *23*
Morrill, Leslie H(olt) 1934-2003 .... *48*
   Brief entry *33*
   Obituary *148*
   See also SAAS *22*
Morris, Chris(topher Crosby) 1946- *66*
Morris, Deborah 1956- *91*
Morris, Desmond 1928- *14*
Morris, Desmond John
   See Morris, Desmond
Morris, Don 1954- *83*

Morris, Gerald 1963- *150*
   Earlier sketch in SATA *107*
Morris, Gerald Paul
   See Morris, Gerald
Morris, Gilbert (Leslie) 1929- *104*
Morris, Jackie *151*
Morris, Janet (Ellen) 1946- *66*
Morris, Jay
   See Tatham, Julie Campbell
Morris, (Margaret) Jean 1924- *98*
Morris, Jeffrey B(randon) 1941- *92*
Morris, Jennifer E. 1969- *179*
Morris, Jill 1936- *165*
   Earlier sketch in SATA *119*
Morris, Juddi *85*
Morris, Judy K. 1936- *61*
Morris, Oradel Nolen *128*
Morris, Robert A(da) 1933- *7*
Morris, William 1913-1994 .... *29*
Morrison, Bill 1935- *66*
   Brief entry *37*
Morrison, Chloe Anthony Wofford
   See Morrison, Toni
Morrison, Dorothy Nafus *29*
Morrison, Gordon 1944- *128*
   Earlier sketch in SATA *87*
Morrison, Joan 1922- *65*
Morrison, Lillian 1917- *108*
   Earlier sketch in SATA *3*
Morrison, Lucile Phillips 1896- *17*
Morrison, Martha A. 1948- *77*
Morrison, Meighan 1966- *90*
Morrison, Richard
   See Lowndes, Robert A(ugustine) W(ard)
Morrison, Robert
   See Lowndes, Robert A(ugustine) W(ard)
Morrison, Roberta
   See Webb, Jean Francis (III)
Morrison, Susan Dudley
   See Gold, Susan Dudley
Morrison, Taylor 1971- *159*
   Earlier sketch in SATA *95*
Morrison, Toni 1931- *144*
   Earlier sketch in SATA *57*
   See also CLR *99*
Morrison, Velma Ford 1909- *21*
Morrison, Wilbur Howard 1915- *64*
Morrison, William
   See Samachson, Joseph
Morriss, James E(dward) 1932- *8*
Morrow, Barbara Olenyik 1952- *167*
Morrow, Betty
   See Bacon, Elizabeth
Morse, Carol
   See Yeakley, Marjory Hall
Morse, Flo 1921- *30*
Morse, Tony 1953- *129*
Mort, Vivian
   See Cromie, Alice Hamilton
Mortensen, Denise Dowling *179*
Mortimer, Anne 1958- *116*
Morton, Alexandra (Hubbard) 1957- *144*
Morton, Anthony
   See Arthur, Robert, (Jr.)
Morton, Jane 1931- *50*
Morton, Joseph C. 1932- *156*
Morton, Lee Jack, Jr. 1928- *32*
Morton, Miriam 1918(?)-1985 .... *9*
   Obituary *46*
Mosatche, Harriet (S.) 1949- *122*
Moscow, Alvin 1925- *3*
Mosel, Arlene (Tichy) 1921-1996 .... *7*
Moseley, James W(illett) 1931- *139*
Moseng, Elisabeth 1967- *90*
Moser, Barry (A.) 1940- *138*
   Earlier sketches in SATA *56, 79*
   See also CLR *49*
   See also SAAS *15*
Moser, Don(ald Bruce) 1932- *31*
Moses, Sheila P. 1961- *168*

Moses, Will 1956- 178
   Earlier sketch in SATA *120*
Mosesson, Gloria R(ubin) 24
Mosher, Richard 1949- 120
Moskin, Marietta D(unston) 1928- 23
Moskof, Martin Stephen 1930- 27
Mosley, Francis 1957- 57
Moss, Don(ald) 1920- 11
Moss, Elaine (Dora) 1924- 57
   Brief entry 31
Moss, Jeff(rey) 1942-1998 73
   Obituary 106
Moss, Marissa 1959- 163
   Earlier sketches in SATA *71, 104*
Moss, Miriam 1955- 140
   Earlier sketch in SATA *76*
Moss, Thylias 1954- 108
Moss, Thylias Rebecca Brasier
   See Moss, Thylias
Most, Bernard 1937- 134
   Brief entry 40
   Earlier sketches in SATA *48, 91*
Mott, Evelyn Clarke 1962- 133
   Earlier sketch in SATA *75*
Motz, Lloyd 1909- 20
Mould, Edwin
   See Whitlock, Ralph
Mouly, Francoise 155
Mountain, Robert
   See Montgomery, Raymond A. (Jr.)
Mountfield, David
   See Grant, Neil
Moussard, Jacqueline 1924- 24
Mowat, Claire (Angel Wheeler) 1933- 123
Mowat, Farley 1921- 55
   Earlier sketch in SATA *3*
   See also CLR *20*
Mowat, Farley McGill
   See Mowat, Farley
Mowry, Jess 1960- 131
   Autobiography Feature 131
   Earlier sketch in SATA *109*
   See also CLR *65*
Moxley, Sheila 1966- 96
Moyer, Terry J. 1937- 94
Moyes, Patricia 63
   See Haszard, Patricia Moyes
Moyler, Alan (Frank Powell) 1926- 36
Mozelle, Shirley 179
Mozley, Charles 1915- 43
   Brief entry 32
Mphahlele, Es'kia
   See Mphahlele, Ezekiel
Mphahlele, Ezekiel 1919- 119
   See Mphahlele, Es'kia
Mr. McGillicuddy
   See Abisch, Roslyn Kroop
Mr. Sniff
   See Abisch, Roslyn Kroop
Mr. Tivil
   See Lorkowski, Thomas V(incent)
Mr. Wizard
   See Herbert, Don
Mrs. Fairstar
   See Horne, Richard Henry Hengist
Muchamore, Robert 1972- 175
Muchmore, Jo Ann 1937- 103
Mude, O.
   See Gorey, Edward (St. John)
Mudgeon, Apeman
   See Mitchell, Adrian
Mueller, Jorg 1942- 67
   See also CLR *43*
Mueller, Virginia 1924- 28
Muggs
   See Watkins, Lois
Muir, Diana
   See Appelbaum, Diana Muir Karter
Muir, Frank (Herbert) 1920-1998 30
Muir, Helen 1937- 65

Mukerji, Dhan Gopal 1890-1936 40
   See also CLR *10*
Mulcahy, Lucille Burnett 12
Mulford, Philippa G. 1948- 112
   Earlier sketch in SATA *43*
Mulford, Philippa Greene
   See Mulford, Philippa G.
Mulila, Vigad G.
   See Maillu, David G(ian)
Mullen, Michael 1937- 122
Muller, Billex
   See Ellis, Edward S(ylvester)
Muller, Jorg
   See Mueller, Jorg
Muller, (Lester) Robin 1953- 86
Mullin, Caryl Cude 1969- 130
Mullins, Edward S(wift) 1922- 10
Mullins, Hilary 1962- 84
Mulock, Dinah Maria
   See Craik, Dinah Maria (Mulock)
Mulvihill, William Patrick 1923- 8
Mumford, Ruth 1919- 86
   See Dallas, Ruth
Mumy, Bill 1954- 112
Mun
   See Leaf, (Wilbur) Munro
Munari, Bruno 1907-1998 15
   See also CLR *9*
Munce, Ruth Hill 1898- 12
Mundy, Simon 1954- 64
Mundy, Simon Andrew James Hainault
   See Mundy, Simon
Munger, Nancy 170
Munowitz, Ken 1935-1977 14
Munoz, William 1949- 92
   Earlier sketch in SATA *42*
Munro, Alice 1931- 29
Munro, Alice Anne
   See Munro, Alice
Munro, Eleanor 1928- 37
Munro, Roxie 1945- 136
   Earlier sketch in SATA *58*
Munsch, Bob
   See Munsch, Robert (Norman)
Munsch, Robert (Norman) 1945- 120
   Brief entry 48
   Earlier sketches in SATA *50, 83*
   See also CLR *19*
Munsinger, Lynn 1951- 177
   Earlier sketches in SATA *33, 94*
Munson, Derek 1970- 139
Munson, R. W.
   See Karl, Jean E(dna)
Munson-Benson, Tunie 1946- 15
Munsterberg, Peggy 1921- 102
Munthe, Nelly 1947- 53
Munves, James (Albert) 1922- 30
Munzer, Martha E. 1899-1999 4
Murch, Mel
   See Manes, Stephen
Murdoch, David H(amilton) 1937- 96
Murhall, J(acqueline) J(ane) 1964- 143
Murphy, Barbara Beasley 1933- 130
   Earlier sketch in SATA *5*
Murphy, Claire Rudolf 1951- 137
   Earlier sketch in SATA *76*
Murphy, E(mmett) Jefferson 1926- 4
Murphy, Jill (Frances) 1949- 142
   Earlier sketches in SATA *37, 70*
   See also CLR *39*
Murphy, Jim 1947- 124
   Brief entry 32
   Earlier sketches in SATA *37, 77*
   See also CLR *53*
Murphy, Joseph E., Jr. 1930- 65
Murphy, Kelly 1977- 143
Murphy, Louise 1943- 155
Murphy, Pat
   See Murphy, E(mmett) Jefferson
Murphy, Patricia J. 1963- 132
Murphy, Rita 180

Murphy, Robert (William) 1902-1971 10
Murphy, Shirley Rousseau 1928- 126
   Earlier sketches in SATA *36, 71*
   See also SAAS *18*
Murphy, Stuart J. 1942- 157
   Earlier sketch in SATA *115*
Murphy, Tim
   See Murphy, Jim
Murray, John 1923- 39
Murray, Kirsty 1960- 165
   Earlier sketch in SATA *108*
Murray, Marguerite 1917- 63
Murray, Marian 5
Murray, Martine 1965- 125
Murray, (Judith) Michele (Freedman)
   1933-1974 7
Murray, Ossie 1938- 43
Murray, Peter
   See Hautman, Pete
Murrow, Liza Ketchum 1946- 78
   See Ketchum, Liza
Musgrave, Florence 1902-1999 3
Musgrove, Margaret W(ynkoop) 1943- 124
   Earlier sketch in SATA *26*
Mussey, Virginia Howell
   See Ellison, Virginia H(owell)
Mussey, Virginia T.H.
   See Ellison, Virginia H(owell)
Mutel, Cornelia F. 1947- 74
Muth, Jon J. 165
Mutz
   See Kuenstler, Morton
Mwangi, Meja 1948- 174
My Brother's Brother
   See Chekhov, Anton (Pavlovich)
Myers, Anna 160
Myers, Arthur 1917- 91
   Earlier sketch in SATA *35*
Myers, Bernice 81
   Earlier sketch in SATA *9*
Myers, Caroline Elizabeth Clark 1887-1980
   28
Myers, Christopher 1975-
   See CLR *97*
Myers, Edward 1950- 172
   Earlier sketch in SATA *96*
Myers, Elisabeth P(erkins) 1918- 36
Myers, (Mary) Hortense (Powner) 1913-1987
   10
Myers, Jack 1913-2006 83
   Obituary 178
Myers, Jack Edgar
   See Myers, Jack
Myers, Lou 1915-2005 81
   Obituary 171
Myers, Louis
   See Myers, Lou
Myers, R.E. 1924- 119
Myers, Robert Eugene
   See Myers, R.E.
Myers, Tim 1953- 176
   Earlier sketch in SATA *147*
Myers, Timothy Joseph
   See Myers, Tim
Myers, Walter Dean 1937- 157
   Brief entry 27
   Earlier sketches in SATA *41, 71, 109*
   See also CLR *110*
   See also SAAS *2*
   See Myers, Walter M.
Myers, Walter M.
   See Myers, Walter Dean
Myller, Rolf 1926-2006 27
   Obituary 175
Myra, Harold L(awrence) 1939- 46
   Brief entry 42
Myracle, Lauren 1969- 162
Myrus, Donald (Richard) 1927- 23
Mysterious Traveler, The
   See Arthur, Robert, (Jr.)

N

Na, An *149*
Naaslund, Goorel Kristina 1940- *170*
Nadel, Laurie 1948- *74*
Naden, Corinne J. 1930- *166*
  Earlier sketch in SATA *79*
Nagel, Andreas Fischer
  See Fischer-Nagel, Andreas
Nagel, Heiderose Fischer
  See Fischer-Nagel, Heiderose
Nagle, Shane *176*
Naidoo, Beverley 1943- *180*
  Earlier sketches in SATA *63, 135*
  See also CLR *29*
Naipaul, Shivadhar Srinivasa
  See Naipaul, Shiva
Nakae, Noriko 1940- *59*
Nakatani, Chiyoko 1930-1981 .... *55*
  Brief entry *40*
  See also CLR *30*
Nally, Susan W. 1947- *90*
Namioka, Lensey 1929- *157*
  Autobiography Feature *116*
  Earlier sketches in SATA *27, 89*
  See also CLR *48*
  See also SAAS *24*
Nanji, Shenaaz 1954- *131*
Nanogak Agnes 1925- *61*
Napier, Mark
  See Laffin, John (Alfred Charles)
Napoli, Donna Jo 1948- *137*
  Earlier sketch in SATA *92*
  See also CLR *51*
  See also SAAS *23*
Narahashi, Keiko 1959- *115*
  Earlier sketch in SATA *79*
Narayan, Rasipuram Krishnaswami
  See Narayan, R.K.
Narayan, R.K. 1906-2001 .... *62*
Nascimbene, Yan 1949- *173*
  Earlier sketch in SATA *133*
Nash, Bruce M(itchell) 1947- *34*
Nash, Linell
  See Smith, Linell Nash
Nash, Mary (Hughes) 1925- *41*
Nash, (Fredric) Ogden 1902-1971 .... *46*
  Earlier sketch in SATA *2*
Nash, Renea Denise 1963- *81*
Nast, Elsa Ruth
  See Watson, Jane Werner
Nast, Thomas 1840-1902 .... *51*
  Brief entry *33*
Nastick, Sharon 1954- *41*
Nathan, Amy *155*
  Earlier sketch in SATA *104*
Nathan, Dorothy (Goldeen) (?)-1966 .... *15*
Nathan, Robert (Gruntal) 1894-1985 .... *6*
  Obituary *43*
Nathanson, Laura Walther 1941- *57*
Natti, Susanna 1948- *125*
  Earlier sketch in SATA *32*
Naughtie, Eleanor
  See Updale, Eleanor
Naughton, Bill
  See Naughton, William John (Francis)
Naughton, James Franklin 1957- *85*
Naughton, Jim
  See Naughton, James Franklin
Naughton, William John (Francis) 1910-1992
  .... *86*
  See Naughton, Bill
Navarra, John Gabriel 1927- *8*
Naylor, Penelope 1941- *10*
Naylor, Phyllis 1933-
  See Naylor, Phyllis Reynolds

Naylor, Phyllis Reynolds 1933- *152*
  Autobiography Feature *152*
  Earlier sketches in SATA *12, 66, 102*
  See also CLR *17*
  See also SAAS *10*
  See Naylor, Phyllis
Nazarian, Nikki
  See Nichols, Cecilia Fawn
Nazaroff, Alexander I(vanovich) 1898-1981 . *4*
Neal, Harry Edward 1906-1993 .... *5*
  Obituary *76*
Neal, Michael
  See Teitelbaum, Michael
Nearing, Penny 1916- *47*
  Brief entry *42*
Nebel, Gustave E. *45*
  Brief entry *33*
Nebel, Mimouca
  See Nebel, Gustave E.
Nee, Kay Bonner *10*
Needham, Kate 1962- *95*
Needle, Jan 1943- *98*
  Earlier sketch in SATA *30*
  See also CLR *43*
  See also SAAS *23*
Needleman, Jacob 1934- *6*
Neel, David 1960- *82*
Neel, Preston 1959- *93*
Negri, Rocco 1932- *12*
Neier, Aryeh 1937- *59*
Neigoff, Anne *13*
Neigoff, Mike 1920- *13*
Neilson, Frances Fullerton (Jones) 1910-2001
  .... *14*
Neimark, Anne E. 1935- *145*
  Earlier sketch in SATA *4*
Neimark, Paul G. 1934- *80*
  Brief entry *37*
Neitzel, Shirley 1941- *134*
  Earlier sketch in SATA *77*
Nell
  See Hanna, Nell(ie L.)
Nelscott, Kris
  See Rusch, Kristine Kathryn
Nelson, Blake 1960- *177*
Nelson, Catherine Chadwick 1926- *87*
Nelson, Cordner (Bruce) 1918- *54*
  Brief entry *29*
Nelson, Drew 1952- *77*
Nelson, Esther L. 1928- *13*
Nelson, Jim A.
  See Stotter, Mike
Nelson, Julie L. 1970- *117*
Nelson, Kadir *181*
  Earlier sketch in SATA *154*
Nelson, Kris
  See Rusch, Kristine Kathryn
Nelson, Marilyn 1946- *180*
  Autobiography Feature *180*
  Earlier sketch in SATA *151*
  See Waniek, Marilyn Nelson
Nelson, Mary Carroll 1929- *23*
Nelson, O. Terry 1941- *62*
Nelson, Peter N. 1953- *73*
Nelson, Richard K(ing) 1941- *65*
Nelson, Robin Laura 1971- *141*
Nelson, Roy Paul 1923- *59*
Nelson, S.D. *181*
Nelson, Sharlene (P.) 1933- *96*
Nelson, Ted (W.) 1931- *96*
Nelson, Theresa 1948- *143*
  Autobiography Feature *143*
  Earlier sketch in SATA *79*
Nerlove, Miriam 1959- *53*
  Brief entry *49*
Nesbit, E. 1858-1924 .... *100*
  See also YABC *1*
  See also CLR *70*
Nesbit, Edith
  See Nesbit, E.

Nesbit, Troy
  See Folsom, Franklin (Brewster)
Nespojohn, Katherine V(eronica) 1912-1975
  .... *7*
Ness, Evaline (Michelow) 1911-1986 .... *26*
  Obituary *49*
  Earlier sketch in SATA *1*
  See also CLR *6*
  See also SAAS *1*
Nestor, Larry 1940- *149*
Nestor, William P(rodromos) 1947- *49*
Nethery, Mary *93*
Neubecker, Robert *170*
Neuberger, Julia (Babette Sarah) 1950- *142*
  Earlier sketch in SATA *78*
Neufeld, John (Arthur) 1938- *131*
  Autobiography Feature *131*
  Earlier sketches in SATA *6, 81*
  See also CLR *52*
  See also SAAS *3*
Neuhaus, David 1958- *83*
Neumeyer, Peter F(lorian) 1929- *13*
Neurath, Marie (Reidemeister) 1898-1986 .... *1*
Neuschwander, Cindy 1953- *157*
  Earlier sketch in SATA *107*
Neusner, Jacob 1932- *38*
Neville, Charles
  See Bodsworth, (Charles) Fred(erick)
Neville, Emily Cheney 1919- *1*
  See also SAAS *2*
Neville, Mary
  See Woodrich, Mary Neville
Nevins, Albert (Francis) J(erome) 1915-1997
  .... *20*
Newberger, Devra
  See Speregen, Devra Newberger
Newberry, Clare Turlay 1903-1970 .... *1*
  Obituary *26*
Newbery, John 1713-1767 .... *20*
Newbery, Linda 1952- *142*
Newcombe, Jack *45*
  Brief entry *33*
  See Newcombe, Eugene A.
Newcome, Robert 1955- *91*
Newcome, Zita 1959- *88*
Newell, Crosby
  See Bonsall, Crosby Barbara (Newell)
Newell, Edythe W(eatherford) 1910-1989 .. *11*
Newell, Hope Hockenberry 1896-1965 .... *24*
Newfeld, Frank 1928- *26*
Newlon, (Frank) Clarke 1905(?)-1982 .... *6*
  Obituary *33*
Newman, Daisy 1904-1994 .... *27*
  Obituary *78*
Newman, Gerald 1939- *46*
  Brief entry *42*
Newman, Jerry 1935- *82*
Newman, Leslea 1955- *134*
  Earlier sketches in SATA *71, 128*
Newman, Margaret
  See Potter, Margaret (Newman)
Newman, Marjorie *146*
Newman, Matthew (Harrison) 1955- *56*
Newman, Nanette 1934- *162*
Newman, Robert (Howard) 1909-1988 .... *87*
  Obituary *60*
  Earlier sketch in SATA *4*
Newman, Shirlee P(etkin) *144*
  Earlier sketches in SATA *10, 90*
Newsom, Carol 1948- *92*
  Earlier sketch in SATA *40*
Newsom, Tom 1944- *80*
Newth, Mette 1942- *140*
Newton, David E(dward) 1933- *67*
Newton, James R(obert) 1935- *23*
Newton, Suzanne 1936- *77*
  Earlier sketch in SATA *5*
Ney, John 1923- *43*
  Brief entry *33*
Nez, John *155*
Ng, Franklin *82*

Nichol, B(arrie) P(hillip) 1944-1988 .... *66*
Nicholas, Louise D.
  See Watkins, Dawn L.
Nicholls, Judith (Ann) 1941- *61*
Nichols, Cecilia Fawn 1906-1987 .... *12*
Nichols, Grace 1950- *164*
  Earlier sketch in SATA *98*
Nichols, Janet (Louise) 1952- *67*
Nichols, Judy 1947- *124*
Nichols, Leigh
  See Koontz, Dean R.
Nichols, Paul
  See Hawks, Robert
Nichols, Peter
  See Youd, (Christopher) Samuel
Nichols, (Joanna) Ruth 1948- *15*
Nicholson, C. R.
  See Nicole, Christopher (Robin)
Nicholson, Christina
  See Nicole, Christopher (Robin)
Nicholson, Joyce Thorpe 1919- *35*
Nicholson, Lois P. 1949- *88*
Nicholson, Robin
  See Nicole, Christopher (Robin)
Nicholson, William *180*
Nicholson, William 1872-1949
  See CLR *76*
Nickell, Joe 1944- *167*
  Earlier sketch in SATA *73*
Nickelsburg, Janet 1893-1983 .... *11*
Nickerson, Elizabeth *14*
  See Nickerson, Betty
Nickl, Barbara (Elisabeth) 1939- *56*
Nicklaus, Carol *62*
  Brief entry *33*
Nickle, John *181*
Nickless, Will 1902-1979(?) *66*
Nic Leodhas, Sorche
  See Alger, Leclaire (Gowans)
Nicol, Ann
  See Turnbull, Ann (Christine)
Nicolas
  See Mordvinoff, Nicolas
Nicolay, Helen 1866-1954
  See YABC *1*
Nicole, Christopher (Robin) 1930- *5*
Nicoll, Helen 1937- *87*
Nicolson, Cynthia Pratt 1949- *141*
Ni Dhuibhne, Eilis 1954- *91*
Niehaus, Paddy Bouma
  See Bouma, Paddy
Nields, Nerissa 1967- *166*
Nielsen, Kay (Rasmus) 1886-1957 .... *16*
  See also CLR *16*
Nielsen, Laura F(arnsworth) 1960- *93*
Nielsen, Nancy J. 1951- *77*
Nielsen, Virginia
  See McCall, Virginia Nielsen
Nieuwsma, Milton J(ohn) 1941- *142*
Nightingale, Sandy 1953- *76*
Nikolajeva, Maria 1952- *127*
Nikola-Lisa, W. 1951- *180*
  Earlier sketch in SATA *71*
Niland, Deborah 1951- *172*
  Earlier sketch in SATA *27*
Niland, Kilmeny *75*
Nilsen, Anna 1948- *174*
  Earlier sketch in SATA *96*
Nilsson, Eleanor 1939- *117*
  Earlier sketch in SATA *81*
  See also SAAS *23*
Nilsson, Per 1954- *159*
Nimmo, Jenny 1944- *144*
  Earlier sketch in SATA *87*
  See also CLR *44*
Niven, Larry 1938- *171*
  Earlier sketch in SATA *95*
  See Niven, Laurence VanCott
Niven, Laurence VanCott
  See Niven, Larry

Nivola, Claire A. 1947- *140*
  Earlier sketch in SATA *84*
Nix, Garth 1963- *143*
  Earlier sketch in SATA *97*
  See also CLR *68*
Nixon, Hershell Howard 1923- *42*
Nixon, Joan Lowery 1927-2003 .... *115*
  Obituary *146*
  Earlier sketches in SATA *8, 44, 78*
  See also CLR *24*
  See also SAAS *9*
Nixon, K.
  See Nixon, Kathleen Irene (Blundell)
Nixon, Kathleen Irene (Blundell) 1894-1988(?)
  .... *14*
  Obituary *59*
Nobisso, Josephine 1953- *121*
  Earlier sketch in SATA *78*
Noble, Iris (Davis) 1922-1986 .... *5*
  Obituary *49*
Noble, Marty 1947- *125*
  Earlier sketch in SATA *97*
Noble, Trinka Hakes *123*
  Brief entry *37*
Noda, Takayo 1961- *168*
Nodelman, Perry 1942- *101*
Nodset, Joan L.
  See Lexau, Joan M.
Noel Hume, Ivor 1927- *65*
Noestlinger, Christine
  See Nostlinger, Christine
Noguere, Suzanne 1947- *34*
Nolan, Dennis 1945- *166*
  Brief entry *34*
  Earlier sketches in SATA *42, 92*
Nolan, Han 1956- *157*
  Earlier sketch in SATA *109*
Nolan, Janet 1956- *145*
Nolan, Jeannette Covert 1897-1974 .... *2*
  Obituary *27*
Nolan, Paul T(homas) 1919- *48*
Nolan, William F(rancis) 1928- *88*
  Brief entry *28*
Nolen, Jerdine 1953- *157*
  Earlier sketch in SATA *105*
Noll, Sally 1946- *82*
Noonan, Diana 1960- *146*
Noonan, Julia 1946- *148*
  Earlier sketches in SATA *4, 95*
Norac, Carl 1960- *166*
Nordan, Robert W(arren) 1934-2004 .... *133*
Nordhoff, Charles Bernard 1887-1947 .... *23*
Nordlicht, Lillian *29*
Nordstrom, Ursula 1910-1988 .... *3*
  Obituary *57*
Nordtvedt, Matilda 1926- *67*
Norling, Beth 1969- *149*
Norman, Charles 1904-1996 .... *38*
  Obituary *92*
Norman, Howard
  See Norman, Howard A.
Norman, Howard A. 1949- *81*
Norman, James
  See Schmidt, James Norman
Norman, Jay
  See Arthur, Robert, (Jr.)
Norman, Lilith 1927- *120*
  Earlier sketch in SATA *86*
Norman, Mary 1931- *36*
Norman, Steve
  See Pashko, Stanley
Norment, Lisa 1966- *91*
Norris, Gunilla Brodde 1939- *20*
North, Andrew
  See Norton, Andre
North, Anthony
  See Koontz, Dean R.
North, Captain George
  See Stevenson, Robert Louis (Balfour)
North, Captain George
  See Stevenson, Robert Louis (Balfour)

North, Howard
  See Trevor, Elleston
North, Joan 1920- *16*
North, Milou
  See Erdrich, Louise
North, Robert
  See Withers, Carl A.
North, Sara
  See Bonham, Barbara Thomas
  and Hager, Jean
North, Sterling 1906-1974 .... *45*
  Obituary *26*
  Earlier sketch in SATA *1*
Northeast, Brenda V(ictoria) 1948- *106*
Northmore, Elizabeth Florence 1906-1974
  .... *122*
Norton, Alice Mary *43*
  Earlier sketch in SATA *1*
  See Norton, Andre
Norton, Andre 1912-2005 .... *91*
  See also CLR *50*
  See Norton, Alice Mary
Norton, Browning
  See Norton, Frank R. B(rowning)
Norton, Frank R. B(rowning) 1909-1989 .... *10*
Norton, Mary 1903-1992 .... *60*
  Obituary *72*
  Earlier sketch in SATA *18*
  See also CLR *6*
Nosredna, Trebor
  See Anderson, Bob
Nostlinger, Christine 1936- *162*
  Brief entry *37*
  Earlier sketch in SATA *64*
  See also CLR *12*
Nourse, Alan E(dward) 1928-1992 .... *48*
  See also CLR *33*
Novak, Matt 1962- *165*
  Brief entry *52*
  Earlier sketches in SATA *60, 104*
Novelli, Luca 1947- *61*
Nowell, Elizabeth Cameron *12*
Noyes, Deborah
  See Wayshak, Deborah Noyes
Nugent, Nicholas 1949- *73*
Numeroff, Laura Joffe 1953- *142*
  Earlier sketches in SATA *28, 90*
  See also CLR *85*
Nunes, Lygia Bojunga 1932- *154*
  Earlier sketch in SATA *75*
  See Bojunga, Lygia
Nunn, Laura (Donna) Silverstein 1968- *124*
Nurnberg, Maxwell 1897-1984 .... *27*
  Obituary *41*
Nussbaumer, Paul (Edmund) 1934- *16*
Nutt, Ken 1951- *163*
  Earlier sketch in SATA *97*
Nuygen, Mathieu 1967- *80*
Nyberg, (Everett Wayne) Morgan 1944- *87*
Nyce, (Nellie) Helene von Strecker 1885-1969
  .... *19*
Nyce, Vera 1862-1925 .... *19*
Nye, Naomi Shihab 1952- *147*
  Earlier sketch in SATA *86*
  See also CLR *59*
Nye, Robert 1939- *6*
Nyikos, Stacy A. 1969- *164*
Nystrom, Carolyn 1940- *130*
  Earlier sketch in SATA *67*

O

Oakes, Elizabeth H. 1964- *132*
Oakes, Vanya 1909-1983 .... *6*
  Obituary *37*
Oakley, Don(ald G.) 1927- *8*
Oakley, Graham 1929- *84*
  Earlier sketch in SATA *30*
  See also CLR *7*

Oakley, Helen (McKelvey) 1906- .... _10_
Oana, Katherine 1929- .... _53_
  Brief entry .... _37_
Oates, Eddie H. 1943- .... _88_
Oates, Joyce Carol 1938- .... _159_
Oates, Stephen B(aery) 1936- .... _59_
Obed, Ellen Bryan 1944- .... _74_
Oberle, Joseph 1958- .... _69_
Oberman, Sheldon 1949-2004 .... _85_
  Autobiography Feature .... _114_
  Obituary .... _153_
  See also CLR 54
  See also SAAS 26
Obligado, Lilian (Isabel) 1931- .... _61_
  Brief entry .... _45_
Obrant, Susan 1946- .... _11_
O'Brian, E. G.
  See Clarke, Arthur C.
O'Brien, Anne Sibley 1952- .... _80_
  Brief entry .... _48_
  Earlier sketch in SATA _53_
O'Brien, Robert C.
  See CLR 2
  See Conly, Robert Leslie
O'Brien, Thomas C(lement) 1938- .... _29_
O'Callaghan, Julie 1954- .... _113_
O'Callahan, Jay 1938- .... _88_
O'Carroll, Ryan
  See Markun, Patricia Maloney
Ochiltree, Dianne 1953- .... _117_
Ockham, Joan Price
  See Price, Joan
O'Connell, Margaret F(orster) 1935-1977 .. _30_
  Obituary .... _30_
O'Connell, Peg
  See Ahern, Margaret McCrohan
O'Connell, Rebecca 1968- .... _130_
O'Connor, Barbara 1950- .... _154_
O'Connor, Francine M(arie) 1930- .... _90_
O'Connor, Genevieve A. 1914- .... _75_
O'Connor, Jane 1947- .... _150_
  Brief entry .... _47_
  Earlier sketches in SATA _59, 103_
O'Connor, Karen 1938- .... _89_
  Earlier sketch in SATA _34_
O'Connor, Patrick
  See Wibberley, Leonard (Patrick O'Connor)
O'Conor, Jane 1958- .... _78_
Odaga, Asenath (Bole) 1937- .... _130_
  Earlier sketch in SATA _67_
  See also SAAS 19
O Danachair, Caoimhin
  See Danaher, Kevin
Odanaka, Barbara .... _159_
O'Daniel, Janet 1921- .... _24_
O'Day, Cathy
  See Crane, Barbara (Joyce)
O'Dell, Scott 1898-1989 .... _134_
  Earlier sketches in SATA _12, 60_
  See also CLR 16
Odenwald, Robert P(aul) 1899-1965 .... _11_
Odgers, Sally
  See Odgers, Sally Farrell
Odgers, Sally Farrell 1957- .... _139_
  Earlier sketch in SATA _72_
O'Donnell, Dick
  See Lupoff, Richard A(llen)
  and Thompson, Don(ald Arthur)
Oechsli, Kelly 1918-1999 .... _5_
Oesterle, Virginia Rorby
  See Rorby, Ginny
Ofek, Uriel 1926- .... _36_
  See also CLR 28
Offenbacher, Ami 1958- .... _91_
Offit, Sidney 1928- .... _10_
Ofosu-Appiah, L(awrence) H(enry) 1920- .. _13_
Ogan, George F. 1912-1983 .... _13_
Ogan, M. G.
  See Ogan, George F.
  and Ogan, Margaret E. (Nettles)
Ogan, Margaret E. (Nettles) 1923-1979 ...... _13_

Ogburn, Charlton (Jr.) 1911-1998 .... _3_
  Obituary .... _109_
Ogburn, Jacqueline K. .... _162_
Ogilvie, Elisabeth May 1917-2006 .... _40_
  Brief entry .... _29_
  Obituary .... _176_
Ogilvy, Gavin
  See Barrie, J(ames) M(atthew)
Ogilvy, Ian 1943- .... _177_
Ogilvy, Ian Raymond
  See Ogilvy, Ian
Ogletree, Charles J. 1952- .... _175_
O'Green, Jennifer
  See Roberson, Jennifer
O'Green, Jennifer Roberson
  See Roberson, Jennifer
O'Hagan, Caroline 1946- .... _38_
O'Hanlon, Jacklyn
  See Meek, Jacklyn O'Hanlon
O'Hara, Elizabeth
  See Ni Dhuibhne, Eilis
O'Hara, Kenneth
  See Morris, (Margaret) Jean
O'Hara, Mary
  See Alsop, Mary O'Hara
O'Hara (Alsop), Mary
  See Alsop, Mary O'Hara
O'Hare, Jeff(rey A.) 1958- .... _105_
Ohi, Ruth 1964- .... _95_
Ohiyesa
  See Eastman, Charles A(lexander)
Ohlsson, Ib 1935- .... _7_
Ohmi, Ayano 1959- .... _115_
Ohtomo, Yasuo 1946- .... _37_
o huigin, sean 1942- .... _138_
  See also CLR 75
Oiseau
  See Moseley, James W(illett)
Oke, Janette 1935- .... _97_
O'Keefe, Susan Heyboer .... _176_
  Earlier sketch in SATA _133_
O'Keeffe, Frank 1938- .... _99_
O'Kelley, Mattie Lou 1908-1997 .... _97_
  Earlier sketch in SATA _36_
Okimoto, Jean Davies 1942- .... _103_
  Earlier sketch in SATA _34_
Okomfo, Amasewa
  See Cousins, Linda
Olaleye, Isaac O. 1941- .... _96_
  See also SAAS 23
Olcott, Frances Jenkins 1872(?)-1963 .... _19_
Old, Wendie C(orbin) 1943- .... _154_
Old Boy
  See Hughes, Thomas
Oldenburg, E(gbert) William 1936-1974 ..... _35_
Older, Effin 1942- .... _114_
Older, Jules 1940- .... _156_
  Earlier sketch in SATA _114_
Oldfield, Jenny 1949- .... _140_
Oldfield, Margaret J(ean) 1932- .... _56_
Oldfield, Pamela 1931- .... _86_
Oldham, June .... _70_
Oldham, Mary 1944- .... _65_
Olds, Elizabeth 1896-1991 .... _3_
  Obituary .... _66_
Olds, Helen Diehl 1895-1981 .... _9_
  Obituary .... _25_
Oldstyle, Jonathan
  See Irving, Washington
O'Leary, Brian (Todd) 1940- .... _6_
O'Leary, Patsy B(aker) 1937- .... _97_
Oliphant, B. J.
  See Tepper, Sheri S.
Oliver, Burton
  See Burt, Olive Woolley
Oliver, Chad
  See Oliver, Symmes C(hadwick)
Oliver, John Edward 1933- .... _21_
Oliver, Marilyn Tower 1935- .... _89_
Oliver, Narelle 1960- .... _152_
Oliver, Shirley (Louise Dawkins) 1958- ..... _74_

Oliver, Symmes C(hadwick) 1928-1993 ... _101_
  See Oliver, Chad
Oliviero, Jamie 1950- .... _84_
Olmsted, Lorena Ann 1890-1989 .... _13_
Olney, Ross R. 1929- .... _13_
Olschewski, Alfred (Erich) 1920- .... _7_
Olsen, Barbara .... _148_
Olsen, Carol 1945- .... _89_
Olsen, Ib Spang 1921- .... _81_
  Earlier sketch in SATA 6
Olsen, Violet (Mae) 1922-1991 .... _58_
Olson, Arielle North 1932- .... _67_
Olson, Gene 1922- .... _32_
Olson, Helen Kronberg .... _48_
Olson, Kay Melchisedech 1948- .... _175_
Olson, Marianne
  See Mitchell, Marianne
Olugebefola, Ademole 1941- .... _15_
Oluonye, Mary N(kechi) 1955- .... _111_
Om
  See Gorey, Edward (St. John)
O'Malley, Kevin 1961- .... _157_
Oman, Carola (Mary Anima) 1897-1978 .... _35_
O'Mara, Carmel 1965- .... _166_
O'Mara-Horwitz, Carmel
  See O'Mara, Carmel
O'Meara, Walter (Andrew) 1897-1989 .... _65_
Ommanney, F(rancis) D(ownes) 1903-1980
  .... _23_
O Mude
  See Gorey, Edward (St. John)
Oneal, Elizabeth 1934- .... _82_
  Earlier sketch in SATA _30_
  See Oneal, Zibby
O'Neal, Reagan
  See Jordan, Robert
Oneal, Zibby
  See CLR 13
  See Oneal, Elizabeth
O'Neill, Amanda 1951- .... _111_
O'Neill, Gerard K(itchen) 1927-1992 .... _65_
O'Neill, Judith (Beatrice) 1930- .... _34_
O'Neill, Mary L(e Duc) 1908(?)-1990 .... _2_
  Obituary .... _64_
Onslow, Annette Rosemary MacArthur
  See MacArthur-Onslow, Annette Rosemary
Onyefulu, Ifeoma 1959- .... _157_
  Earlier sketches in SATA _81, 115_
Opie, Iona (Margaret Balfour) 1923- .... _118_
  Earlier sketches in SATA _3, 63_
  See also SAAS 6
Opie, Peter (Mason) 1918-1982 .... _118_
  Obituary .... _28_
  Earlier sketches in SATA _3, 63_
Oppel, Kenneth 1967- .... _153_
  Earlier sketch in SATA _99_
Oppenheim, Joanne 1934- .... _174_
  Earlier sketches in SATA _5, 82, 136_
Oppenheim, Shulamith Levey 1928- .... _177_
Oppenheimer, Joan L(etson) 1925- .... _28_
Oppong, Joseph Ransford 1953- .... _160_
Optic, Oliver
  See Adams, William Taylor
  and Stratemeyer, Edward L.
Oram, Hiawyn 1946- .... _101_
  Earlier sketch in SATA _56_
Orbach, Ruth Gary 1941- .... _21_
Orczy, Emma
  See Orczy, Baroness Emmuska
Orczy, Emma Magdalena Rosalia Maria Josefa
  See Orczy, Baroness Emmuska
Orczy, Emmuska
  See Orczy, Baroness Emmuska
Orczy, Baroness Emmuska 1865-1947 .... _40_
  See Orczy, Emma
Orde, A. J.
  See Tepper, Sheri S.
O'Reilly, Jackson
  See Jordan, Robert
Orenstein, Denise Gosliner 1950- .... _157_

Pokeberry, P.J.
  See Mitchell, B.J.
POLA
  See Watson, Pauline
Polacco, Patricia 1944- *180*
  Earlier sketches in SATA *74, 123*
  See also CLR *40*
Polacco, Patricia Ann
  See Polacco, Patricia
Polak, Monique 1960- *178*
Polatnick, Florence T. 1923- *5*
Polder, Markus
  See Kruss, James
Polese, Carolyn 1947- *58*
Polese, James 1914- *87*
Polette, Nancy (Jane) 1930- *42*
Polhamus, Jean Burt 1928- *21*
Policoff, Stephen Phillip 1948- *77*
Polikoff, Barbara G. 1929- *162*
  Earlier sketch in SATA *77*
Polikoff, Barbara Garland
  See Polikoff, Barbara G.
Polisar, Barry Louis 1954- *134*
  Earlier sketch in SATA *77*
Politi, Leo 1908-1996 .... *47*
  Obituary *88*
  Earlier sketch in SATA *1*
  See also CLR *29*
Polking, Kirk 1925- *5*
Pollack, Jill S. 1963- *88*
Polland, Barbara K(ay) 1939- *44*
Polland, Madeleine A(ngela Cahill) 1918- .. *68*
  Earlier sketch in SATA *6*
  See also SAAS *8*
Pollema-Cahill, Phyllis 1958- *123*
Pollock, Bruce 1945- *46*
Pollock, Mary
  See Blyton, Enid (Mary)
Pollock, Penny 1935- *137*
  Brief entry *42*
  Earlier sketch in SATA *44*
Pollowitz, Melinda Kilborn 1944- *26*
Polner, Murray 1928- *64*
Polonsky, Arthur 1925- *34*
Polseno, Jo *17*
Pomaska, Anna 1946- *117*
Pomerantz, Charlotte 1930- *177*
  Earlier sketches in SATA *20, 80*
Pomeroy, Pete
  See Roth, Arthur J(oseph)
Pond, Alonzo W(illiam) 1894-1986 .... *5*
Pontiflet, Ted 1932- *32*
Poole, Gray Johnson 1906- *1*
Poole, Josephine *5*
  See also SAAS *2*
  See Helyar, Jane Penelope Josephine
Poole, (Jane Penelope) Josephine
  See Helyar, Jane Penelope Josephine
Poole, Lynn 1910-1969 .... *1*
Poole, Peggy 1925- *39*
Poortvliet, Rien 1932- *65*
  Brief entry *37*
Pope, Elizabeth Marie 1917- *38*
  Brief entry *36*
Popescu, Christine
  See Pullein-Thompson, Christine
Poploff, Michelle 1956- *67*
Popp, K. Wendy *91*
Poppel, Hans 1942- *71*
Portal, Colette 1936- *6*
Porte, Barbara Ann 1943- *152*
  Brief entry *45*
  Earlier sketches in SATA *57, 93*
Porter, A(nthony) P(eyton) 1945- *68*
Porter, Connie (Rose) 1959(?)- *129*
  Earlier sketch in SATA *81*
Porter, Donald Clayton
  See Gerson, Noel Bertram
Porter, Eleanor H(odgman) 1868-1920
  See CLR *110*

Porter, Gene(va Grace) Stratton
  See Stratton-Porter, Gene(va Grace)
Porter, Janice Lee 1953- *108*
  Earlier sketch in SATA *68*
Porter, Katherine Anne 1890-1980 .... *39*
  Obituary *23*
Porter, Kathryn
  See Swinford, Betty (June Wells)
Porter, Sheena 1935- *24*
  See also SAAS *10*
Porter, Sue
  See Limb, Sue
Porter, Sue 1951- *76*
Porter, William Sydney 1862-1910
  See YABC *2*
  See Henry, O.
Porto, Tony 1960- *153*
Posell, Elsa Z(eigerman) -1995 .... *3*
Posten, Margaret L(ois) 1915- *10*
Posthuma, Sieb 1960- *150*
Potok, Chaim 1929-2002 .... *106*
  Obituary *134*
  Earlier sketch in SATA *33*
  See also CLR *92*
Potok, Herbert Harold -2002
  See Potok, Chaim
Potok, Herman Harold
  See Potok, Chaim
Potter, Beatrix 1866-1943 .... *132*
  Earlier sketch in SATA *100*
  See also YABC *1*
  See also CLR *73*
Potter, Giselle *150*
Potter, Helen Beatrix
  See Potter, Beatrix
Potter, Margaret (Newman) 1926-1998 .... *21*
  Obituary *104*
  See Betteridge, Anne
Potter, Marian 1915- *9*
Potter, Miriam Clark 1886-1965 .... *3*
Poulin, Stephane 1961- *98*
  See also CLR *28*
Poulton, Kimberly 1957(?)- *136*
Pournelle, Jerry (Eugene) 1933- *161*
  Earlier sketches in SATA *26, 91*
Povelite, Kay 1955- *102*
Pow, Tom 1950- *163*
Powe-Allred, Alexandra
  See Allred, Alexandra Powe
Powell, A. M.
  See Morgan, Alfred P(owell)
Powell, Consie *174*
Powell, E. Sandy 1947- *72*
Powell, E.S.
  See Powell, E. Sandy
Powell, Pamela 1960- *78*
Powell, Patricia Hruby 1951- *136*
Powell, Randy 1956- *118*
Powell, Richard Stillman
  See Barbour, Ralph Henry
Powell, Robert (Stephenson Smyth) Baden
  See Baden-Powell, Robert (Stephenson Smyth)
Powell, Stephanie 1953- *93*
Power, Margaret (M.) 1945- *125*
  Earlier sketch in SATA *75*
Powers, Anne
  See Schwartz, Anne Powers
Powers, Bill 1931- *52*
  Brief entry *31*
Powers, Daniel 1959- *164*
Powers, Margaret
  See Heal, Edith
Powers, Tim 1952- *107*
Powers, Timothy Thomas
  See Powers, Tim
Powledge, Fred 1935- *37*
Poynter, Margaret 1927- *27*
Prachaticka, Marketa
  See Kolibalova, Marketa

Prachatika, Marketa
  See Kolibalova, Marketa
Prager, Arthur *44*
Prager, Ellen J. 1962- *136*
Prange, Beckie *172*
Prap, Lila 1955- *177*
Pratchett, Terry 1948- *139*
  Earlier sketch in SATA *82*
  See also CLR *64*
Prater, John 1947- *149*
  Earlier sketches in SATA *72, 103*
Pratt, (Murray) Fletcher 1897-1956 .... *102*
Pratt, Kristin Joy 1976- *87*
Pratt, Pierre 1962- *166*
  Earlier sketch in SATA *95*
Preiss, Byron 1953-2005 .... *166*
  Brief entry *42*
  Earlier sketch in SATA *47*
Preiss, Byron Cary
  See Preiss, Byron
Preller, James 1961- *88*
Prelutsky, Jack 1940- *171*
  Earlier sketches in SATA *22, 66, 118*
  See also CLR *115*
Prentice, Amy
  See Kaler, James Otis
Prescott, Casey
  See Morris, Chris(topher Crosby)
Presnall, Judith (Ann) Janda 1943- *96*
Pressler, Mirjam 1940- *155*
Preston, Douglas 1956- *113*
Preston, Edna Mitchell *40*
Preston, Lillian Elvira 1918- *47*
Preussler, Otfried 1923- *24*
Price, Beverley Joan 1931- *98*
Price, Christine (Hilda) 1928-1980 .... *3*
  Obituary *23*
Price, Jennifer
  See Hoover, Helen (Drusilla Blackburn)
Price, Joan 1931- *124*
Price, Jonathan (Reeve) 1941- *46*
Price, Karen 1957- *125*
Price, Kathy Z. 1957- *172*
Price, Lucie Locke
  See Locke, Lucie
Price, Olive 1903-1991 .... *8*
Price, Susan 1955- *128*
  Earlier sketches in SATA *25, 85*
Price, Willard 1887-1983 .... *48*
  Brief entry *38*
Price-Groff, Claire *127*
Priceman, Marjorie 1958- *168*
  Earlier sketches in SATA *81, 120*
Prichard, Katharine Susannah 1883-1969 ... *66*
Prideaux, Tom 1908-1993 .... *37*
  Obituary *76*
Priestley, Alice 1962- *95*
Priestley, Lee (Shore) 1904-1999 .... *27*
Priestly, Doug 1954- *122*
Priestly, Douglas Michael
  See Priestly, Doug
Prieto, Mariana Beeching 1912-1999 .... *8*
Primavera, Elise 1954- *109*
  Brief entry *48*
  Earlier sketch in SATA *58*
Prime, Derek (James) 1931- *34*
Prince, Alison (Mary) 1931- *86*
  Earlier sketch in SATA *28*
Prince, April Jones 1975- *180*
Prince, J(ack) H(arvey) 1908- *17*
Prince, Maggie *102*
Pringle, Eric *138*
Pringle, Laurence P. 1935- *154*
  Earlier sketches in SATA *4, 68, 104*
  See also CLR *57*
  See also SAAS *6*
Pringle, Laurence Patrick
  See Pringle, Laurence P.
Prinz, Yvonne 1960- *175*
Prior, Natalie Jane 1963- *106*
Pritchett, Elaine H(illyer) 1920- *36*

Pritchett, Laura 1971- *178*
Pritchett, Laura Rose
  See Pritchett, Laura
Pritts, Kim Derek 1953- *83*
Prochazkova, Iva 1953- *68*
Proctor, Everitt
  See Montgomery, Rutherford George
Proeysen, Alf 1914-1970
  See CLR *24*
  See Proysen, Alf
Professor Scribbler
  See Hollingsworth, Mary
Proimos, James 1955- *173*
Prose, Francine 1947- *149*
  Earlier sketch in SATA *101*
Provensen, Alice 1918- *147*
  Earlier sketches in SATA *9, 70*
  See also CLR *11*
Provensen, Martin (Elias) 1916-1987 .... *70*
  Obituary *51*
  Earlier sketch in SATA *9*
  See also CLR *11*
Provenzo, Eugene (F., Jr.) 1949- *142*
  Earlier sketch in SATA *78*
Provost, Gail Levine 1944- *65*
Provost, Gary (Richard) 1944-1995 .... *66*
Proysen, Alf *67*
  See Proeysen, Alf
Pruett, Candace (J.) 1968- *157*
Pryor, Bonnie H. 1942- *69*
Pryor, Boori (Monty) 1950- *112*
Pryor, Helen Brenton 1897-1972 .... *4*
Pryor, Michael 1957- *153*
Pucci, Albert John 1920- *44*
Pudney, John (Sleigh) 1909-1977 .... *24*
Pugh, Ellen (Tiffany) 1920- *7*
Pullein-Thompson, Christine 1925-2005 ..... *82*
  Obituary *172*
  Earlier sketch in SATA *3*
Pullein-Thompson, Diana *3*
  See Farr, Diana (Pullein-Thompson)
Pullein-Thompson, Josephine (Mary
  Wedderburn) *82*
  Earlier sketch in SATA *3*
Pullman, Philip 1946- *150*
  Earlier sketches in SATA *65, 103*
  See also CLR *84*
  See also SAAS *17*
Pullman, Philip Nicholas
  See Pullman, Philip
Pulver, Harry, Jr. 1960- *129*
Pulver, Robin 1945- *133*
  Earlier sketch in SATA *76*
Puner, Helen W(alker) 1915-1989 .... *37*
  Obituary *63*
Purdy, Carol 1943- *120*
  Earlier sketch in SATA *66*
Purdy, Susan G(old) 1939- *8*
Purmell, Ann 1953- *147*
Purnell, Idella 1901-1982 .... *120*
Purscell, Phyllis 1934- *7*
Purtill, Richard L. 1931- *53*
Pushker, Gloria 1927- *162*
  Earlier sketch in SATA *75*
Pushker, Gloria Teles
  See Pushker, Gloria
Pushkin, Aleksandr Sergeevich
  See Pushkin, Alexander (Sergeyevich)
Pushkin, Alexander (Sergeyevich) 1799-1837
  .... *61*
  See Pushkin, Aleksandr Sergeevich
Putnam, Alice 1916- *61*
Putnam, Arthur Lee
  See Alger, Horatio, Jr.
Putnam, Peter B(rock) 1920-1998 .... *30*
  Obituary *106*
Puttock, Simon *178*
Pyle, Howard 1853-1911 .... *100*
  Earlier sketch in SATA *16*
  See also CLR *117*
Pyle, Katharine 1863-1938 .... *66*

Pyne, Mable Mandeville 1903-1969 .... *9*
Pyrnelle, Louise-Clarke 1850-1907 .... *114*

Q

Quackenbush, Robert M(ead) 1929- *133*
  Autobiography Feature *133*
  Earlier sketches in SATA *7, 70*
  See also CLR *122*
  See also SAAS *7*
Qualey, Marsha 1953- *124*
  Earlier sketch in SATA *79*
Qualls, Sean *177*
Quammen, David 1948- *7*
Quark, Jason
  See Eldin, Peter
Quarles, Benjamin (Arthur) 1904-1996 .... *12*
Quatermass, Martin
  See Carpenter, John (Howard)
Quattlebaum, Mary 1958- *134*
  Earlier sketch in SATA *88*
Quay, Emma *173*
  Earlier sketch in SATA *119*
Queen, Ellery
  See Deming, Richard
  and Dannay, Frederic
  and Davidson, Avram (James)
  and Fairman, Paul W.
  and Flora, Fletcher
  and Hoch, Edward D(entinger)
  and Kane, Henry
  and Lee, Manfred B.
  and Marlowe, Stephen
  and Powell, (Oval) Talmage
  and Sheldon, Walter J(ames)
  and Sturgeon, Theodore (Hamilton)
  and Tracy, Don(ald Fiske)
  and Vance, Jack
Queen, Ellery, Jr.
  See Dannay, Frederic
  and Holding, James (Clark Carlisle, Jr.)
  and Lee, Manfred B.
Quennell, Marjorie Courtney 1884-1972 .... *29*
Quentin, Brad
  See Bisson, Terry
Quest, (Edna) Olga W(ilbourne) Hall
  See Hall-Quest, (Edna) Olga W(ilbourne)
Quick, Annabelle 1922-1986 .... *2*
Quill, Monica
  See McInerny, Ralph
Quin-Harkin, Janet 1941- *165*
  Earlier sketches in SATA *18, 90, 119*
Quin-Harkin, Janet Elizabeth
  See Quin-Harkin, Janet
Quinlan, Susan E. 1954- *88*
Quinlan, Susan Elizabeth
  See Quinlan, Susan E.
Quinn, Elisabeth 1881-1962 .... *22*
Quinn, Pat 1947- *130*
Quinn, Patrick 1950- *73*
Quinn, Rob 1972- *138*
Quinn, Theodora K.
  See Kroeber, Theodora (Kracaw)
Quinn, Vernon
  See Quinn, Elisabeth
Quintano, D.M.
  See Sheldon, Dyan
Quirk, Anne (E.) 1956- *99*
Quixley, Jim 1931- *56*
Quyth, Gabriel
  See Jennings, Gary (Gayne)

R

Ra, Carol F. 1939- *76*
Raab, Evelyn 1951- *129*
Rabe, Berniece (Louise) 1928- *148*
  Autobiography Feature *148*
  Earlier sketches in SATA *7, 77*
  See also SAAS *10*

Rabe, Olive H(anson) (?)-1968 .... *13*
Rabin, Staton 1958- *162*
  Earlier sketch in SATA *84*
Rabinowich, Ellen 1946- *29*
Rabinowitz, Sandy 1954- *52*
  Brief entry *39*
Rachlin, Carol K(ing) 1919- *64*
Rachlin, Harvey 1951- *47*
Rachlin, Harvey Brant
  See Rachlin, Harvey
Rachlin, Nahid *64*
Rackham, Arthur 1867-1939 .... *100*
  Earlier sketch in SATA *15*
  See also CLR *57*
Raczka, Bob 1963- *163*
Radencich, Marguerite C. 1952-1998 .... *79*
Radford, Ruby L(orraine) 1891-1971 .... *6*
Radin, Ruth Yaffe 1938- *107*
  Brief entry *52*
  Earlier sketch in SATA *56*
Radlauer, David 1952- *28*
Radlauer, Edward 1921- *15*
Radlauer, Ruth Shaw 1926- *98*
  Earlier sketch in SATA *15*
Radley, Gail 1951- *112*
  Earlier sketch in SATA *25*
Radunsky, Vladimir *177*
Rae, Gwynedd 1892-1977 .... *37*
Raebeck, Lois 1921- *5*
Rael, Elsa Okon 1927-
  See CLR *84*
Raffi
  See Cavoukian, Raffi
Raftery, Gerald (Bransfield) 1905-1986 ...... *11*
Ragan-Reid, Gale 1956- *90*
Rahaman, Vashanti 1953- *98*
Rahn, Joan Elma 1929- *27*
Rai, Bali 1971- *152*
Raible, Alton (Robert) 1918- *35*
Raiff, Stan 1930- *11*
Raines, Shirley C(arol) 1945- *128*
Rainey, W. B.
  See Blassingame, Wyatt Rainey
Rake, Jody 1961- *157*
Ralston, Jan
  See Dunlop, Agnes M. R.
Ramal, Walter
  See de la Mare, Walter (John)
Ramanujan, A(ttipat) K(rishnaswami)
  1929-1993 .... *86*
Ramstad, Ralph L. 1919- *115*
Rana, Indi
  See Rana, Indira Higham
Rana, Indira Higham 1944- *82*
Ranadive, Gail 1944- *10*
Rand, Ann (Binkley) *30*
Rand, Gloria 1925- *156*
  Earlier sketch in SATA *101*
Rand, Paul 1914-1996 .... *6*
Randall, Carrie
  See Ransom, Candice F.
Randall, David 1972- *167*
Randall, Florence Engel 1917-1997 .... *5*
Randall, Janet
  See Young, Janet Randall
  and Young, Robert W(illiam)
Randall, Robert
  See Garrett, (Gordon) Randall (Phillip)
  and Silverberg, Robert
Randall, Ruth (Elaine) Painter 1892-1971 .... *3*
Randell, Beverley
  See Price, Beverley Joan
Randle, Kristen D. 1952- *92*
  Autobiography Feature *119*
  See also SAAS *24*
Randle, Kristen Downey
  See Randle, Kristen D.
Randolph, Boynton M.D.
  See Ellis, Edward S(ylvester)
Randolph, Ellen
  See Rawn, Melanie

Randolph, Geoffrey
  See Ellis, Edward S(ylvester)
Randolph, J. H.
  See Ellis, Edward S(ylvester)
Randolph, Lieutenant J. H.
  See Ellis, Edward S(ylvester)
Rands, William Brighty 1823-1882 .... *17*
Raney, Ken 1953- *74*
Rankin, Joan 1940- *148*
  Earlier sketch in SATA *88*
Rankin, Laura 1953(?)- *176*
Ranney, Agnes V. 1916-1985 .... *6*
Ransom, Candice F. 1952- *135*
  Brief entry *49*
  Earlier sketches in SATA *52, 89*
Ransome, Arthur (Michell) 1884-1967 .... *22*
  See also CLR *8*
Ransome, James E. 1961- *178*
  Earlier sketches in SATA *76, 123*
  See also CLR *86*
Rant, Tol E.
  See Longyear, Barry B(rookes)
Raphael, Elaine *23*
  See Bolognese, Elaine (Raphael Chionchio)
Rapp, Adam 1968(?)- *148*
Rappaport, Doreen *151*
Rappaport, Eva 1924- *6*
Rappoport, Ken 1935- *167*
  Earlier sketch in SATA *89*
Rarick, Carrie 1911-2002 .... *41*
Raschka, Chris 1959- *166*
  Earlier sketches in SATA *80, 117*
Raschka, Christopher
  See Raschka, Chris
Rascol, Sabina I. *159*
Rash, Andy *162*
Raskin, Edith Lefkowitz 1908-1987 .... *9*
Raskin, Ellen 1928-1984 .... *139*
  Earlier sketches in SATA *2, 38*
  See also CLR *12*
Raskin, Joseph 1897-1982 .... *12*
  Obituary *29*
Rathjen, Carl Henry 1909-1984 .... *11*
Rathmann, Peggy 1953- *157*
  Earlier sketch in SATA *94*
  See Crosby, Margaret
Ratliff, Thomas M. 1948- *118*
Rattigan, Jama Kim 1951- *99*
Ratto, Linda Lee 1952- *79*
Rattray, Simon
  See Trevor, Elleston
Ratz de Tagyos, Paul 1958- *76*
Rau, Dana Meachen 1971- *167*
  Earlier sketch in SATA *94*
Rau, Margaret 1913- *168*
  Earlier sketch in SATA *9*
  See also CLR *8*
Raucher, Herman 1928- *8*
Raum, Elizabeth 1949- *155*
RavenWolf, Silver 1956- *155*
Ravielli, Anthony 1916-1997 .... *3*
  Obituary *95*
Ravilious, Robin 1944- *77*
Rawding, F(rederick) W(illiam) 1930- *55*
Rawlings, Marjorie Kinnan 1896-1953 ..... *100*
  See also YABC *1*
  See also CLR *63*
Rawlinson, Julia *175*
Rawls, (Woodrow) Wilson 1913-1984 .... *22*
  See also CLR *81*
Rawlyk, George Alexander 1935- *64*
Rawn, Melanie 1954- *98*
Rawn, Melanie Robin
  See Rawn, Melanie
Ray, Carl 1943-1978 .... *63*
Ray, Deborah *8*
  See Kogan Ray, Deborah
Ray, Delia 1963- *179*
  Earlier sketch in SATA *70*
Ray, Irene
  See Sutton, Margaret Beebe

Ray, Jane 1960- *152*
  Earlier sketch in SATA *72*
Ray, JoAnne 1935- *9*
Ray, Mary (Eva Pedder) 1932- *127*
  Earlier sketch in SATA *2*
Ray, Mary Lyn 1946- *154*
  Earlier sketch in SATA *90*
Rayban, Chloe 1944- *167*
Rayevsky, Robert 1955- *81*
Raymond, Robert
  See Alter, Robert Edmond
Rayner, Hugh *151*
Rayner, Mary 1933- *87*
  Earlier sketch in SATA *22*
  See also CLR *41*
Rayner, Shoo
  See Rayner, Hugh
Rayner, William 1929- *55*
  Brief entry *36*
Raynor, Dorka *28*
Rayson, Steven 1932- *30*
Razzell, Arthur (George) 1925- *11*
Razzell, Mary (Catherine) 1930- *102*
Razzi, James 1931- *10*
Read, Elfreida 1920- *2*
Read, Nicholas 1956- *146*
Read, Piers Paul 1941- *21*
Reade, Deborah 1949- *69*
Reader, Dennis 1929- *71*
Reading, Richard P(atrick) 1962- *161*
Readman, Jo 1958- *89*
Ready, Kirk L(ewis) 1943- *39*
Reaney, James 1926- *43*
Reaver, Chap 1935-1993 .... *69*
  Obituary *77*
Reaver, Herbert R.
  See Reaver, Chap
Reaves, J. Michael
  See Reaves, (James) Michael
Reaves, (James) Michael 1950- *99*
Redding, Robert Hull 1919- *2*
Redekopp, Elsa *61*
Redlich, Ben 1977- *181*
Redway, Ralph
  See Hamilton, Charles (Harold St. John)
Redway, Ridley
  See Hamilton, Charles (Harold St. John)
Reece, Colleen L. 1935- *116*
Reece, Gabrielle 1970- *108*
Reed, Betty Jane 1921- *4*
Reed, E.
  See Evans, Mari
Reed, Gwendolyn E(lizabeth) 1932- *21*
Reed, Kit 1932- *116*
  Earlier sketch in SATA *34*
Reed, Lynn Rowe *171*
Reed, Neil 1961- *99*
Reed, Talbot Baines 1852-1893
  See CLR *76*
Reed, Thomas (James) 1947- *34*
Reed, William Maxwell 1871-1962 .... *15*
Reeder, Carolyn 1937- *97*
  Earlier sketch in SATA *66*
  See also CLR *69*
Reeder, Colin (Dawson) 1938- *74*
Reeder, Colonel Red
  See Reeder, Russell P(otter), Jr.
Reeder, Russell P(otter), Jr. 1902-1998 .... *4*
  Obituary *101*
Reeder, Stephanie Owen 1951- *102*
Reed-Jones, Carol 1955- *112*
Reef, Catherine 1951- *128*
  Earlier sketch in SATA *73*
Reekie, Jocelyn (Margaret) 1947- *145*
Reeman, Douglas Edward 1924- *63*
  Brief entry *28*
Rees, Celia 1949- *124*
Rees, David (Bartlett) 1936-1993 .... *69*
  Obituary *76*
  Earlier sketch in SATA *36*
  See also SAAS *5*

Rees, Douglas 1947- *169*
Rees, Ennis (Samuel, Jr.) 1925- *3*
Rees, (George) Leslie (Clarence) 1905-2000
  .... *105*
  Obituary *135*
Reese, Bob
  See Reese, Robert A.
Reese, Della 1931(?)- *114*
Reese, Lyn
  See Reese, Carolyn Johnson
Reese, Robert A. 1938- *60*
  Brief entry *53*
Reese, (John) Terence 1913-1996 .... *59*
Reeve, Joel
  See Cox, William R(obert)
Reeve, Kirk 1934- *117*
Reeve, Philip *170*
Reeves, Faye Couch 1953- *76*
Reeves, James *15*
  See Reeves, John Morris
Reeves, Jeni 1947- *111*
Reeves, John Morris 1909-1978 .... *87*
  See Reeves, James
Reeves, Joyce 1911- *17*
Reeves, Lawrence F. 1926- *29*
Reeves, Ruth Ellen
  See Ranney, Agnes V.
Regan, Dian Curtis 1950- *149*
  Autobiography Feature *149*
  Earlier sketches in SATA *75, 133*
Regehr, Lydia 1903-1991 .... *37*
Reger, James P. 1952- *106*
Reggiani, Renee 1925- *18*
Rehm, Karl M. 1935- *72*
Reich, Ali
  See Katz, Bobbi
Reich, Susanna 1954- *113*
Reiche, Dietlof 1941- *159*
Reichert, Mickey Zucker
  See Reichert, Miriam Zucker
Reichert, Miriam Zucker 1962- *85*
Reichert, Renee *172*
Reichhold, Jane(t E.) 1937- *147*
Reid, Alastair 1926- *46*
Reid, Barbara 1922- *21*
Reid, Barbara (Jane) 1957- *93*
  See also CLR *64*
Reid, Desmond
  See Moorcock, Michael
  and McNeilly, Wilfred (Glassford)
Reid, Eugenie Chazal 1924- *12*
Reid, John Calvin *21*
Reid, (Thomas) Mayne 1818-1883 .... *24*
Reid, Meta Mayne 1905-1991 .... *58*
  Brief entry *36*
Reid, Robin (Nicole) 1969- *145*
Reid Banks, Lynne 1929- *165*
  Earlier sketches in SATA *22, 75, 111*
  See also CLR *24*
  See Banks, Lynne Reid
Reider, Katja 1960- *126*
Reid Jenkins, Debra 1955- *87*
Reiff, Stephanie Ann 1948- *47*
  Brief entry *28*
Reig, June 1933- *30*
Reigot, Betty Polisar 1924- *55*
  Brief entry *41*
Reim, Melanie (K.) 1956- *104*
Reinach, Jacquelyn (Krasne) 1930-2000 ..... *28*
Reiner, Carl 1922- *151*
Reiner, William B(uck) 1910-1976 .... *46*
  Obituary *30*
Reinfeld, Fred 1910-1964 .... *3*
Reinhardt, Dana 1971- *175*
Reinhart, Matthew *161*
Reiniger, Lotte 1899-1981 .... *40*
  Obituary *33*
Reinsma, Carol 1949- *91*
Reinstedt, Randall A. 1935- *101*
Reinstedt, Randy
  See Reinstedt, Randall A.

Reisberg, Mira 1955- 82
Reisberg, Veg
  See Reisberg, Mira
Reiser, Lynn 1944- 180
  Earlier sketches in SATA *81, 138*
Reiser, Lynn Whisnant
  See Reiser, Lynn
Reisgies, Teresa (Maria) 1966- 74
Reiss, Johanna (de Leeuw) 1929(?)- 18
  See also CLR *19*
Reiss, John J. 23
Reiss, Kathryn 1957- 144
  Earlier sketch in SATA *76*
Reit, Seymour Victory 1918-2001 21
  Obituary 133
Reit, Sy
  See Reit, Seymour Victory
Relf, Patricia 1954- 134
  Earlier sketch in SATA *71*
Remi, Georges 1907-1983 13
  Obituary 32
  See Herge
Remington, Frederic S(ackrider) 1861-1909
  41
Remkiewicz, Frank 1939- 152
  Earlier sketch in SATA *77*
Remy, Georges
  See Remi, Georges
Renaud, Bernadette 1945- 66
Renault, Mary
  See Challans, Mary
Rendell, Joan 28
Rendina, Laura (Jones) Cooper 1902- 10
Rendon, Marcie R. 1952- 97
Rendon, Maria 1965- 116
Renee, Janina 1956- 140
Renfro, Ed 1924- 79
Renick, Marion (Lewis) 1905-1983 1
Renken, Aleda 1907- 27
Renlie, Frank H. 1936- 11
Rennert, Richard Scott 1956- 67
Rennison, Louise 1951- 149
Reno, Dawn E(laine) 1953- 130
Rensie, Willis
  See Eisner, Will
Renton, Cam
  See Armstrong, Richard
Renvoize, Jean 5
Resciniti, Angelo G. 1952- 75
Resnick, Michael David
  See Resnick, Mike
Resnick, Mike 1942- 159
  Earlier sketches in SATA *38, 106*
Resnick, Seymour 1920- 23
Retla, Robert
  See Alter, Robert Edmond
Reuter, Bjarne (B.) 1950- 142
  Earlier sketch in SATA *68*
Reuter, Carol (Joan) 1931- 2
Revena
  See Wright, Betty Ren
Revsbech, Vicki
  See Liestman, Vicki
Rey, H(ans) A(ugusto) 1898-1977 100
  Earlier sketches in SATA *1, 26, 69*
  See also CLR *93*
Rey, Margret (Elisabeth) 1906-1996 86
  Obituary 93
  Earlier sketch in SATA *26*
  See also CLR *93*
Reyher, Becky
  See Reyher, Rebecca Hourwich
Reyher, Rebecca Hourwich 1897-1987 18
  Obituary 50
Reynolds, C. Buck 1957- 107
Reynolds, Jan 1956- 180
Reynolds, John
  See Whitlock, Ralph
Reynolds, Madge
  See Whitlock, Ralph

Reynolds, Malvina 1900-1978 44
  Obituary 24
Reynolds, Marilyn (M.) 1935- 121
  See also SAAS *23*
Reynolds, Marilynn 1940- 141
  Earlier sketch in SATA *80*
Reynolds, Pamela 1923- 34
Reynolds, Peter H. 1961- 128
Reynolds, Peter J. 1961- 179
Reynolds, Susan 179
Rhine, Richard
  See Silverstein, Alvin
  and Silverstein, Virginia B(arbara Opshelor)
Rhoades, Diane 1952- 90
Rhodes, Bennie (Loran) 1927- 35
Rhodes, Donna McKee 1962- 87
Rhodes, Frank Harold Trevor 1926- 37
Rhue, Morton
  See Strasser, Todd
Rhyne, Nancy 1926- 66
Rhynes, Martha E. 1939- 141
Ribbons, Ian 1924- 37
  Brief entry 30
  See also SAAS *3*
Ricciuti, Edward R(aphael) 1938- 10
Rice, Alice (Caldwell) Hegan 1870-1942 ... 63
Rice, Bebe Faas 1932- 89
Rice, Dale R. 1948- 42
Rice, Dale Richard
  See Rice, Dale R.
Rice, Dick
  See Rice, R. Hugh
Rice, Earle (Wilmont), Jr. 1928- 151
  Earlier sketch in SATA *92*
Rice, Edward 1918-2001 47
  Brief entry 42
Rice, Elizabeth 1913-1976 2
Rice, Eve 1951- 91
  Earlier sketch in SATA *34*
Rice, Eve Hart
  See Rice, Eve
Rice, Inez 1907- 13
Rice, James 1934- 93
  Earlier sketch in SATA *22*
Rice, John F. 1958- 82
Rice, R. Hugh 1929- 115
Rice, Richard H.
  See Rice, R. Hugh
Rich, Barbara
  See Graves, Robert
Rich, Elaine Sommers 1926- 6
Rich, Josephine Bouchard 1912- 10
Rich, Louise Dickinson 1903-1991 54
  Obituary 67
Richard, Adrienne 1921- 5
  See also SAAS *9*
Richard, James Robert
  See Bowen, Robert Sydney
Richards, Chuck 1957- 170
Richards, Frank
  See Hamilton, Charles (Harold St. John)
Richards, Hilda
  See Hamilton, Charles (Harold St. John)
Richards, Jackie 1925- 102
Richards, Jean 1940- 135
Richards, Justin 169
Richards, Kay
  See Baker, Susan (Catherine)
Richards, Laura E(lizabeth Howe) 1850-1943
  See YABC *1*
  See also CLR *54*
Richards, Leigh
  See King, Laurie R.
Richards, Norman 1932- 48
Richards, R(onald) C(harles) W(illiam) 1923-
  59
  Brief entry 43
Richardson, Andrew (William) 1986- 120
Richardson, Carol 1932- 58
Richardson, Grace Lee
  See Dickson, Naida

Richardson, Jean (Mary) 59
Richardson, Judith Benet 1941- 77
Richardson, Robert S(hirley) 1902-1981 8
Richardson, Sandy 1949- 116
Richardson, Willis 1889-1977 60
Richelson, Geraldine 1922- 29
Richemont, Enid 1940- 82
Richler, Mordecai 1931-2001 98
  Brief entry 27
  Earlier sketch in SATA *44*
  See also CLR *17*
Richman, Sophia 1941- 142
Rich-McCoy, Lois
  See McCoy, Lois (Rich)
Richmond, Robin 1951- 75
Richoux, Pat(ricia) 1927- 7
Richter, Alice 1941- 30
Richter, Conrad (Michael) 1890-1968 3
Richter, Hans Peter 1925-1993 6
  See also CLR *21*
  See also SAAS *11*
Rickard, Graham 1949- 71
Riddell, Chris 1962- 166
  Earlier sketch in SATA *114*
Riddell, Christopher Barry
  See Riddell, Chris
Riddell, Edwina 1955- 82
Ridden, Brian (John) 1934- 123
Riddle, Tohby 1965- 151
  Earlier sketch in SATA *74*
Riddles, Libby 1956- 140
Ridge, Antonia (Florence) (?)-1981 7
  Obituary 27
Ridge, Martin 1923-2003 43
Ridley, Philip 171
  Earlier sketch in SATA *88*
Ridlon, Marci 22
  See Balterman, Marcia Ridlon
Riedman, Sarah R(egal) 1902-1995 1
Riehecky, Janet 1953- 164
Riesenberg, Felix, Jr. 1913-1962 23
Rieu, E(mile) V(ictor) 1887-1972 46
  Obituary 26
Riffenburgh, Beau 1955- 175
Rigg, Sharon
  See Creech, Sharon
Riggio, Anita 1952- 148
  Earlier sketch in SATA *73*
Riggs, Stephanie 1964- 138
Rigney, James Oliver, Jr.
  See Jordan, Robert
Rikhoff, Jean 1928- 9
Rikki
  See Ducornet, Erica
Riley, James A. 1939- 97
Riley, James Whitcomb 1849-1916 17
Riley, Jocelyn 1949- 60
  Brief entry 50
Riley, Jocelyn Carol
  See Riley, Jocelyn
Riley, Linda Capus 1950- 85
Riley, Martin 1948- 81
Rimes, (Margaret) LeAnn 1982- 154
Rinaldi, Ann 1934- 161
  Brief entry 50
  Earlier sketches in SATA *51, 78, 117*
  See also CLR *46*
Rinard, Judith E(llen) 1947- 140
  Earlier sketch in SATA *44*
Rinder, Lenore 1949- 92
Ring, Elizabeth 1920- 79
Ringdahl, Mark
  See Longyear, Barry B(rookes)
Ringgold, Faith 1930- 114
  Earlier sketch in SATA *71*
  See also CLR *30*
Ringi, Kjell (Arne Soerensen) 1939- 12
Rinkoff, Barbara Jean (Rich) 1923-1975 4
  Obituary 27
Rinn, Miriam 1946- 127
Riordan, James 1936- 95

Riordan, Rick 174
Rios, Tere
  See Versace, Marie Teresa Rios
Ripken, Cal, Jr. 1960- 114
Ripken, Calvin Edward, Jr.
  See Ripken, Cal, Jr.
Ripley, Catherine 1957- 82
Ripley, Elizabeth Blake 1906-1969 5
Ripper, Charles L(ewis) 1929- 3
Ripper, Chuck
  See Ripper, Charles L(ewis)
Riq
  See Atwater, Richard (Tupper)
Rish, David 1955- 110
Riskind, Mary 1944- 60
Rissinger, Matt 1956- 93
Rissman, Art
  See Sussman, Susan
Rissman, Susan
  See Sussman, Susan
Ritchie, Barbara Gibbons 14
Ritter, Felix
  See Kruss, James
Ritter, John H. 1951- 137
  Earlier sketch in SATA 129
Ritter, Lawrence S(tanley) 1922-2004 58
  Obituary 152
Ritthaler, Shelly 1955- 91
Ritz, Karen 1957- 80
Rivera, Geraldo (Miguel) 1943- 54
  Brief entry 28
Rivers, Elfrida
  See Bradley, Marion Zimmer
Rivers, Karen 1970- 131
Riverside, John
  See Heinlein, Robert A.
Rivkin, Ann 1920- 41
Rivoli, Mario 1943- 10
Roach, Marilynne K. 1946- 9
Roach, Marilynne Kathleen
  See Roach, Marilynne K.
Roach, Portia
  See Takakjian, Portia
Robb, Laura 1937- 95
Robbins, Frank 1917-1994(?) 42
  Brief entry 32
Robbins, Ken 1945- 147
  Brief entry 53
  Earlier sketch in SATA 94
Robbins, Raleigh
  See Hamilton, Charles (Harold St. John)
Robbins, Ruth 1917(?)- 14
Robbins, Tony
  See Pashko, Stanley
Robbins, Wayne
  See Cox, William R(obert)
Robel, S. L.
  See Fraustino, Lisa Rowe
Roberson, Jennifer 1953- 72
Roberson, John R(oyster) 1930- 53
Robert, Adrian
  See St. John, Nicole
Roberts, Bethany 133
Roberts, Bruce (Stuart) 1930- 47
  Brief entry 39
Roberts, Charles G(eorge) D(ouglas)
  1860-1943 88
  Brief entry 29
  See also CLR 33
Roberts, David
  See Cox, John Roberts
Roberts, Elizabeth 1944- 80
Roberts, Elizabeth Madox 1886-1941 33
  Brief entry 27
  See also CLR 100
Roberts, Jim
  See Bates, Barbara S(nedeker)
Roberts, John G(aither) 1913-1993 27
Roberts, Judy I. 1957- 93
Roberts, Katherine 1962- 152

Roberts, M. L.
  See Mattern, Joanne
Roberts, Nancy Correll 1924- 52
  Brief entry 28
Roberts, Terence
  See Sanderson, Ivan T(erence)
Roberts, Willo Davis 1928-2004 150
  Autobiography Feature 150
  Obituary 160
  Earlier sketches in SATA 21, 70, 133
  See also CLR 95
  See also SAAS 8
Robertson, Barbara (Anne) 1931- 12
Robertson, Don 1929-1999 8
  Obituary 113
Robertson, Dorothy Lewis 1912- 12
Robertson, Ellis
  See Ellison, Harlan
  and Silverberg, Robert
Robertson, Janet (E.) 1935- 68
Robertson, Jennifer Sinclair 1942-1998 12
Robertson, Jenny
  See Robertson, Jennifer Sinclair
Robertson, Keith (Carlton) 1914-1991 85
  Obituary 69
  Earlier sketch in SATA 1
  See also SAAS 15
Robertson, Stephen
  See Walker, Robert W(ayne)
Robertus, Polly M. 1948- 73
Robeson, Kenneth
  See Dent, Lester
  and Goulart, Ron(ald Joseph)
Robeson, Kenneth
  See Johnson, (Walter) Ryerson
Robinet, Harriette Gillem 1931- 104
  Earlier sketch in SATA 27
  See also CLR 64
Robins, Deri 1958- 166
  Earlier sketch in SATA 117
Robins, Patricia
  See Clark, Patricia Denise
Robins, Rollo, Jr.
  See Ellis, Edward S(ylvester)
Robins, Seelin
  See Ellis, Edward S(ylvester)
Robinson, Adjai 1932- 8
Robinson, Aminah Brenda Lynn 1940- 159
  Earlier sketch in SATA 77
Robinson, Barbara (Webb) 1927- 84
  Earlier sketch in SATA 8
Robinson, C(harles) A(lexander), Jr. 1900-1965
  36
Robinson, Charles 1870-1937 17
Robinson, Charles 1931- 6
Robinson, Dorothy W. 1929- 54
Robinson, Eve
  See Tanselle, Eve
Robinson, Glen 1953- 92
Robinson, Glendal P.
  See Robinson, Glen
Robinson, Jan M. 1933- 6
Robinson, Jean O. 1934- 7
Robinson, Joan (Mary) G(ale Thomas)
  1910-1988 7
Robinson, Kim Stanley 1952- 109
Robinson, Lee 1948- 110
Robinson, Lloyd
  See Silverberg, Robert
Robinson, Lynda S(uzanne) 1951- 107
Robinson, Marileta 1942- 32
Robinson, Maudie Millian Oller 1914- 11
Robinson, Nancy K(onheim) 1942-1994 91
  Brief entry 31
  Obituary 79
  Earlier sketch in SATA 32
Robinson, Ray(mond Kenneth) 1920- 23
Robinson, Shari
  See McGuire, Leslie (Sarah)
Robinson, Sharon 1950- 162
Robinson, Spider 1948- 118

Robinson, Sue
  See Robinson, Susan Maria
Robinson, Susan Maria 1955- 105
Robinson, Suzanne
  See Robinson, Lynda S(uzanne)
Robinson, T(homas) H(eath) 1869-1950 17
Robinson, (Wanda) Veronica 1926- 30
Robinson, W(illiam) Heath 1872-1944 17
Robison, Bonnie 1924- 12
Robison, Nancy L(ouise) 1934- 32
Robles, Harold E. 1948- 87
Robottom, John 1934- 7
Robson, Eric 1939- 82
Roche, A. K.
  See Abisch, Roslyn Kroop
  and Kaplan, Boche
Roche, Denis (Mary) 1967- 99
Roche, Luane 1937- 170
Roche, P(atricia) K. 1935- 57
  Brief entry 34
Roche, Terry
  See Poole, Peggy
Rochman, Hazel 1938- 105
Rock, Lois
  See Joslin, Mary
Rock, Maxine 1940- 108
Rocker, Fermin 1907- 40
Rocklin, Joanne 1946- 134
  Earlier sketch in SATA 86
Rockwell, Anne F. 1934- 162
  Earlier sketches in SATA 33, 71, 114
  See also SAAS 19
Rockwell, Anne Foote
  See Rockwell, Anne F.
Rockwell, Bart
  See Pellowski, Michael (Joseph)
Rockwell, Harlow 1910-1988 33
  Obituary 56
Rockwell, Norman (Percevel) 1894-1978 ... 23
Rockwell, Thomas 1933- 70
  Earlier sketch in SATA 7
  See also CLR 6
Rockwood, Joyce 1947- 39
Rockwood, Roy 67
  Earlier sketch in SATA 1
  See McFarlane, Leslie (Charles)
  and Stratemeyer, Edward L.
Rodanas, Kristina 1952- 155
Rodari, Gianni 1920-1980
  See CLR 24
Rodd, Kathleen Tennant 57
  Obituary 55
  See Rodd, Kylie Tennant
Rodda, Emily 1948- 146
  Earlier sketch in SATA 97
  See also CLR 32
Roddenberry, Eugene Wesley 1921-1991 45
  Obituary 69
  See Roddenberry, Gene
Roddenberry, Gene
  Obituary 69
  See Roddenberry, Eugene Wesley
Roddie, Shen 153
Roddy, Lee 1921- 57
Rodenas, Paula 73
Rodgers, Frank 1944- 69
Rodgers, Mary 1931- 130
  Earlier sketch in SATA 8
  See also CLR 20
Rodman, Emerson
  See Ellis, Edward S(ylvester)
Rodman, Eric
  See Silverberg, Robert
Rodman, Maia
  See Wojciechowska, Maia (Teresa)
Rodman, (Cary) Selden 1909-2002 9
Rodowsky, Colby 1932- 164
  Earlier sketches in SATA 21, 77, 120
  See also SAAS 22
Rodowsky, Colby F.
  See Rodowsky, Colby

Rodriguez, Alejo 1941- *83*
Rodriguez, Christina 1981- *177*
Rodriguez, Luis J. 1954- *125*
Rodriguez, Rachel *180*
Rodriguez, Rachel Victoria
    See Rodriguez, Rachel
Roeder, Virginia Marsh 1926- *98*
Roehrig, Catharine H. 1949- *67*
Roennfeldt, Robert 1953- *78*
Roessel-Waugh, C. C.
    See Waugh, Carol-Lynn Rossel
    and Waugh, Charles G(ordon)
Roets, Lois F. 1937- *91*
Roever, J(oan) M(arilyn) 1935- *26*
Rofes, Eric 1954-2006 .... *52*
Rofes, Eric Edward 1954-2006
    See Rofes, Eric
Roffey, Maureen 1936- *33*
Rogak, Lisa 1962- *80*
Rogak, Lisa Angowski
    See Rogak, Lisa
Rogasky, Barbara 1933- *144*
    Earlier sketch in SATA *86*
Rogers, (Thomas) Alan (Stinchcombe) 1937-
    .... *81*
    Earlier sketch in SATA *2*
Rogers, Bettye 1858-1919 .... *103*
Rogers, Cindy 1950- *89*
Rogers, Emma 1951- *74*
Rogers, Frances 1888-1974 .... *10*
Rogers, Fred McFeely 1928-2003 .... *33*
    Obituary *138*
Rogers, Hal
    See Sirimarco, Elizabeth
Rogers, Jean 1919- *55*
    Brief entry *47*
Rogers, Matilda 1894-1976 .... *5*
    Obituary *34*
Rogers, Pamela 1927- *9*
Rogers, Paul 1950- *98*
    Earlier sketch in SATA *54*
Rogers, Robert
    See Hamilton, Charles (Harold St. John)
Rogers, W(illiam) G(arland) 1896-1978 ..... *23*
Rohan, M. S.
    See Rohan, Michael Scott
Rohan, Michael Scott 1951- *98*
Rohan, Mike Scott
    See Rohan, Michael Scott
Rohmann, Eric 1957- *171*
    See also CLR *100*
Rohmer, Harriet 1938- *56*
Rohrer, Doug 1962- *89*
Rojan
    See Rojankovsky, Feodor (Stepanovich)
Rojankovsky, Feodor (Stepanovich) 1891-1970
    .... *21*
Rojany, Lisa *94*
Rokeby-Thomas, Anna E(lma) 1911- *15*
Roland, Albert 1925-2002 .... *11*
Roland, Mary
    See Lewis, Mary (Christianna)
Roleff, Tamara L. 1959- *143*
Rolerson, Darrell A(llen) 1946- *8*
Roll, Winifred 1909-1998 .... *6*
Rollins, Charlemae Hill 1897-1979 .... *3*
    Obituary *26*
Rollock, Barbara T(herese) 1924- *64*
Romack, Janice Reed
    See LeNoir, Janice
Romain, Trevor *134*
Romanenko, Vitaliy 1962- *101*
Romano, Louis G. 1921- *35*
Romano, Melora A. 1966- *118*
Romano, Ray 1957- *170*
Romano, Raymond
    See Romano, Ray
Romijn, Johanna Maria Kooyker
    See Kooyker-Romijn, Johanna Maria
Romyn, Johanna Maria Kooyker
    See Kooyker-Romijn, Johanna Maria

Rong, Yu 1970- *174*
Rongen, Bjoern 1906- *10*
Rongen, Bjorn
    See Rongen, Bjoern
Ronson, Mark
    See Alexander, Marc
Rood, Ronald (N.) 1920- *12*
Rook, Sebastian
    See Jeapes, Ben
Rooke, Daphne (Marie) 1914- *12*
Roop, Connie 1951- *167*
    Brief entry *49*
    Earlier sketches in SATA *54, 116*
Roop, Constance Betzer
    See Roop, Connie
Roop, Peter 1951- *167*
    Brief entry *49*
    Earlier sketches in SATA *54, 116*
Roop, Peter G.
    See Roop, Peter
Roop, Peter Geiger
    See Roop, Peter
Roos, Stephen 1945- *128*
    Brief entry *41*
    Earlier sketches in SATA *47, 77*
Roose-Evans, James 1927- *65*
Roosevelt, (Anna) Eleanor 1884-1962 .... *50*
Root, Betty *84*
Root, Phyllis 1949- *145*
    Brief entry *48*
    Earlier sketches in SATA *55, 94*
Roper, Laura (Newbold) Wood 1911-2003 . *34*
    Obituary *150*
Roper, Robert 1946- *142*
    Earlier sketch in SATA *78*
Roraback, Robin (Ellan) 1964- *111*
Rorby, Ginny 1944- *94*
Rorer, Abigail 1949- *85*
Rosamel, Godeleine de 1968- *151*
Roscoe, D(onald) T(homas) 1934- *42*
Rose, Anne *8*
Rose, Deborah Lee 1955- *124*
    Earlier sketch in SATA *71*
Rose, Elizabeth (Jane Pretty) 1933- *68*
    Brief entry *28*
Rose, Florella
    See Carlson, Vada F.
Rose, Gerald (Hembdon Seymour) 1935- ... *68*
    Brief entry *30*
Rose, Malcolm 1953- *168*
    Earlier sketch in SATA *107*
Rose, Nancy A.
    See Sweetland, Nancy A(nn)
Rose, Ted 1940- *93*
Rose, Wendy 1948- *12*
Rosen, Lillian (Diamond) 1928- *63*
Rosen, Marvin 1933- *161*
Rosen, Michael 1946- *181*
    Brief entry *40*
    Earlier sketches in SATA *48, 84, 137*
    See also CLR *45*
Rosen, Michael J(oel) 1954- *86*
Rosen, Michael Wayne
    See Rosen, Michael
Rosen, Sidney 1916- *1*
Rosen, Winifred 1943- *8*
Rosenbaum, Maurice 1907- *6*
Rosenberg, Amye 1950- *74*
Rosenberg, Dorothy 1906- *40*
Rosenberg, Eth(el) Clifford 1915- *3*
    See Clifford, Eth
Rosenberg, Jane 1949- *58*
Rosenberg, Liz 1958- *129*
    Earlier sketch in SATA *75*
Rosenberg, Maxine B(erta) 1939- *93*
    Brief entry *47*
    Earlier sketch in SATA *55*
Rosenberg, Nancy (Sherman) 1931- *4*
Rosenberg, Sharon 1942- *8*
Rosenberry, Vera 1948- *144*
    Earlier sketch in SATA *83*

Rosenblatt, Arthur
    See Rosenblatt, Arthur S.
Rosenblatt, Arthur S. 1938- *68*
    Brief entry *45*
Rosenblatt, Lily 1956- *90*
Rosenbloom, Joseph 1928- *21*
Rosenblum, Richard 1928- *11*
Rosenburg, John M. 1918- *6*
Rosenfeld, Dina 1962- *99*
Rosenthal, Amy Krouse 1965- *177*
Rosenthal, Betsy R. 1957- *178*
Rosenthal, Harold 1914-1999 .... *35*
Rosenthal, M(acha) L(ouis) 1917-1996 .... *59*
Rosenthal, Mark A(lan) 1946- *64*
Rosman, Steven M 1956- *81*
Rosman, Steven Michael
    See Rosman, Steven M
Rosoff, Meg 1956- *160*
Ross, Alan
    See Warwick, Alan R(oss)
Ross, Christine 1950- *172*
    Earlier sketch in SATA *83*
Ross, Clare *111*
    Earlier sketch in SATA *48*
    See Romano, Clare
Ross, Dana Fuller
    See Cockrell, Amanda
    and Gerson, Noel Bertram
Ross, Dave *32*
    See Ross, David
Ross, David 1896-1975 .... *49*
    Obituary *20*
Ross, David 1949- *133*
    See Ross, Dave
Ross, Diana
    See Denney, Diana
Ross, Edward S(hearman) 1915- *85*
Ross, Eileen 1950- *115*
Ross, Frank (Xavier), Jr. 1914- *28*
Ross, Jane 1961- *79*
Ross, John 1921- *45*
Ross, Judy 1942- *54*
Ross, Katharine Reynolds
    See Ross, Kathy
Ross, Kathy 1948- *169*
    Earlier sketch in SATA *89*
Ross, Kent 1956- *91*
Ross, Lillian Hammer 1925- *72*
Ross, Michael Elsohn 1952- *170*
    Earlier sketches in SATA *80, 127*
Ross, Pat(ricia Kienzle) 1943- *53*
    Brief entry *48*
Ross, Ramon R(oyal) 1930- *62*
Ross, Stewart 1947- *134*
    Earlier sketch in SATA *92*
    See also SAAS *23*
Ross, Tom 1958- *84*
Ross, Tony 1938- *176*
    Earlier sketches in SATA *17, 65, 130*
Ross, Wilda 1915- *51*
    Brief entry *39*
Rossel, Seymour 1945- *28*
Rossel-Waugh, C. C.
    See Waugh, Carol-Lynn Rossel
Rossetti, Christina 1830-1894 .... *20*
    See also CLR *115*
Rossetti, Christina Georgina
    See Rossetti, Christina
Rossi, Joyce 1943- *116*
Rossotti, Hazel Swaine 1930- *95*
Rostkowski, Margaret I. 1945- *59*
Roth, Arnold 1929- *21*
Roth, Arthur J(oseph) 1925-1993 .... *43*
    Brief entry *28*
    Obituary *75*
    See also SAAS *11*
Roth, David 1940- *36*
Roth, Julie Jersild *180*
Roth, Matthue 1978(?)- *174*
Roth, Susan L. *181*
    Earlier sketch in SATA *134*

Rothberg, Abraham 1922- 59
Roth-Hano, Renee 1931- 85
Rothkopf, Carol Z. 1929- 4
Rothman, Joel 1938- 7
Rotner, Shelley 1951- 169
  Earlier sketch in SATA 76
Rottman, S(usan) L(ynn) 1970- 157
  Earlier sketch in SATA 106
Roueche, Berton 1911-1994 28
Roughsey, Dick 1921(?)-1985 35
  See also CLR 41
Roughsey, Goobalathaldin
  See Roughsey, Dick
Rounds, Glen (Harold) 1906-2002 112
  Obituary 141
  Earlier sketches in SATA 8, 70
Rourke, Constance Mayfield 1885-1941
  See YABC 1
Rowan, Deirdre
  See Williams, Jeanne
Rowe, Jennifer
  See Rodda, Emily
Rowe, John A. 1949- 146
Rowh, Mark 1952- 90
Rowland, Florence Wightman 1900-1997 8
  Obituary 108
Rowland-Entwistle, (Arthur) Theodore (Henry)
  1925- 94
  Earlier sketch in SATA 31
Rowling, J.K. 1965- 174
  Earlier sketch in SATA 109
  See also CLR 112
Rowling, Joanne Kathleen
  See Rowling, J.K.
Rowsome, Frank (Howard), Jr. 1914-1983 . 36
Roy, Gabrielle 1909-1983 104
Roy, Jacqueline 1954- 74
Roy, Jennifer
  See Roy, Jennifer Rozines
Roy, Jennifer Rozines 1967- 178
Roy, Liam
  See Scarry, Patricia (Murphy)
Roy, Ron(ald) 1940- 110
  Brief entry 35
  Earlier sketch in SATA 40
Roybal, Laura 1956- 85
Roybal, Laura Husby
  See Roybal, Laura
Royds, Caroline 1953- 55
Royston, Angela 1945- 169
  Earlier sketch in SATA 120
Rozakis, Laurie E. 1952- 84
Rubel, Nicole 1953- 181
  Earlier sketches in SATA 18, 95, 135
Rubin, Eva Johanna 1925- 38
Rubin, Susan Goldman 1939- 132
  Earlier sketch in SATA 84
Rubinetti, Donald 1947- 92
Rubinstein, Gillian 1942- 158
  Autobiography Feature 116
  Earlier sketches in SATA 68, 105
  See also CLR 35
  See also SAAS 25
Rubinstein, Gillian Margaret
  See Rubinstein, Gillian
Rubinstein, Patricia (Giulia Caulfield Kate)
  -2003 29
  Obituary 149
  See Forest, Antonia
Rubinstein, Robert E(dward) 1943- 49
Rublowsky, John M(artin) 1928- 62
Rubright, Lynn 1936- 171
Ruby, Laura 181
  Earlier sketch in SATA 155
Ruby, Lois (F.) 1942- 95
  Autobiography Feature 105
  Brief entry 34
  Earlier sketch in SATA 35
Ruchlis, Hy(man) 1913-1992 3
  Obituary 72
Rucker, Mike 1940- 91

Ruckman, Ivy 1931- 93
  Earlier sketch in SATA 37
Ruck-Pauquet, Gina 1931- 40
  Brief entry 37
Rudley, Stephen 1946- 30
Rudolph, Marguerita 1908- 21
Rudomin, Esther
  See Hautzig, Esther Rudomin
Rue, Leonard Lee III 1926- 142
  Earlier sketch in SATA 37
Ruedi, Norma Paul
  See Ainsworth, Norma
Ruelle, Karen Gray 1957- 126
  Earlier sketch in SATA 84
Ruemmler, John D(avid) 1948- 78
Ruepp, Krista 1947- 143
Ruffell, Ann 1941- 30
Ruffins, Reynold 1930- 125
  Earlier sketch in SATA 41
Rugoff, Milton 1913- 30
Ruhen, Olaf 1911-1989 17
Rumbaut, Hendle 1949- 84
Rumford, James 1948- 116
Rumsey, Marian (Barritt) 1928- 16
Rumstuckle, Cornelius
  See Brennan, J(ames) H(erbert)
Runnerstroem, Bengt Arne 1944- 75
Runyan, John
  See Palmer, Bernard (Alvin)
Runyon, Catherine 1947- 62
Ruoff, A. LaVonne Brown 1930- 76
Rusch, Kris
  See Rusch, Kristine Kathryn
Rusch, Kristine Kathryn 1960- 113
Rush, Alison 1951- 41
Rush, Peter 1937- 32
Rushford, Patricia H(elen) 1943- 134
Rushmore, Helen 1898-1994 3
Rushmore, Robert (William) 1926-1986 8
  Obituary 49
Ruskin, Ariane
  See Batterberry, Ariane Ruskin
Ruskin, John 1819-1900 24
Russ, Lavinia (Faxon) 1904-1992 74
Russell, Charlotte
  See Rathjen, Carl Henry
Russell, Ching Yeung 1946- 107
Russell, Franklin (Alexander) 1926- 11
Russell, Gertrude Barrer
  See Barrer-Russell, Gertrude
Russell, Helen Ross 1915- 8
Russell, James 1933- 53
Russell, Jim
  See Russell, James
Russell, Joan Plummer 1930- 139
Russell, P(hilip) Craig 1951- 162
  Earlier sketch in SATA 80
Russell, Patrick
  See Sammis, John
Russell, Paul (Gary) 1942- 57
Russell, Sarah
  See Laski, Marghanita
Russell, Sharman Apt 1954- 123
Russell, Solveig Paulson 1904-1985 3
Russo, Marisabina 1950- 151
  Earlier sketch in SATA 106
Russo, Monica J. 1950- 83
Russo, Susan 1947- 30
Russon, Penni 1974- 179
Rutgers van der Loeff, An
  See Rutgers van der Loeff-Basenau, An(na)
  Maria Margaretha
Rutgers van der Loeff-Basenau, An(na) Maria
  Margaretha 1910- 22
Ruth, Rod 1912-1987 9
Rutherford, Douglas
  See McConnell, James Douglas Rutherford
Rutherford, Meg 1932- 34
Ruthin, Margaret 4
  See Catherall, Arthur
Rutledge, Jill Zimmerman 1951- 155

Rutz, Viola Larkin 1932- 12
Ruurs, Margriet 1952- 147
  Earlier sketch in SATA 97
Ruzzier, Sergio 1966- 159
Ryan, Betsy
  See Ryan, Elizabeth (Anne)
Ryan, Cheli Duran 20
Ryan, Darlene 1958- 176
Ryan, Elizabeth (Anne) 1943- 30
Ryan, Jeanette
  See Mines, Jeanette
Ryan, John (Gerald Christopher) 1921- 22
Ryan, Margaret 1950- 166
  Earlier sketch in SATA 78
Ryan, Mary E. 1953- 61
Ryan, Mary Elizabeth
  See Ryan, Mary E.
Ryan, Pam(ela) Munoz 134
Ryan, Patrick 1957- 138
Ryan, Peter (Charles) 1939- 15
Ryan-Lush, Geraldine 1949- 89
Rybakov, Anatoli (Naumovich) 1911-1998 . 79
  Obituary 108
  See Rybakov, Anatolii (Naumovich)
Rybakov, Anatolii (Naumovich)
  See Rybakov, Anatoli (Naumovich)
Rybolt, Thomas R. 1954- 62
Rybolt, Thomas Roy
  See Rybolt, Thomas R.
Rybolt, Tom
  See Rybolt, Thomas R.
Rydberg, Ernest E(mil) 1901-1993 21
Rydberg, Lou(isa Hampton) 1908- 27
Rydell, Katy 1942- 91
Rydell, Wendell
  See Rydell, Wendy
Rydell, Wendy 4
Ryden, Hope 91
  Earlier sketch in SATA 8
Ryder, Joanne (Rose) 1946- 163
  Brief entry 34
  Earlier sketches in SATA 65, 122
  See also CLR 37
Ryder, Pamela
  See Lamb, Nancy
Rye, Anthony
  See Youd, (Christopher) Samuel
Rylant, Cynthia 1954- 160
  Brief entry 44
  Earlier sketches in SATA 50, 76, 112
  See also CLR 86
  See also SAAS 13
Rymer, Alta May 1925- 34

S

S. L. C.
  See Clemens, Samuel Langhorne
S., Svend Otto
  See Soerensen, Svend Otto
Saaf, Donald W(illiam) 1961- 124
Saal, Jocelyn
  See Sachs, Judith
Sabbeth, Carol (Landstrom) 1957- 125
Saberhagen, Fred 1930-2007 89
  Earlier sketch in SATA 37
Saberhagen, Fred Thomas
  See Saberhagen, Fred
Sabin, Edwin L(egrand) 1870-1952
  See YABC 2
Sabin, Francene 27
Sabin, Lou
  See Sabin, Louis
Sabin, Louis 1930- 27
Sabre, Dirk
  See Laffin, John (Alfred Charles)
Sabuda, Robert 1965- 170
Sabuda, Robert (James) 1965- 120
  Earlier sketch in SATA 81

Sabuda, Robert James
  See Sabuda, Robert
Sachar, Louis 1954- *154*
  Brief entry *50*
  Earlier sketches in SATA *63, 104*
  See also CLR *79*
Sachs, Elizabeth-Ann 1946- *48*
Sachs, Judith 1947- *52*
  Brief entry *51*
Sachs, Marilyn 1927- *164*
  Autobiography Feature *110*
  Earlier sketches in SATA *3, 68*
  See also CLR *2*
  See also SAAS *2*
Sachs, Marilyn Stickle
  See Sachs, Marilyn
Sackett, S(amuel) J(ohn) 1928- *12*
Sackson, Sid 1920- *16*
Sacre, Antonio 1968- *152*
Saddler, Allen
  See Richards, R(onald) C(harles) W(illiam)
Saddler, K. Allen
  See Richards, R(onald) C(harles) W(illiam)
Sadie, Stanley (John) 1930-2005 .... *14*
Sadiq, Nazneen 1944- *101*
Sadler, Catherine Edwards 1952- *60*
  Brief entry *45*
Sadler, Marilyn (June) 1950- *79*
Sadler, Mark
  See Lynds, Dennis
Saffer, Barbara *144*
Sagan, Carl 1934-1996 .... *58*
  Obituary *94*
Sagan, Carl Edward
  See Sagan, Carl
Sage, Juniper
  See Brown, Margaret Wise
  and Hurd, Edith Thacher
Sagsoorian, Paul 1923- *12*
Said, S.F. 1967- *174*
Said, S.F. 1967- *174*
Saidman, Anne 1952- *75*
Saint, Dora Jessie 1913- *10*
St. Anthony, Jane *175*
St. Antoine, Sara L. 1966- *84*
Saint-Exupery, Antoine de 1900-1944 ...... *20*
  See also CLR *10*
Saint-Exupery, Antoine Jean Baptiste Marie
  Roger de
  See Saint-Exupery, Antoine de
St. George, Judith 1931- *161*
  Earlier sketches in SATA *13, 99*
  See also CLR *57*
  See also SAAS *12*
St. James, Blakely
  See Gottfried, Theodore Mark
  and Platt, Charles
St. James, Blakely
  See Griffin, W.E.B.
Saint James, Synthia 1949- *152*
  Earlier sketch in SATA *84*
St. John, Nicole *143*
  Autobiography Feature *143*
  Earlier sketch in SATA *89*
  See also CLR *46*
  See also SAAS *7*
  See Johnston, Norma
St. John, Philip
  See del Rey, Lester
St. John, Wylly Folk 1908-1985 .... *10*
  Obituary *45*
St. Max, E. S.
  See Ellis, Edward S(ylvester)
St. Meyer, Ned
  See Stratemeyer, Edward L.
St. Mox, E. A.
  See Ellis, Edward S(ylvester)
St. Myer, Ned
  See Stratemeyer, Edward L.
St. Tamara
  See Kolba, St. Tamara

Saito, Michiko
  See Fujiwara, Michiko
Sakers, Don 1958- *72*
Sakharnov, S.
  See Sakharnov, Svyatoslav
Sakharnov, Svyatoslav 1923- *65*
Sakharnov, Svyatoslav Vladimirovich
  See Sakharnov, Svyatoslav
Saksena, Kate *148*
Sakurai, Gail 1952- *153*
  Earlier sketch in SATA *87*
Salassi, Otto R(ussell) 1939-1993 .... *38*
  Obituary *77*
Salat, Cristina *82*
Saldutti, Denise 1953- *39*
Sale, Tim 1956- *153*
Salem, Kay 1952- *92*
Salerno, Steven *176*
Salinger, J.D. 1919- *67*
  See also CLR *18*
Salinger, Jerome David
  See Salinger, J.D.
Salisbury, Graham 1944- *161*
  Earlier sketches in SATA *76, 108*
Salisbury, Joyce E(llen) 1944- *138*
Salkey, (Felix) Andrew (Alexander) 1928-1995
  .... *118*
  Earlier sketch in SATA *35*
Salley, Coleen *166*
Sallis, Susan (Diana) 1929- *55*
Salmon, Annie Elizabeth 1899- *13*
Salsi, Lynn 1947- *130*
Salsitz, R. A. V.
  See Salsitz, Rhondi Vilott
Salsitz, Rhondi Vilott *115*
  See Salsitz, R. A. V.
Salten, Felix
  See Salzmann, Siegmund
Salter, Cedric
  See Knight, Francis Edgar
Saltman, Judith 1947- *64*
Saltzberg, Barney 1955- *135*
Saltzman, David (Charles Laertes) 1967-1990
  .... *86*
Salvadori, Mario (George) 1907-1997 .... *97*
  Earlier sketch in SATA *40*
Salwood, F. K.
  See Kilworth, Garry
Salzer, L. E.
  See Wilson, Lionel
Salzman, Marian 1959- *77*
Salzmann, Siegmund 1869-1945 .... *25*
  See Salten, Felix
Samachson, Dorothy (Mirkin) 1914-1997 ..... *3*
Samachson, Joseph 1906-1980 .... *3*
  Obituary *52*
Sammis, John 1942- *4*
Sampson, Emma (Keats) Speed 1868-1947
  .... *68*
Sampson, Fay (Elizabeth) 1935- *151*
  Brief entry *40*
  Earlier sketch in SATA *42*
Sampson, Michael 1952- *143*
  Earlier sketch in SATA *95*
Samson, Anne S(tringer) 1933- *2*
Samson, Joan 1937-1976 .... *13*
Samson, Suzanne M. 1959- *91*
Samuels, Charles 1902-1982 .... *12*
Samuels, Cynthia K(alish) 1946- *79*
Samuels, Gertrude 1910(?)-2003 .... *17*
  Obituary *147*
Sanborn, Duane 1914-1996 .... *38*
Sancha, Sheila 1924- *38*
Sanchez, Alex 1957- *151*
Sanchez, Sonia 1934- *136*
  Earlier sketch in SATA *22*
  See also CLR *18*
Sanchez-Silva, Jose Maria 1911- *132*
  Earlier sketch in SATA *16*
  See also CLR *12*
Sand, George X. *45*

Sandak, Cass R(obert) 1950-2001 .... *51*
  Brief entry *37*
Sandberg, (Karin) Inger 1930- *15*
Sandberg, Karl C. 1931- *35*
Sandberg, Lasse (E. M.) 1924- *15*
Sandburg, Carl (August) 1878-1967 .... *8*
  See also CLR *67*
Sandburg, Charles
  See Sandburg, Carl (August)
Sandburg, Charles A.
  See Sandburg, Carl (August)
Sandburg, Helga 1918- *3*
  See also SAAS *10*
Sandell, Lisa Ann 1977- *175*
Sander, Heather L. 1947- *157*
Sanderlin, George 1915- *4*
Sanderlin, Owenita (Harrah) 1916- *11*
Sanders, Betty Jane
  See Monthei, Betty
Sanders, Nancy I. 1960- *141*
  Earlier sketch in SATA *90*
Sanders, Scott Russell 1945- *109*
  Earlier sketch in SATA *56*
Sanders, Winston P.
  See Anderson, Poul
Sanderson, Irma 1912- *66*
Sanderson, Ivan T(erence) 1911-1973 .... *6*
Sanderson, Margaret Love
  See Keats, Emma
  and Sampson, Emma (Keats) Speed
Sanderson, Ruth 1951- *172*
  Earlier sketches in SATA *41, 109*
Sanderson, Ruth L.
  See Sanderson, Ruth
Sandin, Joan 1942- *153*
  Earlier sketches in SATA *12, 94*
Sandison, Janet
  See Cameron, Elizabeth Jane
Sandler, Martin W. *160*
Sandoz, Mari(e Susette) 1900-1966 .... *5*
Sanford, Agnes (White) 1897-1976 .... *61*
Sanford, Doris 1937- *69*
Sanger, Marjory Bartlett 1920- *8*
San Jose, Christine 1929- *167*
Sankey, Alice (Ann-Susan) 1910- *27*
San Souci, Daniel *96*
San Souci, Robert D. 1946- *158*
  Earlier sketches in SATA *40, 81, 117*
  See also CLR *43*
Santiago, Esmeralda 1948- *129*
Santos, Helen
  See Griffiths, Helen
Santrey, Louis
  See Sabin, Louis
Santucci, Barbara 1948- *130*
Sapergia, Barbara 1943- *181*
Sapieyevski, Anne Lindbergh 1940-1993 ... *78*
  Earlier sketch in SATA *35*
  See Feydy, Anne Lindbergh
  and Lindbergh, Anne
Saport, Linda 1954- *123*
Sapp, Allen 1929- *151*
Sarac, Roger
  See Caras, Roger A(ndrew)
Sarah, Duchess of York
  See Ferguson, Sarah
Sarasin, Jennifer
  See Sachs, Judith
Sarg, Anthony Frederick
  See Sarg, Tony
Sarg, Tony 1882-1942
  See YABC *1*
Sargent, Pamela 1948- *78*
  Earlier sketch in SATA *29*
Sargent, Robert 1933- *2*
Sargent, Sarah 1937- *44*
  Brief entry *41*
Sargent, Shirley 1927-2004 .... *11*
Sarnoff, Jane 1937- *10*
Saroyan, William 1908-1981 .... *23*
  Obituary *24*

Sarton, Eleanor May
See Sarton, May
Sarton, May 1912-1995 .... *36*
  Obituary *86*
Saseen, Sharon (Dillon) 1949- *59*
Sasek, Miroslav 1916-1980 .... *16*
  Obituary *23*
  See also CLR 4
Sasso, Sandy Eisenberg 1947- *162*
  Earlier sketches in SATA *86, 116*
Sathre, Vivian 1952- *133*
  Earlier sketch in SATA *79*
Satterfield, Charles
  See del Rey, Lester
  and Pohl, Frederik
Sattgast, L. J.
  See Sattgast, Linda J.
Sattgast, Linda J. 1953- *91*
Sattler, Helen Roney 1921-1992 .... *74*
  Earlier sketch in SATA *4*
  See also CLR 24
Sauer, Julia Lina 1891-1983 .... *32*
  Obituary *36*
Sauerwein, Leigh 1944- *155*
Saul, Carol P. 1947- *117*
  Earlier sketch in SATA *78*
Saul, John (W. III) 1942- *98*
Saul, (Ellen) Wendy 1946- *42*
Saulnier, Karen Luczak 1940- *80*
Saunders, Caleb
  See Heinlein, Robert A.
Saunders, Dave 1939- *85*
Saunders, Julie 1939- *85*
Saunders, (William) Keith 1910-1994 .... *12*
Saunders, Rubie (Agnes) 1929- *21*
Saunders, Susan 1945- *96*
  Brief entry *41*
  Earlier sketch in SATA *46*
Saunders-Smith, Gail 1952- *169*
Sauvain, Philip Arthur 1933- *111*
Savadier, Elivia 1950- *164*
  Earlier sketch in SATA *79*
Savage, Alan
  See Nicole, Christopher (Robin)
Savage, Blake
  See Goodwin, Harold L(eland)
Savage, Candace (M.) 1949- *142*
Savage, Deborah 1955- *76*
Savage, Jeff 1961- *97*
Savageau, Cheryl 1950- *96*
Savery, Constance (Winifred) 1897-1999 ..... *1*
Saville, Andrew
  See Taylor, Andrew
Saville, (Leonard) Malcolm 1901-1982 ...... *23*
  Obituary *31*
Saviozzi, Adriana
  See Mazza, Adriana
Savitt, Sam 1917(?)-2000 .... *8*
  Obituary *126*
Savitz, Harriet May 1933- *72*
  Earlier sketch in SATA *5*
  See also SAAS 26
Sawicki, Mary 1950- *90*
Sawyer, (Frederick) Don(ald) 1947- *72*
Sawyer, Kem Knapp 1953- *84*
Sawyer, Robert J. 1960- *149*
  Earlier sketch in SATA *81*
Sawyer, Robert James
  See Sawyer, Robert J.
Sawyer, Ruth 1880-1970 .... *17*
  See also CLR 36
Saxby, H. M.
  See Saxby, (Henry) Maurice
Saxby, (Henry) Maurice 1924- *71*
Saxon, Andrew
  See Arthur, Robert, (Jr.)
Saxon, Antonia
  See Sachs, Judith
Say, Allen 1937- *161*
  Earlier sketches in SATA *28, 69, 110*
  See also CLR 22

Sayers, Frances Clarke 1897-1989 .... *3*
  Obituary *62*
Sayles, Elizabeth 1956- *163*
  Earlier sketch in SATA *108*
Saylor-Marchant, Linda 1963- *82*
Sayre, April Pulley 1966- *131*
  Earlier sketch in SATA *88*
Sazer, Nina 1949- *13*
Scabrini, Janet 1953- *13*
Scagell, Robin 1946- *107*
Scagnetti, Jack 1924- *7*
Scamander, Newt
  See Rowling, J.K.
Scamell, Ragnhild 1940- *180*
  Earlier sketch in SATA *77*
Scanlon, Marion Stephany *11*
Scannell, Vernon 1922- *59*
Scarborough, Elizabeth *171*
  See Scarborough, Elizabeth Ann
Scarborough, Elizabeth Ann 1947- *171*
  Earlier sketch in SATA *98*
  See Scarborough, Elizabeth
Scarf, Maggi
  See Scarf, Maggie
Scarf, Maggie 1932- *5*
Scariano, Margaret M. 1924- *86*
Scarlett, Susan
  See Streatfeild, (Mary) Noel
Scarry, Huck
  See Scarry, Richard McClure, Jr.
Scarry, Patricia (Murphy) 1924- *2*
Scarry, Patsy
  See Scarry, Patricia (Murphy)
Scarry, Richard (McClure) 1919-1994 .... *75*
  Obituary *90*
  Earlier sketches in SATA *2, 35*
  See also CLR 41
Scarry, Richard McClure, Jr. 1953- *35*
Schachner, Judith Byron 1951- *178*
  Earlier sketch in SATA *88*
Schachner, Judy
  See Schachner, Judith Byron
Schachtel, Roger 1949- *38*
Schachtel, Roger Bernard
  See Schachtel, Roger
Schaedler, Sally *116*
Schaefer, Carole Lexa *173*
Schaefer, Jack (Warner) 1907-1991 .... *66*
  Obituary *65*
  Earlier sketch in SATA *3*
Schaefer, Lola M. 1950- *144*
  Earlier sketch in SATA *91*
Schaeffer, Mead 1898- *21*
Schaeffer, Susan Fromberg 1941- *22*
Schaer, Brigitte 1958- *112*
Schaller, George B(eals) 1933- *30*
Schanzer, Rosalyn (Good) 1942- *138*
  Earlier sketch in SATA *77*
Schatell, Brian *66*
  Brief entry *47*
Schechter, Betty (Goodstein) 1921- *5*
Schecter, Ellen 1944- *85*
Scheeder, Louis 1946- *141*
Scheer, Julian (Weisel) 1926-2001 .... *8*
Scheffer, Victor B(lanchard) 1906- *6*
Scheffler, Axel 1957- *180*
Scheffler, Ursel 1938- *81*
Scheffrin-Falk, Gladys 1928- *76*
Scheidl, Gerda Marie 1913- *85*
Scheier, Michael 1943- *40*
  Brief entry *36*
Schell, Mildred 1922- *41*
Schell, Orville (Hickok) 1940- *10*
Scheller, Melanie 1953- *77*
Schellie, Don 1932- *29*
Schembri, Jim 1962- *124*
Schemm, Mildred Walker 1905-1998 .... *21*
  Obituary *103*
  See Walker, Mildred
Schenker, Dona 1947- *133*
  Earlier sketch in SATA *68*

Scher, Paula 1948- *47*
Scherf, Margaret 1908-1979 .... *10*
Schermer, Judith (Denise) 1941- *30*
Schertle, Alice 1941- *145*
  Earlier sketches in SATA *36, 90*
Schick, Alice 1946- *27*
Schick, Eleanor 1942- *144*
  Earlier sketches in SATA *9, 82*
Schick, Joel 1945- *31*
  Brief entry *30*
Schields, Gretchen 1948- *75*
Schiff, Ken(neth Roy) 1942- *7*
Schiller, Andrew 1919- *21*
Schiller, Barbara (Heyman) 1928- *21*
Schiller, Pamela (Byrne) *127*
Schindel, John 1955- *115*
  Earlier sketch in SATA *77*
Schindelman, Joseph 1923- *67*
  Brief entry *32*
Schindler, S.D. 1952- *171*
  Brief entry *50*
  Earlier sketches in SATA *75, 118*
Schindler, Steven D.
  See Schindler, S.D.
Schinto, Jeanne 1951- *93*
Schisgall, Oscar 1901-1984 .... *12*
  Obituary *38*
Schlaepfer, Gloria G. 1931- *154*
Schlee, Ann 1934- *44*
  Brief entry *36*
Schleichert, Elizabeth 1945- *77*
Schlein, Miriam 1926-2004 .... *130*
  Obituary *159*
  Earlier sketches in SATA *2, 87*
  See also CLR 41
Schlesinger, Arthur M., Jr. 1917-2007 .... *61*
  Obituary *181*
  See Schlesinger, Arthur Meier
Schlesinger, Arthur Meier 1888-1965
Schlessinger, Laura (Catherine) 1947- *160*
  Earlier sketch in SATA *110*
Schloat, G. Warren, Jr. 1914-2000 .... *4*
Schmid, Eleonore 1939- *126*
  Earlier sketches in SATA *12, 84*
Schmiderer, Dorothy 1940- *19*
Schmidt, Annie M. G. 1911-1995 .... *67*
  Obituary *91*
  See also CLR 22
Schmidt, Diane 1953- *70*
Schmidt, Elizabeth 1915- *15*
Schmidt, Gary D. 1957- *135*
  Earlier sketch in SATA *93*
Schmidt, James Norman 1912-1983 .... *21*
Schmidt, Karen Lee 1953- *94*
Schmidt, Lynette 1952- *76*
Schneider, Antonie 1954- *167*
  Earlier sketch in SATA *89*
Schneider, Christine M. 1972(?)- *171*
  Earlier sketch in SATA *120*
Schneider, Dick
  See Schneider, Richard H.
Schneider, Elisa
  See Kleven, Elisa
Schneider, Herman 1905-2003 .... *7*
  Obituary *148*
Schneider, Howie -2007 .... *181*
Schneider, Laurie
  See Adams, Laurie
Schneider, Nina 1913- *2*
Schneider, Rex 1937- *44*
Schneider, Richard H. 1922- *171*
Schneider, Richard Henry
  See Schneider, Richard H.
Schnirel, James R. 1931- *14*
Schnitter, Jane T. 1958- *88*
Schnitzlein, Danny *134*
Schnur, Steven 1952- *144*
  Earlier sketch in SATA *95*
Schoberle, Cecile 1949- *80*
Schock, Pauline 1928- *45*
Schoell, William 1951- *160*

Schoen, Barbara (Taylor) 1924-1993 .... *13*
Schoenherr, Ian *177*
Schoenherr, John (Carl) 1935- *66*
    Earlier sketch in SATA *37*
    See also SAAS *13*
Schofield, Sandy
    See Rusch, Kristine Kathryn
Scholastica, Sister Mary
    See Jenkins, Marie M(agdalen)
Scholefield, A. T.
    See Scholefield, Alan
Scholefield, Alan 1931- *66*
Scholefield, Edmund O.
    See Griffin, W.E.B.
Scholey, Arthur 1932- *28*
Schone, Virginia *22*
Schongut, Emanuel 1936- *52*
    Brief entry *36*
Schoonover, Frank (Earle) 1877-1972 .... *24*
Schoor, Gene 1921- *3*
Schories, Pat 1952- *164*
    Earlier sketch in SATA *116*
Schott, Jane A. 1946- *172*
Schotter, Roni *149*
    Earlier sketch in SATA *105*
Schraff, Anne E(laine) 1939- *92*
    Earlier sketch in SATA *27*
Schram, Peninnah 1934- *119*
Schrecengost, Maity 1938- *118*
Schrecengost, S. Maitland
    See Schrecengost, Maity
Schrecker, Judie 1954- *90*
Schreiber, Elizabeth Anne (Ferguson) 1947-
    .... *13*
Schreiber, Ralph W(alter) 1942- *13*
Schreiner, Samuel A(gnew), Jr. 1921- *70*
Schroeder, Alan 1961- *98*
    Earlier sketch in SATA *66*
Schroeder, Binette
    See Nickl, Barbara (Elisabeth)
Schroeder, Russell (K.) 1943- *146*
Schubert, Dieter 1947- *101*
    Earlier sketch in SATA *62*
Schubert, Leda 1950(?)- *181*
Schubert-Gabrys, Ingrid 1953- *101*
    Earlier sketch in SATA *62*
Schuerger, Michele R. *110*
Schuett, Stacey 1960- *168*
    Earlier sketch in SATA *75*
Schulke, Flip Phelps Graeme 1930- *57*
Schulman, Arlene 1961- *105*
Schulman, Janet 1933- *137*
    Earlier sketch in SATA *22*
Schulman, L(ester) M(artin) 1934- *13*
Schulte, Elaine L(ouise) 1934- *36*
Schultz, Betty K(epka) 1932- *125*
Schultz, Gwendolyn *21*
Schultz, James Willard 1859-1947
    See YABC *1*
Schultz, Pearle Henriksen 1918- *21*
Schulz, Charles M. 1922-2000 .... *10*
    Obituary *118*
Schulz, Charles Monroe
    See Schulz, Charles M.
Schumaker, Ward 1943- *96*
Schuman, Michael A. 1953- *134*
    Earlier sketch in SATA *85*
Schur, Maxine
    See Schur, Maxine Rose
Schur, Maxine Rose 1948- *135*
    Autobiography Feature *135*
    Brief entry *49*
    Earlier sketches in SATA *53, 98*
Schurfranz, Vivian 1925- *13*
Schutzer, A. I. 1922- *13*
Schuyler, Pamela R. 1948- *30*
Schwager, Tina 1964- *110*
Schwandt, Stephen (William) 1947- *61*
Schwark, Mary Beth 1954- *51*

Schwartz, Alvin 1927-1992 .... *56*
    Obituary *71*
    Earlier sketch in SATA *4*
    See also CLR *89*
Schwartz, Amy 1954- *131*
    Brief entry *41*
    Earlier sketches in SATA *47, 83*
    See also CLR *25*
    See also SAAS *18*
Schwartz, Anne Powers 1913-1987 .... *10*
Schwartz, Carol 1954- *77*
Schwartz, Charles W(alsh) 1914- *8*
Schwartz, David M. 1951- *110*
    Earlier sketch in SATA *59*
Schwartz, David Martin
    See Schwartz, David M.
Schwartz, Elizabeth Reeder 1912- *8*
Schwartz, Ellen 1949- *117*
Schwartz, Jerome L.
    See Lawrence, Jerome
Schwartz, Joel L. 1940- *54*
    Brief entry *51*
Schwartz, Joyce R. 1950- *93*
Schwartz, Julius 1907-2004 .... *45*
Schwartz, Perry 1942- *75*
Schwartz, Sheila (Ruth) 1929- *27*
Schwartz, Stephen (Lawrence) 1948- *19*
Schwartz, Virginia Frances 1950- *131*
Schwarz, (Silvia Tessa) Viviane 1977- *141*
Schweitzer, Byrd Baylor
    See Baylor, Byrd
Schweitzer, Iris *59*
    Brief entry *36*
Schweninger, Ann 1951- *168*
    Earlier sketches in SATA *29, 98*
Schwerin, Doris H(alpern) 1922- *64*
Scieszka, Jon 1954- *160*
    Earlier sketches in SATA *68, 105*
    See also CLR *107*
Scillian, Devin *128*
Scioscia, Mary (Hershey) 1926- *63*
Scofield, Penrod 1933- *62*
    Obituary *78*
Scoggin, Margaret C(lara) 1905-1968 .... *47*
    Brief entry *28*
Scoltock, Jack 1942- *141*
    Earlier sketch in SATA *72*
Scoppettone, Sandra 1936- *92*
    Earlier sketch in SATA *9*
    See Early, Jack
Scot, Michael
    See Rohan, Michael Scott
Scot-Bernard, P.
    See Bernard, Patricia
Scotland, Jay
    See Jakes, John
Scott, Alastair
    See Allen, Kenneth S.
Scott, Ann Herbert 1926- *140*
    Autobiography Feature *140*
    Brief entry *29*
    Earlier sketches in SATA *56, 94*
Scott, Bill
    See Scott, William N(eville)
Scott, Cora Annett (Pipitone) 1931- *11*
Scott, Dan
    See Barker, S(quire) Omar
Scott, Elaine 1940- *164*
    Earlier sketches in SATA *36, 90*
Scott, Jack Denton 1915-1995 .... *83*
    Earlier sketch in SATA *31*
    See also CLR *20*
    See also SAAS *14*
Scott, Jane (Harrington) 1931- *55*
Scott, Jessica
    See De Wire, Elinor
Scott, John 1912-1976 .... *14*
Scott, John Anthony 1916- *23*
Scott, John M(artin) 1913- *12*
Scott, Mary
    See Mattern, Joanne

Scott, Melissa 1960- *109*
Scott, Richard
    See Rennert, Richard Scott
Scott, Roney
    See Gault, William Campbell
Scott, Sally 1909-1978 .... *43*
Scott, Sally 1948- *44*
Scott, Sally Elisabeth
    See Scott, Sally
Scott, W. N.
    See Scott, William N(eville)
Scott, Sir Walter 1771-1832
    See YABC *2*
Scott, Warwick
    See Trevor, Elleston
Scott, William N(eville) 1923- *87*
Scotti, Anna
    See Coates, Anna
Scotton, Rob 1960- *177*
Scribner, Charles, Jr. 1921-1995 .... *13*
    Obituary *87*
Scribner, Joanne L. 1949- *33*
Scribner, Kimball 1917- *63*
Scrimger, Richard 1957- *164*
    Earlier sketch in SATA *119*
Scroder, Walter K. 1928- *82*
Scruggs, Sandy 1961- *89*
Scudder, Brooke 1959- *154*
Scull, Marie-Louise 1943-1993 .... *77*
Scuro, Vincent 1951- *21*
Seabrooke, Brenda 1941- *148*
    Earlier sketches in SATA *30, 88*
Seaman, Augusta Huiell 1879-1950 .... *31*
Seamands, Ruth 1916- *9*
Searcy, Margaret Zehmer 1926- *54*
    Brief entry *39*
Searight, Mary W(illiams) 1918- *17*
Searle, Kathryn Adrienne 1942- *10*
Searle, Ronald (William Fordham) 1920- ... *70*
    Earlier sketch in SATA *42*
Sears, Stephen W. 1932- *4*
Sebastian, Lee
    See Silverberg, Robert
Sebestyen, Igen
    See Sebestyen, Ouida
Sebestyen, Ouida 1924- *140*
    Earlier sketch in SATA *39*
    See also CLR *17*
    See also SAAS *10*
Sebrey, Mary Ann 1951- *62*
Sechrist, Elizabeth Hough 1903-1991 .... *2*
Sedges, John
    See Buck, Pearl S(ydenstricker)
Sedgwick, Marcus 1968- *160*
Seed, Cecile Eugenie 1930- *86*
    See Seed, Jenny
Seed, Jenny *8*
    See also CLR *76*
    See Seed, Cecile Eugenie
Seeger, Laura Vaccaro *172*
Seeger, Pete 1919- *139*
    Earlier sketch in SATA *13*
Seeger, Peter R.
    See Seeger, Pete
Seeley, Laura L. 1958- *71*
Seever, R.
    See Reeves, Lawrence F.
Sefozo, Mary 1925- *82*
Sefton, Catherine
    See Waddell, Martin
Segal, John *178*
Segal, Joyce 1940- *35*
Segal, Lore 1928- *163*
    Earlier sketches in SATA *4, 66*
    See also SAAS *11*
Segal, Lore Groszmann
    See Segal, Lore
Segar, E(lzie) C(risler) 1894-1938 .... *61*
Seguin, Marilyn W(eymouth) 1951- *91*
Seguin-Fontes, Marthe 1924- *109*

Seibold, J. Otto 1960- 149
  Earlier sketch in SATA 83
  See also SAAS 22
Seidel, Ross 95
Seidelman, James Edward 1926- 6
Seiden, Art(hur) 107
  Brief entry 42
Seidler, Ann (G.) 1925- 131
Seidler, Tor 1952- 149
  Brief entry 46
  Earlier sketches in SATA 52, 98
Seidman, Laurence Ivan 1925- 15
Seigel, Kalman 1917-1998 12
  Obituary 103
Seignobosc, Françoise 1897-1961 21
Seinfeld, Jerry 1954- 146
Seitz, Jacqueline 1931- 50
Seixas, Judith S. 1922- 17
Sejima, Yoshimasa 1913- 8
Selberg, Ingrid (Maria) 1950- 68
Selden, George
  See CLR 8
  See Thompson, George Selden
Selden, Neil R(oy) 1931- 61
Self, Margaret Cabell 1902-1996 24
Selig, Sylvie 1942- 13
Sellers, Naomi
  See Flack, Naomi John White
Selman, LaRue W. 1927- 55
Selsam, Millicent E(llis) 1912-1996 29
  Obituary 92
  Earlier sketch in SATA 1
  See also CLR 1
Seltzer, Meyer 1932- 17
Seltzer, Richard 1946- 41
Seltzer, Richard Warren, Jr.
  See Seltzer, Richard
Selvadurai, Shyam 1965(?)- 171
Selway, Martina 1940- 169
  Earlier sketch in SATA 74
Selznick, Brian 1966- 171
  Earlier sketches in SATA 79, 117
Semel, Nava 1954- 107
Semloh
  See Holmes, Peggy
Sendak, Jack 1924(?)-1995 28
Sendak, Maurice 1928- 165
  Earlier sketches in SATA 1, 27, 113
  See also CLR 74
Sendak, Maurice Bernard
  See Sendak, Maurice
Sender, Ruth M(insky) 1926- 62
Sengler, Johanna 1924- 18
Senisi, Ellen B. 1951- 116
Senisi, Ellen Babinec
  See Senisi, Ellen B.
Senn, J(oyce) A(nn) 1941- 115
Senn, Steve 1950- 60
  Brief entry 48
Serage, Nancy 1924- 10
Seredy, Kate 1899-1975 1
  Obituary 24
  See also CLR 10
Seroff, Victor I(ilyitch) 1902-1979 12
  Obituary 26
Serraillier, Ian (Lucien) 1912-1994 73
  Obituary 83
  Earlier sketch in SATA 1
  See also CLR 2
  See also SAAS 3
Serros, Michele 175
Serros, Michele M.
  See Serros, Michele
Servello, Joe 1932- 10
Service, Pamela F. 1945- 64
Service, Robert
  See Service, Robert W(illiam)
Service, Robert W(illiam) 1874(?)-1958 20
  See Service, Robert
Serwadda, W(illiam) Moses 1931- 27

Serwer-Bernstein, Blanche L(uria) 1910-1997
  10
Sescoe, Vincent E. 1938- 123
Seth, Mary
  See Lexau, Joan M.
Seton, Anya 1904(?)-1990 3
  Obituary 66
Seton, Ernest (Evan) Thompson 1860-1946
  18
  See also CLR 59
Seton-Thompson, Ernest
  See Seton, Ernest (Evan) Thompson
Seuling, Barbara 1937- 145
  Earlier sketches in SATA 10, 98
  See also SAAS 24
Seuss, Dr.
  See Dr. Seuss
  and Geisel, Theodor Seuss
  and LeSieg, Theo.
  and Stone, Rosetta
Severn, Bill
  See Severn, William Irving
Severn, David
  See Unwin, David S(torr)
Severn, William Irving 1914- 1
Sewall, Marcia 1935- 119
  Earlier sketches in SATA 37, 69
Seward, Prudence 1926- 16
Sewell, Anna 1820-1878 100
  Earlier sketch in SATA 24
  See also CLR 17
Sewell, Helen (Moore) 1896-1957 38
Sexton, Anne (Harvey) 1928-1974 10
Seymour, Alta Halverson 10
Seymour, Jane 1951- 139
Seymour, Tres 1966- 164
  Earlier sketch in SATA 82
Shachtman, Tom 1942- 49
Shackleton, C. C.
  See Aldiss, Brian W.
Shader, Rachel
  See Sofer, Barbara
Shadow, Jak
  See Sutherland, Jon
Shadyland, Sal
  See Cooper, Louise
Shafer, Robert E(ugene) 1925- 9
Shaffer, Terea 1968- 79
Shahan, Sherry 1949- 134
  Earlier sketch in SATA 92
Shahn, Bernarda Bryson
  See Bryson, Bernarda
Shaik, Fatima 114
Shalant, Phyllis 1949- 150
Shan, Darren 1972- 168
  Earlier sketch in SATA 129
Shanberg, Karen
  See Shragg, Karen (I.)
Shane, Harold Gray 1914-1993 36
  Obituary 76
Shange, Ntozake 1948- 157
Shanks, Ann Zane (Kushner) 10
Shannon, David 1959- 152
  Earlier sketch in SATA 107
  See also CLR 87
Shannon, George (William Bones) 1952- . 143
  Earlier sketches in SATA 35, 94
Shannon, Jacqueline 63
Shannon, Margaret
  See Silverwood, Margaret Shannon
Shannon, Monica 1905(?)-1965 28
Shannon, Terry 21
  See Mercer, Jessie
Shannon, Terry Miller 1951- 148
Shapiro, Irwin 1911-1981 32
Shapiro, Milton J. 1926- 32
Shapiro, Tricia
  See Andryszewski, Tricia
Shapp, Martha Glauber 1910- 3
Sharfman, Amalie 14
Sharma, Partap 1939- 15

Sharma, Rashmi
  See Singh, Rashmi Sharma
Sharman, Alison
  See Leonard, Alison
Sharmat, Marjorie Weinman 1928- 133
  Earlier sketches in SATA 4, 33, 74
Sharmat, Mitchell 1927- 127
  Earlier sketch in SATA 33
Sharp, Anne Wallace 1947- 144
Sharp, Luke
  See Alkiviades, Alkis
Sharp, Margery 1905-1991 29
  Obituary 67
  Earlier sketch in SATA 1
  See also CLR 27
Sharpe, Jon
  See Duncan, Alice
  and Knott, William C(ecil, Jr.)
  and Messman, Jon
Sharpe, Mitchell R(aymond) 1924- 12
Sharpe, Susan 1946- 71
Sharratt, Nick 1962- 153
  Earlier sketch in SATA 104
Shasha, Mark 1961- 80
Shattuck, Roger 1923-2005 64
  Obituary 174
Shattuck, Roger Whitney
  See Shattuck, Roger
Shaw, Arnold 1909-1989 4
  Obituary 63
Shaw, Carolyn V. 1934- 91
Shaw, Charles (Green) 1892-1974 13
Shaw, Evelyn S. 1927- 28
Shaw, Flora Louisa
  See Lugard, Flora Louisa Shaw
Shaw, Janet 1937- 146
  Earlier sketch in SATA 61
  See also CLR 96
Shaw, Janet Beeler
  See Shaw, Janet
Shaw, Lisa
  See Rogak, Lisa
Shaw, Margret 1940- 68
Shaw, Mary 1965- 180
Shaw, Nancy 1946- 162
  Earlier sketch in SATA 71
Shaw, Ray 7
Shaw, Richard 1923- 12
Shawn, Frank S.
  See Goulart, Ron(ald Joseph)
Shay, Art
  See Shay, Arthur
Shay, Arthur 1922- 4
Shay, Lacey
  See Shebar, Sharon Sigmond
Shea, George 1940- 54
  Brief entry 42
Shea, Pegi Deitz 1960- 172
  Earlier sketches in SATA 77, 137
Shearer, John 1947- 43
  Brief entry 27
  See also CLR 34
Shearer, Ted 1919- 43
Shebar, Sharon Sigmond 1945- 36
Shecter, Ben 1935- 16
Shedd, Warner 1934- 147
  Earlier sketch in SATA 87
Sheedy, Alexandra Elizabeth 1962- 39
  Earlier sketch in SATA 19
Sheehan, Ethna 1908-2000 9
Sheehan, Patty 1945- 77
Sheehan, Sean 1951- 154
  Earlier sketch in SATA 86
Sheen, Barbara 1949- 143
Shefelman, Janice Jordan 1930- 129
  Earlier sketch in SATA 58
Shefelman, Tom (Whitehead) 1927- 58
Sheffer, H. R.
  See Abels, Harriette S(heffer)
Sheffield, Charles 1935-2002 109
Sheffield, Janet N. 1926- 26

Sheikh, Nazneen
  See Sadiq, Nazneen
Shekerjian, Regina Tor 16
Shelby, Anne 1948- 85
  Autobiography Feature 121
  See also SAAS 26
Sheldon, Ann 67
  Earlier sketch in SATA 1
Sheldon, Ann
  See Antle, Nancy
Sheldon, Aure 1917-1976 12
Sheldon, Dyan 181
Sheldon, John
  See Bloch, Robert (Albert)
Sheldon, Muriel 1926- 45
  Brief entry 39
Shell, Barry 1951- 176
Shelley, Frances
  See Wees, Frances Shelley
Shelley, Mary Wollstonecraft (Godwin)
  1797-1851 29
Shelton, William Roy 1919-1995 5
  Obituary 129
Shemie, Bonnie (Jean Brenner) 1949- 96
Shemin, Margaretha (Hoeneveld) 1928- 4
Shen, Michele 1953- 173
Shenker, Michele
  See Shen, Michele
Shenton, Edward 1895-1977 45
Shepard, Aaron 1950- 113
  Earlier sketch in SATA 75
Shepard, Ernest Howard 1879-1976 100
  Obituary 24
  Earlier sketches in SATA 3, 33
  See also CLR 27
Shepard, James R.
  See Shepard, Jim
Shepard, Jim 1956- 164
  Earlier sketch in SATA 90
Shepard, Mary
  See Knox, (Mary) Eleanor Jessie
Shephard, Esther 1891-1975 5
  Obituary 26
Shepherd, Donna Walsh
  See Walsh Shepherd, Donna
Shepherd, Elizabeth 4
Shepherd, Irana 173
Shepherd, Roni
  See Shepherd, Irana
Shepperson, Rob 178
Sherburne, Zoa (Lillian Morin) 1912-1995 ... 3
  See also SAAS 18
Sherlock, Patti 71
Sherman, D(enis) R(onald) 1934- 48
  Brief entry 29
Sherman, Diane (Finn) 1928- 12
Sherman, Elizabeth
  See Friskey, Margaret (Richards)
Sherman, Harold (Morrow) 1898-1987 37
  Obituary 137
Sherman, Josepha 163
  Earlier sketch in SATA 75
Sherman, Michael
  See Lowndes, Robert A(ugustine) W(ard)
Sherman, Nancy
  See Rosenberg, Nancy (Sherman)
Sherman, Pat 174
Sherman, Peter Michael
  See Lowndes, Robert A(ugustine) W(ard)
Sherrard, Valerie (Anne) 1957- 141
Sherrod, Jane
  See Singer, Jane Sherrod
Sherry, Clifford J. 1943- 84
Sherry, (Dulcie) Sylvia 1932- 122
  Earlier sketch in SATA 8
Sherwan, Earl 1917- 3
Sherwood, Jonathan
  See London, Jonathan (Paul)
Shetterly, Will 1955- 78
  Autobiography Feature 106

Shetterly, William Howard
  See Shetterly, Will
Shiefman, Vicky 1942- 22
Shields, Brenda Desmond (Armstrong) 1914-
  37
Shields, Carol Diggory 174
Shields, Charles 1944- 10
Shiels, Barbara
  See Adams, Barbara Johnston
Shiffman, Lena 1957- 101
Shiina, Makoto 1944- 83
Shimin, Symeon 1902-1984 13
Shine, Andrea 1955- 104
Shine, Deborah 1932- 71
Shinn, Everett 1876-1953 21
Shinn, Sharon 1957- 164
  Earlier sketch in SATA 110
Shippen, Katherine B(inney) 1892-1980 1
  Obituary 23
  See also CLR 36
Shippey, T(homas) A(lan) 1943- 143
Shipton, Eric Earle 1907-1977 10
Shiraz, Yasmin 173
Shirer, William L(awrence) 1904-1993 45
  Obituary 78
Shirley, Gayle C 1955- 96
Shirley, Gayle Corbett
  See Shirley, Gayle C
Shirley, Jean 1919- 70
Shirreffs, Gordon D(onald) 1914-1996 11
Shirts, Morris A(lpine) 1922- 63
Shlichta, Joe 1968- 84
Shmurak, Carole B. 1944- 118
Shore, Diane Z. 179
Shore, Diane ZuHone
  See Shore, Diane Z.
Shore, June Lewis 30
Shore, Nancy 1960- 124
Shore, Robert 1924- 39
Short, Michael 1937- 65
Short, Roger
  See Arkin, Alan
Shortall, Leonard W. 19
Shortt, Tim(othy Donald) 1961- 96
Shotwell, Louisa Rossiter 1902-1993 3
Shoup, Barbara 1947- 156
  Earlier sketch in SATA 86
  See also SAAS 24
Showalter, Jean B(reckinridge) 12
Showell, Ellen Harvey 1934- 33
Showers, Paul C. 1910-1999 92
  Obituary 114
  Earlier sketch in SATA 21
  See also CLR 6
  See also SAAS 7
Shpakow, Tanya 1959(?)- 94
Shpitalnik, Vladimir 1964- 83
Shragg, Karen (I.) 1954- 142
Shreeve, Elizabeth 1956- 156
Shreve, Susan
  See Shreve, Susan Richards
Shreve, Susan Richards 1939- 152
  Brief entry 41
  Earlier sketches in SATA 46, 95
Shriver, Jean Adair 1932- 75
Shriver, Maria 1955- 134
Shriver, Maria Owings
  See Shriver, Maria
Shrode, Mary
  See Hollingsworth, Mary
Shtainmets, Leon 32
Shub, Elizabeth 1915(?)-2004 5
Shuken, Julia 1948- 84
Shulevitz, Uri 1935- 165
  Earlier sketches in SATA 3, 50, 106
  See also CLR 61
Shulman, Alix Kates 1932- 7
Shulman, Dee 1957- 146
Shulman, Irving 1913-1995 13
Shulman, Neil B(arnett) 1945- 89

Shumsky, Zena
  See Collier, Zena
Shura, Mary Francis
  See Craig, Mary (Francis) Shura
Shusterman, Neal 1962- 140
  Autobiography Feature 140
  Earlier sketches in SATA 85, 121
Shuter, Jane (Margaret) 1955- 151
  Earlier sketch in SATA 90
Shuttlesworth, Dorothy Edwards 3
Shwartz, Susan (Martha) 1949- 94
Shyer, Christopher 1961- 98
Shyer, Marlene Fanta 13
Siberell, Anne 29
Sibley, Don 1922- 12
Siburt, Ruth 1951- 121
Siculan, Daniel 1922- 12
Sidgwick, Ethel 1877-1970 116
Sidjakov, Nicolas 1924- 18
Sidman, Joyce 1956- 181
  Earlier sketch in SATA 145
Sidney, Frank
  See Warwick, Alan R(oss)
Sidney, Margaret
  See Lothrop, Harriet Mulford Stone
Siegal, Aranka 1930- 88
  Brief entry 37
Siegel, Beatrice 36
Siegel, Helen
  See Siegl, Helen
Siegel, Robert (Harold) 1939- 39
Siegelson, Kim L. 1962- 114
Siegl, Helen 1924- 34
Siepmann, Mary Aline
  See Wesley, Mary (Aline)
Sierra, Judy 1945- 162
  Earlier sketch in SATA 104
Sieswerda, Paul L. 1942- 147
Sievert, Terri
  See Dougherty, Terri (L.)
Silas
  See McCay, (Zenas) Winsor
Silcock, Sara Lesley 1947- 12
Sill, Cathryn 1953- 141
  Earlier sketch in SATA 74
Sill, John 1947- 140
  Earlier sketch in SATA 74
Sillitoe, Alan 1928- 61
Sills, Leslie (Elka) 1948- 129
Silly, E. S.
  See Kraus, (Herman) Robert
Silsbe, Brenda 1953- 73
Silva, Joseph
  See Goulart, Ron(ald Joseph)
Silver, Ruth
  See Chew, Ruth
Silverberg, Robert 1935- 91
  Autobiography Feature 104
  Earlier sketch in SATA 13
  See also CLR 59
Silverman, Erica 1955- 165
  Earlier sketches in SATA 78, 112
Silverman, Janis L. 1946- 127
Silverman, Mel(vin Frank) 1931-1966 9
Silverman, Robin L. 1954- 96
Silverman, Robin Landew
  See Silverman, Robin L.
Silverstein, Alvin 1933- 124
  Earlier sketches in SATA 8, 69
  See also CLR 25
Silverstein, Herma 1945- 106
Silverstein, Robert Alan 1959- 124
  Earlier sketch in SATA 77
Silverstein, Shel 1932-1999 92
  Brief entry 27
  Obituary 116
  Earlier sketch in SATA 33
  See also CLR 96
Silverstein, Sheldon Allan
  See Silverstein, Shel

Stock, Catherine 1952- *158*
Earlier sketches in SATA *65, 114*
Stockdale, Susan 1954- *98*
Stockham, Peter (Alan) 1928- *57*
Stockton, Francis Richard 1834-1902 .... *44*
See Stockton, Frank R.
Stockton, Frank R.
Brief entry *32*
See Stockton, Francis Richard
Stockwell-Moniz, Marc J. 1954- *164*
Stoddard, Edward G. 1923- *10*
Stoddard, Hope 1900-1987 .... *6*
Stoddard, Sandol 1927- *98*
See Warburg, Sandol Stoddard
Stoehr, Shelley 1969- *107*
Stoeke, Janet Morgan 1957- *136*
Earlier sketch in SATA *90*
Stohner, Anu 1952- *179*
Stoiko, Michael 1919- *14*
Stojic, Manya 1967- *156*
Stoker, Abraham 1847-1912 .... *29*
See Stoker, Bram
Stoker, Bram
See Stoker, Abraham
Stokes, Cedric
See Beardmore, George
Stokes, Jack (Tilden) 1923- *13*
Stokes, Olivia Pearl 1916- *32*
Stolz, Mary 1920-2006 .... *133*
Obituary *180*
Earlier sketches in SATA *10, 71*
See also SAAS *3*
Stolz, Mary Slattery
See Stolz, Mary
Stone, Alan
See Svenson, Andrew E(dward)
Stone, David K(arl) 1922- *9*
Stone, David Lee 1978- *166*
Stone, Eugenia 1879-1971 .... *7*
Stone, Gene
See Stone, Eugenia
Stone, Helen V(irginia) *6*
Stone, Idella Purnell
See Purnell, Idella
Stone, Ikey
See Purnell, Idella
Stone, Irving 1903-1989 .... *3*
Obituary *64*
Stone, Jeff *178*
Stone, Jon 1931-1997 .... *39*
Obituary *95*
Stone, Josephine Rector
See Dixon, Jeanne
Stone, Lesley
See Trevor, Elleston
Stone, Peter 1930-2003 .... *65*
Obituary *143*
Stone, Phoebe *134*
Stone, Raymond *1*
Stone, Rosetta
See Dr. Seuss
and Geisel, Theodor Seuss
and LeSieg, Theo.
and Seuss, Dr.
Stonehouse, Bernard 1926- *140*
Earlier sketches in SATA *13, 80*
Stones, (Cyril) Anthony 1934- *72*
Stong, Phil(ip Duffield) 1899-1957 .... *32*
Stoops, Erik D(aniel) 1966- *142*
Earlier sketch in SATA *78*
Stoppelmoore, Cheryl Jean
See Ladd, Cheryl (Jean)
Stops, Sue 1936- *86*
Storad, Conrad J. 1957- *119*
Storey, Margaret 1926- *9*
Storey, Victoria Carolyn 1945- *16*
Storme, Peter
See Stern, Philip Van Doren
Storr, Catherine (Cole) 1913-2001 .... *87*
Obituary *122*
Earlier sketch in SATA *9*

Story, Josephine
See Loring, Emilie (Baker)
Stotko, Mary-Ann 1960- *154*
Stott, Dorothy (M.) 1958- *99*
Earlier sketch in SATA *67*
Stott, Dot
See Stott, Dorothy (M.)
Stotter, Mike 1957- *108*
Stout, William 1949- *132*
Stoutenburg, Adrien (Pearl) 1916-1982 .... *3*
Stoutland, Allison 1963- *130*
Stover, Allan C(arl) 1938- *14*
Stover, Jill (Griffin) 1958- *82*
Stover, Marjorie Filley 1914- *9*
Stowe, Harriet (Elizabeth) Beecher 1811-1896
See YABC *1*
Stowe, Leland 1899-1994 .... *60*
Obituary *78*
Stowe, Rosetta
See Ogan, George F.
and Ogan, Margaret E. (Nettles)
Strachan, Ian 1938- *85*
Strachan, Linda *167*
Strachan, Margaret Pitcairn 1908-1998 .... *14*
Strahinich, H. C.
See Strahinich, Helen C.
Strahinich, Helen C. 1949- *78*
Strait, Treva Adams 1909- *35*
Strand, Mark 1934- *41*
Stranger, Joyce
See SAAS *24*
See Wilson, Joyce M(uriel Judson)
Strangis, Joel 1948- *124*
Strannigan, Shawn 1956- *93*
Strannigan, Shawn Alyne
See Strannigan, Shawn
Strasser, Todd 1950- *153*
Earlier sketches in SATA *41, 45, 71, 107*
See also CLR *11*
Stratemeyer, Edward L. 1862-1930 .... *100*
Earlier sketches in SATA *1, 67*
See Adams, Harrison
and Appleton, Victor
and Dixon, Franklin W.
and Keene, Carolyn
and Rockwood, Roy
and Young, Clarence
Stratford, Philip 1927- *47*
Stratton, Allan 1951- *178*
Stratton, J. M.
See Whitlock, Ralph
Stratton, Thomas
See Coulson, Robert S(tratton)
and DeWeese, Thomas Eugene
Stratton-Porter, Gene(va Grace) 1863-1924
.... *15*
See also CLR *87*
See Porter, Gene(va Grace) Stratton
Strauss, Gwen 1963- *77*
Strauss, Joyce 1936- *53*
Strauss, Linda Leopold 1942- *127*
Strauss, Susan (Elizabeth) 1954- *75*
Strayer, E. Ward
See Stratemeyer, Edward L.
Streano, Vince(nt Catello) 1945- *20*
Streatfeild, (Mary) Noel 1897(?)-1986 .... *20*
Obituary *48*
See also CLR *83*
Street, Janet Travell 1959- *84*
Street, Julia Montgomery 1898-1993 .... *11*
Streissguth, Thomas 1958- *116*
Strelkoff, Tatiana 1957- *89*
Stren, Patti 1949- *88*
Brief entry *41*
See also CLR *5*
Strete, Craig Kee 1950- *96*
Earlier sketch in SATA *44*
Stretton, Barbara (Humphrey) 1936- *43*
Brief entry *35*
Strickland, (William) Brad(ley) 1947- *142*
Earlier sketches in SATA *83, 137*

Strickland, Craig (A.) 1956- *102*
Strickland, Dorothy S(alley) 1933- *89*
Strickland, Michael R. 1965- *144*
Earlier sketch in SATA *83*
Strickland, Tessa *173*
Striegel, Jana 1955- *140*
Striegel-Wilson, Jana
See Striegel, Jana
Striker, Lee
See Clark, Margaret (D.)
Striker, Susan 1942- *63*
Stringer, Lauren 1957- *129*
Stroeyer, Poul 1923- *13*
Stromoski, Rick 1958- *111*
Strong, Charles
See Epstein, Beryl (M. Williams)
and Epstein, Samuel
Strong, David
See McGuire, Leslie (Sarah)
Strong, Jeremy 1949- *175*
Earlier sketches in SATA *36, 105*
Strong, J.J.
See Strong, Jeremy
Strong, Pat
See Hough, Richard (Alexander)
Strong, Stacie 1965- *74*
Stroud, Bettye 1939- *165*
Earlier sketch in SATA *96*
Stroud, Jonathan 1970- *159*
Earlier sketch in SATA *102*
Stroyer, Poul
See Stroeyer, Poul
Strug, Kerri 1977- *108*
Stryker, Daniel
See Morris, Chris(topher Crosby)
and Stump, Jane Barr
Stuart, David
See Hoyt, Edwin P(almer), Jr.
Stuart, Derek
See Foster, John L(ouis)
Stuart, Forbes 1924- *13*
Stuart, Ian
See MacLean, Alistair (Stuart)
Stuart, Jesse (Hilton) 1906-1984 .... *2*
Obituary *36*
Stuart, Ruth McEnery 1849(?)-1917 .... *116*
Stuart, Sheila
See Baker, Mary Gladys Steel
Stuart-Clark, Christopher (Anthony) 1940- . *32*
Stubis, Talivaldis 1926- *5*
Stubley, Trevor (Hugh) 1932- *22*
Stucky, Naomi R. 1922- *72*
Stucley, Elizabeth
See Northmore, Elizabeth Florence
Stultifer, Morton
See Curtis, Richard (Alan)
Sture-Vasa, Mary
See Alsop, Mary O'Hara
Sturges, Philemon *174*
Sturtevant, Katherine 1950- *180*
Earlier sketch in SATA *130*
Sturton, Hugh
See Johnston, H(ugh) A(nthony) S(tephen)
Sturtzel, Howard A(llison) 1894-1985 .... *1*
Sturtzel, Jane Levington 1903-1996 .... *1*
Stutley, D(oris) J(ean) 1959- *142*
Stutson, Caroline 1940- *104*
Stuve-Bodeen, Stephanie 1965- *158*
Earlier sketch in SATA *114*
Stux, Erica 1929- *140*
Styles, (Frank) Showell 1908- *10*
Stynes, Barbara White *133*
Suba, Susanne *4*
Subond, Valerie
See Grayland, Valerie (Merle Spanner)
Sudbery, Rodie 1943- *42*
Suen, Anastasia 1956(?)- *157*
Sufrin, Mark 1925- *76*
Sugarman, Joan G. 1917- *64*
Sugarman, Tracy 1921- *37*
Sugita, Yutaka 1930- *36*

Suhl, Yuri (Menachem) 1908-1986 8
    Obituary 50
    See also CLR 2
    See also SAAS 1
Suhr, Joanne 129
Suid, Murray 1942- 27
Sullivan, George (Edward) 1927- 147
    Earlier sketches in SATA 4, 89
Sullivan, Jody
    See Rake, Jody
Sullivan, Kathryn A. 1954- 141
Sullivan, Mary Ann 1954- 63
Sullivan, Mary W(ilson) 1907- 13
Sullivan, Pat
    See Messmer, Otto
Sullivan, Paul 1939- 106
Sullivan, Sarah G. 1953- 179
Sullivan, Silky
    See Makowski, Silvia Ann
Sullivan, Sue
    See Sullivan, Susan E.
Sullivan, Susan E. 1962- 123
Sullivan, Thomas Joseph, Jr. 1947- 16
Sullivan, Tom
    See Sullivan, Thomas Joseph, Jr.
Sully, Tom 1959- 104
Sumichrast, Jozef 1948- 29
Sumiko
    See Davies, Sumiko
Summerforest, Ivy B.
    See Kirkup, James
Summers, James L(evingston) 1910-1973 .. 57
    Brief entry 28
Summertree, Katonah
    See Windsor, Patricia
Sun, Chyng Feng 1959- 90
Sunderlin, Sylvia (S.) 1911-1997 28
    Obituary 99
Sung, Betty Lee 26
Supeene, Shelagh Lynne 1952- 153
Supraner, Robyn 1930- 101
    Earlier sketch in SATA 20
Supree, Burt(on) 1941-1992 73
Surface, Mary Hall 1958- 126
Surge, Frank 1931- 13
Susac, Andrew 1929- 5
Susi, Geraldine Lee 1942- 98
Sussman, Cornelia Silver 1914-1999 59
Sussman, Irving 1908-1996 59
Sussman, Susan 1942- 48
Sutcliff, Rosemary 1920-1992 78
    Obituary 73
    Earlier sketches in SATA 6, 44
    See also CLR 37
Sutcliffe, Jane 1957- 138
Sutherland, Colleen 1944- 79
Sutherland, Efua (Theodora Morgue)
    1924-1996 25
Sutherland, Jon 1958- 167
Sutherland, Jonathan D.
    See Sutherland, Jon
Sutherland, Margaret 1941- 15
Sutherland, Zena Bailey 1915-2002 37
    Obituary 137
Suttles, Shirley (Smith) 1922- 21
Sutton, Ann (Livesay) 1923- 31
Sutton, Eve(lyn Mary) 1906-1992 26
Sutton, Felix 1910(?)-1973 31
Sutton, Jane 1950- 52
    Brief entry 43
Sutton, Larry M(atthew) 1931- 29
Sutton, Margaret Beebe 1903-2001 1
    Obituary 131
Sutton, Myron Daniel 1925- 31
Sutton, Roger 1956- 93
Suzanne, Jamie
    See Hawes, Louise
    and Lantz, Francess L(in)
    and Singleton, Linda Joy
    and Zach, Cheryl (Byrd)
Suzuki, David T(akayoshi) 1936- 138

Svendsen, Mark 1962- 181
    Earlier sketch in SATA 120
Svendsen, Mark Nestor
    See Svendsen, Mark
Svenson, Andrew E(dward) 1910-1975 2
    Obituary 26
Swain, Carol 1962- 172
Swain, Gwenyth 1961- 134
    Earlier sketch in SATA 84
Swain, Ruth
    See Swain, Ruth Freeman
Swain, Ruth Freeman 1951- 161
    Earlier sketch in SATA 119
Swain, Su Zan (Noguchi) 1916- 21
Swallow, Pamela Curtis 178
Swamp, Jake 1941- 98
Swan, Susan 1944- 108
    Earlier sketch in SATA 22
Swann, Brian (Stanley Frank) 1940- 116
Swann, E. L.
    See Lasky, Kathryn
Swann, Ruth Rice 1920- 84
Swanson, Helen M(cKendry) 1919- 94
Swanson, June 1931- 76
Swanson, Wayne 1942- 167
Swarthout, Glendon (Fred) 1918-1992 26
Swarthout, Kathryn 1919- 7
Swayne, Sam(uel F.) 1907- 53
Swayne, Zoa (Lourana) 1905- 53
Sweat, Lynn 1934- 168
    Earlier sketch in SATA 57
Swede, George 1940- 67
Sweeney, James B(artholomew) 1910-1999
    21
Sweeney, Joyce 1955- 167
    Earlier sketches in SATA 65, 68, 108
Sweeney, Joyce Kay
    See Sweeney, Joyce
Sweeney, Karen O'Connor
    See O'Connor, Karen
Sweeney, Matthew (Gerard) 1952- 156
Sweet, Melissa 1956- 172
Sweet, Sarah C.
    See Jewett, (Theodora) Sarah Orne
Sweetland, Nancy A(nn) 1934- 48
Swenson, Allan A(rmstrong) 1933- 21
Swenson, May 1919-1989 15
Swentzell, Rina 1939- 79
Swiatkowska, Gabi 1971(?)- 180
Swift, Bryan
    See Knott, William C(ecil, Jr.)
Swift, David
    See Kaufmann, John
Swift, Jonathan 1667-1745 19
    See also CLR 53
Swift, Merlin
    See Leeming, Joseph
Swiger, Elinor Porter 1927- 8
Swinburne, Laurence (Joseph) 1924- 9
Swinburne, Stephen R. 1952- 150
Swinburne, Steve
    See Swinburne, Stephen R.
Swindells, Robert (Edward) 1939- 150
    Brief entry 34
    Earlier sketches in SATA 50, 80
    See also SAAS 14
Swinford, Betty (June Wells) 1927- 58
Swinford, Bob
    See Swinford, Betty (June Wells)
Swithen, John
    See King, Stephen
Switzer, Ellen 1923- 48
Swope, Sam 156
Swope, Samuel
    See Swope, Sam
Sybesma, Jetske
    See Ironside, Jetske
Sydney, Frank
    See Warwick, Alan R(oss)
Sylvester, Natalie G(abry) 1922- 22

Syme, (Neville) Ronald 1913-1992 87
    Earlier sketch in SATA 2
Symes, R. F. 77
Symes, Ruth Louise 1962- 179
Symons, (Dorothy) Geraldine 1909- 33
Symons, Stuart
    See Stanley, George Edward
Symynkywicz, Jeffrey B. 1954- 87
Symynkywicz, Jeffrey Bruce
    See Symynkywicz, Jeffrey B.
Synge, (Phyllis) Ursula 1930- 9
Sypher, Lucy Johnston 1907- 7
Szasz, Suzanne (Shorr) 1915-1997 13
    Obituary 99
Szekeres, Cyndy 1933- 157
    Autobiography Feature 157
    Earlier sketches in SATA 5, 60, 131
    See also SAAS 13
Szekessy, Tanja 98
Szpura, Beata 1961- 93
Szudek, Agnes S(usan) P(hilomena) 57
    Brief entry 49
Szulc, Tad 1926-2001 26
Szydlow, Jarl
    See Szydlowski, Mary Vigliante
Szydlowski, Mary Vigliante 1946- 94
Szymanski, Lois 1957- 91

T

Taback, Simms 1932- 170
    Brief entry 36
    Earlier sketches in SATA 40, 104
    See also CLR 100
Tabor, Nancy Maria Grande 1949- 161
    Earlier sketch in SATA 89
Tabrah, Ruth Milander 1921- 14
Tackach, James 1953- 123
Tadgell, Nicole 1969- 177
Tafuri, Nancy (E.) 1946- 130
    Earlier sketches in SATA 39, 75
    See also CLR 74
    See also SAAS 14
Tagg, Christine Elizabeth 1962- 138
Tagliaferro, Linda 173
Taha, Karen T(erry) 1942- 156
    Earlier sketch in SATA 71
Tai, Sharon O. 1963- 153
Tait, Douglas 1944- 12
Takabayashi, Mari 1960- 156
    Earlier sketch in SATA 115
Takahashi, Rumiko 1957- 163
Takakjian, Portia 1930- 15
Takashima, Shizuye 1928- 13
Takayama, Sandi 1962- 106
Takeda, Pete(r M.) 1964- 148
Tal, Eve 1947- 176
Talbert, Marc (Alan) 1953- 154
    Autobiography Feature 154
    Earlier sketches in SATA 68, 99
Talbot, Charlene Joy 1928- 10
Talbot, Toby 1928- 14
Talbott, Hudson 1949- 131
    Earlier sketch in SATA 84
Talifero, Gerald 1950- 75
Talker, T.
    See Rands, William Brighty
Tallarico, Tony 1933- 116
Tallcott, Emogene 10
Tallis, Robyn
    See Coville, Bruce
    and Doyle, Debra
    and Macdonald, James D.
    and Smith, Sherwood
    and Zambreno, Mary Frances
Tallon, Robert 1939- 43
    Brief entry 28
Talmadge, Marian 14

Tamar, Erika 1934- *150*
  Earlier sketches in SATA *62, 101*
Tamarin, Alfred H. 1913-1980 .... *13*
Tamburine, Jean 1930- *12*
Tames, Richard (Lawrence) 1946- *102*
  Earlier sketch in SATA *67*
Tamminga, Frederick W(illiam) 1934- *66*
Tan, Amy 1952- *75*
Tan, Amy Ruth
  See Tan, Amy
Tanaka, Beatrice 1932- *76*
Tanaka, Shelley *136*
Tang, Charles 1948- *81*
Tang, Greg *172*
Tang, You-Shan 1946- *53*
Tania B.
  See Blixen, Karen (Christentze Dinesen)
Tannen, Mary 1943- *37*
Tannenbaum, Beulah Goldstein 1916- *3*
Tannenbaum, D(onald) Leb 1948- *42*
Tanner, Jane 1946- *74*
Tanner, Louise S(tickney) 1922-2000 .... *9*
Tanobe, Miyuki 1937- *23*
Tanselle, Eve 1933- *125*
Tapio, Pat Decker
  See Kines, Pat Decker
Tapp, Kathy Kennedy 1949- *88*
  Brief entry *50*
Tarbescu, Edith 1939- *107*
Tarkington, (Newton) Booth 1869-1946 ..... *17*
Tarpley, Natasha A(nastasia) 1971- *147*
Tarr, Judith 1955- *149*
  Earlier sketch in SATA *64*
Tarry, Ellen 1906- *16*
  See also CLR *26*
  See also SAAS *16*
Tarshis, Jerome 1936- *9*
Tarsky, Sue 1946- *41*
Tashjian, Janet 1956- *151*
  Earlier sketch in SATA *102*
Tashjian, Virginia A. 1921- *3*
Tasker, James 1908- *9*
Tate, Don(ald E.) *159*
Tate, Eleanora E(laine) 1948- *94*
  Earlier sketch in SATA *38*
  See also CLR *37*
Tate, Ellalice
  See Hibbert, Eleanor Alice Burford
Tate, Joan 1922- *86*
  Earlier sketch in SATA *9*
  See also SAAS *20*
Tate, Mary Anne
  See Hale, Arlene
Tate, Nikki *134*
Tate, Richard
  See Masters, Anthony (Richard)
Tate, Suzanne 1930- *91*
Tatham, Betty *142*
Tatham, Campbell
  See Elting, Mary
Tatham, Julie
  See Tatham, Julie Campbell
Tatham, Julie Campbell 1908-1999 .... *80*
Tavares, Matt *159*
Tavares, Victor 1971- *176*
Taves, Isabella 1915- *27*
Taylor, Alastair 1959- *130*
Taylor, Andrew 1951- *70*
Taylor, Andrew John Robert
  See Taylor, Andrew
Taylor, Ann 1782-1866 .... *41*
  Brief entry *35*
Taylor, Audilee Boyd 1931- *59*
Taylor, Barbara J. 1927- *10*
Taylor, Ben
  See Strachan, Ian
Taylor, Carl 1937- *14*
Taylor, Cheryl Munro 1957- *96*
Taylor, Cora (Lorraine) 1936- *103*
  Earlier sketch in SATA *64*
  See also CLR *63*

Taylor, Dave 1948- *78*
Taylor, David
  See Taylor, Dave
Taylor, David 1900-1965 .... *10*
Taylor, Debbie A. 1955- *169*
Taylor, Elizabeth 1912-1975 .... *13*
Taylor, Florance Walton *9*
Taylor, Florence M(arian Tompkins) 1892-1983
  .... *9*
Taylor, G(raham) P(eter) 1959(?)- *156*
Taylor, Gage 1942-2000 .... *87*
Taylor, Graham
  See Taylor, G(raham) P(eter)
Taylor, Herb(ert Norman, Jr.) 1942-1987 .... *22*
  Obituary *54*
Taylor, J. David
  See Taylor, Dave
Taylor, Jane 1783-1824 .... *41*
  Brief entry *35*
Taylor, Jerry D(uncan) 1938- *47*
Taylor, John Robert
  See Taylor, Andrew
Taylor, Judy
  See Hough, Judy Taylor
Taylor, Kenneth N. 1917-2005 .... *26*
Taylor, Kenneth Nathaniel
  See Taylor, Kenneth N.
Taylor, Kim *180*
Taylor, L(ester) B(arbour), Jr. 1932- *27*
Taylor, Lois Dwight Cole
  See Cole, Lois Dwight
Taylor, Louise Todd 1939- *47*
Taylor, Margaret 1950- *106*
Taylor, Mark 1927- *32*
  Brief entry *28*
Taylor, Mildred D. 1943- *135*
  See also CLR *90*
  See also SAAS *5*
Taylor, Mildred Delois
  See Taylor, Mildred D.
Taylor, Paula (Wright) 1942- *48*
  Brief entry *33*
Taylor, Robert Lewis 1912-1998 .... *10*
Taylor, Sydney (Brenner) 1904(?)-1978 ...... *28*
  Obituary *26*
  Earlier sketch in SATA *1*
Taylor, Theodore 1921-2006 .... *128*
  Obituary *177*
  Earlier sketches in SATA *5, 54, 83*
  See also CLR *30*
  See also SAAS *4*
Taylor, William 1938- *164*
  Earlier sketches in SATA *78, 113*
  See also CLR *63*
Tazewell, Charles 1900-1972 .... *74*
Tchana, Katrin Hyman 1963- *177*
  Earlier sketch in SATA *125*
Tchekhov, Anton
  See Chekhov, Anton (Pavlovich)
Tchen, Richard *120*
Tchudi, Stephen N. 1942- *55*
Teague, Bob
  See Teague, Robert
Teague, Mark 1963- *170*
  Earlier sketches in SATA *68, 99*
Teague, Mark Christopher
  See Teague, Mark
Teague, Robert 1929- *32*
  Brief entry *31*
Teal, Val(entine M.) 1902-1997 .... *10*
  Obituary *114*
Teale, Edwin Way 1899-1980 .... *7*
  Obituary *25*
Teasdale, Sara 1884-1933 .... *32*
Tebbel, John (William) 1912-2004 .... *26*
Teensma, Lynne Bertrand
  See Bertrand, Lynne
Tee-Van, Helen Damrosch 1893-1976 .... *10*
  Obituary *27*
Tegner, Bruce 1928- *62*

Teitelbaum, Michael 1953- *116*
  Earlier sketch in SATA *59*
Tejima
  See Tejima, Keizaburo
Tejima, Keizaburo 1931- *139*
  See also CLR *20*
Telander, Todd (G.) 1967- *88*
Teleki, Geza 1943- *45*
Telemaque, Eleanor Wong 1934- *43*
Telescope, Tom
  See Newbery, John
Temkin, Sara Anne Schlossberg 1913-1996
  .... *26*
Temko, Florence *13*
Templar, Maurice
  See Groom, Arthur William
Temple, Charles 1947- *79*
Temple, Frances (Nolting) 1945-1995 .... *85*
Temple, Herbert 1919- *45*
Temple, Paul
  See McConnell, James Douglas Rutherford
Temple, William F(rederick) 1914-1989 ... *107*
Tenggren, Gustaf 1896-1970 .... *18*
  Obituary *26*
Tennant, Kylie *6*
  See Rodd, Kylie Tennant
Tennant, Veronica 1947- *36*
Tenneshaw, S. M.
  See Beaumont, Charles
  and Garrett, (Gordon) Randall (Phillip)
  and Silverberg, Robert
Tenniel, John 1820-1914 .... *74*
  Brief entry *27*
  See also CLR *18*
Tepper, Sheri S. 1929- *113*
Terada, Alice M. 1928- *90*
Terban, Marvin 1940- *54*
  Brief entry *45*
ter Haar, Jaap 1922- *6*
  See Haar, Jaap ter
Terhune, Albert Payson 1872-1942 .... *15*
Terkel, Susan N(eiburg) 1948- *103*
  Earlier sketch in SATA *59*
Terlouw, Jan (Cornelis) 1931- *30*
Terris, Susan 1937- *77*
  Earlier sketch in SATA *3*
Terry, Luther L(eonidas) 1911-1985 .... *11*
  Obituary *42*
Terry, Margaret
  See Dunnahoo, Terry Janson
Terry, Walter 1913-1982 .... *14*
Terzian, James P. 1915- *14*
Tessendorf, K(enneth) C(harles) 1925-2003
  .... *75*
  Obituary *142*
Tessler, Stephanie Gordon
  See Gordon, Stephanie Jacob
Tester, Sylvia Root 1939- *64*
  Brief entry *37*
Tether, (Cynthia) Graham 1950- *46*
  Brief entry *36*
Tetzner, Lisa 1894-1963 .... *169*
Thacher, Mary McGrath 1933- *9*
Thackeray, William Makepeace 1811-1863
  .... *23*
Thaler, Michael C.
  See Thaler, Mike
Thaler, Mike 1936- *93*
  Brief entry *47*
  Earlier sketch in SATA *56*
Thaler, Shmuel 1958- *126*
  Earlier sketch in SATA *72*
Thamer, Katie 1955- *42*
Thane, Elswyth 1900-1984(?) *32*
Tharp, Louise (Marshall) Hall 1898-1992 .... *3*
  Obituary *129*
Thayer, Ernest Lawrence 1863-1940 .... *60*
Thayer, Jane
  See Woolley, Catherine
Thayer, Marjorie 1908-1992 .... *74*
  Brief entry *37*

Thayer, Peter
  See Wyler, Rose
Thelwell, Norman 1923-2004 .... *14*
Themerson, Stefan 1910-1988 .... *65*
Thermes, Jennifer 1966- *155*
Theroux, Paul 1941- *109*
  Earlier sketch in SATA *44*
Theroux, Paul Edward
  See Theroux, Paul
Thesman, Jean *124*
  Earlier sketch in SATA *74*
Thieda, Shirley Ann 1943- *13*
Thiele, Colin 1920-2006 .... *125*
  Earlier sketches in SATA *14, 72*
  See also CLR *27*
  See also SAAS *2*
Thiele, Colin Milton
  See Thiele, Colin
Thiesing, Lisa 1958- *159*
  Earlier sketch in SATA *95*
Thiry, Joan (Marie) 1926- *45*
Thistlethwaite, Miles 1945- *12*
Thollander, Earl 1922- *22*
Thomas, Abigail 1941- *112*
Thomas, Andrea
  See Hill, Margaret (Ohler)
Thomas, Art(hur Lawrence) 1952- *48*
  Brief entry *38*
Thomas, Carroll
  See Ratliff, Thomas M.
  and Shmurak, Carole B.
Thomas, Dylan (Marlais) 1914-1953 .... *60*
Thomas, Egbert S.
  See Ellis, Edward S(ylvester)
Thomas, Estelle Webb 1899-1982 .... *26*
Thomas, Frances 1943- *171*
  Earlier sketch in SATA *92*
Thomas, H. C.
  See Keating, Lawrence A.
Thomas, Ianthe 1951- *139*
  Brief entry *42*
  See also CLR *8*
Thomas, Jane Resh 1936- *171*
  Earlier sketches in SATA *38, 90*
Thomas, Jerry D. 1959- *91*
Thomas, Joan Gale
  See Robinson, Joan (Mary) G(ale Thomas)
Thomas, Joyce Carol 1938- *137*
  Autobiography Feature *137*
  Earlier sketches in SATA *40, 78, 123*
  See also CLR *19*
  See also SAAS *7*
Thomas, Lowell Jackson, Jr. 1923- *15*
Thomas, Margaret
  See Thomas, Peggy
Thomas, Meredith 1963- *119*
Thomas, Michael
  See Wilks, Michael Thomas
Thomas, Patricia J. 1934- *51*
Thomas, Peggy *174*
Thomas, Rob 1965- *97*
Thomas, Scott 1959- *147*
Thomas, Velma Maia 1955- *171*
Thomas, Vernon (Arthur) 1934- *56*
Thomas, Victoria
  See DeWeese, Thomas Eugene
  and Kugi, Constance Todd
Thomasma, Kenneth R. 1930- *90*
Thomassie, Tynia 1959- *92*
Thompson, Brenda 1935- *34*
Thompson, Carol 1951- *85*
Thompson, China
  See Lewis, Mary (Christianna)
Thompson, Colin (Edward) 1942- *163*
  Earlier sketch in SATA *95*
Thompson, David H(ugh) 1941- *17*
Thompson, Eileen
  See Panowski, Eileen Thompson

Thompson, George Selden 1929-1989 .... *73*
  Obituary *63*
  Earlier sketch in SATA *4*
  See Selden, George
Thompson, Harlan (Howard) 1894-1987 .... *10*
  Obituary *53*
  See Holt, Stephen
Thompson, Hilary 1943- *56*
  Brief entry *49*
Thompson, Julian F(rancis) 1927- *155*
  Brief entry *40*
  Earlier sketches in SATA *55, 99*
  See also CLR *24*
  See also SAAS *13*
Thompson, K(athryn Carolyn) Dyble 1952-
  .... *82*
Thompson, Kay 1912(?)-1998 .... *16*
  See also CLR *22*
Thompson, Lauren 1962- *174*
  Earlier sketch in SATA *132*
Thompson, Lauren Stevens
  See Thompson, Lauren
Thompson, Ruth Plumly 1891-1976 .... *66*
Thompson, Sharon 1952- *119*
Thompson, Sharon Elaine
  See Thompson, Sharon
Thompson, Stith 1885-1976 .... *57*
  Obituary *20*
Thompson, Vivian L(aubach) 1911- *3*
Thomson, Celia
  See Lynn, Tracy
Thomson, David (Robert Alexander)
  1914-1988 .... *40*
  Obituary *55*
Thomson, Pat 1939- *122*
  Earlier sketch in SATA *77*
Thomson, Peggy 1922- *31*
Thomson, Sarah L. *178*
Thon, Melanie Rae 1957- *132*
Thong, Roseanne *174*
Thorn, John 1947- *59*
Thorndyke, Helen Louise *67*
  Earlier sketch in SATA *1*
  See Benson, Mildred (Augustine Wirt)
Thorne, Ian
  See May, Julian
Thorne, Jean Wright
  See May, Julian
Thornhill, Jan 1955- *148*
  Earlier sketch in SATA *77*
Thornton, Hall
  See Silverberg, Robert
Thornton, W. B.
  See Burgess, Thornton Waldo
Thornton, Yvonne S(hirley) 1947- *96*
Thorpe, E(ustace) G(eorge) 1916- *21*
Thorpe, J. K.
  See Nathanson, Laura Walther
Thorvall, Kerstin 1925- *13*
Thorvall-Falk, Kerstin
  See Thorvall, Kerstin
Thrasher, Crystal (Faye) 1921- *27*
Threadgall, Colin 1941- *77*
Three Little Pigs
  See Lantz, Francess L(in)
Thum, Gladys 1920- *26*
Thum, Marcella *28*
  Earlier sketch in SATA *3*
Thundercloud, Katherine
  See Witt, Shirley Hill
Thurber, James (Grover) 1894-1961 .... *13*
Thurlo, Aimee *161*
Thurlo, David *161*
Thurman, Judith 1946- *33*
Thurman, Mark (Gordon Ian) 1948- *63*
Thwaite, Ann (Barbara Harrop) 1932- *14*
Tibbetts, Peggy *127*
Tibbles, Jean-Paul 1958- *115*
Tibo, Gilles 1951- *107*
  Earlier sketch in SATA *67*
Tiburzi, Bonnie 1948- *65*

Ticheburn, Cheviot
  See Ainsworth, William Harrison
Tichenor, Tom 1923-1992 .... *14*
Tichnor, Richard 1959- *90*
Tichy, William 1924- *31*
Tickle, Jack
  See Chapman, Jane
Tiegreen, Alan F. 1935- *94*
  Brief entry *36*
Tierney, Frank M. 1930- *54*
Tierney, Tom 1928- *113*
Tiffault, Benette W. 1955- *77*
Tiller, Ruth L. 1949- *83*
Tilly, Nancy 1935- *62*
Tilton, Madonna Elaine 1929- *41*
Tilton, Rafael
  See Tilton, Madonna Elaine
Timberlake, Amy *156*
Timberlake, Carolyn
  See Dresang, Eliza (Carolyn Timberlake)
Timmins, William F(rederick) *10*
Tiner, John Hudson 1944- *32*
Tingle, Dolli (?)-
  See Brackett, Dolli Tingle
Tingle, Rebecca *174*
Tingum, Janice 1958- *91*
Tinkelman, Murray 1933- *12*
Tinkle, (Julien) Lon 1906-1980 .... *36*
Tinling, Marion (Rose) 1904- *140*
Tipene, Tim 1972- *141*
Tippett, James S(terling) 1885-1958 .... *66*
Tirone Smith, Mary-Ann 1944- *143*
Titler, Dale M(ilton) 1926- *35*
  Brief entry *28*
Titmarsh, Michael Angelo
  See Thackeray, William Makepeace
Titus, Eve 1922- *2*
Tjong Khing, The 1933- *76*
Tobias, Katherine
  See Gottfried, Theodore Mark
Tobias, Tobi 1938- *82*
  Earlier sketch in SATA *5*
  See also CLR *4*
Todd, Anne Ophelia
  See Dowden, Anne Ophelia Todd
Todd, Barbara 1961- *173*
Todd, Barbara K(eith) 1917- *10*
Todd, H(erbert) E(atton) 1908-1988 .... *84*
  Earlier sketch in SATA *11*
Todd, Loreto 1942- *30*
Todd, Pamela 1950- *124*
Todd, Peter
  See Hamilton, Charles (Harold St. John)
Toews, Miriam 1964- *165*
Tofel, Richard J. 1957- *140*
Toft, Kim Michelle 1960- *170*
Tolan, Stephanie S. 1942- *142*
  Earlier sketches in SATA *38, 78*
Toland, John (Willard) 1912-2004 .... *38*
Tolbert, Steve 1944- *143*
Tolkien, John Ronald Reuel
  See Tolkien, J.R.R
Tolkien, J.R.R 1892-1973 .... *100*
  Obituary *24*
  Earlier sketches in SATA *2, 32*
  See also CLR *56*
Toll, Emily
  See Cannon, Eileen E(mily)
Toll, Nelly S. 1935- *78*
Tolland, W. R.
  See Heitzmann, William Ray
Tolles, Martha 1921- *76*
  Earlier sketch in SATA *8*
Tolliver, Ruby C(hangos) 1922- *110*
  Brief entry *41*
  Earlier sketch in SATA *55*
Tolmie, Kenneth Donald 1941- *15*
Tolstoi, Lev
  See Tolstoy, Leo (Nikolaevich)
Tolstoy, Leo (Nikolaevich) 1828-1910 ...... *26*
  See Tolstoi, Lev

Tolstoy, Count Leo
  See Tolstoy, Leo (Nikolaevich)
Tomalin, Ruth 29
Tomaselli, Rosa
  See Pausacker, Jenny
Tomecek, Steve 172
Tomes, Margot (Ladd) 1917-1991 70
  Brief entry 27
  Obituary 69
  Earlier sketch in SATA 36
Tomey, Ingrid 1943- 77
Tomfool
  See Farjeon, Eleanor
Tomkins, Jasper
  See Batey, Tom
Tomline, F. Latour
  See Gilbert, W(illiam) S(chwenck)
Tomlinson, Jill 1931-1976 3
  Obituary 24
Tomlinson, Theresa 1946- 165
  Earlier sketch in SATA 103
  See also CLR 60
Tompert, Ann 1918- 139
  Earlier sketches in SATA 14, 89
Toner, Raymond John 1908-1986 10
Tong, Gary S. 1942- 66
Took, Belladonna
  See Chapman, Vera (Ivy May)
Tooke, Louise Mathews 1950- 38
Tooke, Susan 173
Toonder, Martin
  See Groom, Arthur William
Toothaker, Roy Eugene 1928- 18
Tooze, Ruth (Anderson) 1892-1972 4
Topek, Susan Remick 1955- 78
Topping, Audrey R(onning) 1928- 14
Tor, Regina
  See Shekerjian, Regina Tor
Torbert, Floyd James 1922- 22
Torgersen, Don Arthur 1934- 55
  Brief entry 41
Torley, Luke
  See Blish, James (Benjamin)
Torres, Daniel 1958- 102
Torres, John A. 1965- 163
  Earlier sketch in SATA 94
Torres, John Albert
  See Torres, John A.
Torres, Laura 1967- 146
  Earlier sketch in SATA 87
Torres, Leyla 1960- 155
Torrie, Malcolm
  See Mitchell, Gladys (Maude Winifred)
Toten, Teresa 1955- 99
Totham, Mary
  See Breinburg, Petronella
Touponce, William F. 1948- 114
Tournier, Michel 1924- 23
Tournier, Michel Edouard
  See Tournier, Michel
Towle, Wendy 1963- 79
Towne, Mary
  See Spelman, Mary
Townley, Rod
  See Townley, Roderick
Townley, Roderick 1942- 177
Townsend, Brad W. 1962- 91
Townsend, John Rowe 1922- 132
  Autobiography Feature 132
  Earlier sketches in SATA 4, 68
  See also CLR 2
  See also SAAS 2
Townsend, Sue 93
  Brief entry 48
  Earlier sketch in SATA 55
  See Townsend, Susan Lilian
Townsend, Thomas L. 1944- 59
Townsend, Tom
  See Townsend, Thomas L.
Townson, Hazel 134
Toye, William Eldred 1926- 8

Traherne, Michael
  See Watkins-Pitchford, Denys James
Trahey, Jane 1923-2000 36
  Obituary 120
Trapani, Iza 1954- 116
  Earlier sketch in SATA 80
Trapp, Maria Augusta von 16
  See von Trapp, Maria Augusta
Travers, P(amela) L(yndon) 1899-1996 100
  Obituary 90
  Earlier sketches in SATA 4, 54
  See also CLR 93
  See also SAAS 2
Travis, Lucille 133
  Earlier sketch in SATA 88
Treadgold, Mary 1910- 49
Trease, (Robert) Geoffrey 1909-1998 60
  Obituary 101
  Earlier sketch in SATA 2
  See also CLR 42
  See also SAAS 6
Treat, Lawrence 1903-1998 59
Tredez, Alain 1926- 17
Tredez, Denise 1930- 50
Treece, Henry 1912-1966 2
  See also CLR 2
Tregarthen, Enys
  See Sloggett, Nellie
Tregaskis, Richard 1916-1973 3
  Obituary 26
Treherne, Katie Thamer 1955- 76
Trell, Max 1900-1996 14
  Obituary 108
Tremain, Ruthven 1922- 17
Trembath, Don 1963- 168
  Earlier sketch in SATA 96
Tremens, Del
  See MacDonald, Amy
Trent, Robbie 1894-1988 26
Trent, Timothy
  See Malmberg, Carl
Treseder, Terry Walton 1956- 68
Tresilian, (Cecil) Stuart 1891-(?) 40
Tresselt, Alvin 1916-2000 7
  See also CLR 30
Trevino, Elizabeth B(orton) de 1904- 29
  Earlier sketch in SATA 1
  See also SAAS 5
Trevor, Elleston 1920-1995 28
  See Hall, Adam
Trevor, Frances
  See Teasdale, Sara
Trevor, Glen
  See Hilton, James
Trevor, (Lucy) Meriol 1919-2000 113
  Obituary 122
  Earlier sketch in SATA 10
Trez, Alain
  See Tredez, Alain
Trez, Denise
  See Tredez, Denise
Trezise, Percy (James) 1923-
  See CLR 41
Triggs, Tony D. 1946- 70
Trimble, Marshall I(ra) 1939- 93
Trimby, Elisa 1948- 47
  Brief entry 40
Tripp, Eleanor B(aldwin) 1936- 4
Tripp, Janet 1942- 108
Tripp, John
  See Moore, John Travers
Tripp, Nathaniel 1944- 101
Tripp, Paul 1916-2002 8
  Obituary 139
Tripp, Valerie 1951- 168
  Earlier sketch in SATA 78
Tripp, Wallace (Whitney) 1940- 31
Trivelpiece, Laurel 1926- 56
  Brief entry 46
Trivett, Daphne Harwood 1940- 22
Trivizas, Eugene 1946- 84

Trnka, Jiri 1912-1969 43
  Brief entry 32
Trollope, Anthony 1815-1882 22
Trost, Lucille W(ood) 1938- 149
  Earlier sketch in SATA 12
Trott, Betty 1933- 91
Trotter, Grace V(iolet) 1900-1991 10
Trottier, Maxine 1950- 175
  Earlier sketch in SATA 131
Troughton, Joanna (Margaret) 1947- 37
Trout, Kilgore
  See Farmer, Philip Jose
Trout, Richard E. 123
Trudeau, Garretson Beekman
  See Trudeau, G.B.
Trudeau, Garry
  See Trudeau, G.B.
Trudeau, Garry B.
  See Trudeau, G.B.
Trudeau, G.B. 1948- 168
  Earlier sketch in SATA 35
  See Trudeau, Garry B.
Trueit, Trudi
  See Trueit, Trudi Strain
Trueit, Trudi Strain 179
Trueman, Terry 1947- 178
  Earlier sketch in SATA 132
Truesdell, Judy
  See Mecca, Judy Truesdell
Truesdell, Sue
  See Truesdell, Susan G.
Truesdell, Susan G. 108
  Brief entry 45
Trumbauer, Lisa (Trutkoff) 1963- 149
Truss, Jan 1925- 35
Tryon, Leslie 139
Tubb, Jonathan N. 1951- 78
Tubby, I. M.
  See Kraus, (Herman) Robert
Tucker, Caroline
  See Nolan, Jeannette Covert
Tudor, Tasha 1915- 160
  Earlier sketches in SATA 20, 69
  See also CLR 13
Tuerk, Hanne 1951- 71
Tulloch, Richard 1949- 180
  Earlier sketch in SATA 76
Tulloch, Richard George
  See Tulloch, Richard
Tulloch, Shirley 169
Tully, John (Kimberley) 1923- 14
Tumanov, Vladimir A. 1961- 138
Tung, Angela 1972- 109
Tunis, Edwin (Burdett) 1897-1973 28
  Obituary 24
  Earlier sketch in SATA 1
  See also CLR 2
Tunis, John R(oberts) 1889-1975 37
  Brief entry 30
Tunnell, Michael
  See Tunnell, Michael O('Grady)
Tunnell, Michael O('Grady) 1950- 157
  Earlier sketch in SATA 103
Tunnicliffe, C(harles) F(rederick) 1901-1979
  62
Turck, Mary C. 1950- 144
Turk, Hanne
  See Tuerk, Hanne
Turk, Ruth 1917- 82
Turkle, Brinton 1915- 79
  Earlier sketch in SATA 2
Turlington, Bayly 1919-1977 5
  Obituary 52
Turnbull, Agnes Sligh 1888-1982 14
Turnbull, Ann (Christine) 1943- 160
  Earlier sketch in SATA 18
Turner, Alice K. 1940- 10
Turner, Ann 1945- 178
  Earlier sketches in SATA 14, 77, 113
Turner, Ann Warren
  See Turner, Ann

Turner, Bonnie 1932- 75
Turner, Elizabeth 1774-1846
  See YABC 2
Turner, Glennette Tilley 1933- 71
Turner, Josie
  See Crawford, Phyllis
Turner, Megan Whalen 1965- 174
  Earlier sketch in SATA 94
Turner, Philip (William) 1925- 83
  Earlier sketch in SATA 11
  See also CLR 89
  See also SAAS 6
Turner, Robyn 1947- 77
Turngren, Ellen (?)-1964 3
Turska, Krystyna (Zofia) 1933- 31
  Brief entry 27
Turteltaub, H.N.
  See Turtledove, Harry
Turtledove, Harry 1949- 166
  Earlier sketch in SATA 116
Turtledove, Harry Norman
  See Turtledove, Harry
Tusa, Tricia 1960- 111
  Earlier sketch in SATA 72
Tusiani, Joseph 1924- 45
Twain, Mark
  See CLR 66
  See Clemens, Samuel Langhorne
Tweit, Susan J 1956- 94
Tweit, Susan Joan
  See Tweit, Susan J
Tweton, D. Jerome 1933- 48
Twinem, Neecy 1958- 92
Tworkov, Jack 1900-1982 47
  Obituary 31
Tyche
  See Papademetriou, Lisa
Tyers, Jenny 1969- 89
Tyers, Kathy 1952- 82
Tyler, Anne 1941- 173
  Earlier sketches in SATA 7, 90
Tyler, Linda
  See Tyler, Linda W(agner)
Tyler, Linda W(agner) 1952- 65
Tyler, Vicki 1952- 64
Tyne, Joel
  See Schembri, Jim
Tyrrell, Frances 1959- 107

U

Ubell, Earl 1926-2007 4
Uchida, Yoshiko 1921-1992 53
  Obituary 72
  Earlier sketch in SATA 1
  See also CLR 56
  See also SAAS 1
Udall, Jan Beaney 1938- 10
Uden, (Bernard Gilbert) Grant 1910- 26
Uderzo, Albert 1927-
  See CLR 37
Udry, Janice May 1928- 152
  Earlier sketch in SATA 4
Uegaki, Chieri 1969- 153
Ueno, Noriko
  See Nakae, Noriko
Uhlberg, Myron 174
Uhlig, Susan 1955- 129
Ulam, S(tanislaw) M(arcin) 1909-1984 51
Ullman, James Ramsey 1907-1971 7
Ulm, Robert 1934-1977 17
Ulmer, Louise 1943- 53
Ulyatt, Kenneth 1920- 14
Umansky, Kaye 1946- 158
Unada
  See Gliewe, Unada (Grace)
Uncle Carter
  See Boucher, (Clarence) Carter

Uncle Eric
  See Maybury, Richard J.
Uncle Gus
  See Rey, H(ans) A(ugusto)
Uncle Ray
  See Coffman, Ramon Peyton
Uncle Shelby
  See Silverstein, Shel
Underhill, Alice Mertie (Waterman) 1900-1971
  10
Underhill, Liz 1948- 53
  Brief entry 49
Unger, Harlow G. 1931- 75
Unger, Jim 1937- 67
Ungerer, (Jean) Thomas 1931- 106
  Earlier sketches in SATA 5, 33
  See Ungerer, Tomi
Ungerer, Tomi 1931-
  See CLR 77
  See Ungerer, (Jean) Thomas
Unkelbach, Kurt 1913-1992 4
Unnerstad, Edith (Totterman) 1900-1982 ... 3
  See also CLR 36
Unobagha, Uzo 139
Unrau, Ruth 1922- 9
Unstead, R(obert) J(ohn) 1915-1988 12
  Obituary 56
Unsworth, Walt(er) 1928- 4
Untermeyer, Bryna Ivens 1909-1985 61
Untermeyer, Louis 1885-1977 37
  Obituary 26
  Earlier sketch in SATA 2
Unwin, David S(torr) 1918- 14
Unwin, Nora S(picer) 1907-1982 3
  Obituary 49
Unzner, Christa 1958- 141
  Earlier sketch in SATA 80
Unzner-Fischer, Christa
  See Unzner, Christa
Updale, Eleanor 1953- 175
Updyke, Rosemary K. 1924- 103
Upitis, Alvis 109
Urban, Helle (Denise) 1957- 149
Ure, Jean 1943- 129
  Earlier sketches in SATA 48, 78
  See also CLR 34
  See also SAAS 14
U'Ren, Andrea 1968- 142
Uris, Leon 1924-2003 49
  Obituary 146
Uris, Leon Marcus
  See Uris, Leon
Ursu, Anne 177
Ury, Allen B. 1954- 98
Uschan, Michael V. 1948- 129
Usher, Margo Scegge
  See McHargue, Georgess
Uslan, Michael E. 1951- 169
Uston, Ken(neth Senzo) 1935-1987 65
Uttley, Alice Jane (Taylor) 1884-1976 88
  Obituary 26
  Earlier sketch in SATA 3
  See Uttley, Alison
Uttley, Alison
  See Uttley, Alice Jane (Taylor)
Utz, Lois (Marie) 1932-1986 5
  Obituary 50

V

Vaeth, J(oseph) Gordon 1921- 17
Vagin, Vladimir (Vasilevich) 1937- 142
Vail, Rachel 1966- 163
  Earlier sketch in SATA 94
Vainio, Pirkko 1957- 123
  Earlier sketch in SATA 76
Valen, Nanine 1950- 21
Valencak, Hannelore 42
  See Mayer, Hannelore Valencak

Valens, Amy 1946- 70
Valens, E(vans) G(ladstone), Jr. 1920-1992 .. 1
Valentine, Johnny 72
Valerio, Geraldo 1970- 180
Valgardson, W(illiam) D(empsey) 1939- .. 151
  Earlier sketch in SATA 101
Valleau, Emily 1925- 51
Van Abbe, Salaman 1883-1955 18
Van Allsburg, Chris 1949- 156
  Earlier sketches in SATA 37, 53, 105
  See also CLR 113
Van Anrooy, Francine 1924- 2
Van Anrooy, Frans
  See Van Anrooy, Francine
Vanasse, Deb 1957- 170
Vance, Eleanor Graham 1908-1985 11
Vance, Gerald
  See Garrett, (Gordon) Randall (Phillip)
  and Silverberg, Robert
Vance, Marguerite 1889-1965 29
VanCleave, Janice 1942- 116
  Autobiography Feature 123
  Earlier sketch in SATA 75
Vandenburg, Mary Lou 1943- 17
Vander Boom, Mae M. 14
Vander-Els, Betty 1936- 63
van der Linde, Laurel 1952- 78
van der Meer, Ron 1945- 98
Van der Veer, Judy 1912-1982 4
  Obituary 33
Vanderwerff, Corrine 1939- 117
Vander Zee, Ruth 159
Vande Velde, Vivian 1951- 141
  Earlier sketches in SATA 62, 95
Vandivert, Rita (Andre) 1905-1986 21
Van Draanen, Wendelin 122
Van Dusen, Chris 173
Van Duyn, Janet 1910- 18
Van Dyne, Edith
  See Baum, L(yman) Frank
  and Sampson, Emma (Keats) Speed
  and van Zantwijk, Rudolf (Alexander Marinus)
Vane, Mitch
  See Vane, Mitchelle
Vane, Mitchelle 176
van Frankenhuyzen, Gijsbert 1951- 132
Van Genechten, Guido 1957- 165
Van Hook, Beverly H. 1941- 99
Van Horn, William 1939- 43
van Hout, Mies 1962- 178
Van Iterson, S(iny) R(ose) 26
Van Kampen, Vlasta 1943- 163
  Earlier sketch in SATA 54
Van Laan, Nancy 1939- 105
van Lawick-Goodall, Jane
  See Goodall, Jane
Van Leeuwen, Jean 1937- 141
  Autobiography Feature 141
  Earlier sketches in SATA 6, 82, 132
  See also SAAS 8
van Lhin, Erik
  See del Rey, Lester
Van Loon, Hendrik Willem 1882-1944 18
VanOosting, James 1951- 170
Van Orden, M(erton) D(ick) 1921- 4
Van Rensselaer, Alexander (Taylor Mason)
  1892-1962 14
Van Riper, Guernsey, Jr. 1909-1995 3
van Rossum, Heleen 1962- 174
Van Rynbach, Iris 1952- 102
Vansant, Rhonda Joy Edwards 1950- 92
Van Steenwyk, Elizabeth (Ann) 1928- 89
  Earlier sketch in SATA 34
Van Stockum, Hilda 1908-2006 5
  Obituary 179
Van Tuyl, Barbara 1940- 11
van Vogt, A(lfred) E(lton) 1912-2000 14
  Obituary 124
Van Woerkom, Dorothy (O'Brien) 1924-1996
  21

Van Wormer, Joe
  See Van Wormer, Joseph Edward
Van Wormer, Joseph Edward 1913-1998 .... *35*
Van Wright, Cornelius *173*
Van Zwienen, Ilse Charlotte Koehn 1929-1991
  .... *34*
  Brief entry *28*
  Obituary *67*
Van Zyle, Jon 1942- *176*
  Earlier sketch in SATA *84*
Varela, Barry *180*
Varga, Judy
  See Stang, Judit
Varley, Dimitry V. 1906-1984 .... *10*
Varley, Susan 1961- *134*
  Earlier sketch in SATA *63*
Vasileva, Tatiana
  See Wassiljewa, Tatjana
Vasiliev, Valery 1949- *80*
Vasilieva, Tatiana
  See Wassiljewa, Tatjana
Vasiliu, Mircea 1920- *2*
Vass, George 1927- *57*
  Brief entry *31*
Vaughan, Carter A.
  See Gerson, Noel Bertram
Vaughan, Harold Cecil 1923- *14*
Vaughan, Marcia (K.) 1951- *159*
  Earlier sketches in SATA *60, 95*
Vaughan, Richard 1947- *87*
Vaughan, Sam(uel) 1928- *14*
Vaughn, Ruth 1935- *14*
Vautier, Ghislaine 1932- *53*
Vavra, Robert James 1935- *8*
Vecsey, George Spencer 1939- *9*
Vedral, Joyce L(auretta) 1943- *65*
Vega, Denise B. *174*
  See Vega, Denise
Veglahn, Nancy (Crary) 1937- *5*
Velasquez, Gloria (Louise) 1949- *113*
  See Velasquez(-Trevino), Gloria (Louise)
Velthuijs, Max 1923-2005 .... *110*
  Obituary *160*
  Earlier sketch in SATA *53*
Venable, Alan (Hudson) 1944- *8*
Venezia, Mike 1945- *150*
Ventura, Anthony
  See Pellowski, Michael (Joseph)
Ventura, Piero (Luigi) 1937- *61*
  Brief entry *43*
  See also CLR *16*
Vequin, Capini
  See Quinn, Elisabeth
Verba, Joan Marie 1953- *78*
Verboven, Agnes 1951- *103*
verDorn, Bethea (Stewart) 1952- *76*
Verissimo, Erico (Lopes) 1905-1975 .... *113*
Verne, Jules (Gabriel) 1828-1905 .... *21*
  See also CLR *88*
Verney, John 1913-1993 .... *14*
  Obituary *75*
Verniero, Joan C. 1949- *181*
Vernon, (Elda) Louise A(nderson) 1914- *14*
Vernon, Rosemary
  See Smith, Susan Vernon
Vernor, D.
  See Casewit, Curtis W(erner)
Verr, Harry Coe
  See Kunhardt, Edith
Verral, Charles Spain 1904-1990 .... *11*
  Obituary *65*
Versace, Marie Teresa Rios 1917- *2*
Vertreace, Martha M(odena) 1945- *78*
Vesey, A(manda) 1939- *62*
Vesey, Mark (David) 1958- *123*
Vesey, Paul
  See Allen, Samuel W(ashington)
Vestergaard, Hope *178*
Vestly, Anne-Cath(arina) 1920- *14*
  See also CLR *99*

Vevers, (Henry) Gwynne 1916-1988 .... *45*
  Obituary *57*
Viator, Vacuus
  See Hughes, Thomas
Vicar, Henry
  See Felsen, Henry Gregor
Vick, Helen Hughes 1950- *88*
Vicker, Angus
  See Felsen, Henry Gregor
Vickers, Sheena 1960- *94*
Vickery, Kate
  See Kennedy, T.A.
Victor, Edward 1914- *3*
Victor, Joan Berg 1942- *30*
Vidrine, Beverly Barras 1938- *103*
Viereck, Ellen K. 1928- *14*
Viereck, Phillip 1925- *3*
Viertel, Janet 1915- *10*
Vigliante, Mary
  See Szydlowski, Mary Vigliante
Vigna, Judith 1936- *102*
  Earlier sketch in SATA *15*
Viguers, Ruth Hill 1903-1971 .... *6*
Villasenor, Edmundo
  See Villasenor, Victor
Villasenor, Victor 1940- *171*
Villasenor, Victor E. 1940-
  See Villasenor, Victor
Villasenor, Victor Edmundo
  See Villasenor, Victor
Villiard, Paul 1910-1974 .... *51*
  Obituary *20*
Villiers, Alan (John) 1903-1982 .... *10*
Vilott, Rhondi
  See Salsitz, Rhondi Vilott
Vincent, Eric Douglas 1953- *40*
Vincent, Felix 1946- *41*
Vincent, Gabrielle 1928-2000 .... *121*
  Earlier sketch in SATA *61*
  See also CLR *13*
Vincent, Mary Keith
  See St. John, Wylly Folk
Vincent, William R.
  See Heitzmann, William Ray
Vinegar, Tom
  See Gregg, Andrew K.
Vinest, Shaw
  See Longyear, Barry B(rookes)
Vinge, Joan (Carol) D(ennison) 1948- *113*
  Earlier sketch in SATA *36*
Vining, Elizabeth Gray 1902-1999 .... *6*
  Obituary *117*
  See Gray, Elizabeth Janet
Vinson, Kathryn 1911-1995 .... *21*
Vinton, Iris 1906(?)-1988 .... *24*
  Obituary *55*
Viola, Herman J(oseph) 1938- *126*
Viorst, Judith 1931- *172*
  Earlier sketches in SATA *7, 70, 123*
  See also CLR *90*
Vip
  See Partch, Virgil Franklin II
Vipont, Charles
  See Foulds, Elfrida Vipont
Vipont, Elfrida
  See Foulds, Elfrida Vipont
Viscott, David S(teven) 1938-1996 .... *65*
Visser, W(illem) F(rederik) H(endrik)
  1900-1968 .... *10*
Vitale, Stefano 1958- *180*
  Earlier sketch in SATA *114*
Vivas, Julie 1947- *96*
Vivelo, Jackie 1943- *63*
Vivelo, Jacqueline J.
  See Vivelo, Jackie
Vivelo, Jacqueline Jean
  See Vivelo, Jackie
Vizzini, Ned 1981- *179*
  Earlier sketch in SATA *125*
Vlahos, Olivia 1924- *31*

Vlasic, Bob
  See Hirsch, Phil
Voake, Charlotte *180*
  Earlier sketch in SATA *114*
Voake, Steve 1961- *178*
Vo-Dinh, Mai 1933- *16*
Vogel, Carole Garbuny 1951- *105*
  Earlier sketch in SATA *70*
Vogel, Ilse-Margret 1918- *14*
Vogel, John H., Jr. 1950- *18*
Vogt, Esther Loewen 1915-1999 .... *14*
Vogt, Gregory L. *94*
Vogt, Marie Bollinger 1921- *45*
Voight, Virginia Frances 1909-1989 .... *8*
Voigt, Cynthia 1942- *160*
  Brief entry *33*
  Earlier sketches in SATA *48, 79, 116*
  See also CLR *48*
Voigt, Erna 1925- *35*
Voigt-Rother, Erna
  See Voigt, Erna
Vojtech, Anna 1946- *108*
  Earlier sketch in SATA *42*
Vollstadt, Elizabeth Weiss 1942- *121*
Volponi, Paul *175*
Volting, Dr. R.E.
  See Lerangis, Peter
Von Ahnen, Katherine 1922- *93*
Vondra, Josef (Gert) 1941- *121*
Von Gunden, Kenneth 1946- *113*
Von Hagen, Victor Wolfgang 1908-1985 .... *29*
von Klopp, Vahrah
  See Malvern, Gladys
von Schmidt, Eric 1931-2007 .... *50*
  Brief entry *36*
  Obituary *181*
von Storch, Anne B. 1910- *1*
von Ziegesar, Cecily 1970- *161*
Vos, Ida 1931- *121*
  Earlier sketch in SATA *69*
  See also CLR *85*
Vosburgh, Leonard (W.) 1912- *15*
Voyle, Mary
  See Manning, Rosemary (Joy)
Vriens, Jacques 1946- *151*
Vugteveen, Verna Aardema *107*
  Obituary *119*
  Earlier sketches in SATA *4, 68*
  See also CLR *17*
  See also SAAS *8*
  See Aardema, Verna
Vulture, Elizabeth T.
  See Gilbert, Suzie
Vuong, Lynette Dyer 1938- *110*
  Earlier sketch in SATA *60*

W

Waas, Uli
  See Waas-Pommer, Ulrike
Waas-Pommer, Ulrike 1949- *85*
Waber, Bernard 1924- *155*
  Brief entry *40*
  Earlier sketches in SATA *47, 95*
  See also CLR *55*
Wachtel, Shirley Russak 1951- *88*
Wachter, Oralee (Roberts) 1935- *61*
  Brief entry *51*
Waddell, Evelyn Margaret 1918- *10*
Waddell, Martin 1941- *129*
  Autobiography Feature *129*
  Earlier sketches in SATA *43, 81, 127*
  See also CLR *31*
  See also SAAS *15*
Waddy, Lawrence (Heber) 1914- *91*
Wade, Mary Dodson 1930- *151*
  Earlier sketch in SATA *79*
Wade, Suzanne
  See Kirby, Susan E.

Wade, Theodore E., Jr. 1936- 37
Wademan, Peter John 1946- 122
Wademan, Spike
  See Wademan, Peter John
Wadsworth, Ginger 1945- 157
  Earlier sketch in SATA 103
Wagenheim, Kal 1935- 21
Wagner, Michele R. 1975- 157
Wagner, Sharon B. 1936- 4
Wagoner, David (Russell) 1926- 14
Wahl, Jan (Boyer) 1933- 132
  Earlier sketches in SATA 2, 34, 73
  See also SAAS 3
Waide, Jan 1952- 29
Wainscott, John Milton 1910-1981 53
Wainwright, Richard M. 1935- 91
Wainwright, Ruth
  See Symes, Ruth Louise
Wait, Lea 1946- 137
Waite, Judy 174
Waite, Judy Bernard
  See Bernard, Patricia
Waite, Michael P(hillip) 1960- 101
Waite, P(eter) B(usby) 1922- 64
Waitley, Douglas 1927- 30
Wakefield, Jean L.
  See Laird, Jean E(louise)
Wakin, Daniel (Joseph) 1961- 84
Wakin, Edward 1927- 37
Walden, Amelia Elizabeth 3
Waldherr, Kris 1963- 76
Waldman, Bruce 1949- 15
Waldman, Neil 1947- 142
  Earlier sketches in SATA 51, 94
Waldron, Ann Wood 1924- 16
Waldron, Kathleen Cook 176
Walgren, Judy 1963- 118
Walker, Addison
  See Walker, (Addison) Mort
Walker, Alice 1944- 31
Walker, Alice Malsenior
  See Walker, Alice
Walker, Barbara (Jeanne) K(erlin) 1921- 80
  Earlier sketch in SATA 4
Walker, Barbara M(uhs) 1928- 57
Walker, (James) Braz(elton) 1934-1983 45
Walker, David G(ordon) 1926- 60
Walker, David Harry 1911-1992 8
  Obituary 71
Walker, Diana 1925- 9
Walker, Diane Marie Catherine
  See Walker, Kate
Walker, Dick
  See Pellowski, Michael (Joseph)
Walker, Frank 1931-2000 36
Walker, Holly Beth
  See Bond, Gladys Baker
Walker, Kate 1950- 165
  Earlier sketch in SATA 82
Walker, Kathrine Sorley
  See Sorley Walker, Kathrine
Walker, Lou Ann 1952- 66
  Brief entry 53
Walker, Mary Alexander 1927- 61
Walker, Mildred
  See Schemm, Mildred Walker
Walker, (Addison) Mort 1923- 8
Walker, Pamela 1948- 142
  Earlier sketch in SATA 24
Walker, Paul Robert 1953- 154
Walker, Robert W(ayne) 1948- 66
Walker, Sally M(acArt) 1954- 135
Walker, Stephen J. 1951- 12
Walker-Blondell, Becky 1951- 89
Wallace, Barbara Brooks 1922- 136
  Earlier sketches in SATA 4, 78
  See also SAAS 17
Wallace, Beverly Dobrin 1921- 19
Wallace, Bill 1947- 169
  Brief entry 47
  Earlier sketches in SATA 53, 101

Wallace, Daisy
  See Cuyler, Margery S(tuyvesant)
Wallace, Ian 1950- 141
  Earlier sketches in SATA 53, 56
  See also CLR 37
Wallace, John 1966- 155
  Earlier sketch in SATA 105
Wallace, John A(dam) 1915-2004 3
  Obituary 155
Wallace, Karen 1951- 139
  Earlier sketch in SATA 83
Wallace, Nancy Elizabeth 1948- 141
Wallace, Nigel
  See Hamilton, Charles (Harold St. John)
Wallace, Paula S. 153
Wallace, Rich 1957- 158
  Earlier sketch in SATA 117
Wallace, Robert 1932-1999 47
  Brief entry 37
Wallace, William Keith
  See Wallace, Bill
Wallace-Brodeur, Ruth 1941- 169
  Brief entry 41
  Earlier sketches in SATA 51, 88
Wallenta, Adam 1974- 123
Waller, Leslie 1923-2007 20
Walley, Byron
  See Card, Orson Scott
Wallis, Diz 1949- 77
Wallis, G. McDonald
  See Campbell, Hope
Wallner, Alexandra 1946- 156
  Brief entry 41
  Earlier sketches in SATA 51, 98
Wallner, John C. 1945- 133
  Earlier sketches in SATA 10, 51
Wallower, Lucille 11
Walsh, Ann 1942- 176
  Earlier sketch in SATA 62
Walsh, Ellen Stoll 1942- 147
  Earlier sketches in SATA 49, 99
Walsh, George Johnston 1889-1981 53
Walsh, Gillian Paton
  See Paton Walsh, Jill
Walsh, Jill Paton
  See CLR 65
  See Paton Walsh, Jill
Walsh, Lawrence 1942- 170
Walsh, Mary Caswell 1949- 118
Walsh, Suella 170
Walsh, V. L.
  See Walsh, Vivian
Walsh, Vivian 1960- 120
Walsh Shepherd, Donna 1948- 78
Walter, Frances V. 1923- 71
Walter, Mildred Pitts 1922- 133
  Brief entry 45
  Earlier sketch in SATA 69
  See also CLR 61
  See also SAAS 12
Walter, Villiam Christian
  See Andersen, Hans Christian
Walter, Virginia 134
  See Walter, Virginia A.
Walters, Audrey 1929- 18
Walters, Celeste 1938- 126
Walters, Eric (Robert) 1957- 155
  Earlier sketch in SATA 99
Walters, Hugh
  See Hughes, Walter (Llewellyn)
Walther, Thomas A. 1950- 31
Walther, Tom
  See Walther, Thomas A.
Waltner, Elma 1912-1987 40
Waltner, Willard H. 1909- 40
Walton, Darwin McBeth 1926- 119
Walton, Fiona L. M. 1959- 89
Walton, Richard J. 1928- 4
Walton, Rick 1957- 151
  Earlier sketch in SATA 101
Waltrip, Lela (Kingston) 1904-1995 9

Waltrip, Mildred 1911- 37
Waltrip, Rufus (Charles) 1898-1988 9
Walworth, Nancy Zinsser 1917- 14
Wangerin, Walter, Jr. 1944- 98
  Brief entry 37
  Earlier sketch in SATA 45
Waniek, Marilyn Nelson 1946- 60
  See Nelson, Marilyn
Wannamaker, Bruce
  See Moncure, Jane Belk
Warbler, J. M.
  See Cocagnac, Augustin Maurice(-Jean)
Warburg, Sandol Stoddard 14
  See Stoddard, Sandol
Ward, E. D.
  See Gorey, Edward (St. John)
  and Lucas, E(dward) V(errall)
Ward, Ed
  See Stratemeyer, Edward L.
Ward, Helen 1962- 144
  Earlier sketch in SATA 72
Ward, Jennifer 1963- 146
Ward, John (Stanton) 1917- 42
Ward, Jonas
  See Ard, William (Thomas)
  and Cox, William R(obert)
  and Garfield, Brian (Francis Wynne)
Ward, Lynd (Kendall) 1905-1985 36
  Obituary 42
  Earlier sketch in SATA 2
Ward, Martha (Eads) 5
Ward, Melanie
  See Curtis, Richard (Alan)
  and Lynch, Marilyn
Ward, Tom
  See Stratemeyer, Edward L.
Wardell, Dean
  See Prince, J(ack) H(arvey)
Wardlaw, Lee 1955- 115
  Earlier sketch in SATA 79
Ware, Cheryl 1963- 101
Ware, Chris 1967- 140
Ware, Leon (Vernon) 1909-1976 4
Wargin, Kathy-jo 1965- 145
Warner, Frank A. 67
  Earlier sketch in SATA 1
Warner, Gertrude Chandler 1890-1979 9
  Obituary 73
Warner, J(ohn) F. 1929- 75
Warner, Lucille Schulberg 30
Warner, Matt
  See Fichter, George S.
Warner, Oliver (Martin Wilson) 1903-1976
  29
Warner, Sally 1946- 131
Warner, Sunny (B.) 1931- 108
Warnes, Tim 1971- 166
  Earlier sketch in SATA 116
Warnes, Timothy
  See Warnes, Tim
Warnick, Elsa 1942- 113
Warren, Andrea 1946- 98
Warren, Betsy
  See Warren, Elizabeth Avery
Warren, Billy
  See Warren, William Stephen
Warren, Cathy 1951- 62
  Brief entry 46
Warren, Elizabeth
  See Supraner, Robyn
Warren, Elizabeth Avery 1916- 46
  Brief entry 38
Warren, Jackie M. 1953- 135
Warren, Joshua P(aul) 1976- 107
Warren, Joyce W(illiams) 1935- 18
Warren, Mary Phraner 1929- 10
Warren, Robert Penn 1905-1989 46
  Obituary 63
Warren, Scott S. 1957- 79
Warren, William Stephen 1882-1968 9
Warrick, Patricia Scott 1925- 35

Warsh
  See Warshaw, Jerry
Warshaw, Jerry 1929- 30
Warshaw, Mary 1931- 89
Warshofsky, Fred 1931- 24
Warshofsky, Isaac
  See Singer, Isaac Bashevis
Wartski, Maureen (Ann Crane) 1940- 50
  Brief entry 37
Warwick, Alan R(oss) 1900-1973 42
Wa-Sha-Quon-Asin
  See Belaney, Archibald Stansfeld
Wa-sha-quon-asin
  See Belaney, Archibald Stansfeld
Washburn, Bradford 1910-2007 38
  Obituary 181
Washburn, Henry Bradford, Jr.
  See Washburn, Bradford
Washburn, Jan(ice) 1926- 63
Washburne, Carolyn Kott 1944- 86
Washburne, Heluiz Chandler 1892-1970 10
  Obituary 26
Washington, Booker T(aliaferro) 1856-1915
  28
Washington, Donna L. 1967- 159
  Earlier sketch in SATA 98
Wasserstein, Wendy 1950-2006 94
  Obituary 174
Wassiljewa, Tatjana 1928- 106
Watanabe, Shigeo 1928- 131
  Brief entry 32
  Earlier sketch in SATA 39
  See also CLR 8
Waters, John F(rederick) 1930- 4
Waters, Tony 1958- 75
Waterton, Betty (Marie) 1923- 99
  Brief entry 34
  Earlier sketch in SATA 37
Watkins, Dawn L. 126
Watkins, Gloria Jean
  See hooks, bell
Watkins, Lois 1930- 88
Watkins, Peter 1934- 66
Watkins, Yoko Kawashima 1933- 93
Watkins-Pitchford, Denys James 1905-1990
  87
  Obituary 66
  Earlier sketch in SATA 6
  See also SAAS 4
Watling, James 1933- 117
  Earlier sketch in SATA 67
Watson, Aldren A(uld) 1917- 42
  Brief entry 36
Watson, Amy Zakrzewski 1965- 76
Watson, B. S.
  See Teitelbaum, Michael
Watson, Carol 1949- 78
Watson, Clyde 1947- 68
  Earlier sketch in SATA 5
  See also CLR 3
Watson, James 1936- 106
  Earlier sketch in SATA 10
Watson, Jane Werner 1915- 54
  Earlier sketch in SATA 3
Watson, John H.
  See Farmer, Philip Jose
Watson, Mary 1953- 117
Watson, N. Cameron 1955- 81
Watson, Nancy Dingman 32
Watson, Pauline 1925- 14
Watson, Richard F.
  See Silverberg, Robert
Watson, Richard Jesse 1951- 62
Watson, Sally (Lou) 1924- 3
Watson, Wendy (McLeod) 1942- 142
  Earlier sketches in SATA 5, 74
Watson Taylor, Elizabeth 1915- 41
Watt, Melanie 1975- 136
Watt, Thomas 1935- 4
Wattenberg, Jane 174
Watterson, Bill 1958- 66

Watt-Evans, Lawrence
  See Evans, Lawrence Watt
Watts, (Anna) Bernadette 1942- 103
  Earlier sketch in SATA 4
Watts, Ephraim
  See Horne, Richard Henry Hengist
Watts, Franklin (Mowry) 1904-1978 46
  Obituary 21
Watts, Irene N(aemi) 1931- 111
  Earlier sketch in SATA 56
Watts, Isaac 1674-1748 52
Watts, James K(ennedy) M(offitt) 1955- 59
Watts, Jeri Hanel 1957- 170
Watts, Julia 1969- 103
Watts, Leander 1956- 146
Watts, Leslie Elizabeth 1961- 168
Watts, Mabel Pizzey 1906-1994 11
Watts, Nigel 1957-1999 121
Waugh, C. C. Roessel
  See Waugh, Carol-Lynn Rossel
  and Waugh, Charles G(ordon)
Waugh, Carol-Lynn Rossel 1947- 41
Waugh, Dorothy -1996 11
Waugh, Sylvia 1935- 169
Waugh, Virginia
  See Sorensen, Virginia
Wax, Wendy A. 1963- 163
  Earlier sketch in SATA 73
Wayland, April Halprin 1954- 143
  Earlier sketch in SATA 78
  See also SAAS 26
Wayne, (Anne) Jenifer 1917-1982 32
Wayne, Kyra Petrovskaya 1918- 8
Wayne, Richard
  See Decker, Duane
Wayshak, Deborah Noyes 1965- 145
Waystaff, Simon
  See Swift, Jonathan
Weales, Gerald (Clifford) 1925- 11
Weary, Ogdred
  See Gorey, Edward (St. John)
Weatherford, Carole Boston 1956- 181
  Earlier sketch in SATA 138
Weatherly, Myra (S.) 1926- 130
Weaver, Harriett E. 1908-1993 65
Weaver, John L. 1949- 42
Weaver, Robyn
  See Conley-Weaver, Robyn
Weaver, Robyn M.
  See Conley-Weaver, Robyn
Weaver, Ward
  See Mason, F(rancis) van Wyck
Weaver, Will 1950- 161
  Earlier sketches in SATA 88, 109
Weaver, William Weller
  See Weaver, Will
Weaver-Gelzer, Charlotte 1950- 79
Webb, Christopher
  See Wibberley, Leonard (Patrick O'Connor)
Webb, Jacqueline
  See Pearce, Margaret
Webb, Jacquelyn
  See Pearce, Margaret
  and Pearce, Margaret
Webb, Jean Francis (III) 1910-1991 35
Webb, Kaye 1914- 60
Webb, Lois Sinaiko 1922- 82
Webb, Margot 1934- 67
Webb, Sharon 1936- 41
Webb, Sophie 1958- 135
Webber, Andrew Lloyd
  See Lloyd Webber, Andrew
Webber, Desiree Morrison 1956- 170
Webber, Irma E(leanor Schmidt) 1904-1995
  14
Weber, Alfons 1921- 8
Weber, Bruce 1942- 120
  Earlier sketch in SATA 73
Weber, Debora 1955- 58
Weber, EdNah New Rider 1919(?)- 168
Weber, Jill 1950- 127

Weber, Judith E(ichler) 1938- 64
Weber, Ken(neth J.) 1940- 90
Weber, Lenora Mattingly 1895-1971 2
  Obituary 26
Weber, Michael 1945- 87
Weber, Sandra 1961- 158
Weber, William J(ohn) 1927- 14
Webster, Alice Jane Chandler 1876-1916 ... 17
Webster, David 1930- 11
Webster, Frank V. 67
  Earlier sketch in SATA 1
Webster, Gary
  See Garrison, Webb B(lack)
Webster, James 1925-1981 17
  Obituary 27
Webster, Jean
  See Webster, Alice Jane Chandler
Wechter, Nell (Carolyn) Wise 1913-1989 . 127
  Earlier sketch in SATA 60
Weck, Thomas L. 1942- 62
Wedd, Kate
  See Gregory, Philippa
Weddle, Ethel Harshbarger 1897-1996 11
Weeks, Sarah 158
Weems, David B(urnola) 1922- 80
Wees, Frances Shelley 1902-1982 58
Weevers, Peter 1944- 59
Wegen, Ronald 1946-1985 99
Wegman, William (George) 1943- 135
  Earlier sketches in SATA 78, 129
Wegner, Fritz 1924- 20
Weidhorn, Manfred 1931- 60
Weidt, Maryann N. 1944- 85
Weigel, Jeff 1958- 170
Weigelt, Udo 1960- 168
Weihs, Erika 1917- 107
  Earlier sketch in SATA 15
Weik, Mary Hays 1898(?)-1979 3
  Obituary 23
Weil, Ann Yezner 1908-1969 9
Weil, Lisl 1910- 7
Weilerstein, Sadie Rose 1894-1993 3
  Obituary 75
Weill, Cynthia 1959- 167
Wein, Elizabeth E(ve) 1964- 151
  Earlier sketch in SATA 82
Weinberg, Larry
  See Weinberg, Lawrence (E.)
Weinberg, Lawrence (E.) 92
  Brief entry 48
Weinberger, Tanya 1939- 84
Weiner, Sandra 1922- 14
Weingarten, Violet (Brown) 1915-1976 3
  Obituary 27
Weingartner, Charles 1922- 5
Weinstein, Nina 1951- 73
Weir, Bob 1947- 76
Weir, Diana (R.) Loiewski 1958- 111
Weir, Joan S(herman) 1928- 99
Weir, LaVada 2
Weir, Rosemary (Green) 1905-1994 21
Weir, Wendy 1949- 76
Weis, Margaret 1948- 164
  Earlier sketches in SATA 38, 92
Weisberger, Bernard A(llen) 1922- 21
Weiser, Marjorie P(hillis) K(atz) 1934- 33
Weisgard, Leonard (Joseph) 1916-2000 85
  Obituary 122
  Earlier sketches in SATA 2, 30
  See also SAAS 19
Weiss, Adelle 1920- 18
Weiss, Ann E(dwards) 1943- 69
  Earlier sketch in SATA 30
  See also SAAS 13
Weiss, Edna
  See Barth, Edna
Weiss, Ellen 1953- 44
Weiss, Harvey 1922- 76
  Earlier sketches in SATA 1, 27
  See also CLR 4
  See also SAAS 19

Weiss, Jaqueline Shachter 1926- 65
Weiss, Malcolm E. 1928- 3
Weiss, Margaret Edith
  See Weis, Margaret
Weiss, Miriam
  See Schlein, Miriam
Weiss, Mitch 1951- 123
Weiss, Nicki 1954- 86
  Earlier sketch in SATA 33
Weiss, Renee Karol 1923- 5
Weissberger, Ela 1930- 181
Weissberger, Ela Stein
  See Weissberger, Ela
Weitzman, David L. 1936- 172
  Earlier sketch in SATA 122
Wekesser, Carol A. 1963- 76
Welber, Robert 26
Welch, Amanda (Jane) 1945- 75
Welch, Jean-Louise
  See Kempton, Jean Welch
Welch, Pauline
  See Bodenham, Hilda Morris
Welch, Ronald
  See Felton, Ronald Oliver
Welch, Sheila Kelly 1945- 130
Welch, Willy 1952- 93
Welford, Sue 1942- 75
Weller, George 1907-2002 31
  Obituary 140
Weller, George Anthony
  See Weller, George
Welling, Peter J. 1947- 135
Wellington, Monica 1957- 157
  Earlier sketches in SATA 67, 99
Wellman, Alice 1900-1984 51
  Brief entry 36
Wellman, Manly Wade 1903-1986 6
  Obituary 47
Wellman, Paul I(selin) 1898-1966 3
Wellman, Sam(uel) 1939- 122
Wells, H(erbert) G(eorge) 1866-1946 20
  See also CLR 64
Wells, Helen
  See Campbell, Hope
Wells, Helen 1910-1986 49
  Earlier sketch in SATA 2
Wells, J. Wellington
  See de Camp, L(yon) Sprague
Wells, June
  See Swinford, Betty (June Wells)
Wells, Robert
  See Welsch, Roger L(ee)
Wells, Rosemary 1943- 156
  Earlier sketches in SATA 18, 69, 114
  See also CLR 69
  See also SAAS 1
Wells, Susan (Mary) 1951- 78
Wels, Byron G(erald) 1924-1993 9
Welsbacher, Anne 1955- 89
Welsch, Roger L(ee) 1936- 82
Welsh, David
  See Hills, C.A.R.
Weltner, Linda R(iverly) 1938- 38
Welton, Jude 1955- 143
  Earlier sketch in SATA 79
Welty, S. F.
  See Welty, Susan F.
Welty, Susan F. 1905- 9
Wendelin, Rudolph 1910-2000 23
Wentworth, Robert
  See Hamilton, Edmond
Werlin, Nancy 1961- 161
  Earlier sketches in SATA 87, 119
Werner, Elsa Jane
  See Watson, Jane Werner
Werner, Herma 1926- 47
  Brief entry 41
Werner, Jane
  See Watson, Jane Werner
Werner, K.
  See Casewit, Curtis W(erner)

Wersba, Barbara 1932- 58
  Autobiography Feature 103
  Earlier sketch in SATA 1
  See also CLR 78
  See also SAAS 2
Werstein, Irving 1914(?)-1971 14
Werth, Kurt 1896-1983 20
Wesley, Alison
  See Barnes, Michael
Wesley, Kathryn
  See Rusch, Kristine Kathryn
Wesley, Mary (Aline) 1912-2002 66
Wesley, Valerie Wilson 1947- 168
  Earlier sketch in SATA 106
West, Andrew
  See Arthur, Robert, (Jr.)
West, Anna 1938- 40
West, Barbara
  See Price, Olive
West, Betty 1921- 11
West, Bruce 1951- 63
West, C. P.
  See Wodehouse, P(elham) G(renville)
West, Dorothy
  See Benson, Mildred (Augustine Wirt)
West, Emily Govan 1919- 38
West, Emmy
  See West, Emily Govan
West, James
  See Withers, Carl A.
West, Jerry
  See Svenson, Andrew E(dward)
West, John
  See Arthur, Robert, (Jr.)
West, Owen
  See Koontz, Dean R.
Westall, Robert (Atkinson) 1929-1993 69
  Obituary 75
  Earlier sketch in SATA 23
  See also CLR 13
  See also SAAS 2
Westaway, Jane 1948- 121
Westcott, Nadine Bernard 1949- 130
Westerberg, Christine 1950- 29
Westerduin, Anne 1945- 105
Westerfeld, Scott 161
Westervelt, Virginia Veeder 1914-2005 10
Westheimer, David 1917-2005 14
  Obituary 170
Westheimer, David Kaplan
  See Westheimer, David
Westmacott, Mary
  See Christie, Agatha (Mary Clarissa)
Westman, Barbara 70
Westman, Paul (Wendell) 1956- 39
Westmoreland, William C. 1914-2005 63
Westmoreland, William Childs
  See Westmoreland, William C.
Weston, Allen
  See Hogarth, Grace (Weston Allen)
  and Norton, Andre
Weston, Carol 1956- 135
Weston, John (Harrison) 1932- 21
Weston, Martha 1947- 119
  Earlier sketch in SATA 53
Westphal, Arnold Carl 1897- 57
Westrup, Hugh 102
Westwood, Jennifer 1940- 10
Wexler, Jerome (LeRoy) 1923- 14
Weyland, Jack 1940- 81
Weyn, Suzanne 1955- 164
  Earlier sketches in SATA 63, 101
Weyr, Garret
  See Freymann-Weyr, (Rhoda) Garret
  (Michaela)
Wezyk, Joanna 1966- 82
Whaley, Joyce Irene 1923- 61
Whalin, W. Terry 1953- 93
Wharf, Michael
  See Weller, George
Wharmby, Margot 63

Whatley, Bruce 1954- 177
Wheatley, Arabelle 1921- 16
Wheatley, Nadia 1949- 147
Wheeler, Cindy 1955- 49
  Brief entry 40
Wheeler, Deborah (Jean Ross) 1947- 83
Wheeler, Janet D. 1
Wheeler, Jill C. 1964- 136
  Earlier sketch in SATA 86
Wheeler, Jody 1952- 148
  Earlier sketch in SATA 84
Wheeler, Lisa 1963- 162
Wheeler, Opal 1898- 23
Whelan, Elizabeth M(urphy) 1943- 14
Whelan, Gloria 1923- 178
  Earlier sketches in SATA 85, 128
  See also CLR 90
Whelan, Gloria Ann
  See Whelan, Gloria
Whipple, A(ddison) B(eecher) C(olvin) 1918-
  64
Whipple, Cal
  See Whipple, A(ddison) B(eecher) C(olvin)
Whisp, Kennilworthy
  See Rowling, J.K.
Whistler, Reginald John 1905-1944 30
Whistler, Rex
  See Whistler, Reginald John
Whitcher, Susan (Godsil) 1952- 96
Whitcomb, Jon 1906-1988 10
  Obituary 56
Whitcomb, Laura 171
White, Anne Terry 1896-1980 2
White, Carolyn 1948- 130
White, Dale
  See Place, Marian T(empleton)
White, Dori 1919- 10
White, E. B. 1899-1985 100
  Obituary 44
  Earlier sketches in SATA 2, 29
  See also CLR 107
White, Eliza Orne 1856-1947
  See YABC 2
White, Elwyn Brooks
  See White, E. B.
White, Florence M(eiman) 1910- 14
White, Laurence B(arton), Jr. 1935- 10
White, Lee 176
White, Martin 1943- 51
White, Nancy 1942- 126
White, Ramy Allison 67
  Earlier sketch in SATA 1
White, Robb 1909-1990 83
  Earlier sketch in SATA 1
  See also CLR 3
  See also SAAS 1
White, Ruth C. 1942- 165
  Earlier sketches in SATA 39, 117
White, T(erence) H(anbury) 1906-1964 12
White, Tekla N. 1934- 115
White, Timothy (Thomas Anthony) 1952-2002
  60
White, Tom 1923- 148
White, William, Jr. 1934- 16
Whitehead, Don(ald) F. 1908-1981 4
Whitehead, Kathy 1957- 176
Whitehouse, Arch
  See Whitehouse, Arthur George Joseph
Whitehouse, Arthur George Joseph 1895-1979
  14
  Obituary 23
Whitehouse, Elizabeth S(cott) 1893-1968 ... 35
Whitehouse, Jeanne 29
  See Peterson, Jeanne Whitehouse
Whitelaw, Nancy 1933- 166
  Earlier sketch in SATA 76
Whitesel, Cheryl Aylward 162
Whitinger, R. D.
  See Place, Marian T(empleton)
Whitley, Mary Ann
  See Sebrey, Mary Ann

Whitley, Peggy 1938- 140
Whitlock, Ralph 1914-1995 35
Whitman, Alice
    See Marker, Sherry
Whitman, Sylvia (Choate) 1961- 135
    Earlier sketch in SATA 85
Whitman, Walt(er) 1819-1892 20
Whitmore, Arvella 1922- 125
Whitney, Alex(andra) 1922- 14
Whitney, David C(harles) 1921- 48
    Brief entry 29
Whitney, Kim Ablon 162
Whitney, Phyllis A(yame) 1903- 30
    Earlier sketch in SATA 1
    See also CLR 59
Whitney, Sharon 1937- 63
Whitney, Thomas P(orter) 1917- 25
Whittington, Mary K(athrine) 1941- 75
Whitworth, John 1945- 123
Whybrow, Ian 132
Whyte, Mal(colm Kenneth, Jr.) 1933- 62
Whyte, Mary 1953- 148
    Earlier sketch in SATA 94
Whytock, Cherry 177
Wiater, Stanley 1953- 84
Wibbelsman, Charles J(oseph) 1945- 59
Wibberley, Leonard (Patrick O'Connor)
    1915-1983 45
    Obituary 36
    Earlier sketch in SATA 2
    See also CLR 3
    See Holton, Leonard
Wiberg, Harald (Albin) 1908- 93
    Brief entry 40
Wick, Walter 1953- 148
Wickens, Elaine 86
Wickstrom, Sylvie 1960- 169
Widdemer, Mabel Cleland 1902-1964 5
Widener, Terry 1950- 105
Widerberg, Siv 1931- 10
Wiebe, Rudy 1934- 156
Wiebe, Rudy Henry
    See Wiebe, Rudy
Wieler, Diana (Jean) 1961- 109
Wiener, Lori 1956- 84
Wier, Ester (Alberti) 1910-2000 3
Wiese, Kurt 1887-1974 36
    Obituary 24
    Earlier sketch in SATA 3
    See also CLR 86
Wiesel, Elie 1928- 56
Wiesel, Eliezer
    See Wiesel, Elie
Wiesner, David 1956- 181
    Earlier sketches in SATA 72, 117, 139
    See also CLR 84
Wiesner, Portia
    See Takakjian, Portia
Wiesner, William 1899-1984 5
Wiggers, Raymond 1952- 82
Wiggin, Eric E. 1939- 167
    Earlier sketch in SATA 88
Wiggin, Eric Ellsworth 1939-
    See Wiggin, Eric E.
Wiggin (Riggs), Kate Douglas (Smith)
    1856-1923
    See YABC 1
    See also CLR 52
Wiggins, VeraLee (Chesnut) 1928-1995 89
Wight, James Alfred 1916-1995 55
    Brief entry 44
    See Herriot, James
Wignell, Edel 1936- 69
Wijnberg, Ellen 85
Wikland, Ilon 1930- 93
    Brief entry 32
Wikler, Madeline 1943- 114
Wilber, Donald N(ewton) 1907-1997 35
Wilbur, C. Keith 1923- 27
Wilbur, Frances 1921- 107

Wilbur, Richard 1921- 108
    Earlier sketch in SATA 9
Wilbur, Richard Purdy
    See Wilbur, Richard
Wilburn, Kathy 1948- 68
Wilcox, Charlotte 1948- 72
Wilcox, R(uth) Turner 1888-1970 36
Wilcox, Roger
    See Collins, Paul
Wild, Jocelyn 1941- 46
Wild, Margaret 1948- 151
Wild, Robin (Evans) 1936- 46
Wild, Robyn 1947- 117
Wilde, D. Gunther
    See Hurwood, Bernhardt J.
Wilde, Oscar (Fingal O'Flahertie Wills)
    1854(?)-1900 24
    See also CLR 114
Wilder, Buck
    See Smith, Tim(othy R.)
Wilder, Laura (Elizabeth) Ingalls 1867-1957
    100
    Earlier sketches in SATA 15, 29
    See also CLR 111
Wildsmith, Brian 1930- 124
    Earlier sketches in SATA 16, 69
    See also CLR 52
    See also SAAS 5
Wiles, Deborah 171
Wilhelm, Hans 1945- 135
    Earlier sketch in SATA 58
    See also CLR 46
    See also SAAS 21
Wilkie, Katharine E(lliott) 1904-1980 31
Wilkin, Eloise 1904-1987 49
    Obituary 54
Wilkins, Frances 1923- 14
Wilkins, Kim 147
Wilkins, Marilyn (Ruth) 1926- 30
Wilkins, Marne
    See Wilkins, Marilyn (Ruth)
Wilkins, Mary Huiskamp 1926- 139
    Earlier sketch in SATA 84
    See Calhoun, Mary
Wilkins, Mary Huiskamp Calhoun
    See Wilkins, Mary Huiskamp
Wilkins, Rose 180
Wilkinson, (Thomas) Barry 1923- 50
    Brief entry 32
Wilkinson, Beth 1925- 80
Wilkinson, Brenda 1946- 91
    Earlier sketch in SATA 14
    See also CLR 20
Wilkinson, (John) Burke 1913-2000 4
Wilkinson, Sylvia 1940- 56
    Brief entry 39
Wilkon, Jozef 1930- 133
    Earlier sketches in SATA 31, 71
Wilks, Michael Thomas 1947- 44
Wilks, Mike
    See Wilks, Michael Thomas
Will
    See Lipkind, William
Willard, Barbara (Mary) 1909-1994 74
    Earlier sketch in SATA 17
    See also CLR 2
    See also SAAS 5
Willard, Mildred Wilds 1911-1978 14
Willard, Nancy 1936- 127
    Brief entry 30
    Earlier sketches in SATA 37, 71
    See also CLR 5
Willcox, Isobel 1907-1996 42
Willems, Mo 180
    Earlier sketch in SATA 154
    See also CLR 114
Willett, Edward (C.) 1959- 115
Willey, Margaret 1950- 86
Willey, Robert
    See Ley, Willy
Willhoite, Michael A. 1946- 71

Williams, Kate
    See Armstrong, Jennifer
Williams, Arlene 171
Williams, Barbara 1925- 107
    Earlier sketch in SATA 11
    See also CLR 48
    See also SAAS 16
Williams, Barbara 1937- 62
Williams, Beryl
    See Epstein, Beryl (M. Williams)
Williams, Brian (Peter) 1943- 54
Williams, Carol Lynch 1959- 110
Williams, Charles
    See Collier, James Lincoln
Williams, Clyde C. 1881-1974 8
    Obituary 27
Williams, Coe
    See Harrison, C(hester) William
Williams, Colleen Madonna Flood 1963- . 156
Williams, Cynthia G. 1958- 123
Williams, Dar 1967- 168
Williams, Donna Reilly 1945- 83
Williams, (Marcia) Dorothy 71
    See Williams, Marcia (Dorothy)
Williams, Dorothy
    See Williams, Marcia (Dorothy)
Williams, Dorothy Snowden
    See Williams, Dar
Williams, Eric (Ernest) 1911-1983 14
    Obituary 38
Williams, Ferelith Eccles 22
    See Eccles Williams, Ferelith
Williams, Frances B.
    See Browin, Frances Williams
Williams, Garth (Montgomery) 1912-1996 . 66
    Obituary 90
    Earlier sketch in SATA 18
    See also CLR 57
    See also SAAS 7
Williams, Guy R(ichard) 1920- 11
Williams, Hawley
    See Heyliger, William
Williams, Helen 1948- 77
Williams, J. R.
    See Williams, Jeanne
Williams, J. Walker
    See Wodehouse, P(elham) G(renville)
Williams, Jay 1914-1978 41
    Obituary 24
    Earlier sketch in SATA 3
    See also CLR 8
Williams, Jeanne 1930- 5
Williams, Jenny 1939- 60
Williams, Karen Lynn 1952- 99
    Earlier sketch in SATA 66
Williams, Kit 1946(?)- 44
    See also CLR 4
Williams, Laura E. 180
Williams, Laura Ellen
    See Williams, Laura E.
Williams, L.E.
    See Williams, Laura Ellen
Williams, Leslie 1941- 42
Williams, Linda 1948- 59
Williams, Lynn
    See Hale, Arlene
Williams, Marcia (Dorothy) 1945- 159
    Earlier sketch in SATA 97
    See Williams, (Marcia) Dorothy
Williams, Margery
    See Bianco, Margery Williams
Williams, Mark
    See Arthur, Robert, (Jr.)
Williams, Mark London 1959- 140
Williams, Maureen 1951- 12
Williams, Michael
    See St. John, Wylly Folk
Williams, Patrick J.
    See Griffin, W.E.B.
Williams, Pete
    See Faulknor, Cliff(ord Vernon)

Williams, S. P.
  See Hart, Virginia
Williams, Sam *177*
  Earlier sketch in SATA *124*
Williams, Selma R(uth) 1925- *14*
Williams, Sherley Anne 1944-1999 .... *78*
  Obituary *116*
Williams, Sheron 1955- *77*
Williams, Shirley
  See Williams, Sherley Anne
Williams, Slim
  See Williams, Clyde C.
Williams, Sophy 1965- *135*
Williams, Suzanne (Bullock) 1953- *71*
Williams, Ursula Moray *3*
  See Moray Williams, Ursula
Williams, Vera B(aker) 1927- *102*
  Brief entry *33*
  Earlier sketch in SATA *53*
  See also CLR *9*
Williams-Andriani, Renee 1963- *98*
Williams-Ellis, (Mary) Amabel (Nassau
  Strachey) 1894-1984 .... *29*
  Obituary *41*
Williams-Garcia, Rita 1957- *160*
  Earlier sketch in SATA *98*
  See also CLR *36*
Williamson, Gwyneth 1965- *109*
Williamson, Henry (William) 1895-1977 .... *37*
  Obituary *30*
Williamson, Joanne S(mall) 1926- *122*
  Earlier sketch in SATA *3*
Willis, Charles
  See Clarke, Arthur C.
Willis, Connie 1945- *110*
  See also CLR *66*
Willis, Jeanne 1959- *123*
  Earlier sketch in SATA *61*
Willis, Jeanne Mary
  See Willis, Jeanne
Willis, Meredith Sue 1946- *101*
Willis, Nancy Carol 1952- *139*
  Earlier sketch in SATA *93*
Willis, Paul J. 1955- *113*
Willms, Russ *95*
Willoughby, Lee Davis
  See Avallone, Michael (Angelo, Jr.)
  and Brandner, Gary (Phil)
  and Deming, Richard
  and DeAndrea, William L(ouis)
  and Laymon, Richard (Carl)
  and Streib, Dan(iel Thomas)
  and Toombs, John
  and Webb, Jean Francis (III)
Willson, Robina Beckles *27*
  See Beckles Willson, Robina (Elizabeth)
Wilma, Dana
  See Faralla, Dana
Wilson, April *80*
Wilson, Barbara Ker
  See Ker Wilson, Barbara
Wilson, Beth P(ierre) *8*
Wilson, Budge 1927- *55*
  See Wilson, Marjorie
Wilson, Carletta 1951- *81*
Wilson, Carter 1941- *6*
Wilson, Charles Morrow 1905-1977 .... *30*
Wilson, Darryl B(abe) 1939- *90*
Wilson, Diane Lee *172*
Wilson, Dirk
  See Pohl, Frederik
Wilson, Dorothy Clarke 1904-2003 .... *16*
Wilson, Edward A(rthur) 1886-1970 .... *38*
Wilson, Ellen (Janet Cameron) (?)-1976 ...... *9*
  Obituary *26*
Wilson, Eric (H.) 1940- *34*
  Brief entry *32*
Wilson, Erica *51*
Wilson, Forrest 1918- *27*
Wilson, Gahan 1930- *35*
  Brief entry *27*

Wilson, Gina 1943- *85*
  Brief entry *34*
  Earlier sketch in SATA *36*
Wilson, (Leslie) Granville 1912- *14*
Wilson, Hazel (Hutchins) 1898-1992 .... *3*
  Obituary *73*
Wilson, J(erry) M. 1964- *121*
Wilson, Jacqueline 1945- *153*
  Brief entry *52*
  Earlier sketches in SATA *61, 102*
Wilson, John 1922- *22*
Wilson, Johnniece Marshall 1944- *75*
Wilson, Jonathan 1950- *181*
Wilson, Joyce M(uriel Judson) *84*
  Earlier sketch in SATA *21*
  See Stranger, Joyce
Wilson, Karma *174*
Wilson, Leslie 1952- *166*
Wilson, Linda Miller 1936- *116*
Wilson, Lionel 1924-2003 .... *33*
  Brief entry *31*
  Obituary *144*
Wilson, Marjorie
  Brief entry *51*
  See Wilson, Budge
Wilson, Maurice (Charles John) 1914- *46*
Wilson, Nancy Hope 1947- *138*
  Earlier sketch in SATA *81*
Wilson, Nick
  See Ellis, Edward S(ylvester)
Wilson, Phil 1948- *181*
Wilson, Ron(ald William) 1941- *38*
Wilson, Sarah 1934- *142*
  Earlier sketch in SATA *50*
Wilson, Tom 1931- *33*
  Brief entry *30*
Wilson, Troy 1970- *169*
Wilson, Walt(er N.) 1939- *14*
Wilson-Max, Ken 1965- *170*
  Earlier sketch in SATA *93*
Wilton, Elizabeth 1937- *14*
Wilwerding, Walter Joseph 1891-1966 .... *9*
Wimmer, Mike 1961- *70*
Winborn, Marsha (Lynn) 1947- *75*
Winch, John 1944- *165*
  Earlier sketch in SATA *117*
Winchester, James H(ugh) 1917-1985 .... *30*
  Obituary *45*
Winchester, Stanley
  See Youd, (Christopher) Samuel
Windawi, Thura al- 1983(?)- *165*
Winders, Gertrude Hecker -1987 .... *3*
Windham, Basil
  See Wodehouse, P(elham) G(renville)
Windham, Kathryn T(ucker) 1918- *14*
Windling, Terri 1958- *151*
Windrow, Martin
  See Windrow, Martin Clive
Windrow, Martin C.
  See Windrow, Martin Clive
Windrow, Martin Clive 1944- *68*
Windsor, Claire
  See Hamerstrom, Frances
Windsor, Linda 1950- *124*
Windsor, Patricia 1938- *78*
  Earlier sketch in SATA *30*
  See also SAAS *19*
Wineman-Marcus, Irene 1952- *81*
Winer, Yvonne 1934- *120*
Winerip, Michael *175*
Winfield, Arthur M.
  See Stratemeyer, Edward L.
Winfield, Edna
  See Stratemeyer, Edward L.
Winfield, Julia
  See Armstrong, Jennifer
Wing, Natasha (Lazutin) 1960- *82*
Winick, Judd 1970- *124*
Winks, Robin William 1930-2003 .... *61*
Winn, Alison
  See Wharmby, Margot

Winn, Chris 1952- *42*
Winn, Janet Bruce 1928- *43*
Winn, Marie 1936(?)- *38*
Winnick, Karen B(eth) B(inkoff) 1946- *51*
Winslow, Barbara 1947- *91*
Winstead, Rosie *180*
Winston, Clara 1921-1983 .... *54*
  Obituary *39*
Winston, Richard 1917-1979 .... *54*
Winter, Janet 1926- *126*
Winter, Jeanette 1939- *151*
Winter, Jonah 1962- *179*
Winter, Milo (Kendall) 1888-1956 .... *21*
Winter, Paula Cecelia 1929- *48*
Winter, R. R.
  See Winterbotham, R(ussell) R(obert)
Winterbotham, R(ussell) R(obert) 1904-1971
  .... *10*
Winterbotham, Russ
  See Winterbotham, R(ussell) R(obert)
Winterfeld, Henry 1901-1990 .... *55*
Winters, J. C.
  See Cross, Gilbert B.
Winters, Jon
  See Cross, Gilbert B.
Winters, Katherine 1936- *153*
  Earlier sketch in SATA *103*
Winters, Kay
  See Winters, Katherine
Winters, Nina 1944- *62*
Winters, Paul A. 1965- *106*
Winterton, Gayle
  See Adams, William Taylor
Winthrop, Elizabeth *164*
  Autobiography Feature *116*
  Earlier sketches in SATA *8, 76*
  See also CLR *89*
  See Mahony, Elizabeth Winthrop
Winton, Ian (Kenneth) 1960- *76*
Winton, Tim 1960- *98*
Wintz-Litty, Julie
  See Litty, Julie
Wirt, Ann
  See Benson, Mildred (Augustine Wirt)
Wirt, Mildred A.
  See Benson, Mildred (Augustine Wirt)
Wirtenberg, Patricia Z(arrella) 1932- *10*
Wirth, Beverly 1938- *63*
Wirths, Claudine (Turner) G(ibson) 1926-2000
  .... *104*
  Earlier sketch in SATA *64*
Wise, Lenny
  See Wise, Leonard
Wise, Leonard 1940- *167*
Wise, Leonard A.
  See Wise, Leonard
Wise, Leonard Allan
  See Wise, Leonard
Wise, William 1923- *163*
  Earlier sketch in SATA *4*
Wise, Winifred E. *2*
Wiseman, Ann (Sayre) 1926- *31*
Wiseman, B(ernard) 1922-1995 .... *4*
Wiseman, David 1916- *43*
  Brief entry *40*
Wishinsky, Frieda 1948- *166*
  Earlier sketches in SATA *70, 112*
Wisler, G(ary) Clifton 1950- *103*
  Brief entry *46*
  Earlier sketch in SATA *58*
Wismer, Donald (Richard) 1946- *59*
Wisner, Bill
  See Wisner, William L.
Wisner, William L. 1914(?)-1983 .... *42*
Wisniewski, David 1953-2002
  See Wisniewski, David
Wisniewski, David 1953-2002 .... *95*
  Obituary *139*
  See also CLR *51*
Wister, Owen 1860-1938 .... *62*
Witham, (Phillip) Ross 1917- *37*

Withers, Carl A. 1900-1970 .... *14*
Withrow, Sarah 1966- *124*
Witt, Dick 1948- *80*
Witt, Shirley Hill 1934- *17*
Wittanen, Etolin 1907- *55*
Wittels, Harriet Joan 1938- *31*
Wittig, Susan
  See Albert, Susan Wittig
Wittlinger, Ellen 1948- *122*
  Autobiography Feature *128*
  Earlier sketch in SATA *83*
Wittman, Sally (Anne Christensen) 1941- .. *30*
Witty, Paul 1898-1976 .... *50*
  Obituary *30*
Wodehouse, P(elham) G(renville) 1881-1975
  .... *22*
Wodge, Dreary
  See Gorey, Edward (St. John)
Woelfle, Gretchen 1945- *145*
Wohlberg, Meg 1905-1990 .... *41*
  Obituary *66*
Wohlrabe, Raymond A. 1900-1977 .... *4*
Wojciechowska, Maia (Teresa) 1927-2002 . *83*
  Autobiography Feature *104*
  Obituary *134*
  Earlier sketches in SATA *1, 28*
  See also CLR *1*
  See also SAAS *1*
Wojciechowski, Susan *126*
  Earlier sketch in SATA *78*
Wolcott, Patty 1929- *14*
Wold, Allen L. 1943- *64*
Wold, Jo Anne 1938- *30*
Woldin, Beth Weiner 1955- *34*
Wolf, Bernard 1930- *102*
  Brief entry *37*
Wolf, Erica (Van Varick) 1978- *156*
Wolf, Gita 1956- *101*
Wolf, Janet 1957- *78*
Wolf, Sallie 1950- *80*
Wolfe, Art 1952- *76*
Wolfe, Burton H. 1932- *5*
Wolfe, Gene 1931- *165*
  Earlier sketch in SATA *118*
Wolfe, Gene Rodman
  See Wolfe, Gene
Wolfe, Louis 1905-1985 .... *8*
  Obituary *133*
Wolfe, Rinna (Evelyn) 1925- *38*
Wolfenden, George
  See Beardmore, George
Wolfer, Dianne 1961- *167*
  Autobiography Feature *117*
  Earlier sketch in SATA *104*
Wolff, Alexander (Nikolaus) 1957- *137*
  Earlier sketch in SATA *63*
Wolff, Ashley 1956- *155*
  Earlier sketches in SATA *50, 81*
Wolff, Diane 1945- *27*
Wolff, Ferida 1946- *164*
  Earlier sketch in SATA *79*
Wolff, Jennifer Ashley
  See Wolff, Ashley
Wolff, Robert Jay 1905-1977 .... *10*
Wolff, Sonia
  See Levitin, Sonia (Wolff)
Wolff, Virginia Euwer 1937- *137*
  Earlier sketch in SATA *78*
  See also CLR *62*
Wolfman, Judy 1933- *138*
Wolfson, Evelyn 1937- *62*
Wolitzer, Hilma 1930- *31*
Wolkoff, Judie (Edwards) *93*
  Brief entry *37*
Wolkstein, Diane 1942- *138*
  Earlier sketches in SATA *7, 82*
Wolny, P.
  See Janeczko, Paul B(ryan)
Wolters, Richard A. 1920-1993 .... *35*
Wondriska, William 1931- *6*

Wong, Jade Snow 1922-2006 .... *112*
  Obituary *175*
Wong, Janet S. 1962- *148*
  Earlier sketch in SATA *98*
  See also CLR *94*
Wood, Anne (Savage) 1937- *64*
Wood, Audrey *139*
  Brief entry *44*
  Earlier sketches in SATA *50, 81*
  See also CLR *26*
Wood, Catherine
  See Etchison, Birdie L(ee)
Wood, David 1944- *87*
Wood, Don 1945- *50*
  Brief entry *44*
  See also CLR *26*
Wood, Douglas 1951- *180*
  Earlier sketches in SATA *81, 132*
Wood, Douglas Eric
  See Wood, Douglas
Wood, Edgar A(llardyce) 1907-1998 .... *14*
Wood, Esther
  See Brady, Esther Wood
Wood, Frances Elizabeth *34*
Wood, Frances M. 1951- *97*
Wood, James Playsted 1905- *1*
Wood, Jenny 1955- *88*
Wood, John Norris 1930- *85*
Wood, June Rae 1946- *120*
  Earlier sketch in SATA *79*
  See also CLR *82*
Wood, Kerry
  See Wood, Edgar A(llardyce)
Wood, Kim Marie *134*
Wood, Laura N.
  See Roper, Laura (Newbold) Wood
Wood, Linda C(arol) 1945- *59*
Wood, Marcia 1956- *80*
Wood, Marcia Mae
  See Wood, Marcia
Wood, Nancy
  See Wood, Nancy C.
Wood, Nancy C. 1936- *178*
  Earlier sketch in SATA *6*
Wood, Nuria
  See Nobisso, Josephine
Wood, Owen 1929- *64*
Wood, Phyllis Anderson 1923- *33*
  Brief entry *30*
Wood, Richard 1949- *110*
Wood, Tim(othy William Russell) 1946- *88*
Woodard, Carol 1929- *14*
Woodburn, John Henry 1914- *11*
Woodbury, David Oakes 1896-1981 .... *62*
Woodford, Peggy 1937- *25*
Woodhouse, Barbara (Blackburn) 1910-1988
  .... *63*
Wooding, Chris 1977- *166*
Wooding, Sharon
  See Wooding, Sharon L(ouise)
Wooding, Sharon L(ouise) 1943- *66*
Woodman, Allen 1954- *76*
Woodrich, Mary Neville 1915- *2*
Woodruff, Elvira 1951- *162*
  Earlier sketches in SATA *70, 106*
Woodruff, Joan Leslie 1953- *104*
Woodruff, Marian
  See Goudge, Eileen
Woodruff, Noah 1977- *86*
Woods, George A(llan) 1926-1988 .... *30*
  Obituary *57*
Woods, Geraldine 1948- *111*
  Brief entry *42*
  Earlier sketch in SATA *56*
Woods, Harold 1945- *56*
  Brief entry *42*
Woods, Lawrence
  See Lowndes, Robert A(ugustine) W(ard)
Woods, Margaret 1921- *2*
Woods, Nat
  See Stratemeyer, Edward L.

Woodson, Jack
  See Woodson, John Waddie Jr.
Woodson, Jacqueline 1964- *139*
  Earlier sketch in SATA *94*
  See also CLR *49*
Woodson, Jacqueline Amanda
  See Woodson, Jacqueline
Woodson, John Waddie Jr. 1913- *10*
Woodtor, Dee
  See Woodtor, Delores Parmer
Woodtor, Dee Parmer 1945(?)-2002
  See Woodtor, Delores Parmer
Woodtor, Delores Parmer 1945-2002 .... *93*
Wood-Trost, Lucille
  See Trost, Lucille W(ood)
Woodward, (Landon) Cleveland 1900-1986
  .... *10*
  Obituary *48*
Woodworth, Chris 1957- *168*
Woodworth, Viki 1952- *127*
Woody, Regina Jones 1894-1983 .... *3*
Woog, Adam 1953- *125*
  Earlier sketch in SATA *84*
Wooldridge, Connie Nordhielm 1950- *143*
  Earlier sketch in SATA *92*
Wooldridge, Frosty 1947- *140*
Wooldridge, Rhoda 1906-1988 .... *22*
Wooley, Susan Frelick 1945- *113*
Woolf, Paula 1950- *104*
Woolfe, Angela 1976- *169*
Woolley, Catherine 1904-2005 .... *3*
  Obituary *166*
Woolman, Steven 1969-2004 .... *163*
  Earlier sketch in SATA *90*
Woolsey, Janette 1904-1989 .... *3*
  Obituary *131*
Worcester, Donald E(mmet) 1915- *18*
Word, Reagan 1944- *103*
Work, Virginia 1946- *57*
  Brief entry *45*
Worline, Bonnie Bess 1914- *14*
Wormell, Christopher 1955- *154*
  Earlier sketch in SATA *103*
Wormell, Mary 1959- *96*
Wormser, Richard 1933- *106*
  Autobiography Feature *118*
  See also SAAS *26*
Wormser, Sophie 1897-1979 .... *22*
Worth, Richard 1945- *59*
  Brief entry *46*
Worth, Valerie -1994 .... *70*
  Earlier sketch in SATA *8*
  See also CLR *21*
  See Bahlke, Valerie Worth
Wortis, Avi 1937- *14*
  See Avi
  and Wortis, Edward (Irving)
Wortis, Edward (Irving) *156*
  See Wortis, Avi
Wosmek, Frances 1917- *29*
Woychuk, Denis 1953- *71*
Wrede, Patricia C(ollins) 1953- *146*
  Earlier sketch in SATA *67*
Wriggins, Sally Hovey 1922- *17*
Wright, Alexandra 1979- *103*
Wright, Betty Ren *109*
  Brief entry *48*
  Earlier sketch in SATA *63*
Wright, Cliff 1963- *168*
  Earlier sketch in SATA *76*
Wright, Courtni
  See Wright, Courtni C(rump)
Wright, Courtni C(rump) 1950- *84*
Wright, Courtni Crump
  See Wright, Courtni C(rump)
Wright, Dare 1914(?)-2001 .... *21*
  Obituary *124*
Wright, David K. 1943- *112*
  Earlier sketch in SATA *73*
Wright, Enid Meadowcroft (LaMonte)
  1898-1966 .... *3*

Wright, Esmond 1915-2003 .... *10*
Wright, Frances Fitzpatrick 1897-1982 .... *10*
Wright, J. B.
  See Barkan, Joanne
Wright, Judith 1915-2000 .... *14*
  Obituary *121*
Wright, Judith Arundell
  See Wright, Judith
Wright, Katrina
  See Gater, Dilys
Wright, Kenneth
  See del Rey, Lester
Wright, Kit 1944- *87*
Wright, Leslie B(ailey) 1959- *91*
Wright, Nancy Means *38*
Wright, R(obert) H(amilton) 1906- *6*
Wright, Rachel *134*
Wright, Susan Kimmel 1950- *97*
Wrightfrierson
  See Wright-Frierson, Virginia (Marguerite)
Wright-Frierson, Virginia (Marguerite) 1949-
  .... *110*
  Earlier sketch in SATA *58*
Wrightson, (Alice) Patricia 1921- *112*
  Earlier sketches in SATA *8, 66*
  See also CLR *14*
  See also SAAS *4*
Wroble, Lisa A. 1963- *134*
Wronker, Lili
  See Wronker, Lili Cassel
Wronker, Lili Cassel 1924- *10*
Wryde, Dogear
  See Gorey, Edward (St. John)
Wu, Norbert 1961- *155*
  Earlier sketch in SATA *101*
Wulffson, Don (L.) 1943- *155*
  Earlier sketches in SATA *32, 88*
Wunderli, Stephen 1958- *79*
Wunsch, Josephine (McLean) 1914- *64*
Wuorio, Eva-Lis 1918- *34*
  Brief entry *28*
Wurts, Janny 1953- *98*
Wyatt, B. D.
  See Robinson, Spider
Wyatt, Jane
  See Bradbury, Bianca (Ryley)
Wyatt, Melissa 1963- *177*
Wyeth, Betsy James 1921- *41*
Wyeth, N(ewell) C(onvers) 1882-1945 .... *17*
  See also CLR *106*
Wyler, Rose 1909-2000 .... *18*
  Obituary *121*
Wylie, Betty Jane *48*
Wylie, Laura
  See Matthews, Patricia
Wylie, Laurie
  See Matthews, Patricia
Wyllie, Stephen *86*
Wyman, Andrea *75*
Wyman, Carolyn 1956- *83*
Wymer, Norman (George) 1911- *25*
Wynard, Talbot
  See Hamilton, Charles (Harold St. John)
Wyndham, John
  See Harris, John (Wyndham Parkes Lucas)
  Beynon
Wyndham, Lee
  See Hyndman, Jane Andrews Lee
Wyndham, Robert
  See Hyndman, Robert Utley
Wynne-Jones, Tim 1948- *136*
  Autobiography Feature *136*
  Earlier sketches in SATA *67, 96*
  See also CLR *58*
Wynne-Jones, Timothy
  See Wynne-Jones, Tim
Wynter, Edward (John) 1914- *14*
Wynyard, Talbot
  See Hamilton, Charles (Harold St. John)

Wyss, Johann David Von 1743-1818 .... *29*
  Brief entry *27*
  See also CLR *92*
Wyss, Thelma Hatch 1934- *140*
  Earlier sketch in SATA *10*

X

Xavier, Father
  See Hurwood, Bernhardt J.
Xuan, YongSheng 1952- *116*
  Autobiography Feature *119*

Y

Yaccarino, Dan *141*
Yadin, (Rav-Aloof) Yigael 1917-1984 .... *55*
Yaffe, Alan
  See Yorinks, Arthur
Yagher, Kevin 1962- *143*
Yakovetic, (Joseph Sandy) 1952- *59*
Yakovetic, Joe
  See Yakovetic, (Joseph Sandy)
Yamaguchi, Marianne (Illenberger) 1936- *7*
Yamaka, Sara 1978- *92*
Yamanaka, Lois-Ann 1961- *166*
Yancey, Diane 1951- *138*
  Earlier sketch in SATA *81*
Yang, Belle 1960- *170*
Yang, Jay 1941- *12*
Yang, Mingyi 1943- *72*
Yarbrough, Camille 1938- *79*
  See also CLR *29*
Yaroslava
  See Mills, Yaroslava Surmach
Yashima, Taro
  See CLR *4*
  See Iwamatsu, Jun Atsushi
Yates, Elizabeth 1905-2001 .... *68*
  Obituary *128*
  Earlier sketch in SATA *4*
  See also SAAS *6*
Yates, Janelle K(aye) 1957- *77*
Yates, John 1939- *74*
Yates, Philip 1958- *149*
  Earlier sketch in SATA *92*
Yates, Raymond F(rancis) 1895-1966 .... *31*
Yaukey, Grace S(ydenstricker) 1899-1994 .. *80*
  Earlier sketch in SATA *5*
Ye, Ting-xing 1952- *106*
Yeakley, Marjory Hall 1908- *21*
Yeatman, Linda 1938- *42*
Yee, Brenda Shannon *133*
Yee, Lisa 1959- *160*
Yee, Paul (R.) 1956- *143*
  Earlier sketches in SATA *67, 96*
  See also CLR *44*
Yee, Wong Herbert 1953- *172*
  Earlier sketches in SATA *78, 115*
Yeh, Chun-Chan 1914- *79*
  See Ye Junjian
Ye Junjian
  See Yeh, Chun-Chan
Yenawine, Philip 1942- *85*
Yensid, Retlaw
  See Disney, Walt(er Elias)
Yeo, Wilma (Lethem) 1918-1994 .... *81*
  Earlier sketch in SATA *24*
Yeoman, John 1934- *80*
  Earlier sketch in SATA *28*
  See also CLR *46*
Yep, Laurence 1948- *176*
  Earlier sketches in SATA *7, 69, 123*
  See also CLR *54*
Yep, Laurence Michael
  See Yep, Laurence
Yepsen, Roger B(ennet), Jr. 1947- *59*
Yerian, Cameron John *21*

Yerian, Margaret A. *21*
Yerxa, Leo 1947- *181*
Yetska
  See Ironside, Jetske
Ylvisaker, Anne 1965(?)- *172*
Yoder, Carolyn P(atricia) 1953- *149*
Yoder, Dorothy Meenen 1921- *96*
Yoder, Dot
  See Yoder, Dorothy Meenen
Yoder, Walter D. 1933- *88*
Yolen, Jane 1939- *158*
  Autobiography Feature *111*
  Earlier sketches in SATA *4, 40, 75, 112*
  See also CLR *44*
  See also SAAS *1*
Yolen, Jane Hyatt
  See Yolen, Jane
Yonge, Charlotte (Mary) 1823-1901 .... *17*
Yoo, Paula 1969(?)- *174*
Yorinks, Adrienne 1956- *171*
Yorinks, Arthur 1953- *144*
  Earlier sketches in SATA *33, 49, 85*
  See also CLR *20*
York, Alison
  See Nicole, Christopher (Robin)
York, Andrew
  See Nicole, Christopher (Robin)
York, Carol Beach 1928- *77*
  Earlier sketch in SATA *6*
York, Rebecca
  See Buckholtz, Eileen (Garber)
  and Glick, Ruth (Burtnick)
York, Simon
  See Heinlein, Robert A.
Yoshida, Toshi 1911- *77*
Yoshikawa, Sachiko *181*
Youd, C. S.
  See SAAS *6*
  See Youd, (Christopher) Samuel
Youd, (Christopher) Samuel 1922- *135*
  Brief entry *30*
  Earlier sketch in SATA *47*
  See Christopher, John
  and Youd, C. S.
Young, Bob
  See Young, Robert W(illiam)
  and Young, James Robert
Young, Carol 1945- *102*
Young, Catherine
  See Olds, Helen Diehl
Young, Clarence *67*
  Earlier sketch in SATA *1*
  See Stratemeyer, Edward L.
Young, Collier
  See Bloch, Robert (Albert)
Young, Dan 1952- *126*
Young, Dianne 1959- *88*
Young, Dorothea Bennett 1924- *31*
Young, Ed 1931- *173*
  Earlier sketches in SATA *10, 74, 122*
  See also CLR *27*
Young, Ed Tse-chun
  See Young, Ed
Young, Edward
  See Reinfeld, Fred
Young, Elaine L.
  See Schulte, Elaine L(ouise)
Young, James
  See Graham, Ian
Young, Jan
  See Young, Janet Randall
Young, Janet Randall 1919-1994 .... *3*
Young, Jeff C. 1948- *132*
Young, John
  See Macintosh, Brownie
Young, Judy 1956- *155*
Young, Judy (Elaine) Dockrey 1949- *72*
Young, Karen Romano 1959- *168*
  Earlier sketch in SATA *116*
Young, Ken 1956- *86*
Young, Lois Horton 1911-1981 .... *26*

Young, Louisa *161*
Young, Louise B. 1919- *64*
Young, Margaret B(uckner) 1922- *2*
Young, Mary 1940- *89*
Young, Miriam 1913-1974 .... *7*
Young, Noela 1930- *89*
Young, (Rodney Lee) Patrick (Jr.) 1937- *22*
Young, Percy M(arshall) 1912-2004 .... *31*
  Obituary *154*
Young, Richard Alan 1946- *72*
Young, Robert W(illiam) 1916-1969 .... *3*
Young, Ross B. 1955- *150*
Young, Ruth 1946- *67*
Young, Scott A. 1918-2005 .... *5*
Young, Scott Alexander
  See Young, Scott A.
Young, Vivien
  See Gater, Dilys
Younger, Barbara 1954- *108*
Youngs, Betty 1934-1985 .... *53*
  Obituary *42*
Younkin, Paula 1942- *77*
Yount, Lisa (Ann) 1944- *124*
  Earlier sketch in SATA *74*
Yourgrau, Barry *179*
Yuditskaya, Tatyana 1964- *75*
Yumoto, Kazumi 1959- *153*

Z

Zach, Cheryl (Byrd) 1947- *98*
  Brief entry *51*
  Earlier sketch in SATA *58*
  See also SAAS *24*
Zacharias, Gary L. 1946- *153*
Zaffo, George J. (?)-1984 .... *42*
Zagwyn, Deborah Turney 1953- *138*
  Earlier sketch in SATA *78*
Zahn, Timothy 1951- *156*
  Earlier sketch in SATA *91*
Zaid, Barry 1938- *51*
Zaidenberg, Arthur 1908(?)-1990 .... *34*
  Obituary *66*
Zalben, Jane Breskin 1950- *170*
  Earlier sketches in SATA *7, 79, 120*
  See also CLR *84*
Zallinger, Jean (Day) 1918- *115*
  Earlier sketches in SATA *14, 80*
Zallinger, Peter Franz 1943- *49*
Zambreno, Mary Frances 1954- *140*
  Earlier sketch in SATA *75*
Zanderbergen, George
  See May, Julian
Zappa, Ahmet 1974- *180*
Zappa, Ahmet Emuukha Rodan
  See Zappa, Ahmet
Zappler, Lisbeth 1930- *10*
Zarchy, Harry 1912-1987 .... *34*
Zarin, Cynthia 1959- *108*
Zaring, Jane (Thomas) 1936- *40*
Zarins, Joyce Audy *57*
  See dos Santos, Joyce Audy
Zaslavsky, Claudia 1917- *36*
Zaugg, Sandra L. 1938- *118*
Zaugg, Sandy
  See Zaugg, Sandra L.

Zaunders, Bo 1939- *137*
Zawadzki, Marek 1958- *97*
Zebra, A.
  See Scoltock, Jack
Zebrowski, George 1945- *67*
Zebrowski, George T.
  See Zebrowski, George
Zeck, Gerald Anthony 1939- *40*
Zeck, Gerry
  See Zeck, Gerald Anthony
Zed, Dr.
  See Penrose, Gordon
Zei, Alki 1925- *24*
  See also CLR *6*
Zeier, Joan T(heresa) 1931- *81*
Zeinert, Karen 1942-2002 .... *137*
  Earlier sketch in SATA *79*
Zeises, Lara M. 1976- *145*
Zelazny, Roger 1937-1995 .... *57*
  Brief entry *39*
Zelazny, Roger Joseph
  See Zelazny, Roger
Zeldis, Malcah 1931- *146*
  Earlier sketch in SATA *86*
Zelinsky, Paul O. 1953- *154*
  Brief entry *33*
  Earlier sketches in SATA *49, 102*
  See also CLR *55*
Zellan, Audrey Penn *22*
  See Penn, Audrey
Zemach, Harve *3*
  See Fischtrom, Harvey
Zemach, Kaethe 1958- *149*
  Brief entry *39*
  Earlier sketch in SATA *49*
Zemach, Margot 1931-1989 .... *70*
  Obituary *59*
  Earlier sketch in SATA *21*
Zemach-Bersin, Kaethe
  See Zemach, Kaethe
Zeman, Ludmila 1947- *153*
Zephaniah, Benjamin 1958- *140*
  Earlier sketch in SATA *86*
Zephaniah, Benjamin Obadiah Iqbal
  See Zephaniah, Benjamin
Zerman, Melvyn Bernard 1930- *46*
Zettner, Pat 1940- *70*
Zevin, Gabrielle *176*
Zhang, Christopher Zhong-Yuan 1954- *91*
Zhang, Song Nan 1942- *170*
  Earlier sketch in SATA *85*
Ziefert, Harriet 1941- *154*
  Earlier sketch in SATA *101*
Ziegler, Jack (Denmore) 1942- *60*
Ziemienski, Dennis (Theodore) 1947- *10*
Ziliox, Marc
  See Fichter, George S.
Zillah
  See Macdonald, Zillah K(atherine)
Zim, Herbert S(pencer) 1909-1994 .... *30*
  Obituary *85*
  Earlier sketch in SATA *1*
  See also CLR *2*
  See also SAAS *2*
Zima, Gordon 1920- *90*
Zimelman, Nathan 1921- *65*
  Brief entry *37*

Zimmer, Dirk 1943- *147*
  Earlier sketch in SATA *65*
Zimmer, Tracie Vaughn *169*
Zimmerman, Andrea Griffing 1950- *123*
Zimmerman, H. Werner 1951- *101*
Zimmerman, Heinz Werner
  See Zimmerman, H. Werner
Zimmerman, Naoma 1914-2004 .... *10*
Zimmermann, Arnold E. 1909- *58*
Zimmett, Debbie
  See Becker, Deborah Zimmett
Zimmy
  See Stratemeyer, Edward L.
Zimnik, Reiner 1930- *36*
  See also CLR *3*
Zindel, Bonnie 1943- *34*
Zindel, Paul 1936-2003 .... *102*
  Obituary *142*
  Earlier sketches in SATA *16, 58*
  See also CLR *85*
Ziner, Feenie
  See Ziner, Florence
Ziner, Florence 1921- *5*
Zingara, Professor
  See Leeming, Joseph
Zinger, Yitskhok
  See Singer, Isaac Bashevis
Zion, Eugene 1913-1975 .... *18*
Zion, Gene
  See Zion, Eugene
Zohorsky, Janet R. 1958- *148*
Zolkower, Edie Stoltz *171*
Zolkowski, Cathy (A.) 1969- *121*
Zolotow, Charlotte (Gertrude) S(hapiro) 1915-
  .... *138*
  Earlier sketches in SATA *1, 35, 78*
  See also CLR *77*
Zonderman, Jon 1957- *92*
Zonia, Dhimitri 1921- *20*
Zonta, Pat 1951- *143*
Zubrowski, Bernard 1939- *90*
  Earlier sketch in SATA *35*
Zubrowski, Bernie
  See Zubrowski, Bernard
Zucker, Miriam S.
  See Reichert, Miriam Zucker
Zudeck, Darryl 1961- *61*
Zupa, G. Anthony
  See Zeck, Gerald Anthony
Zupancic, Lilijana Praprotnik
  See Prap, Lila
Zurbo, Matt(hew) 1967- *98*
Zurhorst, Charles (Stewart, Jr.) 1913-1989 . *12*
Zurlo, Tony 1941- *145*
Zuromskis, Diane
  See Stanley, Diane
Zuromskis, Diane Stanley
  See Stanley, Diane
Zusak, Markus 1975- *149*
Zwahlen, Diana 1947- *88*
Zweifel, Frances W. 1931- *14*
Zwerger, Lisbeth 1954- *130*
  Earlier sketch in SATA *66*
  See also CLR *46*
  See also SAAS *13*
Zwinger, Ann (H.) 1925- *46*
Zymet, Cathy Alter 1965- *121*